LOUISIANA
CODE OF CIVIL PROCEDURE

2022 Edition

As amended through the
2021 Regular and Veto Sessions
of the Legislature

Edited by
GUY HOLDRIDGE
Judge, Louisiana First Circuit Court of Appeal and
Adjunct Professor of Law, Louisiana State University Law Center

THOMSON REUTERS

Mat #42723625

ISBN: 978–1–539–22083–1

TABLE OF CONTENTS

DEDICATION

This edition of the Code of Civil Procedure is dedicated to my wife, Jackie, and my three children, Adrienne, Aimee, and Reed, and my beautiful new granddaughter, Elle.

PREFACE

This edition of the Louisiana Code of Civil Procedure was prepared with the practicing attorney and the trial judge in mind. Hopefully, it will be a quick resource for questions and problems concerning procedural issues in Louisiana courts.

Many major and new changes were passed in the 2021 Legislative session. New articles on recusal were added, as well as the elimination of the preliminary default. Delays for answering were extended and notice to attorneys prior to default judgments being granted were added. Judges may now raise the objection of prescription in certain cases to prevent default judgments from being rendered if the case appears from the pleadings to be prescribed. All attorneys who file pleadings must now have an email address and service may be made electronically using their email address. Many other articles were amended. Please refer to the section on new legislation for an overview of all of the 2021 changes to the Code of Civil Procedure.

Included in this edition are many checklists which will help both the trial judge and attorney. Of particular interest is the checklist for the motion for summary judgment, which has been updated with recent cases and new legislation. Also included is a Table of Delays and Required Security which must be posted. Both are intended as a quick reference and not a substitute for reading the actual articles.

The Editor's Notes under the various articles are my personal opinion, and are limited deliberately to my evaluation of what authority or analysis beyond the article itself is needed to apply the provisions of the article correctly. Many more Official Comments were added for articles, which hopefully will aid in the application and understanding of the provisions.

The appendix of statutory provisions at the end of the volume is comprised of those statutes that in my judgment the members of the Bar most often consult in conjunction with procedural problems. The district court rules are listed first and should be referred to in connection with the code articles. The civil code articles which are listed next contain most of the substantive law used in filing pleadings in accordance with the code of civil procedure. In many cases, the editor's notes will direct you to the appropriate statutory provision, which is necessary for a full understanding of the code article.

I would like to thank my law clerks, Chaylon Mendolia, Karen Merrifield, and Lauren Falcon, and Mallory Waller of the Louisiana State Law Institute for their help on this project.

Guy Holdridge

Judge, Louisiana First Circuit Court of
Appeal and Adjunct Professor of Law,
Louisiana State University Law Center

December, 2021

LEGISLATIVE CHANGES IN THE 2021 REGULAR SESSION

I. Louisiana Code of Civil Procedure article 151 et seq. (Recusal)

i. Act 143 of the 2021 Legislative Session amended and added new articles on recusal that were drafted by the Louisiana State Law Institute in response to growing concerns from the courts and members of the bar with respect to inconsistencies between the Code of Civil Procedure and the Code of Judicial Conduct regarding recusal. Specifically, Canon 3C of the Code of Judicial Conduct provides that a judge should recuse himself when "the judge's impartiality might reasonably be questioned," but this language does not appear in current Code of Civil Procedure article 151.

ii. While returning the former grounds for recusal, the revisions to C.C.P. art. 151 add a new "catchall" ground for recusal when a substantial and objective basis exists that would reasonably be expected to prevent the judge from conducting any aspect of the cause in a fair and impartial manner. This ground for recusal is mandatory and is intended to incorporate a clearer, more objective standard than the language of Canon 3C.

iii. The additional ground for recusal in C.C.P. art. 151(B) states:

> A judge of any trial or appellate court shall also be recused when there exists a substantial and objective basis that would reasonably be expected to prevent the judge from conducting any aspect of the cause in a fair and impartial manner.

iv. The permissive grounds for recusal under former C.C.P. art. 151(B) have been deleted, and their substance has been moved to C.C.P. art. 152 to provide for mandatory disclosures that must be made to all attorneys and unrepresented parties. C.C.P. art. 152(A)(5) is a slight expansion of former C.C.P. art. 151(B)(4) in that it requires the judge to make a disclosure if his immediate family member has a substantial economic interest in the matter in all cases, as opposed to only when one of these relatives lives in the judge's household. An amendment was also added to C.C.P. art. 152(A)(4)(b) to require the judge to disclose if he is related not only to an attorney or the spouse of an attorney, but also to any member of the attorney's law firm within the second degree. Upon disclosure, any party may file a motion that sets forth a ground for recusal under C.C.P. art. 151.

v. Louisiana Code of Civil Procedure article 152—disclosures as amended reads:

A. A judge of any trial or appellate court shall disclose, to the best of his information and belief, the existence of any of the following to all attorneys and unrepresented parties in the cause:

1. The judge has been associated with an attorney during the latter's employment in the cause.
2. At the time of the hearing of any contested issue in the cause, the judge has continued to employ, to represent him personally, the attorney actually handling the cause or a member of that attorney's firm.
3. The judge performed a judicial act in the cause in another court.
4. The judge is related to any of the following:

   a. A party or the spouse of a party, within the fourth degree.

   b. An attorney employed in the cause, the spouse of the attorney, or any member of the attorney's law firm, within the second degree.

5. The judge's spouse, parent, child, or immediate family member has a substantial economic interest in the subject matter in controversy.

B. Upon disclosure, any party may file a motion that sets forth a ground for recusal under Article 151.

vi. The revisions to C.C.P. art. 153 add a new provision requiring a judge who self-recuses to provide written reasons for the recusal and to provide copies to the judicial administrator of the Supreme Court. These changes are intended to balance the judge's duty to sit against his obligation to recuse when a valid ground for doing so exists. See In re Lemoine, 96-2116 (La. 1/14/97), 686 So.2d 837, 840 (which stated that a judge is not at liberty, nor does he have the right, to take himself out of a case and burden another judge with his responsibility without good and legal cause.)

vii. The cause shall not be allotted to another judge until the order of recusal and written reasons containing the factual basis for the recusal are filed into the record.

viii. Louisiana Code of Civil Procedure article 153(C) as amended reads:

Prior to the cause being allotted to another judge, a judge who recuses himself for any reason shall contemporaneously file in the record the order of recusal and written reasons that provide the factual basis for recusal under Article 151. The judge shall also provide a copy of the recusal and the written reasons therefor to the judicial administrator of the supreme court.

ix. The revisions to C.C.P. art. 154(A) add a time requirement for filing a motion to recuse. Now, a motion to recuse shall be filed no later than 30 days after discovery of the facts constituting the ground for recusal, but in all cases prior to the scheduling of the matter for trial, or if these facts occur or are discovered after the matter is scheduled for trial, immediately thereafter. These changes are intended to prevent the parties from delaying the proceedings by using a late-filed motion to recuse as a continuance.

x. Louisiana Code of Civil Procedure article 154(A) as amended reads:

A party desiring to recuse a judge of a district court shall file a written motion therefor assigning the ground for recusal under Article 151. This motion shall be filed no later than thirty days after discovery of the facts constituting the ground upon which the motion is based, but in all cases prior to the scheduling of the matter for trial. In the event that the facts constituting the ground upon which the motion to recuse is based occur after the matter is scheduled for trial or the party moving for recusal could not, in the exercise of due diligence, have discovered such facts, the motion to recuse shall be filed immediately after such facts occur or are discovered.

xi. The revisions to C.C.P. art. 154(B) require a district judge who is the subject of a motion to recuse to either recuse himself or to request in writing that the Supreme Court appoint an ad hoc judge to hear the motion to recuse. If, however, the motion to recuse is not timely filed or fails to set forth a ground for recusal, new Paragraph C provides that the judge who is the subject of the motion may deny it, provided that he gives written reasons for doing so. A party who disagrees with such denial may apply for a supervisory writ seeking review of the decision. While this section only applies to district judges, appellate judges may adopt this rule in either the Uniform Rules, Courts of Appeal, or in the rules of their individual court.

xii. Louisiana Code of Civil Procedure article 154(C) as amended reads:

If the motion to recuse is not timely filed in accordance with Paragraph A of this Article or fails to set forth a ground for recusal under Article 151, the judge may deny the motion without the appointment of an ad hoc judge or a hearing but shall provide written reasons for the denial.

xiii. The revisions to C.C.P. art. 155 provide that once a motion to recuse has been referred for hearing, the motion shall be heard by an ad hoc judge appointed by the Supreme Court, as opposed to another judge of the same court. This change is intended to increase confidence in the judiciary by reducing or eliminating the potential for impartiality or bias. Similarly, the revisions to C.C.P. art. 156 provide that once a judge has been recused, the case shall be randomly assigned to another division or section of the court or, in courts where there is only one judge, the Supreme Court shall appoint an ad hoc judge to hear the case.

xiv. Louisiana Code of Civil Procedure article 155(A) — Selection of judge to try motion to recuse as amended reads:

Once a motion that sets forth a ground for recusal under Article 151 is referred for hearing, the supreme court shall appoint an ad hoc judge to hear the motion to recuse, and only the ad hoc judge to whom the motion is assigned shall have the power and authority to act in the cause pending disposition of the motion.

xv. The articles on recusal of a supreme court justice or court of appeal judge have also been updated. Motions to recuse court of appeal judges shall be heard by an ad hoc judge appointed by the supreme court rather than the other judges on the panel or all of the judges sitting en banc. And if a court of appeal judge is recused, the court shall randomly allot another of its judges to sit on the panel in place of the recused judge.

xvi. Finally, the provisions on recusal of judges in city and parish courts and of justices of the peace have been updated for purposes of consistency.

II. Louisiana Code of Civil Procedure articles 1918, 1951, 2088 (Judgments and Appeals)

i. Act 259 of the 2021 Legislative Session amended several articles dealing with judgments, decretal language, amending judgments, and trial court jurisdiction after an order of appeal is signed. The amended articles are an attempt to overturn the recent practice of the courts of appeal to dismiss an appeal of a judgment that does not contain the proper decretal language. See St. Romain v. Delta S. Co., Inc., 2020-1252 (La. App. 1 Cir. 6/16/21), 2021 WL 2451713, at *4 (unpublished); Advanced Leveling & Concrete Sols. v. Lathan Co., Inc., 2017-1250 (La. App. 1 Cir. 12/20/18), 268 So.3d 1044, 1046.

ii. Louisiana Code of Civil Procedure article 1918 was amended to provide that a final judgment in accordance with C.C.P. art. 1841 (decides the merits of a case in whole or in part) must contain the proper decretal language. In the event the final judgment does not contain the proper decretal language, the court of appeal is authorized to remand the case to the trial court instead of dismissing the appeal. The court of appeal shall set a time period for the trial court to amend the judgment.

iii. Louisiana Code of Civil Procedure article 1918(A) as amended reads:

A final judgment in accordance with Article 1841 shall be identified as such by appropriate language; shall be signed and dated; and shall, in its decree, identify the name of the party in whose favor the relief is awarded, the name of the party against whom the relief is awarded, and the relief that is awarded. If appealed, a final judgment that does not contain the appropriate decretal language shall be remanded to the trial court, which shall amend the judgment in accordance with Article 1951 within the time set by the appellate court.

iv. Louisiana Code of Civil Procedure article 1951 was changed to clarify that a final judgment may be amended to correct any deficiency in the decretal language. This would allow a trial court to amend its judgment to add the proper decretal language in accordance with C.C.P. art. 1918. In those cases, the court of appeal would not be required to dismiss the appeal from a final judgment that lacks the proper decretal language. C.C.P. art. 1918 was further amended to retain the current law that the trial court cannot make a change to the substance of a final judgment. See Denton v. State Farm Mut. Auto. Ins. Co., 2008-0483 (La. 12/12/08), 998 So.2d 48, 52; Bourgeois v. Kost, 2002-2785 (La. 5/20/03), 846 So.2d 692, 695.

v. Louisiana Code of Civil Procedure article 1951 as amended reads:

> On motion of the court or any party, a final judgment may be amended at any time to alter the phraseology of the judgment or to correct deficiencies in the decretal language or errors of calculation. The judgment may be amended only after a hearing with notice to all parties, except that a hearing is not required if all parties consent or if the court or the party submitting the amended judgment certifies that it was provided to all parties at least five days before the amendment and that no opposition has been received. A final judgment may not be amended under this Article to change its substance.

vi. Louisiana Code of Civil Procedure article 2088 was also amended to add that after the jurisdiction of the appellate court attaches, the trial court retains jurisdiction to set attorney's fees, certify a partial judgment as appealable under C.C.P. art. 1915(B), and to amend a final judgment to provide the proper decretal language. The amendment to La. C.C.P. art. 2088 codifies the holding in In re Interdiction of Gambino, 2020-00312 (La. 6/3/20), 296 So.3d 1046 (per curiam), in which the Louisiana Supreme Court held that the trial court retained jurisdiction to certify a partial judgment under C.C.P. art. 1915(B) as a final, appealable judgment, even after the trial court had signed the order of appeal and the appeal was lodged with the court of appeal.)

III. Louisiana Code of Civil Procedure articles 5183 (In forma pauperis proceedings)

i. Act 416 of the 2021 Legislative Session amended C.C.P. art. 5183 in an attempt to clarify and to ensure consistent application of the in forma pauperis proceedings. The changes were drafted by the Louisiana State Law Institute and were requested by the Louisiana State Bar Association's access to Justice Committee. C.C.P. art. 5183(B)(1) requires the court to do one of three things with respect to an application to proceed in forma pauperis: grant the application, deny the application and provide written reasons for the denial, or set the matter for contradictory hearings. The revision is intended to address the problem of applications to proceed in forma pauperis being denied without explanation as to whether the reason for the denial is substantive (that the application does not qualify because the applicant's income or assets are too high) or procedural (that the application is deficient or does not contain enough information to make a determination).

ii. Louisiana Code of Civil Procedure article 5183(B)(1) as amended reads, in part:

> Upon the filing of the completed application and supporting affidavits, the court shall render an order that does one of the following:
>
> (a) Grants the application and allows the applicant to litigate or to continue the litigation without paying the costs in advance.

(b) Denies the application with written reasons for such denial.

(c) Sets the matter for a contradictory hearing.

iii. Louisiana Code of Civil Procedure article 5183(B)(2) was also amended to require the court to give written reasons if it finds that the presumption that the applicant is entitled to proceed in forma pauperis has been rebutted. C.C.P. art. 5183(B)(2) as amended reads:

The submission by the applicant of supporting documentation that the applicant is receiving public assistance benefits or that the applicant's income is less than or equal to one hundred twenty-five percent of the federal poverty level shall create a rebuttable presumption that the applicant is entitled to the privilege granted in this Chapter. If the court finds that the presumption has been rebutted, it shall provide written reasons for its finding.

iv. The revisions to C.C.P. art. 5185 provide that the party proceeding in forma pauperis has the right to have any judgment or order filed and to receive a certified copy of the judgment or order. Under present law, the party proceeding in forma pauperis is only entitled to obtain copies of pleadings, not orders or judgments. This revision is intended to address the problem of parties proceeding in forma pauperis being unable to obtain a copy of orders or judgments rendered in the case because the other party failed to pay the court costs. This issue often arises in family law cases and prevents the party proceeding in forma pauperis from, for example, obtaining a copy of the judgment of divorce. The proposed revisions also provide for the order to proceed in forma pauperis to be rescinded or to expire, since some courts provide for the expiration of the order within a certain period of time.

v. Louisiana Code of Civil Procedure article 5185(A)(4) as amended reads, in part:

A. When an order of court permits a party to litigate without the payment of costs until this order is rescinded or expires, the party is entitled to:

(4) The right to have any judgment or order filed and to receive one certified copy of the judgment or order.

IV. Louisiana Code of Civil Procedure articles 193, 194, 195, 863, 891, 1313 (Changes in Technology & Modernization of the Code of Civil Procedure; Attorneys shall provide an e-mail address)

i. Act 68 of the 2021 Legislative Session adopted several provisions drafted by the Louisiana Supreme Court's Technology Commission, which identified certain articles that needed to be updated and changed. The Louisiana State Law Institute studied the proposals and the proposed articles were adopted by the legislature.

ii. A major change was adopted in C.C.P. arts. 863 and 891, which will now require that pleadings including petitions contain an e-mail address of the attorney in addition to the physical and designated mailing address for service of process. However, a self-represented litigant with no e-mail address can continue to provide only a physical or designated mailing address for service. By requiring every attorney that files a pleading to include their e-mail address, C.C.P. art. 1313(C) was amended to allow the service of a pleading or order that sets a trial date by electronic means as long as the sender receives an electronic confirmation of delivery (which can be, but is not necessarily, a "read receipt"). This change is intended to ensure that parties receive notice of court dates as quickly as possible, which has become particularly important in light of the recent delays with mail and commercial courier services. However, if the requisite confirmation is not received, the sender will need to use one of the other alternatives provided by existing law (registered or certified mail, commercial courier, or service by the sheriff.)

iii. Louisiana Code of Civil Procedure article 1313(C) as amended reads:

> Notwithstanding Paragraph A of this Article, if a pleading or order sets a court date, then service shall be made by registered or certified mail or as provided in Article 1314, by actual delivery by a commercial courier, or by emailing the document to the email address designated by counsel or the party. Service by electronic means is complete upon transmission, provided that the sender receives an electronic confirmation of delivery.

iv. Act 68 revised C.C.P. art. 193 by removing outdated provisions allowing courts to call special sessions during vacation and requiring rules adopted by district courts to be printed in pamphlet form. The revisions to C.C.P. art. 194 allow certain orders and judgments that can be presently be signed by the district judge in chambers to be signed wherever the judge is physically located, including via electronic signature in accordance with existing provisions of the Code (C.C.P. arts. 253(C) and 1911(A)). The revisions to C.C.P. art. 195 allow any proceedings that can presently be conducted by the district judge in chambers to be conducted by audio-visual means. The revisions to C.C.P. art. 196.1 remove the limitation on a judge's power to sign orders and judgments while outside of the court's territorial jurisdiction only during emergencies and disasters, and instead allow this to occur at any time. These changes are intended to ensure that the Code of Civil Procedure is consistent with the current practices of district court judges, particularly in light of the challenges presented by the COVID-19 pandemic.

v. The revisions to R.S. 9:2603 remove an outdated reference to the UCC and extend the applicability of LUETA to family law cases, a change that has also become important in light of the COVID-19 pandemic. The repeal of C.C.P. art. 196 removes an outdated provision concerning the power of district courts to act "in vacation."

vi. The effective date of the changes provided for by Act 68 is January 1, 2022.

V. Louisiana Code of Civil Procedure articles 1701, 1702, 1702.1 (Elimination of Preliminary Defaults, Extension of time to file Responsive Pleading, and New Rules on Default Judgments)

i. In response to House Resolution 50 of the 2020 Legislative Session, a study was conducted by the Louisiana State Law Institute, which concluded that preliminary defaults serve little practical purpose and therefore should be eliminated. Act 174 of the 2021 Legislative Session adopts the proposals made by the Louisiana State Law Institute and repeals and deletes several articles to reflect the removal of the use of preliminary defaults. Louisiana Code of Civil Procedure article 1701 (preliminary defaults) was repealed in its entirety to eliminate the concept of preliminary defaults from the Code of Civil Procedure. Various other articles were amended to facilitate the elimination of the preliminary default. Louisiana Code of Civil Procedure article 1001 was amended to extend the time period within which the defendant must answer from fifteen to twenty-one days, which is consistent with the Federal Rules of Civil Procedure. If, however, a discovery request is served with the petition, the defendant would have thirty days within which to answer the petition and respond to the discovery request, a change that is intended to eliminate confusion, particularly for self-represented litigants, by making both time periods consistent. This change does not apply to answering in city, parish, or justice of the peace courts.

ii. Louisiana Code of Civil Procedure article 1001 as amended reads:

A. A defendant shall file his answer within twenty-one days after service of citation upon him, except as otherwise provided by law. If the plaintiff files and serves a discovery request with his petition, the defendant shall file his answer to the petition within thirty days after service of citation and service of discovery request.

B. When an exception is filed prior to answer and is overruled or referred to the merits, or is sustained and an amendment of the petition [is] ordered, the answer shall be filed within fifteen days after the exception is overruled or referred to the merits, or fifteen days after service of the amended petition.

C. The court may grant additional time for answering.

iii. Louisiana Code of Civil Procedure articles 1702, 4904, and 4921 were amended to establish the rules which must be followed to obtain a default judgment in district, city, parish, and justice of the peace courts. In all trial courts, if the defendant fails to answer or file other pleadings within the time prescribed by law, and the plaintiff establishes a prima facie case by competent and admissible evidence, a default judgment may be rendered in favor of the plaintiff.

iv. Under C.C.P. art. 1702, in district court, the competent and admissible evidence necessary to obtain a default judgment must be admitted on the record for a default judgment to be rendered. Louisiana Code of Civil Procedure article 1702 was further amended to provide notice to a party who fails to answer in the following cases:

i. If a party who fails to answer has made an appearance of record in the case, notice that the plaintiff intends to obtain a default judgment shall be sent by certified mail to counsel of record for the party, or if there is no counsel of record, to the party, at least seven days before a default judgment may be rendered.

ii. If an attorney for a party who fails to answer has contacted the plaintiff or the plaintiff's attorney in writing concerning the action after it has been filed, notice that the plaintiff intends to obtain a default judgment shall be sent by certified mail to the party's attorney at least seven days before a default judgment may be rendered.

iii. In cases involving delictual actions where neither Subparagraph (i) or (ii) of this Paragraph applies, notice that the plaintiff intends to obtain a default judgment shall be sent by regular mail to the party who fails to answer at the address where service was obtained at least seven days before a default judgment may be rendered.

(The new time periods are seven days, not the seven days exclusive of holidays which was the time period prior to the amendment)

v. R.S. 23:1316.1(A) was amended to make the changes in C.C.P. art. 1702 applicable to the workers' compensation cases.

vi. Louisiana Code of Civil Procedure article 1702 was also amended to provide for a special procedure to obtain a C.C. art. 103(1) divorce. The article provides that if the defendant by sworn affidavit acknowledges receipt of a certified copy of the petition for divorce and waives formal citation, service of process, all legal delays, notice of trial, and appearance at trial, a default judgment may be entered against the defendant, two days, exclusive of legal holidays, after the affidavit is filed.

vii. Other technical changes were made to various articles and revised statutes to eliminate the preliminary default and confirmation of default language.

viii. The effective date of these changes is January 1, 2022.

VI. Louisiana Code of Civil Procedure articles 1702, 4904, 4921, 927(B), and Louisiana Civil Code article 3452 (Prescription Sua Sponte)

i. Act 259 of the 2021 Legislative Session made changes to the Code of Civil Procedure and the Civil Code to allow the trial court to raise the issue of prescription sua sponte in certain limited situations. The proposed changes were made in response to concurrent resolutions asking the Louisiana State Law Institute to study the issue of third-party debt collectors suing on prescribed debts and the court being powerless to raise the prescription objection. Louisiana Code of Civil Procedure article 1702 was amended to allow the court to raise an objection of prescription before entering a final default judgment when the demand is based upon a right by assignment in an open account, promissory note, or other negotiable instrument. Evidence that the demand is prescribed should appear in the pleadings or evidence submitted. Once the court raises the prescription objection, the default judgment shall not be entered until the plaintiff presents prima facie proof that the action is not barred by prescription. Upon the plaintiff's request, the court shall hold a hearing for the submission of proof. The comments add that the court is only authorized to deny the request for a default judgment, but is not to dismiss the case.

ii. Louisiana Code of Civil Procedure article 1702(D) as amended reads:

> When the demand is based upon a right acquired by assignment in an open account, promissory note, or other negotiable instrument, the court may raise an objection of prescription before entering a default judgment if the grounds for the objection appear from the pleadings or from the evidence submitted by the plaintiff. If the court raises an objection of prescription, it shall not enter the default judgment unless the plaintiff presents prima facie proof that the action is not barred by prescription. Upon the plaintiff's request, the court shall hold a hearing for the submission of such proof.

iii. Louisiana Civil Code article 3452 and Louisiana Code of Civil Procedure article 927(B) were also amended to allow the objection of prescription to be raised sua sponte. Louisiana Code of Civil Procedure articles 4904 and 4921 made the provisions applicable in parish, city courts, and justice of the peace courts.

VII. Louisiana Code of Civil Procedure article 1561 (Consolidation)

i. Act 259 amended C.C.P. art. 1561 to allow the consolidation of cases for trial and other limited purposes such as discovery. The prior article did not allow cases to be consolidated only for discovery purposes. See Boh v. James Indus. Contractors, L.L.C., 2003-1211 (La. App. 4 Cir. 2/11/04), 868 So.2d 180, writ denied, 2004-0456 (La. 3/5/04), 869 So.2d 801.

ii. Louisiana Code of Civil Procedure article 1561(A) as amended reads, in part:

> When two or more separate actions are pending in the same court, the section or division of the court in which the first filed action is pending may order consolidation of the actions for trial or other limited purposes after a contradictory hearing[.]

iii. Louisiana Code of Civil Procedure article 253.2 was also amended to reflect that a consolidation of cases may be for trial or other limited purposes.

VIII. Louisiana Code of Civil Procedure articles 1793, 1795 (Jury Trials)

i. Louisiana Code of Civil Procedure article 1793 was amended by Act 259 to delete the previous language that the jury could receive "any object or document received in evidence when a physical examination thereof is required ... ." This provision was in error and conflicted with C.C.P. art. 1794(B), which stated that "the court may allow the jury to take with them any object or writing received in evidence, except depositions and except as otherwise provided in the Louisiana Code of Evidence."

ii. Louisiana Code of Civil Procedure article 1795 was also amended to clarify that when the jury retires for deliberation and later requests review of certain testimony, the jury must be "... conducted to the courtroom. After giving notice to the parties, the court may have the requested testimony read to the jury."

IX. Louisiana Code of Civil Procedure articles 1974, 4907 (Delay for New Trial)

i. A technical amendment was made by Act 259 to C.C.P. art. 1974 to eliminate any prior confusion or misinterpretation, and to clarify that "[a] party may file a motion for new trial not later than seven days, exclusive of legal holidays, after the clerk has mailed or the sheriff has served the notice of judgment as required by article 1913."

X. Louisiana Code of Civil Procedure article 5001 (Appeals from Baton Rouge City Court)

i. Louisiana Code of Civil Procedure article 5001 was amended by Act 259 to eliminate the provision that appeals from the Baton Rouge City Court would be filed in the Nineteenth Judicial District. With the amendment, appeals from all city courts in the state shall now be taken to their respective appellate courts.

XI. Louisiana Code of Civil Procedure article 592 (Class Actions)

i. A technical amendment was made to C.C.P. art. 592 by Act 259 to remove the prohibition against the court resolving determinative motions and exceptions prior to the certification of the class. Now, the court, in accordance with prior jurisprudence, may hear and decide motions and exceptions, which are dispositive of common and determinative issues, prior to the certification of the class. See Cooper v. CVS Caremark Corp., 2014-1797 (La. App. 1 Cir. 6/17/15), 176 So.3d 422.

XII. Louisiana Revised Statutes 13:3661 (Witness Fees)

i. R.S. 13:3661 was amended by Act 259 to increase the witness fees for their travel expenses "at a rate equal to the rate in effect for state officials" and "an attendance fee of fifty dollars for each day that the witness is required to appear in court." The statute was also amended to provide that "in cases of exceptional hardship, the court may increase the travel expenses paid to the witness."

XIII. Louisiana Code of Civil Procedure article 893 (Pleading of Damages)

i. Louisiana Code of Civil Procedure article 893 was amended by Act 259 to allow the court to award attorney fees and costs against the person who signed the petition, the party on whose behalf the petition was filed, or both. Before the amendment, attorney fees and costs could only be awarded against the party who filed the petition. This amendment is intended to make the imposition of attorney fees and costs consistent with C.C.P. arts. 893 and 863.

XIV. Louisiana Code of Civil Procedure article 1352 (Restriction on Subpoena)

i. Louisiana Code of Civil Procedure article 1352 was amended by Act 259 to allow witnesses who are subpoenaed to get paid in accordance with R.S. 13:3661 regardless of whether they live more than twenty-five miles from the courthouse.

XV. Louisiana Code of Civil Procedure articles 2254, 2721 (Seizures)

i. Act 259 also made technical amendments to C.C.P. arts. 2254 and 2721 to remove the outdated reference to Chapter 9 of the Louisiana Commercial laws.

XVI. Louisiana Code of Civil Procedure article 3943 (Appeal from Judgments in Support cases)

i. Louisiana Code of Civil Procedure article 3943 was amended by Act 259 to clarify that the appeal from a judgment awarding, modifying, or denying custody shall be taken only within thirty days from the expiration of the delay for applying for a new trial or judgment notwithstanding the verdict or the date of the mailing of the notice of the court's denying the motion. Prior to the amendment, there was a question as to whether the delay for filing an appeal from a judgment denying a request for support was thirty or sixty days.

XVII. Louisiana Code of Civil Procedure article 3947 (Name Confirmation)

i. Louisiana Code of Civil Procedure article 3947 was amended by Act 259 to make clear that an order confirming the name of a person in a divorce proceeding applied to all spouses and not only to a married woman.

XVIII. Louisiana Code of Civil Procedure article 80 (Action Involving Immovable Property)

i. A technical amendment to C.C.P. art. 80 by Act 259 removed the phrase, "except as provided in article 72" since a defendant can no longer convert a personal action into an in rem action by objecting to venue.

XIX. Miscellaneous Changes to the Code of Civil Procedure

i. Louisiana Code of Civil Procedure article 4912(A)(3) was amended by Act 25 to provide that a justice of the peace shall have jurisdiction over suits for possession and ownership of a manufactured home, as defined by R.S. 9:1149.2, not exceeding five thousand dollars in value. R.S. 9:3259.2 was added to include detailed provisions for a privilege for unpaid lease payments, abandoned manufactured homes and abandoned movable property. A special procedure was enacted for the enforcement of this privilege. Definitions were included for abandoned manufactured home, manufactured homes, and abandoned movable property.

ii. Louisiana Code of Civil Procedure article 4843(H) was amended by Act 251 to increase the civil jurisdiction of the City Court of Sulphur to fifty thousand dollars.

iii. Louisiana Code of Civil Procedure article 4566 was amended by Act 163 to specifically provide that a curator shall have authority to access deposit accounts in the name of the interdict and the authority to establish and maintain deposit accounts in the name of the 'curator on behalf of the interdict' unless expressly prohibited by the letters of curatorship.

iv. Louisiana Code of Civil Procedure article 2331 was amended by Act 264 to add that if a judicial sale of immovable property is cancelled or postponed and rescheduled for a later date, notice of the sale of the property under a writ of fieri facias shall be published only once (as opposed to twice in the original publication).

v. Payment of Interpreter—C.C.P. art. Article 192.2(B) (Act 207 of the 2021 Legislative Session)

- **i.** Notwithstanding any other provision of the law to the contrary, the court shall order payment to the interpreter for his service at a fixed reasonable amount, and that amount shall be paid out of the appropriate court fund.

vi. Partition by Licitation or by Private Sale—C.C. art. 811, C.C.P. arts. 4607, 4622, 4624, 2625

- **i.** Act 27 of the 2021 Legislative Session made changes to C.C. art. 811 by amending it to make it mandatory on the court to order a partition by private sale even if the co-owners are absentees or have not consented to the partition by private sale. The article further requires that first priority to the private sale shall be between the existing owner of the property as of date of the petition for partition is filed. Louisiana Code of Civil Procedure article 4607 was amended to provide that when the partition is made by private sale without the consent of all co-owners, the sale shall be for the appraised value of the property and the sale documents shall be executed on behalf of the absentee or nonconsenting co-owner by a court appointed representative.
- **ii.** Louisiana Code of Civil Procedure article 4622 was amended to provide that the partition for private sale between co-owners shall have "first priority status" and shall identify if the purchaser is a co-owner or a third-party.

vii. Small Succession—C.C.P. art. 3434 (Act 44 of the 2021 Legislative Session)

- **i.** Article 3434 adopts the amendment to R.S. 6:325(E) that authorizes a small succession affidavit to constitute "full and sufficient authority for the payment or delivery of any money or property, including property held in a safety deposit box" to the heirs, legatees, or a surviving spouse of the deceased customer. The statute further provides that no person shall have a "right or cause of action against the bank paying the money or delivery the property pursuant to ... this Subsection."

CIVIL JUSTICE REFORM ACT

I. Civil Justice Reform Act of 2020

(Act 37–2020 First Extraordinary Session) The Act shall become effective January 1, 2021 and shall not apply to causes of action arising or pending prior to January 1, 2021.

1. La. C.C.P. art. 1732 (lowers the jury threshold to $10,000.00)

A. A trial by jury shall not be available in:

1. A suit where the amount of no individual petitioner's cause of action exceeds $10,000.00 dollars exclusive of interest and costs, except as follows:

a. If the petitioner judicially admits 60 days or more that his claim does not exceed $10,000.00.

b. If the petitioner stipulates or judicially admits less than 60 days before trial that his cause of action does not exceed $10,000.00, any other party may retain the right to a jury trial if they had otherwise complied with the requirements for a jury trial.

c. If, as a result of a dismissal or compromise, a petitioner stipulates within 60 days of trial his claim is less than $10,000.00, a remaining defendant is not entitled to a jury trial.

B. The rules in paragraph (1) above apply to delictual or quasi-delictual cases in suits commenced in a parish or city court. (Other cases may be heard in Parish or City Courts up to their jurisdictional limits.)

2. La. C.C.P. art. 1733 (cash deposit for cases between $10,000.00 and $50,000.00)

(2)(a) In a suit for damages arising from a delictual or quasi-delictual action where an individual petitioner stipulates or otherwise judicially admits that his cause of action exceeds $10,000.00 and is less than $50,000.00, a party may obtain a trial by jury by filing a pleading demanding a trial by jury and providing a cash deposit of $5,000.00 no later than 60 days after filing the request for a trial by jury. Failure to post the cash deposit as required by this Subparagraph shall constitute a waiver of the trial by jury. This cash deposit shall be subject to Article 1734.1(E).

(b) When the case is set for trial, the court may additionally provide for a supplemental bond or cash deposit in accordance with Article 1734 or 1734.1.

(If the claim is valued over $50,000.00, presumably the rules of La. C.C.P. arts. 1734 and 1734.1 would apply for posting a bond or cash deposit.)

3. La. C.C.P. art. 4873 (Transfer to District Court for jury trial)

A. A party entitled thereto under the provisions of Article 4872 may transfer the action to the district court in the following manner:

1. Within the delay allowed for answer in the trial court of the limited jurisdiction, or within ten days after an answer has been filed, he shall file a motion to transfer with the clerk of court in which the suit is pending. The motion shall include a declaration that the matter is one to which the defendant would have been entitled to trial by jury if commenced in district court, and the defendant desires trial by jury. If a party fails to file a motion to transfer within the delays required by this paragraph, the matter shall not be transferred.

4. Code of Evidence Article 411 (Evidence of Liability Insurance)

B. The existence of insurance coverage shall not be communicated to the jury unless one of the following apply:

1. A factual dispute related to an issue of coverage is an issue which the jury will decide.

2. The existence of insurance would be admissible to attack the credibility of a witness pursuant to Code of Evidence art. 607.

3. Cause of action is brought against the insurer only when permitted by the direct action statute or is a bad faith claim.

C. The identity of the insurer shall not be communicated to the jury unless the identity of the insurer would be admissible to attack the credibility of the witness.

At the opening and closing of a jury trial against an insurer under the direct action statute or for a bad faith claim, the court shall read instructions to the jury that there is insurance coverage for the damages claimed by the plaintiff.

5. Collateral Source (La. R.S. 9:2800.27 - The 40% Rule)

A. Past medical expenses

1. Where medical expenses have been paid, in whole or in part, by a health insurer or Medicare, the plaintiff's recovery is limited to the amount actually paid to the healthcare provider by the health insurer or Medicare plus any co-pay or deductible paid or owed by the claimant and in addition to this amount, the court shall award 40% of the difference between the amount billed by the provider and the amount paid by the insurer unless the defendant proves that recovery of this amount would make the award unreasonable. The stated purpose of the 40% award is to compensate the plaintiff for the loss of procurement of the insurance.

2. The recovery of past medical expenses other than by a health insurer or Medicare shall be limited to the amounts paid to the medical provider by or on behalf of the claimant and any amounts remaining owed to a medical provider (including amounts subject to a lien).

3. In a jury trial, the jury shall be informed only of the amount billed by a medical provider for medical treatment. Whether any person, health insurance insurer or Medicare has paid or has agreed to pay, in whole or in part, any of a claimant's medical expenses, shall not be disclosed to the jury.

a. After the jury's verdict is rendered, the court may receive evidence related to the limitations of recoverable past medical expenses provided for in Subsection B (the 40% rule for Medicare and medical insurance) or subsection D (actual amounts actually paid and amounts remaining owed).

b. In a judge trial, the court may consider such evidence during the trial.

4. This provision does not apply to the Governmental Liability Act or Medical Malpractice Act.

5. Repeal of La. R.S. 32:295.1(E) (Evidence of wearing a seatbelt allowed).

La. R.S. 32:295.1(E) did not allow the failure to wear a seatbelt to be considered as evidence of comparative fault or to be admitted to mitigate damages. This provision has been repealed.

GOVERNOR'S PROCLAMATIONS AND SUPPLEMENTAL ORDER EXTENDING DEADLINES 2021

I. Proclamation Number JBE 170-2021

A. Legal

Legal deadlines applicable to legal proceedings in all courts, administrative agencies, and boards, are hereby suspended until September 24, 2021, including, but not limited to, any such deadlines set forth by law within the following:

1) Louisiana Civil Code;

2) Louisiana Code of Civil Procedure;

3) Louisiana Children's Code;

4) Title 9 of Louisiana Revised Statutes, Civil Code Ancillaries;

5) Title 13 of the Louisiana Revised Statutes, Courts and Judicial Procedure

The provisions of this section shall not suspend any prescriptive, preemptive (preemptive) or abandonment time periods over which the Louisiana Supreme Court has suspension authority pursuant to C.C.P. arts. 562, 3472.1, and C.C. art. 3472.1.

II. Supreme Court order dated August 31, 2021

A. Acting under the authority of Louisiana Civil Code Article 3472.1 and Louisiana Code of Civil Procedure Article 562, and considering the state of emergency declared statewide by Governor John Bel Edwards as a result of then-Tropical Storm Ida in Proclamation 165 JBE 2021 on August 26, 2021 and the catastrophic damage that Hurricane IDA has caused in the state,

IT IS HEREBY ORDERED THAT:

1. <u>Emergency suspension of prescription and preemption</u>: All prescriptive and preemptive periods are hereby suspended statewide for a period of thirty days commencing form the Governor's August 26, 2021 declaration of state emergency.

2. <u>Emergency suspension of abandonment</u>: All periods of abandonment are hereby suspended statewide for thirty days commencing from the Governor's August 26, 2021 declaration of state emergency.

(Note: In both C.C. art. 3472.1 and C.C.P. art. 562, the right to file any pleading subject to suspension shall terminate 60 days after the termination of suspension.)

2021 RECENT DEVELOPMENTS

I. ARTICLES 2 AND 925(6) – LACK OF SUBJECT MATTER JURISDICTION

Ballard v. Ballard, 321 So.3d 517 (La. App. 2 Cir. 5/26/21).

Monroe City Court lacks subject matter jurisdiction to determine an eviction proceeding where the court must determine real rights in immovable property. Under La. C.C.P. art. 4847(a)(1), the city court has no jurisdiction in a case involving the title to immovable property. The objection to the lack of subject matter jurisdiction may be raised at any stage of the action even by the Court of Appeal on its own motion.

See also LeCompte v. St. Tammy Parish School Board, 2020-0333 (La. App. 1 Cir. 4/26/21), 2021 WL 1609241, which held that the Office of Workers' Compensation has original subject matter jurisdiction to hear the merits of a workers' compensation claim from a teacher/coach/athletic director who claimed he was injured by mold-exposure at his workplace at Mandeville High School.

II. ARTICLE 44 – VENUE

Ameriprint, LLC v. Canon Solutions America, Inc., 21-94 (La. App. 5 Cir. 5/24/21), 2021 WL 2093283.

A forum selection clause in a lease agreement was enforceable. Even though Article 44 states that an objection to venue may not be waived prior to the institution of suit, the Louisiana Supreme Court has made it clear that forum selection clauses are not per se violative of public policy. *Shelter Mut. Ins. Co. v. Rimkus Consulting Grp., Inc. of La.*, 2013-1977 (La. 7/1/14), 148 So.3d 871, 881. They are favored because they eliminate uncertainties regarding the location of the litigation. The Court emphasized that forum selection clauses are unenforceable only in "very limited circumstances." *Creekstone Juban I, L.L.C. v. XL Ins. Am., Inc.*, 2018-0748 (La. 5/8/19), 282 So.3d 1042, 1048. When consent to the forum selection clause is called into question, the party challenging the forum selection clause as adhesionary must prove that the non-drafting party did not consent to the terms or any consent was vitiated by error.

Deaville v. Exxon Mobil Corp., 2021-0240 (La. App. 4 Cir. 5/3/21), 319 So.3d 381.

Plaintiff sued twenty defendants for occupational exposure to asbestos, which led to his developing mesothelioma. Over a month before trial, plaintiff filed a motion to voluntarily dismiss claims against one Orleans Parish defendant without prejudice, and the court granted the motion. The night before trial, plaintiff's counsel emailed a motion for partial dismissal, moving to dismiss claims against the only remaining defendant with a registered office in Orleans Parish. The trial court granted the motion. Defendant Exxon filed a declinatory exception raising the objection of improper venue and a motion to transfer. Exxon argued that the dismissed defendants had been sued only as a basis for establishing proper venue in Orleans Parish. The trial court denied the motion and overruled the exception, holding that plaintiff's claims against the dismissed defendant were compromised by an agreement to dismiss in exchange for a waiver of costs. La C.C.P. art. 73(B) provides as follows: "If the action against this defendant is compromised prior to judgment, or dismissed after a trial on the merits, the venue shall remain proper as to the other defendants, unless the joinder was made for the sole purpose of establishing venue as to the other defendants." The Fourth Circuit reversed and held that the claims against the dismissed Orleans Parish defendants were not compromised. Defendants were dismissed without prejudice. There were no settlement documents as to the two dismissed Orleans Parish defendants. The court held that the alleged agreement for waiver of court costs included in the motion to dismiss was inadequate to establish a compromise. The motion provided only that each party would bear its own costs. Finding no compromises, the exception to the general venue rules provided by La. C.C.P. art. 73(B) was inapplicable, and venue was improper in Orleans Parish.

III. ARTICLE 532 – MOTION TO STAY

Loeb v. Vergara, 2020-0261 (La. App. 4 Cir. 1/27/21), 313 So.3d 346, *writ denied*, 2021-00314 (La. 4/20/21), 313 So.3d 1257.

La. C.C.P. art. 532 applies when a suit is filed in another state or in federal court first, and then an action is filed in a Louisiana state court. Unlike article 531 (lis pendens, where two suits are pending in Louisiana courts), article 532 does not permit the Louisiana court to dismiss the action; rather, it grants the court discretion to stay the Louisiana lawsuit until the first-filed action has been discontinued or brought to a final judgment.

IV. ARTICLE 561 – ABANDONMENT

Williams v. Mongomery, 2020-01120 (La. 5/13/21), 2021 WL 1921078, *reh'g denied* (La. 6/29/21).

Plaintiff filed a petition for slip-and-fall damages against defendant and her insurer on May 2, 2014. Plaintiff requested service on the insurer, but service was withheld on the individual while the parties negotiated. Defendant insurer filed an answer to plaintiffs' petition for damages on February 2, 2017. On August 8, 2017, defendant insurer filed a motion for abandonment and requested that the trial court enter a formal order of dismissal as to the other defendant—its insured—because plaintiff took no formal step in the prosecution of her action against the insured in the trial court for more than three years. The trial court granted the motion to dismiss the claim as abandoned. The Court of Appeal reversed. The Supreme Court reversed the Court of Appeal and found that service and an answer on one defendant did not interrupt the running of the three-year abandonment period on the unserved defendants. The Court found that there is a logical distinction between served and unserved defendants because "[i]mplicit in the abandonment jurisprudence is the necessity of notice and the right of a defendant to adequately defend himself." The court further noted that the dismissal of the suit on the basis of abandonment was without prejudice. The Court remanded the matter to the trial court to determine if the action against the dismissed defendant was prescribed since a suit against one solidary or joint defendant interrupts prescription as to all defendants. La. C.C. art. 1799.

Jacobs v. Metzler-Brenckle, 2020-0585 & 2020-0607 (La. App. 4 Cir. 5/26/21), 2021 WL 2134299.

A motion to set a status conference is a step in the prosecution of an action that stops the tolling of the abandonment period. The court found that "motions to set status conferences are likewise attempts to hasten the matter to judgment because the motions specify that the purpose of the status conferences is to have the trial court set pretrial deadlines and select a trial date." This is so regardless of whether the conference is held.

Provenza v. City of Bossier City, 54,002 (La. App. 2 Cir. 6/30/21), 2021 WL 2677824.

An ex parte motion to continue a trial, without a date, is not a step in the prosecution of the action that interrupts abandonment. The Second Circuit held that it was joining the First, Third, and Fifth Circuits and declining to follow the Fourth Circuit. The Court reasoned that a "step" is a formal action before the trial court intended to hasten the action to judgment or the taking of formal discovery. Continuance of a case without date, even if the motion is joint or unopposed, does not hasten the action to judgment.

V. ARTICLE 861 – PLEADING SPECIAL DAMAGES

St. Germain v. St. Germain, 2020-0146 (La. App. 4 Cir. 3/17/21), 315 So.3d 443.

The trial court awarded Mr. St. Germain damages from being excluded from the enjoyment of using a co-owned home. The Court of Appeal reversed and found that the claim for damages for the loss of the use of the home was a claim for special damages. La. C.C.P. art. 861 requires that special damages be specifically pleaded. In this case, the ex-husband admitted that he did not specifically plead the item of damages for loss of use and enjoyment of the home but his ex-wife was on notice of the claim because it was included in his pre-trial memorandum and his descriptive list. Noting that a memorandum or a detailed descriptive list are not pleadings in accordance with La. C.C.P. art. 852, the court held that Mr. St. Germain did not specifically plead his claim for damages and reversed the award of the trial court.

VI. ARTICLE 925(5) – OBJECTION OF LACK OF PERSONAL JURISDICTION

Robinson v. Jeopardy Prods., Inc., 2019-1095 (La. App. 1 Cir. 10/21/20), 315 So.3d 273, *writ denied*, 2020-01343 (La. 1/20/21), 308 So.3d 1166.

The gameshow Jeopardy's principal place of business is in California. The Secretary of the Louisiana Department of Revenue sued to collect corporate and franchise taxes from the nonresident television production company. Jeopardy contracted with two third parties that negotiated the broadcasting of the "Jeopardy!" game show at television stations across the United States, as well as agreements for merchandise reflecting the Jeopardy trademark or logo. Jeopardy had no contacts with Louisiana, but the two third parties did. Jeopardy filed the declinatory exception raising the objection of lack of personal jurisdiction. The trial court granted the exception, noting that "Jeopardy had no physical presence in Louisiana; Jeopardy made no business decisions in Louisiana; Jeopardy did not carry out any direct business activity in Louisiana; Jeopardy had no employees in Louisiana; and Jeopardy did not render any services in Louisiana." The Court of Appeal affirmed. The Court of Appeal discussed specific and general jurisdiction under the Louisiana long-arm statute and concluded that plaintiff failed to prove any minimum contacts of defendant with Louisiana. The court observed that Jeopardy had "zero contacts" with Louisiana other than the contacts of the third parties with whom it contracted. The court found neither general nor specific jurisdiction applied. "[T]he random, fortuitous, and attenuated contacts with Louisiana, that were initiated by the independent activities of third parties, were simply not sufficient to establish personal jurisdiction over Jeopardy in Louisiana."

VII. ARTICLE 926(1) – OBJECTION OF PRESCRIPTION (FAX-FILING)

Petit-Blanc v. Charles, 2021-00094 (La. 4/20/21), 313 So.3d 1245 (per curiam).

In an automobile accident case, the Clerk of Court received plaintiff's petition by facsimile on November 13, 2019. The Clerk of Court subsequently received the original petition and the accompanying filing fee on November 25, 2019. Defendant filed the peremptory exception of prescription based on noncompliance with the fax-filing statute, which requires that the original be delivered to the Clerk of Court within seven (7) days of receipt of the fax-filing.

Plaintiff argued that she mailed the original petition to the Clerk of Court on November 14, 2019, and it must have been delivered to the Clerk of Court sometime before November 25. The Court of Appeal held that the original petition was not timely delivered to the Clerk of Court within the meaning of the Louisiana fax-filing statute when it was mailed at some time and then received by the Clerk of Court 12 days after the fax-filing. The fax-filing statute, La. R.S. 13:850(B) as amended in 2016, requires delivery of the original pleading to the Clerk of Court within seven (7) days, exclusive of holidays, of the facsimile transmission. The Court explained, "Considering the 2016 amendment to the statute, we must conclude merely transmitting an original document within the deadline is insufficient; rather, the litigant must establish the document was delivered to the clerk within the deadline." In this case, plaintiff could not establish that the Clerk of Court was in actual or constructive possession of the original at any time prior to November 25.

Davis v. State through Louisiana Racing Commission, 2020-01020 (La. 5/13/21), 2021 WL 1920976, *reh'g denied*, 2020-01020 (La. 6/29/21).

In a suit against the state, plaintiff failed to request service within 90 days and the suit was dismissed for insufficient service of process. Plaintiff filed his second suit before dismissal of the first. Defendant filed an objection of prescription. Generally, La. C.C. arts. 3462 and 3463 provide that prescription is interrupted when the action is commenced, and interruption continues as long as the suit is pending. However, the more specific provision, La. R.S. 13:5107(D)(3), provides that when a suit against the state is dismissed for failure to request service within 90 days, the running of prescription against the state, state agency, or political subdivision is not interrupted or suspended. Therefore, the Supreme Court held that the case was prescribed.

Three justices dissented: Justices Hughes, Genovese, and Griffin. Justice Hughes wrote that "[g]enerally, prescription statutes are strictly construed against prescription and in favor of the claim sought to be extinguished by it; thus, of two possible constructions, that which favors maintaining, as opposed to barring an action, should be adopted."

Hawthorne v. Norfolk Southern Corp., 2020-0439 (La. App. 4 Cir. 4/28/21), 2021 WL 1679305.

Plaintiff fax-filed petition on October 9, 2019. She mailed the original hard copy of the petition to the Clerk of Court on October 15, 2019, and the Clerk of Court received the original on October 30, 2019. Defendant filed an objection of prescription, and the trial court granted it. The Court of Appeal affirmed, finding that plaintiff's mailing of the original petition failed to satisfy the requirement of La. R.S. 13:850(B) that the original be "delivered" to the Clerk of Court within seven days of the date of the fax-filing. Under the fax-filing statute, the term "shall be delivered" requires that the Clerk of Court be in possession of the original petition. Under that interpretation, the petition was not delivered to the Clerk of Court until October 30, 2019, and the prior fax-filing had no force or effect and did not interrupt prescription. Plaintiff's claim prescribed before the filing of her original petition.

VIII. ARTICLE 926(1), 1153 – OBJECTION OF PRESCRIPTION (RELATING BACK)

Watson v. Woldenberg Village, Inc., 2020-0453 (La. App. 4 Cir. 7/7/21), 2021 WL 2820469.

Plaintiff, administrator of the decedent's estate, filed wrongful death and survival actions against defendant assisted living/rehabilitation facility. Defendant filed the exception of no right of action, contending that the administrator of the estate had no right to bring wrongful death and survival actions. In response, plaintiff filed an amended petition that named the decedent's children as the proper plaintiffs. Defendant filed the peremptory exception of prescription regarding the amended petition naming the children as plaintiffs. The trial court granted both exceptions. The Court of Appeal affirmed, holding that in accordance with the Louisiana Supreme Court in order for an amending petition to relate back under La. C.C.P. art. 1153, the original petition must contain a legally viable claim in order for the late-filed pleading to relate back. Since plaintiff lacked a right of action to bring in the original petition, there was no legally viable claim to which the late-filed claim could relate back (citing Naghi v. Brener, 2008-2527 (La. 6/26/09), 17 So.3d 919, 925).

IX. ARTICLE 927(1) – OBJECTION OF PRESCRIPTION

Medical Review Panel for Claim of Richard Bush, 2020-0468 (La. App. 4 Cir. 6/2/21), 2021 WL 2217464.

The Fourth Circuit found that *contra non valentem* discovery doctrine applied to both medical malpractice survival and wrongful death actions. Prior appellate court decisions conducted hearings to determine if the parties to the wrongful death action had enough information to timely file their claims without having to rely on *contra non valentem* to avoid prescription. The appellate court disagreed with the trial court's finding that the delay in bringing the survival action was reasonable, but the delay in bringing the wrongful death action was unreasonable. The court reasoned that it would be contradictory to have two different factual findings regarding when sufficient knowledge existed to commence the prescriptive period for each cause of action.

X. ARTICLE 927(4) – NONJOINDER OF A PARTY

Minot v. Waffle House, Inc., 2020-0444 (La. App. 4 Cir. 10/2/20), 2020 WL 5868328, *writ denied*, 2020-01277 (La. 1/12/21), 308 So.3d 714.

Decedent was shot and killed outside a Waffle House in New Orleans. Two wrongful death and survival actions were filed by different children of decedent—one in Georgia and one in Louisiana. In the Louisiana lawsuit, defendant filed the peremptory exception raising the objection of nonjoinder and a motion to dismiss based on *forum non conveniens*. The trial court overruled the exception and denied the motion. The Court of Appeal affirmed, holding that the wrongful death actions and right to damages were based on the relationship and the support derived from the father. Plaintiffs in Georgia would have distinct and separate evidence, and their nonjoinder in the Louisiana would not affect or prejudice their rights to seek damages. Furthermore, one of the Georgia plaintiffs was a Georgia resident and not subject to personal jurisdiction in Louisiana. A survival action is a separate and distinct cause of action from a wrongful death action. Joinder of all parties granted a right of action under La. C.C. art. 2315.1 in a single action is not required because a survival action is divisible among the beneficiaries. Because it is divisible, the beneficiaries may sue separately to recover their virile shares. Considering both the private interest and public interest factors, the court concluded that Orleans Parish was a more convenient forum than a Georgia court and the trial court correctly denied the motion.

Johnson v. Strange, 21-12 (La. App. 3 Cir. 6/9/21), 2021 WL 2350892.

Plaintiff sued defendant for money owed on a promissory note for the financing of land purchased by defendant. Defendant had bought the land from Mr. and Mrs. Duck. Mr. and Mrs. Duck divorced. Defendant paid the balance of $31,226.92 with a certified check made payable to Mr. Duck. Mr. Duck negotiated the check, marked the note "Paid in Full," and returned it to defendant who had the mortgage on the property cancelled. Thereafter, Mr. Duck's ex-wife (then Johnson) sued defendant, claiming that she had not received any of the balance paid to Mr. Duck and that she was owed $15,613.46. At trial, the court determined that the debt was divisible with each of the former spouses being owed half. The trial court awarded plaintiff $5,994.98, which was half the amount defendant owed for payments on the promissory note, which was not prescribed. The Court of Appeal found that the ex-husband was a party whose joinder was needed under La. C.C.P. art. 641. The court reasoned that neither plaintiff nor defendant could obtain full relief without the joinder of the ex-husband. This result was dictated by Louisiana's negotiable instruments law, which provides that on an instrument made payable to two persons, only the two acting together can enforce or negotiate the instrument. The court went on to decide that joinder of the ex-husband was feasible because the trial court could exercise personal jurisdiction over him. Because he was a necessary party, the judgment was a nullity, and the appellate court vacated the judgment and remanded for joinder of the absent party and retrial.

XI. ARTICLE 927(5) – OBJECTION OF NO CAUSE OF ACTION

Dodson & Hooks, APLC v. La. Community Development Capital Fund, Inc., 2020-01002 (La. 2/17/21), 310 So.3d 553 (per curiam).

Plaintiffs sued law firm for allegedly charging fees it had not earned, obtaining and recording a lien for nonpayment, and wrongfully refusing to remove the lien. The Court of Appeal affirmed the granting of the peremptory exception of no cause of action. The Supreme Court reversed and found that plaintiff stated a claim in tort. In deciding the objection of no cause of action, a "court reviews the petition and accepts well pleaded allegations of fact as true, and the issue at the trial of the exception is whether, on the face of the petition, the plaintiff is legally entitled to the relief sought." Based on that liberal standard, the Court held that plaintiff had alleged sufficient facts to state a cause of action.

Hovell v. Origin Bank, 2020-01417 (La. 3/2/21), 311 So.3d 340 (per curiam).

The Louisiana Credit Agreement Statute precludes actions for damages based on oral credit agreements. Plaintiff alleged, beyond the written loan documentation, that defendant bank was supposed to obtain additional collateral to secure a loan. Although plaintiff attached documents related to the sale and loan, there was no writing expressing the alleged agreement to secure additional collateral. Neither party alleged that such a written agreement existed. Because plaintiff's allegations were about an oral credit agreement, which was expressly prohibited by statute, the trial court properly granted defendant's exception of no cause of action.

Daniels v. State, 2020-0175 (La. App. 4 Cir. 10/21/20), 2020 WL 6156387, *writ denied*, 2021-00008 (La. 3/2/21), 311 So.3d 1055.

Putative class action by parents of high school students against Orleans Parish School Boards for elementary and secondary education. Plaintiffs asserted, in part, mismanagement of records and lack of oversight causing students not to be able to graduate on schedule. Defendant school boards filed peremptory exception raising the objection of no cause of action based on the affirmative defense of statutory immunity under La. R.S. 17:3993(B). The trial court granted the exception. The Court of Appeal reversed. In its reasoning, the court explained, "[T]he statute requires an analysis of the charter agreement, which was not attached to either petition, and cannot be considered on an exception of no cause of action." Defendants also argued that the exception could be sustained because the petition included no specific allegations implicating the school boards in any of the conduct plaintiffs alleged caused the claimed damages. The court rejected that argument: "[I]t does not appear beyond doubt that Plaintiffs can prove no set of facts in support of any claim which would entitle them to relief."

Cambre v. Cambre, 2020-0135 (La. App. 4 Cir. 10/21/20), 307 So.3d 243.

Putative class action by parents of high school students against Orleans Parish School Boards for elementary and secondary education. Plaintiffs asserted, in part, mismanagement of records and lack of oversight causing students not to be able to graduate on schedule. Defendant school boards filed peremptory exception raising the objection of no cause of action based on the affirmative defense of statutory immunity under La. R.S. 17:3993(B). The trial court granted the exception. The Court of Appeal reversed. In its reasoning, the court explained, "[T]he statute requires an analysis of the charter agreement, which was not attached to either petition, and cannot be considered on an exception of no cause of action." Defendants also argued that the exception could be sustained because the petition included no specific allegations implicating the school boards in any of the conduct plaintiffs alleged caused the claimed damages. The court rejected that argument: "[I]t does not appear beyond doubt that Plaintiffs can prove no set of facts in support of any claim which would entitle them to relief."

Parker v. Paladin Contractors, LLC, 2020-0492 (La. App. 4 Cir. 3/3/21), 314 So.3d 1128.

The Court of Appeal reversed the granting of a partial no cause of action objection. The Court of Appeal observed, "The jurisprudence of this state 'has long disfavored the granting of partial exceptions of no cause of action.' " In this case, the court found that "the operative facts of one transaction or occurrence give rise to [plaintiff's] right to assert the entire action." This case does not present a situation in which the granting of a partial objection of no cause of action is permissible. Therefore, the Court of Appeal reversed the trial court's judgment dismissing some, but not all, of plaintiff's causes of action. (This is contrary to the language in La. C.C.P. art. 1915(B)(1) "[w]hen a court ... sustains an exception in part, as to one or more but less than all of the claims, demands, issues, or theories against a party ... the judgment shall not constitute a final judgment unless it is designated as a final judgment by the court after an express determination that there is no just reason for delay.")

Beem v. Beem, 2020-0897 (La. App. 1 Cir. 4/20/21), 2021 WL 1540545

Generally, the exception is triable solely on the face of the petition and any attached documents, and no evidence may be introduced at any time to support or controvert the objection that the petition fails to state a cause of action. However, the jurisprudence recognizes an exception to this rule, which allows the court to consider evidence admitted without objection. In those instances, the pleadings are considered to have been enlarged.

XII. ARTICLE 927(6) – OBJECTION OF NO RIGHT OF ACTION

Rismiller v. Gemini Ins. Co., 2020-00313 (La. 6/30/21), 2021 WL 2679552, *rev'g*, 2020 WL 7310506 (La. 12/11/20).

Adult children of the decedent who were given in adoption when they were minors sued defendants in wrongful death and survival actions for the death of their biological father and biological half siblings. The trial court granted defendants' peremptory exception raising the objection of no right of action. The Supreme Court reversed and held that children given in adoption are not included in the list of those who can bring survival and wrongful death actions under La. C.C. arts. 2315.1 and 2315.2. The Supreme Court stated the following:

> [A]s a result of their adoption, in which "the adopting parent becomes the parent of the child for all purposes" and the previous "filiation between the child and his legal parent is terminated" (La. C.C. art. 199), and the plain text of La. C.C. arts. 2315.1 and 2315.2, plaintiffs have no right to assert a survival and wrongful death action in connection with the death of their biological father and half-siblings. Any relevant legal relationship

between the children given in adoption and the biological relatives whose deaths are the subject of these tort cases has been terminated.

Justice Griffin dissented and would have adhered to the Court's decision in the original hearing, reasoning as follows: "[W]hile both Articles expressly expand the term 'child or children of the deceased' to include children by adoption, there is no language excluding biological children of the deceased who were given in adoption."

XIII. ARTICLE 966, 967 – SUMMARY JUDGMENTS

A) EXPERT AFFIDAVITS

Sketchler v. Hernandez, 2020-01475 (La. 3/2/21), 311 So.3d 343 (per curiam)

Plaintiffs were in a vehicle on the interstate and were struck by another vehicle that crossed the median. One of the defendants sued by plaintiffs claimed that the vehicle that crossed the interstate rear-ended his vehicle and then crossed the median. Plaintiffs argued that defendant's vehicle swerved in front of that other vehicle on the shoulder causing it to cross the median and eventually collide with plaintiffs' vehicle. Defendant driver moved for summary judgment, and the trial court granted the summary judgment, reasoning that plaintiffs did not offer sufficient evidence to show that the accident was not a rear-end collision and that they did not rebut the presumption of fault on the following driver in the accident. On appeal, plaintiffs argued, in part, that the trial court erred in disregarding their expert's affidavit, on the ground that there was an insufficient basis for his opinion, without following the procedures in La. C.C.P. art. 1425(F). The expert was a registered professional civil engineer specializing in traffic and transportation engineering and accident reconstructionist. The Court of Appeal held that, even if the expert's affidavit was admissible and accepted as true, it did not create genuine issues of material fact that the defendant's actions contributed to the accident causing plaintiffs' injuries. Judge Holdridge dissented, reasoning that plaintiff's expert in his affidavit created a genuine issue of material fact by asserting that the defendant's movement to the left was a contributing factor in causing the median-crossing vehicle's driver to lose control. Thus, the trial court and the Court of Appeal majority could reach a conclusion that there was no genuine issue of material fact only by giving no credibility to the expert's affidavit. "While a trial court may totally disregard the opinion of an expert at the trial on the merits, this is not the rule for appellate courts in deciding a motion for summary judgment upon de novo review." The Supreme Court reversed based on the reasoning of Judge Holdridge in his Court of Appeal dissent:

> Per La. C.E. 702, the expert affidavits were provided by a competent expert, based on sufficient facts and data, utilizing reliable principles and methods, which the expert reliably applied to the facts of the case. We find that the affidavits and depositions produced by the applicant sufficiently proved the existence of genuine issues of material fact, precluding the granting of summary judgment.

Thomas v. Dalal, 2020-0065 (La. App. 3 Cir. 10/28/20), 306 So.3d 507.

In plaintiff's medical malpractice action, defendant filed a motion for summary judgment. In opposition to the motion, plaintiff filed several documents, including the affidavit of a doctor who stated that defendant did breach the standard of care and that breach caused the injury. Defendant argued that the doctor's affidavit was inadmissible because the doctor failed to identify the documents he reviewed in arriving at his opinion. The trial court granted summary judgment, dismissing all claims.

The Court of Appeal reversed and held that the trial court improperly granted the summary judgment. If an expert's summary judgment affidavit contains opinions that lack an adequate factual basis, are not sufficiently reliable, or are otherwise inadmissible, the opposing party must object to the affidavit. An objection to an affidavit is made in a timely filed reply memorandum. Defendant in this case did not object. If an opposing party fails to object to an expert's opinions, the trial court shall consider the expert's opinions. (La. C.C.P. art. 966(D)(2).) However, a court may consider an affidavit to which no objection is made and conclude that the affidavit is insufficient to defeat summary judgment. In this case, the doctor's affidavit did create a genuine issue of material fact on the issue of breach and causation.

Marks v. Schultz, 2020-0197 (La. App. 1 Cir. 12/10/20), 316 So.3d 534.

Plaintiff sued store for injuries when she caught her foot on a produce display and fell. Defendant merchant filed a motion for summary judgment, arguing that the display was not unreasonably dangerous because it was open and obvious. Plaintiff filed a memorandum in opposition with an expert's opinion in an affidavit that the condition was not open and obvious. The trial court heard the motion and granted summary judgment. The Court of Appeal reversed and held that: (1) the court cannot make credibility determinations on a motion for summary judgment; (2) the court must not attempt to evaluate the persuasiveness of competing scientific studies, and in performing its gatekeeping analysis, the court must focus solely on the principles and methodology, not on the conclusions they generate; (3) the court must draw those inferences from the undisputed facts which are most favorable to the party opposing the motion; and (4) most importantly, because summary judgments deprive the litigants of the opportunity to present their evidence to a jury, they should be granted only when the evidence presented at the motion for summary judgment, including admissible expert opinion evidence, establishes that there is no genuine issue of material fact in dispute. In this case, defendants did not challenge the qualifications, methodology or conclusions of customer's expert, nor did they raise objection to expert's affidavit. "[I]n the absence of an objection, the trial court is statutorily obligated to consider the expert's opinions under [La. C.C.P.] art. 966(D)(2). At that point, in determining whether the evidence creates a genuine issue of material fact, the trial court cannot make credibility determinations, evaluate testimony, or otherwise weigh the evidence.... The trial court must assume all affiants are credible...."

B) DOCUMENTS

Huggins v. Amtrust Ins. Co. of Kansas, Inc., 2020-0516 (La. App. 1 Cir. 12/30/20), 319 So. 3d 362.

In cross motions for summary judgment, the appellate record did not include the exhibits attached to affidavits, which were the evidence supporting the motion for summary judgment. The exhibits were insurance policies, which were in the record, but the appellate record did not clearly indicate that the exhibits were attached to the motion when it was filed in the trial court. Counsel for the moving party admitted that the exhibits were not in the appellate record but argued that they were in the trial court record from previous filings. The trial court granted the motion for summary judgment. The Court of Appeal reversed finding that the court could not consider exhibits that were not contained in the appellate record even though they may have been contained in connection with other pleadings in the trial court. La. C.C.P. art. 966(D)(2) clearly provides that the only documents that may be considered on summary judgment are documents filed in support of or in opposition to the motion. Accordingly, the Court of Appeal reversed the granting of summary judgment.

In a concurring opinion, it was noted that:

> When parties file cross motions for summary judgment, the parties are free to file a joint written stipulation in accordance with La. C.C.P. art. 966(A)(4), in which the parties would

stipulate that any documents filed in connection with a motion for summary judgment or opposition in one case may be used in the cross motion without the necessity of the party re-filing the same documents. A joint written stipulation would avoid the expense of re-filing the same documents, as well as allowing this court, in its *de novo* review, to consider all documents filed in both cross motions for summary judgment.

C) SUMMARY JUDGMENT DEADLINES

Bell v. Puyau, 2020-0265 (La. App. 1 Cir. 12/3/20), 318 So.3d 178.

The trial court granted a continuance on a motion for summary judgment. The trial court later granted summary judgment, apparently finding that plaintiff's expert's affidavit in opposition to summary judgment was not timely filed because it was filed after the original deadline. The Court of Appeal reversed, holding that under *Reed v. Restorative Home Health Care, LLC*, 2019-01974 (La. 2/26/20), 289 So.3d 1028, *reh'g denied*, 2019-01974 (La. 6/3/20), 296 So.3d 1064, the 15-day deadline for filing opposition documents and other deadlines reset when the trial court granted a continuance. Thus, the affidavit in opposition to summary judgment was timely filed and should have been considered.

D) CONTINUANCES

Francois v. Ports America La., LLC, 2020-0440 (La. App. 4 Cir. 3/10/21), 314 So.3d 894, *writ denied*, 2021-00496 (La. 6/1/21), 316 So.3d 830.

The trial court granted defendants' motion for summary judgment although plaintiff opposed the summary judgment, arguing that discovery was not complete and the defendants had not been cooperative in obtaining the discovery and identifying a person involved in the hit-and-run accident. The Court of Appeal reversed finding that La. C.C.P. art. 966 does not give a party an absolute right to delay a hearing on a summary judgment motion, but it does require that the parties be given a fair opportunity to present their case. The Fourth Circuit has identified the following factors to guide a court's exercise of its discretion: (1) whether the party was ready to go to trial; (2) whether the party indicated what additional discovery was needed; (3) whether the party took any steps to conduct additional discovery during the period between the filing of the motion and the hearing on it; and (4) whether the discovery issue was raised in the trial court before the entry of the summary judgment. (citing *Roadrunner Transportation Sys. v. Brown*, 2017-0040 (La. App. 4 Cir. 5/10/17), 219 So.3d 1265, 1273). Applying those factors, the Court of Appeal held that the trial court abused its discretion in hearing the motion rather than granting a continuance in a case in which no trial date had been set, defendants had not filed an answer, defendants' exception of vagueness had not been resolved, and no depositions had been taken. The Court of Appeal stated that "a scant nine months" had elapsed between the filing of the petition and the filing of the motion for summary judgment.

Laforge v. Golden Nugget Lake Charles, LLC, 2020-0110 (La. App. 3 Cir. 11/4/20), 307 So.3d 266.

Summary judgment motion was filed by alleged owners of casino seeking to dismiss negligence claim made by patron, who was allegedly injured when she fell in the casino. Plaintiff opposed the summary judgment and urged that the motion was premature because of insufficient time to conduct adequate discovery. The trial court granted summary judgment in favor of defendants. The Court of Appeal reversed, finding that the issues presented by patron's claims were not purely legal, and only limited discovery had been conducted. The patron was unable to conduct adequate discovery before the trial court heard alleged casino owner's motion for summary judgment. A continuance was justified prior to the trial court deciding a summary judgment motion in favor of owners, where no trial date had been set and litigation was pending in the trial court for less than three months, due to a remand from federal court, before the motion was filed; patron propounded discovery to all opposing parties upon receipt of the motion; responses to limited discovery revealed potential liability of the owners; and patron's opposition to the motion urged the need for additional discovery and documented how the ability to conduct discovery had been hampered.

State Farm Fire & Casualty Co. v. Dean Flores Real Estate, LLC, 2020-1087 (La. App. 1 Cir. 5/12/21), 2021 WL 1897088.

The trial court continued a summary judgment hearing due to the pandemic. The minute entry did not indicate, and the record did not show, that the parties were notified of the rescheduled hearing date. The trial court held the hearing, only the movant attended, and the trial court granted the partial summary judgment, dismissing the moving party. The Clerk of Court mailed notice of the judgment to the plaintiff, State Farm. State Farm filed a motion for new trial and to set aside the judgment with an attached affidavit of counsel stating that she did not receive notice of the rule resetting the motion for hearing. At the hearing, the trial court had the Clerk of Court verify that State Farm had been notified via mail of the rescheduled hearing and that the court had read the Notice of Rule on the record and made it part of the record. The appellate record did not include the Notice of Rule. The trial court denied the motion for new trial. State Farm appealed, claiming a violation of its procedural due process rights. The Court of Appeal reversed. In addition to proof that the moving party is entitled to summary judgment under the substantive law, the moving party must prove that it secured the judgment in accordance with procedural law. Although the minute entry from the hearing stated that the clerk served State Farm "via mail," it did not specify that the notice was sent via registered mail, certified mail, or a commercial courier as required by La. C.C.P. arts. 966(C) and 1313(C). Furthermore, although the minute entry indicated that the court made the notice part of the record, the appellate record did not include the notice of rule. Finally, although the minute entry indicated that the court read the notice of rule on the record, the appellate record did not include a transcript of the hearing documenting what the court read. The moving party had the burden to prove it was entitled to summary judgment, and it failed to prove that it obtained the judgment in accordance with procedural law. The Court of Appeal held that the trial court abused its discretion in denying the motion for new trial, reversed the partial summary judgment, and remanded.

E) SUBJECTIVE FACTS

Wroten v. Ferriday Auto Ventures, LLC, 2020-387 (La. App. 3 Cir. 12/16/20), 310 So.3d 621, *writ denied*, 2021-00085 (La. 3/9/21), 312 So.3d 585.

Plaintiff alleged that car dealership intentionally misrepresented material facts to get purchaser to sign agreement to purchase car. Insurer of dealership moved for summary judgment, arguing that there was no coverage because of the intentional act exclusion in the policy. The trial court granted the summary judgment, dismissing the insurance company. The Court of Appeal reversed, finding that "Summary judgment is rarely appropriate for disposition of a case requiring judicial determination of subjective facts such as intent, motive, malice, good faith, or knowledge." "[T]he issue of subjective intent is fact-intensive and is an issue to be determined by the totality of the circumstances examined on a case-by-case basis."

See also Priority Hospital Group, Inc. v. Manning, 53,564 (La. App. 2 Cir. 9/23/20), 303 So.3d 1106, *writ denied*, 2020-01238 (La. 1/20/21), 308 So.3d 1160. ("Summary judgment is seldom appropriate for determinations based on subjective facts of motive, intent, good faith, knowledge, or malice, yet it may be granted on such issues when no issue of material fact exists concerning the pertinent intent.").

Thompson v. Cenac Towing Co., L.L.C., 2019-1185 (La. App. 1 Cir. 3/25/21), 322 So.3d 852, *writ denied*, 2021-00766 (La. 10/1/21).

The trial court should assess plaintiff's credibility at a trial and not at summary judgment. Subjective facts such as knowledge, intent, fear, and emotional injuries that are personal to the party, and which require the trial court to make credibility determinations and weigh the evidence, are generally improper evidence upon which to grant summary judgment. It would be an improper use of summary judgment to determine the level of fear experienced by an African-American worker when seeing a noose on a tugboat upon which he would have to work for 28 days.

F) IMMUNITY

Simmons v. Hughes, 2019-1389 (La. App. 1 Cir. 11/25/20), 316 So.3d 488.

The trial court granted summary judgment finding that the police officers were not liable in a lawsuit against police officers and the city for use of excessive force by arresting police officers. The Court of Appeal affirmed, holding that under La. R.S. 9:2798.1, qualified immunity applies and prevents liability unless the officers' use of force constitutes "acts or omissions which constitute criminal, fraudulent, malicious, intentional, willful, outrageous, reckless, or flagrant misconduct." On a motion for summary judgment, after the mover has presented sufficient documentary evidence, the burden shifts to the plaintiff to show that there are genuine issues of fact that preclude qualified immunity from applying. Plaintiff presented no facts supporting the proposition that the police officers' conduct rose to the level required by the statute to defeat the immunity.

G) ISSUES OF FACT

Rivault v. American Homeland, LLC, 2021-00708 (La. 10/12/21), 2021 WL 4739310.

In a case involving whether building restrictions were still valid or had been abandoned, the Supreme Court reversed the trial court and the court of appeal and found that the defendant, American Homeland, had produced sufficient factual support to establish a genuine issue of fact with respect to the question of whether or not the building restrictions at issue were abandoned. The Court found that the court of appeal erred by weighing the evidence presented with the motion and opposition.

Wyrick v. Golden Nugget Lake Charles, LLC, 2020-0665 (La. App. 1 Cir. 12/30/20), 317 So.3d 708.

Casino patron was injured when, while operating a scooter, she ran into the sharp corner of a slot machine and cut her leg. Plaintiff sued under La. R.S. 9:2800.6. Defendant casino moved for summary judgment. "[Plaintiff] could not say how or when the base's sharp edge came to be, i.e., whether the slot machine base was in its original condition or had been altered or damaged during its time at the casino. She likewise had no knowledge of whether Golden Nugget had any actual notice of the base's hazardous condition." The trial court granted summary judgment, finding that plaintiff could not make a positive showing that the casino had either actual or constructive notice of the condition. The Court of Appeal reversed, finding that all factual inferences drawn from the evidence must be construed in favor of the party opposing a motion for summary judgment. Examining the evidence supporting and opposing the motion for summary judgment, the Court of Appeal held that there was a genuine issue of material fact as to whether the defendant casino had created the condition or had constructive notice of it.

H) BURDEN OF PROOF

Broussard v. Blount, 2020-544 (La. App. 3 Cir. 5/5/21), 319 So.3d 389.

Plaintiffs sued defendants for injuries suffered in an automobile collision. Defendants moved for summary judgment. In the motion, defendants attempted to point out that plaintiffs lacked factual support for their negligence claim. Defendants stated as follows: "Plaintiffs cannot satisfy their burden of proof in the instant suit as [P]laintiffs have failed to demonstrate any liability and/or causation in the instant matter and further have failed to produce any expert testimony to establish one or all of the necessary elements of their claim[s]." The trial court granted the summary judgment. The Court of Appeal reversed holding that "[T]he jurisprudence is clear that the defendant moving for summary judgment does not carry his initial burden when he simply points out by motion or brief that there is a lack of factual support for an essential element of the plaintiff's claim." In this case, none of the supporting documents negated an essential element of plaintiffs' negligence claims. Defendants did not attach any affidavits to support the motion for summary judgment. Second, the documents did not demonstrate that plaintiffs lacked evidence to support an essential element of their claim. Defendants argued in their memorandum that plaintiffs' responses to discovery were inadequate to demonstrate any evidence of causation, but none of the discovery responses were attached to defendants' motion. Defendants further failed to identify the portions of their supporting documents that demonstrated an absence of a genuine issue of material fact. Article 966(D)(1) states that the burden of proof rest with the mover. Only after the motion for summary judgment has been properly supported does the burden shift to the non-moving party.

Heirs of John Beckwith, LLC v. Sims, 2020-0476 (La. App. 4 Cir. 3/10/21), 315 So.3d 306.

The trial court erred in permitting late-filed opposition affidavit to be considered in summary judgment hearing.

XIV. ARTICLE 971 – MOTION TO STRIKE

LaCerte v. State, 2019-1401 (La. App. 1 Cir. 1/4/21), 317 So.3d 763, *writ denied*, 2021-00193 (La. 3/23/21), 313 So.3d 272.

Article 971 (Special Motion to Strike) protects a person's right of petition and free speech from lawsuits that infringe upon those rights. The State of Louisiana, the Legislative Auditor, and the Inspector General do not have constitutional rights and cannot engage in First Amendment-protected speech because they are juridical persons rather than natural persons; therefore, trial court erred by granting their La. C.C.P. art. 971 motion.

XV. ARTICLE 1151 – AMENDING PETITIONS

Kendrick v. Estate of Barre, 2020-0474 (La. App. 4 Cir. 6/9/21), 2021 WL 2370725.

Plaintiff, as an individual and as tutor of her minor son, filed a petition for filiation and child support. Plaintiff later filed a pleading styled as an "amended and supplemental petition." The amended petition deleted claims against two parties named in the original petition. The trial court dismissed those parties from the action. The court of appeal reversed and held that La. C.C.P. art. 1671 provides that "[a] judgment dismissing an action without prejudice shall be rendered upon application of the plaintiff." The filing of an amended petition not naming the parties was not an adequate basis for dismissing the parties and causes of action. The proper procedure was for plaintiff to file a motion for voluntary dismissal. Moreover, plaintiff could not amend the petition as of right and did not file a motion for leave of court to file an amended petition as required by La. C.C.P. art. 1151. Accordingly, the amended petition is without effect and is treated as never having been filed.

XVI. ARTICLE 1155 – SUPPLEMENTAL PLEADINGS

Jones v. Dynamic Indus., Inc., 2020-528 (La. App. 3 Cir. 5/26/21), 2021 WL 2132844.

Decedent was injured and filed a timely suit. He died on July 14, 2017. On April 12, 2019, his wife filed a supplemental petition asserting a wrongful death action. Defendants filed the peremptory exception of prescription, asserting that the wrongful death action had prescribed, and the trial court granted the exception finding that the supplemental petition asserting the wrongful death action did not relate back to the timely filed petition asserting the personal injury claim. The court of appeal affirmed, making the distinction between an amending petition and a supplemental petition. Amending pleadings involve matters that occurred before the original petition was filed but that were overlooked or unknown at the time. Supplemental pleadings address matters that have arisen since the original petition was filed and which relate to the matters asserted in the original petition. The newly asserted wrongful death action did not relate back. Although plaintiff styled her pleading a "supplemental and amending petition," it actually was a supplemental petition, and supplemental petitions do not relate back under La. C.C.P. arts. 1153 and 1155.

XVII. ARTICLES 1201, 925(2) – REQUEST OF SERVICE WITHIN 90 DAYS

Freeman v. Ochsner Clinic Found, 20-283 (La. App. 5 Cir. 11/10/20), 307 So.3d 335.

In a medical malpractice case, defendant doctor filed in accordance with La. C.C.P. article 925(2) an exception of insufficiency of service of process for plaintiff's failure to request service of process on defendant doctor within ninety (90) days of filing the petition. Plaintiff argued that she had good cause because the doctor lived in the United Arab Emirates, and plaintiff attached as an exhibit a screen shot of a computer screen that showed an internet search for an address. The trial court found that plaintiff established good cause and denied the exception. The Court of Appeal reversed. The exhibits were not offered or admitted into evidence and thus could not be considered by the trial or appellate courts. Even if the exhibits were considered, the court should have granted the exception for the following reasons: (1) service was not requested until eight months after the expiration of the 90 days; (2) the defendant's counsel before the medical review panel was not asked for a current address for service; (3) no request for service at last known address was made; (4) no long-arm service was attempted; and (5) no timely request was made for appointment of a curator.

Walker v. GoAuto Ins. Co., 2020-0331 (La. App. 4 Cir. 6/10/21), 2021 WL 2384843.

Plaintiff filed a petition and a request to proceed in forma pauperis. When the request was denied, the Clerk of Court notified plaintiff's counsel that the request was denied and advised of fees due, but did not inform counsel of service fees due to the sheriff. Counsel sent a check for the requested amount. A year later, when counsel checked on service and discovered that it had not been made, the Clerk of Court's office informed counsel that the sheriff's office was holding service because service fees were due to the sheriff. When service finally was made, defendants filed a declinatory exception raising the objection of insufficiency of service for failure to request service of process within 90 days of filing the action. The trial court sustained the exception and dismissed the action. The court of appeal reversed. Plaintiff satisfied the requirement of La. C.C.P. art. 1201 that service be requested within 90 days. The ordinary meaning of the word "request," according to the Louisiana Supreme Court is "a two-party transaction involving one who asks that something be done and one who does what is asked[.]" (quoting Tranchant v. State, 2008-0978 (La. 1/21/09), 5 So.3d 832, 836.) Thus, service of the citation is deemed requested when the Clerk of Court receives service instructions from plaintiff.

Methvien v. Our Lady of the Lake, 2020-1081 (La. App. 1 Cir. 4/16/21), 318 So.3d 329.

The Court of Appeal held that valid of service of process was not requested within 90 days on Our Lady of the Lake (OLOL) as prescribed by La. C.C.P. art. 1201(C) when plaintiff requested service on OLOL in his petition but did not timely pay the fee to the sheriff's office for service of process. Service is not requested until the Clerk of Court receives a request for service and payment of fees or an order granting pauper status. In this case, plaintiff did not pay the fees until she was served with defendant's exception.

The court further found that plaintiff did not show good cause for the failure to request the service under La. C.C.P. art. 1672(C). Although the record did not prove that plaintiff's attorney received the Clerk of Court's message regarding payment of additional fees, defendant was not served until about seven months after the petition was filed. The jurisprudence places some responsibility on the party and attorney, and they should have taken steps to verify service after the passage of that much time. The trial court was not manifestly erroneous in finding that good cause was not established.

XVIII. ARTICLES 1201, 1231 – SERVICE

KCREW Invs., LLC v. Clark, 54,003 (La. App. 2 Cir. 6/30/21), 2021 WL 2677640.

Defendant's estranged wife was served at a house. Thereafter, a default judgment was rendered against defendant. On appeal, defendant argued that the judgment was a nullity because of ineffective domiciliary service. There was no sheriff's return in the record and plaintiff could not prove that the defendant resided at the residence where domicilary service was allegedly made. The court of appeal reversed the judgment finding that the evidence in the record did not establish proper domiciliary service. Personal service and domiciliary service have the same effect under La. C.C.P. article 1231. However, domicilary service requires service on one of suitable age and discretion residing in defendant's dwelling house or usual place of abode. The court additionally noted, "[V]alid domiciliary service depends on the actual and true facts at the time of service and not on information furnished by the defendant at some time prior to service." Accordingly, the Court of Appeal found that there are many reasons a person might list an address other than their actual dwelling house or place of abode. The judgment was reversed.

XIX. ARTICLES 1423, 1470 – DISCOVERY

Thomas v. Waste Management of Louisiana, LLC, 2020-0475 (La. App. 4 Cir. 2/24/21), 314 So.3d 875.

Plaintiff was injured when a door of a waste management container opened and struck plaintiff in the back of the head. Plaintiff sent a request for production of documents (under La. C.C.P. arts. 1461 & 1462) for a copy of all the insurance policies for Waste Management New Orleans Hauling (WM). WM responded by sending to plaintiff "sufficient policies" to cover plaintiff's injuries. After a Motion to Compel was granted, the trial court ordered that WM produce all of its policies. WM produced a $1,000,000 liability policy. After a second Motion to Compel, WM produced a $9,000,000 policy. Plaintiff filed a "motion for constructive contempt" (La. C.C.P. art. 1470) against WM for its failure to produce all of the policies in accordance with the court's order. WM argued that La. C.C.P. art. 1423 only requires defendant to produce the relevant policies (enough to cover defendant's damages). The trial court granted plaintiff's motion, ordered WM to produce all of its policies, and imposed an award of $1,500 in attorney fees. The Court of Appeal affirmed. The plain language of La. C.C.P. art. 1423 indicates that the existence and contents of any policy under which a party may be liable for all or part of a judgment is discoverable. There is no requirement in the article that a party seeking discovery of the existence and contents of policies must first establish the value of its claim. The court explained:

Considering WM's serial noncompliance with the district court's judgments, the deleterious effect failing to comply with article 1423 has had and will have upon [plaintiff], and the vast discretion of the district court, we find that there has been no showing that the district court abused its discretion in granting the Motion for Constructive Contempt, and ordering the production of all applicable insurance policies.

XX. ARTICLE 1424 – DISCOVERY

Gray v. State Farm Mut. Auto. Ins. Co., 2020-407 (La. App. 3 Cir. 2/3/21), 311 So.3d 490.

Plaintiffs filed suit over the death of their wife and mother who died in a car accident. Named as defendants were the owner of the van in the accident and his insurer, State Farm. State Farm filed a subpoena duces tecum to obtain an accident reconstruction report prepared by the State's Office of Risk Management (ORM) (who had prepared the report in connection with the state police because a fatality had occurred). ORM filed a motion to quash the subpoena arguing that the report was subject to the work-product privilege under La. C.C.P. art. 1424 and was protected from discovery under 23 U.S.C. § 409 (reports completed to evaluate highway safety enhancement are not subject to discovery). The trial court and Court of Appeal held that the privilege under La. C.C.P. art. 1424 applies to only an adverse party or his attorney. In this case, ORM was not a party to the suit and therefore could not assert a work-product privilege. Furthermore, the federal restriction did not apply because ORM did not produce any evidence that the report was prepared as part of a highway safety program.

XXI. ARTICLE 1425(F) – ADMISSIBILITY OF EXPERTS

Melerine v. Tom's Marine & Salvage, LLC, 2020-00571 (La. 3/24/21), 315 So.3d 806.

The trial court denied a motion to exclude testimony of expert, pursuant to La. C.C.P. art. 1425(F), contending that he was not qualified to render opinions in specified fields, and that his methodology was not reliable. The Court of Appeal reversed, finding that the witness offered conclusions that were, by his own admission, beyond his area of expertise. Second, the record did not support that his opinions quantifying plaintiff's damages were supported by reliable methodology.

XXII. ARTICLE 1464 – ADDITIONAL MEDICAL EXAMINATIONS

Dao v. Thibodeaux, 21-153 (La. App. 5 Cir. 5/11/21), 2021 WL 1895464.

La. C.C.P. art. 1464 was amended in 2017 to allow for additional medical opinions (which were formerly independent medical exams). The article states that a minor subject to an examination shall have the right to a parent, tutor, or guardian present during the exam. The issue before the court is whether an adult has the right to have a party present during the exam. The Court of Appeal recognized that trial courts have great discretion regarding IME's (the court called it an IME rather than AME). However, the Fifth Circuit held: "[N]owhere in the plain language of the statute does it expressly provide for the right of an adult party to have someone present to record the exam. With regard to the specific question of whether a plaintiff has a right to have legal representatives present during an IME, courts have consistently held that such an accommodation is not proper unless the plaintiff has demonstrated special circumstances to justify the request."

XXIII. ARTICLE 1571 – ANSWER REQUIRED PRIOR TO SETTING FOR TRIAL

Allen v. First Castle Federal Credit Union, 2019-0952 (La. App. 1 Cir. 9/2/20), 312 So.3d 634, *writ denied*, 2020-01285 (La. 1/12/21), 308 So.3d 712.

Default judgment entered on a vendor's reconventional demand for a vehicle purchaser's outstanding loan balance was null and void as premature. Vendor obtained preliminary default against purchaser on the day of trial, but purchaser did not file answer to vendor's demand prior to trial, and purchaser did not appear at trial or take action, which could be considered waiver of answer required by rule for assigning cases for trial. La. C.C.P. art. 1571 does not permit the assignment of ordinary proceedings for trial until after an answer is filed. Valid default judgment could not have been entered on date of trial before answer was filed.

XXIV. ARTICLE 1631 – ADMISSIBILITY OF WITNESSES

Tassin v. State Farm Mut. Auto. Ins. Co., 2020-00652 (La. 10/14/20), 302 So.3d 1098 (per curiam).

In a case for personal injuries caused by defendant's failure to yield at traffic signal, the trial court excluded the testimony of a witness pursuant to a motion to strike. Defendants attempted to add that witness on the eve of trial although she was listed as a witness in the pretrial order by the city/parish and not defendants. The trial court granted the motion to strike the proffered testimony because defendants failed to include her "in their discovery responses, witness lists, or on the pre-trial order." The Supreme Court agreed with the trial court holding that a trial court judge has great discretion in conducting a trial including any questions regarding the admissibility of witness testimony (citing La. C.C.P. art. 1631). The court did not abuse its discretion in excluding the testimony in view of the failure of defendants to list the witness and the fact that her testimony was cumulative of other witnesses' testimony.

Justice Crain dissented, stating that "[a]lthough, a trial judge has great discretion in deciding whether to receive or refuse testimony objected to on the grounds of failure to abide by the pre-trial order, any doubt must be resolved in favor of receiving the information."

XXV. ARTICLE 1702 – DEFAULT JUDGMENTS

Kokowski Plumbing, L.L.C. v. Country Aire MHP, LLC, 2020-0063 (La. App. 3 Cir. 11/12/20), 307 So.3d 291.

There is a presumption that a default judgment is supported by sufficient evidence, but this presumption may be rebutted by the record upon which the judgment is rendered. An affidavit of correctness submitted by plumbing company in its action on an open account against a former customer, in which the manager of the company testified that $7,170.00 was the correct balance for services rendered on behalf of the customer and for attorney's fees incurred by the company in seeking payment, was sufficient to establish a prima facie case. Under La. C.C.P. 1702(C), a suit for an open account may be confirmed without a hearing in open court and plaintiff may submit proof required by law. Defendant seemed to argue that the court erred because the Affidavit of Correctness was attached to plaintiff's petition and not submitted by plaintiff as an attachment with its Motion for Confirmation of Default Judgment. The court labeled this argument "untenable."

Alexander v. Rodgers Homes and Construction, Inc., 53,663 (La. App. 2 Cir. 1/13/21), 310 So.3d 303.

In confirming a default judgment against the insurer, plaintiffs must authenticate the duplicate copy of the insurance policy. The insurance policy contained the terms and conditions that were a critical part of the prima facie case to prove defendant's liability. An unauthenticated insurance policy was insufficient evidence to support the judgment and award of the trial court, and a prima facie showing was not made that plaintiffs were entitled to the judgment rendered. Thus, the trial court erred in confirming the final default judgment.

Vance v. Int'l House of Pancakes, 2020-01373 (La. 2/17/21), 310 So.3d 550 (per curiam), *reh'g denied*, 313 So.3d 1254 (La. 4/20/21).

Plaintiff sued IHOP, alleging that he was injured as a result of a slip and fall in an IHOP restaurant in Natchitoches. When the defendant failed to answer, the plaintiff confirmed a default judgment. The Court of Appeal affirmed. The Supreme Court in a per curiam opinion reversed. The Court found the confirmation of a default judgment requires 'proof of the demand sufficient to establish a prima facie case. La. C.C.P. art. 1702(A). The Court held that even though the plaintiff alleged that "International House of Pancakes, LLC, had care, custody, control, and guard over the bathroom as 'owner and manager' of the restaurant, he offered no evidence proving defendant's ownership, management, control, or other responsibility for the condition of that particular restaurant premises." Thus, plaintiff did not establish a prima facie case under La. R.S. 9:2800.6.

Concurring, Justice Crain explained that "merchant" as defined by La. R.S. 9:2800.6 includes both the nature of the business and the owner of the business. Although plaintiff established the nature of the business as a merchant, he did not establish the owner or custodian of the particular IHOP restaurant.

Reardon v. Global Awnings of Louisiana, L.L.C., 53,622 (La. App. 2 Cir. 11/10/20), 306 So.3d 591.

The trial court confirmed a default judgment for breach of an employment contract although the affidavit of correctness did not adopt or attach the agreement between the parties and the court did not take oral testimony. The Court of Appeal held that the default judgment was not valid. Even though the employment contract was attached to the petition, La. C.C.P. art. 1702.1(A) requires attachment of "any proof required by law[.]" Even if the court were to consider the contract attached to the petition, it could not be determined whether plaintiff complied with the drug and alcohol policy. Plaintiff simply did not establish a prima facie case. Furthermore, the court expressed reservations about a $57,000.00 attorney fee for confirming a default judgment.

Libertas Tax Fund I LLC v. Mompoint, 2020-0105 (La. App. 5 Cir. 10/5/20), 304 So.3d 581, *writ denied*, 2020-01387 (La. 1/26/21), 309 So.3d 348.

The trial court confirmed a default judgment without holding a hearing and obtaining competent evidence sufficient to establish the elements of a prima facie case in order to confirm a tax-sale purchaser's action to quiet title as to certain immovable property and to obtain partition by licitation of property. The confirmation of the default did not fall within the exception of La. C.C.P. art. 1702(B)(1) & (C) governing confirmation of preliminary default allowing for the admission of hearsay evidence without a hearing. The purchaser did not present proof of its demand to establish a prima facie case for confirmation, as exhibits attached to purchaser's motion to confirm the preliminary default judgment were not accepted into evidence by the trial court.

See also ***Precept Credit Opportunities Fund, L.P. v. Brown***, 2020-0114 (La. App. 4 Cir. 7/22/20), 2020 WL 4199728 (no hearing held to introduce and admit evidence in claim to quiet title, and the action did not fit within the exceptions of La. C.C.P. arts. 1702(B)(1) & (C) and 1702.1).

Patin v. Goudeau, 2019-1685 (La. App. 1 Cir. 10/27/20), 315 So.3d 289, *writ not considered*, 2020-01391 (La. 1/26/21), 309 So.3d 348.

The entry of a final default judgment after confirmation of a preliminary default is similar to a trial at which defendant is absent; plaintiff must present admissible and competent evidence that is admitted on the record that establishes a prima facie case, proving both the existence and validity of the claim. Passenger of motor vehicle involved in collision failed to establish a prima facie case against the driver's alleged uninsured/underinsured motor vehicle insurer, in her personal injury action against alleged insurer and others, and thus passenger was not entitled to entry of final default judgment against alleged insurer. Passenger did not introduce a copy of insurance policy into evidence.

XXVI. ARTICLES 1841, 2083 – APPEALABLE JUDGMENTS

Riley v. Plaquemines Parish Sheriff's Office, 2020-0262 (La. App. 4 Cir. 9/9/20), 2020 WL 5405923.

The Court of Appeal lacked jurisdiction under La. C.C.P. arts. 2083 and 1841 to review the trial court's order denying plaintiff's affidavit for *in forma pauperis* status, through which plaintiff sought to avoid pre-paying costs prior to filing an appeal of an order granting peremptory exceptions of no cause of action as to negligent infliction of emotional distress claims brought against the sheriff and cellular telephone companies. The order was not a final judgment that determined the merits of plaintiff's actions or an interlocutory judgment; rather, the order merely determined a preliminary matter in the course of the underlying action.

The court did not convert the appeal to a writ application because the motion for appeal was not filed within the thirty-day time period mandated for filing a supervisory writ application in accordance with Rule 4-3 of the Uniform Rules, Courts of Appeal.

Wachovia Mortgage Corp. v. Hoover, 2019-1520 (La. App. 1 Cir. 9/21/20), 314 So.3d 42.

The First Circuit holds that a judgment awarding "additional amounts accruing thereafter," "reasonable attorney fees," "all expenses," and "fees" without specifying the amounts was not a final and appealable judgment. "A final appealable judgment must name the party in favor of whom the ruling is ordered, the party against whom the ruling is ordered, and the relief that is granted or denied." The indefinite awards rendered the judgment non-appealable.

Harp v. Succession of Bryan, 2019-0062 (La. App. 1 Cir. 9/3/20), 313 So.3d 284.

A trial court's judgment dismissing all claims arising from a contract dispute in favor of the wife of a property owner and the estate of the deceased property owner constituted a valid final judgment, and thus the appellate court had the jurisdiction to consider the merits of an appeal. Although the judgment did not specifically address a reconventional demand and contained surplus language that the judgment was in favor of the owners without affirmatively granting the owners relief, the judgment was issued after a trial on the merits, and there was no indication that any issues remained outstanding. The language dismissing all claims was sufficiently specific to encompass dismissal of the claims asserted in the reconventional demand. "Furthermore, silence in a judgment as to any issue that was placed before the trial court is deemed a rejection of the claim."

Coastal Industries, LLC v. Arkel Constructors, LLC, 2019-1586 (La. App. 1 Cir. 9/21/20), 313 So.3d 1270.

A judgment that confirmed a final arbitration award in favor of a general contractor on a counterclaim against a subcontractor, but which lacked decretal language dismissing the subcontractor's original damages claims against general contractor for breach of contract, was defective and could not be considered a final judgment for the purposes of appeal. The judgment did not resolve the subcontractor's original claim against the contractor, as it did not dismiss these claims, notwithstanding the findings and provisions of the interim and final arbitration awards.

The court declined to convert the improper appeal to an application for supervisory writs and reasoned: "[w]hen the jurisdictional defect lies in the non-finality of a judgment (as opposed to an appeal from an interlocutory judgment), an appellate court will generally refrain from the exercise of its supervisory jurisdiction when an adequate remedy exists by appeal." Thus, the court declined to exercise its discretion to convert the appeal to a writ from a judgment that was not final due to a lack of precise, definite, and certain decretal language.

Parker v. Paladin Contractors, LLC, 2020-0492 (La. App. 4 Cir. 3/3/21), 314 So.3d 1128.

Plaintiff filed a single petition in which she cumulated two actions—a damages action and a derivative action. The trial court granted a peremptory exception raising the objection no right of action dismissing the derivative action and a partial no cause of action exception. Plaintiff appealed. The Court of Appeal held that even though the trial court's granting of the objection of no cause of action dismissed one of the two cumulated actions of plaintiff, it did not dismiss any party. Therefore, the judgment was not appealable under La. C.C.P. art. 1915(A). Since the judgment was not a final judgment for purposes of appeal under La. C.C.P. art. 1915(A), the judgment was appealable under La. C.C.P. art. 1915(B) only if the trial court designated it as final and found no just reason for delay. Since the trial court did not designate it as such, the judgment was a non-appealable partial judgment.

The Court of Appeal converted the appeal to an application for a supervisory writ because two conditions were satisfied: (1) the motion for appeal was filed within the thirty-day time period allowed for the filing of an application for supervisory writs under Rule 4-3 of the Uniform Rules, Courts of Appeal; and (2) the circumstances indicated that an immediate decision of the issue sought to be appealed was necessary to ensure fundamental fairness and judicial efficiency, such as where reversal of the trial court's decision would terminate the litigation.

XXVII. ARTICLE 1915(B) – CERTIFICATION OF A PARTIAL JUDGMENT

In Re Interdiction of Gambino, 2020-00312 (La. 6/3/20), 296 So.3d 1046 (per curiam).

Neither La. C.C.P. art. 1915(B) nor any other provision of Louisiana law establishes a time delay for filing a motion to certify a judgment as final for purposes of appeal. Absent an expression of legislative will, Louisiana courts cannot impose a specific delay for filing a motion to certify a judgment as final for purposes of immediate appeal. Accordingly, a certification order issued after notice of appeal can cure jurisdictional defects in an appeal. (The 2021 amendment to La. C.C.P. art. 2088 codified the holding of Gambino.)

Kosak v. La. Farm Bureau Cas. Ins. Co., 2020-0222 (La. App. 1 Cir. 12/20/20), 316 So.3d 522, *reh'g denied*, (1/11/21).

The trial court granted defendant's exception of prescription and dismissed plaintiffs' amending/supplementing petition for damages alleging bad faith claims against defendant with prejudice. The trial court certified the judgment as final and appealable under La.

C.C.P. art. 1915(B). The Court of Appeal dismissed the appeal, holding that a trial court's designation of a judgment as final and appealable is not dispositive of the appellate court's jurisdiction. An appellate court has the duty *sua sponte* to examine its subject matter jurisdiction. The judgment did not state any reasons why there was "no just reason for delay." Accordingly, the Court of Appeal conducted a *de novo* review to determine whether the trial court's certification was proper. The Court of Appeal considered the factors cited in *R.J. Messinger, Inc. v. Rosenblum*, 2004-1664 (La. 3/2/05), 894 So.2d 1113), and determined that the court lacked jurisdiction because the certification by the trial court was not proper. In this case the overarching inquiry was whether there was no just reason for delay. The Court of Appeal concluded that addressing the issues on appeal at that stage would promote piecemeal appeals; therefore, the court could not conclude that there was no just reason for delay. See also *Belleview Estates, LLC v. Knoll & Dufour Lands, LLC*, 2019-1394 (La. App. 1 Cir. 9/21/20), 315 So.3d 252, 258 (listing the considerations).

Lyons v. Axiall Corp., 2019-733 (La. App. 3 Cir. 5/20/20), 298 So.3d 207.

Defendants sought to file an amended and supplemental answer and a third-party demand. This was denied by the trial court, and the ruling was ultimately affirmed on appeal. Later in the litigation, defendants again tried to amend their answer to add the third parties. Plaintiff filed a motion to strike, which the trial court granted. At the request of the defendant, the trial court designated its ruling on the motion as an appealable final judgment in accordance with La. C.C.P. art. 1915(B). The Court of Appeal reversed, finding that the trial court improperly certified the judgment as final. A judgment on a motion to strike is an interlocutory decree from which no appeal may be taken. The circumstances did not warrant an immediate appeal. Defendant was attempting to have "a second bite" at an issue on which the trial court, court of appeal, and Supreme Court already had denied relief. The trial court did not explain reasons for its certification that there was no just reason for delay, so the court of appeal applied the (nonexclusive) considerations from *R.J. Messinger, Inc. v. Rosenblum*, 2004-1664 (La. 3/2/05), 894 So.2d 1113. The Court of Appeal concluded that the circumstances of the case did not warrant an immediate appeal. Judicial resources would be wasted, especially considering that the case would probably be appealed after trial.

Barnett & Assocs., LLC v. Whiteside, 20-362 (La. App. 5 Cir. 12/11/20), 308 So.3d 1218.

Trial court denied defendants' objections of prescription and peremption. Defendants filed a devolutive appeal. The Court of Appeal held that a denial of a peremptory exception is not appealable. "A trial court judgment which overrules an exception or denies a motion is inherently not an appealable final judgment, but is an interlocutory judgment which is subject only to discretionary review by the courts of appeal through their supervisory jurisdiction." The Fifth Circuit has adopted a policy of not converting jurisdictionally defective appeals into writ applications.

Burgos v. Evans, 2020-0326 (La. App. 4 Cir. 12/16/20), 312 So.3d 1145.

The Fourth Circuit holds that a judgment that enforces a settlement agreement without disposing of the entire matter is not appealable. There were numerous pending matters that remained to be resolved by the trial court. There are four categories of appealable judgments: (1) a final judgment that determines the merits in whole; (2) a partial final judgment that does not require designation as a final judgment pursuant to La. C.C.P. art. 1915(A); (3) a partial judgment that has been properly designated as final pursuant to La. C.C.P. art. 1915(B)(1); and (4) an interlocutory judgment for which the law expressly provides for an appeal pursuant to La. C.C.P. art. 2082(C).

Phipps v. Schupp, 2020-0045 (La. App. 4 Cir. 12/9/20), 310 So.3d 610, *writ denied*, 2021-00048 (La. 3/2/21), 311 So.3d 1052.

Plaintiff voluntarily and unconditionally acquiesced in the judgment dismissing his claims asserting a petitory action and a right of passage under La. C.C. art. 689, with prejudice. The judgment contained the language proposed by plaintiff in his motion for voluntary dismissal. The Court of Appeal held that a party may not appeal from a judgment granting the exact relief for which that party petitions. There is no error to be corrected by the appellate court.

XXVIII. ARTICLE 2252 – EXECUTORY JUDGMENTS

Pitre v. Louisiana Thoroughbred Breeders Association, 21-184 (La. App. 5 Cir. 4/29/21), 2021 WL 1700946.

The trial court granted plaintiff's motion to enforce execution of a judgment prior to the court ruling on a timely filed motion for new trial. The Court of Appeal held that "[t]he language of La. C.C.P. art. 2252 is clear." It prohibits a judgment creditor from taking any steps in the execution of a judgment during the suspensive appeal delays. "It does not require a defendant to have actually taken a suspensive appeal[.]" The judgment will not become executory until 30 days after notice is mailed of the denial of the new trial.

XXIX. ARTICLE 3851 – MANDAMUS

Lowther v. Town of Bastrop, 2020-01231 (La. 5/13/21), 2021 WL 1920977.

Firefighters obtained a judgment against the city for payment of back wages. The firefighters sought to enforce their judgment for about $1.7 million by filing a writ of mandamus. The city filed an exception of no cause of action, arguing that the firefighters were statutorily and constitutionally prohibited from using a writ of mandamus to execute a judgment against a political subdivision. The Supreme Court had to decide whether there is a cause of action for a writ of mandamus compelling a municipality to satisfy a judgment for back wages owed to its firefighter employees. The Supreme Court found that this was a proper case for the use of a mandamus proceeding. "A writ of mandamus is an extraordinary remedy that is directed at a public officer to compel the performance of a ministerial duty required by law." A ministerial duty is one for which no element of discretion is left to the public official. Because the duty of the city to pay the firefighters is statutorily and constitutionally established, it is a ministerial duty. The ministerial nature of the duty of the city to pay the firefighters did not change to discretionary because the firefighters obtained a judgment confirming and quantifying the payment. The Supreme Court relied upon cases where a mandamus proceeding was used to order the appropriation of funds to pay a refund judgment of overpaid taxes and to order the payment of a judgment of damages in an expropriation case.

XXX. ARTICLE 4652 – CONCURSUS PROCEEDING

Jefferson v. State Farm Mutual Ins. Co., 53,849 (La. App. 2 Cir. 5/26/21), 321 So.3d 520, *writ denied*, 2021-00886 (La. 10/12/21).

Counsel for State Farm indicated to the trial court that the matter was settled. Plaintiff refused the settlement stating that he was a resident of Texas and was entitled to receive more than the $30,000.00 policy limits of the State Farm policy. State Farm deposited its $30,000.00 policy limits and invoked a concursus proceeding impleading Mr. Jefferson, the state of Texas, Ms. Bluford, and Dudley DeBosier. Mr. Jefferson filed additional claims against State Farm who responded by filing a peremptory exception raising the objection of no cause of action. The trial court granted the exception and dismissed the plaintiff's claims. The Court of Appeal affirmed, stating that the concursus proceeding is simply a vehicle whereby anyone who admits owing money to others may deposit that money into the registry of the court, thereby relieving himself of the liability for the money so deposited. La. C.C.P. art. 4658. The jurisdiction of the court is limited to disposing of the funds on deposit and relieving the stakeholder from further liability to the impleaded claimants. Once State Farm deposited the money, the plaintiff had no additional actions against it in the concursus proceeding.

XXXI. ARTICLE 4731 – EVICTION

Capers v. NorthPro Properties Management, LLC, 53,919 (La. App. 2 Cir. 5/5/21), 321 So.3d 502.

Defendant filed suit to evict the plaintiff from the house that she was leasing. Two weeks prior to the hearing date on the eviction, defendant hired several men to remove all of the plaintiff's possessions from the house and placed them in a garbage dumpster. Plaintiff filed suit for damages for the value of the property removed from the residence. The Court of Appeal affirmed the trial court and awarded plaintiff $15,000.00. The court found that "it is well-established that a lessor has no right to take possession or in any way disturb the possession of the lessee without first resorting to judicial process." The court further held that the defendant did not prove that the plaintiff had abandoned the property. Abandonment under La. C.C.P. art. 4731 requires both an act of voluntary relinquishment of the premises and a specific intent to abandon on the part of the lessee. In this case, the lessee did not relinquish her keys, had all of her and her children's belongings in the residence and was present in the home the night before her belongings were removed. *See also, In re: Justice of the Peace King*, 2020-01069 (La. 11/19/20), 2020 WL 6789979, where a Justice of the Peace was removed from office where the Supreme Court held that the respondent's "apparent ignorance of certain procedural requirements in eviction proceedings is no excuse for failing to take appropriate action" to have the eviction motion served and set for hearing.

Old Gentilly Lane, LLC / Valverde v. Robles, 2020-0296 (La. App. 4 Cir. 11/25/20), 2020 WL 6937762.

Property owner entered into an oral lease with the defendant. Owner sold the property to plaintiff. Plaintiff filed an eviction proceeding to remove defendant from the property. The trial court affirmed the eviction and ordered that any claim for damages by defendant must be brought in a separate ordinary proceeding. Court of Appeal affirmed and held that under La. C.C. art. 2712, a third person who acquired immovable property is not bound by an unrecorded lease even if he has actual knowledge of the lease. The text messages between defendant and the prior owner do not bind the current owner. The Court of Appeal further found that a lessee's claim for damages must be adjudicated in an ordinary proceeding. "The lessee [cannot] raise these claims during the eviction proceeding because a rule for possession ... is a summary proceeding."

XXXII. MEDICAL MALPRACTICE PROCEDURE – La. R.S. 13:4522

Bergeron v. Richardson, 2020-01409 (La. 6/30/21), 2021 WL 2679021.

Plaintiff filed medical malpractice wrongful death and survival actions for the death of her husband. Almost six years after the suit was filed, defendants filed a bond for cost pursuant to La. R.S. 13:4522 (defendant before pleading in all cases may by motion require plaintiff to give security for costs). The Supreme Court held that a bond for costs must be filed before a defendant files any pleadings. The Supreme Court admitted that defendants seldom incur significant litigation costs before filing an answer, and that could make it difficult to quantify the bond amount at that time. Nonetheless, the language of the statute is clear and unambiguous and to interpret it in any other way would be to read out the "before pleading" language in the statute. The Supreme Court stated that it was overruling, to the extent it was controlling precedent, *Jones v. Williams*, 191 La. 129, 184 So. 565, 566 (La. 1938).

XXXIII. MISCELLANEOUS – JURISPRUDENCE CONSTANTE

Bergeron v. Richardson, 2020-01409 (La. 6/30/21), 2021 WL 2679021.

The Supreme Court affirmed a ruling of the trial court which appeared to apply the language of the statute and deviated from a past Supreme Court case. The court decided that *jurisprudence constante* did not preclude it from overruling *Jones v. Williams*, 191 La. 129, 184 So. 565, 566 (La. 1938). Louisiana civil law does not recognize *stare decisis*. There are only two sources of law in Louisiana: legislation and custom. Judicial decisions are not an authoritative source of law. A long line of cases following the same reasoning in Louisiana forms *jurisprudence constante*. Because the reasoning in *Jones* was confined to a single case, the Court did not assign it the status of *jurisprudence constante* or custom. Furthermore, when a statute's language addresses an issue, a court should not resort to jurisprudence.

Chief Justice Weimer concurred, agreeing with 24th JDC Judge Scott Schlegel that the case epitomized the "beauty of living in a Civilian jurisdiction.' Furthermore, '[w]hile the decisions of this court are persuasive authority and, generally, should be followed in the lower courts to ensure consistency and stability, the district judge correctly noted that, ultimately, in a civilian jurisdiction, legislation is the superior source of law." *Bergeron*, 320 So.3d 1116 (Weimer concurrence). Justice Crichton also concurred, noting the primary role of courts in civil law systems is to interpret statutes and code articles according to their plain meaning.

XXXIV. MISCELLANEOUS – La. R.S. 13:1808 (LONG-ARM SERVICE)

Cochran v. Forman, 2020-01400 (La. 3/9/21), 312 So.3d 263.

Default judgment was entered against father after he did not appear for a hearing when notice of the hearing was sent to him by certified mail in another state but unclaimed. The father moved to annul the judgment, arguing that the mother had not complied with the requirement of the Louisiana long-arm statute that no hearing on a contradictory motion can take place until thirty days after filing of an affidavit showing notice was sent. The trial court denied the petition to annul the default judgment. On appeal, the court reversed, holding that the father had not received proper notice since the hearing was held less than thirty days after service. The Supreme Court held the Court of Appeal erred in annulling the judgment of the trial court based on its finding the non-resident father was not given proper notice of the proceedings pursuant to the provisions of the Uniform Child Custody Jurisdiction and Enforcement Act ("UCCJEA"). The relevant provision of the UCCJEA provides as follows:

> Notice required for the exercise of jurisdiction when a person is outside this state may be given in a manner prescribed by the law of this state for service of process or by the law of the state in which the service is made. Notice shall be given in a manner reasonably calculated to give actual notice but may be by publication if other means are not effective. La. R.S. 13:1808(A).

The Court of Appeal held that the UCCJEA provision did not incorporate the requirements of the Louisiana long-arm statute. The long-arm statute requires that a hearing be held at least 30 days after service is made by registered mail and an affidavit is filed into the record. "La.

R.S. 13:1808 mandates only that notice be given in a manner 'reasonably calculated to give actual notice' and does not mandate compliance with the Louisiana Long-Arm Statute." *Cochran*, 312 So.3d at 265. Therefore, the thirty-day requirement of the long arm statute does not apply to proceedings under the Uniform Child Custody Act.

XXXV. MISCELLANEOUS – La. R.S. 13:5107 (SERVICE ON THE STATE)

Brown v. Chesson, 2020-00730 (La. 3/24/21), 315 So.3d 834.

Plaintiff filed a malpractice suit against the individual physician who was employed by the state. Plaintiff served defendant individually pursuant to La. C.C.P. art. 1232. Defendant filed a declinatory exception raising the objection of insufficiency of citation and service of process, arguing that in a claim against a qualified state health care provider, service is proper pursuant to La. R.S. 13:5107 and La. R.S. 39:1538, which require service on three entities: (1) the head of the department for the Board of Supervisors of the Louisiana State University Agricultural and Mechanical College; (2) the Office of Risk Management; and (3) the Attorney General. The trial court denied the exception, but the appellate court reversed. The Supreme Court reversed the Court of Appeal's reversal and reinstated the trial court judgment, holding that it is sufficient to request service solely on a qualified state health care provider when that individual is the only named defendant in a medical malpractice suit. Plaintiff's request for service was sufficient pursuant to La. R.S. 13:5107(D) because that section does not specify the method of service required. La. R.S. 13:5107(D) clearly states that "[i]f not waived, a request for service of citation upon the defendant shall be considered timely if requested on the defendant within the time period provided by this Section[.]" The only defendant in this case was the named physician. Therefore, the court concluded, "If a medical malpractice plaintiff may name an individual physician state health care provider as a defendant, it is axiomatic that service may be requested on this individual pursuant to La. C.C.P. art. 1232."

XXXVI. MISCELLANEOUS – La. R.S. 13:5107 (SERVICE ON THE STATE)

Dominick v. Grambling State Univ., 2019-1402 (La. App. 1 Cir. 7/24/20), 309 So.3d 384.

Plaintiff, who alleged he was shot in his dorm room at Grambling, sued the Board of Supervisors for the University of Louisiana System. Plaintiff's request for service of process as follows: "Please Serve: / Attorney General/ Board of Supervisors/ University System of Louisiana." It provided no address for service. The Board filed the declinatory exception raising the objection of insufficiency of service of process. The trial court sustained the exception and dismissed the action. The Court of Appeal affirmed. La. R.S. 13:5107(D) requires that service on state defendant's shall be requested within ninety (90) days of the commencement of the action or be subject to dismissal. Plaintiff argued that the trial court erred because failing to provide an address for service is not the same as failing to request service. The Court of Appeal explained, "[f]or service to be requested and effectuated, the clerk must be provided with the correct name and address of those persons to be served. The plain language of La. R.S. 13:5107(D)(1), without more, requires that the clerk receive this information before it can be considered 'requested.' " The Court of Appeal did not find "good cause" under La. C.C.P. art. 1672(C) to excuse the failure to serve. The good cause requirement is strictly construed. Neither inadvertence nor confusion over service information satisfied good cause.

XXXVII. MISCELLANEOUS – JUDICIAL CONFESSION

Harris v. Boh Bros. Constr. Co., L.L.C., 2021-00084 (La. 3/16/21), 312 So.3d 565 (per curiam).

The trial court granted summary judgment, finding that defendant was not liable because it qualified for immunity from suit under the government contractor immunity. The Court of Appeal reversed, finding that defendant failed to submit a copy of its plans and specifications, which were approved by the Corps of Engineers, which would entitle defendant to claim the immunity. The Louisiana Supreme Court reversed and held that plaintiff judicially confessed that the "government approved the specifications." A filing in the trial court indicated the "[p]laintiff does not dispute the first prong of the Affirmative Defense of Governmental Contractor Immunity applies." Thus, there was no need to discuss that issue. An admission by a party in a judicial proceeding is a judicial confession and is full proof against the party making it. La. C.C. art. 1853. This admission has the effect of waiving evidence in the summary judgment proceeding as to the approval by the corps since it was the subject of a judicial confession.

TABLE OF TIME DELAYS FOR CIVIL PROCEDURE

(Consult full text of articles cited. Also consult District Court Rules in Statutory Appendix for changes in time requirements, e.g., Rules 9.9(d) and 9.10. Where security is required, see Required Security Which Must Be Posted, ante, for the amount of security.)

ALIMONY, CUSTODY, VISITATION, SUPPORT

Appeal, Judgment Awarding Article 3942	30 days from applicable date provided in Art. 2087(A). (CAVEAT: This appeal cannot be suspensive, C.C.P. Art. 3943.) (This rule may not apply to a judgment denying custody, visitation, or support)

AMENDMENTS

Answer Article 1151	Within 15 days after it has been served, defendant may amend answer once without leave of court.
Petition Article 1151	Amend petition without leave of court any time before answer is served.
Supplemental Pleading Article 1151	On motion, with notice to opposing party and leave of court.

ANSWER

Petition, District Court Article 1001	Within 21 days from service of citation (or, exception may be filed, with 15 days to answer if exception overruled, or 15 days after service of amended petition). However, see Article 1002 below. However, if discovery requests are filed with the petition, delay for answering is 30 days.
Article 1002	Answer may be filed at any time prior to confirmation of default.
Amended Pleading Article 1151	Within time remaining for pleading to the original pleading, or within 10 days after service of amended petition, whichever period is longer.
Incidental Demand Article 1035	Within the delay allowed by Article 1001, or any time prior to a judgment by default against the defendant in the incidental action.
Appeal	(See APPEALS).
Garnishment Interrogatories	(See GARNISHMENT).
Interrogatories	(See DISCOVERY).

TABLE OF TIME DELAYS

Concursus Article 4655	Same delay as for ordinary proceedings, but if no timely answer, then further time not exceeding 10 days from service or publication of order, Article 4657.
Eviction, Rule For Articles 4733 and 4735	Prior to rule, must plead affirmative defenses and answer under oath to preserve appeal.
Parish and City Courts Article 4903	Within 10 days of service of citation, except if service through Secretary of State, then 15 days after service.
APPEAL	
Devolutive Article 2087	Appellant has 60 days from expiration of new trial delays; or from denial of new trial **timely** applied for; or through Article 1914 notice of court's refusal to grant new trial. Delays suspended on filing notice of removal. (See Article 2087(C)). Appellee has 10 days to appeal after the mailing by clerk of notice of devolutive appeal **timely** taken.
Suspensive Article 2123	30 days from expiration of new trial delays; or from denial of new trial **timely** applied for; or from Article 1914 notice of court's refusal to grant new trial. Delays suspended on filing notice of removal. (See also Art. 2123(B)). **(Security required)**
Answer to Appeal Article 2133	15 days after return day or lodging of record, whichever is later. Other parties have 15 days after appellee's action for similar answers.
Motion to Dismiss Appeal for Irregularity Article 2161	Three days exclusive of holidays after return date, or lodging of record, whichever is later.
Partial Final Judgments Article 1915(B)	Only appealable if the judgment is certified by trial court that there is no just reason for delay.
Rehearing, Court of Appeal Article 2166	Within 14 days of **transmission** of notice of judgment and opinion.
Rehearing, Supreme Court Article 2167	Within 14 days of **transmission** of notice of judgment.
Certiorari, Application for Writ to Louisiana Supreme Court Article 2166	Within 30 days of **transmission** of notice of judgment and opinion of Court of Appeals; or within 30 days of transmission of notice of denial of **timely** application for rehearing by any party; or 10 days after transmission of notice by clerk of opponent's application.

City and Parish Courts Article 5002	10 days from the date of judgment or from the service of the notice of judgment, when such notice is necessary; or from the denial of new trial or service of notice thereof. (CAVEAT: Myles v. Turner, 612 So.2d 32 (La.1993), holds that this delay runs from **receipt** of the notice, not from mailing.)
Costs, Appeal, Payment Article 2126	Within 20 days of the mailing of notice of estimated costs by the clerk.

CONCURSUS

Articles 4655, 4657	(See ANSWER).

DEFAULT

(CAVEAT: See District Court Rule 9.19)

Confirmation of Default Article 1702	Anytime after the delays for answering or filing other responsive pleading notice must be sent and default judgment cannot be obtained until 7 days. After mailing if a party makes an appearance of record, Attorney contacts defendant after the suit is filed or is a delicitual case.
Parish and City Courts Article 4904	If defendant fails to answer timely, final judgment may be rendered.
Justice of the Peace Article 4921	Final judgment shall be rendered if defendant fails to answer timely; no preliminary default is necessary.

DISCOVERY

Deposition on Oral Examination Article 1437	Leave of court required only if taken prior to expiration of 15 days from service of citation on any defendant.
Interrogatories, Answer Article 1458	30 days after service; in family law cases 15 days after service, but 30 days if discovery is served with the original petition.
Medical Records, Request for Release of Article 1465.1	30 days after service of request for medical records' release.
Production of Documents and Things Article 1462	30 days after service of the request; in family law cases 15 days after service, but 30 days if production request is served with original petition.

DIVORCE, ANNULMENT

Alimony, Custody, Visitation	(See that heading)

Appeal, Suspensive Article 3942	30 days from applicable dates provided in Article 2087(A).

EVICTION

Lessee Article 4701	5 day notice to vacate if lease terminated or lease provision violated; if no fixed term, 10 day notice to terminate, which shall constitute notice to vacate.
Occupant Article 4702	5 day notice to vacate.
Rule for Possession Article 4732	Returnable not earlier than 3rd day after service of rule for possession.
Warrant For Possession Article 4733	Issues immediately if lessee or occupant does not comply within 24 hours.
Appeal, Judgment of Eviction Article 4735	Within 24 hours after the rendition of judgment of eviction only if the appellant answered the rule under oath.

EXECUTION OF JUDGMENT

Execution of Judgment Article 2252	Creditor may proceed only after delay for suspensive appeal has elapsed (and no suspensive appeal has been perfected).

EXECUTORY PROCEEDING, APPEAL FROM WRIT OF SEIZURE AND SALE

Articles 2642, 2751-2754	Within 15 days of the service of the notice of seizure directing the issuance of a writ of seizure and sale. (Article 2721) **(Security required)**

GARNISHMENT

Interrogatories, Delay For Answering Article 2412	Within 15 days from service of interrogatories.
Article 2414	Traversing Answer of Garnishee within 15 days of service of notice of filing answer.

HABEAS CORPUS

Appeal Article 3831	Within 30 days from applicable dates provided in Article 2087(A)(1) and (2). (A devolutive appeal does not suspend the execution of the judgment.)

TABLE OF TIME DELAYS

INCIDENTAL DEMAND	
(reconvention, intervention, third-party demand, crossclaim)	
Answer	(See ANSWER).
Filing Article 1033	Without leave of court, any time up to and including time answer is filed to principal demand; thereafter, with leave of court.
INJUNCTION	
Dissolution Article 3607	Temporary restraining order or preliminary injunction, upon 2 days' notice, or such shorter notice as court may prescribe.
Proof at hearings Article 3609	Affidavits must be served on adverse party 24 hours in advance of hearing if proof is upon verified pleadings or supporting affidavits.
Appeal, Preliminary Injunction Article 3612	Within 15 days, and bond furnished, from date of the order. **(Security required)** Suspensive effect only if court so orders.
Appeal, Final Injunction Article 3612	Same delays as for other final judgments, but suspensive appeal allowed only on order of court. (It is implicit in Art. 3612 that an appeal from a final injunction is subject to ordinary delays under Art. 2087. An appeal is not suspensive unless the court so orders. It is not clear, but it would seem that to be ordered suspensive, an appeal would be taken subject to the delays of Art. 2123.)
INTERDICTION	
Appeal, Appointment or Removal of Curator Article 4555	Within 30 days of the applicable dates provided in Article 2087(A)(1) and (2). Only a devolutive appeal, does not suspend order or judgment.
Curator, Appointment Article 4562	Court may revoke appointment if person appointed does not qualify within 10 days. **(Security required)**
JNOV	
Article 1811	Within 7 days, exclusive of legal holidays, after mailing or service of notice of judgment under Article 1913.
JUDGMENT DEBTOR EXAMINATION, APPEARANCE	
Article 2453	Court shall order appearance of debtor not less than 5 days from personal service of motion and order.

TABLE OF TIME DELAYS

MOTIONS	
Judgment on Offer of Judgment Article 970	Any time more than 20 days before trial date. 10 days after offer is accepted, either party may move for judgment.
Judgment on the Pleadings Article 965	After the answer is filed.
Strike, Motion to Article 964	After service of the pleading upon the mover. (No time limit on the motion)
Summary Judgment Article 966	A plaintiff's motion may be filed any time after answer; a defendant's motion may be filed at any time. The following time periods are mandatory: (1) motion filed & served at least 65 days prior to trial; (2) hearing at least 30 days after filing and 30 days prior to trial; (3) opposition filed & served 15 days prior to hearing; and (4) reply 5 days prior to hearing.
Special Motion to Strike Article 971	Within 90 days of service of the petition or any later time, in the court's discretion.
NEW TRIAL, APPLICATION	
Article 1974	Within 7 days, exclusive of legal holidays, from service of notice of judgment under Article 1913.
NEW TRIAL, APPLICATION, CITY AND PARISH COURTS	
Article 4907(B)	Shall be 7 days, exclusive of legal holidays, commences to run on the day "after the clerk has mailed, or the sheriff has served, the notice of judgment."
NULLITY OF JUDGMENTS	
Article 2002	For absolute nullities, may be brought at any time by summary or ordinary proceedings unless prohibited by Article 2003.
Article 2004	For unconscionability, fraud or ill practices, must be brought by ordinary process within 1 year from discovery of the fraud or ill practice. (Peremptive period)
PARTITION	
Absentee Article 4624	Absent defendant has 15 days from publication of notice to answer petition or judge can order sale of property.
POSSESSORY ACTION	
Relief Granted	Court may order defendant to assert petitory

Article 3662	action within 60 days from date judgment becomes executory.
Suspensive Appeal Article 3662	Within 30 days from the delays provided in Article 2123. **(Security required)**
Devolutive Appeal Article 3662	Within 30 days of applicable dates provided in Article 2087(A)(1) and (2). (Note: This is a shortened devolutive appeal delay.)

REHEARING—(See APPEALS)

REVIVAL OF JUDGMENT

Article 2031	File ex parte motion to revive any time before it prescribes. (Also file a reinscription of mortgage in accordance with La. C.C. art. 3359)

SEIZURE, EXCESSIVE, REDUCTION

Article 2296	By contradictory motion not less than 10 days before day fixed for sale.

SERVICE OF PROCESS

State as defendant R.S. 13:5107	Within 90 days of the commencement of the action. (If dismissed, prescription not interrupted, La. R.S. 13:5107(D)(3))
All other defendants Article 1201(C)	Within 90 days of the commencement of the action. Prescription is interrupted unless Plaintiff in bad faith. La. R.S. 9:5801.
La. C.C. Art. 102 Divorce, C.C.P. Art. 395	Within 90 days of the commencement of the action.

SUCCESSION PROCEEDINGS

Claims Against Succession Article 3242	Within 30 days of receipt thereof, the succession shall acknowledge or reject the claim.
Payment of Debts of Succession Article 3302	Upon expiration of 3 months from death of decedent, succession representative shall proceed to pay debts.
Homologation of Petition To Pay Debts Article 3304	Can be homologated after the expiration of 7 days from publication of notice of filing petition, unless opposition is filed.
Account of Succession Representation, Homologation Article 3335	May be homologated after expiration of 10 days from date of service on each heir or legatee unless opposition is filed.

Probate, Opposition Article 2901	If objection made orally to ex parte probate, opponent is allowed 10 days to file opposition. Written opposition may be filed any time prior to probate.
Succession, Independent Administration Proceedings Article 3396.2, 3396.4, 3396.5	Court shall grant independent administrator if provided for in testament. If not, all heirs or legatees must approve.

TUTORSHIP

Opposition to Application Article 4067	10 days from publication or mailing of notice of application for appointment for legal or dative tutor.
Appeal, From Appointment of Article 4068	Within 30 days from applicable dates provided in Article 2087(A)(1) and (2). Only a devolutive appeal, does not suspend judgment.
Tutor Appointment Article 4067	Within 10 days of the publication or date of mailing of notice, court shall appoint the applicant or tutor. **(Security required)**

REQUIRED SECURITY WHICH MUST BE POSTED

The following orders may be signed if all legal requirements have been met and security is posted. Under C.C.P. art. 5121, when a party to a judicial proceeding is required to furnish security, any bond so furnished shall be payable to the clerk of the trial court. No property seized shall be released from seizure unless the bond is executed by a surety company licensed to do business in this state or has been approved by the sheriff. (C.C.P. art. 5127)

A. Security for a suspensive appeal bond

1. If the judgment is for a sum of money - security is equal to the judgment amount plus interest. (C.C.P. art. 2124(B)(1))
    a. If it is a surety bond, security can be 150% of the amount of the judgment plus interest for good cause shown. (C.C.P. art 2124(D)).
2. Judgment over $150 million - security may be set after motion and hearing in an amount sufficient to protect the judgment creditor. The time period for taking a suspensive appeal is suspended until court sets the amount. (C.C.P. art 2124(B)(1)).
3. In all other cases, an amount to assure satisfaction of the judgment and any damages caused by the suspension of the execution. (C.C.P. art. 2124(B)(3).

B. Security for a Suspensive Appeal or a Temporary Restraining Order or Preliminary Injunction in an Executory Process Suit **(there is no TRO to arrest the sale of immovable property in executory process suits. C.C.P. art. 2751)**

1. There is no security required if it is alleged that:
    a. The debt is extinguished or prescribed.
    b. Enforcement of the debt is premature.
    c. Debtor's signature was procured by fraud, violence, or other unlawful means.
    d. Defendant has a liquidated claim to plead in compensation against the debt.
    e. The order of seizure and sale was rendered without sufficient authentic evidence.
2. If security is required, it is in any amount fixed by the court to indemnify the person wrongfully restrained for the costs incurred and damages sustained. (C.C.P. arts. 2753, 3610)
3. Security for a suspensive appeal from an order directing a writ of seizure and sale shall be for an amount exceeding by one-half the balance due on the debt secured by the mortgage or privilege including principal, interest, and attorney fees, but not costs. (C.C.P. art. 2642(B))

C. Administrator of a Succession

1. An amount exceeding by one-fourth of the total value of all of the property of the succession as shown in the inventory or detailed descriptive list. (C.C.P. art. 3151)

D. Provisional Administrator of a Succession

1. An amount determined by the court to protect the heirs, legatees, surviving spouse in community, and succession creditors. (C.C.P. art. 3152)

E. Testamentary Executor

1. No security unless the will specifically requires the executor to furnish security. (C.C.P. art. 3153)

F. Independent Administrator

1. No security unless court orders security after a contradictory hearing upon interested party's request. (C.C.P. art. 3396.14)

G. Writ of Attachment

1. Amount of plaintiff's demands, exclusive of interest and costs.
2. Non-resident writ of attachment, not more than $250. (C.C.P. art. 3544)
3. The defendant may obtain release of seized property by furnishing security for the satisfaction of any judgment that may be rendered against him. (C.C.P. art 3507)
4. Plaintiff may obtain the release of property seized by showing proof of ownership, posting security in an amount exceeding by one-fourth the value of the property seized, and paying costs of seizure. (C.C.P. arts. 3507.1, 3508)
5. A third party may intervene to have the seized property released if he can show that he is the owner, pledgee, or consignee of the property and post security in an amount to satisfy judgment which may be rendered. (C.C.P. arts. 3509, 3507)

H. Writ of Sequestration

1. An amount determined by the court to protect the defendant against any wrongfully issued sequestration. (C.C.P. art. 3574)
2. No security is required for a sequestration in connection with an action to enforce a lessor's privilege. (C.C.P. arts. 3574, 3575)
3. See numbers 3-5 under "G. Writ of Attachment" for the amount of security for the release of property subject to a writ of sequestration. (C.C.P. art. 3576)

I. Temporary Restraining Order and Preliminary Injunction

1. An amount fixed by the court to indemnify the person wrongfully restrained or enjoined for payment of costs and damages sustained. (C.C.P. art. 3610)
2. No security is required for a TRO or injunction in the following matters:
   a. TROs or injunctions seeking protection from domestic abuse, dating violence, stalking, or sexual assault. (C.C.P. art. 3610)
   b. Prohibiting the disposition or encumbrance of community property. (C.C.P. art. 3944; R.S. 9:371)
   c. Allowing the removal of personal property. (C.C.P. art. 3944; R.S. 9:373)
   d. Granting the possession or use of the family residence. (C.C.P. art. 3944; R.S. 9:374)

J. Natural Tutor

1. Does not have to post security but may file a certificate with clerk in the mortgage records where he is domiciled. (C.C.P. art. 4134)
2. If minor has no assets or if the only asset is a contested claim, no certificate is needed until the claim is recovered. (C.C.P. art. 4134(A))
3. The recordation operates as a legal mortgage for the amount of the certificate in favor of the minor on all immovable property of the tutor. (C.C.P. art. 4134(C))

K. All Other Tutors

1. Security shall be set in an amount equal to the total value of the minor's moveable property unless it is shown that the amount is substantially in excess of what is needed for the protection of the minor. (C.C.P. art. 4131)
2. If minor's only asset is a contested claim for damages, no security is needed until the claim is recovered. (C.C.P. art. 4131(D))
3. Provisional tutors shall furnish security in an amount determined by the court as adequate for the protection of the minor. (C.C.P. art. 4071)

L. Curators

1. Security shall be set in an amount equal to the total value of the interdict's moveable property. (C.C.P. arts. 4563, 4131)

M. Evictions

1. The amount of the suspensive appeal bond or security shall be determined by the court to protect the lessor against all such damage he may sustain as a result of the appeal. (C.C.P. art. 4735)

CHECKLIST FOR SUMMARY JUDGMENT UNDER C.C.P. Arts. 966-967

(This document was printed with the permission of the Louisiana Judicial College and Professor William Corbett of the LSU Law Center.)

WHO MAY MOVE AND WHEN? Art. 966(A)(1)

Plaintiff—any time after answer filed

Defendant—any time

MAY A COURT RENDER A PARTIAL SUMMARY JUDGMENT? Yes. **Art. 966(E)**

WHEN SHOULD A SUMMARY JUDGMENT BE RULED ON RATHER THAN A CONTINUANCE GRANTED? "after an *opportunity* for adequate discovery" **Art. 966(A)(3)**

— These words were deliberately chosen—not adequate discovery completed but opportunity for adequate discovery.

— Factors to consider in granting summary judgment or instead granting a continuance—Roadrunner Transp. Sys. v. Brown, 2017-0040 (La. App. 4 Cir. 5/10/17), 219 So.3d 1265, 1273: (1) whether the party was ready to go to trial; (2) whether the party indicated what additional discovery was needed; (3) whether the party took any steps to conduct additional discovery during the period between filing the motion and the hearing; and (4) whether the discovery was raised in the trial court before entry of summary judgment. Plaintiff should be afforded the opportunity to obtain the deposition of an alleged eyewitness before the motion for summary judgment is heard. Milton-Gustain v. Salvage Store, Inc., 2019-01854 (La. 2/10/20), 289 So.3d 48 (per curiam); see also, Laforge v. Golden Nugget Lake Charles, LLC, 2020-100 (La. App. 3 Cir. 11/4/20), 307 So.3d 266.

WHAT IS THE STANDARD FOR GRANTING? Art. 966(A)(3)

Two questions:

1) Is the law in favor of the party moving?

2) Is it true that there is no "genuine issue of material fact"?

— This standard requires identification of the key elements that a party must prove on a cause of action or an affirmative defense.

WHAT DOES THE STANDARD FOR SUMMARY JUDGMENT HAVE TO DO WITH BURDENS AT TRIAL? Art. 966(D)

— If a party would not have the two burdens at trial, then as a party moving for summary judgment, that party has a relatively lower standard—show that the other party cannot produce sufficient evidence so that reasonable people could find for that party. This is the position of a defendant moving for summary judgment on plaintiff's claims or a plaintiff moving for summary judgment on defendant's affirmative defenses.

— On the other hand, if a party would have the burdens of production and persuasion at trial, then that party has a high burden on summary judgment. A plaintiff moving for summary judgment on her claims would have to exceed preponderance of the evidence (standard is reasonable people could not disagree) for summary judgment to be granted. This is the position of a plaintiff moving for summary judgment on her claims or a defendant moving for summary judgment on her affirmative defenses.

— A moving party always must file supporting documents to carry its initial burden of production. If the moving party will not have the burdens at trial, the point of the documents will be to show that the other party lacks evidence on essential element(s). See answers to next question.

HOW DOES THE SHIFTING OF BURDENS WORK AND WHAT MUST BE FILED? Art. 966(D)(1)

— The burden of proof is on the party filing a motion for summary judgment.

— The mover can meet this burden by filing supporting documentary evidence as permitted by **Art. 966(A)(4)**.

— The mover's supporting documentary evidence must prove the essential facts necessary to carry the mover's burden. In deciding the motion, it must first be determined whether the supporting documents presented by the mover are sufficient to resolve all material factual issues. Broussard v. Blount, 2020-544 (La. App. 3 Cir. 5/5/21), 319 So.3d 389; Crockerham v. Louisiana Med. Mut. Ins. Co., 2017-1590 (La. App. 1 Cir. 6/21/18), 255 So.3d 604, 608.

— Once the mover properly establishes the material facts by its supporting documents, the mover does not have to negate all of the essential elements of the adverse party's claim, action, or defense. **Art. 966(D)(1)**.

— The moving party must only point out to the court the absence of factual support for one or more elements essential to the adverse party's claim, action or defense.

— The burden then shifts to the non-moving party to produce factual support, through the use of proper documentary evidence attached to its opposition, which establishes the existence of a genuine issue of material fact or the mover is not entitled to judgment as a matter of law.

— If the non-moving party fails to produce sufficient factual support in its opposition and attached documents, which proves the existence of a genuine issue of material fact or that mover is not entitled to judgment as a matter of law, summary judgment shall be granted. Jenkins v. Hernandez, 2019-0874 (La. App. 1 Cir. 6/3/20), 305 So.3d 365, writ denied, 2020-00835 (La. 10/20/20), 303 So.3d 315.

WHAT DOCUMENTS MAY BE FILED IN SUPPORT OF OR OPPOSITION TO AND WHEN? Art. 966(A)(4)

— Only pleadings, memoranda, affidavits, depositions, answers to interrogatories, certified medical records, written stipulations, and admissions.

— If a document is not in this list, then it will need to be accompanied by an affidavit. **Comment to Art. 966** (added in 2018); Thibodeaux v. Allstate Insurance Co., 19-458 (La. App. 5 Cir. 3/20/20), 293 So.3d 797, writ denied, 2020-00515 (La. 6/22/20), 297 So.3d 762; Cryer v. Tangi Pines Nursing Ctr., 2017-0697 (La. App. 1 Cir. 12/21/17), 240 So.3d 975; Raborn v. Albea, 2016-1468 (La. App. 1 Cir. 5/11/17), 221 So.3d 104, 111.

WHEN MAY DOCUMENTS BE FILED IN SUPPORT OF OR IN OPPOSITION TO?

— Only with the motion and the opposition. No additional documents may be filed with the reply, and there are no stages beyond the reply. **Art. 966(B)(3).**

EXCLUSION OF DOCUMENTS FILED IN SUPPORT OF OR IN OPPOSITION TO.

How does a party object and request exclusion of documents?

— If objecting to form of the affidavit under **Art. 967**, include an objection in the opposition or the reply. **Art. 966(D)(2).**

— If objecting to the qualifications or methodology of an expert, file a motion in limine and request a *Daubert/Foret* hearing under **Art. 1425(F).**

— If a party does not file a *Daubert/Foret* motion, then court must consider expert testimony reliable and credible. Hickman v. Exxon Mobil Corp., 2017-0235 (La. App. 1 Cir. 7/18/18), 255 So.3d 1097, writ denied, 2018-1463 (La. 11/20/18), 256 So.3d 996.

— An expert's opinion must be based on sufficient "factual foundation" for it to create a genuine issue of material fact to preclude the granting of summary judgment. Murphy v. Savannah, 2018-C-0991 (La 5/8/19), 282 So.3d 1034. If an expert's affidavit is competent and based on sufficient facts and data, the court cannot make a credibility determination that the affidavit does not create a genuine issue of material fact. Sketchler v. Hernandez, 2020-01475 (La. 3/2/21), 311 So.3d 343 (per curiam).

— Court must state on the record or in writing if it declines to consider any document filed. **Art. 966(D)(2).**

COURT SHALL CONSIDER ANY DOCUMENTS TO WHICH NO OBJECTION IS MADE. Art. 966(D)(2)

— After considering a document, a court may give no evidentiary value to it if the document would not be admissible at trial. Cryer v. Tangi Pines Nursing Ctr., 2017-0697 (La. App. 1 Cir. 12/21/17), 240 So.3d 975.

COURT MAY NOT CONSIDER ANYTHING IN THE RECORD THAT IS NOT FILED BY THE PARTIES IN SUPPORT OF OR IN OPPOSITION TO. Art. 966(D)(2); Forstall v. City of New Orleans, 2017-0414 (La. App. 4 Cir. 1/17/18), 238 So.3d 465; Cryer v. Tangi Pines Nursing Ctr., 2017-0697 (La. App. 1 Cir. 12/21/17), 240 So.3d 975.

ONLY ISSUES ON WHICH COURT MAY GRANT OR DENY SUMMARY JUDGMENT ARE THOSE RAISED IN THE MOTION FOR SUMMARY JUDGMENT. Art. 966(F): Cutrone v. English Turn Property Owners Ass'n, 2019-0896 (La. App. 4 Cir. 3/4/20), 293 So.3d 1209.

SUMMARY JUDGMENT IS RARELY APPROPRIATE IN CASES REQUIRING JUDICIAL DETERMINATION OF SUBJECTIVE FACTS SUCH AS INTENT, MOTIVE, MALICE, GOOD FAITH, OR KNOWLEDGE. Wroten v. Ferriday Auto Ventures, LLC, 20-387 (La. App. 3 Cir. 12/16/20), 310 So.3d 621, writ denied, 2021-00085 (La. 3/9/21), 312 So.3d 585; Priority Hospital Group, Inc. v. Manning, 53,564 (La. App. 2 Cir. 9/23/20), 303 So.3d 1106.

CHECKLIST FOR SUMMARY JUDGMENT UNDER C.C.P. ARTS. 966–967

TIMING OF PARTIES' FILINGS Art. 966(B)

Unless extended by the court AND agreed to by all parties

— MOTION FOR SUMMARY JUDGMENT and supporting documents filed not later than 65 days before trial.

— OPPOSITION TO SUMMARY JUDGMENT and supporting documents filed not later than 15 days before hearing of motion.

— REPLY not later than 5 days before hearing of motion.

— If last day is a legal holiday, then next day that is not a legal holiday.

— When the court grants a motion to continue a hearing on a motion for summary judgment, the filing deadlines are reset. Reed v. Restorative Home Health Care, LLC, 2019-01974 (La. 2/26/20), 289 So.3d 1028 (per curiam).

TIMING OF COURT ACTIONS Art. 966(C)

Unless otherwise agreed to by all parties AND the court

— CONTRADICTORY HEARING on motion held not less than 30 days after motion filed and not less than 40 days before trial.

— NOTICE OF HEARING served on parties (sheriff's service **Art. 1314** or registered or certified mail, actual delivery by commercial courier, or electronic service to attorney's email address on pleading **Art. 1313(C)**) not less than 30 days before hearing.

— JUDGMENT ON MOTION not less than 20 days before trial.

JUDGMENT Art. 966(C)(4)

— Court shall state on the record or in writing reasons for granting or denying.

— If in writing AND designated as final and appealable under **Art. 1915**, reasons must be in a separate document than judgment. **Art. 1918**.

ARE SUMMARY JUDGMENTS FINAL AND APPEALABLE? Art. 1915

— If dismisses entire case, yes. **Art. 1915(A)(3).**

— If dismisses a party, yes. **Art. 1915(A)(1).**

— If partial summary judgment, no unless designated as final after determination that there is not just reason for delay under **Art. 1915(B).**

— A denial of a summary judgment is never appealable.

MAY A PARTY FILE A SECOND MOTION FOR SUMMARY JUDGMENT? Yes. Talbert v. Restoration Hardware, Inc., 2017-0986 (La. App. 1 Cir. 5/31/18), 251 So.3d 532, writ denied, 2018-1102 (La. 10/15/18), 253 So.3d 1304.

IS A CONTRADICTORY HEARING REQUIRED ON A MOTION FOR SUMMARY JUDGMENT? Yes. **Art. 966(C)(1)(a)**; Viering v. Liberty Mut. Ins. Co., 2017-0204 (La. App. 1 Cir. 9/27/17), 232 So.3d 598, writ denied, 2017-1821 (La. 12/15/17), 231 So.3d 637.

CHECKLIST FOR SUCCESSION PROCEDURE

I. SIMPLE SUCCESSION

A. Petition (C.C.P. art. 3002) by all of the heirs (C.C.P. art. 3001, if all are competent, accept the succession and succession is relatively free of debt.)

1. Petition shall include:
   a. Competency of petitioners
      1. Heirs
      2. Surviving spouse
         a. Must state facts showing that she is the surviving spouse.
   b. Date of Death
   c. Facts on which jurisdiction and venue is based
      1. Venue is jurisprudential. (C.C.P. arts. 2811, 44)
   d. Facts showing that petitioners are sole heirs
   e. Succession is relatively free of debt (C.C.P. art. 3001)
      1. Only has:
         a. Administrative expenses
         b. Mortgages not in arrears
         c. Debts small in comparison with assets
2. Must be verified by the affidavit of at least one of the petitioners. (C.C.P. art. 3002)

B. Affidavit of Death and Heirship (C.C.P. arts. 3003, 2821-2823)

1. Also can be provided by official certificates (C.C.P. art. 2821)
   (Cannot use affidavits if there is a dispute or contradictory hearing. (C.C.P. art. 2824)

C. Detailed Descriptive List (C.C.P. art. 3136)

1. Sworn to and subscribed by person filing it.
2. Shows the location of all items of property.
3. Set forth the fair market value of each item at the time of death.

D. Judgment of Possession

1. Ex parte judgment immediately signed by Judge. (C.C.P. arts. 3301, 3004, 3061)
2. Should include:
   a. Recognize heirs and/or surviving spouse and send them into possession (C.C.P. art. 3061)
   b. The last known address of at least one of the heirs or surviving spouse.
3. It is prima facie proof of their right to possession of the estate of the deceased. (C.C.P. art. 3062)

4. Describe all property carefully - especially stocks and VIN numbers on movables.
5. Send certified copies to banks, agents for stock transfer, etc.

II. SIMPLE SUCCESSION WITH A WILL

A. Petition for probate of will (C.C.P. art. 2851)

B. Petition for affidavit of death and heirship (C.C.P. art. 2852)
   1. Can be provided by official certificates (C.C.P. arts. 2821-22)
      a. Cannot use affidavits if there is a dispute or contradictory hearing. (C.C.P. art. 2824)

C. Original Will (C.C.P. art. 2853)
   1. Must present it to the court even though you do not think it is valid.
      a. Search for will - if the will cannot be located. Order to inspect bank boxes, safety deposit boxes. (C.C.P. art. 2854)
      b. Appoint notary and notary makes return even if search unsuccessful. (C.C.P. art. 2855)

D. Must present will within 5 years of the opening of the succession of the deceased. (C.C.P. art. 2893).

E. If no objection, court probates will ex parte. (C.C.P. art. 2881)
   1. If the will is a notarial testament, statutory testament, or nuncupative testament by public act, no proof is necessary, court shall order it filed and executed. (C.C.P. art. 2891)
   2. If olographic will, must be proved by two credible witnesses.
      a. This may be done by affidavits. (C.C.P. art. 2883)
      b. This may be done by deposition. (C.C.P. art. 2889)

F. Procès Verbal of Probate (C.C.P. art. 2890)
   1. If live witnesses or depositions or videotape, a procès verbal must be prepared and signed by judge describing what happened at the probate hearing.

G. Procès Verbal Not Necessary (C.C.P. art. 2890(B))
   1. If only written affidavits are used, procès verbal shall be dispensed with and court <u>shall</u> enter a written order finding that:
      a. Will has been proved or
      b. Refusing to probate the testament and giving the reasons therefore.

H. Once will is probated, do the same steps as a simple succession except legatees may only be sent into possession if the person named as executor joins in the petition. (C.C.P. art. 3033)

III. SIMPLE SUCCESSION WITH A CONTESTED WILL

A. Petition for Probate (C.C.P. art. 2851)

B. Affidavit of death and heirship (C.C.P. art. 2852)

C. File the purported testament (C.C.P. art. 2853)

D. Objection to the will
  1. Must be filed prior to hearing or orally at the hearing (C.C.P. art. 2881)
    a. If an objection is made orally, court will allow up to 10 days to file written opposition (C.C.P. art. 2901)
    b. Opposition must contain (C.C.P. art. 2972)
      1. Name, surname and domicile of opponent.
      2. Interest of opponent in filing the opposition.
      3. Grounds for the opposition.
      4. Prayer for appropriate relief.
    c. Opposition must be served on petitioner for probate (C.C.P. art. 2902)

E. Contradictory hearing
  1. Proponent (petitioner for probate usually) bears the burden of proving the authenticity of the testament and compliance with all formal requirements (C.C.P. art. 2903)
  2. Videotape of the execution of the will is admissible (C.C.P. art. 2904)
    a. Testator must be sworn and oath must be recorded on videotape - the execution and reading of the will may be used for:
      1. Proper execution of will.
      2. Intentions of testator.
      3. Mental state or capacity of testator.
      4. Authenticity of will.
      5. Any relevant matters determined by court.

F. Procès Verbal (C.C.P. art. 2890)
  1. After hearing, a procès verbal is prepared and judge signs a probated will or an order refusing to probate the will and gives his reasons therefore.

G. Appeals
  1. Same as in ordinary proceedings. (C.C.P. art. 2974)

H. Proceed with the same steps as simple succession.

IV. ATTACKING WILL AFTER IT IS PROBATED

A. Petition to Annul Probated Testament (C.C.P. art. 2931)

1. File a direct action against:
   a. Legatees
   b. Residuary heir
   c. Executor, if appointed and has not been discharged.
2. Prescriptive Period is 5 years. (C.C. art. 3497)
3. Burden of Proof (C.C.P. art. 2932)
   a. Plaintiff - if the action is brought more than 3 months after will is probated.
   b. Defendants (legatees, heirs, executor) if the action to annul is brought within 3 months of the will being probated. (Same as C.C.P. art. 2903)
   c. If it is notarial will, statutory will, or nuncupative will by public act, plaintiff always has the burden (C.C.P. art. 2932(B)).

CHECKLIST FOR A REGULAR PARTITION ACTION

I. Petition to Partition (by kind or licitation). (C.C.P. art. 4603)

a. May request an inventory. (C.C.P. art. 4604)

II. Service on all owners in indivision.

III. Answer

IV. Trial

a. To determine co-ownership.

b. To determine if property is to be divided in kind or by licitation.

V. Judgment ordering Partition and the Appointment of Notary. (C.C.P. art. 4605)

a. Unless the property is indivisible or cannot be divided, the Court shall order the partition to be made in kind. (C.C.P. art. 4606)

VI. In Kind Partition. (C.C. art. 810)

a. Property is divided into lots of nearly equal value; and

b. The value of the aggregate lots is approximately equal in value to the value of the whole.

VII. By Private Sale or Licitation. (C.C. art. 811, C.C.P. art. 4605)

a. When the thing held indivision is not susceptible to partition in kind, the Court shall decree a partition by licitation or by private sale.

b. The court shall give first priority to the private sale between the existing co-owners over the sale by licitation or to third parties.

c. If by licitation, a public auction after advertisements and notice to all attorneys of record. (C.C.P. art. 4607)

d. If the sale of the thing to a third person is excluded by the provision agreement, an auction is conducted among the co-owners.

e. If the partition is by private sale without the consent of all co-owners, the sale shall not be less than for the appraised value.

f. The documents shall be executed on behalf of the non-consenting co-owners by a court-appointed representative.

VIII. Notary prepares and files Procès Verbal. (C.C.P. art. 4609)

IX. Any party may file a rule to show cause why the partition (procès verbal) should not be homologated or rejected. (C.C.P. art. 4609)

a. Service on all parties of the rule to show cause.

X. If no opposition is filed within ten (10) days - Judgment of Partition is homologated. (C.C.P. art. 4610).

XI. If an opposition is filed a <u>hearing</u> to determine partition is held.

a. If the partition is rejected- go back to same or different notary to prepare a supplementary act of partition. (C.C.P. art. 4611)

b. If sustained, court signs the homologation judgment.

CHECKLIST FOR A PARTITION BY LICITATION WHEN ONE OF THE CO-OWNERS IS AN ABSENTEE

I. Petition for Partition by Licitation or Private Sale (C.C.P. art. 4621)

a. Facts showing an absent and unrepresented defendant.

b. Allegations that partition by private sale between co-owners will have first priority.

c. Name of the proposed co-owner purchasers.

d. If judgment of court ordering the sale, payment shall be made within twenty-four hours using cash or certified funds. Affidavit of plaintiff or attorney.

e. Order appointing an attorney to represent the absentee defendant (C.C.P. art. 4623)

f. Order ordering the publication of notice of institution of the proceedings to partition.

II. Service

a. Regular service on all defendants.

b. Service on attorney appointed to represent absentee defendant.

III. Publication in the parish where the partition proceeding was instituted stating the primary terms and if by private sale. (C.C.P. art. 4624)

IV. Trial (C.C.P. art. 4625)

a. If no opposition or if absentee does not appear in court, the court renders a judgment ordering the private sale between co-owners for cash or certified funds, the private sale to a third-party, or a public sale of the property for cash.

b. If the absentee has an attorney, maybe a partition in kind. (C.C.P. art. 4630)

V. Judgment

a. Ordering the private sale to co-owners at appraised value.

b. Ordering the private sale to a third-party.

c. Ordering the sale of the property at public auction for cash.

d. Order reimbursement of co-owner of amount he has proved he is due for taxes and expenses.

e. Payment due to co-owner of amount due to him from fruits and revenues.

f. If a private sale is ordered the court shall appoint a court-appointed representative to sign the sale for the absentee (C.C.P. art. 4625)

VI. After Sale- amount due absentee is placed in the registry of the court not to be withdrawn without court approval. (C.C.P. art. 4628)

CHECKLIST FOR DIVORCE

Form G	**LA. C.C. ART. 102 DIVORCE CHECKLIST**

This form is from the Family Court of the Nineteenth Judicial District Court which granted permission for the form to be used herein.

______________________________ **NO:** ________________ **DIV:** _____

(PETITIONER)

VERSUS **THE FAMILY COURT**

PARISH OF

______________________________ **STATE OF LOUISIANA**

(DEFENDANT)

THE PETITION

- Date the parties were married: _________________
- Date the petition was filed: _________________
- Does the petition have a verifying affidavit? ______
- Does the petition contain allegations of jurisdiction and venue? ______
- Date the parties began living separate and apart: _________________
- Service / waiver of petition (*select one*):

  ____ Personal / domiciliary service on: _________________

  ____ Waiver was executed on: __________ and filed on: ____________

  ____ Long arm service delivery on: __________ and affidavit filed: ____

THE RULE TO SHOW CAUSE

- Date the rule was filed: _________________
- Does the rule have a verifying affidavit? ______
- Does the rule allege proper service / waiver of the petition? ______
- The requisite period of time to live separate and apart (select one):

  _____ 180 days- there are no minor children of the marriage

  _____ 365 days- there are minor children of the marriage at the time the rule to show cause is filed
- Does the rule allege the requisite period of time has elapsed since service / waiver? ______
- Does the rule allege the parties have lived separate and apart for the requisite period of time? ______
- Service / waiver of rule (*select one*):

  ____ Personal / domiciliary service on: _________________

CHECKLIST FOR DIVORCE—FORM G

_____ Waiver was executed on: ____________ and filed on: ______________

_____ Long arm service delivery on: ____________ and affidavit filed: ____

MOVER'S AFFIDAVIT

- Was the final affidavit executed by the mover after the rule was filed? _______
- Does the affidavit state the parties have lived separate and apart for the requisite period of time prior to the filing of the rule? _______
- Does the affidavit state the parties still live separate and apart, and that the mover desires to be divorced? _______

CERTIFICATION OF ATTORNEY

I certify that the information I have provided above is correct after an examination of the record.

_______________________________ _____________________

ATTORNEY SIGNATURE DATE

THE FAMILY COURT FORM G REVISED: AUG 2014

Form 1	DEFAULT CONFIRMATION OF LA. C.C. ART. 103 DIVORCE PURSUANT TO LA. C.C.P. ART. 1702(E) CHECKLIST

This form is from the Family Court of the Nineteenth Judicial District Court which granted permission for the form to be used herein.

________________________ **NO:** ________________ **DIV:** ____

(PETITIONER)

VERSUS

THE FAMILY COURT

PARISH OF

STATE OF LOUISIANA

____

(DEFENDANT)

- Date the parties were married: ________________
- For La. C.C. art. 103(1): date the parties began living separate and apart: ________________________________
- The requisite period of time to live separate and apart (*select one*):
  ____ 180 days- there are no minor children of the marriage
  ____ 365 days- there are minor children of the marriage
- For La. C.C. art. 103(5): date that a protective order or injunction was issued against the defendant to protect the petitioner or a child of one of the spouses from abuse: ________________
- Date the petition was filed: ________________
- Service / waiver (*select one*):
  ____ Personal / domiciliary service on: ________________
  ____ Waiver was executed on: __________ and filed on: __________
  ____ Long arm service delivery on: __________ and affidavit filed: ____
- Is there two days exclusive of holidays from the date the affidavit waiving all legal delays was filed in a 103(1) divorce. See 1702(E)(2).
- Is there an affidavit specifically attesting to and testifying as to the truth of all of the factual allegations contained in the petition? ________

CHECKLIST FOR DIVORCE—FORM 1

CERTIFICATION OF ATTORNEY

I certify that the information I have provided above is correct after an examination of the record.

______________________________ ____________________

ATTORNEY SIGNATURE DATE

CERTIFICATION OF MINUTE CLERK

I certify that after examining the record, no answer or opposition has been filed in the proceeding.

______________________________ ____________________

MINUTE CLERK SIGNATURE DATE

Form 2	UNCONTESTED LA. C.C. ART. 103 DIVORCE PURSUANT TO LA. C.C.P. ART. 969(B) CHECKLIST

This form is from the Family Court of the Nineteenth Judicial District Court which granted permission for the form to be used herein.

_______________________________ **NO:** _______________ **DIV:** ____

(PETITIONER)

VERSUS **THE FAMILY COURT**

PARISH OF

_______________________________ **STATE OF LOUISIANA**

(DEFENDANT)

- Date the parties were married: _______________
- Date the parties began living separate and apart: _______________
- The requisite period of time to live separate and apart (select one):
  ____ 180 days- there are no minor children of the marriage
  ____ 365 days- there are minor children of the marriage
- Date the petition was filed: _______________
- Does the petition have a verifying affidavit? ______
- Is the petitioner represented by an attorney? ______
- Service / waiver (*select one*):
  ____ Personal / domiciliary service on: _______________
  ____ Waiver was executed on: __________ and filed on: __________
  ____ Long arm service delivery on: __________ and affidavit filed: ____
- Date the answer was filed: _______________
- Is the defendant represented by an attorney? __________
- Is there a joint stipulation of facts, request for judgment, and sworn verification by each party filed by counsels for both parties? __________

CHECKLIST FOR DIVORCE—FORM 2

- Is there a proposed judgment containing a certification that both counsels and both parties agree to its terms? ______________

CERTIFICATION OF ATTORNEY

I certify that the information I have provided above is correct after an examination of the record.

______________________________ ______________________

ATTORNEY SIGNATURE DATE

CHECKLIST FOR INTERDICTION PROCEEDINGS
(C.C.P. arts. 4541-4570)

I. Regular Interdiction Proceedings

A. Verified Petition (filed by any person) containing the following: (C.C.P. art. 4541)

1. Name, domicile, age and current address of the petitioner and relationship to the defendant.
2. Name, domicile, age and current address of the defendant, and where the petitioner proposes the defendant will reside.
3. Reasons why the interdiction is necessary.
4. If full interdiction is requested, why limited interdiction is inappropriate.
5. If limited interdiction is requested, the capacity sought to be removed.
6. Name and address of the spouse of the defendant (if not the petitioner).
7. Name and address of adult children, or if he has none, name and address of parents and siblings, or if he has none, name and address of nearest adult relative.
8. Name and address of any legal representative or previous curator.
9. Name, domicile, age, education, and current address of the proposed curator and reasons why the proposed curator should be appointed.
10. A description of the petitioner's efforts to use less restrictive means before seeking interdiction, including all of the following:
    - (a) The less restrictive means for meeting the defendant's needs that were considered or implemented.
    - (b) If a less restrictive means was not considered or implemented, the reason that the less restrictive means was not considered or implemented.
    - (c) The reason a less restrictive means is insufficient to meet the needs of the defendant.

B. Service (C.C.P. art. 4543)

1. Must be personal
2. Within 3 days of filing of petition, petitioner must send by certified mail, return receipt requested, notice to all persons named in the petition.
3. File notarized affidavit in the record affirming personal delivery.

C. If defendant does not answer within 15 days after service, petitioner must apply to court to have an attorney appointed to represent the defendant. (C.C.P. art. 4544)

D. Petitioner may ask court to appoint a doctor to examine the defendant. (C.C.P. art. 4545)

E. Petitioner shall request the court to set an interdiction hearing. (C.C.P. art. 4546)

F. Notice of hearing must be personally served on the defendant. (C.C.P. art. 4546)

G. All parties listed in the petition shall receive notice of the hearing by regular mail at least 10 days prior to the hearing.

H. Defendant has right to be present and the court cannot have a hearing without the defendant unless there is good cause. (C.C.P. art. 4547)

I. After hearing, court issues a judgment of interdiction which shall contain: (C.C.P. art. 4551)
1. Appointment of a curator.
2. Appointment of an undercurator.
3. Powers of curator to commence upon qualification.
4. Direct clerk to record judgment in mortgage and conveyance records.
5. Set forth the name, domicile, age, and current address of the defendant.
6. Must state whether it is a full or limited interdiction.

J. Curator must:
1. File Detailed Descriptive List/Inventory (C.C.P. art. 4563)
2. Post Security (C.C.P. arts. 4563, 4131) in an amount equal to the interdict's movable property.
3. Take an oath. (C.C.P. art. 4562)
4. Obtain from the Clerk of Court Letters of Curatorship. (C.C.P. art. 4564)
5. Within fifteen days of his qualification, the curator shall cause the judgment of interdiction to be recorded in the conveyance and mortgage records of every other parish in which the interdict owns immovable property. (C.C.P. art. 4552)

K. Undercurator must take oath. (C.C.P. art. 4565)

II. Interdiction Proceedings with Temporary & Preliminary Interdiction

A. Verified Petition for Interdiction containing all of the elements of C.C.P. art. 4541 and additionally:
1. Request for an order of temporary interdiction included with a Verified Petition or affidavit showing immediate and irreparable injury, loss, or damage will result to the person or property of the defendant before a hearing can be held and the defendant and/or his attorney can be heard.
2. Affidavit by a licensed physician or psychologist attesting to the fact that there is a substantial likelihood that the grounds for interdiction exist and substantial harm to the health, safety, or property of the person sought to be interdicted is imminent. (C.C.P. art. 4549, C.C. art. 391)

3. Affidavit of the petitioner or his attorney attesting to the efforts made to give notice to the defendant or reasons why notice should not be given.

B. Ex parte judgment of temporary interdiction which includes:
1. A date for the preliminary interdiction hearing (which can be no more than 10 days from the signing but can be extended for an additional 10 days).
2. Why the order was granted without notice and without adversarial hearing.
3. An order appointing an attorney to represent the defendant. (C.C.P. art. 4549(A))

C. No later than 72 hours prior to preliminary injunction hearing, all orders, pleadings, and supporting documents must be served upon the defendant and his attorney.
1. Reasonable notice of preliminary injunction hearing shall be given to all parties listed in the petition, if possible.

D. Adversarial hearing on Preliminary Interdiction. (C.C.P. art. 4549(B)(1))

E. Judgment of Preliminary Interdiction (expires 30 days after signed but may be extended for an additional 30 days. C.C. art. 397) and (must set forth date of termination C.C.P. art. 4551(C))

F. Steps D-K as above.

CHECKLIST FOR TUTORSHIP PROCEEDINGS

I. Natural tutor (C.C. arts. 250-256; C.C.P. arts. 4061-4061.1)

A. Verified petition to be recognized/confirmed as tutor (C.C.P. art. 4031)

B. Inventory/detailed descriptive list (C.C.P. arts. 4101, 4462)

C. Recordation of clerk's certificate (C.C.P. art. 4134) (C.C. art. 322-legal mortgage in favor of minor)

   1. Bond or special mortgage instead of legal mortgage (C.C.P. art. 4135)

D. Order appointing tutor and undertutor (C.C.P. art. 4201)

E. Oath by tutor and undertutor (C.C.P. arts. 4061, 4171, 4201)

F. Issuance of letters of tutorship by clerk (C.C.P. art. 4172)

II. Tutorship by will (C.C. arts. 257-262; C.C.P. art. 4062)

A. Verified petition to be recognized/confirmed as tutor (C.C.P. art. 4031)

B. Will or other notarial act designating the tutor

C. Inventory/detailed descriptive list (C.C.P. arts. 4101, 4462)

D. Furnish security in an amount equal to the total value of the minor's movable property. (C.C.P. art. 4131)

   1. If the asset is only a claim for damages, court may postpone the posting of security until the claim is recovered. (C.C.P. art. 4131(D))

   2. Security can be (C.C.P. art. 4132)

      a. Surety bond (C.C.P. art. 4132(A)(1))

      b. State or municipal bonds or certificates of deposit (C.C.P. art. 4132(A)(2))

      c. Two personal sureties who are residents of state and have unencumbered property sufficient to meet the bond amount. C.C.P. art. 4132(A)(3))

      d. Special mortgage on immovable property, which is unencumbered and approved by court. (C.C.P. art. 4133)

E. Order appointing tutor and undertutor (C.C.P. art. 4201)

F. Oath by tutor and undertutor (C.C.P. arts. 4171, 4201)

G. Issuance of letters of tutorship by clerk (C.C.P. art. 4172)

   1. Tutor may not be appointed if he is

      a. Disqualified from being a tutor (C.C.P. art. 4231)

      b. Appointment is not in the best interest of the minor (C.C.P. art. 4062)

III. Tutorship by law (C.C. art. 263; C.C.P. art. 4063) or dative tutor (C.C. art. 270; C.C.P. art. 4064)

A. Verified petition to be confirmed as to tutor and undertutor
   1. Affidavit annexed to the petition listing
      a. Minor's ascendants and collaterals within the 3rd degree (C.C.P art. 4065)
      b. Surviving spouse of mother or father dying last who reside in the state (C.C.P art. 4065)
   2. Copy of the petition must be mailed by registered or certified mail to each person listed on the affidavit (C.C.P. art. 4065)

B. Notice of application shall be published once in the parish where the petition is filed. (C.C.P. art. 4065)

C. Opposition can be filed and heard in a summary proceeding. (C.C.P. arts. 4066-4067)

D. If no opposition after 10 days from publication or date of mailing of notice, whichever is longer, court shall appoint petitioner as tutor. (C.C.P. art. 4067)

E. Furnish security (same as tutorship by will). (C.C.P. arts. 4131, 4132)

F. Order appointing tutor and undertutor. (C.C.P. art. 4201)

G. Oath by tutor and undertutor (C.C.P. arts. 4171, 4201)

H. Issuance of letter of tutorship by clerk (C.C.P. art. 4172)

CHECKLIST FOR JUDICIAL SALE AFTER JUDGMENT

1. Executory judgment (C.C.P. art. 2252)
   a. Only after all suspensive appeal delays have expired. Motion for new trial - 7 days exclusive of holidays (C.C.P. art. 1974) & suspensive appeal - 30 days (C.C.P. art. 2123).

2. Letter to clerk (C.C.P. art. 2253)
   a. Asking clerk to issue writ of fifa to sheriff to seize property of the judgment debtor.

3. Writ of fifa (C.C.P. arts. 2253, 2291)
   a. Directed to sheriff commanding him to seize property of judgment debtor.
   b. Can be issued to any sheriff in any parish of more than 1 sheriff. (C.C.P. art. 2253)
   c. Only good for 1 year (C.C.P. art. 2294) except Orleans Parish city court writs are only good for 6 months. (C.C.P. art. 2294.1)
   d. If determined unsatisfied, may issue another writ. (C.C.P. art. 2297)

4. Notice of seizure (C.C.P. art. 2293(B))
   a. Must be served on judgment debtor by personal (C.C.P. art. 1232) or domiciliary service (C.C.P. art. 1234).
      1. If cannot serve judgment debtor, may serve his attorney.
      2. If can't serve either, must serve an attorney appointed to represent the judgment debtor.
   b. Must serve occupants of seized property.
      1. Service by personal (C.C.P. art. 1232) or domiciliary service (C.C.P. art. 1234).
      2. If cannot make, may post on the main entrance; if over 10 units, can serve by posting a sign.

5. Designate order of sale (C.C.P. art. 2295)

6. Motion to release excess property seized (C.C.P. art. 2296)

7. Injunction prohibiting the sale (C.C.P. art. 2298)

8. Advertisement (C.C.P. art. 2331)
   a. Once at least 10 days before the sale for movable (R.S. 43:203(1))
   b. Twice, at least 30 days prior to the sheriff's sale for the first advertisement and not earlier than 7 days for the second advertisement before the sale (R.S. 43:203(2))
   c. Before advertisement, 3 days exclusive of holidays must have elapsed after service of notice

d. If the judicial sale is cancelled or postponed and rescheduled for a later date, notice of sale of property under a writ of fifa shall be published once in a manner provided by law. (C.C.P. art. 2331)

9. Appraisal (C.C.P. art. 2332)
   a. Each party can name an appraiser (R.S. 13:4363)

10. Sale (C.C.P. arts. 2334-2338, 2295, 2296)
    a. 2/3 for 1st sale if with appraisement, 2nd sale for any price.
    1. Debt reduced at 2nd sale, 1/2 of appraisal value minus superior liens or bid amount that exceeds superior liens, whichever is greater.

11. Not sold if bid does not exceed costs plus superior liens (C.C.P. art. 2337).

12. Act of sale (C.C.P. art. 2342)
    a. Sheriff's deed to be passed within 15 days of the sheriff's sale.

13. Distribution of proceeds (C.C.P. arts. 2372-2377)
    a. After costs are taken out, sheriff pays:
       1. Seizing creditor (if he is the 1st lienholder)
       2. Holders of inferior liens
       3. Judgment debtor - anything remaining

CODE OF CIVIL PROCEDURE
ANALYSIS

BOOK I—COURTS, ACTIONS, AND PARTIES

TITLE I—COURTS

CHAPTER 1. JURISDICTION

CHAPTER 2. VENUE

SECTION 1. GENERAL DISPOSITIONS

SECTION 2. EXCEPTIONS TO GENERAL RULES

TITLE IV—PRE–TRIAL PROCEDURE

TITLE V—TRIAL

CHAPTER 1. CONSOLIDATION OF CASES AND SEPARATE TRIALS OF ISSUES OF LIABILITY AND DAMAGES

TITLE IV—FOREIGN JUDGMENTS

BOOK V—SUMMARY AND EXECUTORY PROCEEDINGS

TITLE I—SUMMARY PROCEEDINGS

TITLE II—EXECUTORY PROCEEDINGS

CHAPTER 1. GENERAL DISPOSITIONS

CHAPTER 2. PROCEEDING AGAINST SURVIVING SPOUSE, SUCCESSION, OR HEIR

CHAPTER 3. PROCEEDINGS WHEN PROPERTY IN POSSESSION OF THIRD PERSON

CHAPTER 4. EXECUTION OF WRIT OF SEIZURE AND SALE

BOOK VII—SPECIAL PROCEEDINGS

TITLE I—PROVISIONAL REMEDIES

CHAPTER 1. ATTACHMENT AND SEQUESTRATION

SECTION 1. GENERAL DISPOSITIONS

SECTION 2. ATTACHMENT

SECTION 3. SEQUESTRATION

CHAPTER 2. INJUNCTION

TITLE II—REAL ACTIONS

CHAPTER 1. ACTIONS TO DETERMINE OWNERSHIP OR POSSESSION

CHAPTER 2. BOUNDARY ACTION

CHAPTER 3. HYPOTHECARY ACTION

SECTION 1. GENERAL DISPOSITIONS

SECTION 2. HYPOTHECARY ACTION AGAINST THIRD PERSON

TITLE II—DEFINITIONS

LOUISIANA CODE OF CIVIL PROCEDURE

ACTS 1960, NO. 15

AN ACT to revise the Code of Practice of the State of Louisiana by adopting a system of laws consolidating the procedural rules applicable generally to civil actions and proceedings, to be known as the Louisiana Code of Civil Procedure; to provide for the continuous revision thereof; to repeal the Code of Practice of the State of Louisiana, and all other laws in conflict or inconsistent with the provisions of the code hereby adopted; to provide that the provisions of this act shall prevail over the conflicting provisions of any other act adopted at this legislative session; and to provide the effective date of this act.

BE IT ENACTED BY THE LEGISLATURE OF LOUISIANA:

SECTION 1. The Louisiana Code of Civil Procedure, as set forth hereinafter in this section, is hereby adopted and enacted into law:

BOOK I

COURTS, ACTIONS, AND PARTIES

TITLE I. COURTS

INTRODUCTION TO 1960 CODE OF CIVIL PROCEDURE

The concept of jurisdiction, under the Codes of Practice of 1825 and 1870, was subdivided into "jurisdiction ratione materiae" and "jurisdiction ratione personae". This classification was patterned upon the "compétence ratione materiae" and "compétence ratione personae" of French procedure. Comment, Jurisdiction Ratione Materiae et Personae in Louisiana, 12 La.L.Rev. 210 (1951). These twin concepts of Louisiana procedure correspond closely with the "jurisdiction over subject matter" and "venue" of Anglo-American law.

Prior to 1878, the problems solved by the Anglo-American concept of "jurisdiction over the person" were solved by Louisiana procedure, under a different approach, by an application of the code requirements of citation and service of process. Cf. Art. 206, Louisiana Codes of Practice of 1825 and 1870. The decision of the United States Supreme Court in Pennoyer v. Neff, 95 U.S. 714, 24 L.Ed. 565 (1878), not only engrafted the concept of "jurisdiction over the person" onto our procedural system, as requirements of due process of law and full faith and credit, but also introduced the by-products of this concept, the classification of "jurisdiction in personam", "jurisdiction in rem", and "jurisdiction quasi in rem". A modern Louisiana codification of procedural law would be unrealistic if it failed to give recognition to all of these important procedural concepts.

Recent decisions of the Louisiana courts have served to obscure to some extent the line of demarcation between the twin civilian concepts of jurisdiction ratione materiae and jurisdiction ratione personae. Cf. Bercegeay v. Techeland Oil Corporation, 209 La. 33, 24 So.2d 242 (1945), noted 7 La.L.Rev. 437 (1947). See also, Mitcham v. Mitcham, 186 La. 641, 173 So. 132 (1937); Johnston v. Burton, 202 La. 182, 11 So.2d 513 (1942); and Comment, Jurisdiction Ratione Materiae et Personae in Louisiana, 12 La.L.Rev. 210 (1951). Additional confusion might possibly result from the majority opinion in Tanner v. Beverly Country Club, 217 La. 1043, 47 So.2d 906 (1950), noted 25 Tul.L.Rev. 399 (1951), in which the civilian concept of jurisdiction ratione personae was treated as if identical with the Anglo-American "jurisdiction over the person".

For these reasons, this Code adopts the Anglo-American concepts of jurisdiction, jurisdiction over the subject matter, jurisdiction over the person, and venue. In view of the constitutional requirements of due process of law and full faith and credit, this represents little more than a realistic change of terminology.

CHAPTER 1. JURISDICTION

Article

Art. 1. Jurisdiction defined

Jurisdiction is the legal power and authority of a court to hear and determine an action or proceeding involving the legal relations of the parties, and to grant the relief to which they are entitled.

Official Revision Comments—1960

(a) See Introduction to this Title.

(b) In this article there is presented a definition of sufficient accuracy to include all elements of the term, and yet of sufficient breadth and flexibility to avoid undue restraint on the courts in their empirical development of the concept of jurisdiction, and its application to new remedies.

For the derivation of the word "jurisdiction" and a general definition thereof, see Wedding v. Meyler, 192 U.S. 573, 24 S.Ct. 122, 48 L.Ed. 570, 66 L.R.A. 833 (1904); Central R. Co. v. Jersey City, 209 U.S. 473, 28 S.Ct. 592, 52 L.Ed. 896 (1909); Nielson v. State of Oregon, 212 U.S. 315, 29 S.Ct. 833, 53 L.Ed. 528 (1910).

Aside from the indirect source provision of this article and Succession of Weigel, 17 La.Ann. 70 (1865), the Louisiana law afforded little help in providing an accurate definition of jurisdiction. See State ex rel. Phelps v. Judge, 45 La.Ann. 1250, 14 So. 310 (1893); Allen v. Shreveport Mut. Bldg. Ass'n, 183 La. 521, 164 So. 328 (1935); and 7 La.L.Rev. 437, 439, n. 9 (1947).

Some courts define jurisdiction merely in terms of judicial power. See Johnson v. McKinnon, 54 Fla. 221, 45 So. 23 (1907) and cases cited. One of the most complete definitions of the term is to be found in Black on Judgments (2d ed.) 322 (1902). But it is entirely too complex and lengthy to serve as the predicate of a code definition. The majority of cases define the term as "the power to hear and determine a cause" or "the authority to hear and determine a cause." See the cases cited in 23 Words & Phrases (Perm.ed.) 367 (1940). See, also, General Invest. Co. v. New York Cent. R. Co., 271 U.S. 228, 46 S.Ct. 497, 70 L.Ed. 920 (1926); State ex rel. Shoemaker v. Hall, 257 S.W. 1047 (Mo.1924); United Cemeteries Co. v. Strother, 119 S.W.2d 764 (Mo.1938); Clark v. Arizona Mut. Savings & Loan Ass'n, 217 F. 640 (D.C.Ariz.1914).

One element of the definition of this term not usually recognized expressly in the cases, but necessarily implied, is that it is the *legal* power and authority of a court. This means authority under the constitutions and laws of both the state and the United States. Withers v. Patterson, 27 Tex. 491, 86 Am.Dec. 643 (1864); In re Harkness' Estate, 83 Okla. 107, 204 P. 911 (1921). Another important limitation on the definition of the term is that the action or proceeding must involve the legal relations of the parties. Stumberg, Principles of Conflict of Laws (2d ed.) 59 (1951).

There is not included within this definition the power to enforce execution of the judgment rendered by the court, which is considered an integral part of the definition by some courts. See Worcester v. Georgia, 6 Pet. 515, 8 L.Ed. 483 (1832); In re Ferguson, 9 John. 239 (N.Y.1812); and Dickson Fruit Co. v. District Court of Sac County, 203 Iowa 1028, 213 N.W. 803 (1927). Aside from the fact that such a definition might cause difficulty with respect to the declaratory and other types of judgments which require no enforcement, there are many valid judgments which courts have jurisdiction to render, but which they may be powerless to enforce, *e.g.*, a judgment against a nonresident who owns no property in the state and who was served with process personally while transiently in the state. In this Code the power of a court to enforce its judgment is no element of jurisdiction except to the extent that such power is included within the phrase "legal power and authority."

(c) The articles of this Title differentiate sharply the concepts of jurisdiction and venue. Generally, jurisdiction denotes the power or authority of a court to adjudicate; while venue signifies the place where the action or proceeding is to be brought and tried. . . .

Notwithstanding the fact that prior Louisiana decisions have often obscured the line of demarcation between jurisdiction ratione materiae and jurisdiction ratione personae, every effort has been made in the articles in this Title to keep the line of demarcation between jurisdiction and venue as clear and as distinct as possible. There are, however, some instances where public policy requires the institution of certain actions or proceedings in certain parishes only, under penalty of the nullity of the judgments. These exceptional cases are enumerated in the second paragraph of Art. 44, *infra*.

Art. 2. Jurisdiction over subject matter

Jurisdiction over the subject matter is the legal power and authority of a court to hear and determine a particular class of actions or proceedings, based upon the object of the demand, the amount in dispute, or the value of the right asserted.

Editor's Notes

There is no subject matter jurisdiction over Indian Tribes who have not expressly waived their sovereign immunity. Bonnett v. Tunica-Biloxi Indians, 873 So.2d 1 (La. App. 3d Cir., 2003).

Ortego v. Tunica Biloxi Indians of La., 865 So.2d 985 (La. App. 3 Cir. 2004). State Workers' Compensation Office has no jurisdiction over Workers' Compensation claims as to employer-tribe casino, which has to date not waived tribal sovereign immunity with the State.

Meyer & Assoc. v. Coushatta Tribe of La., 992 So.2d 446 (La. 2008), Indian tribe had executed waivers of sovereign immunity so that state district court was free to go on with trial rather than wait for further tribal court action to determine jurisdiction.

See also, Simon v. Board of Com'rs of New Orleans, 875 So.2d 102 (La. App. 4 Cir. 2004), no subject matter jurisdiction over Civil Service dispute, subject exclusively to jurisdiction of Civil Service Commission.

Art. 3. Same; cannot be conferred by consent

The jurisdiction of a court over the subject matter of an action or proceeding cannot be conferred by consent of the parties. A judgment rendered by a court which has no jurisdiction over the subject matter of the action or proceeding is void.

Art. 4. Same; determination when dependent on amount in dispute or value of right asserted

When the jurisdiction of a court over the subject matter of an action depends upon the amount in dispute, or value of the right asserted, it shall be determined by the amount demanded, including damages pursuant to Civil Code Articles 2315.3 and 2315.4, or value asserted in good faith by the plaintiff, but the amount in dispute does not include interest, court costs, attorney fees, or penalties, whether provided by agreement or by law.

Amended by Acts 1995, No. 409, § 1.

Comment–1995

The amendment has two purposes. First, it eliminates the conflict between Article 4 and Article 4841 as to whether penalties and attorney fees are to be included in calculating the amount in dispute by amending Article 4 to provide that the amount in dispute does not include penalties and attorney fees. Second, the amendment provides that damages pursuant to C.C. Arts. 2315.3 and 2315.4 are to be included in calculating the amount in dispute. This eliminates the uncertainty as to whether damages pursuant to C.C. Arts. 2315.3 and 2315.4 were to be treated as penalties and excluded from the calculation.

Editor's Notes

See C.C.P. art. 4841 as to parish and city courts and C.C.P. art 4911 as to justice of the peace courts.

Art. 5. Same; effect of reduction of claim

When a plaintiff reduces his claim on a single cause of action to bring it within the jurisdiction of a court and judgment is rendered thereon, he remits the portion of his claim for which he did not pray for judgment, and is precluded thereafter from demanding it judicially.

Editor's Notes

Cf. C.C.P. art. 425, pleading all causes of action arising out of the transaction or occurrence and cases cited there.

Art. 6. Jurisdiction over the person

A. Jurisdiction over the person is the legal power and authority of a court to render a personal judgment against a party to an action or proceeding. The exercise of this jurisdiction requires:

(1) The service of process on the defendant, or on his agent for the service of process, or the express waiver of citation and service under Article 1201.

(2) The service of process on the attorney at law appointed by the court to defend an action or proceeding brought against an absent or incompetent defendant who is domiciled in this state.

(3) The submission of the party to the jurisdiction of the court by commencing an action or by the waiver of objection to jurisdiction by failure to timely file the declinatory exception.

B. In addition to the provisions of Paragraph A, a court of this state may exercise personal jurisdiction over a nonresident on any basis consistent with the constitution of this state and with the Constitution of the United States. —Long Arm Jurisdiction

Amended by Acts 1997, No. 578, § 1; Acts 1999, No. 1263, § 1, eff. Jan. 1, 2000.

Official Revision Comments—1960

(a) The Anglo-American concept of jurisdiction over the person was brought into the procedural law of Louisiana as one of the requirements of due process of law by Pennoyer v. Neff, 95 U.S. 714, 24 L.Ed. 565 (1878). See Introduction to this Title.

The language of the above article, while couched in terms giving effect to the principles of procedural law peculiar to Louisiana, such as those providing for the appointment of an attorney to defend the suit when the defendant is absent or incompetent, are well within the permissible legal limits of due process of law. See Restatement of Conflict of Laws, § 42(1).

(b) For a definition of "agent for the service of process", see Art. 5251, *infra*. The words in that article, "designated . . . by law" refer to those statutes which provide that the doing of an act is deemed equivalent to the appointment of the secretary of state as the agent for the service of process in all actions brought against the person in connection with the doing of the act. See former R.S. 13.3471(5)(c), 13:3474, 13:3475, 13:3479–13:3482, and R.S. 22:1253.

(c) Art. 6(2) is declaratory of the prior law which recognized that valid service of process might be made on an attorney at law appointed by the court to defend the suit when the defendant is either an absentee or an incompetent. See Arts. 116, 294, 964, Code of Practice of 1870; Civil Code, Art. 56; former R.S. 13:3471(14). In personal actions, this substituted service is valid only as to Louisiana domiciliaries. Restatement of Conflict of Laws, § 42(1). See Art. 5091, *infra*.

(d) Art. 6(3) is declaratory of the former procedural law. See comments under Art. 7, *infra*.

(e) Since the objection to the court's lack of jurisdiction over the person of the defendant is waivable, this objection must be pleaded through the declinatory exception. Art. 925, *infra*.

(f) The service of process contemplated by this article includes either personal or domiciliary service on the defendant. See Arts. 1233 and 1234, *infra*.

(g) This article is broad enough to include the extension of the limits of jurisdiction over the person recently made by McGee v. International Life Ins. Co., 355 U.S. 220, 78 S.Ct. 199, 2 L.Ed.2d 223 (1957).

(h) See, also, Comments under Arts. 422, 925, *infra*.

Comment—1997

This amendment simplifies waiver of objection to jurisdiction by providing that a waiver only occurs through the failure to timely file the declinatory exception. The amendment eliminates the waiver through a general appearance.

Comment—1999

The 1999 amendment specifies what constitutes a party's "submission" to the court's jurisdiction. "Commencing an action" is taken from Code of Civil Procedure Article 421. Waiver of the declinatory exception is provided in Code of Civil Procedure Article 928.

Editor's Notes

La. C.C.P. art. 6 and the long-arm statute, La. R.S. 13:3201, extends personal jurisdiction of a Louisiana court to the fullest extent allowed by constitutional due process. Southeast Wireless Network, Inc. v. U.S. Telemetry Corp., 2006-1736 (La. 4/11/07), 954 So.2d 120. The United States Supreme Court has recognized two types of personal jurisdiction, general and specific jurisdiction. When the state exercises personal jurisdiction over a defendant in a suit arising out of or related to the defendant's contacts with the forum, the state is exercising specific jurisdiction over the defendant. When the states exercise personal jurisdiction over a defendant in a suit not arising out of or related to the defendant's contacts with the forum, the state is exercising general jurisdiction over the defendant. Burger King Corp. v. Rudzewicz, 471 U.S. 462, 105 S.Ct. 2174, 85 L.Ed.2d 528 (1985).

In Louisiana, in both specific and general jurisdiction cases, a two-part analysis applies. First, the plaintiff has the burden of showing minimum contacts with the forum state and then the burden shifts to the opposing party to prove that the assertion of jurisdiction would be so unreasonable in light of traditional notions of fair play and substantial justice to overcome the presumption of reasonableness created by the defendant's minimum contact with the forum. de Reyes v. Marine Mgmt. & Consulting, Ltd., 586 So.2d 103, 105 (La. 1991).

See Hensgens v. Pelican Beach Resort, 2012-268 (La. App. 3 Cir. 10/10/12), 100 So.3d 371, 372 (Florida resort had no minimum contacts with Louisiana even though it had a booking website available to Louisiana residents.); Delahoussaye v. Boelter, 2015-1790, (La. App. 1 Cir. 7/28/16), 199 So.3d 633, 635, writ denied, 2016-01626 (La. 11/18/16), 210 So.3d 290, (no minimum contacts with the defendant, a resident of Wisconsin, who sold a bicycle on e-bay three years before the accident.) See also Canon v. Towns, 2012-243 (La. App. 3 Cir. 10/3/12), 99 So.3d 1122, 1126; Lewis v. Pine Belt Multipurpose Community Action Acquisition Agency, Inc., 48,827, (La. App. 2 Cir. 4/9/14), 138 So.3d 776, 780, writ denied, 2014-0965 (La. 8/25/14), 147 So.3d 1119; Witter v. Sanibel Yacht & Slip, LLC, 2019-1031 (La. App. 1 Cir. 6/24/20), 307 So.3d 1053, 1057 (which found that the defendants lacked minimum contacts with Louisiana); see also La. R.S. 13:3201, long-arm jurisdiction, and La. R.S. 13:3474 et seq., Secretary of State as agent for a non-resident motorist, La. R.S. 13:3479, for a non-resident water-craft operator.

Art. 7. Repealed by Acts 1997, No. 578, § 5

Art. 8. Jurisdiction over property; in rem

A court which is otherwise competent under the laws of this state has jurisdiction to enforce a right in, to, or against property having a situs in this state, claimed or owned by a nonresident.

Amended by Acts 1995, No. 1104, § 1.

Art. 9. Same; quasi in rem; attachment

A court which is otherwise competent under the laws of this state has jurisdiction to render a money judgment against a nonresident if the action is commenced by an attachment of his property in this state. Unless the nonresident subjects himself personally to the jurisdiction of the court, the judgment may be executed only against the property attached.

Amended by Acts 1995, No. 1104, § 1.

Comment—1995

Former Articles 8 and 9 could only be applied if the non-resident was "not subject personally to the jurisdiction of the court". But the U.S. Supreme Court held in *Shaffer v. Heitner*, 433 U.S. 186 (1977) that quasi in rem jurisdiction could not be asserted if the non-resident did not have sufficient contact with the forum to support *in personam* jurisdiction. As a result, the articles could not be constitutionally applied. This amendment eliminates the problem by dropping the requirement that the non-resident not be subject personally to the jurisdiction of the court.

Art. 10. Jurisdiction over status

A. A court which is otherwise competent under the laws of this state has jurisdiction of the following actions or proceedings only under the following conditions:

(1) An adoption proceeding in accordance with Title XII of the Children's Code, if the surrendering parent of the child, a prospective adoptive parent, the adoptive parent or parents, or any parent of the child has been domiciled in this state for at least eight months, or if the child is in the custody of the Department of Children and Family Services; and an adoption proceeding in accordance with Civil Code Article 212, if either party to the adoption of an adult is domiciled in this state.

(2) An emancipation proceeding if the minor is domiciled in this state.

(3) An interdiction proceeding brought pursuant to the provisions of the Louisiana Uniform Adult Guardianship and Protective Proceedings Jurisdiction Act.

(4) A tutorship or curatorship proceeding if the minor or absentee, as the case may be, is domiciled in this state or has property herein.

(5) A proceeding to obtain the legal custody of a minor if he is domiciled in, or is in, this state.

(6) An action to annul a marriage if one or both of the parties are domiciled in this state.

(7) An action of divorce, if, at the time of filing, one or both of the spouses are domiciled in this state.

(8) Unless otherwise provided by law, an action to establish parentage and support or to disavow parentage if the child is domiciled in or is in this state, and was either born in this state, born out of state while its mother was domiciled in this state, or acknowledged in this state. However, regardless of the location of the child or its place of birth, an action to disavow may be brought if the person seeking to disavow was domiciled in this state at the time of conception and birth and is presumed to be its parent under the laws of this state.

(9) A proceeding for support of an adult child with a disability, as provided in R.S. 9:315.22(E), if he is domiciled in, or is in, this state.

B. For purposes of Subparagraphs (6) and (7) of Paragraph A of this Article, if a spouse has established and maintained a residence in a parish of this state for a period of six months, there shall be a rebuttable presumption that he has a domicile in this state in the parish of such residence.

Amended by Acts 1968, No. 172, § 1; Acts 1980, No. 764, § 1; Acts 1990, No. 1009, § 4, eff. Jan. 1, 1991; Acts 1999, No. 1243, § 1, eff. Jan. 1, 2000; Acts 1999, No. 1263, § 1, eff. Jan. 1, 2000; Acts 2001, No. 567, § 2; Acts 2001, No. 1064, § 1; Acts 2008, No. 351, § 2, eff. Jan. 1, 2009; Acts 2015, No. 379, § 2, eff. Aug. 1, 2016; Acts 2016, No. 333, § 2.

Comments—1990

(a) Subparagraph A(7) of this Article was amended to delete reference to the place of occurrence of the grounds for a divorce in accord with the new divorce laws implemented by Acts 1990, No. 1009.

(b) Paragraph (B) was amended to provide a rebuttable presumption of domicile after six months' residency instead of the former twelve month period.

Comments—1999

The 1999 amendment tightens the requirements for jurisdiction in adoption cases to eliminate the practice of baby selling in Louisiana.

Revision Comment—2008

Article 10(A)(1) was amended by Acts 2008, No. 351 to include a provision relative to jurisdiction for an adult adoption proceeding in accordance with Civil Code Article 212 as revised by Acts 2008, No. 351.

Editor's Notes

Uniform Child Custody Jurisdiction and Enforcement Act, R.S. 13:1801. Family court for East Baton Rouge Parish, jurisdiction, R.S. 13:1401 et seq. Liquidation and partition of the community remains under the jurisdiction of the 19th Judicial District Court, R.S. 13:1401. Orleans Parish, see R.S. 13:1138 to 13:1140 domestic relations section. Adoption venue, R.S. 9:423. Habeas corpus venue, C.C.P. art. 3822. Custody and support venue, C.C.P. art. 74.2. Filiation venue, C.C.P. art. 74.1. Tutorship venue, C.C.P. arts. 4031 to 4034.

Art. 11. Military personnel

For the purpose of status jurisdiction provided for in Article 10, a person not domiciled elsewhere in this state who is serving in the armed forces of the United States and has been stationed at one or more military installations in this state for at least six months and has resided in the parish where an action has been filed in which he is a party, for at least ninety days immediately preceding the filing of such action, is considered to be a domiciliary of this state and of the parish during the period of his service at such installations.

Added by Acts 2008, No. 801, § 2, eff. Jan. 1, 2009.

CHAPTER 2. VENUE

SECTION 1. GENERAL DISPOSITIONS

Article

SECTION 2. EXCEPTIONS TO GENERAL RULES

SECTION 1. GENERAL DISPOSITIONS

Art. 41. Definition

Venue means the parish where an action or proceeding may properly be brought and tried under the rules regulating the subject.

Art. 42. General rules

The general rules of venue are that an action against:

(1) An individual who is domiciled in the state shall be brought in the parish of his domicile; or if he resides but is not domiciled in the state, in the parish of his residence.

(2) A domestic corporation, a domestic insurer, or a domestic limited liability company shall be brought in the parish where its registered office is located.

(3) A domestic partnership, or a domestic unincorporated association, shall be brought in the parish where its principal business establishment is located.

(4) A foreign corporation or foreign limited liability company licensed to do business in this state shall be brought in the parish where its principal business establishment is located as designated in its application to do business in the state, or, if no such designation is made, then in the parish where its primary place of business in the state is located.

(5) A foreign corporation or a foreign limited liability company not licensed to do business in the state, or a nonresident who has not appointed an agent for the service of process in the manner provided by law, other than a foreign or alien insurer, shall be brought in the parish of the plaintiff's domicile or in a parish where the process may be, and subsequently is, served on the defendant.

(6) A nonresident, other than a foreign corporation or a foreign or alien insurer, who has appointed an agent for the service of process in the manner provided by law, shall be brought in the parish of the designated post office address of an agent for the service of process.

(7) A foreign or alien insurer shall be brought in the parish of East Baton Rouge.

Amended by Acts 1961, No. 23, § 1; Acts 1990, No. 487, § 1; Acts 1999, No. 145, § 2; Acts 2001, No. 23, § 1; Acts 2003, No. 545, § 1; Acts 2012, No. 126, § 1.

Editor's Notes

The rules on domicile are found in La. C.C. arts. 38-46 in the statutory appendix.

See Fair Debt Collection Practices Act, 15 U.S. C. § 1692a, et seq. Prior to initiating any debt collection process, including promissory notes, contracts and the foreclosure of mortgages, extreme care must be exercised to conform to the exacting requirements of the Fair Debt Collection Practices Act. See the elaborate forms in West's LSA Civil Procedure, Vol. 12, Forms 1589a, et seq. The penalties against the attorney for violation are serious, $1,000.00 per violation, heard and enforced in the Federal District Court.

The Act specifies the venue that may be used in a collection suit. The Act's venue provision preempts the venue provided in this Code of Procedure.

Venue in direct action against insurer, R.S. 22:1269. Davis v. Hanover Insurance Company, 289 So.2d 292 (3d 1974) holds that R.S. 22:1269 provides additional venue rules. See also notes to C.C.P. art. 77, *infra*. Par. (6) does not apply to a nonresident for whom the Secretary of State is appointed agent by operation of law, Comment (d). See also Surridge v. Benanti, *infra*, C.C.P. art. 77, holding that C.C.P. art. 42(7) is not exclusive; but see Meyers v. Smith, 419 So.2d 449 (1982), overruling Surridge. Venue under long-arm jurisdiction, see R.S. 13:3203. Requirement that wife's domicile be that of husband was deleted from C.C. art. 39 by Acts 1985, No. 272.

The procedural needs of the limited liability company were provided for by amendment to C.C.P. arts 42(2), (4), (5), 690, 691, 692, 739, 740, 5091(A)(2)(b), 5251(11) and (12), R.S. 13:3206 and 3471(1); and by enactment of C.C.P. art 1266.

See R.S. 13:5104 for venue of suits filed against the state, state agency, political subdivisions.

Art. 43. Exceptions to general rules

The general rules of venue provided in Article 42 are subject to the exceptions provided in Section 2 of Chapter 2 of Title 1 of Book 1 of this Code and otherwise provided by law.

Amended by Acts 1982, No. 649, § 1; Acts 2013, No. 78, § 1.

Art. 44. Waiver of objections to venue

A. An objection to the venue may not be waived prior to the institution of the action.

B. The venue provided in Articles 2006, 2811, 2812, 3941, 3993, 4031 through 4034, and 4542 may not be waived.

C. Except as otherwise provided in this article or by other law, any objection to the venue, including one based on any article in this Chapter, is waived by the failure of the defendant to plead the declinatory exception timely as provided in Article 928.

Amended by Acts 1961, No. 23, § 1; Acts 2010, No. 185, § 1.

Editor's Notes

In Shelter Mutual Ins. Co. v. Rimkus Consulting Group, Inc. of Louisiana, 2013-1977 (La. 7/1/14), 148 So.3d 871, the Louisiana Supreme Court held that contractual forum selection clauses are generally enforceable and not per se violative of public policy. The provision of article 44 which states that an objection to venue cannot be waived only prohibits the waiver of objections prior to the institution of suit. The court specifically overruled the holding in Thompson Tree & Spraying Serv. Inc. v. White-Spunner Const. Inc. 68 So.3d 1142 (La. App. 3 Cir. 2011).

Art. 45. Conflict between two or more articles in Chapter

The following rules determine the proper venue in cases where two or more articles in this Chapter may conflict:

(1) Article 78, 79, 80, 81, 82, 83, 84, 86, or 87 governs the venue exclusively, if this article conflicts with any of Articles 42 and 71 through 77;

(2) If there is a conflict between two or more of Articles 78, 79, 80, 81, 82, 83, 84, 86, or 87, the plaintiff may bring the action in any venue provided by any applicable article; and

(3) If Articles 78, 79, 80, 81, 82, 83, 84, 86, and 87 are not applicable, and there is a conflict between two or more of Articles 42 and 71 through 77, the plaintiff may bring the action in any venue provided by any applicable article.

Amended by Acts 2013, No. 78, § 1.

Comment—2013

Articles added to the Code of Civil Procedure after its 1960 enactment were not included in Article 45. The 2013 amendment adds Articles 84, 86, and 87 to the list of those articles governing venue exclusively if they conflict with the general venue articles. Article 85, providing for actions against domestic corporations with a revoked charter and franchise, has not been included because it provides for multiple venues including Article 42(2) and its exceptions provided in Article 43.

SECTION 2. EXCEPTIONS TO GENERAL RULES

Art. 71. Action against individual who has changed domicile

An action against an individual who has changed his domicile from one parish to another may be brought in either parish for a period of one year from the date of the change, unless he has filed a declaration of intention to change his domicile, in the manner provided by law.

Art. 72. Certain actions involving property

An action in which a sequestration is sought, or an action to enforce a mortgage or privilege by an ordinary proceeding, may be brought in the parish where the property, or any portion thereof, is situated.

Amended by Acts 1997, No. 1055, § 1.

Editor's Notes

This applies when foreclosure is via ordinaria, not by executory process.

Art. 73. Action against joint or solidary obligors

A. An action against joint or solidary obligors may be brought in a parish of proper venue, under Article 42 only, as to any obligor who is made a defendant provided that an action for the recovery of damages for an offense or quasi-offense against joint or solidary obligors may be brought in the parish where the plaintiff is domiciled if the parish of plaintiff's domicile would be a parish of proper venue against any defendant under either Article 76 or R.S. 13:3203.

B. If the action against this defendant is compromised prior to judgment, or dismissed after a trial on the merits, the venue shall remain proper as to the other defendants, unless the joinder was made for the sole purpose of establishing venue as to the other defendants.

Amended by Acts 1989, No. 117, § 1.

Comments—1989 [1]

This Article is amended to provide that the reference to Article 42 does not include the exceptions under Articles 71 through 85.

It also provides that venue is proper in plaintiff's domicile in an action for an offense or quasi offense against solidary or joint obligors if it is proper venue against any defendant under Article 76 or R.S. 13:3203.

[1] The 1989 Comment was revised after the enactment of Acts 1989, No. 117, to reflect changes made by the legislature to the original Law Institute proposal, Senate Bill No. 213.

Editor's Notes

Civil Code article 3462 provides that prescription is interrupted when an action is commenced in a court of competent jurisdiction and venue. If liability is not solidarily, then liability for damages caused by two or more persons shall be a joint and divisible obligation. Civil Code article 2324. Interruptions of prescription against one joint tortfeasor is effective against all joint tortfeasors. Civil code article 2324(C).

Art. 74. Action on offense or quasi offense

An action for the recovery of damages for an offense or quasi offense may be brought in the parish where the wrongful conduct occurred, or in the parish where the damages were sustained. An action to enjoin the commission of an offense or quasi offense may be brought in the parish where the wrongful conduct occurred or may occur.

As used herein, the words "offense or quasi offense" include a nuisance and a violation of Article 667 of the Civil Code.

Amended by Acts 1962, No. 92, § 1.

Art. 74.1. Action to establish or disavow filiation

An action to establish filiation and support of a child may be brought in the parish: (1) of the domicile of the child, (2) where conception occurred, (3) where either parent resided at the time of conception, (4) where an act of acknowledgement of the child occurred, or (5) where the birth of the child occurred.

An action to disavow filiation may be brought in the parish of the child's birth, or where either parent resided at the time of that birth.

Added by Acts 1980, No. 764, § 3. Amended by Acts 1981, No. 722, § 1.

Editor's Notes

See C.C. arts. 178, 179, 199, 200, as to definition and establishing of filiation.

Art. 74.2. Custody proceedings; support; forum non conveniens

A. A proceeding to obtain the legal custody of a child or to establish an obligation of support may be brought in the parish where a party is domiciled or in the parish of the last matrimonial domicile.

B. A proceeding for change of custody may be brought in the parish where the person awarded custody is domiciled or in the parish where the custody decree was rendered. If the person awarded custody is no longer domiciled in the state, the proceeding for change of custody may be brought in the parish where the person seeking a change of custody is domiciled or in the parish where the custody decree was rendered.

C. A proceeding for modification of support may be brought in any of the following:

(1) The parish where the person awarded support is domiciled if the award has been registered in that parish pursuant to the provisions of Article 2785 et seq., regardless of the provisions of Article 2786(A) relative to the domicile of the parties.

(2) The parish where the support award was rendered if it has not been registered and confirmed in another court of this state, pursuant to the provisions of Article 2785 et seq.

(3) The parish where the support award was last registered if registered in multiple courts of this state.

(4) Any of the following, if the person awarded support is no longer domiciled in the state:

(a) The parish where the other person is domiciled.

(b) The parish where the support award was rendered if not confirmed in another court of this state pursuant to Article 2785 et seq.

(c) The parish where the support order was last confirmed pursuant to the provisions of Article 2785 et seq.

D. A proceeding to register a child support, medical support, and income assignment order, or any such order issued by a court of this state for modification, may be brought in the parish where the person awarded support is domiciled.

E. For the convenience of the parties and the witnesses and in the interest of justice, a court, upon contradictory motion or upon its own motion after notice and hearing, may transfer the custody or support proceeding to another court where the proceeding might have been brought.

F. Notwithstanding any other provision of law, if after August 26, 2005, and before August 15, 2007, a party has changed his domicile within the state and the other party resided in another state prior to the hurricanes, the custody or support proceeding shall be transferred to the parish of the domicile, upon motion made prior to December 31, 2007.

Added by Acts 1983, No. 62, § 1. Amended by Acts 1986, No. 982, § 1; Acts 1987, No. 417, § 1; Acts 1997, No. 603, § 1; Acts 2007, No. 99, § 1; Acts 2010, No. 689, § 1, eff. June 29, 2010; Acts 2015, No. 379, § 2, eff. Aug. 1, 2016.

Comments—1987

(a) Paragraph (A) allows a party seeking to establish support to bring the action in the parish where either party is domiciled or in the parish of the last matrimonial domicile, thus making support venue track that of divorce. For clarity, the word "original" has been deleted from Paragraph (B) of this revision.

(b) Paragraph (C) has been inserted to give separate treatment for a proceeding for modification of support. It allows a party seeking modification of support against a resident to bring the action in the parish of the awardee or in the original court. If the party awarded custody is a nonresident, the action for modification of support may be brought in the parish of residence of the "other" party, that is, the parish of the party not awarded support, or in the parish of the original decree.

(c) Paragraph (D), former Paragraph (C), providing forum non conveniens, has been changed to include support proceedings.

(d) "Support", as used in this Article, includes both child and spousal support.

Art. 74.3. Marriage of persons related by adoption

Persons related by adoption seeking judicial authorization to marry in accordance with Civil Code Article 90 shall request authorization of the district court in the parish of either party's domicile.

Added by Acts 1987, No. 886, § 2, eff. Jan. 1, 1988.

Art. 74.3.1. Marriage of persons; waiver of certain information

A. A person applying for a marriage license who is unable to provide a birth certificate, letter required by R.S. 9:227, a valid and unexpired passport, or visa accompanied by Form I–94 as issued by the United States may provide a Certificate of Naturalization by the U.S. Citizenship and Immigration Authority. A person applying for a marriage license who is unable to provide a social security number may provide a driver's license, a government issued identification card, a passport, a visa issued by the United States Department of State, or a Certificate of Naturalization issued by the United States Citizenship and Immigration Services. A person applying for a marriage license who is unable to comply with the requirements of this Article may seek judicial authorization for waiver of the requirements of this Article. The court may grant the waiver and order the issuance of the marriage license if, after hearing and good cause shown, the court finds that such relief is appropriate and that the person has complied with other legal requirements for the marriage license. The hearing may be conducted in camera, and before a duty judge. The written order granting the waiver shall be attached to the marriage license application. If the court denies the waiver, the court shall provide reasons for the denial of the waiver.

B. The judicial authorization may be granted by the district court, parish court, family court, or juvenile court, in the parish in which the marriage license application is made, or by the First or Second City Court of the City of New Orleans if such application is made within their territorial jurisdiction, or by a justice of the peace court or city court if the issuing official is located within the justice of the peace or city court's territorial jurisdiction.

C. The provisions of this Article are in addition to any other right or remedy provided by law, are notwithstanding any other provision of law to the contrary, and shall supersede and control to the extent of conflict with any other provision of law.

Added by Acts 2017, No. 419, § 1.

Art. 74.4. Action on an open account or a promissory note

A. An action to collect an open account may be brought in the parish where the open account was created or where the services that formed the basis of such open account were performed, or in the parish of the domicile of the debtor.

B. An action on a promissory note may be brought in the parish where the promissory note was executed or in the parish of the domicile of the debtor.

Added by Acts 2007, No. 433, § 1. Amended by Acts 2008, No. 357, § 1, eff. June 21, 2008.

Art. 74.5. Adult adoption

An action to authorize an adult adoption in accordance with the second paragraph of Civil Code Article 212 may be brought in the parish of the domicile of either party to the adoption.

Added by Acts 2008, No. 351, § 2, eff. Jan. 1, 2009.

For Official Comments and Annotative Materials,

Editor's Notes

See C.C. arts. 178, 179, 199, and 200 as to filiation, adoption, and adoption of minors and effect thereof on filiation.

Art. 74.6. Actions to seek court approval by parents during marriage

During the marriage of a minor's parents, an action to seek court approval to alienate, encumber, or lease the property of the minor, incur an obligation of the minor, or compromise a claim of the minor may be brought in the domicile of the minor, or if the parents seek to compromise a claim of the minor in a pending action, in that action.

Added by Acts 2015, No. 260, § 2, eff. Jan. 1, 2016.

Art. 75. Action on judicial bond

A. An action against the principal or surety, or both, on a bond filed in a judicial proceeding may be brought in the court where the bond was filed.

B. An action against a legal surety may be brought in any parish where the principal obligor may be sued.

Amended by Acts 1987, No. 409, § 2, eff. Jan. 1, 1988.

Art. 76. Action on insurance policy

An action on a life insurance policy may be brought in the parish where the deceased died, the parish where he was domiciled, or the parish where any beneficiary is domiciled.

An action on a health and accident insurance policy may be brought in the parish where the insured is domiciled, or in the parish where the accident or illness occurred.

An action on any other type of insurance policy may be brought in the parish where the loss occurred or the insured is domiciled.

Art. 76.1. Action on contract

An action on a contract may be brought in the parish where the contract was executed or the parish where any work or service was performed or was to be performed under the terms of the contract.

Added by Acts 1991, No. 217, § 2.

Art. 77. Action against person doing business in another parish

An action against a person having a business office or establishment in a parish other than that where he may be sued under Article 42 only, on a matter over which this office or establishment had supervision, may be brought in the parish where this office or establishment is located.

Amended by Acts 1989, No. 117, § 1.

Comment—1989 [1]

This Article is amended to provide that the reference to Article 42 does not include the exceptions under Articles 71 through 85.

[1] The 1989 Comment was revised after the enactment of Acts 1989, No. 117, to reflect changes made by the legislature to the original Law Institute proposal, Senate Bill No. 213.

Art. 78. Action against partners of existing partnership

Except as provided in Article 79, an action against a partner of an existing partnership on an obligation of the latter, or on an obligation growing out of the partnership, shall be brought in any parish of proper venue as to the partnership.

Art. 79. Action to dissolve partnership

An action for the dissolution of a partnership shall be brought in the parish where it has or had its principal business establishment.

Art. 80. Action involving immovable property

A. The following actions may be brought in the parish where the immovable property is situated or in the parish where the defendant in the action is domiciled:

(1) An action to assert an interest in immovable property, or a right in, to, or against immovable property.

(2) An action to partition immovable property, except as otherwise provided in Articles 81, 82, and 83.

(3) An action arising from the breach of a lease of immovable property, including the enforcing of a lessor's privilege or seeking the payment of rent. The venue authorized by this Subparagraph shall be in addition to any other venue provided by law for such action.

B. If the immovable property, consisting of one or more tracts, is situated in more than one parish, the action may be brought in any of these parishes.

C. Any action by the sheriff after rendition of judgment shall be by the sheriff of the parish in which the immovable property is situated; however, if the immovable property, consisting of one or more tracts, is situated in more than one parish, the action may be brought by the sheriff of any of the parishes in which a portion of the immovable property is situated.

D. Any action to revoke a donation of immovable property shall be brought in the parish in which the property is located. If the property is located in more than one parish, the action may be brought in any one of them. When such an action is filed a notice of pendency shall be filed in accordance with the provisions of Article 3751.

Amended by Acts 1984, No. 732, § 1; Acts 1989, No. 393, § 1; Acts 1989, No. 541, § 1; Acts 2021, No. 259, § 2.

Art. 81. Action involving succession

When a succession has been opened judicially, until rendition of the judgment of possession, the following actions shall be brought in the court in which the succession proceeding is pending:

(1) A personal action by a creditor of the deceased; but an action brought against the deceased prior to his death may be prosecuted against his succession representative in the court in which it was brought;

(2) An action to partition the succession;

(3) An action to annul the testament of the deceased; and

(4) An action to assert a right to the succession of the deceased, either under his testament or by effect of law.

Art. 82. Action to partition community property

A. Except as otherwise provided in this Article, an action to partition community property and to settle the claims between the parties arising from either a matrimonial regime or from co-ownership of former community property shall be brought either as an incident of the action which would result in the termination of the community property regime or as a separate action in the parish where the judgment terminating the community property regime was rendered.

B. If the spouses own community immovable property, the action to partition the community property, movable and immovable, and to settle the claims between the parties arising either from a matrimonial regime or from co-ownership of former community property may be brought in the parish in which any of the community immovable property is situated.

C. If the spouses do not own community immovable property, the action to partition the community property and to settle the claims between the parties arising either from a matrimonial regime or from co-ownership of former community property may be brought in the parish where either party is domiciled.

Amended by Acts 1997, No. 1055, § 1.

Comment—1997

This amendment provides venue for claims between parties arising from a matrimonial regime or from co-ownership of former community property and an additional venue for an action to partition community property where there is no immovable community property. The new provisions would apply, for example, when, after the parties were divorced in California, the wife sues the husband in Louisiana, where he is domiciled, to partition community property in the form of military retirement benefits. *Hill v. Hill,* 575 So.2d 886 (2nd Cir., 1991).

Art. 83. Action to partition partnership property

Except as otherwise provided in the second paragraph of this article, an action to partition partnership property shall be brought either as an incident of the action to dissolve the partnership, or as a separate action in the court which rendered the judgment dissolving the partnership.

If the partnership owns immovable property, the action to partition the partnership property, movable and immovable, may be brought in the parish where any of the immovable property is situated.

Art. 84. Action involving certain retirement systems and employee benefit programs

Actions involving the Louisiana State Employees' Retirement System, Office of Group Benefits, State Police Pension and Relief Fund, Louisiana School Employees' Retirement System, Louisiana School Lunch Employees' Retirement System, Teachers' Retirement System of Louisiana, Assessors' Retirement Fund, Clerks of Court Retirement and Relief Fund, District Attorneys' Retirement System, Municipal Employees' Retirement System of Louisiana, Parochial Employees' Retirement System of Louisiana, Registrar of Voters Employees' Retirement System, Sheriffs' Pension and Relief Fund, Municipal Police Employees' Retirement System, or the Firefighters' Retirement System shall be brought in the parish of East Baton Rouge or in the parish of the domicile of the retirement system or employee benefit program.

Added by Acts 1980, No. 164, § 1. Amended by Acts 1982, No. 103, § 1; Acts 2001, No. 1178, § 8, eff. June 29, 2001.

Art. 85. Action against domestic corporation; charter revoked by secretary of state

An action against a domestic corporation, the charter and franchise of which have been administratively revoked by the secretary of state in accordance with R.S. 12:163, may be brought in any parish where the suit could have been brought prior to revocation.

Added by Acts 1982, No. 649, § 1.

Art. 86. Action involving voting trusts

An action against a voting trust or trustee of the voting trust, or both, may be brought:

(1) In the parish or parishes where the document or documents creating the voting trust were executed.

(2) If stock transferred to the voting trust was held by an inter vivos trust, in the parish or parishes where the inter vivos trust documents were executed.

(3) If stock transferred to the voting trust was held by a mortis causa trust, in the parish having jurisdiction over the settlor's estate.

Added by Acts 1998, 1st Ex.Sess., No. 102, § 2, eff. May 5, 1998.

Art. 87. Repealed by Acts 2019, No. 121, § 2

SECTION 3. CHANGE OF VENUE

Art. 121. Action brought in improper venue; transfer

When an action is brought in a court of improper venue, the court may dismiss the action, or in the interest of justice transfer it to a court of proper venue.

Editor's Notes

When a plaintiff does not knowingly file suit in the wrong venue, transfer to the correct venue rather than dismissal of the action is proper. See e. g. Perniciaro v. McInnis, 16-740 (La. App. 5 Cir. 5/31/17) 222 So.3d 987. However, the transfer of the case to a court of proper venue does not deprive the defendant of the right to urge an exception of prescription because the filing of the original action in an improper venue would not interrupt prescription. See e. g. Harris v. Angelina Cas. Co. 559 So.2d 545 (La. App. 2 Cir. 1990).

Art. 122. Change of proper venue

Any party by contradictory motion may obtain a change of venue upon proof that he cannot obtain a fair and impartial trial because of the undue influence of an adverse party, prejudice existing in the public mind, or some other sufficient cause. If the motion is granted, the action shall be transferred to a parish wherein no party is domiciled.

Art. 123. Forum non conveniens

A. (1) For the convenience of the parties and the witnesses, in the interest of justice, a district court upon contradictory motion, or upon the court's own motion after contradictory hearing, may transfer a civil case to another district court where it might have been brought; however, no suit brought in the parish in which the plaintiff is domiciled, and in a court which is otherwise a court of competent jurisdiction and proper venue, shall be transferred to any other court pursuant to this Article.

(2) For purposes of Subparagraph (1) of this Paragraph, domicile shall be the location pursuant to Article 42 where the plaintiff would be subject to suit had he been a defendant.

B. Upon the contradictory motion of any defendant in a civil case filed in a district court of this state in which a claim or cause of action is predicated upon acts or omissions originating outside the territorial boundaries of this state, when it is shown that there exists a more appropriate forum outside of this state, taking into account the location where the acts giving rise to the action occurred, the convenience of the parties and witnesses, and the interest of justice, the court may dismiss the suit without prejudice; however, no suit in which the plaintiff is domiciled in this state, and which is brought in a court which is otherwise a court of competent jurisdiction and proper venue, shall be dismissed pursuant to this Article.

C. In the interest of justice, and before the rendition of the judgment of dismissal, the court shall require the defendant or defendants to file with the court a waiver of any defense based upon prescription that has matured since the commencement of the action in Louisiana, provided that a suit on the same cause of action or on any cause of action arising out of the same transaction or occurrence is commenced in a court of competent jurisdiction in an appropriate foreign forum within sixty days from the rendition of the judgment of dismissal. Such waiver shall be null and of no effect if such suit is not filed within this sixty-day period. The court may further condition the judgment of dismissal to allow for reinstatement of the same cause of action in the same forum in the event a suit on the same cause of action or on any cause of action arising out of the same transaction or occurrence is commenced in an appropriate foreign forum within sixty days after the rendition of the judgment of dismissal and such foreign forum is unable to assume jurisdiction over the parties or does not recognize such cause of action or any cause of action arising out of the same transaction or occurrence.

Added by Acts 1970, No. 294, § 1. Amended by Acts 1988, No. 818, § 1, eff. July 18, 1988; Acts 1999, No. 536, § 1, eff. June 30, 1999; Acts 2012, No. 713, § 1.

Art. 124. Forum non conveniens; transfer to city court

If a party has filed separate suits in a district court and a city court within the territorial jurisdiction of the district court relating to the same cause of action but placing a claim for property damage in one court and a claim for personal injury in the other court, the district court upon contradictory motion, or upon the court's own motion after contradictory hearing, may transfer the suit in its court to the city court if the transfer serves the convenience of the parties and the witnesses and is in the interest of justice.

Added by Acts 1985, No. 600, § 1.

Editor's Notes

C.C.P. art. 4852 provides a parallel provision in the rules governing trial courts of limited jurisdiction.

CHAPTER 3. RECUSAL OF JUDGES

Article

Art. 151. Grounds

A. A judge of any trial or appellate court shall be recused upon any of the following grounds:

(1) The judge is a witness in the cause.

(2) The judge has been employed or consulted as an attorney in the cause or has previously been associated with an attorney during the latter's employment in the cause, and the judge participated in representation in the cause.

(3) The judge is the spouse of a party, or of an attorney employed in the cause or the judge's parent, child, or immediate family member is a party or attorney employed in the cause.

(4) The judge is biased, prejudiced, or interested in the cause or its outcome or biased or prejudiced toward or against the parties or the parties' attorneys or any witness to such an extent that the judge would be unable to conduct fair and impartial proceedings.

B. A judge of any trial or appellate court shall also be recused when there exists a substantial and objective basis that would reasonably be expected to prevent the judge from conducting any aspect of the cause in a fair and impartial manner.

C. In any cause in which the state or a political subdivision thereof is interested, the fact that the judge is a citizen of the state or a resident of the political subdivision, or pays taxes thereto, is not a ground for recusal. In any cause in which a religious body or religious corporation is interested, the fact that the judge is a member of the religious body or religious corporation is not alone a ground for recusal.

Acts 2021, No. 143, § 1.

Editor's Notes

See C.C.P. art. 4861 for special provisions relating to city and parish courts, and justices of the peace.

Art. 152. Disclosures

A. A judge of any trial or appellate court shall disclose, to the best of his information and belief, the existence of any of the following to all attorneys and unrepresented parties in the cause:

(1) The judge has been associated with an attorney during the latter's employment in the cause.

(2) At the time of the hearing of any contested issue in the cause, the judge has continued to employ, to represent him personally, the attorney actually handling the cause or a member of that attorney's firm.

(3) The judge performed a judicial act in the cause in another court.

(4) The judge is related to any of the following:

(a) A party or the spouse of a party, within the fourth degree.

(b) An attorney employed in the cause, the spouse of the attorney, or any member of the attorney's law firm, within the second degree.

(5) The judge's spouse, parent, child, or immediate family member has a substantial economic interest in the subject matter in controversy.

B. Upon disclosure, any party may file a motion that sets forth a ground for recusal under Article 151.

Acts 2021, No. 143, § 1.

Art. 153. Recusal on court's own motion

A. A judge may recuse himself in any cause in which a ground for recusal exists, whether or not a motion for his recusal has been filed by a party.

B. A district judge may recuse himself in any cause objecting to the candidacy or contesting the election for any office in which the district or jurisdiction of such office lies wholly within the judicial district of the court on which the district judge serves.

C. Prior to the cause being allotted to another judge, a judge who recuses himself for any reason shall contemporaneously file in the record the order of recusal and written reasons that provide the factual basis for recusal under Article 151. The judge shall also provide a copy of the recusal and the written reasons therefor to the judicial administrator of the supreme court.

Acts 2021, No. 143, § 1.

Art. 154. Procedure for recusal of district court judge

A. A party desiring to recuse a judge of a district court shall file a written motion therefor assigning the ground for recusal under Article 151. This motion shall be filed no later than thirty days after discovery of the facts constituting the ground upon which the motion is based, but in all cases prior to the scheduling of the matter for trial. In the event that the facts constituting the ground upon which the motion to recuse is based occur after the matter is scheduled for trial or the party moving for recusal could not, in the exercise of due diligence, have discovered such facts, the motion to recuse shall be filed immediately after such facts occur or are discovered.

B. If the motion to recuse sets forth a ground for recusal under Article 151, the judge shall either recuse himself or make a written request to the supreme court for the appointment of an ad hoc judge as provided in Article 155.

C. If the motion to recuse is not timely filed in accordance with Paragraph A of this Article or fails to set forth a ground for recusal under Article 151, the judge may deny the motion without the appointment of an ad hoc judge or a hearing but shall provide written reasons for the denial.

Acts 2021, No. 143, § 1.

Editor's Notes

A motion to recuse the trial judge after the trial was completed, but before judgment was signed, was timely under this article, Radcliffe 10, L.L.C. v. Zip Tube Systems of Louisiana, 942 So.2d 1071 (La. 2006).

Art. 155. Selection of judge to try motion to recuse

Once a motion that sets forth a ground for recusal under Article 151 is referred for hearing, the supreme court shall appoint an ad hoc judge to hear the motion to recuse, and only the ad hoc judge to whom the motion is assigned shall have the power and authority to act in the cause pending disposition of the motion.

Acts 2021, No. 143, § 1.

Art. 156. Selection of judge after recusal

A. When a district court judge of a court having two or more judges voluntarily recuses himself or is recused after a motion to recuse is heard, the cause shall be randomly assigned to another division or section of that court.

B. When a district court judge in a single-judge district voluntarily recuses himself, the judge shall make a written request to the supreme court for the appointment of an ad hoc judge to hear the cause. When an ad hoc judge appointed by the supreme court to hear a recusal grants the motion to recuse, that judge shall request that an ad hoc judge be appointed to hear the cause.

Acts 2021, No. 143, § 1.

Art. 157. Recusal of supreme court justice

A. A party desiring to recuse a justice of the supreme court shall file a written motion therefor assigning the ground for recusal under Article 151. When a written motion is filed to recuse a justice of the supreme court, the justice may recuse himself or the motion shall be heard by the other justices of the court.

B. When a justice of the supreme court recuses himself or is recused, the court may do one of the following:

(1) Have the cause argued before and disposed of by the other justices.

(2) Appoint a sitting or retired judge of a district court or a court of appeal having the qualifications of a justice of the supreme court to act for the recused justice in the hearing and disposition of the cause.

Acts 2021, No. 143, § 1.

Art. 158. Recusal of judge of court of appeal

A. A party desiring to recuse a judge of a court of appeal shall file a written motion therefor assigning the ground for recusal under Article 151. When a written motion is filed to recuse a judge of a court of appeal, the judge may recuse himself or the motion shall be heard by an ad hoc judge appointed by the supreme court.

B. When a judge of a court of appeal recuses himself or is recused, the court shall randomly allot another of its judges to sit on the panel in place of the recused judge.

Acts 2021, No. 143, § 1.

Art. 159. Recusal of ad hoc judge

An ad hoc judge appointed to try a motion to recuse a judge, or appointed to try the cause, may be recused on the grounds and in the manner provided in this Chapter for the recusal of judges.

Acts 2021, No. 143, § 1.

CHAPTER 4. POWER AND AUTHORITY

SECTION 1. GENERAL DISPOSITIONS

Article

SECTION 1. GENERAL DISPOSITIONS

Art. 191. Inherent judicial power

A court possesses inherently all of the power necessary for the exercise of its jurisdiction even though not granted expressly by law.

Art. 192. Appointment of expert witnesses; expenses

A. The appointment of expert witnesses is controlled by Louisiana Code of Evidence Article 706.

B. The reasonable fees and expenses of these experts shall be taxed as costs of court.

Amended by Acts 1988, No. 515, § 2, eff. Jan. 1, 1989.

Comment—1988

The subject of court appointed experts is now generally covered by Code of Evidence Article 706. See comments thereunder. The former provision that fees and expenses are taxed as costs of court has been retained in this Article.

Art. 192.1. Interpreters for deaf and severely hearing-impaired persons

A. In all civil cases and in the taking of any deposition where a party or a witness is a deaf or severely hearing-impaired person, the proceedings of the trial shall be interpreted to him in a language that he can understand by a qualified interpreter appointed by the court. The qualification of an interpreter as an expert is governed by the Louisiana Code of Evidence.

B. In any case in which an interpreter is required to be appointed by the court under the provisions of this Article, the court shall not commence proceedings until the appointed interpreter is in court. The interpreter so appointed shall take an oath or affirmation that he will make a true interpretation to the deaf or severely hearing-impaired person of all the proceedings of the case in a language that he understands, and that he will repeat the deaf or severely hearing-impaired person's answer to questions to counsel, court or jury to the best of his skill and judgment.

C. (1) Interpreters appointed in accordance with the provisions of this Article shall be paid an amount determined by the judge presiding. In the event travel of the interpreter is necessary, all of the actual expenses of travel, lodging, and meals incurred by the interpreter in connection with the case at which the interpreter is appointed to serve shall be paid at the same rate applicable to state employees.

(2) The costs of such interpreter shall be borne by the court.

Added by Acts 1968, No. 319, § 1. Amended by Acts 1988, No. 515, § 2, eff. Jan. 1, 1989; Acts 1989, No. 109, § 1; Acts 1995, No. 285, § 1, eff. June 14, 1995.

Comment—1988

The last sentence of Paragraph A was added to make clear that the qualification of an interpreter as an expert is governed by the Code of Evidence. See Code of Evidence Art. 604.

Art. 192.2. Appointment of interpreter for non-English-speaking persons

A. If a non-English-speaking person who is a principal party in interest or a witness in a proceeding before the court has requested an interpreter, a judge shall appoint, after consultation with the non-English-speaking person or his attorney, a competent interpreter to interpret or to translate the proceedings to him and to interpret or translate his testimony.

B. Notwithstanding any other provision of law to the contrary, the court shall order payment to the interpreter for his services at a fixed reasonable amount, and that amount shall be paid out of the appropriate court fund.

C. In a proceeding alleging abuse under R.S. 46:2134 et seq., an interpreter if necessary shall be appointed prior to a rule to show cause hearing.

Added by Acts 2008, No. 882, § 1. Amended by Acts 2019, No. 406, § 1, eff. June 20, 2019; Acts 2021, No. 207, § 1, eff. June 11, 2021.

Art. 193. Power to adopt local rules; publication

A. A court may adopt rules for the conduct of judicial business before it, including those governing matters of practice and procedure that are not contrary to the rules provided by law. When a court has more than one judge, its rules shall be adopted or amended by a majority of the judges thereof, sitting en banc.

B. The rules shall be entered on the minutes of the court. Rules adopted by an appellate court shall be published in the manner that the court considers most effective and practicable.

Amended by Acts 2021, No. 68, § 1, eff. Jan. 1, 2022.

Art. 194. Power of district court to act; signing orders and judgments

The following orders and judgments may be signed by the district judge in any place where the judge is physically located:

(1) Order directing the taking of an inventory; judgment decreeing or homologating a partition, when unopposed; judgment probating a testament ex parte; order directing the execution of a testament; order confirming or appointing a legal representative, when unopposed; order appointing an undertutor or an undercurator; order appointing an attorney at law to represent an absent, incompetent, or unrepresented person, or an attorney for an absent heir; order authorizing the sale of property of an estate administered by a legal representative; order directing the publication of the notice of the filing of a tableau of distribution, or of an account, by a legal representative; judgment recognizing heirs or legatees and sending them into possession, when unopposed; all orders for the administration and settlement of a succession, or for the administration of an estate by a legal representative.

(2) Order to show cause; order directing the issuance and providing the security to be furnished by a party for the issuance of a writ of attachment or sequestration; order directing the release of

property seized under a writ of attachment or sequestration and providing the security to be furnished therefor; order for the issuance of a temporary restraining order and providing the security therefor; order for the issuance of a writ, or alternative writ, of habeas corpus, mandamus, or quo warranto.

(3) Order for the seizure and sale of property in an executory proceeding.

(4) Order for the taking of testimony by deposition; for the production of documentary evidence; for the production of documents and things for inspection, copying, or photographing; for permission to enter land for the purpose of measuring, surveying, or photographing.

(5) Order or judgment deciding or otherwise disposing of an action, proceeding, or matter that may be tried or heard in chambers.

(6) Order or judgment that may be granted on ex parte motion or application, except an order of appeal on an oral motion.

(7) Any other order or judgment not specifically required by law to be signed in open court.

Amended by Acts 2018, No. 195, § 1; Acts 2021, No. 68, § 1, eff. Jan. 1, 2022.

Comments—2018

Subparagraph (6) of this Article has been amended to remove the exception requiring a judgment granting or confirming a default to be signed in open court. Rather, a district judge is permitted to sign in chambers a final default judgment confirming a preliminary default pursuant to Subparagraph (7) of this Article.

Art. 195. Judicial proceedings in chambers

The following judicial proceedings may be conducted by the district judge in chambers or by any audio-visual means:

(1) Hearing on an application by a legal representative for authority, whether opposed or unopposed, and on a petition for emancipation.

(2) Homologation of a tableau of distribution, or of an account, filed by a legal representative, so far as unopposed.

(3) Trial of a rule to determine the nonexempt portion of wages, salaries, or commissions seized under garnishment and to direct the payment thereof periodically by the garnishee to the sheriff.

(4) Examination of a judgment debtor.

(5) Trial of or hearing on any other action, proceeding, or matter that the law expressly provides may be tried or heard in chambers.

Amended by Acts 2021, No. 68, § 1, eff. Jan. 1, 2022.

Art. 196. Repealed by Acts 2021, No. 68, § 3, eff. Jan. 1, 2022

Art. 196.1. Power of judges to sign orders and judgments while outside of the court's territorial jurisdiction

The judge of a district court or a court of limited jurisdiction may sign orders and judgments while outside of the court's territorial jurisdiction.

Added by Acts 2018, No. 275, § 1. Amended by Acts 2021, No. 68, § 1, eff. Jan. 1, 2022.

Art. 197. Testimony of inmates

A. As used in this Article, "inmate" means a person confined in any prison, jail, correctional or training institution operated by the state, any of its political subdivisions, or any sheriff either while awaiting disposition of contemplated or pending criminal charges, pursuant to a sentence imposed by a court following the conviction of a crime, or pursuant to the judgment of a juvenile court.

B. When in any judicial proceeding the testimony of an inmate is required by law to be given in open court, when an inmate is a party to a judicial proceeding under circumstances giving him the legal right to be present in open court at any stage of the proceeding, or when the presence of an inmate witness in open court is requested timely by a party to litigation and is justified under the facts and circumstances of the case, the trial judge, in his discretion, may order any of the following:

(1) The court be convened and the testimony of the inmate be taken or the proceedings conducted at the institution wherein the inmate is confined.

(2) The testimony of the inmate be taken, or the proceedings conducted, by teleconference, video link, or other available remote technology approved by the judge, or by telephone if agreed to by all parties and approved by the judge.

(3) If the interests of justice require the presence of the inmate in open court and if no other methodology authorized hereunder is feasible, the court may order that the prisoner be transported to the courthouse pursuant to R.S. 15:706(D).

Added by Acts 1975, No. 403, § 1. Amended by Acts 2001, No. 842, § 1, eff. June 26, 2001.

SECTION 2. POWER TO PUNISH FOR CONTEMPT

Art. 221. Kinds of contempt

A contempt of court is any act or omission tending to obstruct or interfere with the orderly administration of justice, or to impair the dignity of the court or respect for its authority.

Contempts of court are of two kinds, direct and constructive.

Editor's Notes

See R.S. 13:4611.

Art. 222. Direct contempt

A direct contempt of court is one committed in the immediate view and presence of the court and of which it has personal knowledge, or a contumacious failure to comply with a subpoena or summons, proof of service of which appears of record.

Any of the following acts constitutes a direct contempt of court:

(1) Contumacious, insolent, or disorderly behavior toward the judge, or an attorney or other officer of the court, tending to interrupt or interfere with the business of the court, or to impair its dignity or respect for its authority;

(2) Breach of the peace, boisterous conduct, or violent disturbance tending to interrupt or interfere with the business of the court, or to impair its dignity or respect for its authority;

(3) Use of insulting, abusive, or discourteous language by an attorney or other person in open court, or in a pleading, brief, or other document filed with the court in irrelevant criticism of another attorney or of a judge or officer of the court;

(4) Violation of a rule of the court adopted to maintain order and decorum in the court room;

(5) Contumacious failure to comply with a subpoena, proof of service of which appears of record, or refusal to take the oath or affirmation as a witness, or refusal of a witness to answer a non-incriminating question when ordered to do so by the court; and

(6) Contumacious failure to attend court to serve as a juror after being accepted as such, or to attend court as a member of a jury venire, when proof of service of the summons appears of record.

Art. 222.1. Direct contempt; fingerprinting and photographing; exception

No person arrested or found guilty for the first offense of direct contempt of court either for failure to attend court as a member of a jury venire when proof of service of the summons appears on the record or for failure to comply with a subpoena to attend court to serve as a witness when proof of service of the subpoena appears on the record shall be subject to fingerprinting or have his photograph taken in any arrest or postsentence procedure.

Added by Acts 1985, No. 937, § 1.

Art. 223. Same; procedure for punishing

A person who has committed a direct contempt of court may be found guilty and punished therefor by the court forthwith, without any trial other than affording him an opportunity to be heard orally by way of defense or mitigation. The court shall render an order reciting the facts constituting the contempt, adjudging the person guilty thereof, and specifying the punishment imposed.

Art. 224. Constructive contempt

A constructive contempt of court is any contempt other than a direct one.

Any of the following acts constitutes a constructive contempt of court:

(1) Wilful neglect or violation of duty by a clerk, sheriff, or other person elected, appointed, or employed to assist the court in the administration of justice;

(2) Wilful disobedience of any lawful judgment, order, mandate, writ, or process of the court;

(3) Removal or attempted removal of any person or property in the custody of an officer acting under authority of a judgment, order, mandate, writ, or process of the court;

(4) Deceit or abuse of the process or procedure of the court by a party to an action or proceeding, or by his attorney;

(5) Unlawful detention of a witness, party, or his attorney, while going to, remaining at, or returning from the court where the action or proceeding is to be tried;

(6) Improper conversation by a juror or venireman with a party to an action which is being, or may be, tried by a jury of which the juror is a member, or of which the venireman may be a member, or with any person relative to the merits of such an action; or receipt by a juror or venireman of a communication from any person with reference to such an action, without making an immediate disclosure to the court of the substance thereof;

(7) Assuming to act as a juror, or as an attorney or other officer of the court, without lawful authority;

(8) Comment by a newspaper or other medium for the dissemination of news upon a case or proceeding, then pending and undecided, which constitutes a clear, present, and imminent danger of obstructing or interfering with the orderly administration of justice, by either influencing the court to reach a particular decision, or embarrassing it in the discharge of its judicial duties;

(9) Wilful disobedience by an inferior court, judge, or other officer thereof, of the lawful judgment, order, mandate, writ, or process of an appellate court, rendered in connection with an appeal from a judgment or order of the inferior court, or in connection with a review of such judgment or order under a supervisory writ issued by the appellate court; and

(10) Any other act or omission punishable by law as a contempt of court, or intended to obstruct or interfere with the orderly administration of justice, or to impair the dignity of the court or respect for its authority, and which is not a direct contempt.

(11) Knowingly making a false statement or representation of a material fact or knowingly failing to disclose a material fact in order to apply for or receive support enforcement services for the purpose of securing an order of paternity, child support, medical support, an income assignment order, or a notice of income assignment against another person.

Amended by Acts 2004, No. 159, § 1, eff. June 10, 2004.

Art. 225. Same; procedure for punishing

A. Except as otherwise provided by law, a person charged with committing a constructive contempt of court may be found guilty thereof and punished therefor only after the trial by the judge of a rule against him to show cause why he should not be adjudged guilty of contempt and punished accordingly. The rule to show cause may issue on the court's own motion or on motion of a party to the action or proceeding and shall state the facts alleged to constitute the contempt. A person charged with committing a constructive contempt of a court of appeal may be found guilty thereof and punished therefor after receiving a notice to show cause, by brief, to be filed not less than forty-eight hours from the date the person receives such notice why he should not be found guilty of contempt and punished accordingly. The person so charged shall be granted an oral hearing on the charge if he submits a written request to the clerk of the appellate court within forty-eight hours after receiving notice of the charge. Such notice from the court of appeal may be sent by registered or certified mail or may be served by the sheriff. In all other cases, a certified copy of the motion, and of the rule to show cause, shall be served upon the person charged with contempt in the same manner as a subpoena at least forty-eight hours before the time assigned for the trial of the rule.

B. If the person charged with contempt is found guilty the court shall render an order reciting the facts constituting the contempt, adjudging the person charged with contempt guilty thereof, and specifying the punishment imposed.

Amended by Acts 1984, No. 530, § 2.

Art. 226. Same; imprisonment until performance

When a contempt of court consists of the omission to perform an act which is yet in the power of the person charged with contempt to perform, he may be imprisoned until he performs it, and in such a case this shall be specified in the court's order.

Art. 227. Punishment for contempt

A person may not be adjudged guilty of a contempt of court except for misconduct defined as such, or made punishable as such, expressly by law.

The punishment which a court may impose upon a person adjudged guilty of contempt of court is provided in R.S. 13:4611.

CHAPTER 5. CLERKS

SECTION 1. GENERAL DISPOSITIONS

Article

SECTION 1. GENERAL DISPOSITIONS

Art. 251. Custodian of court records; certified copies; records public

A. The clerk of court is the legal custodian of all of its records and is responsible for their safekeeping and preservation. He may issue a copy of any of these records, certified by him under the seal of the court to be a correct copy of the original. Except as otherwise provided by law, he shall permit any person to examine, copy, photograph, or make a memorandum of any of these records at any time during which the clerk's office is required by law to be open. However, notwithstanding the provisions of this Paragraph or R.S. 44:31 et seq., the use, placement, or installation of privately owned copying, reproducing, scanning, or any other such imaging equipment, whether hand-held, portable, fixed, or otherwise, within the offices of the clerk of court is prohibited unless ordered by a court of competent jurisdiction.

B. Notwithstanding the provisions of Paragraph A of this Article, a judge issuing a court order may certify a copy of that order for service of process, if the order is issued in an emergency situation and at a time when the clerk of court's office is not open. A determination of when an emergency situation exists shall be made by the judge issuing the order.

Amended by Acts 1986, No. 218, § 1; Acts 1995, No. 372, § 1, eff. July 1, 1995; Acts 2005, No. 193, § 1.

Art. 252. Issuance of process

The clerk of a court shall issue all citations, writs, mandates, summons, subpoenas, and other process of the court in the name of the State of Louisiana. He shall indicate thereon the court from which they issue, sign them in his official capacity, and affix the seal of the court thereto. If service by the sheriff is required, the clerk shall deliver or mail them to the sheriff who is to make the service.

Art. 253. Pleadings, documents, and exhibits to be filed with clerk

A. All pleadings or documents to be filed in an action or proceeding instituted or pending in a court, and all exhibits introduced in evidence, shall be delivered to the clerk of the court for such purpose. The clerk shall endorse thereon the fact and date of filing and shall retain possession thereof for inclusion in the record, or in the files of his office, as required by law. The endorsement of the fact and date of filing shall be made upon receipt of the pleadings or documents by the clerk and shall be made without regard to whether there are orders in connection therewith to be signed by the court.

B. The filings as provided in Paragraph A of this Article and all other provisions of this Chapter may be transmitted electronically in accordance with a system established by a clerk of court or by Louisiana Clerks' Remote Access Authority. When such a system is established, the clerk of court shall adopt and implement procedures for the electronic filing and storage of any pleading, document, or exhibit. The official record shall be the electronic record. A pleading or document filed electronically is deemed filed on the date and time stated on the confirmation of electronic filing sent from the system, if the clerk of court accepts the electronic filing. Public access to electronically filed pleadings and documents shall be in accordance with the rules governing access to written filings.

C. A judge or justice presiding over a court in this state may sign a court order, notice, official court document, and other writings required to be executed in connection with court proceedings, by use of an electronic signature as defined by R.S. 9:2602. The various courts shall provide by court rule for the method of electronic signature to be used and to ensure the authenticity of the electronic signature.

D. Any pleading or document in a traffic or criminal action may be filed with the court by facsimile transmission in compliance with the provision of the Code of Criminal Procedure Article 14.1.

E. The clerk shall not refuse to accept for filing any pleading or other document signed by electronic signature, as defined by R.S. 9:2602, and executed in connection with court proceedings, or which complies with the procedures for electronic filing implemented pursuant to this Article, if any applicable fees for filing and transmission are paid, solely on the ground that it was signed by electronic signature.

F. If the filing party fails to comply with any requirement of this Article, the electronic filing shall have no force or effect. The district courts may provide by court rule for other matters related to filings by electronic transmission.

G. The clerk of court may procure equipment, services, and supplies necessary to accommodate electronic filings out of the clerk's salary fund.

H. All electronic filings shall include an electronic signature. For the purpose of this Article, "electronic signature" means an electronic symbol or process attached to or logically associated with a record and executed or adopted by a person with the intent to sign the record.

Amended by Acts 1980, No. 355, § 1; Acts 1985, No. 457, § 1; Acts 2001, No. 319, § 2; Acts 2010, No. 461, § 1; Acts 2014, No. 606, § 1; Acts 2017, No. 419, § 4, eff. Jan. 1, 2018; Acts 2020, No. 264, § 3.

Comments—2017

Paragraph E is new; however, nothing in this provision is intended to abrogate any specific legislation requiring that certain documents be signed by other than electronic means.

Art. 253.1. Pleadings; random assignment of cases

All pleadings filed shall be randomly assigned to a particular section or division of the court by either of the following methods:

(1) By drawing indiscriminately from a pool containing designations of all sections or divisions of court in the particular jurisdiction in which the case is filed.

(2) By use of a properly programmed electronic device or computer programmed to randomly assign cases to any one of the sections or divisions of court in the particular jurisdiction in which the case is filed.

Added by Acts 1995, No. 829, § 1.

Editor's Notes

See Rule 9.3, Allotment; Signing of Pleadings in Alloted or Non-Alloted Cases, District Court Rules.

Art. 253.2. Transfer and reassignment of pending cases

After a case has been assigned to a particular section or division of the court, it may not be transferred from one section or division to another section or division within the same court, unless agreed to by all parties, or unless it is being transferred to effect a consolidation pursuant to Article 1561. However, the supreme court, by rule, may establish uniform procedures for reassigning cases under circumstances where an expeditious disposition of cases may be effectuated.

Added by Acts 1997, No. 968, § 1. Amended by Acts 2021, No. 259, § 2.

Art. 253.3. Duty judge exceptions; authority to hear certain matters

A. In any case assigned pursuant to Article 253.1, a duty judge shall only hear and sign orders or judgments for the following:

(1) Domestic relations emergency matters and protective orders concerning physical safety.

(2) Temporary restraining orders.

(3) Default judgments, stipulated matters, examination of judgment debtors, orders to proceed in forma pauperis, orders allowing the filing of supplemental and amending petitions when no trial date has been assigned, orders allowing incidental demands when no trial date has been assigned, orders allowing additional time to answer, and judicial commitments.

(4) Uncontested cases in which all parties other than the plaintiff are represented by an attorney appointed by the court.

(5) Uncontested judgments of divorce pursuant to Civil Code Article 102.

(6) Orders directing the taking of an inventory; judgments decreeing or homologating a partition, when unopposed; judgments probating a testament ex parte; orders directing the execution of a testament; orders confirming or appointing a legal representative, when unopposed; orders appointing an undertutor or an undercurator; orders appointing an attorney at law to represent an absent, incompetent, or unrepresented person, or an attorney for an absent heir; orders authorizing the sale of property of an estate administered by a legal representative; orders directing the publication of the notice of the filing of a tableau of distribution, or of an account, by a legal representative; judgments recognizing heirs or legatees and sending them into possession, when unopposed; and all orders for the administration and settlement of a succession, or for the administration of an estate by a legal representative.

(7) Orders for the seizure and sale of property in an executory proceeding.

B. In any case assigned pursuant to Article 253.1, a duty judge shall only sign orders for issuing the following: orders to show cause; orders directing the issuance and providing the security to be furnished by a party for the issuance of a writ of attachment or sequestration; orders directing the release of property seized under a writ of attachment or sequestration and providing the security to be furnished therefor; orders for the issuance of a writ, or alternative writ, of habeas corpus, mandamus, or quo warranto; and orders for appeal.

C. In any case assigned pursuant to Article 253.1, a duty judge may sign any order specifically and expressly authorized by the judge to whom the case is assigned.

D. When a duty judge hears any matter or signs any order or judgment pursuant to this Article, he shall not acquire jurisdiction over additional matters in the case. Following the ruling of the duty judge, the judge assigned pursuant to Article 253.1 shall hear the other matters in the case, including but not limited to discovery matters, preliminary injunctions, and injunctions.

Added by Acts 2000, 1st Ex.Sess., No. 24, § 1. Amended by Acts 2017, No. 419, § 1; Acts 2021, No. 174, § 1, eff. Jan. 1, 2022.

Comments—2017

The purpose of the amendment to Subparagraph (A)(4) of this Article was to align the provision with Article 5091 by replacing "a curator ad hoc" with "an attorney appointed by the court."

Editor's Notes

See Rules 3.2 and 9.2, Duty Judges, District Court Rules.

Art. 254. Docket and minute books

A. In addition to other record books required by law, each court shall keep docket and minute books.

B. The clerk of the court shall enter in the docket book the number and title of each action or proceeding filed in the court, the date of filing of the petition, exceptions, answers, and other pleadings, and the court costs paid by and the names of counsel of record for each of the parties.

C. All orders and judgments rendered, all motions made, all proceedings conducted, and all judicial acts of the court during each day it is in session shall be entered in the minute book.

D. An electronic record of the minutes which is not capable of alteration without indication that a change has been made may be maintained in lieu of a written entry.

Amended by Acts 1995, No. 1003, § 1.

Art. 255. Deputy clerks and other employees

Except as otherwise provided by law, a deputy clerk of a court possesses all of the powers and authority granted by law to the clerk, and may perform any of the duties and exercise any of the functions of the clerk.

Deputy clerks and other employees of a clerk of court are subject to his direction and supervision, and shall perform the duties assigned to them by law, the court, and the clerk.

The clerk of a court is responsible for the performance or nonperformance of their official duties by his deputies and other employees.

Art. 256. Minute clerk

The minute clerk of a court shall keep the minutes of the court daily when in session and transcribe them into the minute book, as required by Article 254; shall file all pleadings and documents tendered for filing in open court; and shall perform such other duties as are assigned to him by law, the court, and the clerk with the approval of the court.

The minute clerk of a trial court shall administer the oath to jurors and witnesses and shall file all exhibits offered in evidence, when directed to do so by the court. If there are two or more judges on a trial court, its rules may require a minute clerk for each division thereof.

When a court has no minute clerk, and there is no deputy clerk available for such duty, the clerk shall perform all of the duties of the minute clerk.

Art. 257. Neglect, failure, or refusal of clerk, deputy, or other employee to perform duty subjects him to punishment for contempt

The neglect, failure, or refusal of a clerk, deputy clerk, or other employee of a clerk of court to perform any ministerial duty subjects him to punishment for contempt of court.

Art. 258. Electronic filing and recording of written instruments

A. Notwithstanding any provision of law to the contrary, a clerk of court, as ex officio recorder, the Orleans Parish register of conveyances, or its successor, or the Orleans Parish recorder of mortgages or its successor, hereinafter referred to as "recorder", is authorized to adopt and implement a published plan which shall include a written contract between the clerk of court, the Orleans Parish register of conveyances, or its successor, or the Orleans Parish recorder of mortgages, or its successor, and the filer, which complies with the Louisiana Uniform Electronic Transactions Act, R.S. 9:2601 et seq., and which provides for the acceptance of an electronic record of any recordable written instrument except original maps, plats, property descriptions, or photographs as related to the work of a professional surveyor engaged in the "Practice of Land Surveying" as defined in R.S. 37:682 for filing and recording submitted by any person, department, political subdivision, agency, branch, entity, or instrumentality of Louisiana or of the federal government or of a state-chartered or federally chartered financial institution insured by the Federal Deposit Insurance Corporation or the National Credit Union Administration. The filer of such an electronic record shall certify to the recorder that the written instrument from which the electronic record is taken conforms to all applicable laws relating to the form and content of instruments which are submitted in writing.

B. Immediately after acceptance of an electronic record for filing, the recorder shall endorse such record with the date, hour, and minute it is filed. An electronic filing received on a legal holiday or at any time other than during the normal business hours of the recorder shall be accepted for filing on the next business day by the same procedure followed when a paper document is received in the mail of the recorder at any time other than during normal business hours.

C. An electronic record shall be effective with respect to a third person from the time of its filing in the same manner as if the written instrument had been filed.

D. On or before January 1, 2022, each clerk of court, including the Orleans Parish register of conveyances or its successor and the Orleans Parish recorder of mortgages or its successor, shall adopt and implement a plan for recording electronic documents in accordance with Paragraph A of this Article.

Added by Acts 2005, No. 125, § 1. Amended by Acts 2008, No. 368, § 1; Acts 2017, No. 173, § 5.

Editor's Notes

See also, R.S. 13:850. Facsimile filing of motion for new trial was of no effect for failure to pay the filing and transmission fees within five days of the filing, Malbrough v. Dunn, 956 So.2d 179 (3 Cir., 2007).

In Stevenson v. Progressive Security Ins. Co., no. 2019-C-00637 (La. 4/3/2020) 2020 WL 1671565, the Louisiana Supreme Court held that a petition for damages may be fax-filed until midnight of the last day of the prescriptive period in order to interrupt prescription. Even though the Clerk of Court turned off her fax machine at 4:30 p. m. the fax by the plaintiff's attorney that was not received until the next day interrupted prescription since the clerk of court failed to make its fax equipment available as required by the statute.

Art. 259. Liability of clerk of court

The clerk of court shall not be liable for any damages caused by any third party to any information included in pleadings or documents filed of record by the clerk of court.

Added by Acts 2017, No. 173, § 5.

SECTION 2. CLERKS OF DISTRICT COURTS

Art. 281. Certain articles not applicable to Civil District Court for the Parish of Orleans

The provisions of Articles 282 through 286 do not apply to the clerk and the deputy clerks of the Civil District Court for the Parish of Orleans.

Art. 282. Acts which may be done by district court clerk

The clerk of a district court may:

(1) Grant an appeal and fix the return day thereof; fix the amount of the bond for an appeal, or for the issuance of a writ of attachment or of sequestration, or for the release of property seized under any writ, unless fixed by law; appoint an attorney at law to represent a nonresident, absent, incompetent, or unrepresented defendant; or dismiss without prejudice, on application of plaintiff, an action or proceeding in which no exception, answer, or intervention has been filed; and

(2) Probate a testament, when there is no opposition thereto; homologate an inventory; confirm or appoint a tutor, undertutor, undertutor ad hoc, curator, undercurator, undercurator ad hoc, administrator, executor, or dative testamentary executor, when there is no opposition thereto; appoint

an attorney for absent heirs; and approve and accept the bond required of a legal representative for the faithful performance of his duties.

Art. 283. Orders and judgments which may be signed by district court clerk

A. The clerk of a district court may sign any of the following orders or judgments:

(1) An order or judgment effecting or evidencing the doing of any of the acts authorized in Article 282;

(2) An order for the issuance of executory process, of a writ of attachment or of sequestration, or of garnishment process under a writ of fieri facias, attachment, or of sequestration; the release under bond of property seized under a writ of attachment or of sequestration; or to permit the filing of an intervention;

(3) An order for the execution of a probated testament; the affixing of seals; the taking of an inventory; the public sale of succession property to pay debts, on the written application of the succession representative accompanied by a list of the debts of the succession; the advertisement of the filing of a tableau of distribution or of an account by a legal representative; or requiring a legal representative to file an account; or

(4) An order to permit a party to institute and prosecute, or to defend, a suit without the payment of costs, under the provisions of Articles 5181 through 5188.

B. When an order signed by the clerk requires the services of a notary, the clerk shall appoint the notary suggested by the party obtaining the order.

Amended by Acts 2010, No. 175, § 1.

Art. 284. Judicial powers of district court clerk

The clerk of a district court may render and sign default judgments or judgments by confession in cases where the jurisdiction of the court is concurrent with that of justices of the peace, as provided in Article 5011.

Amended by Acts 1979, No. 46, § 2, eff. Jan. 1, 1980; Acts 2017, No. 419, § 1; Acts 2021, No. 174, § 1, eff. Jan. 1, 2022.

Art. 285. Powers of district court clerk may be exercised whether judge absent from parish or not

The powers and authority granted to the clerk of a district court under Articles 282 through 284 may be exercised by him whether the judge of the district court is absent from the parish or not.

Art. 286. Powers of district court clerk which may not be exercised by deputy; powers of chief deputy clerk

A. No deputy clerk of a district court, except the chief deputy clerk, may exercise any of the powers and authority granted to the clerk of the district court under Articles 282 and 283.

B. Whether the judge or the clerk, or both, are absent from the parish or not, the chief deputy clerk of a district court may exercise all of the powers and authority granted to the clerk of a district court under Articles 282 and 283.

Amended by Acts 1991, No. 174, § 1.

Art. 287. District court clerk ex officio notary

The clerk of a district court is ex officio a notary; and, as such, may administer oaths and exercise all of the other functions, powers, and authority of a notary.

Art. 288. Functions which district court clerk may exercise on holiday

The only functions which a clerk of a district court may exercise on a legal holiday are:

(1) The signing of an order for the issuance of a writ of attachment or of sequestration by a clerk of a district court other than the Civil District Court for the Parish of Orleans; and

(2) The issuance of a writ of attachment, sequestration, or injunction.

CHAPTER 6. SHERIFFS

Article

Art. 321. Executive officer of district court; serves process, executes writs and mandates directed to him by courts

The sheriff is the executive officer of the district court.

He shall serve citations, summons, subpoenas, notices, and other process, and shall execute writs, mandates, orders, and judgments directed to him by the district courts, the courts of appeal, and the supreme court.

Art. 322. Exercises civil functions only in own parish; exception

Except as otherwise provided in Article 1291, the sheriff may exercise his civil functions only in the parish for which he was elected.

Art. 323. Writs executed on holiday

The sheriff shall not execute any writ, mandate, order, or judgment of a court in a civil case on a legal holiday, except a writ of attachment, sequestration, fieri facias, or seizure and sale under executory process, or an injunction.

Amended by Acts 1978, No. 169, § 1.

Art. 324. Returns on process served, and writs and judgments executed

The sheriff shall make a return to the issuing court on citations, summons, subpoenas, notices, and other process, and on writs, mandates, orders, and judgments, showing the date on which and the manner in which they were served or executed.

Art. 325. Right of entry for execution; may require assistance of others if resistance offered or threatened

In the execution of a writ, mandate, order, or judgment of a court, the sheriff may enter on the lands, and into the residence or other building, owned or occupied by the judgment debtor or defendant. If necessary to effect entry, he may break open any door or window. If resistance is offered or threatened, he may require the assistance of the police, of neighbors, and of persons present or passing by.

Art. 326. Protection and preservation of property seized

The sheriff shall take actual possession of all movable property seized which is susceptible of actual possession and may remove it to a warehouse or other place of safekeeping.

He may take actual possession of all immovable property seized, unless it is under lease or occupied by an owner.

He shall safeguard, protect, and preserve all property seized of which he has taken or is required to take actual possession; and for such purposes may appoint a keeper of the property.

Art. 327. Seizure of rents, fruits, and revenue of property under seizure

The seizure of property by the sheriff effects the seizure of the fruits and issues which it produces while under seizure. The sheriff shall collect all rents and revenue produced by property under seizure.

Art. 328. Power of administration of property under seizure

The sheriff has the power of administration of all property under seizure, regardless of the type of writ or mandate under authority of which the property was seized.

If immovable property is not occupied by an owner and is not under lease, the sheriff may lease it for a term not beyond the date of judicial sale. He cannot lease movable property under seizure unless authorized by the court with the consent of the parties.

The sheriff may, and if the necessary funds therefor are advanced or satisfactory security is furnished him by any interested person shall, continue the operation of any property under seizure, including a business, farm, or plantation. For such purposes, the sheriff may employ a manager and such other employees as he may consider necessary.

Art. 329. Disbursements for protection, preservation, and administration of seized property

The sheriff may make all necessary disbursements for the protection, preservation, and administration of property under seizure, which shall be taxed as costs of the seizure.

Art. 330. Collection of fines from, and imprisonment of, persons found guilty of contempt of court

The sheriff shall collect the fines which persons found guilty of contempt of court are sentenced to pay, and pay them over to the official entitled by law to receive them. He shall take into custody and imprison individuals found guilty of contempt of court and sentenced to imprisonment in the parish jail.

Art. 331. Deputy sheriffs and other employees

Except as otherwise provided by law, a deputy sheriff possesses all of the powers and authority granted by law to the sheriff, and may perform any of the duties and exercise any of the functions of the sheriff.

Deputy sheriffs and other employees of the sheriff are subject to his direction and supervision, and shall perform the duties assigned to them by law, and by the sheriff.

The sheriff is responsible for the performance or nonperformance of their official duties by his deputies and other employees.

Art. 332. Service or execution by constable or marshal

When authorized to do so by the sheriff, a constable of a justice of the peace court, or a constable or marshal of a city court, within the territorial jurisdiction of his court, may serve any process and execute any writ or mandate which the sheriff is authorized to serve or execute.

For such purpose, the constable or marshal possesses the powers and authority of the sheriff; a service or execution so made has the same effect as if made by the sheriff; and the latter is responsible for the performance or nonperformance of his duties by a constable or marshal in such cases.

Art. 333. Crier

The crier of a court shall attend all sessions thereof; under the direction of the judge shall open and close court at each session, and maintain order and decorum in the court room; and shall perform such other duties as are assigned to him by law, the court, or the sheriff.

The crier of a trial court, when requested to do so, shall call all witnesses in the building whose testimony is desired by the court or by a party.

When a court has no crier, and there is no deputy sheriff available for such duty, the sheriff shall perform the duties of crier.

Editor's Notes

See District Court Rule 6.0, The Opening of Court, form for "Oyez...."

Art. 334. Neglect, failure, or refusal of sheriff, deputy sheriff, or employee to perform duty subjects him to punishment for contempt

The neglect, failure, or refusal of a sheriff, deputy sheriff, or other employee of a sheriff to perform any ministerial duty subjects him to punishment for contempt of court.

CHAPTER 7. OTHER OFFICERS OF THE COURT

Article

Art. 371. Attorney

An attorney at law is an officer of the court. He shall conduct himself at all times with decorum, and in a manner consistent with the dignity and authority of the court and the role which he himself should play in the administration of justice.

He shall treat the court, its officers, jurors, witnesses, opposing party, and opposing counsel with due respect; shall not interrupt opposing counsel, or otherwise interfere with or impede the orderly dispatch of judicial business by the court; shall not knowingly encourage or produce false evidence; and shall not knowingly make any misrepresentation, or otherwise impose upon or deceive the court.

For a violation of any of the provisions of this article, the attorney at law subjects himself to punishment for contempt of court, and such further disciplinary action as is otherwise provided by law.

Art. 372. Court reporter

A. The court reporter of a trial court, when directed by the court, shall report verbatim in shorthand by stenography or stenotype, or by voice recording or any other recognized manner when the equipment therefor has been approved by the court, the testimony of all witnesses, the other evidence introduced or offered, the objections thereto, and the rulings of the court thereon, on the trial of any appealable civil case or matter.

B. When the court so directs, or the fees therefor have been paid or secured, or when an appeal has been granted in cases in which a party has been permitted to litigate without the payment of costs, he shall transcribe verbatim in a manner approved by the supreme court, all of his notes taken at the trial, or such portion thereof as is designated. He shall file one copy of the transcript in the trial court; shall deliver a copy thereof to each of the parties who has paid therefor; and, when an appeal has been granted, he shall furnish to the clerk of the trial court the number of copies of the transcript required by law.

C. The court reporter shall retain all notes and tape recordings in civil cases for a period of not less than five years after the end of the trial. However, if the record of the trial is fully transcribed, the court reporter shall retain all notes and tape recordings which have been fully transcribed for a period of not less than two years after transcription is completed. The court reporter shall destroy any notes and tape recordings of any matter upon order of a court of competent jurisdiction.

D. The notes and tape recordings of any civil case which are retained by a court reporter pursuant to the provisions of this Article shall be the property of the court in which the case was heard. The court reporter shall have the duty to retain and maintain all such notes and tape recordings pursuant to the provisions of this Article, although the notes and tape recordings shall remain the property of the court.

E. He shall perform such other duties as are assigned to him by law or by the court.

F. When a party to a proceeding requests a transcript and has paid for the transcript, the court reporter shall provide that party with an electronic copy of the transcript along with a paper copy of the transcript at no additional charge or cost to the requesting party.

Amended by Acts 1986, No. 545, § 1; Acts 2006, No. 820, § 1, eff. July 5, 2006.

See West's Louisiana Statutes Annotated

Editor's Notes

See Rule 4.0, Court Reporters, District Court Rules.

Art. 373. Expert appointed by court

An expert appointed by a trial court to assist it in the adjudication of a case in which his special skill and knowledge may aid the court is an officer of the court from the time of his qualification until the rendition of final judgment in the case.

Art. 374. Legal representative

A legal representative appointed or confirmed by a court is an officer of this court from the time of his qualification for the office until his discharge.

Art. 375. Neglect, failure, or refusal of expert or legal representative to perform a legal duty when ordered to do so, subjects him to punishment for contempt of court

The neglect, failure, or refusal of an expert appointed by the court, or a legal representative appointed or confirmed by the court, to perform a legal duty when ordered to do so by the court, subjects him to punishment for contempt of the court.

Art. 376. Limitation of immunity

Any immunity which may extend to an expert appointed by the court pursuant to Code of Civil Procedure Article 373 shall not extend to those acts of the expert which constitute perjury, as provided in R.S. 14:123.

Added by Acts 2001, No. 571, § 1.

Arts. 377 to 420. [Reserved]

TITLE II. ACTIONS

CHAPTER 1. GENERAL DISPOSITIONS

Causes of action

Article

Art. 421. Civil action; commencement; amicable demand unnecessary

A civil action is a demand for the enforcement of a legal right. It is commenced by the filing of a pleading presenting the demand to a court of competent jurisdiction. Amicable demand is not a condition precedent to a civil action, unless specifically required by law.

Editor's Notes

Civil Code article 3462 provides that prescription is interrupted when an action is commenced in a court of competent jurisdiction and venue. If liability is not solidarily, then liability for damages caused by two or more persons shall be a joint and divisible obligation. Civil Code article 2324. Interruptions of prescription against one joint tortfeasor is effective against all joint tortfeasors. Civil code article 2324(C).

Art. 422. Personal, real, mixed actions

A personal action is one brought to enforce an obligation against the obligor, personally and independently of the property which he may own, claim, or possess.

A real action is one brought to enforce rights in, to, or upon immovable property.

A mixed action is one brought to enforce both rights in, to, or upon immovable property, and a related obligation against the owner, claimant, or possessor thereof.

Art. 423. Implied right to enforce obligation; prematurity

An obligation implies a right to enforce it which may or may not accrue immediately upon the creation of the obligation. When the obligation allows a term for its performance, the right to enforce it does not accrue until the term has elapsed. If the obligation depends upon a suspensive condition, the right to enforce it does not accrue until the occurrence or performance of the condition.

When an action is brought on an obligation before the right to enforce it has accrued, the action shall be dismissed as premature, but it may be brought again after this right has accrued.

Editor's Notes

Prematurity must be urged through the dilatory exception if the term for performance has not expired; if the obligation is dependent upon a suspensive condition that may not occur, the objection must be raised through the peremptory exception, Halbert v. Klauer Mfg. Co., App. 2 Cir.1938, 181 So. 75. See C.C. art. 1767, suspensive and resolutory conditions as to obligations, and C.C. art. 1777, as to obligations with a term.

Art. 424. Cause of action as a defense

A person who has a right to enforce an obligation also has a right to use his cause of action as a defense.

Except as otherwise provided herein, a prescribed obligation arising under Louisiana law may be used as a defense if it is incidental to, or connected with, the obligation sought to be enforced by the plaintiff. A prescribed cause of action arising under The Federal Consumer Credit Protection Act may not be used as a defense even if it is incidental to, or connected with, the obligation sought to be enforced by the plaintiff.

However, in connection with the enforcement of a negotiable instrument the defense of redhibition may not be used if it has otherwise prescribed.

Amended by Acts 1976, No. 710, § 1; Acts 1977, No. 254, § 1.

Editor's Notes

This article recognizes the positive law of Louisiana adopted form the Roman law maxim: Quae temporalia sunt ad agendum perpetua sunt ad exeipiendum (things which are temporary for attack are permanent for the purposes of defense.) Under this maxim, the courts have repeatedly held that a cause of action which would be prescribed if the obligee attempted to sue the obligor can nevertheless be used a as defense to an action. In such cases, there must be a connexity between the obligation sued on by the plaintiff and the prescribed obligation interposed as a defense.

Art. 425. Preclusion by judgment

A. A party shall assert all causes of action arising out of the transaction or occurrence that is the subject matter of the litigation.

B. Paragraph A of this Article shall not apply to an action for divorce under Civil Code Article 102 or 103, an action for determination of incidental matters under Civil Code Article 105, an action for contributions to a spouse's education or training under Civil Code Article 121, and an action for partition of community property and settlement of claims between spouses under R.S. 9:2801.

Amended by Acts 1990, No. 521, § 2, eff. Jan. 1, 1991; Acts 1991, No. 367, § 2.

Comment—1990

This amendment expands the scope of this Article to reflect the changes made in the defense of res judicata and puts the parties on notice that all causes of action arising out of the transaction or occurrence that is the subject matter of the litigation must be raised.

Comment—1991

Paragraph B is added to this Article in order to make it clear that a party to a divorce action is not required to raise the actions commonly associated with divorce actions, such as claims for spousal and child support, in the divorce action itself. Such claims historically have been assertable after the divorce action has been concluded by judgment, and the added phrase makes it clear that this Article does not change the law in that respect.

Editor's Notes

See, also, C.C.P. art. 5, remission of part of claim by reducing claim on single cause of action. This article helps to implement our rule of res judicata under R.S. 13:4231. Note that nothing in the text of the article refers to "res judicata" or "preclusion by judgment."

Claims not pleaded were waived, Westerman v. State Farm Mut. Auto Ins. Co., 834 So.2d 445 (App. 1 Cir. 2002); but see Spires v. State Farm Mut. Auto Ins. Co., 996 So.2d 696 (App. 3 Cir. 2008), contra.

Art. 426. Transmission of action and of right to enforce obligation

An action to enforce an obligation is the property of the obligee which on his death is transmitted with his estate to his heirs, universal legatees, or legatees under a universal title, except as otherwise provided by law. An action to enforce an obligation is transmitted to the obligee's legatee under a particular title only when it relates to the property disposed of under the particular title.

These rules apply also to a right to enforce an obligation, when no action thereon was commenced prior to the obligee's death.

Editor's Notes

See C.C. arts. 1585 to 1588 for legatee definitions. See notes to C.C.P. art. 428.

Art. 427. Action against obligor's heirs or legatees

An action to enforce an obligation, if the obligor is dead, may be brought against the heirs, universal legatees, or general legatees, who have accepted his succession, except as otherwise provided by law. The liability of these heirs and legatees is determined by the provisions of the Civil Code.

Amended by Acts 1997, No. 1421, § 3, eff. July 1, 1999.

Art. 428. No abatement on death of party

An action does not abate on the death of a party. The only exception to this rule is an action to enforce a right or obligation which is strictly personal.

Editor's Notes

This article, in conjunction with C.C. art. 2315, preserves, among other actions, the survivors' action provided for in C.C. art. 2315.1, Comment (a). See Nathan v. Touro Infirmary, 512 So.2d 352 (La.1987), holding that survival action does not abate on victim's death and vests in succession representative or heirs in absence of listed beneficiaries. See C.C. art 2315.1(B), vesting survival action in succession representative in absence of other beneficiaries. See C.C.P. art. 421, definition of "action".

CHAPTER 2. CUMULATION OF ACTIONS

Article

Art. 461. Cumulation of actions defined

Cumulation of actions is the joinder of separate actions in the same judicial demand, whether by a single plaintiff against a single defendant, or by one or more plaintiffs against one or more defendants.

Editor's Notes

Under La. C.C.P. art. 1038, the court may withhold signing a final judgment until all actions have been tried. Cumulation is the joining of actions and parties in a single suit. Consolidation is the joining of two or more separate actions pending in the same court for trial or other limited purpose. La. C.C.P. art. 1561.

Art. 462. Cumulation by single plaintiff against single defendant

A plaintiff may cumulate against the same defendant two or more actions even though based on different grounds, if:

(1) Each of the actions cumulated is within the jurisdiction of the court and is brought in the proper venue; and

(2) All of the actions cumulated are mutually consistent and employ the same form of procedure.

Except as otherwise provided in Article 3657, inconsistent or mutually exclusive actions may be cumulated in the same judicial demand if pleaded in the alternative.

Art. 463. Cumulation, plural plaintiffs or defendants

Two or more parties may be joined in the same suit, either as plaintiffs or as defendants, if:

(1) There is a community of interest between the parties joined;

(2) Each of the actions cumulated is within the jurisdiction of the court and is brought in the proper venue; and

(3) All of the actions cumulated are mutually consistent and employ the same form of procedure.

Except as otherwise provided in Article 3657, inconsistent or mutually exclusive actions may be cumulated in the same suit if pleaded in the alternative.

Editor's Notes

Community of interest explained, Gill v. City of Lake Charles, 43 So. 897 (1907), *i.e.*, presenting same factual and legal issues, Comment (b) and (c).

In Underwood v. Lane Memorial Hospital, et al., 714 So.2d 715 (La. 1998), survival and wrongful death actions arose out of two successive injuries caused by separate acts or omissions of different tortfeasors. Both the initial tortfeasor and the health care provider who treated the tort victim for the injury were political subdivisions of the state, and each was located in a different parish, hence calling for separate venues, but by applying ancillary venue both actions could be brought in one of the two parishes proper for the two political subdivisions.

An action for damages may be cumulated with the action for injunction under art. 3601, Abadie v. Cassidy, 581 So.2d 657 (La. 1991).

Art. 464. Improper cumulation, effect

When the court lacks jurisdiction of, or when the venue is improper as to, one of the actions cumulated, that action shall be dismissed.

When the cumulation is improper for any other reason, the court may: (1) order separate trials of the actions; or (2) order the plaintiff to elect which actions he shall proceed with, and to amend his petition so as to delete therefrom all allegations relating to the action which he elects to discontinue. The penalty for noncompliance with an order to amend is a dismissal of plaintiff's suit.

Art. 465. Separate trials of cumulated actions

When the court is of the opinion that it would simplify the proceedings, would permit a more orderly disposition of the case, or would otherwise be in the interest of justice, at any time prior to trial, it may order a separate trial of cumulated actions, even if the cumulation is proper.

Art. 466. Repealed by Acts 1983, No. 534, § 11

CHAPTER 3. LIS PENDENS

Article

Art. 531. Suits pending in Louisiana court or courts

When two or more suits are pending in a Louisiana court or courts on the same transaction or occurrence, between the same parties in the same capacities, the defendant may have all but the first suit dismissed by excepting thereto as provided in Article 925. When the defendant does not so except, the plaintiff may continue the prosecution of any of the suits, but the first final judgment rendered shall be conclusive of all.

Amended by Acts 1990, No. 521, § 2, eff. Jan. 1, 1991.

Comment—1990

This Article is amended to conform to the changes made in the defense of res judicata by R.S. 13:4231 and 4232.

Art. 532. Motions to stay in suits pending in Louisiana and federal or foreign court

When a suit is brought in a Louisiana court while another is pending in a court of another state or of the United States on the same transaction or occurrence, between the same parties in the same capacities, on motion of the defendant or on its own motion, the court may stay all proceedings in the second suit until the first has been discontinued or final judgment has been rendered.

Amended by Acts 1990, No. 521, § 2, eff. Jan. 1, 1991; Acts 2017, No. 419, § 1.

Comment—1990

This Article is amended to conform to the changes made in the defense of res judicata by R.S. 13:4231 and 4232.

CHAPTER 4. ABANDONMENT OF ACTION

Article

Art. 561. Abandonment in trial and appellate court

A. (1) An action, except as provided in Subparagraph (2) of this Paragraph, is abandoned when the parties fail to take any step in its prosecution or defense in the trial court for a period of three years, unless it is a succession proceeding:

(a) Which has been opened;

(b) In which an administrator or executor has been appointed; or

(c) In which a testament has been probated.

(2) Terminated by Acts 2007, No. 361, § 1, eff. Aug. 26, 2010.

(3) This provision shall be operative without formal order, but, on ex parte motion of any party or other interested person by affidavit which provides that no step has been timely taken in the prosecution or defense of the action, the trial court shall enter a formal order of dismissal as of the date of its abandonment. The sheriff shall serve the order in the manner provided in Article 1314, and shall execute a return pursuant to Article 1292.

(4) A motion to set aside a dismissal may be made only within thirty days of the date of the sheriff's service of the order of dismissal. If the trial court denies a timely motion to set aside the dismissal, the clerk of court shall give notice of the order of denial pursuant to Article 1913(A) and shall file a certificate pursuant to Article 1913(D).

(5) An appeal of an order of dismissal may be taken only within sixty days of the date of the sheriff's service of the order of dismissal. An appeal of an order of denial may be taken only within sixty days of the date of the clerk's mailing of the order of denial.

(6) The provisions of Subparagraph (2) of this Paragraph shall become null and void on August 26, 2010.

B. Any formal discovery as authorized by this Code and served on all parties whether or not filed of record, including the taking of a deposition with or without formal notice, shall be deemed to be a step in the prosecution or defense of an action.

C. An appeal is abandoned when the parties fail to take any step in its prosecution or disposition for the period provided in the rules of the appellate court.

Amended by Acts 1966, No. 36, § 1; Acts 1982, No. 186, § 1; Acts 1983, No. 670, § 1; Acts 1987, No. 149, § 1; Acts 1997, No. 1221, § 1, eff. July 1, 1998; Acts 2003, No. 545, § 1; Acts 2007, No. 361, § 1, eff. July 9, 2007.

Editor's Notes

Voluntary dismissal, C.C. art. 3463, replacing C.C. art. 3519; abatement, C.C.P. art. 428; dismissal for abandonment, C.C.P. art. 2162; interruption of prescription, C.C. art. 3462, et seq., replacing R.S. 9:5801; involuntary dismissal, C.C.P. art. 1672. Steps taken by plaintiff after abandonment has accrued are ineffective, Semel v. Green, 211 So.2d 300 (1968). "Any steps in its prosecution or defense" means a formal move or action before the trial court intended to hasten judgment, Gros v. Houma Medical and Surgical Clinic, App. 1 Cir.1977, 343 So.2d 1115.

As to par. B above, see Art. 1446(D) and Art. 1474(4), both specifically stating that the taking of a deposition or serving of "discovery materials" shall be considered a step in the prosecution or defense of an action for the purposes of Art. 561.

Caveat: See District Court Rule 10.1 as to "discovery motions."

The 1997 amendment sets the period for abandonment at three years (rather than the previous period of five years), and provides specifically that formal discovery is a step in the prosecution preventing abandonment. Paragraph C was previously designated as Paragraph B.

Paternostro v. Falgoust, 897 So.2d 19 (La. App. 1 Cir. 2004). Abandonment against the plaintiff patient was maintained against his suit brought in medical malpractice. Discovery during the three-year allowed period was not served on all parties and therefore did not satisfy "as a step in the prosecution of the action". Motion to enroll counsel, motion to terminate counsel were not steps in the prosecution. Actions taken by plaintiff after abandonment has accrued are without effect and cannot revive an abandoned action.

Bell v. Kreider, 890 So.2d 648 (La. App. 5 Cir. 2004). Defendant's filing answer after accrual of abandonment was a waiver of defendant's right to plead abandonment, contrary to the rule as to a plaintiff.

See Rule 2–8.6 for rule of abandonment in Courts of Appeal.

Art. 562. Emergency suspension of abandonment

A. Notwithstanding any other provisions of law to the contrary, in the event the governor declares a state of emergency or disaster pursuant to R.S. 29:721 through 772, the Supreme Court of Louisiana may enter an order or series of orders as deemed necessary and appropriate to suspend the period of abandonment for a period of time not to exceed ninety days. Thereafter, should the need for continuing suspension be necessary to preserve access to the courts, the governor may issue executive orders as deemed appropriate. The period of suspension authorized by the provisions of this Article shall terminate upon the earlier of an order of the Supreme Court of Louisiana or upon termination of the declared state of disaster or emergency. Nothing in this Article limits the authority of the governor or the legislature to act in accordance with its authority.

B. The right to file any pleading subject to the suspension as provided by Paragraph A of this Article shall terminate sixty days after the termination of the suspension as provided by Paragraph A of this Article.

Added by Acts 2020, 1st Ex.Sess., No. 3, § 2, eff. June 25, 2020.

CHAPTER 5. CLASS AND DERIVATIVE ACTIONS

SECTION 1. CLASS ACTIONS

Article

SECTION 2. DERIVATIVE ACTIONS

SECTION 1. CLASS ACTIONS

Editor's Notes

Caveat: Class Action Fairness Act, 28 U.S.C.A. § 1332(d)(2)(A) grants Federal jurisdiction of the action if any one plaintiff is a citizen of a state different from any defendant, subject to some exceptions.

Art. 591. Prerequisites; maintainable class actions

A. One or more members of a class may sue or be sued as representative parties on behalf of all, only if:

(1) The class is so numerous that joinder of all members is impracticable.

(2) There are questions of law or fact common to the class.

(3) The claims or defenses of the representative parties are typical of the claims or defenses of the class.

(4) The representative parties will fairly and adequately protect the interests of the class.

(5) The class is or may be defined objectively in terms of ascertainable criteria, such that the court may determine the constituency of the class for purposes of the conclusiveness of any judgment that may be rendered in the case. This prerequisite shall not be satisfied if it is necessary for the court to inquire into the merits of each potential class member's cause of action to determine whether an individual falls within the defined class.

B. An action may be maintained as a class action only if all of the prerequisites of Paragraph A of this Article are satisfied, and in addition:

(1) The prosecution of separate actions by or against individual members of the class would create a risk of:

(a) Inconsistent or varying adjudications with respect to individual members of the class which would establish incompatible standards of conduct for the party opposing the class, or

(b) Adjudications with respect to individual members of the class which would as a practical matter be dispositive of the interests of the other members not parties to the adjudications or substantially impair or impede their ability to protect their interests; or

(2) The party opposing the class has acted or refused to act on grounds generally applicable to the class, thereby making appropriate final injunctive relief or corresponding declaratory relief with respect to the class as a whole; or

(3) The court finds that the questions of law or fact common to the members of the class predominate over any questions affecting only individual members, and that a class action is superior to other available methods for the fair and efficient adjudication of the controversy. The matters pertinent to these findings include:

(a) The interest of the members of the class in individually controlling the prosecution or defense of separate actions;

(b) The extent and nature of any litigation concerning the controversy already commenced by or against members of the class;

(c) The desirability or undesirability of concentrating the litigation in the particular forum;

(d) The difficulties likely to be encountered in the management of a class action;

(e) The practical ability of individual class members to pursue their claims without class certification;

(f) The extent to which the relief plausibly demanded on behalf of or against the class, including the vindication of such public policies or legal rights as may be implicated, justifies the costs and burdens of class litigation; or

(4) The parties to a settlement request certification under Subparagraph B(3) for purposes of settlement, even though the requirements of Subparagraph B(3) might not otherwise be met.

For Official Comments and Annotative Materials,

C. Certification shall not be for the purpose of adjudicating claims or defenses dependent for their resolution on proof individual to a member of the class. However, following certification, the court shall retain jurisdiction over claims or defenses dependent for their resolution on proof individual to a member of the class.

Acts 1997, No. 839, § 1, eff. July 1, 1997. Amended by Acts 2013, No. 254, § 1.

Editor's Notes

Stevens v. Board of Trustees of Police Pension Fund, 309 So.2d 144 (1975), interprets this action according to Fed.Rule Civ.Proc. 23. Williams v. State of Louisiana, 350 So.2d 131 (1977), requires reasonable notice to all members of the class. See, in general, McCastle v. Rollins Environmental Services, 456 So.2d 612 (La.1984).

The 1997 legislation completely rewrites the Louisiana Class Action provisions. The expanded provisions appear to incorporate much of the jurisprudence, as set forth in McCastle v. Rollins, *supra.*

See, also, Banks v. New York Life Ins. Co., 737 So.2d 1275 (La. 1999), Ford v. Murphy Oil U.S.A., Inc., 703 So.2d 542 (La. 1997), and Price v. Martin, 79 So.3d 960 (La. 2011), for full analysis of criteria for certifying class action.

Caveat: Class Action Fairness Act, 28 U.S.C.A. § 1332(d)(2)(A), grants Federal jurisdiction of the action if any one plaintiff is a citizen of a state different from any defendant, subject to some exceptions.

Art. 592. Certification procedure; notice; judgment; orders

A. (1) Within ninety days after service on all adverse parties of the initial pleading demanding relief on behalf of or against a class, the proponent of the class shall file a motion to certify the action as a class action. The delay for filing the motion may be extended by stipulation of the parties or on motion for good cause shown.

(2) If the proponent fails to file a motion for certification within the delay allowed by Subparagraph (1) of this Paragraph, any adverse party may file a notice of the failure to move for certification. On the filing of such a notice and after hearing thereon, the demand for class relief may be stricken. If the demand for class relief is stricken, the action may continue between the named parties alone. A demand for class relief stricken under this Subparagraph may be reinstated upon a showing of good cause by the proponent.

(3)(a) No motion to certify an action as a class action shall be granted prior to a hearing on the motion. Such hearing shall be held as soon as practicable, but in no event until after both of the following have occurred:

(i) All named adverse parties have been served with the pleading containing the demand for class relief or have made an appearance or, with respect to unserved defendants who have not appeared, the proponent of the class has made due and diligent effort to perfect service of such pleading.

(ii) The parties have had a reasonable opportunity to obtain discovery on class certification issues, on such terms and conditions as the court deems necessary, which may include expert witness testimony or evidence. The admissibility of expert witness testimony or evidence for class certification purposes shall also be governed by Article 1425(F), although the court in its discretion may change the deadlines for filing or hearing a motion as set forth in Article 1425(F) provided such deadlines are prior to or contemporaneous with the class certification hearing.

(b) At the hearing on the motion to certify an action as a class action, the proponent of the class shall have the burden of proof to establish that all requirements of Article 591 have been satisfied.

(c) If the court finds that the action should be maintained as a class action, it shall certify the action accordingly. If the court finds that the action should not be maintained as a class action, the action may continue between the named parties. In either event, the court shall give in writing its findings of fact and reasons for judgment provided a request is made not later than ten days after notice of the order or judgment. A suspensive or devolutive appeal, as provided in Article 2081 et seq., may be taken as a matter of right from an order or judgment provided for herein.

(d) In the process of class certification, or at any time thereafter before a decision on the merits of the common issues, the court may alter, amend, or recall its initial ruling on certification and may enlarge, restrict, or otherwise redefine the constituency of the class or the issues to be maintained in the class action.

B. (1) In any class action maintained under Article 591(B)(3), the court shall direct to the members of the class the best notice practicable under the circumstances, including individual notice to all members who can be identified through reasonable effort. This notice, however given, shall be given as soon as practicable after certification, but in any event early enough that a delay provided for the class members to exercise an option to be excluded from the class will have expired before commencement of the trial on the merits of the common issues.

(2) The notice required by Subparagraph (1) of this Paragraph shall include:

(a) A general description of the action, including the relief sought, and the names and addresses of the representative parties or, where appropriate, the identity and location of the source from which the names and addresses of the representative parties can be obtained.

(b) A statement of the right of the person to be excluded from the action by submitting an election form, including the manner and time for exercising the election.

(c) A statement that the judgment, whether favorable or not, will include all members who do not request exclusion.

(d) A statement that any member who does not request exclusion may, if the member desires, enter an appearance through counsel at that member's expense.

(e) A statement advising the class member that the member may be required to take further action as the court deems necessary, such as submitting a proof of claim in order to participate in any recovery had by the class.

(f) A general description of any counterclaim brought against the class.

(g) The address of counsel to whom inquiries may be directed.

(h) Any other information that the court deems appropriate.

(3) Unless the parties agree otherwise, the proponents of the class shall bear the expense of the notification required by this Paragraph. The court may require the party opposing the class to cooperate in securing the names and addresses of the persons within the class defined by the court for the purpose of providing individual notice, but any additional costs reasonably incurred by the party opposing the class in complying with this order shall be paid by the proponent of the class. The court may tax all or part of the expenses incurred for notification as costs.

C. The judgment in an action maintained as a class action under Article 591(B)(1) or (2), whether or not favorable to the class, shall include and describe those whom the court finds to be members of the class. The judgment in an action maintained as a class action under Article 591(B)(3), whether or not favorable to the class, shall include and specify or describe those to whom the notice provided in Paragraph B of this Article was directed, and who have not requested exclusion, and whom the court finds to be members of the class.

D. When appropriate an action may be brought or maintained as a class action with respect to particular issues, or a class may be divided into subclasses and each subclass treated as a class, and the provisions of Article 591 and this Article shall then be construed and applied accordingly.

E. In the conduct of actions to which Article 591 and this Article apply, the court may make any of the following appropriate orders:

(1) Determining the course of proceedings or prescribing measures to prevent undue repetition or complication in the presentation of evidence or argument.

(2) Requiring, for the protection of the members of the class or otherwise for the fair conduct of the action, that notice be given in such manner as the court may direct to members of the class of any step in the action, or of the proposed extent of the judgment, or of the opportunity of members to signify whether they consider the representation fair and adequate, to intervene and present claims or defenses, or otherwise to come into the action.

(3) Imposing conditions on the representative parties or on intervenors.

(4) Requiring that the pleadings be amended to eliminate therefrom allegations as to representation of absent persons, and that the action proceed accordingly.

(5) Dealing with similar procedural matters, including but not limited to case management orders providing for consolidation, duties of counsel, the extent and the scheduling of and the delays for pre-certification and post-certification discovery, and other matters which affect the general order of proceedings; however, the court shall not order the class-wide trial of issues dependent for their resolution on proof individual to a member of the class, including but not limited to the causation of the member's injuries, the amount of the member's special or general damages, the individual knowledge or reliance of the member, or the applicability to the member of individual claims or defenses.

(6) Any of the orders provided in this Paragraph may be combined with an order pursuant to Article 1551, and may be altered or amended as may be desirable from time to time.

Acts 1997, No. 839, § 1, eff. July 1, 1997. Amended by Acts 2005, No. 205, § 1, eff. Jan. 1, 2006; Acts 2012, No. 115, § 1; Acts 2013, No. 254, § 1; Acts 2021, No. 259, § 2.

Editor's Notes

The 1997 amendment requires proponents of the class action to move for certification of the class within 90 days of service.

Art. 593. Venue

A. An action brought on behalf of a class shall be brought in a parish of proper venue as to the defendant.

B. An action brought against a class shall be brought in a parish of proper venue as to any member of the class named as a defendant.

Acts 1997, No. 839, § 1, eff. July 1, 1997.

Art. 593.1. Class actions; lis pendens

A. When two or more actions requesting the certification of a class pursuant to Article 591 are filed in two or more Louisiana courts regarding the same transaction or occurrence at the same location, and such classes, if certified, would encompass one or more of the same plaintiffs suing in the same capacities against one or more of the same defendants in the same capacities, the defendant may, by excepting as provided in Article 925, have all such actions transferred to the district court where the transaction or occurrence occurred.

B. When two or more actions requesting the certification of a class pursuant to Article 591 are filed in two or more Louisiana courts regarding multiple related transactions or occurrences in different locations and such classes, if certified, would encompass one or more of the same plaintiffs suing in the same capacities against one or more of the same defendants in the same capacities, the defendant may, by excepting as provided in Article 925, have all such actions transferred to the district court where the first suit was brought.

Added by Acts 2012, No. 713, § 1.

Art. 593.2. Class actions; forum non conveniens

Notwithstanding the provisions of Article 123, within thirty days of the certification of a class under Article 591 by a different Louisiana court regarding the same transaction or occurrence and encompassing one or more of the same plaintiffs suing in the same capacities against one or more of the same defendants in the same capacities, any court where a related putative class action is pending may, upon contradictory motion, in the interests of justice and for good cause shown, transfer the putative class action to the district where the related action has been certified.

Added by Acts 2012, No. 713, § 1.

Art. 594. Dismissal or compromise

A. (1) An action previously certified as a class action shall not be dismissed or compromised without the approval of the court exercising jurisdiction over the action.

(2) Notice of the proposed dismissal of an action previously certified as a class action shall be provided to all members of the class, together with the terms of any proposed compromise that the named parties have entered into. Notice shall be given in such manner as the court directs.

B. After notice of the proposed compromise has been provided to the members of the class, the court shall order a hearing to determine whether the proposed compromise is fair, reasonable, and adequate for the class. At such hearing, all parties to the action, including members of the class, shall be permitted an opportunity to be heard.

C. The court shall retain the authority to review and approve any amount paid as attorney fees pursuant to the compromise of a class action, notwithstanding any agreement to the contrary.

D. Any agreement entered by the parties to a class action that provides for the payment of attorney fees is subject to judicial approval.

E. If the terms of the proposed compromise provide for the adjudged creation of a settlement fund to be disbursed to and among members of the class in accordance with the terms thereof, the court having jurisdiction over the class action is empowered to approve the compromise settlement of the class action as a whole and issue a final judgment accordingly, following a finding that the compromise is fair, reasonable, and adequate for the class, and to order the distribution of the settlement fund accordingly, without the necessity of prior qualification of representatives of minors, interdicts, successions, or other incompetents or absentees, or prior approval of the terms of the settlement or the distribution thereof by another court; provided, that in such cases the court having jurisdiction over the class action shall include in the orders of settlement and distribution of the settlement fund appropriate provisions to ensure that all funds adjudicated to or for the benefit of such incompetents, successions, or absentees are placed in appropriate safekeeping pending the completion of appointment, qualification, and administrative procedures otherwise applicable in this Code to the interests and property of incompetents, successions, and absentees.

Acts 1997, No. 839, § 1, eff. July 1, 1997.

Art. 595. Award of expenses of litigation; security for costs

A. The court may allow the representative parties their reasonable expenses of litigation, including attorney's fees, when as a result of the class action a fund is made available, or a recovery or compromise is had which is beneficial, to the class.

B. The court, on contradictory motion at any stage of the proceeding in the trial court prior to judgment, may require the plaintiff in a class action to furnish security for the court costs which a defendant may be compelled to pay. This security for costs may be increased or decreased by the court, on contradictory motion of any interested party, on a showing that the security furnished has become inadequate or excessive.

Art. 596. Prescription; suspension

A. Liberative prescription on the claims arising out of the transactions or occurrences described in a petition brought on behalf of a class is suspended on the filing of the petition as to all members of the class as defined or described therein. Prescription which has been suspended as provided herein, begins to run again:

(1) As to any person electing to be excluded from the class, thirty days from the submission of that person's election form;

(2) As to any person excluded from the class pursuant to Article 592, thirty days after mailing or other delivery or publication of a notice to such person that the class has been restricted or otherwise redefined so as to exclude him; or

(3) As to all members, thirty days after mailing or other delivery or publication of a notice to the class that the action has been dismissed, that the demand for class relief has been stricken pursuant to Article 592, or that the court has denied a motion to certify the class or has vacated a previous order certifying the class.

B. The time periods in Subparagraphs (A)(2) and (3) of this Article commence upon the expiration of the delay for taking an appeal if there is no appeal, or when an appeal becomes final and definitive. The notice required by Subparagraphs (A)(2) and (3) of this Article shall contain a statement of the delay periods provided herein.

Acts 1997, No. 839, § 1, eff. July 1, 1997. Amended by Acts 2010, No. 185, § 1.

Editor's Notes

The 1997 amendment provides for suspension of prescription upon filing the action. See C.C. arts. 3469 and 3472 for the definition and effect of suspension, Taranto v. Louisiana Citizens Property Ins., 62 So.3d 721 (La. 2011), contractual time limitation in policy did not prevail over prescription rules of C.C. art. 3457.

Art. 597. Effect of judgment

A definitive judgment on the merits rendered in a class action concludes all members of the class, whether joined in the action or not, if the members who were joined as parties fairly insured adequate representation of all members of the class.

SECTION 2. DERIVATIVE ACTIONS

Art. 611. Derivative actions; prerequisites

A. When a corporation or unincorporated association refuses to enforce a right of the corporation or unincorporated association, a shareholder, partner, or member thereof may bring a derivative action to enforce the right on behalf of the corporation or unincorporated association. A derivative action may be maintained as a class action when the persons constituting the class are so numerous as to make it impracticable for all of them to join or be joined as parties. In the case of a derivative class action, Articles 594 and 595 shall apply.

B. If a derivative action is a "derivative proceeding" as defined in the Business Corporation Act, the action is exempt from the provisions of this Chapter other than this Subsection, and is subject instead to the provisions of the Business Corporation Act concerning derivative proceedings.

Acts 1997, No. 839, § 1, eff. July 1, 1997. Amended by Acts 2014, No. 328, § 4, eff. Jan. 1, 2015.

Comment—2014

The last sentence of Article 611 was added in connection with Louisiana's adoption in 2014 of the Business Corporation Act. The added language causes a derivative action that is filed on behalf of a Louisiana business corporation or, to the limited extent provided in R.S. 12:1–747, on behalf of a foreign corporation to be governed by the derivative proceeding provisions of the Business Corporation Act instead of the class and derivative actions chapter of the Code of Civil Procedure. See R.S. 12:1–740(1). A derivative proceeding that is governed by the Business Corporation Act is exempted only from this Chapter, however, and otherwise remains subject to the provisions of the Code of Civil Procedure.

Art. 612. Representation

One or more members of the class, who will fairly ensure the adequate representation of all members, may sue or be sued in a derivative class action on behalf of all members.

Acts 1997, No. 839, § 1, eff. July 1, 1997.

Art. 613. Procedure

After commencement of a derivative action by or on behalf of parties alleged to be members of a class, the court, on its own motion, or on the motion of any party or on trial of any exception directed to such issue, shall determine whether the action may be properly maintained as a class action as a prerequisite to any further proceedings therein. If the court finds that the action should be maintained as a class action, it shall certify the action accordingly. If not, the court may permit amendment of the pleadings in the action to permit maintenance thereof as a proceeding on behalf of parties expressly named therein under Article 616.

Acts 1997, No. 839, § 1, eff. July 1, 1997.

Art. 614. Venue

A derivative action of a shareholder, partner, or member to enforce a right of a corporation or unincorporated association shall be brought in the parish of proper venue as to the corporation or unincorporated association.

Acts 1997, No. 839, § 1, eff. July 1, 1997.

Art. 615. Petition in shareholder's derivative action

The petition in a class action brought by a shareholder, partner, or member of a corporation or unincorporated association because it refuses to enforce a right which it may enforce shall:

(1) Allege that the plaintiff was a shareholder, partner, or member at the time of the occurrence or transaction of which he complains, or that his share, partnership, or membership thereafter devolved on him by operation of law.

(2) Allege with particularity the efforts of the plaintiff to secure from the managing directors, governors, or trustees and, if necessary, from the shareholders, partners, or members, the enforcement of the right and the reasons for his failure to secure such enforcement, or the reason for not making such an effort to secure enforcement of the right.

(3) Join as defendants the corporation or unincorporated association and the obligor against whom the obligation is sought to be enforced.

(4) Include a prayer for judgment in favor of the corporation or unincorporated association and against the obligor on the obligation sought to be enforced.

(5) Be verified by the affidavit of the plaintiff or his counsel.

Acts 1997, No. 839, § 1, eff. July 1, 1997.

Art. 616. Shareholder's derivative action when not impracticable to join all shareholders, partners, or members

A. When it is not impracticable for all of the shareholders, partners, or members of a corporation or unincorporated association to join or to be joined as parties to a derivative action to enforce a right of the corporation or unincorporated association which it refuses to enforce, such action shall not be maintained as a class action. Instead, all of the shareholders, partners, or members who refuse or fail to join as plaintiffs in such an action shall be joined as defendants.

B. Derivative actions governed by this Article shall be subject to Articles 614 and 615.

Acts 1997, No. 839, § 1, eff. July 1, 1997.

Art. 617. Unincorporated association; definition; applicability

As used in Articles 611 through 616, the term "unincorporated association" shall include any unincorporated business association that is treated by controlling substantive law as a separate juridical person.

Acts 1997, No. 839, § 1, eff. July 1, 1997.

TITLE III. PARTIES

CHAPTER 1. JOINDER

Article

Art. 641. Joinder of parties needed for just adjudication

A person shall be joined as a party in the action when either:

(1) In his absence complete relief cannot be accorded among those already parties.

(2) He claims an interest relating to the subject matter of the action and is so situated that the adjudication of the action in his absence may either:

(a) As a practical matter, impair or impede his ability to protect that interest.

(b) Leave any of the persons already parties subject to a substantial risk of incurring multiple or inconsistent obligations.

Amended by Acts 1995, No. 662, § 1.

Comment—1995

The amendments to Articles 641 through 646, 926 and 927, codify the holding of the Louisiana Supreme Court in State Department of Highways v. Lamar Advertising Co. of La., Inc., 279 So.2d 671 (La.1973), that courts determine whether a party should be joined and whether the action could proceed if the party could not be joined by a factual analysis of the interests involved. The factors to be considered are set out in the amendments to Articles 641 and 642 and replace the formal classification of parties as necessary or indispensable based solely on the interests of the party to be joined. The failure to join a party may be raised at any time through the peremptory exception.

Art. 642. Determination by court whenever joinder not feasible

If a person described in Article 641 cannot be made a party, the court shall determine whether the action should proceed among the parties before it, or should be dismissed. The factors to be considered by the court include:

(1) To what extent a judgment rendered in the person's absence might be prejudicial to him or those already present.

(2) The extent to which the prejudice can be lessened or avoided by protective provisions in the judgment, by the shaping of relief, or by other measures.

(3) Whether a judgment rendered in the person's absence will be adequate.

(4) Whether the plaintiff will have an adequate remedy if the action is dismissed for nonjoinder.

Amended by Acts 1995, No. 662, § 1.

Art. 643. Solidary obligees and obligors; joinder

One or more solidary obligees may sue to enforce a solidary right, and one or more solidary obligors may be sued to enforce a solidary obligation, without the necessity of joining all others in the action.

Amended by Acts 1995, No. 662, § 1.

Editor's Notes

C.C. art. 2324(B) provides that joint tortfeasors are joint and divisible obligors, under C.C. art. 1789, not in solido. C.C. art. 2324(A) provides that intentional tortfeasors who conspire to commit the tort are in solido.

C.C. 1790 defines solidary obligees; C.C. 1794 defines solidary obligors.

Art. 644. Party plaintiff who refuses or fails to sue

If a party subject to the jurisdiction of the court should join as a plaintiff but refuses or fails to do so, he may be joined as a defendant and required to assert his rights in the action or be precluded thereafter from asserting them.

Amended by Acts 1995, No. 662, § 1.

Editor's Notes

Tropicana Pools South, Inc. v. Chamberlain, 324 So.2d 29 (2d 1975), joins non-resident indispensable party.

Art. 645. Pleading nonjoinder of a party

The failure to join a party to an action may be pleaded in the peremptory exception, or may be noticed by the trial or appellate court on its own motion.

Amended by Acts 1995, No. 662, § 1.

Editor's Notes

Vision Aviation v. Airport Aut. for Airport, 33 So.3d 423 (La.App. 3 Cir. 2010). Bank holding a mortgage on the leasehold was a necessary party as a beneficiary of a stipulation "pour autrui". In an action to terminate lease agreement with lessee after judgment was rendered in favor of lessor terminating the lease, lessee appealed and filed a peremptory exception to join bank as necessary party. There were stipulations in the mortgage clearly to the benefit of the bank, requiring remand of the whole proceedings to make bank a party, the prior judgment of the trial court being an absolute nullity.

Art. 646. Amendment of petition to join a party

When the failure to join a party is pleaded successfully in or noticed by a trial court, the latter may permit amendment of the petition so as to make him a party, and may reopen the case if it has been submitted and further evidence is necessary. When such failure is pleaded successfully in or noticed by an appellate court, the latter may remand the case for such amendment and further evidence.

Amended by Acts 1995, No. 662, § 1.

Art. 647. Permissive joinder governed by rules of cumulation of actions

The permissive joinder of two or more plaintiffs or defendants in the same suit is governed by the rules regulating the cumulation of actions provided in Articles 463 through 465.

CHAPTER 2. PARTIES PLAINTIFF

Article

Art. 681. Real and actual interest required

Except as otherwise provided by law, an action can be brought only by a person having a real and actual interest which he asserts.

Art. 682. Individuals having procedural capacity

A competent major and a competent emancipated minor have the procedural capacity to sue.

Art. 683. Unemancipated minor

A. An unemancipated minor has no procedural capacity to sue.

B. All persons having parental authority over an unemancipated minor must join as proper plaintiffs to sue to enforce a right of the minor, unless a joint custody implementation order otherwise applies. Nevertheless, with permission of the court, any person having parental authority may represent the minor whenever the other person having parental authority fails or refuses to do so.

C. During tutorship, the tutor is the proper plaintiff to sue to enforce a right of the unemancipated minor.

D. Notwithstanding the provisions of Paragraph A, B, or C of this Article, an attorney appointed by the court having jurisdiction over an unemancipated minor who is in the legal custody of the Department of Children and Family Services is the proper plaintiff to sue to enforce a right of an unemancipated minor. Upon application of the tutor or a person having parental authority who would otherwise be the proper plaintiff to sue pursuant to Paragraph B or C of this Article, the court shall appoint or substitute as the proper plaintiff the best qualified among the tutor, a person having parental authority, or the appointed attorney.

Amended by Acts 1992, No. 106, § 1, eff. June 5, 1992; Acts 1993, No. 867, § 1, eff. June 23, 1993; Acts 1995, No. 268, § 1, eff. June 14, 1995; Acts 2004, No. 26, § 2; Acts 2012, No. 741, § 1; Acts 2015, No. 260, § 2, eff. Jan. 1, 2016.

Comment—2012

Article 686(B) has been amended to remove the words "appointed by a court of this state" in order to conform with Article 4061.1, which provides that a natural tutor may file an action for damages based on a delictual obligation without obtaining court approval.

Revision Comments—2015

(a) This Article changes the law in part. Under this Article, while the regime of parental authority is in existence, all persons having parental authority must join as plaintiffs to file suit to enforce the right of an unemancipated minor. Either parent during the marriage has parental authority of the child unless extraordinary circumstances exist, such as if one parent is mentally incompetent, committed, interdicted, imprisoned, or is an absent person. See C.C. Art. 232 (Rev. 2015). Additionally, an ascendant of the minor, other than the parent, who is awarded custody during the marriage of the parents, has parental authority. See C.C. Art. 234 (Rev. 2015). Therefore, under this revision, all persons having parental authority must be joined, but one person may act alone if extraordinary circumstances exist, see C.C. Art. 232, or with court approval when the other person fails or refuses to act. Under prior law, the father was the proper plaintiff to sue and only if the father was mentally incompetent, committed, interdicted, imprisoned, or an absent person was the mother the proper plaintiff to sue. See Article 683 (as amended prior to 2015).

(b) The failure to join all persons having parental authority can be raised by the peremptory exception of nonjoinder of a party. See C.C.P. Art. 927.

Editor's Notes

Cf. C.C.P. arts. 4265, 4271, requirements for approval by court.

Art. 684. Mental incompetent; interdict

A. A mental incompetent does not have the procedural capacity to sue.

B. Except as otherwise provided in Articles 4431, 4554, and 4566, the curator is the proper plaintiff to sue to enforce a right of an interdict.

Art. 685. Succession

Except as otherwise provided by law, the succession representative appointed by a court of this state is the proper plaintiff to sue to enforce a right of the deceased or of his succession, while the latter is under administration. The heirs or legatees of the deceased, whether present or represented in the state or not, need not be joined as parties, whether the action is personal, real, or mixed.

Art. 686. Marital community

Either spouse is the proper plaintiff, during the existence of the marital community, to sue to enforce a community right; however, if one spouse is the managing spouse with respect to the community right sought to be enforced, then that spouse is the proper plaintiff to bring an action to enforce the right.

When doubt exists whether the right sought to be enforced is a community right or is the separate right of the plaintiff spouse, that spouse may sue in the alternative to enforce the right.

When only one spouse sues to enforce a community right, the other spouse is a necessary party. Where the failure to join the other spouse may result in an injustice to that spouse, the trial court may order the joinder of that spouse on its own motion.

Amended by Acts 1970, No. 344, § 1; Acts 1979, No. 711, § 3, eff. Jan. 1, 1980.

Art. 687. Person doing business under trade name

A person who does business under a trade name shall sue in his own name to enforce a right created by or arising out of the doing of such business.

Art. 688. Partnership

A partnership has the procedural capacity to sue to enforce its rights in the partnership name, and appears through and is represented by an authorized partner.

Editor's Notes

Cf. C.C. art. 2801, a partnership is a juridical person.

Art. 689. Unincorporated association

An unincorporated association has the procedural capacity to sue to enforce its rights in its own name, and appears through and is represented by its president or other authorized officer.

Editor's Notes

R.S. 12:501–520 allows unincorporated associations to appoint agent with authority to acquire or sell property for the association, and limits liability of members.

Art. 690. Domestic corporation; insurer; limited liability company

Except as otherwise provided in Articles 692 and 693, a domestic corporation, a domestic insurer, and a domestic limited liability company has the procedural capacity to sue to enforce its rights in the corporate or company name.

Amended by Acts 1999, No. 145, § 2.

Art. 691. Foreign corporation; foreign limited liability company; foreign or alien insurance corporation

Except as otherwise provided in Articles 692 and 693, a foreign corporation, a foreign or alien insurer, and a foreign limited liability company has the procedural capacity to sue to enforce its rights in the corporate or company name.

Amended by Acts 1999, No. 145, § 2.

Editor's Notes

Foreign corporation doing business in the state, but not licensed, may not sue in state court on intrastate transaction, R.S. 12:314.

Art. 692. Corporation, limited liability company, or partnership in receivership or liquidation

A. Except as otherwise provided by law, the receiver or liquidator appointed for a domestic or foreign corporation, limited liability company, or partnership by a court of this state is the proper plaintiff to sue to enforce a right of the corporation, limited liability company, or partnership, or of its receiver or liquidator. These rules apply whether, under the law of its domicile, the existence of the corporation, limited liability company, or partnership continues or is terminated.

B. The receiver or liquidator may institute and prosecute any action without special authorization from the court which appointed him.

Amended by Acts 1999, No. 145, § 2.

Art. 693. Insurer in receivership

The receiver appointed by a court of this state for a domestic insurer is the proper plaintiff to sue to enforce a right of the domestic insurer, or of its receiver.

Except as otherwise provided by law, the ancillary receiver appointed by a court of this state for a foreign or alien insurer is the proper plaintiff to sue to enforce a right of the foreign or alien insurer, or of its domiciliary or ancillary receiver.

As used herein and in Article 741, "receiver" includes liquidator, rehabilitator, and conservator.

Art. 694. Agent

An agent has the procedural capacity to sue to enforce a right of his principal, when specially authorized to do so.

For all procedural purposes, the principal is considered the plaintiff in such an action. The defendant may assert any defense available against the principal, and may enforce his rights against the principal in a reconventional demand.

Editor's Notes

C.C. art. 2997, express and special power required for agent.

Art. 695. Absent or mentally incompetent managing spouse

If the managing spouse with respect to the community right sought to be enforced is an absentee or a mental incompetent, then the other spouse is the proper plaintiff to enforce that community right.

Added by Acts 1979, No. 711, § 4, eff. Jan. 1, 1980.

Art. 696. Pledgor and pledgee

The pledgee of a real right, or of a negotiable instrument or other incorporeal right, is the proper plaintiff to sue to enforce the pledged right.

The pledgee may enforce the entire right judicially, unless it is an obligation of the pledgor, in which event it may be enforced only to the extent of the indebtedness secured by the pledge.

Editor's Notes

See R.S. 10:9–101 et seq. See also La. C.C. art. 3141 et seq. for the definition of pledge.

Art. 697. Subrogor and subrogee

An incorporeal right to which a person has been subrogated, either conventionally or by effect of law, shall be enforced judicially by:

(1) The subrogor and the subrogee, when the subrogation is partial; or

(2) The subrogee, when the entire right is subrogated.

Art. 698. Assignor and assignee

An incorporeal right which has been assigned, whether unconditionally or conditionally for purposes of collection or security, shall be enforced judicially by:

(1) The assignor and the assignee, when the assignment is partial; or

(2) The assignee, when the entire right is assigned.

Editor's Notes

See the cross references listed under C.C. art. 2642. R.S. 9:3051, transfer of claims for collection.

Art. 699. Trust estate

Except as otherwise provided by law, the trustee of an express trust is the proper plaintiff to sue to enforce a right of the trust estate.

Editor's Notes

R.S. 9:1721, Trust Code.

Art. 700. Authority or qualification of plaintiff suing in representative capacity

When a plaintiff sues as an agent to enforce a right of his principal, or as a legal representative, his authority or qualification is presumed, unless challenged by the defendant by the timely filing of the dilatory exception. When so challenged, the plaintiff shall prove his authority or qualification on the trial of the exception.

CHAPTER 3. PARTIES DEFENDANT

Article

Art. 731. Individuals having procedural capacity

A competent major and a competent emancipated minor have the procedural capacity to be sued.

Editor's Notes

See La. C.C. arts. 365–371 and La. C.C. art. 2318 in the statutory appendix for the provisions on emancipation.

Art. 732. Unemancipated minor

A. An unemancipated minor has no procedural capacity to be sued.

B. Any person having parental authority over an unemancipated minor is a proper defendant in an action to enforce an obligation against the minor.

C. During tutorship, the tutor is the proper defendant in an action to enforce an obligation against the unemancipated minor. If a minor has no tutor, the action may be brought against the minor, but the court shall appoint an attorney to represent him until a tutor is appointed for the minor.

D. Notwithstanding the provisions of Paragraph A, B, or C of this Article, an attorney appointed by the court having jurisdiction over an unemancipated minor who is in the legal custody of the Department of Children and Family Services is the proper defendant in an action to enforce an obligation against an unemancipated minor. Upon application of the tutor or person having parental authority who would otherwise be the proper defendant to be sued pursuant to Paragraph B or C of this Article, the court shall appoint or substitute as the proper defendant the best qualified among the tutor, a person having parental authority, or the appointed attorney.

Amended by Acts 1992, No. 106, § 1, eff. June 5, 1992; Acts 1993, No. 867, § 1, eff. June 23, 1993; Acts 2004, No. 26, § 2; Acts 2015, No. 260, § 2, eff. Jan. 1, 2016.

Revision Comments—2015

This Article changes the law in part. When parents are married, any person having parental authority can be the proper defendant in an action to enforce an obligation against an unemancipated minor. Either parent during the marriage has parental authority of the child unless extraordinary circumstances exist. See C.C. Art. 232 (Rev. 2015). Additionally, an ascendant of the minor, other than the parent, who is awarded custody during the marriage of the parents, has parental authority. See C.C. Art. 234 (Rev. 2015). Under prior law, the father was the proper party to be sued and only if the father was mentally incompetent, committed, interdicted, imprisoned, or an absent person was the mother the proper party to sue. See Article 732 (as amended prior to 2015).

Editor's Notes

See C.C.P. art. 4031, et seq.; C.C. art. 246 et seq. See also C.C.P. art. 4061.1, allowing natural tutor to file suit for delictual obligation without qualifying.

Art. 733. Mental incompetent; interdict

A. A mental incompetent has no procedural capacity to be sued.

B. Except as otherwise provided in Articles 732, 4431, and 4566, the curator appointed by a court of this state is the proper defendant in an action to enforce an obligation against a mental incompetent or an interdict. If an incompetent has no curator, but is interdicted, or committed to or confined in a mental institution, the action shall be brought against him, but the court shall appoint an attorney at law to represent him.

Editor's Notes

See C.C.P. art. 4541, et seq., C.C. art. 389 et seq.

Art. 734. Succession

Except as otherwise provided by law, including but not limited to Articles 2641 and 2674, the succession representative appointed by a court of this state is the proper defendant in an action to enforce an obligation of the deceased or of his succession, while the latter is under administration. The heirs or legatees of the deceased, whether present or represented in the state or not, need not be joined as parties, whether the action is personal, real, or mixed.

Amended by Acts 1991, No. 229, § 1.

Editor's Notes

See C.C.P. art. 3241, et seq.

Art. 735. Marital community

Either spouse is the proper defendant, during the existence of the marital community, in an action to enforce an obligation against community property; however, if one spouse is the managing spouse with respect to the obligation sought to be enforced against the community property, then that spouse is the proper defendant in an action to enforce the obligation.

When doubt exists whether the obligation sought to be enforced is a community obligation or the separate obligation of the defendant spouse, that spouse may be sued in the alternative.

When only one spouse is sued to enforce an obligation against community property, the other spouse is a necessary party. Where the failure to join the other spouse may result in an injustice to that spouse, the trial court may order the joinder of that spouse on its own motion.

Amended by Acts 1979, No. 711, § 3, eff. Jan. 1, 1980.

Editor's Notes

See C.C. arts. 2359 to 2364; See, also, Matrimonial Regimes generally, C.C. art. 2325, et seq.

Art. 736. Person doing business under trade name

A person who does business under a trade name is the proper defendant in an action to enforce an obligation created by or arising out of the doing of such business.

Art. 737. Partnership; partners

A partnership has the procedural capacity to be sued in its partnership name.

The partners of an existing partnership may not be sued on a partnership obligation unless the partnership is joined as a defendant.

Art. 738. Unincorporated association; members

An unincorporated association has the procedural capacity to be sued in its own name. The members of an unincorporated association may be sued jointly on an obligation of the association and the association may be joined as a defendant in such an action.

Editor's Notes

See notes for C.C.P. art. 689, infra.

Art. 739. Corporation; limited liability company; insurer

Except as otherwise provided in Articles 740 and 741, a domestic or foreign corporation, a domestic or foreign limited liability company, or a domestic, foreign, or alien insurer has the procedural capacity to be sued in its corporate or company name.

Amended by Acts 1999, No. 145, § 2.

Art. 740. Corporation; limited liability company; partnership in receivership or liquidation

A. Except as otherwise provided by law, the receiver or liquidator of a domestic or foreign corporation, a domestic or foreign limited liability company, or a domestic or foreign partnership, appointed by a court of this state is the proper defendant in an action to enforce an obligation of the corporation, limited liability company, or partnership, or of its receiver or liquidator.

B. The receiver or liquidator may be sued without the necessity of obtaining permission therefor from the court which appointed him.

Amended by Acts 1999, No. 145, § 2.

Art. 741. Insurer in receivership

The receiver appointed by a court of this state for a domestic insurer is the proper defendant in an action to enforce an obligation of the insurer, or of its receiver.

Except as otherwise provided by law, the ancillary receiver appointed by a court of this state for a foreign or alien insurer is the proper defendant in an action to enforce an obligation of the insurer, or of its domiciliary or ancillary receiver.

Art. 742. Trust estate

The trustee of an express trust is the proper defendant in an action to enforce an obligation against a trust estate.

Art. 743. Absent or mentally incompetent managing spouse

If the managing spouse with respect to the obligation sought to be enforced against community property is an absentee or a mental incompetent, then the other spouse is the proper defendant in a suit to enforce that obligation.

Added by Acts 1979, No. 711, § 4, eff. Jan. 1, 1980.

CHAPTER 4. PARTIES TO INCIDENTAL DEMANDS

Article

Art. 771. Rules applicable

Articles 641 through 742 and 801 through 821 are applicable to the parties to an incidental demand.

CHAPTER 5. SUBSTITUTION OF PARTIES

SECTION 1. IN TRIAL COURTS

Article

822 to 850. [Reserved].

SECTION 1. IN TRIAL COURTS

Art. 801. Voluntary substitution for deceased party; legal successor

When a party dies during the pendency of an action which is not extinguished by his death, his legal successor may have himself substituted for the deceased party, on ex parte written motion supported by proof of his quality.

As used in Articles 801 through 804, "legal successor" means:

(1) The survivors designated in Article 2315.1 of the Civil Code, if the action survives in their favor; and

(2) Otherwise, it means the succession representative of the deceased appointed by a court of this state, if the succession is under administration therein; or the heirs and legatees of the deceased, if the deceased's succession is not under administration therein.

Amended by Acts 1962, No. 92, § 1.

Editor's Notes

C.C.P. arts. 426 to 428; C.C. art. 2315.1.

Art. 802. Compulsory substitution for deceased party; summons

On ex parte written motion of any other party, supported by an affidavit of the truth of the facts alleged, the court may order the issuance of a summons to the legal successor to appear and substitute himself for the deceased party. This summons shall show the title and docket number of the action, and the name and address of the court where the action is pending.

Art. 803. Same; service or publication of summons

A. When the name and address of the legal successor is known, and he is a resident of the state, he shall be summoned to appear and substitute himself for the deceased party within thirty days of the date the summons is served on him.

B. When the name and address of the legal successor is known, but he is a nonresident or absentee, he shall be summoned to appear and substitute himself for the deceased party within sixty days of the receipt of the summons through registered or certified mail.

C. If the name or address of the legal successor is unknown, the summons shall be by two publications not less than fifteen days apart in a newspaper published in the parish where the action is pending and in the parish of the domicile of the deceased party, which shall summon him to appear and substitute himself for the deceased party within sixty days of the first publication. The summons shall be addressed to the legal successor by name, if the latter is known; and otherwise shall be addressed to "The legal successor of ____________, deceased".

Amended by Acts 1987, No. 146, § 1.

Art. 804. Same; effect or failure of legal successor to appear

When the legal successor fails to appear and substitute himself for the deceased party within the delay allowed in the summons, on ex parte written motion of any other party, the court may:

(1) Dismiss the action as to the deceased party, with or without prejudice, if the deceased was a plaintiff; or

(2) When the legal successor of a deceased defendant has not been served by personal or domiciliary service with summons to appear and substitute, appoint an attorney at law to represent such legal successor, and the action shall be proceeded with contradictorily against the attorney at law.

Amended by Acts 1968, No. 123, § 1.

Comments—1968

Amended upon recommendation of the Louisiana State Law Institute to avoid the necessity of appointing an attorney at law to represent a legal successor of a deceased defendant when service of the summons to appear and substitute has been made in Louisiana by personal or domiciliary service on the legal successor. Appointment of an attorney at law would be necessary only in such cases where it is impossible to serve the legal successor by personal or domiciliary service in Louisiana because he is out of the state or he cannot be found.

Art. 805. Legal representative; successor

Articles 801 through 804 apply to the substitution of a legal representative of any party other than a deceased person, and to the substitution of the successor of any legal representative appointed by a court of this state, except that the term "legal successor", as used therein, shall be considered as referring to such legal representative, or successor, as the case may be.

When an action has been commenced by a proper representative on behalf of an incompetent person and such person thereafter becomes competent, the authority of the representative shall continue until substitution is made in accordance with the provisions of this article.

Amended by Acts 1968, No. 124, § 1.

Comments—1968

Amended on the recommendation of the Louisiana State Law Institute to overcome whatever effect the case of Butler v. State Farm Mutual Ins. Co., 195 So.2d 314 (1967) may have as to cases not on the appellate level. Art. 821 still provides that the substitution articles (801–807) do not apply as to substitutions on the appellate level. Such substitutions are regulated by Rule 13 of the rules of the Supreme Court and of the courts of appeal, which, however, apply only in case of death.

The formerly incompetent person can, of course, immediately substitute himself and thus prevent the "representative" from further controlling the litigation. The amendment applies to persons who were incompetent because of minority but who reach the age of majority during the litigation or become emancipated, and it applies to other incompetents who regain competency and are declared to be competent.

Art. 806. Public officer

When an officer of the state, or of a municipality, parish, political subdivision, agency, or public corporation, who is a party dies, resigns, or otherwise ceases to hold office, his successor may be substituted therefor on ex parte written motion of the successor or any other party, supported by an affidavit of the truth of the facts alleged. A copy of the order substituting the successor shall be served on the adverse party by mail.

Art. 807. Transfer of interest

When a party to an action transfers an interest in the subject matter thereof, the action shall be continued by or against such party, unless the court directs that the transferee be substituted for or joined with the transferor.

SECTION 2. IN APPELLATE COURTS

Art. 821. Rules of Chapter applicable to district courts; rules of other appellate courts applicable

Articles 801 through 807 govern the substitution of parties in a case pending in a district court on appeal from a justice of the peace or city court.

The substitution of parties in an action pending in the supreme court or in a court of appeal is governed by the rules of the appellate court.

Arts. 822 to 850. [Reserved]

BOOK II

ORDINARY PROCEEDINGS

TITLE I. PLEADING

CHAPTER 1. GENERAL DISPOSITIONS

Art. 851. Three modes of procedure; Book II governs ordinary proceedings

Three different modes of procedure are used in civil matters in the trial courts of this state: ordinary, summary, and executory.

The articles in this Book govern ordinary proceedings, which are to be used in the district courts in all cases, except as otherwise provided by law.

Summary and executory proceedings are regulated by the provisions of Book V.

Art. 852. Pleadings allowed; replicatory pleadings prohibited

The pleadings allowed in civil actions, whether in a principal or incidental action, shall be in writing and shall consist of petitions, exceptions, written motions, and answers. No replicatory pleadings shall be used and all new matter alleged in exceptions, contradictory motions, and answers, whether in a principal or incidental action, shall be considered denied or avoided.

Art. 853. Caption of pleadings; adoption by reference; exhibits

Every pleading shall contain a caption setting forth the name of the court, the title and number of the action, and a designation of the pleading. The title of the action shall state the name of the first party on each side with an appropriate indication of other parties.

A statement in a pleading may be adopted by reference in a different part of the same pleading or in another pleading in the same court. A copy of any written instrument that is an exhibit to a pleading is a part thereof.

Amended by Acts 2018, No. 195, § 1.

Comments—2018

The amendment to this Article eliminates the phrase "for all purposes" to resolve a conflict that previously existed between this provision and Article 966(A)(4), which provides the exclusive list of documents that may be filed in support of or in opposition to a motion for summary judgment. Under Article 966(A)(4), a copy of a written instrument that is an exhibit to a pleading may not be filed in connection with a motion for summary judgment unless the written instrument itself is properly authenticated. See Article 966, Comment (c) (2015); see also *Raborn v. Albea*, 221 So. 3d 104, 111 (La. App. 1 Cir. 2017).

Art. 854. Form of pleading

No technical forms of pleading are required.

All allegations of fact of the petition, exceptions, or answer shall be simple, concise, and direct, and shall be set forth in numbered paragraphs. As far as practicable, the contents of each paragraph shall be limited to a single set of circumstances.

Art. 855. Pleading special matters; capacity

Except as otherwise provided by law, it is not necessary to allege the capacity of a party to sue or be sued or the authority of a party to sue or be sued in a representative capacity or the legal existence of a legal entity or an organized association of persons made a party. Such procedural capacity shall be presumed, unless challenged by the dilatory exception.

Amended by Acts 2018, No. 195, § 1.

Editor's Notes

See article 4061.1 which requires a natural tutor filing an action for damages based on a delictual obligation to "set forth the facts, including the relationship to the minor child, entitling the petitioner to act as tutor."

Art. 856. Same; fraud, mistake, or condition of the mind

In pleading fraud or mistake, the circumstances constituting fraud or mistake shall be alleged with particularity. Malice, intent, knowledge, and other condition of mind of a person may be alleged generally.

Editor's Notes

Mayer v. Valentine Sugars, Inc., 444 So.2d 618 (La.1984), applies this provision to the intentional act exception to Workers' Compensation immunity, as set forth in Bazley v. Tortorich, 397 So.2d 475 (La. 1981).

Art. 857. Same; suspensive conditions

In pleading the performance or occurrence of suspensive conditions, it is sufficient to allege generally that all such conditions have been performed or have occurred. A denial of performance or occurrence shall be alleged specifically and with particularity.

Art. 858. Same; official document or act

In pleading an official document or official act, it is sufficient to allege that the document was issued or the act done in compliance with law.

Art. 859. Same; judgment or decision

In pleading a judgment of a domestic or foreign court, or a decision of a judicial or quasi judicial tribunal, or of a board, commission, or officer, it is sufficient to allege the judgment or decision without setting forth matter showing jurisdiction to render it.

Art. 860. Same; time and place

For the purpose of testing the sufficiency of a pleading, allegations of time and place are material and shall be considered as all other allegations of material matter.

Art. 861. Same; special damage

When items of special damage are claimed, they shall be specifically alleged.

Editor's Notes

Lost wages, medical expenses and property damages are examples, *e.g.*, Lanier Business Products, Inc. v. First Nat. Bank of Rayville, 388 So.2d 442 (2d 1980), which also announces the rule against recovery of items not pleaded. Should hedonic damages be specially pleaded? According to McGee v. AC and S, Inc., 933 So.2d 770 (La. 2006), ". . . loss of enjoyment of life is recoverable as a separate element of general damages that may be included as a separate item on a jury verdict form . . .", p. 772.

Art. 862. Relief granted under pleadings; sufficiency of prayer

Except as provided in Article 1703, a final judgment shall grant the relief to which the party in whose favor it is rendered is entitled, even if the party has not demanded such relief in his pleadings and the latter contain no prayer for general and equitable relief.

Official Revision Comments—1960

(a) This article eliminates the necessity for the prayer for general and equitable relief, as it automatically performs the function of such prayer. The exception to the rule established to protect a person against whom a default judgment is rendered accords with the strict requirement imposed upon a plaintiff who takes judgment by default against the defendant. *Cf.* Louisiana State Bank v. Senecal, 9 La. 225 (1836).

(b) Even more important, this article, together with Art. 1154, *infra,* suppresses the harsh and unduly technical "theory of the case" doctrine in Louisiana, under which the litigant must select a theory of his case or defense and adhere to it throughout the litigation and which has been severely criticized. See Hubert, The Theory of a Case in Louisiana, 24 Tul.L.Rev. 66 (1949). Rules 8(e), 15(b), and 54(c) of the Federal Rules of Civil Procedure, from which the above article is taken were likewise intended to abrogate the "theory of the case" doctrine in the federal courts. See Matarese v. Moore-McCormack Lines, 158 F.2d 631 (2 Cir.1946); Nester v. Western Union Tel. Co., 25 F.Supp. 478 (D.C.Cal.1938); Mitchell

Novelty Co. v. United Manufacturing Co., 94 F.Supp. 612 (D.C.Ill.1950). See also Clark on Code Pleading (2d ed.) 234 (1947); Commentary, Pleading of "Theory" of Recovery, 3 Fed. Rules Serv. 667 (1940).

Art. 863. Signing of pleadings; effect

A. Every pleading of a party represented by an attorney shall be signed by at least one attorney of record in his individual name, whose physical address and email address for service of process shall be stated. A party who is not represented by an attorney shall sign his pleading and state his physical address and email address, if he has an email address, for service of process. If mail is not received at the physical address for service of process, a designated mailing address shall also be provided.

B. Pleadings need not be verified or accompanied by affidavit or certificate, except as otherwise provided by law, but the signature of an attorney or party shall constitute a certification by him that he has read the pleading, and that to the best of his knowledge, information, and belief formed after reasonable inquiry, he certifies all of the following:

(1) The pleading is not being presented for any improper purpose, such as to harass, cause unnecessary delay, or needlessly increase the cost of litigation.

(2) Each claim, defense, or other legal assertion in the pleading is warranted by existing law or by a nonfrivolous argument for the extension, modification, or reversal of existing law.

(3) Each allegation or other factual assertion in the pleading has evidentiary support or, for a specifically identified allegation or factual assertion, is likely to have evidentiary support after a reasonable opportunity for further investigation or discovery.

(4) Each denial in the pleading of a factual assertion is warranted by the evidence or, for a specifically identified denial, is reasonably based on a lack of information or belief.

C. If a pleading is not signed, it shall be stricken unless promptly signed after the omission is called to the attention of the pleader.

D. If, upon motion of any party or upon its own motion, the court determines that a certification has been made in violation of the provisions of this Article, the court shall impose upon the person who made the certification or the represented party, or both, an appropriate sanction which may include an order to pay to the other party the amount of the reasonable expenses incurred because of the filing of the pleading, including reasonable attorney fees.

E. A sanction authorized in Paragraph D shall be imposed only after a hearing at which any party or his counsel may present any evidence or argument relevant to the issue of imposition of the sanction.

F. A sanction authorized in Paragraph D shall not be imposed with respect to an original petition which is filed within sixty days of an applicable prescriptive date and then voluntarily dismissed within ninety days after its filing or on the date of a hearing on the pleading, whichever is earlier.

G. If the court imposes a sanction, it shall describe the conduct determined to constitute a violation of the provisions of this Article and explain the basis for the sanction imposed.

Amended by Acts 1988, No. 442, § 1, eff. Jan. 1, 1989; Acts 2010, No. 540, § 1; Acts 2020, No. 13, § 1; Acts 2021, No. 68, § 1, eff. Jan. 1, 2022.

Editor's Notes

First American Bank v. First Guar. Bank, App. 1 Cir.1993, 615 So.2d 1060, holds that advancing novel legal argument or theory with good-faith argument for change is not a violation of this article. Sanctions against attorney allowed for his falsely certifying domicile of client in divorce action, Mathis v. Mathis, 964 So.2d 426 (App. 4 Cir. 2007).

See Rule 9.7, District Court Rules, Signing of Pleading.

Art. 864. Attorney subject to disciplinary action

An attorney may be subjected to appropriate disciplinary action for a wilful violation of any provision of Article 863, or for the insertion of scandalous or indecent matter in a pleading.

Editor's Notes

The attorney functions as an officer of the court, C.C.P. art. 371.

Art. 865. Construction of pleadings

Every pleading shall be so construed as to do substantial justice.

CHAPTER 2. PETITION

Article

Art. 891. Form of petition

A. The petition shall comply with Articles 853, 854, and 863, and, whenever applicable, with Articles 855 through 861. It shall set forth the name, surname, and domicile of the parties; shall contain a short, clear, and concise statement of all causes of action arising out of, and of the material facts of, the transaction or occurrence that is the subject matter of the litigation; shall designate a physical address, not a post office box, and an email address for receipt of service of all items involving the litigation; and shall conclude with a prayer for judgment for the relief sought. Relief may be prayed for in the alternative.

B. For petitions involving domestic violence brought pursuant to R.S. 46:2131 et seq., R.S. 9:361 et seq., Children's Code Article 1564 et seq., or Code of Civil Procedure Article 3601 et seq., the address and parish of the residence of each petitioner and each person on whose behalf the petition is filed may remain confidential with the court.

Amended by Acts 1990, No. 521, § 2, eff. Jan. 1, 1991; Acts 1991, No. 48, § 1; Acts 1997, No. 1156, § 2; Acts 2021, No. 68, § 1, eff. Jan. 1, 2022.

Comment—1990

This Article is amended to reflect the changes made in the defense of res judicata. Except as otherwise provided by law, the plaintiff is required to set forth the facts of the transaction or occurrence that is the subject matter of the litigation, and not merely the facts supporting the cause of action asserted, because all causes of action arising out of that transaction or occurrence are considered to have been submitted for adjudication and will be barred or merged in the judgment.

Editor's Notes

Fact pleading is retained through this article, Comment (a). See R.S. 13:4231 and 4232, statutory provisions for res judicata.

The 1997 amendment added the last sentence, to conform to the extensive amendments of the Children's Code by Act 1156 of 1997.

Under the Fed. Rules of Civ. Proc., as interpreted by the opinion in Iqbal, 129 S.Ct. 1937 (2009) a complaint must allege sufficient facts to state a plausible claim for relief; otherwise, it is vulnerable to a motion to dismiss. The claim is plausible when the court can draw a reasonable inference that the defendant is liable for the alleged misconduct. This requirement of plausibility requires more than the mere possibility that the defendant acted wrongfully.

Art. 892. Alternative causes of action

Except as otherwise provided in Article 3657, a petition may set forth two or more causes of action in the alternative, even though the legal or factual bases thereof may be inconsistent or mutually exclusive. In such cases all allegations shall be made subject to the obligations set forth in Article 863.

Art. 893. Pleading of damages

A. (1) No specific monetary amount of damages shall be included in the allegations or prayer for relief of any original, amended, or incidental demand. The prayer for relief shall be for such damages as are reasonable in the premises except that if a specific amount of damages is necessary to establish the jurisdiction of the court, the right to a jury trial, the lack of jurisdiction of federal courts due to insufficiency of damages, or for other purposes, a general allegation that the claim exceeds or is less than the requisite amount is required. By interrogatory, an opposing party may seek specification of the amount sought as damages, and the response may thereafter be supplemented as appropriate.

(2) If a petition is filed in violation of this Article, the claim for a specific monetary amount of damages shall be stricken upon the motion of an opposing party, and the court may award attorney fees and costs against the person who signed the petition, the party on whose behalf the petition was filed, or both.

B. The provisions of Paragraph A of this Article shall not be applicable to a suit on a conventional obligation, promissory note, open account, or other negotiable instrument, for alimony or child support, on a tax claim, or in a garnishment proceeding.

C. The prohibitions in Paragraph A of this Article apply only to an original, amended, or incidental demand. Evidence at trial or hearing of a specific monetary amount of damages shall be adduced in accordance with the Louisiana Code of Evidence or other applicable law.

Added by Acts 1988, No. 443, § 1, eff. Jan. 1, 1989. Amended by Acts 1989, No. 724, § 1, eff. July 8, 1989; Acts 1992, No. 332, § 1; Acts 2004, No. 334, § 1; Acts 2021, No. 259, § 2.

CHAPTER 3. EXCEPTIONS

Article

Art. 921. Exception defined

An exception is a means of defense, other than a denial or avoidance of the demand, used by the defendant, whether in the principal or an incidental action, to retard, dismiss, or defeat the demand brought against him.

Art. 922. Kinds of exceptions

Three exceptions and no others shall be allowed: the declinatory exception, the dilatory exception, and the peremptory exception.

Art. 923. Functions of exceptions

The function of the declinatory exception is to decline the jurisdiction of the court, while the dilatory exception merely retards the progress of the action, but neither exception tends to defeat the action. The function of the peremptory exception is to have the plaintiff's action declared legally nonexistent, or barred by effect of law, and hence this exception tends to dismiss or defeat the action.

Art. 924. Form of exceptions

All exceptions shall comply with Articles 853, 854, and 863, and, whenever applicable, with Articles 855 through 861. They shall set forth the name and surname of the exceptor, shall state with particularity the objections urged and the grounds thereof, and shall contain a prayer for the relief sought.

Art. 925. Objections raised by declinatory exception; waiver

A. The objections which may be raised through the declinatory exception include but are not limited to the following:

(1) Insufficiency of citation.

(2) Insufficiency of service of process, including failure to request service of citation on the defendant within the time prescribed by Article 1201(C), or failure to request service of petition within the time prescribed by Article 3955.

(3) Lis pendens under Article 531.

(4) Improper venue.

(5) The court's lack of jurisdiction over the person of the defendant.

(6) The court's lack of jurisdiction over the subject matter of the action.

B. When two or more of these objections are pleaded in the declinatory exception, they need not be pleaded in the alternative or in any particular order.

C. All objections which may be raised through the declinatory exception, except the court's lack of jurisdiction over the subject matter of the action, are waived unless pleaded therein.

Amended by Acts 1990, No. 521, § 2, eff. Jan. 1, 1991; Acts 1997, No. 578, § 1; Acts 2006, No. 750, § 1; Acts 2010, No. 407, § 1; Acts 2017, No. 419, § 1.

See West's Louisiana Statutes Annotated

Comments—2017

Subparagraph (A)(3) of this Article was amended to clarify that, although Article 532 appears in Chapter 3 of Title II of Book I, entitled "Lis Pendens," the declinatory exception of lis pendens may be raised only under Article 531. Article 532 permits the court to stay the proceedings of a second suit pending resolution of the first suit but does not permit the court to dismiss the second suit by granting an exception of lis pendens.

Editor's Notes

The list is illustrative, not restrictive. All declinatory objections must be pleaded at the same time, under last paragraph of this article.

The 1997 amendment deleted the phrase "When a defendant makes an appearance" from paragraph C, to conform to the elimination of "general appearance" by the repeal of C.C.P. art. 7.

Art. 926. Objections raised by dilatory exception; waiver

A. The objections which may be raised through the dilatory exception include but are not limited to the following:

(1) Prematurity.

(2) Want of amicable demand.

(3) Unauthorized use of summary proceeding.

(4) Nonconformity of the petition with any of the requirements of Article 891.

(5) Vagueness or ambiguity of the petition.

(6) Lack of procedural capacity.

(7) Improper cumulation of actions, including improper joinder of parties.

(8) Discussion.

B. All objections which may be raised through the dilatory exception are waived unless pleaded therein.

Amended by Acts 1995, No. 662, § 1.

Editor's Notes

The list is illustrative, not restrictive. All dilatory exceptions must be pleaded at the same time.

Art. 927. Objections raised by peremptory exception

A. The objections which may be raised through the peremptory exception include but are not limited to the following:

(1) Prescription.

(2) Peremption.

(3) Res judicata.

(4) Nonjoinder of a party under Articles 641 and 642.

(5) No cause of action.

(6) No right of action, or no interest in the plaintiff to institute the suit.

(7) Discharge in bankruptcy.

B. Except as otherwise provided by Articles 1702(D), 4904(D), and 4921(C), the court may not supply the objection of prescription, which shall be specially pleaded. The nonjoinder of a party, peremption, res judicata, the failure to disclose a cause of action or a right or interest in the plaintiff to institute the suit, or discharge in bankruptcy, may be noticed by either the trial or appellate court on its own motion.

Amended by Acts 1995, No. 662, § 1; Acts 2008, No. 824, § 1, eff. Jan. 1, 2009; Acts 2021, No. 259, § 2.

Editor's Notes

The list is illustrative, not restrictive. If a petition contains multiple, severable causes of action, one or more may be subjected to "partial no cause of action", Everything on Wheels Subaru, Inc. v. Subaru South, Sup.1993, 616 So.2d 1234, and C.C.P. art. 1915.

Art. 928. Time of pleading exceptions

A. The declinatory exception and the dilatory exception shall be pleaded prior to or in the answer and, prior to or along with the filing of any pleading seeking relief other than entry or removal of the name of an attorney as counsel of record, extension of time within which to plead, security for costs, or dissolution of an attachment issued on the ground of the nonresidence of the defendant, and in any event, prior to the signing of a default judgment. When both exceptions are pleaded, they shall be filed at the same time, and may be incorporated in the same pleading. When filed at the same time or in the same pleading, these exceptions need not be pleaded in the alternative or in a particular order.

B. The peremptory exception may be pleaded at any stage of the proceeding in the trial court prior to a submission of the case for a decision and may be filed with the declinatory exception or with the dilatory exception, or both.

Amended by Acts 1983, No. 60, § 1; Acts 1997, No. 1055, § 1; Acts 1999, No. 983, § 1, eff. July 1, 2000; Acts 2017, No. 419, § 1; Acts 2021, No. 174, § 1, eff. Jan. 1, 2022.

Editor's Notes

If declinatory and dilatory are not filed together, the late-filed one is waived. See Polmer v. Spencer, 256 So.2d 766 (App. 1 Cir. 1971). See C.C.P. art. 2163, filing peremptory in appellate court. Bickham v. Sub Sea International, Inc., Sup.1993, 617 So.2d 483, holds that filing a declinatory exception of improper venue in the same pleading with the answer does not waive that exception, and that a general appearance subsequent to filing an exception of improper venue does not waive the pending exception. See notes to LSA–C.C.P. Forms Nos. 401 and 404.

The 1999 amendment conforms this article to the revision of C.C.P. art. 6 and the repeal of C.C.P. art. 7, as to the mode of establishing personal jurisdiction by waiving (failing to file timely) the declinatory exception. It statutorily implements the rule of Bickham and retains the concept of former C.C.P. art. 7 by listing the pleadings that may be filed prior to the declinatory or dilatory exceptions without waiving those exceptions.

Caveat: Rule 9.13, Withdrawal as Counsel of Record, District Court Rules, contains elaborate provisions governing withdrawal. See Spiers v. Roye, 927 So.2d 1158 (1st Cir. 2006).

Art. 929. Time of trial of exceptions

A. The declinatory exception, the dilatory exception, and the peremptory exception when pleaded before or in the answer shall be tried and decided in advance of the trial of the case.

B. If the peremptory exception has been filed after the answer, but at or prior to the trial of the case, it shall be tried and disposed of either in advance of or on the trial of the case. If the peremptory exception has been pleaded after the trial of the case, the court may rule thereon at any time unless the party against whom it has been pleaded desires and is entitled to introduce evidence thereon. In the latter event, the peremptory exception shall be tried specially.

Amended by Acts 1987, No. 169, § 1; Acts 1997, No. 1055, § 1.

Art. 930. Evidence on trial of declinatory and dilatory exceptions

On the trial of the declinatory exception, evidence may be introduced to support or controvert any of the objections pleaded, when the grounds thereof do not appear from the petition, the citation, or return thereon.

On the trial of the dilatory exception, evidence may be introduced to support or controvert any of the objections pleaded, when the grounds thereof do not appear from the petition.

Art. 931. Evidence on trial of peremptory exception

On the trial of the peremptory exception pleaded at or prior to the trial of the case, evidence may be introduced to support or controvert any of the objections pleaded, when the grounds thereof do not appear from the petition.

When the peremptory exception is pleaded in the trial court after the trial of the case, but prior to a submission for a decision, the plaintiff may introduce evidence in opposition thereto, but the defendant may introduce no evidence except to rebut that offered by plaintiff.

No evidence may be introduced at any time to support or controvert the objection that the petition fails to state a cause of action.

Art. 932. Effect of sustaining declinatory exception

A. When the grounds of the objections pleaded in the declinatory exception may be removed by amendment of the petition or other action of plaintiff, the judgment sustaining the exception shall order the plaintiff to remove them within the delay allowed by the court; if the court finds, on sustaining the objection that service of citation on the defendant was not requested timely, it may either dismiss the action as to that defendant without prejudice or, on the additional finding that service could not have been timely requested, order that service be effected within a specified time.

B. If the grounds of the objection cannot be so removed, or if the plaintiff fails to comply with an order requiring such removal, the action, claim, demand, issue, or theory subject to the exception shall be dismissed; except that if an action has been brought in a court of improper jurisdiction or venue, the court may transfer the action to a proper court in the interest of justice.

Amended by Acts 2003, No. 545, § 1; Acts 2006, No. 750, § 1.

Art. 933. Effect of sustaining dilatory exception

A. If the dilatory exception pleading want of amicable demand is sustained, the judgment shall impose all court costs upon the plaintiff. If the dilatory exception pleading prematurity is sustained, the premature action, claim, demand, issue or theory shall be dismissed.

B. When the grounds of the other objections pleaded in the dilatory exception may be removed by amendment of the petition or other action by plaintiff, the judgment sustaining the exception shall order plaintiff to remove them within the delay allowed by the court; and the action, claim, demand, issue or theory subject to the exception shall be dismissed only for a noncompliance with this order.

Amended by Acts 2003, No. 545, § 1.

Art. 934. Effect of sustaining peremptory exception

When the grounds of the objection pleaded by the peremptory exception may be removed by amendment of the petition, the judgment sustaining the exception shall order such amendment within the delay allowed by the court. If the grounds of the objection raised through the exception cannot be so removed, or if the plaintiff fails to comply with the order to amend, the action, claim, demand, issue, or theory shall be dismissed.

Amended by Acts 2003, No. 545, § 1.

CHAPTER 4. WRITTEN MOTIONS

Article

Editor's Notes

CAVEAT: See the elaborate provisions for the filing and support of ex parte, contradictory, or unopposed motions, Rules 9.8 and 9.9, District Court Rules.

Art. 961. Written motion required; exception

An application to the court for an order, if not presented in some other pleading, shall be by motion which, unless made during trial or hearing or in open court, shall be in writing.

Art. 962. Form of written motion

A written motion shall comply with Articles 853 and 863, and shall state the grounds therefor, and the relief or order sought. It must also comply with Article 854 if the motion is lengthy, and whenever applicable, with Articles 855 through 861.

Art. 963. Ex parte and contradictory motions; rule to show cause

If the order applied for by written motion is one to which mover is clearly entitled without supporting proof, the court may grant the order ex parte and without hearing the adverse party.

If the order applied for by written motion is one to which the mover is not clearly entitled, or which requires supporting proof, the motion shall be served on and tried contradictorily with the adverse party.

The rule to show cause is a contradictory motion.

Art. 964. Motion to strike

The court on motion of a party or on its own motion may at any time and after a hearing order stricken from any pleading any insufficient demand or defense or any redundant, immaterial, impertinent, or scandalous matter.

Amended by Acts 1997, No. 1055, § 1.

Comment—1997

The amendment eliminates the requirement that the motion must be filed within 10 days of service of the pleading. This expands the usefulness of the motion to strike.

Editor's Notes

See the "Comment—1997" above.

Art. 965. Motion for judgment on pleadings

Any party may move for judgment on the pleadings after the answer is filed, or if an incidental demand has been instituted after the answer thereto has been filed, but within such time as not to delay the trial. For the purposes of this motion, all allegations of fact in mover's pleadings not denied by the adverse party or by effect of law, and all allegations of fact in the adverse party's pleadings shall be considered true.

Editor's Notes

Hygrade Investment, Inc. v. Leonard, App. 4 Cir.1967, 197 So.2d 702, generally.

Art. 966. Motion for summary judgment; procedure

A. (1) A party may move for a summary judgment for all or part of the relief for which he has prayed. A plaintiff's motion may be filed at any time after the answer has been filed. A defendant's motion may be filed at any time.

(2) The summary judgment procedure is designed to secure the just, speedy, and inexpensive determination of every action, except those disallowed by Article 969. The procedure is favored and shall be construed to accomplish these ends.

(3) After an opportunity for adequate discovery, a motion for summary judgment shall be granted if the motion, memorandum, and supporting documents show that there is no genuine issue as to material fact and that the mover is entitled to judgment as a matter of law.

(4) The only documents that may be filed in support of or in opposition to the motion are pleadings, memoranda, affidavits, depositions, answers to interrogatories, certified medical records, written stipulations, and admissions. The court may permit documents to be filed in any electronically stored format authorized by court rules or approved by the clerk of the court.

B. Unless extended by the court and agreed to by all of the parties, a motion for summary judgment shall be filed, opposed, or replied to in accordance with the following provisions:

(1) A motion for summary judgment and all documents in support of the motion shall be filed and served on all parties in accordance with Article 1313 not less than sixty-five days prior to the trial.

(2) Any opposition to the motion and all documents in support of the opposition shall be filed and served in accordance with Article 1313 not less than fifteen days prior to the hearing on the motion.

(3) Any reply memorandum shall be filed and served in accordance with Article 1313 not less than five days prior to the hearing on the motion. No additional documents may be filed with the reply memorandum.

(4) If the deadline for filing and serving a motion, an opposition, or a reply memorandum falls on a legal holiday, the motion, opposition, or reply is timely if it is filed and served no later than the next day that is not a legal holiday.

C. (1) Unless otherwise agreed to by all of the parties and the court:

(a) A contradictory hearing on the motion for summary judgment shall be set not less than thirty days after the filing and not less than thirty days prior to the trial date.

(b) Notice of the hearing date shall be served on all parties in accordance with Article 1313(C) or 1314 not less than thirty days prior to the hearing.

(2) For good cause shown, the court may order a continuance of the hearing.

(3) The court shall render a judgment on the motion not less than twenty days prior to the trial.

(4) In all cases, the court shall state on the record or in writing the reasons for granting or denying the motion. If an appealable judgment is rendered, a party may request written reasons for judgment as provided in Article 1917.

D. (1) The burden of proof rests with the mover. Nevertheless, if the mover will not bear the burden of proof at trial on the issue that is before the court on the motion for summary judgment, the mover's burden on the motion does not require him to negate all essential elements of the adverse party's claim, action, or defense, but rather to point out to the court the absence of factual support for one or more elements essential to the adverse party's claim, action, or defense. The burden is on the adverse party to produce factual support sufficient to establish the existence of a genuine issue of material fact or that the mover is not entitled to judgment as a matter of law.

(2) The court may consider only those documents filed in support of or in opposition to the motion for summary judgment and shall consider any documents to which no objection is made. Any objection to a document shall be raised in a timely filed opposition or reply memorandum. The court shall consider all objections prior to rendering judgment. The court shall specifically state on the record or in writing which documents, if any, it held to be inadmissible or declined to consider.

E. A summary judgment may be rendered dispositive of a particular issue, theory of recovery, cause of action, or defense, in favor of one or more parties, even though the granting of the summary judgment does not dispose of the entire case as to that party or parties.

F. A summary judgment may be rendered or affirmed only as to those issues set forth in the motion under consideration by the court at that time.

G. When the court grants a motion for summary judgment in accordance with the provisions of this Article, that a party or non-party is not negligent, is not at fault, or did not cause in whole or in part the injury or harm alleged, that party or non-party shall not be considered in any subsequent allocation of fault. Evidence shall not be admitted at trial to establish the fault of that party or non-party. During the course of the trial, no party or person shall refer directly or indirectly to any such fault, nor shall that party or non-party's fault be submitted to the jury or included on the jury verdict form.

H. On review, an appellate court shall not reverse a trial court's denial of a motion for summary judgment and grant a summary judgment dismissing a case or a party without assigning the case for briefing and permitting the parties an opportunity to request oral argument.

Amended by Acts 1966, No. 36, § 1; Acts 1983, No. 101, § 1, eff. June 24, 1983; Acts 1984, No. 89, § 1; Acts 1992, No. 71, § 1; Acts 1996, 1st Ex.Sess., No. 9, § 1, eff. May 1, 1996; Acts 1997, No. 483, § 1, eff. July 1, 1997; Acts 2001, No. 771, § 1; Acts 2003, No. 867, § 1; Acts 2010, No. 690, § 1; Acts 2012, No. 257, § 1; Acts 2012, No. 741, § 1; Acts 2013, No. 391, § 1; Acts 2014, No. 187, § 1; Acts 2015, No. 422, § 1, eff. Jan. 1, 2016.

Comments—2015

(a) Subparagraphs (A)(1) and (2) do not change the law.

(b) Subparagraph (A)(3) does not change the law. It makes clear that a motion for summary judgment should be heard and granted only after there has been an opportunity for adequate discovery. See Broussard v. Winters, 123 So.3d 902 (La. App. 3d Cir. 2013). A continuance should be granted to a party who has not had adequate time to conduct discovery relating to the issues in the motion. The legal standard to be used by the court in granting a motion for summary judgment remains unchanged.

(c) Subparagraph (A)(4), which is new, contains the exclusive list of documents that may be filed in support of or in opposition to a motion for summary judgment. This Subparagraph intentionally does not allow the filing of documents that are not included in the exclusive list, such as photographs, pictures, video images, or contracts, unless they are properly authenticated by an affidavit or deposition to which they are attached. Although a memorandum is not a pleading or evidence, it is a proper document that can be used by a party to advance his arguments in support of or in opposition to the motion. See, e.g., Meaux v. Galtier, 972 So.2d 1137 (La. 2008). An opinion of the medical review panel cannot be filed in support of or in opposition to the motion unless it is properly authenticated and attached to the affidavit or deposition. Article 1458 requires that interrogatories be answered under oath, and only answers that are made under oath may be filed in support of or in opposition to a motion for summary judgment. This Subparagraph continues the rule that no oral testimony shall be allowed at a hearing on a motion for summary judgment, even if all parties agree. See Mapp Construction, LLC v. Amerisure Mutual Insurance Co., 143 So.3d 520 (La. App. 1st Cir. 2014). All supporting documents may be filed electronically if provided for by local rules or the clerk of court.

(d) Subparagraphs (B)(1), (B)(2) and (B)(3) are new. They establish the time periods for filing or opposing motions for summary judgment. These provisions supersede Rule 9.9 of the District Court Rules but at the same time recognize the ability of the trial court and all of the parties to enter in to a case management or scheduling order or other order to establish deadlines different from those provided by this Article. Nevertheless, these orders may not shorten the period of time allowed for a party to file or oppose a motion for summary judgment under this Article. The Article makes clear that all motions, memoranda, and supporting documents shall be served on all parties and filed with the clerk of court. This Article continues the rule that no new documents may be filed with a reply memorandum. Unless provided otherwise by an order agreed upon by all of the parties and the court, the motion, any opposition, and any reply shall be served by the methods provided for in Article 1313 (e.g., mailing, delivering a copy, or by electronic means).

(e) Subparagraph (B)(4) is new. This Subparagraph follows Article 5059 and its interpretation in Becnel v. Northrop Grumman Ship Sys., Inc., 18 So.3d 1269 (La. 2009). It establishes the rule that, if the date for filing the motion, opposition, or reply memorandum falls on a legal holiday, the party has until the next day that is not a legal holiday to file the pleading and supporting documents. This is significant because the trial court has vast discretion whether to consider late-filed affidavits or documents in support of an opposition. See, e.g., Buggage v. Volks Constructors, 928 So.2d 536 (La. 2006).

(f) Subparagraphs (C)(1) and (2) are new. A motion for summary judgment shall be set for hearing more than thirty days after filing. The notice of the date of the hearing shall be served in accordance with Article 1313(C) (i.e., by certified mail or commercial courier) or 1314 (i.e., by the sheriff) to ensure that a party receives timely notice of the hearing date. The hearing on the motion shall be set at least thirty days prior to the trial date.

(g) Subparagraph (C)(2) establishes the rule that if a party has a good cause for failing to meet this deadline, the court may order a continuance of the hearing on the motion so that the parties and the court can comply with the applicable deadlines.

(h) Subparagraph (C)(3), which is new, changes the law. This time period requires the court to decide a motion for summary judgment sufficiently in advance of the trial to allow a party to apply for supervisory writs without interrupting the trial setting.

(i) Subparagraph (C)(4) is new. The court shall state either on the record or in writing the reasons for granting or denying the motion. Nevertheless, the court does not have to address every reason or argument, and the form and detail of the reasons are left to the discretion of the court. Cf. Federal Rules of Civil Procedure, Rule 56(a).

(j) Subparagraph (D)(1) does not change the law. It is consistent with Section 4 of Acts 1997, No. 483, which declares that "all cases inconsistent with" Hayes v. Autin, 685 So.2d 691 (La. App. 3d Cir. 1996) are legislatively overruled. Hayes holds that Celotex v. Catrett, 477 U.S. 317, 106 S.Ct. 2548, 91 L.Ed.2d 265 (1986), correctly states the law for our summary judgment procedure. In accordance with Celotex and Babin v. Winn–Dixie Louisiana Inc. 764 So.2d 37 (La. 2000), once the motion for summary judgment has been properly supported by the moving party, the non-moving party must produce evidence of the existence of a material factual dispute or demonstrate that the mover is not entitled to judgment as a matter of law.

(k) Subparagraph (D)(2) maintains most of the recent legislative changes to this Article, which change the law. Subparagraph (D)(2) makes clear that the court can consider only those documents filed in support of or in opposition to the motion. This rule differs from Federal Rules of Civil Procedure, Rule 56(c)(3), which allows the court to consider other materials in the record. This Subparagraph also maintains the requirement that any objection to any supporting document must be raised in a timely-filed opposition or reply memorandum. The provision changes prior law by specifically removing the motion to strike as a means of raising an objection to a document offered by an adverse party in support of or in opposition to a motion for summary judgment and does not allow a party to file that motion. This Subparagraph also makes explicit that an oral objection to any document cannot be raised at the hearing on the motion for summary judgment and that a court must consider all documents to which there is no objection. This Subparagraph adds the provision that the court shall specifically state either on the record or in writing what evidence it deems to be inadmissible or declines to consider. The court may, in accordance with Code of Judicial Conduct Canon 3, make a reasonable effort for a self-represented litigant to be fairly heard, attempt to make the legal concepts understandable, and provide information about the proceeding and the evidentiary and foundational requirements.

(*l*) Paragraphs E and F do not change the law, except that Paragraph F makes clear that, in deciding a motion for summary judgment, a court can consider only the issues raised in the motion or opposition filed by the parties. The court cannot rule on issues not raised by the parties.

(m) Paragraph G, which is new, adopts the rule from prior Article 966(G)(1) that if a person is found in a summary judgment not to be negligent, not at fault, not to have caused the injury or harm, that person cannot be considered in any allocation of fault. The requirement of former Article 966(G)(2) is removed. The trial judge does not have to specifically provide in the judgment on the motion that the person is not to be part of any allocation of fault at trial for this rule to apply. The Paragraph also establishes the rule that, at trial, evidence of that person's fault shall not be admitted, nor shall that person's fault be referred to by any person or be submitted to the jury on the jury verdict form.

(n) Paragraph H is new. This provision requires the appellate court to assign the matter for briefing and to permit the parties an opportunity to request oral argument if the court intends to reverse a lower court decision that denied a motion for summary judgment. If a summary judgment is granted at the trial level dismissing a party or a case, the losing party is entitled to an appeal. See Article 1915(A). However, under prior law, if the appellate court, on a supervisory writ, reversed the lower court and granted the motion for summary judgment dismissing a party or the case, the losing party was denied an appeal. This Paragraph changes the law and provides a party against whom summary judgment may be rendered at the appellate level an opportunity to brief his case and to request oral argument on his case.

Comments—2018

Under Subparagraph (A)(4) of this Article, which provides the exclusive list of documents that may be filed in support of or in opposition to a motion for summary judgment, a copy of a written instrument that is an exhibit to a pleading may not be filed in connection with a motion for summary judgment unless the written instrument itself is properly authenticated. See Comment (c) (2015); see also *Raborn v. Albea*, 221 So. 3d 104, 111 (La. App. 1 Cir. 2017).

Editor's Notes

See the checklist for Summary Judgment in the preliminary material of this publication.

Art. 967. Same; affidavits

A. Supporting and opposing affidavits shall be made on personal knowledge, shall set forth such facts as would be admissible in evidence, and shall show affirmatively that the affiant is competent to testify to the matters stated therein. The supporting and opposing affidavits of experts may set forth such experts' opinions on the facts as would be admissible in evidence under Louisiana Code of Evidence Article 702, and shall show affirmatively that the affiant is competent to testify to the matters stated therein. Sworn or certified copies of all papers or parts thereof referred to in an affidavit shall be attached thereto or served therewith. The court may permit affidavits to be supplemented or opposed by depositions, answers to interrogatories, or by further affidavits.

B. When a motion for summary judgment is made and supported as provided above, an adverse party may not rest on the mere allegations or denials of his pleading, but his response, by affidavits or as otherwise provided above, must set forth specific facts showing that there is a genuine issue for trial. If he does not so respond, summary judgment, if appropriate, shall be rendered against him.

C. If it appears from the affidavits of a party opposing the motion that for reasons stated he cannot present by affidavit facts essential to justify his opposition, the court may refuse the application for judgment or may order a continuance to permit affidavits to be obtained or depositions to be taken or discovery to be had or may make such other order as is just.

D. If it appears to the satisfaction of the court at any time that any of the affidavits presented pursuant to this Article are presented in bad faith or solely for the purposes of delay, the court immediately shall order the party employing them to pay to the other party the amount of the reasonable expenses which the filing of the affidavits caused him to incur, including reasonable attorney fees. Any offending party or attorney may be adjudged guilty of contempt.

Amended by Acts 1966, No. 36, § 1; Acts 2003, No. 545, § 1.

Editor's Notes

Affidavit (except for experts) must be on personal knowledge, Walker v. Firemen's Insurance Company, 264 So.2d 277 (1972).

As to affidavits by experts, this article was judicially amended to exclude them from the requirement of "personal knowledge" in Independent Fire Ins. Co. v. Sunbeam Corp., 755 So.2d 226 (La. 2000), subject to the Daubert test.

Caveat: See specific requirements for serving opposing affidavits, Rule 9.10, District Court Rules.

Art. 968. Effect of judgment on pleadings and summary judgment

Judgments on the pleadings, and summary judgments, are final judgments and shall be rendered and signed in the same manner and with the same effect as if a trial had been had upon evidence regularly adduced. If the judgment does not grant mover all of the relief prayed for, jurisdiction shall be retained in order to adjudicate on mover's right to the relief not granted on motion.

An appeal does not lie from the court's refusal to render any judgment on the pleading or summary judgment.

Art. 969. Judgment on pleadings and summary judgment not permitted in certain cases; exception

A. Judgments on the pleadings and summary judgments shall not be granted in any action for divorce or annulment of marriage, nor in any case where the community, paraphernal, or dotal rights may be involved in an action between husband and wife.

B. (1) Notwithstanding the provisions of Paragraph A, judgments on the pleadings and summary judgments may be granted without hearing in any action for divorce under Civil Code Article 103(1) under the following conditions:

(a) All parties are represented by counsel;

(b) Counsel for each party, after answer is filed, file a written joint stipulation of facts, request for judgment, and sworn verification by each party; and

(c) Counsel for each party file a proposed judgment containing a certification that counsel and each party agree to the terms thereof.

(2) The court may render and sign such judgments in chambers without a hearing and without the taking of testimony.

Amended by Acts 1986, No. 219, § 2; Acts 1987, No. 271, § 1; Acts 1990, No. 1009, § 4, eff. Jan. 1, 1991.

Art. 970. Motion for judgment on offer of judgment

A. At any time more than twenty days before the time specified for the trial of the matter, without any admission of liability, any party may serve upon an adverse party an offer of judgment for the purpose of settling all of the claims between them. The offer of judgment shall be in writing and state that it is made under this Article; specify the total amount of money of the settlement offer; and specify whether that amount is inclusive or exclusive of costs, interest, attorney fees, and any other amount which may be awarded pursuant to statute or rule. Unless accepted, an offer of judgment shall remain confidential between the offeror and offeree. If the adverse party, within ten days after service, serves written notice that the offer is accepted, either party may move for judgment on the offer. The court shall grant such judgment on the motion of either party.

B. An offer of judgment not accepted shall be deemed withdrawn and evidence of an offer of judgment shall not be admissible except in a proceeding to determine costs pursuant to this Article.

C. If the final judgment obtained by the plaintiff-offeree is at least twenty-five percent less than the amount of the offer of judgment made by the defendant-offeror or if the final judgment obtained against the defendant-offeree is at least twenty-five percent greater than the amount of the offer of judgment made by the plaintiff-offeror, the offeree must pay the offeror's costs, exclusive of attorney fees, incurred after the offer was made, as fixed by the court.

D. The fact that an offer is made but not accepted does not preclude a subsequent offer or a counter offer. When the liability of one party to another has been determined by verdict, order, or judgment, but the amount or extent of the damages remains to be determined by future proceedings, either party may make an offer of judgment, which shall have the same effect as an offer made before trial if it is served within a reasonable time not less than thirty days before the start of hearings to determine the amount or extent of damages.

E. For purposes of comparing the amount of money offered in the offer of judgment to the final judgment obtained, which judgment shall take into account any additur or remittitur, the final judgment obtained shall not include any amounts attributable to costs, interest, or attorney fees, or to any other amount which may be awarded pursuant to statute or rule, unless such amount was expressly included in the offer.

F. A judgment granted on a motion for judgment on an offer of judgment is a final judgment when signed by the judge; however, an appeal cannot be taken by a party who has consented to the judgment.

Added by Acts 1996, 1st Ex.Sess., No. 60, § 1, eff. May 9, 1996. Amended by Acts 1997, No. 354, § 1; Acts 2012, No. 557, § 1.

Art. 971. Special motion to strike

A. (1) A cause of action against a person arising from any act of that person in furtherance of the person's right of petition or free speech under the United States or Louisiana Constitution in connection with a public issue shall be subject to a special motion to strike, unless the court determines that the plaintiff has established a probability of success on the claim.

(2) In making its determination, the court shall consider the pleadings and supporting and opposing affidavits stating the facts upon which the liability or defense is based.

(3) If the court determines that the plaintiff has established a probability of success on the claim, that determination shall be admissible in evidence at any later stage of the proceeding.

B. In any action subject to Paragraph A of this Article, a prevailing party on a special motion to strike shall be awarded reasonable attorney fees and costs.

C. (1) The special motion may be filed within ninety days of service of the petition, or in the court's discretion, at any later time upon terms the court deems proper.

(2) If the plaintiff voluntarily dismisses the action prior to the running of the delays for filing an answer, the defendant shall retain the right to file a special motion to strike within the delays provided by Subparagraph (1) of this Paragraph, and the motion shall be heard pursuant to the provisions of this Article.

(3) The motion shall be noticed for hearing not more than thirty days after service unless the docket conditions of the court require a later hearing.

D. All discovery proceedings in the action shall be stayed upon the filing of a notice of motion made pursuant to this Article. The stay of discovery shall remain in effect until notice of entry of the order ruling on the motion. Notwithstanding the provisions of this Paragraph, the court, on noticed motion and for good cause shown, may order that specified discovery be conducted.

E. This Article shall not apply to any enforcement action brought on behalf of the state of Louisiana by the attorney general, district attorney, or city attorney acting as a public prosecutor.

F. As used in this Article, the following terms shall have the meanings ascribed to them below, unless the context clearly indicates otherwise:

(1) "Act in furtherance of a person's right of petition or free speech under the United States or Louisiana Constitution in connection with a public issue" includes but is not limited to:

(a) Any written or oral statement or writing made before a legislative, executive, or judicial proceeding, or any other official proceeding authorized by law.

(b) Any written or oral statement or writing made in connection with an issue under consideration or review by a legislative, executive, or judicial body, or any other official body authorized by law.

(c) Any written or oral statement or writing made in a place open to the public or a public forum in connection with an issue of public interest.

(d) Any other conduct in furtherance of the exercise of the constitutional right of petition or the constitutional right of free speech in connection with a public issue or an issue of public interest.

(2) "Petition" includes either a petition or a reconventional demand.

(3) "Plaintiff" includes either a plaintiff or petitioner in a principal action or a plaintiff or petitioner in reconvention.

(4) "Defendant" includes either a defendant or respondent in a principal action or a defendant or respondent in reconvention.

Added by Acts 1999, No. 734, § 1. Amended by Acts 2004, No. 232, § 1; Acts 2012, No. 449, § 1.

Editor's Notes

This article appears to establish a specialized defense motion akin to a motion for summary judgment for defamation and other actions, allowing a more liberal time for bringing the motion than the motion for summary judgment allows. It appears that witnesses can be heard. See Lee v. Pennington, 830 So.2d 1037, (App. 4 Cir. 2002).

Davis v. Benton, 874 So.2d 185 (La. App. 1 Cir. 2004). Special motion to strike was granted in favor of landlord against defamation suit brought by police officer alleging defamation by landlord in writing a letter to the police chief alleging misconduct. The officer could not establish a probability of success on her defamation claim. The special motion was granted, including the award of $5,000 in attorney fees to the landlord.

Darden v. Smith, 879 So.2d 390 (La. App. 3 Cir. 2004). Special motion to strike was properly applied against police jury member who filed suit with defamation and other claims, such as emotional distress, against developer regarding plaintiff's official conduct. A public official plaintiff cannot recover for a defamatory statement relating to her official conduct even if it is false unless plaintiff proves actual malice by clear and convincing evidence. This article is broad enough to include claims other than defamation. C.C.P. art. 971.

Succession of Carroll, 72 So.3d 384 (App. 2 Cir. 2011), writing a will was exercise of free speech for attorney.

Arts. 972 to 1000. Reserved for future legislation

CHAPTER 5. ANSWER

Article

Art. 1001. Delay for answering

A. A defendant shall file his answer within twenty-one days after service of citation upon him, except as otherwise provided by law. If the plaintiff files and serves a discovery request with his petition, the defendant shall file his answer to the petition within thirty days after service of citation and service of discovery request.

B. When an exception is filed prior to answer and is overruled or referred to the merits, or is sustained and an amendment of the petition ordered, the answer shall be filed within fifteen days after the exception is overruled or referred to the merits, or fifteen days after service of the amended petition.

C. The court may grant additional time for answering.

Amended by Acts 2021, No. 174, § 1, eff. Jan. 1, 2022.

Comments—2021

(a) The revision to Paragraph A of this Article extends the time within which the defendant must file an answer from fifteen to twenty-one days after service of citation. If the plaintiff files a discovery request with his petition, the delays for answering the petition and for responding to the discovery request will be thirty days. See Articles 1458(A), 1462(B)(1), and 1467(A). This change is intended to eliminate confusion, particularly for self-represented litigants who are served with a discovery request along with the petition, since the delays for responding to both are now the same.

(b) The revision to Paragraph B of this Article extends the time within which the defendant must file an answer to fifteen days after an exception is overruled or referred to the merits, or fifteen days after service of an amended petition when an exception is sustained and an amendment is ordered.

Art. 1002. Answer or other pleading filed prior to signing of default judgment

Notwithstanding the provisions of Article 1001, the defendant may file his answer or other pleading at any time prior to the signing of a default judgment against him.

Amended by Acts 2017, No. 419, § 1; Acts 2021, No. 174, § 1, eff. Jan. 1, 2022.

Comments—2017

This Article has been amended to clarify that the defendant may file an answer or other pleading at any time prior to the actual signing of the final default judgment. See *Martin v. Martin*, 680 So. 2d 759 (La. App. 1st Cir. 1996).

Art. 1003. Form of answer

The answer shall comply with Articles 853, 854, and 863 and, whenever applicable, with Articles 855 through 861. It shall admit or deny the allegations of the petition as required by Article 1004, state in short and concise terms the material facts upon which the defenses to the action asserted are based, and shall set forth all affirmative defenses as required by Article 1005. It shall also contain a prayer for the relief sought. Relief may be prayed for in the alternative.

Editor's Notes

See C.C.P. arts. 856, 892, 1154.

Art. 1004. Denials

The answer shall admit or deny the allegations of fact contained in each paragraph of the petition, and all such allegations, other than those as to the amount of damages, are admitted if not denied in the answer. If the defendant is without knowledge or information sufficient to justify a belief as to the truth of an allegation of fact made in the petition, he shall so state and this shall have the effect of a denial. Denials shall fairly meet the substance of the allegations denied. When the defendant intends in good faith to deny only a part of or to qualify an allegation of fact, he shall admit so much of it as is true and material and shall deny or qualify the remainder.

Art. 1005. Affirmative defenses

The answer shall set forth affirmatively negligence, or fault of the plaintiff and others, duress, error or mistake, estoppel, extinguishment of the obligation in any manner, failure of consideration, fraud, illegality, injury by fellow servant, and any other matter constituting an affirmative defense. If a party has mistakenly designated an affirmative defense as a peremptory exception or as an incidental demand, or a peremptory exception as an affirmative defense, and if justice so requires, the court, on such terms as it may prescribe, shall treat the pleading as if there had been a proper designation.

Amended by Acts 2008, No. 824, § 1, eff. Jan. 1, 2009.

Editor's Notes

Paxton v. Ballard, 289 So.2d 85 (1974) and Webster v. Rushing, 316 So.2d 111 (1975), standard for pleading affirmative defenses. Webster gives definition and nature of affirmative defense. The existence of additional liability insurance covering the allegedly underinsured defendant, thus rendering UM coverage inapplicable, is not an affirmative defense, Keller v. Amedeo, 512 So.2d 385 (La.1987). Sudden unconsciousness is affirmative defense, Brannon v. Sheltor Mut. Ins. Co., 507 So.2d 194 (La.1987). Assumption of risk abolished, and "comparative fault" recognized as affirmative defense encompassing both contributory negligence and what was assumption of risk, Murray v. Ramada Inns, 521 So.2d 1123 (La.1988); see, also, Howard v. Allstate Ins. Co., 520 So.2d 715 (La.1988), comparative "causation" must be used to compare strict liability and contributory negligence. In suit against political subdivision or state, showing constructive or actual knowledge of dangerous condition is part of plaintiff's burden, not an affirmative defense, Boudoin v. City of Kenner, 556 So.2d 123 (La.App. 5 Cir.1990). Damages "cap" for State not affirmative defense, Mitchell v. State through DOTD, (App. 3 Cir.1992) 596 So.2d 353; same, as to "interest cap" (R.S.13:5112), Salter v. State through DHHR, (App. 1 Cir.1992) 612 So.2d 163.

Art. 1006. Alternative defenses

An answer may set forth two or more defenses in the alternative, even though the factual or legal bases thereof may be inconsistent or mutually exclusive. All allegations in such cases are made subject to the obligations set forth in Article 863.

CHAPTER 6. INCIDENTAL ACTIONS

SECTION 1. GENERAL DISPOSITIONS

Art. 1031. Incidental demands allowed

A. A demand incidental to the principal demand may be instituted against an adverse party, a co-party, or against a third person.

B. Incidental demands are reconvention, cross-claims, intervention, and the demand against third parties.

Amended by Acts 1983, No. 63, § 1.

For Official Comments and Annotated Materials,

Comment—1983

This amendment adds a cross-claim to the list of incidental actions and provides that an incidental demand can be asserted against a co-party.

Art. 1032. Form of petition

An incidental demand shall be commenced by a petition which shall comply with the requirements of Articles 891, 892 and 893. An incidental demand instituted by the defendant in the principal action may be incorporated in his answer to the principal demand. In this event, the caption shall indicate appropriately the dual character of the combined pleading.

Amended by Acts 1988, No. 443, § 2, eff. Jan. 1, 1989.

Art. 1033. Delay for filing incidental demand

An incidental demand may be filed without leave of court at any time up to and including the time the answer to the principal demand is filed.

An incidental demand may be filed thereafter, with leave of court, if it will not retard the progress of the principal action, or if permitted by Articles 1066 or 1092.

An incidental demand that requires leave of court to file shall be considered as filed as of the date it is presented to the clerk of court for filing if leave of court is thereafter granted.

Amended by Acts 1970, No. 473, § 1.

Art. 1034. Exceptions and motions

A defendant in an incidental action may plead any of the exceptions available to a defendant in a principal action, and may raise any of the objections enumerated in Articles 925 through 927, except that an objection of improper venue may not be urged if the principal action has been instituted in the proper venue. Exceptions pleaded by the defendant in an incidental action shall be subject to all of the provisions of Articles 924 through 934.

A party to an incidental action may plead any of the written motions available to a party to a principal action, subject to the provisions of Articles 961 through 969.

Art. 1035. Answer

The answer in an incidental action shall be filed within the delay allowed by Article 1001, and shall be subject to all of the rules set forth in Articles 1001 and 1003 through 1006.

Amended by Acts 2014, No. 655, § 1.

Comment—2014

The 2014 amendment to this Article conforms with the rules for answering incidental demands to those provided for the principal demand.

Art. 1036. Jurisdiction; mode of procedure

A. Except as otherwise provided in Article 4845, a court shall have jurisdiction over an incidental demand only if it would have had jurisdiction over the demand had it been instituted in a separate suit. The only exceptions to this rule are those provided in the state constitution.

B. The mode of procedure employed in the incidental action shall be the same as that used in the principal action, except as otherwise provided by law.

Amended by Acts 1995, No. 202, § 1.

Editor's Notes

Parish and city courts, C.C.P. art. 4845.

Art. 1037. Action instituted separately

When a person does not assert in an incidental demand the action which he has against a party to the principal action or a third person, he does not thereby lose his right of action, except as provided in Article 1113, and except as provided in Article 1061.

Amended by Acts 1990, No. 521, § 2, eff. Jan. 1, 1991.

Comment—1990

This Article is amended to conform to the 1990 amendment of Article 1061. Acts 1990, No. 521.

Art. 1038. Separate trial; separate judgment

The court may order the separate trial of the principal and incidental actions, either on exceptions or on the merits; and after adjudicating the action first tried, shall retain jurisdiction for the adjudication of the other.

When the principal and incidental actions are tried separately, the court may render and sign separate judgments thereon. When in the interests of justice, the court may withhold the signing of the judgment on the action first tried until the signing of the judgment on the other.

Art. 1039. Effect of dismissal of principal action

If an incidental demand has been pleaded prior to motion by plaintiff in the principal action to dismiss the principal action, a subsequent dismissal thereof shall not in any way affect the incidental action, which must be tried and decided independently of the principal action.

Art. 1040. Words "plaintiff" and "defendant" include plaintiff and defendant in an incidental action

Unless the context clearly indicates otherwise, wherever the words "plaintiff" and "defendant" are used in this Code, they respectively include a plaintiff and a defendant in an incidental demand.

Art. 1041. When prescribed incidental or third party demand is not barred

An incidental demand is not barred by prescription or peremption if it was not barred at the time the main demand was filed and is filed within ninety days of date of service of main demand or in the case of a third party defendant within ninety days from service of process of the third party demand.

Redesignated from C.C.P. art. 1067 by Acts 2017, No. 419, § 5. Added by Acts 1970, No. 472, § 1. Amended by Acts 1974, No. 86, § 1.

Editor's Notes

Incidental demands allowed in the interest of judicial efficiency under the liberal view of Gallin, Gehr, Bellow, and Travelers, cited in notes to C.C.P. art. 1091, *infra,* may not warrant the extended time conferred by this article; but see C.C.P. arts. 1071 through 1073, cross-claims. This article, for extension of time, applies only to incidental demand, not to main demand, Randall v. Feducia, Sup.1987, 507 So.2d 1237.

Reggio v. E.T.I., 15 So.3d 951 (La. 2008). "In sum, we find that the prescriptive period on a claim for indemnity does not begin to run until NOAB is cast in judgment, regardless of the applicable theory of indemnity. Thus we expressly overrule the holding of Lawyer v. Succession of Kountz, supra."

"An action for indemnity is a separate substantive cause of action, independent of the underlying tort. The action for indemnity does not accrue until the City of New Orleans is responsible for a judgment or actually discharges a liability for which NOAB is responsible. Thus, NOAB's action against E.T.I. is neither premature nor prescribed."

The city had filed its claim for indemnity in the suit against it more than three years after the beginning of the suit. Defendant said it was prescribed under C.C.P. art. 1067 requiring third party demands to be filed within 90 days after the main demand. That limitation was held not to apply in this case in which the third party demand was for indemnity.

SECTION 2. RECONVENTION

Art. 1061. Actions pleaded in reconventional demand; compulsory

A. The defendant in the principal action may assert in a reconventional demand any causes of action which he may have against the plaintiff in the principal action, even if these two parties are domiciled in the same parish and regardless of connexity between the principal and reconventional demands.

B. The defendant in the principal action, except in an action for divorce under Civil Code Article 102 or 103 or in an action under Civil Code Article 186, shall assert in a reconventional demand all causes of action that he may have against the plaintiff that arise out of the transaction or occurrence that is the subject matter of the principal action.

Amended by Acts 1990, No. 521, § 2, eff. Jan. 1, 1991; Acts 1991, No. 367, § 2; Acts 2006, No. 344, § 2, eff. June 13, 2006.

Comments—1990

(a) Judicial efficiency is served by requiring the defendant through a compulsory reconventional demand to assert all causes of action he may have against the plaintiff that arise out of the transaction or occurrence that is the basis for the plaintiff's action.

(b) Furthermore, if the defendant has a cause of action arising out of the subject matter of the plaintiff's action, then the defense of res judicata will prevent relitigation of issues common to both causes of action except as otherwise provided by law. The requirement of a compulsory reconventional demand therefore also serves the interest of fairness by giving the defendant notice that he must assert his related cause of action.

Comment—1991

The phrase beginning with "except" in Paragraph B of this Article is added in order to make it clear that a defendant in a divorce action is not required to raise the actions commonly associated with divorce actions, such as claims for spousal and child support, in his reconventional demand, if one is filed. Such claims historically have been assertable after the divorce action has been concluded by judgment, and the added phrase makes it clear that this Article does not change the law in that respect.

Editor's Notes

See C.C.P. art. 1731, jury trial of compulsory reconventional demand when it qualifies for jury trial, but the principal demand does not.

Compulsory reconvention must be filed in the same action (main demand), Hy-Octane Investments v. G & B Oil Products, 702 So.2d 1057, (3rd Cir. 1997).

Reconventional demand could not be filed in the same action, which was filed as summary proceeding in city court, Horacek v. Watson, 934 So.2d 908 (3rd Cir. 2006).

Art. 1062. Pleading compensation

Compensation may be asserted in the reconventional demand.

Editor's Notes

Compensation is also an affirmative defense, Comment (b).

Art. 1063. Service of reconventional demand; citation unnecessary

The petition in reconvention, whether incorporated in the answer to the principal action or filed separately, shall be served on the plaintiff in the principal action in the manner prescribed by Article 1314. Citation of the plaintiff in the principal action shall not be necessary.

Amended by Acts 1972, No. 662, § 1.

Art. 1064. Additional parties

Persons other than those made parties to the original action may be made parties to the reconventional demand.

Amended by Acts 1995, No. 858, § 1.

Comment—1995

The amendment clarifies the law by providing for the permissive and compulsory joinder of parties in a reconventional demand. This has been the approach taken by the courts, e.g., Lawton v. Cain, 172 So.2d 734 (2nd Cir.1964), but the language of the article seemed to suggest that it was limited to compulsory joinder.

Art. 1065. Reconventional demand exceeding principal demand

The reconventional demand may or may not diminish or defeat the recovery sought in the principal demand. It may claim relief exceeding in amount that sought in the principal demand.

Art. 1066. Action matured or acquired after pleading

An action which either matured or was acquired by the defendant in the principal action after answer may be presented, with the permission of the court, as a reconventional demand by supplemental pleading.

Art. 1067. Redesignated as C.C.P. art. 1041 by Acts 2017, No. 419, § 5

SECTION 3. CROSS–CLAIMS

Art. 1071. Cross-claims

A party by petition may assert as a cross-claim a demand against a co-party arising out of the transaction or occurrence that is the subject matter either of the original action or a reconventional demand or relating to any property that is the subject matter of the original action. The cross-claim may include a demand that the party against whom it is asserted is or may be liable to the cross-claimant for all or part of the demand asserted in the action against the cross-claimant.

Added by Acts 1983, No. 63, § 1.

Comment—1983

This Article would allow a party to assert a demand against a co-party provided the demand arose out of the transaction or occurrence that is the subject matter of the original action or of a reconventional demand. The addition of the cross-claim serves the interest of judicial economy and convenience as to the other incidental actions.

Art. 1072. Service of cross-claim, citation unnecessary

The petition in a cross-claim shall be served on the co-party in the manner prescribed by Article 1314. Citation of the co-party shall not be necessary.

Added by Acts 1983, No. 63, § 1.

Comment—1983

Since a cross-claim is asserted against a co-party, citation is unnecessary and service by the sheriff under Article 1314 assures adequate notice.

Art. 1073. Additional parties

Persons other than those made parties to the original action may be made parties to a cross-claim.

Added by Acts 1983, No. 63, § 1.

Comment—1983

This Article provides that persons other than those who are parties to the original action may be made parties to the cross-claim provided that the demand against them arises out of the transaction or occurrence that is the subject matter of the original action or of the reconventional demand. The joinder is subject to the articles governing incidental actions (Articles 1031–1040). The ordinary rules for citation and service of process would apply.

Editor's Notes

See Patterson v. State, Dept. of Transportation and Development, App. 3 Cir.1987, 509 So.2d 505.

SECTION 4. INTERVENTION

Art. 1091. Third person may intervene

A third person having an interest therein may intervene in a pending action to enforce a right related to or connected with the object of the pending action against one or more of the parties thereto by:

(1) Joining with plaintiff in demanding the same or similar relief against the defendant;

(2) Uniting with defendant in resisting the plaintiff's demand; or

(3) Opposing both plaintiff and defendant.

Editor's Notes

For construction of term "object", see Gallin v. Travelers Ins. Co., App. 4 Cir.1975, 323 So.2d 908; Bellow v. New York Fire & Marine Underwriters, Inc., App. 3 Cir.1968, 215 So.2d 350; Gehr v. Department of Highways, App. 4 Cir.1976, 337 So.2d 691; and Travelers Insurance Company v. Sonnier,

App. 4 Cir.1977, 344 So.2d 73. These interpretations are liberal and probably beyond the intent of the articles on incidental demand; but consider C.C.P. arts. 1071 through 1073, cross-claims, a more suitable vehicle for those demands.

Art. 1092. Third person asserting ownership of, or mortgage or privilege on, seized property

A third person claiming ownership of, or a mortgage or privilege on, property seized may assert his claim by intervention. If the third person asserts ownership of the seized property, the intervention may be filed at any time prior to the judicial sale of the seized property, and the court may grant him injunctive relief to prevent such sale before an adjudication of his claim of ownership.

If the third person claims a mortgage or privilege on the entire property seized, whether superior or inferior to that of the seizing creditor, the intervention may be filed at any time prior to the distribution by the sheriff of the proceeds of the sale of the seized property, and the court shall order the sheriff to hold such proceeds subject to its further orders. When the intervener claims such a mortgage or privilege only on part of the property seized, and the intervention is filed prior to the judicial sale, the court may order the separate sale of the property on which the intervener claims a mortgage or privilege; or if a separate sale thereof is not feasible or necessary, or the intervener has no right thereto, the court may order the separate appraisement of the entire property seized and of the part thereof on which the intervener claims a mortgage or privilege.

An intervener claiming the proceeds of a judicial sale does not thereby admit judicially the validity, nor is he estopped from asserting the invalidity, of the claim of the seizing creditor.

Amended by Acts 1962, No. 92, § 1.

Editor's Notes

Comment (d) says that this article requires a joinder of all parties to the principal action, where the intervention asserts ownership of, or a mortgage or privilege on, the seized property.

Art. 1093. Service of petition; citation unnecessary

When the intervention asserts ownership of, or a mortgage or privilege on, the seized property, the petition shall be served on the sheriff and all parties to the principal action as provided in Article 1313. Any other petition of intervention shall be served on all parties to the principal action as provided in Article 1314. Citation is not necessary in intervention.

Art. 1094. Intervener accepts proceedings

An intervener cannot object to the form of the action, to the venue, or to any defects and informalities personal to the original parties.

Editor's Notes

An intervener takes the proceedings as he finds them, Comment.

SECTION 5. DEMAND AGAINST THIRD PARTY

Art. 1111. Defendant may bring in third person

The defendant in a principal action by petition may bring in any person, including a codefendant, who is his warrantor, or who is or may be liable to him for all or part of the principal demand.

In such cases the plaintiff in the principal action may assert any demand against the third party defendant arising out of or connected with the principal demand. The third party defendant thereupon shall plead his objections and defenses in the manner prescribed in Articles 921 through 969, 1003 through 1006, and 1035. He may reconvene against the plaintiff in the principal action or the third party plaintiff, on any demand arising out of or connected with the principal demand, in the manner prescribed in Articles 1061 through 1066.

Editor's Notes

The defendant may bring in a third party defendant as of right any time up to and including the filing of answer, Comment. See notes to C.C.P. art. 1091.

Art. 1112. Defendant in reconvention may bring in third person

The defendant in reconvention likewise may bring in his warrantor, or any person who is or may be liable to him for all or part of the reconventional demand, and the rules provided in Articles 1111, and 1113 through 1115 shall apply equally to such third party actions.

Art. 1113. Effect of failure to bring in third party

A defendant who does not bring in as a third party defendant a person who is liable to him for all or part of the principal demand does not on that account lose his right or cause of action against such person, unless the latter proves that he had means of defeating the action which were not used, because the defendant either failed to bring him in as a third party defendant, or neglected to apprise him that the suit had been brought. The same rule obtains with respect to a defendant in reconvention who fails to bring in as a third party defendant a person who is liable to him for all or part of the reconventional demand.

Art. 1114. Service of citation and pleadings

A citation and a certified copy of the third party petition shall be served on the third party defendant in the manner prescribed by Articles 1231 through 1293. Unless previously served on or filed by the third party defendant, certified copies of the following pleadings shall also be served on him in the same manner: the petition in the principal demand; the petition in the reconventional demand, if any; and the answers to the principal and reconventional demands filed prior to the issuance of citation in the third party action.

Amended by Acts 1964, No. 4, § 1.

Art. 1115. Defenses of original defendant available to third party defendant

The third party defendant may assert against the plaintiff in the principal action any defenses which the third party plaintiff has against the principal demand.

Art. 1116. Third party defendant may bring in third person

A third party defendant may proceed under Articles 1111 through 1115 against any person who is or may be liable to him for all or any part of the third party demand.

CHAPTER 7. AMENDED AND SUPPLEMENTAL PLEADINGS

Article

Art. 1151. Amendment of petition and answer; answer to amended petition

A plaintiff may amend his petition without leave of court at any time before the answer thereto is served. He may be ordered to amend his petition under Articles 932 through 934. A defendant may amend his answer once without leave of court at any time within ten days after it has been served. Otherwise, the petition and answer may be amended only by leave of court or by written consent of the adverse party.

A defendant shall plead in response to an amended petition within the time remaining for pleading to the original pleading or within ten days after service of the amended petition, whichever period is longer, unless the time is extended under Article 1001.

Art. 1152. Amendment of exceptions

A defendant may amend his declinatory or dilatory exceptions by leave of court or with the written consent of the adverse party, at any time prior to the trial of the exceptions, so as to amplify or plead more particularly an objection set forth or attempted to be set forth in the original exception. A declinatory or a dilatory exception may not be amended so as to plead an objection not attempted to be set forth in the original exception.

A defendant may amend his peremptory exception at any time and without leave of court, so as to either amplify an objection set forth or attempted to be set forth in the original exception, or to plead an objection not set forth therein.

Editor's Notes

The last sentence of the first paragraph is consistent with the anti-stringing-out rule as to dilatory and declinatory exceptions, C.C.P. arts. 925, 926, and 928.

Art. 1153. Amendment relates back

When the action or defense asserted in the amended petition or answer arises out of the conduct, transaction, or occurrence set forth or attempted to be set forth in the original pleading, the amendment relates back to the date of filing the original pleading.

Editor's Notes

Ray v. Alexandria Mall, 434 So.2d 1083 (1983), as to late–added defendants, and Giroir v. South La. Medical Ctr., Etc., 475 So.2d 1040 (La.1985), as to late–added plaintiffs, summarize "relating back" for prescription purposes. Use of fictitious names for unknown defendants ineffective to interrupt prescription, Bankston v. B & H Air Tools, Inc., App. 1 Cir.1986, 486 So.2d 199.

Perempted claim cannot relate back, Naghi v. Brener, No. 08–CC–2527, June 26, 2009, S.Ct. Prescribed medical malpractice claim late-added will not relate back, Warren v. La. Med. Mut. Ins. Group, No. 2007–CC–0492, June 26, 2008, S.Ct.

Art. 1154. Amendment to conform to evidence

When issues not raised by the pleadings are tried by express or implied consent of the parties, they shall be treated in all respects as if they had been raised by the pleading. Such amendment of the pleadings as may be necessary to cause them to conform to the evidence and to raise these issues may be made upon motion of any party at any time, even after judgment; but failure to so amend does not affect the result of the trial of these issues. If evidence is objected to at the trial on the ground that it is not within the issues made by the pleadings, the court may allow the pleadings to be amended and shall do so freely when the presentation of the merits of the action will be subserved thereby, and the objecting party fails to satisfy the court that the admission of such evidence would prejudice him in maintaining his action or defense on the merits. The court may grant a continuance to enable the objecting party to meet such evidence.

Editor's Notes

The third sentence does not contemplate the *adding* of an issue not pleaded, but rather allows the pleading of material facts for an issue pleaded only generally or as a legal conclusion, Comment (c).

Art. 1155. Supplemental pleadings

The court, on motion of a party, upon reasonable notice and upon such terms as are just, may permit mover to file a supplemental petition or answer setting forth items of damage, causes of action or defenses which have become exigible since the date of filing the original petition or answer, and which are related to or connected with the causes of action or defenses asserted therein.

Art. 1156. Amended and supplemental pleadings in incidental action

The petition, the answer, and the exceptions filed in an incidental action may be amended or supplemented in the manner provided in Articles 1151 through 1155.

Arts. 1157 to 1200. Reserved for future legislation

TITLE II. CITATION AND SERVICE OF PROCESS

CHAPTER 1. CITATION

Article

PRELIMINARY STATEMENT [Acts 1960, No. 15]

Most of the concepts contained in the 1870 Code of Practice and the Service of Process Act, former R.S. 13:3471, have been retained in this Chapter although somewhat modified in form. In addition, some new rules have been incorporated. Only a few provisions of the 1870 Code have been deleted as unnecessary; and the provision of Arts. 181, 183, and 184 of that Code which fix the duties of the clerk in connection with citation and service have been included in Arts. 251 through 288, *supra*, dealing with court officers and their duties.

This Chapter provides the basic general law governing citation in ordinary proceedings. However, special provisions of law providing for a particular mode of citation and service are not affected.

Art. 1201. Citation; waiver; delay for service

A. Citation and service thereof are essential in all civil actions except summary and executory proceedings, divorce actions under Civil Code Article 102, and proceedings under the Children's Code. Without them all proceedings are absolutely null.

B. The defendant may expressly waive citation and service thereof by any written waiver made part of the record.

C. Service of the citation shall be requested on all named defendants within ninety days of commencement of the action. When a supplemental or amended petition is filed naming any additional defendant, service of citation shall be requested within ninety days of its filing. The defendant may expressly waive the requirements of this Paragraph by any written waiver. The requirement provided by this Paragraph shall be expressly waived by a defendant unless the defendant files, in accordance with the provisions of Article 928, a declinatory exception of insufficiency of service of process specifically alleging the failure to timely request service of citation.

D. If not waived, a request for service of citation upon the defendant shall be considered timely if requested on the defendant within the time period provided by this Article, notwithstanding insufficient or erroneous service.

Amended by Acts 1991, No. 367, § 2; Acts 1997, No. 518, § 2, eff. Jan. 1, 1998; Acts 2003, No. 545, § 1; Acts 2006, No. 750, § 1; Acts 2014, No. 379, § 2, eff. May 30, 2014.

For Official Comments and Annotated Materials,

Comment—1991

The form of initial notice that is required in divorce actions brought under Article 102 of the Civil Code is exclusively set forth in R.S. 13:3491 (1990). Often, however, such a divorce action will be accompanied by an ordinary action, such as a claim for partition of community property, that requires service of citation under this Article. In such cases both the notice required by R.S. 13:3491 and the citation required by this Article will have to be served on the defendant, unless those services are waived.

Editor's Notes

La. R.S. 13:5107(A)(1), in all suits filed against the State of Louisiana or a state agency may be obtained by citation and service through the attorney general. La. R.S. 13:5107(A)(2), service shall be requested upon the attorney general within 90 days of filing suit.

Art. 1202. Form of citation

The citation must be signed by the clerk of the court issuing it with an expression of his official capacity and under the seal of his office; must be accompanied by a certified copy of the petition, exclusive of exhibits, even if made a part thereof; and must contain the following:

(1) The date of issuance;

(2) The title of the cause;

(3) The name of the person to whom it is addressed;

(4) The title and location of the court issuing it; and

(5) A statement that the person cited must either comply with the demand contained in the petition or make an appearance, either by filing a pleading or otherwise, in the court issuing the citation within the delay provided in Article 1001 under penalty of default.

Art. 1203. Citation to legal representative of multiple defendants

When one person is the legal representative of several persons made defendant in the same cause, only one citation need be addressed to such representative.

CHAPTER 2. SERVICE ON PERSONS

Article

PRELIMINARY STATEMENT [Acts 1960, No. 15]

This Chapter deals with personal and domiciliary service, and these two types cover all possible situations.

Art. 1231. Types of service; time of making

Service of citation or other process may be either personal or domiciliary, and except as otherwise provided by law, each has the same effect.

Service, whether personal or domiciliary, may be made at any time of day or night, including Sundays and holidays.

Editor's Notes

Sheriff's rules for service, C.C.P. arts. 321, 322, 324, 1291. See also R.S. 13:3471, 13:3472, 13:3475, and 13:3484.

Art. 1232. Personal service

Personal service is made when a proper officer tenders the citation or other process to the person to be served.

Editor's Notes

"Tendering" is distinguished from "delivered", Comment (b).

Art. 1233. Same; where made

Personal service may be made anywhere the officer making the service may lawfully go to reach the person to be served.

Editor's Notes

Service through fraudulent enticement is invalid, Comment, and see Fidelity & Deposit Co. of Md., 22 So.2d 562 (1945). See, also, C.Cr.P. art. 743, exemption from service of process while present in state in response to summons in criminal case.

Art. 1234. Domiciliary service

Domiciliary service is made when a proper officer leaves the citation or other process at the dwelling house or usual place of abode of the person to be served with a person of suitable age and discretion residing in the domiciliary establishment.

Amended by Acts 1985, No. 355, § 1.

Editor's Notes

The 1985 amendment deletes the requirement that person served be a "member" of the domiciliary establishment.

Art. 1235. Service on representative

A. Service is made on a person who is represented by another by appointment of court, operation of law, or mandate, through personal or domiciliary service on such representative.

B. Service on an attorney, as a representative of a client, is proper when the attorney's secretary is served in the attorney's office.

C. For the purposes of this Article "secretary" shall be defined as the person assigned to a particular attorney and who is charged with the performance of that part of the attorney's business concerned with the keeping of records, the sending and receiving of correspondence, and the preparation and monitoring of the attorney's appointments calendar.

Amended by Acts 1991, No. 45, § 1.

Art. 1235.1. Service on incarcerated person

A. Service is made on a person who is incarcerated in a jail or detention facility through personal service on the warden or his designee for that shift. The warden or his designee shall in turn make personal service on the person incarcerated.

B. When requested by the petitioner or mover, proof of service may be made by filing in the record the affidavit of the person serving the citation and pleadings on the person who is incarcerated.

C. Personal service on the person incarcerated as required by Paragraph A of this Article shall be made promptly, but in no event shall it be made later than ten days after service upon the warden or his designee. If, for reasons beyond the control of the warden, such personal service cannot be accomplished by the tenth day, then on the next day or as soon as it is apparent that such personal service cannot be accomplished, the warden or his designee shall note the inability to serve on the citation or pleadings and return the citation or pleadings to the issuing court.

D. Service as provided in Paragraph A of this Article shall be deemed to be accomplished on the date of personal service shown by the affidavit specified in Paragraph B of this Article, or if no such affidavit is timely received, nor a return by the warden or his designee in Paragraph C of this Article indicating a lack of personal service, then service is deemed to be accomplished ten days after service upon the warden or his designee under Paragraph A of this Article.

Added by Acts 1991, No. 46, § 1. Amended by Acts 2004, No. 744, § 1.

Art. 1236. Service on clerical employees of physicians

Service on any physician, when not a party to an action, may be made at his or her office through personal service on any clerical employee of such physician.

Added by Acts 1975, No. 778, § 1. Amended by Acts 1997, No. 1056, § 1.

Comment—1997

This amendment clarifies the article by eliminating reference to service of citation. The article is intended to apply to service on a physician who is not a party but service of citation would make the physician a party and is thus inconsistent with the intent of the article.

Art. 1237. Service on individual in multiple capacities

In cases wherein an individual is named in pleadings in more than one capacity, personal service on that individual is sufficient to constitute service of process on that individual in all capacities, including but not limited to as an individual, tutor, or a representative of a legal or quasi legal entity, when it is clear from the pleadings or service instructions the capacities in which the individual is being served.

Added by Acts 1995, No. 851, § 1; Acts 1995, No. 1257, § 1.

CHAPTER 3. SERVICE ON LEGAL AND QUASI LEGAL ENTITIES

Article

Art. 1261. Domestic or foreign corporation

A. Service of citation or other process on a domestic or foreign corporation is made by personal service on any one of its agents for service of process.

B. If the corporation has failed to designate an agent for service of process, if there is no registered agent by reason of death, resignation, or removal, or if the person attempting to make service certifies that he is unable, after due diligence, to serve the designated agent, service of the citation or other process may be made by any of the following methods:

(1) By personal service on any officer, or director, or on any person named as such in the last report filed with the secretary of state.

(2) By personal service on any employee of suitable age and discretion at any place where the business of the corporation is regularly conducted.

(3) By service of process under the provisions of R.S. 13:3204, if the corporation is subject to the provisions of R.S. 13:3201.

C. Service of citation or other process on a bank is made pursuant to R.S. 6:285(C).

Amended by Acts 1988, No. 37, § 1, eff. June 10, 1988; Acts 1991, No. 656, § 2; Acts 1995, No. 859, § 1; Acts 1995, No. 1257, § 1.

Editor's Notes

Foreign insurers, see R.S. 22:1253; list of agents by Secretary of State, R.S. 13:3473.

Service abroad under the Hague Convention, see Appendix to this volume setting forth part of Rule 4, F.R.C.V.P., West's U.S.C.A., Title 28. See also the excellent Commentary on jurisdiction and service in the 1996 pocket part of Title 28, Rule 4, F.R.C.V.P.

Art. 1262. Same; secretary of state

If the officer making service certifies that he is unable, after diligent effort, to have service made as provided in Article 1261, then the service may be made personally on the secretary of state, or on a person in his office designated to receive service of process on corporations. The secretary of state shall forward this citation to the corporation at its last known address.

Art. 1263. Partnership

Service of citation or other process on a partnership is made by personal service on a partner. Service of citation or other process on a partnership in commendam is made by personal service on a general partner. When the officer certifies that he is unable, after diligent effort, to make service in this manner, he may make personal service on any employee of suitable age and discretion at any place where the business of the partnership or partnership in commendam is regularly conducted.

Amended by Acts 2001, No. 512, § 1.

Art. 1264. Unincorporated association

Service on an unincorporated association is made by personal service on the agent appointed, if any, or in his absence, upon a managing official, at any place where the business of the association is regularly conducted. In the absence of all officials from the place where the business of the association is regularly conducted, service of citation or other process may be made by personal service upon any member of the association.

Art. 1265. Political entity; public officer

Service of citation or other process on any political subdivision, public corporation, or state, parochial or municipal board or commission is made at its office by personal service upon the chief executive officer thereof, or in his absence upon any employee thereof of suitable age and discretion.

A public officer, sued as such, may be served at his office either personally, or in his absence, by service upon any of his employees of suitable age and discretion.

If the political entity or public officer has no established office, then service may be made at any place where the chief executive officer of the political entity or the public officer to be served may be found.

Editor's Notes

But see the specific provisions of R.S. 39:1538 for service of process on the State for tort actions, in addition to the provisions of R.S. 13:5107, which is the general requirement for service on the State.

Art. 1266. Limited liability company

A. Service of citation or other process on a domestic or foreign limited liability company is made by personal service on any one of its agents for service of process.

B. If the limited liability company has failed to designate an agent for service of process, if there is no registered agent by reason of death, resignation, or removal, or if the person attempting to make service certifies that he is unable, after due diligence, to serve the designated agent, service of the citation or other process may be made by any of the following methods:

(1) Personal service on any manager if the management of the limited liability company is vested in one or more managers or if management is not so vested in managers, then on any member.

(2) Personal service on any employee of suitable age and discretion at any place where the business of the limited liability company is regularly conducted.

(3) Service of process under the provisions of R.S. 13:3204, if the limited liability company is subject to the provisions of R.S. 13:3201.

(4) Repealed by Acts 2001, No. 407, § 2.

Added by Acts 1999, No. 145, § 1.

Editor's Notes

This is the comprehensive service of process article for the limited liability company. Additional service provisions are in R.S. 13:3471(1). Other provisions are: venue, C.C.P. art. 42; procedural capacity, C.C.P. arts. 690–692, 739, 740; appointment of attorney, C.C.P. art. 5091; non-resident, R.S. 13:3206; definition of "person", C.C.P. art. 5251.

Art. 1267. Same; service on secretary of state

If the officer making service certifies that he is unable, after diligent effort, to have service made as provided in Article 1266, then the service may be made personally on the secretary of state, or on a person in his office designated to receive service of process on limited liability companies. The secretary of state shall forward this citation to the limited liability company at its last known address.

Added by Acts 2001, No. 407, § 1.

CHAPTER 4. PERSONS AUTHORIZED TO MAKE SERVICE

Article

Art. 1291. Service by sheriff

Except as otherwise provided by law, service shall be made by the sheriff of the parish where service is to be made or of the parish where the action is pending.

Editor's Notes

R.S. 13:3471, supplemental rules for service on foreign corporations. Return on service is conclusive unless attacked directly, R.S. 13:3471(5); see, also, R.S. 13:3484, mailing of process to serving officer. Cf. C.C.P. 322, sheriff exercises civil functions only in his parish.

Art. 1292. Sheriff's return

A. The sheriff shall endorse on a copy of the citation or other process the date, place, and method of service and sufficient other data to show service in compliance with law. He shall sign and return the copy promptly after the service to the clerk of court who issued it. The return, when received by the clerk, shall form part of the record, and shall be considered prima facie correct. The court, at any time and upon such terms as are just, may allow any process or proof of service thereof to be amended, unless it clearly appears that material prejudice would result to the substantial rights of the party against whom the process issued.

B. In addition to the provisions of Paragraph A of this Article, when the citation or other process is a temporary restraining order, protective order, preliminary injunction, permanent injunction, or court-approved consent agreement as referenced in R.S. 46:2136.2(B), the person making the service, or his designee, shall transmit proof of service to the judicial administrator's office, Louisiana Supreme Court, for entry into the Louisiana Protective Order Registry, as provided in R.S. 46:2136.2(A), by facsimile transmission or direct electronic input as expeditiously as possible, but no later than the end of the next business day after making service, exclusive of weekends and holidays. This proof shall include, at a minimum, the case caption, docket number, type of order, serving agency and officer, and the date and time service was made.

Amended by Acts 2018, No. 679, § 1.

Art. 1293. Service by private person

A. When the sheriff has not made service within ten days after receipt of the process or when a return has been made certifying that the sheriff has been unable to make service, whichever is earlier, on motion of a party the court shall appoint a person over the age of majority, not a party and residing within the state whom the court deems qualified to perform the duties required, to make service of process in the same manner as is required of sheriffs. Service of process made in this manner shall be proved like any other fact in the case. Any person who is a Louisiana licensed private investigator shall be presumed qualified to perform the duties required to make service.

B. In serving notice of a summary proceeding as provided by Article 2592 or a subpoena which is related to the proceeding, on motion of a party the court shall have the discretion to appoint any person over the age of majority, not a party and residing within the state, to make service of process, notices, and subpoenas in the same manner as is required of sheriffs, without first requiring the sheriff to attempt service. The party making such a motion shall include the reasons, verified by affidavit, necessary to forego service by the sheriff, which shall include but not be limited to the urgent emergency nature of the hearing, knowledge of the present whereabouts of the person to be served, as well as any other good cause shown.

C. In addition to those natural persons who the court may appoint to make service of process pursuant to Paragraph A or B of this Article, the court may also appoint a juridical person which may then select an employee or agent of that juridical person to make service of process, provided the employee or agent perfecting service of process is a natural person who qualifies as an agent for service of process pursuant to Paragraph A or B of this Article.

D. In addition to the provisions of Paragraph A of this Article, when the citation or other process is a temporary restraining order, protective order, preliminary injunction, permanent injunction, or court-approved consent agreement as referenced in R.S. 46:2136.2(B), the person making the service, or his designee, shall transmit proof of service to the judicial administrator's office, Louisiana Supreme Court, for entry into the Louisiana Protective Order Registry, as provided in R.S. 46:2136.2(A), by facsimile transmission or direct electronic input as expeditiously as possible, but no later than the end of the next business day after making service, exclusive of weekends and holidays. This proof shall include, at a minimum, the case caption, docket number, type of order, serving agency and officer, and the date and time service was made.

Amended by Acts 1984, No. 210, § 1; Acts 2006, No. 704, § 1, eff. June 29, 2006; Acts 2010, No. 185, § 1; Acts 2010, No. 466, § 1, eff. June 22, 2010; Acts 2012, No. 521, § 1; Acts 2018, No. 679, § 1.

Editor's Notes

See C.C.P. art. 1355 for rule as to service of subpoena by private person.

CHAPTER 5. SERVICE OF PLEADINGS

Article

Art. 1311. Service of copy of exhibit to pleading unnecessary

A copy of any written instrument which is an exhibit to a pleading need not be served upon the adverse party unless the party who files the pleading expressly prays for such service.

Art. 1312. Service of pleadings subsequent to petition; exceptions

Except as otherwise provided in the second paragraph hereof, every pleading subsequent to the original petition shall be served on the adverse party as provided by Article 1313 or 1314, whichever is applicable.

No service on the adverse party need be made of a motion or petition for an appeal, of a petition for the examination of a judgment debtor, of a petition for the issuance of garnishment interrogatories in the execution of a final judgment, or of any pleading not required by law to be in writing.

Art. 1313. Service by mail, delivery, or electronic means

A. Except as otherwise provided by law, every pleading subsequent to the original petition, and every pleading which under an express provision of law may be served as provided in this Article, may be served either by the sheriff or by:

(1) Mailing a copy thereof to the counsel of record, or if there is no counsel of record, to the adverse party at his last known address, this service being complete upon mailing.

(2) Delivering a copy thereof to the counsel of record, or if there is no counsel of record, to the adverse party.

(3) Delivering a copy thereof to the clerk of court, if there is no counsel of record and the address of the adverse party is not known.

(4) Transmitting a copy by electronic means to counsel of record, or if there is no counsel of record, to the adverse party, at the number or addresses expressly designated in a pleading or other writing for receipt of electronic service. Service by electronic means is complete upon transmission but is not effective and shall not be certified if the serving party learns the transmission did not reach the party to be served.

B. When service is made by mail, delivery, or electronic means, the party or counsel making the service shall file in the record a certificate of the manner in which service was made.

C. Notwithstanding Paragraph A of this Article, if a pleading or order sets a court date, then service shall be made by registered or certified mail or as provided in Article 1314, by actual delivery by a commercial courier, or by emailing the document to the email address designated by counsel or the party. Service by electronic means is complete upon transmission, provided that the sender receives an electronic confirmation of delivery.

D. For purposes of this Article, a "commercial courier" is any foreign or domestic business entity having as its primary purpose the delivery of letters and parcels of any type, and that:

(1) Acquires a signed receipt from the addressee, or the addressee's agent, of the letter or parcel upon completion of delivery.

(2) Has no direct or indirect interest in the outcome of the matter to which the letter or parcel concerns.

Amended by Acts 1997, No. 249, § 1; Acts 1999, No. 1263, § 1, eff. Jan. 1, 2000; Acts 2010, No. 185, § 1; Acts 2012, No. 741, § 1; Acts 2021, No. 68, § 1, eff. Jan. 1, 2022.

Comment—2010

Subparagraph (A)(4) and Paragraph B have been amended and broadened to authorize service by "electronic means," which is intended to include e-mail and facsimile transmissions. The prior version of the Article limited electronic service to facsimile transmissions. Service by electronic means must be made to the number or addresses expressly designated for service by electronic means in a pleading filed by the adverse party or in a writing agreed to by the parties. Service is not effective if the serving party learns that the electronic transmission did not reach the party to be served. See FRCP Rule 5(b)(2)(E). This Article also applies to serving discovery requests and responses. See Art. 1474(A).

Editor's Notes

This article allows all pleadings subsequent to the petition to be served by mail, fax, or electronic means, "except as otherwise provided by law". Some exceptions to the rule are: the reconvention, C.C.P. art. 1063; cross-claim, C.C.P. art. 1072; most interventions, C.C.P. art. 1093; third-party demand, C.C.P. art. 1114; presumably subpoenas, C.C.P. art. 1355 (and C.C.P. arts. 1231-36); rules to show cause, see C.C.P. art. 2594 and C.C.P. art. 1313(C); habeas corpus, C.C.P. art. 3824; mandamus and quo warranto, see C.C.P. arts. 2594 and 1313(C). While the latter three are summary proceedings that are initiated by petition, they might be part of a broader suit and thus be "subsequent" to the original petition.

Art. 1314. Same; service by sheriff

A. A pleading which is required to be served, but which may not be served under Article 1313, shall be served by the sheriff by either of the following:

(1) Service on the adverse party in any manner permitted under Articles 1231 through 1266.

(2)(a) Personal service on the counsel of record of the adverse party or delivery of a copy of the pleading to the clerk of court, if there is no counsel of record and the address of the adverse party is not known.

(b) Except as otherwise provided in Article 2293, service may not be made on the counsel of record after a final judgment terminating or disposing of all issues litigated has been rendered, the delays for appeal have lapsed, and no timely appeal has been taken.

B. Personal service on a partner or office associate of a counsel of record, including a secretary, receptionist, legal staff, administrative staff, or paralegal in the employ of the counsel of record, at the office address of record of the counsel of record shall constitute valid service under Paragraph A of this Article.

Amended by Acts 1968, No. 125, § 1; Acts 1997, No. 268, § 1; Acts 1997, No. 1056, § 1; Acts 1999, No. 1263, § 1, eff. Jan. 1, 2000; Acts 2001, No. 512, § 1; Acts 2012, No. 242, § 1.

TITLE III. PRODUCTION OF EVIDENCE

CHAPTER 1. SUBPOENAS

CAVEAT: See District Court Rule 9.15 as to subpoenas.

Art. 1351. Issuance; form

The clerk or judge of the court wherein the action is pending, at the request of a party, shall issue subpoenas for the attendance of witnesses at hearings or trials. A subpoena shall issue under the seal of the court. It shall state the name of the court, the title of the action, and shall command the attendance of the witness at a time and place specified, until discharged.

Art. 1352. Restrictions on subpoena

A witness, whether a party or not, who resides or is employed in this state may be subpoenaed to attend a trial or hearing wherever held in this state. No subpoena shall issue to compel the attendance of such a witness unless the provisions of R.S. 13:3661 are complied with.

Amended by Acts 1961, No. 23, § 1; Acts 2021, No. 259, § 2.

Art. 1353. Prepayment of fees

No subpoena shall issue until the party who wishes to subpoena the witness first deposits with the clerk of court a sum of money sufficient to pay all fees and expenses to which the witness is entitled by law.

Editor's Notes

Witnesses and fees, R.S. 13:3661.

Art. 1354. Subpoena duces tecum

A. A subpoena may order a person to appear and produce at the trial, deposition, or hearing, books, papers, documents, any other tangible things, or electronically stored information, in his possession or under his control, if a reasonably accurate description thereof is given. A subpoena may specify the form or forms in which electronically stored information is to be produced. A party or an attorney requesting the issuance and service of a subpoena shall take reasonable steps to avoid imposing undue burden or cost on a person subject to that subpoena. The court in which the action is pending in its discretion may vacate or modify the subpoena if it is unreasonable or oppressive. Except when otherwise required by order of the court, certified copies, extracts, or copies of books, papers, and documents may be produced in obedience to the subpoena duces tecum instead of the originals thereof. If the party or attorney requesting the subpoena does not specify that the named person shall be ordered to appear, the person may designate another person having knowledge of the contents of the books, papers, documents, other things, or electronically stored information, to appear as his representative.

B. A person commanded to respond to a subpoena duces tecum may within fifteen days after service of the subpoena or before the time specified for compliance, if such time is less than fifteen days after service, send to the party or attorney designated in the subpoena written objections, with supporting reasons, to any or all of the requests, including objection to the production of electronically stored information in the form or forms requested. If objection is so made, the party serving the subpoena may file a motion to compel compliance with the subpoena and may move for sanctions for failure to reasonably comply.

C. A person responding to a subpoena to produce books, papers, or documents shall produce them as they are kept in the usual course of business or may organize and label them to correspond with the categories in the demand.

D. If a subpoena does not specify the form or forms for producing electronically stored information, a person responding to a subpoena may produce the information in a form or forms in which the person ordinarily maintains it or in a form or forms that are reasonably useable.

E. A person responding to a subpoena need not produce the same electronically stored information in more than one form.

F. A person responding to a subpoena need not produce books, papers, documents, or electronically stored information from sources that the person identifies as not reasonably accessible because of undue burden or cost. On motion to compel production or to quash, the person from whom production is sought shall show that the information sought is not reasonably accessible because of undue burden or cost. If that showing is made, the court may nonetheless order production from such sources if the requesting party shows good cause. The court may specify conditions, including an allocation of the costs, for the production.

G. When the person subpoenaed is an adverse party, the party requesting the subpoena duces tecum may accompany his request with a written request under oath as to what facts he believes the books, papers, documents, electronically stored information, or tangible things will prove, and a copy of such statement shall be attached to the subpoena. If the party subpoenaed fails to comply with the subpoena, the facts set forth in the written statement shall be taken as confessed, and in addition the party subpoenaed shall be subject to the penalties set forth in Article 1357.

H. Subpoenas duces tecum shall reproduce in full the provisions of this Article.

Amended by Acts 1978, No. 593, § 1; Acts 2008, No. 824, § 2, eff. Jan. 1, 2009.

Comment—2008

(a) Consistent with the 2007 amendments to Articles 1461 and 1462, pertaining to requests for production of electronically stored information directed to parties, Article 1354 has been amended in a number of respects to provide more detailed governing procedures for the production of electronically stored information in response to a subpoena.

(b) Paragraph B has been added to clarify that a party served with a subpoena may respond by sending written objections to the party or attorney issuing the subpoena; thus, a motion to quash, though still an option, is no longer required. If objections are made on a timely basis, a motion to compel may be filed and served and a court order must be obtained to compel compliance with all or part of the subpoena which is subject to objection.

(c) In order to inform the subpoenaed person of the procedures for objecting to a subpoena duces tecum, Paragraph H adds the requirement that all subpoenas duces tecum reproduce the provisions of this Article. It is suggested that the subpoena forms include a prominent notice that Article 1354 appears in full on the back of the form.

Editor's Notes

The production of documents, etc., is an adjunct to appearance by the subpoenaed witness, Comment (b). See C.C.P. art. 1463(B), subpoena duces tecum to non-party for production other than at trial or hearing.

Art. 1355. Service of subpoena

A. Except as provided in Paragraph B of this Article, a subpoena shall be served and a return thereon made in the same manner and with the same effect as a service of and return on a citation. When a party is summoned as a witness, service of the subpoena may be made by personal service on the witness' attorney of record.

B. Except as otherwise provided by law, when the sheriff has not made service of a subpoena within five days after its receipt or when a return has been made certifying that the sheriff has been unable to make service, any person over the age of majority, not a party and residing within the state, may make service of the subpoena in the same manner as is required by the sheriff. Proof of service by a private person shall be made by filing with the clerk of the court by which the subpoena is issued a notarized return showing the title of the action and the name of the court issuing it, the date and manner of service, and the name of the person served, signed by the person who made the service.

Amended by Acts 2008, No. 824, § 3, eff. Jan. 1, 2009.

Comments—2008

(a) Due to the difficulty in locating and serving some witnesses with a subpoena for trial or depositions, and to expedite the process, the Article has been amended to authorize a private person to serve subpoenas without the need of a motion and order provided that the sheriff has been unable to serve the subpoena within five working days of its receipt or when the sheriff has made a return that he's unable to make service. A notarized return of service signed by the person making service must be filed in the court which issued the subpoena. The change in the Article is intended to apply only to service of subpoenas and does not affect the procedures for serving citations and pleadings.

(b) Service of subpoenas in a summary proceeding filed pursuant to Article 2592(6) or (8) is provided in Article 1293(B).

Editor's Notes

A witness without knowledge of the domiciliary service of a subpoena has a "reasonable excuse" for non-compliance as protection against contempt, Comment (b).

Caveat: Rule 9.15, Subpoenas, District Court Rules, sets specific deadlines for the issuance of subpoenas.

Art. 1355.1. Reissuance of subpoena; service by certified or registered mail

When a subpoena that has been personally served is ordered reissued due to continuance or passage of the trial or hearing, the party requesting such reissuance may have the subpoena served in accordance with Article 1355 or may serve the subpoena by mailing a copy of the original subpoena, together with a notice of the new date and time for attendance, to the witness at his dwelling house or usual place of abode, or to a representative of the witness if personal service of the original subpoena was made on such representative. The mailing shall be by registered or certified mail, return receipt requested. The date of mailing shall be not less than thirty-five days prior to the date on which the witness is subpoenaed to appear. A copy of the documents mailed to the witness and the signed return receipt shall be filed by the party in the record as proof of service. If the registered or certified mail is unclaimed, service of the subpoena shall be as otherwise provided by law.

Added by Acts 1988, No. 283, § 1.

Art. 1356. Subpoenas and subpoenas duces tecum for depositions or inspection

A. Proof of service of a notice to take a deposition or of a notice of inspection under Article 1463 constitutes sufficient authorization for issuance by the clerk or judge of the district court wherein the action is pending of subpoenas and subpoenas duces tecum.

B. Subpoenas and subpoenas duces tecum compelling the appearance of a witness who is not a party shall be served within a reasonable period of time before the time specified for the deposition.

C. All provisions applicable to subpoenas and subpoenas duces tecum shall apply to subpoenas and subpoenas duces tecum issued under the provisions of this Article, except as otherwise provided by law.

Amended by Acts 1968, No. 116, § 1; Acts 1995, No. 410, § 1; Acts 1995, No. 1068, § 1, eff. June 29, 1995.

Editor's Notes

See note to C.C.P. art. 1355.

Art. 1357. Failure to comply with subpoena

A person who, without reasonable excuse, fails to obey a subpoena may be adjudged in contempt of the court which issued the subpoena. The court may also order a recalcitrant witness to be attached and brought to court forthwith or on a designated day.

CHAPTER 2. PROOF OF OFFICIAL RECORDS

Article

Art. 1391. Repealed by Acts 1988, No. 515, § 7, eff. Jan. 1, 1989

Comment—1988

This Article, providing for judicial notice of laws, is repealed effective January 1, 1989, by the enactment of the Code of Evidence. Chapter 2 of the Code of Evidence provides the rules on judicial notice. See also Code of Evidence Article 1101 for the applicability of the Code in this area, particularly Article 1101(D).

Art. 1392. Proof of statutes

The court shall take judicial notice of the laws of the United States, of every state, territory, and other jurisdiction of the United States as provided by Code of Evidence Article 202.

Amended by Acts 2018, No. 184, § 1.

Arts. 1393 to 1397. Repealed by Acts 1988, No. 515, § 7, eff. Jan. 1, 1989

See West's Louisiana Statutes Annotated

CHAPTER 3. DISCOVERY

SECTION 1. GENERAL PROVISIONS GOVERNING DISCOVERY

SECTION 2. DEPOSITIONS: GENERAL DISPOSITIONS

SECTION 1. GENERAL PROVISIONS GOVERNING DISCOVERY

Art. 1420. Signing of discovery requests, responses, or objections

A. Every request for discovery, or response or objection thereto, made by a party represented by an attorney shall be signed by at least one attorney of record in his individual name, whose address shall be stated. A party who is not represented by an attorney shall sign the request, response, or objection and state his address.

B. The signature of an attorney or party constitutes a certification by him that he has read the request, response, or objection and that to the best of his knowledge, information, and belief formed after reasonable inquiry the request, response, or objection is:

(1) Consistent with all the rules of discovery and is warranted by existing law or a good faith argument for the extension, modification, or reversal of existing law;

(2) Not interposed for any improper purpose, such as to harass or to cause unnecessary or needless increase in the cost of litigation; and

(3) Not unreasonable, unduly burdensome, or expensive, given the needs of the case, the discovery already had in the case, the amount in controversy, and the importance of the issues at stake in the litigation.

C. If a request, response, or objection is not signed, it shall be stricken unless promptly signed after the omission is called to the attention of the person whose signature is required. A party shall not be obligated to take any action with respect to the request, response, or objection until it is signed.

D. If, upon motion of any party or upon its own motion, the court determines that a certification has been made in violation of the provisions of this Article, the court shall impose upon the person who made the certification or the represented party, or both, an appropriate sanction which may include an order to pay to the other party or parties the amount of the reasonable expenses incurred because of the filing of the request, response, or objection, including a reasonable attorney's fee.

E. A sanction authorized in Paragraph D shall be imposed only after a hearing at which any party or his counsel may present any evidence or argument relevant to the issue of imposition of the sanction.

Added by Acts 1988, No. 442, § 1, eff. Jan. 1, 1989.

Editor's Notes

Rule 10.1, Discovery Motions, District Court Rules, requires a conference with opposing party before filing a discovery motion.

Art. 1421. Discovery methods

Parties may obtain discovery by one or more of the following methods: depositions upon oral examination or written questions; written interrogatories; production of documents or things or permission to enter upon land or other property, for inspection and other purposes; physical and mental examinations, including additional medical opinions under Article 1464; request for release of medical records; and requests for admission. Unless the court orders otherwise under Article 1426, the frequency of use of these methods is not limited.

Acts 1976, No. 574, § 1. Amended by Acts 1993, No. 823, § 1; Acts 2017, No. 381, § 1, eff. June 23, 2017.

Art. 1421.1. [Blank]

Art. 1422. Scope of discovery; in general

Unless otherwise limited by order of the court in accordance with this Chapter, the scope of discovery is as set forth in this Article and in Articles 1423 through 1425.

Parties may obtain discovery regarding any matter, not privileged, which is relevant to the subject matter involved in the pending action, whether it relates to the claim or defense of the party seeking discovery or to the claim or defense of any other party, including the existence, description, nature, custody, condition, and location of any books, documents, or other tangible things and the identity and location of persons having knowledge of any discoverable matter. It is not ground for objection that the information sought will be inadmissible at the trial if the information sought appears reasonably calculated to lead to the discovery of admissible evidence.

Acts 1976, No. 574, § 1.

Art. 1422.1. Scope of discovery; records of the Louisiana Bureau of Criminal Identification and Information

In civil proceedings, the records of the Louisiana Bureau of Criminal Identification and Information as defined in R.S. 15:577 shall be privileged and shall not be subject to discovery by third parties. The term "records" as used in this Article shall include but not be limited to "rap sheets", fingerprint records, or any other record created by or maintained by the bureau.

Added by Acts 2003, No. 1199, § 1.

Art. 1423. Scope of discovery; insurance agreements

A party may obtain discovery of the existence and contents of any insurance agreement under which any person carrying on an insurance business may be liable to satisfy part or all of a judgment which may be entered in the action or to indemnify or reimburse for payments made to satisfy the judgment.

Acts 1976, No. 574, § 1.

Art. 1424. Scope of discovery; trial preparation; materials

A. The court shall not order the production or inspection of any writing, or electronically stored information, obtained or prepared by the adverse party, his attorney, surety, indemnitor, or agent in anticipation of litigation or in preparation for trial unless satisfied that denial of production or inspection will unfairly prejudice the party seeking the production or inspection in preparing his claim or defense or will cause him undue hardship or injustice. Except as otherwise provided in Article 1425(E)(1), the court shall not order the production or inspection of any part of the writing, or electronically stored information, that reflects the mental impressions, conclusions, opinions, or theories of an attorney.

B. A party may obtain without the required showing a statement concerning the action or its subject matter previously made by that party. Upon request, a person not a party may obtain without the required showing a statement concerning the action or its subject matter previously made by that person. If the request is refused, the person may move for a court order. The provisions of Article 1469(4) apply to the award of expenses incurred in relation to the motion. For purposes of this Paragraph, a statement previously made is a written statement signed or otherwise adopted or approved by the person making it, or a stenographic, mechanical, electronically stored, or other recording, or a transcription thereof, which is a substantially verbatim recital of an oral statement by the person making it and contemporaneously recorded.

C. When a party withholds information otherwise discoverable under these rules by claiming that it is privileged or subject to protection as trial preparation material, the party shall make the claim expressly and shall describe the nature of the documents, communications, or things not produced or disclosed in a manner that, without revealing information itself privileged or protected, will enable other parties to assess the applicability of the privilege or protection.

D. A disclosure of a communication or information covered by the attorney-client privilege or work product protection does not operate as a waiver if the disclosure is inadvertent and is made in connection with litigation or administrative proceedings, and if the person entitled to assert the privilege or work product protection took reasonably prompt measures, once the holder knew of the disclosure, to notify the receiving party of the inadvertence of the disclosure and the privilege asserted. Once notice is received, the receiving party shall either return or promptly safeguard the inadvertently disclosed material, but with the option of asserting a waiver. Even without notice of the inadvertent disclosure from the sending party, if it is clear that the material received is privileged and inadvertently produced, the receiving party shall either return or promptly safeguard the material, and shall notify the sending party of the material received, but with the option of asserting a waiver.

Acts 1976, No. 574, § 1. Amended by Acts 2003, No. 545, § 1; Acts 2007, No. 140, § 1.

Editor's Notes

In Wolford v. Joellen Smith Psych. Hosp., 693 So.2d 1164 (La. 1997) the court held that the attorney work product exception to general discovery refers only to writing and does not cover videotapes or other tangible things. The existence of surveillance materials is discoverable and the defendant must respond as to the existence thereof, though the defendant may take the deposition of the plaintiff before turning over the tapes.

Art. 1425. Experts; pretrial disclosures; scope of discovery

A. A party may through interrogatories or by deposition require any other party to identify each person who may be used at trial to present evidence under Articles 702 through 705 of the Louisiana Code of Evidence.

B. Upon contradictory motion of any party or on the court's own motion, an order may be entered requiring that each party that has retained or specially employed a person to provide expert testimony in the case or whose duties as an employee of the party regularly involve giving expert testimony provide a written report prepared and signed by the witness. The report shall contain a complete statement of all opinions to be expressed and the basis and reasons therefor and the data or other information considered by the witness in forming the opinions. The parties, upon agreement, or if ordered by the court, shall include in the report any or all of the following: exhibits to be used as a summary of or support for the opinions; the qualifications of the witness, including a list of all publications authored by the witness within the preceding ten years; the compensation to be paid for the study and testimony; a listing of any other cases in which the witness has testified as an expert at trial or by deposition within the preceding four years.

C. If the court orders the disclosures of Paragraph B of this Article, they shall be made at the times and in the sequence directed by the court. In the absence of directions from the court or stipulation by the parties, the disclosures ordered pursuant to Paragraph B of this Article shall be made at least ninety days before the trial date or, if the evidence is intended solely to contradict or rebut evidence on the same subject matter identified by another party under Paragraph B of this Article, within thirty days after the disclosure made by the other party. The parties shall supplement these disclosures when required by Article 1428.

D. (1) Except as otherwise provided in Paragraph E of this Article, a party may, through interrogatories, deposition, and a request for documents and tangible things, discover facts known or opinions held by any person who has been identified as an expert whose opinions may be presented at trial. If a report from the expert is required under Paragraph B, the deposition shall not be conducted until after the report is provided.

(2) A party may, through interrogatories or by deposition, discover facts known by and opinions held by an expert who has been retained or specially employed by another party in anticipation of litigation or preparation for trial and who is not expected to be called as a witness at trial, only as provided in Article 1465 or upon a showing of exceptional circumstances under which it is impracticable for the party seeking discovery to obtain facts or opinions on the same subject by other means.

(3) Unless manifest injustice would result, the court shall require that the party seeking discovery pay the expert a reasonable fee for time spent in responding to discovery under this Paragraph; and with respect to discovery obtained under Subparagraph (2) of this Paragraph, the court shall also require the party seeking discovery to pay the other party a fair portion of the fees and expenses reasonably incurred by the latter party in obtaining facts and opinions from the expert.

E. (1) The expert's drafts of a report required under Paragraph B of this Article, and communications, including notes and electronically stored information or portions thereof that would reveal the mental impressions, opinions, or trial strategy of the attorney for the party who has retained the expert to testify, shall not be discoverable except, in either case, on a showing of exceptional circumstances under which it is impractical for the party seeking discovery to obtain facts or opinions on the same subject by other means.

(2) Nothing in this Article shall preclude opposing counsel from obtaining any facts or data the expert is relying on in forming his opinion, including that coming from counsel, or from otherwise

inquiring fully of an expert into what facts or data the expert considered, whether the expert considered alternative approaches, or into the validity of the expert's opinions.

F. (1) Any party may file a motion for a pretrial hearing to determine whether a witness qualifies as an expert or whether the methodologies employed by such witness are reliable under Articles 702 through 705 of the Louisiana Code of Evidence. The motion shall be filed not later than sixty days prior to trial and shall set forth sufficient allegations showing the necessity for these determinations by the court.

(2) The court shall hold a contradictory hearing and shall rule on the motion not later than thirty days prior to the trial. At the hearing, the court shall consider the qualifications and methodologies of the proposed witness based upon the provisions of Articles 104(A) and 702 through 705 of the Louisiana Code of Evidence. For good cause shown, the court may allow live testimony at the contradictory hearing.

(3) If the ruling of the court is made at the conclusion of the hearing, the court shall recite orally its findings of fact, conclusions of law, and reasons for judgment. If the matter is taken under advisement, the court shall render its ruling and provide written findings of fact, conclusions of law, and reasons for judgment not later than five days after the hearing.

(4) The findings of facts, conclusions of law, and reasons for judgment shall be made part of the record of the proceedings. The findings of facts, conclusions of law, and reasons for judgment shall specifically include and address:

(a) The elements required to be satisfied for a person to testify under Articles 702 through 705 of the Louisiana Code of Evidence.

(b) The evidence presented at the hearing to satisfy the requirements of Articles 702 through 705 of the Louisiana Code of Evidence at trial.

(c) A decision by the judge as to whether or not a person shall be allowed to testify under Articles 702 through 705 of the Louisiana Code of Evidence at trial.

(d) The reasons of the judge detailing in law and fact why a person shall be allowed or disallowed to testify under Articles 702 through 705 of the Louisiana Code of Evidence.

(5) A ruling of the court pursuant to a hearing held in accordance with the provisions of this Paragraph shall be subject to appellate review as provided by law.

(6) Notwithstanding the time limitations in Subparagraphs (1), (2), and (3) of this Paragraph, by unanimous consent of the parties, and with approval by the court, a motion under this Paragraph may be filed, heard, and ruled upon by the court at any time prior to trial. The ruling by the court on such motion shall include findings of fact, conclusions of law, and reasons for judgment complying with the provisions of Subparagraph (4) of this Paragraph.

(7) The provisions of this Paragraph shall not apply to testimony in an action for divorce or annulment of marriage, or to a separation in a covenant marriage, to a property partition, or to an administration of a succession, or to testimony in any incidental or ancillary proceedings or matters arising from such actions.

(8) All or a portion of the court costs, including reasonable expert witness fees and costs, incurred when a motion is filed in accordance with this Paragraph may, in the discretion of the court, be assessed to the non-prevailing party as taxable costs at the conclusion of the hearing on the motion.

Acts 1976, No. 574, § 1. Amended by Acts 2003, No. 545, § 1; Acts 2007, No. 140, § 1; Acts 2008, No. 787, § 1, eff. Jan. 1, 2009; Acts 2014, No. 655, § 1.

Comment—2003

(a) The amendments to Article 1425 remove its restrictions on the discovery of testifying expert witnesses. It is an anomaly that any aspect of expert testimony can be admissible at trial but shielded from discovery. The prior distinctions between discovery of facts, opinions, and writings of testifying experts applied in cases such as *Weidenbacher v. St. Paul Fire and Marine*, 347 So.2d 1160 (La. 1977), have been eliminated.

(b) Broadening the scope of discovery of testifying experts is consistent with (i) the application of Code of Evidence Article 705, which permits cross-examination of an adverse expert at trial as to the "underlying facts or data;" (ii) Article 1450(A)(5), which grants the trial court authority to accept depositions of experts at hearings in lieu of live testimony; and (iii) Article 967(A) which permits expert depositions to be used in connection with motions for summary judgment. It also facilitates the pretrial assessment of the admissibility of expert testimony pursuant to the policy set forth in *Daubert v. Merrell Dow Pharms.*, 509 U.S. 579 (1993) and *State v. Foret*, 628 So.2d 1116 (La. 1993).

(c) The grant of authority to the court in Paragraph B to order the parties to provide written reports for testifying expert witnesses is new. The practice has previously been utilized by some trial courts pursuant to their authority in Article 1551(5) to regulate the use of expert testimony through pre-trial orders. See *Southern Casing of Louisiana, Inc. v. Houma Avionics, Inc.*, 809 So.2d 1040 (La. App. 1 Cir, 2001). The new provision should not be interpreted to mean that expert reports should be required in all cases. To the contrary, the court should always consider the complexity of the case, amount in controversy, and the limitations on the financial resources of the parties in determining whether the added expense to the parties in providing an expert report is justified.

Furthermore, court orders requiring the exchange of reports of testifying experts should not apply to every witness who may be entitled to express an opinion at trial. For example, when a witness, such as a treating physician or other persons with particular professional or other knowledge, will testify to facts and opinions developed because of their treatment, observations, perception or connection to a party or event (i.e. coroner, investigating officer, etc.) and have not been specially retained or employed to provide expert testimony, he or she should not be required to generate a report solely for the purposes of the litigation.

(d) In contrast to the changes in Article 1425(D)(1), Article 1425(D)(2) provides for restrictions on the discovery of the identity of, facts known to, writings of, and opinions held by an expert hired or consulted in anticipation of litigation or preparation for trial and who is not expected to testify at trial. This information may only be obtained by order of the court and under exceptional circumstances. This eliminates the distinctions discussed as to facts and opinions in *State Dept. of Transp. & Develop. v. Stumpf* 458 So.2d 448 (La. 1984).

Comment—2007

Paragraph E was added in 2007 to protect from discovery drafts of required expert reports and communications with testifying experts that would reveal the attorney's mental impressions, opinions, or trial strategy, without sacrificing full discoverability of facts and data supporting the expert's opinions. If documents or electronically stored information contain both facts and protected material of an attorney, the court may order production subject to redaction.

Comment—2014

(a) Contrary to *Quillian v. The Dixie Bonded Warehouse*, 105 So.3d 71 (La. App. 2d Cir. 8/29/12), Article 1425 does not require a party, absent a discovery request or an order requiring an expert report, to identify testifying experts.

(b) The identification of testifying expert witnesses is obtained by interrogatories, depositions, requirements in a scheduling order entered pursuant to Article 1551(A)(5) or (8), or by court order under Paragraph B. The preparation and submission of reports of testifying experts is required only if ordered by the court pursuant to Paragraph (B). If expert reports are ordered, the court should set production deadlines in the order; however, if there is no deadline set in the order, then the sequence provided in Paragraph (C) applies by default.

Art. 1426. Protective orders

A. Upon motion by a party or by the person from whom discovery is sought, and for good cause shown, the court in which the action is pending or alternatively, on matters relating to a deposition, the court in the district where the deposition is to be taken may make any order which justice requires to protect a party or person from annoyance, embarrassment, oppression, or undue burden or expense, including one or more of the following:

(1) That the discovery not be had.

(2) That the discovery may be had only on specified terms and conditions, including a designation of the time or place.

(3) That the discovery may be had only by a method of discovery other than that selected by the party seeking discovery.

(4) That certain matters not be inquired into, or that the scope of the discovery be limited to certain matters.

(5) That discovery be conducted with no one present except persons designated by the court.

(6) That a deposition after being sealed be opened only by order of the court.

(7) That a trade secret or other confidential research, development, or commercial information not be disclosed or be disclosed only in a designated way.

(8) That the parties simultaneously file specified documents or information enclosed in sealed envelopes to be opened as directed by the courts.

B. If the motion for a protective order is denied in whole or in part, the court may, on such terms and conditions as are just, order that any party or person provide or permit discovery. The provisions of Article 1469 apply to the award of expenses incurred in relation to the motion.

C. No provision of this Article authorizes a court to issue a protective order preventing or limiting discovery or ordering records sealed if the information or material sought to be protected relates to a public hazard or relates to information which may be useful to members of the public in protecting themselves from injury that might result from such public hazard, unless such information or material sought to be protected is a trade secret or other confidential research, development, or commercial information.

D. Any portion of an agreement or contract which has the purpose or effect of concealing a public hazard, any information relating to a public hazard, or any information which may be useful to members of the public in protecting themselves from injury that might result from a public hazard is null and shall be void and unenforceable as contrary to public policy, unless such information is a trade secret or other confidential research, development, or commercial information.

E. Any substantially affected person or any representative of the news media has standing to contest any order or judgment that violates the provisions of Paragraph C of this Article or any agreement or contract contrary to public policy pursuant to Paragraph D of this Article.

Acts 1976, No. 574, § 1. Amended by Acts 1995, No. 49, § 1.

Art. 1426.1. Stay of discovery in civil matters by a district attorney in a related criminal matter

A. Upon motion of the district attorney in a criminal proceeding, a court having jurisdiction over any related pending civil action or proceeding may, in the interests of justice and for good cause shown after a contradictory hearing with all parties in the civil action, stay all or a portion of discovery sought in such civil action or proceeding. The contradictory hearing shall be held by the court in the civil action within thirty days of the filing of the motion. Good cause shall include but not be limited to a finding by the court that such discovery will adversely affect the ability of the district attorney to conduct a related criminal investigation or the prosecution of a related felony criminal case.

B. No provision of this Article shall prohibit a party to the stayed discovery proceeding from moving to have the stay subsequently lifted for good cause.

C. Within thirty days after disposition in the trial court of the related criminal prosecution, in any matter where a stay has issued, the district attorney shall file an ex parte motion consenting to the termination of the stay.

D. The time during which the civil proceeding is stayed pursuant to this Article shall not be used to compute the three-year abandonment period of the civil matter.

E. Repealed by Acts 2017, No. 91, § 1.

Added by Acts 2012, No. 664, § 1.

Art. 1427. Sequence and timing of discovery

Unless the court upon motion, for the convenience of parties and witnesses and in the interest of justice, orders otherwise, methods of discovery may be used in any sequence and the fact that a party is conducting discovery, whether by deposition or otherwise, shall not operate to delay any other party's discovery.

Acts 1976, No. 574, § 1.

Art. 1428. Supplementation of responses

A party who has responded to a request for discovery with a response that was complete when made is under no duty to supplement his response to include information thereafter acquired, except as follows:

(1) A party is under a duty seasonably to supplement his response with respect to any question directly addressed to the identity and location of persons having knowledge of discoverable matters, and the identity of each person expected to be called as an expert witness at trial, the subject matter on which he is expected to testify, and the substance of his testimony.

(2) A party is under a duty seasonably to amend a prior response if he obtains information upon the basis of which he knows that the response was incorrect when made, or he knows that the response though correct when made is no longer true and the circumstances are such that a failure to amend the response is in substance a knowing concealment.

(3) A duty to supplement responses may be imposed by order of the court, agreement of the parties, or at any time prior to trial through new requests for supplementation of prior responses.

Acts 1976, No. 574, § 1.

SECTION 2. DEPOSITIONS: GENERAL DISPOSITIONS

Art. 1429. Perpetuation of testimony; petition

A person who desires to perpetuate his own testimony or that of another person regarding any matter that may be cognizable in any court of this state may file a verified petition in a court in which the anticipated action might be brought. The petition shall be entitled in the name of the petitioner and shall show:

(1) That the petitioner expects to be a party to an action cognizable in a court of this state but is presently unable to bring it or cause it to be brought.

(2) The subject matter of the expected action and his interest therein.

(3) The facts which he desires to establish by the proposed testimony and his reasons for desiring to perpetuate it.

(4) The names or a description of the persons he expects will be adverse parties and their addresses so far as known.

(5) The names and addresses of the persons to be examined and the substance of the testimony which he expects to elicit from each, and shall ask for an order authorizing the petitioner to take the depositions of the persons to be examined named in the petition, for the purpose of perpetuating their testimony.

Acts 1976, No. 574, § 1.

Art. 1430. Notice and service of petition; perpetuation of testimony

The petitioner shall thereafter serve a notice upon each person named in the petition as an expected adverse party, together with a copy of the petition, stating that the petitioner will apply to the court, at a time and place named therein, for the order described in the petition. At least twenty days before the date of hearing the notice shall be served as provided in Article 1314; but if such service cannot with due diligence be made upon any expected adverse party named in the petition, the court may make such order as is just for service by publication or otherwise, and shall appoint, for persons not served in the manner provided in Article 1314, an attorney who shall represent them, and, in case they are not otherwise represented, shall cross examine the deponent. If any expected adverse party is a minor or incompetent the court shall appoint an attorney to represent him.

Acts 1976, No. 574, § 1.

Art. 1430.1. Ex parte order; death or incapacitating illness

A. Notwithstanding the provisions of Article 1430, the court may by ex parte order grant the perpetuation of testimony as provided in Article 1431 if:

(1) The facts set forth in the petition show the desire to perpetuate testimony is based upon a reasonable belief that there is a substantial possibility that the person whose testimony is sought will die or be too incapacitated to testify before a contradictory hearing can be held; and

(2) The interest of justice requires the immediate perpetuation of the testimony.

B. Should the court grant perpetuation of testimony in accordance with this Article, the petitioner shall give reasonable notice in writing to an expected adverse party of the time and place for perpetuating the testimony, manner of perpetuation, name and address of the person whose testimony is to be perpetuated, and the subject matter of the testimony.

C. If an expected adverse party is a minor or incompetent, the court shall appoint an attorney to represent him, and the notice shall be sent to the attorney.

D. No appeal shall lie from the granting or denial of an ex parte order under this Article. The admissibility at trial or other proceeding of any testimony perpetuated under this Article shall be governed by the Louisiana Code of Evidence.

E. The procedure authorized by this Article shall be in addition to any other procedure provided by law for the perpetuation of testimony.

Added by Acts 1989, No. 53, § 1.

Art. 1431. Order and examination; perpetuation of testimony

If the court is satisfied that the perpetuation of the testimony may prevent a failure or delay of justice, it shall make an order designating or describing the persons whose depositions may be taken and specifying the subject matter of the examination and whether the depositions shall be taken upon oral examination or written interrogatories. The depositions may then be taken in accordance with this Chapter; and the court may make orders of the character provided for by Articles 1461 through 1465. For the purpose of applying the provisions of this Chapter to depositions for perpetuating testimony, each reference therein to the court in which the action is pending shall be deemed to refer to the court in which the petition for such deposition was filed.

Acts 1976, No. 574, § 1.

Art. 1432. Use of deposition

A deposition to perpetuate testimony taken under Articles 1429 through 1431 may be used in any action involving the same subject matter subsequently brought in any court of this state, in accordance with the provisions of Article 1450.

Acts 1976, No. 574, § 1.

Art. 1433. Deposition after trial

A. If an appeal has been taken from a judgment of a district court or before the taking of an appeal if the time has not expired, the district court in which the judgment was rendered may allow the taking of the depositions of witnesses to perpetuate their testimony for use in the event of further proceedings in the district court. In such case the party who desires to perpetuate the testimony may make a motion in the district court for leave to take the depositions, upon the same notice and service thereof as if the action was pending in the district court. The motion shall show:

(1) The names and addresses of persons to be examined and the substance of the testimony which he expects to elicit from each.

(2) The reasons for perpetuating their testimony.

B. If the court finds that the perpetuation of the testimony is proper to avoid a failure or delay of justice, it may make an order allowing the depositions to be taken and may make orders of the character provided for in Articles 1461 through 1465, and thereupon the depositions may be taken and used in the same manner and under the same conditions as are prescribed in this Chapter for depositions taken in actions pending in the court.

C. In aid of execution of the judgment, the district court in which the judgment was rendered may, upon motion of the judgment creditor, allow the taking of a third person's deposition, as provided in Article 2451, upon the same notice and service thereof as if the action was pending in the district court. The person whose deposition is so ordered shall be reimbursed by the judgment creditor for the reasonable costs incurred or to be incurred in the course of complying with the order, including document reproduction costs and travel expenses.

Acts 1976, No. 574, § 1. Amended by Acts 1990, No. 1000, § 1.

Art. 1434. Person before whom deposition taken

A. (1) A deposition shall be taken before an officer authorized to administer oaths, who is not an employee or attorney of any of the parties or otherwise interested in the outcome of the case.

(2) For purposes of this Article, an employee includes a person who has a contractual relationship with a party litigant to provide shorthand reporting or other court reporting services and also includes a person employed part or full time under contract or otherwise by a person who has a contractual relationship with a party litigant to provide shorthand reporting or other court reporting services. A party litigant does not include federal, state, or local governments, and the subdivisions thereof, or parties in proper person.

B. "Officer" as used in this Article means a certified shorthand or general reporter currently holding a valid certificate issued by the Board of Examiners of Certified Shorthand Reporters pursuant to the provisions of R.S. 37:2551 et seq., and an official court reporter, and a deputy official court reporter, as defined in R.S. 37:2555(B)(1) and (2).

C. In a video deposition, the deponent can be sworn by anyone authorized to take oaths. The oath shall be recorded on tape.

Acts 1976, No. 574, § 1. Amended by Acts 1990, No. 295, § 1; Acts 1990, No. 842, § 1, eff. July 24, 1990; Acts 1995, No. 1145, § 1.

Art. 1435. Deposition taken in another state, or in a territory, district, or foreign jurisdiction

If the witness whose deposition is to be taken is found in another state, or in a territory, district, or foreign jurisdiction, the law of the place where the deposition is to be taken shall govern the compulsory process to require the appearance and testimony of witnesses, but otherwise the provisions of this Chapter or of R.S. 13:3823 shall be applicable to such a deposition.

Acts 1976, No. 574, § 1.

Art. 1436. Stipulations; manner of taking; modification of procedures

Unless the court orders otherwise and except as provided by Article 1425, the parties may by written stipulation provide that depositions may be taken before any person, at any time or place, upon any notice, and in any manner and when so taken may be used like other depositions, and modify the procedures provided by these rules for other methods of discovery.

A witness who is a resident of this state may be required to attend an examination to take his deposition only in the parish in which he resides or is employed or transacts his business in person, or at such other convenient place as may be fixed by order of court. A witness who is a nonresident of this state, but is temporarily in this state, may be required to attend an examination to take his deposition only in the parish where he is served with a subpoena or at such other convenient place as may be fixed by order of court.

Acts 1976, No. 574, § 1.

Art. 1436.1. Depositions by telephone

If agreed upon by every party to a suit or if ordered by the court, a deposition may be taken by telephone or other remote electronic means.

Added by Acts 1986, No. 205, § 1. Amended by Acts 2003, No. 545, § 1.

Art. 1437. Deposition upon oral examination; when deposition may be taken

After commencement of the action, any party may take the testimony of any person, including a party, by deposition upon oral examination. Leave of court, granted with or without notice, must be obtained only if the plaintiff seeks to take a deposition prior to the expiration of fifteen days after service of citation upon any defendant, except that leave is not required if a defendant has served a notice of taking deposition or otherwise sought discovery, or if special notice is given as provided in Article 1439. The attendance of witnesses may be compelled by the use of subpoena as for witnesses in trials. The deposition of a person confined in prison may be taken only by leave of court on such terms as the court prescribes.

Acts 1976, No. 574, § 1.

Art. 1438. Notice of examination; time and place; subpoena duces tecum

A party desiring to take the deposition of any person upon oral examination shall give reasonable notice in writing to every other party to the action. The notice shall state the time and place for taking the deposition and the name and address of each person to be examined, if known, and, if the name is not known, a general description sufficient to identify him or the particular class or group to which he belongs. If a subpoena duces tecum is to be served on the person to be examined, the designation of the materials to be produced as set forth in the subpoena shall be attached to or included in the notice.

The court may for cause shown lengthen or shorten the time for taking the deposition.

Acts 1976, No. 574, § 1.

Art. 1439. Special notice

Leave of court is not required for the taking of a deposition by plaintiff if the notice states that the person to be examined is about to go out of the state and will be unavailable for examination unless his deposition is taken before expiration of the fifteen-day period, and sets forth facts to support the statement. The plaintiff's attorney shall sign the notice, and his signature constitutes a certification by him that to the best of his knowledge, information, and belief the statement and supporting facts are true. The sanctions provided by Articles 863 and 864 are applicable to the certification.

If a party shows that when he was served with notice under this Article he was unable through the exercise of diligence to obtain counsel to represent him at the taking of the deposition, the deposition may not be used against him.

Acts 1976, No. 574, § 1.

Art. 1440. Nonstenographic recordation of testimony

The testimony at a deposition may be recorded by other than stenographic means, in which event the notice shall designate the manner of recording, preserving, and filing the deposition, and shall include other provisions to assure that the recorded testimony will be accurate and trustworthy. A videotaped deposition may be taken and used without court order just as any other deposition. A certified shorthand reporter shall be present at the time of any videotaped deposition taken without a court order unless waived by all parties. A party may nevertheless arrange to have a stenographic transcription made at his own expense.

Acts 1976, No. 574, § 1. Amended by Acts 1990, No. 295, § 1.

Art. 1441. Production of documents and things

The notice to a party deponent may be accompanied by a request made in compliance with Article 1461 for the production of documents and tangible things at the taking of the deposition. The procedure of Articles 1461 through 1463 shall apply to the request.

Acts 1976, No. 574, § 1.

Art. 1442. Deposition of an organization

A party may in his notice name as the deponent a public or private corporation or a partnership or association or governmental agency and designate with reasonable particularity the matters on which examination is requested. The organization so named shall designate one or more officers, directors, or managing agents, or other persons who consent to testify on its behalf, and may set forth, for each person designated, the matters on which he will testify. The persons so designated shall testify as to matters known or reasonably available to the organization. This Article does not preclude taking a deposition by any other procedure authorized in this Chapter.

Acts 1976, No. 574, § 1.

Art. 1443. Examination and cross-examination; record of examination; oath; objections

A. Examination and cross-examination of witnesses may proceed as permitted at the trial under the provisions of the Louisiana Code of Evidence. The officer before whom the deposition is to be taken shall administer an oath or affirmation to the witness and shall personally, or by someone acting under his direction and in his presence, record the testimony of the witness. The testimony shall be taken stenographically or recorded by any other means. If requested by one of the parties, the testimony shall be transcribed.

B. All objections made at the time of the examination to the qualifications of the officer taking the deposition, or to the manner of taking it, or to the evidence presented, or to the conduct of any party, and any other objection to the proceedings, shall be noted by the officer upon the deposition. The officer shall cease or suspend recordation of the testimony, questions, objections, or any other statements only upon agreement of all counsel and parties present at the deposition, or upon termination or suspension of the deposition pursuant to Code of Civil Procedure Article 1444. Any objection during a deposition shall be stated concisely and in a non-argumentative and non-suggestive manner. Evidence objected to shall be taken subject to the objections. Counsel shall cooperate with and be courteous to each other and to the witness and otherwise conduct themselves as required in open court and shall be subject to the power of the court to punish for contempt. In lieu of participating in the oral examination, parties may serve written questions in a sealed envelope on the party taking the deposition, and he shall transmit them to the officer, or anyone authorized to take oaths, who shall propound them to the witness and record the answers verbatim.

C. "Officer" as used in this Article means a certified shorthand reporter currently holding a valid certificate issued by the Board of Examiners of Certified Shorthand Reporters pursuant to the provisions of R.S. 37:2551 et seq., and an official court reporter, and a deputy official court reporter, as defined in R.S. 37:2555 (C) and (D).

D. Unless otherwise stipulated or as provided in Article 1455, objections are considered reserved until trial or other use of the deposition. A party may instruct a deponent not to answer only when necessary to preserve a privilege, to enforce a limitation on evidence imposed by the court, to prevent harassing or repetitious questions, or to prevent questions which seek information that is neither admissible at trial nor reasonably calculated to lead to the discovery of admissible evidence.

E. If the court finds that an objection made during a deposition taken for trial purposes is in violation of this Article, the court shall order the party in violation to pay for the editing or redacting of the transcript or video, along with any other costs or sanctions the court deems appropriate unless good cause is shown.

Acts 1976, No. 574, § 1. Amended by Acts 1988, No. 515, § 2, eff. Jan. 1, 1989; Acts 1990, No. 295, § 1; Acts 1990, No. 842, § 1, eff. July 24, 1990; Acts 1997, No. 1056, § 1; Acts 2004, No. 365, § 1; Acts 2010, No. 456, § 1; Acts 2010, No. 458, § 1.

Comment—1988

The language of this Article has been changed to conform to Code of Evidence Article 603. See also Code of Civil Procedure Art. 1633.

Comment—1997

The amendment restricts the general practice of instructing a deponent not to answer by providing that such an instruction may only be given for the limited purposes set out in the article.

Comments—2004

(a) A sentence has been added to Paragraph B providing that objections at a deposition must be made in a concise and non-argumentative and non-suggestive manner. The purpose of this amendment is to curtail a practice of using lengthy or "speaking" objections designed to coach the witness or berate or argue with opposing counsel or the witness. The language was taken from Fed. R. Civ. P. Rl. 30(d)(1). Many other states have enacted a similar procedural rule. See Phelps Gay, Professionalism in Depositions: The Sound of Silence, 54 Fed. Def. & Corp. Counsel Quarterly, p. 213 (Spring 2004).

(b) A second sentence has been added to Paragraph B codifying the obligation of all counsel attending a deposition to treat each other and the witness and otherwise conduct themselves in a professional manner as though they were in open court. Since depositions are taken without the presence of a judge, abusive and unprofessional conduct may occur which would not be permitted in open court. Article 221 broadly defines a contempt of court as "any act or omission tending to obstruct or interfere with the orderly administration of justice. . ." Accordingly, the court has the power to treat improper behavior at depositions as a constructive contempt of court and invoke sanctions in accordance with Article 225.

(c) The first sentence in Paragraph D has been amended to modify its prior provision that "all objections are considered reserved until trial." This provision conflicted with Article 1455 which provides that certain objections which could be made at a deposition, such as to the form of the question, are waived for trial purposes unless "seasonably made at the taking of the deposition."

(d) The word "only" has been added to the second sentence of Paragraph D to make it clear that the grounds for instructing a witness not to answer a question set forth in the paragraph are exclusive and not illustrative.

Art. 1444. Motion to terminate; limit examination

At any time during the taking of the deposition, on motion of a party or of the deponent and upon a showing that the examination is being conducted in bad faith or in such manner as unreasonably to annoy, embarrass, or oppress the deponent or party, the court in which the action is pending may order the officer conducting the examination to cease forthwith from taking the deposition, or may limit the scope and manner of the taking of the deposition as provided in Article 1426. If the order made terminates the examination, it shall be resumed thereafter only upon the order of the court. Upon demand of the objecting party or deponent, the taking of the deposition shall be suspended for the time necessary to make a motion for an order. The provisions of Article 1469 apply to the award of expenses incurred in relation to the motion.

Acts 1976, No. 574, § 1.

Art. 1445. Submission to witness; changes; signing

When the testimony is fully transcribed the deposition shall be submitted to the witness for examination and shall be read to or by him, unless such examination and reading are waived by the witness and by the parties. Any changes in form or substance which the witness desires to make shall be entered upon the deposition by the officer with a statement of the reasons given by the witness for making them. The deposition shall then be signed by the witness unless the parties by stipulation waive the signing or the witness is ill or is absent from the parish where the deposition was taken or cannot be found or refuses to sign. If the deposition is not signed by the witness within thirty days of its submission to him, the officer shall sign it and state on the record the fact of the waiver or of the illness or absence of the witness or the fact of the refusal to sign together with the reason, if any, given therefor; and the deposition may then be used as fully as though signed unless on a motion to suppress under Article 1456 the court holds that the reasons given for the refusal to sign require rejection of the deposition in whole or in part. A video deposition does not have to comply with the requirements of reading and signing by the deponents.

Acts 1976, No. 574, § 1. Amended by Acts 1990, No. 295, § 1.

Art. 1446. Certification by officer; custody of deposition; exhibits; copies; notice of availability for inspection or copying; cost of originals and copies of transcripts

A. (1)(a) The officer as defined in Article 1434(B) shall certify on the deposition that the witness was duly sworn and that the deposition is a true record of the testimony given by the witness.

(b) The officer shall do either of the following:

(i) Securely seal the deposition in an envelope endorsed with the title of the action and marked "Deposition of (here insert name of witness)" and shall promptly and simultaneously send it by United States mail or by courier to the party at whose request the deposition was taken, who shall become the custodian of the deposition, and to all other parties to the action who have ordered a copy of the deposition transcript.

(ii) At the request of the parties, seal the deposition electronically by secure electronic means approved by rules promulgated by the Louisiana Board of Examiners of Certified Shorthand Reporters and shall promptly and simultaneously deliver the deposition electronically to the party at whose request the deposition was taken and to all other parties to the action who have ordered a copy of the deposition transcript. The party at whose request the deposition was taken shall then become the custodian of the deposition.

(c) The original of the deposition shall not be filed in the record, but shall be made available to all other parties in the matter for inspection or copying. The failure or lack of filing such original in the record shall not affect the use or admissibility of the original at trial or by the court if otherwise authorized or provided by law.

(2) Documents and things produced for inspection during the examination of the witness shall, upon the request of a party, be marked for identification and annexed to and returned with the deposition, and may be inspected and copied by any party, except that the person producing the materials may substitute copies to be marked for identification, if he affords to all parties fair opportunity to verify the copies by comparison with the originals, and if the person producing the materials requests their return, the officer shall mark them, give each party an opportunity to inspect and copy them, and return them to the person producing them, and the materials may then be used in the same manner as if annexed to and returned with the deposition. Any party may move for an order that the original be annexed to and returned with the deposition to the court, pending final disposition of the case.

B. (1) Upon payment of reasonable charges therefor, the officer as defined in Article 1434(B) shall furnish a copy of the deposition to any party or to the deponent.

(2) Except as provided by Subparagraph (4) of this Paragraph, an attorney who takes a deposition, the attorney's firm, and the client are liable in solido for a certified shorthand reporter's charges for the reporting of the deposition, transcribing the deposition, and each copy of the deposition transcript requested by the attorney.

(3) Except as provided by Subparagraph (4) of this Paragraph, an attorney who appears at a deposition, the attorney's firm, and the client are liable in solido for the certified shorthand reporter's charges for each copy of the deposition transcript provided by the certified shorthand reporter at the request of the attorney.

(4) Prior to the taking of any deposition, a determination of the person who will pay for the deposition costs shall be agreed upon by the parties in writing or be made on the record, if an attorney is unwilling to be bound by the provisions of Subparagraphs (2) or (3) of this Paragraph. If this determination is made in writing instead of on the record, the certified shorthand reporter shall give a copy of the written determination to all the parties.

(5) In this Paragraph "firm" means a partnership organized for the practice of law in which an attorney is a partner or with which an attorney is associated, or a professional corporation organized for the practice of law of which an attorney is a shareholder or employee. An attorney "takes" a deposition if the attorney obtains the deponent's appearance through an informal request of the deponent directly or through his attorney, or obtains the deponent's appearance through a formal means, including a notice of deposition or subpoena.

(6) Nothing contained in this Paragraph shall preclude the court from awarding the charges of the certified shorthand reporter as a court cost.

C. The party taking the deposition shall give prompt notice to all other parties of its availability for inspection or copying.

D. The taking of a deposition shall be considered a step in the prosecution or defense of an action for the purposes of Article 561, notwithstanding that the deposition is not filed in the record of the proceedings.

Acts 1976, No. 574, § 1. Amended by Acts 1989, No. 388, § 1, eff. June 30, 1989; Acts 1992, No. 336, § 1; Acts 1992, No. 1002, §§ 1, 2, eff. Sept. 1, 1992; Acts 2017, No. 268, § 1.

Art. 1447. Failure to attend or to serve subpoena; expenses

A. If the party giving the notice of the taking of a deposition fails to attend and proceed therewith and another party attends in person or by attorney pursuant to the notice, the court may order the party giving the notice to pay to such other party the reasonable expenses incurred by him and his attorney in attending, including reasonable attorney's fees.

B. If the party giving the notice of the taking of a deposition of a witness fails to serve a subpoena upon him and the witness because of such failure does not attend, and if another party attends in person or by attorney because he expects the deposition of that witness to be taken, the court may order the party giving the notice to pay to such other party the reasonable expenses incurred by him and his attorney in attending, including reasonable attorney's fees.

Acts 1976, No. 574, § 1.

Art. 1448. Serving written questions; notice

A. After commencement of the action, any party may take the testimony of any person, including a party, by deposition upon written questions. The attendance of witnesses may be compelled by the use of subpoena as for witnesses in trials. The deposition of a person confined in prison may be taken only by leave of court on such terms as the court prescribes.

B. A party desiring to take a deposition upon written questions shall serve them upon every other party with a notice stating the name and address of the person who is to answer them, if known, and if the name is not known, a general description sufficient to identify him or the particular class or group to which he belongs, and the name or descriptive title and address of the officer before whom the deposition is to be taken. A deposition upon written questions may be taken of a public or private corporation or a partnership or association or governmental agency in accordance with the provisions of Article 1442.

C. Within thirty days after the notice and written questions are served, a party may serve cross questions upon all other parties. Within ten days after being served with cross questions, a party may serve redirect questions upon all other parties. Within ten days after being served with redirect questions, a party may serve recross questions upon all other parties. The court may for cause shown enlarge or shorten the time.

Acts 1976, No. 574, § 1.

Art. 1449. Taking of testimony; preparation of record; notice of filing

A copy of the notice and copies of all questions served shall be delivered by the party taking the deposition to the officer designated in the notice, who shall proceed promptly, in the manner provided by Articles 1443, 1445, and 1446, to take the testimony of the witness in response to the questions and to prepare, certify, and file or mail the deposition, attaching thereto the copy of the notice and the questions received by him.

When the deposition is filed the party taking it shall promptly give notice thereof to all other parties.

Acts 1976, No. 574, § 1.

Art. 1450. Use of depositions

A. At the trial or upon the hearing of a motion or an interlocutory proceeding, any part or all of a deposition, so far as admissible under the Louisiana Code of Evidence applied as though the witnesses were then present and testifying, may be used against any party who was present or represented at the taking of the deposition or who had reasonable notice thereof, in accordance with any of the following provisions:

(1) Any deposition may be used by any party for the purpose of contradicting or impeaching the testimony of deponent as a witness.

(2) The deposition of a party or of anyone who at the time of taking the deposition was an officer, director, or managing agent, or a person designated under Article 1442 or 1448 to testify on behalf of a public or private corporation, partnership, or association, or governmental agency which is a party may be used by an adverse party for any purpose.

(3) The deposition of a witness, whether or not a party, may be used by any party for any purpose if the court finds:

(a) That the witness is unavailable;

(b) That the witness resides at a distance greater than one hundred miles from the place of trial or hearing or is out of the state, unless it appears that the absence of the witness was procured by the party offering the deposition; or

(c) Upon application and notice, that such exceptional circumstances exist as to make it desirable, in the interest of justice and with due regard to the importance of presenting the testimony of witnesses orally in open court, to allow the deposition to be used.

(4) If only part of a deposition is offered in evidence by a party, an adverse party may require him to introduce any other part which, in fairness, should be considered with the part introduced, and any party may introduce any other parts.

(5) However, any party may use the deposition of an expert witness for any purpose upon notice to all counsel of record, any one of whom shall have the right within ten days to object to the deposition, thereby requiring the live testimony of an expert. The objecting counsel of record shall pay in advance the fee, reasonable expenses, and actual costs of such expert witness associated with such live testimony. The fees, expenses, and costs specified in this Subparagraph shall be subject to the approval of the court. The provisions of this Subparagraph do not supersede Subparagraph (A)(3) nor Code of Evidence Article 804(A). However, the court may permit the use of the expert's deposition, notwithstanding the objection of counsel to the use of that deposition, if the court finds that, under the circumstances, justice so requires.

B. Substitution of parties does not affect the right to use depositions previously taken; and, when an action in any court of this state, or the United States or of any state has been dismissed and another action involving the same subject matter is afterward brought between the same parties or their representatives or successors in interest, all depositions lawfully taken and duly filed in the former action may be used in the latter as if originally taken therefor.

C. Conflicts between this Article and Code of Evidence Article 804, regarding the use of depositions, shall be resolved by the court in its discretion.

Acts 1976, No. 574, § 1. Amended by Acts 1988, No. 515, § 2, eff. Jan. 1, 1989; Acts 1990, No. 134, § 1; Acts 1991, No. 304, § 1, eff. July 3, 1991; Acts 1992, No. 645, § 1; Acts 1999, No. 1263, § 1, eff. Jan. 1, 2000.

Comment—1988

(a) The introductory paragraph of this Article was amended by the enactment of the Code of Evidence to make specific reference to that Code. This change makes it clear that the admissibility of depositions is limited by the requirements of that Code.

(b) The former provisions of Paragraph (3) relating to use of depositions under certain specified circumstances, such as illness of the witness, death of the witness, etc., has been replaced with a general reference to unavailability so as to align this Article with the Code of Evidence. See Code of Evidence Art. 804.

(c) Former Subparagraph (3)(b), relating to the use of a deposition when the witness is over one hundred miles from the place of the trial or hearing, has been deleted. See now general rule on unavailability, Code of Evidence Art. 804.

Art. 1451. Objections to admissibility

Subject to the provisions of R.S. 13:3823 and Article 1455, objection may be made at the trial or hearing to receiving in evidence any deposition or part thereof for any reason which would require the exclusion of the evidence if the witness were then present and testifying.

Acts 1976, No. 574, § 1.

Art. 1452. Effect of taking or using depositions; deposing attorneys of record

A. A party does not make a person his own witness for any purpose by taking his deposition. The introduction in evidence of the deposition or any part thereof for any purpose other than that of contradicting or impeaching the deponent makes the deponent the witness of the party introducing the deposition, but this shall not apply to the use by an adverse party of a deposition as described in Article 1450(2). At the trial or hearing any party may rebut any relevant evidence contained in a deposition whether introduced by him or by any other party.

B. No attorney of record representing the plaintiff or the defendant shall be deposed except under extraordinary circumstances and then only by order of the district court after contradictory hearing.

Acts 1976, No. 574, § 1. Amended by Acts 1981, No. 767, § 1.

Art. 1453. Objection to irregularities in notice; waiver

All errors and irregularities in the notice for taking a deposition are waived unless written objection is promptly served upon the party giving the notice.

Acts 1976, No. 574, § 1.

Art. 1454. Objections as to disqualification of officer; waiver

An objection to taking a deposition because of disqualification of the officer before whom it is to be taken is waived unless made before the taking of the deposition begins or as soon thereafter as the disqualification becomes known or could be discovered with reasonable diligence.

Acts 1976, No. 574, § 1.

Art. 1455. Objections, competency of witnesses; relevancy of testimony; manner or form of taking deposition

Objections to the competency of a witness or to the competency, relevancy, or materiality of testimony are not waived by failure to make them before or during the taking of the deposition, unless the ground of the objection is one which might have been obviated or removed if presented at that time.

Objections to errors and irregularities occurring at the oral examination in the manner of taking the deposition, in the form of the questions or answers, in the oath or affirmation, or in the conduct of parties, and errors of any kind which might be obviated, removed, or cured if promptly presented, are waived unless seasonably made at the taking of the deposition.

Objections to the form of written questions submitted under Articles 1448 and 1449 are waived unless served in writing upon the party propounding them within the time allowed for serving the succeeding cross questions and within five days after service of the last questions authorized.

Acts 1976, No. 574, § 1.

Art. 1456. Objection as to completion and return of deposition

Errors and irregularities in the manner in which the testimony is transcribed or the deposition is prepared, signed, certified, sealed, endorsed, transmitted, filed, or otherwise dealt with by the officer under Articles 1437 through 1449 are waived unless a motion to suppress the deposition or some part thereof is made with reasonable promptness after such defect is, or with due diligence might have been, ascertained.

Acts 1976, No. 574, § 1.

Art. 1457. Interrogatories to parties; availability; additional, hearing required

A. Any party may serve upon any other party written interrogatories to be answered by the party served or, if the party served is a public or private corporation or a partnership or association or governmental agency, by any officer or agent, who shall furnish such information as is available to the party. Interrogatories may accompany the petition or be served after commencement of the action and without leave of court.

B. During an entire proceeding, written interrogatories served in accordance with Paragraph A shall not exceed thirty-five in number, including subparts, without leave of court. Additional interrogatories, not to exceed thirty-five in number including subparts, shall be allowed upon ex parte motion of any party. Thereafter, any party desiring to serve additional interrogatories shall file a written motion setting forth the proposed additional interrogatories and the reasons establishing good cause why they should be allowed to be filed. The court after contradictory hearing and for good cause shown may allow the requesting party to serve such additional interrogatories as the court deems appropriate. Local rules of court may provide a greater restriction on the number of written interrogatories.

Acts 1976, No. 574, § 1. Amended by Acts 1993, No. 416, § 1; Acts 1997, No. 1315, § 1.

Art. 1458. Interrogatories to parties; procedures for use

A. Each interrogatory shall be answered separately and fully in writing under oath, unless it is objected to, in which event the reasons for objection shall be stated in lieu of an answer. The written answer or reasons for objection to each interrogatory shall immediately follow a restatement of the interrogatory to which the answer or objection is responding. The answers are to be signed by the person making them. When interrogatories are served on a specific party, that party shall verify he has read and confirmed the answers and objections. The party upon whom the interrogatories have been served shall serve a copy of the answers, and objections if any, within thirty days after the service of the interrogatories, except as set forth in Paragraph B of this Article. The court may allow a shorter or longer time. The party submitting the interrogatories may move for an order under Article 1469 with respect to any objection to or other failure to answer an interrogatory.

B. The delay for serving a copy of the answers to interrogatories in family law cases, including divorce, custody, spousal and child support, community property, and matters incidental to family law proceedings, shall be fifteen days after service of the discovery, unless the interrogatories are served with an original petition, in which case the party who has been served shall have thirty days from the date of service to serve a copy of the answers to interrogatories.

Acts 1976, No. 574, § 1. Amended by Acts 1993, No. 416, § 1; Acts 2010, No. 682, § 1, eff. Jan. 1, 2011; Acts 2016, No. 132, § 1; Acts 2018, No. 135, § 1.

Art. 1459. Interrogatories to parties; scope; use at trial

Interrogatories may relate to any matters which can be inquired into under Articles 1422 through 1425, and the answers may be used at trial to the extent permitted by rules of evidence.

Acts 1976, No. 574, § 1.

Art. 1460. Option to produce business records

When the answer to an interrogatory may be derived or ascertained from the business records, including electronically stored information, of the party upon whom the interrogatory has been served or from an examination, audit, or inspection of such business records, including a compilation, abstract, or summary based thereon, and the burden of deriving or ascertaining the answer is substantially the same for the party serving the interrogatory as for the party served, it is a sufficient answer to such interrogatory to specify the records from which the answer may be derived or ascertained and to afford to the party serving the interrogatory reasonable opportunity to examine, audit, or inspect such records and to make copies, compilations, abstracts, or summaries. A specification shall be in sufficient detail to permit the interrogating party to locate and to identify, as readily as can the party served, the records from which the answer may be ascertained.

Acts 1976, No. 574, § 1. Amended by Acts 1982, No. 450, § 1; Acts 2007, No. 140, § 1.

Art. 1461. Production of documents and things; entry upon land; scope

Any party may serve on any other party a request (1) to produce and permit the party making the request, or someone acting on his behalf, to inspect, copy, test, and sample any designated documents or electronically stored information, including writings, drawings, graphs, charts, photographs, phono-records, sound recordings, images, and other data or data compilations in any medium from which information can be obtained, translated, if necessary, by the respondent through detection and other devices into reasonably usable form, or except as provided in Article 1462(E), to inspect and copy, test, or sample any tangible things which constitute or contain matters within the scope of Articles 1422 through 1425 and which are in the possession, custody, or control of the party upon whom the request is served; or (2) except as provided in Article 1462(E), to permit entry upon designated land or other property in the possession or control of the party upon whom the request is served for the purpose of inspection and measuring, surveying, photographing, testing, or sampling the property or any designated object or operation thereon, within the scope of Articles 1422 through 1425.

Acts 1976, No. 574, § 1. Amended by Acts 2007, No. 140, § 1.

Comments—2007

(a) Prior to their amendments, Articles 1461 and 1462 allowed requests for production of documents and other designated materials and direct access to inspect, test and sample any operations or tangible things in the control of the responding party which contained the requested information. The Articles were enacted in 1976 and made no reference to procedures for the discovery of the now widely used electronic storage of information on computers. The 2007 changes to Articles 1461 and 1462 make it clear that a requesting party may, within the scope of Articles 1422 through 1425, inspect and copy the product of a computer such as a printout of electronically stored information on paper or on a disc resulting from the translation of the stored information. This authorization does not require a responding party to produce electronically stored information from sources that are shown not to be reasonably accessible because of undue burden or cost. When the responding party presents a valid objection to production on this basis the court may consider production under more convenient and less burdensome conditions and with an allocation of the cost of production between the parties. See Article 1426(A) and Fed. R. Civ. P. 26(b)(2).

(b) Because direct access to a computer may present novel and difficult problems and risks for the responding party, including the burden of locating and segregating the requested information and protecting from disclosure proprietary, privileged, personal, or irrelevant material, the amended Articles do not give the requesting party the right initially to conduct the actual search of the responding party's computer.

(c) Article 1462(E) now permits direct access during discovery to computers and other types of the devices to inspect, copy, test, and sample the requested electronically stored information which such devices may contain only after the responding party has had an opportunity to search for and produce the information in a reasonably usable form. Absent an agreement between the parties, a requesting party, dissatisfied with an initial response, must successfully prosecute a motion to compel discovery under Article 1469 and obtain an order permitting direct access to the responding parties computer in the form of an inspection, copying, testing or sampling of its contents to determine if there has been a failure to comply with the discovery request. Such an order should be granted only when the requesting party has shown good cause that the initial production of electronically stored information for inspection and copying may not have been in compliance with an appropriate discovery request, and after alternative and less burdensome forms of production have been considered by the court. Furthermore, the order should provide for protections of the type set forth in Article 1426 as to the manner and scope of the search necessary to protect the responding party from an undue burden and disclosure of protected information. As stated in the Advisory Committee Notes to the 2006 amendments to Fed. R. Civ. P. 34(a), the parallel provision of the amended Article, "courts should guard against undue intrusiveness resulting from inspecting and testing" computer systems. See *In Re Ford Motor Co.*, 345 F.3d 1315 (11th Cir. 2003).

Art. 1462. Production of documents and things; entry upon land; procedure

A. The request under Article 1461 may, without leave of court, be served upon the plaintiff after commencement of the action and upon any other party with or after service of the petition upon that party. The request shall set forth the items to be inspected either by individual item or by category, and describe each item and category with reasonable particularity. The request shall specify a reasonable time, place, and manner of making the inspection and performing the related acts. The request may specify the form or forms in which information, including electronically stored information, is to be produced.

B. (1) The party upon whom the request is served shall serve a written response within thirty days after service of the request, except as set forth in Subparagraph (2) of this Paragraph. The court may allow a shorter or longer time. With respect to each item or category, the response shall state that inspection and related activities will be permitted as requested, unless the request is objected to, in which event the reasons for objection shall be stated. If objection is made to part of an item or category, the part shall be specified. The written answer or reasons for objection to each request for production of documents shall immediately follow a restatement of the request for production of documents to which the answer or objection is responding. The party submitting the request may move for an order under Article 1469 with respect to any objection to or other failure to respond to the request, or any part thereof, or any failure to permit inspection as requested. If objection is made to the requested form or forms for producing information, including electronically stored information, or if no form was specified in the request, the responding party shall state in its response the form or forms it intends to use.

(2) The delay for serving a copy of the responses to requests in family law cases, including divorce, custody, spousal and child support, community property, and matters incidental to family law proceedings, shall be fifteen days after service of the discovery, unless the request is served with an original petition, in which case the party who has been served shall have thirty days from the date of service to serve a copy of the answers to the request.

(3) A party need not provide discovery of electronically stored information from sources that the party identifies as not reasonably accessible because of undue burden or cost. On motion to compel discovery or for a protective order, the party from whom discovery is sought shall show that the information is not reasonably accessible because of undue burden or cost. If that showing is made, the court may nonetheless order discovery from such sources if the requesting party shows good cause. The court may specify conditions for the discovery considering the criteria and limitations of Article 1426.

C. A party who produces documents for inspection shall produce them as they are kept in the usual course of business or shall organize and label them to correspond with the categories of the request. If a request does not specify the form or forms for producing information, including electronically stored information, a responding party shall produce the information in a form or forms in which it is ordinarily maintained or in a form or forms that are reasonably usable. When electronically stored information is produced, the responding party shall identify the specific means for electronically accessing the information.

D. Unless otherwise ordered by the court, a party need not produce the same information, including electronically stored information, in more than one form.

E. If the requesting party considers that the production of designated electronically stored information is not in compliance with the request, the requesting party may move under Article 1469 for an order compelling discovery, and in addition to the other relief afforded by Article 1469, upon a showing of good cause by the requesting party, the court may order the responding party to afford access under specified conditions and scope to the requesting party, the representative of the requesting party, or the designee of the court to the computers or other types of devices used for the electronic storage of information to inspect, copy, test, and sample the designated electronically stored information within the scope of Articles 1422 and 1425.

Acts 1976, No. 574, § 1. Amended by Acts 1982, No. 451, § 1; Acts 2007, No. 140, § 1; Acts 2010, No. 185, § 1; Acts 2010, No. 682, § 1, eff. Jan. 1, 2011; Acts 2014, No. 655, § 1; Acts 2016, No. 132, § 1; Acts 2018, No. 135, § 1.

Comment—2010

(a) A new subparagraph modeled on FRCP 26(b)(2)(B) has been added to Paragraph B authorizing the trial court to weigh and, if appropriate, shift all or part of the cost or burden of producing electronically stored information to the requesting party when considering a motion to compel. A similar provision in Article 1354(F) applies to subpoenas duces tecum.

(b) To avoid the type of confusion illustrated in *Evangelist v. Dept. of Police*, 32 So. 3d 815, 2009 (La. App. 4 Cir.) a sentence has been added to Article 1462(C) requiring the responding party to identify the "means" (*e.g.*, the software program and hardware) which the receiving party must use to fully and accurately access the electronically stored information being produced.

Comment—2014

The 2014 amendment to Paragraph B extends the period for the state and its political subdivisions to respond to a request from fifteen days to thirty days so as to coincide with the period provided in Article 1458 for responses to interrogatories.

Art. 1463. Production of documents and things; entry upon land, persons not parties

A. Articles 1461 and 1462 do not preclude an independent action against a person not a party for production of documents and things and permission to enter upon land.

B. In addition, a party may have a subpoena duces tecum served on a person not a party directing that person to produce documents and things for inspection and copying or to permit entry onto and inspection of land, provided that a reasonably accurate description of the things to be produced, inspected, or copied is given. A reasonable notice of the intended inspection, specifying date, time, and place shall be served on all other parties and shall specify that the other parties may attend and participate in the inspection and copying of the things to be produced. The rules applicable to depositions and subpoenas duces tecum issued and served in connection with depositions shall apply except to the extent inconsistent with this Paragraph.

Acts 1976, No. 574, § 1. Amended by Acts 1995, No. 410, § 1.

Art. 1464. Order for an additional medical opinion for physical or mental examination of persons

A. When the mental or physical condition of a party, or of a person in the custody or under the legal control of a party, is in controversy, the court in which the action is pending may order the party to submit to an additional medical opinion regarding physical or mental examination by a physician or to produce for examination the person in his custody or legal control, except as provided by law. In addition, the court may order the party to submit to an additional medical opinion regarding an examination by a vocational rehabilitation expert or a licensed clinical psychologist who is not a physician, provided the party has given notice of intention to use such an expert. The order may be made only on motion for good cause shown and upon notice to the person to be examined and to all parties and shall specify the time, place, manner, conditions, and scope of the examination and the person or persons by whom it is to be made.

B. Regardless of the number of defendants, a plaintiff shall not be ordered to submit to multiple examinations by multiple physicians within the same field of specialty for the same injury except for good cause shown.

C. A minor subject to examination under the provisions of this Article shall have the right to have a parent, tutor, or legal guardian present during the examination. If such person cannot be present, the court shall order the examination to be videotaped at the expense of the party being examined. The court shall consider the best interests of the minor and may impose conditions upon videotaping, including that it be done in a manner least harmful to the minor and without disclosure to the minor.

Acts 1976, No. 574, § 1. Amended by Acts 1991, No. 324, § 1; Acts 1997, No. 1056, § 1; Acts 2017, No. 381, § 1, eff. June 23, 2017.

Comment—1997

The amendment expands the category of examiner to include a licensed clinical psychologist if the other party has given notice of an intent to use such an expert.

Art. 1465. Report of examining physician

A. If requested by the party against whom an order is made under Article 1464 or by the person examined, the party causing the examination to be made shall deliver to him a copy of a detailed written report of the examining physician setting out his findings, including results of all tests made, diagnoses, and conclusions, together with like reports of all earlier examinations of the same condition. After delivery the party causing the examination shall be entitled upon request to receive from the party against whom the order is made a like report of any examination, previously or thereafter made, of the same condition, unless, in the case of a report of examination of a person not a party, the party shows that he is unable to obtain it. The court on motion may make an order against a party requiring delivery of a report on such terms as are just, and if a physician fails or refuses to make a report the court may exclude his testimony if offered at the trial.

B. By requesting and obtaining a report of the examination so ordered or by taking the deposition of the examiner, the party examined waives any privilege he may have in that action or any other involving the same controversy, regarding the testimony of every other person who has examined or may thereafter examine him in respect of the same mental or physical condition.

C. This Article applies to examinations made by agreement of the parties, unless the agreement expressly provides otherwise. This Article does not preclude discovery of a report of an examining physician or the taking of a deposition of the physician in accordance with the provisions of any other rule.

Acts 1976, No. 574, § 1. Amended by Acts 1993, No. 619, § 1.

Art. 1465.1. Requests for release of medical records

A. Any party may serve upon the plaintiff or upon any other party whose medical records are relevant to an issue in the case a request that the plaintiff or other authorized person sign a medical records release authorizing the health care provider to release to the requesting party the medical records of the party whose medical condition is at issue. The release shall be directed to a specific health care provider, shall authorize the release of medical records only, and shall state that the release does not authorize verbal communications by the health care provider to the requesting party.

B. The party upon whom the request is served, within thirty days after service of the request, shall provide to the requesting party releases signed by the plaintiff or other authorized person unless the request is objected to, in which event the reasons for the objection shall be stated. The party requesting the release of medical records may move for an order under Article 1469 with respect to any objection or other failure to respond to the request.

C. The party requesting the medical records shall provide to the party whose medical records are being sought or to his attorney, if he is represented by an attorney, a copy of the request directed to the health care provider, which copy shall be provided contemporaneously with the request directed to the health care provider.

D. The party requesting the medical records shall provide to the party whose medical records are being sought or to his attorney, within seven days of receipt, a copy of all documents obtained by the requesting party pursuant to the release.

Added by Acts 1993, No. 823, § 1. Amended by Acts 2016, No. 132, § 1.

Art. 1466. Requests for admission; service of request

A party may serve upon any other party a written request for the admission, for purposes of the pending action only, of the truth of any matters within the scope of Articles 1422 through 1425 set forth in the request or of the truth of any relevant matters of fact, including the genuineness of any documents described in the request. Copies of documents shall be served with the request unless they have been or are otherwise furnished or made available for inspection and copying. The request may, without leave of court, be served upon the plaintiff after commencement of the action and upon any other party with or after service of the petition upon that party.

Acts 1976, No. 574, § 1.

Art. 1467. Requests for admission; answers and objections

A. Each matter of which an admission is requested shall be separately set forth. The matter is admitted unless, within thirty days after service of the request, or within such shorter or longer time as the court may allow, the party to whom the request is directed serves upon the party requesting the admission a written answer or objection addressed to the matter, signed by the party or by his attorney. The written answer or reasons for objection to each request for admission shall immediately follow a restatement of the request for admission to which the answer or objection is responding. If objection is made, the reasons therefor shall be stated. The answer shall specifically deny the matter or set forth in detail the reasons why the answering party cannot truthfully admit or deny the matter. A denial shall fairly meet the substance of the requested admission, and when good faith requires that a party qualify his answer or deny only a part of the matter of which an admission is requested, he shall specify so much of it as is true and qualify or deny the remainder. An answering party may not give lack of information or knowledge as a reason for failure to admit or deny unless he states that he has made reasonable inquiry and that the information known or readily obtainable by him is insufficient to enable him to admit or deny. A party who considers that a matter of which an admission has been requested presents a genuine issue for trial may not, on that ground alone, object to the request; he may, subject to the provisions of Article 1472, deny the matter or set forth reasons why he cannot admit or deny it.

B. The party who has requested the admissions may move to determine the sufficiency of the answers or objections. Unless the court determines that an objection is justified, it shall order that an answer be served. If the court determines that an answer does not comply with the requirements of this rule, it may order either that the matter is admitted or that an amended answer be served. The court may, in lieu of these orders, determine that final disposition of the request be made at a pretrial conference or at a designated time prior to trial. The provisions of Article 1469 apply to the award of expenses incurred in relation to the motion.

Acts 1976, No. 574, § 1. Amended by Acts 2010, No. 682, § 1, eff. Jan. 1, 2011; Acts 2016, No. 132, § 1.

Art. 1468. Requests for admissions; effect of admission

Any matter admitted under this rule is conclusively established unless the court on motion permits withdrawal or amendment of the admission. Subject to the provisions of Article 1551 governing amendment of a pretrial order, the court may permit withdrawal or amendment when the presentation of the merits of the action will be subserved thereby and the party who obtained the admission fails to satisfy the court that withdrawal or amendment will prejudice him in maintaining his action or defense on the merits. Any admission made by a party under Articles 1466 and 1467 is for the purpose of the pending action only and is not an admission by him for any other purpose nor may it be used against him in any other proceeding.

Acts 1976, No. 574, § 1.

Art. 1469. Motion for order compelling discovery

A party, upon reasonable notice to other parties and all persons affected thereby, may apply for an order compelling discovery as follows:

(1) An application for an order to a party or a deponent who is not a party may be made to the court in which the action is pending.

(2) If a deponent fails to answer a question propounded or submitted under Articles 1437 or 1448, or a corporation or other entity fails to make a designation under Articles 1442 or 1448, or a party fails to answer an interrogatory submitted under Article 1457, or if a party, in response to a request for inspection submitted under Article 1461, fails to respond that inspection will be permitted as requested or fails to permit inspection as requested, the discovering party may move for an order compelling an answer, or a designation, or an order compelling inspection in accordance with the request. When taking a deposition on oral examination, the proponent of the question may complete or adjourn the examination before he applies for an order.

If the court denies the motion in whole or in part, it may make such protective order as it would have been empowered to make on a motion made pursuant to Article 1426.

(3) For purposes of this Subdivision an evasive or incomplete answer is to be treated as a failure to answer.

(4) If the motion is granted, the court shall, after opportunity for hearing, require the party or deponent whose conduct necessitated the motion or the party or attorney advising such conduct or both of them to pay to the moving party the reasonable expenses incurred in obtaining the order, including attorney's fees, unless the court finds that the opposition to the motion was substantially justified or that other circumstances make an award of expenses unjust.

If the motion is denied, the court shall, after opportunity for hearing, require the moving party or the attorney advising the motion or both of them to pay to the party or deponent who opposed the motion the reasonable expenses incurred in opposing the motion, including attorney's fees, unless the court finds that the making of the motion was substantially justified or that other circumstances make an award of expenses unjust.

If the motion is granted in part and denied in part, the court may apportion the reasonable expenses incurred in relation to the motion among the parties and persons in a just manner.

(5) An application for an order compelling discovery to a member or former member of the legislature in his capacity as a state lawmaker, or a legislative employee in his official capacity, when the legislature or either body thereof is not a party to the proceeding may be made to the court in which the action is pending, but no order compelling discovery shall issue except in strict conformity with the provisions of R.S. 13:3667.3(C). For purposes of this Article "legislative employee" means the clerk of the House of Representatives, the secretary of the Senate, or an employee of the House of Representatives, the Senate, or the Legislative Bureau.

Acts 1976, No. 574, § 1. Amended by Acts 2006, No. 690, § 1, eff. June 29, 2006; Acts 2008, No. 374, § 1, eff. June 21, 2008; Acts 2012, No. 519, § 1.

Editor's Notes

Office Furniture Outlet, Inc., v. Grau, 12 So.3d 1065 (La. App. 2 Cir. 2009). Defendant was sanctioned for $32,000 in attorney's fees for repeated failures to comply with motions to compel discovery. The sanctions for failure to comply were rendered under C.C.P. art. 1469(4). The partial judgment is appealable under C.C.P. art. 863 and 1915(A)(6).

Art. 1469.1. Order compelling discovery of medical records

No order, subpoena, or subpoena duces tecum for the purpose of obtaining or compelling the production or inspection of medical, hospital, or other records relating to a person's medical treatment, history, or condition, including a subpoena or order issued under Article 1463 and including a subpoena compelling the attendance of the custodian of records or other employee of the health care provider, either by name, title, or position, in connection with such production, shall be granted or issued except as provided in R.S. 13:3715.1.

Added by Acts 1986, No. 1046, § 1. Amended by Acts 1988, No. 980, § 1; Acts 1995, No. 1250, § 1.

Art. 1469.2. Order compelling discovery of financial records; notice

An order or subpoena duces tecum compelling the production of records of a bank, a savings and loan association, a company issuing credit cards, or a business offering credit relating to the financial or credit information of its customers, whether pursuant to Articles 1421 through 1474, Articles 2451, et seq., or otherwise, shall not be enforceable, unless the person seeking production of such records has complied with the provisions of R.S. 9:3571 or R.S. 6:333, as applicable, requiring that a copy of the subpoena or order also be served on the person whose records are being sought.

Added by Acts 1989, No. 157, § 2; Acts 1989, No. 779, § 3, eff. July 9, 1989. Amended by Acts 1990, No. 1000, § 1.

Art. 1470. Failure to comply with order compelling discovery; contempt

If a party or other witness refuses to be sworn or refuses to answer any question after being directed to do so by the court in which the action is pending or in which the judgment was originally rendered, the refusal shall be considered a contempt of the court of the parish where the deposition is being taken.

Acts 1976, No. 574, § 1.

Art. 1471. Failure to comply with order compelling discovery; sanctions

A. If a party or an officer, director, or managing agent of a party or a person designated under Article 1442 or 1448 to testify on behalf of a party fails to obey an order to provide or permit discovery, including an order made under Article 1464 or 1469, the court in which the action is pending may make such orders in regard to the failure as are just, including any of the following:

(1) An order that the matters regarding which the order was made or any other designated facts shall be taken to be established for the purposes of the action in accordance with the claim of the party obtaining the order.

(2) An order refusing to allow the disobedient party to support or oppose designated claims or defenses, or prohibiting him from introducing designated matters in evidence.

(3) An order striking out pleadings or parts thereof, or staying further proceedings until the order is obeyed, or dismissing the action or proceeding or any part thereof, or rendering a default judgment against the disobedient party upon presentation of proof as required by Article 1702.

(4) In lieu of any of the foregoing orders or in addition thereto, an order treating as a contempt of court the failure to obey any orders except an order to submit to a physical or mental examination.

(5) Where a party has failed to comply with an order under Article 1464, requiring him to produce another for examination, such orders as are listed in Subparagraphs (1), (2), and (3) of this

Paragraph, unless the party failing to comply shows that he is unable to produce such person for examination.

B. Absent exceptional circumstances, a court may not impose sanctions under this Article on a person or party for failing to provide electronically stored information lost as a result of the routine. good-faith operation of an electronic information system.

C. In lieu of any of the foregoing orders or in addition thereto, the court shall require the party failing to obey the order or the attorney advising him or both to pay the reasonable expenses, including attorney fees, caused by the failure, unless the court finds that the failure was substantially justified or that other circumstances make an award of expenses unjust.

Acts 1976, No. 574, § 1. Amended by Acts 2008, No. 824, § 3, eff. Jan. 1, 2009; Acts 2018, No. 195, § 1; Acts 2021, No. 174, § 1, eff. Jan. 1, 2022.

Editor's Notes

Lane v. Kennan, 901 So.2d 630 (La. App. 4 Cir. 2005). Trial court's dismissal with prejudice of plaintiff's suit for failure to comply with discovery was amended to dismissal without prejudice, considering as mitigating circumstances plaintiff's residence in another state and the absence of proof in the record that plaintiff had received actual notice of the various discovery procedures. (Two vigorous dissents from the mitigation).

Art. 1472. Failure to admit; expenses

If a party fails to admit the genuineness of any document or the truth of any matter as requested under Article 1466, and if the party requesting the admissions thereafter proves the genuineness of the document or the truth of the matter, he may apply to the court for an order requiring the other party to pay him the reasonable expenses incurred in making that proof, including reasonable attorney's fees. The court shall make the order unless it finds that the request was held objectionable pursuant to Article 1467, or the admission sought was of no substantial importance, or the party failing to admit had reasonable ground to believe that he might prevail on the matter, or there was other good reason for the failure to admit.

Acts 1976, No. 574, § 1.

Art. 1473. Failure to attend deposition, serve answers or respond to request for inspection

If a party or an officer, director, or managing agent of a party or a person designated under Articles 1442 or 1448 to testify on behalf of a party fails to appear before the officer who is to take his deposition, after being served with a proper notice, or to serve answers or objections to interrogatories submitted under Article 1457, after proper service of the interrogatories, or to serve a written response to a request for inspection submitted under Article 1461, after proper service of the request, the court in which the action is pending on motion may make such orders in regard to the failure as are just, and among others it may take any action authorized under Paragraphs (1), (2), and (3) of Article 1471. In lieu of any order or in addition thereto, the court shall require the party failing to act or the attorney advising him or both to pay the reasonable expenses, including attorney's fees, caused by the failure, unless the court finds that the failure was substantially justified or that other circumstances make an award of expenses unjust.

The failure to act described in this Article may not be excused on the ground that the discovery sought is objectionable unless the party failing to act has applied for a protective order as provided by Article 1426.

Acts 1976, No. 574, § 1.

Art. 1474. Service of written objections, notices, requests, affidavits, interrogatories, and answers thereto

A. Except as otherwise provided by Article 1430, all of the objections, notices, requests, affidavits, interrogatories, and answers to interrogatories, required by any Article in this Chapter to be in writing and served on an adverse party, may be served as provided in Article 1313.

B. Interrogatories and the answers thereto, requests for production or inspection, and requests for admissions and the responses thereto authorized by Article 1421 shall be served upon other counsel or parties, but shall not be filed in the record of the proceedings, unless filing is required under the provisions of Paragraph C of this Article or unless ordered to be filed by the court. The failure or lack of filing such items shall not affect the use or admissibility at trial or by the court if otherwise authorized or provided by law. The party responsible for service of the discovery materials shall retain the original and become the custodian of such materials.

C. (1) If relief is sought under Article 1467 or 1469 with regard to any interrogatories, requests for production or inspection, requests for admissions, answers to interrogatories, or responses to requests for admissions, copies of the portions of the interrogatories, requests, answers, or responses in dispute shall be filed with the court contemporaneously with any motion filed under such Articles.

(2) If interrogatories, requests, answers, or responses are to be used at trial or are necessary to a pretrial motion which might result in a final order on any issue, the portions to be used shall be filed in the proceedings at the outset of the trial or at the filing of the motion insofar as their use can be reasonably anticipated.

(3) When documentation of discovery not previously in the record is needed for appeal purposes, upon an application and order of the court, or by stipulation of counsel, the necessary discovery materials shall be filed in the proceedings.

(4) The serving of any discovery materials pursuant to the provisions of this Article shall be considered a step in the prosecution or defense of an action for purposes of Article 561, notwithstanding that such discovery materials are not filed in the record of the proceedings.

D. The provisions of this Article shall not be construed to preclude the filing of any discovery materials as exhibits or as evidence in connection with a motion or at trial.

Acts 1976, No. 574, § 1. Amended by Acts 1989, No. 388, § 1, eff. June 30, 1989.

Art. 1475. Affidavit for medical cost; counter affidavit; service

A. (1) Unless a controverting affidavit is filed as provided for in this Article, an affidavit establishing medical services and costs shall be sufficient evidence to support a finding of fact by a judge or jury that the bill is authentic.

(2) The affidavit shall be made either by the person who provided the medical service or by the official custodian in charge of the medical records. The affidavit shall be accompanied by an itemized statement which shall set forth with specificity the medical service provided and the corresponding charge.

(3) The party submitting the affidavit in evidence shall file the affidavit with the clerk of court and serve a copy of the affidavit on other parties and all persons affected thereby at least thirty days before the trial.

B. (1) Any party intending to contravene the affidavit shall file a counter affidavit with the clerk of court and serve a copy of the counter affidavit on the other party or party's attorney of record not later than fifteen days after receipt of a copy of the affidavit and at least ten days before the trial or at any time before the trial with leave of court.

(2) The counter affidavit shall establish a reasonable basis on which the party intends to controvert the claim set forth in the initial affidavit and shall be made by a person who is qualified either by knowledge, skill, experience, training, or education, to testify in contravention of all or part of any matters contained in the initial affidavit.

C. If a counter affidavit is filed, and after opportunity for hearing, a party who fails to establish to the court's satisfaction that the medical statements are not authentic shall be required to pay to the initial affiant all costs and expenses incurred as a result of the hearing. The court may waive assessment of costs and expenses if it finds that the counter affidavit was substantially justified or that other circumstances make an award of expenses unjust.

Added by Acts 1997, No. 72, § 1.

Editor's Notes

This article was enacted by 1997 legislation.

Arts. 1476 to 1490. [Blank]

Arts. 1491 to 1496. [Blank]

Arts. 1497 to 1510. [Blank]

Arts. 1511 to 1515. [Blank]

Arts. 1516 to 1550. [Reserved]

TITLE IV. PRE-TRIAL PROCEDURE

Art. 1551. Pretrial and scheduling conference; order

A. In any civil action in a district court the court may in its discretion direct the attorneys for the parties to appear before it for conferences to consider any of the following:

(1) The simplification of the issues, including the elimination of frivolous claims or defenses.

(2) The necessity or desirability of amendments to the pleadings.

(3) What material facts and issues exist without substantial controversy, and what material facts and issues are actually and in good faith controverted.

(4) Proof, stipulations regarding the authenticity of documents, and advance rulings from the court on the admissibility of evidence.

(5) Limitations or restrictions on or regulation of the use of expert testimony under Louisiana Code of Evidence Article 702.

(6) The control and scheduling of discovery including any issues relating to disclosure or discovery of electronically stored information, and the form or forms in which it should be produced.

(7) Any issues relating to claims of privilege or protection of trial preparation material, and whether the court should include agreements between counsel relating to such issues in an order.

(8) The identification of witnesses, documents, and exhibits.

(9) The presentation of testimony or other evidence by electronic devices.

(10) Such other matters as may aid in the disposition of the action.

B. The court shall render an order which recites the action taken at the conference, the amendments allowed to the pleadings, and the agreements made by the parties as to any of the matters considered, and which limits the issues for trial to those not disposed of by admissions or agreements of counsel. Such order controls the subsequent course of the action, unless modified at the trial to prevent manifest injustice.

C. If a party's attorney fails to obey a pretrial order, or to appear at the pretrial and scheduling conference, or is substantially unprepared to participate in the conference or fails to participate in good faith, the court, on its own motion or on the motion of a party, after hearing, may make such orders as are just, including orders provided in Article 1471 (2), (3), and (4). In lieu of or in addition to any other sanction, the court may require the party or the attorney representing the party or both to pay the reasonable expenses incurred by noncompliance with this Paragraph, including attorney fees.

D. If a suit has been pending for more than one year since the date of filing of the original petition and no trial date has been assigned, upon motion of any party, the court shall set the matter for conference for the purpose of resolving all matters subject to the provisions of this Article, including the scheduling of discovery, assignment for trial, and any other matters that will expedite the resolution of the suit. The conference may be conducted in chambers, by telephone, or by video teleconference.

Amended by Acts 1997, No. 1056, § 1; Acts 2008, No. 824, § 3, eff. Jan. 1, 2009; Acts 2018, No. 254, § 1.

Comment—1997

This amendment strengthens the authority of the trial court at the pretrial conference, and provides a more useful procedure for preparing the case for trial. It allows the court to impose sanctions on an attorney who is unprepared or fails to participate in good faith.

Caveat: See Rule 9.14, Fixing for Trial or Hearing; Scheduling Orders; Contact with Jurors, District Court Rules, for additional regulations for fixing for trial or hearing.

Editor's Notes

Eanes v. McKnight, 265 So.2d 220 (1972), pretrial generally; also, see Vernon v. Wade Correctional Institute, App. 2 Cir.1994, 642 So.2d 684.

See the "Comment—1997". This article is substantially revised.

Art. 1552. Environmental management orders

Upon the request of any party in any civil action alleging environmental damage pursuant to R.S. 30:29, or the Department of Natural Resources, office of conservation, the court shall direct the attorneys for the parties to appear before the court to develop an environmental management order. The environmental management order shall authorize all parties to access the property allegedly impacted to perform inspections and environmental testing. The order shall require that all test results be submitted to all parties and the Department of Natural Resources, office of conservation, within thirty days of receipt thereof. Failure by a party to provide the results of testing to the other parties shall preclude that party from admitting those results into evidence in the civil action. The environmental management order shall include reasonable terms for all of the following:

(1) Access to the property.

(2) Investigation and environmental testing.

(3) Sampling and testing protocols.

(4) Specific time frames within which to conduct such testing and sampling.

Added by Acts 2012, No. 754, § 1.

TITLE V. TRIAL

CHAPTER 1. CONSOLIDATION OF CASES AND SEPARATE TRIALS OF ISSUES OF LIABILITY AND DAMAGES

Art. 1561. Consolidation for trial or other limited purposes

A. When two or more separate actions are pending in the same court, the section or division of the court in which the first filed action is pending may order consolidation of the actions for trial or other limited purposes after a contradictory hearing, upon a finding that common issues of fact and law predominate, and, in the event a trial date has been set in a subsequently filed action, upon a finding that consolidation is in the interest of justice. The contradictory hearing may be waived upon the certification by the mover that all parties in all cases to be consolidated consent to the consolidation.

B. Consolidation shall not be ordered if it would do any of the following:

(1) Cause jury confusion.

(2) Prevent a fair and impartial trial.

(3) Give one party an undue advantage.

(4) Prejudice the rights of any party.

Amended by Acts 1997, No. 968, § 1; Acts 2008, No. 824, § 4, eff. Jan. 1, 2009; Acts 2012, No. 194, § 1; Acts 2021, No. 259, § 2.

Art. 1562. Separate trials of issues of insurance coverage, liability, and damages

A. If it would simplify the proceedings or would permit a more orderly disposition of the case or otherwise would be in the interest of justice, at any time prior to trial the court may order, with the consent of all parties, separate trials on the issues of liability and damages, whether or not there is to be a jury trial on either issue.

B. If a defendant has been found liable by a jury, the court shall proceed with the trial on the remaining issues before the same jury unless all parties consent to a trial before a different jury.

C. Notwithstanding the provisions of Paragraph B of this Article, in a jury trial, the court may order, with the consent of all the parties, that a separate trial on the issue of damages shall precede a trial on the issue of liability.

D. If it would simplify the proceedings or would permit a more orderly disposition of the case or otherwise would be in the interest of justice, at any time prior to trial on the merits, the court may order, with the consent of all parties, a separate trial on the issue of insurance coverage, unless a factual dispute that is material to the insurance coverage issue duplicates an issue relative to liability or damages. The issue of insurance coverage shall be decided by the court alone, whether or not there is to be a jury trial on the issue of liability or damages.

Added by Acts 1983, No. 534, § 2. Amended by Acts 1985, No. 289, § 1, eff. July 8, 1985; Acts 1992, No. 72, § 1.

Art. 1563. Limited admission of liability in environmental damage lawsuits; effect

A. (1) If any party admits liability for environmental damage pursuant to R.S. 30:29, that party may elect to limit this admission of liability for environmental damage to responsibility for implementing the most feasible plan to evaluate, and if necessary, remediate all or a portion of the contamination that is the subject of the litigation to applicable regulatory standards, hereinafter referred to as a "limited admission". A limited admission shall not be construed as an admission of liability for damages under R.S. 30:29(H), nor shall a limited admission result in a waiver of any rights or defenses of the admitting party.

(2) Upon the expiration of the delay in which a party may file a limited admission under Subparagraph (5) of this Paragraph, and if one or more of the defendants have made a timely limited admission, the court shall refer the matter to the Department of Natural Resources, office of conservation, hereinafter referred to as the "department", to conduct a public hearing to approve or structure a plan which the department determines to be the most feasible plan to evaluate or remediate the environmental damage under the applicable regulatory standards pursuant to the provisions of R.S. 30:29. There shall be a rebuttable presumption that the plan approved or structured by the department, after consultation with the Department of Environmental Quality as appropriate, shall be the most feasible plan to evaluate or remediate the environmental damage under the applicable regulatory standards pursuant to the provisions of R.S. 30:29. For cases tried by a jury, the court shall instruct the jury regarding this presumption if requested by a party.

(3) The limited admission, the plan approved by the department, and all written comments provided by the agencies pursuant to R.S. 30:29(C)(3)(b) shall be admissible subject to the Code of Evidence Articles 702 through 705 and Code of Civil Procedure Article 1425 as evidence in any action.

(4) At any time after the filing of a civil action subject to the provisions of R.S. 30:29 and, absent good cause shown, no later than ninety days after the completion of the environmental testing set forth in the environmental management order issued by the court pursuant to the Code of Civil Procedure Article 1552, any party may make a limited admission by filing the same into the record of the court proceeding.

(5) Any other party who intends to make a limited admission for the same or any other environmental damage shall file it into the record of the court proceeding within sixty days of the filing of the first limited admission by another party. Any limited admission filed by another party after the first limited admission is filed shall be filed no later than ninety days following the completion of the environmental testing set forth in the environmental management order.

(6) The party making a limited admission shall be required to deposit with the department sufficient funds to cover the cost of the department's review of the plans or submittals under R.S. 30:29, including the cost of holding a public hearing to approve or structure the feasible plan. The initial payment of these costs shall be in an amount of one hundred thousand dollars. This initial payment shall be deposited prior to or along with the submission of the plan by the admitting party. The admitting party shall be entitled to reimbursement of any portion of the deposit that is unused by the department. Within thirty days of the department's filing of the plan, the party admitting

responsibility for implementing the most feasible plan shall reimburse the plaintiff for those costs which the court determines to be recoverable under R.S. 30:29(E)(1).

B. The provisions of this Article shall not establish primary jurisdiction with the Department of Natural Resources.

Added by Acts 2012, No. 754, § 1. Amended by Acts 2014, No. 400, § 2.

CHAPTER 2. ASSIGNMENT OF CASES FOR TRIAL

Article

Art. 1571. Assignment by court rule

A. (1) The district courts shall prescribe the procedure for assigning cases for trial, by rules which shall:

(a) Require adequate notice of trial to all parties; and

(b) Prescribe the order of preference in accordance with law.

(2) These rules shall not allow the assignment of ordinary proceedings for trial except after answer filed.

B. A party who appears in proper person before the court shall advise the court of his current address and any change of address during the pendency of the proceedings. The address and change of address shall be entered in the record of the proceedings. The failure of a party to provide such information does not affect the validity of any judgment rendered if notice of trial or other matters was sent to the party's last known address of record.

Amended by Acts 1989, No. 284, § 1.

Editor's Notes

Watson v. Lane Memorial Hospital, 743 So.2d 676 (La. 1999), a medical malpractice plaintiff may not file a petition to get a case number for conducting discovery and then use the same docket (and division of court) for the suit itself, which must be randomly alloted as a new suit.

Caveat: See Rule 9.14, Fixing for Trial or Hearing; Scheduling Orders; Contact with Jurors, District Court Rules, for additional regulations for fixing for trial or hearing.

Art. 1572. Written request for notice of trial

The clerk shall give written notice of the date of the trial whenever a written request therefor is filed in the record or is made by registered mail by a party or counsel of record. This notice shall be mailed by the clerk, by certified mail, properly stamped and addressed, at least ten days before the date fixed for the trial. The provisions of this article may be waived by all counsel of record at a pre-trial conference.

Amended by Acts 1980, No. 460, § 1.

Art. 1573. Assignment of trials; preference; terminally ill

The court shall give preference in scheduling upon the motion of any party to the action who presents to the court documentation to establish that the party has reached the age of seventy years or who presents to the court medical documentation that the party suffers from an illness or condition because of which he is not likely to survive beyond six months, if the court finds that the interests of justice will be served by granting such preference.

Added by Acts 1990, No. 106, § 1.

CHAPTER 3. CONTINUANCE

Article

Art. 1601. Discretionary grounds

A continuance may be granted in any case if there is good ground therefor.

Art. 1602. Peremptory grounds

A continuance shall be granted if at the time a case is to be tried, the party applying for the continuance shows that he has been unable, with the exercise of due diligence, to obtain evidence material to his case; or that a material witness has absented himself without the contrivance of the party applying for the continuance.

Amended by Acts 1966, No. 186, § 1.

Art. 1603. Motion for continuance

A motion for a continuance shall set forth the grounds upon which it is based, and if in writing shall comply with the provisions of Article 863.

Art. 1604. Prevention of continuance by admission of adverse party

When a party applies for a continuance on account of the absence of a material witness, the adverse party may require him to disclose on oath what facts he intends to prove by such witness, and if the adverse party admits that if the witness were present he would testify as stated in the affidavit, the court shall proceed to the trial of the case.

Art. 1605. Trial of motion; order

Every contested motion for a continuance shall be tried summarily and contradictorily with the opposite party.

CHAPTER 4. TRIAL PROCEDURE

Article

Art. 1631. Power of court over proceedings; exclusion of witnesses; mistrial

A. The court has the power to require that the proceedings shall be conducted with dignity and in an orderly and expeditious manner, and to control the proceedings at the trial, so that justice is done.

B. The exclusion of witnesses is governed by Louisiana Code of Evidence Article 615.

C. The court on its own motion, or on the motion of any party, after hearing, may grant a mistrial.

Amended by Acts 1966, No. 36, § 1; Acts 1988, No. 515, § 2, eff. Jan. 1, 1989; Acts 1995, No. 411, § 1.

Comment—1988

The second paragraph of this Article, providing for the exclusion of witnesses from the courtroom upon motion or in the interest of justice, has been replaced by Code of Evidence Article 615.

Art. 1632. Order of trial

The normal order of trial shall be as follows:

(1) The opening statements by the plaintiff and the defendant, in that order;

(2) The presentation of the evidence of the plaintiff and of the defendant, in that order;

(3) The presentation of the evidence of the plaintiff in rebuttal; and

(4) The argument of the plaintiff, of the defendant, and of the plaintiff in rebuttal, in that order.

This order may be varied by the court when circumstances so justify.

When an action involves parties in addition to the plaintiff and the defendant, the court shall determine the order of trial as to them and the plaintiff and the defendant.

Art. 1633. Oath or affirmation of witnesses; refusal to testify

A. Before testifying, every witness shall be required to declare that he will testify truthfully, by oath or affirmation administered in a form calculated to awaken his conscience and impress his mind with his duty to do so.

B. A witness who appears but refuses to testify without proper cause shall be considered in contempt of court.

Amended by Acts 1988, No. 515, § 2, eff. Jan. 1, 1989.

Comment—1988

This Article was amended to conform to the Code of Evidence, with retention of the provision for contempt for failure to testify. See Code of Evidence Art. 603 and comments thereunder.

Art. 1633.1. Live trial testimony by video

The court may order, upon a showing of appropriate safeguards, live testimony of a witness to be presented in open court by teleconference, video link, or other visual remote technology, if the witness is beyond the subpoena power of the court or when compelling circumstances are shown. The order may be entered at a pretrial conference or, in exceptional circumstances, on motion set for hearing at least ten days prior to trial or at another time that does not prejudice the parties.

Added by Acts 2007, No. 140, § 1.

Art. 1634. Cross-examination of a party or person identified with a party

A party or a person identified with a party may be called as a witness and examined by the adverse party in accordance with Louisiana Code of Evidence Articles 607 and 611.

Amended by Acts 1970, No. 406, § 1; Acts 1988, No. 515, § 2, eff. Jan. 1, 1989.

Comment—1988

The former provisions of this Article on cross-examination have been replaced by the Code of Evidence. The cross-reference to the pertinent articles of that Code is an aid to the practitioner.

Art. 1635. Exceptions unnecessary

Formal exceptions to rulings or orders of the court are unnecessary. For all purposes it is sufficient that a party, at the time the ruling or order of the court is made or sought, makes known to the court the action which he desires the court to take or his objection to the action of the court and his grounds therefor; and, if a party has no opportunity to object to a ruling or order at the time it is made, the absence of an objection does not thereafter prejudice him.

Art. 1636. Evidence held inadmissible; record or statement as to nature thereof

A. When the court rules against the admissibility of any evidence, it shall either permit the party offering such evidence to make a complete record thereof, or permit the party to make a statement setting forth the nature of the evidence.

B. At the request of any party, the court may allow any excluded evidence to be offered, subject to cross-examination: on the record during a recess or such other time as the court shall designate; or by deposition taken before a person authorized by Article 1434 within thirty days subsequent to the exclusion of any such evidence or the completion of the trial or hearing, whichever is later. When the record is completed during a recess or other designated time, or by deposition, there will be no necessity for the requesting party to make a statement setting forth the nature of the evidence.

C. In all cases, the court shall state the reason for its ruling as to the inadmissibility of the evidence. This ruling shall be reviewable on appeal without the necessity of further formality.

D. If the court permits a party to make a complete record of the evidence held inadmissible, it shall allow any other party the opportunity to make a record in the same manner of any evidence bearing upon the evidence held to be inadmissible.

Amended by Acts 1993, No. 985, § 1.

Art. 1637. Completion of trial; pronouncement of judgment

After the trial is completed, the court may immediately pronounce judgment or take the case under advisement.

CHAPTER 5. DISMISSAL

Art. 1671. Voluntary dismissal

A judgment dismissing an action without prejudice shall be rendered upon application of the plaintiff and upon his payment of all costs, if the application is made prior to any appearance of record by the defendant. If the application is made after such appearance, the court may refuse to grant the judgment of dismissal except with prejudice.

Amended by Acts 1997, No. 578, § 1.

Comment—1997

For comments regarding the repeal of general appearance, see the 1997 Comment to Article 6 of the Code of Civil Procedure. Appearance of record includes filing a pleading, appearing at a hearing, and formally enrolling as counsel of record.

Art. 1672. Involuntary dismissal

A. (1) A judgment dismissing an action shall be rendered upon application of any party, when the plaintiff fails to appear on the day set for trial. In such case, the court shall determine whether the judgment of dismissal shall be with or without prejudice.

(2) The court, on its own motion, may dismiss an action without prejudice when all the parties thereto fail to appear on the day set for trial; however, when a case has been dismissed pursuant to this provision and it is claimed that there is a pending settlement, either party may reinstate the suit within sixty days of receipt of the notice of dismissal, and any cause of action which had not prescribed when the case was originally filed shall be fully reinstated as though the case had never been dismissed.

B. In an action tried by the court without a jury, after the plaintiff has completed the presentation of his evidence, any party, without waiving his right to offer evidence in the event the motion is not granted, may move for a dismissal of the action as to him on the ground that upon the facts and law, the plaintiff has shown no right to relief. The court may then determine the facts and render judgment against the plaintiff and in favor of the moving party or may decline to render any judgment until the close of all the evidence.

C. A judgment dismissing an action without prejudice shall be rendered as to a person named as a defendant for whom service has not been requested within the time prescribed by Article 1201(C) or 3955 upon the sustaining of a declinatory exception filed by such defendant, or upon contradictory motion of any other party, unless good cause is shown why service could not be requested, in which case the court may order that service be effected within a specified time.

Amended by Acts 1983, No. 534, § 9; Acts 1997, No. 518, § 2, eff. Jan. 1, 1998; Acts 1997, No. 1058, § 1; Acts 2006, No. 750, § 1; Acts 2010, No. 407, § 1.

Comment—1983

Paragraph B of former Art. 1810 did not belong in the section dealing with jury trials and was transferred to Art. 1672 by Acts 1983 No. 534.

Art. 1673. Effect of dismissal with or without prejudice

A judgment of dismissal with prejudice shall have the effect of a final judgment of absolute dismissal after trial. A judgment of dismissal without prejudice shall not constitute a bar to another suit on the same cause of action.

Editor's Notes

The term "final" refers to C.C.P. art. 1841.

CHAPTER 6. DEFAULT

Article

Art. 1701. Repealed by Acts 2021, No. 174, § 6, eff. Jan. 1, 2022

Art. 1702. Default judgment

A. (1) If a defendant in the principal or incidental demand fails to answer or file other pleadings within the time prescribed by law or by the court, and the plaintiff establishes a prima facie case by competent and admissible evidence that is admitted on the record, a default judgment in favor of the plaintiff may be rendered, provided that notice that the plaintiff intends to obtain a default judgment is sent if required by this Paragraph, unless such notice is waived. The court may permit documentary evidence to be filed in the record in any electronically stored format authorized by the local rules of the district court or approved by the clerk of the district court for receipt of evidence.

(2) If a party who fails to answer has made an appearance of record in the case, notice that the plaintiff intends to obtain a default judgment shall be sent by certified mail to counsel of record for the party, or if there is no counsel of record, to the party, at least seven days before a default judgment may be rendered.

(3) If an attorney for a party who fails to answer has contacted the plaintiff or the plaintiff's attorney in writing concerning the action after it has been filed, notice that the plaintiff intends to obtain a default judgment shall be sent by certified mail to the party's attorney at least seven days before a default judgment may be rendered.

(4) In cases involving delictual actions where neither Subparagraph (2) or (3) of this Paragraph applies, notice that the plaintiff intends to obtain a default judgment shall be sent by regular mail to the party who fails to answer at the address where service was obtained at least seven days before a default judgment may be rendered.

B. (1) When a demand is based upon a conventional obligation, affidavits and exhibits annexed thereto that contain facts sufficient to establish a prima facie case shall be admissible, self-authenticating, and sufficient proof of such demand. The court may, under the circumstances of the case, require additional evidence in the form of oral testimony before entering a default judgment.

(2) When a demand is based upon a delictual obligation, the testimony of the plaintiff with corroborating evidence, which may be by affidavits and exhibits annexed thereto containing facts sufficient to establish a prima facie case, shall be admissible, self-authenticating, and sufficient proof of such demand. The court may, under the circumstances of the case, require additional evidence in the form of oral testimony before entering a default judgment.

(3) When the sum due is on an open account or a promissory note or other negotiable instrument, an affidavit of the correctness thereof shall be prima facie proof. When the demand is based upon a promissory note or other negotiable instrument, no proof of any signature thereon shall be required.

C. In those proceedings in which the sum due is on an open account or a promissory note, other negotiable instrument, or other conventional obligation, or a deficiency judgment derived therefrom, including those proceedings in which one or more mortgages, pledges, or other security for the open account, promissory note, negotiable instrument, conventional obligation, or deficiency judgment derived therefrom is sought to be enforced, maintained, or recognized, or in which the amount sought is that authorized by R.S. 9:2782 for a check dishonored for nonsufficient funds, a hearing in open court shall not be required unless the judge, in his discretion, directs that such a hearing be held. The plaintiff shall submit to the court the proof required by law and the original and not less than one copy of the proposed default judgment. The judge shall, within seventy-two hours of receipt of such submission from the clerk of court, sign the proposed default judgment or direct that a hearing be held. The clerk of court shall certify that no answer or other pleading has been filed by the defendant. The minute clerk shall make an entry showing the dates of receipt of proof, review of the record, and rendition of the default judgment. A certified copy of the signed default judgment shall be sent to the plaintiff by the clerk of court, and notice of the signing of the default judgment shall be given as provided in Article 1913.

D. When the demand is based upon a right acquired by assignment in an open account, promissory note, or other negotiable instrument, the court may raise an objection of prescription before entering a default judgment if the grounds for the objection appear from the pleadings or from the evidence submitted by the plaintiff. If the court raises an objection of prescription, it shall not enter the default judgment unless the plaintiff presents prima facie proof that the action is not barred by prescription. Upon the plaintiff's request, the court shall hold a hearing for the submission of such proof.

E. When the demand is based upon a claim for a personal injury, a sworn narrative report of the treating physician or dentist may be offered in lieu of his testimony.

F. (1) Notwithstanding any other provisions of law to the contrary, when the demand is for divorce under Civil Code Article 103(1) or (5), whether or not the demand contains a claim for relief incidental or ancillary thereto, a hearing in open court shall not be required unless the judge, in his discretion, directs that a hearing be held. The plaintiff shall submit to the court an affidavit specifically attesting to and testifying as to the truth of all of the factual allegations contained in the petition, the original and not less than one copy of the proposed default judgment, a certification indicating the type of service made on the defendant and the date of service, and a certification by the clerk that the record was examined by the clerk, including the date of the examination, and a statement that no answer or other pleading has been filed. If the demand is for divorce under Civil Code Article 103(5), a certified copy of the protective order or injunction rendered after a contradictory hearing or consent decree shall also be submitted to the court. If no answer or other pleading has been filed by the defendant, the judge shall review the submitted affidavit, proposed default judgment, and certification and render and sign the proposed default judgment or direct that a hearing be held. The minutes shall reflect rendition and signing of the default judgment.

(2) If the demand is for divorce under Civil Code Article 103(1) and the defendant, by sworn affidavit, acknowledges receipt of a certified copy of the petition and waives formal citation, service of process, all legal delays, notice of trial, and appearance at trial, a default judgment of divorce may be entered against the defendant two days, exclusive of legal holidays, after the affidavit is filed. The affidavit of the defendant may be prepared or notarized by any notary public.

Amended by Acts 1968, No. 88, § 1; Acts 1983, No. 266, § 1, eff. Jan. 1, 1984; Acts 1986, No. 219, § 1; Acts 1986, No. 285, § 1; Acts 1986, No. 430, § 1; Acts 1987, No. 182, § 1; Acts 1987, No. 271, § 1; Acts 1990, No. 1009, § 4, eff. Jan. 1, 1991; Acts 1992, No. 292, § 1; Acts 2001, No. 512, § 1; Acts 2008, No. 354, § 1, eff. June 21, 2008; Acts 2013, No. 78, § 1; Acts 2014, No. 791, § 20; Acts 2015, No. 221, § 2; Acts 2017, No. 419, § 1; Acts 2021, No. 174, § 5, eff. Jan. 1, 2022; Acts 2021, No. 259, § 2.

Comments—2013

(a) The 2013 amendment to the first sentence in Article 1702(A) adds a new requirement that all of the proof required to establish a *prima facie* case supporting confirmation of a default judgment must be placed into the court record prior to judgment. The change follows La. Const. Art. 1 § 19, which grants litigants "the right of judicial review based upon a complete record of all evidence upon which the judgment is based." The amendment is also consistent with jurisprudence holding that "to prevent reversal on appeal, both the plaintiff and the trial judge should be vigilant to assure that the judgment rests on admissible evidence that establishes a *prima facie* case." *Arias v. Stolthaven New Orleans, LLC*, 9 So.3d 815, 820 (La. 2009).

(b) Although there is a presumption that a default judgment is supported by sufficient admissible evidence, this presumption may be rebutted through the defendant's utilization of appellate review of the record upon which the judgment was rendered. Without a complete record of the evidence presented to the trial court, meaningful appellate review of default judgments may be impaired. Prior jurisprudence holding that a simple recitation in the default judgment that "the court reviewed the proof of the demands" is a substitute for the introduction in the record of the evidence considered by the trial court in rendering the judgment is no longer valid.

(c) To avoid encumbering the court records with documentary evidence, the 2013 amendment provides an option to the trial court to admit documentary evidence in the record in an electronically stored form. See Code of Evidence, Article 1003.1.

Comments—2021

(a) Subparagraph (A)(3) of this Article adopts a new rule that, prior to the rendition of a default judgment, notice must be sent to a party's attorney who has contacted the plaintiff or the plaintiff's attorney in writing about the case. The term "in writing" includes electronic means as well as any other type of writing. If such notice is not given, any default judgment rendered shall be a nullity similar to that arising from a lack of the notice required by

Subparagraph (A)(2). See, e.g., *First Bank & Trust v. Bayou Land and Marine Contractors, Inc.*, 103 So. 3d 1148 (La. App. 5 Cir. 2012).

(b) Subparagraph (A)(4) of this Article is also new. In all delictual cases that do not fall under Subparagraph (A)(2) or (3), this provision requires the plaintiff to send written notice by regular mail at least seven days prior to obtaining a default judgment against a defendant. Similar to Subparagraphs (A)(2) and (3), if the required notice is not given, any default judgment rendered in the delictual case shall be a nullity. See, e.g., First Bank & Trust v. Bayou Land and Marine Contractors, Inc., 103 So. 3d 1148 (La. App. 5 Cir. 2012). For purposes of consistency with Subparagraphs (A)(3) and (4), the time period provided by Subparagraph (A)(2) was shortened from "seven days, exclusive of holidays" to "seven days."

(c) Paragraph D of this Article is new and provides that in limited cases, a court may raise an objection of prescription before entering a default judgment if the grounds for the objection appear from the pleadings or from the submitted evidence. If the plaintiff seeks to obtain the default judgment by oral testimony in open court, the court may raise the objection of prescription at the hearing, and the plaintiff must present prima facie proof that the action is not barred by prescription. If the plaintiff seeks to obtain the default judgment without a hearing in accordance with Article 1702(B)(1) and (C) and Article 1702.1, the court may raise the objection of prescription and allow the plaintiff to present prima facie proof by affidavits and exhibits that the action is not barred by prescription. Upon the plaintiff's request, the court shall hold a hearing for the submission of such proof. If the plaintiff fails to submit sufficient proof that the action is not barred by prescription, the court shall deny the plaintiff's request for a default judgment but shall not dismiss the case on its own motion. See, e.g., Gorman v. Miller, 136 So. 3d 834 (La. App. 1 Cir. 2013) ("[I]f the plaintiff fails to present sufficient evidence to confirm a preliminary default judgment . . . the trial court is effectively prevented from dismissing the plaintiff's suit on its own motion. . . . [T]he trial court's authority is limited to a denial of the request to confirm the preliminary default judgment.").

(d) Paragraph F of this Article continues the authorization under former Articles 1701 and 1702(E) for a judgment of divorce under Civil Code Article 103(1) to be granted without a hearing in open court two days, exclusive of holidays, after the filing of the defendant's affidavit waiving all legal delays, and for a judgment of divorce under Civil Code Article 103(5) to be rendered without a hearing in open court after the delays for answering have expired.

Editor's Notes

Paragraph E requires that for confirmation of a Civil Code article 103(5) divorce, in addition to an affidavit, a certified copy of the protective order or injunction rendered after a contradictory hearing or a consent decree shall be submitted.

Art. 1702.1. Default judgment without hearing in open court; required information; certifications

A. When the plaintiff seeks a default judgment without appearing for a hearing in open court as provided in Article 1702(B)(1) and (C), the plaintiff shall file a written request for default judgment containing a certification that the suit is on an open account, promissory note, or other negotiable instrument, on a conventional obligation, or on a check dishonored for nonsufficient funds, and that the necessary invoices and affidavit, note and affidavit, or check or certified reproduction thereof are attached, along with any proof required by law and a proposed default judgment. If attorney fees are sought under R.S. 9:2781 or 2782, the attorney shall certify that fact and the fact that the number of days required by R.S. 9:2781(A) or 2782(A), respectively, have elapsed since demand was made upon the defendant.

B. The certification shall indicate the type of service made on the defendant and the date of service and shall also include a certification by the clerk that the record was examined by the clerk, including therein the date of the examination and a statement that no answer or other pleading has been filed within the time prescribed by law or by the court.

Added by Acts 1984, No. 507, § 1. Amended by Acts 1987, No. 182, § 1; Acts 1992, No. 292, § 1; Acts 2001, No. 1075, § 2; Acts 2017, No. 419, § 1; Acts 2021, No. 174, § 1, eff. Jan. 1, 2022.

Editor's Notes

A written request is required if the plaintiff seeks a default judgment without appearing for a hearing in open court. The invoices and the affidavit must be offered into evidence for prima facie proof of the claim, Sessions & Fishman v. Liquid Air Corp., Sup.1993, 616 So.2d 1254.

Art. 1703. Scope of judgment

A default judgment shall not be different in kind from that demanded in the petition. The amount of damages awarded shall be the amount proven to be properly due as a remedy.

Amended by Acts 1988, No. 443, § 2, eff. Jan. 1, 1989; Acts 2017, No. 419, § 1; Acts 2021, No. 174, § 1, eff. Jan. 1, 2022.

Art. 1704. Default judgment in suits against the state or a political subdivision

A. Notwithstanding any other provision of law to the contrary, prior to the rendition of a default judgment against the state or any of its departments, offices, boards, commissions, agencies, or instrumentalities, the plaintiff or the plaintiff's attorney shall send notice of the plaintiff's intent to obtain a default judgment, together with a certified copy of the petition or other demand, to the attorney general by registered or certified mail, or shall be served by the sheriff personally upon the attorney general or the first assistant attorney general at the office of the attorney general. If the notice and petition are served on the attorney general by mail, the person mailing such items shall execute and file in the record an affidavit stating that these items have been enclosed in an envelope properly addressed to the attorney general with sufficient postage affixed, and stating the date on which such envelope was deposited in the United States mail. The return receipt shall be attached to the affidavit that is filed in the record.

B. If no answer or other pleading is filed during the twenty-one days immediately following the date on which the attorney general or the first assistant attorney general received notice of the intent to obtain a default judgment as provided in Paragraph A of this Article, a default judgment against the state or any of its departments, offices, boards, commissions, agencies, or instrumentalities may be rendered upon proof as required by Article 1702.

C. Notwithstanding any other provision of law to the contrary, prior to the rendition of a default judgment against a political subdivision of the state or any of its departments, offices, boards, commissions, agencies, or instrumentalities, the plaintiff or the plaintiff's attorney shall send notice of the plaintiff's intent to obtain a default judgment, together with a certified copy of the petition or other demand, by registered or certified mail to the proper agent or person for service of process at the office of that agent or person. The person mailing such items shall execute and file in the record an affidavit stating that these items have been enclosed in an envelope properly addressed to the proper agent or person for service of process, with sufficient postage affixed, and stating the date on which such envelope was deposited in the United States mail. The return receipt shall be attached to the affidavit that is filed in the record.

D. If no answer or other pleading is filed during the twenty-one days immediately following the date on which the agent or person for service of process received notice of the intent to obtain a default judgment as provided in Paragraph C of this Article, a default judgment against the political subdivision of the state or any of its departments, offices, boards, commissions, agencies, or instrumentalities may be rendered upon proof as required by Article 1702.

Added by Acts 1978, No. 149, § 1, eff. June 29, 1978. Amended by Acts 1986, No. 155, § 1, eff. June 28, 1986; Acts 2017, No. 419, § 1; Acts 2021, No. 174, § 1, eff. Jan. 1, 2022.

Comments—2021

Article 1704 continues the requirement that, prior to a default judgment being rendered against the state of Louisiana or any of its departments, offices, boards, commissions, agencies, or instrumentalities, the office of the attorney general must receive notice of the plaintiff's intent to obtain the default judgment along with a certified copy of the petition or other demand. A similar notice requirement applies to any political subdivision of the state.

Editor's Notes

Failure to comply with this notice requirement rendered judgment null under C.C.P. art. 2002, Bonnette v. Caldwell Parish Police Jury, App. 2 Cir.1982, 415 So.2d 247.

CHAPTER 7. JURY TRIAL

SECTION 1. RIGHT TO TRIAL BY JURY

Article

SECTION 2. SELECTION OF JURY

SECTION 3. PROCEDURE FOR CALLING AND EXAMINING JURORS

SECTION 4. PROCEDURE IN JURY TRIALS

SECTION 1. RIGHT TO TRIAL BY JURY

Art. 1731. Issues triable by jury

A. Except as limited by Article 1732, the right of trial by jury is recognized.

B. Except as otherwise provided, the nature and amount of the principal demand shall determine whether any issue in the principal or incidental demand is triable by jury.

C. If the compulsory reconventional demand is triable by a jury, but the principal demand is not, the compulsory reconventional demand may be tried by a jury.

Acts 1983, No. 534, § 1. Amended by Acts 1995, No. 661, § 1.

Editor's Notes

The right to a jury trial depends on the good faith amount in dispute and not necessarily on the amount initially demanded by the plaintiff, Cambridge Corner Corp. v. Menard, 525 So.2d 527 (La.1988).

For an exhaustive analysis of the judge-trial, jury-trial procedure (bifurcation) see Fontenot v. Patterson Ins., 997 So.2d 529 (La. 2008).

Art. 1732. Limitation upon jury trials

A trial by jury shall not be available in:

(1) A suit where the amount of no individual petitioner's cause of action exceeds ten thousand dollars exclusive of interest and costs, except as follows:

(a) If an individual petitioner stipulates or otherwise judicially admits sixty days or more prior to trial that the amount of the individual petitioner's cause of action does not exceed ten thousand dollars exclusive of interest and costs, a defendant shall not be entitled to a trial by jury.

(b) If an individual petitioner stipulates or otherwise judicially admits for the first time less than sixty days prior to trial that the amount of the individual petitioner's cause of action does not exceed ten thousand dollars exclusive of interest and costs, any other party may retain the right to a trial by jury if that party is entitled to a trial by jury pursuant to this Article and has otherwise complied with the procedural requirements for obtaining a trial by jury.

(c) Notwithstanding Subsubparagraphs (a) and (b) of this Subparagraph, if, as a result of a compromise or dismissal of one or more claims or parties which occurs less than sixty days prior to trial, an individual petitioner stipulates or otherwise judicially admits that the amount of the individual petitioner's cause of action does not exceed ten thousand dollars exclusive of interest and costs, a defendant shall not be entitled to a trial by jury.

(2)(a) A suit commenced in a parish or city court, wherein the individual petitioner stipulates or otherwise judicially admits that the amount of the individual petitioner's cause of action does not exceed the amount in dispute to which the jurisdiction of the court is limited by Articles 4842 and 4843, exclusive of interest, penalties, attorney fees, and costs.

(b) The provisions of this Subparagraph shall not apply to delictual or quasi-delictual actions, which shall be governed by the provisions of Subparagraph (1) of this Article.

(3) A suit on an unconditional obligation to pay a specific sum of money, unless the defense thereto is forgery, fraud, error, want, or failure of consideration.

(4) A summary, executory, probate, partition, mandamus, habeas corpus, quo warranto, injunction, concursus, workers' compensation, emancipation, tutorship, interdiction, curatorship, filiation, annulment of marriage, or divorce proceeding.

(5) A proceeding to determine custody, visitation, alimony, or child support.

(6) A proceeding to review an action by an administrative or municipal body.

(7) All cases where a jury trial is specifically denied by law.

Acts 1983, No. 534, § 1. Amended by Acts 1984, No. 301, § 1; Acts 1987, No. 766, § 1; Acts 1988, No. 147, § 1; Acts 1989, No. 107, § 1; Acts 1990, No. 361, § 1, eff. Jan. 1, 1991; Acts 1993, No. 661, § 1; Acts 1999, No. 1363, § 1; Acts 2004, No. 26, § 2; Acts 2013, No. 391, § 1; Acts 2020, 1st Ex.Sess., No. 37, § 2, eff. Jan. 1, 2021.

Art. 1733. Demand for jury trial; bond for costs

A. (1) Except as provided in Subparagraph (2) of this Paragraph, a party may obtain a trial by jury by filing a pleading demanding a trial by jury and a bond in the amount and within the time set by the court pursuant to Article 1734.

(2)(a) In a suit for damages arising from a delictual or quasi-delictual action where an individual petitioner stipulates or otherwise judicially admits that his cause of action exceeds ten thousand dollars and is less than fifty thousand dollars, a party may obtain a trial by jury by filing a pleading demanding a trial by jury and providing a cash deposit of five thousand dollars no later than sixty days after filing the request for a trial by jury. Failure to post the cash deposit as required by this Subparagraph shall constitute a waiver of the trial by jury. This cash deposit shall be subject to Article 1734.1(E).

(b) When the case is set for trial, the court may additionally provide for a supplemental bond or cash deposit in accordance with Article 1734 or 1734.1.

B. A motion to withdraw a demand for a trial by jury shall be in writing.

C. The pleading demanding a trial by jury shall be filed not later than ten days after either the service of the last pleading directed to any issue triable by a jury, or the granting of a motion to withdraw a demand for a trial by jury.

Acts 1983, No. 534, § 1. Amended by Acts 2020, 1st Ex.Sess., No. 37, § 2, eff. Jan. 1, 2021.

Art. 1734. Fixing the bond; calling the jury venire

A. Except as otherwise provided by R.S. 13:3105 et seq., when the case has been set for trial, the court shall fix the amount of the bond to cover all costs estimated by the court related to the trial by jury and shall fix the time for filing the bond, which shall be no later than sixty days prior to trial. Notice of the fixing of the bond shall be served on all parties. If the bond is not filed timely, any other party shall have an additional ten days to file the bond.

B. When the bond has been filed, the clerk of court shall order the jury commission to draw a sufficient number of jurors to try and determine the cause, such drawing to be made in accordance with R.S. 13:3044.

Acts 1983, No. 534, § 1. Amended by Acts 1987, No. 148, § 1; Acts 1995, No. 148, § 1; Acts 2005, No. 28, § 1; Acts 2021, No. 382, § 1.

Art. 1734.1. Cash deposit; procedure

A. When the case has been set for trial, the court may order, in lieu of the bond required in Article 1734, a deposit for costs, which shall be a specific amount estimated by the court, and the court shall fix the time for making the deposit, which shall be no later than thirty days prior to trial. The deposit shall include sufficient funds for payment of all costs associated with a jury trial, including juror fees and expenses and charges of the jury commission, clerk of court, and sheriff. The required deposit shall not exceed five thousand dollars for the first day, and one thousand dollars per day for each additional day the court estimates the trial will last. Notice of the fixing of the deposit shall be served on all parties. If the deposit is not timely made, any other party shall have an additional ten days to make the required deposit. Failure to post the deposit shall constitute a waiver of a trial by jury. However, no deposit shall be required of an applicant for a jury trial under the provisions of this Article if waived or an order is rendered, pursuant to Chapter 5 of Title I of Book IX of this Code, permitting the applicant to litigate or continue to litigate without payment of costs in advance or furnishing security therefor.

B. When the deposit has been filed, the clerk of court shall order the jury commission to draw a sufficient number of jurors to try and determine the cause, such drawing to be made in accordance with R.S. 13:3044.

C. The clerk of court may disburse funds from the cash deposit for payment of all or a part of the jury costs as such costs accrue. The clerk shall keep a record of funds disbursed from the deposit.

D. The court may require an additional deposit to be filed during the trial if the original amount of the deposit is insufficient to pay jury costs.

E. The funds disbursed from the cash deposit for payment of jury costs shall be assessed as costs of court.

F. After payment of all jury costs, any unexpended amounts remaining on deposit shall be refunded by the clerk of court to the party or attorney filing the deposit.

Added by Acts 1987, No. 937, § 2. Amended by Acts 1989, No. 307, § 1; Acts 1995, No. 148, § 1; Acts 2004, No. 840, § 2; Acts 2021, No. 382, § 1.

Art. 1735. Specification of issues

In his demand a party may specify the issues which he wishes to be tried by jury; otherwise, he shall be considered to have demanded trial by jury for all the issues so triable. If he has demanded trial by jury for only some of the issues, any other party, within ten days after service of the demand, may demand trial by jury of any or all of the other issues in the action.

Acts 1980, No. 598, § 2. Amended by Acts 1983, No. 534, § 1.

Art. 1736. Trial of less than all issues; stipulation

The trial of all issues for which a jury trial has been requested shall be by jury, unless the parties stipulate that the jury trial shall be as to certain issues only or unless the right to trial by jury as to certain issues does not exist; however, except as otherwise provided under the provisions of Article 1562, there shall be but one trial.

Acts 1983, No. 534, § 1.

SECTION 2. SELECTION OF JURY

Art. 1751. Qualification and exemptions of jurors

The qualification and exemptions of jurors and the method of choosing and summoning the general venire are provided by special laws.

Amended by Acts 1983, No. 534, § 4.

Comment—1983

The amendment of Art. 1751 by Acts 1983 No. 534 provides a stylistic change by eliminating the phrase "in jury cases" following the word "venire".

Editor's Notes

R.S. 13:3041 et seq., juries; and Supreme Court Rule XXV (Vol. 8, LSA–R.S.), exemption of jurors.

SECTION 3. PROCEDURE FOR CALLING AND EXAMINING JURORS

Art. 1761. Procedure in general

A. In cases to be tried by jury, twelve jurors summoned in accordance with law shall be chosen by lot to try the issues specified unless the parties stipulate that the case shall be tried by six jurors. The method of calling and drawing by lot shall be at the discretion of the court.

B. The parties may stipulate that if one or more jurors die or become disqualified the remaining jurors shall try the issues specified.

Amended by Acts 1983, No. 534, § 5.

Art. 1762. Swearing of juror before examination

Before being examined, every prospective juror shall be sworn or shall affirm to answer truthfully such questions as may be propounded to him.

Amended by Acts 1983, No. 534, § 5.

Comment—1983

The amendment of this article by Acts 1983 No. 534 allows a juror to make an affirmation instead of taking an oath. Article 1633 gives a witness at trial the same choice.

Art. 1763. Examination of juror

A. The court shall examine prospective jurors as to their qualifications and may conduct such further examination as it deems appropriate.

B. The parties or their attorneys shall individually conduct such examination of prospective jurors as each party deems necessary, but the court may control the scope of the examination to be conducted by the parties or their attorneys.

Amended by Acts 1983, No. 534, § 5; Acts 1990, No. 603, § 1.

Comments—1983

(a) This article as amended by Acts 1983 No. 534, expresses the former law that parties have a right to examine prospective jurors. It also makes it explicit that the court can control the examination to prevent unfair or prejudicial questioning. This authority has been recognized in the cases—Morgan v. Liberty Mutual Ins. Co., 323 So.2d 855 (4th Cir.1975) and Trahan v. Odell Vinson Oil Field Contractors, 295 So.2d 224 (3rd Cir.1974).

(b) This article eliminates the restriction in the former language that the examination by the court is limited to ascertaining the qualifications of the juror. Such a limitation is too restrictive because the judge has a right to excuse a juror for cause on his own motion—Art. 1767—and thus should be given the same scope in examining a prospective juror as is enjoyed by the parties.

Art. 1764. Peremptory challenges

A. If trial is by a jury of six, each side is allowed three peremptory challenges. If there is more than one party on any side, the court may allow each side additional peremptory challenges, not to exceed two.

B. If trial is by a jury of twelve, each side is allowed six peremptory challenges. If there is more than one party on any side, the court may allow each side additional peremptory challenges, not to exceed four.

C. Each side shall be allowed an equal number of peremptory challenges. If the parties on a side are unable to agree upon the allocation of peremptory challenges among themselves, the allocation shall be determined by the court before the examination on the voir dire.

Amended by Acts 1983, No. 534, § 5.

Art. 1765. Challenges for cause

A juror may be challenged for cause based upon any of the following:

(1) When the juror lacks a qualification required by law;

(2) When the juror has formed an opinion in the case or is not otherwise impartial, the cause of his bias being immaterial;

(3) When the relations whether by blood, marriage, employment, friendship, or enmity between the juror and any party or his attorney are such that it must be reasonably believed that they would influence the juror in coming to a verdict;

(4) When the juror served on a previous jury, which tried the same case or one arising out of the same facts;

(5) When the juror refuses to answer a question on the voir dire examination on the ground that his answer might tend to incriminate him.

Art. 1766. Time for challenges; method

A. After a juror has been examined as provided in Article 1763, the court may excuse the juror and if the court does not do so, either party may challenge the juror for cause.

B. If a juror has not been excused for cause, a peremptory challenge may be made by any party. The court shall alternate between the sides when making initial inquiry as to whether any party wishes to exercise a peremptory challenge to that juror.

C. After the entire jury has been accepted and sworn, no party has a right to challenge peremptorily.

D. Peremptory challenges of jurors shall be made and communicated to the court in a side bar conference of the judge, the attorneys conducting the examination and selection of jurors, and the plaintiff or defendant in a case in which the plaintiff or defendant chooses to represent himself. The conference shall be conducted in a manner that only the court, the attorneys, and the plaintiff or defendant in a case in which the plaintiff or defendant chooses to represent himself, are aware of the challenges made until the court announces the challenges without reference to any party or attorney in the case. The side bar conference shall be conducted on the record and out of the presence of the prospective jurors.

Amended by Acts 1983, No. 534, § 5; Acts 1990, No. 703, § 1.

Comments—1983

(a) Former Art. 1766 made no provision for the order of making challenges except to provide that a peremptory challenge could not be made after the entire jury had been accepted and sworn. All other questions were left to the control of the court.

(b) The amendment to Art. 1766 by Acts 1983 No. 534 attempts to achieve a certain degree of uniformity in this area. It prescribes that the challenges for cause should first be made by the court and, if not made by the court, then by the parties. This promotes efficiency and reduces the risk of prejudice to a party that might result from an unsuccessful challenge. See C.Cr.P. Art. 788 and ABA Standards Trial by Jury § 2.5.

(c) Paragraph B calls for exercising the peremptory challenge after a juror has been passed for cause.

Art. 1767. Challenging or excusing jurors after acceptance

Although the entire jury may have been accepted and sworn, up to the beginning of the taking of evidence, a juror may be challenged for cause by either side or be excused by the court for cause or by consent of both sides, and the panel completed in the ordinary course.

Amended by Acts 1976, No. 212, § 1; Acts 1977, No. 377, § 1; Acts 1983, No. 534, § 5.

Comment—1983

Acts 1983 No. 534 amends this article by restoring it to what it had been before the amendments in 1976 and 1977.

Art. 1768. Swearing of jurors; selection of foreman

When the jury has been accepted by all parties, the jurors shall be sworn to try the case in a just and impartial manner, to the best of their judgment, and to render a verdict according to the law and the evidence. When the jury has retired, the jurors shall select a foreman to preside over them and sign the verdict which they may render.

Art. 1769. Alternate jurors

A. The court may direct that one or more jurors, in addition to the regular panel, be called and empanelled to sit as alternate jurors.

B. Alternate jurors, in the order in which they are called, shall replace jurors who, prior to the time the jury retires to consider its verdict, become unable or disqualified to perform their duties.

C. Alternate jurors shall be drawn in the same manner, shall have the same qualifications, shall be subject to the same examination and challenges, shall take the same oath, and shall have the same functions, powers, facilities, and privileges as the principal jurors.

D. An alternate juror who does not replace a principal juror shall be discharged when the jury retires to consider its verdict.

E. If one or more alternate jurors are called, each side shall have an equal number of additional peremptory challenges. The court shall determine how many challenges shall be allowed and shall allocate them among the parties on each side. The additional peremptory challenges may be used only against an alternate juror, and the other peremptory challenges allowed by law shall not be used against the alternate jurors.

Amended by Acts 1983, No. 534, § 5.

Comment—1983

Acts 1983 No. 534 changes this article to allow for "one or more" alternate jurors instead of the "one or two" formerly provided.

Editor's Notes

Taken from Fed.Rules of Civ.Proc. 47(b).

SECTION 4. PROCEDURE IN JURY TRIALS

Art. 1791. Comment on facts by judge prohibited

The judge in the presence of the jury shall not comment upon the facts of the case, either by commenting upon or recapitulating the evidence, repeating the testimony of any witness, or giving an opinion as to what has been proved, not proved, or refuted.

Acts 1983, No. 534, § 7.

Comment—1983

This revision is based on Code of Criminal Procedure Article 772 and expands the scope of former Art. 1792 which was limited to the judge's charge to the jury.

Art. 1792. Charge to the jury

A. At any time during the trial, the court may instruct the jury on the law applicable to any issue in the case.

B. After the trial of the case and the presentation of all the evidence and arguments, the court shall instruct the jurors on the law applicable to the cause submitted to them. The court shall reduce such instructions to writing. The court shall further instruct the jury that it may take with it or have sent to it a written copy of all instructions and charges and any object or document received in evidence when a physical examination thereof is required to enable the jury to reach its verdict.

C. This charge shall be in writing and available to the parties and to jurors in their deliberations.

Acts 1983, No. 534, § 7. Amended by Acts 1997, No. 668, § 1.

Comments—1983

(a) Paragraph A, as enacted by Acts 1983, No. 534, is new and expressly recognizes the authority of the judge to give instructions to the jury during the course of the trial. These instructions would be particularly helpful to a jury in a complex or lengthy trial.

(b) Paragraphs B and C make no change in the law and were contained in Arts. 1791 and 1792 prior to the 1983 amendment.

Editor's Notes

The 1997 amendment allows the jury to have with it [in the jury room] a written copy of the jury charges and any object or document received in evidence.

Adams v. Rhodia, Inc., 983 So.2d 798 (La. 2008), is a complete treatise for adequate jury instructions.

Art. 1793. Instructions to jury; objections

A. At the close of the evidence, or at such earlier time as the court reasonably directs, a party may file written requests that the court instruct the jury on the law as set forth in the requests.

B. The court shall inform the parties of its proposed action on the written requests and shall also inform the parties of the instructions it intends to give to the jury at the close of the evidence within a reasonable time prior to their arguments to the jury.

C. A party may not assign as error the giving or the failure to give an instruction unless he objects thereto either before the jury retires to consider its verdict or immediately after the jury retires, stating specifically the matter to which he objects and the grounds of his objection. If he objects prior to the time the jury retires, he shall be given an opportunity to make the objection out of the hearing of the jury.

D. The jury may take with it or have sent to it a written copy of all instructions and charges.

Acts 1983, No. 534, § 7. Amended by Acts 1987, No. 699, § 1; Acts 1997, No. 668, § 1; Acts 2021, No. 259, § 2.

Comments—1983

(a) Paragraph A as amended by Acts 1983 No. 534 broadens the period for filing written requests. The former provision referred to "an earlier time during the trial". The amendment recognizes the authority of the court to direct the filing of written requests even before trial begins.

(b) Article 1793 as amended in 1983, requires the court to inform the parties of its decision upon their written requests. The 1983 amendment also requires the court to inform the parties of the instructions it intends to give to the jury. In addition, this information is to be given to the parties in sufficient time to enable them to make the appropriate arguments to the jury.

(c) Paragraph C, as amended in 1983, makes no change in the law.

Art. 1794. Taking evidence to jury room

A. Jurors shall be permitted to take notes. The court shall provide the needed writing implements. Jurors may, but need not, take notes and such notes as are taken may be used during the jury's deliberations but shall not be preserved for review on appeal. The trial judge shall ensure the confidentiality of the notes during the course of the trial and the jury's deliberations. At each recess prior to jury deliberation, the court shall collect and maintain any and all notes made by each juror and upon reconvening, the court shall return to each juror his individual notes and shall cause the notes to be destroyed immediately upon return of the verdict.

B. The court may allow the jury to take with them any object or writing received in evidence, except depositions and except as otherwise provided in the Louisiana Code of Evidence.

Acts 1983, No. 534, § 7. Amended by Acts 1988, No. 515, § 2, eff. Jan. 1, 1989; Acts 1997, No. 668, § 1.

Comments—1983

(a) This article, as amended by Acts 1983 No. 534 retains the restriction in former Art. 1794 that jurors may not rely on notes taken during the trial (N.B. see 1997 Act changing this restriction), but it gives the trial judge discretion to allow the jury to take any object or writing received in evidence if it would aid them in their deliberations. The judge is to consider how helpful such an examination might be and the risk of misuse by the jury and possible prejudice to any party. Examination of depositions is expressly excluded.

(b) The 1983 revision is based on ABA Standards, Trial by Jury § 5.1.

Comment—1988

This Article was amended to accommodate the Code of Evidence. As examples of materials that may not be taken into the jury room, see Code of Evidence Art. 803(5) and (18).

Art. 1795. Jury request to review testimony

If the jury, after retiring for deliberation, requests a review of certain testimony, they shall be conducted to the courtroom. After giving notice to the parties, the court may have the requested testimony read to the jury.

Acts 1983, No. 534, § 7. Amended by Acts 2021, No. 259, § 2.

Comments—1983

(a) This article is new and addresses the problem of a request by the jury to refresh its memory about testimony or to clear up questions about materials admitted into evidence. The court is given the discretion to grant the request. Any reexamination of testimony is to be done in the courtroom and in the presence of the parties if they choose to be present after being properly notified.

(b) Under this article the judge may allow the jury to examine objects and writings only in the courtroom, or he may allow the jury to take the objects or writings to the jury room under Art. 1794.

(c) "Read" is intended to include not only repeating testimony from a transcript or reporter's notes, but also playing back the testimony from any recording.

Art. 1796. Additional instructions

A. If the jury, after retiring for deliberation, desires to receive information on any point of law, they shall be conducted to the courtroom.

B. After giving notice to the parties, the court may give the appropriate instructions.

C. The court, after giving notice to the parties, may recall the jury after they have retired:

(1) To correct or withdraw an erroneous instruction.

(2) To clarify an ambiguous instruction.

(3) To inform the jury on a point of law which should have been covered in the original instructions.

(4) To give such further instructions as may be appropriate.

Acts 1983, No. 534, § 7.

Comments—1983

(a) This article is new and deals with additional instructions to the jury on their request and when the court on its own believes additional instructions are appropriate.

(b) The rights of the parties are protected by giving them notice and an opportunity to object to the additional instructions.

(c) This article is based on ABA Standards, Trial by Jury § 5.3 and C.Cr.P. Art. 808.

Art. 1797. Number required for verdict

A. If trial is by a jury of six, five of the jurors must concur to render a verdict unless the parties stipulate otherwise.

B. If trial is by a jury of twelve, nine of the jurors must concur to render a verdict unless the parties stipulate otherwise.

C. If the parties have stipulated pursuant to Article 1761(B) that the remaining jurors shall try the issues specified if members of the jury die or become disqualified, they also shall stipulate as to the number of jurors who must concur to render a verdict.

Acts 1983, No. 534, § 7.

SECTION 5. VERDICTS

Art. 1810. Directed verdicts; motion to dismiss at close of plaintiff's evidence

A party who moves for a directed verdict at the close of the evidence offered by an opponent may offer evidence in the event that the motion is not granted, without having reserved the right so to do and to the same extent as if the motion had not been made. A motion for a directed verdict that is not granted is not a waiver of trial by jury even though all parties to the action have moved for directed verdicts. A motion for a directed verdict shall state the specific grounds therefor. The order of the court granting a motion for a directed verdict is effective without any assent of the jury.

Acts 1983, No. 534, § 8.

Comments—1983

(a) This article as amended by Acts 1983 No. 534 reproduces paragraph A of former Art. 1810.

(b) Paragraph B of former Art. 1810 does not belong in the section dealing with jury trials and it has been moved to Art. 1672 which governs involuntary dismissals. The provisions of Paragraph B of former Art. 1810 are taken from Federal Rule of Civil Procedure 41b which governs involuntary dismissals.

Art. 1810.1. Repealed by Acts 1983, No. 534, § 11

Art. 1811. Motion for judgment notwithstanding the verdict

A. (1) Not later than seven days, exclusive of legal holidays, after the clerk has mailed or the sheriff has served the notice of judgment under Article 1913, a party may move for a judgment notwithstanding the verdict. If a verdict was not returned, a party may move for a judgment notwithstanding the verdict not later than seven days, exclusive of legal holidays, after the jury was discharged.

(2) A motion for a new trial may be joined with this motion, or a new trial may be prayed for in the alternative.

B. If a verdict was returned the court may allow the judgment to stand or may reopen the judgment and either order a new trial or render a judgment notwithstanding the verdict. If no verdict was returned, the court may render a judgment or order a new trial.

C. (1) If the motion for a judgment notwithstanding the verdict is granted, the court shall also rule on the motion for a new trial, if any, by determining whether it should be granted if the judgment is thereafter vacated or reversed and shall specify the grounds for granting or denying the motion for a new trial. If the motion for a new trial is thus conditionally granted, the order thereon does not affect the finality of the judgment.

(2) If the motion for a new trial has been conditionally granted and the judgment is reversed on appeal, the new trial shall proceed unless the appellate court orders otherwise.

(3) If the motion for a new trial has been conditionally denied and the judgment is reversed on appeal, subsequent proceedings shall be in accordance with the order of the appellate court.

D. The party whose verdict has been set aside on a motion for a judgment notwithstanding the verdict may move for a new trial pursuant to Articles 1972 and 1973. The motion for a new trial shall be filed no later than seven days, exclusive of legal holidays, after the clerk has mailed or the sheriff has served the notice of the signing of the judgment notwithstanding the verdict under Article 1913. The motion shall be served pursuant to Articles 1976 and 1314.

E. If the motion for a judgment notwithstanding the verdict is denied, the party who prevailed on that motion may, as appellee, assert grounds entitling him to a new trial in the event the appellate court concludes that the trial court erred in denying the motion for a judgment notwithstanding the verdict. If the appellate court reverses the judgment, nothing in this Article precludes the court from determining that the appellee is entitled to a new trial or from directing the trial court to determine whether a new trial shall be granted.

F. The motion for a judgment notwithstanding the verdict may be granted on the issue of liability or on the issue of damages or on both issues.

Acts 1983, No. 534, § 8. Amended by Acts 1984, No. 40, § 1; Acts 1999, No. 1263, § 1, eff. Jan. 1, 2000.

Comment—1983

The amendment of this article by Acts 1983 No. 534 contains the provisions of former Art. 1810.1 with a few changes in style and a change in when the motion for a judgment notwithstanding the verdict must be filed. The former article gave a party seven days from mailing or serving notice of judgment. The new article sets the period at seven days from the signing of the judgment unless notice must be given under Art. 1913. Unlike the delay for filing a motion for a new trial, the period for filing a motion for a judgment notwithstanding the verdict includes legal holidays. See Art. 5059.

Comments—1984

This amendment makes two changes in Article 1811.

First, the delay for filing a motion for a judgment notwithstanding the verdict is changed from seven days to seven days exclusive of legal holidays in order to make the delay under this Article the same as that presently provided for a motion for a new trial under Article 1974. The periods should be the same to eliminate confusion especially since a motion for new trial may be joined with a motion for a judgment notwithstanding the verdict.

The same change is made in Paragraph D in connection with the motion for new trial which may be filed after the court grants the motion for a judgment notwithstanding the verdict.

Second, Paragraph F is added to overrule Rougeau v. Commercial Union Insurance Company, 432 So.2d 1162 (3rd Cir.1983), which held that a trial court could not grant a judgment N.O.V. on the issue of quantum and could only use the procedure of additur and remittitur. The decision seems incorrect because additur and remittitur are intended to be a substitute for a new trial, which may be granted where the verdict is clearly contrary to the weight of the evidence; but, a judgment N.O.V. is based on a different standard—namely, that based on the evidence there is no genuine issue of fact. Thus where the trial court is convinced that, under the evidence, reasonable minds could not differ as to the amount of damages, it should have the authority to grant the appropriate judgment notwithstanding the verdict.

Comment—1999

See the 1999 Comment to Article 1913.

Editor's Notes

The 1999 amendment to par. A(1) provides that the delay for moving for a JNOV runs from service of the notice of judgment as provided in C.C.P. art. 1913. The same rule under par. D applies to the delay for applying for a new trial after the JNOV.

Smith v. State, DOTD, 899 So.2d 518 (La. 2005). The Supreme Court reiterated the proper standard for granting a JNOV, previously articulated by the court in several cases cited on page 524 of this opinion. The justification for a JNOV is found when reasonable persons could not reach a different conclusion, not merely when there is a preponderance of evidence for the mover.

Art. 1812. Special verdicts

A. The court may require a jury to return only a special verdict in the form of a special written finding upon each issue of fact. In that event, the court may submit to the jury written questions susceptible of categorical or other brief answer, or may submit written forms of the several special findings which might properly be made under the pleadings and evidence, or may use any other appropriate method of submitting the issues and requiring the written findings thereon. The court shall give to the jury such explanation and instruction concerning the matter submitted as may be necessary to enable the jury to make its findings upon each issue. If the court omits any issue of fact raised by the pleadings or by the evidence, each party waives his right to a trial by jury of the issue omitted unless, before the jury retires, he demands its submission to the jury. As to an issue omitted without such demand the court may make a finding, or if it fails to do so, it shall be presumed to have made a finding in accord with the judgment on the special verdict.

B. The court shall inform the parties within a reasonable time prior to their argument to the jury of the special verdict form and instructions it intends to submit to the jury and the parties shall be given a reasonable opportunity to make objections.

C. In cases to recover damages for injury, death, or loss, the court at the request of any party shall submit to the jury special written questions inquiring as to:

(1) Whether a party from whom damages are claimed, or the person for whom such party is legally responsible, was at fault, and, if so:

(a) Whether such fault was a legal cause of the damages, and, if so:

(b) The degree of such fault, expressed in percentage.

(2)(a) If appropriate under the facts adduced at trial, whether another party or nonparty, other than the person suffering injury, death, or loss, was at fault, and, if so:

(i) Whether such fault was a legal cause of the damages, and, if so:

(ii) The degree of such fault, expressed in percentage.

(b) For purposes of this Paragraph, nonparty means a person alleged by any party to be at fault, including but not limited to:

(i) A person who has obtained a release from liability from the person suffering injury, death, or loss.

(ii) A person who exists but whose identity is unknown.

(iii) A person who may be immune from suit because of immunity granted by statute.

(3) If appropriate, whether there was negligence attributable to any party claiming damages, and, if so:

(a) Whether such negligence was a legal cause of the damages, and, if so:

(b) The degree of such negligence, expressed in percentage.

(4) The total amount of special damages and the total amount of general damages sustained as a result of the injury, death, or loss, expressed in dollars, and, if appropriate, the total amount of exemplary damages to be awarded.

D. The court shall then enter judgment in conformity with the jury's answers to these special questions and according to applicable law.

Acts 1983, No. 534, § 8. Amended by Acts 1985, No. 143, § 1; Acts 1996, 1st Ex.Sess., No. 65, § 1, eff. May 9. 1996.

Comments—1983

(a) The 1983 amendment adds the requirements that the court inform the parties of the verdict form it intends to use and that the parties be given an opportunity to make objections. This is presently done with respect to jury instructions, and the same principles of fairness should apply to verdict forms. See Smith v. Tiblier, 374 So.2d 685 (4th Cir.1979); Smith v. Danyo, 585 F.2d 83 (3rd Cir.1978).

(b) Paragraph B of former Art. 1811 provided that in actions to recover for death, injury or loss the court was required to submit certain written questions to the jury.

(c) The phrase "whether party or not" was added by the 1983 amendment to clarify the meaning of question 2 in paragraph C.

Editor's Notes

Assumption of risk abolished, and "comparative fault" recognized as affirmative defense encompassing both contributory negligence and what was assumption of risk, Murray v. Ramada Inns, 521 So.2d 1123 (La.1988); see, also, Howard v. Allstate Ins. Co., 520 So.2d 715 (La.1988), comparative "causation" must be used to compare strict liability and contributory negligence. This article was revised to implement the allocation of fault rules under C.C. arts 2323 and 2324. See also C.C.P. art. 1005, affirmative defenses, and Notes thereto.

Art. 1813. General verdict accompanied by answer to interrogatories

A. The court may submit to the jury, together with appropriate forms for a general verdict, written interrogatories upon one or more issues of fact the decision of which is necessary to a verdict. The court shall give such explanation or instruction as may be necessary to enable the jury both to make answers to the interrogatories and to render a general verdict, and the court shall direct the jury both to make written answers and to render a general verdict.

B. The court shall inform the parties within a reasonable time prior to their arguments to the jury of the general verdict form and instructions it intends to submit to the jury, and the parties shall be given a reasonable opportunity to make objections.

C. When the general verdict and the answers are harmonious, the court shall direct the entry of the appropriate judgment upon the verdict and answers.

D. When the answers are consistent with each other but one or more is inconsistent with the general verdict, the court may direct the entry of judgment in accordance with the answers, notwithstanding the general verdict, or may return the jury for further consideration of its answers and verdict, or may order a new trial.

E. When the answers are inconsistent with each other and one or more is likewise inconsistent with the general verdict, the court shall not direct the entry of judgment but may return the jury for further consideration of its answers or may order a new trial.

Acts 1983, No. 534, § 8.

Comment—1983

The 1983 revision adds the requirements that the court inform the parties of the verdict form it intends to use and that the parties be given an opportunity to make objections. This is presently done with respect to jury instructions, and the same principles of fairness should apply to verdict forms. See Smith v. Tiblier, 374 So.2d 685 (4th Cir.1979); Smith v. Danyo, 585 F.2d 83 (3rd Cir.1978).

Art. 1814. Remittitur or additur as alternative to new trial; reformation of verdict

If the trial court is of the opinion that the verdict is so excessive or inadequate that a new trial should be granted for that reason only, it may indicate to the party or his attorney within what time he may enter a remittitur or additur. This remittitur or additur is to be entered only with the consent of the plaintiff or the defendant as the case may be, as an alternative to a new trial, and is to be entered only if the issue of quantum is clearly and fairly separable from other issues in the case. If a remittitur or additur is entered, then the court shall reform the jury verdict or judgment in accordance therewith.

Added by Acts 1989, No. 173, § 1.

Comments—1989

(a) This Article reproduces verbatim the language of former Art. 1814 prior to its repeal by Acts 1988, No. 452, § 1.

(b) The purpose of this legislation is to reinstate Article 1814 which is considered to be a necessary part of the provisions for jury trials in Louisiana. It serves judicial efficiency by allowing the parties to avoid a possibly unnecessary new trial and then to seek appellate review of the correctness of the judgment reformed by additur or remittitur.

Editor's Notes

The judgment reformed in accordance with remittitur or additur is appealable, C.C.P. art 2083.

Arts. 1815 to 1840. Reserved for future legislation

TITLE VI. JUDGMENTS

CHAPTER 1. GENERAL DISPOSITIONS

Article

Art. 1841. Judgments, interlocutory and final

A judgment is the determination of the rights of the parties in an action and may award any relief to which the parties are entitled. It may be interlocutory or final.

A judgment that does not determine the merits but only preliminary matters in the course of the action is an interlocutory judgment.

A judgment that determines the merits in whole or in part is a final judgment.

Editor's Notes

See C.C.P. art. 2083, judgment must be "final" to be appealable, and C.C.P. arts. 1915A and B, partial final judgments. Also see C.C.P. art. 1911, rendition; C.C.P. art. 2252, execution. See C.C.P. arts. 1562, 966(C), and 1915(A)(5) as to final judgment on issue of liability alone; See C.C.P. arts. 2166 and 2167 as to "final and definitive".

Art. 1842. Repealed by Acts 1990, No. 521, § 3, eff. Jan. 1, 1991

Art. 1843. Default judgment

A default judgment is that which is rendered against a defendant who fails to plead within the time prescribed by law.

Amended by Acts 2017, No. 419, § 1; Acts 2021, No. 174, § 1, eff. Jan. 1, 2022.

Art. 1844. Judgment of dismissal; effect

A judgment of dismissal with or without prejudice shall be rendered and the effects thereof shall be regulated in accordance with the provisions of Articles 1671 through 1673.

CHAPTER 2. DECLARATORY JUDGMENTS

Article

Art. 1871. Declaratory judgments; scope

Courts of record within their respective jurisdictions may declare rights, status, and other legal relations whether or not further relief is or could be claimed. No action or proceeding shall be open to objection on the ground that a declaratory judgment or decree is prayed for; and the existence of another adequate remedy does not preclude a judgment for declaratory relief in cases where it is appropriate. The declaration shall have the force and effect of a final judgment or decree.

Art. 1872. Interested parties may obtain declaration of rights, status, or other legal relations

A person interested under a deed, will, written contract or other writing constituting a contract, or whose rights, status, or other legal relations are affected by a statute, municipal ordinance, contract or franchise, may have determined any question of construction or validity arising under the instrument, statute, ordinance, contract, or franchise and obtain a declaration of rights, status, or other legal relations thereunder.

Editor's Notes

C.C.P. arts. 1872 to 1883 are taken virtually verbatim from the Uniform Declaratory Judgments Act, Comment.

Art. 1873. Construction of contract

A contract may be construed either before or after there has been a breach thereof.

Art. 1874. Interested person may obtain declaration of rights; purpose

A person interested as or through an executor, administrator, trustee, guardian, or other fiduciary, creditor, devisee, legatee, heir, next of kin, or cestui que trust, in the administration of a trust, or of the estate of a decedent, an infant, lunatic, or insolvent, may have a declaration of rights or legal relations in respect thereto:

(1) To ascertain any class of creditors, devisees, legatees, heirs, next of kin or others;

(2) To direct the executors, administrators, or trustees to do or abstain from doing any particular act in their fiduciary capacity; or

(3) To determine any question arising in the administration of the estate or trust, including questions of construction of wills and other writings.

Art. 1875. Powers enumerated not exclusive

The enumeration in Articles 1872 through 1874 does not limit or restrict the exercise of the general powers conferred in Article 1871 in any proceeding where declaratory relief is sought, in which a judgment or decree will terminate the controversy or remove an uncertainty.

Art. 1876. Court may refuse declaratory judgment

The court may refuse to render a declaratory judgment or decree where such judgment or decree, if rendered, would not terminate the uncertainty or controversy giving rise to the proceeding.

Art. 1877. Review of judgments and decrees

All orders, judgments, and decrees under Articles 1871 through 1883 may be reviewed as other orders, judgments, and decrees.

Art. 1878. Supplemental relief; expedited hearing for constitutional determination; effect of pendency of other proceedings

A. Further relief based on a declaratory judgment or decree may be granted whenever necessary or proper. The application therefor shall be by petition to a court having jurisdiction to grant the relief. If the application is considered sufficient, the court, on reasonable notice, shall require any adverse party whose rights have been adjudicated by the declaratory judgment or decree, to show cause why further relief should not be granted forthwith.

B. In any action or proceeding seeking a declaratory judgment as to the constitutionality of the expenditure of state funds, the court shall set the matter with preference and proceed to hear and determine the matter as expeditiously as the ends of justice may require, notwithstanding resolution of a pending petition for injunction sought pursuant to Article 3601 or a petition for mandamus sought pursuant to Article 3862.

Amended by Acts 2014, No. 41, § 1.

Art. 1879. Trial and determination of issue of fact

When a proceeding under Articles 1871 through 1883 involves the determination of an issue of fact, such issue may be tried and determined in the same manner as issues of fact are tried and determined in other civil actions in the court in which the proceeding is pending.

Art. 1880. Parties

When declaratory relief is sought, all persons shall be made parties who have or claim any interest which would be affected by the declaration, and no declaration shall prejudice the rights of persons not parties to the proceeding. In a proceeding which involves the validity of a municipal ordinance or franchise, such municipality shall be made a party, and shall be entitled to be heard. If the statute, ordinance, or franchise is alleged to be unconstitutional, the attorney general of the state shall also be served with a copy of the proceeding and be entitled to be heard.

Art. 1881. Construction

Articles 1871 through 1883 are declared to be remedial. Their purpose is to settle and afford relief from uncertainty and insecurity with respect to rights, status, and other legal relations, and they are to be liberally construed and administered.

Art. 1882. Provisions independent and severable

Articles 1873 through 1883 are declared independent and severable, and the invalidity, if any, of any part or feature thereof shall not affect or render the remainder of the articles invalid or inoperative.

Art. 1883. Uniformity of interpretation

Articles 1871 through 1882 shall be interpreted and construed so as to effectuate their general purpose to make uniform the law of those states which enact them, and to harmonize, as far as possible, with federal laws and regulations on the subject of declaratory judgments and decrees.

CHAPTER 3. RENDITION

Article

Art. 1911. Final judgment; partial final judgment; signing; appeals

A. Except as otherwise provided by law, every final judgment shall contain the typewritten or printed name of the judge and be signed by the judge. Any judgment that does not contain the typewritten or printed name of the judge shall not be invalidated for that reason. Judgments may be signed by the judge by use of electronic signature. The various courts shall provide by court rule for the method of electronic signature to be used and to ensure the authenticity of the electronic signature.

B. For the purpose of an appeal as provided in Article 2083, no appeal may be taken from a final judgment until the requirement of this Article has been fulfilled. No appeal may be taken from a partial final judgment under Article 1915(B) until the judgment has been designated a final judgment under Article 1915(B). An appeal may be taken from a final judgment under Article 1915(A) without the judgment being so designated.

Amended by Acts 1974, No. 87, § 1; Acts 1979, No. 618, § 1; Acts 1999, No. 1263, § 1, eff. Jan. 1, 2000; Acts 2014, No. 144, § 1; Acts 2014, No. 606, § 1.

Editor's Notes

Maximum delay for rendering judgment taken under advisement, R.S. 13:4207. See Overmier v. Taylor, 475 So.2d 1094 (1985), which states: "An appeal granted before the signing of a final judgment is subject to dismissal until the final judgment is signed." See note under C.C.P. art. 2121, particularly Traigle, as to difference between suspensive and devolutive appeals.

The last two sentences of the article were added by the 1999 amendment to make it absolutely clear that final judgments under C.C.P. art. 1915(A) are appealable without certification by the trial court, while a *partial* final judgment under C.C.P. art. 1915(B) must be *designated* as a final judgment to be appealable.

See Rule 9.5, District Court Rules, Court's Signature.

Art. 1912. Final judgment; multi-parish districts, signing in any parish in the state

A final judgment may be signed in any parish within the state and shall be sent to the clerk of the parish in which the case is pending.

Amended by Acts 1974, No. 242, § 1.

Art. 1913. Notice of judgment

A. Except as otherwise provided by law, notice of the signing of a final judgment, including a partial final judgment under Article 1915, is required in all contested cases, and shall be mailed by the clerk of court to the counsel of record for each party, and to each party not represented by counsel.

B. Notice of the signing of a default judgment against a defendant on whom citation was not served personally, or on whom citation was served through the secretary of state, and who filed no exception, answer, or other pleading, shall be served on the defendant by the sheriff, by either personal or domiciliary service, or in the case of a defendant originally served through the secretary of state, by service on the secretary of state.

C. Except when service is required under Paragraph B of this Article, notice of the signing of a default judgment shall be mailed by the clerk of court to the defendant at the address where personal service was obtained or to the last known address of the defendant.

D. The clerk shall file a certificate in the record showing the date on which, and the counsel and parties to whom, notice of the signing of the judgment was mailed.

E. Repealed by Acts 2008, No. 824, § 5, eff. Jan. 1, 2009.

Amended by Acts 1961, No. 23, § 1; Acts 1968, No. 127, § 1; Acts 1990, No. 1000, § 1; Acts 1992, No. 700, § 1; Acts 1999, No. 1263, § 1, eff. Jan. 1, 2000; Acts 2001, No. 512, § 1; Acts 2006, No. 337, § 1; Acts 2017, No. 419, § 1; Acts 2018, No. 195, § 1; Acts 2021, No. 174, § 1, eff. Jan. 1, 2022.

Art. 1914. Interlocutory judgments; notice; delay for further action

A. Except as provided in Paragraphs B and C of this Article, the rendition of an interlocutory judgment in open court constitutes notice to all parties.

B. The interlocutory judgment shall be reduced to writing if the court so orders, if a party requests within ten days of rendition in open court that it be reduced to writing, or if the court takes the interlocutory matter under advisement. The clerk shall mail notice of the subsequent judgment to each party.

C. If the interlocutory judgment is one refusing to grant a new trial or a judgment notwithstanding the verdict, the clerk shall mail notice to each party regardless of whether the motion is taken under advisement. The delay for appealing the final judgment commences to run only from the date of the mailing of the notice, as provided in Articles 2087 and 2123.

D. Except as provided in Paragraph C of this Article, each party shall have ten days either from notice of the interlocutory judgment, or from the mailing of notice when required to take any action or file any pleadings in the trial court; however, this provision does not suspend or otherwise affect the time for applying for supervisory writs, nor does it affect the time for appealing an interlocutory judgment under Article 2083.

E. The provisions of this Article do not apply to an interlocutory injunctive order or judgment.

Amended by Acts 1983, No. 61, § 1; Acts 1995, No. 657, § 1; Acts 2003, No. 545, § 1.

Editor's Notes

C.C.P. art. 1979, time within which court must decide motion for new trial.

Art. 1915. Partial final judgment; partial judgment; partial exception; partial summary judgment

A. A final judgment may be rendered and signed by the court, even though it may not grant the successful party or parties all of the relief prayed for, or may not adjudicate all of the issues in the case, when the court:

(1) Dismisses the suit as to less than all of the parties, defendants, third party plaintiffs, third party defendants, or intervenors.

(2) Grants a motion for judgment on the pleadings, as provided by Articles 965, 968, and 969.

(3) Grants a motion for summary judgment, as provided by Articles 966 through 969, but not including a summary judgment granted pursuant to Article 966(E).

(4) Signs a judgment on either the principal or incidental demand, when the two have been tried separately, as provided by Article 1038.

(5) Signs a judgment on the issue of liability when that issue has been tried separately by the court, or when, in a jury trial, the issue of liability has been tried before a jury and the issue of damages is to be tried before a different jury.

(6) Imposes sanctions or disciplinary action pursuant to Article 191, 863, or 864 or Code of Evidence Article 510(G).

B. (1) When a court renders a partial judgment or partial summary judgment or sustains an exception in part, as to one or more but less than all of the claims, demands, issues, or theories against a party, whether in an original demand, reconventional demand, cross-claim, third-party claim, or intervention, the judgment shall not constitute a final judgment unless it is designated as a final judgment by the court after an express determination that there is no just reason for delay.

(2) In the absence of such a determination and designation, any such order or decision shall not constitute a final judgment for the purpose of an immediate appeal and may be revised at any time prior to rendition of the judgment adjudicating all the claims and the rights and liabilities of all the parties.

C. If an appeal is taken from any judgment rendered under the provisions of this Article, the trial court shall retain jurisdiction to adjudicate the remaining issues in the case.

Amended by Acts 1983, No. 534, § 3; Acts 1992, No. 71, § 1; Acts 1997, No. 483, § 2, eff. July 1, 1997; Acts 1999, No. 89, § 1; Acts 1999, No. 1263, § 1, eff. Jan. 1, 2000; Acts 2001, No. 553, § 1; Acts 2013, No. 391, § 1.

Comment—1983

The enactment of this article by Acts 1983, No. 534 reflects the intent of the last paragraph of former Art. 466, that the court may render a final judgment on the issue of liability alone when that issue has been tried separately.

Comment—1999

The language in 1915(B)(1) is amended to eliminate confusion with Article 1915(A) by the elimination of "parties" from (B)(1). A partial final judgment under Article 1915(B) is appealable only if so designated by the court. See Banks v. State Farm, 708 So.2d 523 (2 Cir. 1998). A final judgment under Article 1915(A) is appealable without being so designated, except for a partial summary judgment under Article 966(E). A partial summary judgment under Article 966(E) is covered under Article 1915(B). See C.C.P. Art. 1911.

Editor's Notes

The 1999 amendment makes it clear that a judgment under C.C.P. art. 1915(A), except for C.C.P. art. 966(E), is a *final* judgment subject to appeal as any other final judgment; while a *partial* final judgment under C.C.P. 1915(B)(1) must be *designated* as a final judgment to be appealable. The C.C.P. art. 1915(B)(1) *partial* final judgments, of course, may nonetheless be the suitable subject for an application for supervisory writs.

Subparagraph (A)(6) was added to make the imposition of sanctions or disciplinary action a *final* appealable judgment.

Bloodworth v. Wilson, 891 So.2d 15 (La. App. 5 Cir. 2004). (See this case for appeal of partial judgment under C.C.P. art. 1915.)

R.J. Messinger, Inc. v. Rosenblum, 894 So.2d 1113 (La. 2005). Appeal from partial summary judgment under C.C.P. art. 1915, subd. B, would not be dismissed for failure of trial court to state that there was no reason for delay of the appeal. Prior jurisprudence to the contrary was overruled, the court finding that "the trial court should give explicit reasons, either oral or written for its determination that there is no just reason for delay. However, if the trial court fails to do so, we find the appellate court cannot summarily dismiss the appeal." The Court of Appeal should examine the record to see whether the justification for appeal is apparent. (This opinion is an excellent "book" on the appeal of partial summary judgments under C.C.P. art. 1915B).

Art. 1916. Jury cases; compromise agreements; signature of judgment by the court

A. After a trial by jury, the court shall prepare and sign a judgment in accordance with the verdict of the jury within ten days of the rendition of the verdict, or the court may order counsel for a party in the case to prepare and submit a judgment to the court for signature within ten days of the rendition of the verdict, in accordance with the rules for Louisiana district courts.

B. When the parties to a contested matter reach a compromise agreement which is recited in open court and on the record capable of being transcribed, the court may order counsel for a party to prepare and submit a judgment to the court for signature, in accordance with the rules for Louisiana district courts, within twenty days of the recital.

Amended by Acts 2006, No. 474, § 1; Acts 2008, No. 824, § 3, eff. Jan. 1, 2009.

Art. 1917. Findings of the court and reasons for judgment

A. In all appealable contested cases, other than those tried by a jury, the court when requested to do so by a party shall give in writing its findings of fact and reasons for judgment, provided the request is made not later than ten days after the mailing of the notice of the signing of the judgment.

B. In nonjury cases to recover damages for injury, death, or loss, whether or not requested to do so by a party, the court shall make specific findings that shall include those matters to which reference is made in Paragraph C of Article 1812 of this Code. These findings need not include reasons for judgment.

Amended by Acts 1979, No. 431, § 3, eff. Aug. 1, 1980; Acts 1980, No. 111, § 1, eff. Aug. 1, 1980; Acts 1980, No. 112, § 1, eff. June 26, 1980; Acts 2005, No. 205, § 1, eff. Jan. 1, 2006.

Art. 1918. Form of final judgment

A. A final judgment in accordance with Article 1841 shall be identified as such by appropriate language; shall be signed and dated; and shall, in its decree, identify the name of the party in whose favor the relief is awarded, the name of the party against whom the relief is awarded, and the relief that is awarded. If appealed, a final judgment that does not contain the appropriate decretal language shall be remanded to the trial court, which shall amend the judgment in accordance with Article 1951 within the time set by the appellate court.

B. When written reasons for the judgment are assigned, they shall be set out in an opinion separate from the judgment.

Amended by Acts 2021, No. 259, § 2.

See West's Louisiana Statutes Annotated

Art. 1919. Judgment affecting immovable property; particular description

All final judgments which affect title to immovable property shall describe the immovable property affected with particularity.

This article does not apply to judgments in succession proceedings recognizing heirs or legatees and sending them into possession.

Art. 1920. Costs; parties liable; procedure for taxing

Unless the judgment provides otherwise, costs shall be paid by the party cast, and may be taxed by a rule to show cause.

Except as otherwise provided by law, the court may render judgment for costs, or any part thereof, against any party, as it may consider equitable.

Art. 1921. Interest allowed by the judgment

The court shall award interest in the judgment as prayed for or as provided by law.

Editor's Notes

Actions ex delicto, judicial interest runs from date of judicial demand, R.S. 13:4203; C.C. art. 2924, rates of interest; C.C. art. 2000 et seq., kinds of interest and other provisions regulating interest. See also limitation of interest in actions against state or political subdivisions, R.S. 13:5112(C).

Art. 1922. Money judgments; judgment debtor; date of birth; social security number

A. A final judgment for the payment of money shall include the date of birth of all parties against whom it is rendered, if the date of birth is known by the attorney preparing the judgment. However, the failure to include the date of birth of the judgment debtors shall not affect the validity of the judgment.

B. (1) A final judgment for the payment of money shall also include the last four digits of the social security number of the judgment debtors, if known by the attorney preparing the judgment. However, the failure to include such information shall not affect the validity of the judgment.

(2) A recorded lien having the effect of a money judgment shall also include the last four digits of the social security number of the debtor, or the Internal Revenue Service taxpayer identification number of the debtor in the case of a debtor doing business other than as an individual, if known by the attorney preparing the lien. However, the failure to include such information shall not affect the validity of the lien.

C. (1) The recorder shall not refuse to record a money judgment or lien which does not include the information required by Paragraph B of this Article. If any judgment or lien being recorded does not include the information required by this Article, the recorder shall be entitled to collect a fee not to exceed twenty-five dollars per debtor in addition to the applicable fee set forth in R.S. 13:841.

(2) The fee authorized by Subparagraph (1) of this Paragraph shall not apply if, at the time of recording the judgment, the creditor attaches to and records with the judgment an affidavit setting forth the information required by Paragraph B of this Article or by Civil Code Article 3352(A)(5).

(3) A person recording an affidavit of distinction pursuant to R.S. 9:5501 through 5503 shall not be required to pay a fee for recording the affidavit of distinction.

(4) The provisions of Subparagraph (3) of this Paragraph shall not apply to an affidavit of distinction recorded in order to distinguish the affiant from a debtor named in a judgment or lien which was recorded prior to July 1, 2012.

Added by Acts 1995, No. 1295, § 1. Amended by Acts 2003, No. 599, § 1; Acts 2007, No. 11, § 1, eff. June 18, 2007; Acts 2012, No. 20, § 1, eff. July 1, 2012.

Arts. 1923 to 1950. [Blank]

CHAPTER 4. MODIFICATION IN TRIAL COURT

SECTION 1. AMENDMENT

Article

SECTION 2. NEW TRIAL

SECTION 3. ACTION OF NULLITY

SECTION 1. AMENDMENT

Art. 1951. Amendment of judgment

On motion of the court or any party, a final judgment may be amended at any time to alter the phraseology of the judgment or to correct deficiencies in the decretal language or errors of calculation. The judgment may be amended only after a hearing with notice to all parties, except that a hearing is not required if all parties consent or if the court or the party submitting the amended judgment certifies that it was provided to all parties at least five days before the amendment and that no opposition has been received. A final judgment may not be amended under this Article to change its substance.

Amended by Acts 2013, No. 78, § 1; Acts 2021, No. 259, § 2.

Comment—2013

Article 1951 has been changed to require a hearing before a final judgment may be amended, unless the parties consent to the amendment or no opposition is filed after notice. The notice referenced in the Article is to counsel for named parties and self-represented parties entitled to notice under Article 1913. The court may direct notice to other interested persons, such as those entitled to notice in succession proceedings under Article 3305 and 3335.

Editor's Notes

A second judgment with substantive difference from first judgment was a nullity under this article, Oreman v. Oreman, 926 So.2d 709 (App. 5th Cir., 2006).

SECTION 2. NEW TRIAL

Art. 1971. Granting of new trial

A new trial may be granted, upon contradictory motion of any party or by the court on its own motion, to all or any of the parties and on all or part of the issues, or for reargument only. If a new trial is granted as to less than all parties or issues, the judgment may be held in abeyance as to all parties and issues.

Editor's Notes

C.C.P. arts. 1813, 1814, jury trials.

Art. 1972. Peremptory grounds

A new trial shall be granted, upon contradictory motion of any party, in the following cases:

(1) When the verdict or judgment appears clearly contrary to the law and the evidence.

(2) When the party has discovered, since the trial, evidence important to the cause, which he could not, with due diligence, have obtained before or during the trial.

(3) When the jury was bribed or has behaved improperly so that impartial justice has not been done.

Amended by Acts 1983, No. 534, § 10.

Art. 1973. Discretionary grounds

A new trial may be granted in any case if there is good ground therefor, except as otherwise provided by law.

Editor's Notes

The granting of a default judgment may be a discretionary "good ground" to grant a new trial. See e.g., Pollock v. Talco Midstream Assets, Ltd., 44,629 (La. App. 2 Cir. 9/23/09), 22 So.3d 1033, 1034; Bates v. Legion Indem. Co., 2001-0552 (La. App. 1 Cir. 2/27/02), 818 So.2d 176, 178.

Art. 1974. Delay for applying for new trial

A party may file a motion for a new trial not later than seven days, exclusive of legal holidays, after the clerk has mailed or the sheriff has served the notice of judgment as required by Article 1913.

Amended by Acts 1961, No. 23, § 1; Acts 1974, No. 520, § 1; Acts 1999, No. 1263, § 1, eff. Jan. 1, 2000; Acts 2021, No. 259, § 2.

Editor's Notes

The 1999 amendment makes the delay commence to run in *all* cases on the day after *service* of the notice of judgment under C.C.P. art. 1913, rather than from the signing of the judgment.

Art. 1975. Application for new trial; verifying affidavit

A motion for a new trial shall set forth the grounds upon which it is based. When the motion is based on Article 1972(2) and (3), the allegations of fact therein shall be verified by the affidavit of the applicant.

Art. 1976. Service of notice

Notice of the motion for new trial and of the time and place assigned for hearing thereon must be served upon the opposing party as provided by Article 1314.

Art. 1977. Assignment of new trial

When a new trial is granted, it shall be assigned for hearing in accordance with the rules and practice of the court.

Art. 1978. Procedure in new trial

It shall not be necessary in a non-jury trial to resummon the witnesses or to hear them anew at a new trial if their testimony has once been reduced to writing, but all such testimony and evidence received on the former trial shall be considered as already in evidence. Any party may call new witnesses or offer additional evidence, and with the permission of the court recall any witness for further examination or cross-examination as the case may be. However, the parties shall not be precluded from producing new proofs, on the ground they have not been offered on the first trial. When a new trial is granted for reargument only, no evidence shall be adduced.

Amended by Acts 1988, No. 515, § 2, eff. Jan. 1, 1989.

Comment—1988

The provision of this Article relative to admission in a new trial of former testimony that has been reduced to writing has been limited to bench trials to accommodate the unavailability requirement of the Code of Evidence. Art. 804(B)(1) of that Code states that the unavailability of a witness is a general prerequisite to the admissibility of his former testimony. See Code of Evidence Art. 804(B)(1) and comments thereunder.

Art. 1979. Summary decision on motion; maximum delays

The court shall decide on a motion for a new trial within ten days from the time it is submitted for decision. The time may be extended for a specified period upon the written consent or stipulation of record by the attorneys representing all parties. When the court grants a motion for a new trial, it shall specify each of its reasons in the order.

Amended by Acts 2013, No. 78, § 1.

Comment—2013

The last sentence was added to require the court to state all of its reasons in an order granting a new trial. The change was taken from a similar provision in FRCP 59(d). The specification of reasons for granting a new trial may facilitate appellate review by supervisory writ or subsequent trial court proceedings.

Editor's Notes

C.C.P. art. 1914; see notes to C.C.P. art. 1973.

SECTION 3. ACTION OF NULLITY

Art. 2001. Grounds in general

The nullity of a final judgment may be demanded for vices of either form or substance, as provided in Articles 2002 through 2006.

Art. 2002. Annulment for vices of form; time for action

A. A final judgment shall be annulled if it is rendered:

(1) Against an incompetent person not represented as required by law.

(2) Against a defendant who has not been served with process as required by law and who has not waived objection to jurisdiction, or against whom a valid default judgment has not been taken.

(3) By a court which does not have jurisdiction over the subject matter of the suit.

B. Except as otherwise provided in Article 2003, an action to annul a judgment on the grounds listed in this Article may be brought at any time.

Amended by Acts 1997, No. 578, § 1; Acts 2017, No. 419, § 1; Acts 2021, No. 174, § 1, eff. Jan. 1, 2022.

Editor's Notes

An action of nullity on these grounds may be asserted collaterally and at any time, Comment (e).

The 1997 amendment of par. (2) presumably would include "submission of the party to the exercise of jurisdiction over him personally by the court...", under C.C.P. art. 6 as sufficient to obviate the nullity, as well as the waiver of objection by failure to file the declinatory exception timely. For an example of "submission" apart from "waiver", see DeFatta v. DeFatta, 352 So.2d 287 (2nd Cir.1997).

Art. 2003. Same; action lost through acquiescence

A defendant who voluntarily acquiesced in the judgment, or who was present in the parish at the time of its execution and did not attempt to enjoin its enforcement, may not annul the judgment on any of the grounds enumerated in Article 2002.

Art. 2004. Annulment for vices of substance; peremption of action

A. A final judgment obtained by fraud or ill practices may be annulled.

B. An action to annul a judgment on these grounds must be brought within one year of the discovery by the plaintiff in the nullity action of the fraud or ill practices.

C. The court may award reasonable attorney fees incurred by the prevailing party in an action to annul a judgment on these grounds.

Amended by Acts 2001, No. 512, § 1.

Editor's Notes

These grounds must be asserted in a direct action, not collaterally, Comment (d). See Kem Search, Inc. v. Sheffield, 434 So.2d 1067 (1983), holding that the requirements for nullity are satisfied when enforcement of the judgment would be inequitable or unconscionable. The one-year period in par. B is peremptive. Knox v. West Baton Rouge Cred., Inc., 9 So.3d 1020 (App. 1 Cir. 2009).

Art. 2005. Annulment of judgments; effect of appeal

A judgment may be annulled prior to or pending an appeal therefrom, or after the delays for appealing have elapsed.

A judgment affirmed, reversed, amended, or otherwise rendered by an appellate court may be annulled only when the ground for nullity did not appear in the record of appeal or was not considered by the appellate court.

An action of nullity does not affect the right to appeal.

Art. 2006. Court where action brought

An action to annul a judgment must be brought in the trial court, even though the judgment sought to be annulled may have been affirmed on appeal, or even rendered by the appellate court.

Editor's Notes

The action must be brought in the court that rendered the judgment, Comment. See Licoho Enterprises, Inc. v. Succession of Champagne, 283 So.2d 217 (1973).

CHAPTER 5. REVIVAL

Article

Art. 2031. Revival of judgments

A. A money judgment may be revived at any time before it prescribes by an interested party by the filing of an ex parte motion brought in the court and suit in which the judgment was rendered. The filing of the motion to revive interrupts the prescriptive period applicable to the judgment. The motion to revive judgment shall be accompanied by an affidavit of the holder and owner of the judgment, stating that the original judgment has not been satisfied. A judgment shall thereupon be rendered reviving the original judgment. No citation or service of process of the motion to revive shall be required. The court may order the judgment debtor to pay additional court costs and reasonable attorney fees in connection with the judgment revival action. Notice of signing of the judgment of revival shall be mailed by the clerk of court to the judgment debtor at his last known address as reflected in the suit record.

B. At any time after the signing of the judgment of revival, the judgment debtor may, by contradictory motion, have the judgment of revival annulled, upon showing that the judgment which has been revived was in fact satisfied prior to the signing of the judgment of revival. If the judgment debtor proves that the judgment has been satisfied prior to the filing of the motion to revive the judgment, the holder or owner of the judgment shall pay all court costs, fees, and attorney fees incurred by the judgment debtor in opposing the ex parte order of revival and the cancellation of the judgment from the mortgage records.

Amended by Acts 2003, No. 806, § 1; Acts 2005, No. 205, § 1, eff. Jan. 1, 2006.

Editor's Notes

See C.C. art. 3501, money judgment prescribes in ten years; a revived judgment prescribes in ten years from revival.

See also C.C. arts. 3362 to 3365, reinscription of mortgages, including judicial mortgage (to be synchronized with revival).

Arts. 2032 to 2080. Reserved for future legislation

BOOK III

PROCEEDINGS IN APPELLATE COURTS

TITLE I. APPELLATE PROCEDURE

CHAPTER 1. GENERAL DISPOSITIONS

Art. 2081. Applicability of Title

The provisions of this Title are applicable to all appeals to the supreme court and the courts of appeal, except as otherwise provided by law.

Editor's Notes

See Uniform Rules—Courts of Appeal, and Supreme Court Rules, Volume 8, West's LSA–Revised Statutes (following Title 13).

Art. 2082. Definition of appeal

Appeal is the exercise of the right of a party to have a judgment of a trial court revised, modified, set aside, or reversed by an appellate court.

Art. 2083. Judgments appealable

A. A final judgment is appealable in all causes in which appeals are given by law, whether rendered after hearing, by default, or by reformation under Article 1814.

B. In reviewing a judgment reformed in accordance with a remittitur or additur, the court shall consider the reasonableness of the underlying jury verdict.

C. An interlocutory judgment is appealable only when expressly provided by law.

Amended by Acts 1984, No. 59, § 1; Acts 1989, No. 173, § 1; Acts 2005, No. 205, § 1, eff. Jan. 1, 2006.

Comments—2005

(a) Article 2083(C) has been amended to provide that interlocutory judgments are appealable only when expressly provided by legislation such as Code of Civil Procedure Article 3612 and 592(A)(3)(b). Appellate review of all other interlocutory judgments should now be applied for pursuant to the appellate court's supervisory authority set forth in Article 2201, the Uniform Rules, Courts of Appeal, and the Rules of the Supreme Court of Louisiana.

(b) The prior cases recognizing a right to appeal interlocutory judgments based on the irreparable injury standard set forth in the previous version of Article 2083(A) are no longer valid. However, the change is not intended to create any new substantive grounds to be applied by the appellate courts in screening writ applications. Irreparable injury continues to be an important (but not exclusive) ingredient in an application for supervisory writs. See *Herlitz Const. Co., Inc. v. Hotel Investors of New Iberia, Inc.*, 396 So.2d 878 (La. 1981); *Tatum, Revisiting the Supervisory Powers, 41 Louisiana Bar Journal*, Vol. 41, No. 5 (Feb.1994).

(c) The 2005 amendment to Article 2083 was made for several reasons. First, it eliminates the uncertainty of selection between an interlocutory appeal and supervisory writ as the proper procedure when the overlapping and ill-defined irreparable injury standard is thought to be applicable to the trial court's ruling. See *Maraist and Lemmon*, Vol. I, Louisiana Civil Law Treatise, § 14.17. Secondly, the procedures inherent in an interlocutory appeal often created unnecessary delay in the progress of a lawsuit at the trial court level. See *Hamilton Medical Group v. Ochsner Health Plan*, 550 So.2d 290, 292 (La. App. 3 Cir. 1989). Finally, the amendment promotes uniformity and clarity in appellate practice in that there is now one delay period provided in Uniform Rules—Courts of Appeal § 4.3 for seeking appellate review of all interlocutory judgments except those for which an appeal is expressly provided, rather than multiple periods under the prior system when both a supervisory writ and an appeal were options.

(d) The amendment does not change the appealability of partial final judgments pursuant to Article 1915(B).

Art. 2084. Legal representative may appeal

A legal representative may appeal any appealable judgment rendered against him or affecting the property which he is administering, for the benefit of the person whose property he administers or whom he represents, whenever he considers an appeal necessary or advisable.

Art. 2085. Limitations on appeals

An appeal cannot be taken by a party who confessed judgment in the proceedings in the trial court or who voluntarily and unconditionally acquiesced in a judgment rendered against him. Confession of or acquiescence in part of a divisible judgment or in a favorable part of an indivisible judgment does not preclude an appeal as to other parts of such judgment.

Art. 2086. Right of third person to appeal

A person who could have intervened in the trial court may appeal, whether or not any other appeal has been taken.

Art. 2087. Delay for taking devolutive appeal

A. Except as otherwise provided in this Article or by other law, an appeal which does not suspend the effect or the execution of an appealable order or judgment may be taken within sixty days of any of the following:

(1) The expiration of the delay for applying for a new trial or judgment notwithstanding the verdict, as provided by Article 1974 and Article 1811, if no application has been filed timely.

(2) The date of the mailing of notice of the court's refusal to grant a timely application for a new trial or judgment notwithstanding the verdict, as provided under Article 1914.

B. When a devolutive appeal has been taken timely, an appellee who seeks to have the judgment appealed from modified, revised, or reversed as to any party may take a devolutive appeal therefrom within the delays allowed in Paragraph A of this Article or within ten days of the mailing by the clerk of the notice of the first devolutive appeal in the case, whichever is later.

C. When one or more parties file motions for new trial or for judgment notwithstanding the verdict, the delay periods specified herein shall commence for all parties at the time they commence for the party whose motion is last to be acted upon by the trial court.

D. An order of appeal is premature if granted before the court disposes of all timely filed motions for new trial or judgment notwithstanding the verdict. The order becomes effective upon the denial of such motions.

E. The time within which to take a devolutive appeal under the provisions of this Article is interrupted for all parties upon the filing of a notice of removal in a district court of the United States, pursuant to the provisions of 28 U.S.C. 1446, and commences anew on the date the proceeding is remanded.

Amended by Acts 1962, No. 92, § 1; Acts 1976, No. 201, § 1; Acts 1977, No. 174, § 1, eff. Jan. 1, 1978; Acts 1987, No. 695, § 1; Acts 1995, No. 658, § 1; Acts 1997, No. 609, § 1; Acts 1997, No. 1056, § 1.

Comment—1997

The amendment makes it clear that an appeal granted before disposition of timely motions for new trial or judgment notwithstanding the verdict is premature and that it becomes effective upon the denial of such motion(s).

Art. 2088. Divesting of jurisdiction of trial court

A. The jurisdiction of the trial court over all matters in the case reviewable under the appeal is divested, and that of the appellate court attaches, on the granting of the order of appeal and the timely filing of the appeal bond, in the case of a suspensive appeal or on the granting of the order of appeal, in the case of a devolutive appeal. Thereafter, the trial court has jurisdiction in the case only over those matters not reviewable under the appeal, including the right to do any of the following:

(1) Allow the taking of a deposition, as provided in Article 1433.

(2) Extend the return day of the appeal, as provided in Article 2125.

(3) Make, or permit the making of, a written narrative of the facts of the case, as provided in Article 2131.

(4) Correct any misstatement, irregularity, informality, or omission of the trial record, as provided in Article 2132.

(5) Test the solvency of the surety on the appeal bond as of the date of its filing or subsequently, consider objections to the form, substance, and sufficiency of the appeal bond, and permit the curing thereof, as provided in Articles 5123, 5124, and 5126.

(6) Grant an appeal to another party.

(7) Execute or give effect to the judgment when its execution or effect is not suspended by the appeal.

(8) Enter orders permitting the deposit of sums of money within the meaning of Article 4658.

(9) Impose the penalties provided by Article 2126, or dismiss the appeal, when the appellant fails to timely pay the estimated costs or the difference between the estimated costs and the actual costs of the appeal.

(10) Set and tax costs, expert witness fees, and attorney fees.

(11) Certify a partial judgment or partial summary judgment in accordance with Article 1915(B).

(12) Amend a judgment to provide proper decretal language under Article 1918 or 1951.

B. In the case of a suspensive appeal, when the appeal bond is not timely filed and the suspensive appeal is thereby not perfected, the trial court maintains jurisdiction to convert the suspensive appeal to a devolutive appeal, except in an eviction case.

Amended by Acts 1964, No. 4, § 1; Acts 1968, No. 128, § 1; Acts 1977, No. 175, § 1, eff. Jan. 1, 1978; Acts 1983, No. 126, § 1; Acts 2008, No. 658, § 1; Acts 2021, No. 259, § 2.

Art. 2089. Description required of immovable property affected by judgments or decrees

All judgments and decrees which affect title to immovable property shall describe with particularity the immovable property affected.

CHAPTER 2. PROCEDURE FOR APPEALING

Article

Art. 2121. Method of appealing

An appeal is taken by obtaining an order therefor, within the delay allowed, from the court which rendered the judgment.

An order of appeal may be granted on oral motion in open court, on written motion, or on petition. This order shall show the return day of the appeal in the appellate court and shall provide the amount of security to be furnished, when the law requires the determination thereof by the court.

When the order is granted, the clerk of court shall mail a notice of appeal to counsel of record of all other parties, to the respective appellate court, and to other parties not represented by counsel. The failure of the clerk to mail the notice does not affect the validity of the appeal.

Amended by Acts 1961, No. 23, § 1; Acts 1976, No. 202, § 1.

Editor's Notes

But see Traigle v. Gulf Coast Aluminum Corp., 399 So.2d 183 (1981), approving order of devolutive appeal signed after delays have run, when motion for appeal was timely filed. Footnote 18 of the opinion specifically limits the holding to devolutive appeals. CAVEAT: See the footnote itself as to suspensive appeals. Also, Overmier v. Traylor, 475 So.2d 1094 (1985), states: "An appeal granted before the signing of a final judgment is subject to dismissal until the final judgment is signed."

Art. 2122. Appointment or removal of legal representative not suspended by appeal; effect of vacating appointment on appeal

A judgment or order of a trial court appointing or removing a legal representative shall be executed provisionally notwithstanding an appeal therefrom.

A judgment rendered on appeal vacating a judgment or order of the trial court appointing a legal representative does not invalidate any of his official acts performed prior to the rendition of the judgment of the appellate court.

Art. 2123. Delay for taking suspensive appeal

A. Except as otherwise provided by law, an appeal that suspends the effect or the execution of an appealable order or judgment may be taken, and the security therefor furnished, only within thirty days of any of the following:

(1) The expiration of the delay for applying for a new trial or judgment notwithstanding the verdict, as provided by Article 1974 and Article 1811, if no application has been filed timely.

(2) The date of the mailing of notice of the court's refusal to grant a timely application for a new trial or judgment notwithstanding the verdict, as provided under Article 1914.

B. Whenever one or more parties file motions for a new trial or for judgment notwithstanding the verdict, the delay periods specified herein commence for all parties at the time they commence for the party whose motion is last to be acted upon by the trial court.

C. An order of appeal is premature if granted before the court disposes of all timely filed motions for new trial or judgment notwithstanding the verdict. The order becomes effective upon the denial of such motions.

D. The time within which to take a suspensive appeal under the provisions of this Article is interrupted for all parties upon the filing of a notice of removal in a district court of the United States, pursuant to the provisions of 28 U.S.C. 1446, and commences anew on the date the proceeding is remanded.

Amended by Acts 1974, No. 129, § 1; Acts 1987, No. 695, § 1; Acts 1995, No. 658, § 1; Acts 1997, No. 609, § 1; Acts 1997, No. 1056, § 1.

Official Revision Comments—1960

(a) The principal change made by this article was to increase the delay for taking a suspensive appeal from "ten days, not including Sundays" under the source provisions, to fifteen days. The primary reason for this change was the fact that the majority of suspensive appeal bonds today are surety company bonds, and more time is needed to obtain this type of bond.

(b) One of the principal exceptions to the general rule of this article is set forth in Art. 2122, *supra*, prohibiting a suspensive appeal from any judgment or order appointing or removing a legal representative. Other important exceptions to the general rule of this article are appeals from judgments or orders: awarding alimony or custody of children in divorce or judicial separation cases; ordering the release of a person in custody, or awarding his custody to another; granting interim allowance to surviving spouse, heirs, or legatees of deceased persons; issuing temporary restraining orders and preliminary injunction; and expropriating property of a defendant. See Arts. 3321, 3612, 3831, and 3943, *infra*; Art. 2634, Civil Code; and R.S. 19:13.

(c) See, also, Comments under Arts. 2087, 2121, *supra*, and Art. 2252, *infra*.

Comment—1995

The amendments to Articles 2087 and 2123 make it clear that a motion for a judgment notwithstanding the verdict affects the delays for taking an appeal, and that only the motions for new trial and judgment notwithstanding the verdict affect the delays for appeal. The former language "post-judgment motions" could be misinterpreted as including a motion to amend a judgment under Article 1951.

Comment—1997

The amendment makes it clear that an appeal granted before disposition of timely motions for new trial or judgment notwithstanding the verdict is premature and that it becomes effective upon the denial of such motion(s).

Editor's Notes

In accordance with La. Code of Civ. Proc. Art. 2088, in a case of a suspensive appeal, when the appeal bond is not timely filed and the suspensive appeal is thereby not perfected, the trial court maintains jurisdiction to convert the suspensive appeal to a devolutive appeal, except in an eviction case.

Art. 2124. Security to be furnished for an appeal

A. No security is required for a devolutive appeal.

B. The security to be furnished for a suspensive appeal is determined in accordance with the following rules:

(1) When the judgment is for a sum of money, the amount of the security shall be equal to the amount of the judgment, including the interest allowed by the judgment to the date the security is furnished, exclusive of the costs.

(a) However, in all cases, except litigation related to the Tobacco Master Settlement Agreement, or any litigation where the state is a judgment creditor, where the amount of the judgment exceeds one hundred fifty million dollars, the trial court, upon motion and after a hearing, may, in the exercise of its broad discretion, fix the security in an amount sufficient to protect the rights of the judgment creditor while at the same time preserving the favored status of appeals in Louisiana.

(b) The time for taking the suspensive appeal under Article 2123 shall be interrupted for judgments pursuant to Article 2124(B)(1)(a) until the trial court fixes the amount of the security and commences anew on the date the security is fixed.

(2) When the judgment distributes a fund in custodia legis, only security sufficient to secure the payment of costs is required.

(3) In all other cases, the security shall be fixed by the trial court at an amount sufficient to assure the satisfaction of the judgment, together with damages for the delay resulting from the suspension of the execution.

C. Where the party seeking to appeal from a judgment for a sum of money is aggrieved by the amount of the security fixed by the trial court, the party so aggrieved may seek supervisory writs to review the appropriateness of the determination of the trial court in fixing the security. The application for supervisory writ shall be heard by the court of appeal on a priority basis. The time for taking a suspensive appeal under Article 2123 shall be interrupted until the appellate court acts on the supervisory writs to review the determination of the trial court in fixing the security and commences anew on the date the action is taken.

D. For good cause shown, the trial judge in the case of the appeal of a money judgment to be secured by a surety bond may fix the amount of the security at an amount not to exceed one hundred fifty percent of the amount of the judgment, including the interest allowed by the judgment to the date the security is furnished, exclusive of the costs.

E. A suspensive appeal bond shall provide, in substance, that it is furnished as security that the appellant will prosecute his appeal, that any judgment against him will be paid or satisfied from the proceeds of the sale of his property, or that otherwise the surety is liable for the amount of the judgment.

Amended by Acts 1977, No. 176, § 1, eff. Jan. 1, 1978; Acts 1988, No. 444, § 1, eff. Jan. 1, 1989; Acts 1989, No. 307, § 2; Acts 2001, No. 450, § 1, eff. June 19, 2001.

Art. 2125. Return day

The return day of the appeal shall be thirty days from the date estimated costs are paid if there is no testimony to be transcribed and lodged with the record and forty-five days from the date such costs are paid if there is testimony to be transcribed, unless the trial judge fixes a lesser period. The trial court may grant only one extension of the return day and such extension shall not be more than thirty days. A copy of the extension shall be filed with the appellate court. Subsequent extensions of the return day may be granted by the appellate court for sufficient cause or at the request of the court reporter as provided in Article 2127.2.

Amended by Acts 1976, No. 426, § 2; Acts 1977, No. 177, § 1, eff. Jan. 1, 1978; Acts 1984, No. 937, § 1.

Art. 2125.1. Notice of extension of return day granted by clerk of trial court

When a subsequent extension of the return day is granted by the appellate court in accordance with the provisions of Article 2125, notice thereof shall be given by mail by the clerk of the trial court to counsel of record of all parties, and to parties not represented by counsel. The failure of the clerk of the trial court to mail such notice does not affect the validity of the appeal, nor does any error or defect that is not imputable to the appellant affect the validity of the appeal.

Added by Acts 1976, No. 708, § 1.

Art. 2126. Payment of costs

A. The clerk of the trial court, immediately after the order of appeal has been granted, shall estimate the cost of the preparation of the record on appeal, including the fee of the court reporter for preparing the transcript and the filing fee required by the appellate court. The clerk shall send notices of the estimated costs by certified mail to the appellant and by first class mail to the appellee.

B. Within twenty days of the mailing of notice, the appellant shall pay the amount of the estimated costs to the clerk. The trial court may grant one extension of the period for paying the amount of the estimated costs for not more than an additional twenty days upon written motion showing good cause for the extension.

C. The appellant may question the excessiveness of the estimated costs by filing a written application for reduction in the trial court within the first twenty-day time limit, and the trial court may order reduction of the estimate upon proper showing. If an application for reduction has been timely filed, the appellant shall have twenty days to pay the costs beginning from the date of the action by the trial court on application for reduction.

D. After the preparation of the record on appeal has been completed, the clerk of the trial court shall, as the situation may require, either refund to the appellant the difference between the estimated costs and the actual costs if the estimated costs exceed the actual costs, or send a notice by certified mail to the appellant of the amount of additional costs due, if the actual costs exceed the estimated costs. If the payment of additional costs is required, the appellant shall pay the amount of additional costs within twenty days of the mailing of the notice.

E. If the appellant fails to pay the estimated costs, or the difference between the estimated costs and the actual costs, within the time specified, the trial judge, on his own motion or upon motion by the clerk or by any party, and after a hearing, shall:

(1) Enter a formal order of dismissal on the grounds of abandonment; or

(2) Grant a ten day period within which costs must be paid in full, in default of which the appeal is dismissed as abandoned.

F. If the appellant pays the costs required by this Article, the appeal may not be dismissed because of the passage of the return day without an extension being obtained or because of an untimely lodging of the record on appeal.

Amended by Acts 1976, No. 708, § 2; Acts 1977, No. 198, § 2, eff. Jan. 1, 1978; Acts 1978, No. 449, § 1, eff. Jan. 1, 1979; Acts 1984, No. 937, § 1; Acts 1995, No. 105, § 1.

Art. 2127. Record on appeal; preparation

The clerk of the trial court shall have the duty of preparing the record on appeal. He shall cause it to be lodged with the appellate court on or before the return day or any extension thereof. Failure of the clerk to prepare and lodge the record on appeal either timely or correctly shall not prejudice the appeal.

Amended by Acts 1977, No. 178, § 1, eff. Jan. 1, 1978; Acts 1984, No. 525, § 1; Acts 1984, No. 528, § 3; Acts 1984, No. 937, § 1.

Art. 2127.1. Same; certified and dated

A. All records and supplemental records prepared for filing in any appellate court shall be certified and dated by the clerk upon completion. The certification shall include the date any transcript was received for inclusion in the record.

B. All transcripts or parts thereof completed for inclusion in the record shall be dated and certified by the court reporter who prepares them. The date of certification by the court reporter shall be the date on which the transcript was concluded and furnished to the clerk for inclusion in the record.

Added by Acts 1984, No. 528, § 3.

Art. 2127.2. Same; preparation and delivery of transcript

A. Except as provided in Paragraph B of this Article, each court reporter assigned to prepare any transcript designated to be transcribed and necessary to complete the record shall deliver the transcript to the clerk of the trial court with the duty of preparing the record for appeal no later than five days before the return day.

B. Whenever the court reporter cannot deliver the transcript to the clerk of the trial court by the date required in Paragraph A, the reporter shall draft and file a request for an extension of the return day with the trial court or court of appeal as provided by law. Whenever a court reporter has not delivered a transcript by the fifth day prior to the return day, the clerk of the trial court shall file a certificate with the court of appeal advising that the record is ready for lodging except for the lack of delivery of the transcript. In such certificate the clerk shall include the names and addresses of each court reporter who has failed to deliver a transcript, the date estimated costs were paid, and whether any of the named court reporters have requested an extension of the return day.

C. Upon the request of the court of appeal when the transcript has not been delivered to the clerk of court but the record is otherwise ready for lodging, the record shall be lodged. The clerk of the trial court shall include with the record a certificate stating the names and addresses of each court reporter who is required to prepare and deliver a transcript of the case and a statement of the date on which estimated costs and, if relevant, additional costs were paid. Thereafter, the court of appeal may issue appropriate orders to any named court reporter to expedite preparation and delivery of any necessary transcripts.

Added by Acts 1984, No. 937, § 1. Amended by Acts 1997, No. 409, § 1.

Art. 2127.3. Same; contempt

The failure of the court reporter to file the transcript with the clerk no later than five days before the return date or any extension thereof shall subject such reporter to prosecution for contempt of court. Such contempt charges may be initiated by the trial judge or by the court of appeal on the court's own motion or on the motion of any party.

Added by Acts 1984, No. 525, § 1. Amended by Acts 1997, No. 409, § 1.

Art. 2128. Same; determination of content

The form and content of the record on appeal shall be in accordance with the rules of the appellate court, except as provided in the constitution and as provided in Article 2128.1. However, within three days, exclusive of holidays, after taking the appeal the appellant may designate in a writing filed with the trial court such portions of the record which he desires to constitute the record on appeal. Within five days, exclusive of holidays, after service of a copy of this designation on the other party, that party may also designate in a writing filed with the trial court such other portions of the record as he considers necessary. In such cases the clerk shall prepare the record on appeal as so directed, but a party or the trial court may cause to be filed thereafter any omitted portion of the record as a supplemental record. When no designation is made, the record shall be a transcript of all the proceedings as well as all documents filed in the trial court.

Amended by Acts 2012, No. 171, § 1.

Art. 2128.1. Depositions

Depositions made a part of the record on appeal may be attached in a reduced format consisting of no more than four pages of deposition testimony per physical page or in any electronic format approved by the court.

Added by Acts 2012, No. 171, § 1.

Art. 2129. Assignment of errors unnecessary; exception

An assignment of errors is not necessary in any appeal. Where the appellant designates only portions of the record as the record on appeal, he must serve with his designation a concise statement of the points on which he intends to rely, and the appeal shall be limited to those points.

Editor's Notes

Rule VII, Section 4(3), Supreme Court Rules, and Rule 2–12.4, Uniform Rules—Courts of Appeal (Volume 8, LSA–R.S.).

Art. 2130. Record on appeal; statement of facts

A party may require the clerk to cause the testimony to be taken down in writing and this transcript shall serve as the statement of facts of the case. The parties may agree to a narrative of the facts in accordance with the provisions of Article 2131.

Art. 2131. Same; narrative of facts

If the testimony of the witnesses has not been taken down in writing the appellant must request the other parties to join with him in a written and signed narrative of the facts, and in cases of disagreement as to this narrative or of refusal to join in it, at any time prior to the lodging of the record in the appellate court, the judge shall make a written narrative of the facts, which shall be conclusive.

Art. 2132. Same; correction

A record on appeal which is incorrect or contains misstatements, irregularities or informalities, or which omits a material part of the trial record, may be corrected even after the record is transmitted to the appellate court, by the parties by stipulation, by the trial court or by the order of the appellate court. All other questions as to the content and form of the record shall be presented to the appellate court.

Art. 2133. Answer of appellee; when necessary

A. An appellee shall not be obliged to answer the appeal unless he desires to have the judgment modified, revised, or reversed in part or unless he demands damages against the appellant. In such cases, he must file an answer to the appeal, stating the relief demanded, not later than fifteen days after the return day or the lodging of the record whichever is later. The answer filed by the appellee shall be equivalent to an appeal on his part from any portion of the judgment rendered against him in favor of the appellant and of which he complains in his answer. Additionally, however, an appellee may by answer to the appeal, demand modification, revision, or reversal of the judgment insofar as it did not allow or consider relief prayed for by an incidental action filed in the trial court. If an appellee files such an answer, all other parties to the incidental demand may file similar answers within fifteen days of the appellee's action.

B. A party who does not seek modification, revision, or reversal of a judgment in an appellate court, including the supreme court, may assert, in support of the judgment, any argument supported by the record, although he has not appealed, answered the appeal, or applied for supervisory writs.

Amended by Acts 1968, No. 129, § 1; Acts 1970, No. 474, § 1; Acts 1989, No. 121, § 1.

For Official Comments and Annotative Materials,

Official Revision Comments—1960

(a) Arts. 591 and 592 of the 1870 Code of Practice seem to require an answer by appellee in all cases. Likewise, Arts. 886 through 889 of the 1870 Code seem to contemplate a formal answer by appellee even if he merely seeks confirmation of the judgment as rendered. However, all of these articles are negated by Arts. 890 and 891 of the 1870 Code. The result is that no answer by appellee is required under Louisiana law unless the appellee desires some modification of the judgment or damages for a frivolous appeal. The above article preserves the system set up by the 1870 Code. It may be noted that the courts adhere strictly to the time limitation on filing the answer. Ford v. Leonard Truck Lines, 26 So.2d 309 (La.App.1946).

(b) Under Louisiana jurisprudence if an appellant takes a limited appeal, this does not preclude the appellee from raising any other points on appeal by answer, even though such points are not embraced in the appellant's appeal as taken. Allengi v. Hartford Acc. & Indemnity Co., 183 La. 847, 165 So. 8 (1935); Shreveport v. Kahn, 194 La. 55, 193 So. 461 (1939). The above article is declaratory of this jurisprudential rule.

However, there is a division of authority on the question of whether defendant's answer to plaintiff's appeal brings up for appellate review a reconventional demand rejected by the lower court. Earlier cases held that in such a case, a distinct appeal by the defendant was necessary. The later cases take the position that an answer to the appeal is sufficient. See cases cited in McMahon 1023, n. 180. The above article is declaratory of the rule of the later cases.

(c) Art. 890 of the Code of Practice of 1870 required that the answer to an appeal be filed at least three days before the argument, and in the circuit courts of appeal permitted this answer to be filed prior to argument within the first three days of the term. This rule caused difficulty, as it permitted the answer to the appeal to be filed after the briefs had been filed, and usually required the appellant to file another brief in reply to the issues raised in the answer to the appeal.

For this reason, the above article requires the answer to the appeal to be filed "not later than fifteen days after the return day or the lodging of the record, whichever is later."

(d) See, also, Comments under Art. 2164, *infra*.

Comments—1970

Amended on the recommendation of the Louisiana State Law Institute to provide for appellate review of a judgment insofar as it did not allow or consider relief prayed for by an incidental demand.

CHAPTER 3. PROCEDURE IN APPELLATE COURT

Article

Art. 2161. Dismissal for irregularities

An appeal shall not be dismissed because the trial record is missing, incomplete or in error no matter who is responsible, and the court may remand the case either for retrial or for correction of the record. An appeal shall not be dismissed because of any other irregularity, error or defect unless it is imputable to the appellant. Except as provided in Article 2162, a motion to dismiss an appeal because of any irregularity, error, or defect which is imputable to the appellant must be filed within three days, exclusive of holidays, of the return day or the date on which the record on appeal is lodged in the appellate court, whichever is later.

Amended by Acts 1972, No. 531, § 1.

Editor's Notes

See La. R.S. 13:4433 as to the two-day period for the appellant to fix any irregularities in transcript, exhibits, or any errors on the part of the clerk of court or any purely technical reasons without the appeal being dismissed.

Art. 2162. Dismissal by consent of parties, or because of lack of jurisdiction or right to appeal, or abandonment; transfer

An appeal can be dismissed at any time by consent of all parties, or for lack of jurisdiction of the appellate court, or because there is no right to appeal, or if, under the rules of the appellate court, the appeal has been abandoned.

If an appeal is taken to an appellate court which has no jurisdiction over it, the court may transfer the appeal to the proper court, upon such terms and conditions as it may prescribe. If an appeal is transferred to the supreme court in error, the supreme court may transfer or retransfer it to the proper court.

Art. 2163. Peremptory exception filed in appellate court; remand if prescription pleaded

The appellate court may consider the peremptory exception filed for the first time in that court, if pleaded prior to a submission of the case for a decision, and if proof of the ground of the exception appears of record.

If the ground for the peremptory exception pleaded in the appellate court is prescription, the plaintiff may demand that the case be remanded to the trial court for trial of the exception.

Editor's Notes

C.C.P art. 928.

Art. 2164. Scope of appeal and action to be taken; costs

The appellate court shall render any judgment which is just, legal, and proper upon the record on appeal. The court may award damages, including attorney fees, for frivolous appeal or application for writs, and may tax the costs of the lower or appellate court, or any part thereof, against any party to the suit, as in its judgment may be considered equitable.

Amended by Acts 2010, No. 184, § 1.

Art. 2164.1. Assignment of appellate panels

The provisions of R.S. 13:319 shall be applicable to assignment of appellate panels.

Added by Acts 2018, No. 658, § 2.

Art. 2165. Appeals deemed abandoned

An appeal is abandoned when the parties fail to take any step in its prosecution or disposition for the period provided in the rules of the appellate court.

Amended by Acts 1966, No. 36, § 1; Acts 1982, No. 186, § 2.

Art. 2166. Court of appeal judgment rehearing; finality; stay

A. Within fourteen days of the transmission of the notice of the judgment of the court of appeal, a party may apply to the court of appeal for a rehearing. Within thirty days of the transmission of the notice of the judgment of the court of appeal, a party may apply to the supreme court for a writ of certiorari. The judgment of a court of appeal becomes final and definitive if neither an application to the court of appeal for rehearing nor an application to the supreme court for a writ of certiorari is timely filed.

B. When any party files a timely application to the court of appeal for a rehearing, the time within which any other party may apply to the supreme court for a writ of certiorari shall be extended until thirty days of the transmission of the notice of a denial of rehearing.

C. When a timely application for rehearing has been filed in the court of appeal and the court of appeal denies the application, the judgment becomes final and definitive unless an application for writ of certiorari to the supreme court is filed within thirty days of the transmission of the notice of a denial of rehearing.

D. When a party files a timely application for a writ of certiorari to the supreme court within the delays provided in this Article, any other party may also apply for certiorari to the supreme court within thirty days of the transmission of the notice of judgment of the court of appeal or within ten days of the transmission by the supreme court clerk of the notice of first application for certiorari in the case, whichever is later.

E. When an application for certiorari to the supreme court is timely filed, a judgment of the court of appeal becomes final and definitive after a delay of five days, exclusive of legal holidays, commencing to run on the day after the clerk has mailed the denial by the supreme court of the application for certiorari. The supreme court may stay the execution of the judgment of the court of appeal pending a timely application for certiorari or an appeal to the United States Supreme Court.

F. For the purposes of this Article, "transmission of the notice" means the sending of the notice via the United States Postal Service, electronic mail, or facsimile.

Amended by Acts 1977, No. 179, § 1, eff. Jan. 1, 1978; Acts 1982, No. 163, § 1; Acts 1983, No. 451, § 2; Acts 2001, No. 587, § 1; Acts 2012, No. 290, § 1, eff. Jan. 1, 2013; Acts 2012, No. 741, § 1.

Editor's Notes

Rule IX, Supreme Court Rules, and Rule 2–18, Uniform Rules—Courts of Appeal (Volume 8, LSA–R.S.), provide for the delays and requirements for rehearing in the appellate courts.

Art. 2167. Supreme court judgment rehearing; finality; stay

A. Within fourteen days of the transmission of the notice of judgment in the supreme court, a party may apply to the court for a rehearing.

B. A judgment of the supreme court becomes final and definitive when the delay for application for rehearing has expired and no timely application therefor has been made.

C. When an application for rehearing has been applied for timely, a judgment of the supreme court becomes final and definitive when the application is denied. The supreme court may stay the execution of the judgment pending a timely application for certiorari or an appeal to the United States Supreme Court.

D. For the purposes of this Article, "transmission of the notice" means the sending of the notice via the United States Postal Service, electronic mail, or facsimile.

Amended by Acts 1977, No. 180, § 1, eff. Jan. 1, 1978; Acts 1982, No. 163, § 1; Acts 2012, No. 290, § 1, eff. Jan. 1, 2013.

Editor's Notes

Rule X, Supreme Court Rules, application for writs.

Art. 2168. Posting of unpublished opinions; citation

A. The unpublished opinions of the supreme court and the courts of appeal shall be posted by such courts on the Internet websites of such courts.

B. Opinions posted as required in this Article may be cited as authority and, if cited, shall be cited by use of the case name and number assigned by the posting court.

Added by Acts 2006, No. 644, § 1.

TITLE II. SUPERVISORY PROCEDURE

Art. 2201. Supervisory writs

Supervisory writs may be applied for and granted in accordance with the constitution and rules of the supreme court and other courts exercising appellate jurisdiction.

Editor's Notes

Rule X, Supreme Court Rules, and Rule 4, Uniform Rules—Courts of Appeal (Volume 8, LSA-R.S.).

Arts. 2202 to 2250. [Reserved]

BOOK IV

EXECUTION OF JUDGMENTS

TITLE I. GENERAL DISPOSITIONS

Article

Art. 2251. Execution only in trial court; appellate court judgment

A judgment can be executed only by a trial court.

A party seeking to execute a judgment of an appellate court must first file a certified copy with the clerk of the trial court. This filing may be made without prior notice to the adverse party.

Official Revision Comments—1960

(a) Unnecessary language has been eliminated from the source provisions. For example, that portion of Art. 620, Code of Practice of 1870, giving the clerk power to receive, file and record judgments of the supreme court and issue process thereon is superfluous since clerks have that power without specific authority.

(b) The district court's functions in connection with recordation of appellate court judgments prior to execution is not changed; such functions are merely ministerial. Trial courts have no discretion to refuse to record appellate court judgments. State ex rel. Villavaso v. Judge of Second Judicial Dist. Ct., 20 La.Ann. 521 (1868); Gajan v. Patout & Burguieres, 135 La. 156, 65 So. 17 (1914).

(c) When a judgment is rendered after a change of venue, under R.S. 13:3276, the clerk of the court returns the file of the proceedings to the parish where the suit originated so that it can be executed there. The above article effects no change in that procedure. Likewise, this article does not affect R.S. 13:4434 through 13:4436, which provide that registry of the decree of an appellate court in the mortgage office creates a judicial mortgage.

(d) Arts. 588 and 589, Code of Practice of 1870, provide that where the appellant fails to file his record timely in the appellate court, the appellee can obtain a certificate from the clerk to the effect that the record has not been brought up, and upon filing the certificate in the district court, have execution issue.

Art. 2127, *supra*, places on the clerk the duty of preparing the record and filing it timely. Thus, the appellant's only duty is to pay the necessary costs, and failure to file a record timely will no longer be a ground for dismissal of an appeal. Therefore, the procedure of procuring a certificate from the appellate court that the record is not filed is no longer necessary.

(e) No mention is made of the execution of judgments rendered by the supreme court in the exercise of its original jurisdiction under Const. Art. VII, § 10. Such judgments are not subject to execution in the ordinary sense of the term, since the court's original jurisdiction extends only to disbarment cases, suits for removal of judges, and questions of fact involving its appellate jurisdiction.

(f) The choice of the term "judgment" for use in this article was the subject of considerable debate and research. Despite the fact that "judgment" and "decree" have been used interchangeably in Louisiana as well as in other jurisdictions as applied to appellate and trial court judgments, "judgment" was considered the more comprehensive term. Therefore, it is used in the above article.

Editor's Notes

R.S. 13:4434, registration of appellate decree in mortgage or conveyance records whether or not application for writs or rehearing has been made; R.S. 13:4435, effect of registry of appellate decree, as judicial mortgage, recognition of title, or otherwise. But such a decree, for which application for writs or rehearing may still be timely made, is not executory, Creech v. Capitol Mack, Inc., App. 1 Cir.1974, 296 So.2d 387.

Art. 2252. Delay before proceeding with execution

A judgment creditor may proceed with the execution of a judgment only after the delay for a suspensive appeal therefrom has elapsed; however, recordation of a judgment in the mortgage records prior to the lapsing of the delay for a suspensive appeal does not begin proceedings for the execution of the judgment.

Amended by Acts 1985, No. 523, § 1, eff. July 12, 1985.

Official Revision Comments—1960

(a) Art. 624, Code of Practice of 1870, provides, in effect, that no execution can issue until the expiration of the time for taking a suspensive appeal. Arts. 2123 and 2124, *supra*, relate to the suspension of execution of judgments and the requirements for a suspensive appeal bond. Under Art. 2123, *supra*, the delay within which to file the suspensive appeal bond has been increased to fifteen days.

(b) There is jurisprudence to the effect that an execution issued before the expiration of the delay for a suspensive appeal is not ipso facto null; the defendant ratifies the premature execution when he fails to appeal suspensively. Sowle v. Pollard, 14 La.Ann. 287 (1859); Wheeling Pottery Co. v. Levi, 48 La.Ann. 777, 19 So. 752 (1896); O'Keefe & Simpson Main Street Pharmacy, 8 La.App. 443 (1927).

A premature seizure under a writ of fieri facias is valid as between the judgment creditor and judgment debtor, but it creates no right in the seizing creditor as against a third person who may levy a seizure which is not premature. Kimber-Murphy Mfg. Co. v. Vestal, Inc., 43 So.2d 508 (La.App.1950). The rules of these cases are not changed by the above article. *Cf.* Art. 2292, *infra.*

(c) Art. 622 of the 1870 Code of Practice provides that judgments not appealable or judgments rendered on confession of judgment may be executed immediately after the close of the term of court. No provision similar to this article has been included because it was considered unnecessary and obsolete.

(d) Where property is sold under a writ of fieri facias and the judgment is subsequently reversed after a devolutive appeal, the validity of the sale is not affected by subsequent reversal of the judgment, and the defendant-appellant's only remedy is to sue the original judgment creditor for the return of the price for which the property was sold. Bomarito v. Barnett Furniture Co., 177 La. 1010, 150 So. 2 (1933); State v. Mutual Inv. Co., 214 La. 356, 37 So.2d 817 (1948). These cases are based upon Art. 578 of the 1870 Code of Practice which provides that a devolutive appeal does not stay the execution of judgment. Arts. 2087 and 2124, *supra*, furnish adequate basis for the retention of the above jurisprudential rule, although no provision similar to Art. 578, Code of Practice of 1870, has been included in this Code.

(e) See, also, Comments under Art. 2292, *infra*.

Editor's Notes

(CAVEAT: Fair Debt Collection Practices Act, 15 U.S. C. § 1692, et seq. Prior to initiating any debt collecting process, including promissory notes, contracts and the foreclosure of mortgages, extreme care must be exercised to conform to the exacting requirements of the Fair Debt Collection Practices Act. See the elaborate forms in West's LSA Civil Procedure, Vol. 12, Forms 1589a, et seq. The penalties against the attorney for violation are serious, $1,000.00 per violation, heard and enforced in the Federal District Court).

C.C.P. arts. 2123 and 2292. See Comment (b) under C.C.P. art. 2252 and Comment (c) under C.C.P. art. 2292, as to premature seizure.

Art. 2253. Writ from clerk to sheriff

At the request of a judgment creditor, the clerk shall issue a writ bearing his signature, the seal of the court, and the date, and directing the sheriff of the parish where the judgment is to be executed to enforce it in the manner set forth in the writ. Concurrent writs may be directed to sheriffs of several parishes.

Official Revision Comments—1960

(a) This article is a consolidation of the source articles. Art. 627 of the 1870 Code of Practice, requiring the sheriff to endorse on the order of execution the date on which it was delivered to him, has been relegated to those articles dealing with the duties of court officers generally. See Art. 324, *supra*.

(b) Art. 629 of the 1870 Code of Practice, which provides that the court, whether appellate or inferior, which has rendered the judgment must take cognizance of the manner of its execution, has been deleted as unnecessary in view of its interpretation by the supreme court as contemplating the exercise of the court's supervisory jurisdiction. Brown v. Pontchartrain Land Co., 49 La.Ann. 1779, 23 So. 292 (1896); Globe Realty Co. v. Vix, 120 La. 95, 44 So. 997 (1907).

(c) Art. 642 of this 1870 Code provides that the writ of fieri facias is directed to the sheriff of the parish where the property is situated and also permits several writs to exist in various parishes at the same time. The last sentence in the above article represents a change in the law in so far as it is made applicable to all types of execution.

(d) Under this article, a judgment rendered in one parish may be executed in another parish by sending the appropriate writ to the sheriff of the parish where the judgment is to be executed.

(e) See, also, Comments under Arts. 2254, 2291, 2416, *infra*.

Art. 2254. Execution by sheriff; return; wrongful seizure

A. The sheriff shall proceed promptly to execute the writ and make a return to the clerk who issued it, stating the manner in which it was executed.

B. The sheriff shall have no liability to the debtor or to any third party for wrongful or improper seizure of the debtor's or third party's property of the same general type as described in the debtor's security agreement. If necessary, the sheriff shall request the secured creditor to identify the property subject to the security agreement and shall act pursuant to the secured creditor's instructions. The debtor's and other owner's sole remedy for the wrongful or improper seizure of the property shall be for actual losses sustained under R.S. 10:9–625 against the secured creditor on whose behalf and pursuant to whose instructions the sheriff may act.

Amended by Acts 1989, No. 137, § 18, eff. Sept. 1, 1989; Acts 2021, No. 259, § 2.

Editor's Notes

Acts 1989, 1st Ex.Sess., No. 12, § 1, and Acts 1989, No. 135, § 12, provide for a January 1, 1990 effective date for Chapter 9 of the Louisiana Commercial Laws (R.S. 10:9–101, et seq.). Acts 1989, No. 137, implementing Chapter 9, provides a September 1, 1989 effective date for the affected Code of Civil Procedure articles and certain other amended statutes (see § 22 of Act 137). See Acts 1989, No. 135, §§ 10 and 11, and Acts 1989, No. 137, § 20 for provisions on application of security device laws prior to January 1, 1990. See, also, Acts 1989, No. 598, § 9.

TITLE II. MONEY JUDGMENTS

CHAPTER 1. WRIT OF FIERI FACIAS

Art. 2291. Money judgment; fieri facias

A judgment for the payment of money may be executed by a writ of fieri facias directing the seizure and sale of property of the judgment debtor.

Editor's Notes

Exemptions from seizure, R.S. 13:3881; homestead exemption, R.S. 20:1.

Art. 2292. Privilege of creditor on seized property; successive seizures

A. To the extent not otherwise governed under Chapter 9 of the Louisiana Commercial Laws (R.S. 10:9–101, et seq.), a seizing creditor, by the mere act of seizure, acquires a privilege on the property seized, which entitles him to a preference over ordinary creditors.

B. When several seizures of the same property are made by ordinary creditors, the seizing creditors acquire a privilege and are entitled to a preference among themselves according to the order of their seizures.

Amended by Acts 1989, No. 137, § 18, eff. Sept. 1, 1989.

Editor's Notes

See notes to C.C.P. art. 2252, *infra.* Board of Supervisors of LSU v. Hart, 26 So.2d 361 (1946), privilege relating back to time of seizure, after judgment taken.

Art. 2293. Notice to judgment debtor; appointment of attorney

A. Upon making a seizure of immovable property, the sheriff shall file with the recorder of mortgages of the parish in which the immovable property is located a notice of seizure setting forth the title and docket number of the action out of which the writ issued, the judicial district and parish in which the action is pending, and a description of the immovable property.

B. (1) After the seizure of property, the sheriff shall serve promptly upon the judgment debtor a written notice of the seizure and a list of the property seized, in the manner provided for service of citation. Such notice of seizure shall be accomplished by personal service or domiciliary service. If service cannot be made on the judgment debtor or his attorney of record, the court shall appoint an attorney upon whom service may be made. The notice of seizure shall include information concerning the availability of housing counseling services, as well as the time, date, and place of the sheriff's sale, in accordance with the form provided in R.S. 13:3852(B).

(2) In addition to the written notice of seizure to be served on the judgment debtor as provided in Subparagraph (1) of this Paragraph, the sheriff shall also serve upon the occupants of the seized property a written notice stating that the subject property has been seized. Such service shall be accomplished by directing the notice to "occupants" of the seized premises and if the notice cannot be served personally or by domiciliary service upon the occupants, such service shall be accomplished by posting the notice upon the main entrance to the seized premises. The failure to serve the notices as provided herein shall not invalidate the sheriff's sale; however, such failure shall prevent the purchaser at the sheriff's sale from availing himself of the provisions of R.S. 13:4346 as it applies to the ejectment or eviction of any occupants of the seized premises other than the judgment debtor. The failure to serve the notices required in this Paragraph shall not affect the rights of the foreclosing creditor or of the purchaser at the sheriff's sale under Code of Civil Procedure Articles 4701 et seq.

(3)(a) If the premises foreclosed upon consists of more than ten units, instead of giving notice as provided in Subparagraph (2) of this Paragraph, the foreclosing creditor shall have the option of causing a sign or signs to be posted by the sheriff measuring not less than two feet high and three feet wide posted in such a manner as to notify residents of the building containing the following language or words to this effect: "________ JUDICIAL DISTRICT COURT FOR THE PARISH OF ________, DOCKET NUMBER ________. THIS PROPERTY HAS BEEN SEIZED AND SHALL BE SOLD IN ACCORDANCE WITH LAW ON OR AFTER ________, 200__/s/ SHERIFF ________, PARISH. Any person who removes or damages this notice is subject to prosecution in accordance with R.S. 14:56." The cost of preparation of such sign shall be borne by the foreclosing creditor and the fee of the sheriff in connection with the posting of such sign shall be determined in accordance with the provisions of R.S. 13:5530(A)(14).

(b) An affidavit of the creditor shall be filed of record in the foreclosure proceeding stating that such sign was posted, which affidavit shall be prima facie evidence that the sign was posted in accordance with this Subparagraph.

(4) The provisions of Subparagraphs (2) and (3) of this Paragraph shall apply only to foreclosure proceedings on immovable property which is occupied or intended for occupancy as a residence and shall not apply to foreclosure proceedings on property subject to time share operations, hotels, motels, inns, guest houses, rooming houses, bed and breakfasts, camp sites, campgrounds, and other lodging establishments intended for the temporary housing of guests.

C. After the seizure of property, the sheriff shall give notice of the seizure to persons other than the judgment debtor in the manner and to the extent provided by R.S. 13:3886. The sheriff shall file with the clerk who issued the writ his affidavit setting forth the name of each person to whom the notices were given and the address or addresses to which the notices were sent. The affidavit, when received by the clerk, shall form part of the record and shall be considered prima facie correct.

D. Cancellation of a mortgage, whether legal, judicial, or conventional, shall allow any interested party to cancel the notice of seizure of property affected by the mortgage upon submitting a request to cancel evidencing that the mortgage has been cancelled and upon submission of proof that all costs due the clerk of court and the sheriff have been paid. Nevertheless, a notice of seizure shall prescribe ten years after the date of recordation unless reinscribed in the same manner as an instrument creating a mortgage under Civil Code Article 3362. Any interested party may obtain cancellation of the notice of seizure on the basis of prescription of ten years without submitting evidence that all costs due to the clerk of court and sheriff have been paid in full.

Amended by Acts 1974, No. 88, § 1; Acts 1991, No. 662, § 1, eff. Jan. 1, 1992; Acts 1995, No. 614, § 1; Acts 2004, No. 877, § 1; Acts 2005, No. 216, § 1; Acts 2008, No. 828, § 1; Acts 2012, No. 395, § 1; Acts 2013, No. 339, § 2.

Official Revision Comments—1960

(a) The source article provides that notice shall be delivered to the debtor in person or left at his place of ordinary residence. The above article effects a change in this respect inasmuch as it provides that service of the notice shall be made in the manner provided for service of citation.

(b) A sale without notice of seizure is null. Lamorandier v. Meyer, 8 Rob. 152 (La.1844); Birch v. Bates, 22 La.Ann. 198 (1867); Graff v. Moylan, 28 La.Ann. 75 (1873). Under certain conditions the nullity may be cured by the prescription of five years. R.S. 9:5642. There is no intention to change these rules.

Editor's Notes

The forms to be used by the sheriff to serve the notice of seizure is provided in La. R.S. 13:3852 for both a seizure by virtue of a writ of fifa and a writ of seizure and sale in an executory process proceeding. See La. R.S. 13:3852 in the statutory appendix. See also La. R.S. 13:3851.1 which prohibits the seizure and sale of the homestead of the judgment debtor in the execution of a judgment for consumer credit card charges.

Art. 2294. Time for seizure; return

A seizure may be made under a writ of fieri facias only within one year from the date of its issuance.

At the expiration of that time the sheriff shall make a return on the writ unless a seizure has been made within the time. If a seizure has been made the sheriff shall proceed with the sale and thereupon make a return.

Editor's Notes

R.S. 13:4287, duty of officers to return writs of fieri facias.

Art. 2294.1. Time for seizure; return; city courts in Orleans Parish

A. A seizure may be made under a writ of fieri facias issued by a city court in Orleans Parish, only within six months from the date of its issuance.

B. At the expiration of that time the constable shall make a return on the writ unless a seizure has been made within the time. If a seizure has been made the constable shall proceed with the sale and thereupon make a return.

Added by Acts 1978, No. 366, § 1. Amended by Acts 1991, No. 289, § 1; Acts 2011, 1st Ex.Sess., No. 29, § 1.

Art. 2295. Order of sale; sale in globo

If several items of property have been seized, or if one item of property which is divisible into portions has been seized, the judgment debtor, at any time prior to the first advertisement, may designate the order in which the items or portions of property will be sold, except that the judgment creditor can direct the sale of property on which he has a mortgage, or a privilege other than that resulting from the seizure.

If the judgment debtor does not designate the order of sale, the order of sale shall be at the discretion of the sheriff.

When property is offered by items or portions and the total price bid is insufficient to satisfy the judgment, with interest and costs, or if the judgment debtor so requests, the property shall be offered in globo and thus sold if a higher bid is obtained.

Art. 2296. Reduction of excessive seizure

If several items of property have been seized, or if one item of property which is divisible into portions has been seized, and if the value of the property seized exceeds what is reasonably necessary to satisfy the judgment, including interest and costs, the judgment debtor may obtain the release of the excess items or portion by contradictory motion filed not less than ten days before the day fixed for the sale.

The judgment debtor may not obtain the release of property on which the judgment creditor has a mortgage, or a privilege other than that resulting from the seizure.

Editor's Notes

Damages for excessive seizure, R.S. 13:4290.

Art. 2297. Alias fieri facias

After a writ of fieri facias has been returned unsatisfied, another writ of fieri facias may be issued.

Art. 2298. Injunction prohibiting sale; damages

Injunctive relief prohibiting the sheriff from proceeding with the sale of property seized under a writ of fieri facias shall be granted to the judgment debtor or to a third person claiming ownership of the seized property:

(1) When the sheriff is proceeding with the execution contrary to law;

(2) When subsequent to the judgment payment has been made, or compensation has taken place against the judgment, or it has been otherwise extinguished. If the payment, compensation, or extinguishment is for a part of the judgment, the injunction shall be granted to that extent, and the execution shall continue for the amount of the excess;

(3) When the judgment is for the payment of the purchase price of property sold to the judgment debtor and a suit for recovery of the property has been filed by an adverse claimant; or

(4) When the judgment sought to be executed is absolutely null.

In the event injunctive relief is granted to the judgment debtor or third party claiming ownership of the seized property, if the court finds the seizure to be wrongful, it may allow damages. Attorney's fees for the services rendered in connection with the injunction may be included as an element of the damages.

Amended by Acts 1981, No. 301, § 1.

Editor's Notes

Governs the issuance of an injunction and the bond therefor under this Article, C.C.P. art. 3601, et seq. See Comment (a).

Art. 2299. Order prohibiting payment of proceeds of sale

When a third person has intervened and asserted a privilege on the property seized superior to that of the judgment creditor, the court shall order the sheriff to withhold a portion of the proceeds of the judicial sale of the property sufficient to satisfy the intervener's claim, subject to the further orders of the court.

Amended by Acts 1961, No. 23, § 1.

Editor's Notes

Third party claiming *ownership,* R.S. 13:3874.

CHAPTER 2. JUDICIAL SALE UNDER FIERI FACIAS

Article

Art. 2331. Publication of notice of sale

A. Notice of the sale of property under a writ of fieri facias shall be published at least once for movable property, and at least twice for immovable property, in the manner provided by law. The court may order additional publications.

B. Notwithstanding the requirements of Paragraph A of this Article, if a judicial sale of immovable property is cancelled or postponed and rescheduled for a later date, notice of sale of property under a writ of fieri facias shall be published once in the manner provided by law.

C. The sheriff shall not order the advertisement of the sale of the property seized until three days, exclusive of holidays, have elapsed after service on the judgment debtor of the notice of seizure, as provided in Article 2293.

Amended by Acts 2021, No. 469, § 1.

Editor's Notes

See the checklist for Judicial Sale in the preliminary material of this publication. See La. R.S. 43:203 which provides if there is only one publication, the newspaper notice shall be published at least 10 days before the date of the judicial sale. If two publications are required, the first notice shall be published at least 30 days before the date of the sale and the second shall be published not earlier than 7 days before and not later than the day before the judicial sale. See also, La. R.S. 13:4341 et seq. for the time and place of judicial sale.

Art. 2332. Appraisal

A. The property seized must be appraised according to law prior to the sale. However, when the property seized is subject to a mortgage, security agreement, or other document creating a privilege in which the debtor has waived the right to appraisal and the judgment recites that the right of the judgment creditor to enforce the judgment is limited to the collateral or security for the amount of such judgment, there shall be no requirement that the property seized be appraised prior to the sale. If a mortgage on immovable property contains a waiver of appraisal and is sought to be enforced under a writ of fieri facias and the plaintiff prays for a sale without appraisal, the sale shall be conducted without appraisal.

B. If the personal obligation is also secured by other mortgages or security interests not recognized in the judgment, the judicial sale of any property securing the personal obligation in accordance with Paragraph A shall not prevent the enforcement in rem of such other mortgages or security interests.

C. There is no requirement that collateral subject to a security interest under Chapter 9 of the Louisiana Commercial Laws be appraised prior to the sale.

Amended by Acts 1991, No. 377, § 1, eff. Jan. 1, 1992; Acts 2001, No. 588, § 1; Acts 2003, No. 1072, § 1.

Editor's Notes

R.S. 13:4363, appointment of appraisers.

Art. 2333. Sale of perishable property

The court, at the request of a party, may order the immediate sale at public auction, without advertisement or appraisement, of property that is perishable and subject to loss or deterioration pending compliance with the usual formalities. Notice of the time and place of the sale shall be given to all parties. The property shall be sold for cash to the highest bidder.

Art. 2334. Reading of advertisement and certificates

A. At the time and place designated for the sale, the sheriff shall read aloud all or part of the advertisement describing the property in such sufficiency as to reasonably provide notice to the public of the property then being offered for sale, which, at a minimum, shall include the lot and subdivision or municipal number or by section, township, and range, including some identifying mark, if appropriate, and a reference to the conveyance or mortgage recordation. The sheriff shall also read aloud a mortgage certificate and any other certificate required by law or otherwise provide, at least twenty-four hours prior to the sale, a copy of such certificates to the public by means of public posting, written copies, electronic means, or by any other method.

B. The failure of the sheriff to procure, read aloud, or provide a copy of any certificate as required by this Article shall not impact the validity of the sale and shall not give rise to any cause of action against the sheriff, the seizing creditor, or the purchaser arising out of such failure.

Amended by Acts 2019, No. 415, § 1; Acts 2021, No. 309, § 1.

Editor's Notes

R.S. 13:4344, R.S. 13:4345, certificates.

Art. 2335. Superior mortgage or privilege

The sheriff shall announce that the property is to be sold for cash subject to any security interest, mortgage, lien, or privilege thereon superior to that of the seizing creditor.

Amended by Acts 1989, No. 137, § 18, eff. Sept. 1, 1989.

Editor's Notes

Goldking Properties Co. v. Primeaux, 477 So.2d 76 (1985), a judgment debtor who perfects a suspensive appeal may have the inscription of the judgment cancelled. See C.C. art. 3304 and R.S. 13:4434 to 13:4435 for statutory implementation of Goldking.

Art. 2336. Minimum price; second offering

Except as provided in Article 2332, the property shall not be sold if the price bid by the highest bidder is less than two-thirds of the appraised value. In that event, the sheriff shall re-advertise the sale of the property in the same manner as for an original sale, and the same delay must elapse. At the second offering, the property shall be sold for cash for whatever it will bring, except as provided in Article 2337. The debt owed to the seizing creditor shall not be reduced by the costs of the sale, but shall be reduced by the greater of either one-half of the appraised value, less superior security interests, mortgages, liens, and privileges, or the amount by which the price bid exceeds superior security interests, mortgages, liens, and privileges.

Amended by Acts 1995, No. 1023, § 1; Acts 2001, No. 588, § 1.

Editor's Notes

See R.S. 13:4108.1 for special provisions relating to appraisal and deficiency judgment.

Art. 2337. Price insufficient to discharge superior privileges; property not sold

If the price offered by the highest bidder at the first or subsequent offering is not sufficient to discharge the costs of the sale and the security interests, mortgages, liens, and privileges superior to that of the seizing creditor, the property shall not be sold.

Amended by Acts 1989, No. 137, § 18, eff. Sept. 1, 1989.

Art. 2338. Judgment creditor having superior privilege; price insufficient to satisfy inferior mortgage

A. If the security interest, mortgage, lien, or privilege of the seizing creditor is superior to other security interests, mortgages, liens, and privileges on the property, he may require that the property be sold, even though the price is not sufficient to satisfy his or the inferior security interests, mortgages, liens, and privileges.

B. If the seizing creditor is not present or represented at the sale, the property shall not be sold for less than the amount necessary to fully satisfy his writ plus the costs.

Amended by Acts 1987, No. 939, § 1; Acts 1989, No. 137, § 18, eff. Sept. 1, 1989.

Editor's Notes

Mennonite Board of Missions v. Adams, 462 U.S. 791 (1983), held that a tax sale is null if an inferior mortgage holder on the property sold fails to receive notice of the sale. Tulsa Professional Collection Services v. Pope, 108 S.Ct. 1340 (1988), held to the same general effect as to creditors of a succession who fail to receive notice that the debts of the succession are being paid. (See Notes under C.C.P. art. 3304). Magee v. Amiss, Sup.1987, 502 So.2d 568, held that a judicial sale divesting the ownership interest of the wife in community property was null for failure to give her notice of the sale. Davis Oil v. Mills, C.A.5 (La.)1989, 873 F.2d 774, holds that R.S. 13:3886, Louisiana's request-notice statute, does not remedy the constitutional insufficiency of its constructive notice provision for foreclosures and a creditor who avails itself of state foreclosure procedures is constitutionally obligated to provide notice reasonably calculated to apprise interested parties of the pendency of the action, so that a party with an interest in property does not waive its due process rights by failing to request notice under the Louisiana statute. A creditor therefore retains the duty to provide notice to interested parties whose identity is reasonably ascertainable or actually known. Small Engine Shop, Inc. v. Cascio, C.A.5 (La.)1989, 878 F.2d 883, held that a foreclosing creditor must give notice not only to those who buy subject to the mortgage, but also to those who assume the mortgage, so that actual notice is required, and a creditor may not fail to search the public records and give notice because R.S. 13:3886 is only a supplement to the constructive notice scheme of Louisiana, available to creditors who want notice of foreclosure and file a request for the notice in the public records.

Sterling v. Block, C.A.5 (La.)1989, 953 F.2d 198, holds that Davis is retroactive.

While R.S. 13:3886 was enacted to put the burden of getting notice of the judicial sale on the third party having an interest in the property sold, the foregoing cases seem to hold that this statutory scheme for notice cannot be relied upon as the sole provision for the protection of the inferior creditor through notice.

Art. 2339. Judgment debtor and creditor may bid

The judgment debtor and the seizing creditor may bid for the property.

Art. 2340. Payment of debt prior to adjudication

The sale of the property may be prevented at any time prior to the adjudication by payment to the sheriff of the judgment, with interest and costs.

Art. 2341. Sale when installment not due

When the seizing creditor has a security interest, mortgage, lien, or privilege on the property seized, for a debt of which all the installments are not due, he may demand that the property be sold for the entire debt, on the same terms for the payment of unmatured installments as provided in the original contract.

Amended by Acts 1989, No. 137, § 18, eff. Sept. 1, 1989.

Art. 2342. Act of sale by sheriff

Within fifteen days after the adjudication, the sheriff shall pass an act of sale to the purchaser, in the manner and form provided by law.

The act of sale adds nothing to the force and effect of the adjudication, but is only intended to afford proof of it.

Amended by Acts 1986, No. 992, § 1.

Editor's Notes

R.S. 13:4353 et seq.; R.S. 9:5622; C.C. arts. 2618 to 2621; R.S. 9:5642, prescription on sheriff's deeds; R.S. 13:4112, executory process.

Art. 2343. Sheriff's return after sale

The sheriff shall make a signed return to the clerk who issued the writ, showing that all formalities have been complied with and stating the manner in which the writ was executed, a description of the property sold, the name of the purchaser, the purchase price, and the disposition thereof.

CHAPTER 3. THE ADJUDICATION AND ITS EFFECT

Article

Art. 2371. Effect of adjudication

The adjudication transfers to the purchaser all the rights and claims of the judgment debtor as completely as if the judgment debtor had sold the property.

Editor's Notes

C.C. arts. 2618 to 2621.

Art. 2372. Sale subject to superior real charge or lease

The property is sold subject to any real charge or lease with which it is burdened, superior to any security interest, mortgage, lien, or privilege of the seizing creditor.

Amended by Acts 1989, No. 137, § 18, eff. Sept. 1, 1989.

Editor's Notes

See C.C.P. arts. 2334 and 2335; R.S. 13:4344, R.S. 13:4345.

Art. 2373. Distribution of proceeds of sale

After deducting the costs, the sheriff shall first pay the amount due the seizing creditor, then the inferior security interests, mortgages, liens, and privileges on the property sold, and shall pay to the debtor whatever surplus may remain.

Amended by Acts 1989, No. 137, § 18, eff. Sept. 1, 1989.

Art. 2374. Property subject to superior mortgage; payment of price

If there is a security interest, mortgage, lien, or privilege on the property superior to that of the seizing creditor, the purchaser shall pay to the sheriff only that portion of the sale price which exceeds the amount of the superior security interest, mortgage, lien, or privilege.

Amended by Acts 1989, No. 137, § 18, eff. Sept. 1, 1989.

Art. 2375. Purchaser's liability; property subject to inferior mortgages

The purchaser is liable for nothing beyond the purchase price. He shall pay the full purchase price to the sheriff, despite the existence of a mortgage, lien, or privilege on the property inferior to that of the seizing creditor.

Art. 2376. Release of inferior mortgages, liens, and privileges

The sheriff shall give the purchaser a release from the security interest, mortgage, lien, or privilege of the seizing creditor, and from all inferior security interests, mortgages, liens, and privileges, and he shall direct the clerk of court or proper filing officer to cancel or partially release their inscriptions insofar as they affect the property sold.

Amended by Acts 1989, No. 137, § 18, eff. Sept. 1, 1989; Acts 2018, No. 452, § 1.

Art. 2377. Inferior mortgages; payment; reference to proceeds

The sheriff shall pay the inferior security interests, mortgages, liens, and privileges, after payment of the costs and the amount due the seizing creditor. When the sum remaining after payment of the costs and the amount due the seizing creditor is insufficient to pay such inferior claims in full, the sheriff may deposit the remainder with the court and proceed by contradictory motion against the inferior creditors to have their claims referred to the proceeds of the sale.

Amended by Acts 1989, No. 137, § 18, eff. Sept. 1, 1989.

Art. 2378. Enforcement of mortgage or privilege superior to that of seizing creditor

When the purchaser fails to pay a security interest or mortgage superior to the security interest, mortgage, lien, or privilege of the seizing creditor, the superior security interest or mortgage may be enforced under any of the applicable provisions of Articles 3721 through 3743, or as otherwise provided under applicable law.

Amended by Acts 1989, No. 137, § 18, eff. Sept. 1, 1989.

Editor's Notes

C.C.P. art. 3741 et seq.

Art. 2379. Rights of buyer in case of eviction

The purchaser who has been evicted from property sold under a writ of fieri facias shall have his recourse for reimbursement against the judgment debtor and the seizing creditor. If judgment is obtained against both, the purchaser shall issue execution first against the judgment debtor, and if his judgment remains unsatisfied, he may issue execution against the seizing creditor. The purchaser's right of reimbursement against the seizing creditor shall be limited to the value received by the seizing creditor from the sheriff's sale conducted to sell the property under the writ of fieri facias.

Amended by Acts 2012, No. 19, § 1.

Editor's Notes

Phillips v. Kathman-Landry, Inc., 154 So.2d 363 (1963), purchaser may proceed against judgment creditor without joining judgment debtor.

Art. 2380. Loss of recourse when purchaser fails to give judgment debtor timely notice

The purchaser shall lose the right granted him by Article 2379 if a suit is filed to evict him and he neglects to notify the judgment debtor in time for him to defend the suit, and if the debtor could have successfully defended the suit.

Art. 2381. Action by seizing creditor who has been compelled to reimburse purchaser

The seizing creditor may recover from his judgment debtor whatever he has had to pay to the purchaser who has been evicted.

CHAPTER 4. GARNISHMENT UNDER A WRIT OF FIERI FACIAS

Article

Art. 2411. Garnishee; effect of service; financial institutions

A. The judgment creditor, by petition and after the issuance of a writ of fieri facias, may cause a third person to be cited as a garnishee to declare under oath what property he has in his possession or under his control belonging to the judgment debtor and in what amount he is indebted to him, even though the debt may not be due. He may require the third person to answer categorically and under oath the interrogatories annexed to the petition within the delay provided by Article 2412.

B. (1) The seizure shall take effect upon service of the petition, citation, interrogatories, and a notice of seizure, as required by Article 2412(A)(1).

(2) For wage garnishments subject to the provisions of R.S. 13:3921 et seq., if the garnishee or judgment debtor files no opposition to the garnishment proceedings, and the garnishee answers the garnishment interrogatories affirmatively as to the employment of the judgment debtor by the garnishee, and the garnisher fails to obtain a garnishment judgment within one hundred eighty days of the filing of the answers to the interrogatories, all effects of the seizure by garnishment shall automatically cease upon the lapse of the one hundred eightieth day, and the garnisher shall be required to re-serve the garnishee pursuant to R.S. 13:3923 and 3924.

C. Other than as provided in R.S. 13:3921 et seq. applicable to garnishments of wages, a garnishment shall not be continuing in nature and the garnishee need only respond as to property of the judgment debtor that the garnishee has in his possession or under his control at the time the garnishment interrogatories are served on him.

D. Notwithstanding any other law to the contrary, when the garnishee is a bank, savings and loan association, or credit union, the garnishee may continue to pay checks and drafts drawn on the judgment debtor's deposit accounts maintained with the garnishee that are presented for payment in the ordinary course of business on the day garnishment interrogatories are served upon the garnishee or on the next business day thereafter, without incurring any liability or obligation in favor of the judgment creditor or any other third party.

Amended by Acts 1989, No. 742, § 1; Acts 1999, No. 887, § 1; Acts 2004, No. 18, § 1.

Editor's Notes

Wage garnishment statute, R.S. 13:3921, et seq.; Sun Sales Co. v. Hodges, 237 So.2d 684 (1970); R.S. 13:3881 (exemption); federal standards and prohibition against firing, 15 U.S.C.A. § 1672, et seq.; exemption of wages earned out-of-state, R.S. 13:3951.

The 1999 amendment makes clear that a garnishment is not continuing in nature, except against wages. See also R.S. 13:3913, to same effect.

Art. 2412. Method of service; delay for answering

A. (1) The sheriff shall serve upon the garnishee the citation and a copy of the petition and of the interrogatories, together with a notice that a seizure is thereby effected against any property of or indebtedness to the judgment debtor.

(2) The judgment creditor shall send to the judgment debtor written notice of the filing of the garnishment petition by mail or electronic means. However, the notice provided to the judgment debtor shall have no effect on the validity of the seizure.

B. Service of garnishment petitions against the wages, salaries, or commissions of employees employed within the executive branch of state government shall be made in the following manner:

(1) For employees paid through the office of statewide uniform payroll of the division of administration, service shall be made on the said office.

(2) For all other employees not covered by Subparagraph (1) of this Paragraph, service shall be made only on the secretary of the department employing the debtor or on his designee.

C. Service shall be made in the manner provided for service of citation, except that if the garnishee is an individual, service must be personal. If the garnishee has concealed or absented himself with the purpose of avoiding personal service, the court may order that service be made in any other manner provided by law.

D. The garnishee shall file his sworn answers to the interrogatories within fifteen days from the date of service made pursuant to this Article.

Amended by Acts 1999, No. 886, § 1; Acts 2001, No. 250, § 1; Acts 2004, No. 741, § 1.

Editor's Notes

The 1999 amendment requires service on the secretary of the department employing the debtor, par. B.

Art. 2413. Effect of garnishee's failure to answer

A. If the garnishee fails to answer within the delay provided by Article 2412, the judgment creditor may proceed by contradictory motion against the garnishee for the amount of the unpaid judgment, with interest and costs. When the garnishee is a state agency or department within the executive branch of state government, the party designated for service of garnishment petitions in Article 2412(B) shall be notified of the intent to file such a motion by certified mail at least fifteen days prior to the filing of the motion. The failure of the garnishee to answer prior to the filing of such a contradictory motion is prima facie proof that he has property of or is indebted to the judgment debtor to the extent of the judgment, interest, and costs.

B. Judgment shall be rendered against the garnishee on trial of the motion unless he proves that he had no property of and was not indebted to the judgment debtor. If on the trial of such motion, the garnishee proves the amount of such property or indebtedness, the judgment against the garnishee shall be limited to the delivery of the property or payment of the indebtedness, as provided in Article 2415.

C. Regardless of the decision on the contradictory motion, the court shall render judgment against the garnishee for the costs and a reasonable attorney fee for the motion.

Amended by Acts 1999, No. 886, § 1; Acts 2001, No. 250, § 1.

Editor's Notes

See La. R.S. 13:3923 which allows the garnishee to request the court to reopen the garnishment case where a judgment is rendered against the garnishee for the amount owed by the judgment debtor. See Zurich Ins. Co. v. Harmon, 95-0297 (La. App. 1 Cir. 10/6/95), 671 So.2d 383, 384.

Art. 2414. Notice of answer; traversing

The clerk shall cause written notice of the filing of the garnishee's answer to be served promptly upon the seizing creditor in the manner provided by Article 1314.

Unless the creditor files a contradictory motion traversing the answer of the garnishee within fifteen days after service upon him of the notice of the filing of the garnishee's answer, any property of the judgment debtor in the possession of the garnishee and any indebtedness to the judgment debtor which the garnishee has not admitted holding or owing shall be released from seizure. A new seizure may be made of such property or indebtedness by filing a supplemental petition and serving additional interrogatories.

Art. 2415. Delivery of property or payment of indebtedness to sheriff

When the garnishee admits in his answer, or when on trial of a contradictory motion under Article 2413 or Article 2414 it is found that he has in his possession property belonging to the judgment debtor or is indebted to him, the court shall order the garnishee to deliver the property immediately to the sheriff or to pay him the indebtedness when due. Delivery or payment to the sheriff discharges the garnishee's obligation to the judgment debtor to the extent of the delivery or payment.

This article does not apply to garnishment of wages, salaries, or commissions.

Art. 2416. Venue of garnishment proceedings

The venue of a garnishment proceeding under a writ of fieri facias is the parish where the garnishee may be sued under Article 42 only or Article 77.

The venue of a garnishment proceeding under a writ of attachment or sequestration, in an action against a resident of the state, is any parish where the defendant may be sued.

Amended by Acts 1964, No. 4, § 1; Acts 1989, No. 117, § 1.

Comment—1989

This Article is amended to provide that the reference to Article 42 does not include the exceptions under Articles 71 through 85.

Art. 2417. Garnishment in court other than one which rendered judgment

The procedure in garnishment proceedings under the writ of fieri facias in a court other than that which rendered the judgment shall be the same as if the garnishment were in the court where the judgment was rendered, except:

(1) The judgment must be made executory in the court where the garnishment proceedings are filed, as provided in Article 2782; and

(2) The writ of fieri facias directed to the sheriff, constable, or marshal of the court where the garnishment proceedings are filed may be issued either by the court which rendered the judgment or by the court which made the judgment executory.

Amended by Acts 1961, No. 23, § 1.

CHAPTER 5. EXAMINATION OF JUDGMENT DEBTOR

Article

Art. 2451. Examination of judgment debtor and third parties; depositions

A. In aid of execution the judgment creditor may examine the judgment debtor, his books, papers, or documents, upon any matter relating to his property, either as provided in Articles 1421 through 1515 or as provided in Articles 2452 through 2456.

B. In aid of execution of the judgment, the judgment creditor may also examine any person upon any matter relating to the judgment debtor's property, as provided in Articles 1421 through 1474.

Amended by Acts 1990, No. 1000, § 1.

Art. 2451.1. [Blank]

Art. 2452. Court where motion filed and examination conducted

A. Except as provided in Paragraph B, the written motion for the examination of a judgment debtor shall be filed, and the proceedings conducted, in the court which rendered the judgment.

B. If the judgment debtor is an individual who is domiciled in the state but not in the parish where the judgment was rendered, or who has changed his domicile to another parish after the institution of the suit, the written motion for his examination shall be filed, and the examination conducted, in a court of competent jurisdiction in the parish of his then domicile or where the judgment was rendered or where the debt that has been reduced to judgment was incurred. If the judgment debtor is a nonresident, the petition for his examination shall be filed, and the examination conducted, in a court of competent jurisdiction in any parish where he may be found, or in the court which rendered the judgment. In any case mentioned in this Paragraph, a certified copy of the judgment shall be attached to the written motion for examination.

Amended by Acts 1988, No. 37, § 1, eff. June 10, 1988; Acts 2007, No. 433, § 1.

Editor's Notes

"Found" means any parish in which proper service may be, and subsequently is, effected, Strange v. Imperial Pools, Inc., 506 So.2d 1205 (La.1987).

Art. 2453. Motion; order; service

On ex parte written motion of the judgment creditor, personally or through his attorney, the court shall order the judgment debtor to appear in court for examination at a time fixed by the court, not less than five days from the date of service of the motion and order on the judgment debtor or his counsel of record, and to produce any books, papers, and other documents relating to the judgment debtor's property described in the motion.

Amended by Acts 2006, No. 12, § 1.

Art. 2454. Oath; testimony not used in criminal proceedings

The debtor shall be sworn to tell the truth in the same manner as a witness in a civil action.

No testimony given by a debtor shall be used in any criminal proceeding against him, except for perjury committed at such examination.

Art. 2455. Costs

Court costs in connection with the examination shall be taxed against the judgment debtor, except that if the court determines that the creditor invoked the remedy needlessly, the court may tax the costs against the creditor.

Art. 2456. Contempt

If the motion and order have been served personally on the judgment debtor, as provided by law or if service is obtained pursuant to Article 1261, and the judgment debtor refuses to appear for the examination or to produce his books, papers, or other documents when ordered to do so, or if he refuses to answer any question held pertinent by the court, the judgment debtor may be punished for contempt.

Amended by Acts 1988, No. 37, § 1, eff. June 10, 1988.

TITLE III. JUDGMENTS OTHER THAN MONEY JUDGMENTS

Art. 2501. Judgment ordering delivery of possession; writ of possession

A party in whose favor a judgment of possession has been rendered may obtain from the clerk a writ of possession directing the sheriff to seize and deliver the property to him if it is movable property, or to compel the party in possession to vacate the property by use of force, if necessary, if it is immovable.

Editor's Notes

R.S. 13:4346, writ of possession to put adjudicatee in possession of immovable property. See C.C.P. arts. 4733, 4734 for warrant of possession under judgment of eviction as to leased premises.

Art. 2502. Writ of distringas; contempt; damages

If a judgment orders the delivery of a thing and the sheriff cannot seize it because the defendant has concealed or removed it from the jurisdiction of the court, or when the judgment orders a defendant to do or refrain from doing an act other than the delivery of a thing, and he refuses or neglects to comply with the order, the party entitled to performance may obtain by contradictory motion the following remedies:

(1) A writ to distrain the property of the defendant;

(2) An order adjudging the disobedient party in contempt; or

(3) A judgment for any damages he may have sustained. He may likewise sue for damages in a separate action.

Art. 2503. Distringas, execution and revocation

In the execution of the writ of distringas, the sheriff shall seize the property of the defendant and retain it in his possession subject to the orders of the court.

The court shall revoke the writ, and order the sheriff to release and return to the defendant all property seized thereunder, when the defendant proves that he has complied with the judgment sought to be enforced through the distringas, and has also satisfied any judgment for damages which the plaintiff may have obtained against him because of his noncompliance with the judgment first mentioned.

Perishable property seized under a writ of distringas may be sold as provided in Article 2333. The proceeds of such a sale shall be held by the sheriff subject to the orders of the court.

Art. 2504. Specific performance; court directing performance by third party

If a judgment directs a party to perform a specific act, and he fails to comply within the time specified, the court may direct the act to be done by the sheriff or some other person appointed by the court, at the cost of the disobedient party, and with the same effect as if done by the party.

TITLE IV. FOREIGN JUDGMENTS

Art. 2541. Execution of foreign judgments

A. A party seeking recognition or execution by a Louisiana court of a judgment or decree of a court of the United States or a territory thereof, or of any other state, or of any foreign country may bring an ordinary proceeding against the judgment debtor in the proper Louisiana court, to have the judgment or decree recognized and made the judgment of the Louisiana court.

B. A duly authenticated copy of the judgment or decree must be annexed to the petition.

C. A judgment, decree, or order of a court of the United States or any other court that is entitled to full faith and credit in this state may also be enforced pursuant to R.S. 13:4241.

Amended by Acts 1985, No. 464, § 2; Acts 2016, No. 132, § 1.

Comments—2016

Article 2541 was amended to clarify that La. R.S. 13:4241 does not authorize ex parte enforcement of the judgments of foreign countries in a Louisiana state court. See Baker & Mckenzie Advokatbyra v. Thinkstream, 20 So. 3d 1109 (La. App. 1 Cir. 2009).

Editor's Notes

For alternative method of enforcing foreign judgments, see R.S. 13:4241.

Art. 2542. Grounds for recognition of foreign defamation judgments

A. For the purposes of this Section, "foreign defamation judgment" means a judgment or decree rendered in a jurisdiction outside of any state or territory of the United States which was founded on a cause of action arising from allegations of defamation, libel, or slander.

B. A foreign defamation judgment is not conclusive if any of the following apply:

(1) The judgment was rendered under a system which does not provide impartial tribunals or procedures compatible with the requirements of due process of law.

(2) The foreign court did not have personal jurisdiction over the defendant.

(3) The foreign court did not have jurisdiction over the subject matter.

C. A foreign defamation judgment need not be recognized if any of the following apply:

(1) The defendant in the proceedings in the foreign court did not receive notice of the proceedings in sufficient time to enable him to provide a defense.

(2) The judgment was obtained by fraud.

(3) The cause of action or claim for relief on which the judgment is based is repugnant to the public policy of this state.

(4) The judgment conflicts with another final and conclusive order.

(5) The proceeding in the foreign court was contrary to an agreement between the parties under which the dispute in question was to be settled otherwise than by proceedings in that court.

(6) In the case of jurisdiction based only on personal service, the foreign court was an inconvenient forum for the trial of the action.

(7) The foreign jurisdiction where judgment was rendered would not give recognition to a similar judgment rendered in this state.

(8) The court sitting in this state before which the matter is brought determines that the defamation law applied in the adjudication by the foreign court failed to provide at least as much protection for freedom of speech and press in that case as would be provided by the constitutions of this state and the United States.

D. For the purposes of rendering declaratory relief with respect to the liability of a person for a foreign defamation judgment and determining whether the foreign defamation judgment should be deemed recognizable pursuant to this Section, the courts of this state shall have personal jurisdiction over any person who obtains a judgment in a defamation proceeding outside the United States against any of the following persons:

(1) A resident of this state.

(2) A person or entity amenable to the jurisdiction of this state.

(3) A person who has assets in this state.

(4) A person who may have to take action in this state to comply with the judgment.

Added by Acts 2010, No. 712, § 1; Acts 2010, No. 878, § 1.

BOOK V

SUMMARY AND EXECUTORY PROCEEDINGS

TITLE I. SUMMARY PROCEEDINGS

Art. 2591. Proceedings conducted with rapidity

Summary proceedings are those which are conducted with rapidity, within the delays allowed by the court, and without citation and the observance of all the formalities required in ordinary proceedings.

Official Revision Comments—1960

(a) The clause "within the delays allowed by the court" is declaratory of Louisiana procedural law. In the case of the extraordinary writs, this statement is in accord with the rule of Arts. 813, 841, 851, and 869 of the 1870 Code. Under the jurisprudence, the court always fixes the return day of rules to show cause and other contradictory motions.

(b) Art. 1201, *supra*, provides that "Citation and service thereof are essential in all civil actions except summary and executory proceedings." This goes beyond Art. 206 of the 1870 Code in so far as the exact language is concerned, but is in accord with prior law. *Cf.* Art. 98, Code of Practice of 1870.

(c) It has been consistently held that summary procedure is not unconstitutional, and clearly falls within the due process of law requirements of the Constitutions of Louisiana and of the United States. Kennard v. State of Louisiana, 92 U.S. 480, 23 L.Ed. 478 (1875); City of New Orleans v. Cannon, 10 La.Ann. 764 (1855); State ex rel. Morgan v. Kennard, 25 La.Ann. 238 (1873). Notice of the trial is required under Art. 2594, *infra*, to meet the requirements of due process.

Art. 2592. Use of summary proceedings

Summary proceedings may be used for trial or disposition of the following matters only:

(1) An incidental question arising in the course of judicial proceedings, including the award of and the determination of reasonableness of attorney fees.

(2) An application for a new trial.

(3) An issue which may be raised properly by an exception, contradictory motion, or rule to show cause.

(4) An action against the surety on a judicial bond after judgment has been obtained against the principal, or against both principal and surety when a summary proceeding against the principal is permitted.

(5) The homologation of a judicial partition, of a tableau of distribution or account filed by a legal representative, or of a report submitted by an auditor, accountant, or other expert appointed by the court; and an opposition to any of the foregoing, to the appointment of a legal representative, or to a petition for authority filed by a legal representative.

(6) A habeas corpus, mandamus, or quo warranto proceeding.

(7) The determination of the rank of mortgages, liens, and privileges on property sold judicially, and of the order of distribution of the proceeds thereof.

(8) The original granting of, subsequent change in, or termination of custody, visitation, and support for a child; support for a spouse; injunctive relief; support between ascendants and descendants; use and occupancy of the family home or use of community movables or immovables; or use of personal property.

(9) An action to compel an accounting at termination of parental authority; and an action to seek court approval to alienate, encumber, or lease the property of a minor, to incur an obligation of a minor, or to compromise the claim of a minor.

(10) An action to annul a probated testament under Article 2931.

(11) An action to enforce the right to a written accounting provided for in R.S. 9:2776.

(12) An action for dissolution or specific performance of a compromise entered pursuant to Article 1916(B) or by consent judgment.

(13) All other matters in which the law permits summary proceedings to be used.

Amended by Acts 1964, No. 4, § 1; Acts 1974, No. 130, § 1; Acts 1976, No. 321, § 1; Acts 1984, No. 90, § 1; Acts 1986, No. 116, § 1; Acts 1987, No. 565, § 2; Acts 1988, No. 817, § 3, eff. July 18, 1988; Acts 1989, No. 118, § 1; Acts 1990, No. 1008, § 4, eff. Jan. 1, 1991; Acts 1990, No. 1009, § 4, eff. Jan. 1, 1991; Acts 1992, No. 688, § 1, eff. July 6, 1992; Acts 2008, No. 824, § 3, eff. Jan. 1, 2009; Acts 2015, No. 260, § 2, eff. Jan. 1, 2016; Acts 2015, No. 379, § 2, eff. Aug. 1, 2016.

Comment—1989

Article 2592(1) is amended to provide a simple and expeditious procedure for the determination of the reasonableness of attorney's fees. See *Leenerts Farms, Inc. v. Rogers,* 421 So.2d 216 (La.1982) and *Central Progressive Bank v. Bradley,* 502 So.2d 1017 (La.1987).

Comment—1990

Paragraph (8) relief may be sought as an incident to a termination of marriage action or after a judgment has been granted in such an action. The phrase "injunctive relief" applies to family-related injunctions under Code Title V of Title 9 of the Revised Statutes.

Editor's Notes

State Dept. of Highways v. Lamar Adv. Co. of La., Inc., 279 So.2d 671 (1973), use of summary proceedings, C.C.P. art. 2592 list is exclusive. C.C.P. art. 2931 provides that the action to annul a probated testament "shall" be tried as a summary proceeding. Claim of unreasonable attorney fees in mortgage or privilege enforcement proceedings shall be tried summarily, C.C.P. art. 2753(C). See C.C.P. arts. 3604(B), (C), and 3607, injunctions in domestic and family matters. Use summary proceedings to enforce settlement, Howard v. Louisiana Citizens Property Ins., 65 So.3d 697 (App. 4 Cir. 2011).

Art. 2593. Pleadings

A summary proceeding may be commenced by the filing of a contradictory motion or by a rule to show cause, except as otherwise provided by law.

Exceptions to a contradictory motion, rule to show cause, opposition, or petition in a summary proceeding shall be filed prior to the time assigned for, and shall be disposed of at, the trial. An answer is not required, except as otherwise provided by law.

No responsive pleadings to an exception are permitted.

Amended by Acts 2010, No. 861, § 1A.

Official Revision Comments—1960

(a) One of the difficulties concerning the use of summary procedure in Louisiana has been the absence of specific rules in the 1870 Code of Practice. The necessary rules are to be found in the jurisprudence, it is true, but it is important that they be made readily accessible from the provisions of the procedural code itself.

(b) Specific reference was made to the rule to show cause for the reason indicated in Comment (d) of Art. 2592, *supra*.

(c) The second paragraph of the above article is in accord with the practice and jurisprudence of Louisiana, except as stated in Comment (e), *infra*.

Under Arts. 810, 842, and 869, respectively, Code of Practice of 1870, an answer is required in habeas corpus, mandamus and quo warranto proceedings. Except for these and similar special provisions in the statutes, no answer is required under summary procedure, and if the defendant fails to appear at the trial, plaintiff may introduce his evidence immediately and secure whatever relief is justified thereby, without the necessity of taking a default. Succession of Porter, 5 Rob. 96 (La.1843); State v. McDonnell, 13 La.Ann. 231 (1858).

(d) The defendant waives any objection to the improper use of summary procedure if he enters upon the trial without excepting to the summary procedure. Butchert v. Ricker, 11 La.Ann. 489 (1856); Younger Bros. v. Spell, 194 La. 16, 193 So. 354 (1939); Alfonso v. Ruiz, 2 So.2d 480 (La.App.1941); Roper v. Brooks, 9 So.2d 497 (La.App.1941); Cryer v. Cryer, 44 So.2d 517 (La.App.1950). See, also, Dussin v. Delaroderie, 5 Rob. 202 (La.1843); LeBouef v. Merle, 1 La.Ann. 144 (1846); Conery v. Heno, 9 La.Ann. 587 (1854); Succession of Moore, 18 La.Ann. 512 (1866); Succession of Esteves, 182 La. 604, 162 So. 194 (1935); Bloomenstiel v. Tridico, 156 So. 793 (La.App.1934); Foret v. Stark, 16 So.2d 79 (La.App.1943). All other exceptions which, under ordinary procedure, are required to be filed prior to answer or default should be filed prior to the commencement of the summary trial, since there is no default in summary proceedings.

(e) Despite the well settled rule stated in Comment (d), *supra*, it has been held that, if the defendant does not make an appearance at the trial, he may appeal and urge his objections to the summary procedure in the appellate court. Sharp v. Bright, 14 La.Ann. 390 (1859); Succession of Esteves, *supra*. This rule appears undesirable for at least four reasons: (1) an appeal should be a review of the proceedings below, and if this issue was not presented to the trial judge, it should not be considered on appeal; (2) the rule throws an unnecessarily heavy burden upon the appellate courts, as it forces them to determine issues which were never presented to the trial courts; (3) there is no basis for different rules on the same subject; and (4) the rule militates against the expeditious settlement of the controversy, which is the very object of summary procedure. For these reasons, this article requires a defendant in a summary proceeding to urge his objections to the use of summary process by the dilatory exception filed prior to the commencement of the trial, under penalty of waiver, whether he appears at the trial or not. See Comment (d), *supra*, and Art. 926, *supra*.

Editor's Notes

C.C.P. art. 3781 et seq., special rules for mandamus, habeas corpus, quo warranto; see also, Int'l Matex v. Systemfuels, 393 So.2d 104 (1981), filing of exceptions together in summary proceedings approved; *cf.* C.C.P. art. 928.

Art. 2594. Service of process

Citation and service thereof are not necessary in a summary proceeding. A copy of the contradictory motion, rule to show cause, or other pleading filed by the plaintiff in the proceeding, and of any order of court assigning the date and hour of the trial thereof, shall be served upon the defendant.

Art. 2595. Trial; decision

Upon reasonable notice a summary proceeding may be tried in open court or in chambers, in term or in vacation; and shall be tried by preference over ordinary proceedings, and without a jury, except as otherwise provided by law.

The court shall render its decision as soon as practicable after the conclusion of the trial of a summary proceeding and, whenever practicable, without taking the matter under advisement.

Art. 2596. Rules of ordinary proceedings applicable; exceptions

The rules governing ordinary proceedings are applicable to summary proceedings, except as otherwise provided by law.

TITLE II. EXECUTORY PROCEEDINGS

CHAPTER 1. GENERAL DISPOSITIONS

Article

Art. 2631. Use of executory proceedings

Executory proceedings are those which are used to effect the seizure and sale of property, without previous citation and judgment, to enforce a mortgage or privilege thereon evidenced by an authentic act importing a confession of judgment, and in other cases allowed by law.

Editor's Notes

See La. R.S. 10:9-101 for security interest on movables.

Art. 2632. Act importing a confession of judgment

An act evidencing a mortgage or privilege imports a confession of judgment when the obligor therein acknowledges the obligation secured thereby, whether then existing or to arise thereafter, and confesses judgment thereon if the obligation is not paid at maturity.

Editor's Notes

C.C.P art. 3723.

Art. 2633. Venue

An executory proceeding to enforce a mortgage or privilege may be brought either in the parish where the property is situated, or as provided in the applicable provision of Article 42 only.

Amended by Acts 1989, No. 117, § 1.

Comment—1989

This Article is amended to provide that the reference to Article 42 does not include the exceptions under Articles 71 through 85.

Editor's Notes

An executory proceeding to enforce a mortgage or privilege affecting a tract of land situated in different parishes at the option of the plaintiff may be brought at the domicile of the defendant or in any parish where a portion of the tract is located. La R.S. 13:4112.

Art. 2634. Petition

A person seeking to enforce a mortgage or privilege on property in an executory proceeding shall file a petition therefor, praying for the seizure and sale of the property affected by the mortgage or privilege. This petition shall comply with Article 891, and the plaintiff shall submit therewith the exhibits mentioned in Article 2635.

Editor's Notes

Rule 9.11 of the district court rules requires that parties who file suit for executory process should clearly highlight or emphasize the language in the attached exhibits necessary for executory process, such as "confession of judgment" and "waiver of demand for payment." A failure to comply with the rule may result in a delay while the pleadings are amended to conform to the rule.

Art. 2635. Authentic evidence submitted with petition

A. In order for a plaintiff to prove his right to use executory process to enforce the mortgage, security agreement, or privilege, it is necessary only for the plaintiff to submit with his petition authentic evidence of:

(1) The note, bond, or other instrument evidencing the obligation secured by the mortgage, security agreement, or privilege.

(2) The authentic act of mortgage or privilege on immovable property importing a confession of judgment.

(3) The act of mortgage or privilege on movable property importing a confession of judgment whether by authentic act or by private signature duly acknowledged.

B. This requirement of authentic evidence is necessary only in those cases, and to the extent, provided by law. A variance between the recitals of the note and of the mortgage or security agreement regarding the obligation to pay attorney's fees shall not preclude the use of executory process.

Amended by Acts 1981, No. 210, § 1; Acts 1982, No. 259, § 1; Acts 1989, No. 137, § 18, eff. Sept. 1, 1989.

Editor's Notes

See Miller, Lyon & Co. v. Cappel, 36 La.Ann. 264 (1884); and Louisiana National Bank of Baton Rouge v. Heroman, 280 So.2d 362 (1st 1973); correction of errors, R.S. 13:4104, 13:4105.

Art. 2636. Authentic evidence

The following documentary evidence shall be deemed to be authentic for purposes of executory process:

(1) The note, bond, or other instrument evidencing the obligation secured by the mortgage, security agreement, or privilege, paraphed for identification with the act of mortgage or privilege by

the notary or other officer before whom it is executed, with the exception that a paraph is not necessary in connection with a note secured by a security agreement subject to Chapter 9 of the Uniform Commercial Code or a copy of the note, bond, or other instrument evidencing the obligation certified as such by the notary before whom the act of mortgage, security agreement, or privilege was executed.

(2) A certified copy or a duplicate original of an authentic act.

(3) A certified copy of any judgment, judicial letters, or order of court.

(4) A copy of a resolution of the board of directors, or other governing board of a corporation, authorizing or ratifying the execution of a mortgage on its property, certified in accordance with the provisions of R.S. 13:4103.

(5)(a) A security agreement subject to Chapter 9 of the Uniform Commercial Code, which need not be executed or acknowledged before a notary.

(b) A reproduction of a security agreement described in Subsubparagraph (a) of this Subparagraph or a reproduction of a single writing that evidences both an obligation to pay and a security agreement described in Subsubparagraph (a) of this Subparagraph, that is certified by a representative of a financial institution in the manner provided for in R.S. 13:3733.1(E).

(6) A certified copy of the limited liability company's articles of organization filed with the secretary of state or a written consent or extract of minutes of a meeting of the persons specified in R.S. 13:4103.1, in each case authorizing or ratifying the execution of an act of mortgage on its property and in the form required by R.S. 13:4103.1, certified as provided in R.S. 12:1317(C).

(7) A certified copy of the contract of partnership authorizing the execution of an act of mortgage filed for registry with the secretary of state.

(8) All other documentary evidence recognized by law as authentic evidence, including R.S. 9:5555, R.S. 10:9–629, and R.S. 13:3733.1 and 3733.2.

(9) A promissory note or other evidence of indebtedness evidencing the obligation secured by the mortgage, security agreement or privilege, containing an electronic signature in accordance with the Louisiana Uniform Electronic Transactions Act, R.S. 9:2601 et seq. and accompanied by a certification in accordance with R.S. 13:3733.2.

Amended by Acts 1982, No. 177, § 1; Acts 1982, No. 185, § 1; Acts 1989, No. 137, § 18, eff. Sept. 1, 1989; Acts 1993, No. 475, § 2, eff. June 9, 1993; Acts 2003, No. 1072, § 1; Acts 2011, No. 90, § 1; Acts 2012, No. 505, § 2; Acts 2014, No. 440, § 3, eff. July 1, 2014; Acts 2015, No. 84, § 1.

Official Revision Comments—1960

(a) Paragraph (1) of this article reflects the prevailing custom and practice in Louisiana under which the mortgage note issued in connection with a mortgage, and identified therewith, is considered self-proving. This mortgage note must be annexed to the petition. See cases cited in Comment (c) under Art. 2635, *supra*.

(b) See Comment (d) under Art. 2635, *supra*. See also Dosson v. Sanders, 12 Rob. 238 (La.1845); Dobel v. Delavallade, 30 La.Ann. 604 (1878); and *cf.* Bank of Leesville v. Wingate, 123 La. 386, 48 So. 1005 (1909).

"Authentic evidence" is not limited to certified copies of authentic acts, as defined by Art. 2234 of the Civil Code. The term "authentic evidence" includes copies of any public act, certified as required by law. Woods v. Jastremski, 201 La. 1092, 11 So.2d 4 (1942).

(c) Paragraph (5) of this article is designed to include the following statutes: (1) R.S. 6:762, providing that the certificate of the secretary or assistant secretary of a building and loan association that the borrower, or the person who has assumed the borrower's loan, is in arrears, shall be considered authentic evidence of the default and arrears; (2) R.S. 6:763, providing that the certificate of the secretary or assistant secretary of a building and loan association, certifying the amount of advances made to the borrower, shall constitute authentic evidence of this indebtedness; (3) Art. 3159 of the Civil Code, providing that an act of pledge in favor of any bank passed before its cashier, is "authentic proof"; and, (4) R.S. 13:4104 and 13:4105 permitting the correction of any variance between the provisions of the act of mortgage and the mortgage note.

Comments—1982

(a) See comments to original article.

(b) Louisiana Civil Code Article 2814 as amended in 1981 provides that "any person authorized to execute a mortgage on behalf of a partnership shall, for purposes of executory process, have authority to execute a confession of judgment in the act of mortgage without execution of the articles of partnership by authentic act."

A contract of partnership must be filed in the Central Registry for Contracts of Partnership maintained by the secretary of state in order to affect third persons. (See R.S. 9:3401–3408, R.C.C. Arts. 2806 and 2841.) This amendment provides that a certified copy issued by the secretary of state of the contract of partnership authorizing the execution of an act of mortgage and filed in the Central Registry for Contracts of Partnerships shall be deemed authentic evidence of the authority to execute the mortgage and therefore, pursuant to Civil Code Article 2814, authentic evidence of the authority to execute a confession of judgment.

Editor's Notes

See C.C. art. 1833, definition of authentic act. See, also, R.S. 10:9–508 for requirements for authentic evidence as to security interests governed by Louisiana Commercial Laws (R.S. 10:9–101 et seq.). See, also, R.S. 9:5555, as to collateral mortgages, and vendor's privilege; and R.S. 13:4103A(2), as to corporate authority to execute mortgage; and R.S. 13:4103 generally.

Section 8 of Acts 1993, No. 475, provides that the enactment of par. (6) of Article 2636 "is remedial in nature and applies to existing mortgages, collateral mortgages, and security agreements previously granted by limited liability companies."

Art. 2637. Evidence which need not be authentic

A. Evidence as to the proper party defendant, or as to the necessity for appointing an attorney at law to represent an unrepresented defendant, or of any agreement to extend or modify the obligation to pay or of written notification of default, or of the breach or occurrence of a condition of the act of mortgage, or of the security agreement, or privilege securing the obligation, or of advances made by the holder of a collateral mortgage note or note for future advances, or of an obligation secured under Chapter 9 of the Uniform Commercial Code, need not be submitted in authentic form. These facts may be proved by the verified petition, or supplemental petition, or by affidavits submitted therewith.

B. If a mortgage sought to be enforced secures the repayment of any advances for the payment of taxes, insurance premiums, or special assessments on, or repairs to, or maintenance of, the property affected by the mortgage or security agreement, the existence, date, and amount of these advances may be proved by the verified petition, or supplemental petition, or by affidavits submitted therewith.

C. If a mortgage sought to be enforced is a collateral mortgage, or if the conventional mortgage or security agreement sought to be enforced secures multiple or future indebtedness of the debtor, the existence of the actual indebtedness may be proved by verified original or supplemental petition, or by an affidavit submitted with the original or supplemental petition, along with the original or reproduction of the note, bond, handnote, or other evidence representing the actual indebtedness, attached as an exhibit. A reproduction of the note, bond, handnote, or other evidence representing the actual indebtedness shall be certified by a representative of a financial institution pursuant to the provisions of R.S. 13:3733.1(E).

D. Evidence of a name change, merger, purchase and assumption, or similar disposition or acquisition, of a financial or lending institution may be proved by a verified petition or supplemental petition, or by an affidavit or affidavits submitted therewith by an appropriate officer of the successor entity.

E. Evidence of the name change or death of any party need not be submitted in authentic form, but may be proved by verified petition or supplemental petition, or by affidavit submitted therewith.

F. Evidence as to the proper party plaintiff entitled to enforce the obligation secured by the note, bond, handnote, or other instrument, including those that are electronically signed, evidencing the obligation of which a copy or reproduction is submitted in accordance with Article 2636(8) or Paragraph C of this Article, may be proved by verified original or supplemental petition, or by an affidavit submitted therewith.

Amended by Acts 1964, No. 4, § 1; Acts 1982, No. 260, § 1; Acts 1983, No. 185, § 1; Acts 1987, No. 408, § 1; Acts 1989, No. 137, § 18, eff. Sept. 1, 1989; Acts 1989, No. 161, § 1, eff. June 22, 1989; Acts 2014, No. 440, § 3, eff. July 1, 2014; Acts 2015, No. 84, § 1.

Editor's Notes

See Notes under C.C.P. art. 2636. Under par. C. above, the court has held that the handnote must be attached to the petition. See Bank of Coushatta v. King, 522 So. 2d 1328 (2d Cir. 1988). Also, the signatories to the mortgage note, but not to the handnote, were not indebted under the handnote. See Commercial Nat'l. Bank of Shreveport v. Succ. of Rogers, 628 So.2d 33 (2d Cir. 1993), but see Ruston State Bank v. Colvin, 28,490 (La.App. 2 Cir. 6/26/96), 679 So.2d 162, 1996 WL 348092, writ denied 96–1869 (La. 10/25/96), 679 So.2d 162, contra.

The collateral mortgage note does not represent a personal debt, Diamond Services Corp. v. Benoit, 780 So.2d 367 (La. 2001), putting all the conjecture to rest.

Art. 2638. Order for issuance of writ of seizure and sale

If the plaintiff is entitled thereto, the court shall order the issuance of a writ of seizure and sale commanding the sheriff to seize and sell the property affected by the mortgage or privilege, as prayed for and according to law.

Official Revision Comments—1960

Under recent Louisiana practice, the order rendered by the court on the petition and exhibits submitted therewith is either for the issuance of a writ of seizure and sale, or for the issuance of executory process; and the actual seizure and sale is made by the sheriff under authority of the "writ of seizure and sale" issued to him by the clerk of court. See Flemming's Formulary 520 (1933).

In the absence of any injunction to arrest the seizure and sale, the order rendered by the court directing the seizure and sale of the property is the only action taken by the court in an executory proceeding. It is the closest analogy to a judgment which can be found in executory procedure; and this is the order from which an appeal must be taken. *Cf.* State ex rel. Feibleman v. Judge, 45 La.Ann. 1426, 14 So. 428 (1893).

Art. 2639. Repealed by Acts 2003, No. 1072, § 2

Art. 2640. Citation unnecessary

Citation is not necessary in an executory proceeding.

Amended by Acts 2006, No. 498, § 1.

Editor's Notes

(CAVEAT: Fair Debt Collection Practices Act, 15 U.S. C. § 1692a, et seq. Prior to initiating any debt collection process, including promissory notes, contracts and the foreclosure of mortgages, extreme care must be exercised to conform to the exacting requirements of the Fair Debt Collection Practices Act. See the elaborate forms in West's LSA Civil Procedure, Vol. 12, Forms 1589a, et seq. The penalties against the attorney for violation are serious, $1,000.00 per violation, heard and enforced in the Federal District Court).

Art. 2641. Service upon, and seizure and sale prosecuted against, attorney for unrepresented defendant

In all cases governed by Article 2674, all demands, notices, and other documents required to be served upon the defendant in an executory proceeding shall be served upon the attorney at law appointed by the court to represent him, against whom the seizure and sale shall be prosecuted contradictorily.

Art. 2642. Assertion of defenses; appeal

A. Defenses and procedural objections to an executory proceeding may be asserted either through an injunction proceeding to arrest the seizure and sale as provided in Articles 2751 through 2754, or a suspensive appeal from the order directing the issuance of the writ of seizure and sale, or both.

B. A suspensive appeal from an order directing the issuance of a writ of seizure and sale shall be taken within fifteen days of service of the notice of seizure as provided in Article 2721. The appeal is governed by the provisions of Articles 2081 through 2086, 2088 through 2122, and 2124 through 2167, except that the security therefor shall be for an amount exceeding by one-half the balance due on the debt secured by the mortgage or privilege sought to be enforced, including principal, interest to date of the order of appeal, and attorney fees, but exclusive of court costs.

Amended by Acts 1964, No. 4, § 1; Acts 2016, No. 132, § 1.

Official Revision Comments—1960

(a) The whole theory on which the civilian executory proceeding rests is that a seizure of the property subject to the mortgage or privilege may be made immediately on the order of the court issued on the ex parte application of the creditor. It is not a contradictory proceeding at all; but an ex parte one. The defendant can assert any valid defenses to the seizure, but he must do so either through an opposition to arrest the seizure and sale, or through an appeal from the order directing the seizure and sale. See Engelmann-Millar, A History of Continental Civil Procedure 498–501 (1927); General Motors Acceptance Corp. v. Anzelmo, 222 La. 1019, 64 So.2d 417 (1953), noted 14 La.L.Rev. 289 (1953); and Boatmen's Savings Bank v. Wagenspack, 12 F. 66, 4 Woods 130 (5 Cir.1882).

(b) The second paragraph announces the Louisiana rule. State ex rel. Feibleman v. Judge, 45 La.Ann. 1426, 14 So. 428 (1893).

(c) Although theoretically a devolutive appeal from an order directing the issuance of a writ of seizure and sale is available to the defendant in an executory proceeding, if the property is sold prior to the time of the hearing on appeal, the appeal will be dismissed as presenting only a moot question. Bank of LaFourche v. Barrios, 167 La. 215, 118 So. 893 (1928). For this reason in this Code no devolutive appeal is permitted from an order directing the issuance of the writ of seizure and sale.

Comments—1964

(a) See Comments under original article.

(b) Amended on the recommendation of the Louisiana State Law Institute to set forth precisely the delay for a suspensive appeal from an order directing the issuance of a writ of seizure and sale. The reference to Article 2123 on this point in the original article was not clear, since there can be no application for a new trial in an executory proceeding.

Art. 2643. Third person claiming mortgage, security interest, or privilege on property seized

A third person claiming a mortgage, security interest, or privilege on the property seized in an executory proceeding may assert his right to share in the distribution of the proceeds of the sale of the property by intervention, as provided in Article 1092. The intervention shall be served as provided in Article 1093 and shall be tried summarily.

Amended by Acts 1962, No. 92, § 1; Acts 1989, No. 137, § 18, eff. Sept. 1, 1989.

Art. 2644. Conversion to ordinary proceeding

The plaintiff in an executory proceeding may convert it into an ordinary proceeding by amending his petition so as to pray that the defendant be cited and for judgment against him on the obligation secured by the mortgage or privilege.

The plaintiff in an ordinary proceeding may not convert it into an executory proceeding.

Editor's Notes

C.C.P. art. 3721.

CHAPTER 2. PROCEEDING AGAINST SURVIVING SPOUSE, SUCCESSION, OR HEIR

Article

Art. 2671. Proceeding against surviving spouse in community

When a mortgage, security interest, or privilege has been granted on community property to secure an obligation of the community, and one of the spouses in community has died subsequently, an executory proceeding to enforce the mortgage, security agreement, or privilege may be brought against the surviving spouse in community. It shall not be necessary to make the succession representative, heirs, or legatees of the deceased spouse parties to the proceeding.

Amended by Acts 1989, No. 137, § 18, eff. Sept. 1, 1989.

Art. 2672. Proceeding against heirs or legatees

When the original debtor is dead, and his heirs or legatees have accepted his succession, the executory proceeding may be brought against his heirs or legatees.

If an heir or legatee is dead, incompetent, or absent, his heirs, legatees, succession, or legal representative may be made a party defendant to the executory proceeding as provided above and in Articles 2673 and 2674, as the case may be.

Art. 2673. Proceeding against legal representative

When the property of the original debtor is under the administration of a legal representative, the executory proceeding may be brought against his legal representative, and no other person need be made a party to the proceeding.

Art. 2674. Attorney appointed to represent unrepresented defendant

The court shall appoint an attorney at law to represent the unrepresented defendant in an executory proceeding under the following circumstances:

(1) When the defendant is an absentee;

(2) When the debtor is dead, no succession representative has been appointed, and his heirs and legatees have not been sent into possession;

(3) When the debtor's property is under the administration of a legal representative, but the latter has died, resigned, or been removed from office, and no successor thereof has qualified;

(4) When the defendant is a corporation or a partnership upon which process cannot be served for any reason; and

(5) When the defendant is a minor, or a mental incompetent, who has no legal representative at the time of the institution of the proceeding.

Art. 2675. Case falling within application of two or more articles; plaintiff may bring proceeding under any applicable article

If a case falls within the provisions of two or more of Articles 2671 through 2674, the plaintiff may bring the executory proceeding under any applicable article.

CHAPTER 3. PROCEEDINGS WHEN PROPERTY IN POSSESSION OF THIRD PERSON

Article

Art. 2701. Alienation of property to third person disregarded

A mortgage or privilege evidenced by authentic act importing a confession of judgment, affecting property sold by the original debtor or his legal successor to a third person, may be enforced against the property without reference to any sale or alienation to the third person. The executory proceeding may be brought against the original debtor, his surviving spouse in community, heirs, legatees, or legal representative, as the case may be. The third person who then owns and is in possession of the property need not be made a party to the proceeding.

Art. 2702. Rights of third person who has acquired property and assumed indebtedness

When property sold or otherwise alienated by the original debtor or his legal successor has been seized and is about to be sold under executory process, a person who has acquired the property and assumed the indebtedness secured by the mortgage or privilege thereon may:

(1) Pay the balance due on the indebtedness, in principal, interest, attorney's fees, and costs; or

(2) Arrest the seizure and sale on any of the grounds mentioned in Article 2751.

Art. 2703. Rights of third possessor

When property sold or otherwise alienated by the original debtor or his legal successor has been seized and is about to be sold under executory process, a person who has acquired the property subject to the mortgage or privilege thereon and who has not assumed the payment of the indebtedness secured thereby may:

(1) Pay the balance due on the indebtedness, in principal, interest, attorney's fees, and costs;

(2) Arrest the seizure and sale on any of the grounds mentioned in Article 2751, or on the ground that the mortgage or privilege was not recorded, or that the inscription of the recordation thereof had perempted; or,

(3) Intervene in the executory proceeding to assert any claim which he has to the enhanced value of the property due to improvements placed on the property by him, or by any prior third possessor through whom he claims ownership of the property. This intervention shall be a summary proceeding initiated by a petition complying with Article 891.

CHAPTER 4. EXECUTION OF WRIT OF SEIZURE AND SALE

Article

Art. 2721. Seizure of property; notice

A. The sheriff shall seize the property affected by the mortgage, security agreement, or privilege immediately upon receiving the writ of seizure and sale.

B. The sheriff shall serve upon the defendant a written notice of the seizure of the property. Such notice of seizure shall be accomplished by personal service or domiciliary service. The notice of seizure shall reproduce in full the provisions of Article 2642 and include information concerning the availability of housing counseling services, as well as the time, date, and place of the sheriff's sale, in accordance with the form provided in R.S. 13:3852(B).

C. The sheriff shall have no liability to the debtor or to any third party for wrongful or improper seizure of the debtor's or third party's property of the same general type as described in the debtor's security agreement. If necessary, the sheriff shall request the secured creditor to identify the property subject to the security agreement and shall act pursuant to the secured creditor's instructions. The debtor's and other owner's sole remedy for the wrongful or improper seizure of the property shall be for actual losses sustained under R.S. 10:9–625 against the secured creditor on whose behalf and pursuant to whose instructions the sheriff may act.

Amended by Acts 1989, No. 137, § 18, eff. Sept. 1, 1989; Acts 2001, No. 128, § 17, eff. July 1, 2001 at 12:01 A.M; Acts 2006, No. 498, § 1; Acts 2013, No. 339, § 2; Acts 2016, No. 132, § 1; Acts 2021, No. 259, § 2.

Editor's Notes

The notice of seizure is not waivable, see Comment (b).

Acts 1989, 1st Ex.Sess., No. 12, § 1, and Acts 1989, No. 135, § 12, provide for a January 1, 1990 effective date for Chapter 9 of the Louisiana Commercial Laws (R.S. 10:9–101, et seq.). Acts 1989, No. 137, implementing Chapter 9, provides a September 1, 1989 effective date for the affected Code of Civil Procedure articles and certain other amended statutes (see § 22 of Act 137). See Acts 1989, No. 135, §§ 10 and 11, and Acts 1989, No. 137, § 20 for provisions on application of security device laws prior to January 1, 1990. See, also, Acts 1989, No. 598, § 9.

Art. 2722. Advertisement of sale

After the seizure of the property, the sheriff shall proceed to advertise the sale of the property, in accordance with the provisions of the first paragraph of Article 2331.

Editor's Notes

Advertising requirements, R.S. 43:203.

Art. 2723. Appraisal of property, unless waived

Prior to the sale, the property seized must be appraised in accordance with law, unless appraisal has been waived in the act evidencing the mortgage, the security agreement, or the document creating the privilege and plaintiff has prayed that the property be sold without appraisal, and the order directing the issuance of the writ of seizure and sale has directed that the property be sold as prayed for. There is no requirement that seized property subject to a security interest under Chapter 9 of the Louisiana Commercial Laws (R.S. 10:9–101, et seq.), be appraised prior to the judicial sale thereof.

Amended by Acts 1989, No. 137, § 18, eff. Sept. 1, 1989.

Editor's Notes

But see R.S. 13:4106, deficiency judgment is precluded if no appraisal.

Art. 2724. Articles relating to sales under fieri facias applicable

A. The provisions of Paragraphs A through C of Article 2293, Articles 2333 through 2335, and 2337 through 2381, relating to a sale of property under the writ of fieri facias, shall apply to a sale of property under the writ of seizure and sale.

B. The provisions of Article 2336 shall also apply to a sale of property under the writ of seizure and sale, unless appraisement has been waived, as provided in Article 2723.

Amended by Acts 1991, No. 662, § 1, eff. Jan. 1, 1992; Acts 2012, No. 127, § 1.

Art. 2725. Seizure and sale of a motor vehicle out-of-state; procedure

A. When a secured party enforces his right to seizure and sale of a motor vehicle located out of this state, he may, in addition to any remedy provided under Louisiana law, proceed under the procedural laws governing seizure and sale of the state in which the property is located. An action to proceed under the laws of another state shall not affect the rights of the secured party granted under Louisiana law, including but not limited to the right to obtain a deficiency judgment upon showing compliance with the laws of the state in which the property was seized.

B. When a secured party seizes a motor vehicle under the procedural laws governing seizure of the state in which the motor vehicle is located, he may, at his option, return the motor vehicle to

Louisiana and sell same at public or private sale without appraisal, provided that the mortgage authorizes a sale without appraisal.

Added by Acts 1984, No. 126, § 1. Amended by Acts 1985, No. 39, § 1; Acts 1986, No. 106, § 1; Acts 1989, No. 137, § 18, eff. Sept. 1, 1989; Acts 2001, No. 128, § 17, eff. July 1, 2001 at 12:01 A.M.

CHAPTER 5. INJUNCTION TO ARREST SEIZURE AND SALE

Article

Art. 2751. Grounds for arresting seizure and sale; damages

The defendant in the executory proceeding may arrest the seizure and sale of the property by injunction when the debt secured by the security interest, mortgage, or privilege is extinguished, or is legally unenforceable, or if the procedure required by law for an executory proceeding has not been followed.

Amended by Acts 1981, No. 302, § 1; Acts 1989, No. 137, § 18, eff. Sept. 1, 1989.

Editor's Notes

A rule to set aside may not be used to arrest the seizure and sale; Comment (a) to C.C.P. art. 2752.

The language below in italics was deleted by amendment of Art. 2751 by Acts 1989, No. 137, § 18, eff. September 1, 1989, and is provided for informational purposes only.

"In the event injunctive relief is granted to the defendant, if the court finds the seizure in the executory proceeding to be wrongful, it may allow damages to the defendant. Attorney's fees for the services rendered in connection with the injunction may be included as an element of the damages."

Acts 1989, 1st Ex.Sess., No. 12, § 1, and Acts 1989, No. 135, § 12, provide for a January 1, 1990 effective date for Chapter 9 of the Louisiana Commercial Laws (R.S. 10:9–101, et seq.). Acts 1989, No. 137, implementing Chapter 9, provides a September 1, 1989 effective date for the affected Code of Civil Procedure articles and certain other amended statutes (see § 22 of Act 137). See Acts 1989, No. 135, §§ 10 and 11, and Acts 1989, No. 137, § 20 for provisions on application of security device laws prior to January 1, 1990. See, also, Acts 1989, No. 598, § 9.

Art. 2752. Injunction procedure

A. The petition for injunction shall be filed in the court where the executory proceeding is pending, either in the executory proceeding or in a separate suit. The injunction proceeding to arrest a seizure and sale shall be governed by the provisions of Articles 3601 through 3609 and 3612, except as provided in Article 2753. However, a temporary restraining order shall not issue to arrest the seizure and sale of immovable property, but the defendant may apply for a preliminary injunction in accordance with Article 3602. In the event the defendant does apply for a preliminary injunction the hearing for such shall be held before the sale of the property.

B. If the court finds that the temporary restraining order or preliminary injunction was wrongfully issued, the court, unless the proceedings are stayed, in addition to the damages authorized under Article 3608, may allow the sheriff to proceed with the sale by virtue of the prior advertisement, if not expired.

Amended by Acts 1987, No. 139, § 1; Acts 1988, No. 812, § 1.

Official Revision Comments—1960

(a) It is well established in the jurisprudence that the seizure and sale can be arrested only by a petition for an injunction, and not by a rule to set aside the order of seizure and sale. Clement v. Oakey, 2 Rob. 90 (La.1842); Minot v. Bank of the United States, 4 Rob. 490 (La.1843); Merchants Bank of Baltimore v. Bank of the United States, 4 Rob. 493 (La.1843); Koch v. Godchaux, 46 La.Ann. 1382, 16 So. 181 (1894). *Cf.* State v. Judge of the Fourth District Court, 18 La.Ann. 110 (1866); Levi v. Converse, 20 La.Ann. 558 (1868).

(b) Apparently no issue has been raised in the reported cases as to whether the petition for injunctive relief to arrest a seizure and sale should be filed in the executory proceedings or in a separate suit. Both practices appear to have been followed at one time or another in various sections of the state. The point is technical, and of no real importance, as long as it is settled definitely. The above article permits either practice.

(c) It is now settled that former R.S. 13:4062 through R.S. 13:4071, regulating interlocutory injunctive orders, are applicable to injunctive relief granted to arrest the seizure and sale in an executory proceeding. American Nat. Bank v. Bauman, 173 La. 336, 137 So. 54 (1931). See, also, 17 Tul.L.Rev. 630 (1943).

(d) The exception as to Art. 2753, *infra*, is intended to preserve the exceptions embodied in Art. 739 of the 1870 Code permitting injunction without bond in certain cases.

(e) See, also, Comments under Arts. 2298, 2751, *supra*.

Art. 2753. Security not required in certain cases

A. The original debtor, his surviving spouse in community, heirs, legatees, and legal representative are not required to furnish security for the issuance of a temporary restraining order or preliminary injunction to arrest a seizure and sale, when the injunctive relief is applied for solely on one or more of the following grounds:

(1) The debt secured by the mortgage, security agreement, or privilege is extinguished or prescribed;

(2) The enforcement of the debt secured by the mortgage, security agreement, or privilege is premature, either because the original term allowed for payment, or any extension thereof granted by the creditor, had not expired at the time of the institution of the executory proceeding;

(3) The act evidencing the mortgage or privilege or the security agreement is forged, or the debtor's signature thereto was procured by fraud, violence, or other unlawful means;

(4) The defendant in the executory proceeding has a liquidated claim to plead in compensation against the debt secured by the mortgage, security agreement, or privilege; or

(5) The order directing the issuance of the writ of seizure and sale was rendered without sufficient authentic evidence having been submitted to the court, or the evidence submitted was not actually authentic.

B. Notwithstanding any of the provisions of this Chapter to the contrary, a claim or an action in redhibition shall not be grounds for the issuance of a temporary restraining order or preliminary injunction to arrest a seizure and sale, without security as provided by law.

C. Notwithstanding any of the provisions of this Chapter to the contrary, a claim that the attorney's fees established in the mortgage, security agreement, or privilege to be enforced are unreasonable shall not be grounds for the issuance of a temporary restraining order or preliminary injunction to arrest a seizure and sale. Any such claim may only be urged either:

(1) Prior to the sale by means of a rule to show cause filed not later than ten days, exclusive of holidays, prior to the sale, and tried summarily prior to the date of the sale, or

(2) In conjunction with a proceeding seeking a deficiency judgment to satisfy the debt for which the property was sold.

Amended by Acts 1979, No. 92, § 1; Acts 1983, No. 341, § 1; Acts 1987, No. 304, § 1; Acts 1989, No. 137, § 18, eff. Sept. 1, 1989.

Art. 2754. Security otherwise required

Except as provided in Article 2753, no temporary restraining order or preliminary injunction shall issue to arrest a seizure and sale unless the applicant therefor furnishes security as provided in Article 3610.

CHAPTER 6. DEFICIENCY JUDGMENT

Article

Art. 2771. When deficiency judgment obtainable

Unless otherwise provided by law, the creditor may obtain a judgment against the debtor for any deficiency due on the debt after the distribution of the proceeds of the judicial sale only if the property has been sold under the executory proceeding after appraisal in accordance with the provisions of Article 2723.

Amended by Acts 1989, No. 137, § 18, eff. Sept. 1, 1989.

Editor's Notes

Deficiency Judgment Act, R.S. 13:4106. First Guaranty Bank, Hammond, Louisiana v. Baton Rouge Petroleum Center, Inc., Sup.1988, 529 So.2d 834 (on rehearing), after judicial sale and distribution of proceeds, a deficiency judgment may not be defeated on grounds of lack of authentic evidence in the executory proceeding. Guaranty Bank of Mamou v. Community Rice Mill, Sup.1987, 502 So.2d 1067, holds that the Deficiency Judgment Act applies solely to foreclosure by executory process, not to ordinary process. See, also, R.S. 13:4108.1 for special provisions relating to appraisal and deficiency judgment with "giving in payment" (dation en paiement).

A deficiency judgment may be precluded by "fundamental flaws" in the executory proceeding. A failure to serve notice to appoint an appraiser is a fundamental flaw, Citizens Sav. and Loan Ass'n v. Kinchen, Sup.1993, 622 So.2d 662. Security Homestead Ass'n v. Fuselier, Sup.1991, 591 So.2d 335, held that it was a fundamental flaw to fail to serve notice to appoint appraisers or to fail to give notice of seizure. First Fed. Sav. & Loan v. Moss, Sup.1993, 616 So.2d 648, held that the in globo appraisal of the property covered by two separate mortgages was unauthorized and barred a deficiency judgment. The in globo appraisal of the properties covered in the same mortgage in cross-collateralization was authorized, First Bank of Natchitoches v. Chenault, App. 3 Cir.1991, 576 So.2d 1123. Bank of Coushatta v. King, App. 2 Cir.1988, 522 So.2d 1328, held that, in the executory process to enforce a collateral mortgage, the handnote must be attached to the petition, as set forth in C.C.P. art. 2637(C).

Art. 2772. Procedure to obtain deficiency judgment

A creditor may obtain a deficiency judgment against the debtor either by converting the executory proceeding into an ordinary proceeding as provided in Article 2644, or by a separate suit.

In either case, the defendant must be cited, and all of the delays and formalities required in ordinary proceedings must be observed.

CHAPTER 7. MAKING JUDGMENTS OF OTHER LOUISIANA COURTS EXECUTORY

SECTION 1. IN GENERAL

SECTION 1. IN GENERAL

Art. 2781. When judgments may be made executory by other courts

A judgment rendered in a Louisiana court may be made executory in any other Louisiana court of competent jurisdiction, if its execution has not been and may not be suspended by appeal.

Editor's Notes

A Louisiana judgment must be made executory for garnishment under fieri facias if garnishee domiciled in another parish—C.C.P. art. 2416; and in examination of judgment debtor domiciled in a parish other than where judgment rendered—C.C.P. art. 2452. [Comment (b)].

Sears, Roebuck and Co. v. Dennis, 870 So.2d 1080 (La. App. 5 Cir. 2004). A detailed analysis of the electronic record of an open account under a Sears charge card. Sears collected, R.S. 9:2781.

Art. 2782. Procedure; execution of executory judgment

A creditor wishing to have a judgment of a Louisiana court made executory, as provided in Article 2781, may file an ex parte petition complying with Article 891, with a certified copy of the judgment annexed, praying that the judgment be made executory. The court shall immediately render and sign its judgment making the judgment of the other Louisiana court executory.

The judgment thus made executory may be executed or enforced immediately as if it had been a judgment of that court rendered in an ordinary proceeding.

Editor's Notes

See Comment for bond requirements.

Art. 2783. Injunction to arrest execution of judgment made executory

The execution of a judgment made executory under the provisions of Article 2782 may be arrested by injunction if the judgment is extinguished, prescribed, or is otherwise legally unenforceable. No temporary restraining order or a preliminary writ of injunction may be issued, however, unless the applicant therefor furnishes security as provided in Article 3610.

SECTION 2. INTRASTATE REGISTRATION OF SUPPORT ORDERS FOR MODIFICATION AND ENFORCEMENT

SUBSECTION A. GENERAL PROVISIONS

Art. 2785. Definitions

For purposes of this Section:

(1) "Confirmed registered support order" means a support order registered pursuant to the provisions of Article 2786 and subsequently confirmed by a registering court or operation of law pursuant to the provisions of Article 2788(A)(2) or (B) or Article 2793(A)(2), (A)(3), or (B).

(2) "Rendering court" means the district or, if applicable, family or juvenile court which rendered the support order.

(3) "Registering court" means the district or, if applicable, family or juvenile court in which a support obligation rendered by another court of this state has been filed.

(4) "Support order" means a judgment, decree, or order, whether temporary, final, or subject to modification, for the benefit of a child, a spouse, or a former spouse, which provides for monetary support, health care, arrearages, or reimbursement, and may include related costs and fees, interest, income withholding, attorney fees, and other relief.

(5) "Party to a support order" means the obligee of a support order, or the state of Louisiana, Department of Children and Family Services, or similar agency of another jurisdiction or state when supplying support services as defined in or substantially similar to R.S. 46:236.1(A)(7),[1] or under the Uniform Interstate Family Support Act (UIFSA), or in performance of its official duties under Title IV, Subchapter D of the Social Security Act as stated in 45 C.F.R. 301.1.

Added by Acts 1997, No. 603, § 2. Amended by Acts 1999, No. 210, § 1.

[1] House Bill 1145, 1999 Reg. Sess., which was introduced to enact R.S. 46:236.1(A)(7), did not pass.

Editor's Notes

The 1997 legislation enacted C.C.P. arts. 2785 to 2794 as the Intrastate Registration of Support Orders for Modification and Enforcement.

The 1999 legislation amended C.C.P. arts. 2786(B) and (2), (C)(3), and (D), 2787, 2789(B), 2790(A), 2791(B)(2) and (C)(3) and 2792; and enacted C.C.P. arts. 2785(5), 2786(C)(4) and 2795.

SUBSECTION B. MODIFICATION

Art. 2786. Registration of support orders for modification

A. A support order rendered by a court of this state may be registered for modification in another court of this state if all parties to the order are no longer domiciled in the parish of the rendering court.

B. A party to a support order seeking to register the support order pursuant to the provisions of this Subsection shall transmit to the clerk of the registering court all of the following:

(1) A certified copy of the support order.

(2) A verified statement of support or a federally approved URESA or UIFSA form, signed by a party to the support order, indicating all of the following:

(a) The name and street address of the obligee.

(b) The name, last known place of residence, and post office or street address of the obligor.

(c) A list of all the jurisdictions in which the order is registered.

C. Upon receipt of these documents, the clerk of court shall:

(1) Treat the documents as if they were a petition seeking relief relative to a family law matter by assigning a docket number and, if applicable, designate a division to which the matter is allotted.

(2) Register the support order by stamping or making a notation thereof on the certified copy of the support order in substantially the following form: "REGISTERED FOR MODIFICATION by the Clerk of the [District, Family, or Juvenile] Court in and for the Parish of [name of parish] on [date]."

(3)(a) Send a copy of the registered support order, by certified or registered mail, to the obligor at the address provided in the verified statement of support, or

(b) Issue service of process as permitted by law and notice of registration in lieu of citation, which shall be served by ordinary process.

(4) Issue notice of the registration to the rendering court or, if the support order has been previously registered and confirmed for modification in another court of this state, to the last registering court.

D. The filing of a support order in compliance with the provisions hereof constitutes registration of the support order for modification, and if subsequently confirmed, shall divest the rendering court, or if registered in another court for modification, the court of last registration, of jurisdiction to modify the support order.

Added by Acts 1997, No. 603, § 2. Amended by Acts 1999, No. 210, § 1.

Art. 2787. Objections to registration of support order for modification

An objection for any purpose to the registration of the support order must be filed by the obligor with the registering court within twenty days from the date of mailing of the notice required in Article 2786(C)(3) (a), or within twenty days from the date of service required in Article 2786(C)(3)(b).

Added by Acts 1997, No. 603, § 2. Amended by Acts 1999, No. 210, § 1.

Art. 2788. Confirmation of registered support order for modification

A. If the obligor files a timely objection and, after a hearing, the court finds:

(1) There exists a legitimate basis for objecting to the registration, the court shall issue an order vacating the registration of the support order.

(2) There exists no legitimate basis for objecting to the registration, the court shall issue an order confirming the registration of the support order.

B. If the obligor fails to file a timely objection, the registered support order is confirmed by operation of law and becomes executory in all respects.

Added by Acts 1997, No. 603, § 2.

Art. 2789. Confirmed registered support order for modification; effect

A. Upon confirming the registration of the support order, the registering court shall have continuing jurisdiction to modify the support order.

B. The clerk of the registering court shall issue notice of the confirmation to the rendering court or, if the support order has been previously registered and confirmed for modification in another court of this state, to the last registering court. Upon receipt of the notice, the rendering court or, if applicable, the last registering court shall cause the notice to be filed in the proceedings in which the support order was rendered or registered and that court shall be divested of jurisdiction to modify the support order retroactively to the original notice of registration filed therein unless it is subsequently registered therein for modification.

C. When confirmed, the registered support order shall be treated in the same manner and have the same effect as a support order issued by the registering court. Additionally, the confirmed registered support order is subject to the same procedures, defenses, and proceedings for modifying, vacating, or staying as a support order of the rendering court, and may be enforced and satisfied in a like manner.

Added by Acts 1997, No. 603, § 2. Amended by Acts 1999, No. 210, § 1.

Art. 2790. Confirmed registered support order; enforcement

A. At a hearing to enforce a confirmed registered support order, the obligor may present only matters that would be available to him as defenses in an action to enforce the support order in the rendering court. If he shows to the court that an appeal from the order is pending or will be taken or that a stay of execution has been granted, the court shall stay enforcement of the order until the appeal has been concluded, the time for appeal has expired, or the stay order has been vacated, upon satisfactory proof that the obligor has furnished security for payment of the support ordered as required by the rendering court. If he shows to the court any ground upon which enforcement of the confirmed registered support order may be stayed, the court shall stay enforcement of the order for an appropriate period if the obligor furnishes the security for payment of the support ordered that is required by law.

B. Arrearages which accrue prior to registration of a support order shall not be modified unless there is a pending petition for modification at the time of registration of the support order. Any such modification shall be retroactive only to the date of filing of the petition for modification.

Added by Acts 1997, No. 603, § 2. Amended by Acts 1999, No. 210, § 1.

SUBSECTION C. ENFORCEMENT

Art. 2791. Registration of support orders for enforcement only

A. A support order rendered by a court of this state may be registered for enforcement in another court of this state.

B. An obligee of a support order seeking to register a support order pursuant to the provisions of this Paragraph shall transmit to the clerk of the registering court all of the following:

(1) A certified copy of the support order.

(2) A verified statement of support or a federally approved URESA or UIFSA form, signed by a party to the support order, indicating all of the following:

(a) The name and street address of the obligee.

(b) The name, last known place of residence, and post office or street address of the obligor.

(c) The total amount of arrearages owed pursuant to the support order which have not been reduced to a judgment.

(d) A list of all the jurisdictions in which the order is registered.

C. Upon receipt of these documents, the clerk of court shall:

(1) Treat the documents as if they were a petition seeking relief relative to a family law matter by assigning a docket number and, if applicable, designate a division to which the matter is allotted.

(2) Register the support order by stamping or making a notation thereof on the certified copy of the support order in substantially the following form: "REGISTERED FOR ENFORCEMENT by the Clerk of the [District, Family, or Juvenile] Court in and for the Parish of [name of parish] on [date]."

(3)(a) Send a copy of the registered support order and verified statement of support, by certified or registered mail, to the obligor at the addresses provided in the verified statement of support, or

(b) Issue service of process as permitted by law and notice of registration in lieu of citation, which shall be served by ordinary process.

D. The filing of a support order in compliance with the provisions hereof constitutes registration of the support order for enforcement.

Added by Acts 1997, No. 603, § 2. Amended by Acts 1999, No. 210, § 1.

Art. 2792. Objections to registration of support order for enforcement

An objection for any purpose to the registration of the support order must be filed by the obligor with the registering court within twenty days from the date of mailing of the notice required in Article 2791(C)(3)(a), or within twenty days from the date of service required in Article 2791(C)(3)(b).

Added by Acts 1997, No. 603, § 2. Amended by Acts 1999, No. 210, § 1.

Art. 2793. Confirmation of registered support order for enforcement

A. If the obligor files a timely objection and, after a hearing, the court finds:

(1) There exists a legitimate basis for objecting to the registration, other than the amount of arrearages alleged to be owed, the court shall issue an order vacating the registration of the support order for enforcement.

(2) There exists no legitimate basis for objecting to the registration, other than the amount of arrearages alleged to be owed, the court shall issue an order confirming the registration of the support order for enforcement.

(3) There exists no legitimate basis for objecting to the registration and there is no dispute as to the amount of arrearages owed as stated in the verified statement of support, the court shall issue an order confirming the registration of the support order for enforcement and render a judgment making the arrearages executory.

B. If the obligor fails to file a timely objection, the registered support order is confirmed by operation of law and the amount of arrearages alleged to be owed in the verified statement of support becomes executory in all respects.

Added by Acts 1997, No. 603, § 2.

Art. 2794. Confirmed registered support order; enforcement

A. When confirmed, the registered support order shall be enforced in the same manner as a support order issued by the registering court. It is subject to the same procedures, defenses, and proceedings for enforcing or staying as a support order of the rendering court.

B. At a hearing to enforce a confirmed registered support order for enforcement, the obligor may present matters that would be available to him as defenses in an action to enforce the support order in the rendering court. If he shows to the court that an appeal from the order is pending or will be taken or that a stay of execution has been granted, the court shall stay enforcement of the order until the appeal has been concluded, the time for appeal has expired, or the stay order has been vacated, upon satisfactory proof that the obligor has furnished security for payment of the support ordered as required by the rendering court. If he shows to the court any ground upon which enforcement of the confirmed registered support order may be stayed, the court shall stay enforcement of the order for an appropriate period if the obligor furnishes the security for payment of the support ordered that is required by law.

Added by Acts 1997, No. 603, § 2.

Art. 2795. Joinder of actions

Nothing herein shall be construed as prohibiting a party from asserting multiple remedies hereunder nor requesting additional proceedings for enforcement or modification of the support order at the time of the filing of the order for registration.

Added by Acts 1999, No. 210, § 1.

Arts. 2796 to 2810. [Reserved]

BOOK VI

PROBATE PROCEDURE

TITLE I. GENERAL DISPOSITIONS

CHAPTER 1. JURISDICTION

Art. 2811. Court in which succession opened

A proceeding to open a succession shall be brought in the district court of the parish where the deceased was domiciled at the time of his death.

If the deceased was not domiciled in this state at the time of his death, his succession may be opened in the district court of any parish where:

(1) Immovable property of the deceased is situated; or,

(2) Movable property of the deceased is situated, if he owned no immovable property in the state at the time of his death.

Official Revision Comments—1960

(a) Prior to 1952, probate jurisdiction could be alternatively established: (1) in the parish of the domicile of the deceased; (2) in the parish where deceased left immovable property, or in the parish of the situs of the principal immovable if he left immovables in more than one parish; or (3) in the parish where the deceased had died, if he had no domicile in the state. The last alternative was applicable in cases where the deceased had no Louisiana domicile, but died in Louisiana leaving movable property in the state. 1870 Code of Practice Art. 929; Civil Code Art. 935.

There was no provision, however, covering cases in which a decedent, domiciled in another state, had died in another jurisdiction, leaving only movable property in Louisiana. To remove this hiatus, Art. 929 of the Code of Practice of 1870 was amended by La.Act 87 of

1952 to provide that the succession could be opened in any parish where decedent had left movable property, if at the time of his death he was domiciled elsewhere and had left no immovable property in Louisiana.

The 1952 amendment also provided that if decedent had no domicile or property in Louisiana, his succession could be opened in the parish where he died, if death occurred in this state. It is clear, however, that this last provision could serve no useful purpose since the courts of Louisiana would have no jurisdiction to open a succession unless the decedent was either domiciled in this state at the time of his death, or had property in this state. Goodrich, Conflict of Laws (3rd ed.) 535 *et seq.* (1949). If the deceased was domiciled in Louisiana, or had property in this state at the time of his death, then paragraph 4 of Art. 929 of the 1870 Code of Practice could not be applied. Conversely, if there was neither domicile nor property in this state, then the Louisiana courts would not be vested with jurisdiction to open the succession. For these reasons, paragraph 4 of Art. 929 of the 1870 Code, as amended, was not retained in the above article.

(b) Nothing in the above article conflicts with or modifies the provisions of Art. 2315 of the Civil Code, as amended.

(c) See, also, Comments under Arts. 2812, 4031, 4032, 4033, *infra*.

Editor's Notes

Succession is opened by death, C.C. art. 934. Venue not waivable, C.C.P. art. 44. See succession pleading forms, Vol. 11, LSA–C.C.P.

Art. 2812. Proceedings in different courts; stay; adoption of proceedings by court retaining jurisdiction

If proceedings to open the succession of a deceased person who was not domiciled in this state at the time of his death are brought in two or more district courts of competent jurisdiction, the court in which the proceeding was first brought shall retain jurisdiction over the succession, and the other courts shall stay their proceedings.

The court retaining jurisdiction may adopt by ex parte order any of the proceedings taken in any other Louisiana court of competent jurisdiction, with the same force and effect as if these proceedings had been taken in the adopting court.

CHAPTER 2. EVIDENCE OF JURISDICTION AND HEIRSHIP

Article

Art. 2821. Evidence of jurisdiction, death, and relationship

The deceased's domicile at the time of his death, his ownership of property in this state, and all other facts necessary to establish the jurisdiction of the court may be evidenced by affidavits.

The deceased's death, his marriage, and all other facts necessary to establish the relationship of his heirs may be evidenced either by official certificates issued by the proper public officer, or by affidavits.

Art. 2822. Requirements of affidavit evidence

The affidavits referred to in Article 2821 shall be executed by two persons having knowledge of the facts sworn to. These affidavits shall be filed in the record of the succession proceeding.

Official Revision Comments—1960

(a) See Comments under Art. 2821, *supra.*

(b) The rationale of the custom of proving the facts in an ex parte succession by affidavits is that the latter constitute the depositions of "two good and credible witnesses." Since at the time this custom was adopted the parties to any judicial proceeding were deemed incompetent to testify, there was implicit in the customary practice the requirement that the affidavits annexed to the petition be those of disinterested witnesses. However, there is no requirement in the above article that the affiants be disinterested. In the case of old people, dying with few or no relatives here, the heirs and the attorney are often the only persons who can swear to the facts showing the relationship of the heirs. Furthermore, in certain parts of the state the practice heretofore has not been to require disinterested affiants, and if any requirement is made that the affidavits be those of disinterested witnesses doubt might be cast in many cases upon the legality of judgments of possession based upon completely accurate recitals of fact.

(c) See, also, Comments under Art. 3061, *infra.*

Art. 2823. Additional evidence

In any case in which evidence by affidavit is permitted under Article 2821, the court may require further evidence of any fact sworn to therein by the introduction of evidence as in ordinary cases.

Art. 2824. No affidavit evidence of factual issues

No fact which is an issue in a contradictory proceeding in a succession may be proved by affidavit under Articles 2821 and 2822. In all such contradictory proceedings, issues of fact shall be determined on the trial thereof only by evidence introduced as in ordinary cases.

Art. 2825. Costs

In all succession proceedings conducted ex parte, the court costs are to be paid as administration expenses. In all contradictory succession proceedings, the court costs are to be paid by the party cast, unless the court directs otherwise.

Amended by Acts 1997, No. 1421, § 3, eff. July 1, 1999.

Art. 2826. Definition of certain terms used in Book VI

Except where the context clearly indicates otherwise, as used in the Articles of this Book:

(1) "Residuary legatee" includes a recipient of a universal legacy or a general legacy, and also includes a residuary heir.

(2) "Residuary heir" is a successor who inherits the residue of a testamentary succession in default of a valid disposition thereof by the testator.

(3) "Succession representative" includes an administrator, provisional administrator, administrator of a vacant succession, executor, and dative testamentary executor.

Amended by Acts 1997, No. 1421, § 3, eff. July 1, 1999.

CHAPTER 3. PROBATE AND REGISTRY OF TESTAMENTS

SECTION 1. PROCEDURE PRELIMINARY TO PROBATE

Article

SECTION 1. PROCEDURE PRELIMINARY TO PROBATE

Art. 2851. Petition for probate

If the deceased is believed to have died testate, any person who considers that he has an interest in opening the succession may petition a court of competent jurisdiction for the probate and execution of the testament.

Official Revision Comments—1960

This article does not change the probate procedure of Louisiana and does not require an actual justiciable interest, but permits the probate of the testament to be requested by any person who considers that he has an interest in its probate.

See, also, Comments under Art. 3095, *infra*.

Art. 2852. Documents submitted with petition for probate

A. The petitioner shall submit with his petition evidence of the death of the decedent, and of all other facts necessary to establish the jurisdiction of the court.

B. If the testament is one other than a statutory testament, a notarial testament, or a nuncupative testament by public act, and is in the possession of the petitioner, he shall present it to the court, and pray that it be probated and executed.

Amended by Acts 1997, No. 1421, § 3, eff. July 1, 1999.

Art. 2853. Purported testament must be filed, though possessor doubts validity

If a person has possession of a document purporting to be the testament of a deceased person, even though he believes that the document is not the valid testament of the deceased, or has doubts concerning the validity thereof, he shall present it to the court with his petition praying that the document be filed in the record of the succession proceeding.

A person so presenting a purported testament to the court shall not be deemed to vouch for its authenticity or validity, nor precluded from asserting its invalidity.

Official Revision Comment—1960

This article covers the case of a person in possession of what purports to be the testament of the deceased of which the possessor doubts the validity or authenticity. In such a case the person in possession should file the instrument in court, but his act in filing the purported testament does not impose upon him the penalty of being considered as having vouched for its authenticity or validity.

Art. 2854. Search for testament

If the testament is not in the possession of the petitioner, he shall pray that the court direct that a search be made for the testament by a notary of the parish. In its order directing the search, the court may order any person having in his possession or under his control any books, papers, or documents of the deceased, or any bank box, safety deposit vault, or other receptacle likely to contain the testament of the deceased, to permit the examination of the books, papers, and documents, and of the contents of the bank box, safety deposit vault, or other receptacle, by the notary.

Editor's Notes

LSA–C.C.P. Form 810a; access to safety deposit boxes, R.S. 6:321 et seq.

Art. 2855. Return to order to search for testament

If the notary finds any document which purports to be a testament of the deceased, he shall take possession of it, and produce it in court with his written return to the order directing the search. The original petitioner, or any other interested person, may petition for the probate of the testament so produced.

If the search is unsuccessful, despite diligent effort, the notary shall make his written return to this effect to the court.

Editor's Notes

LSA–C.C.P. Form 810f.

Art. 2856. Probate hearing; probate forthwith if witness present

When a testament that is required to be probated has been produced, the court shall order it presented for probate on a date and hour assigned. If all necessary witnesses are present in court at the time the testament is produced, the court may order it presented for probate forthwith.

Amended by Acts 1997, No. 1421, § 3, eff. July 1, 1999.

Art. 2857. Proponent must produce witnesses; subpoenas

The petitioner for the probate of the testament shall produce all necessary witnesses at the time assigned for the probate hearing, and may cause them to be subpoenaed to appear and testify.

SECTION 2. EX PARTE PROBATE OF TESTAMENTS

Art. 2881. Ex parte probate if no objection

The court shall proceed to probate the testament ex parte as provided in Article 2882, unless an objection thereto is made at the hearing.

An objection to the ex parte probate of a testament may be presented in an opposition, or made orally at the hearing. The opposition must comply with the provisions of Article 2902, and must be filed prior to the hearing. The oral objection must specify the grounds of invalidity of the testament asserted, and must be urged immediately after the objector has had an opportunity to examine the purported testament.

Official Revision Comments—1960

(a) The 1870 Code does not expressly state that when an objection is made to the ex parte probate of a testament, the court shall refuse to proceed further, and assign a date and hour for the probate hearing at which the parties may introduce evidence. Yet, it has been recognized that the very purpose of requiring notice to the presumptive heirs living in the parish under Art. 935 of the 1870 Code of Practice, is to afford them an opportunity to oppose the probate. Succession of McDonogh, 18 La.Ann. 419 (1866); Succession of Theriot, 114 La. 611, 38 So. 471 (1905); Succession of Hagan, 150 La. 934, 91 So. 303 (1922); Succession of Wadsworth, 152 La. 131, 92 So. 760 (1922).

(b) Neither the 1870 Code provisions nor the jurisprudence provide the manner of opposing the ex parte probate of a testament. In most of the decided cases, the objections of the opponents have been set forth in an opposition filed prior to the commencement of the probate hearing. Yet there may be cases in which the opponent of the testament has no opportunity for determining in advance of the hearing whether the purported testament is either genuine or valid, particularly when it is sealed in an envelope and opened for the first time at the probate hearing. For this reason, under the above article an oral objection to the ex parte probate of a purported testament suffices to require the court to assign a date and hour for the contradictory probate thereof.

(c) The term "depositions" of the witnesses employed in Art. 939 of the Code of Practice of 1870 has not been retained either in this or in subsequent articles on the same subject matter. Actually, the reference in Art. 939 is to a recital in the procès verbal of the probate proceedings as to the declarations of the witnesses, not to the testimony of witnesses taken by deposition. Succession of Lewis, 177 La. 212, 148 So. 29 (1933).

(d) See, also, Comments under Art. 2883, *infra.*

Editor's Notes

See the checklist for the Succession procedure for a Simple Succession with Probate of a Will in the preliminary material of this publication.

Art. 2882. Proceedings at probate hearing

At the probate hearing the court shall open the testament, if it is enclosed in a sealed envelope, receive proof of the making of the testament as provided in Articles 2883 through 2889, may read the testament to those present, and shall paraph the top and bottom of each page of the testament by inscribing it "ne varietur" over the judicial signature.

Amended by Acts 1968, No. 130, § 1.

Art. 2883. Olographic testament

A. The olographic testament must be proved by the testimony of two credible witnesses that the testament was entirely written, dated, and signed in the testator's handwriting. The court must satisfy itself, through interrogation or from the written affidavits or the depositions of the witnesses, that the handwriting and signature are those of the testator, and except as provided in Article 2890, must mention these facts in its proces verbal.

B. A person's testimony for the purpose of this Article may be given in the form of an affidavit executed after the death of the testator stating that the olographic will was entirely written, dated, and signed in the testator's handwriting, unless the court in its discretion requires the person to appear and testify orally. All affidavits accepted by the court in lieu of oral testimony shall be filed in the probate proceedings. This Paragraph does not apply to testimony with respect to the genuineness of a will that is judicially attacked.

Amended by Acts 1983, No. 594, § 1; Acts 1984, No. 393, § 1; Acts 1999, No. 85, § 1.

Editor's Notes

The 1999 amendment deleted the requirement that this affidavit be executed before a notary and two witnesses. (N.B. The title to Act 85, effecting this amendment, states that the amendment is "to authorize witnesses to give testimony in the form of an affidavit in lieu of an authentic act...". The affidavit would then be in the conventional form, executed before a notary, but without the two witnesses.)

Art. 2884. Nuncupative testament by private act

A. Except as provided in Article 2886, the nuncupative testament by private act must be proved by the testimony of at least three of the competent witnesses present when it was made. These witnesses must testify, in substance:

(1) That they recognize the testament presented to them as being the same that was written in their presence by the testator, or by another person at his direction, or which the testator had written or caused to be written out of their presence and which he declared to them contained his testament; and

(2) That they recognize their signatures and that of the testator, if they signed it, or the signature of him who signed for them, respectively, if they did not know how to sign their names.

B. A person's testimony for the purpose of this Article may be given in the form of an affidavit executed after the death of the testator, unless the court in its discretion requires the person to appear and testify orally. All affidavits accepted by the court in lieu of oral testimony shall be filed in the probate proceedings. This Paragraph does not apply to testimony with respect to the genuineness of a will that is judicially attacked.

Amended by Acts 1987, No. 270, § 1; Acts 1999, No. 85, § 1.

Editor's Notes

LSA–C.C.P. Form 828a. See Notes to C.C.P. art. 2883.

Art. 2885. Mystic testament

A. Except as provided in Article 2886, the mystic testament must be proved by the testimony of at least three of the witnesses who were present at the act of superscription. These witnesses shall testify, in substance:

(1) That they recognize the sealed envelope presented to them to be the same that the testator delivered to the notary in their presence, declaring to the latter that it contained the testator's testament; and

(2) That they recognize their signatures and that of the notary in the act of superscription, if they signed it, or the signature of the notary and of the person who signed for them, if the witnesses did not know how to sign their names.

B. The notary before whom the act of superscription has been passed may testify as one of the three witnesses required above.

C. A person's testimony for the purpose of this Article may be given in the form of an affidavit executed after the death of the testator, unless the court in its discretion requires the person to appear and testify orally. All affidavits accepted by the court in lieu of oral testimony shall be filed in the probate proceedings. This Paragraph does not apply to testimony with respect to the genuineness of a will that is judicially attacked.

Amended by Acts 1987, No. 270, § 1; Acts 1999, No. 85, § 1.

Editor's Notes

See Notes to C.C.P. art. 2883.

Art. 2886. Probate of nuncupative testament by private act; mystic testament, when witnesses dead, absent, or incapacitated

A. If some of the witnesses to the nuncupative testament by private act, or to the act of superscription of the mystic testament, are dead, absent from the state, incapacitated, or cannot be located, so that it is not possible to procure the prescribed number of witnesses to prove the testament, it may be proved by the testimony of those witnesses then residing in the state and available.

B. If the notary and all of the subscribing witnesses are dead, absent from the state, incapacitated, or cannot be located, the testament may be proved by the testimony of two credible witnesses who recognize the signature of the testator, or of the notary before whom the act of superscription of the mystic testament was passed, or the signatures of two of the witnesses to the nuncupative testament by private act, or to the act of superscription of the mystic testament.

C. A person's testimony for the purpose of this Article may be given in the form of an affidavit executed after the death of the testator, unless the court in its discretion requires the person to appear and testify orally. All affidavits accepted by the court in lieu of oral testimony shall be filed in the probate proceedings. This Paragraph does not apply to testimony with respect to the genuineness of a will that is judicially attacked.

Amended by Acts 1980, No. 106, § 2; Acts 1987, No. 270, § 1; Acts 1999, No. 85, § 1.

Editor's Notes

See Notes to C.C.P. art. 2883.

Art. 2887. Repealed by Acts 1997, No. 1421, § 8, eff. July 1, 1999

Art. 2888. Foreign testament

A written testament subscribed by the testator and made in a foreign country, or in another state, or a territory of the United States, in a form not valid in this state, but valid under the law of the place where made, or under the law of the testator's domicile, may be probated in this state by producing the evidence required under the law of the place where made, or under the law of the testator's domicile, respectively.

Art. 2889. Depositions of witnesses

A petitioner for the probate of a testament under the provisions of Articles 2882 through 2888 may obtain leave of court ex parte for the taking of the deposition of any witness whose testimony otherwise would not be available. The provisions of Articles 1426, 1434 through 1436, 1443 through 1446, 1449, 1452, and 1469 through 1471, so far as applicable, shall govern the taking of such deposition.

Amended by Acts 1985, No. 26, § 1.

Art. 2890. Procès verbal of probate

A. A procès verbal of the hearing shall be prepared, signed by the judge or by the clerk, and by the witnesses who testified at the hearing, which shall be a record of the succession proceeding, and which shall recite or include:

(1) The opening of the testament, and the manner in which proof of its authenticity and validity was submitted;

(2) The names and surnames of the witnesses testifying, either personally or by affidavit or deposition; the substance of the testimony of the witnesses who testify personally at the hearing; and that any affidavits or depositions used are made a part thereof by attachment or by reference;

(3) The paraphing of the testament by the court, as set forth in Article 2882;

(4) An order that the testament be recorded, filed, and executed, if the court finds that it has been proved in accordance with law; or an order refusing to probate the testament, giving the substance of the court's reasons therefor.

B. If written affidavits only are used to prove a will under Articles 2883 through 2887, the proces verbal shall be dispensed with, and the court shall render a written order that the testament be recorded, filed, and executed, if the court finds that it has been proved in accordance with law, or a written order refusing to probate the testament, giving the substance of the court's reasons therefor.

Amended by Acts 1968, No. 130, § 1; Acts 1970, No. 475, § 1; Acts 1984, No. 393, § 1; Acts 1987, No. 270, § 1.

Art. 2891. Notarial testament, nuncupative testament by public act, and statutory testament executed without probate

A notarial testament, a nuncupative testament by public act, and a statutory testament do not need to be proved. Upon production of the testament, the court shall order it filed and executed and this order shall have the effect of probate.

Amended by Acts 1997, No. 1421, § 3, eff. July 1, 1999.

Editor's Notes

Prior to July 1, 1999 see, C.C. art. 1647 (no probate required) Following July 1, 1999, see C.C. art. 1605 et seq.

Art. 2892. Use of probate testimony in subsequent action

When a testament has been probated in accordance with law, the record of the substance of the testimony of any witness at the hearing, and the deposition of any witness taken under Article 2889, shall be admissible in evidence in any subsequent action in which it is sought to annul the testament, if at the time of trial thereof the witness has died, or for any other reason his testimony cannot be taken again either by subpoenaing him to appear at the trial, or by deposition.

Art. 2893. Period within which will must be probated

No testament shall be admitted to probate unless a petition therefor has been filed in a court of competent jurisdiction within five years after the judicial opening of the succession of the deceased.

Amended by Acts 1981, No. 316, § 1, eff. Sept. 1, 1983; Acts 1986, No. 247, § 1.

Editor's Notes

See R.S. 9:5643, to same effect.

SECTION 3. CONTRADICTORY PROBATE OF TESTAMENTS

Art. 2901. Contradictory trial required; time to file opposition

If an objection is made to the ex parte probate of a testament, as provided in Article 2881, the testament may be probated only at a contradictory trial of the matter. If only an oral objection is made to the ex parte probate, the court shall allow the opponent a reasonable delay, not exceeding ten days, to file his opposition.

Editor's Notes

See art. 2904 authorizing videotape evidence in probate or nullity proceeding.

Art. 2902. Opposition to petition for probate

The opposition to the petition for the probate of a testament shall comply with Article 2972, shall allege the grounds of invalidity of the testament relied on by the opponent, and shall be served upon the petitioner for the probate of the testament.

Art. 2903. Proponent bears burden of proof

At the contradictory trial to probate a testament, its proponent bears the burden of proving the authenticity of the testament, and its compliance with all of the formal requirements of law.

Art. 2904. Admissibility of videotape of execution of testament

A. In a contradictory trial to probate a testament under Article 2901 or an action to annul a probated testament under Article 2931, and provided the testator is sworn by a person authorized to take oaths and the oath is recorded on the videotape, the videotape of the execution and reading of the testament by the testator may be admissible as evidence of any of the following:

(1) The proper execution of the testament.

(2) The intentions of the testator.

(3) The mental state or capacity of the testator.

(4) The authenticity of the testament.

(5) Matters that are determined by a court to be relevant to the probate of the testament.

B. For purposes of this Article, "videotape" means the visual recording on a magnetic tape, film, videotape, compact disc, digital versatile disc, digital video disc, or by other electronic means together with the associated oral record.

Added by Acts 2005, No. 79, § 1.

CHAPTER 4. ANNULMENT OF PROBATED TESTAMENTS

Article

Art. 2931. Annulment of probated testament by direct action; defendants; summary proceeding

A probated testament may be annulled only by a direct action brought in the succession proceeding against the legatees, the residuary heir, if any, and the executor, if he has not been discharged. The action shall be tried as a summary proceeding.

Amended by Acts 1984, No. 90, § 2.

Official Revision Comments—1960

(a) Neither the Code of Practice nor the Civil Code prescribes the procedure for the annulment of a probated testament. The rules set forth in the above article are those established by Succession of Hagan, 150 La. 934, 91 So. 303 (1922) and cases cited therein. Cf. Succession of Wadsworth, 152 La. 131, 92 So. 760 (1922); Succession of Lirette, 5 So.2d 197 (La.App.1942).

(b) The action to annul the probated testament is a new suit, requiring citation and service on all defendants, who have the same delay for answering as in any other ordinary proceeding. The requirement that the action be brought in the succession proceeding permits the judge who probated the testament to try the nullity action. All of these aspects of this article were observed in the cases cited in Comment (a) above.

(c) See, also, Comments under Art. 2826, *supra*.

Comment—1984

This amendment allows an action to annul a probated testament to be tried through the more expeditious summary proceeding.

Editor's Notes

See the checklist for Succession Procedure for a Succession with a Contested Probate of a Will in the preliminary material of this publication.

Art. 2932. Burden of proof in action to annul

A. The plaintiff in an action to annul a probated testament has the burden of proving the invalidity thereof, unless the action was instituted within three months of the date the testament was probated. In the latter event, the defendants have the burden of proving the authenticity of the testament, and its compliance with all of the formal requirements of the law.

B. In an action to annul a notarial testament, a nuncupative testament by public act, or a statutory testament, however, the plaintiff always has the burden of proving the invalidity of the testament.

Amended by Acts 1997, No. 1421, § 3, eff. July 1, 1999.

Art. 2933. Repealed by Acts 1997, No. 1421, § 8, eff. July 1, 1999

CHAPTER 5. PAYMENT OF STATE INHERITANCE TAXES

Article

Art. 2951. Repealed by Acts 2010, No. 175, § 6

Art. 2952. Descriptive list of property, if no inventory

A. If no inventory of the property left by the deceased has been taken, any heir, legatee, or other interested party shall file in the succession proceeding a detailed descriptive list, sworn to and subscribed by him, of all items of property composing the succession of the deceased, stating the actual cash value of each item at the time of the death of the deceased.

B. The detailed descriptive list shall be sealed upon the request of an heir or legatee.

C. If the detailed descriptive list is sealed, a copy shall be provided to the decedent's universal successors and surviving spouse. Upon motion of any successor, surviving spouse, or creditor of the estate, the court may furnish relevant information contained in the detailed descriptive list regarding assets and liabilities of the estate.

Amended by Acts 2020, No. 19, § 2.

Arts. 2953, 2954. Repealed by Acts 2010, No. 175, § 6

CHAPTER 6. GENERAL RULES OF PROCEDURE

Article

Art. 2971. Pleading and service of process

Except as otherwise provided by law, the rules of pleading and service of process applicable in ordinary proceedings shall apply to succession proceedings.

A certified copy of the petition, opposition, contradictory motion, or rule initiating a contradictory succession proceeding shall be served on the adverse party; but citation is necessary only in those cases in which it is specifically required by law.

An opposition may be served upon the adverse party as provided in Article 1313.

Official Revision Comments—1960

(a) Under the applicable articles in both the Code of Practice and the Civil Code, succession proceedings utilize both ordinary and summary process. No departure from this rule is made in this Code. Thus, the above article provides that the rules of pleading applicable to ordinary proceedings are likewise applicable to succession proceedings, except when summary process is expressly authorized.

(b) Service of process is necessary in all contradictory succession proceedings, but it is only in the rare case, such as the action to annul a probated testament under Art. 2931, *supra*, in which the issuance and service of citation are necessary.

(c) The last sentence of this article eliminates all doubts as to the validity of the service of an opposition made in accordance with Art. 1313, *supra*.

(d) See, also, Comments under Art. 2902, *supra*.

Art. 2972. Oppositions

An opposition to the petition, motion, or other application of a party to a succession proceeding for an order or judgment of the court shall be in writing and be filed within the delay allowed. It shall comply with the provisions of Articles 853 through 863; shall state the name, surname, and domicile of the opponent; shall allege the interest of opponent in filing the opposition, and the grounds for opposing the petition, motion, or other application; and shall conclude with a prayer for appropriate relief.

Official Revision Comments—1960

(a) Although the Civil Code and the Code of Practice frequently refer to the opposition to be filed in a succession proceeding, there are no provisions relating to its form except those of Arts. 971 and 972 of the Code of Practice dealing with oppositions to applications for the appointment of administrators. The above article supplies this deficiency. Its requirements are, in general, those of all other pleadings, and, in particular, those matters which relate peculiarly to the opposition.

(b) No person should be permitted to file an opposition in a succession proceeding unless he has a justiciable interest in doing so. The definition of this interest has been left for the determination of the courts, and the requirement has been stated only implicitly in the term "interested person."

(c) The delay allowed for the filing of an opposition may be: (1) provided by Code provision, (2) determined by the court, or (3) as under Art. 2901, *supra*, a maximum delay which the court has discretion to shorten. The term "within the delay allowed" is intended to cover all three types of delay.

Art. 2973. Responsive pleadings to opposition

Responsive pleadings to an opposition may be filed as provided in Article 2593.

Art. 2974. Appeals

Appeals from orders or judgments rendered in succession proceedings shall be governed by the rules applicable to appeals in ordinary proceedings, except that an order or judgment confirming, appointing, or removing a succession representative, or granting an interim allowance under Article 3321 shall be executed provisionally, notwithstanding appeal.

The acts of a succession representative shall not be invalidated by the annulment of his appointment on appeal.

TITLE II. ACCEPTANCE OF SUCCESSIONS WITHOUT ADMINISTRATION

CHAPTER 1. INTESTATE SUCCESSIONS

Art. 3001. Sending into possession without administration when all heirs are competent and accept

A. The heirs of an intestate decedent shall be recognized by the court, and sent into possession of his property without an administration of the succession, on the ex parte petition of all of the heirs, when all of them are competent and accept the succession, and the succession is relatively free of debt. A succession shall be deemed relatively free of debt when its only debts are administration expenses, mortgages not in arrears, and debts of the decedent that are small in comparison with the assets of the succession.

B. The surviving spouse in community of an intestate decedent shall be recognized by the court on ex parte petition as entitled to the possession of an undivided half of the community, and of the other undivided half to the extent that he has the usufruct thereof, without an administration of the succession, when the succession is relatively free of debt, as provided above.

Amended by Acts 1979, No. 711, § 3, eff. Jan. 1, 1980; Acts 1997, No. 1421, § 3, eff. July 1, 1999.

Editor's Notes

See the checklist for the Succession procedure for a Simple Succession in the preliminary material of this publication.

Art. 3002. Same; petition for possession

The petition of the heirs for possession under Article 3001 shall include allegations as to: the competency of the petitioners; the date of death of the deceased, and all other facts on which the jurisdiction of the court is based; the facts showing that petitioners are the sole heirs of the deceased; and that the succession is relatively free of debt, as provided in Article 3001.

The petition of the surviving spouse in community for possession under Article 3001 shall include all of the above allegations except those relating to heirship; shall allege the facts showing that he is the surviving spouse in community; shall state what property belonged to the community; and if he claims the usufruct of any interest in the community property, shall allege the fact showing that he is entitled thereto.

The allegations of the petition for possession shall be verified by the affidavit of at least one of the petitioners.

Amended by Acts 1979, No. 711, § 3, eff. Jan. 1, 1980.

Official Revision Comments—1960

(a) See Comments under Art. 3001, *supra*.

(b) Since the petition for possession in an intestate succession in which all of the competent heirs accept unconditionally is usually the only pleading filed in the succession proceeding, it is necessary that it include all the allegations required in the above article. In a few cases, additional allegations may be necessary.

(c) Nothing in the probate procedure of Louisiana heretofore required the verifying affidavit of at least one of the petitioners, since the provisions of former R.S. 13:3601(5) were not applicable to petitions for possession. Under local practices, however, the verifying affidavit of at least one of the petitioners has usually been attached to the petition for possession.

This article requires some evidence of the acceptance of the community by the surviving widow in those instances where she did not execute any verifying affidavit to the petition for possession. This requirement is based upon the obvious advantage of having the record reflect expressly her acceptance of the community.

Editor's Notes

LSA–C.C.P. Form 802a.

Art. 3003. Same; evidence of allegations of petition for possession

Evidence of the allegations of the petition for possession, under Articles 3002 or 3005, as to the death of the deceased, jurisdiction of the court, marriage of the spouses, and relationship of the petitioners to the deceased, shall be submitted to the court as provided by Articles 2821 through 2823.

Art. 3004. Discretionary power to send heirs and surviving spouse into possession

A. The heirs of an intestate decedent may be recognized by the court, and sent into possession of his property without an administration of his succession when none of the creditors of the succession has demanded its administration, on the ex parte petition of any of the following:

(1) Those of the heirs who are competent, if all of them accept the succession.

(2) The legal representative of the incompetent heirs, if all of the heirs are incompetent and a legal representative has been appointed therefor.

(3) The surviving spouse in community of the decedent, if all of the heirs are incompetent and no legal representative has been appointed for some or all of them.

B. In such cases, the surviving spouse in community of the decedent may be recognized by the court as entitled to the possession of the community property, as provided in Article 3001.

Amended by Acts 1961, No. 23, § 1; Acts 1997, No. 1421, § 3, eff. July 1, 1999.

Editor's Notes

See, prior to July 1, 1999, C.C. art. 977 (minor's acceptance with benefit of inventory). Following July 1, 1999, see C.C. arts. 947, 948 under acceptance and renunciation of successions.

Art. 3005. Same; petition for possession; evidence

The petition of the heirs for possession under Article 3004 shall include allegations as to: the competency of the petitioners; the date of death of the intestate, and all other facts on which the jurisdiction of the court is based; and the facts showing that petitioners and the incompetent heirs named in the petition, if any, are the sole heirs of the intestate.

The petition of the surviving spouse in community for possession under Article 3004 shall include all of the pertinent allegations of Article 3002.

The allegation of the petition for possession shall be verified by the affidavit of at least one of the petitioners.

The allegations of the petition for possession shall be proved as provided in Article 3003.

Amended by Acts 1979, No. 711, § 3, eff. Jan. 1, 1980.

Art. 3006. Same; when one of competent heirs cannot join in petition for possession

If a competent heir of an intestate resides out of the state and cannot be located, or his whereabouts are unknown, the other competent heirs may be sent into possession of the property without an administration of the succession, as provided herein and in Articles 3004 and 3005.

Upon the filing of the petition for possession, the court shall appoint an attorney at law to represent the absent heir, and shall order him to show cause why the heirs of the intestate should not be recognized, and sent into possession of the property of the intestate without an administration of the succession.

After a hearing on the rule against the attorney for the absentee, if the court concludes that the succession is thoroughly solvent and that there is no necessity for an administration, it may send all the heirs of the intestate, including the absentee, into possession.

Art. 3007. Creditor may demand security when heirs sent into possession

When the heirs of an intestate, or the heirs and the surviving spouse thereof, have been sent into possession of the property of the intestate under Articles 3001 or 3004, any creditor having a claim against the succession may file in the succession proceeding, within three months of the date of the judgment of possession, a contradictory motion against all parties sent into possession to compel them to furnish security for the payment of his claim.

On the trial of this motion, the court may order the parties sent into possession to furnish such security as it deems necessary to protect the claimant.

Art. 3008. Administration in default of security

If the security required by the court under Article 3007 is not furnished within the delay allowed, on ex parte motion of the creditor, the court shall render a judgment annulling the judgment of possession, directing the cancellation of all inscriptions of the registry thereof, ordering an administration of the succession, and ordering the parties sent into possession to surrender to the administrator to be appointed thereafter all of the property of the deceased which they have received, and which they have not alienated.

Conventional mortgages and other encumbrances placed by the heirs, legatees, or surviving spouse in community on property so surrendered, and recorded prior to the cancellation of the inscription of the registry of the judgment of possession, shall retain their initial force and effect despite the administration of the succession.

CHAPTER 2. TESTATE SUCCESSIONS

Art. 3031. Sending legatees into possession without administration

A. When a testament has been probated or given the effect of probate, and subject to the provisions of Article 3033, the court may send all of the legatees into possession of their respective legacies without an administration of the succession, on the ex parte petition of all of the general and universal legatees, if each of them is either competent or is acting through a qualified legal representative, and each of them accepts the succession, and none of the creditors of the succession has demanded its administration.

B. In such cases, the surviving spouse in community of the testator may be recognized by the court as entitled to the possession of the community property, as provided in Article 3001.

Amended by Acts 1997, No. 1421, § 3, eff. July 1, 1999.

Official Revision Comments—1960

(a) Succession of Dupuy, 4 La.Ann. 570 (1849) and Succession of Walker, 32 La.Ann. 321 (1880) support the proposition that the legatees may be sent into possession without any administration of the succession, if none of the creditors demands an administration. These cases, however, were expressly overruled by Succession of Serres, 135 La. 1005, 66 So. 342 (1914), holding that even though the testate succession is completely free of debt, and the residuary legatees are willing to accept it unconditionally, there must be an administration if only to permit the executor to execute the testament by delivering the legacies. In the Serres case, the petition of the legatees for possession was opposed by the person named in the testament as executor; and it is probable that the decision would have been otherwise, had the person named as executor waived his commission and joined with the legatees in the petition for possession. However, if none of the creditors demands an administration, and the residuary legatee is willing to deliver the particular legacies, there is no reason why the residuary legatee should be burdened with the unnecessary costs of administration, if the person named as executor has either waived his compensation or the residuary legatee is willing to pay it.

For this reason, the above article makes it discretionary with the court to send the legatees into possession without an administration, if the latter would be unnecessary and would only impose useless costs upon the residuary legatee.

(b) The requirement that all incompetent legatees be represented by their qualified legal representatives is necessary to permit the residuary legatee to receive a valid receipt for the delivery of particular legacies.

(c) When the testator makes only a few particular legacies, intending that the remainder of his estate should go to his heirs under the laws of descent and distribution, the procedure for permitting the residuary heir to be sent into possession is the same, under the above article, as in the case of the residuary legatee.

(d) See, also, Comments under Art. 2826, *supra*.

Art. 3032. Same; petition for possession; evidence

The petition of the legatees for possession under Article 3031 shall include allegations that all of the petitioners are either competent or are acting through their qualified legal representatives. The person named as executor in the testament shall join in the petition, except as otherwise provided by Article 3033.

The petition of the surviving spouse in community for possession under Article 3031 shall comply with all of the pertinent provisions of Article 3002.

The allegations of the petition for possession shall be verified by the affidavit of at least one of the petitioners.

The allegations of the petition for possession shall be proved as provided in Article 3003.

Amended by Acts 1979, No. 711, § 3, eff. Jan. 1, 1980.

Art. 3033. Same; compensation of executor

If the testament is dated prior to January 1, 1961, the person named therein as executor shall be entitled to the full compensation allowed by law for an executor's services in administering a testate succession, even though he may not have been confirmed as executor.

If the testament is dated subsequent to December 31, 1960, the person named therein as executor shall be entitled to reasonable compensation for the services which he has rendered, whether he has been confirmed as executor or not.

Except as provided hereinafter, the legatees may be sent into possession only if the person named in the testament as executor joins in the petition thereof.

If the residuary legatee and the person named in the testament as executor cannot agree upon the compensation due him, or for any other reason he refuses to join in the petition for possession, the residuary legatee may rule him into court to show cause why the compensation due should not be determined judicially, and why the legatees should not be sent into possession of their legacies. The court shall not send the legatees into possession until satisfactory proof has been submitted that the compensation determined to be due the person named in the testament as executor has been paid.

Art. 3034. Creditor may demand security when legatees sent into possession; administration in default of security

When the legatees of a testator, or the legatees and the surviving spouse in community thereof, have been sent into possession of his property under Article 3031, any creditor having a claim against the succession may compel the parties sent into possession to furnish security for the payment of his claim, and may require an administration of the succession in default of such security, as provided by Articles 3007 and 3008.

Art. 3035. Particular legatee may demand security for delivery of legacy; administration in default of security

A particular legatee who has not received his legacy after being sent into possession by judgment may demand that the residuary legatee furnish security for the delivery of his legacy and may require an administration of the succession in default of such security, as provided by Articles 3007 and 3008.

Editor's Notes

Privilege of particular legatee, R.S. 9:5011.

CHAPTER 3. JUDGMENTS OF POSSESSION

Article

Art. 3061. Judgment rendered and signed immediately

A. The court shall render and sign immediately a judgment of possession, if it finds from an examination of the petition for possession, and from the record of the proceeding, that the petitioners are entitled to the relief prayed for.

B. The judgment shall recognize the petitioners as the heirs, legatees, surviving spouse in community, or usufructuary, as the case may be, of the deceased, send the heirs or legatees into possession of the property owned by the deceased at the time of his death, and recognize the surviving spouse in community as entitled to the possession of an undivided one-half of the community property, and of the other undivided one-half to the extent that he has the usufruct thereof. The judgment shall include the last known address of at least one of the heirs or legatees or the surviving spouse, as the case may be, sent into possession of the property of the deceased. The failure to include the address of at least one of the heirs or legatees or the surviving spouse shall not affect the validity of the judgment.

C. A judgment sending one or more petitioners into possession under a testamentary usufruct or trust automatically incorporates all the terms of the testamentary usufruct or trust without the necessity of stating the terms in the judgment.

Amended by Acts 1972, No. 326, § 2, eff. Jan. 1, 1973; Acts 2001, No. 641, § 1; Acts 2006, No. 314, § 1; Acts 2010, No. 175, § 1; Acts 2010, No. 226, § 1.

Editor's Notes

LSA–C.C.P. Form 811e.

Art. 3062. Effect of judgment of possession

The judgment of possession rendered in a succession proceeding shall be prima facie evidence of the relationship to the deceased of the parties recognized therein, as heir, legatee, surviving spouse in community, or usufructuary, as the case may be, and of their right to the possession of the estate of the deceased.

Editor's Notes

Transfer of assets to heirs and legatees by banks, R.S. 6:325; savings and loans, R.S. 6:767; corporations, R.S. 12:603; federal homestead, R.S. 6:902; mandamus by administratrix to compel transfer, Thorn v. Whitney Natl. Bank of New Orleans, App. 4 Cir.1976, 326 So.2d 606.

TITLE III. ADMINISTRATION OF SUCCESSIONS

CHAPTER 1. QUALIFICATION OF SUCCESSION REPRESENTATIVES

SECTION 1. EXECUTORS

SECTION 2. ADMINISTRATORS

SECTION 3. PROVISIONAL ADMINISTRATORS

SECTION 4. ADMINISTRATORS OF VACANT SUCCESSIONS

SECTION 5. INVENTORY OF SUCCESSION PROPERTY

SECTION 1. EXECUTORS

Art. 3081. Petition for confirmation

After the probate of the testament, or after its production into court as provided by Article 2891 if it is a nuncupative testament by public act, the person named as executor therein may petition the court for confirmation, and for the issuance of letters testamentary. If he files the original petition for the execution of the testament, he may pray therein for the issuance of letters.

Editor's Notes

LSA–C.C.P. Form 835a.

Art. 3082. Order of confirmation; letters

Unless the person named in the testament as executor is disqualified on any of the grounds assigned in Article 3097, the court shall render an order upon his petition for confirmation, confirming him as testamentary executor and directing the issuance of letters testamentary to him after he has taken his oath of office and furnished security, if required.

Editor's Notes

LSA–C.C.P. Form 835b.

Art. 3083. Appointment of dative testamentary executor

If no executor has been named in the testament, or if the one named is dead, disqualified, or declines the trust, on its own motion or on motion of any interested party, the court shall appoint a dative testamentary executor, in the manner provided for the appointment of an administrator of an intestate succession.

Editor's Notes

LSA–C.C.P. Form 839a.

SECTION 2. ADMINISTRATORS

Art. 3091. Petition for notice of application for appointment

An interested person desiring to be notified of the filing of an application for appointment as administrator, at any time after the death of the deceased, may petition the court in which the succession has been opened, or may be opened, for such notice.

A petition for such notice shall comply with Article 3092, shall bear the number and caption of the succession proceeding, and shall be docketed and filed by the clerk in the record thereof.

When a petition for such notice has been filed within ten days of the death of the deceased, or prior to the application for appointment as administrator, the applicant for appointment shall serve the notice prayed for, as provided in Article 3093.

Editor's Notes

Succ. of Houssiere, 174 So.2d 521 (1965), appointment generally; LSA–C.C.P. Form 818a.

Art. 3092. Form of petition for notice of application for appointment

A petition for notice under Article 3091 shall not be effective unless it is signed by the petitioner or his attorney, and sets forth: (1) the name, surname, and domicile of petitioner; (2) a statement of the interest of the petitioner; (3) the name, surname, and mailing address of the person to whom the requested notice shall be given; and (4) a prayer that the requested notice be given.

Art. 3093. Notice in compliance with petition

When notice has been petitioned for as provided in Article 3091, the applicant for appointment as administrator shall mail or deliver to the person designated to receive such notice a copy of his application for appointment, and shall notify him of the date and hour assigned by the court for a hearing thereon.

Art. 3094. Order on application for appointment

The court shall order the taking of an inventory, or the filing of a descriptive list as provided in Article 3136, of the property of the deceased upon the filing of an application for appointment as administrator.

If notice of the application for appointment is required under Articles 3091 through 3093, the court shall assign a date and hour for a hearing on the application, which shall be held not earlier than the eleventh day after the mailing or delivery of such notice. If no such notice is required, and ten days have elapsed since the death of the deceased, the court may appoint the applicant as administrator forthwith, unless he is disqualified under Article 3097.

Art. 3095. Opposition to application for appointment

The opposition to an application for appointment as administrator shall be filed prior to the hearing on the application and shall be served on the applicant for appointment. This opposition shall comply with Article 2972, and shall allege the prior right of opponent to the appointment, or the grounds on which it is claimed the applicant is disqualified. If the opposition is based on a prior right to the appointment, the opponent shall pray that he be appointed administrator.

Editor's Notes

Succ. of Houssiere, *supra,* C.C.P. art. 3091; LSA–C.C.P. Form 819e.

Art. 3096. Appointment when no opposition; appointment after trial of opposition

At the hearing on the application for appointment as administrator, if no opposition thereto has been filed, the court shall appoint the applicant, unless he is disqualified under Article 3097.

If an opposition to the application for appointment has been filed prior to the hearing thereon, the court shall assign the opposition for trial. After this trial, the court shall appoint as administrator the qualified claimant having the highest priority of appointment.

If all of the claimants are disqualified under Article 3097, the court shall appoint a qualified person who is willing to accept the administration of the succession.

Art. 3097. Disqualifications

A. No person may be confirmed as testamentary executor, or appointed dative testamentary executor, provisional administrator, or administrator who is:

(1) Under eighteen years of age;

(2) Interdicted, or who, on contradictory hearing, is proved to be mentally incompetent;

(3) A convicted felon, under the laws of the United States or of any state or territory thereof;

(4) A nonresident of the state who has not appointed a resident agent for the service of process in all actions and proceedings with respect to the succession, and caused such appointment to be filed in the succession proceeding;

(5) A corporation not authorized to perform the duties of the office in this state; or

(6) A person who, on contradictory hearing, is proved to be unfit for appointment because of bad moral character.

B. No person may be appointed dative testamentary executor, provisional administrator, or administrator who is not the surviving spouse, heir, legatee, legal representative of an heir or legatee, or a creditor of the deceased or a creditor of the estate of the deceased, or the nominee of the surviving spouse, heir, legatee, or legal representative of an heir or legatee of the deceased, or a co-owner of immovable property with the deceased.

Amended by Acts 1964, No. 4, § 1; Acts 1972, No. 347, § 1; Acts 1985, No. 528, § 1, eff. July 12, 1985.

Art. 3098. Priority of appointment

A. When the appointment as administrator or dative testamentary executor is claimed by more than one qualified person, except as otherwise provided by law, preference in the appointment shall be given by the court in the following order to:

(1) The best qualified among the surviving spouse, competent heirs or legatees, or the legal representatives of any incompetent heirs or legatees of the deceased.

(2) The best qualified of the nominees of the surviving spouse, of the competent heirs or legatees, or of the legal representatives of any incompetent heirs or legatees of the deceased.

(3) The best qualified of the creditors of the deceased or a creditor of the estate of the deceased, or a co-owner of immovable property with the deceased.

B. "Best qualified", as used in this Article, means the claimant best qualified personally, and by training and experience, to administer the succession.

Amended by Acts 1964, No. 4, § 1; Acts 1985, No. 528, § 2, eff. July 12, 1985; Acts 1992, No. 778, § 1; Acts 1993, No. 29, § 1.

SECTION 3. PROVISIONAL ADMINISTRATORS

Art. 3111. Appointment

The court may appoint a provisional administrator of a succession, pending the appointment of an administrator or the confirmation of an executor, when it deems such appointment necessary to preserve, safeguard, and operate the property of the succession. On the application of an interested party, or on its own motion, when such an appointment is deemed necessary, the court may appoint a qualified person as provisional administrator forthwith.

Art. 3112. Security; oath; tenure; rights and duties

A provisional administrator shall furnish security and take the oath of office required by Articles 3152 and 3158, respectively. He shall continue in office until an administrator or executor has been qualified, or until the heirs or legatees have been sent into possession.

Except as otherwise provided by law, a provisional administrator has all of the authority and rights of an administrator, and is subject to the same duties and obligations, in the discharge of his functions of preserving, safeguarding, and operating the property and business of the succession.

Art. 3113. Inventory taken or descriptive list filed when appointment made

When the court appoints a provisional administrator, it shall order the taking of an inventory of the property of the succession as provided in Article 3131 or the filing of a descriptive list of the succession property as provided in Article 3136, unless either has been ordered taken before.

Amended by Acts 1972, No. 665, § 1.

SECTION 4. ADMINISTRATORS OF VACANT SUCCESSIONS

Art. 3121. Attorney appointed as administrator of vacant successions; exceptions

When no qualified person has petitioned for appointment as administrator of a vacant succession within three months of the death of the deceased, the court may appoint an attorney at law as administrator thereof and set his compensation. Said attorney shall be selected, on a rotating basis, from a list of attorneys currently practicing in the parish in which the succession is to be opened.

The attorney shall be required to furnish security as required by law. Otherwise, all of the provisions of law relating to the administrator of a succession apply to the attorney when appointed administrator of a vacant succession.

This article does not apply to any parish for which a public administrator has been appointed.

Amended by Acts 1961, No. 23 § 1; Acts 1974, No. 530, § 1.

Editor's Notes

Vacant succession definition, C.C. art. 1095.

Art. 3122. Public administrator as administrator of vacant successions in certain parishes

In parishes for which a public administrator has been appointed, he shall be appointed administrator of all successions of which, under Article 3121, an attorney at law in other parishes may be appointed administrator.

All provisions of law relating to the administrator of a succession apply to the public administrator, except as otherwise provided by R.S. 9:1581 through 9:1589.

Amended by Acts 1961, No. 23, § 1; Acts 1974, No. 530, § 1.

SECTION 5. INVENTORY OF SUCCESSION PROPERTY

Art. 3131. Notary appointed for inventory in each parish

When the court orders the taking of an inventory of the property of the succession, it shall appoint a notary of each parish in which the deceased left property to take the inventory of such property in that parish.

Editor's Notes

Descriptive list in lieu of inventory, C.C.P. art. 3136; LSA–C.C.P. Form 825a, et seq.; minor's inventory, C.C.P. art. 4102.

Art. 3132. Public inventory

The public inventory of the property of a deceased person, or of other estates under the administration of the court, shall be taken by a notary appointed by the court, in the presence of at least two competent witnesses, assisted by two competent appraisers appointed and sworn by the notary. The witnesses and appraisers need not be residents of the parish where the inventory is taken.

The taking of the inventory may be attended by any person interested in the estate to be administered, or by his attorney; and when timely requested to do so, the notary shall give such person, or his attorney, notice by ordinary mail of the time and place thereof.

Art. 3133. Procès verbal of inventory

The public inventory shall be evidenced by the notary's procès verbal of the proceedings, subscribed by him, and signed by the appraisers, witnesses, and other persons who have attended. This procès verbal shall contain:

(1) The names, surnames, domiciles, and qualities of the notary taking the inventory, of the witnesses thereto, of the appraisers who have valued the property, and of any other interested persons who have attended;

(2) The dates when and places where the inventory was taken;

(3) A description of the manner in which the inventory was taken;

(4) An adequate description of each item of property belonging to the estate and found in the parish where the inventory was taken, and the fair market value thereof estimated by the appraisers;

(5) An adequate description of all of the titles, account books, and written evidences of indebtedness due the estate, found during the taking of the inventory, and the amounts of the indebtedness, and the name, surname, and address of each debtor, as shown therein;

(6) An adequate description of any property owned in whole or in part by third persons, or claimed by third persons as having been left on loan, deposit, consignment, or otherwise; and

(7) A recapitulation of the aggregate value of all movable property, the aggregate value of all immovable property, and the total value of all property owned by the estate.

Art. 3134. Return of procès verbal of inventory

The notary who took the inventory, or the party at whose instance it was taken, shall make duplicate copies of the procès verbal, the original procès verbal shall be returned into the court which ordered it taken, immediately upon its completion and signing. The duplicate copy shall be certified and filed with the collector of revenue. A certified copy of the procès verbal of any inventory taken in Orleans Parish may be returned in the same manner, and with the same effect as the original.

Amended by Acts 1972, No. 326, § 2, eff. Jan. 1, 1973.

Art. 3135. Procès verbal of inventory prima facie proof; traverse

The procès verbal of a public inventory returned into court as provided in Article 3134 shall be accepted as prima facie proof of all matters shown therein, without homologation by the court.

An interested person at any time may traverse the procès verbal of a public inventory by contradictory motion served upon the notary and the person at whose instance the inventory was made.

If a descriptive list is amended or successfully traversed a copy of the amended or traversed procès verbal shall be filed with the Collector of Revenue.

Amended by Acts 1972, No. 326, § 2, eff. Jan. 1, 1973.

Art. 3136. Descriptive list of property in lieu of inventory

Whenever an inventory of succession property otherwise would be required by law, the person at whose instance the inventory would be taken may file with the Department of Revenue and in the succession proceeding, in lieu of an inventory complying with articles 3131 through 3135, a detailed, descriptive list of all succession property. This list shall be sworn to and subscribed by the person filing it, shall show the location of all items of succession property, and shall set forth the fair market value of each item thereof at the date of the death of the deceased.

The privilege of filing a descriptive list of succession property, in lieu of an inventory thereof, may be exercised without judicial authority.

Amended by Acts 1972, No. 326, § 2, eff. Jan. 1, 1973.

Editor's Notes

LSA–C.C.P. Form 823a, et seq.; formal inventory required for minor's property, see Comment to C.C.P. art. 4102.

Art. 3137. Descriptive list prima facie correct; amendment or traverse; reduction or increase of security

The descriptive list of succession property authorized by Article 3136 shall be accepted as prima facie proof of all matters shown therein, unless amended or traversed successfully.

The court may amend the descriptive list at any time to correct errors therein, on ex parte motion of the person filing it. Any interested person may traverse the descriptive list at any time, on contradictory motion served on the person filing it. If a descriptive list is amended, or successfully traversed a copy of the amended or traversed descriptive list shall be filed with the Department of Revenue. The court may order the reduction or increase of the security required of a succession representative to conform to the corrected total value of the property of the succession.

Amended by Acts 1972, No. 326, § 2, eff. Jan. 1, 1973.

SECTION 6. SECURITY, OATH, AND LETTERS OF SUCCESSION REPRESENTATIVE

Art. 3151. Security of administrator

Except as otherwise provided by law, the person appointed administrator shall furnish security for the faithful performance of his duties in an amount exceeding by one-fourth the total value of all property of the succession as shown by the inventory or descriptive list.

The court may reduce the amount of this security, on proper showing, whenever it is proved that the security required is substantially in excess of that needed for the protection of the heirs and creditors.

Editor's Notes

Sureties generally, C.C. art. 3035 et seq.; sureties' qualifications, C.C. art. 3065; premium on bond, R.S. 9:3901; special mortgage in lieu of bond, C.C.P. art. 3157.

Art. 3152. Security of provisional administrator

The person appointed provisional administrator shall furnish security for the faithful performance of his duties in an amount determined by the court as being adequate for the protection of the heirs, legatees, surviving spouse in community, and creditors of the succession.

Art. 3153. Security of testamentary executor

The person appointed dative testamentary executor shall furnish the same security as is required of the administrator under Article 3151.

The person named by the testator as executor is not required to furnish security, except when required by the testament or as provided in Articles 3154 through 3155.

Art. 3154. Forced heirs and surviving spouse in community may compel executor to furnish security

Forced heirs and the surviving spouse in community of the testator may compel the executor to furnish security by an ex parte verified petition therefor. If the court finds that the petitioner is a forced heir, or the surviving spouse in community, it shall order the executor to furnish security within ten days of the service of the order, in an amount determined by the court as adequate to protect the interest of the petitioner.

Art. 3154.1. Repealed by Acts 2004, No. 158, § 2

Art. 3155. Creditor may compel executor to furnish security

A person having a pecuniary claim against a testate succession, whether liquidated or not, or claiming the ownership of specific items of property in the possession of the succession, may compel the executor to furnish security in an amount exceeding by one-fourth the amount of the claim, or the value of the property as shown on the inventory or the descriptive list. His verified petition for security may be presented ex parte to the court, which shall order the executor to furnish such security within ten days of the service of the order upon him.

Art. 3155.1. Repealed by Acts 1997, No. 1421, § 8, eff. July 1, 1999

Art. 3156. Maximum security of executor

The executor cannot be compelled to furnish security, under the provisions of Articles 3153 through 3155, in an amount in excess of the maximum security required of the administrator under Article 3151.

Art. 3157. Special mortgage in lieu of bond

The person appointed or confirmed as succession representative may give a special mortgage on unencumbered immovable property within the parish where the succession has been opened, in lieu of the security required by Articles 3151 through 3155. The mortgage shall be for the same amount as the security required, and shall be approved by the court before letters may be issued to him.

Editor's Notes

General and special mortgages, C.C. art. 3288.

Art. 3158. Oath of succession representative

Before the person appointed or confirmed as succession representative enters upon the performance of his official duties, he must take an oath to discharge faithfully the duties of his office.

Art. 3159. Issuance of letters to succession representative

After the person appointed or confirmed as succession representative has qualified by furnishing the security required of him by law, and by taking his oath of office, the clerk shall issue to him letters of administration or letters testamentary, as the case may be.

These letters, issued in the name and under the seal of the court, evidence the confirmation or appointment of the succession representative, his qualification, and his compliance with all requirements of law relating thereto.

Editor's Notes

Authority to collect assets, see notes to C.C.P. art. 3062, *supra*.

CHAPTER 2. ATTORNEY FOR ABSENT HEIRS AND LEGATEES

Article

Art. 3171. Appointment

If it appears from the record, or is otherwise proved by an interested party, that an heir of an intestate, or a legatee or presumptive legal heir of a deceased testator, is an absentee, and there is a necessity for such appointment, the court shall appoint an attorney at law to represent the absent heir or legatee.

Editor's Notes

Absentee defined, C.C.P. art. 5251; see also, C.C.P. art. 5091, attorneys appointed for absentees and others, generally.

Art. 3172. Duties

The attorney at law appointed to represent an absent heir or legatee shall:

(1) Make all necessary efforts to determine the identity and address of the absent heir or legatee, and to inform him of the death of the deceased and of his interest in the succession;

(2) Represent the absent heir or legatee in the succession, and defend his interests in all contradictory proceedings brought against him therein; and

(3) Take any conservatory action necessary to protect the interests of the absent heir or legatee, including the filing of all necessary suits.

Art. 3173. Removal; appointment of successor

The attorney at law appointed to represent an absent heir or legatee may be relieved by the court of his trust for any lawful reason, shall be removed by the court for nonperformance of duty, and his office shall terminate when the absent heir or legatee by proper pleading advises the court of his appointment of an attorney in fact, or of the selection of his own counsel.

If the attorney appointed to represent an absent heir or legatee, as provided in Article 3171, is removed, resigns, or dies, the court may appoint another attorney at law to succeed him.

Editor's Notes

Substitution of parties, successor to legal representative, C.C.P. art. 805.

Art. 3174. Compensation

The court may allow the attorney at law appointed to represent an absent heir or legatee, upon the completion of his duties, reasonable compensation for the services rendered, payable out of the share of the absent heir or legatee in the succession.

If the person whom the attorney has been appointed to represent is not entitled to any share in the succession, or such share is insufficient to compensate him adequately for his services, his reasonable compensation shall be taxed as costs of court against the mass of the succession.

Such compensation may be determined judicially by contradictory motion against the absent heir or legatee, if he has appeared through counsel or an attorney in fact, or otherwise against the succession representative.

CHAPTER 3. REVOCATION OF APPOINTMENT, AND REMOVAL OF SUCCESSION REPRESENTATIVE

Article

Art. 3181. Revocation of appointment or confirmation; extension of time to qualify

If a person appointed or confirmed as succession representative fails to qualify for the office within ten days after his appointment or confirmation, on its own motion or on motion of any interested person, the court may revoke the appointment or confirmation, and appoint another qualified person to the office forthwith.

The delay allowed herein for qualification may be extended by the court for good cause shown.

Art. 3182. Removal

The court may remove any succession representative who is or has become disqualified, has become incapable of discharging the duties of his office, has mismanaged the estate, has failed to perform any duty imposed by law or by order of court, has ceased to be a domiciliary of the state without appointing an agent as provided in Article 3097(4), or has failed to give notice of his application for appointment when required under Article 3093.

The court on its own motion may, and on motion of any interested party shall, order the succession representative sought to be removed to show cause why he should not be removed from office. The removal of a succession representative from office does not invalidate any of his official acts performed prior to his removal.

CHAPTER 4. GENERAL FUNCTIONS, POWERS, AND DUTIES OF SUCCESSION REPRESENTATIVE

SECTION 1. GENERAL DISPOSITIONS

Article

SECTION 1. GENERAL DISPOSITIONS

Art. 3191. General duties; appointment of agent

A. A succession representative is a fiduciary with respect to the succession, and shall have the duty of collecting, preserving, and managing the property of the succession in accordance with law. He shall act at all times as a prudent administrator, and shall be personally responsible for all damages resulting from his failure so to act.

B. A nonresident succession representative may execute a power of attorney appointing a resident of the state to represent him in all acts of his administration. A resident succession representative who will be absent from the state temporarily similarly may appoint an agent to act for him during his absence. In either case, the power of attorney appointing the agent shall be filed in the record of the succession proceeding.

C. Subject to any restrictions provided in a valid testament of a decedent or an order of a court of competent jurisdiction, a succession representative shall have the power and authority to take control of, handle, conduct, continue, distribute, or terminate any digital account of the decedent.

D. (1) Except as provided in Subparagraph (2) of this Paragraph and to the extent permitted by federal law, any person that electronically stores, maintains, manages, controls, operates, or administers the digital accounts of a decedent shall transfer, deliver, or provide a succession representative access or possession of any digital account of a decedent within thirty days after receipt of letters testamentary, letters of administration, or letters of independent administration evidencing the appointment of the succession representative.

(2) Notwithstanding any other provision of law to the contrary, R.S. 6:325 or 767 shall control how federally insured financial institutions provide Internet or other electronic access to an authorized succession representative for the administration of a decedent's estate.

E. This Article supersedes any contrary provision in the terms and conditions of any service agreement and a succession representative shall be considered an authorized user with lawful consent of the decedent for purposes of accessing or possessing the decedent's digital accounts.

F. The authority provided in this Article shall be specifically subject to copyright law and shall not increase the scope of the license granted in the terms of service of any digital account. The agent, representative or fiduciary shall be personally responsible for any infringement of third party copyrights that occurs in the transfer or distribution of any digital account or its contents.

G. No cause of action shall lie in any court under the law of this state against any provider of digital account service, including its officers, directors, employees, agents, members, or other specified persons, for any actions taken to disclose or otherwise provide access to the contents of a digital account pursuant to this Article.

H. For purposes of this Article, the term "digital account" shall include any account of the decedent on any social networking Internet website, web log Internet website, microblog service Internet website, short message service Internet website, electronic mail service Internet website, financial account Internet website, or any similar electronic services or records, together with any words, characters, codes, or contractual rights necessary to access such digital assets and any text, images, multimedia information, or other personal property stored by or through such digital account.

Amended by Acts 1964, No. 4, § 1; Acts 2014, No. 758, § 1.

Editor's Notes

LSA–C.C.P. Form 846a, et seq., petitions for authority to do various acts.

Art. 3192. Duties and powers of multiple representatives

If there are several succession representatives, all action by them shall be taken jointly, unless:

(1) The testator has provided otherwise; or

(2) The representatives have filed in the record a written authorization to a single representative to act for all.

Art. 3193. Powers of surviving representatives

Every power exercised by joint succession representatives may be exercised by the survivor of them in case of the death or termination of appointment of one or more of them, unless the testator has provided otherwise.

Art. 3194. Contracts between succession representative and succession prohibited; penalties for failure to comply

A succession representative cannot in his personal capacity or as representative of any other person make any contracts with the succession of which he is a representative. He cannot acquire any property of the succession, or interest therein, personally or by means of third persons, except as provided in Article 3195.

All contracts prohibited by this article are voidable and the succession representative shall be liable to the succession for all damages resulting therefrom.

Art. 3195. Contracts between succession representative and succession; exceptions

The provisions of Article 3194 shall not apply when a testament provides otherwise or to a succession representative who is:

(1) The surviving spouse of the deceased;

(2) A partner of the deceased, with respect to the assets and business of the partnership;

(3) A co-owner with the deceased, with respect to the property owned in common;

(4) An heir or legatee of the deceased; or

(5) A mortgage creditor or holder of a vendor's privilege, with respect to property subject to the mortgage or privilege.

Amended by Acts 1961, No. 23, § 1.

Art. 3196. Procedural rights of succession representative

In the performance of his duties, a succession representative may exercise all procedural rights available to a litigant.

Art. 3197. Duty to close succession

It shall be the duty of a succession representative to close the succession as soon as advisable.

Art. 3198. Compromise and modification of obligations

A succession representative may:

(1) Effect a compromise of an action or right of action by or against the succession; or

(2) Extend, renew, or in any manner modify the terms of any obligation owed by or to the succession.

Any action taken under this article must be approved by the court after notice as provided by Article 3229.

Editor's Notes

Definition of compromise, C.C. art. 3071.

SECTION 2. COLLECTION OF SUCCESSION PROPERTY

Art. 3211. Duty to take possession; enforcement of claims and obligations

A succession representative shall be deemed to have possession of all property of the succession and shall enforce all obligations in its favor.

Editor's Notes

See notes to C.C.P. art. 3062, *supra*.

SECTION 3. PRESERVATION AND MANAGEMENT OF SUCCESSION PROPERTY

Art. 3221. Preservation of succession property

A succession representative shall preserve, repair, maintain, and protect the property of the succession.

Art. 3222. Deposit of succession funds; unauthorized withdrawals prohibited; penalty

A succession representative shall deposit all moneys collected by him as soon as received, in a bank account in his official capacity, in a state or national bank in this state, and shall not withdraw the deposits or any part thereof, except in accordance with law.

On failure to comply with the provisions of this article, the court may render a judgment against the succession representative and his surety in solido to the extent of twenty percent interest per annum on the amount not deposited or withdrawn without authority, such sum to be paid to the succession. He may also be adjudged liable for all special damage suffered, and may be dismissed from office.

Art. 3223. Investment of succession funds

When it appears to the best interest of the succession, and subject to the representative's primary duty to preserve the estate for prompt distribution and to the terms of the testament, if any, the court may authorize a succession representative to invest the funds of the succession and make them productive.

Unless the testator has provided otherwise, such investments shall be restricted to the kinds of investments permitted to trustees by the laws of this state.

Editor's Notes

Trustees are subject to ordinary prudence rule, R.S. 9:2090; see LSA–C.C.P. Forms 853a, 853b.

Art. 3224. Continuation of business

When it appears to the best interest of the succession, and after compliance with Article 3229, the court may authorize a succession representative to continue any business of the deceased for the benefit of the succession; but if the deceased died testate and his succession is solvent, the order of court shall be subject to the provisions of the testament. This order may contain such conditions, restrictions, regulations, and requirements as the court may direct.

Art. 3224.1. Continuation of corporation or partnership in which decedent held a majority interest

A. The succession representative of an estate owning a majority interest in a corporation or partnership shall provide notice as provided in Articles 3272 and 3282 prior to alienating, encumbering, or disposing of any real property of a corporation or partnership in which the decedent held a majority interest at the time of his death. The notification required herein shall be by certified mail to the last known address of the heirs or legatees. The heirs and legatees may waive this notification.

B. Upon motion by an heir or legatee, and contradictory hearing thereon, the court may require that a succession representative of an estate owning a majority interest in a corporation or partnership seek court approval prior to alienating, encumbering, or disposing of any or all of the real property belonging to the corporation or partnership.

Added by Acts 1988, No. 549, § 1. Amended by Acts 1992, No. 999, § 1.

See West's Louisiana Statutes Annotated

Art. 3225. Continuation of business; interim order unappealable

When an application to continue business has been filed, the court may issue an interim ex parte order to the succession representative to continue the business immediately until such time as the procedure provided for by Article 3229 may be complied with. The order granted herein shall expire at the end of forty-five days unless extended by the court.

No appeal shall lie from the granting or denial of the interim order.

Amended by Acts 1972, No. 666, § 1.

Art. 3226. Lease of succession property

When it appears to the best interest of the succession, the court may authorize a succession representative to grant a lease upon succession property after compliance with Article 3229. No lease may be granted for more than one year, except with the consent of the heirs and interested legatees.

The court may also authorize the granting of mineral leases on succession property after compliance with Article 3229. The leases may be for a period greater than one year as may appear reasonable to the court. A copy of the proposed lease contract shall be attached to the application for the granting of a mineral lease, and the court may require alterations as it deems proper.

The order of the court shall state the minimum bonus, if any, to be received by the executor or administrator of the estate under the lease and the minimum royalty to be reserved to the estate, which in no event shall be less than one-eighth royalty on the oil and such other terms as the court may embody in its order.

Amended by Acts 1974, No. 131, § 1.

Editor's Notes

LSA–C.C.P. Forms 847a to 847e.

Art. 3227. Execution of contracts

If a person dies before performing an executory contract evidenced by writing, the court may authorize the succession representative to perform the contract, after compliance with Article 3229.

Editor's Notes

The provisions relating to private sale, C.C.P. art. 3281, et seq., are inapplicable here; Comment (b).

Art. 3228. Loans to succession representative for specific purposes; authority to encumber succession property as security therefor

When it appears to the best interest of the succession, and after compliance with Article 3229, the court may authorize a succession representative to borrow money for the purposes of preserving the property or the orderly administration of the estate, of paying estate debts, and for expenditures in the regular course of business conducted in accordance with Article 3224. As security for the loans the court may authorize the succession representative to encumber succession property upon the terms and conditions as it may direct.

Amended by Acts 1995, No. 203, § 1; Acts 1997, No. 1421, § 3, eff. July 1, 1999; Acts 2010, No. 175, § 1.

Art. 3229. Notice by publication of application for court order; opposition

A. When an application is made for an order under Articles 3198, and 3224 through 3228, notice of the application shall be published once in the parish where the succession proceeding is pending in the manner provided by law. When an application is made for an order under Article 3226 to grant a mineral lease, the notice shall also be published in the parish or parishes in which the affected property is located.

B. A court order shall not be required for the publication of the notice. The notice shall state that the order may be issued after the expiration of seven days from the date of publication and that an opposition may be filed at any time prior to the issuance of the order. If no opposition is filed, the court may grant the authority requested at any time after the expiration of the seven days from the date of publication.

C. An opposition shall be tried as a summary proceeding.

Amended by Acts 1974, No. 131, § 2; Acts 1981, No. 317, § 1; Acts 1987, No. 269, § 1.

CHAPTER 5. ENFORCEMENT OF CLAIMS AGAINST SUCCESSIONS

Article

Art. 3241. Presenting claim against succession

A creditor of a succession under administration may submit his claim to the succession representative for acknowledgment and payment in due course of administration.

Except for the purposes of Article 3245, no particular form is required for the submission of a claim by a creditor of the succession other than that it be in writing.

Editor's Notes

Parol proof of debt of decedent, R.S. 13:3721, 13:3722. See, also, C.C. arts. 1832, 1847.

Art. 3242. Acknowledgment or rejection of claim by representative

The succession representative to whom a claim against the succession has been submitted, within thirty days thereof, shall either acknowledge or reject the claim, in whole or in part. This acknowledgment or express rejection shall be in writing, dated, and signed by the succession representative, who shall notify the claimant of his action. Failure of the succession representative either to acknowledge or reject a claim within thirty days of the date it was submitted to him shall be considered a rejection thereof.

Art. 3243. Effect of acknowledgment of claim by representative

The acknowledgment of a claim by the succession representative, as provided in Article 3242, shall:

(1) Entitle the creditor to have his claim included in the succession representative's petition for authority to pay debts, or in his tableau of distribution, for payment in due course of administration;

(2) Create a prima facie presumption of the validity of the claim, even if it is not included in the succession representative's petition for authority to pay debts, or in his tableau of distribution; and

(3) Suspend the running of prescription against the claim as long as the succession is under administration.

Editor's Notes

An acknowledgment works in conjunction with R.S. 13:3721 in proving debt of deceased, Comment (d).

Art. 3244. Effect of inclusion of claim in petition or in tableau of distribution

The inclusion of the claim of a creditor of the succession in the succession representative's petition for authority to pay debts or in his tableau of distribution creates a prima facie presumption of the validity of the claim; and the burden of proving the invalidity thereof shall be upon the person opposing it.

Editor's Notes

The rule as to prescription in C.C.P. art. 3243 applies to this article; Comment (a).

Art. 3245. Submission of formal proof of claim to suspend prescription

A. A creditor may suspend the running of prescription against his claim for up to ten years:

(1) By delivering personally or by certified or registered mail to the succession representative, or his attorney of record, a formal written proof of the claim.

(2) By filing a formal written proof of the claim in the record of the succession proceeding, if the succession has been opened and no person has been appointed or confirmed as succession representative and no judgment of possession has been signed.

(3) By filing a formal written proof of the claim in the mortgage records of the appropriate parish as provided in Article 2811, in the absence of a proceeding to open the succession.

B. Such proof of claim shall be sworn to by the claimant and shall set forth:

(1) The name and address of the creditor;

(2) The amount of the claim, and a short statement of facts on which it is based; and

(3) If the claim is secured, a description of the security and of any property affected thereby.

C. If the claim is based on a written instrument, a copy thereof with all endorsements must be attached to the proof of the claim. The original instrument must be exhibited to the succession representative on demand, unless it is lost or destroyed, in which case its loss or destruction must be stated in the claim.

D. The submission of this formal proof of claim, even though it be rejected subsequently by the succession representative, shall suspend the running of prescription against the claim as long as the succession is under administration or, if the succession has been opened and no person has been appointed or confirmed as succession representative and no judgment of possession has been signed, submission of the formal proof of claim shall suspend the running of prescription against the claim as long as no judgment of possession has been signed. In the absence of a proceeding to open the succession, submission of the formal proof of claim shall suspend the running of prescription against the claim for five years, commencing from the date of submission of the proof of claim.

Amended by Acts 1987, No. 693, § 1; Acts 1993, No. 481, § 1.

For Official Comments and Annotated Materials,

Art. 3246. Rejection of claim; prerequisite to judicial enforcement

A creditor of a succession may not sue a succession representative to enforce a claim against the succession until the succession representative has rejected the claim.

If the claim is rejected in whole or in part by the succession representative, the creditor to the extent of the rejection may enforce his claim judicially.

Editor's Notes

Presentation of claim is informal, as in C.C.P. art. 3241; claim is considered rejected if succession representative takes no action for 30 days; this article applies to all claims, including damage suits; Comment (a), (b), (d).

Art. 3247. Execution against succession property prohibited

Execution shall not issue against any property of a succession under administration to enforce a judgment against the succession representative, or one rendered against the deceased prior to his death.

Art. 3248. Enforcement of conventional mortgage or pledge

The provisions of Articles 3246 and 3247 shall not prevent the enforcement of a conventional mortgage on or a pledge of movable or immovable property of the succession in a separate proceeding.

Art. 3249. Succession representative as party defendant

The succession representative shall defend all actions brought against him to enforce claims against the succession, and in doing so may exercise all procedural rights available to a litigant.

CHAPTER 6. ALIENATION OF SUCCESSION PROPERTY

SECTION 1. GENERAL DISPOSITIONS

Article

SECTION 2. PUBLIC SALE

SECTION 3. PRIVATE SALE

SECTION 4. EXCHANGE OF SUCCESSION PROPERTY

SECTION 5. GIVING IN PAYMENT; PROCEDURE

SECTION 1. GENERAL DISPOSITIONS

Art. 3261. Purpose of sale

A succession representative may sell succession property in order to pay debts and legacies, or for any other purpose, when authorized by the court as provided in this Chapter.

Editor's Notes

This article does not apply to sales in continuation of business under C.C.P. art. 3224, Comment (b).

Art. 3262. No priority as between movables and immovables

There shall be no priority in the order of sale as between movable and immovable property.

Art. 3263. Terms of sale

Sales of succession property shall be for cash, unless upon the petition of the succession representative the court authorizes a credit sale. When a credit sale is authorized, the order shall specify the terms of the sale and the security.

Art. 3264. Perishable property; crops

Upon the petition of the succession representative as provided in Articles 3263 and 3271, the court may order the immediate sale of perishable property and growing crops either at public auction or private sale, without appraisal, and without advertisement, or with such advertisement as the court may direct.

Editor's Notes

LSA–C.C.P. Form 841a.

Art. 3265. Prima facie proof of publication

When a publication of notice is required by this Title, prima facie proof may be made either by an affidavit of publication by the official journal or newspaper which published the notice, reciting the date or dates of publication and the text of the notice, or by the original newspaper tear sheet showing both the text of the notice and its date of publication, accompanied by an affidavit by the moving party or the party's attorney, attesting to the publication and its date or dates.

Added by Acts 1993, No. 26, § 1, eff. May 18, 1993.

Art. 3266. Issuance of certificates of no opposition

When no opposition has been filed to an application by a succession representative for an order or judgment of the court, pursuant to an Article of this Title, the clerk of court shall issue a certificate that no opposition has been filed. No further proof shall be required.

Added by Acts 1993, No. 27, § 1, eff. May 18, 1993.

SECTION 2. PUBLIC SALE

Art. 3271. Petition; order

A succession representative desiring to sell succession property at public auction shall file a petition setting forth a description of the property and the reasons for the sale.

The court shall render an order authorizing the sale at public auction after publication, when it considers the sale to be to the best interests of the succession.

Editor's Notes

Persons authorized to make judicial sales, R.S. 9:3001. The court may refuse to allow the sale if it is unnecessary; the court may not on its own motion order a private, rather than public, sale, Comment (b). LSA–C.C.P. Form 842a, et seq.

Art. 3272. Publication of notice of sale; place of sale

Notice of the sale shall be published at least once for movable property, and at least twice for immovable property, in the manner provided by law. The court may order additional publications.

The notice of sale shall be published in the parish where the succession proceeding is pending. When immovable property situated in another parish is to be sold, the notice shall also be published in the parish where the property is situated. When movable property situated in another parish is to be sold, the court may require the notice to be published also in the parish where the property is situated.

The sale shall be conducted in the parish where the succession proceeding is pending, unless the court orders that the sale be conducted in the parish where the property is situated.

Editor's Notes

R.S. 13:4341, R.S. 13:4351, place of holding the sale.

Art. 3273. Minimum price; second offering

The property shall not be sold if the price bid by the last and highest bidder is less than two-thirds of the appraised value in the inventory. In that event, on the petition of the succession representative, the court shall order a readvertisement in the same manner as for an original sale, and the same delay must elapse. At the second offering the property shall be sold to the last and highest bidder regardless of the price.

SECTION 3. PRIVATE SALE

Art. 3281. Petition for private sale

A. A succession representative who desires to sell succession property at private sale shall file a petition setting forth a description of the property, the price and conditions of and the reasons for the proposed sale. If an agreement to sell has been executed in accordance with Paragraph B of this Article, a copy of such agreement shall be annexed to the petition.

B. A succession representative may execute, without prior court authority, an agreement to sell succession property at private sale, subject to the suspensive condition that the court approve the proposed sale.

C. The succession representative shall be obligated to file a petition in accordance with Paragraph A of this Article within thirty (30) days of the date of execution of such an agreement to sell.

Amended by Acts 1980, No. 369, § 1.

Art. 3282. Publication

Notice of the application for authority to sell succession property at private sale shall be published at least once for movable property, and at least twice for immovable property, in the manner provided by law. A court order shall not be required for the publication of the notice.

The notice shall be published in the parish in which the succession proceeding is pending. When immovable property situated in another parish is to be sold, the notice shall also be published in the parish in which the property is situated. When movable property situated in another parish is to be sold, the notice may be published also in the parish in which the property is situated, without necessity of a court order for the publication; however, the court may order the notice to be published in the parish where the movable property is situated.

The notice shall state that any opposition to the proposed sale must be filed within seven days from the date of the last publication.

Amended by Acts 1972, No. 626, § 1; Acts 1976, No. 364, § 1.

Editor's Notes

Requirements of publication, R.S. 43:203.

Art. 3283. Who may file opposition

An opposition to a proposed private sale of succession property may be filed only by an heir, legatee, or creditor.

Art. 3284. Order; hearing

A. If no opposition has been filed timely and the court considers the sale to be to the best interests of the succession, the court shall render an order authorizing the sale and shall fix the minimum price to be accepted. The price may be fixed exactly as the appraised value, as a fraction of the appraised value, as more than the appraised value, or as not less than the appraised value of the property. If an agreement to sell has been executed as provided in Article 3281 and the price and conditions fixed by the court are the price and conditions set in the agreement, the order of court authorizing the sale under such agreement shall fulfill the suspensive condition of the agreement, which thereafter shall be enforceable by the parties to the agreement.

B. Nothing contained in this Article shall affect the general duties of a succession representative.

C. An opposition shall be tried as a summary proceeding.

D. This Article is remedial and shall be retroactive to January 1, 1961. All sales of succession property on and after January 1, 1961, made in compliance with the provisions of this Article are hereby validated.

Amended by Acts 1968, No. 203, §§ 1, 2; Acts 1980, No. 369, § 1.

Art. 3285. Bonds and stocks

A succession representative may sell bonds and shares of stock at private sale at rates prevailing in the open market, by obtaining a court order authorizing the sale. No advertisement is necessary, and the order authorizing the sale may be rendered upon the filing of the petition.

The endorsement of the succession representative and a certified copy of the court order authorizing the sale shall be sufficient warrant for the transfer.

Art. 3286. Court may authorize listing

A succession representative who desires to list succession property for sale shall file a petition to which shall be annexed the proposed listing agreement, which shall contain a provision that any offer to purchase submitted under such agreement to the succession representative shall be subject to the suspensive condition that the court approve the proposed sale. The court shall render an order, ex parte, authorizing the execution of the listing agreement by the succession representative when it considers such agreement to be in the best interests of the succession.

Added by Acts 1980, No. 369, § 2.

Art. 3287. Household goods

A succession representative may sell household goods at prices not less than the appraised value of such goods in the succession inventory or descriptive list by obtaining an order authorizing sales, from time to time, for such prices as the succession representative shall determine. No advertisement shall be necessary, and the order authorizing such sales may be rendered upon the filing of the petition. Household goods shall include furniture, furnishings, appliances, linen, and clothing. If the succession representative desires to sell household goods for less than the appraised value, advertisement shall be required.

Added by Acts 1985, No. 724, § 1.

Art. 3288. Motor vehicles; sale at appraised value

A. A succession representative may sell motor vehicles at prices not less than the appraised value of such motor vehicles in the succession inventory or descriptive list by obtaining an order authorizing sales, from time to time, for such prices as the succession representative shall determine. No advertisement shall be necessary, and the order authorizing such sales may be rendered upon the filing of the petition. If the succession representative desires to sell motor vehicles for less than the appraised value, advertisement shall be required.

B. For purposes of this Article, "motor vehicles" shall include automobiles, two-axle trucks, and motorcycles.

Added by Acts 1986, No. 237, § 1.

SECTION 4. EXCHANGE OF SUCCESSION PROPERTY

Art. 3291. Court may authorize exchange

The court may authorize an exchange of succession property, on the petition of the succession representative, for a consideration to be paid in corporate stock or other property, or partly therein and partly in cash, if advantageous to the heirs and legatees and not prejudicial of the rights of the succession creditors.

Added by Acts 1962, No. 92, § 3.

Art. 3292. Petition for authority to exchange

The petition of the succession representative for authority to exchange succession property for other property, or for other property and cash, shall set forth a description of both properties, the petitioner's opinion of the values thereof, the conditions of the exchange, and the reasons why such an exchange would be advantageous to the heirs and legatees, and would not prejudice the rights of succession creditors.

Added by Acts 1962, No. 92, § 3.

Art. 3293. Copy of petition for authority to be served on heirs and legatees; exception

A certified copy of the succession representative's petition for authority to exchange succession property shall be served, as provided in Article 1314, on all heirs and legatees of the deceased who have not joined in this petition. The petition need not be served on a legatee who has received all of his legacies as provided in the testament.

Added by Acts 1962, No. 92, § 3. Amended by Acts 1988, No. 578, § 1.

Art. 3294. Publication of notice; opposition; hearing; order

The provisions of Articles 3282 through 3284 shall apply to the publication of notice of the application for authority to exchange succession property, opposition thereto, and the hearing and order thereon.

Added by Acts 1962, No. 92, § 3.

SECTION 5. GIVING IN PAYMENT; PROCEDURE

Art. 3295. Giving in payment of succession property

The executor or administrator may transfer by a giving in payment any succession property in satisfaction of secured or unsecured debts. The property may be taken in indivision by the secured or unsecured creditors, or both.

R.S. 9:1471. Amended by Acts 1988, No. 564, § 1. Redesignated as C.C. P. art. 3295 by Acts 1997, No. 1421, § 7, eff. July 1, 1999. Amended by Acts 2003, No. 545, § 1.

Art. 3296. Petition

A. To this end, he shall present to the judge a petition setting forth the nature of the property, the amount of the encumbrances if any, and the reasons why he deems it in the best interest of the succession to convey the property in satisfaction of the debt or debts.

B. A copy of the petition shall be served by the executor or administrator on each creditor of the succession who has requested notification, together with a notice requiring that any opposition to the granting of the application be filed within seven days from date of service. Service of the petition as set forth herein may be made by registered or certified mail, return receipt requested.

R.S. 9:1472. Amended by Acts 1988, No. 564, § 1. Redesignated as C.C.P. art. 3296 by Acts 1997, No. 1421, § 7, eff. July 1, 1997

Art. 3297. Publication

Notice of the application shall be published in the manner prescribed for judicial advertisements, requiring all whom it may concern, including the heirs, to make opposition, if they have any, to the granting of the application, within seven days from the day whereon the last publication appears.

R.S. 9:1473. Amended by Acts 1981, No. 314, § 1. Redesignated as C.C.P. art. 3297 pursuant to Acts 1997, No. 1421, § 7, eff. July 1, 1999.

Art. 3298. Hearing; order

If no opposition should be made within the time, the judge may grant to the administrator or executor the authority applied for, after the debt is proven, but if opposition should be made, he shall hear the matter and determine thereon in a summary manner.

R.S. 9:1474. Amended by Acts 1988, No. 564, § 1. Redesignated as C.C. P. art. 3298 by Acts 1997, No. 1421, § 7, eff. July 1, 1999.

CHAPTER 7. PAYMENT OF ESTATE DEBTS

Article

Art. 3301. Payment of estate debts; court order

A succession representative may pay an estate debt only with the authorization of the court, except as provided by Articles 3224 and 3302.

Amended by Acts 1997, No. 1421, § 3, eff. July 1, 1999.

Editor's Notes

See the "Preliminary Statement" in the official volume (LSA–C.C.P. Volume 1) for an excellent summary; LSA–C.C.P. Form 856b.

Art. 3302. Time of payment of estate debts; urgent estate debts

A. Upon the expiration of three months from the death of the decedent, the succession representative shall proceed to pay the estate debts as provided in this Chapter.

B. At any time and without publication the court may authorize the payment of estate debts the payment of which should not be delayed.

Amended by Acts 1997, No. 1421, § 3, eff. July 1, 1999.

Editor's Notes

Priority of claims, C.C. art. 3276.

Art. 3303. Petition for authority; tableau of distribution

A. When a succession representative desires to pay estate debts, he shall file a petition for authority and shall include in or annex to the petition a tableau of distribution listing those estate debts to be paid. A court order shall not be required for the publication of the notice of filing of a tableau of distribution.

B. If the funds in his hands are insufficient to pay all the estate debts in full, the tableau of distribution shall show the total funds available and shall list the proposed payments according to the rank of the privileges and mortgages of the creditors.

Amended by Acts 1986, No. 204, § 1; Acts 1997, No. 1421, § 3, eff. July 1, 1999.

Editor's Notes

Privilege defined, C.C. art. 3186; rank, C.C. art. 3254; action of unpaid new creditors against paid creditors, C.C. art. 1188.

Art. 3304. Notice of filing of petition; publication

Notice of the filing of a petition for authority to pay an estate debt shall be published once in the parish where the succession proceeding is pending in the manner provided by law. The notice shall state that the petition can be homologated after the expiration of seven days from the date of publication and that any opposition to the petition must be filed prior to homologation.

Amended by Acts 1980, No. 280, § 1; Acts 1989, No. 116, § 1; Acts 1990, No. 65, § 1, eff. June 27, 1990; Acts 1997, No. 1421, § 3, eff. July 1, 1999.

Editor's Notes

The repeal in 1990 of former paragraph A raises a question of the constitutionality of this notice provision. Former paragraph A and its comment were adopted by Acts 1989, No. 116, § 1, and read as follows:

"A. Notice of the filing of a petition for authority to pay debts and charges shall be sent by mail to all creditors who have not filed claims and who are known or who could be known by reasonably diligent efforts. The notice shall state that the petition can be homologated after the expiration of seven days from the date of mailing or publication, whichever is later, and that any opposition to the petition must be filed prior to homologation. Proof of mailing is sufficient; no proof of receipt is required. If notice of the petition has not been mailed when required under this Article, a judgment homologating the petition shall have no effect against the creditor entitled to such notice."

"Comment—1989

"Article 3304 is amended to meet the notice requirements established by the U.S. Supreme Court decision of *Tulsa Professional Collection Services v. Pope*, 108 S.Ct. 1340 (1988). In that case the Supreme Court held that notice must be given to creditors whose interests might be adversely affected by the proceedings and who are known or who could be known by reasonably diligent efforts. Notice under this Article is not required for creditors who have already filed claims because they will receive notice under Article 3242."

Requirements of publication of notice, R.S. 43:203.

Art. 3305. Petition for notice of filing of tableau of distribution

An interested person may petition the court for notice of the filing of a tableau of distribution.

The petition for such notice shall be signed by the petitioner or by his attorney, and shall set forth: (1) the name, surname, and address of the petitioner; (2) a statement of the interest of petitioner; (3) the name, surname, and office address of the attorney at law licensed to practice law in this state to whom the notice prayed for shall be mailed; and (4) a prayer that petitioner be notified, through his attorney, of the filing of the tableau of distribution.

A copy of this petition shall be served upon the succession representative, as provided in Article 1314.

Art. 3306. Notice of filing of tableau of distribution; effect of failure to serve

When notice has been requested in accordance with Article 3305, the succession representative, without the necessity for a court order thereon, shall send a notice of the filing of a tableau of distribution by mail to the attorney designated by the person praying for notice at the address designated. Proof of mailing is sufficient; no proof of receipt is required.

If no notice of the filing of a tableau of distribution has been mailed when required under this article, a judgment homologating the tableau of distribution shall have no effect against the person praying for such notice.

For Official Comments and Annotated Materials,

Amended by Acts 1962, No. 92, § 1.

Art. 3307. Homologation; payment

A. An opposition may be filed at any time before homologation, and shall be tried as a summary proceeding. If no opposition has been filed, the succession representative may have the tableau of distribution homologated and the court may grant the authority requested at any time after the expiration of seven days from the date of publication or from the date the notice required by Article 3306 is mailed, whichever is later.

B. If an opposition has been taken under advisement by the court after the trial thereof, notice of the signing of the judgment homologating the tableau of distribution, as originally submitted or as amended by the court, need be mailed by the clerk of court only to counsel for the opponent, or to the opponent if not represented by counsel.

C. After the delay for a suspensive appeal from the judgment of homologation has elapsed, the succession representative shall pay the debts approved by the court.

Amended by Acts 1961, No. 23, § 1; Acts 1980, No. 280, § 1; Acts 1989, No. 116, § 1; Acts 1990, No. 65, § 1, eff. June 27, 1990.

Editor's Notes

See Notes under C.C.P. art. 3304.

Art. 3308. Appeal

Only a suspensive appeal as provided in Article 2123 shall be allowed from a judgment homologating a tableau of distribution. The appeal bond shall comply with Article 2124.

The succession representative shall retain a sum sufficient to pay the amount in dispute on appeal until a definitive judgment is rendered. He shall distribute the remainder among the creditors whose claims have been approved and are not in dispute on appeal.

CHAPTER 8. INTERIM ALLOWANCE TO HEIRS AND LEGATEES

Article

Art. 3321. Interim allowance for maintenance during administration

When a succession is sufficiently solvent, the surviving spouse, heirs, or legatees shall be entitled to a reasonable periodic allowance in money for their maintenance during the period of administration, if the court concludes that such an allowance is necessary, provided the sums so advanced to the spouse, heirs, or legatees are within the amount eventually due them. Such payments shall be charged to the share of the person receiving them.

A surviving spouse, heir, or legatee may compel the payment of an allowance during the administration by contradictory motion against the succession representative.

Notice of the filing of a petition for authority to pay an allowance, or of a contradictory motion to compel the payment of an allowance, shall be published once in the manner provided by law. The notice shall state that any opposition must be filed within ten days from the date of publication.

Editor's Notes

This article does not affect rights of widow in necessitous circumstances, C.C. arts. 2432 and 3252, or the authority of banks and depositories to pay a portion of deposits to surviving spouse, R.S. 9:1513 to R.S. 9:1514; same, employers, R.S. 9:1515; R.S. 6:765, certificates in two names.

CHAPTER 9. ACCOUNTING BY SUCCESSION REPRESENTATIVE

Article

Art. 3331. Time for filing account

A succession representative shall file an account annually and at any other time when ordered by the court on its own motion or on the application of any interested person.

Editor's Notes

LSA–C.C.P. Form 857a.

Art. 3332. Final account

A. A succession representative may file a final account of his administration at any time after homologation of the final tableau of distribution and the payment of all estate debts and legacies as set forth in the tableau.

B. The court shall order the filing of a final account upon the application of an heir or residuary legatee who has been sent into possession or upon the rendition of a judgment ordering the removal of a succession representative.

Amended by Acts 1997, No. 1421, § 3, eff. July 1, 1999.

Art. 3333. Contents of account

An account shall show the money and other property received by and in the possession of the succession representative at the beginning of the period covered by the account, the revenue, other receipts, disbursements, and disposition of property during the period, and the remainder in his possession at the end of the period.

Art. 3334. Failure to file account; penalty

An interested person may proceed by contradictory motion to remove a succession representative who has failed to file an account after being ordered to do so by the court and may obtain the remedies provided by Article 2502.

Art. 3335. Notice to heirs and residuary legatees

A copy of any account filed by a succession representative shall be served upon each heir or residuary legatee, together with a notice that the account may be homologated after the expiration of ten days from the date of service and that any opposition thereto must be filed before homologation.

In the case of any account other than the final account, service on either a resident or nonresident may be made by ordinary mail.

In the case of a final account, service may be made:

(a) In accordance with the provisions of Article 1314; or

(b) By certified or registered mail on either a resident or nonresident. The certificate of the attorney for the succession representative that the notice and final account were mailed to the heir or legatee, together with the return receipt signed by the addressee shall be filed in the succession proceeding prior to homologation of the final account.

Amended by Acts 1966, No. 36, § 1.

Art. 3336. Opposition; homologation

An opposition to an account may be filed at any time before homologation. An opposition shall be tried as a summary proceeding.

When no opposition has been filed, or to the extent to which the account is unopposed, the succession representative may have the account homologated at any time after the expiration of ten days from the date of service as provided in Article 3335.

Art. 3337. Effect of homologation

A judgment homologating any account other than a final account shall be prima facie evidence of the correctness of the account.

A judgment homologating a final account has the same effect as a final judgment in an ordinary action.

Art. 3338. Deceased or interdicted succession representative

If a succession representative dies or is interdicted, an account of his administration may be filed by his heirs or by his legal representative; and upon the petition of an interested person the court shall order the filing of such an account.

CHAPTER 10. COMPENSATION OF SUCCESSION REPRESENTATIVE

Article

Art. 3351. Amount of compensation; when due

An executor shall be allowed as compensation for his services such reasonable amount as is provided in the testament in which he is appointed. An administrator for his services in administering a succession shall be allowed such reasonable amount as is provided by the agreement between the administrator and the surviving spouse, and all competent heirs or legatees of the deceased.

In the absence of a provision in the testament or an agreement between the parties, the administrator or executor shall be allowed a sum equal to two and one-half percent of the amount of the inventory as compensation for his services in administering the succession. The court may increase the compensation upon a proper showing that the usual commission is inadequate.

A provisional administrator or an administrator of a vacant succession shall be allowed fair and reasonable compensation by the court for his services.

The compensation of a succession representative shall be due upon the homologation of his final account. The court may allow an administrator or executor an advance upon his compensation at any time during the administration.

Amended by Acts 1982, No. 281, § 1.

Editor's Notes

LSA–C.C.P. Form 894.

Art. 3351.1. Amount of compensation; limitation when serving as attorney, corporate officer, or managing partner

A. Unless expressly stated in the testament appointing the succession representative, if the succession representative, in discharging his duties as succession representative, is or becomes an officer of a corporation, in which the majority of outstanding shares were owned by the decedent at the time of his death, or is or becomes the managing partner of a partnership in which the decedent at the time of his death owned a majority interest, the succession representative shall not receive compensation both as a succession representative and as an officer of the corporation, or managing partner of the partnership; however, the compensation of a succession representative shall be reduced by the amount of compensation which he received and which was attributable to the performance of his duties as an officer of the corporation or managing partner of the partnership.

B. Unless expressly stated in the testament appointing the succession representative, if the succession representative serves as an attorney for the succession or for the succession representative, the succession representative shall not receive compensation both as a succession representative and as an attorney for the succession or for the succession representative; however, the compensation of a succession representative shall be reduced by the amount of compensation received and which was attributable to the performance of the duties as attorney for the succession or for the succession representatives.

C. The provisions of Paragraphs A and B of this Article limiting compensation received by a succession representative may be waived upon written approval by the heirs and legatees of the decedent owning a two-thirds interest in the succession.

D. Any compensation paid or due to a succession representative under the provisions of this Article shall not be paid unless approved by the court.

Added by Acts 1988, No. 548, § 1. Amended by Acts 1992, No. 484, § 1.

Art. 3352. More than one succession representative

If there is more than one succession representative, the compensation provided by Article 3351 shall be apportioned among them as the court shall direct.

Art. 3353. Legacy to executor

A testamentary executor who is a legatee shall be entitled to compensation, unless the testament provides to the contrary. If the legacy and the compensation of the executor together exceed the disposable portion, the executor shall receive only the disposable portion.

CHAPTER 11. SENDING HEIRS AND LEGATEES INTO POSSESSION

SECTION 1. INTESTATE SUCCESSION

Article

SECTION 2. TESTATE SUCCESSION

For Official Comments and Annotated Materials,

SECTION 1. INTESTATE SUCCESSION

Art. 3361. After homologation of final tableau of distribution

At any time after the homologation of the final tableau of distribution, an heir of an intestate succession may file a petition to be sent into possession alleging the facts showing that he is an heir. Upon the filing of such a petition, the court shall order the administrator to show cause why the petitioner should not be sent into possession.

Amended by Acts 1997, No. 1421, § 3, eff. July 1, 1999.

Art. 3362. Prior to homologation of final tableau of distribution

At any time prior to the homologation of the final tableau of distribution, a majority of the heirs of an intestate decedent whose succession is under administration may be sent into possession of all or part of the property of the succession upon their filing a petition for possession as provided in Articles 3001 through 3008 excluding any provisions of Article 3004 to the contrary, except that the proceeding shall be contradictory with the administrator. Upon the filing of such a petition the court shall order the administrator to show cause why the petitioners should not be sent into possession, and shall order that the petitioners be sent into possession unless the administrator or any heir shows that irreparable injury would result, and upon a showing that adequate assets will be retained in the succession to pay all claims, charges, debts, and obligations of the succession. If a majority of the heirs are sent into possession of a part of the property, the administrator shall continue to administer the remainder.

Amended by Acts 1986, No. 209, § 1; Acts 1997, No. 1421, § 3, eff. July 1, 1999.

Editor's Notes

If heirs or legatees are sent into possession prior to completion of administration it constitutes an unconditional acceptance and C.C.P. arts. 3001 to 3062 must be complied with, Caveat preceding C.C.P. art. 3361. This would not apply to putting into possession under C.C.P. art. 3361, Comment. But see R.S. 9:1421, limiting liability under unconditional acceptance.

SECTION 2. TESTATE SUCCESSION

Art. 3371. After homologation of final tableau of distribution

A. At any time after the homologation of the final tableau of distribution, a legatee or an heir may file a petition to be sent into possession, alleging the facts showing that he is a legatee or an heir. Upon the filing of such a petition, the court shall order the executor to show cause why the petitioner should not be sent into possession.

B. Evidence of the allegations in the petition for possession showing that the petitioner is a legatee or an heir shall be submitted to the court as provided by Articles 2821 through 2823.

Amended by Acts 1997, No. 1421, § 3, eff. July 1, 1999.

Editor's Notes

Analogous to C.C.P. art. 3361, Comment.

Art. 3372. Prior to homologation of final tableau of distribution

At any time prior to the homologation of the final tableau of distribution, the legatees in a testate succession may be sent into possession of all or part of their respective legacies upon filing a petition for possession as provided in Articles 3031 through 3035, except that the proceeding shall be contradictory with the executor. Upon the filing of such a petition, the court shall order the executor to show cause why the legatees should not be sent into possession. If the legatees are sent into possession of a part of their respective legacies, the executor shall continue to administer the remainder.

Editor's Notes

Analogous to C.C.P. art. 3362. Comment (a).

SECTION 3. JUDGMENT OF POSSESSION

Art. 3381. Judgment of possession

A judgment of possession shall be rendered and signed as provided in Article 3061. The judgment shall be rendered and signed only after a hearing contradictory with the succession representative, unless he joins in the petition, in which event the judgment shall be rendered and signed immediately.

CHAPTER 12. DISCHARGE OF SUCCESSION REPRESENTATIVE

Article

Art. 3391. Discharge of succession representative

After homologation of the final account, or upon proof that the heirs have waived a final account, the succession representative may petition for discharge.

Upon the filing of receipts or other evidence satisfactory to the court, showing that the creditors have been paid and that the balance of the property in the possession of the succession representative has been distributed to the heirs and legatees, the court shall render a judgment discharging the succession representative and cancelling his bond.

Art. 3392. Effect of judgment of discharge

The judgment discharging the succession representative relieves him of further duty, responsibility, and authority as succession representative.

Editor's Notes

Succession of Quaglino, 65 So.2d 127 (1953), is illustrative. Prescription, acts of succession representative, R.S. 9:5621.

Art. 3393. Reopening of succession

A. After a succession representative has been discharged, if other property of the succession is discovered or for any other proper cause, upon the petition of any interested person, the court, without notice or upon such notice as it may direct, may order that the succession be reopened. The court may reappoint the succession representative or appoint another succession representative. The procedure provided by this Code for an original administration shall apply to the administration of a reopened succession in so far as applicable.

B. After formal or informal acceptance by the heirs or legatees or rendition of a judgment of possession by a court of competent jurisdiction, if other property is discovered, or for any other proper cause, upon the petition of any interested person, the court, without notice or upon such notice as it may direct, may order that the succession be opened or reopened, as the case may be, regardless of whether or not, theretofore, any succession proceedings had been filed in court. The court may appoint or reappoint the succession representative, if any, or may appoint another, or new, succession representative. The procedure provided by this Code, for an original administration, shall apply to the administration of successions formally or informally accepted by heirs or legatees and in successions where a judgment of possession has been rendered, in so far as same is applicable.

C. The reopening of a succession shall in no way adversely affect or cause loss to any bank, savings and loan association or other person, firm or corporation, who has in good faith acted in accordance with any order or judgment of a court of competent jurisdiction in any previous succession proceedings.

Amended by Acts 1970, No. 644, § 1; Acts 1997, No. 1421, § 3, eff. July 1, 1999.

Art. 3394. Refusal or inability to accept funds; deposit in bank

A. When an heir, legatee, or creditor is unwilling or unable to accept and receipt for the amount due him, on contradictory motion against the heir, legatee, or creditor the court may order that the succession representative deposit in a state or national bank or in the registry of the court to the credit of the person entitled thereto the amount due him.

B. A receipt showing the deposit shall be sufficient in the discharge of the succession representative to the same extent as though distribution to the person entitled thereto had been made.

Amended by Acts 1997, No. 1421, § 3, eff. July 1, 1999.

Art. 3395. Disposition of movables not accepted by heir

If the succession representative has in his possession corporeal movable property the delivery of which an heir, legatee, or creditor is unwilling or unable to accept and receipt for, the succession representative may make such disposition thereof as the court may direct.

CHAPTER 13. INDEPENDENT ADMINISTRATION OF ESTATES

Article

See West's Louisiana Statutes Annotated

Art. 3396. Definitions

In this Chapter:

(1) "Independent administration" means the administration of an estate in accordance with the provisions of this Chapter.

(2) "Independent administrator" means the succession representative authorized by the court to administer a succession in accordance with the provisions of this Chapter. The term "independent administrator" means and includes "independent executor".

(3) "Independent executor" means and includes an independent administrator.

(4) "Letters of independent administration" means letters testamentary or letters of administration that signify that the administration of a succession by the designated succession representative is authorized pursuant to the provisions of this Chapter. The term "letters of independent administration" includes "letters of independent executorship", and the term "letters of independent executorship" includes "letters of independent administration". Such letters have the same force and effect as letters of administration or letters testamentary in a succession that is administered in accordance with the other provisions of this Book.

Added by Acts 2001, No. 974, § 1.

Revision Comment—2001

The concept of "independent administration" of an estate employs new terms of art that are used throughout Chapter 13. This Article defines those terms and clarifies that some of the terms may be used interchangeably. For the definition of "succession representative," see Article 5251(14).

Art. 3396.1. Scope

Upon qualification of a succession representative and compliance with the provisions of this Chapter, the clerk shall issue letters of independent administration or letters of independent executorship, as appropriate, certifying that the independent administrator has been duly qualified.

Added by Acts 2001, No. 974, § 1. Amended by Acts 2020, No. 107, § 1, eff. June 9, 2020.

Revision Comments—2001

(a) This Article uses the mandatory "shall" to establish that, at the outset, independent administration is not discretionary with the court. When a succession representative "qualifies" and "complies" with the provisions of this Chapter, the court is required to issue the appropriate "letters of administration" certifying that the independent administrator has been duly qualified. Subsequent events may result in a reversal of that appointment. See Article 3396.20.

(b) In order for a succession representative to be appointed an Independent Administrator, the succession record must contain the documentation required by the other provisions of Book VI with regard to filing or probate of a testament, establishment of the jurisdiction of the court, affidavit of death, domicile and heirship, and oath of the succession representative.

Art. 3396.2. Provision for independent administration by testator

A. When a testament provides for independent administration of an estate, the court shall enter an appropriate order granting independent administration of the estate.

B. A statement in a testament to the effect that the succession representative may act as an "independent administrator" or "independent executor" is sufficient to constitute authorization for independent administration of an estate.

Added by Acts 2001, No. 974, § 1.

Revision Comment—2001

This Article deals with independent administration of a testate succession when the testator himself has provided for independent administration of the estate. This Article clarifies that a testament need not contain magic words or specific language in order to make such a provision. In the same manner that the Trust Code permits a settlor to use the word "spendthrift" in a trust instrument and thereby bring into play all the rules of Trust Code Section 2007, this Article permits a similar short-hand method for a testator to provide for independent administration.

Art. 3396.3. Designation of executor but failure to provide for independent administration by testator

When a decedent dies testate and his testament designates an executor, but his testament does not provide for independent administration of the estate as provided in this Chapter, all of the general or universal legatees of the decedent may agree to have an independent administration and in the application for filing for probate of the decedent's testament, or thereafter, collectively designate the person named in the testament to serve as independent executor. In such case, the court shall enter an order granting independent administration and appointing the person designated in the application as independent executor.

Added by Acts 2001, No. 974, § 1.

Revision Comments—2001

(a) This Article sets forth the procedure required to obtain independent administration of a testate succession when the testament designates a succession representative, but does not expressly authorize independent administration of the estate.

(b) This Article purposefully uses the words "or thereafter" to clarify that it is not necessary that the person designated as executor qualify as an "independent" executor when the testament is filed for probate. The application may be made at that time, or at any time "thereafter". Thus, the fact that the succession begins with a regular administration does not preclude the parties from subsequently agreeing to convert to independent administration and proceed under the provisions of this chapter. Furthermore, the Article does not impose a time limit within which the parties may agree to independent administration.

Art. 3396.4. Failure to designate an executor

When the decedent dies testate but his testament fails to designate an executor, or the person designated is unwilling or unable to serve, all of the general or universal legatees of the decedent may agree on the advisability of having an independent administration and collectively designate a qualified person to serve as dative independent executor. In such case, the court shall enter an order granting independent administration and appointing the person designated in the application as dative independent executor.

Added by Acts 2001, No. 974, § 1.

Revision Comment—2001

This Article sets forth the procedure required to obtain independent administration of a testate succession when no executor is designated, or, if designated, the person designated as executor is unwilling or unable to serve.

Art. 3396.5. Independent administration when decedent dies intestate

When a decedent dies intestate, all of the intestate successors may agree on the advisability of having an independent administration and collectively designate, in the application for administration of the decedent's estate, or thereafter, a qualified person to serve as independent administrator. In such case, the court shall enter an order granting independent administration and appointing the person designated in the application as independent administrator.

Added by Acts 2001, No. 974, § 1.

Revision Comments—2001

(a) The immediately preceding Articles (3396.2 through 3396.4) apply to testate successions only. When the succession is intestate, the successors are not precluded from having an independent administration. This Article permits the intestate successors to agree to have an independent administration, but only if they act unanimously. Like Article 3396.1, this Article uses the mandatory "shall," and provides that the court "shall" enter an order granting independent administration if the requirements of Article 3396.5 are met.

(b) This Article, like Code of Civil Procedure Article 3396.3, purposefully uses the words "or thereafter" to clarify that there is no time limit imposed on the parties to elect to have independent administration. The administration of the estate may commence as an independent administration or it may be converted to independent administration at any time in the proceedings. See Revision Comments to Code of Civil Procedure Article 3396.3, *supra.*

Art. 3396.6. Independent administration when estate is part testate, part intestate

When a decedent dies partially testate and partially intestate, all of the successors whose concurrence is required in Articles 3396.3, 3396.4, and 3396.5 must concur in the request for independent administration of the estate, and in the designation of the person to serve as independent administrator.

Added by Acts 2001, No. 974, § 1.

Revision Comment—2001

This Article covers a gap that would otherwise exist in the procedures set forth in the preceding Articles when the succession is part testate and part intestate. When a decedent dies leaving a testament that only disposes of a portion of the estate, so that some of the estate passes by testacy and some passes by intestacy, this Article permits independent administration of the estate and sets forth the requirements to implement it.

Art. 3396.7. Trusteeships

If a trust is created in the testament or a trustee is a legatee, and if concurrence in having an independent administration is required, the trustee shall be deemed to be the legatee authorized to consent to independent administration on behalf of the trust.

Added by Acts 2001, No. 974, § 1.

Revision Comment—2001

When concurrence is required in order to have an independent administration, and property is left in trust, this Article removes any doubt as to whose concurrence is required. The consent of the trustee only, not the beneficiary, is required.

Art. 3396.8. Usufruct

When the testament creates a usufruct and concurrence in having an independent administration is required, or when the usufruct arises by operation of law, the concurrence of the usufructuary and the naked owner is required.

Added by Acts 2001, No. 974, § 1.

Revision Comment—2001

When concurrence is required, whether the usufruct is created by testament or by operation of law, this Article requires the consent of the usufructuary and of the naked owner. See C.C. Art. 890 (rev. 1996). If there are more than one usufructuary or naked owner, the consent of all of them is required. The concurrence of the usufructuary alone is not sufficient, and conversely, the concurrence of all the naked owners, without the consent of the usufructuary, would not suffice, either.

Art. 3396.9. Interdict or unemancipated minor

A. If a successor whose concurrence is required is an unemancipated minor, the concurrence may be made on his behalf by the administrator of his estate or his natural tutor, as appropriate, without the need for a formal tutorship proceeding or concurrence of an undertutor.

B. If a successor whose concurrence is required is an interdict, the concurrence may be made on his behalf by the curator without the need for court authorization in the interdiction proceeding or concurrence of the undercurator.

Added by Acts 2001, No. 974, § 1. Amended by Acts 2016, No. 86, § 2.

Revision Comment—2001

When concurrence is needed, and the successor is a minor, this Article authorizes the administrator of the minor's estate, or his natural tutor , to concur on behalf of the minor. To simplify matters, the Article expressly provides for that concurrence to be granted without the need of a formal tutorship proceeding.

Art. 3396.10. Survivorship

If the testament contains a provision that a legatee must survive the decedent by a prescribed period of time in order to take under the testament, the legatee living at the time of filing of the application for independent administration shall be the legatee authorized to consent to independent administration.

Added by Acts 2001, No. 974, § 1.

Revision Comment—2001

Civil Code Article 1521 permits a testator to impose a short-term survivorship requirement as a suspensive condition for a legatee to take under the testament. In that situation, when concurrence is required, this Article resolves the question of whose concurrence is needed so that it is not necessary to wait until the term of the condition has expired.

Art. 3396.11. Possibility of renunciation

A. The subsequent renunciation of an heir or legatee who has consented to an independent administration shall have no effect on the validity of the independent administration, and the consent of those persons who receive an interest in the succession by reason of the renunciation is not required.

B. A successor who concurs in the application for independent administration of an estate shall not be considered, for that reason, as having formally or informally accepted the succession.

Added by Acts 2001, No. 974, § 1.

Revision Comment—2001

Under substantive succession law, a successor is not required to accept an inheritance or legacy, but may renounce. The purpose of this Article is to validate a concurrence by the appropriate successor when concurrence is granted and the successor subsequently renounces. This Article protects the independent administration of the estate by providing that the subsequent renunciation has no effect on the validity of the independent administration. In addition, in order to remove any concern that a successor might be considered as having formally or informally accepted the succession by concurring in the application for independent administration, this Article expressly provides that the concurrence will not be considered as a formal or informal acceptance by the successor.

Art. 3396.12. Death of successor

If a successor dies before the filing of an application for independent administration and the share of the successor is transmitted to his estate, then the deceased successor's universal successors, or the succession representative if one has qualified as such, may sign the application for independent administration of the decedent's estate.

Added by Acts 2001, No. 974, § 1.

Revision Comment—2001

When a successor dies and transmits his share to his own successors before he concurs in the independent administration the universal successors, or the succession representative, of the now-deceased successor may sign the application for independent administration in place of the successor who has died.

Art. 3396.13. Testamentary prohibition of independent administration

A testator may expressly provide that no independent administration of his estate may be allowed. In such case, his estate, if administered, shall be administered in accordance with the other provisions of Book VI.

Added by Acts 2001, No. 974, § 1.

Revision Comment—2001

Because independent administration of the estate significantly relaxes the procedural rules, a testator may desire that his estate not be administered by independent administration, even if his successors agree. Although this situation may be rare, this Article makes it a matter of public policy that the testator himself may prohibit an independent administration of his estate.

Art. 3396.14. Security of independent administrator

Except where the testament provides otherwise, an independent administrator shall not be required to provide security for the administration of the estate. If an interested person, such as an heir, legatee, or creditor of the estate requests security, then upon application by such party, and after a contradictory hearing, the court may order the independent administrator to furnish security as the court determines to be adequate.

Added by Acts 2001, No. 974, § 1.

Revision Comments—2001

(a) In most testate successions, it is customary to relieve the succession representative of the obligation of posting security. This Article implements the same rule for an independent administration, but, in fairness, because of the relaxed nature of the procedure, this Article authorizes an heir, legatee or creditor to request security. In many instances, a surviving spouse may request security as an "interested person" under this Article. In that instance, the court must have a hearing and may order the administrator to furnish security in whatever manner the court determines to be adequate under all circumstances.

(b) This Article is intentionally worded to clarify that the court need not necessarily order a bond to be posted. There are any number of remedies that may be appropriate to protect the parties. Even when a bond is appropriate, the court may reduce the penal sum of the bond to an amount that the court considers satisfactory. See Civil Code Article 1514, regarding the security furnished by a usufructuary. See Also C.C.P. Art. 3152.

Art. 3396.15. Rights, powers, and duties; performance without court authority

Except as expressly provided otherwise in this Chapter, an independent administrator shall have all the rights, powers, authorities, privileges, and duties of a succession representative provided in Chapters 4 through 12 of this Title, but without the necessity of delay for objection, or application to, or any action in or by, the court.

Added by Acts 2001, No. 974, § 1.

Revision Comments—2001

(a) This Article sets out the broad scope of authority permitted a succession representative who serves as an independent administrator. The primary function of independent administration is to permit the succession representative to act without the expense or delays involved in publishing notices and waiting for the time to run after the notice has been published before securing court approval, which is often perfunctory at best. When all of the successors are in agreement, the necessity for publishing requests for approval to alienate or encumber property, or to pay debts, serves little or no purpose and significantly increases the cost of probate. The more formal rules that apply in other successions are generally not necessary to protect the successors or the creditors. Further, all of the successors and creditors have the opportunity to oppose an independent administration at the outset, and to request more formal administration after an independent administration has already begun.

(b) This Article is at the very heart of independent administration. It allows the succession representative to assume the role of succession representative and proceed to act without being encumbered by all of the more formalistic procedural rules that are in most cases unrealistic and impractical. This new approach should significantly reduce the time involved in administering an estate, as well as many of the legal fees and out-of-pocket costs incurred in administering the estate. Although the procedural rules are relaxed, the succession representative is a fiduciary and is responsible for his actions.

(c) This Article sets forth the primary duties of an independent administrator, which are also specified in Code of Civil Procedure Articles 3221 et seq. All of those duties are not repeated here, since they are subsumed under the express provisions in this Article for collection of the assets, preservation and management of the assets, and authorization of the succession representative to discharge estate debts or "make arrangements" for the discharge of such debts.

(d) An independent administrator has all the rights, powers, authority and privileges of other succession representatives but without the necessity of obtaining court approval to exercise them. These rights include the power to borrow money and incur obligations and secure such obligations by encumbering property of the estate, and to sell or exchange movable and immovable property upon such terms and conditions, and to do so for such a duration of time, as the independent executor, in his discretion, determines to be proper. All such loans, obligations, encumbrances, leases, sales, and exchanges are valid and enforceable against the estate and against successors who take possession of property of the estate.

(e) One of the paramount functions of independent administration is to permit a succession representative to perform all of those duties without having to apply to the court or obtain court approval. The succession representative must, in due course, distribute assets of the estate to those persons entitled to receive them. There are requirements spelled out in Chapter 13 that provide for the designation of the assets on a sworn descriptive list, proof that the inheritance tax has been paid on such assets, and a judgment of possession, whether final or partial, before the succession representative may make distribution.

(f) Because the independent executor has "all the rights, powers [and] authorities...of a succession representative," he has the authority needed to pay debts, borrow funds, sell movable and immovable property, settle lawsuits, and so forth. It is not necessary for the court to approve those actions, as this Article expressly provides that no action "in or by the court" is required. One beneficial result of this Article is that, unlike an ordinary administration, it is not necessary to publish notice of the "application for authority" to sell property provided for in the Code of Civil Procedure Article 3282, since the independent executor already has the "authority" to sell and does not need to "apply" for a court order granting it.

Art. 3396.16. Enforcement of claims against estate

Any person having a claim against the estate may enforce the payment or performance of the claim against an independent administrator in the same manner and to the same extent provided for the assertion of such rights in this Code.

Added by Acts 2001, No. 974, § 1.

Revision Comment—2001

This Article incorporates by reference the provisions contained elsewhere in the Code of Civil Procedure for enforcing claims against an estate. Those procedures are adequate and appropriate, even in the context of independent administration.

Art. 3396.17. Accounting

An independent administrator is not required to file an interim accounting. Nevertheless, any person interested in the estate may demand an annual accounting from the independent administrator as provided in Article 3331. Further, the court on application of any interested person may require an independent administrator to furnish accountings at more frequent intervals.

Added by Acts 2001, No. 974, § 1.

Revision Comment—2001

Under existing rules a succession representative is required to render an annual accounting of receipts and disbursements. This Article relaxes that requirement for independent administration. Nevertheless, the article imposes an obligation on the independent administrator to account before he is discharged. To protect successors and creditors, this Article further provides that any person interested in the estate may demand an annual accounting, which is all that would be obtained under the other rules on succession procedure. The article further authorizes the court, on application of "any interested person," to require accountings at more frequent intervals.

Art. 3396.18. Inventory or sworn descriptive list

A. Before the succession can be closed, a judgment of possession rendered, and the independent administrator discharged, there shall be filed an inventory or sworn detailed descriptive list of assets and liabilities of the estate verified by the independent administrator.

B. The detailed descriptive list shall be sealed upon the request of an independent administrator, heir, or legatee.

C. If the detailed descriptive list is sealed, a copy shall be provided to the decedent's universal successors and surviving spouse. Upon motion of any successor, surviving spouse, or creditor of the estate, the court may furnish relevant information contained in the detailed descriptive list regarding assets and liabilities of the estate.

Added by Acts 2001, No. 974, § 1. Amended by Acts 2010, No. 175, § 1; Acts 2017, No. 198, § 1; Acts 2020, No. 19, § 2.

Revision Comment—2001

Because of the relaxed nature of the proceedings in independent administration, this Article affords a measure of protection to successors, and to creditors, by requiring a sworn descriptive list of assets and liabilities, verified by the succession representative, as well as a petition for possession and a final judgment of possession. The chief function of independent administration is to reduce expenses and remove some of the potholes and roadblocks along the way when the succession representative is performing his functions of collecting the assets, ascertaining the liabilities, discharging the liabilities, and ultimately turning property over t o the persons who are entitled to receive it. Once those tasks are completed, there must be sufficient information in the succession record for successors and creditors to determine the assets and liabilities of the estate.

Revision Comments—2017

(a) The 2017 revision changes the law insofar as it attempts to strike an appropriate balance between publicity regarding the assets and liabilities of a decedent and privacy of the decedent and his successors.

(b) Paragraph A maintains the prior law requiring the production and filing of the detailed descriptive list. Under Paragraph B of the revision, however, the independent administrator or an heir or legatee of the decedent may request that the detailed descriptive list be sealed and therefore shielded from general availability to the public.

(c) Paragraph C recognizes that the privacy of the parties requesting the sealing of the detailed descriptive list cannot prejudice the rights of those parties with a legitimate interest in the assets and liabilities of the succession. Therefore, if sealed, copies of the detailed descriptive list must be provided to all of the decedent's universal successors as well as the surviving spouse. Even after the sealing of the detailed descriptive list, these same parties may have a need for the information at a later time. Other parties, such as particular legatees or creditors of the estate, may also have a legitimate interest in relevant information regarding the assets and liabilities of the decedent. Consequently, upon appropriate motion of any successor, surviving spouse, or creditor of the estate, a court may provide information that, in the court's discretion, is relevant to the party's request. The appropriate information to be furnished to the requesting party is likely to differ depending upon the requesting party and the reason for the request. In some instances, it may be appropriate for the court to furnish the entire detailed descriptive list to the requesting party, but in other instances a redacted version or excerpted portion may be more appropriate.

Comments—2020

This revision clarifies the law by definitively stating that the rendition of a judgment of possession is still necessary even when a succession is independently administered. The 2017 amendments did not intend to repeal the requirement of a judgment of possession, even though independent administrators have "all the rights, powers, authorities, privileges, and duties of a succession representative provided in Chapters 4 through 12" of Title III of Book VI of the Code of Civil Procedure. See Article 3395.15. Nothing in this Article affects the rendition of a partial judgment of possession pursuant to Article 3362 or 3372.

Art. 3396.19. Final account

Unless the heirs and legatees waive a final accounting, the independent administrator shall file a final account with the court. After homologation of that account, the court shall enter an order discharging the succession representative. The final account shall be served in accordance with Chapter 9 of Title III of Book VI [1].

Added by Acts 2001, No. 974, § 1.

[1] Chapter 9, Title III, Book VI, see C.C.P. art. 3331 et seq.

Revision Comment—2001

Although the rules do not require annual accountings, unless demand is made for them and the court orders them, this Article preserves the requirement of a final accounting. As in other succession proceedings, however, a final account may be waived. It is reasonable to assume that a final account likely will be waived in most instances where independent administration is employed. In the absence of a waiver, however, a final account must be filed with the court and must be homologated.

Art. 3396.20. Removal of succession representative and termination of independent administration

The court on motion of any interested person, after a contradictory hearing, may remove an independent administrator for any of the reasons provided in Book VI for which a succession representative may be removed from office. In addition, the court on motion of any interested person, after a contradictory hearing, may for good cause order that the letters of independent administration be withdrawn and that the succession thereafter be administered under the procedures set forth elsewhere in Book VI, other than those contained in this Chapter.

Added by Acts 2001, No. 974, § 1.

Revision Comments—2001

(a) This Article protects successors and creditors by providing for removal of an independent administrator and also for termination of the independent administration itself. In the hands of trustworthy succession representatives, the ease and efficiency of independent administration is not merely appropriate but highly desirable. When a question is raised about the propriety of actions of an independent administrator or whether a succession representative should be removed for any reason, this Article provides a basis for removal of the representative. It also provides that the court may order the independent administration to cease. In that event, the succession would thereafter be administered in accordance with the rules by which successions are administered with all the formalities required by the Code of Civil Procedure.

(b) Acts taken on behalf of the succession by the independent administrator prior to his removal or prior to the withdrawal of letters of independent administration remain valid and enforceable by and against the succession.

Editor's Notes

See the relevant Forms for Independent Administration in the pocket part of Volume 11 of West's LSA–Code of Civil Procedure, Form Nos. 900a to 900d.

TITLE IV. ANCILLARY PROBATE PROCEDURE

Art. 3401. Jurisdiction; procedure

When a nonresident dies leaving property situated in this state, a succession proceeding may be instituted in a court of competent jurisdiction in accordance with Article 2811.

Except as otherwise provided in this Title, the procedure in such a succession shall be the same as provided by law for the succession of a Louisiana domiciliary.

Art. 3402. Foreign representative; qualification

A succession representative appointed by a court outside Louisiana may act with respect to property situated in Louisiana only after qualifying in a court of competent jurisdiction in Louisiana. He shall furnish bond upon the application of any interested person for good cause shown in the same amount as an administrator, even though in the case of a testamentary succession the testament dispenses with bond.

After such qualification the succession representative may exercise all of the rights and privileges of and has the same obligation as a succession representative originally qualified in Louisiana.

Editor's Notes

Foreign executor may sue here for wrongful death without qualifying, R.S. 13:3331.

Art. 3403. Capacity to sue

Except as otherwise provided by law, a succession representative appointed by a court outside Louisiana has no capacity to appear in court on behalf of the succession without first qualifying in a court of competent jurisdiction in Louisiana.

Editor's Notes

The first clause allows for R.S. 13:3331, Comment.

Art. 3404. Priority in appointment

When a succession representative has been appointed by a court of the decedent's domicile outside Louisiana, priority shall be given to him in the appointment of a representative in Louisiana, unless he is disqualified under Article 3097. Otherwise, priority shall be given in the appointment of a representative as provided in Article 3098.

Art. 3405. Testament probated outside Louisiana

A testament admitted to probate outside Louisiana shall be governed by the provisions of R.S. 9:2421 through 9:2425.

Editor's Notes

Uniform Wills Law, R.S. 9:2401, for wills executed out-of-state. If tendered for probate here, C.C.P. art. 2888.

TITLE V. SMALL SUCCESSIONS

CHAPTER 1. GENERAL DISPOSITIONS

See West's LSA Civil Procedure Forms, Vol. 11 Form No. 884.

Article

Art. 3421. Small successions defined

A. A small succession, within the meaning of this Title, is the succession or the ancillary succession of a person who at any time has died and the decedent's property in Louisiana has a gross value of one hundred twenty-five thousand dollars or less valued as of the date of death or, if the date of death occurred at least twenty years prior to the date of filing of a small succession affidavit as authorized in this Title, leaving property in Louisiana of any value.

B. A small succession shall also include a succession of a person who has died testate, leaving no immovable property, and probate of the testament of the deceased would have the same effect as if the deceased had died intestate.

Amended by Acts 1976, No. 187, § 1, eff. Jan. 1, 1977; Acts 1979, No. 71, § 1, eff. Jan. 1, 1980; Acts 1980, No. 582, § 1; Acts 2009, No. 81, § 1, eff. June 18, 2009; Acts 2011, No. 323, § 1, eff. June 29, 2011; Acts 2012, No. 618, § 1, eff. June 7, 2012; Acts 2017, No. 96, § 1; Acts 2020, No. 173, § 1.

Art. 3422. Court costs; compensation

In judicial proceedings under this Title, the following schedule of costs, compensation, and fees shall prevail:

(1) Court costs for successions valued less than one hundred twenty-five thousand dollars shall be one-half the court costs in similar proceedings in larger successions, but the minimum costs in any case shall be five dollars; and

(2) The compensation of the succession representative shall be not more than five percent of the gross assets of the succession.

Amended by Acts 2017, No. 96, § 1; Acts 2018, No. 422, § 1.

Art. 3422.1. Small succession immovable property damaged by disaster or catastrophe

A. The provisions of this Article shall apply to immovable property, subject to a small succession proceeding, that is damaged by a disaster or catastrophe for which a declaration of emergency or federal declaration of disaster or emergency was issued.

B. In the absence of a written agreement between co-owners for the use and management of such immovable recorded in the mortgage records for the parish in which the immovable is situated, any public entity or agent of such entity may conclusively presume that a co-owner in possession of the immovable for more than one year has been appointed by all co-owners to manage, administer, repair, reconstruct, and restore the immovable, and to receive, disburse and account for funds given to him by the public entity solely for the purposes of such repair, reconstruction, and restoration.

C. The power of the managing co-owner shall include the power to execute mortgages to secure funds not exceeding the amount necessary to repair, reconstruct, and restore the immovable, and also to encumber the immovable with such restrictions as may be required by the public entity, without the need to obtain the concurrence of all co-owners.

D. Possession of the immovable by the managing co-owner shall continue during any period the managing co-owner has been forced to leave the immovable due to fire, hurricane, flood, or other disaster or catastrophe.

E. The management of the immovable by the co-owner shall be subject to the laws of negotiorum gestio and mandate applicable to co-owners. However, the provisions of this Article shall control to the extent of any conflict.

F. It is the intent of the legislature that the provisions of this Article be liberally construed to allow the maximum possible repair, reconstruction, and restoration of immovable property in this state, subject to a small succession proceeding, that has been damaged by disaster or catastrophe.

G. Repealed by Acts 2012, No. 618, § 2, eff. June 7, 2012.

Added by Acts 2011, No. 323, § 1, eff. June 29, 2011.

CHAPTER 2. WHEN JUDICIAL PROCEEDINGS UNNECESSARY

Article

Art. 3431. Small successions; judicial opening unnecessary

A. It shall not be necessary to open judicially the small succession of a person domiciled in Louisiana who died intestate or testate as provided by Article 3421(B), or domiciled outside of Louisiana who died intestate or whose testament has been probated by court order of another state, and whose sole heirs are the following:

(1) His descendants.

(2) His ascendants.

(3) His brothers or sisters, or descendants thereof.

(4) His surviving spouse.

(5) His legatees under a testament.

B. Any person appointed as public administrator by the governor may use the affidavit procedure of this Chapter to take possession of the estate of the deceased for transmittal to the state provided there is no surviving spouse or other heir present or represented in the state, and provided he has advertised one time in the official journal of the parish where a succession would have been opened under Article 2811, and verifies that he has received no notice of opposition.

C. The legal notice required in Paragraph B of this Article shall read as follows:

"Notice is hereby given to any heirs or creditors of ________ that ________, Public Administrator for the parish of ____________, intends to administer the intestate succession of ______________, under the provisions of Small Successions as set forth in Chapter 2 of Title V of Book VI of the Code of Civil Procedure.

Anyone having an objection to such administration of the succession should notify ____________ at ____________."

D. Repealed by Acts 2011, No. 323, § 2, eff. June 29, 2011.

Amended by Acts 1984, No. 623, § 1, eff. July 12, 1984; Acts 1990, No. 701, § 1; Acts 1995, No. 111, § 1; Acts 2006, No. 257, § 1, eff. June 8, 2006; Acts 2009, No. 81, § 1, eff. June 18, 2009; Acts 2011, No. 323, § 1, eff. June 29, 2011; Acts 2012, No. 618, § 1, eff. June 7, 2012; Acts 2020, No. 173, § 1.

Art. 3432. Affidavit for small succession; contents

A. When it is not necessary under the provisions of Article 3431 to open judicially a small succession, at least two persons, including the surviving spouse, if any, and one or more competent major heirs of the deceased, may execute one or more multiple originals of an affidavit, duly sworn before any officer or person authorized to administer oaths in the place where the affidavit is executed, setting forth:

(1) The date of death of the deceased, and his domicile at the time thereof;

(2) The fact that the deceased died intestate;

(3) The marital status of the deceased, the location of the last residence of the deceased, and the name of the surviving spouse, if any, and the surviving spouse's address, domicile, and location of last residence;

(4) The names and last known addresses of the heirs of the deceased, their relationship to the deceased, and the statement that an heir not signing the affidavit (a) cannot be located after the exercise of reasonable diligence, or (b) was given ten days notice by U.S. mail of the affiants' intent to execute an affidavit for small succession and did not object;

(5) A description of the property left by the deceased, including whether the property is community or separate, and which in the case of immovable property must be sufficient to identify the property for purposes of transfer;

(6) A showing of the value of each item of property, and the aggregate value of all such property, at the time of the death of the deceased;

(7) A statement describing the respective interests in the property which each heir has inherited and whether a legal usufruct of the surviving spouse attaches to the property;

(8) An affirmation that, by signing the affidavit, the affiant, if an heir, has accepted the succession of the deceased; and

(9) An affirmation that, by signing the affidavit, the affiants swear under penalty of perjury that the information contained in the affidavit is true, correct and complete to the best of their knowledge, information, and belief.

B. If the deceased had no surviving spouse, the affidavit must be signed by at least two heirs. If the deceased had no surviving spouse and only one heir, the affidavit must also be signed by a second person who has actual knowledge of the matters stated therein.

C. In addition to the powers of a natural tutor otherwise provided by law, a natural tutor may also execute the affidavit on behalf of a minor child without the necessity of filing a petition pursuant to Article 4061.

Amended by Acts 1974, No. 524, § 1; Acts 2009, No. 81, § 1, eff. June 18, 2009; Acts 2011, No. 323, § 1, eff. June 29, 2011; Acts 2012, No. 618, § 1, eff. June 7, 2012.

Editor's Notes

Optional procedure for small successions, R.S. 47:2410.

Art. 3432.1. Affidavit for small succession for a person who died testate; contents

A. When it is not necessary under the provisions of Article 3431 to open judicially a small succession, at least two persons, including the surviving spouse, if any, and one or more competent legatees of the deceased, may execute one or more multiple originals of an affidavit, duly sworn before any officer or person authorized to administer oaths in the place where the affidavit is executed, setting forth all of the following:

(1) The date of death of the deceased, and his domicile at the time thereof.

(2) The fact that the deceased died testate.

(3) The marital status of the deceased, the location of the last residence of the deceased, and the name of the surviving spouse, if any, and the surviving spouse's address, domicile, and location of last residence, together with the names and last known addresses of the legal heirs of the deceased, and identifying those of the legal heirs who are also forced heirs of the deceased.

(4) The names and last known addresses of the legatees of the deceased, and the statement that a legatee not signing the affidavit was given ten days notice by U.S. mail of the affiants' intent to execute an affidavit for small succession and did not object.

(5) A description of the property left by the deceased, including whether the property is community or separate, and which, in the case of immovable property, must be sufficient to identify the property for purposes of transfer.

(6) A showing of the value of each item of property subject to the jurisdiction of the courts of Louisiana, and the aggregate value of all such property, at the time of the death of the deceased.

(7) A statement describing the respective interests in the property which each legatee has inherited and whether a legal usufruct of the surviving spouse attaches to the property.

(8) An attachment consisting of certified copies of the testament and, if the testament has been probated by court order of another state, the probate order of the other state.

(9) An affirmation that, by signing the affidavit, the affiant, if a legatee, has accepted the legacy of the deceased.

(10) An affirmation that, by signing the affidavit, the affiants swear under penalty of perjury that the information contained in the affidavit is true, correct, and complete to the best of their knowledge, information, and belief.

B. If the deceased had no surviving spouse, the affidavit must be signed by at least two persons who have actual knowledge of the matters stated therein.

C. In addition to the powers of a natural tutor otherwise provided by law, a natural tutor may also execute the affidavit on behalf of a minor child without the necessity of filing a petition pursuant to Article 4061.

Added by Acts 2012, No. 618, § 1, eff. June 7, 2012. Amended by Acts 2020, No. 173, § 1.

Art. 3433. Repealed by Acts 2009, No. 81, § 2, eff. June 18, 2009

Art. 3434. Endorsed copy of affidavit authority for delivery of property

A. A multiple original of the affidavit authorized by Article 3432 or 3432.1, shall be full and sufficient authority for the payment or delivery of any money or property of the deceased described in the affidavit to the heirs or legatees of the deceased and the surviving spouse in community, if any, in the percentages listed therein, by any federally insured depository institution, financial institution, trust company, warehouseman, or other depositary, or by any person having such property in his possession or under his control. Similarly, a multiple original of an affidavit satisfying the requirements of this Article shall be full and sufficient authority for the transfer to the heirs or legatees of the deceased, and surviving spouse in community, if any, or to their assigns, of any stock or registered bonds in the name of the deceased and described in the affidavit, by any domestic or foreign corporation.

B. The receipt of the persons named in the affidavit as heirs or legatees of the deceased, or surviving spouse in community thereof, constitutes a full release and discharge for the payment of money or delivery of property made under the provisions of this Article. Any creditor, heir, legatee, succession representative, or other person whatsoever shall have no right or cause of action against the person paying the money, or delivering the property, or transferring the stock or bonds, under the provisions of this Article, on account of such payment, delivery, or transfer.

C. (1) A multiple original of the affidavit, to which has been attached a certified copy of the deceased's death certificate, shall be recorded in the conveyance records in the office of the clerk of court in the parish where any immovable property described therein is situated, after at least ninety days have elapsed from the date of the deceased's death.

(2) An affidavit so recorded, or a certified copy thereof, shall be admissible as evidence in any action involving immovable property to which it relates or is affected by the instrument, and shall be prima facie evidence of the facts stated therein, including the relationship to the deceased of the parties recognized as heir, legatee, surviving spouse in community, or usufructuary as the case may be, and of their rights in the immovable property of the deceased.

(3) An action by a person who claims to be a successor of a deceased person, but who has not been recognized as such in an affidavit authorized by Article 3432 or 3432.1, to assert an interest in property formerly owned by the deceased, against a third person who has acquired an interest in the property, or against his successors by onerous title, is prescribed two years from the date of the recording of the affidavit in accordance with this Paragraph.

Amended by Acts 1974, No. 524, § 1; Acts 2009, No. 81, § 1, eff. June 18, 2009; Acts 2011, No. 323, § 1, eff. June 29, 2011; Acts 2021, No. 44, § 2, eff. June 1, 2021.

CHAPTER 3. JUDICIAL PROCEEDINGS

Article

Art. 3441. Acceptance without administration; procedure

Except as otherwise provided by law, all of the rules applicable to the judicial opening of a succession, and its acceptance by the heirs or legatees without an administration, apply to the small succession.

Art. 3442. Administration of successions; procedure

Except as otherwise provided by law, all of the rules applicable to the judicial opening of a succession, its administration, and sending the heirs or legatees into possession on its termination apply to the small succession.

Art. 3443. Sale of succession property; publication of notice of sale

Notice of the public sale of property, movable or immovable, by the succession representative of a small succession shall be published once and only in the parish where the succession is pending, and the property shall be sold not less than ten days nor more than fifteen days after publication.

Notice of the application of the succession representative of a small succession to sell succession property, movable or immovable, at private sale shall be published once and only in the parish where the succession proceeding is pending, and shall state that any opposition to the proposed sale must be filed within ten days of the date of publication.

TITLE VI. PARTITION OF SUCCESSIONS

Art. 3461. Venue; procedure

The petition for the partition of a succession shall be filed in the succession proceeding, as provided in Article 81(2).

In all other respects and except when manifestly inapplicable, the procedure for partitioning a succession is governed by the provisions of Articles 4601 through 4614.

Art. 3462. Partition of succession property

When a succession has been opened judicially, the coheirs and legatees of the deceased cannot petition for a partition of the succession property unless they could at that time be sent into possession of the succession under Articles 3001, 3004, 3006, 3061, 3361, 3362, 3371, 3372, or 3381.

Arts. 3463 to 3500. Reserved for future legislation

BOOK VII

SPECIAL PROCEEDINGS

TITLE I. PROVISIONAL REMEDIES

CHAPTER 1. ATTACHMENT AND SEQUESTRATION

SECTION 1. GENERAL DISPOSITIONS

SECTION 2. ATTACHMENT

SECTION 3. SEQUESTRATION

SECTION 1. GENERAL DISPOSITIONS

Art. 3501. Petition; affidavit; security

A writ of attachment or of sequestration shall issue only when the nature of the claim and the amount thereof, if any, and the grounds relied upon for the issuance of the writ clearly appear from specific facts shown by the petition verified by, or by the separate affidavit of, the petitioner, his counsel or agent.

The applicant shall furnish security as required by law for the payment of the damages the defendant may sustain when the writ is obtained wrongfully.

Official Revision Comments—1960

(a) The petition for a writ of attachment or of sequestration must contain allegations to support the principal cause of action as well as the provisional remedy. This article retains portions of Arts. 243, 245, and 276 of the Code of Practice, and it makes it clear that either a verified petition or an affidavit setting forth the facts will suffice. Except for the requirements of verification in the absence of an affidavit, the provisions of Book II, Title I are applicable to the petition required by this article.

(b) See Arts. 3544 and 3574, *infra*, for the security which the plaintiff must furnish to secure an attachment, and generally to secure a sequestration, respectively. A sequestration to enforce the lessor's privilege issues without security. Art. 3575, *infra*. The qualifications of the surety and other rules relative to the bond are provided in Arts. 5121 through 5127, *infra*. The provision in Art. 276 of the Code of Practice requiring the bond to be made "in favor of the defendant" has not been included because under Art. 5121, *infra*, all bonds are made in favor of the clerk of court.

(c) The words "as required by law" were added after "security" in order to provide for the two types of sequestration under this Code, namely, sequestration with bond, and sequestration without bond, which takes the place of the former provisional seizure.

Editor's Notes

Sequestration authorized when statute refers to provisional seizure, R.S. 13:3957.

Art. 3502. Issuance of writ before petition filed

A writ of attachment or of sequestration may issue before the petition is filed, if the plaintiff obtains leave of court and furnishes the affidavit and security provided in Article 3501. In such a case the petition shall be filed on the first judicial day after the issuance of the writ of attachment or of sequestration, unless for good cause shown the court grants a longer delay.

Art. 3503. Garnishment under writs of attachment or of sequestration

Except as otherwise provided by law and in the second paragraph of this article, garnishment under a writ of attachment or of sequestration is governed by the rules applicable to garnishment under a writ of fieri facias.

In garnishment under a writ of sequestration the only property that can be seized is property the ownership or possession of which is claimed by the plaintiff or on which he claims a privilege.

Official Revision Comments—1960

(a) Arts. 246 and 250 of the Code of Practice authorize a garnishment in connection with a writ of attachment. There is no provision in the Code of Practice authorizing garnishment in connection with sequestration. See Ozan Lbr. Co. v. Goldonna Lbr. Co., 124 La. 1025, 50 So. 839 (1909). There seems to be no good reason to deny a plaintiff who is seeking a writ of sequestration the privilege of using garnishment interrogatories as an auxiliary remedy to determine whether a third party has property of the defendant in his possession.

(b) Property in the hands of a third person can be seized under a writ of sequestration without the necessity of a garnishment, for sequestration is not limited to property in the physical custody of the defendant, but extends to all property which the defendant can control and dispose of. A. F. Flournoy and Co. v. Milling, 15 La.Ann. 473 (1860); Lannes v. Courege, 31 La.Ann. 74 (1879); Blitz v. Guenin, 187 So. 690 (La.App.1939). This article effects no change in the rule set forth in the cited cases; it merely offers the plaintiff the additional procedural remedy of garnishment. Art. 3571, *infra*, recognizes the possibility of a seizure by sequestration when property is in the physical possession of a third person.

(c) In connection with the limitation contained in the second paragraph of this article, see Art. 3571, *infra*, which permits sequestration only when the plaintiff claims the ownership or the right to the possession of, or a privilege on the property.

Art. 3504. Return of sheriff; inventory

The sheriff, after executing a writ of attachment or of sequestration, shall deliver to the clerk of the court from which the writ issued a written return stating the manner in which he executed the writ. He shall annex to the return an inventory of the property seized.

Art. 3505. Reduction of excessive seizure

If the value of the property seized under a writ of attachment or of sequestration exceeds what is reasonably necessary to satisfy the plaintiff's claim, the defendant by contradictory motion may obtain the release of the excess.

Art. 3506. Dissolution of writ; damages

The defendant by contradictory motion may obtain the dissolution of a writ of attachment or of sequestration, unless the plaintiff proves the grounds upon which the writ was issued. If the writ of attachment or of sequestration is dissolved, the action shall then proceed as if no writ had been issued.

The court may allow damages for the wrongful issuance of a writ of attachment or of sequestration on a motion to dissolve, or on a reconventional demand. Attorney's fees for the services rendered in connection with the dissolution of the writ may be included as an element of damages whether the writ is dissolved on motion or after trial on the merits.

Editor's Notes

The burden of proceeding and the burden of proof for the justification of the writ is on the seizing party, Comment (a) and last clause of the first sentence of the article. Defects in issuance not curable, Hancock Bank v. Alexander, 237 So.2d 669 (1970). Voluntary abandonment of writ renders plaintiff liable for damages, Comment (c) to C.C.P. art. 3544.

Art. 3507. Release of property by defendant; security

A defendant may obtain the release of the property seized under a writ of attachment or of sequestration by furnishing security for the satisfaction of any judgment which may be rendered against him.

Editor's Notes

Release bond, C.C.P. art. 5127. Surety on bond is liable to extent of bond, regardless of type of judgment rendered by court, whether property returned or not, Comment. Non-resident submits to jurisdiction by obtaining release of property, Adams v. Ross Amusement Co., 161 So. 601 (1935), and former C.C.P. art. 7 now repealed. See Notes to art. 3514.

Art. 3507.1. Release of property by plaintiff; security

Property seized under a writ of attachment or of sequestration may be released to the plaintiff upon proof of his ownership and upon furnishing security as required by Article 3508. All costs incurred as a result of the seizure shall be paid by the plaintiff prior to the release of the property. A written agreement to hold the seizing authority harmless for wrongful seizure of property which is not seized to enforce a security interest, mortgage, lien or privilege may be substituted in lieu of security at the discretion of the sheriff.

Added by Acts 1985, No. 593, § 1. Amended by Acts 1989, No. 137, § 18, eff. Sept. 1, 1989.

Editor's Notes

See, also, C.C.P. art. 3576, release of property under sequestration.

Art. 3508. Amount of security for release of attached or sequestered property

The security for the release of property seized under a writ of attachment or of sequestration shall exceed by one-fourth the value of the property as determined by the court, or shall exceed by one-fourth the amount of the claim, whichever is the lesser.

Editor's Notes

Clerk may fix amount, C.C.P. art. 282.

Art. 3509. Release of property by third person

When property seized under a writ of attachment or of sequestration is in the possession of one not a party to the action, he may intervene in the action and, upon prima facie showing that he is the owner, pledgee, or consignee of the property, have the property released by furnishing security in the manner and amount, within the same delay, and with the same effect as a defendant.

Editor's Notes

"Possession" means constructive or actual, Comment (a). Right of third party owner to indemnity bond, R.S. 13:3869 et seq.

Art. 3510. Necessity for judgment and execution

Except as provided in Article 3513, a final judgment must be obtained in an action where a writ of attachment or of sequestration has issued before the property seized can be sold to satisfy the claim.

Editor's Notes

Final judgment, C.C.P. arts. 1841, 2166, 2167; executory judgment, C.C.P. art. 2252.

Art. 3511. Attachment and sequestration; privilege

To the extent not otherwise provided under Chapter 9 of the Louisiana Commercial Laws (R.S. 10:9–101, et seq.), a creditor who seizes property under a writ of attachment or of sequestration acquires a privilege from the time of seizure if judgment is rendered maintaining the attachment or sequestration.

Amended by Acts 1989, No. 137, § 18, eff. Sept. 1, 1989.

Editor's Notes

This article codifies rule of Board of Supervisors v. Hart, 26 So.2d 361 (1946), privilege "relates back" to seizure, Comment.

Art. 3512. Release of plaintiff's security

The security required of the plaintiff for the issuance of a writ of attachment or of sequestration shall be released when judgment is rendered in his favor and is affirmed on appeal or when no appeal has been taken and the delay for appeal has elapsed.

Art. 3513. Sale of perishable property

Perishable property seized under a writ of attachment or of sequestration may be sold as provided in Article 2333. The proceeds of such a sale shall be held by the sheriff subject to the orders of the court.

Nothing contained herein shall be construed to prohibit the release of such property upon furnishing of security.

Art. 3514. Release not to affect right to damages

The release of property upon furnishing security under Articles 3507, 3509, or 3576 shall not preclude a party from asserting the invalidity of the seizure, or impair his right to damages because of a wrongful seizure.

Official Revision Comments—1960

(a) The source provision applies only to releases obtained by third persons. The above article applies to all cases where property is released upon the furnishing of security, whether by the plaintiff, the defendant, or a third person. The scope of this article was broadened to preclude an interpretation that a party waives the right to damages by obtaining the release of seized property or by permitting another person to do so.

(b) This article does not affect the rule that a nonresident who obtains the release of property upon furnishing security submits himself to the jurisdiction of the court and permits a personal judgment to be rendered against him. Adams v. Ross Amusement Co., 182 La. 252, 161 So. 601 (1935). See Art. 7, *supra*, with reference to general appearances.

Editor's Notes

Nonresident submits to jurisdiction by obtaining release of property. Adams v. Ross Amusement Co., 161 So. 601 (1935). Comment. See, also, Forbess v. George Morgan Pontiac Co., 135 So.2d 594 (2d, 1961), seeking attorney's fees for dissolution of attachment was appearance under former C.C.P. art. 7, now repealed. The same result may be obtained under C.C.P. art. 6(3), first clause, as to "submission", and under C.C.P. art. 928, by waiver, unless declinatory exception is filed first, or with the request for release. See Notes to C.C.P. art. 3507.

SECTION 2. ATTACHMENT

Art. 3541. Grounds for attachment

A writ of attachment may be obtained when the defendant:

(1) Has concealed himself to avoid service of citation;

(2) Has granted a security interest under Chapter 9 of the Louisiana Commercial Laws (R.S. 10:9–101, et seq.), or has mortgaged, assigned, or disposed of his property or some part thereof, or is about to do any of these acts, with intent to defraud his creditors or give an unfair preference to one or more of them;

(3) Has converted or is about to convert his property into money or evidences of debt, with intent to place it beyond the reach of his creditors;

(4) Has left the state permanently, or is about to do so before a judgment can be obtained and executed against him; or

(5) Is a nonresident who has no duly appointed agent for service of process within the state.

Amended by Acts 1989, No. 137, § 18, eff. Sept. 1, 1989.

Editor's Notes

A person who retains his Louisiana domicile, though residing elsewhere permanently, is not a "nonresident," Comment (b); *cf.* C.C.P. art. 5251(11) nonresident, and 5251(1), absentee. Minimum contacts may be required, Shaffer v. Heitner, 97 S.Ct. 2569, 433 U.S. 186, 53 L.Ed.2d 683 (1977). Unregistered appointment by nonresident individual or partnership of agent for service is no defense, R.S. 13:3485. Personal service on nonresident does not defeat attachment, Bowers v. Greene, 360 So.2d 639 (3d, 1978).

Art. 3542. Actions in which attachment can issue

A writ of attachment may be obtained in any action for a money judgment, whether against a resident or a nonresident, regardless of the nature, character, or origin of the claim, whether it is for a certain or uncertain amount, and whether it is liquidated or unliquidated.

Official Revision Comments—1960

(a) The provision in Art. 256 of the Code requiring the sheriff to seize as much of the defendant's property as may be equal in value to the amount claimed has been deleted. Art. 3505, *supra*, which gives the defendant the right to obtain the release of any property in excess of what is necessary to protect the plaintiff's claim, is the only effective limitation upon the amount of property subject to seizure.

(b) This article changes the rule that an attachment would not lie in a tort action, Barrow v. McDonald, 12 La.Ann. 110 (1857); Childs v. Wilson, 15 La.Ann. 512 (1860); Hodges & Co. v. Pennsylvania R.R. Co., 171 La. 699, 132 So. 115 (1930), except where the defendant was a nonresident, former R.S. 13:3952 (Act 220 of 1932); Jackson State Bank v. Merchants' Bank, 177 La. 975, 149 So. 539 (1933). See also, Sondheimer Co. v. Richland Lumber Company, 121 La. 786, 46 So. 806 (1908); Christie & Lowe v. Pennsylvania Iron Works Co., 128 La. 208, 54 So. 742 (1911).

(c) This article is thus made applicable to all attachments, no matter what may be the basis for the writ. The defendant is protected by the strict requirements of Art. 3541, *supra*.

Art. 3543. Issuance of a writ of attachment before debt due

A writ of attachment may be obtained before the debt sued upon is due. If the debt is paid when it becomes due, the costs of the seizure shall be paid by the plaintiff.

For Official Comments and Annotated Materials,

Art. 3544. Plaintiff's security

The security required for the issuance of a writ of attachment shall be for the amount of the plaintiff's demand, exclusive of interest and costs. If the writ is obtained on the sole ground that the defendant is a nonresident, the security shall not exceed two hundred fifty dollars, but on proper showing the court may increase the security to any amount not exceeding the amount of the demand.

Editor's Notes

When the plaintiff voluntarily abandons an attachment or sequestration, he is liable for damages for the wrongful issuance of the writ. Under this article, failure to furnish an increased bond when ordered to do so will amount to an abandonment of the attachment so as to make the plaintiff liable for damages.

Art. 3545. Nonresident attachment; venue

An action in which a writ of attachment is sought on the sole ground that the defendant is a nonresident may be brought in any parish where the property to be attached is situated.

SECTION 3. SEQUESTRATION

Art. 3571. Grounds for sequestration

When one claims the ownership or right to possession of property, or a mortgage, security interest, lien, or privilege thereon, he may have the property seized under a writ of sequestration, if it is within the power of the defendant to conceal, dispose of, or waste the property or the revenues therefrom, or remove the property from the parish, during the pendency of the action.

Amended by Acts 1989, No. 137, § 18, eff. Sept. 1, 1989.

Editor's Notes

Lessor's privilege follows goods for 15 days after removal from premises, C.C. art. 2710.

Art. 3572. Sequestration before rent due

A sequestration based upon a lessor's privilege may be obtained before the rent is due, if the lessor has good reason to believe that the lessee will remove the property subject to the lessor's privilege. If the rent is paid when it becomes due, the costs shall be paid by the plaintiff.

Editor's Notes

Caveat: This article requires "good reason" prerequisite to seizure, which is not a requirement under C.C.P. art. 3571.

Art. 3573. Sequestration by court on its own motion

The court on its own motion may order the sequestration of property the ownership of which is in dispute without requiring security when one of the parties does not appear to have a better right to possession than the other.

Editor's Notes

Judicial sequestration, C.C. arts. 2979 to 2981.

Art. 3574. Plaintiff's security

An applicant for a writ of sequestration shall furnish security for an amount determined by the court to be sufficient to protect the defendant against any damage resulting from a wrongful issuance, unless security is dispensed with by law.

Art. 3575. Lessor's privilege

A writ of sequestration to enforce a lessor's privilege shall issue without the furnishing of security.

Editor's Notes

Applicability of exemptions under C.C. art. 2705 and R.S. 13:3881, see Oubre v. Hinchman, 365 So.2d 17 (4th, 1978).

Art. 3576. Release of property under sequestration

If the defendant does not effect the release of property seized under a writ of sequestration, as permitted by Article 3507, within ten days of the seizure, the plaintiff may effect the release thereof by furnishing the security required by Article 3508.

Editor's Notes

Applies only to sequestration, not to attachment, Comment (a). Sureties generally, C.C. art. 3035 et seq., qualification of surety, C.C. art. 3065.

CHAPTER 2. INJUNCTION

Article

Art. 3601. Injunction, grounds for issuance; preliminary injunction; temporary restraining order

A. An injunction shall be issued in cases where irreparable injury, loss, or damage may otherwise result to the applicant, or in other cases specifically provided by law; provided, however, that no court shall have jurisdiction to issue, or cause to be issued, any temporary restraining order, preliminary injunction, or permanent injunction against any state department, board, or agency, or any officer, administrator, or head thereof, or any officer of the state of Louisiana in any suit involving the expenditure of public funds under any statute or law of this state to compel the expenditure of state funds when the director of such department, board, or agency or the governor shall certify that the expenditure of such funds would have the effect of creating a deficit in the funds of said agency or be in violation of the requirements placed upon the expenditure of such funds by the legislature.

B. No court shall issue a temporary restraining order in cases where the issuance shall stay or enjoin the enforcement of a child support order when the Department of Children and Family Social

Services is providing services, except for good cause shown by written reasons made a part of the record.

C. During the pendency of an action for an injunction the court may issue a temporary restraining order, a preliminary injunction, or both, except in cases where prohibited, in accordance with the provisions of this Chapter.

D. Except as otherwise provided by law, an application for injunctive relief shall be by petition.

E. The irreparable injury, loss, or damage enumerated in Paragraph A of this Article may result from the isolation of an individual over the age of eighteen years by any other individual, curator, or mandatary, including but not limited to violations of Civil Code Article 2995 or Code of Civil Procedure Article 4566(J).

Amended by Acts 1969, No. 34, § 2; Acts 2004, No. 765, § 1, eff. July 6, 2004; Acts 2016, No. 110, § 2, eff. May 19, 2016.

Editor's Notes

The action is for an injunction; the temporary restraining order and preliminary injunction are ancillary; the right to the permanent injunction must be proved before a preliminary injunction may issue, Equitable Petroleum v. Cent. Transmission, App. 2 Cir.1983, 431 So.2d 1084. LSA–C.C.P. Form 1771 et seq. enjoining enforcement of criminal statute, LaBauve v. Louisiana Wildlife and Fisheries Comm., 289 So.2d 150 (1974). Irreparable damage must be shown to enjoin violation of C.C. art. 667, Salter v. B. W. S. Corp., Inc., 290 So.2d 821 (1974). Gambling house, R.S. 13:4724; drainage district, R.S. 38:1646; labor dispute, R.S. 23:844; house of prostitution, R.S. 13:4712; unfair trade practices (as to Attorney General), R.S. 51:1407. See, further, the extensive list of injunction statutes in West's LSA General Index.

The action for injunction may be cumulated with the action for damages under C.C.P. art. 461, et seq. See Abadie v. Cassidy, 581 So.2d 657 (La. 1991).

Art. 3602. Preliminary injunction; notice; hearing

A preliminary injunction shall not issue unless notice is given to the adverse party and an opportunity had for a hearing.

An application for a preliminary injunction shall be assigned for hearing not less than two nor more than ten days after service of the notice.

Art. 3603. Temporary restraining order; affidavit or affirmation of irreparable injury and notification efforts

A. A temporary restraining order shall be granted without notice when all of the following occur:

(1) It clearly appears from specific facts shown by a verified petition, by supporting affidavit, or by affirmation as provided in Article 3603.1(C)(3) that immediate and irreparable injury, loss, or damage will result to the applicant before the adverse party or his attorney can be heard in opposition.

(2) The applicant's attorney certifies to the court in writing the efforts which have been made to give the notice or the reasons supporting his claim that notice should not be required.

B. The verification or the affidavit may be made by the plaintiff, or by his counsel, or by his agent.

C. No court shall issue a temporary restraining order in cases where the issuance shall stay or enjoin the enforcement of a child support order when the Department of Children and Family Services is providing services, except for good cause shown by written reasons made a part of the record.

Amended by Acts 1985, No. 204, § 1; Acts 2004, No. 765, § 1, eff. July 6, 2004; Acts 2021, No. 394, § 1.

Comments—1985

(a) This amendment changes the requirement for obtaining a temporary restraining order by adding that the applicant's attorney must show the efforts that have been made to give notice or must show why notice should not be required and further that irreparable injury will result before the adverse party or his attorney can be heard in opposition.

(b) The intent of this change is to reduce the practice of issuing ex parte restraining orders without notice of any kind, and to permit the conduct of some type of adversary proceeding before, rather than after, the issuance of injunctive relief. Cf. Rule 65(b), Federal Rules of Civil Procedure.

(c) This proposal makes no change in the law applicable to injunctive relief in domestic relations cases, as set forth in Art. 3944 and in R.S. 9:306 and 307.

Editor's Notes

Either the verification of the petition or of the affidavit will suffice, Comment. Specific facts must be alleged, Town of Logansport v. Copley, 313 So.2d 901 (2d, 1975).

Art. 3603.1. Governing provisions for issuance of protective orders; grounds; notice; court-appointed counsel

A. Notwithstanding any provision of law to the contrary, and particularly the provisions of Domestic Abuse Assistance, Part II of Chapter 28 of Title 46, Post–Separation Family Violence Relief Act and Injunctions and Incidental Orders, Parts IV and V of Chapter 1 of Code Title V of Title 9, Domestic Abuse Assistance, Chapter 8 of Title XV of the Children's Code, and this Chapter, no temporary restraining order or preliminary injunction prohibiting a spouse or other person from harming or going near or in the proximity of another shall issue, unless the complainant has good and reasonable grounds to fear for his or her safety or that of the children, or the complainant has in the past been the victim of domestic abuse by the other spouse.

B. Any person against whom such an order is issued shall be entitled to a court-appointed attorney if the applicant has likewise been afforded a court-appointed attorney, which right shall also be included in any order or notice.

C. (1) A complainant seeking protection from domestic abuse, dating violence, stalking, or sexual assault shall not be required to prepay or be cast with court costs or costs of service of subpoena for the issuance or dissolution of a temporary restraining order, preliminary or permanent injunction, or protective order, or the dismissal of a petition for such, and the clerk of court shall immediately file and process the order issued regardless of the ability of the plaintiff to pay court costs.

(2) When the complainant is seeking protection from domestic abuse, stalking, or sexual assault, the clerk of court shall make forms available for making application for protective orders, provide clerical assistance to the petitioner when necessary, provide the necessary forms, and provide the services of a notary, where available, for completion of the petition.

(3) When a complainant is seeking a temporary restraining order for protection from domestic abuse, dating violence, stalking, or sexual assault, it is sufficient for the petition to contain a written

affirmation signed and dated by the complainant that the facts and circumstances contained in the complaint are true and correct to the best knowledge, information, and belief of the complainant under penalty of perjury pursuant to R.S. 14:123. The affirmation shall be made before a witness who shall sign and print his name.

Added by Acts 1997, No. 1156, § 2. Amended by Acts 1999, No. 1200, § 4; Acts 2001, No. 430, § 1; Acts 2003, No. 750, § 1; Acts 2004, No. 502, § 1; Acts 2014, No. 355, § 1; Acts 2021, No. 394, § 1.

Editor's Notes

Enacted by 1997 legislation [Acts 1997, No. 1156] as part of a revision of the Children's Code as to domestic violence. See, generally, Ch.C. arts. 617, 618, 627, and 1565 to 1570.1, C.Cr.P. arts. 891 and 871.1, C.C.P. arts. 891 and 3607.1, R.S. 9:362 and 9:372, R.S. 13:4243 and 13:4248, R.S. 14:79, R.S. 46:2121.1, 46:2123 to 46:2124.1, and 46:2132 to 46:2138, all also affected by Act 1156.

The 1999 amendment, Act 1200, substituted "court-appointed attorney" for "counsel at no cost" in par. B. See the related amendments to R.S. 14:79(A)(1), R.S. 46:2132(4), 46:2135(A) and (B), 46:2136(F) and 46:2137(A), Ch.C. arts. 1569(B) and 1571(B); and enactment of Ch.C. art. 1570(1) and repeal of Ch.C. art. 1569(G).

Art. 3604. Form, contents, and duration of restraining order

A. A temporary restraining order shall be endorsed with the date and hour of issuance; shall be filed in the clerk's office and entered of record; shall state why the order was granted without notice and hearing; and shall expire by its terms within such time after entry, not to exceed ten days, as the court prescribes. A restraining order, for good cause shown, and at any time before its expiration, may be extended by the court for one or more periods not exceeding ten days each. The party against whom the order is directed may consent that it be extended for a longer period. The reasons for each extension shall be entered of record.

B. Nevertheless, in a suit for divorce, a temporary restraining order issued in conjunction with a rule to show cause for a preliminary injunction shall remain in force until a hearing is held on the rule for the preliminary injunction prohibiting a spouse from:

(1) Disposing of or encumbering community property;

(2) Harming the other spouse or a child; or

(3) Removing a child from the jurisdiction of the court.

C. (1) A temporary restraining order issued in conjunction with a rule to show cause for a protective order filed in an action pursuant to the Protection from Family Violence Act, R.S. 46:2121 et seq., and pursuant to the Protection From Dating Violence Act, R.S. 46:2151, shall remain in force until a hearing is held on the rule for the protective order or for thirty days, whichever occurs first. If the initial rule to show cause is heard by a hearing officer, the temporary restraining order shall remain in force for fifteen days after the hearing or until the judge signs the protective order, whichever occurs last. At any time before the expiration of a temporary restraining order issued pursuant to this Paragraph, it may be extended by the court for a period not exceeding thirty days.

(2) In the event that the hearing on the rule for the protective order is continued by the court because of a declared state of emergency made in accordance with R.S. 29:724, any temporary restraining order issued in the matter shall remain in force for five days after the date of conclusion of the state of emergency. When a temporary restraining order remains in force under this Paragraph, the court shall reassign the rule for a protective order for hearing at the earliest possible time, but no later than five days after the date of conclusion of the state of emergency. The reassignment of the rule shall take precedence over all matters except older matters of the same character.

D. To be effective against a federally insured financial institution, a temporary restraining order or preliminary injunction issued in accordance with Subparagraph (B)(1) of this Article shall be served in accordance with the provisions of R.S. 6:285(C). A temporary restraining order or preliminary injunction granted pursuant to the provisions of this Article shall be effective only against accounts, safe deposit boxes, or other assets listed or held in the name of the following:

(1) One or both of the spouses named in the injunction.

(2) Another party or business entity specifically named in the injunction.

E. A federally insured financial institution shall not be liable for loss or damages resulting from its actions to comply with a temporary restraining order or preliminary injunction provided that the requirements of this Article have been met.

Amended by Acts 1982, No. 770, § 1; Acts 1983, No. 651, § 1; Acts 1990, No. 361, § 1, eff. Jan. 1, 1991; Acts 1999, No. 1336, § 2; Acts 2003, No. 750, § 1; Acts 2012, No. 582, § 2; Acts 2014, No. 618, § 1.

Editor's Notes

The 1999 amendment to par. C makes provision for a TRO issued by a hearing officer to remain in effect until the district judge signs the protective order. See also R.S. 46:2135(I) enacted by same Act, No. 1336, authorizing a hearing officer to conduct initial rule to show cause hearing.

Art. 3605. Content and scope of injunction or restraining order

An order granting either a preliminary or a final injunction or a temporary restraining order shall describe in reasonable detail, and not by mere reference to the petition or other documents, the act or acts sought to be restrained. The order shall be effective against the parties restrained, their officers, agents, employees, and counsel, and those persons in active concert or participation with them, from the time they receive actual knowledge of the order by personal service or otherwise.

Art. 3606. Temporary restraining order; hearing on preliminary injunction

A. When a temporary restraining order is granted, the application for a preliminary injunction shall be assigned for hearing at the earliest possible time, subject to Article 3602, and shall take precedence over all matters except older matters of the same character. The party who obtains a temporary restraining order shall proceed with the application for a preliminary injunction when it comes on for hearing. Upon his failure to do so, the court shall dissolve the temporary restraining order.

B. In the event that the hearing on the issuance of a preliminary injunction is continued by the court because of a declared state of emergency made in accordance with R.S. 29:724, any temporary restraining order issued in the matter shall remain in force for five days after the conclusion of the state of emergency. When a temporary restraining order remains in force under this Paragraph, the court shall reassign the application for a preliminary injunction for hearing at the earliest possible time, but no later than five days after the conclusion of the state of emergency. The reassignment of the application shall take precedence over all matters except older matters of the same character.

Amended by Acts 2014, No. 618, § 1.

Editor's Notes

Louisiana jurisprudence recognizes the difference between a prohibitory injunction and a mandatory injunction. A prohibitory injunction prevents a party from taking an action. A party requesting a prohibitory injunction may be entitled to a temporary restraining order and preliminary injunction in order to preserve the status quo pending a trial on the merits. See e.g., Concerned Citizens for Proper

Planning, LLC v. Par. of Tangipahoa, 2004-0270 (La. App. 1 Cir. 3/24/05), 906 So.2d 660, 664. The mandatory injunction commands the doing of some action. Therefore, neither a temporary restraining order nor a preliminary injunction upon the showing of a prima facie case are available in a mandatory injunction proceeding. A mandatory injunction is only available "after a full evidentiary hearing where the standard of proof is by a preponderance of the evidence." See e.g., Denta-Max v. Maxicare Louisiana, Inc., 95-2128 (La. App. 4 Cir. 3/14/96), 671 So.2d 995, 997; Saer v. New Orleans Reg'l Physician Hosp. Org., 2014-856 (La. App. 5 Cir. 3/25/15), 169 So.3d 617, 620.

Art. 3607. Dissolution or modification of temporary restraining order or preliminary injunction

An interested person may move for the dissolution or modification of a temporary restraining order or preliminary injunction, upon two days' notice to the adverse party, or such shorter notice as the court may prescribe. The court shall proceed to hear and determine the motion as expeditiously as the ends of justice may require.

The court, on its own motion and upon notice to all parties and after hearing, may dissolve or modify a temporary restraining order or preliminary injunction.

Art. 3607.1. Registry of temporary restraining order, preliminary injunction, or permanent injunction

A. Immediately upon rendering a decision granting the petitioner a temporary restraining order or a preliminary or permanent injunction prohibiting a person from harming a family or household member or dating partner, or directing a person accused of stalking to refrain from abusing, harassing, or interfering with the victim of the stalking when the parties are strangers or acquaintances, the judge shall cause to have prepared a Uniform Abuse Prevention Order, as provided in R.S. 46:2136.2(C), shall sign such order, and shall immediately forward it to the clerk of court for filing on the day that the order is issued.

B. When a temporary restraining order, preliminary injunction, or permanent injunction relative to domestic abuse or dating violence, or relative to stalking as provided for in Paragraph A of this Article, is issued, dissolved, or modified, the clerk of court shall transmit the Uniform Abuse Prevention Order to the Judicial Administrator's Office, Louisiana Supreme Court, for entry into the Louisiana Protective Order Registry, as provided in R.S. 46:2136.2(A), by facsimile transmission or direct electronic input as expeditiously as possible, but no later than the end of the next business day after the order is filed with the clerk of court. The clerk of the issuing court shall also send a copy of the Uniform Abuse Prevention Order, as provided in R.S. 46:2136.2(C), or any modification thereof, to the chief law enforcement officer of the parish where the person or persons protected by the order reside by facsimile transmission or direct electronic input as expeditiously as possible, but no later than the end of the next business day after the order is filed with the clerk of court. A copy of the Uniform Abuse Prevention Order shall be retained on file in the office of the chief law enforcement officer until otherwise directed by the court.

Added by Acts 1997, No. 1156, § 2. Amended by Acts 2003, No. 750, § 1; Acts 2014, No. 317, § 5; Acts 2014, No. 355, § 1.

Editor's Notes

Enacted by 1997 legislation [Acts 1997, No. 1156] as part of a revision of the Children's Code as to domestic violence. See notes to C.C.P. art. 3603.1.

Art. 3608. Damages for wrongful issuance of temporary restraining order or preliminary injunction

The court may allow damages for the wrongful issuance of a temporary restraining order or preliminary injunction on a motion to dissolve or on a reconventional demand. Attorney's fees for the services rendered in connection with the dissolution of a restraining order or preliminary injunction may be included as an element of damages whether the restraining order or preliminary injunction is dissolved on motion or after trial on the merits.

Art. 3609. Proof at hearings; affidavits

The court may hear an application for a preliminary injunction or for the dissolution or modification of a temporary restraining order or a preliminary injunction upon the verified pleadings or supporting affidavits, or may take proof as in ordinary cases. If the application is to be heard upon affidavits, the court shall so order in writing, and a copy of the order shall be served upon the defendant at the time the notice of hearing is served.

At least twenty-four hours before the hearing, or such shorter time as the court may order, the applicant shall deliver copies of his supporting affidavits to the adverse party, who shall deliver to the applicant prior to the hearing copies of affidavits intended to be used by such adverse party. The court, in its discretion, and upon such conditions as it may prescribe, may permit additional affidavits to be filed at or after the hearing, and may further regulate the proceeding as justice may require.

Art. 3610. Security for temporary restraining order or preliminary injunction

A temporary restraining order or preliminary injunction shall not issue unless the applicant furnishes security in the amount fixed by the court, except where security is dispensed with by law. The security shall indemnify the person wrongfully restrained or enjoined for the payment of costs incurred and damages sustained. However, no security is required when the applicant for a temporary restraining order or preliminary or permanent injunction is seeking protection from domestic abuse, dating violence, stalking, or sexual assault.

Amended by Acts 2003, No. 750, § 1.

Editor's Notes

No bond is required for a permanent injunction, Comment (c).

Art. 3611. Penalty for disobedience; damages

Disobedience of or resistance to a temporary restraining order or preliminary or final injunction is punishable as a contempt of court. The court may cause to be undone or destroyed whatever may be done in violation of an injunction, and the person aggrieved thereby may recover the damages sustained as a result of the violation.

Art. 3612. Appeals

A. There shall be no appeal from an order relating to a temporary restraining order.

B. An appeal may be taken as a matter of right from an order or judgment relating to a preliminary or final injunction, but such an order or judgment shall not be suspended during the pendency of an appeal unless the court in its discretion so orders.

C. An appeal from an order or judgment relating to a preliminary injunction must be taken, and any bond required must be furnished, within fifteen days from the date of the order or judgment. The court in its discretion may stay further proceedings until the appeal has been decided.

For Official Comments and Annotated Materials,

D. Except as provided in this Article, the procedure for an appeal from an order or judgment relating to a preliminary or final injunction shall be as provided in Book III.

Amended by Acts 2001, No. 512, § 1.

Official Revision Comments—1960

(a) The principal change effected by this article is that a suspensive appeal from a judgment granting a final injunction is made discretionary with the court. Heretofore, the trial court which granted a permanent injunction was compelled to allow a suspensive appeal even though the appeal had the effect of nullifying the judgment. Bujol v. Missouri Pac. R. Co., 207 La. 123, 20 So.2d 608 (1944); Borgnemouth Realty Co. v. Gulf Soap Corp., 211 La. 255, 29 So.2d 841 (1947).

(b) The third paragraph of the above article is limited to preliminary injunctions, and follows former R.S. 13:4070, except that the delay has been extended to fifteen days to coincide with the delay for suspensive appeals. *Cf.* Art. 2123, *supra.* The time for appeals from final injunctions is not affected.

(c) Under the last paragraph of this article, except where specific portions differ from the general procedure for appeals, the general rules are applicable.

(d) *Cf.* Arts. 194, 195, and 196, *supra*, which authorize hearings on the subjects covered by the above article in term time or in vacation, and in open court and in chambers.

(e) See Comments under Arts. 2083, 2087, 2123, 2124, 3611.

Comment—2001

The purpose of the 2001 amendment is to make the Article clear, as interpreted in Killeen v. Jenkins, 752 So.2d 146 (La. 1999), that a bond is not mandatory in all appeals of a preliminary injunction, such as when the proceeding is not stayed pending the appeal.

Editor's Notes

Appeal delays from preliminary and permanent injunctions, Brickman v. Bd. of Directors of West Jefferson General Hosp., 363 So.2d 86 (4th, 1978).

Art. 3613. Jurisdiction not limited

The provisions of this Chapter do not limit the issuance by a court of any writ, process, or order in aid of its jurisdiction.

Editor's Notes

Const. Art. 5, § 2.

TITLE II. REAL ACTIONS

CHAPTER 1. ACTIONS TO DETERMINE OWNERSHIP OR POSSESSION

Article

Art. 3651. Petitory action

The petitory action is one brought by a person who claims the ownership, but who is not in possession, of immovable property or of a real right therein, against another who is in possession or who claims the ownership thereof adversely, to obtain judgment recognizing the plaintiff's ownership.

Amended by Acts 1981, No. 256, § 1.

Editor's Notes

LSA–C.C.P. Form 1801 et seq. For general authorities, see Yiannopoulos, § 134; Pure Oil Co. v. Skinner, 294 So.2d 797 (1974); C.C. arts. 530 to 532, proof of ownership of immovables; see, also, Clayton v. Langston, App. 3 Cir.1975, 311 So.2d 74, ownership decreed though not prayed for; 30 year prescription as peremptory exception of prescription to petitory action, Montgomery v. Breaux, 297 So.2d 185 (1974).

Art. 3652. Same; parties; venue

A. A petitory action may be brought by a person who claims the ownership of only an undivided interest in the immovable property or real right therein, or whose asserted ownership is limited to a certain period which has not yet expired, or which may be terminated by an event which has not yet occurred.

B. A lessee or other person who occupies the immovable property or enjoys the real right therein under an agreement with the person who claims the ownership thereof adversely to the plaintiff may be joined in the action as a defendant.

C. A petitory action shall be brought in the venue provided by Article 80(A)(1), even when the plaintiff prays for judgment for the fruits and revenues of the property, or for damages.

Amended by Acts 1981, No. 256, § 1; Acts 2010, No. 185, § 1.

Art. 3653. Same; proof of title; immovable

To obtain a judgment recognizing his ownership of immovable property or real right therein, the plaintiff in a petitory action shall:

(1) Prove that he has acquired ownership from a previous owner or by acquisitive prescription, if the court finds that the defendant is in possession thereof; or

(2) Prove a better title thereto than the defendant, if the court finds that the latter is not in possession thereof.

When the titles of the parties are traced to a common author, he is presumed to be the previous owner.

Amended by Acts 1981, No. 256, § 1.

Editor's Notes

Pure Oil Co. v. Skinner, *supra;* particularly, comment to C.C. art. 531.

Art. 3654. Proof of title in action for declaratory judgment, concursus, expropriation, or similar proceeding

When the issue of ownership of immovable property or of a real right therein is presented in an action for a declaratory judgment, or in a concursus, expropriation, or similar proceeding, or the issue of the ownership of funds deposited in the registry of the court and which belong to the owner of the immovable property or of the real right therein is so presented, the court shall render judgment in favor of the party:

(1) Who would be entitled to the possession of the immovable property or real right therein in a possessory action, unless the adverse party proves that he has acquired ownership from a previous owner or by acquisitive prescription; or

(2) Who proves better title to the immovable property or real right therein, when neither party would be entitled to the possession of the immovable property or real right therein in a possessory action.

Amended by Acts 1981, No. 256, § 1.

Official Revision Comments—1960 and 1981

(a) This article adopts, implements, and broadens the suggestion made in Zengel, The Real Actions—A Study in Code Revision, 29 Tul.L.Rev. 617, 631 (1955).

(b) As a practical matter, many issues of ownership are involved and adjudicated in concursus proceedings, where oil companies which have mineral leases from adverse claimants of ownership deposit royalties into the registry of the court and implead the adverse claimants. Rules which give effect to the historic role of possession in determining the burden of proof of ownership are needed in these cases.

This article does not constitute legislative approval of California Company v. Price, 234 La. 338, 99 So.2d 743 (1957) on the issue of res judicata, which many members of the legal profession in this state regard as erroneous. As a practical matter, this article would be needed even should the Price case be overruled. It is urgently needed as long as this decision is followed.

(c) In numerous cases, the action for a declaratory judgment has been used to adjudicate the ownership of land and mineral rights. See Horn v. Skelly Oil Co., 221 La. 626, 60 So.2d 65 (1952); Arkansas Louisiana Gas Co. v. Thompson, 222 La. 868, 64 So.2d 202 (1953); Horn v. Skelly Oil Co., 224 La. 709, 70 So.2d 657 (1954); Bierhorst v. Kelly, 225 La. 934, 74 So.2d 168 (1954); Calhoun v. Gulf Refining Company, 104 So.2d 547 (La.1958); Levenson v. Chancellor, 68 So.2d 116 (La.App.1953); Hastings v. McDowell, 75 So.2d 383 (La.App.1954). Since the broad dictum in Burton v. Lester, 227 La. 347, 79 So.2d 333 (1955) has been overruled legislatively in Art. 1871, *supra*, these actions will be used much more frequently for such purposes, and rules to give effect to the role of possession therein are needed.

(d) Much the same problems may be presented in expropriation suits and similar proceedings where adverse claimants of ownership are asserting conflicting claims to the compensation to be paid for the taking of immovable property. These rules are likewise made applicable to such cases.

(e) The possession required of a plaintiff in a possessory action was adopted here as the arbiter of burden of proof to prevent one of the parties from taking possession of the immovable property briefly prior to rendition of judgment, or from dispossessing the rightful possessor, so as to obtain the benefit of the rules as to burden of proof.

(f) See Comment (c) under Art. 3651, *supra*, and the Comment under Art. 3653, *supra*.

Editor's Notes

"The possession required of a plaintiff in a possessory action was adopted here as the arbiter of burden of proof to prevent one of the parties from taking possession of the immovable property briefly prior to rendition of judgment, or from dispossessing the rightful possessor, so as to obtain the benefit of the rules as to burden of proof." Comment.

Art. 3655. Possessory action

The possessory action is one brought by the possessor of immovable property or of a real right therein to be maintained in his possession of the property or enjoyment of the right when he has been disturbed, or to be restored to the possession or enjoyment thereof when he has been evicted.

Amended by Acts 1981, No. 256, § 1.

Editor's Notes

LSA–C.C.P. Form 1824 et seq. For general authority, see Liner v. Louisiana Land and Exploration Company, 319 So.2d 766 (1975), and Yiannopoulos, Vol. 2, § 138.

Art. 3656. Same; parties; venue

A. A plaintiff in a possessory action shall be one who possesses for himself. A person entitled to the use or usufruct of immovable property, and one who owns a real right therein, possesses for himself. A predial lessee possesses for and in the name of his lessor, and not for himself.

B. The possessory action shall be brought against the person who caused the disturbance, and in the venue provided by Article 80(A)(1), even when the plaintiff prays for a judgment for the fruits and revenues of the property, or for damages.

Amended by Acts 2010, No. 185, § 1.

Editor's Notes

See C.C. art. 3440.

Art. 3657. Same; cumulation with petitory action prohibited; conversion into or separate petitory action by defendant

The plaintiff may not cumulate the petitory and the possessory actions in the same suit or plead them in the alternative, and when he does so he waives the possessory action. If the plaintiff brings the possessory action, and without dismissing it and prior to judgment therein institutes the petitory action, the possessory action is abated.

When, except as provided in Article 3661(1)–(3), the defendant in a possessory action asserts title in himself, in the alternative or otherwise, he thereby converts the suit into a petitory action, and judicially confesses the possession of the plaintiff in the possessory action.

If, before executory judgment in a possessory action, the defendant therein institutes a petitory action in a separate suit against the plaintiff in the possessory action, the plaintiff in the petitory action judicially confesses the possession of the defendant therein.

Official Revision Comments—1960

(a) The rules of this article are intended to keep the trial of the issues of possession and ownership as separate as possible, and to encourage the determination of the issue of possession before the institution of the petitory action.

(b) The first sentence of this article makes no change in the law, but is only a consolidation of its indirect sources.

(c) The second sentence of this article makes a change in the law.

Under the prior law, the penalty for the improper cumulation of the two actions was the judicial confession of the possession of the defendant. This not only worked a waiver of the possessory action when the two were cumulated, but it made it impossible for the plaintiff to dismiss the suit, and then to renew the possessory action alone in the second suit. This is too harsh a penalty when the improper cumulation, or alternative pleading, of the two actions results from a mere inadvertence of counsel.

Under the second sentence of this article, and subject to the provisions of Art. 1671, *supra*, where there is an improper cumulation or alternative pleading of the two actions in the same suit, plaintiff may have this suit dismissed without prejudice, and then renew his possessory action alone in a second suit, without being barred by a judicial confession of the possession of the defendant.

(d) The second paragraph of this article makes the procedural rule heretofore applicable to the former jactitory action, applicable to the broadened possessory action. It not only permits the defendant to convert the suit into a petitory action, but provides that he does so whenever he injects the issue of ownership through his answer.

(e) Under the former jactitory action, the defendant could convert the suit into a petitory action: (1) through his answer, Board of Trustees of Ruston Circuit v. Rudy, 192 La. 200, 187 So. 549 (1939); Barrow v. LeBlanc, 35 So.2d 469 (La.App.1948); or (2) through a reconventional demand, Carmody v. Land, 207 La. 625, 21 So.2d 764 (1945); or (3) through a supplemental answer filed after judgment ordering the defendant to institute the petitory action, Sherburne v. Iberville Land Co., 192 La. 1091, 190 So. 227 (1939). It is intended that the word "answer" in the second paragraph of this article includes all three of these methods of converting the suit into a petitory action.

(f) The last paragraph of this article prevents a defendant in a possessory action from defeating the efforts of the plaintiff in the possessory action to have the issue of his possession adjudicated therein, or from relitigating the issue in a petitory action filed in a separate suit, and in which he would allege that the defendant was not in possession.

(g) The provisions of the former R.S. 13:5063 and 13:5064 would have been unnecessary and unworkable under the new procedure, and have been repealed.

Editor's Notes

Possession by other not judicially confessed unless title asserted, Haas Land Co. v. O'Quin, 187 So.2d 208, (3d 1966); see, also, Causeway Land Co., Inc. v. Karno, 317 So.2d 661 (4th 1975).

McCurley v. Burton, 879 So.2d 186 (La. App. 1 Cir. 2004). Owners of dominant estate sought possessory action and injunction against owners of servient estate to prevent their putting a gate across access road based upon servitude of passage. Dominant owners demonstrated that there was no servitude of passage. Servient owners reconvened to assert ownership thereby confessing owners' possession and converting dominant owners' possessory action to a petitory action. C.C.P. art. 3657.

Art. 3658. Same; requisites

To maintain the possessory action the possessor must allege and prove that:

(1) He had possession of the immovable property or real right therein at the time the disturbance occurred;

(2) He and his ancestors in title had such possession quietly and without interruption for more than a year immediately prior to the disturbance, unless evicted by force or fraud;

(3) The disturbance was one in fact or in law, as defined in Article 3659; and

(4) The possessory action was instituted within a year of the disturbance.

Amended by Acts 1981, No. 256, § 1.

Editor's Notes

Requisite character of possession and of disturbance, Liner v. Louisiana Land and Exploration Company, *supra,* C.C.P. art. 3655.

Art. 3659. Same; disturbance in fact and in law defined

Disturbances of possession which give rise to the possessory action are of two kinds: disturbance in fact and disturbance in law.

A disturbance in fact is an eviction, or any other physical act which prevents the possessor of immovable property or of a real right therein from enjoying his possession quietly, or which throws any obstacle in the way of that enjoyment.

A disturbance in law is the execution, recordation, registry, or continuing existence of record of any instrument which asserts or implies a right of ownership or to the possession of immovable property or of a real right therein, or any claim or pretension of ownership or right to the possession thereof except in an action or proceeding, adversely to the possessor of such property or right.

Amended by Acts 1981, No. 256, § 1.

Official Revision Comments—1960 and 1981

(a) The first two paragraphs of this article make no change in the law.

(b) The last paragraph makes an important change in the law which in turn makes it possible to merge the former jactitory action into the broadened possessory action.

The former jactitory action was borrowed from Spanish procedure by the jurisprudence to fill in a hiatus in our prior procedural law. No completely convincing evidence is available to account for this procedural hiatus, but it is not unreasonable to believe that it resulted from the extremely narrow and unrealistic definition of disturbance in law of Art. 52 of the Code of Practice. Under a much broader definition of disturbance in law of French procedure, its possessory action is broad enough to perform the functions of both of our former possessory and jactitory actions. The broadening of this definition in this article makes it possible to broaden the new possessory action so as to perform also the functions of the former jactitory action.

(c) The third paragraph makes another change in the law. Under Art. 52 of the Code of Practice, the institution of the possessory action was a disturbance in law of the defendant's possession, if the latter actually had possession. Under this article, it is not. However, this leaves no hiatus in the new procedure, since the defendant may reconvene and bring the possessory action against the plaintiff, and obtain the same relief as if he had filed a separate possessory action. See Comment (c) under Art. 3662, *infra*. The acts of possession on which the original plaintiff relied to prove his possession would constitute disturbances in fact, and any recorded title to the plaintiff would constitute a disturbance in law, of the original defendant's possession, if the latter actually had possession.

(d) See the Comment under Art. 3655, *supra*.

Art. 3660. Same; possession

A person is in possession of immovable property or of a real right therein, within the intendment of the articles of this Chapter, when he has the corporeal possession thereof, or civil possession thereof preceded by corporeal possession by him or his ancestors in title, and possesses for himself, whether in good or bad faith, or even as a usurper.

Subject to the provisions of Articles 3656 and 3664, a person who claims the ownership of immovable property or of a real right therein possesses through his lessee, through another who occupies the property or enjoys the right under an agreement with him or his lessee, or through a person who has the use or usufruct thereof to which his right of ownership is subject.

Amended by Acts 1981, No. 256, § 1.

Editor's Notes

Possession generally, C.C. art. 3421 et seq.

Art. 3661. Same; title not at issue; limited admissibility of evidence of title

In the possessory action, the ownership or title of the parties to the immovable property or real right therein is not at issue.

No evidence of ownership or title to the immovable property or real right therein shall be admitted except to prove:

(1) The possession thereof by a party as owner;

(2) The extent of the possession thereof by a party; or

(3) The length of time in which a party and his ancestors in title have had possession thereof.

Amended by Acts 1981, No. 256, § 1.

Editor's Notes

But see Clayton v. Langston, *supra,* C.C.P. art. 3651, ownership decreed though not prayed for.

Art. 3662. Same; relief which may be granted successful plaintiff in judgment; appeal

A. A judgment rendered for the plaintiff in a possessory action shall:

(1) Recognize his right to the possession of the immovable property or real right therein, and restore him to possession thereof if he has been evicted, or maintain him in possession thereof if the disturbance has not been an eviction;

(2) Order the defendant to assert his adverse claim of ownership of the immovable property or real right therein in a petitory action to be filed within a delay to be fixed by the court not to exceed sixty days after the date the judgment becomes executory, or be precluded thereafter from asserting the ownership thereof, if the plaintiff has prayed for such relief; and

(3) Award him the damages to which he is entitled and which he has prayed for.

B. A suspensive appeal from the judgment rendered in a possessory action may be taken within the delay provided in Article 2123, and a devolutive appeal may be taken from such judgment only within thirty days of the applicable date provided in Article 2087 (A).

Amended by Acts 1981, No. 256, § 1; Acts 2010, No. 185, § 1.

Editor's Notes

Taking possession generally, C.C. arts. 3421 to 3423; presumption as to common author, C.C. art. 532.

Art. 3663. Sequestration; injunctive relief

Sequestration of immovable property or of a real right therein involved in a possessory or petitory action during the pendency thereof is available under the applicable provisions of Chapter 1 of Title I of Book VII.

Injunctive relief, under the applicable provisions of Chapter 2 of Title I of Book VII, to protect or restore possession of immovable property or of a real right therein, is available to:

(1) A plaintiff in a possessory action, during the pendency thereof; and

(2) A person who is disturbed in the possession which he and his ancestors in title have had for more than a year of immovable property or of a real right therein of which he claims the ownership, the possession, or the enjoyment.

Amended by Acts 1981, No. 256, § 1.

Art. 3664. Mineral rights asserted, protected and defended as other immovables

The owner of a mineral right may assert, protect, and defend his right in the same manner as the ownership or possession of other immovable property, and without the concurrence, joinder, or consent of the owner of the land or mineral rights.

Amended by Acts 1974, No. 547, § 1, eff. Jan. 1, 1975.

Editor's Notes

Possession of mineral rights, Mineral Code Arts. 153 to 158 (R.S. 31:153 to R.S. 31:158).

Art. 3665. When mineral right owner may assert possessory action

If the owner of a mineral right possesses his right by use or exercise according to its nature, he becomes entitled one year and a day from the date of commencement of his possession to assert the possessory action. Thereafter, if there has been no adverse possession sufficient to include mineral rights, his right to assert the possessory action continues for one year from the date on which his right to bring the action matured or from the last day on which he was in possession of his right by use or exercise thereof, whichever is later.

Added by Acts 1974, No. 547, § 2, eff. Jan. 1, 1975.

Art. 3666. Loss of right to bring possessory action by owner of mineral right

If after the owner of a mineral right has ceased possessing it by use or exercise according to its nature there is adverse possession of the land including the mineral right, the adverse possessor becomes entitled to bring the possessory action when he has been in possession quietly and without interruption for more than one year after his possession began or was resumed.

Added by Acts 1974, No. 547, § 2, eff. Jan. 1, 1975.

Art. 3667. When proof of nonuse required in possessory action against owner of mineral right

In a possessory action against the owner of a mineral right subject to the prescription of nonuse, one possessing land as owner under a title which on its face discloses the mineral right in question must allege and prove that he has possessed the surface of the land as owner quietly and without interruption for more than one year prior to the date the action is brought and that for a period of at least ten years before the year preceding the date on which the action is brought the mineral right was not used or exercised according to its nature. The fact that prescription accruing against the mineral right in question may have been suspended or may have been interrupted for some cause other than use is irrelevant to the possessory action and can be utilized by the defendant only as a basis for claiming ownership of the disputed rights in a petitory action.

Added by Acts 1974, No. 547, § 2, eff. Jan. 1, 1975.

Art. 3668. When proof of nonuse not required in possessory action against claimant of mineral right

In all cases other than those specified in Article 3667, one possessing land as owner need only allege and prove his quiet, uninterrupted possession for more than a year prior to assertion of a possessory action against one claiming a mineral right in the land.

Added by Acts 1974, No. 547, § 2, eff. Jan. 1, 1975.

Art. 3669. Possessory action unavailable between owner of mineral servitude and owner of dependent mineral royalty

In the event of a dispute between the owner of a mineral servitude and the owner of a mineral royalty burdening or alleged to burden the servitude in question, the possessory action is unavailable to either party, and the only available real action is the petitory action. The burden of proof on the plaintiff in such an action is that which must be borne by the plaintiff in a petitory action when neither party is in possession.

Added by Acts 1974, No. 547, § 2, eff. Jan. 1, 1975.

Art. 3670. Real actions against mineral lessee unavailable to mineral lessor or possessor bound by lease

One who has granted a mineral lease, or who possesses under a title subject to a mineral lease, whether or not the lease is disclosed by his act of acquisition, cannot assert the real actions against the lessee on account of the termination of the lease by running of the term or occurrence of an express resolutory condition.

Added by Acts 1974, No. 547, § 2, eff. Jan. 1, 1975.

Art. 3671. Real actions involving mineral rights subject to other provisions governing real actions generally

Real actions involving mineral rights are subject to all of the rules established for other real actions by Articles 3651 through 3653 except to the extent that those articles are inconsistent with the express or implied terms of Articles 3664 through 3670.

Added by Acts 1974, No. 547, § 2, eff. Jan. 1, 1975.

CHAPTER 2. BOUNDARY ACTION

Article

Art. 3691. Boundary action

An action to fix the boundary is an ordinary proceeding.

Amended by Acts 1977, No. 169, § 2, eff. Jan. 1, 1978.

Editor's Notes

See Civil Code articles 784-796. The right to compel the fixing of the boundary between contiguous lands is imprescriptible. Civil Code art. 788.

Art. 3692. Appointment of surveyor by court; duties of surveyor

The court may appoint a surveyor to inspect the lands and to make plans in accordance with the prevailing standards and practices of his profession indicating the respective contentions of the parties.

Amended by Acts 1977, No. 169, § 2, eff. Jan. 1, 1978.

Art. 3693. Evidence; judgment

After considering the evidence, including the testimony and exhibits of a surveyor or other expert appointed by the court or by a party, the court shall render judgment fixing the boundary between the contiguous lands in accordance with the ownership or possession of the parties.

Amended by Acts 1977, No. 169, § 2, eff. Jan. 1, 1978.

Editor's Notes

See Civil Code articles 792-796. When both parties rely on titles only. The boundary shall be fixed according to titles. When the parties trace their titles to a common author, preference shall be given to the more ancient title.

CHAPTER 3. HYPOTHECARY ACTION

SECTION 1. GENERAL DISPOSITIONS

SECTION 1. GENERAL DISPOSITIONS

Art. 3721. Methods of enforcing mortgage

A conventional mortgage is enforced by ordinary or executory proceedings.

Editor's Notes

LSA–C.C.P. Form 1861.

Art. 3722. Enforcement by ordinary proceeding

When the mortgagee enforces a conventional mortgage by an ordinary proceeding, he must first obtain a judgment against the mortgagor and then execute the judgment. If it is not possible to obtain a personal judgment against the mortgagor, then the judgment shall be in rem.

Amended by Acts 2003, No. 1072, § 1.

Art. 3723. Enforcement by executory proceeding

When the mortgagee enforces a conventional mortgage by an executory proceeding, he must comply with Articles 2631 through 2724.

SECTION 2. HYPOTHECARY ACTION AGAINST THIRD PERSON

Art. 3741. Right of enforcement

A legal mortgage, after judgment on the original obligation has been obtained, a judicial mortgage, or a conventional mortgage may be enforced without reference to any alienation or transfer of the mortgaged property from the original debtor, and the creditor may cause the property to be seized and sold as though it were still owned by the original debtor and in his possession.

Editor's Notes

Legal mortgage, generally, C.C. art. 3301 et seq.; effects of mortgage, C.C. art. 3307 et seq.; effects of mortgage against third possessors, C.C. art. 3315–3318 et seq.

Art. 3742. Notice of seizure

When property subject to a legal or a judicial mortgage is no longer owned by the original debtor, the seizing creditor shall cause notices of the seizure to be served by the sheriff upon both the original debtor and the present owner.

Editor's Notes

(N.B.: This is not for a conventional mortgage.) This notice of seizure is served upon both the debtor and the present owner, while under the parallel provision for executory process, only the debtor need be served, Comment (b) to C.C.P. art. 2721. But see Notes to Art. 2701, questioning constitutionality of non-notice to third persons.

Art. 3743. Rights of third possessor

When property subject to a legal or a judicial mortgage is seized to enforce the mortgage, or is about to be seized for this purpose, and the property is no longer owned by the original debtor, the third possessor has the following rights:

(1) To arrest the seizure, or threatened seizure, and consequent judicial sale of the property by injunction on the grounds that the mortgage was not recorded, that the inscription of its recordation had perempted, or that the debt secured by the mortgage is prescribed or extinguished, or to plead discussion as provided in Articles 5154 and 5155; and

(2) All of the rights granted a third possessor under Article 2703 (1) and (3).

CHAPTER 4. NOTICE OF PENDENCY OF ACTION

Article

Art. 3751. Notice to be recorded to affect third persons

The pendency of an action or proceeding in any court, state or federal, in this state affecting the title to, or asserting a mortgage or privilege on, immovable property does not constitute notice to a third person not a party thereto unless a notice of the pendency of the action or proceeding is made, and filed or recorded, as required by Article 3752.

Editor's Notes

LSA–C.C.P. Form 1805.

Art. 3752. Requirements of notice; recordation

A. The notice referred to in Article 3751 shall be in writing, signed by the plaintiff, defendant, or other party to the action or proceeding who desires to have the notice recorded, or by a counsel of record for such party showing the name of the persons against whom it is to be effective, the name of the court in which the action or proceeding has been filed, the title, docket number, date of filing, and object thereof, and the description of the property sought to be affected thereby.

B. This notice shall be recorded in the mortgage office of the parish where the property to be affected is situated and has effect from the time of the filing for recordation. The notice shall cease to have effect after ten years from the date of its filing for recordation. Nevertheless, if the action or proceeding is still pending, the notice may be reinscribed by refiling the notice. A reinscription of the notice that is filed before the effect of recordation ceases continues that effect for five years from the day the notice is reinscribed.

Amended by Acts 2005, No. 169, § 3, eff. July 1, 2006; Acts 2006, No. 267, § 1, eff. Aug. 15, 2007.

Editor's Notes

Section 2 of Acts 2006, No. 267 (§ 1 of which amends par. B of C.C.P. Art. 3752) provides:

"Section 2. This Act shall become effective on August 15, 2007. Any notice filed before that date that would have otherwise terminated by the terms of this Act shall continue for an additional ten years from reinscription if such reinscription occurs before August 15, 2007."

Art. 3753. Cancellation of notice of pendency

When judgment is rendered in the action or proceeding against the party who filed the notice of the pendency thereof, the judgment shall order the cancellation of the notice at the expense of the party who filed it, and as part of the costs of the action or proceeding. Nevertheless, the notice of pendency filed in connection with the proceeding which gave rise to the judgment shall be canceled at the request of any interested party if the judgment has been canceled or if the action or proceeding has been dismissed.

Amended by Acts 1999, No. 870, § 1.

Editor's Notes

The 1999 amendment allows "any interested party" to request the cancellation.

TITLE III. EXTRAORDINARY REMEDIES

CHAPTER 1. GENERAL DISPOSITIONS

Art. 3781. Petition; summary trial; issuance of writs

A writ of habeas corpus, mandamus, or quo warranto may be ordered by the court only on petition. The proceedings may be tried summarily and the writ when ordered may be signed by the clerk under the seal of the court, or it may be issued and signed by the judge without further formality.

Editor's Notes

Refer to C.C.P. art. 2591 et seq., for summary procedure generally, but note that these writs must be brought by petition, while C.C.P. art. 2593 specifies contradictory motion or rule to show cause. See LSA–C.C.P. Form 1901 et seq.

Art. 3782. Return date

Except as otherwise provided by law, a petition for a writ of habeas corpus, mandamus, or quo warranto shall be assigned for hearing not less than two or more than ten days after the service of the writ; but, upon proper showing, the court may assign the matter for hearing less than two days after the service of the writ.

Amended by Acts 1964, No. 483, § 1; Acts 1966, No. 36, § 1.

Editor's Notes

Citation is not required, State ex rel. Brenner v. Noe, 171 So. 708 (1936), C.C.P. art. 2594, and State ex rel. Citizens Finance Co. v. James, 207 So.2d 389 (1968). But see the holding of the latter case that if no citation issues then no answer is required, even under the language of C.C.P. art. 3783.

Art. 3783. Answer

A written answer to a petition for a writ shall be filed not later than the time fixed for the hearing.

Editor's Notes

See Notes under C.C.P. art. 3782 as to requirement of answer.

Art. 3784. Hearing

The hearing may be held in open court or in chambers, in term or in vacation.

Art. 3785. Disobedience of writ or judgment; contempt

A person who fails to comply with a writ of habeas corpus, or with a judgment rendered after a hearing on a petition for a writ of habeas corpus, mandamus, or quo warranto may be punished for contempt. When a sentence of imprisonment is imposed for contempt, imprisonment may continue until the defendant obeys the writ or judgment.

Editor's Notes

See general contempt power of court, C.C.P. art. 227.

CHAPTER 2. HABEAS CORPUS

Article

Art. 3821. Definition

Habeas corpus is a writ commanding a person who has another in his custody to produce him before the court and to state the authority for the custody.

Custody, as used in this Chapter, includes detention and confinement.

A petition for a writ of habeas corpus may be filed by the person in custody or by any other person in his behalf.

Editor's Notes

Some examples of civil use are child custody, imprisonment for contempt, confinement for insanity, and detention under health regulation, Comment (b). For criminal proceedings, see LSA–C.Cr.P. art. 351 et seq. Interspousal immunity from suit does not bar habeas corpus in custody action, Stelly v. Montgomery, 347 So.2d 1145 (1977). See, also, Uniform Child Custody Jurisdiction Act. R.S. 13:1801, 1822 et seq.

Art. 3822. Venue

Habeas corpus proceedings may be brought in the parish in which the defendant is domiciled or the parish in which the person detained is in custody.

Art. 3823. Persons authorized to make service; proof of service

A writ of habeas corpus may be served by any person over the age of twenty-one who is capable of testifying.

If the writ is served by someone other than a sheriff, the affidavit of the person who served it shall be prima facie proof of such service.

Art. 3824. Method of service

A writ of habeas corpus shall be served upon the party to whom it is addressed or who has the person in custody in the manner provided by Articles 1232 and 1233. If personal service cannot be made, service may be made by attaching the writ to an entrance door of the residence of the party to be served or to a door of the place where the person is in custody.

Art. 3825. Answer; production of person in custody

The person upon whom the writ has been served, whether it is directed to him or not, shall file an answer stating whether he has custody of the person named in the writ. If the person is in his custody, he shall produce him and state in his answer by what authority he holds the person detained.

Editor's Notes

Answer is required, under express words of the article. LSA–C.C.P. Form 1907. Rule of State ex rel. Citizens Finance Co. v. James, *supra,* C.C.P. art. 3782, would not apply, Comment to C.C.P. art. 3826.

Art. 3826. Transfer of custody; answer

If the person upon whom the writ of habeas corpus is served has transferred the custody of the person detained prior to service of the writ, he shall state in his answer the name and address of the person to whom custody was transferred, the time of and the authority for the transfer, and the place where the person detained is then in custody.

Art. 3827. Inability to produce person in custody

If the person in custody cannot be brought before the court, the reasons therefor shall be stated in the answer. The hearing may proceed as if he had been produced.

Art. 3828. Custody pendente lite

If judgment cannot be rendered immediately, the court may award the custody to a proper person until rendition of the judgment.

Editor's Notes

"Person" includes welfare institution, See Comment under this article in LSA.

Art. 3829. Notice of hearing

When a person is in custody by virtue of a prior court order, or at the request of any person, reasonable written notice of the hearing shall be given to the person who provoked the prior court order or requested the custody.

Art. 3830. Judgment

The judgment may order the person released or placed in the custody of a proper person.

Art. 3831. Appeal not to suspend execution of judgment; delay

An appeal from a judgment ordering the release of a person from custody or placing him in the custody of another person shall not suspend the execution of the judgment.

Such an appeal shall be taken only within thirty days from the applicable dates provided in Article 2087(A).

Amended by Acts 1974, No. 132, § 1.

CHAPTER 3. MANDAMUS

Article

Art. 3861. Definition

Mandamus is a writ directing a public officer, a corporation or an officer thereof, or a limited liability company or a member or manager thereof, to perform any of the duties set forth in Articles 3863 and 3864.

Amended by Acts 2017, No. 419, § 1.

Official Revision Comments—1960

(a) This Chapter treats of mandamus only as an extraordinary writ, not as a supervisory remedy.

(b) Mandamus is defined in the source articles as an "order directing the performance of some specific act"; an order "to individuals or corporations to compel them to perform certain duties prescribed for them by law"; and an order "issued in the name of the state by a tribunal of competent jurisdiction, and addressed to an individual or corporation, or court of inferior jurisdiction, directing it to perform some certain act belonging to the place, duty or quality with which it is clothed." The above article states the essential features of the writ, all unnecessary language in the source articles having been deleted.

(c) This article does not modify the rule that mandamus may not be used to compel performance of contractual obligations. State ex rel. Brown v. United Gas Public Service Co., 197 La. 616, 2 So.2d 41 (1941).

(d) Mandamus may be directed to an officer or board member whose duty it is to perform the act involved. See Knoll v. Levert, 136 La. 241, 66 So. 959 (1914); Michel v. Michel, 151 La. 541, 92 So. 50 (1922).

(e) The term "duty" in this article is limited to those duties specified in Arts. 3863 and 3864, *infra*.

(f) See Comments under Art. 3901, *infra*.

Editor's Notes

Mandamus may not be used to compel performance of contractual obligations, Comment (c). Writ of review by appellate court, Sup.Ct.Rule X; Rule 4, Uniform Rules—Courts of Appeal (Volume 8, LSA–R.S.); Const. Art. 5, § 2.

Art. 3862. Mandamus; issuance of

A writ of mandamus may be issued in all cases where the law provides no relief by ordinary means or where the delay involved in obtaining ordinary relief may cause injustice; provided, however, that no court shall issue or cause to be issued a writ of mandamus to compel the expenditure of state funds by any state department, board or agency, or any officer, administrator or head thereof, or any officer of the state of Louisiana, in any suit or action involving the expenditure of public funds under any statute or law of this state, when the director of such department, board or agency, or the governor shall certify that the expenditure of such funds would have the effect of creating a deficit in the funds of said agency or be in violation of the requirements placed upon the expenditure of such funds by the legislature.

Amended by Acts 1969, No. 34, § 3.

Official Revision Comments—1960

(a) The above article combines the source articles with changes of wording to achieve brevity.

(b) Mandamus will be denied where there has been an unreasonable delay in applying for it. State ex rel. McCabe v. Police Board of City of New Orleans, 107 La. 162, 31 So. 662 (1901); State ex rel. Boudreaux v. Alford, 205 La. 46, 16 So.2d 901 (1944). The same result obtain under this article.

(c) In some cases the distinction between a mandatory injunction and a writ of mandamus may not be clear. It should be noted that injunction is a much broader remedy and requires bond, whereas mandamus is restricted to the cases specified in this Code and no bond is required.

(d) Of necessity, constitutional provisions and special statutes governing the issuance of mandamus in particular cases remain in effect.

Art. 3863. Person against whom writ directed

A writ of mandamus may be directed to a public officer to compel the performance of a ministerial duty required by law, or to a former officer or his heirs to compel the delivery of the papers and effects of the office to his successor.

Official Revision Comments—1960

(a) A typical and probably the most frequent use of the writ against a public officer is in a proceeding to compel the recorder of mortgages to cancel an illegal or unauthorized inscription. See State ex rel. Code v. Code, 215 La. 485, 41 So.2d 62 (1949).

(b) The following rules established by the jurisprudence are retained:

Mandamus will issue only when there is a clear and specific right to be enforced or a duty which ought to be performed. It never issues in doubtful cases. It may be used only to compel the performance of purely ministerial duties. State ex rel. Hutton v. City of Baton Rouge, 217 La. 857, 47 So.2d 665 (1950); State ex rel. Loraine, Inc. v. Adjustment Board, 220 La. 708, 57 So.2d 409 (1952).

(c) It has been held that a citizen taxpayer has no legal standing to enforce performance of a public officer's duty to the public at large, unless clearly shown to have special and peculiar interest, apart from the interest of the general public. Cleveland v. Martin, 29 So.2d 516 (La.App.1947).

Editor's Notes

Mandamus may lie against a political subdivision when the duty to be compelled is ministerial and not discretionary. In Lowther v. Town of Bastrop, 2020-01231 (La. 5/13/21), 320 So.3d 369, 371, the Supreme Court held that the duty to pay firefighters is statutorily and constitutionally mandated and is ministerial in nature. See also, Jazz Casino Co., L.L.C. v. Bridges, 2016-1663 (La. 5/3/17), 223 So.3d 488, 490, which held that appropriation of funds to pay refund judgments for overpaid taxes is a ministerial duty as mandated by La. R.S. 47:1621, and Parish of St. Charles v. R.H. Creager, Inc., 2010-180 (La. App. 5 Cir. 12/14/10), 55 So.3d 884, 887, writ denied, 2011-0118 (La. 4/1/11), 60 So.3d 1250, which held that appropriation of funds to pay judgment of damages in expropriation cases is a ministerial duty.

Art. 3864. Mandamus against corporation or corporate officer; limited liability company or member or manager

A. A writ of mandamus may be directed to a corporation or an officer thereof to compel either of the following:

(1) The holding of an election or the performance of other duties required by the corporation's articles of incorporation or bylaws, or as prescribed by law.

(2) The recognition of the rights of the corporation's members or shareholders.

B. A writ of mandamus may be directed to a limited liability company or a member or manager thereof to compel either of the following:

(1) The holding of an election or the performance of other duties required by the limited liability company's articles of organization or operating agreement, or as prescribed by law.

(2) The recognition of the rights of the limited liability company's members.

Amended by Acts 2017, No. 419, § 1.

Art. 3865. Alternative writ

Upon the filing of a petition for a writ of mandamus, the court shall order the issuance of an alternative writ directing the defendant to perform the act demanded or to show cause to the contrary.

Editor's Notes

The court must order the issuance of the alternative writ, then may or may not make it peremptory after hearing, Naquin v. Iberia Parish School Board, App. 3 Cir.1963, 157 So.2d 287.

Art. 3866. Judgment

After the hearing, the court may render judgment making the writ peremptory.

CHAPTER 4. QUO WARRANTO

Article

Art. 3901. Definition

Quo warranto is a writ directing an individual to show by what authority he claims or holds public office, or office in a corporation or limited liability company, or directing a corporation or limited liability company to show by what authority it exercises certain powers. Its purpose is to prevent usurpation of office or of powers.

Amended by Acts 2017, No. 419, § 1.

Editor's Notes

Intrusion into office act, R.S. 42:76 et seq., action by state; R.S. 42:77, personal right of action.

Art. 3902. Judgment

When the court finds that a person is holding or claiming office without authority, the judgment shall forbid him to do so. It may declare who is entitled to the office and may direct an election when necessary.

When the court finds that a corporation or limited liability company is exceeding its powers, the judgment shall prohibit it from doing so.

Amended by Acts 2017, No. 419, § 1.

TITLE IV. DIVORCE AND ANNULMENT OF MARRIAGE

CHAPTER 1. DIVORCE AND ANNULMENT

Article

Art. 3941. Court where action brought; nullity of judgment of court of improper venue

A. An action for an annulment of marriage or for a divorce shall be brought in a parish where either party is domiciled, or in the parish of the last matrimonial domicile.

B. The venue provided in this Article may not be waived, and a judgment rendered in either of these actions by a court of improper venue is an absolute nullity.

Amended by Acts 1990, No. 1009, § 4, eff. Jan. 1, 1991.

Editor's Notes

The venue in actions for annulments of marriage or divorce is jurisdictional and objections thereto may not be waived. A judgment rendered by a court of improper venue is an absolute nullity. La. C.C.P. art. 3941. See Stewart v. Stewart, 2003-1270 (La. App. 4 Cir. 10/1/03), 859 So.2d 703, 705, wherein venue was not changed where wife did not reside one night in new venue even though she demonstrated her intent to move and change her domicile. For the opposite result, see Sheets v. Sheets, 612 So.2d 842, 843 (La. App. 1 Cir. 1992), wherein the trial court found the wife established her new domicile in a different parish even though she filed suit before she and her son spent their first night in their new apartment.

Art. 3942. Appeal from judgment granting or refusing annulment or divorce

A. An appeal from a judgment granting or refusing an annulment of marriage or a divorce can be taken only within thirty days from the applicable date provided in Article 2087(A).

B. Such an appeal shall suspend the execution of the judgment insofar as the judgment relates to the annulment, divorce, or any partition of community property or settlement of claims arising from the matrimonial regime.

Amended by Acts 1986, No. 225, § 2; Acts 1990, No. 1009, § 4, eff. Jan. 1, 1991.

Art. 3943. Appeal from judgment awarding, modifying, or denying custody, visitation, or support

An appeal from a judgment awarding, modifying, or denying custody, visitation, or support of a person can be taken only within the delay provided in Article 3942. Such an appeal shall not suspend execution of the judgment insofar as the judgment relates to custody, visitation, or support.

Amended by Acts 1993, No. 261, § 3, eff. Jan. 1, 1994; Acts 2021, No. 259, § 2.

Art. 3944. Injunctive relief in divorce actions; bond not required in certain cases

Either party to an action for divorce may obtain injunctive relief as provided in Part V of Chapter 1 of Code Title V of Code Book I of Title 9 (R.S. 9:371 et seq.) of the Revised Statutes without bond.

Amended by Acts 1990, No. 1009, § 4, eff. Jan. 1, 1991.

Editor's Notes

Irreparable injury need not be shown. See, e.g., Fuori v. Fuori, App. 1 Cir.1976, 334 So.2d 488, refusing injunction under this article after judgment of separation, but allowing injunction under C.C.P. art. 3601 on finding irreparable injury; and Fisher v. Fisher, 261 So.2d 85 (3d 1972) refusing injunction under this article after community property settlement and refusing injunction under C.C.P. art. 3601 on finding no showing of irreparable injury. For specific injunction provision, see R.S. 9:371, disposition or encumbrance of community property; R.S. 9:372, abuse of spouse or child; R.S. 9:373, removal of personal property; and R.S. 9:374, possession and use of family residence or community property.

Art. 3945. Incidental order of temporary child custody; injunctive relief; exceptions

A. The injunctive relief afforded either party to an action for divorce or other proceeding which includes a provision for the temporary custody of a minor child shall be governed by the additional provisions of this Article.

B. An ex parte order of temporary custody of a minor child shall not be granted unless:

(1) It clearly appears from specific facts shown by a verified petition or by supporting affidavit that immediate and irreparable injury will result to the child before the adverse party or his attorney can be heard in opposition.

(2) The applicant's attorney certifies to the court, in writing, either:

(a) The efforts which have been made to give the adverse party reasonable notice of the date and time such order is being presented to the court.

(b) The reasons supporting his claim that notice should not be required.

C. An ex parte order of temporary custody shall:

(1) Expire by operation of law within thirty days of signing of the order; however, the order may be extended for good cause shown at any time before its expiration for one period not exceeding fifteen days.

(2) Provide specific provisions for temporary visitation by the adverse party of not less than forty-eight hours during any fifteen-day period, unless the verified petition or supporting affidavit clearly demonstrates that immediate and irreparable injury will result to the child as a result of such visitation.

(3) Be endorsed with the date on which the ex parte order is signed and the date and hour of the rule to show cause.

D. The rule to show cause why the respondent should not be awarded the custody, joint custody, or visitation of the child shall be assigned for hearing not more than thirty days after signing of the ex parte order of temporary custody.

E. Any ex parte order not in compliance with the provisions of this Article is not enforceable, and is null and void.

F. In the event an ex parte order of temporary custody is denied, the court shall specifically allocate between the parents the time which the child shall spend with each parent at the hearing on the rule to show cause set pursuant to Paragraph D of this Article, unless immediate and irreparable injury will result to the child.

G. The provisions of this Article do not apply to any order of custody of a child requested in a verified petition alleging the applicability of the Domestic Abuse Assistance Act, R.S. 46:2131 et seq., Children's Code Article 1564 et seq., or the Post–Separation Family Violence Relief Act, R.S. 9:361 et seq.

Amended by Acts 1990, No. 1008, § 4, eff. Jan. 1, 1991; Acts 1995, No. 1204, § 1; Acts 1997, No. 374, § 1; Acts 2009, No. 379, § 1; Acts 2014, No. 619, § 1.

Editor's Notes

(Caveat: These authorities should continue to be relevant under the 1990 revision.)

Jurisdiction of nonresidents, R.S. 13:3201(A)(6) and (7); LSA–C.C.P. Forms 2031, 2034a; additional sanctions for non-payment of alimony, R.S. 14:75; attorney's fees, R.S. 9:375; legal interest, C.C. art. 2924. Suspensive appeal allowed from arrearages judgment, Lacour v. Lacour, App. 4 Cir.1978, 355 So.2d 1083. See R.S. 46:236.3 and 46:236.4 for provisions relating to enforcement of support obligations through income assignment and to interstate enforcement through withholding from obligor's income. See, also, R.S. 9:313, past due awarded child support is deemed a judgment by operation of law and executory through summary proceedings.

The 1997 legislation enacts new Paragraph F.

Art. 3946. Execution of support and claims for contributions awards in arrears

A. When a payment of support under a judgment is in arrears, the party entitled thereto may proceed by contradictory motion to have the amount of past due support determined and made executory. On the trial of the contradictory motion, the court shall render judgment for the amount of past due support.

B. The same rules and procedures apply when an installment payment of an award for contributions made to a spouse's education or training is in arrears.

Added by Acts 1995, No. 1204, § 1.

Art. 3947. Name confirmation

A. Marriage does not change the name of either spouse. However, a married person may use the surname of either or both spouses as a surname.

B. The court may enter an order confirming the name of a spouse in a divorce proceeding, whether the person is the plaintiff or defendant, which confirmation shall be limited to the name that the person was using at the time of the marriage, or the name of the person's minor children, or the person's surname on the birth certificate, without complying with the provisions of R.S. 13:4751 through 4755. This Article shall not be construed to allow an amendment to a birth certificate with the Bureau of Vital Statistics.

Added by Acts 1987, No. 836, § 1. Amended by Acts 2021, No. 259, § 2.

CHAPTER 2. DIVORCE UNDER CIVIL CODE ARTICLE 102

Article

Art. 3951. Petition for divorce

A petition for divorce under Civil Code Article 102 shall contain allegations of jurisdiction and venue and shall be verified by the affidavit of the petitioner.

Added by Acts 1990, No. 1009, § 5, eff. Jan. 1, 1991.

Comment—1990

This Article, and the remaining Articles of this Chapter, are new and are designed to implement the new divorce law enacted by Acts 1990, No. 1009. Two new requirements are contained herein: first, the petition must contain allegations of jurisdiction and venue; and, second, the petition must be verified by the affidavit of the petitioner. In all other respects, the ordinary rules of pleading are to apply.

Editor's Notes

See Form G; Checklist for a La. C.C. art. 102 Divorce in the preliminary material of this publication.

Art. 3952. Rule to show cause and affidavit

The rule to show cause provided in Civil Code Article 102 shall allege proper service of the initial petition for divorce, that the requisite period of time, in accordance with Civil Code Article 103.1, or more has elapsed since that service, and that the spouses have lived separate and apart continuously for the requisite period of time, in accordance with Civil Code Article 103.1. The rule to show cause shall be verified by the affidavit of the mover and shall be served on the defendant, the defendant's attorney of record, or the duly appointed attorney for the defendant prior to the granting of the divorce, unless service is waived by the defendant.

Added by Acts 1990, No. 1009, § 5, eff. Jan. 1, 1991. Amended by Acts 1995, No. 386, § 2; Acts 2006, No. 743, § 2, eff. Jan. 1, 2007; Acts 2018, No. 195, § 1.

Art. 3953. Nullity of judgment

A judgment rendered in accordance with Civil Code Article 102 shall be an absolute nullity when:

(1) Less than the requisite period of time, in accordance with Article 103.1, has elapsed between service of the petition, or between execution of written waiver of service of the petition, and filing of the rule to show cause.

(2) Less than the requisite period of time, in accordance with Article 103.1, has elapsed between the date the parties commenced living separate and apart and filing of the rule to show cause.

(3) The requirements of this Title with respect to jurisdiction and venue have not been met.

Added by Acts 1990, No. 1009, § 5, eff. Jan. 1, 1991. Amended by Acts 1991, No. 367, § 2; Acts 1995, No. 386, § 2; Acts 2006, No. 743, § 2, eff. Jan. 1, 2007.

Comment—1990

Failure to comply with the mandatory jurisdictional venue provisions, or failure to observe the one hundred and eighty day waiting period provided in the new divorce provisions will result in an absolute nullity. Few formalities are present in the provisions of Acts 1990, No. 1009 but the requirements herein cannot be bypassed.

The reference to "execution of written waiver of service" is added in order to coordinate this provision with new Article 3957 of the Code of Civil Procedure, added in 1991.

Art. 3954. Abandonment of action

A. A divorce action instituted under Civil Code Article 102 is abandoned if the rule to show cause provided by that Article is not filed within two years of the service of the original petition or execution of written waiver of service of the original petition.

B. This provision shall be operative without formal order, but on ex parte motion of any party or other interested person, the trial court shall enter a formal order of dismissal as of the date of abandonment.

Added by Acts 1990, No. 1009, § 5, eff. Jan. 1, 1991. Amended by Acts 1991, No. 367, § 2.

Comment—1991

The reference to "execution of written waiver of service" is added in order to coordinate this provision with new Article 3957 of the Code of Civil Procedure, added in 1991.

Art. 3955. Service of petition

A. When a petition for divorce is filed in accordance with Civil Code Article 102, service of the petition shall be requested on the defendant within ninety days of the filing of the petition.

B. If the defendant is an absentee, the request for appointment of an attorney to represent the absentee defendant within ninety days of commencement of the action constitutes compliance with the requirements of Paragraph A of this Article.

C. The defendant may expressly waive the requirements of Paragraph A of this Article by any written waiver. The requirement provided by Paragraph A of this Article shall be expressly waived by a defendant unless the defendant files, in accordance with the provisions of Article 928, a declinatory exception of insufficiency of service of process specifically alleging the failure to timely request service of the petition, in which case, after due proceedings, the action shall be dismissed.

D. If not waived, a request for service of citation upon the defendant shall be considered timely if requested on the defendant within the time period provided by this Article, notwithstanding insufficient or erroneous service.

Added by Acts 2010, No. 407, § 1. Amended by Acts 2014, No. 379, § 2, eff. May 30, 2014; Acts 2017, No. 419, § 1.

Comments—2017

The purpose of the amendment to Paragraph B of this Article is to align the provision with Article 5091 by replacing "curator ad hoc" with "attorney to represent the absentee defendant."

Art. 3956. Evidence of facts in divorce action

The facts entitling a moving party to a divorce in accordance with Civil Code Article 102 may be established by:

(1) The petition for divorce.

(2)(a) The sheriff's return of service of the petition.

(b) The sheriff's return of service of the petition showing personal service on the defendant if the parties were living together at the time of the filing of the petition.

(c) The return receipt when service is effectuated pursuant to R.S. 13:3204.

(d) Waiver of the service of petition.

(3) The rule to show cause and the affidavit required by Code of Civil Procedure Article 3952.

(4) The sheriff's return of service of the rule, or by a waiver of that service.

(5) The affidavit of the mover, executed after the filing of the rule, that the parties have lived separate and apart continuously for at least the requisite period of time, in accordance with Civil Code Article 103.1, prior to the filing of the rule to show cause and are still living separate and apart and that the mover desires to be divorced.

Added by Acts 1990, No. 1009, § 5, eff. Jan. 1, 1991. Amended by Acts 1991, No. 367, § 2; Acts 1995, No. 386, § 2; Acts 1999, No. 95, § 1; Acts 2006, No. 743, § 2, eff. Jan. 1, 2007.

Comment—1990

This Article provides a convenient means of proof of the prerequisites to a judgment of divorce stated in Civil Code Article 102 and this Chapter when the matter is uncontested.

Comment—1991

The reference to "a waiver of that service" is added in order to coordinate this provision with new Article 3957 of the Code of Civil Procedure, added in 1991.

Editor's Notes

The 1999 amendment substantially changed the mode of proof of service by deleting "waiver of service" from the sheriff's return, and by adding the last clause of (2)(b) and adding (2)(c) and (d).

Art. 3957. Waiver of service of petition and rule to show cause and accompanying notices

A. A party in a divorce action under Civil Code Article 102 may expressly waive service of the petition and accompanying notice by any written waiver executed after the filing of the petition and made part of the record.

B. If there is such a waiver, the periods specified by Civil Code Article 102 and Code of Civil Procedure Articles 3953 and 3954 shall run from the date of execution of the waiver.

C. A party in a divorce action under Civil Code Article 102 may expressly waive service of the rule to show cause why a divorce should not be granted and accompanying notice by any written waiver executed after the filing of the rule to show cause and made part of the record.

Added by Acts 1991, No. 367, § 2.

Comments—1991

(a) This new Article clarifies, but does not change, the law. It is intended to clarify one aspect of the procedure for obtaining a divorce under Civil Code Article 102 as enacted by Acts 1990, No. 1009. Neither that Article nor accompanying Code of Civil Procedure Articles 3951 through 3956 contained any prohibition of a party in such an action waiving the service upon him of the initial divorce petition or of the subsequent rule to show cause why a divorce should not be granted contemplated by Civil Code Article 102, nor of the special notices required to accompany such pleadings by R.S. 13:3491 and 3492.

(b) Paragraph B of this Article and a coordinating amendment to Civil Code Article 102 make it explicit that under the provisions of this Article the period contemplated by Civil Code Article 102 runs from the date of execution of a valid waiver of service of the divorce petition. In such a case the affidavit required by Code of Civil Procedure Article 3952 should recite that 180 or more days have elapsed since the defendant's execution of the waiver of service of the petition.

Art. 3958. Voluntary dismissal

A judgment dismissing a petition for divorce under Civil Code Article 102 shall be rendered upon joint application of the parties and upon payment of all costs, or upon contradictory motion of the plaintiff. A judgment of dismissal rendered under this Article shall be without prejudice to any separation of property decree rendered under Civil Code Articles 2374 and 2375.

Added by Acts 1993, No. 628, § 1.

Editor's Notes

As drafted, the text of this article fails to make joint stipulation or rule to show cause the exclusive methods for dismissing the petition, though the title of the bill shows clearly that it was the intent to make such methods exclusive. The title reads, in part:

"... to provide that no such action may be dismissed without consent of the other party ..." Acts 1993, No. 628.

TITLE V. JUDICIAL EMANCIPATION

Art. 3991. Petition for judicial emancipation

A. A minor age sixteen or older may petition for emancipation individually without the participation of his tutor or administrator. The petition of the minor shall name as parties defendant and shall be served personally on the parents of the minor, if parental authority exists, or his tutor if parental authority does not exist.

B. The parents of a minor age sixteen or older, if parental authority exists, or the tutor of the minor, if parental authority does not exist, may petition for the emancipation of the minor. A petition filed by the parents or tutor of a minor shall name the minor as defendant and shall be served personally on the minor and on an attorney appointed by the court, who shall represent the minor.

C. A joint petition for judicial emancipation may be filed by a minor age sixteen or older and the parents of the minor, if parental authority exists, or the tutor of the minor, if parental authority does not exist. A joint petition need not be served on any party.

Acts 2008, No. 786, § 2, eff. Jan. 1, 2009.

Revision Comments—2008

(a) This Article creates an exception to C.C.P. Art. 683, which provides that an unemancipated minor does not have capacity to sue.

(b) An absent defendant may be served in accordance with Code of Civil Procedure Articles 5091–5098.

(c) When a minor has more than one tutor or administrator, each tutor or administrator must join as a party plaintiff or be joined as a party defendant to any action requiring the participation of the minor's tutor or administrator.

Editor's Notes

See checklist for a Tutorship Proceeding in the preliminary material of this publication.

Art. 3992. Petition requirements

The petition shall be verified by all petitioners and shall set forth the following with particularity:

(1) The name, domicile, age, and, if known, the current address of the minor.

(2) The names and current addresses of the parents and any tutors of the minor, if known.

(3) The reasons why good cause exists for emancipation.

(4) If limited judicial emancipation is requested, the effects of majority sought to be conferred upon the minor.

(5) A descriptive list of the property of the minor, including the location of such property, if known.

Acts 2008, No. 786, § 2, eff. Jan. 1, 2009.

Editor's Notes

A court may emancipate a minor for good cause. Good cause is explained in the comments to La. C.C. art. 366 as:

"Good cause" warranting emancipation may exist when the minor's parents need to be protected. For example, emancipation might be appropriate if a minor has run away from home and cannot be found. Emancipation would protect the minor's parents from liability for the acts of an absent child over whom they have no control.

"Good cause" warranting emancipation may exist when the minor needs the capacity to enter into juridical acts. For example, emancipation might be appropriate if a minor is operating a business and needs to contract with vendors or suppliers without parental assistance.

"Good cause" warranting emancipation may exist if the parents of a mature and responsible minor give the minor "corrupt examples," "ill treat him excessively," or "refuse him support." See La. C.C. art. 368(1870).

Art. 3993. Venue for judicial emancipation

Venue for a judicial emancipation proceeding is the parish where a party is domiciled.

Acts 2008, No. 786, § 2, eff. Jan. 1, 2009.

Art. 3994. Emancipation hearing

A. An emancipation hearing shall be a summary proceeding.

B. Except for good cause shown, the minor shall be present at the hearing and may be called as a witness by the court.

C. With the consent of all parties and the court, judicial emancipation may be granted without a hearing upon a joint petition for emancipation.

Acts 2008, No. 786, § 2, eff. Jan. 1, 2009.

Art. 3995. Judgment of limited emancipation

A judgment of limited emancipation shall specify the effects of majority conferred and shall state that the minor retains all other effects of minority.

Acts 2008, No. 786, § 2, eff. Jan. 1, 2009.

Art. 3996. Appeal

A judgment granting, modifying, or terminating emancipation is not suspended during the pendency of an appeal. The validity of an act of the minor shall not be affected by the subsequent modification or termination of the judgment.

Acts 2008, No. 786, § 2, eff. Jan. 1, 2009.

Art. 3997. Modification or termination of emancipation

On motion of the court or any person, the court for good cause shown may modify or terminate its judgment of emancipation or an act of limited emancipation by authentic act.

Acts 2008, No. 786, § 2, eff. Jan. 1, 2009.

Art. 3998. Recordation

A. The clerk of court shall record every judgment granting, modifying, or terminating emancipation in the conveyance records of the parish in which the judgment was rendered.

B. Within fifteen days of the signing of a judgment granting, modifying, or terminating emancipation, the petitioner shall cause it to be recorded in the conveyance records of every other parish in which the minor owns immovable property.

Acts 2008, No. 786, § 2, eff. Jan. 1, 2009.

Arts. 3999 to 4030. Reserved for future legislation

TITLE VI. TUTORSHIP

CHAPTER 1. COURT WHERE PROCEEDINGS ARE BROUGHT

Article

Art. 4031. Minor domiciled in the state

A. Except as provided in Paragraph B, a petition for the appointment of a tutor of a minor domiciled in the state shall be filed in the district court of the parish where:

(1) The surviving parent is domiciled, if one parent is dead; or

(2) The parent or other person awarded custody of the minor is domiciled, if the parents are divorced or judicially separated; or

(3) The minor resides.

B. If the parents who are divorced or judicially separated are awarded joint custody of a minor:

(1) They shall petition jointly for appointment as cotutors in the district court of the parish in which the proceedings for divorce or judicial separation were instituted, or if the award of joint custody has specified the legal domicile of the minor, in the district court of the parish of the legal domicile of the minor, or in the district court of the parish where the child resides.

(2) With the permission of the judge, either parent may file a petition in the same court as provided in Subparagraph (1) for appointment as tutor for the limited purpose of enforcing a particular right or compromising a particular claim of an unemancipated minor if the other parent fails or refuses to do so.

Amended by Acts 1981, No. 283, § 2; Acts 1990, No. 764, § 1; Acts 1995, No. 268, § 1, eff. June 14, 1995.

Editor's Notes

"The venue in a tutorship proceeding is jurisdictional, and objections thereto may not be waived. Art. 44. All proceedings taken in a court of improper venue are absolute nullities."

Art. 4032. Minor not domiciled in the state

If the minor is not domiciled in the state, a petition for the appointment of a tutor may be filed in any parish where:

(1) Immovable property of the minor is situated; or

(2) Movable property of the minor is situated, if he owns no immovable property in the state.

Art. 4033. Petitions filed in two or more courts; stay of proceedings in second and subsequent courts; adoption of proceedings by first court

If petitions for the appointment of a tutor are filed in two or more competent courts, the court in which a petition was first filed shall proceed to a determination of the issues and the proceedings in the other courts shall be stayed. However, the first court may adopt as its own any of the proceedings taken in the other courts.

Art. 4034. Proceedings subsequent to appointment of tutor

Proceedings relative to a tutorship subsequent to the confirmation or appointment of a tutor who is domiciled in the state shall be brought in the parish of his domicile if he is living at the time or, if he is dead, in the parish where he was last domiciled. If the proceedings are brought in a court other than the one which confirmed or appointed the tutor, the court may require the filing of certified copies of all or any part of the proceedings in the other court.

Proceedings relative to a tutorship subsequent to the confirmation or appointment of a tutor who is not domiciled in this state, or who has left the state permanently, shall be brought in the court which confirmed or appointed him.

Amended by Acts 1964, No. 4, § 1.

CHAPTER 2. APPOINTMENT OF PARTICULAR TUTORS

Article

Art. 4061. Natural tutor; general obligations

Before a natural tutor enters upon the performance of his official duties, he must take an oath to discharge faithfully the duties of his office, cause an inventory to be taken or a detailed descriptive list to be prepared, and cause a legal mortgage in favor of the minor to be inscribed, or furnish security, in the manner provided by law.

Amended by Acts 1983, No. 344, § 1.

Editor's Notes

See Tutorship by Nature, La. C.C. art. 250, et seq. in the statutory appendix.

Art. 4061.1. Natural tutor; action for damages on behalf of child

A. Notwithstanding Article 4061, the natural tutor of a minor child may file an action for damages based on a delictual obligation without the necessity of qualifying as tutor pursuant to Article 4061 and without the necessity of filing a petition pursuant to Article 4031, if the natural tutor is any of the following:

(1) The surviving parent of the minor child.

(2) The parent under whose sole care the minor child has been placed when the parents are divorced or judicially separated from bed and board.

(3) The mother of her child born outside of marriage not acknowledged by the father, or acknowledged by him alone without her concurrence.

B. The petitioner in an action for damages based on a delictual obligation shall allege in the petition that he qualifies under Paragraph A of this Article to act of right as tutor, and the petitioner shall set forth the facts, including the relationship to the minor child, entitling the petitioner to act as tutor.

C. This Article shall not apply to parents who share joint custody of the minor child or to parents who have both acknowledged their child born outside of marriage pursuant to the Civil Code.

Added by Acts 2003, No. 155, § 1. Amended by Acts 2004, No. 26, § 2.

Editor's Notes

See art. 855. Article 4061.1 is an exception to the general rule that it is not necessary to allege capacity to sue. Under article 4061.1(B), the "petitioner shall set forth the facts, including the relationship to the minor child, entitling the petitioner to act as tutor."

Art. 4062. Tutorship by will

The court shall appoint as tutor the person nominated as such in a testament or an authentic act, upon his furnishing security and taking an oath, as provided in Articles 4131 and 4171, unless he is disqualified or unless for some other reason the court determines that the appointment would not be for the best interest of the minor.

Editor's Notes

Tutorship by will. See La. C.C. art. 257, et seq. in the statutory appendix. Also see Tutorship by Will checklist in the preliminary material of this publication.

Art. 4063. Legal tutor

The court shall appoint a legal tutor under the circumstances and according to the rules for priority provided by law, and in the manner provided in Articles 4065 through 4068.

Editor's Notes

Tutorship by effect of law. See La. C.C. art. 263 in the statutory appendix. Also see and the Tutorship by Law checklist in the preliminary material of this publication.

Art. 4064. Dative tutor

The court shall appoint a dative tutor under the circumstances provided by law and in the manner provided in Articles 4065 through 4068.

Editor's Notes

Dative tutorship, C.C. art. 270.

Art. 4065. Legal or dative tutor; petition for appointment; publication of notice

When a petition for appointment as legal or dative tutor is filed, the applicant shall annex an affidavit listing to the best of his knowledge the minor's ascendants and collaterals by blood within the third degree and the surviving spouse of the minor's mother or father dying last who reside in the state. A copy of the petition for appointment shall be mailed by registered or certified mail to each person listed in the affidavit.

Notice of the application shall be published once in the parish where the petition was filed, in the manner provided by law.

Amended by Acts 1976, No. 429, § 3.

Editor's Notes

Publication requirements, R.S. 43:200 et seq.

Art. 4066. Opposition to application of legal or dative tutor

An opposition to an application for appointment as legal or dative tutor may be filed at any time prior to the appointment, as provided in Article 4067. The opposition shall comply with Article 2972 and shall allege the grounds upon which it is claimed that the applicant is disqualified or that it would be in the best interest of the minor for the opponent to be appointed tutor instead of the applicant.

Amended by Acts 1976, No. 429, § 3.

Art. 4067. Appointment of legal or dative tutor

At any time after the expiration of ten days from date of publication or date of mailing of the notice as provided in Article 4065, whichever period is longer, if no opposition has been filed, the court shall appoint the applicant, unless he is disqualified under Article 4231.

If an opposition has been filed, it shall be tried in a summary manner.

Amended by Acts 1976, No. 429, § 3.

Art. 4068. Appeal from judgment confirming, appointing, or removing tutor or undertutor; effect

An appeal from a judgment confirming, appointing, or removing a tutor or an undertutor can only be taken within thirty days from the applicable date provided in Article 2087(A).

Such judgment shall not be suspended during the pendency of an appeal. The acts of a tutor or of an undertutor shall not be invalidated by the annulment of his appointment on appeal.

Art. 4069. Separate tutor of property

A. In exceptional cases and for good cause shown, the court may appoint a bank or another person as administrator or tutor of the property of the minor. This appointment may be made upon the court's own motion or upon the motion of the tutor or other person entitled to the tutorship if no tutor has been previously appointed, or upon motion of any interested person after a contradictory hearing with the tutor, administrator, or person entitled to the tutorship or the administration.

B. If a person is appointed as tutor or administrator of the minor's property, pursuant to this Article or Civil Code Article 258, that person shall furnish security as provided in Article 4131.

Amended by Acts 1974, No. 163, § 1; Acts 1992, No. 680, § 2.

Art. 4070. Provisional tutor

On the application of an interested person or on its own motion, pending the appointment of a tutor, the court may appoint a qualified person as provisional tutor of a minor, if such appointment is necessary for the welfare of the minor or for the preservation of his property.

Official Revision Comments

(a) Heretofore, there has been no statutory basis in Louisiana for the appointment of a temporary tutor, nor any reported decision on the subject. However, Art. 335 of the Civil Code permits an applicant for the tutorship to preserve the minor's property pending the issuance of letters "in cases which admit of no delay."

(b) This article is similar to Art. 3111, *supra*, dealing with provisional administrators.

(c) The article applies not only pending the appointment of a tutor, but also pending the appointment of a successor in the event of a vacancy. There is no corresponding provision for the appointment of a provisional undertutor.

Art. 4071. Security, oath, and tenure of provisional tutor

A provisional tutor shall take an oath to discharge faithfully the duties of his office and shall furnish security as provided in Article 4132 for the faithful performance of his duties, in an amount determined by the court as adequate for the protection of the minor.

A provisional tutor shall continue in office until his appointment is terminated by the court or until a tutor has been qualified.

Official Revision Comment

The basis for the fixing of the bond of a provisional tutor is the same as that approved for a provisional administrator's bond, Art. 3152, *supra*. Since no inventory will have been taken at this stage of the proceeding, the amount of the bond is left to the court's discretion.

Art. 4072. Inventory or detailed descriptive list on appointment of provisional tutor

When the court appoints a provisional tutor, it shall order the taking of an inventory or the preparation of a detailed descriptive list of the minor's property as provided in Articles 4101 and 4102.

Amended by Acts 1983, No. 344, § 1.

Art. 4073. Functions, duties, and authority of provisional tutor

The functions of a provisional tutor are limited to the care of the person of the minor and the preservation of his rights and property. In the performance of his functions, a provisional tutor has the same authority, and is subject to the same duties and obligations, as a tutor.

Under specific authority of the court which appointed him, a provisional tutor may:

(1) Institute and prosecute an action to enforce judicially a right of the minor; and

(2) Operate a business belonging to the minor.

A provisional tutor shall file an account upon the termination of his authority.

Official Revision Comments

(a) This article is based partly upon Art. 3112, *supra,* dealing with provisional administrators. The provisional tutor's job is to keep matters in the status quo pending the appointment and qualification of a permanent tutor.

(b) A provisional tutor is a tutor within the intendment of Art. 683, *supra.*

CHAPTER 3. INVENTORY OF MINOR'S PROPERTY

Article

Art. 4101. Inventory and appraisement or descriptive list

A. When any person applies to be appointed as tutor, the court shall order either the taking of an inventory and an appraisal of the minor's property or the preparation of a detailed descriptive list of his property in accordance with Article 4462.

B. If an inventory is ordered, it shall be begun not later than ten days after the order is signed. The court shall appoint a notary of each parish in which property of the minor has a situs to take the inventory of such property in that parish.

Amended by Acts 1983, No. 344, § 1.

Editor's Notes

Expense of administration, tutor's bond, R.S. 9:3901.

Art. 4102. Procedure for inventory; procès verbal; return

In so far as applicable, Articles 3131 through 3134 shall govern the procedure for the taking of the inventory, procès verbal, and the return and effect of the procès verbal.

CHAPTER 4. SECURITY OF TUTOR

Article

Art. 4131. Amount

A. The person appointed tutor, except the natural tutor, shall furnish security for the faithful performance of his duties in an amount equal to the total value of the minor's movable property as shown by the inventory or detailed descriptive list, plus such additional sum as the court may consider sufficient to cover any loss or damage which may be caused by the bad administration of the tutor.

B. Upon proper showing that the security required is substantially in excess of that needed for the protection of the minor, the court may fix the security at any amount which it considers sufficient for the protection of the minor.

C. The court may order the security to be increased or diminished at any time as the movable property may increase or diminish in value, or for other circumstances which the court may consider proper.

D. When the only asset of the minor is a contested claim for damages, the court may postpone the furnishing of security until the claim is recovered, at which time the tutor shall provide security as required by this Article.

Amended by Acts 1983, No. 344, § 1; Acts 1985, No. 146, § 1.

Editor's Notes

Effect of legal mortgage, C.C. art. 3320.

Art. 4132. Nature of security

A. The security required by Article 4131 shall be in the form of a bond, to be approved by the court, and secured by:

(1) A surety company authorized to do business in this state;

(2) Bonds of this state or of any political subdivision or any municipality thereof, or of the United States, or certificates of deposit in any bank, savings bank, or trust company chartered under the laws of Louisiana or National Banking Association domiciled in this state and insured by the Federal Deposit Insurance Corporation, or shares of any building or loan or homestead association domiciled in this state and insured by an agency of the United States, in an amount at par value equal at least to the amount of the security required; or

(3) No less than two personal sureties signing in solido who are residents of this state and who each have unencumbered property located in this state in an amount amply sufficient to secure the amount of the bonds notwithstanding the provisions of Civil Code Article 3042 or any other law to the contrary.

B. Bonds or homestead shares or certificates of deposit of a bank posted as security shall be deposited for safekeeping with the clerk of court or in a bank or other recognized depository as directed by the court, and may not be withdrawn without an order of court. The form of the act under which such bonds or shares are given in security shall be substantially that of a bond, in which the principal binds himself and declares that instead of furnishing sureties, he deposits, as directed by the court, such bonds or shares to be subject to any claim the minor may have.

C. Insured homestead shares or certificates of deposit of a bank may not be furnished as security in excess of the amount insured.

D. The bond shall not be recorded in the mortgage records nor operate as a mortgage.

Amended by Acts 1977, No. 192, § 1, eff. July 5, 1977; Acts 1985, No. 136, § 1.

Art. 4133. Special mortgage instead of bond

A. Instead of the security required by Articles 4131 and 4132, the tutor may furnish a special mortgage in favor of the minor on immovable property otherwise unencumbered. The mortgage shall be for the same amount as the security required by Article 4131 and shall be approved by the court as provided in Article 4271.

B. The costs occasioned by the furnishing of a special mortgage shall be borne by the tutor.

C. The special mortgage shall include the date of birth of the minor. The failure to include the date of birth of the minor shall not invalidate the mortgage.

Amended by Acts 2005, No. 62, § 1.

Art. 4134. Natural tutor; bond; recordation of certificate of inventory or detailed descriptive list

A. Except as provided in Article 4135, a natural tutor shall not be required to furnish bond, but shall record in the mortgage records of the parish of his domicile a certificate of the clerk setting forth the date of birth of the minor, the last four digits of the social security number of the tutor and the total value of the minor's property according to the inventory or detailed descriptive list filed in the tutorship proceeding. If the minor has no assets, then no certificate need be filed until he acquires assets. If the only asset is a contested claim, then no certificate need be filed until the claim is recovered, as provided in Article 4131(D). A certificate of the recorder of mortgages setting forth the recordation of the clerk's certificate shall be filed in the tutorship proceedings before the tutor is appointed or letters of tutorship are issued.

B. Within thirty days after his appointment, the natural tutor shall cause the clerk's certificate to be recorded in the mortgage records of every other parish in the state in which he owns immovable property.

C. The recordation operates as a legal mortgage for the amount of the certificate in favor of the minor on all the immovable property of the tutor situated within any parish where recorded. A certificate recorded in the amount of zero dollars shall not create a legal mortgage. If the certificate does not contain the information required by Paragraph A of this Article, it will not be effective against third parties.

D. The legal mortgage shall prescribe four years after the minor reaches majority and shall be canceled from the mortgage record upon the request of any interested party.

Amended by Acts 1983, No. 344, § 1; Acts 2003, No. 728, § 1; Acts 2004, No. 322, § 1; Acts 2014, No. 189, § 1.

Art. 4135. Security instead of legal mortgage

Instead of the legal mortgage provided in Article 4134, a natural tutor may furnish bond in the amount provided by Article 4131 and of the nature provided by Article 4132, or a special mortgage as provided in Article 4133.

If the court determines that the legal mortgage will not be sufficient protection for the minor, and that substantial loss to the minor may result unless a bond is furnished, the court may order that the natural tutor furnish a bond or a special mortgage instead of the legal mortgage.

Art. 4136. Substitution of one kind of security for another

Any tutor who desires to give bond or security and thus release from an existing general or special mortgage the whole or a portion of the property covered thereby may do so with the approval of the court as provided in Article 4271, provided the bond or security tendered fully protects the minor.

Any of the securities enumerated in Articles 4132 and 4133 may be substituted at any time either in whole or in part for any other kind, at the option of the tutor, and with the approval of the court as provided in Article 4271, which shall enter the necessary orders to render the substitutions effective. If other security has been furnished instead of a general mortgage, the tutor may not revert to a general mortgage.

When a bond or security is substituted only in part for the general or special mortgage, the amount thereof may be proportionately smaller based on the value of the property to be released from mortgage.

Art. 4137. Subordination of legal mortgage to conventional mortgage

The legal mortgage provided in Article 4134 may be subordinated to a conventional mortgage or other security to be given on the property of the tutor, provided such subordination is authorized by the court after proof that such would be to the best interest of the minor and provided the concurrence of the undertutor is first obtained.

Added by Acts 1980, No. 389, § 1.

CHAPTER 5. OATH AND LETTERS OF TUTORSHIP

Article

Art. 4171. Oath

Before the person appointed as tutor enters upon the performance of his official duties, he must take an oath to discharge faithfully the duties of his office. A natural tutor shall include in his oath a list of the parishes in which he owns immovable property.

Art. 4172. Issuance of letters

After the person appointed as tutor has qualified by furnishing the security required of him by law, and by taking his oath of office, the clerk shall issue to him letters of tutorship.

These letters, issued in the name and under the seal of the court, evidence the appointment of the tutor, his qualification, and his compliance with all requirements of law relating thereto.

CHAPTER 6. UNDERTUTOR

Article

Art. 4201. Appointment; oath

At the time judgment is rendered appointing a tutor, the court shall also appoint a responsible person as undertutor.

Before entering upon the performance of his official duties, the undertutor must take an oath to discharge faithfully the duties of his office.

Official Revision Comments

(a) The Civil Code does not prescribe any qualifications for the undertutor. The above article provides for the appointment of a "responsible person" as undertutor whose office differs from that of the tutor in that it is always dative, compulsory to no one, and there are no preferences by reason of relationship. See State v. Judge, 2 Rob. 418 (La.1842); Undertutor of Walker, 14 La.Ann. 631 (1859).

(b) Civil Code Art. 273 indicates that the appointment of an undertutor should be made "at the time the letters of tutorship are certified for the tutor." In practice, the appointment is made at the same time as the appointment of the tutor, and this is the procedure contemplated by the above article.

(c) Under Louisiana law, an undertutor has never been required to furnish bond. No change is made in this respect.

Editor's Notes

Undertutor, C.C. art. 273 et seq.

Art. 4202. General duties of undertutor

The undertutor shall express his concurrence or nonconcurrence in action suggested by the tutor to the court, as set forth in Article 4271, and shall act for the minor whenever the minor's interest is opposed to that of the tutor.

Art. 4203. Compelling tutor to account

The undertutor shall apply to the court for an order compelling the tutor to file an account whenever the tutor has failed to file his annual account or at any other time when the circumstances indicate that an account should be filed.

Official Revision Comment

Because one of the tutor's most important duties is to file accounts, the duty of the undertutor to compel the tutor to do so is set forth specifically. In Art. 4391, *infra,* the court is empowered to order an account at any time, and to implement it this article makes it the duty of the undertutor to cause an order to issue whenever circumstances indicate that an account is necessary.

Art. 4204. Security of tutor, undertutor's duty regarding sufficiency

The undertutor shall:

(1) Cause the natural tutor to record the legal mortgage in favor of the minor as provided in Article 4134;

(2) Require the tutor to furnish evidence that he has a valid and merchantable title to property offered as security under a special mortgage instead of bond and that the value of the property is at least equal to the amount of security required; otherwise the undertutor shall oppose the tutor's application to furnish a special mortgage; and

(3) Apply to the court for an order compelling the tutor to furnish additional security whenever the security has become insufficient for any reason.

Editor's Notes

Undertutor's liability concerning minor's legal mortgage, C.C. art. 278.

Art. 4205. Vacancy in tutorship, duty of undertutor

The tutorship does not devolve upon the undertutor when it is vacant. If a vacancy occurs, the undertutor shall apply to the court for the appointment of a new tutor.

Art. 4206. Termination of duties

The undertutor is relieved of further duty and authority as undertutor when the minor reaches majority or is fully emancipated. However, his liability for acts prior thereto shall not be affected.

Editor's Notes

Termination, C.C. art. 280.

CHAPTER 7. DISQUALIFICATION, REVOCATION OF APPOINTMENT, RESIGNATION, AND REMOVAL

Article

Art. 4231. Disqualification of tutor

A. No person may be appointed tutor who is:

(1) Under eighteen years of age;

(2) Interdicted, or who, on contradictory hearing, is proved to be mentally incompetent;

(3) A convicted felon, under the laws of the United States or of any state or territory thereof;

(4) Indebted to the minor, unless he discharges the debt prior to the appointment;

(5) An adverse party to a suit to which the minor is a party; or

(6) A person who, on contradictory hearing, is proved to be incapable of performing the duties of the office, or to be otherwise unfit for appointment because of his physical or mental condition or bad moral character.

B. Except as provided in Paragraph C of this Article, the provisions of Subparagraphs (1), (3), (4), and (5) of Paragraph A do not apply to the parent of the minor.

C. The provisions of Paragraph B of this Article shall not apply to a natural parent of the minor who is convicted of a felony involving theft of funds or misappropriation of funds, a crime of violence as defined in R.S. 14:2(B), a sex offense as defined in R.S. 15:542 or R.S. 46:1844, or any other crime against an individual under the age of eighteen years.

Amended by Acts 1974, No. 573, § 1; Acts 2001, No. 741, § 1.

Art. 4232. Revocation of appointment; extension of time to qualify

If a person who is not a parent of the minor is appointed tutor and fails to qualify for the office within ten days from his appointment, on its own motion or on motion of any interested person, the court may revoke the appointment and appoint another qualified person to the office forthwith.

The delay allowed in this article for qualification may be extended by the court for good cause shown.

Art. 4233. Resignation of tutor

A tutor other than a parent of the minor may resign when authorized by the court under Article 4271:

(1) If subsequent to his appointment as tutor he has been invested with an office or engaged in a service or occupation which excuses him from the obligation of serving as tutor;

(2) If he has reached the age of seventy years;

(3) If because of infirmity he has become incapable of discharging the duties of his office; or

(4) For any other reason which the court in its discretion may deem sufficient.

The resignation by a tutor shall become effective when a successor is appointed, as provided in Article 4237, and when his final account has been filed and homologated.

Amended by Acts 1974, No. 163, § 1.

Art. 4234. Removal of tutor

The court may remove any tutor who is or has become disqualified; is a nonresident who has not appointed, or has left the state permanently without appointing, an agent to represent him as required by Article 4273; has become incapable of discharging the duties of his office; has mismanaged the minor's property; has failed to perform any duty imposed by law or by order of court; or if such removal would be in the best interests of the minor.

The court on its own motion may order, and on motion of any interested party shall order the tutor to show cause why he should not be removed from office. If service of this order cannot be made on the tutor for any reason, the court shall appoint an attorney at law to represent him, on whom service shall be made and against whom the proceeding shall be conducted contradictorily.

The removal of a tutor from office does not invalidate any of his official acts performed prior to his removal.

Amended by Acts 1964, No. 4, § 1; Acts 1976, No. 429, § 3.

Art. 4235. Authority and liability of tutor after resignation or removal

A tutor who has resigned or has been removed shall have no further authority as such, and no further duty except as provided by Article 4392. However, his liability for acts prior to his resignation or removal shall not be affected thereby.

Art. 4236. Undertutor, grounds for disqualification, revocation, or removal

The grounds for disqualification, revocation, and removal provided in Articles 4231, 4232, and 4234, other than indebtedness to the minor, apply also to an undertutor.

An undertutor may resign at any time with the approval of the court, but the resignation shall not be effective until a successor has been appointed and qualified.

Art. 4237. Appointment of successor tutor or undertutor

When a tutor or undertutor dies, is removed, or resigns, another tutor or undertutor shall be appointed in his place in the manner provided for an original appointment.

Art. 4238. Heirs of tutor; responsibility

Tutorship is a personal trust, which does not descend to the heirs of the tutor upon his death. However, the representative of the tutor's succession or the major heirs who have accepted his succession are responsible for the administration of the minor's property until another tutor has been appointed.

CHAPTER 8. GENERAL FUNCTIONS, POWERS, AND DUTIES OF TUTOR

Article

Art. 4261. Care of person of minor; expenses

The tutor shall have custody of and shall care for the person of the minor. He shall see that the minor is properly reared and educated in accordance with his station in life.

The expenses for the support and education of the minor should not exceed the revenue from the minor's property. However, if the revenue is insufficient to support the minor properly or to procure him an education, with the approval of the court as provided in Article 4271, the tutor may expend the minor's capital for these purposes.

Art. 4262. Administration of minor's property

The tutor shall take possession of, preserve, and administer the minor's property. He shall enforce all obligations in favor of the minor and shall represent him in all civil matters. He shall act at all times as a prudent administrator, and shall be personally responsible for all damages resulting from his failure so to act.

Natural cotutors shall be bound *in solido* except as to damages arising from the administration of all or a part of the minor's property by one of the cotutors individually pursuant to an order of the court or an agreement between the cotutors approved by the court.

Amended by Acts 1981, No. 283, § 2; Acts 1982, No. 307, § 2, eff. Jan. 1, 1983.

Art. 4263. Contracts between tutor and minor

A tutor cannot in his personal capacity or as representative for any other person make any contracts with the minor. He cannot acquire any property of the minor, or interest therein, personally or by means of a third person, except as otherwise provided by law.

Contracts prohibited by this article shall be null, and the tutor shall be liable to the minor for damages resulting therefrom.

Editor's Notes

Prescription of minor's action against tutor, C.C. art. 340. Adjudication of minor's property to tutor, C.C.P. art. 4361.

Art. 4264. Tutor's administration in his own name; procedural rights

The tutor acts in his own name as tutor, and without the concurrence of the minor. The tutor may act through a mandatary or attorney in fact outside of the parish of his residence or as provided in Article 4273.

In the performance of his duties, the tutor may exercise all procedural rights available to a litigant.

Amended by Acts 1964, No. 4, § 1.

Editor's Notes

Party defendant, C.C.P. art. 732; party plaintiff, C.C.P. art. 683.

Art. 4265. Compromise and modification of obligations

With the approval of the court as provided in Article 4271, a tutor may compromise an action or right of action by or against the minor, or extend, renew, or in any manner modify the terms of an obligation owed by or to the minor.

Editor's Notes

Bowen v. Smith, 885 So.2d 1 (La. App. 4 Cir. 2004). Court nullified settlement of minor's automobile accident claim by natural tutor who entered the settlement without court approval. Money for legal fees and other funds had to be returned. Insurer's deposit of funds into a concursus did not relieve insurer of obligation to defend after nullification of settlement. C.C. art. 1921, 2000, 2033, R.S. 9:196, C.C.P. art. 4658 et seq.

Art. 4266. Continuation of business

The court may authorize a tutor to continue any business in which the minor has an interest, when it appears to the best interest of the minor, and after compliance with Article 4271. The order of court may contain such conditions, restrictions, regulations and requirements as the court may direct.

Art. 4267. Loans to tutor for specific purposes; authority to mortgage and pledge minor's property

When it appears to the best interest of the minor, and after compliance with Article 4271, the court may authorize a tutor to borrow money for the purpose of preserving or administering the property, of paying debts, for expenditures in the regular course of a business conducted in accordance with Article 4266, or for the care, maintenance, training, or education of the minor. As security for such a loan, the court may authorize the tutor to mortgage or pledge property of the minor upon such terms and conditions as it may direct. Before authorizing a loan, the court may require the tutor to furnish additional security in an amount fixed by the court.

Art. 4268. Lease of minor's property; mineral contracts

When it appears to the best interest of the minor, and after compliance with Article 4271, the court may authorize a tutor to grant a lease upon property of the minor. The term of the lease may extend beyond the anticipated duration of the tutorship.

In addition to the requirements of Article 4271, the petition of the tutor shall set forth the terms and conditions of the proposed lease.

This article applies to mineral leases.

A tutor may execute such other contracts as are authorized by law affecting the whole or any part of the share of his ward in oil, gas, or other minerals, either discovered or undiscovered in the manner provided herein.

Amended by Acts 1974, No. 133, § 1.

Editor's Notes

LSA–C.C.P. Form 929a et seq.

Art. 4269. Investment and management of minor's property

In acquiring, investing, reinvesting, exchanging, retaining, selling, and managing property for the benefit of a minor, a tutor shall exercise the judgment and care, under the circumstances then prevailing, which men of prudence, discretion, and intelligence exercise in the management of their own affairs, not in regard to speculation but in regard to the permanent disposition of their funds, considering the probable income as well as the probable safety of their capital. Within the limitations of the foregoing standard, a tutor is authorized to acquire and retain every kind of property and every kind of investment, specifically including but not by way of limitation, bonds, debentures, and other corporate obligations, and stocks, preferred or common, and securities of any open-end or closed-end management type investment company or investment trust registered under 15 U.S.C. §§ 80a–1 through 80a–52, as from time to time amended, which men of prudence, discretion, and intelligence acquire or retain for their own account.

Editor's Notes

Building and loan shares, R.S. 6:763; federal farm loan bonds, R.S. 9:733. Withdrawal of minor's deposits, R.S. 6:313.

Art. 4269.1. Placement of minor's property in trust

At any time during his administration a tutor may apply to the court for authorization to place some or all of the minor's property in trust for administration, management and investment in accordance with the Louisiana Trust Code. The trust instrument shall name the minor as sole beneficiary of the trust, shall name a trustee, shall impose maximum spendthrift restraints, and shall be subject to termination at the option of the beneficiary upon attaining the age of majority or, should he fail to attain majority, at the option of his heirs or legatees. The court may, upon application, make such changes in the trust instrument as may be advisable. Upon creation of the trust, the tutor shall be entitled to no further commissions with respect to the trust property.

Added by Acts 1980, No. 276, § 1.

Art. 4270. Procedure for investing, reinvesting, or withdrawing funds; checking account on behalf of minor

A. An investment, reinvestment, or withdrawal of funds of a minor may be made only with the approval of the court after compliance with Article 4271.

B. Notwithstanding the provisions of Paragraph A, the court may authorize a tutor to open and maintain a checking account in the name of the "tutor on behalf of the minor" and to write checks on the account for necessary expenses of the minor without the necessity of obtaining prior approval from the court. However, such approval is necessary in order to transfer funds into the checking account, the total of which transfers shall not exceed five thousand dollars a year, except for good cause shown. All sums deposited into the checking account and all checks written on the account shall be reflected in the annual accounting in accordance with Article 4391 et seq.

C. The provisions of this Article do not create an affirmative duty on any financial institution to open, monitor, regulate, or close any account in the name of the tutor on behalf of the minor and any act by the tutor with respect to such account is a full release and discharge of the financial institution for any cause of action alleging a violation of a provision of this Chapter or any other duty of a tutor.

Amended by Acts 1995, No. 122, § 1; Acts 1995, No. 1143, § 1.

Art. 4271. Court approval of action affecting minor's interest

The tutor shall file a petition setting forth the subject matter to be determined affecting the minor's interest, with his recommendations and the reasons therefor, and with a written concurrence by the undertutor. If the court approves the recommendations, it shall render a judgment of homologation. The court may require evidence prior to approving the recommendations.

If the undertutor fails to concur in the tutor's recommendations, the tutor shall proceed by contradictory motion against him. After such hearing and evidence as the court may require, the court shall decide the issues summarily and render judgment.

Art. 4272. Court approval of payments to minor

Court approval of payments to a minor shall be governed by the provisions of Article 4521.

Amended by Acts 1993, No. 867, § 1, eff. June 23, 1993; Acts 1995, No. 122, § 1; Acts 2008, No. 716, § 1; Acts 2018, No. 607, § 1.

Art. 4273. Appointment of agent

A tutor who is a nonresident, or who is about to leave the state permanently, shall execute a power of attorney appointing a resident of this state to receive service of process in any action brought against him in his capacity as tutor; and may authorize this agent to represent him in all matters relating to the tutorship. A tutor who is domiciled in the state and who will be absent temporarily therefrom may similarly appoint such an agent for either or both of these purposes. In all cases, the power of attorney shall be filed in the tutorship proceeding.

Amended by Acts 1964, No. 4, § 1.

Art. 4274. Compensation of tutor

The court shall allow the tutor reasonable compensation for his services annually, which shall not exceed ten percent of the annual revenues of the minor's property, unless increased by the court upon proper showing that this would be inadequate.

Amended by Acts 1966, No. 36, § 1.

Art. 4275. Donations to or by minor

The tutor may accept donations made to the minor, but he cannot make donations of any property of the minor.

Editor's Notes

Acceptance of successions by minors, C.C. art. 977. Unemancipated minor's authorization to donate by marriage contract, C.C. art. 1748.

CHAPTER 9. ALIENATION OF MINOR'S PROPERTY

SECTION 1. GENERAL DISPOSITIONS

Article

SECTION 1. GENERAL DISPOSITIONS

Art. 4301. Purpose of sale or exchange

A tutor may sell or exchange any interest of a minor in property, owned either in its entirety or in indivision, for any purpose, when authorized by the court as provided in Article 4271.

Editor's Notes

Sale of property in which absentee minor owns an interest, R.S. 9:603.

Art. 4302. Terms of sale

A sale of minor's property shall be for cash, unless upon the petition of the tutor the court authorizes a credit sale. When a credit sale is authorized, the order shall specify the terms of the sale and the security.

Art. 4303. Perishable property; crops

Upon the petition of the tutor as provided in Article 4321 or 4341, the court may order the immediate sale of perishable property and growing crops either at public auction or private sale, without appraisal, and without advertisement, or with such advertisement as the court may direct.

Art. 4304. Additional bond prior to sale of immovables

Before authorizing a sale of a minor's immovable property, the court may require the tutor to furnish additional security in an amount fixed by the court.

SECTION 2. PUBLIC SALE

Art. 4321. Petition; order

In addition to the requirements of Article 4271, a petition for authority to sell property of a minor at public sale shall set forth a description of the property and the reasons which make it advantageous to the minor to sell at public sale.

The court shall render an order authorizing the sale at public auction after publication, when it considers the sale to be to the best interest of the minor. The order shall specify the minimum price to be accepted.

Editor's Notes

LSA–C.C.P. Form 941a et seq.

Art. 4322. Publication; place of sale

Notice of the sale shall be published in the parish in which the tutorship proceeding is pending, at least twice for immovable property and at least once for movable property, in the manner provided by law. The court may order additional advertisements.

When immovable property situated in another parish is to be sold, the notice shall also be published in the parish where the property is situated. When movable property situated in another parish is to be sold, the court may require the notice to be published also in the parish where the property is situated.

The sale shall be conducted in the parish in which the tutorship proceeding is pending, unless the court orders that the sale be conducted in the parish where the property is situated.

Art. 4323. Minimum price; subsequent offering

The property shall not be sold if the price bid by the last and highest bidder is less than the minimum price fixed by the court. In that event, on the petition of the tutor, the court may order another offering, with the same formalities as for an original offering, at a lower minimum price.

SECTION 3. PRIVATE SALE

Art. 4341. Petition

In addition to the requirements of Article 4271, a petition for authority to sell property of a minor at private sale shall set forth a description of the property, the price and conditions of the proposed sale, and the reasons which make it advantageous to the minor to sell at private sale.

Editor's Notes

LSA–C.C.P. Form 935a et seq.

Art. 4342. Bonds and stocks

A tutor may sell bonds and stocks of the minor at rates prevailing in the open market, after compliance with Article 4271, by obtaining a court order authorizing the sale.

The endorsement of the tutor and a certified copy of the court order authorizing the sale shall be sufficient warrant for the transfer.

Amended by Acts 1962, No. 92, § 1.

Editor's Notes

LSA–C.C.P. Form 937a et seq.

SECTION 4. ADJUDICATION TO PARENT

Art. 4361. Adjudication of minor's interest to parent co-owner

The parent of a minor who owns property in common with him may obtain a judgment adjudicating the share of the minor either in all of the property or any part thereof to the parent at a price fixed under oath by experts appointed by the court. The adjudication may be made even though there are other co-owners. The proposed adjudication must be approved by the court after compliance with Article 4271.

Editor's Notes

Judgment of court operates as sale without necessity of an act of sale, Krone v. Krone, 70 So. 605 (1916), Comment (b).

Art. 4362. Recordation of judgment; mortgage in favor of minor

A. A judgment adjudicating immovable property shall be effective only after it is recorded in the conveyance records of the parish where the property is situated. If the price of the adjudication has not been paid, the minor shall have a vendor's privilege against the property adjudicated for the unpaid price, and the judgment of adjudication shall also be recorded in the mortgage records of such parish.

B. The provisions of this Article shall apply only to adjudications made six months from and after July 1, 2006. Those made before such time shall continue to be regulated by the provisions of this Article as it existed prior to July 1, 2006.

Amended by Acts 2005, No. 169, § 3, eff. July 1, 2006.

Art. 4363. Security instead of mortgage

Instead of the mortgage provided in Article 4362, the parent may furnish security as provided in Article 4132 or a special mortgage as provided in Article 4133. The amount of the security or special mortgage shall be equal to the price of the adjudication.

SECTION 5. EXCHANGE

Art. 4371. Petition for authority to exchange

In addition to the requirements of Article 4271, a petition for authority to exchange the property of a minor for other property, or for other property and cash, shall set forth a description of both properties, the tutor's opinion of the values thereof, the conditions of the exchange, and the reasons why such an exchange would be advantageous to the minor.

Added by Acts 1962, No. 92, § 5.

CHAPTER 10. ACCOUNTING BY TUTOR

Article

Art. 4391. Duty to account; annual accounts

A tutor shall file an account annually, reckoning from the day of his appointment, and at any other time when ordered by the court on its own motion or on the application of any interested person.

Editor's Notes

Criminal penalty for failure to file account, R.S. 14:354.

Art. 4392. Final account

A tutor may file a final account at any time after expiration of the tutorship.

The court shall order the filing of a final account upon the application of the former minor after the expiration of the tutorship, or upon the rendition of a judgment ordering the removal of a tutor or authorizing his resignation.

Editor's Notes

LSA–C.C.P. Form 951a et seq.

Art. 4393. Contents of account

The account of a tutor shall contain the same matters required by Article 3333 for an account of a succession representative.

Art. 4394. Service of account

A copy of an account filed by a tutor, together with a notice that the account can be homologated after the expiration of ten days from the date of service and that any opposition must be filed before homologation, shall be served in the manner provided for service of citation:

(1) Upon the undertutor, if an annual account or other interim account is ordered by the court;

(2) Upon the former minor, if a final account is rendered after expiration of the tutorship; or

(3) Upon the successor tutor, if a final account is rendered after removal, resignation, death, or interdiction of a tutor.

Art. 4395. Opposition; homologation

An opposition to an account may be filed any time prior to homologation. An opposition shall be tried as a summary proceeding.

If no opposition has been filed, the court may homologate the account at any time after the expiration of ten days from the date of service as provided in Article 4394.

Art. 4396. Effect of homologation

A judgment homologating any account other than a final account shall be prima facie evidence of the correctness of the account.

A judgment homologating a final account has the same effect as a final judgment in an ordinary action.

Art. 4397. Deceased or interdicted tutor

If a tutor dies, an account of his administration may be filed by his succession representative or heirs. If a tutor is interdicted, such an account may be filed by his curator.

The court shall order the filing of such an account in either case, on the petition of an interested person.

Art. 4398. Cost of accounting

Accounts filed by a tutor are at the expense of the minor, except that an account filed by a tutor who has been removed or an account not filed timely is at the expense of the tutor.

CHAPTER 11. ANCILLARY TUTORSHIP PROCEDURE

Article

Art. 4431. Foreign tutor; authority and powers

Upon producing proof of his appointment, a tutor or guardian of a minor residing outside Louisiana, appointed by a court outside Louisiana, may appear in court on behalf of the minor without qualifying as tutor according to the law of Louisiana, when no tutor has been appointed in this state. He may perform acts affecting the minor's property in Louisiana, when authorized by the court of the parish in which the property is situated, in the same manner as a tutor appointed by a court in Louisiana.

Whenever the action of an undertutor would be necessary, an undertutor ad hoc shall be appointed by the court.

Art. 4432. Possession or removal of property from state

In order to take possession of the minor's property, or to remove any of it from the state, a tutor or guardian appointed by a court outside Louisiana shall file a petition for authority to do so in the court of the parish where the property, or any of it, is situated. The court shall render a judgment granting the authority prayed for, if the foreign tutor or guardian alleges in his petition that there are no Louisiana creditors of the minor, or that all such known creditors have been paid; and attaches to his petition an irrevocable power of attorney appointing a resident of this state to receive service of process in any action or proceeding brought in Louisiana to enforce a claim against the minor, or against any of the minor's property in this state.

Amended by Acts 1966, No. 36, § 1.

Art. 4433. Foreign tutor qualifying in Louisiana; authority

A tutor or guardian of a minor residing outside Louisiana, appointed by a court outside Louisiana, may be appointed as tutor by a court of competent jurisdiction in Louisiana, as provided in Article 4032.

The procedure shall be the same as provided by law for the tutorship of a minor residing in Louisiana.

After such qualification the tutor has the same rights and responsibility as a tutor originally qualified in Louisiana.

CHAPTER 12. SMALL TUTORSHIPS

Article

Art. 4461. Small tutorship defined

For the purposes of this Chapter, a small tutorship is the tutorship of a minor whose property in Louisiana has a gross value of fifty thousand dollars or less.

Amended by Acts 1976, No. 437, § 1; Acts 1979, No. 71, § 1, eff. Jan. 1, 1980; Acts 2013, No. 118, § 1, eff. June 5, 2013.

Art. 4462. Inventory dispensed with

In a proceeding under this Chapter, the applicant for the tutorship may file a detailed descriptive list of the property instead of an inventory. The list shall be sworn to and subscribed by the applicant, and shall set forth the location and fair market value of each item of property.

The list has the same effect as an inventory, and an abstract thereof recorded in the mortgage records preserves the legal mortgage of the minor.

Art. 4463. Tutor without bond; undertutor

A. The court may dispense with the furnishing of security by a legal tutor appointed in a proceeding under this Chapter.

B. If the court is satisfied that no one will accept the dative tutorship of a minor in a proceeding under this Chapter and furnish the usual security, if required, it shall appoint a dative tutor, who shall comply with all requirements except that of furnishing security.

C. The court may dispense with the appointment of an undertutor in a proceeding under this Chapter.

Amended by Acts 1990, No. 45, § 1; Acts 2013, No. 118, § 1, eff. June 5, 2013.

Art. 4464. Court costs

In proceedings under this Chapter, court costs shall be one-half of the court costs in similar proceedings in larger tutorships, provided that the minimum costs in any case shall be one hundred dollars.

Amended by Acts 2013, No. 118, § 1, eff. June 5, 2013.

TITLE VII. ADMINISTRATION OF MINOR'S PROPERTY DURING MARRIAGE OF PARENTS

Art. 4501. Rights of parents during marriage over minor's property

A. Except as otherwise provided by law, during marriage, the parents shall seek court approval to alienate, encumber, or lease the property of the minor, incur an obligation of the minor, or compromise a claim of the minor, in the same manner and using the same procedure as a tutor. The parents shall petition jointly, unless one parent is mentally incompetent, interdicted, or imprisoned, or is an absent person, in which case the other parent shall petition alone. One parent may also petition alone, with permission of the court, if the other parent fails or refuses to do so.

B. An ascendant having parental authority shall be considered a parent for the purposes of this Article.

Acts 2015, No. 260, § 2, eff. Jan. 1, 2016.

Revision Comments—2015

(a) This Article changes the law in part. In this Article, when parents are married, the parents must seek court approval to alienate, encumber, or lease property of the minor, incur an obligation of the minor, or compromise a claim of the minor. Under prior law, the father brought the action unless he was mentally incompetent, committed, imprisoned, or an absent person, in which case the mother brought the action. C.C.P. Arts. 4501 and 4502 (as amended prior to 2015). Venue for the action is found in Art. 74.6 (Rev. 2015).

(b) The reference to exceptions otherwise provided by law in Paragraph A of this Article includes the acts that parents may perform without court approval found in R.S. 9:572 (Rev. 2015).

(c) If an ascendant is granted custody during the existence of a marriage, that person has parental authority and will be considered a parent for purposes of this Article. See C.C. Art. 234 (Rev. 2015).

Art. 4502. [Blank]

TITLE VII–A. ADMINISTRATION OF COURT JUDGMENT IN FAVOR OF MINOR

Art. 4521. Payments to minor

A. In approving any proposal by which a minor is to be paid funds as the result of a judgment or settlement, the court may order:

(1) That the funds be paid directly into the registry of the court for the minor's account, to be withdrawn only upon approval of the court. Withdrawn funds shall be invested directly in an interest-bearing investment as approved by the court unless the court for good cause approves another disposition.

(2) That the funds be invested directly in an interest-bearing investment approved by the court, unless the court for good cause approves another disposition.

(3) That the funds be placed in trust in accordance with the Louisiana Trust Code to be administered by an individual or corporate trustee as determined by the court. However, the court shall not order funds which will be paid to an unemancipated minor who is in the legal custody of the Department of Children and Family Services to be placed in trust if the amount of the judgment or settlement is less than fifty thousand dollars.

(4) That the funds be paid under a structured settlement agreement as approved by the court that provides for periodic payments and is underwritten by a financially responsible entity that assumes responsibility for future payments.

(5) Any combination of Subparagraphs (1) through (4) of this Paragraph.

B. In determining whether a proposed periodic payment schedule is in the best interest of the minor, the court shall consider the following factors:

(1) Age and life expectancy of the minor.

(2) Current and anticipated financial needs of the minor.

(3) Income and estate tax implications.

(4) Impact on eligibility for government benefits.

(5) Present value of the proposed payment arrangement and the method by which the value is calculated.

Acts 2015, No. 260, § 2, eff. Jan. 1, 2016. Amended by Acts 2018, No. 607, § 1; Acts 2019, No. 17, § 1, eff. May 24, 2019.

Revision Comment—2015

This Article expounds and consolidates its predecessor articles. See C.C.P. Arts. 4521 and 4522 (as amended prior to 2015). Like its predecessors, this Article provides options to the court to protect the minor when he is paid funds pursuant to a judgment or settlement.

Art. 4522. [Blank]

TITLE VIII. INTERDICTION AND CURATORSHIP OF INTERDICTS

CHAPTER 1. IN GENERAL

Art. 4541. Petition for interdiction

A. Any person may petition for the interdiction of a natural person of the age of majority or an emancipated minor. The petitioner shall verify the petition and, to the extent known, shall set forth the following with particularity:

(1) The name, domicile, age, and current address of the petitioner and his relationship to the defendant.

(2) The name, domicile, age, and current address of the defendant and the place the petitioner proposes the defendant will reside if the relief sought in the petition is awarded.

(3) The reasons why interdiction is necessary, including a brief description of the nature and extent of the alleged infirmities of the defendant.

(4) If full interdiction is requested, the reasons why limited interdiction is inappropriate.

(5) If limited interdiction is requested, the capacity sought to be removed from the limited interdict, and the powers sought to be conferred upon the limited curator.

(6) The name and address of the spouse of the defendant.

(7) The name and address of the adult children of the defendant or, if he has none, of his parents and siblings or, if he has none, of his nearest adult relative.

(8) The name and address of any legal representative of the defendant.

For Official Comments and Annotative Materials,

(9) The name and address of any person previously designated as curator by the defendant in a writing signed by the defendant.

(10) The name, domicile, age, education, and current address of the proposed curator, and the reasons why the proposed curator should be appointed.

(11) A description with particularity of the petitioner's efforts to use less restrictive means before seeking interdiction, including all of the following:

(a) The less restrictive means for meeting the defendant's needs that were considered or implemented.

(b) If a less restrictive means was not considered or implemented, the reason that the less restrictive means was not considered or implemented.

(c) The reason a less restrictive means is insufficient to meet the needs of the defendant.

B. The petitioner shall make a reasonable effort to obtain the information required by this Article.

Acts 2000, 1st Ex.Sess., No. 25, § 3, eff. July 1, 2001. Amended by Acts 2003, No. 1008, § 2; Acts 2020, No. 258, § 1.

Revision Comments—2000

(a) This Article changes the law. Most significantly, it sets forth in detail the required elements of an interdiction petition. Moreover, it requires that every interdiction petition be verified by the petitioner.

(b) Article 10 of the Code of Civil Procedure addresses jurisdiction over interdiction proceedings. See C.C.P. Art. 10. Under that Article, a Louisiana district court has jurisdiction over an interdiction proceeding if the person sought to be interdicted is domiciled in this state, or is present in this state and has property herein. See C.C.P. Art. 10(A)(3).

Editor's Notes

See the Interdiction checklist in the preliminary material of this publication. See also La. C.C. art. 389-399 and comments in the statutory appendix.

Art. 4542. Venue

Venue for an interdiction proceeding is the parish where the defendant is domiciled, where he resides if he has no domicile in this state, or where he is physically present if he has no residence in this state.

Acts 2000, 1st Ex.Sess., No. 25, § 3, eff. July 1, 2001.

Revision Comments—2000

(a) This Article reproduces the substance of Code of Civil Procedure Article 4541 as it existed prior to the 2000 Revision.

(b) An ancillary interdiction proceeding is governed by Code of Civil Procedure Article 4556 (Rev. 2000).

Art. 4543. Service upon defendant and notice to interested persons

A. Service of the citation and petition shall be personal. Nevertheless, if the defendant is domiciled in this state, but is located elsewhere, service may be made by the delivery of a certified copy of the petition, citation, and all attachments, to the defendant personally by any person over the age of eighteen years. Service is effective as of the date a notarized affidavit is filed into the record affirming the personal delivery. Failure to serve the defendant as provided in this Paragraph shall preclude the court from granting the relief sought in the petition.

B. Within three days of filing the petition, the petitioner shall mail a copy of the petition by certified mail, return receipt requested, to the last known address of each other person named in the petition. Failure to mail a copy of the petition to any such person shall not affect the validity of the proceeding, but may subject the petitioner or his attorney to sanctions.

Acts 2000, 1st Ex.Sess., No. 25, § 3, eff. July 1, 2001.

Revision Comments—2000

(a) This Article changes the law. First, it mandates personal service (or delivery) on the defendant in all cases. Formerly, service on an appointed attorney was permissible under certain circumstances. Thus, domiciliary service is not effective in interdiction suits. Second, it requires the mailing of notice to those with a possible interest in the defendant's interdiction.

(b) If the defendant cannot be served in accordance with this Article, the court cannot interdict him. However, if the circumstances warrant it, the court may treat the defendant as an absent person and appoint a curator pursuant to Civil Code Articles 47 through 59 (Rev. 1990).

Art. 4544. Appointment of attorney

A. If the defendant makes no timely appearance through an attorney, the petitioner shall apply for an order appointing an attorney to represent the defendant. Pursuant to such a motion, or on its own motion, the court shall appoint an attorney to represent the defendant. If the defendant either retains his own attorney, or intelligently and voluntarily waives the assistance of an attorney, the court shall discharge the court-appointed attorney. The court-appointed attorney shall represent the defendant until discharged by the court.

B. The attorney representing a defendant shall personally visit the defendant, unless such visit is excused by the court for good cause. To the extent possible, the attorney shall discuss with the defendant the allegations in the petition, the relevant facts and law, and the rights and options of the defendant regarding the disposition of the case. Failure of the attorney to perform any of the duties imposed by this Paragraph shall not affect the validity of the proceeding, but may subject the attorney to sanctions.

Acts 2000, 1st Ex.Sess., No. 25, § 3, eff. July 1, 2001.

Revision Comments—2000

(a) This Article changes the law. Under prior law, every defendant who did not answer an interdiction petition through counsel was afforded an attorney. While this Article continues to mandate the appointment of counsel in all interdiction cases, it requires the petitioner's attorney affirmatively to move for the appointment of counsel if the defendant has either filed no answer or has answered in proper person. Finally, unlike prior law, this Article requires an attorney to personally visit his client and advise him of the allegations made in the petition, the nature of the interdiction proceeding, and the client's rights and options.

(b) If the court previously appointed counsel in connection with a motion for temporary or preliminary interdiction and that attorney has not withdrawn as counsel of record, the court need not appoint or reappoint an attorney under this Article.

(c) An attorney appointed pursuant to this Article is not empowered to accept service of the petition and citation on behalf of a defendant whom the petitioner has failed to serve in accordance with Code of Civil Procedure Article 4543 (Rev. 2000). See Segur v. Pellerin, 16 La. 63 (1840).

Art. 4545. Appointment of examiner

After the filing of a petition for interdiction, the court may appoint an examiner who has training or experience in the type of infirmity alleged. The court may compel the defendant to submit to an examination by the examiner. Not less than seven days prior to a hearing, the examiner shall provide a written report to the court, all counsel of record, and any unrepresented parties. The report shall include such matters as the court directs. The report may consider the infirmities suffered by the defendant, the appropriateness of interdiction, including whether a less restrictive means of intervention is available, the type of interdiction that is appropriate, and any other relevant matters.

Acts 2000, 1st Ex.Sess., No. 25, § 3, eff. July 1, 2001.

Revision Comments—2000

(a) This Article refines prior law. Under Civil Code Article 393 (1870), the court could appoint "any" person, including a health-care professional, to visit and to examine the defendant prior to an interdiction hearing. This Article preserves the substance of prior law but more fully defines the reporting requirements of any such court-appointed examiner. This Article suppresses the requirement that an examiner be appointed when the defendant is located out of this state.

(b) An appointed examiner is considered a court-appointed expert within the meaning of Louisiana Code of Evidence Article 706(A).

Art. 4546. Fixing of hearings or trial

A hearing or trial in an interdiction proceeding shall be fixed and notice shall be served in the manner prescribed for summary proceedings. In addition, such notice shall be served on the defendant in the manner prescribed by Article 4543(A). Except as provided in Article 4549, the petitioner shall mail a copy of the order fixing a hearing or trial by first-class United States mail, postage prepaid, to the last known address of each other person named in the petition at least ten days prior to the hearing. Failure to mail a copy of the order to any such person shall not affect the validity of the proceeding, but may subject the petitioner or his attorney to sanctions.

Acts 2000, 1st Ex.Sess., No. 25, § 3, eff. July 1, 2001.

Revision Comments—2000

(a) This Article changes the law. This Article adds the requirement that the petitioner or movant give notice by first-class mail to other persons with a potential interest in the defendant's interdiction, and to the defendant personally. However, the lack of proper notice to "each other person" will not affect the validity of the interdiction proceeding.

(b) A summary hearing in an interdiction matter may be requested through the filing of a contradictory motion or rule to show cause, and may be fixed by order of the court. See C.C.P. Arts. 2593–2596.

Art. 4547. Hearing

An interdiction proceeding shall be heard summarily and by preference. The defendant has a right to be present at the hearing and the court shall not conduct the hearing in his absence, unless the court determines that good cause exists to do so. The defendant has the right to present evidence, to testify, to cross-examine witnesses, and to otherwise participate at the hearing. If the defendant is unable to come to the courthouse for the hearing, the judge may hold the hearing where the defendant is located. The hearing may be closed for good cause. The court may call witnesses not called by the parties and may require the presence of a proposed curator.

Acts 2000, 1st Ex.Sess., No. 25, § 3, eff. July 1, 2001.

Revision Comments—2000

(a) This Article changes the law. While this Article preserves much of the existing law regarding interdiction hearings, it changes the law by requiring the presence of the defendant, unless the court determines that good cause exists for his absence, and by permitting the court to require the presence of any proposed curator at the interdiction hearing.

(b) The Louisiana rules of evidence apply to interdiction hearings. See Louisiana Code of Evidence Article 1101(A)(1).

Art. 4548. Burden of proof

The petitioner in an interdiction proceeding bears the burden of proof by clear and convincing evidence.

Acts 2000, 1st Ex.Sess., No. 25, § 3, eff. July 1, 2001. Amended by Acts 2003, No. 1008, § 2.

Revision Comments—2000

(a) This Article clarifies the law by making it clear that the burden of proof in all interdiction proceedings is "clear and convincing evidence" rather than a "preponderance of the evidence."

(b) The "clear and convincing" burden of proof applies in all interdiction proceedings, including those in which the petitioner seeks full interdiction, limited interdiction, temporary interdiction, or preliminary interdiction.

Art. 4549. Temporary and preliminary interdiction; attorney

A. Temporary Interdiction: (1) When the court finds that immediate and irreparable injury, loss, or damage will result to the person or property of the defendant before a hearing can be held, the court may order temporary interdiction without notice and without an adversarial hearing. In that order, the court shall state why the order was granted without notice and without an adversarial hearing and shall schedule a preliminary interdiction hearing to be held not more than ten days following the signing of the ex parte judgment of temporary interdiction. On motion of the defendant or for extraordinary reasons shown at a contradictory hearing, the court may continue the hearing for one additional period not to exceed ten days.

(2) A pleading requesting ex parte temporary interdiction shall be accompanied by all of the following:

(a) An affidavit by a licensed physician or psychologist attesting to facts supporting the claim that all grounds for temporary interdiction set forth in Civil Code Article 391 exist.

(b) A verified petition or affidavit attesting to facts supporting the claim that immediate and irreparable injury, loss, or damage will result to the person or property of the defendant before he or his attorney can be heard.

(c) An affidavit by the movant or his attorney attesting to the efforts made to give notice to the defendant or the reasons supporting a claim that notice should not be required.

B. Preliminary Interdiction: (1) The court shall not grant a judgment of preliminary interdiction prior to an adversarial hearing. The court shall conduct a preliminary interdiction hearing within twenty days of signing the order scheduling the hearing.

(2) No later than seventy-two hours prior to a preliminary interdiction hearing, all orders, pleadings, and supporting documents shall be served personally on the defendant and his attorney. To the extent possible, the movant shall give reasonable notice of the preliminary interdiction hearing to all other persons named in the petition.

C. Attorney. In an ex parte judgment of temporary interdiction and in every order scheduling a preliminary interdiction hearing, the court shall appoint an attorney to represent the defendant. If the defendant either retains his own attorney, or intelligently and voluntarily waives the assistance of an attorney, the court shall discharge the court-appointed attorney.

Acts 2000, 1st Ex.Sess., No. 25, § 3, eff. July 1, 2001. Amended by Acts 2003, No. 1008, § 2.

Revision Comments—2000

(a) This Article changes the law. While this Article is substantially similar to the provisions enacted by the legislature in 1997, some differences exist. First, this Article tracks to a greater extent the provisions of the Code of Civil Procedure relating to preliminary injunctions and temporary restraining orders. See C.C.P. Arts. 3601-3613. Indeed, this Article adopts that terminology rather than "provisional interdiction" and "ex parte provisional interdiction." Second, this Article assures that there is no period during which the interdict is not protected by a curator pending a final interdiction hearing.

(b) Civil Code Article 391 (Rev. 2000), sets forth the grounds for temporary interdiction and preliminary interdiction. Civil Code Article 397 (Rev. 2000), prescribes the time at which any judgment of interdiction shall terminate. See C.C. Art. 397(B) (Rev. 2000). This termination date, or any earlier date established by the court, shall appear on any judgment of temporary interdiction or preliminary interdiction.

Art. 4550. Costs and attorney fees

The court may render judgment for costs and attorney fees, or any part thereof, against any party, as the court may consider fair. However, no attorney fees shall be awarded to a petitioner when judgment is granted against the petitioner or the petition is dismissed on the merits.

Acts 2000, 1st Ex.Sess., No. 25, § 3, eff. July 1, 2001.

Revision Comments—2000

(a) This Article resolves a conflict in the law between C.C. Art. 397 (1870) and C.C.P. Art. 4551 as it existed prior to the 2000 Revision.

(b) Costs may include the fees of any examiner or other health-care professional.

(c) This Article applies to all proceedings relating to interdiction, including those taking place after the entry of judgment.

Art. 4551. Judgment

A. In the judgment of interdiction, the court shall:

(1) Appoint a curator.

(2) Appoint an undercurator, unless an undercurator is not required by law.

(3) State that the powers of the curator commence only upon qualification.

(4) Direct the clerk of court to record the judgment in the conveyance and mortgage records of the parish where it was rendered.

(5) Set forth the name, domicile, age, and current address of the defendant.

B. In addition, a judgment of limited interdiction shall confer upon the limited curator only those powers necessitated by the interests of the limited interdict to be protected through limited interdiction and shall state that the limited interdict retains the capacity of a natural person except as expressly limited by the judgment.

C. In addition, a judgment granting or extending temporary or preliminary interdiction shall set forth the date of termination.

Acts 2000, 1st Ex.Sess., No. 25, § 3, eff. July 1, 2001. Amended by Acts 2016, No. 122, § 1.

Revision Comments—2000

(a) This Article changes the law. This Article sets forth all matters that shall be addressed in every judgment of interdiction, including judgments of full interdiction, limited interdiction, temporary interdiction, and preliminary interdiction.

(b) The court shall appoint a curator in every judgment of interdiction. However, if the court believes that additional hearings are necessary regarding the appointment of a more permanent curator, the court can conduct such hearings after entry of the judgment of interdiction.

(c) The court need not appoint an undercurator when it appoints as curator a nonprofit curatorship program. R.S. 9:1031(F): "Notwithstanding any law to the contrary, in cases wherein the program is appointed curator . . ., the appointment of an undercurator . . . is not required."

Art. 4552. Recordation of notice of suit and judgment

A. The clerk of court shall cause to be recorded a notice of the filing of the interdiction suit in the conveyance and mortgage records of the parish in which the interdiction action is pending. The clerk of court shall record every judgment granting, modifying, or terminating interdiction in the conveyance and mortgage records of the parish in which the judgment was rendered.

B. Within fifteen days of his qualification, the curator shall cause the judgment of interdiction to be recorded in the conveyance and mortgage records of every other parish in which the interdict owns immovable property. Within fifteen days from the signing of a judgment modifying or terminating interdiction, the curator shall cause it to be recorded in the conveyance and mortgage records of every other parish in which the interdict owns immovable property.

C. A clerk or curator whose failure to perform his duties causes damage is liable only to those who contract with the interdict and who neither knew nor should have known of the interdiction proceedings or judgment.

Acts 2000, 1st Ex.Sess., No. 25, § 3, eff. July 1, 2001. Amended by Acts 2003, No. 1008, § 2.

Revision Comments—2000

(a) This Article changes the law. This Article requires the clerk of court to record a notice of the filing of an interdiction suit in the mortgage records as well as the conveyance records of the parish in which the interdiction suit is pending. This Article allows a curator fifteen days from his qualification, rather than ten days from his appointment, to record an interdiction judgment in parishes other than the one in which judgment was rendered. This Article relieves the curator of the obligation to record a judgment of interdiction in the parish is which judgment was rendered because the clerk of court has this responsibility.

(b) A petitioner may, but is not required to, file notices of pendency of the interdiction proceeding in parishes in which the interdict owns immovable property in accordance with Code of Civil Procedure Articles 3751 through 3753.

Art. 4553. Post-judgment proceedings

A. Except for good cause shown, the court and division or section rendering an interdiction judgment shall conduct all post-judgment proceedings related to the interdiction.

B. Except for good cause shown, all proceedings for injunction pursuant to Article 3601 et seq., including ancillary proceedings, involving an interdicted person as applicant or as an adverse party, shall be conducted by the court and division or section rendering the interdiction judgment.

C. Any proceeding under this Article pending in any court or division, or section, other than the court and division or section rendering the interdiction judgment, shall be transferred immediately to the court and division or section rendering the interdiction judgment upon motion of any party or upon motion of the court.

Acts 2000, 1st Ex.Sess., No. 25, § 3, eff. July 1, 2001. Amended by Acts 2008, No. 806, § 1, eff. July 7, 2008.

Revision Comments—2000

This Article changes the law in part. The phrase "(e)xcept for good cause shown," clarifies that there is no jurisdictional problem associated with a court other than that which rendered the interdiction judgment conducting a post-judgment proceeding.

Art. 4554. Modification or termination of interdiction

On motion of the court or any person, including the interdict, the court may modify or terminate its judgment when the court finds, by a preponderance of the evidence, that the terms of that judgment are currently either excessive or insufficient or that the ability of the interdict to care for his person or property has so changed as to warrant modification or termination. Except for good cause, the court shall follow substantially the same procedures that apply to an original petition for interdiction before it modifies or terminates an interdiction judgment.

Acts 2000, 1st Ex.Sess., No. 25, § 3, eff. July 1, 2001.

Revision Comments—2000

This Article does not change the law.

Art. 4554.1. [Blank]

Art. 4555. Appeal

An appeal from a judgment of interdiction, an order or judgment appointing or removing a curator or undercurator, or a judgment modifying or terminating interdiction shall be taken within thirty days from the applicable date provided by Article 2087. The order or judgment is not suspended during the pendency of an appeal. The acts of a curator or an undercurator shall not be invalidated by the annulment of his appointment on appeal.

Acts 2000, 1st Ex.Sess., No. 25, § 3, eff. July 1, 2001.

Revision Comments—2000

This Article changes the law in part. This Article does not reproduce the substance of Civil Code Article 396 (1870) that provided for the "hearing of new proofs" in interdiction appeals. This Article does not change the general law of interdiction appeals as provided in Code Civil Procedure Article 4548 as it existed prior to the 2000 Revision.

Art. 4556. Ancillary interdiction procedure

A. Upon producing proof of his appointment, a conservator who was appointed by a court outside of Louisiana may appear in court on behalf of the protected person without qualifying as a curator according to the law of Louisiana when no curator has been appointed in this state. In accordance with the authority set forth in his letters, such a conservator may perform acts affecting the protected person's property in Louisiana when authorized by the court of the parish in which the property is located. Once so authorized, the conservator shall act in the same manner and in accordance with the same procedures as a curator appointed by a court in Louisiana. Whenever the action of an undercurator would be necessary, the court shall appoint an undercurator ad hoc.

B. In order to take possession of the protected person's property, or to remove any of it from the state, a conservator appointed by a court outside Louisiana shall file a petition for authority to do so in the court of the parish in which any of the property is located. The court shall render a judgment granting the authority prayed for if the foreign conservator alleges in the petition that there are no Louisiana creditors of the protected person, or that all such known creditors have been paid, and if the foreign conservator attaches to the petition an irrevocable power of attorney appointing a resident of this state to receive service of process in any action or proceeding brought in Louisiana to enforce a claim against the protected person, or against any of the protected person's property located in this state.

Acts 2000, 1st Ex.Sess., No. 25, § 3, eff. July 1, 2001. Amended by Acts 2016, No. 333, § 2.

Revision Comments—2000

This Article does not change the law.

Arts. 4557 to 4560. [Blank]

CHAPTER 2. CURATORS AND UNDERCURATORS

Article

Art. 4561. Appointment of curator

A. The court shall appoint as curator the qualified person who is best able to fulfill the duties of his office.

B. (1) The following persons are not qualified to serve as a curator of an interdict:

(a) A person under eighteen years of age.

(b) An interdicted person.

(c) A nonresident of the state without a resident agent for service of process.

(2) Except for good cause shown, the following persons are not qualified to serve as a curator of an interdict:

(a) A convicted felon.

(b) A person indebted to the interdict at the time of appointment.

(c) An adverse party in a lawsuit pending against the interdict at the time of appointment.

(d) An owner, operator, or employee of long-term care institutions where the interdict is receiving care, unless he is related to the interdict.

C. (1) The court shall consider the qualified persons in the following order of preference:

(a) A person designated by the defendant in a writing signed by him while he had sufficient ability to communicate a reasoned preference.

(b) The spouse of the defendant.

(c) An adult child of the defendant.

(d) A parent of the defendant.

(e) An individual with whom the defendant has resided for more than six months prior to the filing of the petition.

(f) Any other person.

(2) The court may appoint separate curators for the person and affairs of the interdict pursuant to Article 4069.

D. At any time prior to qualification, the court may revoke the appointment for good cause and appoint another qualified person.

Acts 2000, 1st Ex.Sess., No. 25, § 3, eff. July 1, 2001.

Revision Comments—2000

(a) This Article changes the law. Under this Article, a defendant's preincapacity choice regarding a curator is given priority. Formerly, the defendant's preincapacity choice was given preference only if expressed in a power of attorney. Furthermore, this Article changes the law by enumerating additional persons (other than the defendant's designee and spouse) in the statutory order of preference. This Article preserves the option of appointing separate curators over the person and property of the interdict. This Article changes the law, however, by rendering ineligible for service as a curator (but not as undercurator) the operator of a nursing home or similar facility.

(b) As to what constitutes a signed writing, see Comment (c), Civil Code Article 1837 (Rev. 1984).

(c) The court may appoint a nonprofit curatorship service program to serve as curator. See R.S. 9:1031–9:1034.

Art. 4562. Qualification of curator

A. The person appointed qualifies as curator upon furnishing the security required by law and taking an oath to discharge faithfully the duties of his office.

B. (1) If the person fails to qualify for office within ten days from his appointment or within such other period specified by the court, the court on its own motion, or on motion of any interested person, may revoke the appointment and appoint another qualified person.

(2) The delay allowed for qualification may be extended by the court for good cause.

C. The court rendering an interdiction judgment may issue any protective order necessary to protect the interest of the interdict in the interim between the appointment and qualification of the curator.

Acts 2000, 1st Ex.Sess., No. 25, § 3, eff. July 1, 2001.

Revision Comments—2000

(a) This Article changes the law to permit the extension of the time period allowed for qualification "for good cause."

(b) Code of Civil Procedure Article 4562 (Rev. 2000) states that a court rendering an interdiction judgment may issue protective orders to protect the interdict in the interim between appointment and qualification of the curator.

Art. 4563. Inventory and security

A. The person appointed as the curator shall furnish security conditioned on the faithful discharge of his duties. The rules provided in Articles 4101 through 4102, 4131 through 4133, and 4136 apply to curatorship of interdicts. Provisions establishing special rules for natural tutors and parents shall not apply in the context of interdiction and curatorship.

B. A detailed descriptive list, sworn to and subscribed by the applicant setting forth the fair market value of each item of property of the interdict, shall be permitted in lieu of an inventory in interdiction matters, unless otherwise ordered by the court.

Acts 2000, 1st Ex.Sess., No. 25, § 3, eff. July 1, 2001.

Revision Comments—2000

This Article changes the law by permitting the substitution of a sworn descriptive list for an inventory in all cases. See Cf. C.C.P. Art. 4462. Furthermore, this Article clarifies that the provisions setting forth special security rules for "natural tutors" have no application in the context of interdiction.

Art. 4564. Letters of curatorship

Upon qualification of the appointed curator, the court or clerk thereof shall issue letters of curatorship in the name and under the seal of the court. The letters shall set forth the date of the qualification of the curator and the date, if any, on which the letters expire. Letters of curatorship issued to a limited curator shall also set forth the powers of the limited curator.

Acts 2000, 1st Ex.Sess., No. 25, § 3, eff. July 1, 2001.

Revision Comments—2000

This Article changes the law. This Article requires that letters set forth the date of qualification and the date, if any, on which the letters expire. This Article requires that letters of limited curatorship set forth the powers of the limited curator.

Art. 4565. Undercurators

A. (1) The court shall appoint as undercurator the qualified person best able to fulfill the duties of his office. The person appointed as undercurator qualifies by taking an oath to discharge faithfully the duties of his office.

(2) At any time prior to qualification, the court may revoke the appointment for good cause and appoint another qualified person.

(3) If a person fails to qualify within ten days from his appointment or within the period specified by the court, the court on its own motion or on motion of any interested person, may revoke the appointment and appoint another qualified person. The delay allowed for qualification may be extended by the court for good cause.

B. The undercurator shall:

(1) Notify the court when the curator has failed to qualify timely for office.

(2) Have free access to the interdict and to all records relating to the interdict relevant to his office.

(3) Review all accounts and personal reports filed by the curator.

(4) Notify the court when he has reason to believe that the curator has failed to perform any duties imposed by law, including the duties to file necessary accounts and personal reports, and to maintain adequate security.

(5) Approve or disapprove any transactions that require his concurrence.

(6) Move to appoint a successor for a curator who becomes disqualified or whose office terminates.

(7) Move to appoint a successor for a curator who violates any of the provisions of Article 4566.

C. The undercurator shall have no duties, either express or implied, other than those set forth in this Article and in Civil Code Article 393.

Acts 2000, 1st Ex.Sess., No. 25, § 3, eff. July 1, 2001. Amended by Acts 2016, No. 110, § 2, eff. May 19, 2016.

Revision Comments—2000

(a) This Article changes the law.

(b) Like a curator, an undercurator shall take an oath to discharge faithfully the duties of his office to qualify for office. Under Code of Civil Procedure Article 4565 (Rev. 2000), the undercurator's powers commence upon his qualification.

(c) An undercurator's access to records is limited to those "relevant to his office". For example, an undercurator appointed to monitor a curator of the interdict's property does not need access to the interdict's medical and personal records.

Art. 4566. Management of affairs of the interdict

A. Except as otherwise provided by law, the relationship between interdict and curator is the same as that between minor and tutor. The rules provided by Articles 4261 through 4269, 4270 through 4274, 4301 through 4342, and 4371 apply to curatorship of interdicts. Nevertheless, provisions establishing special rules for natural tutors and parents shall not apply in the context of interdiction.

B. A curator who owns an interest in property with the interdict or who holds a security interest or lien that encumbers the property of the interdict may acquire the property, or any interest therein, from the interdict upon compliance with Article 4271, with prior court authorization, and when it would be in the best interest of the interdict. Except for good cause shown, the court shall appoint an independent appraiser to value the interest to be acquired by the curator.

C. A curator may accept donations made to the interdict. A curator shall not make donations of the property of the interdict except as provided by law.

D. A curator may place the property of the interdict in trust in accordance with the provisions of Article 4269.1. The trust shall be subject to termination at the option of the interdict upon termination of the interdiction, or if the interdict dies during the interdiction, at the option of his heirs or legatees.

E. A curator shall inform the undercurator reasonably in advance of any material changes in the living arrangements of the interdict and any transactions materially affecting his person or affairs.

F. A curator shall not establish or move the place of dwelling of the interdict outside this state without prior court authorization.

G. A curator may not consent to an abortion or sterilization of the interdict without prior court authorization.

H. Neither a curator nor a court shall admit or commit an interdict to a mental health treatment facility except in accordance with the provisions of R.S. 28:50 through 64.

I. A curator appointed in an order of temporary interdiction shall have no authority to admit the defendant to a residential or long- term care facility in the absence of good cause shown at a contradictory hearing.

J. A curator shall allow communication, visitation, and interaction between an interdict who is over the age of eighteen years and a relative of the interdict by blood, adoption, or affinity within the third degree, or another individual who has a relationship with the interdict based on or productive of strong affection if it would serve the best interest of the interdict.

K. Notwithstanding the requirements of Article 4270 or any other provision of law to the contrary, a curator shall have authority to access deposit accounts held in the name of the interdict and authority to establish and maintain deposit accounts in the name of the "curator on behalf of the interdict", unless the letters of curatorship expressly limit such authority.

Acts 2000, 1st Ex.Sess., No. 25, § 3, eff. July 1, 2001. Amended by Acts 2016, No. 110, § 2, eff. May 19, 2016; Acts 2021, No. 163, § 1.

Revision Comments—2000

(a) This Article changes the law. Although this Article retains the basic structure of Code of Civil Procedure Article 4554 as it existed prior to the 2000 Revision (by retaining extensive cross-references to tutorship Articles governing management of a minor's affairs), it omits cross-references that are not necessary or that are made elsewhere in the Revision.

(b) R.S. 9:1022–1024 set forth detailed provisions governing a curator's ability to donate the interdict's property.

Art. 4567. Expenses of interdict and legal dependents

The curator shall expend that portion of the revenue from the property of the interdict as is necessary to care properly for his person or affairs, and with court authorization, to support his legal dependents. If the revenue is insufficient for these purposes, the curator may expend the capital of the interdict, with court authorization in the manner provided by Article 4271.

Acts 2000, 1st Ex.Sess., No. 25, § 3, eff. July 1, 2001.

Revision Comments—2000

This Article does not change the law.

Art. 4568. Removal of a curator or undercurator

On motion of any interested person, or on its own motion, the court may remove a curator or undercurator from office for good cause. Good cause may include but not be limited to a violation of Article 4566(J).

Unless otherwise ordered by the court, removal of the curator or undercurator by the court is effective upon qualification of the appointed successor.

Acts 2000, 1st Ex.Sess., No. 25, § 3, eff. July 1, 2001. Amended by Acts 2016, No. 110, § 2, eff. May 19, 2016.

Revision Comments—2000

(a) This Article changes the law. This Article omits any provision establishing a maximum term of ten years for certain curators. See C.C. Art. 414 (1870). This Article omits cross-references to Code of Civil Procedure Articles 4231–4238 because the substance of those tutorship Articles is set forth in this Article.

(b) In a temporary interdiction or preliminary interdiction, the temporary curator or preliminary curator is removed from office and replaced by the curator appointed in the judgment of interdiction.

(c) Good cause for removal exists when the curator becomes disqualified because he no longer satisfies the requirements set forth in Code of Civil Procedure Article 4561 (Rev. 2000).

(d) R.S. 9:1025 supplements this Article by enumerating several circumstances under which good cause exists for removal.

(e) A curator's office terminates automatically upon his death or upon termination of interdiction. In such cases, "removal" from office is unnecessary.

Art. 4569. Post-judgment monitoring and reporting

A. A curator with responsibility for affairs of the interdict shall file an account annually, upon the termination of his office, and at any other time ordered by the court. A curator with responsibility for the person of an interdict shall file a personal report describing the location and condition of the interdict annually, upon the termination of his responsibilities, and at any other time ordered by the court. At the time of filing, the curator shall send copies of any required account or personal report by first class United States mail postage prepaid to the undercurator and any successor curator. The provisions of Articles 4393 and 4398 shall apply to accounts by curators.

B. The court may appoint an examiner at any time to review an account or personal report of the curator, to interview the interdict, curator, or undercurator, or to make any other investigation. At any time, the court may appoint an attorney to represent the interdict.

Acts 2000, 1st Ex.Sess., No. 25, § 3, eff. July 1, 2001.

Revision Comments—2000

(a) This Article changes the law. This Article omits any cross-reference to Code of Civil Procedure Article 4392, because that Article makes final accounts merely permissive in most cases. This Article changes the law by mandating the filing of a final account or personal report at the termination of every curator's appointment. This Article eliminates the requirement that all accounts be served and homologated in accordance with Code of Civil Procedure Articles 4394 through 4396.

(b) The curator's personal report should, among other things, describe whether there has been a material change in the functional ability of the interdict to care for his person and affairs.

(c) The accounting and personal-reporting requirements applies to all curators, including temporary and preliminary curators.

Art. 4570. Cause of action for visitation with the interdict

A. Any relative of an interdict by blood, adoption, or affinity within the third degree, or an individual who has a relationship with the interdict based on or productive of strong affection may file a rule to show cause seeking visitation, communication, or interaction with an interdict who is over the age of eighteen years.

B. Any person filing a cause of action pursuant to Paragraph A of this Article may request an expedited hearing on the cause of action, and upon showing of good cause, shall be entitled to an expedited hearing.

C. Good cause shall include but is not limited to a showing that the interdict suffers from an illness or condition because of which he is not likely to survive beyond six months.

Added by Acts 2016, No. 110, § 2, eff. May 19, 2016.

TITLE IX. PARTITION BETWEEN CO–OWNERS

CHAPTER 1. GENERAL DISPOSITIONS

Article

Art. 4601. Methods of partition

Partition of property may be made either nonjudicially or judicially.

Editor's Notes

Jury trial not permitted, C.C.P. art. 1732. Basis for partition, C.C. art. 1308. LSA–C.C.P. Form 2101 et seq.

Art. 4602. Judicial partition

Partition must be judicial when:

(1) A party is an unrepresented absentee, minor, or mental incompetent; or

(2) All the interested parties cannot agree upon a nonjudicial partition.

Art. 4603. Same; procedure; venue

A person desiring a judicial partition of property shall petition for it in a court of competent jurisdiction. The partition proceeding shall be brought in the venue provided by Article 80(2) if the property sought to be partitioned is immovables, or both movables and immovables; or in the parish where some of the property is situated, if it consists only of movables.

Except as otherwise provided by law, a partition proceeding is subject to the rules regulating ordinary proceedings.

Art. 4604. Inventory

The court may order that an inventory be made of all property sought to be partitioned, in accordance with the provisions of Articles 3131 through 3137.

Art. 4605. Preference; appointment of notary; discretion of court

A partition proceeding shall be tried with preference over other ordinary proceedings.

After the trial of the proceeding, if the court finds that the plaintiff is entitled to a partition of the property, the court shall appoint a notary to make the partition in accordance with law.

Except as otherwise provided in Article 4606, the court has discretion to direct the manner and conditions of effecting the partition, so that it will be most advantageous and convenient to the parties.

Art. 4606. Partition in kind

Except as otherwise provided by law, or unless the property is indivisible by nature or cannot conveniently be divided, the court shall order the partition to be made in kind.

Art. 4607. Partition by licitation or by private sale

When a partition is to be made by licitation, the sale shall be conducted at public auction and after the advertisements required for judicial sales under execution. When a partition is to be made at private sale without the consent of all co-owners, the sale shall be for not less than the appraised value of the property, and documents required pursuant to a court order shall be executed on behalf of the absentee or nonconsenting co-owner by a court-appointed representative, who may be a co-owner, after the advertisements required for judicial sales under execution are made. All counsel of record, including curators appointed to represent absentee defendants, and persons appearing in proper person shall be given notice of the sale date. At any time prior to the sale, the parties may agree upon a nonjudicial partition.

Amended by Acts 1990, No. 832, § 1; Acts 2020, No. 281, § 2, eff. June 11, 2020; Acts 2021, No. 27, § 2, eff. June 1, 2021.

Art. 4608. Controversy before notary effecting partition

If there should be any controversy between the parties in the course of the proceedings before the notary effecting the partition, he shall record the objections and declarations of the parties in his procès verbal. Unless otherwise ordered by the court, such objections shall not suspend the proceedings before the notary, but any party may present his objections to the court in his opposition to the homologation of the partition.

Art. 4609. Homologation of partition

When the partition has been completed by the notary, he shall file his procès verbal of the partition, or a copy thereof, in the court which ordered the partition. Any party may rule all other parties into court to show cause why the partition should not be homologated or rejected.

Art. 4610. Opposition to homologation

An opposition may be filed at any time prior to the homologation of the partition. If no opposition has been filed, the partition may be homologated at any time after ten days from the service of the rule to show cause.

Art. 4611. Supplementary partition when rule to reject or opposition to homologation sustained

When a rule to reject the partition, or an opposition to its homologation, is sustained in whole or in part, the court shall rectify the partition, or refer the parties to the same or another notary who shall prepare a supplementary act of partition in conformity with the order of the court.

Articles 4609 and 4610 apply to this supplementary partition.

For Official Comments and Annotative Materials,

Art. 4612. Finality of partition when rule to reject or opposition unfounded

When the court finds that a rule to reject the partition, or an opposition to its homologation, is unfounded and that all legal formalities have been observed, it shall homologate the act of partition.

Editor's Notes

Prescription of action for rescission of partition, C.C. arts. 1413, 1414.

Art. 4613. Attorney's fee in uncontested proceedings

When there is no contest of the partition proceeding by any defendant, the court shall allow the attorney for the plaintiff a reasonable fee for his services. Except as provided in the second paragraph of this article, the fee shall be taxed as costs of court and paid out of the mass of the funds or the property partitioned, or the proceeds of the latter if sold.

No portion of the fee may be paid out of the share of any party represented in the proceeding by an attorney, whether appointed by the court or selected by the party.

Art. 4614. Purchase by co-owner of property or interest sold

Any property or interest therein sold to effect a partition, whether by licitation or by private sale, may be purchased by a co-owner.

CHAPTER 2. PARTITION WHEN CO-OWNER AN ABSENTEE

Article

Art. 4621. Partition by licitation or private sale

When one of the co-owners of property sought to be partitioned is an absentee, the partition may be effected by licitation or by private sale, as provided in this Chapter, whether the property is divisible in kind or not.

Amended by Acts 2020, No. 281, § 2, eff. June 11, 2020.

Editor's Notes

Attorney for absentee, C.C.P. art. 5091 et seq.

Art. 4622. Petition

A. The petition for the partition of property in which an absentee owns an interest, under the articles of this Chapter, shall allege the facts showing that the absent and unrepresented defendant is an absentee, as defined in Article 5251, shall describe the property sought to be partitioned and allege the ownership interests thereof, and shall be supported by an affidavit of the petitioner or of his counsel that the facts alleged in the petition are true.

B. (1) If the partition is to be made by private sale, the petition for partition between the co-owners shall have first priority status by the court and shall include all of the following:

(a) The primary terms of the proposed sale.

(b) The name of the proposed purchaser and whether the proposed purchaser is a co-owner or third party in accordance with Civil Code Article 811(B).

(c) The source or location of funds to be used in the sale.

(d) If the proposed purchaser is a juridical entity, including but not limited to corporations, limited liability companies, partnerships, and sole proprietorships, and whether that entity has a relationship with any co-owner.

(e) Whether any costs associated with the sale will be paid to any person related to the petitioning co-owners within the fourth degree or a juridical entity in which the co-owner has a direct or indirect financial interest.

(2) Upon judgment of the court ordering the sale, payment shall be made within twenty-four hours using cash or certified funds.

Amended by Acts 2020, No. 281, § 2, eff. June 11, 2020; Acts 2021, No. 27, § 2, eff. June 1, 2021.

Editor's Notes

LSA–C.C.P. Form 2161a.

Art. 4623. Order; service of citation; contradictory proceedings

When the petition for a partition discloses that the plaintiff is entitled thereto, and that the absent and unrepresented defendant is an absentee who owns an interest in the property, the court shall appoint an attorney at law to represent the absent defendant, and shall order the publication of notice of the institution of the proceeding.

The citation to the absent defendant and all other process shall be served on or service thereof accepted by the attorney at law appointed to represent him, and all proceedings shall be conducted contradictorily against this attorney.

Art. 4624. Publication of notice

Notice of the institution of the proceeding shall be published at least once in the parish where the partition proceeding is instituted, in the manner provided by law. This notice shall set forth the title and docket number of the proceeding, the name and address of the court, a description of the property sought to be partitioned, and the primary terms of the private sale and shall notify the absent defendant that the plaintiff is seeking to have the property partitioned by licitation or by private sale under Civil Code Article 811, this Chapter, and Chapter 1 of this Title, and that the absent defendant has fifteen days from the date of the publication of notice, or of the initial publication of notice if there is more than one publication, to answer the plaintiff's petition.

Amended by Acts 2020, No. 281, § 2, eff. June 11, 2020; Acts 2021, No. 27, § 2, eff. June 1, 2021.

Editor's Notes

The official Caveat states that the publication provisions of R.S. 43:203 are not needed for this article, but that R.S. 43:201, R.S. 43:202, and R.S. 43:204 through R.S. 43:210 do apply.

For Official Comments and Annotative Materials,

Art. 4625. Trial; judgment ordering sale

A. Except as otherwise provided in Article 4630, if the petitioner proves on the trial of the proceeding that he is a co-owner of the property and entitled to the partition thereof and that the defendant is an absentee who owns an interest therein, the court shall render judgment ordering either the public sale of the property for cash by the sheriff to effect a partition, after the advertisement required by law for a sale under execution or the private sale of the property executed on behalf of the absentee or nonconsenting co-owner by a court-appointed representative, who may be a co-owner, under this Chapter and Chapter 1 of this Title, and after the advertisement required by law for a sale under execution.

B. The judgment shall determine the absentee's share in the proceeds of the sale, and award a reasonable fee to the attorney appointed to represent him to be paid from the absentee's share of the proceeds of the sale.

Amended by Acts 2020, No. 281, § 2, eff. June 11, 2020; Acts 2021, No. 27, § 2, eff. June 1, 2021.

Editor's Notes

See Civil Code article 811 which requires the court to order a partition by private sale when one or more of the co-owners are absentees or have not consented to a partition by private sale and that the court shall give priority to the private sale between the existing co-owners over the sale to third parties.

Art. 4626. Judgment ordering reimbursement or payment of amounts due co-owner out of proceeds of public sale

A judgment ordering the public sale of property to effect a partition under the provisions of this Chapter shall order, out of the proceeds of such sale, all of the following:

(1) The reimbursement to a co-owner of the amount proven to be due the co-owner for the payment of taxes on the property, and the expenses of preservation of the property.

(2) The payment to a co-owner of the amount proven to be due the co-owner by another co-owner who has received and retained the fruits and revenues of the property.

Amended by Acts 2020, No. 281, § 2, eff. June 11, 2020.

Art. 4626.1. Judgment ordering reimbursement or payment of amounts due co-owner and payment and allocation of costs of private sale out of proceeds of sale

A judgment ordering the private sale of property to effect a partition under the provisions of this Chapter shall order, out of the proceeds of such sale, all of the following:

(1) The reimbursement to a co-owner of the amount proven to be due the co-owner for the payment of taxes on the property and the expenses of preservation of the property.

(2) The payment to a co-owner of the amount proven to be due the co-owner by another co-owner who has received and retained the fruits and revenues of the property.

(3)(a) The payment of reasonable costs related to the sale, including real estate commissions, brokerage fees, appraisal costs, payments associated with the release of encumbrances and other customary closing costs, and the allocation of such costs to one or more co-owners.

(b) The court in rendering judgment shall consider whether the costs associated with the sale will be paid to any person related to the co-owners within the fourth degree or a juridical entity in which the co-owner has a direct or indirect financial interest.

Added by Acts 2020, No. 281, § 2, eff. June 11, 2020.

Art. 4627. Effect of judgment and sale

The judgment ordering the public sale or private sale of the property to effect a partition, and the sale made in compliance therewith, has the same force and effect as to the absentee, his succession representative and heirs, as if he had been served personally with process and the judgment had been rendered against him personally. Thereafter, the absentee, his succession representative and heirs are precluded from asserting any right, title, or interest in the property partitioned.

Amended by Acts 2020, No. 281, § 2, eff. June 11, 2020.

Art. 4628. Deposit of absentee's share into registry of court

After deducting the portion of the court costs and expenses of the sale to be paid by the absentee, the fee awarded by the court to the attorney appointed to represent him, and any amount required by the judgment to be paid a co-owner, the absentee's share of the proceeds of the sale shall be deposited into the registry of the court for the account of the absentee, his succession representative or heirs. This deposit may be withdrawn only on order of the court, in accordance with the law regulating such deposits.

Art. 4629. Articles applicable to partition by licitation or private sale

Article 4603, the first paragraph of Article 4605, and Articles 4607 and 4614 are applicable to a partition by licitation or a partition by private sale under the provisions of this Chapter.

Amended by Acts 2020, No. 281, § 2, eff. June 11, 2020.

Art. 4630. Partition in kind when defendant appears and prays therefor

If the property sought to be partitioned is divisible in kind, and the defendant timely answers through counsel of his own selection and prays therefor, the court shall render judgment ordering the partition to be made in kind, under the applicable provisions of Chapter 1 of this Title.

CHAPTER 3. PARTITION WHEN CO–OWNER A MINOR OR INTERDICT

Article

Art. 4641. Sale of interest of minor or interdict to effect partition

A. The undivided interest of a minor or interdict in property owned in common with others may be sold to effect a partition, as provided in Articles 4301 through 4304, 4321 through 4323, 4341, 4342, and 4566.

B. The interest of the minor or interdict in the property may be purchased by a co-owner.

Art. 4642. Partition in kind, dispensing with drawing of lots when authorized by court

A. Property may be divided in kind without the necessity of drawing lots therefor when all of the co-owners who are competent agree to the proposed partition, and the court has authorized it on behalf of the incompetent co-owner, as provided in Articles 4271 and 4566.

B. In such event there is no necessity for a judicial partition, and the division of the property may be made by agreement of the co-owners, with the legal representative of an incompetent co-owner executing the act of partition in behalf of the incompetent whom he represents.

Art. 4643. Appointment of attorney for incompetent when interests conflict

A. In any partition of property, whether in kind, by licitation, or by private sale, and whether judicial or conventional, of which an incompetent is a co-owner, and the interests of the incompetent conflict with those of his legal representative, undertutor, or undercurator, as the case may be, the court shall appoint an attorney at law to represent and act for the incompetent in the partition. If two or more incompetent co-owners whose interests conflict have the same legal representative, undertutor, or undercurator, the court shall appoint an attorney at law to represent and act for each of these incompetents in the partition.

B. For the purposes of the partition, the attorney at law so appointed shall act in lieu of, and has all of the power and authority of, the legal representative, undertutor, or undercurator referred to in Paragraph A of this Article.

Added by Acts 1962, No. 92, § 6. Amended by Acts 2020, No. 281, § 2, eff. June 11, 2020.

TITLE X. CONCURSUS PROCEEDINGS

Art. 4651. Definition

A concursus proceeding is one in which two or more persons having competing or conflicting claims to money, property, or mortgages or privileges on property are impleaded and required to assert their respective claims contradictorily against all other parties to the proceeding.

Art. 4652. Claimants who may be impleaded

Persons having competing or conflicting claims may be impleaded in a concursus proceeding even though the person against whom the claims are asserted denies liability in whole or in part to any or all of the claimants, and whether or not their claims, or the titles on which the claims depend, have a common origin, or are identical or independent of each other.

No claimant may be impleaded in a concursus proceeding whose claim has been prosecuted to judgment. No person claiming damages for wrongful death or for physical injuries may be impleaded in a concursus proceeding, except by a casualty insurer which admits liability for the full amount of the insurance coverage, and has deposited this sum into the registry of the court.

Official Revision Comments

(a) The first paragraph of this article removes the jurisprudential limitations on the remedy made possible when La.Act 123 of 1922 introduced the concept of interpleader, and thus paved the way for the recognition of all of the limitations on interpleader in the common law. See American Surety of New York v. Brim, 175 La. 959, 144 So. 727 (1932). The language of this paragraph is based of Fed.Rule 22(1), which combines interpleader with the bill in the nature of interpleader and removes the former limitations and restrictions on the use of the remedy.

Under the first paragraph of the above article, the remedy is no longer limited to a stakeholder, or to an obligor who admits his indebtedness but does not know to whom a fund in his hands should be distributed. The remedy may now be used not only to prevent multiple liability, but to prevent multiple litigation, and thus may be used by a person against whom multiple claims are asserted, although liability on some or all of these claims is denied.

(b) The prohibition against impleading a claimant who has prosecuted his claim to judgment is universal. American Surety Co. of New York v. Brim, *supra*. This prohibition is retained for the protection of a claimant who has prosecuted his claim to judgment, and otherwise would be forced to relitigate the matter, not only with the obligor, but with all other adverse claimants.

(c) The prohibition contained in the last sentence of this article prevents an abuse of the remedy by a tortfeasor or his insurer, so as to deprive claimants for damages for wrongful death or physical injuries of their right of separate suits against the tortfeasor or his insurer, to select the jurisdiction and the venue, and to a trial by jury.

(d) See, also, Comments under Art. 4658, *infra*.

Art. 4653. Parish where proceeding brought

A. Except as provided in the second paragraph of this article, a concursus proceeding may be brought in any parish of proper venue, under Article 42 only, as to any claimant impleaded therein.

B. If the competing or conflicting claims are for money due or claimed to be due on account of, or otherwise involve, any sale, lease, or other transaction affecting or pertaining to immovable property or any character of interest therein, the proceeding shall be brought in the parish where the immovable property or any part thereof is situated.

Amended by Acts 1989, No. 117, § 1.

Comment—1989

This Article is amended to provide that the reference to Article 42 does not include the exceptions under Articles 71 through 85.

Art. 4654. Petition

The petition in a concursus proceeding shall comply with Article 891, shall allege the nature of the competing or conflicting claims, and shall include a prayer that all of the persons having such claims be required to assert their respective claims contradictorily against all other parties to the proceeding.

Official Revision Comments

(a) The cross reference is to the article providing the requisites of the petition in an ordinary proceeding.

(b) In Bland v. Good Citizens Mut. Ben. Ass'n, 64 So.2d 29 (La.App.1953), the court permitted the defendant to convert the suit into a concursus proceeding through what was, in effect, a reconventional demand. There is no intention to overrule this decision or to prohibit the procedure employed. R.S. 45:920 and R.S. 54:17 specifically authorize a defendant to employ this procedure in the cases there provided for. Since none of the provisions ot this Title prohibit such procedure, under Art. 4662, *infra*, a defendant may always convert a suit against him into a concursus proceeding by reconvention. In such a case, his petition in reconvention must comply with the above article.

Art. 4655. Service of process; delay for answer

Service of citation and a copy of the petition in a concursus proceeding shall be made in the same form and manner, and the delays for answering are the same, as in an ordinary proceeding.

Art. 4656. Each defendant both plaintiff and defendant; no responsive pleadings to answer; no default required

Each defendant in a concursus proceeding is considered as being both a plaintiff and a defendant with respect to all other parties. No exceptions or responsive pleadings may be filed to the answer of a defendant, and every fact alleged therein is considered as denied or avoided by effect of law as to all other parties. If a defendant fails to answer, issue need not be joined by default.

Official Revision Comments

(a) This article codifies the jurisprudential rules stated and applied in State v. Alexander, 106 La. 460, 31 So. 60 (1901), and Graphic Arts Bldg. Co. v. Union Indemnity Co., 163 La. 1, 111 So. 470 (1926). From the very nature of the proceeding, and the large number of claimants which may be impleaded, there can be no application of the rules of an ordinary proceeding to the matters covered in the above article. See Comment (a) under Art. 4657, *infra.*

(b) Since every defendant in a concursus proceeding is both a plaintiff and a defendant, his right to the fund deposited, or to the amount claimed to be due by the plaintiff, may be asserted in his answer, and the proper judgment prayed for therein. Hence, since he may not inject issues which are extraneous to the subject matter of the proceeding and with which the other claimants impleaded are not concerned, there is neither a need for nor a possibility of the defendant reconvening.

(c) Nothing in the above article prevents a defendant from excepting to the plaintiff's petition, to raise the objections of lack of jurisdiction, improper venue, no right to implead the defendants, and so forth.

(d) The order in which the plaintiff, and the various claimants, should present their evidence, both in chief and in rebuttal, will vary, and depends to a considerable extent upon the circumstances and issues in the particular case. For this reason, it has been left to the discretion of the trial judge. In more complicated cases where a large number of claimants have been impleaded, this should be done at a pretrial conference.

Art. 4657. Failure of defendant to answer timely

If a defendant fails to answer within the delay allowed by law, any party may move for an ex parte order of court limiting the time in which an answer may be filed in the proceeding. In such event, the court shall order all defendants who have not answered to file their answers within a further delay to be assigned by the court, not exceeding ten days from the service or publication of the order.

If not more than five defendants have failed to answer timely, a copy of this order of court shall be served on each. If more than five defendants have failed to answer timely, a notice of the order of court limiting the delay for answering shall be published once in the parish in which the proceeding was filed, in the manner provided by law.

The failure of a defendant to file an answer within the delay as extended by the court precludes him thereafter from filing an answer, or from asserting his claim against the plaintiff.

Art. 4657.1. Notice to attorney general when the state is a defendant

A. Notwithstanding any other provision of law to the contrary, prior to the taking of a final judgment in any concursus in which one of the defendants is the state or any of its departments, offices, boards, commissions, agencies, or instrumentalities, the notice of the order of court limiting the delay for answer, together with a copy of the petition or other demand, shall be sent by the party moving for the order to the attorney general by registered or certified mail or shall be served by the sheriff personally upon the attorney general or the first assistant attorney general at the office of the attorney general.

B. If the order of court is served on the attorney general by mail, the person mailing such items shall execute and file in the record an affidavit stating that these items have been enclosed in an envelope properly addressed to the attorney general with sufficient postage affixed, and stating the date on which such envelope was deposited in the United States mails. In addition, the return receipt shall be attached to the affidavit which was filed in the record.

C. If no answer is filed within fifteen days immediately following the date on which the attorney general or the first assistant attorney general received notice of the order to answer as provided herein, a judgment may be entered in the concursus proceeding as provided by law.

Added by Acts 1986, No. 480, § 1.

Art. 4658. Deposit of money into registry of court

With leave of court, the plaintiff may deposit into the registry of the court money which is claimed by the defendants, and which plaintiff admits is due one or more of the defendants.

When sums of money due one or more of the defendants accrue from time to time in the hands of the plaintiff after the institution of the proceeding, with leave of court he may deposit the money as it accrues into the registry of the court.

After the deposit of money into the registry of the court, the plaintiff is relieved of all liability to all of the defendants for the money so deposited.

Editor's Notes

Continuously accruing amounts, deposit, R.S. 13:4817. The deposit into the registry of the court is permissive, Comment.

Bowen v. Smith, 885 So.2d 1 (La. App. 4 Cir. 2004). Court nullified settlement of minor's automobile accident claim by natural tutor who entered the settlement without court approval. Insurer's deposit of funds into a concursus did not relieve insurer of obligation to defend after nullification of settlement. C.C. art. 1921, 2000, 2033, R.S. 9:196, C.C.P. art. 4658 et seq.

Art. 4659. Costs

When money has been deposited into the registry of the court by the plaintiff, neither he nor any other party shall be required to pay any of the costs of the proceeding as they accrue, but these shall be deducted from the money on deposit. The court may award the successful claimant judgment for the costs of the proceeding which have been deducted from the money on deposit, or any portion thereof, against any other claimant who contested his right thereto, as in its judgment may be considered equitable.

In all other instances, the court may render judgment for costs as it considers equitable.

Art. 4660. Injunctive relief

The court may grant the plaintiff in a concursus proceeding injunctive relief prohibiting the defendants from instituting or prosecuting in any court of this state or of the United States any other action or proceeding on the claim involved in the concursus proceeding.

Art. 4661. Applicability of articles to proceedings under certain special statutes

Articles 4651 through 4658, and 4662, apply to a concursus proceeding instituted under R.S. 9:4841 or R.S. 38:2243.

Articles 4651 through 4658, 4660, and 4662 apply to a proceeding instituted under R.S. 10:7–603.

Article 4660 does not apply to a proceeding brought under R.S. 9:4841 or R.S. 38:2243. Article 4659 does not apply to any proceeding brought under any of the statutes referred to in this article.

Art. 4662. Rules of ordinary proceeding applicable

Except as otherwise provided in this Title and by law, the rules applicable to an ordinary proceeding apply, so far as practicable, to a concursus proceeding.

TITLE XI. EVICTION OF TENANTS AND OCCUPANTS

CHAPTER 1. GENERAL DISPOSITIONS

Art. 4701. Termination of lease; notice to vacate; waiver of notice

When a lessee's right of occupancy has ceased because of the termination of the lease by expiration of its term, action by the lessor, nonpayment of rent, or for any other reason, and the lessor wishes to obtain possession of the premises, the lessor or his agent shall cause written notice to vacate the premises to be delivered to the lessee. The notice shall allow the lessee not less than five days from the date of its delivery to vacate the leased premises.

If the lease has no definite term, the notice required by law for its termination shall be considered as a notice to vacate under this Article. If the lease has a definite term, notice to vacate may be given not more than thirty days before the expiration of the term.

A lessee may waive the notice requirements of this Article by written waiver contained in the lease, in which case, upon termination of the lessee's right of occupancy for any reason, the lessor or his agent may immediately institute eviction proceedings in accordance with Chapter 2 of Title XI of the Louisiana Code of Civil Procedure.

Amended by Acts 1981, No. 713, § 1.

Editor's Notes

Notice for termination if no fixed term, C.C. art. 2727; presumed duration of predial lease if no fixed term, C.C. art. 2680; presumed duration of house lease, no fixed term, C.C. art. 2680; reconduction of predial lease, C.C. art. 2722; reconduction of house lease, C.C. art. 2723, notice of termination as precluding reconduction, C.C. art. 2721 to 2723, 2728, 2729; lease with fixed term terminates upon expiration, without notice, C.C. art. 2720. One notice can serve both as notice to vacate and as notice to terminate lease, Comment (c); and see generally Tete v. Hardy, 283 So.2d 252 (1973). See, generally, also, other Civil Code provisions, C.C. arts. 2714 to 2728. See R.S. 9:3251, et seq., refund of lease deposit to lessee, attorney fees.

Art. 4702. Notice to occupant other than tenant to vacate

When an owner of immovable property wishes to evict the occupant therefrom, after the purpose of the occupancy has ceased, the owner, or his agent, shall first cause a written notice to vacate the property to be delivered to the occupant.

This notice shall allow the occupant five days from its delivery to vacate the premises.

Editor's Notes

The adjudicatee in a judicial sale can obtain possession under R.S. 13:4346, Comment (c). Injunctive relief against squatters and trespassers, C.C.P. art. 3663 and Comments thereunder.

Art. 4703. Delivery or service when premises abandoned or closed, or whereabouts of tenant or occupant unknown

If the premises are abandoned or closed, or if the whereabouts of the lessee or occupant is unknown, all notices, process, pleadings, and orders required to be delivered or served on the lessee or occupant under this Title may be attached to a door of the premises, and this shall have the same effect as delivery to, or personal service on, the lessee or occupant.

Art. 4704. Definitions

Unless the context clearly indicates otherwise, as used in this Title the following terms have the following meanings:

"Lease" means any oral or written lease, and includes a sublease;

"Lessee" includes a sublessee, whether the person seeking to evict is a lessor or sublessor; and an assignee of a lessee;

"Lessor" includes a sublessor, assignee, or transferee;

"Occupant" includes a sharecropper; half hand; day laborer; former owner; and any person occupying immovable property by permission or accommodation of the owner, former owner, or another occupant, except a mineral lessee, owner of a mineral servitude, or a lessee of the owner;

"Owner" includes a lessee; and

"Premises" includes the land and all buildings and improvements thereon leased by a tenant, or possessed by an occupant.

Art. 4705. Lessors' rights or real actions not affected

Nothing in this Title shall be construed to deprive any lessor of any remedy heretofore allowed him either for the payment of rent due to him or for the seizure of any furniture found on the leased premises; and nothing in this Title shall be construed to conflict with the provisions of Articles 3651 through 3664.

Editor's Notes

Caveat: before proceeding with eviction the lessor's attorney must consider its effects on the right of occupancy and the problem of enforcing the lessor's privilege, and suing for past due and future rents, as set forth, for example, in Henry Rose Mercantile & Mfg. Co. v. Stearns, 98 So. 429 (1923); Morrison v. Faulk, App. 4 Cir.1963, 158 So.2d 837; and as fully analyzed in LSA–C.C.P. Form 376 et seq. and the notes thereto, particularly Note 10.

CHAPTER 2. PROCEDURE

Article

4760 to 4830. Reserved.

Art. 4731. Rule to show cause why possession should not be delivered; abandonment of premises

A. If the lessee or occupant fails to comply with the notice to vacate required under this Title, or if the lessee has waived his right to notice to vacate by written waiver contained in the lease, and has lost his right of occupancy for any reason, the lessor or owner, or agent thereof, may cause the lessee or occupant to be cited summarily by a court of competent jurisdiction to show cause why he should not be ordered to deliver possession of the premises to the lessor or owner. The rule to show cause shall state the grounds upon which eviction is sought.

B. After the required notice has been given, the lessor or owner, or agent thereof, may lawfully take possession of the premises without further judicial process, upon a reasonable belief that the lessee or occupant has abandoned the premises. Indicia of abandonment include a cessation of business activity or residential occupancy, returning keys to the premises, and removal of equipment, furnishings, or other movables from the premises.

Amended by Acts 1981, No. 713, § 1; Acts 1991, No. 684, § 1.

Editor's Notes

An agent must engage an attorney to institute the proceeding, under the provisions of R.S. 37:212, R.S. 37:213 (regulating the practice of law), Comment (b).

Art. 4732. Trial of rule; judgment of eviction

A. The court shall make the rule returnable not earlier than the third day after service thereof, at which time the court shall try the rule and hear any defense which is made.

B. If the court finds the lessor or owner entitled to the relief sought, or if the lessee or occupant fails to answer or to appear at the trial, the court shall render immediately a judgment of eviction ordering the lessee or occupant to deliver possession of the premises to the lessor or owner. The judgment of eviction shall be effective for not less than ninety days.

Amended by Acts 2001, No. 24, § 1.

Art. 4733. Warrant for possession if judgment of eviction not complied with

If the lessee or occupant does not comply with the judgment of eviction within twenty-four hours after its rendition, the court shall issue immediately a warrant directed to and commanding its sheriff, constable, or marshal to deliver possession of the premises to the lessor or owner.

Art. 4734. Execution of warrant

The sheriff, constable, or marshal shall execute a warrant rendered under Article 4733 in the presence of two witnesses, by clearing the premises of any property therein, in order to put the lessor or owner in possession of the premises.

If the sheriff, constable, or marshal finds the windows, doors, or gates of the premises locked or barred, he shall break open any of these when necessary to effect convenient entry into the premises.

Art. 4735. Appeal; bond

An appeal does not suspend execution of a judgment of eviction unless the defendant has answered the rule under oath, pleading an affirmative defense entitling him to retain possession of the premises, and the appeal has been applied for and the appeal bond filed within twenty-four hours after the rendition of the judgment of eviction. The amount of the suspensive appeal bond shall be determined by the court in an amount sufficient to protect the appellee against all such damage as he may sustain as a result of the appeal.

Editor's Notes

The answer to the rule must be signed by the defendant himself (not his attorney) under oath to effect a suspensive appeal, Brewer v. Shiflett, App. 1 Cir.1966, 198 So.2d 704.

Arts. 4736 to 4759. [Blank]

Arts. 4760 to 4830. Reserved for future legislation

BOOK VIII

TRIAL COURTS OF LIMITED JURISDICTION

TITLE I. GENERAL DISPOSITIONS

CHAPTER 1. APPLICABILITY: COURTS OF LIMITED JURISDICTION

Art. 4831. Applicability of Book VIII

The provisions of this Book apply only to suits in trial courts of limited jurisdiction and to suits in the district courts within their jurisdiction concurrent with that of justices of the peace. Except as otherwise provided in this Book, civil proceedings in a trial court of limited jurisdiction, and the enforcement of judgments rendered therein, shall be governed as far as practicable by the other provisions of this Code.

Acts 1979, No. 46, § 1, eff. Jan. 1, 1980.

Art. 4832. Trial courts of limited jurisdiction

Trial courts of limited jurisdiction are parish courts, city courts, and justice of the peace courts.

Acts 1979, No. 46, § 1, eff. Jan. 1, 1980.

Editor's Notes

Uniform Parish Court Jurisdiction and Procedure Act, R.S. 13:1441 et seq.

Arts. 4833 to 4840. [Blank]

CHAPTER 2. CIVIL JURISDICTION

SECTION 1. PARISH COURTS AND CITY COURTS

SECTION 1. PARISH COURTS AND CITY COURTS

Art. 4841. Subject matter jurisdiction

A. The subject matter jurisdiction of parish courts and city courts is limited by the amount in dispute and by the nature of the proceeding, as provided in this Chapter.

B. For the purposes of this Chapter, the amount in dispute is determined by the amount demanded, including damages pursuant to Civil Code Articles 2315.3 and 2315.4, or value asserted in good faith by the plaintiff, but does not include interest, court costs, attorney fees, or penalties, whether provided by agreement or by law.

C. If the demand asserted in an amended or supplemental pleading exceeds the jurisdiction of the court, the court shall transfer the action to a court of proper jurisdiction.

Acts 1986, No. 156, § 1. Amended by Acts 1990, No. 521, § 2, eff. Jan. 1, 1991; Acts 1995, No. 409, § 1.

Comment—1990

This amendment is proposed to legislatively correct the problem presented in Beard v. Circle K, Inc., 554 So.2d 825 (La.App. 1st Cir.1989).

Comment—1995

The amendment has two purposes. First, it eliminates the conflict between Article 4 and Article 4841 as to whether penalties and attorney fees are to be included in calculating the amount in dispute by amending Article 4 to provide that the amount in dispute does not include penalties and attorney fees. Second, the amendment provides that damages pursuant to C.C. Arts. 2315.3 and 2315.4 are to be included in calculating the amount in dispute. This eliminates the uncertainty as to whether damages pursuant to C.C. Arts. 2315.3 and 2315.4 were to be treated as penalties and excluded from the calculation.

Art. 4842. Parish court jurisdiction; amount in dispute; injunctive actions by a political subdivision

A. Except as otherwise provided by law, the civil jurisdiction of a parish court is concurrent with the district court in cases where the amount in dispute, or the value of the property involved, does not exceed twenty thousand dollars.

B. The civil jurisdiction of a parish court is concurrent with the district court in cases or proceedings instituted by the state, a parish, a municipality, or other political subdivision of the state for injunctive relief or other civil relief for the cessation or abatement of any acts or practices which may violate any parish or municipal ordinance or any state law. In such case, the court shall have jurisdiction irrespective of the amount in dispute or the value of the property involved.

Acts 1986, No. 152, § 2, eff. June 28, 1986; Acts 1986, No. 1038, § 1. Amended by Acts 1987, No. 448, § 2, eff. July 9, 1987; Acts 1992, No. 939, § 1; Acts 1995, No. 204, § 1.

Comment—1995

Deletion of "within [the court's] territorial jurisdiction" in Articles 4842, 4843 and 4844 eliminates any connection between the territorial boundaries of city and parish courts and their jurisdiction over subject matter. This is in accord with Article 4841 which limits subject matter jurisdiction by the amount in dispute and the nature of the proceeding.

Editor's Notes

See also parallel provisions, R.S. 13:1443, 13:2561.2, 13:2562.2, and 13:2563.2(A).

Art. 4843. City court jurisdiction; amount in dispute; injunctive actions by state or political subdivision

A. Except as otherwise provided for in this Article, the civil jurisdiction of a city court is concurrent with the district court in cases where the amount in dispute, or the value of the property involved, does not exceed fifteen thousand dollars.

B. The civil jurisdiction of a city court in which the population of the territorial jurisdiction is greater than fifty thousand is concurrent with the district court in cases or proceedings instituted by the state, a parish, a municipality, or other political subdivision of the state for injunctive relief or other civil relief for the cessation or abatement of any acts or practices which may violate a parish or municipal ordinance or state law. In such case, the court has jurisdiction regardless of the amount in dispute or the value of the property involved.

C. In the City Court of Bossier City, and any city court in which the population of the territorial jurisdiction is less than fifty thousand, except as otherwise specifically provided by law, the civil jurisdiction is concurrent with the district court in cases where the amount in dispute, or the value of the property involved, does not exceed fifteen thousand dollars.

D. In the City Court of Houma and the City Court of Lafayette, the civil jurisdiction is concurrent with the district court in cases where the amount in dispute, or the value of the property involved, does not exceed twenty thousand dollars.

E. In the City Court of Bogalusa, the City Court of Bunkie, the City Court of Eunice, the City Court of Marksville, the City Court of Natchitoches, a city court in New Orleans, the City Court of Opelousas, the City Court of Port Allen, the City Court of Ville Platte, and the City Court of Winnsboro, the civil jurisdiction is concurrent with the district court in cases where the amount in dispute, or the value of the property involved, does not exceed twenty-five thousand dollars.

F. In the City Court of Breaux Bridge, the City Court of Crowley, the City Court of Hammond, the City Court of Jeanerette, the City Court of Jennings, the City Court of New Iberia, the City Court of Monroe, the City Court of Oakdale, the City Court of Rayne, and the City Court of Winnfield, the civil jurisdiction is concurrent with the district court in cases where the amount in dispute, or the value of the property involved, does not exceed thirty thousand dollars.

G. In the City Court of Abbeville, the City Court of Baker, the City Court of Baton Rouge, the City Court of Kaplan, the City Court of Leesville, the City Court of Minden, the City Court of Plaquemine, the City Court of Shreveport, the City Court of Springhill, and the City Court of Zachary, the civil jurisdiction is concurrent with the district court in cases where the amount in dispute, or the value of the property involved, does not exceed thirty-five thousand dollars.

H. In the City Court of Alexandria, the Third Ward City Court of Franklin, the City Court of Pineville, the City Court of East St. Tammany, the City Court of Ruston, the City Court of Sulphur, and the City Court of Lake Charles, the civil jurisdiction is concurrent with the district court in cases where the amount in dispute, or the value of the property involved, does not exceed fifty thousand dollars.

Acts 1986, No. 539, § 1; Acts 1986, No. 924, § 1. Amended by Acts 1988, No. 75, § 1; Acts 1988, No. 314, § 1; Acts 1990, No. 186, § 1; Acts 1990, No. 504, § 1, eff. July 18, 1990; Acts 1992, No. 10, § 1; Acts 1992, No. 939, § 1; Acts 1993, No. 541, § 1; Acts 1995, No. 126, § 1; Acts 1995, No. 204, § 1; Acts 1995, No. 311, § 1, eff. June 16, 1995; Acts 1995, No. 466, § 1; Acts 1997, No. 193, § 1, eff. Jan. 1, 1998; Acts 1997, No. 323, § 1; Acts 1997, No. 407, § 1; Acts 1999, No. 504, § 1, eff. Jan. 1, 2000; Acts 1999, No. 644, § 1; Acts 1999, No. 694, § 1; Acts 2001, No. 255, § 1; Acts 2001, No. 343, § 1, eff. Jan. 1, 2001; Acts 2001, No. 357, § 1; Acts 2001, No. 762, § 1, eff. June 25, 2001; Acts 2002, 1st Ex.Sess., No. 58, § 1; Acts 2003, No. 153, § 1; Acts 2003, No. 276, § 1; Acts 2003, No. 435, § 1; Acts 2003, No. 436, § 1; Acts 2003, No. 601, § 1; Acts 2003, No. 905, § 1; Acts 2003, No. 1213, § 2; Acts 2004, No. 205, § 1; Acts 2004, No. 487, § 1; Acts 2004, No. 511, § 1; Acts 2004, No. 538, § 1; Acts 2004, No. 539, § 1; Acts 2004, No. 714, § 1; Acts 2005, No. 31, § 1; Acts 2005, No. 109, § 1; Acts 2005, No. 349, § 1; Acts 2005, No. 353, § 1; Acts 2006, No. 365, § 1; Acts 2006, No. 379, § 1; Acts 2006, No. 575, § 1; Acts 2006, No. 680, § 1; Acts 2006, No. 681, § 1; Acts 2008, No. 44, § 1; Acts 2010, No. 161, § 1; Acts 2010, No. 180, § 1; Acts 2010, No. 228, § 1; Acts 2011, No. 88, § 1; Acts 2011, No. 103, § 1, eff. June 20, 2011; Acts 2012, No. 166, § 1; Acts 2012, No. 331, § 1; Acts 2013, No. 68, § 1; Acts 2014, No. 363, § 1; Acts 2014, No. 843, § 1; Acts 2015, No. 367, § 1; Acts 2015, No. 461, § 1, eff. July 1, 2015; Acts 2019, No. 135, § 1; Acts 2020, No. 205, § 3, eff. June 11, 2020; Acts 2021, No. 251, § 1.

Art. 4844. Amount in dispute; eviction proceedings

A. A parish court or city court shall have jurisdiction, concurrent with the district court, over suits by owners and landlords for the possession of leased premises as follows:

(1) When the lease is by the day and the daily rental is one hundred fifty dollars or less.

(2) When the lease is by the week and the weekly rental is five hundred dollars or less.

(3) When the lease is by the month and the monthly rental is three thousand dollars or less.

(4) When the lease is by the year and the annual rental is thirty-six thousand dollars or less.

(5) When the suit is to evict an occupant as defined by Article 4704, if the annual value of the right of occupancy does not exceed the amount in dispute to which the jurisdiction of the court is limited by Articles 4842 and 4843 or as to the amounts set forth in Subparagraphs (3) and (4) of this Paragraph.

(6) In the City Court of East St. Tammany, the city court shall have the same jurisdictional limit for possession of leased premises in eviction proceedings as provided for in Article 4912 for justice of the peace courts.

B. In computing the jurisdictional amount for purposes of eviction suits, the daily, weekly, monthly, annual, or other rental provided by the lease, exclusive of interest, penalties, or attorney fees, shall determine the amount in dispute.

Acts 1986, No. 156, § 1. Amended by Acts 1995, No. 204, § 1; Acts 1999, No. 102, § 1; Acts 2010, No. 219, § 1; Acts 2020, No. 205, § 3, eff. June 11, 2020.

For Official Comments and Annotative Materials,

Art. 4845. Amount in dispute; jurisdiction of incidental demands; parish, city, and justice of the peace courts; payment of costs of transfer

A. (1) When a parish or city court has subject matter jurisdiction over the principal demand, it may exercise subject matter jurisdiction over any properly instituted incidental action arising out of the same transaction or occurrence from which the principal demand arose, regardless of the amount in dispute in the incidental demand. When a justice of the peace court has jurisdiction over the principal demand, it may exercise subject matter jurisdiction over a good faith incidental demand in the same manner as a parish or city court, except that if the amount in dispute of such incidental demand exceeds its jurisdictional amount, a justice of the peace court may not continue to exercise jurisdiction except for purposes of transferring the entire action as provided in this Section.

(2) When an otherwise properly instituted incidental demand exceeds the subject matter jurisdiction of a parish or city court, the court may transfer the entire action to a court of proper jurisdiction.

B. When a compulsory reconventional demand exceeds the jurisdiction of a parish or city court, and when any good faith incidental demand before a justice of the peace court exceeds the jurisdictional amount of the justice of a peace court, the court shall transfer the entire action to a court of proper jurisdiction. The party filing the incidental demand that causes the justice of the peace court to transfer the action shall be responsible for payment of all costs for the transfer and shall make payment of the costs directly to the clerk of court of the transferee court within fifteen days of the filing of the incidental demand in the justice of the peace court.

Acts 1986, No. 156, § 1. Amended by Acts 1990, No. 521, § 2, eff. Jan. 1, 1991; Acts 1991, No. 676, § 1; Acts 1995, No. 202, § 1; Acts 1999, No. 678, § 1.

Comment—1990

This Article is amended to conform to the 1990 amendment of Article 1061. Acts 1990, No. 521.

Editor's Notes

Incidental demands are intervention, C.C.P. art. 1091 et seq.; cross-claims, C.C.P. art. 1071 et seq.; third party demand, C.C.P. art. 1111 et seq., and reconventional demand, C.C.P. art. 1061 et seq. See Editor's Notes to C.C.P. art. 1091. See parallel provision in R.S. 13:1443(C).

Art. 4845.1. [Blank]

Editor's Notes

C.C.P. art. 4845.1, relative to proceedings for injunctive relief instituted by the state or political subdivisions, was enacted by Acts 1986, No. 152, § 2. Pursuant to the statutory revision authority of the Louisiana State Law Institute, the provisions thus enacted were redesignated as par. B of C.C.P. art. 4842.

Art. 4846. Limitations upon jurisdiction; nature of proceedings

In addition to the limitation by the amount in dispute as set forth above, the jurisdiction of parish courts and city courts is limited by the nature of the proceeding, as set forth in Article 4847.

Acts 1986, No. 156, § 1.

Art. 4847. Limitations upon jurisdiction

A. Except as otherwise provided by law, a parish court or city court has no jurisdiction in any of the following cases or proceedings:

(1) A case involving title to immovable property.

(2) A case involving the right to public office or position.

(3) A case in which the plaintiff asserts civil or political rights under the federal or state constitutions.

(4) A claim for annulment of marriage, divorce, separation of property, or alimony.

(5) A succession, interdiction, receivership, liquidation, habeas corpus, or quo warranto proceeding.

(6) A case in which the state, or a parish, municipal, or other political corporation is a defendant, except for a petition for nullity filed in the City Court of East St. Tammany to nullify a judgment of bond forfeiture rendered by the City Court of East St. Tammany.

(7) Any other case or proceeding excepted from the jurisdiction of these courts by law.

B. In addition, city courts shall not have jurisdiction in tutorship, curatorship, emancipation, and partition proceedings.

Acts 1986, No. 152, § 2, eff. June 28, 1986; Acts 1986, No. 156, § 1. Amended by Acts 1988, No. 670, § 1; Acts 1990, No. 361, § 1, eff. Jan. 1, 1991; Acts 2011, No. 228, § 1; Acts 2020, No. 205, § 3, eff. June 11, 2020.

Art. 4848. Contempt power

A city court and parish court have the same power to punish a contempt of court as a district court.

Acts 1986, No. 156, § 1.

Art. 4849. Jurisdiction over the person

A parish court or a city court may exercise jurisdiction over the person to the same extent, and in the same manner, as a district court.

Acts 1986, No. 156, § 1.

Art. 4850. Jurisdiction in rem or quasi in rem; executory proceedings

A. A parish court or a city court may exercise jurisdiction quasi in rem over movable or immovable property, or jurisdiction in rem over movable property, in the manner provided by law, if the property is situated within the territorial jurisdiction of the court.

B. A parish court or a city court may issue a writ of seizure and sale in an executory proceeding to enforce a privilege or mortgage on movable or immovable property.

Acts 1986, No. 156, § 1.

Art. 4850.1. City Court of Alexandria; in rem and quasi in rem jurisdiction

The City Court of Alexandria may exercise jurisdiction quasi in rem over movable or immovable property, or jurisdiction in rem over movable property, in the manner provided by law, if the property is situated within the territorial jurisdiction of the court and the value of the property and the amount in dispute does not exceed ten thousand dollars. The City Court of Alexandria may issue a writ of seizure and sale in an executory proceeding to enforce a privilege or mortgage on movable or immovable property if the value of the property and the amount in dispute does not exceed ten thousand dollars.

Added by Acts 2003, No. 905, § 1.

Art. 4850.2. First City Court and Second City Court of New Orleans; appellate jurisdiction

The First City Court and the Second City Court shall have jurisdiction over appeals by any person aggrieved by a decision of the Traffic Court of New Orleans concerning a traffic violation enforced by the city of New Orleans' automated traffic enforcement system. Appeals from the traffic court shall extend to the law and the facts and shall be tried upon the records made and the evidence offered in court by the judge to whom the appeal shall be allotted. Any aggrieved person shall file such appeal within thirty days of such decision. The First City Court and the Second City Court shall adopt rules regulating the manner of taking, hearing, and deciding such appeals. All traffic violations on appeal shall maintain their status as civil penalties.

Added by Acts 2012, No. 502, § 1.

Art. 4851. Venue

A. The rules of venue provided in Articles 41 through 45, 71 through 79 and 81, and 121 through 124 apply to suits brought in the parish court.

B. The rules of venue provided in Articles 41 through 45, 71 through 79 and 121 through 124 apply to suits brought in city court, except that where these articles use the word "parish" it shall be construed to mean the territorial jurisdiction of the city court.

Acts 1986, No. 156, § 1.

Art. 4852. Change of venue; city court; forum non conveniens

If a party has filed separate suits in a city court and a district court which has territorial jurisdiction over the city court relating to the same cause of action but placing a claim for property damage in one court and a claim for personal injury in the other court, the city court upon contradictory motion, or upon the court's own motion, after contradictory hearing may transfer the suit in its court to the district court if the transfer serves the convenience of the parties and the witnesses and is in the interest of justice.

Acts 1986, No. 156, § 1.

Editor's Notes

C.C.P. art. 124 was also enacted to have a parallel provision in the rules of procedure governing district courts.

Arts. 4853, 4854. Repealed by Acts 1986, No. 156, § 3

SECTION 2. MUNICIPAL AND TRAFFIC COURTS

Art. 4857. Traffic Court of New Orleans; appellate jurisdiction

The Traffic Court of New Orleans shall have exclusive appellate jurisdiction of all appeals by any person aggrieved by an administrative hearing officer's decision concerning a traffic violation enforced by the city of New Orleans' automated traffic enforcement system. Any aggrieved person shall file such appeal within thirty days after the date of such decision. The traffic court shall have de novo review over such appeals. The traffic court shall adopt rules regulating the manner of taking, hearing, and deciding such appeals. All traffic violations on appeal shall maintain their status as civil penalties.

Added by Acts 2012, No. 502, § 1.

CHAPTER 3. RECUSAL OF JUDGES; APPOINTMENT OF JUDGES AD HOC

Art. 4861. Recusal of judges

A parish court or city court judge or justice of the peace may recuse himself or be recused for the same reasons and on the same grounds as provided in Article 151.

Acts 1979, No. 46, § 1, eff. Jan. 1, 1980. Amended by Acts 2021, No. 143, § 1.

Art. 4862. Motion to recuse

When a written motion is made to recuse a parish court or city court judge or a justice of the peace, the judge or justice of the peace shall either recuse himself, or the motion to recuse shall be tried in the manner provided by Article 4863.

Acts 1979, No. 46, § 1, eff. Jan. 1, 1980. Amended by Acts 2021, No. 143, § 1.

Art. 4863. Determination of recusal; appointment of judge ad hoc

A. In a parish or city court having more than one judge, the motion to recuse shall be tried by another judge of the same court. The manner in which the judge is selected to try the recusal shall be provided by rule of court.

B. In all other cases, the motion shall be tried by an ad hoc judge appointed by the supreme court.

Acts 1979, No. 46, § 1, eff. Jan. 1, 1980. Amended by Acts 2021, No. 143, § 1.

Art. 4864. Appointment of judge ad hoc after recusal

A. When a judge of a parish or city court recuses himself or is recused, another judge of the same court shall be appointed to try the cause, if that court has more than one division. The manner in which the judge is selected to try the cause shall be provided by rule of court. In all other cases, an ad hoc judge shall be appointed by the supreme court to try the cause.

B. When a justice of the peace recuses himself, another justice of the peace shall be appointed by the supreme court to try the cause.

Acts 1979, No. 46, § 1, eff. Jan. 1, 1980. Amended by Acts 2021, No. 143, § 1.

Art. 4865. Appointment of judge ad hoc in event of temporary inability of parish or city court judge to preside

When a parish or city court judge is unable to preside due to temporary absence, incapacity, or inability, he may appoint a judge ad hoc, who may be another judge or who may be a lawyer domiciled in the parish who possesses the qualifications of the judge he replaces. Appointment shall be by order, which shall reflect the term of and reasons for the appointment, and which shall be entered into the minutes of the court.

Acts 1979, No. 46, § 1, eff. Jan. 1, 1980. Amended by Acts 2021, No. 143, § 1.

Art. 4866. Power and authority of judge ad hoc

A judge ad hoc appointed under the provisions of Articles 4861 through 4865 shall have the same power and authority to act on the causes or on the dates to which appointed as the judge whom he replaces would have.

Acts 1979, No. 46, § 1, eff. Jan. 1, 1980. Amended by Acts 2021, No. 143, § 1.

CHAPTER 4. JURY TRIALS PROHIBITED; TRANSFER TO DISTRICT COURT

Article

Art. 4871. Jury trial prohibited

There shall be no trial by jury in any case in a parish court, city court, or justice of the peace court.

Acts 1979, No. 46, § 1, eff. Jan. 1, 1980.

Art. 4872. Transfer to district court

A. Where a principal demand is commenced in a parish or city court in which the defendant would otherwise be entitled to trial by jury under the provisions of Article 1731, or under any other provision of law, the defendant may obtain trial by jury by transferring the action to the district court in the manner provided by Article 4873.

B. Where a principal demand commenced in a parish or city court is one in which the defendant is not entitled to trial by jury under the provisions of Article 1731, a party who files an incidental demand in that court as authorized by Article 4846 waives any right he may have to jury trial on such incidental demand.

Acts 1979, No. 46, § 1, eff. Jan. 1, 1980.

Art. 4873. Transfer to district court; procedure; contest; effect

A party entitled thereto under the provisions of Article 4872 may transfer the action to the district court in the following manner:

(1) Within the delay allowed for answer in the trial court of the limited jurisdiction, or within ten days after answer has been filed, he shall file a motion to transfer with the clerk of the court in which the suit is pending. The motion shall include a declaration that the matter is one to which defendant

would have been entitled to trial by jury if commenced in district court, and that defendant desires trial by jury. If a party fails to file a motion to transfer within the delays required by this Subparagraph, the matter shall not be transferred.

(2) If no opposition is filed within ten days after the filing of the motion to transfer, the judge of the court in which the suit is pending shall order the transfer to the district court. If an opposition is timely filed, it shall be tried summarily.

(3) Where a transfer is ordered, the clerk of the court in which the action was initially filed shall forward to the clerk of court to which the action is transferred a certified copy of the record in the initial court, including pleadings, minute entries, and all other proceedings.

The clerk of the district court shall file the action as a new proceeding in that court, upon payment by the defendant of a filing fee as provided by rule of the district court. All costs accruing thereafter, however, shall be advanced in the same manner as though the action initially had been commenced in the district court by the original plaintiff.

(4) When the matter is docketed by the clerk of the district court, the proceeding shall continue in that court as though originally commenced therein. In the event transfer is effected prior to answer, defendant shall file his answer in the district court within the delays provided by Article 1001, commencing from the date the transferred proceeding is filed in that court.

(5) The disposition of a motion to transfer and any opposition thereto shall not be appealable, but shall be reviewable through the exercise of its supervisory jurisdiction by the court of appeal having appellate jurisdiction over the case.

Acts 1979, No. 46, § 1, eff. Jan. 1, 1980. Amended by Acts 2020, 1st Ex.Sess., No. 37, § 2, eff. Jan. 1, 2021.

Art. 4874. Withdrawal of demand for jury trial after transfer

A motion to transfer pursuant to this Chapter shall constitute a demand by the removing party for trial by jury. He may not subsequently withdraw the demand without the approval of the court and the other party or parties.

Acts 1979, No. 46, § 1, eff. Jan. 1, 1980.

Art. 4875. Entire suit transferred

A. An order to transfer divests the trial court of limited jurisdiction of jurisdiction over all claims and parties cumulated in the suit and the entire suit is transferred to the district court.

B. The right of other parties to trial by jury in the district court shall be determined as if the suit had initially been commenced in that court.

Acts 1979, No. 46, § 1, eff. Jan. 1, 1980.

Arts. 4876 to 4890. [Blank]

Arts. 4891 to 4900. [Blank]

TITLE II. PROCEDURE IN TRIAL COURTS OF LIMITED JURISDICTION

CHAPTER 1. PARISH AND CITY COURTS

Article

Art. 4901. Pleadings in parish and city courts

In suits in a parish court or a city court, written pleadings shall be required; provided, that a court may by rule provide for oral pleadings for suits in which the amount in dispute is two thousand dollars or less, and prescribe the form of such pleadings.[1]

Acts 1986, No. 156, § 1. Amended by Acts 1987, No. 249, § 1.

[1] As appears in enrolled bill.

Art. 4902. Citation in parish and city courts

A. The citation shall summon the defendant to comply with the demand of the plaintiff against him, or to state his answer to the demand, within the delay provided by Article 4903, and shall state the location where the court is to be held.

B. A copy of the petition shall be attached to the citation.

C. The citation shall conform to the requirements for citation issuing out of the district court.

Acts 1986, No. 156, § 1.

Art. 4903. Delay for answering in parish and city courts

The defendant shall answer within ten days of the service of citation, except that when the citation is served through the secretary of state, the delay, as to all defendants, shall be fifteen days after service.

Acts 1986, No. 156, § 1.

Art. 4904. Default judgment in parish and city courts

A. In suits in a parish court or a city court, if the defendant fails to answer timely, or if he fails to appear at the trial, and the plaintiff establishes a prima facie case by competent and admissible evidence, a default judgment in favor of the plaintiff may be rendered.

B. When the suit is for a sum due on an open account, promissory note, negotiable instrument, or other conventional obligation, prima facie proof may be submitted by affidavit. When the demand is based upon a promissory note or other negotiable instrument, no proof of any signature thereon shall be required.

C. When the sum due is on an open account, promissory note, negotiable instrument, or other conventional obligation, a hearing in open court shall not be required unless the judge in his discretion directs that such a hearing be held. The plaintiff shall submit to the court the proof required by law and the original and not less than one copy of the proposed default judgment. The judge shall, within seventy-two hours of receipt of such submission from the clerk of court, sign the proposed default judgment or direct that a hearing be held. The clerk of court shall certify that no answer or other pleading has been filed by the defendant. The minute clerk shall make an entry showing the dates of receipt of proof, review of the record, and rendition of the default judgment. A certified copy of the signed default judgment shall be sent to the plaintiff by the clerk of court, and notice of the signing of the default judgment shall be given as provided in Article 1913.

D. When the demand is based upon a right acquired by assignment in an open account, promissory note, or other negotiable instrument, the court may raise an objection of prescription before entering a default judgment if the grounds for the objection appear from the pleadings or from the evidence submitted by the plaintiff. If the court raises an objection of prescription, it shall not enter the default judgment unless the plaintiff presents prima facie proof that the action is not barred by prescription. Upon the plaintiff's request, the court shall hold a hearing for the submission of such proof.

Acts 1986, No. 156, § 1. Amended by Acts 2017, No. 419, § 1; Acts 2021, No. 174, § 5, eff. Jan. 1, 2022; Acts 2021, No. 259, § 2.

Comments—2021

(a) The change to Paragraph A of this Article makes the burden of proof to obtain a default judgment in parish and city courts consistent with the burden of proof that is imposed in district court pursuant to Article 1702.

(b) Paragraph C of this Article was amended to make this provision consistent with Article 1702(C) concerning the requirements of Article 1913.

(c) Paragraph D of this Article is new and provides that in limited cases, a court may raise an objection of prescription before entering a default judgment if the grounds for the objection appear from the pleadings or from the submitted evidence. If the plaintiff seeks to obtain the default judgment by oral testimony in open court, the court may raise the objection of prescription at the hearing, and the plaintiff must present prima facie proof that the action is not barred by prescription. If the plaintiff seeks to obtain the default judgment without a hearing in accordance with Article 1702(B)(1) and (C) and Article 1702.1, the court may raise the objection of prescription and allow the plaintiff to present prima facie proof by affidavits and exhibits that the action is not barred by prescription. Upon the plaintiff's request, the court shall hold a hearing for the submission of such proof. If the plaintiff fails to submit sufficient proof that the action is not barred by prescription, the court shall deny the plaintiff's request for a default judgment but shall not dismiss the case on its own motion. See, e.g., Gorman v. Miller, 136 So. 3d 834 (La. App. 1 Cir. 2013) ("[I]f the plaintiff fails to present sufficient evidence to confirm a preliminary default judgment . . . the trial court is effectively prevented from dismissing the plaintiff's suit on its own motion. . . . [T]he trial court's authority is limited to a denial of the request to confirm the preliminary default judgment.").

Editor's Notes

See Notes to C.C.P. art. 1702.

Art. 4905. Notice of judgment in parish or city courts

Notice of the signing of a final judgment shall be given as required by Article 1913.

Acts 1986, No. 156, § 1. Amended by Acts 2001, No. 512, § 1.

Art. 4906. Form of judgment in parish or city courts

The judgment shall be in writing, contain the typewritten or printed name of the judge, and be signed by the judge. Any judgment that does not contain the typewritten or printed name of the judge shall not be invalidated for that reason.

Acts 1986, No. 156, § 1. Amended by Acts 2014, No. 144, § 1.

Art. 4907. New trials; delay in parish or city courts

A. After judgment is signed in the parish or city court, a party may make a written request or motion for new trial for any of the grounds provided by Articles 1972 and 1973.

B. The delay for applying for a new trial shall be seven days, exclusive of legal holidays. Where notice of judgment is required, a party may file a motion for a new trial not later than seven days, exclusive of legal holidays, after the clerk has mailed, or the sheriff has served, the notice of judgment.

Acts 1986, No. 156, § 1. Amended by Acts 2010, No. 56, § 1; Acts 2021, No. 259, § 2.

Art. 4908. New trial; procedure in parish or city courts

The application for new trial, and the new trial, when granted, shall be governed by the provisions of Article 1971 and Articles 1975 through 1979.

Acts 1986, No. 156, § 1.

CHAPTER 2. CIVIL JURISDICTION FOR JUSTICE OF THE PEACE COURTS

Article

Art. 4911. Jurisdiction in justice of the peace courts; concurrent with district court; amount in dispute

A. The civil jurisdiction of a justice of the peace court is concurrent with the district court in cases where the amount in dispute does not exceed five thousand dollars.

B. For the purpose of this Chapter, the amount in dispute is determined by the amount demanded or value asserted in good faith by the plaintiff, but does not include interest, court costs, attorney fees, or penalties, whether provided by agreement or by law.

C. If the demand asserted in a good faith amended or supplemental pleading, or in any good faith incidental demand or any other pleading, exceeds the jurisdiction of the court, the court shall transfer the action to a court of proper jurisdiction.

Acts 1986, No. 156, § 1. Amended by Acts 1989, No. 299, § 1; Acts 1992, No. 692, § 1; Acts 1999, No. 151, § 1; Acts 1999, No. 678, § 1; Acts 2005, No. 43, § 1; Acts 2008, No. 338, § 1.

Art. 4912. Possession or ownership of movable property; eviction proceedings; justice of the peace courts

A. (1) A justice of the peace court shall, within its territorial jurisdiction, have jurisdiction, concurrent with the parish or district court, over suits for the possession or ownership of movable property not exceeding five thousand dollars in value and over suits by landowners or lessors for the eviction of occupants or tenants of leased residential premises, regardless of the amount of monthly or yearly rent or the rent for the unexpired term of the lease.

(2) A judgment of ownership of a vehicle ordered by a justice of the peace court shall be recognized by the office of motor vehicles of the Department of Public Safety and Corrections in accordance with the provisions of Chapter 4 of Title 32 of the Louisiana Revised Statutes of 1950.

(3) The provisions of this Paragraph shall also be applicable to suits for possession and ownership of a manufactured home, as defined by R.S. 9:1149.2, not exceeding five thousand dollars in value.

B. A justice of the peace court shall also have jurisdiction over suits by landowners or lessors for the eviction of occupants or tenants of leased commercial premises and leased farmlands where the amount of the monthly rental does not exceed five thousand dollars per month, regardless of the amount of rent due or the rent for the unexpired term of the lease.

Acts 1986, No. 156, § 1. Amended by Acts 1988, No. 587, § 1; Acts 1989, No. 298, § 1; Acts 1991, No. 544, § 1; Acts 2001, No. 713, § 1, eff. June 25, 2001; Acts 2005, No. 43, § 1; Acts 2008, No. 338, § 1; Acts 2021, No. 25, § 2.

Art. 4913. Limitations upon jurisdiction; nature of proceedings; justice of the peace courts

A. In addition to the limitation by the amount in dispute as set forth above, the jurisdiction of justice of the peace courts is limited by the nature of the proceeding, as set forth below.

B. A justice of the peace court has no jurisdiction in any of the following cases or proceedings:

(1) A case involving title to immovable property.

(2) A case involving the right to public office or position.

(3) A case in which the plaintiff asserts civil or political rights under the federal or state constitutions.

(4) A claim for annulment of marriage, separation from bed and board, divorce, separation of property, custody, visitation, spousal support, or child support.

(5) A succession, interdiction, receivership, liquidation, habeas corpus, or quo warranto proceeding.

(6) A case in which the state, or a parish, municipal, or other political corporation is a defendant.

(7) An executory proceeding.

(8) An adoption, tutorship, emancipation, or partition proceeding.

(9) An in rem or quasi in rem proceeding.

(10) Any other case or proceeding excepted from the jurisdiction of these courts by law.

C. In addition, a justice of the peace court may not issue any injunctive order, except to arrest the execution of its own writ and to enforce the execution of a judgment issued by a justice of the peace court or made executory in a justice of the peace court.

Acts 1986, No. 156, § 1. Amended by Acts 1991, No. 545, § 1; Acts 2021, No. 259, § 2.

Art. 4914. Contempt power; justice of the peace courts

A justice of the peace may punish a direct contempt of court, as defined in Article 222, by a fine of not more than fifty dollars, or imprisonment in the parish jail for not more than twenty-four hours, or both.

Acts 1986, No. 156, § 1. Amended by Acts 1991, No. 508, § 3.

Art. 4915. Jurisdiction over the person; justice of the peace courts

A justice of the peace court may exercise jurisdiction over the person to the same extent, and in the same manner, as a district court.

Acts 1986, No. 156, § 1.

Art. 4916. Venue; justice of the peace courts

The rules of venue provided in Articles 41 through 45 and in Articles 71 through 79 apply to suits brought in justice of the peace courts, except where these articles use the word "parish" it shall be construed to mean the territorial jurisdiction of the justice of the peace court.

Acts 1986, No. 156, § 1. Amended by Acts 2012, No. 392, § 1.

Editor's Notes

See Notes to C.C.P. art. 1702.

Art. 4917. Pleadings; justice of the peace courts; district courts with concurrent jurisdiction

A. A party or his attorney may state the claim, exceptions, defenses, or other pleas orally to the justice of the peace or the clerk of court. No written pleadings shall be required.

B. A party may file written pleadings if he so desires, but additional fees resulting from written pleadings not required shall not be imposed upon the party cast as costs of court.

C. A defendant shall include in his answer, whether oral or in writing, all of the exceptions upon which he intends to rely.

Acts 1986, No. 156, § 1.

Art. 4918. Record of the case; subsequent entries; justice of the peace courts; district courts with concurrent jurisdiction

When no written pleadings are required, the justice of the peace or the clerk of court shall record in a permanent book or case file the title of the case, the docket number, the name and address of all parties, a brief statement of the nature and amount of the claim, the issuance and service of citation, the defenses pleaded, motions and other pleas made, the names of witnesses who testified, a list of the documents offered at the trial, the rendition of judgment, and any appeal therefrom.

Acts 1986, No. 156, § 1. Amended by Acts 2004, No. 679, § 1, eff. Jan. 1, 2005.

Art. 4919. Citation; service of citation; justice of the peace courts; district courts with concurrent jurisdiction

A. The citation must be signed by the justice of the peace or the clerk of court issuing it, with an expression of his official capacity and under the seal of his office, must be accompanied by a certified copy of any petition, which has been filed, exclusive of exhibits, even if made a part thereof, and must contain the following:

(1) The date of issuance.

(2) The title of the cause.

(3) The name of the person to whom it is addressed.

(4) The title and location of the court issuing it.

(5)(a) A statement that the person cited must either comply with the demand contained in the pleading filed by the plaintiff against him or make an appearance, either by filing a pleading or otherwise, in the court issuing the citation within the delay provided under Article 4920 under penalty of default.

(b) If the matter is set for hearing pursuant to Article 4921.1(C), the citation must contain a statement that the person cited must either comply with the demand of the plaintiff against him or appear in the court issuing the citation at the time and date provided and that if he fails to appear, judgment may be entered against him.

B. When a written petition has been filed, a copy thereof shall be attached to the citation.

C. When the plaintiff has not filed a written petition, the citation shall:

(1) State the amount and nature of the claim and the year or years in which the indebtedness was contracted or arose and shall describe sufficiently to place the defendant on notice any promissory note or other written evidence of indebtedness on which the demand is based; and

(2) Describe the movable property and state the value thereof, if the suit is for the ownership or possession of movable property.

D. (1) Service of citation or other process may be made by the court by certified mail, with return receipt requested, when costs therefore are posted with the court.

(2) If the properly addressed certified mail return receipt reply form is signed by the addressee who is the defendant, service shall be considered personal service.

(3) If the properly addressed certified mail return receipt reply form is signed by a person other than the defendant, service shall be considered domiciliary service.

Acts 1986, No. 156, § 1. Amended by Acts 2012, No. 666, § 1; Acts 2015, No. 424, § 1.

Art. 4920. Delay for answering; justice of the peace courts; district courts with concurrent jurisdiction

The defendant shall answer within ten days of the service of citation, except that, when the citation is served through the secretary of state, the delay, as to all defendants, shall be fifteen days after service.

Acts 1986, No. 156, § 1.

Art. 4921. Default judgment; justice of the peace courts; district courts with concurrent jurisdiction

A. If the defendant fails to answer timely, or if he fails to appear at the trial, and the plaintiff establishes a prima facie case by competent and admissible evidence, a default judgment in favor of the plaintiff may be rendered.

B. When the suit is for a sum due on an open account, promissory note, negotiable instrument, or other conventional obligation, prima facie proof may be submitted by affidavit. When the demand is based upon a promissory note or other negotiable instrument, no proof of any signature thereon shall be required.

C. When the demand is based upon a right acquired by assignment in an open account, promissory note, or other negotiable instrument, the court may raise an objection of prescription before entering a default judgment if the grounds for the objection appear from the pleadings or from the evidence submitted by the plaintiff. If the court raises an objection of prescription, it shall not enter the default judgment unless the plaintiff presents prima facie proof that the action is not barred by prescription. Upon the plaintiff's request, the court shall hold a hearing for the submission of such proof.

Acts 1986, No. 156, § 1. Amended by Acts 2017, No. 419, § 1; Acts 2021, No. 174, § 5, eff. Jan. 1, 2022; Acts 2021, No. 259, § 2.

Comments—2021

(a) The change to Paragraph A of this Article makes the burden of proof to obtain a default judgment in justice of the peace courts consistent with the burden of proof that is imposed in district court pursuant to Article 1702.

(b) Paragraph C of this Article is new and provides that in limited cases, a court may raise an objection of prescription before entering a default judgment if the grounds for the objection appear from the pleadings or from the submitted evidence. If the plaintiff seeks to obtain the default judgment by oral testimony in open court, the court may raise the objection of prescription at the hearing, and the plaintiff must present prima facie proof that the action is not barred by prescription. If the plaintiff seeks to obtain the default judgment without a hearing in accordance with Article 1702(B)(1) and (C) and Article 1702.1, the court may raise the objection of prescription and allow the plaintiff to present prima facie proof y affidavits and exhibits that the action is not barred by prescription. Upon the plaintiff's request, the court shall hold a hearing for the submission of such proof. If the plaintiff fails to submit sufficient proof that the action is not barred by prescription, the court shall deny the plaintiff's request for a default judgment but shall not dismiss the case on its own motion. See, e.g., Gorman v. Miller, 136 So. 3d 834 (La. App. 1 Cir. 2013) ("[I]f the plaintiff fails to present sufficient evidence to confirm a preliminary default judgment . . . the trial court is effectively prevented from dismissing the plaintiff's suit on its own motion. . . . [T]he trial court's authority is limited to a denial of the request to confirm the preliminary default judgment.").

Art. 4921.1. Demand for trial; abandonment; applicability

A. After the lapse of fifteen days from the date the answer to the suit is filed pursuant to Article 4920, any party may make written demand to have the case set for trial. The judge shall give notice of trial within forty-five days of the answer being filed. The court shall issue notice of trial to be held within forty-five days of that date.

B. Notwithstanding the three-year period for abandonment as provided by Article 561, if the parties fail to take any step in the prosecution or defense of the action for a period of one year, the action shall otherwise be subject to the procedures for abandonment as provided by Article 561, provided that the court has jurisdiction over the subject matter.

C. (1) Notwithstanding the provisions of Paragraph A of this Article, the justice of the peace or clerk may set the matter for trial upon filing of a petition. The date, time, and location of the trial shall be contained in the citation. The first scheduled trial date shall be not more than forty-five days, nor less than ten days, from the service of the citation. If the defendant appears, he need not file an answer unless ordered to do so by the court. If a defendant who has been served with citation fails to appear at the time and place specified in the citation, the judge may enter a default judgment for the plaintiff in the amount proved to be due. If the plaintiff does not appear, the judge may enter an order dismissing the action without prejudice.

(2) If a matter has been set for trial pursuant to Subparagraph (1) of this Paragraph, no default judgment shall be rendered prior to the trial date.

Added by Acts 2005, No. 489, § 1. Amended by Acts 2015, No. 424, § 1; Acts 2017, No. 419, § 1; Acts 2021, No. 174, § 1, eff. Jan. 1, 2022.

Art. 4921.2. Duties of the justice of the peace; trial procedure; rules of evidence; depositions

A. At trial, it is the duty of the justice of the peace to conduct an informal hearing and to develop all of the facts necessary and relevant to an impartial determination of the case. The judge may take testimony, summon any party to appear as a witness in the suit upon his own motion, and do other acts which in his discretion appear necessary to effect a correct judgment and speedy disposition of the case. He may attempt to mediate disputes and encourage fair settlements among the parties.

B. The technical rules of evidence are relaxed, and all relevant evidence is admissible, including hearsay, provided the justice of the peace satisfies himself of its general reliability, and further provided that the judgment is founded upon competent evidence.

C. No depositions shall be taken and no interrogatories or other discovery proceedings shall be used except upon approval of the court. The court shall grant discovery only upon notice and good cause shown, and limited to the necessities of the case.

Added by Acts 2015, No. 424, § 1.

Art. 4922. Notice of judgment; justice of the peace courts; district courts with concurrent jurisdiction

Notice of the signing of any final judgment shall be given as required by Article 1913, except that if the party is personally served with the judgment in open court, no further notice shall be required.

Acts 1986, No. 156, § 1. Amended by Acts 2001, No. 512, § 1; Acts 2015, No. 424, § 1.

Art. 4923. Form of judgment; justice of the peace courts; district courts with concurrent jurisdiction

The judgment shall be in writing and signed by the justice of the peace or the clerk of court.

Acts 1986, No. 156, § 1.

Art. 4924. Appeals from justice of the peace courts; district courts with concurrent jurisdiction

A. Appeal from a judgment rendered by a justice of the peace court or a clerk of court shall be taken to the parish court or, if there is no parish court, to the district court of the parish in which the justice of the peace court is situated.

B. The case is tried de novo on appeal. However, a trial de novo, in the district court from the justice of the peace court, is not subject to the jurisdictional limit of the justice of the peace court.

C. No further appeal from the judgment of the parish or district court is allowed.

D. Supervisory jurisdiction of the proceedings in the parish or district court may be exercised by the court of appeal which otherwise would have had appellate jurisdiction.

Acts 1986, No. 156, § 1. Amended by Acts 1999, No. 678, § 1.

Art. 4925. Delay for appeal; justice of the peace courts; district courts with concurrent jurisdiction

A. The appellant from a judgment rendered by a justice of the peace court or the clerk of court shall file suit for a trial de novo in the district court or the parish court within fifteen days from the date of the judgment or from the service of notice of judgment, when such notice is necessary. A copy of the suit for trial de novo shall be provided to all parties or their attorney of record. A copy of either the notice of suit for trial de novo or the suit pleadings shall also be provided to the justice of the peace court whose judgment is being appealed. The rules of the district court or parish court shall thereafter apply.

B. When an application for new trial is timely filed, however, the delay for appeal commences on the day after the motion is denied, or from service of notice of the order denying a new trial, when such notice is necessary.

Acts 1986, No. 156, § 1. Amended by Acts 2015, No. 424, § 1.

Arts. 4926 to 4940. [Blank]

Arts. 4941, 4942. [Blank]

Arts. 4943 to 4970. [Blank]

Arts. 4971, 4972. [Blank]

CHAPTER 3. APPEALS FROM CITY AND PARISH COURTS

Article

Art. 5001. Appeals from city and parish courts

A. An appeal from a judgment rendered by a parish court or by a city court shall be taken to the court of appeal.

B. Appeal shall be on the record and shall be taken in the same manner as an appeal from the district court.

Acts 1986, No. 156, § 1. Amended by Acts 2001, No. 1134, § 1; Acts 2021, No. 259, § 2.

Art. 5002. Delay for appeal

A. An appeal from a judgment rendered by a city court or a parish court may be taken only within ten days from the date of the judgment or from the service of notice of judgment, when such notice is necessary.

B. When an application for new trial is timely filed, however, the delay for appeal commences on the day after the motion is denied, or from service of notice of the order denying a new trial, when such notice is necessary.

Acts 1986, No. 156, § 1.

Editor's Notes

Myles v. Turner, 612 So.2d 32 (La.1993), the ten-day delay for appeal commences upon receipt of the notice, rather than upon the mailing.

Art. 5003. Procedure for appealing

The appellate procedure provided by Book III for appeals from the district court shall be applicable.

Acts 1986, No. 156, § 1.

Art. 5004. Repealed by Acts 1986, No. 156, § 3

TITLE III. DISTRICT COURTS WHERE JURISDICTION CONCURRENT WITH JUSTICE OF THE PEACE COURTS

Art. 5011. Procedure

The rules provided in Articles 4917 through 4923 apply to a suit in a district court, when a justice of the peace would have concurrent jurisdiction thereof.

Acts 1986, No. 156, § 1.

BOOK IX

MISCELLANEOUS PROVISIONS AND DEFINITIONS

TITLE I. MISCELLANEOUS PROVISIONS

CHAPTER 1. RULES OF CONSTRUCTION

Art. 5051. Liberal construction of articles

The articles of this Code are to be construed liberally, and with due regard for the fact that rules of procedure implement the substantive law and are not an end in themselves.

Art. 5052. Unambiguous language not to be disregarded

When the language of an article is clear and free from ambiguity, its letter is not to be disregarded under the pretext of pursuing its spirit.

Art. 5053. Words and phrases

Words and phrases are to be read in their context, and are to be construed according to the common and approved usage of the language employed.

The word "shall" is mandatory, and the word "may" is permissive.

Art. 5054. Clerical and typographical errors disregarded

Clerical and typographical errors in this Code shall be disregarded when the legislative intent is clear.

Art. 5055. Number; gender

Unless the context clearly indicates otherwise:

(1) Words used in the singular number apply also to the plural; words used in the plural number include the singular; and

(2) Words used in one gender apply also to the others.

Art. 5056. Conjunctive, disjunctive, or both

Unless the context clearly indicates otherwise:

(1) The word "and" indicates the conjunctive;

(2) The word "or" indicates the disjunctive; and

(3) When the article is phrased in the disjunctive, followed by the words "or both", both the conjunctive and disjunctive are intended.

Art. 5057. Headings, source notes, cross references

The headings of the articles of this Code, and the source notes and cross references thereunder, are used for purposes of convenient arrangement and reference, and do not constitute parts of the procedural law.

Art. 5058. References to code articles or statutory sections

Unless the context clearly indicates otherwise:

(1) A reference in this Code to a book, title, chapter, section, or article, without further designation, means a book, title, chapter, section, or article of this Code; and

(2) A reference in this Code to an article of a code, or to a statutory section, applies to all prior and subsequent amendments thereof.

Art. 5059. Computation of time

A. In computing a period of time allowed or prescribed by law or by order of court, the date of the act, event, or default after which the period begins to run is not to be included. The last day of the period is to be included, unless it is a legal holiday, in which event the period runs until the end of the next day which is not a legal holiday.

B. A half-holiday is considered as a legal holiday. A legal holiday is to be included in the computation of a period of time allowed or prescribed, except when:

(1) It is expressly excluded;

(2) It would otherwise be the last day of the period; or

(3) The period is less than seven days.

C. (1) A legal holiday shall be excluded in the computation of a period of time allowed or prescribed to seek rehearing, reconsideration, or judicial review or appeal of a decision or order by an agency in the executive branch of state government.

(2) Subparagraph (1) of this Paragraph shall not apply to the computation of a period of time allowed or prescribed to seek rehearing, reconsideration, or judicial review or appeal of a decision or order by the Department of Revenue, the Department of Environmental Quality, or the Department of Insurance relative to examination reports in R.S. 22:1983.

Amended by Acts 2018, No. 128, § 1; Acts 2019, No. 300, § 1.

Editor's Notes

Legal holidays for the purposes of this article are set forth in R.S. 1:55; computation of time for prescription, see C.C. arts. 3454 to 3456; peremption, C.C. art. 3459.

CHAPTER 2. ATTORNEY APPOINTED TO REPRESENT UNREPRESENTED DEFENDANTS

Article

Art. 5091. Appointment; contradictory proceedings against attorney; improper designation immaterial

A. The court shall appoint an attorney at law to represent the defendant, on the petition or ex parte written motion of the plaintiff, when:

(1) It has jurisdiction over the person or property of the defendant, or over the status involved, and the defendant is:

(a) A nonresident or absentee who has not been served with process, either personally or through an agent for the service of process, and who has not waived objection to jurisdiction.

(b) An unemancipated minor or mental incompetent who has no legal representative, and who may be sued through an attorney at law appointed by the court to represent him.

(c) Deceased and no succession representative has been appointed.

(2) The action of proceeding is in rem and:

(a) The defendant is dead, no succession representative has been appointed, and his heirs and legatees have not been sent into possession judicially.

(b) The defendant is a corporation, a limited liability company, or partnership on which process cannot be served for any reason.

(c) The defendant's property is under the administration of a legal representative, but the latter has died, resigned, or been removed from office and no successor thereof has qualified, or has left the state permanently without appointing someone to represent him.

B. All proceedings against such a defendant shall be conducted contradictorily against the attorney at law appointed by the court to represent him. For the limited purpose of any such action or proceeding, the appointed attorney at law shall be the proper representative of the succession of any such decedent to the same extent as if he were the regularly appointed and duly qualified administrator or executor in such decedent's succession.

C. The improper designation of the attorney appointed by the court to represent such a defendant as curator ad hoc, tutor ad hoc, special tutor, or any other title, does not affect the validity of the proceeding.

D. The improper designation of a defendant for whom an attorney has been appointed by the court in an action or proceeding in rem under Paragraph (A)(2) of this Article shall not affect the validity of the proceedings and any judgment rendered therein shall be binding upon the parties and property involved in the action or proceeding in rem. Therefore, naming an attorney to represent the unopened succession of the defendant, the succession of the defendant, the estate of the defendant, the deceased defendant, or any other similar designation or appellation shall satisfy the requirements of Paragraph (A)(2)(a). The designation of a corporation or a partnership by a name sufficient to identify the same to a reasonably prudent man, regardless of any errors which it might contain, shall satisfy the requirements of Paragraph (A)(2)(b).

Amended by Acts 1964, No. 4, § 1; Acts 1991, No. 366, § 1, eff. July 6, 1991; Acts 1992, No. 584, § 2; Acts 1997, No. 578, § 1; Acts 1999, No. 145, § 2.

Editor's Notes

The court must have jurisdiction over the person, property, or status involved before it may make a valid appointment of an attorney under this article, Comment (b). R.S. 13:3204(B) provides that a C.C.P. art. 5091 attorney may be appointed for the nonresident by order of court.

The 1997 amendment correlated this article with the 1997 repeal of C.C.P. art. 7, and in Paragraph A(1)(a) changes "who has made no general appearance" to "who has not waived objection to jurisdiction". Presumably that requirement would also be satisfied by the submission of the party to the personal jurisdiction of the court over him under C.C.P. art. 6(3).

The 1999 amendment added "limited liability company" to A(2)(b).

Art. 5091.1. Appointment of attorney in disavowal actions

In any action to disavow paternity, the judge shall appoint an attorney to represent the child whose status is at issue, and the attorney so appointed shall not represent any other party in the litigation.

Added by Acts 1976, No. 430, § 3.

Art. 5091.2. Curator ad hoc in adoption cases

In complying with the provisions of the Louisiana Children's Code Articles 1011, 1107, or 1190 and related statutes, the judge of the competent court is authorized to appoint an attorney who shall serve as curator ad hoc who will assist the court in complying with the statutory requirements for maintaining the confidentiality of termination, surrender, adoption, and related records and proceedings.

Added by Acts 1978, No. 450, § 3. Amended by Acts 1997, No. 1056, § 1.

Editor's Notes

R.S. 9:437 and R.S. 40:79, cited within the text of C.C.P. art. 5091.2, were repealed by Acts 1991, No. 235 (the Act which enacted the Louisiana Children's Code), effective January 1, 1992. For disposition of the subject matter of repealed R.S. 9:437, see the Disposition Table preceding Ch.C. Art. 100 in Volume 1 of LSA-Children's Code. See Ch.C. art. 1182 for the subject matter of repealed R.S. 40:79, records of adoption decrees. Acts 1992, No. 705, § 2 enacted a new R.S. 40:79, also concerning records of adoption decrees, and § 6 provided that the provisions of § 2 were retroactive to January 1, 1992.

At the time C.C.P. art. 5091.2 was enacted by Acts 1978, No. 450, R.S. 40:79 provided for a certified copy of the adoption record for the adoptive parents and the sealing of the adoption records and documents. Chapter 2 of Title 40 of the Louisiana Revised Statutes of 1950 was amended and reenacted by Acts 1979, No. 776, and the subject matter of former R.S. 40:79 is now found at R.S. 40:77.

For Official Comments and Annotated Materials,

The section number R.S. 40:81, also cited within the text of C.C.P. art. 5091.2, was vacated by the amendment and reenactment of Chapter 2 of Title 40 of the Louisiana Revised Statutes of 1950 by Acts 1979, No. 776. The amendment and reenactment transferred the subject matter of former R.S. 40:81 to R.S. 40:79.

The 1997 amendment changes the Revised Statute citation to Children's Code citations, and expands the scope of confidentiality by adding "termination", "surrender" and "related".

Art. 5092. Qualifications; suggestions for appointment not permitted

When the court appoints an attorney at law to represent an unrepresented party, it shall appoint an attorney qualified to practice law in this state.

The court shall not accept any suggestion as to the name of the attorney to be appointed, unless manifestly in the interest of the unrepresented party.

Art. 5093. Oath not required; waiver of citation and acceptance of service

An attorney at law appointed by the court to represent an unrepresented party need not take an oath before entering on the performance of his duties, as his oath of office as an attorney applies to all of his professional duties.

An attorney appointed to represent a defendant may waive citation and accept service of process, but may not waive any defense. No further action may be taken by the court after service or acceptance thereof until after the expiration of the delay allowed the defendant to answer, even though the appointed attorney may have filed an exception or answer prior thereto.

Art. 5094. Duties; notice to nonresident or absentee

When an attorney at law is appointed by the court to represent a defendant who is a nonresident or an absentee, the attorney shall use reasonable diligence to communicate with the defendant and inform him of the pendency and nature of the action or proceeding, and of the time available for the filing of an answer or the assertion of a defense otherwise.

Editor's Notes

"(b) The phrase 'the assertion of a defense otherwise' applies to executory proceedings, where no exceptions or answer may be filed, and all defenses must be asserted either in a suit for an injunction to arrest the seizure and sale, or through a suspensive appeal." Comment (b).

Art. 5095. Same; defense of action

A. The attorney at law appointed by the court to represent a defendant shall use reasonable diligence to inquire of the defendant, and to determine from other available sources, what defense, if any, the defendant may have, and what evidence is available in support thereof.

B. Except in an executory proceeding, the attorney may except to the petition, shall file an answer or other pleading in time to prevent a default judgment from being rendered, may plead therein any affirmative defense available, may prosecute an appeal from an adverse judgment, and generally has the same duty, responsibility, and authority in defending the action or proceeding as if he had been retained as counsel for the defendant.

Amended by Acts 2017, No. 419, § 1; Acts 2021, No. 174, § 1, eff. Jan. 1, 2022.

Editor's Notes

"(a) This article is based upon customary practices which are regarded as proper. The appointed attorney has no authority to force the defendant to become the actor by filing a separate suit in his name, or by calling in a third party defendant, or by reconvening. His function, and his sole authority under the law, is to defend the pending action or proceeding, and he may not commit the person he is appointed to represent in any other manner.

"(b) Defenses to an executory proceeding may be raised only through the action to enjoin the seizure and sale, or through a suspensive appeal. The appointed attorney has no legal authority to act for the person he is representing by exercising either remedy. His sole function in an executory proceeding is to receive service of all process and to notify the defendant of the pendency of the proceeding. See Art. 5094, *supra*." Comments.

Art. 5096. Compensation

The court shall allow the attorney at law appointed to represent a defendant a reasonable fee for his services, which shall be paid by the plaintiff, but shall be taxed as costs of court.

The attorney so appointed may require the plaintiff to furnish security for the costs which may be paid by, and the reasonable fee to be allowed, the attorney.

If the attorney so appointed is retained as counsel for the defendant, the attorney shall immediately advise the court and opposing counsel of such employment.

Art. 5097. Attorney appointed to represent claimant in worker's compensation case

Articles 5092, 5093, and 5098 apply to an attorney at law appointed by the court to represent a claimant in a worker's compensation case who seeks authority to compromise or to accept a lump sum settlement.

Art. 5098. Validity of proceeding not affected by failure of attorney to perform duties; punishment of attorney

The failure of an attorney appointed by the court to represent an unrepresented party to perform any duty imposed upon him by, or the violation by any person of, the provisions of Articles 5092 through 5096 shall not affect the validity of any proceeding, trial, order, judgment, seizure, or judicial sale of any property in the action or proceeding, or in connection therewith.

For a wilful violation of any provision of Articles 5092 through 5096 an attorney at law subjects himself to punishment for contempt of court, and such further disciplinary action as is provided by law.

CHAPTER 3. BONDS IN JUDICIAL PROCEEDINGS

Article

Art. 5121. Bond payable to clerk; cash bonds by plaintiffs authorized; person in interest may sue

When a party to a judicial proceeding is required by law or order of court to furnish security, any bond so furnished shall be made payable to the clerk of the trial court in which the proceeding was brought. When the party required to furnish same is a plaintiff, a cash bond may be furnished in lieu of other security, at his option.

Any person in interest may sue thereon. No error, inaccuracy, or omission in naming the obligee on the bond is a defense to an action thereon.

Amended by Acts 1970, No. 492, § 1.

Editor's Notes

Cost bonds, R.S. 13:843; R.S. 13:1215; R.S. 13:4522.

Art. 5121.1. Bond secured by immovable property

Any party to a judicial proceeding who is required by law or court order to provide security may furnish as security a bond secured by immovable property located in this state. The party providing the property bond shall present to a judge of the parish in which the immovable is located an assessment certificate, a homestead exemption waiver if applicable, and a mortgage certificate. Prior to presenting the bond to the court having jurisdiction over the judicial proceeding the bond shall be recorded in the mortgage office of the parish where the immovable is located and the recordation shall be evidenced on the mortgage certificate.

Added by Acts 1984, No. 200, § 2, eff. June 29, 1984.

Art. 5122. Oath of surety and principal on bond

A. Except as otherwise provided in this Article, no bond shall be accepted in a judicial proceeding unless accompanied by affidavits of:

(1) Each surety that he is worth the amount for which he bound himself therein, in assets subject to execution, over and above all of his other obligations.

(2) The party furnishing the bond that he is informed and believes that each surety on the bond is worth the amount for which the surety has bound himself therein, in assets subject to execution, over and above all of the other obligations of the surety.

(3) The party furnishing a bond secured by immovable property under Article 5121.1 that he is worth the amount for which he has bound himself and that the immovable securing the bond contains assets subject to execution, over and above all his other obligations.

B. This Article does not apply to a bond executed by a surety company licensed to do business in this state.

Amended by Acts 1984, No. 200, § 1, eff. June 29, 1984.

Art. 5123. Testing sufficiency and validity of bond

Any person in interest wishing to test the sufficiency, solvency of the surety, or validity of a bond furnished as security in a judicial proceeding shall rule the party furnishing the bond into the trial court in which the proceeding was brought to show cause why the bond should not be decreed insufficient or invalid, and why the order, judgment, writ, mandate, or process conditioned on the furnishing of security should not be set aside or dissolved. If the bond is sought to be held invalid on the ground of the insolvency of a surety other than a surety company licensed to do business in this state, the party furnishing the bond shall prove the solvency of the surety on the trial of the rule.

Art. 5124. Furnishing new or supplemental bond to correct defects of original

Within four days, exclusive of legal holidays, of the rendition of judgment holding the original bond insufficient or invalid, or at any time if no rule to test the original bond has been filed, the party furnishing it may correct any defects therein by furnishing a new or supplemental bond, with either the same surety if solvent, or a new or additional surety.

The new or supplemental bond is retroactive to the date the original bond was furnished, and maintains in effect the order, judgment, writ, mandate, or process conditioned on the furnishing of security.

The furnishing of a supplemental bond, or the furnishing of a new bond by a different surety, does not discharge or release the surety on the original bond; and the sureties on both are liable in solido to the extent of their respective obligations thereon and may be joined in an action on the bond.

Art. 5125. Insufficiency or invalidity of bond; effect on orders or judgments; appeal from order for supplemental bond

No appeal, order, judgment, writ, mandate, or process conditioned on the furnishing of security may be dismissed, set aside, or dissolved on the ground that the bond furnished is insufficient or invalid unless the party who furnished it is afforded an opportunity to furnish a new or supplemental bond, as provided in Articles 5124 and 5126.

No suspensive appeal is allowed from an order or ruling of a trial court requiring or permitting a new or supplemental bond to be furnished as provided in Articles 5124 and 5126.

Art. 5126. Insufficiency or invalidity of new or supplemental bond

The party furnishing a new or supplemental bond under the provisions of Article 5124 may correct an insufficiency or invalidity therein by furnishing a second new or supplemental bond within four days, exclusive of legal holidays, of rendition of judgment holding the new or supplemental bond insufficient or invalid, or at any time if no rule to test the new or supplemental bond has been filed.

If the second new or supplemental bond is insufficient or invalid, the party furnishing it may not correct the defects therein by furnishing a further new or supplemental bond.

Art. 5127. Release bond

No property seized under any order, judgment, writ, mandate, or process of a court may be released from seizure under a release or forthcoming bond unless it is executed by:

(1) A surety company licensed to do business in this state; or

(2) An individual surety, and has been approved by the sheriff after the latter has satisfied himself of the solvency of the surety.

Articles 5121 through 5126 apply to a release or forthcoming bond.

CHAPTER 4. DISCUSSION

Article

Art. 5151. Discussion defined

Discussion is the right of a secondary obligor to compel the creditor to enforce the obligation against the property of the primary obligor or, if the obligation is a legal or judicial mortgage, against other property affected thereby, before enforcing it against the property of the secondary obligor.

Official Revision Comment

The fact that a surety is a secondary obligor is apparent. It is not quite so obvious that a third possessor and the transferee in a revocatory action similarly are secondary obligors. While a third possessor is not liable personally on the principal obligation secured by the legal or judicial mortgage, he is under the obligation of either relinquishing the property so that the creditor might enforce his mortgage against it, or paying the debt due the creditor. He is only a secondary obligor since, of course, the primary obligor is the debtor who owes the principal obligation. The transferee in a revocatory action has a similar obligation, and is also a secondary obligor.

Editor's Notes

Revision Comment. Under the prior law, discussion normally was pleaded as an exception, and there was little need for rules regulating the pleading thereof in a petition; however, the elimination of the hypothecary action (properly speaking) by Arts. 3741 to 3743 now makes the pleading of discussion in a petition necessary. A third possessor may plead discussion in his petition for an injunction to prevent the seizure and consequent judicial sale of property which he purchased subject to a legal or judicial mortgage. Arts. 3743(1), 5154 to 5156.

Art. 5152. Surety's right to plead

When a surety is sued by the creditor on the suretyship obligation, and the right of discussion has been created by contract between the surety and the creditor, the surety may plead discussion to compel the creditor to obtain and execute a judgment against the principal before executing a judgment against the surety.

Amended by Acts 2010, No. 185, § 1.

Comment—2010

This Article was amended to conform with Civil Code Article 3045 which abolishes a surety's plea of discussion by operation of law. However, Civil Code Article 3045 does not prohibit a surety from establishing a right to plead discussion by creation of the right in an agreement with the creditor of the suretyship obligation. See Civil Code Article 3040. In such a case, discussion may be pleaded.

Art. 5153. Transferee in revocatory action; right to plead discussion

When a revocatory action is brought by a creditor to set aside a transfer of property made by his debtor, the transferee may plead discussion to compel the creditor to obtain and execute a judgment against the debtor before setting the transfer aside.

Art. 5154. Third possessor's right to plead

When a legal or judicial mortgage securing an indebtedness due by a former owner of property is sought to be enforced against the property after its acquisition by a third possessor, the latter may plead discussion to compel the mortgagee to enforce the mortgage against other property affected thereby, which is owned by the mortgagor, or which has been acquired from the mortgagor by a third person after the third possessor acquired his property.

Art. 5155. Pleading discussion

A third possessor may plead discussion in an injunction suit to restrain the enforcement of a legal or judicial mortgage against his property. Discussion may be pleaded by a surety or transferee in a revocatory action only in the dilatory exception.

In pleading discussion, the secondary obligor shall:

(1) Point out by a description sufficient to identify it, property in the state belonging to the primary obligor, or otherwise subject to discussion, which is not in litigation, is not exempt from seizure, is free of mortgages and privileges, and is worth more than the total amount of the judgment or mortgage; and

(2) Deposit into the registry of the court, for the use of the creditor, an amount sufficient to defray the costs of executing the judgment or enforcing the mortgage against the property discussed.

Art. 5156. Effect of discussion

When discussion is pleaded successfully by a third possessor, or by the transferee in a revocatory action, the court shall stay proceedings against the third possessor or transferee until the creditor has executed his judgment against the property discussed.

When discussion is pleaded successfully by a surety and the principal is joined, the court may render judgment against both the principal and the surety, but shall order the creditor to execute his judgment against the property discussed. If the principal is not joined in the action initially, the court shall order his joinder if he is subject to its jurisdiction, and may then proceed as provided in this paragraph.

If the creditor is not able to satisfy his judgment out of the proceeds of the judicial sale of the property discussed, he may thereafter proceed as if discussion had not been pleaded.

Editor's Notes

See Caveat under C.C.P. art. 5152. The surety's right to discussion has been abolished, C.C. art. 3047.

CHAPTER 5. WAIVER OF COSTS FOR INDIGENT PARTY

Article

Art. 5181. Privilege of litigating without prior payment of costs

A. Except as provided in Paragraph B of this Article, an individual who is unable to pay the costs of court because of his poverty and lack of means may prosecute or defend a judicial proceeding in any trial or appellate court without paying the costs in advance or as they accrue or furnishing security therefor.

B. In the event any person seeks to prosecute a suit in a court of this state while incarcerated or imprisoned for the commission of a felony without paying the costs in advance as they accrue or furnishing security thereof, the court shall require such person to advance costs in accordance with the following schedule:

Prisoner's Present Assets		Advance Cost To Be Paid	
Minimum Amount	Maximum Amount	Minimum Amount	Maximum Amount
$ 0.00	$ 20.00	$ 0.00	$ 3.00
$ 20.01	$ 45.00	$ 3.00	$ 9.00
$ 45.01	$ 65.00	$ 9.00	$ 15.00
$ 65.01	$ 85.00	$ 15.00	$ 21.00
$ 85.01	$105.00	$ 21.00	$ 27.00
$105.01	$125.00	$ 27.00	$ 33.00
$125.01	$145.00	$ 33.00	$ 39.00
$145.01	$165.00	$ 39.00	$ 45.00
$165.01	$185.00	$ 45.00	$ 51.00
$185.01	$205.00	$ 51.00	$ 57.00
$205.01	$225.00	$ 57.00	$ 63.00
$225.01	$245.00	$ 63.00	$ 69.00
$245.01	$265.00	$ 69.00	$ 75.00
$265.01	$285.00	$ 75.00	$ 81.00
$285.01	$305.00	$ 81.00	$ 87.00
$305.01	$325.00	$ 87.00	$ 93.00
$325.01	$345.00	$ 93.00	$ 99.00
$345.01	$365.00	$ 99.00	$105.00
$365.01	Up	$105.00 to all advance cost.	

C. The court for good cause shown may require a prisoner to pay more or less advance cost than is required by the schedule in Paragraph B of this Article if the court finds that the prisoner's prior financial record makes reliance on his present economic status inappropriate.

Amended by Acts 1964, No. 336, § 1; Acts 1972, No. 663, § 1; Acts 1984, No. 509, § 1.

Editor's Notes

Court reporter, R.S. 13:961, and sections thereafter pertaining to specific judicial districts. Uniform Reciprocal Enforcement of Support Act, R.S. 13:1669, costs and fees.

Art. 5182. Restrictions on privilege

The privilege granted by this Chapter shall be restricted to litigants who are clearly entitled to it, with due regard to the nature of the proceeding, the court costs which otherwise would have to be paid, and the ability of the litigant to pay them or to furnish security therefor, so that the fomentation of litigation by an indiscriminate resort thereto may be discouraged, without depriving a litigant of its benefits if he is entitled thereto.

Art. 5183. Affidavits of poverty; documentation; order

A. A person who wishes to exercise the privilege granted in this Chapter shall apply to the court for permission to do so in his first pleading, or in an ex parte written motion if requested later, to which the applicant shall annex the following:

(1) The applicant's affidavit that the applicant is unable to pay the costs of court in advance, or as they accrue, or to furnish security therefor, because of the applicant's poverty and lack of means, accompanied by any supporting documentation.

(2) The affidavit of a third person other than the applicant's attorney that he knows the applicant, knows the applicant's financial condition, and believes that the applicant is unable to pay the costs of court in advance, or as they accrue, or to furnish security therefor.

(3) A recommendation from the clerk of court's office as to whether or not it feels the litigant is in fact indigent, and thus unable to pay the cost of court in advance, or as they accrue, or to furnish security therefor, if required by local rule of the court.

B. (1) Upon the filing of the completed application and supporting affidavits, the court shall render an order that does one of the following:

(a) Grants the application and allows the applicant to litigate or to continue the litigation without paying the costs in advance.

(b) Denies the application with written reasons for such denial.

(c) Sets the matter for a contradictory hearing.

(2) The submission by the applicant of supporting documentation that the applicant is receiving public assistance benefits or that the applicant's income is less than or equal to one hundred twenty-five percent of the federal poverty level shall create a rebuttable presumption that the applicant is entitled to the privilege granted in this Chapter. If the court finds that the presumption has been rebutted, it shall provide written reasons for its finding.

(3) The court may reconsider its original order granting the application on its own motion at any time in a contradictory hearing.

Amended by Acts 1984, No. 456, § 1; Acts 1997, No. 1122, § 1, eff. July 14, 1997; Acts 1997, No. 1205, § 1; Acts 2021, No. 416, § 1.

Editor's Notes

The 1997 amendment adds "accompanied by any supporting" document to Paragraph A(1). In Paragraph B, the second sentence is added as the rebuttable presumption arising from public assistance benefits or poverty level income. Paragraph A(3) was enacted to require annexation of recommendation from the clerk's office as to whether "it feels" the litigant is indigent.

CAVEAT: Rule 8.2 of the District Court Rules eliminates the requirement of the recommendation from the Clerk's Office, A(3), above.

Art. 5184. Traverse of affidavits of poverty

A. An adverse party or the clerk of the court in which the litigation is pending may traverse the facts alleged in the affidavits of poverty, and the right of the applicant to exercise the privilege granted in this Chapter, by a rule against him to show cause why the order of court permitting him to litigate, or to continue the litigation, without paying the costs in advance, or as they accrue, or furnishing security therefor, should not be rescinded. However, only one rule to traverse the affidavit of poverty shall be allowed, whether the rule is filed by an adverse party or the clerk of court.

B. The court shall rescind its order if, on the trial of the rule to traverse, it finds that the litigant is not entitled to exercise the privilege granted in this Chapter.

Amended by Acts 1990, No. 179, § 1.

Art. 5185. Rights of party permitted to litigate without payment of costs

A. When an order of court permits a party to litigate without the payment of costs until this order is rescinded or expires, the party is entitled to:

(1) All services required by law of a sheriff, clerk of court, court reporter, notary, or other public officer in, or in connection with, the judicial proceeding, including but not limited to the filing of pleadings and exhibits, the issuance of certificates, the certification of copies of notarial acts and

public records, the issuance and service of subpoenas and process, the taking and transcribing of testimony, and the preparation of a record of appeal.

(2)(a) The right to the compulsory attendance of not more than six witnesses for the purpose of testifying, either in court or by deposition, without the payment of the fees, mileage, and other expenses allowed these witnesses by law. If a party has been permitted to litigate without full payment of costs and is unable to pay for witnesses desired by the party, in addition to those summoned at the expense of the parish, the party shall make a sworn application to the court for the additional witnesses. The application shall allege that the testimony is relevant and material and not cumulative and that the defendant cannot safely go to trial without it. A short summary of the expected testimony of each witness shall be attached to the application.

(b) The court shall make a private inquiry into the facts and, if satisfied that the party is entitled to the privilege, shall render an order permitting the party to subpoena additional witnesses at the expense of the parish. If the application is denied, the court shall state the reasons for the denial in writing, which shall become part of the record.

(3) The right to a trial by jury and to the services of jurors, when allowed by law and applied for timely.

(4) The right to have any judgment or order filed and to receive one certified copy of the judgment or order.

(5) The right to a devolutive appeal, and to apply for supervisory writs.

B. The party is not entitled to a suspensive appeal, or to an order or judgment required by law to be conditioned on his furnishing security other than for costs, unless the party furnishes the necessary security therefor.

C. No public officer is required to make any cash outlay to perform any duty imposed on him under any Article in this Chapter, except to pay witnesses summoned at the expense of the parish the witness fee and mileage to which they are entitled.

Amended by Acts 1964, No. 4, § 1; Acts 1984, No. 541, § 1; Acts 2021, No. 416, § 1.

Editor's Notes

There is no statutory provision herein imposing on a court reporter the duty to take depositions out of court, Comment (a).

Art. 5186. Account and payment of costs

An account shall be kept of all costs incurred by a party who has been permitted to litigate without the payment of costs, by the public officers to whom these costs would be payable. If judgment is rendered in favor of the indigent party, the party against whom the judgment is rendered shall be condemned to pay all costs due such officers, who have a privilege on the judgment superior to the rights of the indigent party or his attorney. If judgment is rendered against the indigent plaintiff and he is condemned to pay court costs, an affidavit of the account by an officer to whom costs are due, recorded in the mortgage records, shall have the effect of a judgment for the payment due.

Amended by Acts 1981, No. 545, § 1; Acts 1993, No. 852, § 1; Acts 1997, No. 408, § 1.

Editor's Notes

The 1997 amendment revises the procedure by which public officers shall be paid their costs.

Art. 5187. Compromise; dismissal of proceedings prior to judgment

No compromise shall be effected unless all costs due these officers have been paid. Should any compromise agreement be entered into in violation of this article, each party thereto is liable to these officers for all costs due them at the time.

No judicial proceeding in which a party has been permitted to litigate without the payment of costs shall be dismissed prior to judgment, unless all costs due these public officers have been paid, or there is annexed to the written motion to dismiss the certificates of all counsel of record that no compromise has been effected or is contemplated.

No release of a claim or satisfaction of a judgment shall be effective between the parties to a judicial proceeding in which one of the parties has been permitted to litigate without the payment of costs unless all costs due the clerk of court have been paid. The clerk of court shall have a lien for the payment of such costs superior to that of any other party on any monies or other assets transferred in settlement of such claim or satisfaction of such judgment and shall be entitled to collect reasonable attorney's fees in any action to enforce this lien for the payment of such costs.

Amended by Acts 1982, No. 533, § 1.

Art. 5188. Unsuccessful party condemned to pay costs

Except as otherwise provided by Articles 1920 and 2164, if judgment is rendered against a party who has been permitted to litigate without the payment of costs, he shall be condemned to pay the costs incurred by him, in accordance with the provisions of Article 5186, and those recoverable by the adverse party. The failure of the indigent party to pay the costs specified in this Article shall not prevent entry of a judgment in favor of any party who is not responsible for the costs.

Amended by Acts 1993, No. 852, § 1; Acts 2012, No. 741, § 1.

Comment—2012

Article 5188 was amended to make clear that the court cannot refuse to sign a judgment because an indigent party has failed to satisfy an obligation to the clerk of court in a judgment ordering the payment of court costs.

TITLE II. DEFINITIONS

Art. 5251. Words and terms defined

Except where the context clearly indicates otherwise, as used in this Code:

(1) "Absentee" means a person who is either a nonresident of this state, or a person who is domiciled in but has departed from this state, and who has not appointed an agent for the service of process in this state in the manner directed by law; or a person whose whereabouts are unknown, or who cannot be found and served after a diligent effort, though he may be domiciled or actually present in the state; or a person who may be dead, though the fact of his death is not known, and if dead his heirs are unknown.

(2) "Agent for the service of process" means the agent designated by a person or by law to receive service of process in actions and proceedings brought against him in the courts in this state.

(3) "City court" includes a municipal court which has civil jurisdiction.

(4) "Competent court", or "court of competent jurisdiction", means a court which has jurisdiction over the subject matter of, and is the proper venue for, the action or proceeding.

(5) "Corporation" includes a private corporation, domestic or foreign, a public corporation, and, unless another article in the same Chapter where the word is used indicates otherwise, a domestic, foreign, or alien insurance corporation.

(6) "Foreign corporation" means a corporation organized and existing under the laws of another state or a possession of the United States, or of a foreign country.

(7) "Insurance policy" includes all policies included within the definition in R.S. 22:46, and a life, or a health and accident policy, issued by a fraternal benefit society.

(8) "Insurer" includes every person engaged in the business of making contracts of insurance as provided in R.S. 22:46, and a fraternal benefit society.

(9) "Law" as used in the phrases "unless otherwise provided by law" or "except as otherwise provided by law" means an applicable provision of the constitution, a code, or a statute of Louisiana.

(10) "Legal representative" includes an administrator, provisional administrator, administrator of a vacant succession, executor, dative testamentary executor, tutor, administrator of the estate of a minor child, curator, receiver, liquidator, trustee, and any officer appointed by a court to administer an estate under its jurisdiction.

(11) "Nonresident" means an individual who is not domiciled in this state, a foreign corporation which is not licensed to do business in this state, or a partnership or unincorporated association organized and existing under the laws of another state or a possession of the United States, or of a foreign country and includes a limited liability company which is not organized under the laws of and is not then licensed to do business in this state.

(12) "Person" includes an individual, partnership, unincorporated association of individuals, joint stock company, corporation, or limited liability company.

(13) "Property" includes all classes of property recognized under the laws of this state: movable or immovable, corporeal or incorporeal.

(14) The term "succession representative" includes executor, independent executor, administrator, independent administrator, provisional administrator, together with their successors. The inclusion of the terms "independent executor" and "independent administrator" within the definition

See West's Louisiana Statutes Annotated

of succession representative shall not be construed to subject such a succession representative to control of the court in probate matters with respect to the administration of a succession, except as expressly provided in Chapter 13 of Title III of Book VI [1].

Amended by Acts 1999, No. 145, § 2; Acts 2001, No. 974, § 1.

[1] Chapter 13, Title III, Book VI, see C.C.P. art. 3396 et seq.

Editor's Notes

Absentee submits to the jurisdiction of the court when he appears in the action personally or through his own counsel, Roy O. Martin Lumber Co. v. Strange, 106 So.2d 723 (1958), Comment (a). See the Official Comments under the articles listed for the following terms: agent for service of process, C.C.P. art. 6; competent court, C.C.P. art. 8; insurance policy, C.C.P. art. 76; insurer, C.C.P. arts. 690, 693, 739, 741; legal representative, C.C.P. arts. 194, 195, 374, 805, 2084, 2122, 2637, 2701; nonresident, C.C.P. arts. 5091, 5094; person, C.C.P. arts. 42, 330, 1354, 3097; and property, C.C.P. arts. 8, 326, 2291, 2292, 3541. See other definitions: corporation, R.S. 12:1(G); foreign corporation, R.S. 12:1(K), and R.S. 12:201; insurer, R.S. 22:5 and R.S. 22:757; law, C.C. art. 1; nonresident, R.S. 47:451; and C.C. art. 24 et seq., generally; insurance policy, R.S. 22:624; property, R.S. 14:2, R.S. 19:1, R.S. 47:1702.

The 1999 amendment added "limited liability company" to (11) and (12). See also R.S. 13:3206 and 3471(1), both incorporating the "limited liability company".

SECTION 2. (A) The Louisiana State Law Institute, as the official advisory law revision commission of the State of Louisiana, shall direct and supervise the continuous revision, clarification, and coordination of the Louisiana Code of Civil Procedure in a manner not inconsistent with the provisions of this section.

(B) At the close of each legislative session, the Louisiana State Law Institute shall prepare printer's copy, either for a supplement to the Louisiana Code of Civil Procedure, or for a volume to be called "Louisiana Code of Civil Procedure" containing the text of the Louisiana Code of Civil Procedure as it may have been amended, and omitting therefrom or noting therein those articles which have been repealed. There shall also be incorporated therein, in an appropriate place and classification, the text of all the new procedural legislation applicable generally to civil actions or proceedings, or to those actions or proceedings regulated by the Louisiana Code of Civil Procedure, assigning to these new laws an appropriate book, title, chapter, section, subsection, and article number, and indicating the source of the legislative acts from which they are taken.

(C) In preparing the printer's copy provided in this section, the Louisiana State Law Institute shall not alter the sense, meaning, or effect of any act of the legislature, but it may:

(1) Re-number and re-arrange articles;

(2) Transfer or divide articles or statutory sections so as to give to distinct subject matters a separate article number, but without changing the meaning;

(3) Insert or change the wording of headnotes;

(4) Change reference numbers to agree with the re-numbered articles;

(5) Substitute the proper book, title, chapter, section, subsection, or article number for the terms "this act", "the preceding section", and the like;

(6) Strike out figures where they are merely a repetition of written words and vice-versa;

(7) Change capitalization for the purpose of uniformity;

(8) Correct manifest typographical and grammatical errors; and

(9) Make any other purely formal or clerical changes in keeping with the purposes of the continuous revision.

The Institute shall omit all titles of acts, all enacting, resolving, and repealing clauses, all temporary statutes, all declarations of emergency, and all validity, declaration of policy, and construction clauses, except when the retention thereof is necessary to preserve the full meaning and intent of the law. Whenever any validity, declaration of policy, or construction clause is omitted, proper notation of the omission shall be made.

(D) The printer's copy for any edition of the Louisiana Code of Civil Procedure, or for any supplement thereof, prepared in the manner provided in this section shall be delivered to the secretary of state together with the certification of the Louisiana State Law Institute that each article therein has been compared with the original act enacted after the adoption of the Louisiana Code of Civil Procedure, with the original provisions of the enrolled acts from which the articles were derived, and that with the exception of the changes of form permitted in this section, the articles in the printer's copy are correct. Upon receipt of the printer's copy, the secretary of state shall order the printing of an edition sufficient in number to supply the demand. When the edition has been printed, the secretary of state, after making the necessary comparison with the original printer's copy, shall affix to a copy of the printed edition the Institute's original certificate and file the same for record in his office. All other copies of the same edition may contain a printed facsimile of the Institute's certificate.

(E) Any article in any subsequent edition or supplement of the Louisiana Code of Civil Procedure prepared by the Louisiana State Law Institute may be amended or repealed by reference to the article number, without reference to the legislative act from which the article was taken.

(F) The secretary of state is authorized to enter into contracts with private publishers for the printing, publication, sale, and distribution of any edition or supplement of the Louisiana Code of Civil Procedure prepared by the Louisiana State Law Institute and certified by it pursuant to the provisions of this section. Those editions or supplements so authorized by the secretary of state and containing the printed facsimile of the Institute's certificate of correctness shall be admissible as prima facie evidence of the laws contained therein.

SECTION 3. If, for any reason, any provision of this act, including any provision of the Louisiana Code of Civil Procedure enacted by Section 1 hereof, is declared unconstitutional or invalid, the other separable provisions thereof shall not be affected thereby.

SECTION 4. (A) This act is hereby declared to be remedial legislation.

(B) The provisions of the Louisiana Code of Civil Procedure enacted by Section 1 hereof, so far as applicable, shall govern and regulate the procedure in all civil actions and proceedings:

(1) Instituted on or after the effective date of this act; and

(2) Pending on the effective date of this act, except that none of the provisions thereof shall:

(a) Decrease or shorten any procedural delay granted or allowed by any law in existence immediately prior to, and which had commenced to run but had not yet completely elapsed on, the effective date of this act; or

(b) Affect the validity or change the legal effect of any judicial, official, or procedural act done or attempted, or of any failure to act, prior to the effective date of this act in any civil action or proceeding, including but not limited to any: citation, writ, mandate, summons, subpoena, notice, or other process issued or served; pleading filed; security furnished; oral motion made; testimony taken, by deposition or otherwise; evidence introduced or offered; ruling made by the court; order or judgment rendered; appeal taken or requested; execution of any judgment, writ, or mandate; seizure made by the sheriff or other executive officer of a court; publication of a judicial notice or advertisement; or judicial sale, whether actually completed or not.

SECTION 5. The Code of Practice of the State of Louisiana, and all other laws or parts of laws in conflict or inconsistent with the Louisiana Code of Civil Procedure enacted by Section 1 hereof, are hereby repealed; but nothing contained herein, or in the code enacted hereby, shall be construed to repeal, supersede, or otherwise affect, the provisions of Sections 4438, 4441, 4442, 4445, and 4446 of Title 13 of the Revised Statutes of 1950, as amended or adopted by the Legislature at its Regular Session of 1960.

SECTION 6. In the event of any conflict between the provisions of this act, and those of any other act adopted by the Legislature at its Regular Session of 1960, regardless of which act is adopted later or signed later by the Governor, the provisions of this act, and of the Louisiana Code of Civil Procedure hereby enacted, shall control and prevail on the effective date hereof.

For Official Comments and Annotative Materials,

SECTION 7. All of the provisions of this act shall become effective on January 1, 1961.

Approved June 16, 1960.

STATUTORY APPENDIX

TABLE OF CONTENTS

R.S. 9:301	Court may authorize spouse of military personnel presumed dead to remarry; judgment dissolves marriage
R.S. 9:302	Divorce proceedings; hearings in chambers; procedure
R.S. 9:331 to 9:332	Child Custody; Evaluation and Mediation
R.S. 9:341 to 9:346, 9:348	Child Custody; Protective and Remedial Provisions
R.S. 9:351	Access to Records of Child
R.S. 9:361 to 9:366	Post Separation Family Violence Relief Act
R.S. 9:371 to 9:375	Injunctions and Incidental Actions in Divorce
R.S. 9:572	Person having parental authority; acts that may be performed without court approval
R.S. 9:2781	Open accounts; attorney fees; professional fees; open account owed to the state
R.S. 9:2794	Medical malpractice, burden of proof
R.S. 9:2801 to 9:2801.2	Partition of community property and settlement of claims arising from matrimonial regimes and co-ownership of former community property
R.S. 9:3150	[New Home Warranty Act] Exclusiveness
R.S. 9:3221	Assumption of responsibility by lessee; liability of owner
R.S. 9:3500	Rates of legal and conventional interest; usury
R.S. 9:5011 to 9:5016	Privileges to effect separation of patrimony
R.S. 9:5550 to 9:5557	Authentic evidence, executory process, collateral mortgages, vendor's privileges, and cancellation and release of mortgages
R.S. 9:5604	Actions for accounting malpractice; prescription and peremption
R.S. 9:5605	Actions for legal malpractice; peremption
R.S. 9:5605.1	Theft of client funds; prescription
R.S. 9:5606	Professional insurance agent liability; peremption
R.S. 9:5607	Actions against a professional engineer, surveyor, professional interior designer, architect, real estate developer; peremptive periods
R.S. 9:5608	Actions against home inspectors
R.S. 9:5609	Contracts to buy or sell; peremption of the effect of recordation; prescription for actions
R.S. 9:5610	Actions against real estate appraisers, appraisal management companies, and real estate appraisal companies; prescriptive and peremptive periods
R.S. 9:5622	Informalities in auction sales, two and five year prescription
R.S. 9:5628	Actions for medical malpractice, prescription
R.S. 9:5630	Actions by unrecognized successors against third persons, prescription
R.S. 9:5642	Sheriffs' deeds, prescription
R.S. 9:5801	Failure to timely request service of citation; involuntary dismissal
R.S. 9:5828 to 9:5830	Suspension or extension of prescription and peremption during 2020 COVID-19 public health emergency
R.S. 12:308	Foreign corporation, registered agent, registered office and principal business establishment, keeping of records
R.S. 13:850	Fax filing
R.S. 13:1801 to 13:1842	Uniform Child Custody Jurisdiction and Enforcement Act
R.S. 13:3041	Juries (in part)
R.S. 13:3201 to 13:3207	Long arm statute, personal jurisdiction over non-residents, definitions, procedure
R.S. 13:3471	Supplementary rules of service of process

R.S. 13:3472	Service on foreign corporation through secretary of state
R.S. 13:3474	Operation of motor vehicle by non-resident as appointment of secretary of state as agent for service of process
R.S. 13:3475	Service on secretary of state; sending or delivering notice and copies; filing receipt or affidavit; continuances
R.S. 13:3479	Non-resident watercraft operator, appointment of secretary of state as agent for service of process
R.S. 13:3661	Witness attendance compulsory in civil cases; witnesses within state; deposit
R.S. 13:3661.1	Service of subpoenas on law enforcement officers and fire service personnel
R.S. 13:3721	Parol evidence to prove debt or liability of deceased person; objections not waivable
R.S. 13:3722	Same; evidence required when parol evidence admissible
R.S. 13:3821 to 13:3825	Foreign depositions (Letters rogatory)
R.S. 13:3881	General exemptions from seizure
R.S. 13:3886	Request for notice of seizure on specific property
R.S. 13:3886.1	Seizure, failure to notify lienholder or other interested person
R.S. 13:3921 to 13:3928	Garnishment; procedures
R.S. 13:4101 to 13:4112	Executory process and deficiency judgment act
R.S. 13:4163	Ex parte motion for legislative continuance or extension of time; legislators or employees engaged
R.S. 13:4165	Special masters; appointment; duties and powers; compensation
R.S. 13:4202	Rates of judicial interest
R.S. 13:4231	Res judicata
R.S. 13:4232	Exceptions to the general rule of res judicata
R.S. 13:4241 to 13:4248	Enforcement of Foreign Judgments Act
R.S. 13:4359	Judicial sales, portion of price to be paid on adjudication
R.S. 13:4363	Appointment of appraisers
R.S. 13:4441	Transfer of cases appealed to wrong court; retransfer
R.S. 13:4611	Punishment for contempt of court; defenses
R.S. 13:5101 to 13:5108, 13:5109.1	Suits against the state (in part)
R.S. 13:5200 to 13:5212	Small claims procedures
R.S. 20:1	Declaration of homestead; exemption from seizure and sale; debts excluded from exemption; waiver
R.S. 22:335	Service of process; secretary of state as attorney
R.S. 22:1269	Direct action against insurer; liability policy; insolvency or bankruptcy of insured and inability to effect service of citation or other process
R.S. 22:1892	Payment and adjustment of claims
R.S. 22:1907	Transacting business; constitutes appointment of agent for service of process; workers' compensation claims agent
R.S. 22:1973	Good faith duty; claims settlement practices; cause of action; penalties
R.S. 23:921	Restraint of business prohibited; restraint on forum prohibited; competing business; contracts against engaging in; provision for
R.S. 35:200	Limitation on actions
R.S. 35:701, 35:702	Modification of presence requirement for notary functions performed during 2020 COVID-19 public health emergency
R.S. 39:1538	Claims against the state
R.S. 40:1231.1	Medical malpractice—Definitions and general applications
R.S. 40:1231.8	Medical review panel

STATUTORY APPENDIX

RULES FOR LOUISIANA DISTRICT COURTS AND JUVENILE COURTS AND LOUISIANA FAMILY LAW PROCEEDINGS

TITLE I

RULES FOR PROCEEDINGS IN DISTRICT COURTS, FAMILY COURTS, AND JUVENILE COURTS

CHAPTER 1. CONSTRUCTION, APPLICATION, AND AMENDMENT

Rule 1.0

Rule 1.0. Construction of Rules and Appendices

These Rules and Appendices are intended to govern interaction between the courts, counsel, and litigants, and to ensure the administration of justice in an efficient and effective manner.

Administrative rules governing internal operating procedures of individual courts on topics not otherwise covered by these Rules may be adopted by en banc order of the court.

Such administrative rules shall be made available to the public by filing a copy with the Judicial Council of the Supreme Court and by filing a copy with the clerk of court for the appropriate parish or parishes.

Adopted effective April 1, 2002. Amended November 20, 2009, effective January 1, 2010; Comment amended December 11, 2018, effective January 1, 2019.

Comments

(a) The Louisiana Supreme Court has constitutional authority to promulgate these Rules under' La. Const. art. V, § 5. These Rules are intended to supplement the Codes of Civil and Criminal Procedure. Therefore, a conflict between a Rule and legislation should be resolved by following the legislation.

(b) The Appendices are subordinate to the Rules. Therefore, a conflict between a Rule and an Appendix should be resolved by following the Rule. The information in the Appendices was provided by the various judicial districts and may be revised in accordance with the procedure found in Rule 1.3(b).

(c) Previous district court rules adopted by individual judicial districts often included various rules that duplicated the Code of Civil Procedure and applicable Revised Statutes. No provisions restating existing law have been included in these Rules. The citations to authorities for deleted topics are as follows:

(1) Construction of Pleadings—La. Code Civ. Proc. art. 865.

(2) Form of Pleadings—La. Code Civ. Proc. arts. 853, 854 and 862.

(3) Signing Pleadings—La. Code Civ. Proc. art. 863.

Rule 1.0—Cont'd

(4) Exceptions and Motions—La. Code Civ. Proc. arts. 852–54, 862, 865, 921–24, and 962.

(5) Time of trial of exceptions—La. Code Civ. Proc. art. 929.

(6) Curators ad hoc—La. Code Civ. Proc. arts. 5091–5098; La. R.S. 13:3421–3445; and La. Civ. Code arts. 47–53.

(7) Motions for summary judgment—La. Code Civ. Proc. arts. 966 and 967.

Rule 1.1

Rule 1.1. Application of Rules and Appendices; Citation Form

(a) Title I and Appendices 2.0 through 8.0 apply to all proceedings in district courts, family courts, and juvenile courts.

(b) Title II and Appendices 9.3 through 9.14 apply to all civil proceedings in district courts, except for juvenile proceedings, and as otherwise limited within these Rules.

(c) Title III and Appendices 14.0A through 19.0 apply to criminal proceedings in all district courts.

(d) Title IV applies to all family law proceedings in district courts and in the Family Court for the Parish of East Baton Rouge.

(e) Title V applies to all juvenile proceedings in district courts and in juvenile courts for the Parishes of East Baton Rouge, Orleans, Jefferson, and Caddo.

(f) Title VI applies to all litigation filed by inmates in district courts.

(g) Title I through IV and Title VI of these Rules shall be known as the "Louisiana District Court Rules" and may be officially cited: La. Dist. Ct. R. ____. The Appendices to these Rules may be officially cited: La. Dist. Ct. R. ____, App. ____.

(h) Title V of these Rules shall be known as the "Louisiana Juvenile Court Rules" and may be officially cited: La. Juv. Ct. R. ____. The Appendices to Title V may be officially cited: La. Juv. Ct. R. ____, App. ____.

Adopted April 1, 2002, effective April 1, 2002; amended June 2, 2003, effective July 1, 2003; amended November 3, 2008, effective January 1, 2009; amended November 20, 2009, effective January 1, 2010; amended April 20, 2010, effective June 1, 2010; amended November 21, 2011, effective January 1, 2012; amended April 29, 2014, effective June 1, 2014; amended October 7, 2015, effective January 1, 2016.

Rule 1.2

Rule 1.2. Effective Date

The effective date of the Louisiana Rules for District Courts and all Appendices is April 1, 2002. These rules and all Appendices shall govern all proceedings commenced thereafter and, insofar as just and practicable, all proceedings then pending.

Adopted April 1, 2002, effective April 1, 2002; amended June 2, 2003, effective July 1, 2003.

Rule 1.3

Rule 1.3. Amendment of Rules and Updating Appendices

(a) Proposed rules or amendments to existing Louisiana Rules for District Courts shall be approved by the Supreme Court. Proposed amendments may be submitted by any Louisiana judge

Rule 1.3—Cont'd

or licensed member of the Louisiana bar to the Office of the Judicial Administrator of the Supreme Court.

(b) Amendments to the information contained in the Appendices to the Louisiana Rules for District Courts shall be made by Court Order attached to the Appendix Amendment Form (Appendix 1.3) and submitted to the Office of the Judicial Administrator of the Supreme Court within thirty days of the signing of the Order. The Office of the Judicial Administrator of the Supreme Court shall update the Appendices annually by communication with the chief judge and the clerk of court for each judicial district, family court, or juvenile court.

(c) The Rules and Appendices shall be published annually by West Publishing Company and shall be available on the official website of the Louisiana Supreme Court.

Adopted April 1, 2002, effective April 1, 2002; amended November 3, 2004, effective January 1, 2005; amended November 3, 2008, effective January 1, 2009; amended November 20, 2009, effective January 1, 2010; amended April 20, 2010, effective June 1, 2010; amended May 18, 2016, effective July 1, 2016.

Comment

Amendments to the appendices shall be posted to the Louisiana Supreme Court website as close as possible to the effective date of the amendment.

Rule 1.4

Rule 1.4. Deviations from Rules

An individual judge may, in the interest of justice and upon notice to all parties, permit deviations from these Rules in a particular proceeding. Any such deviation shall be noted on the record in open court in the presence of all parties or by written order filed into the record of the proceedings and mailed to all parties or their counsel of record.

Adopted April 1, 2002, effective April 1, 2002; amended November 20, 2009, effective January 1, 2010.

Rule 1.5

Rule 1.5. Computation of Time

The following rules apply in computing any period of time specified in these Rules provided they do not conflict with legislation:

(a) Exclude the day of the act, event, or default that begins the period.

(b) Exclude intermediate legal holidays when the period is fewer than seven days, unless the period is stated in calendar days.

(c) Include the last day of the period, unless the last day is a legal holiday, in which case the period runs until the end of the next day that is not a legal holiday. *See* La. Code Civ. Proc. art. 966, as amended by House Bill No. 696 of the Louisiana Legislature's 2015 Regular Session, which shall govern the computing times on motions for summary judgment effective January 1, 2016. For example:

(i) When a rule requires an act be done ten days before an event, and the tenth day falls on a Sunday, the act shall be done no later than the preceding Friday (assuming Friday is not a legal holiday). This does not apply to motions for summary judgment—*see* La. Code Civ. Proc. Art. 966.

Rule 1.5—Cont'd

(ii) When a rule requires an act be done ten days after an event, and the tenth day falls on a Sunday, the act shall be done no later than the following Monday (assuming Monday is not a legal holiday).

Adopted June 2, 2003, effective July 1, 2003; amended November 20, 2009, effective January 1, 2010; amended October 7, 2015, effective January 1, 2016.

CHAPTER 2. DATES OF COURT

Rule 2.0

Rule 2.0. Dates of Court

The local holidays observed by each judicial district or court, in addition to legal holidays, are listed in Appendix 2.0 to these Rules.

Adopted April 1, 2002, effective April 1, 2002; amended November 3, 2004, effective January 1, 2005; amended November 20, 2009, effective January 1, 2010; amended April 20, 2010, effective June 1, 2010.

Comments

(a) *See* La. R.S. 1:55 for a listing of legal holidays.

(b) *See* 2004 amendment to La. R.S. 1:55(E)(1)(b) which, by reference to La. R.S. 1:55(B)(1)(a), adds Mardi Gras Day and General Election Day as legal holidays.

CHAPTER 3. JUDGES, FACSIMILE TRANSMISSIONS TO THE COURT, AND TECHNOLOGY-RELATED RULES

Rule 3.0

Rule 3.0. Office Hours

When not on the bench, each judge shall maintain such regular office days and hours as may be necessary to conduct public business.

Adopted April 1, 2002, effective April 1, 2002.

Rule 3.1

Rule 3.1. Divisions or Sections of Court

Courts may, by en banc order, divide into divisions or sections for the purpose of allotting matters within the court's jurisdiction. Those courts that have done so, and their respective methods for assigning judges to divisions or sections, are indicated in Appendix 3.1.

Adopted April 1, 2002, effective April 1, 2002; amended November 20, 2009, effective January 1, 2010; amended April 20, 2010, effective June 1, 2010.

Rule 3.2

Rule 3.2. Duty Judges

Each judicial district or court may designate one or more of its members to act as a duty judge. In civil proceedings, the duties assigned to a duty judge shall comply with La. Code Civ. Proc. art. 253.3. The identity of each duty judge shall be prominently displayed in a manner deemed appropriate by the court. If the court chooses to use multiple duty judges to perform various

Rule 3.2—Cont'd

functions, the delineation of each duty judge's duties shall also be prominently displayed. The length of term and duties of the duty judge shall be at the sole discretion of the judges in each judicial district or court sitting en banc. For those judicial districts or courts that have designated duty judges, the office hours for performance of his or her duties, and the duties assigned, are listed in Appendix 3.2.

Adopted April 1, 2002, effective April 1, 2002; amended November 20, 2009, effective January 1, 2010; amended April 20, 2010, effective June 1, 2010.

Comments

(a) Previous rules of court adopted by individual judicial districts often included various rules dealing with judges, such as selection of a chief judge; courts sitting en banc; duties and powers of judges; duty judges; random allotment; recusal, transfer, and consolidation; accessibility; and judicial accounts. Many of those rules duplicated articles of the Louisiana Constitution, applicable Revised Statutes, or Supreme Court of Louisiana decisions. Furthermore, many of those rules dealt with the internal administration of the court rather than with the interaction of counsel and litigants with the judicial process. No provisions restating existing law have been included in these Rules. The citations to authority for the deleted topics are as follows:

(1) The Court En Banc–La. R.S. 13:472; La. R.S. 13:474; La. R.S. 13:991–999; La. R.S. 13:1221; La.R.S. 13:1312; La. Code Civ. Proc. art. 193.

(2) Chief Judge—La. Const. art. 5, § 17.

(3) Duties and Powers of Judges—La. Code Civ. Proc. art. 191; La. R.S. 13:501.

(4) Random Allotment—*State v. Sprint Communications Co., L.P.*, 96–3094 (La. 9/9/97); 699 So.2d 1058; La. Code Civ. Proc. art. 253.1.

(5) Recusal—La. Code Civ. Proc. arts. 151–158, 161.

(6) Transfer of Actions—*Sprint, supra;* La. Code Civ. Proc. art. 253.2.

(7) Consolidation of Actions—La. Code Civ. Proc. art. 1561.

(8) Cumulation of Actions—La. Code Civ. Proc. arts. 461, et seq.

(b) The constitutional implications of the decision in *Sprint, supra,* regarding random allotment of cases affect a court's ability to appoint duty judges and, more importantly, the designation of duties to such judges. Act 24, § 1 of the 1st Extraordinary Session of the 2000 Legislature enacted La. Code Civ. Proc. art. 253.3, effective June 6, 2000, which clarifies the matters that a duty judge may hear. The Louisiana Constitution and Code of Criminal Procedure govern the appointment of duty judges in criminal proceedings.

(c) Previous rules adopted by individual courts often included various provisions regarding quasi-judicial officers. Many of those rules duplicated applicable revised statutes or code articles.

No provisions restating existing law have been included in these Rules. The citations to authority for the deleted topics are as follows:

(1) Judges Ad Hoc—La. Const. art. 5, §§ 5(A), 22(B); La. Code Civ. Proc. arts. 157, 158, and 161.

(2) Magistrate Commissioners—La. R.S. 13:713.

(3) The clerk of court acting as justice of the peace—La. Code Civ. Proc. art. 284.

(4) Court–Appointed Special Masters—La. R.S. 13:4165.

(d) *See* La. R.S. 13:501 regarding sessions of court.

(e) The constitutional implications of the decision in *State v. Sprint Communications Co., L.P.*, 96–3094 (La. 9/9/97); 699 So.2d 1058, regarding random allotment of cases, affect a

Rule 3.2—Cont'd

court's ability to appoint duty judges and, more importantly, the designation of duties to such judges. Act 24 of the 1st Extraordinary Session of the 2000 Legislature enacted La. Code Civ. Proc. art. 253.3 to clarify the matters that may be heard by a duty judge.

Rule 3.3

Rule 3.3. Facsimile Transmissions to Judges

Any document sent to a judge by facsimile transmission shall not exceed fifteen pages, unless the judge has granted permission for a longer transmission. Before sending a facsimile transmission in excess of fifteen pages, an attorney or party sending such facsimile transmission must contact the court for permission.

Adopted October 29, 2003, effective January 4, 2004; amended November 20, 2009, effective January 1, 2010; amended April 20, 2010, effective June 1, 2010.

Comment

La. R.S. 13:850 allows for facsimile filings and lists the requirements for such filings.

Rule 3.4

Rule 3.4. Use of Electronic Signatures by Judges

See Appendix 3.4 for courts enacting rules related to a judge, justice, or other presiding officer's electronic signature pursuant to La. Code Civ. Proc. arts. 253, 1911, or other applicable law.

Adopted October 7, 2015, effective January 1, 2016.

Rule 3.5. Simultaneous Appearance by a Party or Witness by Audio–Visual Transmission

Courts may authorize simultaneous appearance by a party or witness by audio-visual transmission as allowed by law and/or by order of the Louisiana Supreme Court. *See* Appendix 3.5 for courts enacting rules related to simultaneous appearance by a party or witness by audiovisual transmission.

Adopted effective May 14, 2020.

CHAPTER 4. COURT PERSONNEL

Rule 4.0

Rule 4.0. Court Reporters

The court shall provide a method for making a verbatim recording of all proceedings conducted in open court.

Adopted April 1, 2002, effective April 1, 2002.

Rule 4.1

Rule 4.1. Judicial Administrators

The court en banc may appoint and fix the salary of a judicial administrator to assist the court in fulfilling its administrative obligations. Those judicial districts that have appointed an administrator are listed in Appendix 4.1.

Websites for district courts and clerks of court, where available, are also listed in Appendix 4.1.

Adopted April 1, 2002, effective April 1, 2002; amended November 3, 2008, effective January 1, 2009; amended November 20, 2009, effective January 1, 2010; amended April 20, 2010, effective June 1, 2010.

Rule 4.1—Cont'd

Comments

(a) Previous rules of court adopted by individual judicial districts often included various rules dealing with court reporters, court criers, and bailiffs. Many of those rules duplicated revised statutes or code articles.

(b) No provisions restating existing law have been included in these Rules. The citations to authority for the deleted topics are as follows:

(1) Court Reporters—La. R.S. 13:961, 982; La. Code Civ. Proc. art. 372.

(2) Criers—La. Code Civ. Proc. art. 333.

(3) Docket and Minute Books—La. Code Civ. Proc. arts. 254 and 256.

(4) Costs of transcription, maximum and minimum court reporter fees—La. R.S. 13:961, et seq.

CHAPTER 5. COURTROOM USE, ACCESSIBILITY, AND SECURITY

Rule 5.0

Rule 5.0. Courtroom Use

The name of the judge assigned to a particular courtroom shall be prominently displayed outside the courtroom in a manner deemed appropriate by the court. The clerk of court shall maintain a list of all courtrooms, their locations, and the judges assigned to each.

Adopted April 1, 2002, effective April 1, 2002; amended November 20, 2009, effective January 1, 2010.

Rule 5.1

Rule 5.1. Accessibility to Judicial Proceedings

(a) The facilities, services, and programs of the court shall be readily accessible to persons with disabilities. Attached as Appendix 5.1A is a form that may be used to request reasonable accommodations extended under the ADA. Attached as Appendix 5.1B is a form that may be used to request an interpreter. Attached as Appendix 5.1C is a form that may be used as an interpreter's oath.

(b) In addition to the above requirements, courts having fifty or more employees shall develop, promulgate, and maintain a problem-resolution process and designate a responsible court officer or employee to coordinate access to court programs and services by persons with disabilities and to resolve complaints regarding lack of access for such persons.

Adopted April 1, 2002, effective April 1, 2002; amended November 3, 2008, effective January 1, 2009; amended November 20, 2009, effective January 1, 2010; amended April 20, 2010, effective June 1, 2010.

Rule 5.2

Rule 5.2. Courtroom Security

The sheriff or his or her designated deputies shall provide security for the courtrooms, chambers, judicial offices, and hallways within the courthouse. Security procedures shall be approved by the chief judge of the district court or other court.

Adopted April 1, 2002, effective April 1, 2002; amended November 20, 2009, effective January 1, 2010.

CHAPTER 6. COURTROOM DECORUM AND THE CONDUCT OF ATTORNEYS AND JUDGES

Rule 6.0

Rule 6.0. The Opening of Court

The bailiff shall open each session of court with an appropriate recitation and order, such as the following:

> "Oyez, Oyez, Oyez, Section (or Division) ________, the Honorable ________ Judicial District Court (or other court) of the State of Louisiana, in and for the Parish of ________, is now in session. The Honorable Judge ________ presiding. Order and silence are commanded. God save the State and this Honorable Court."

The bailiff shall direct all persons in the courtroom when they are to rise, in accordance with the directions of the court.

Adopted April 1, 2002, effective April 1, 2002. Amended December 11, 2018, effective January 1, 2019.

Rule 6.1

Rule 6.1. General Courtroom Conduct

(a) No person may engage in any conduct that would be disruptive to the business of the court, including the following:

(1) Using tobacco in any form at any time.

(2) Reading newspapers while court is in session.

(3) Displaying any political advertisement of any nature.

(b) Attorneys, as officers of the court, shall help to maintain the dignity of the court. Male attorneys and clerks of court shall wear coats and ties in the courtroom. Female attorneys and clerks of court shall wear a comparable level of attire.

(c) No one may wear a hat or be barefoot in the courtroom. Witnesses and spectators shall appear neat and clean, within the limits of propriety. The court will make allowances for those who shall appear in work clothes and for those whose attire is dictated by their religion.

(d) No one is allowed inside the rail except for attorneys, litigants, officers of the court, and anyone else that the court specifically authorizes.

(e) A judge should prohibit broadcasting, televising, recording, or the taking of photographs in the courtroom and areas immediately adjacent thereto, at least during sessions of court or recesses between sessions. *See* Code of Judicial Conduct Canon 3A(9).

(f) A judge may prohibit the use of electronic devices, including cellular telephones and recording devices, in a courtroom.

Adopted April 1, 2002, effective April 1, 2002; amended June 2, 2003, effective July 1, 2003; amended November 20, 2009, effective January 1, 2010; amended November 21, 2011, effective January 1, 2012.

Rule 6.2

Rule 6.2. Attorney Conduct

(a) Any attorney who tenders himself or herself before the court and represents that he or she is duly authorized to practice law, but who has been declared ineligible, suspended, or disbarred from practice before the courts of this State, shall be subject to contempt proceedings.

Rule 6.2—Cont'd

(b) No one may represent a party in any proceeding except counsel of record, unless allowed to do so by law.

(c) When an attorney is interested in two or more matters fixed for hearing in different sections or divisions of court on the same day, that attorney shall notify the minute clerk of the section or sections from which he or she expects to be temporarily absent as to his or her presence in another court.

(d) As a general rule, attorneys desiring to address the court while it is in session shall do so while standing. Unless directed otherwise by the judge, all judgments, orders, decrees, or other documents shall be handed to the clerk, who shall hand them to the judge.

(e) Private conversation or conference between attorneys or others in attendance during any court session should not be disruptive to the proceedings.

(f) Attorneys shall address all remarks, objections, and comments to the judge, never to opposing counsel. Impromptu argument or discussion between counsel will not be permitted.

(g) Except with leave of court obtained, only one attorney for each party shall examine any one witness.

(h) Counsel may not approach the witness in the witness chair without first obtaining the court's permission.

(i) Before showing an exhibit to a witness, counsel shall first either show opposing counsel the exhibit or provide opposing counsel with a copy of the exhibit.

(j) Counsel and parties to any litigation shall not send the court copies of correspondence between them.

(k) Attorneys shall abide by the Rules of Professional Conduct and should abide by the Louisiana Code of Professionalism, the latter of which is set forth below:

The Louisiana Code of Professionalism

- My word is my bond.
- I will conduct myself with honesty, dignity, civility, courtesy and fairness and will not engage in any demeaning or derogatory actions or commentary toward others.
- I will not knowingly make statements of fact or law that are untrue or misleading and I will clearly identify for other counsel changes I have made in documents submitted to me.
- I will be punctual in my communication with clients, other counsel and the court. I will honor scheduled appearances and will cooperate with other counsel in all respects.
- I will allow counsel fair opportunity to respond and will grant reasonable requests for extensions of time.
- I will not abuse or misuse the law, its procedures or the participants in me judicial process.
- I will cooperate with counsel and the court to reduce the cost of litigation and will not file or oppose pleadings, conduct discovery or utilize any course of conduct for the purpose of undue delay or harassment of any other counsel or party.
- I will not engage in personal attacks on other counsel or the court or use the threat of sanctions as a litigation tactic.
- I will support my profession's efforts to enforce its disciplinary rules and will not make unfounded allegations of unethical conduct about other counsel.
- I will work to protect and improve the image of the legal profession in the eyes of the public.

Rule 6.2—Cont'd

- I will endeavor to improve our system of justice.
- I will use technology, including social media, responsibly. My words and actions, no matter how conveyed, should reflect the professionalism expected of me as a lawyer.
- I will seek opportunities to be of service to the bench and bar and assist those who cannot afford legal help.
- I will be supportive of new members in the profession.
- I will stay informed about changes in the law, communication, and technology which affect the practice of law.

Adopted April 1, 2002, effective April 1, 2002; amended October 29, 2003, effective January 4, 2004; amended November 20, 2009, effective January 1, 2010; amended effective December 11, 2018.

Comments

(a) The Louisiana Code of Professionalism was authored by the Professionalism and Quality of Life Committee of the Louisiana State Bar Association in 1991. It was adopted by the Louisiana State Bar Association House of Delegates and approved by the Supreme Court of Louisiana in January 1992.

(b) Rule 6.2(j) is not intended to prohibit attaching correspondence between counsel to a pleading where appropriate, such as to show that attempts have been made to schedule a conference to resolve discovery disputes under Rule 10.1.

Rule 6.3

Rule 6.3. Code of Professionalism in the Courts

Attorneys and judges should conform to the Code of Professionalism adopted as Section 11 of Part G, General Administrative Rules, Supreme Court of Louisiana:

The Code of Professionalism in the Courts

PREAMBLE

The following standards are designed to encourage us, the judges and lawyers, to meet our obligations to each other, to litigants and to the system of justice, and thereby achieve the twin goals of professionalism and civility, both of which are hallmarks of a learned profession dedicated to public service.

These standards shall not be used as a basis for litigation or sanctions or penalties. Nothing in these standards alters or detracts from existing disciplinary codes or alters the existing standards of conduct against which judicial or lawyer negligence may be determined.

However, these standards should be reviewed and followed by all judges of the State of Louisiana. Copies may be made available to clients to reinforce our obligation to maintain and foster these standards.

JUDGES' DUTIES TO THE COURT

We will be courteous, respectful, and civil to lawyers, parties, and witnesses. We will maintain control of the proceedings, recognizing that judges have both the obligation and authority to insure that all litigation proceedings are conducted in a civil manner.

We will not employ hostile, demeaning, or humiliating words in opinions or in written or oral communications with lawyers, parties, or witnesses.

We will be punctual in convening all hearings, meetings, and conferences; if delayed, we will notify counsel, if possible.

Rule 6.3—Cont'd

We will be considerate of time schedules of lawyers, parties, and witnesses in scheduling all hearings, meetings and conferences.

We will make all reasonable efforts to decide promptly all matters presented to us for decision.

We will give the issues in controversy deliberate, impartial, and studied analysis and consideration.

While endeavoring to resolve disputes efficiently, we will be considerate of the time constraints and pressures imposed on lawyers by the exigencies of litigation practice.

We recognize that a lawyer has a right and a duty to present a cause fully and properly, and that a litigant has a right to a fair and impartial hearing. Within the practical limits of time, we will allow lawyers to present proper arguments and to make a complete and accurate record.

We will not impugn the integrity or professionalism of any lawyer on the basis of clients whom or the causes which a lawyer represents.

We will do our best to insure that court personnel act civilly toward lawyers, parties, and witnesses.

We will not adopt procedures that needlessly increase litigation expense.

We will bring to lawyers' attention uncivil conduct which we observe.

We will be courteous, respectful, and civil in opinions, ever mindful that a position articulated by another judge is the result of that judge's earnest effort to interpret the law and the facts correctly.

We will abstain from disparaging personal remarks or criticisms, or sarcastic or demeaning comments about another judge in all written and oral communications.

We will endeavor to work with other judges in an effort to foster a spirit of cooperation in our mutual goal of enhancing the administration of justice.

LAWYERS' DUTIES TO THE COURTS

We will speak and write civilly and respectfully in all communications with the court.

We will be punctual and prepared for all court appearances so that all hearings, conferences, and trials may commence on time; if delayed, we will notify the court and counsel, if possible.

We will be considerate of the time constraints and pressures on the court and court staff inherent in their efforts to administer justice.

We will not engage in any conduct that brings disorder or disruption to the courtroom. We will advise our clients and witnesses appearing in court of the proper conduct expected and required there and, to the best of our ability, prevent our clients and witnesses from creating disorder or disruption.

We will not knowingly misrepresent, mischaracterize, misquote, or miscite facts or authorities in any oral or written communication to the court.

We will not engage in *ex parte* communication on any pending action.

We will attempt to verify the availability of necessary participants and witnesses before dates for hearings or trials are set, or if that is not feasible, immediately after such date has been set, so we can promptly notify the court of any likely problems.

We will act and speak civilly to court marshals, clerks, court reporters, secretaries, and law clerks with an awareness that they too, are an integral part of the judicial system.

Adopted April 1, 2002, effective April 1, 2002.

Rule 6.4

Rule 6.4. District Court Standards

The district courts, family and domestic relations courts, and juvenile courts should comply with the District Court Standards adopted as Section 10 of Part G, General Administrative Rules, Supreme Court of Louisiana:

Rule 6.4—Cont'd

I. ACCESS TO JUSTICE

Standard 1.1 Public Proceedings

The court conducts openly its judicial proceedings that are public by law or custom.

Standard 1.2 Safety, Accessibility, and Convenience

The court encourages responsible parties to make court facilities safe, accessible and convenient.

Standard 1.3 Effective Participation

All who appear before the court are given reasonable opportunities to participate effectively without undue hardship or inconvenience.

Standard 1.4 Courtesy, Responsiveness, and Respect

Judges and other trial court personnel are courteous and responsive to the public and accord respect to all with whom they come into contact.

Standard 1.5 Affordable Cost of Access

The court encourages all responsible public bodies and public officers to make the costs of access to the trial court's proceedings and records—whether measured in terms of money, time, or the procedures that must be followed—reasonable, fair, and affordable.

II. EXPEDITION AND TIMELINESS

Standard 2.1 Case Processing

The trial court encourages timely case management and processing.

Standard 2.2 Required Reports and Requests for Information

The trial court promptly provides required reports and responds to requests for information.

Standard 2.3 Prompt Implementation of Law and Procedure

The trial court promptly implements changes in the law and procedure.

III. EQUALITY, FAIRNESS, AND INTEGRITY

Standard 3.1 Fair and Reliable Judicial Process

Trial court procedures faithfully adhere to laws, procedural rules, and established policies.

Standard 3.2 Juries

The jury venire is representative of the jurisdiction from which it is drawn.

Standard 3.3 Court Decisions and Actions

Trial courts give individual attention to cases, deciding them without undue disparity among like cases and upon legally relevant factors.

Standard 3.4 Clarity

Decisions of the trial court address clearly the issues presented to it and, where appropriate, specify how compliance can be achieved.

Standard 3.5 Responsibility for Enforcement

The trial court takes appropriate responsibility for the enforcement of its orders.

Standard 3.6 Production and Preservation of Records

Records of all relevant court decisions and actions are accurate and properly preserved.

Rule 6.4—Cont'd

IV. INDEPENDENCE AND ACCOUNTABILITY

Standard 4.1 Independence and Comity

The trial court maintains its constitutional independence and observes the principle of cooperation with other branches of government.

Standard 4.2 Accountability for Public Resources

The trial court responsibly seeks, uses, and accounts for its public resources.

Standard 4.3 Personnel Practices and Decisions

The trial court uses fair employment practices.

Standard 4.4 Public Education

The trial court informs the community of its structure, function, and programs.

Standard 4.5 Response to Changes

The trial court recognizes new conditions or emergent events and adjusts its operations as necessary.

V. PUBLIC TRUST AND CONFIDENCE

Standard 5.1 Accessibility

The trial court and the justice it renders are perceived by the public as accessible.

Standard 5.2 Fair, Impartial, and Expeditious Court Functions

The trial court functions fairly, impartially, and expeditiously in order that the public has trust and confidence in the integrity of the decisions of the court.

Standard 5.3 Judicial Independence and Accountability

The trial court is perceived to be independent, cooperative with other components of government, and accountable.

Adopted April 1, 2002, effective April 1, 2002; amended November 20, 2009, effective January 1, 2010.

Comment

While many of these standards may be applicable to juvenile and family courts, some of the standards will need to be modified in consideration of the special needs and functions of those specialized jurisdiction courts.

CHAPTER 7. RECORD MANAGEMENT

Rule 7.0

Rule 7.0. Record Management

Each clerk of court shall maintain and destroy records according to law.

Adopted April 1, 2002, effective April 1, 2002. Amended November 20, 2009, effective January 1, 2010.

Comment

No provisions restating existing law have been included in these Rules. The citations to the deleted topics are as follows:

(1) Withdrawal of records—La. R.S. 44:32, et seq., and La. R.S. 13:4681.

(2) Destruction of records—La. R.S. 13:917 and La. R.S. 13:1221.

Rule 7.0—Cont'd

(3) Preservation of records—La. R.S. 44:36.

(4) *See* Title III, Rule 15.0 regarding case records in criminal proceedings.

CHAPTER 8. INDIGENTS AND IN FORMA PAUPERIS

Rule 8.0

Rule 8.0. Uniform In Forma Pauperis Affidavit

A party, other than an inmate, who wishes to proceed in forma pauperis shall complete and file the affidavit in Appendix 8.0.

Adopted April 1, 2002, effective April 1, 2002; amended November 20, 2009, effective January 1, 2010; amended April 20, 2010, effective June 1, 2010.

Rule 8.1

Rule 8.1. Traversal of In Forma Pauperis Status

The court, on its own motion or the motion of any party, may hold a hearing to traverse the right of any litigant to proceed in forma pauperis.

Adopted April 1, 2002, effective April 1, 2002; amended November 20, 2009, effective January 1, 2010.

Rule 8.2

Rule 8.2. No Recommendation from Clerk of Court Required

No recommendation from the clerk of court's office as to whether a litigant is in fact indigent need be attached to an affidavit of poverty submitted by a party wishing to proceed in forma pauperis. No requirement that such a recommendation be attached, pursuant to La. Code Civ. Proc. art. 5183, may be instituted except by amendment to these Rules.

Adopted April 1, 2002, effective April 1, 2002; amended November 20, 2009, effective January 1, 2010; amended April 20, 2010, effective June 1, 2010.

Comments

(a) *See* La. Code Civ. Proc. art. 5181, et seq., for general rules for proceeding in forma pauperis. *See* Chapter 13 of the Louisiana Rules for District Courts for special rules governing civil litigation filed by inmates.

(b) Federal laws, including the Social Security Act and the Privacy Act of 1974, provide that Social Security numbers are confidential and that governmental benefits may not be denied because of a person's refusal to provide that information, unless its provision is required by federal statute. Accordingly, providing the applicant's Social Security number is optional in the affidavit in Appendix 8.0.

TITLE II

RULES FOR CIVIL PROCEEDINGS IN DISTRICT COURTS

CHAPTER 9. PROCEDURE

Rule 9.0

Rule 9.0. Daily Order of Business

To provide for the expeditious administration of justice to the extent practicable, the court shall hear uncontested matters and the trials of motions or exceptions on days on which trials on the merits are not scheduled.

If uncontested matters and the trials of motions or exceptions are heard on days on which trials on the merits are scheduled, the court will, where practicable, maintain the following order of business:

(a) Uncontested matters, including preliminary defaults.

(b) The trial of motions or exceptions that do not require the testimony of witnesses.

(c) The trial of motions or exceptions that require the testimony of witnesses.

(d) Trials on the merits.

Adopted April 1, 2002, effective April 1, 2002; amended November 20, 2009, effective January 1, 2010.

Rule 9.1

Rule 9.1. Matters Scheduled But Not Heard

Whenever practicable, matters should be heard in the order placed on the docket. If the trial of a matter is begun but not concluded before court is adjourned, that trial should take precedence the following day, when practical.

If the court is unable to hear a scheduled matter, the matter should be rescheduled for hearing at the next available date and time.

Adopted April 1, 2002, effective April 1, 2002.

Rule 9.2

Rule 9.2. Matter Heard by Judge to Whom Allotted

Except as allowed by La. Code Civ. Proc. art. 253.3, all contested matters shall be heard by the judge to whom the matter was allotted. The judge to whom the action has been allotted may designate the order-signing judge or any other judge to sign such orders and set such hearings, and in his or her absence, to hear such matters where necessary to comply with law, or when deemed to be an emergency, in accordance with La. Code Civ. Proc. arts. 253.2 and 253.3.

Adopted April 1, 2002, effective April 1, 2002; amended November 20, 2009, effective January 1, 2010; amended November 18, 2010, effective January 1, 2011.

Rule 9.3

Rule 9.3. Allotment; Signing of Pleadings in Allotted or Non–Allotted Cases

All pleadings filed shall be randomly assigned to a particular section or division of the court in accordance with La. Code Civ. Proc. art. 253.1 before presentation of a pleading to any judge. The method of allotment for each district court is set forth in Appendix 9.3. Provided, to the extent allowed by La. Code Civ. Proc. art. 253.3, each district court shall designate in Appendix 9.3: (1) those matters that ordinarily will not be allotted to a particular section or division of the court and instead will be signed by the duty judge or by any judge authorized to sign such pleadings; and (2) those pleadings that, although filed in actions that will be allotted, may be presented for signature to the duty judge or to any judge authorized to sign such pleadings.

Adopted April 1, 2002, effective April 1, 2002. Amended April 20, 2010, effective June 1, 2010.

Comment

See Watson v. Lane Memorial Hospital, 99–0930 (La. 5/28/99); 743 So.2d 676, adopting Judge Shortess' dissent in *Watson*, 98–0273 (La. App. 1 Cir. 3/3/99); 734 So.2d 28, *writ granted* 5/28/99, regarding allotment of medical malpractice actions in which discovery proceedings have been pursued under La. R.S. 40:1299.47.

Rule 9.4

Rule 9.4. Pleadings To Be Filed with Clerk; Prior or Multiple Filings of Pleadings

(a) All pleadings shall be filed with the clerk of court before presentation to the assigned judge. Exceptions to this Rule are noted in Appendix 9.4.

(b) Judge or forum shopping is prohibited. To achieve continuity of case management and avoid the appearance of judge or forum shopping, all subsequent actions asserting the same claim by the same parties, except for cases filed in juvenile courts with concurrent jurisdiction, shall be transferred to the division to which the first case filed was allotted, whether or not the first case is still pending. Any attorney or party who files more than one petition for the same party on the same cause of action shall attach to any subsequent petition a "Notice of Prior Filing or Multiple Filing," regardless of whether any of the previous petitions were dismissed. This notice shall comply with La. Code Civ. Proc. art. 853.

Adopted April 1, 2002, effective April 1, 2002; amended June 2, 2003, effective July 1, 2003; amended November 3, 2008, effective January 1, 2009; amended November 20, 2009, effective January 1, 2010; amended April 20, 2010, effective June 1, 2010; amended May 15, 2013, effective June 1, 2013.

Rule 9.5

Rule 9.5. Court's Signature; Circulation of Proposed Judgment; Request for Reasons for Judgment

(a) All judgments, orders, and rulings requiring the court's signature shall either be presented to the judge for signature when rendered or, if presented later, contain the typewritten name of the judge who rendered the judgment, order, or ruling.

(b) If presented later, the responsible attorney or the self-represented party shall circulate the proposed judgment, order, or ruling to counsel for all parties and to self-represented parties and allow at least five (5) working days for comment before presentation to the court. When submitted, the proposed judgment, order, or ruling shall be accompanied by a Rule 9.5(b) certificate stating: the date of mailing; the method of delivery of the document to other counsel of record and to self-represented

Rule 9.5—Cont'd

parties; whether any opposition was received; and the nature of the opposition. This certificate shall read:

RULE 9.5(b) CERTIFICATE

I certify that I circulated this proposed judgment/order to counsel for all parties and/or to self-represented parties by [insert method of delivery] on [insert date], and that:

___ no opposition was received; or

___ the following opposition was received:

[Insert name of opposing party/attorney and nature of opposition.]

I have allowed at least five (5) working days before presentation to the court.

Certified this ___ day of _________, 20 ___.

____

[Insert typed or printed name]
Attorney for [insert name of party, if applicable]

(c) The page of the judgment, order, or ruling containing the judge's signature line shall reflect the docket number and title(s) of the pleading(s) at issue.

(d) This rule does not apply to judgments by default.

(e) Requests for written reasons pursuant to La. Code Civ. Pro. art. 1917 shall be communicated to the judge either in open court or in writing. If the request is in writing, it shall: (1) contain a completed Rule 9.5(e) certificate (set forth below): and (2) be contemporaneously provided to the ruling judge in chambers, filed with the clerk of court, and served on all counsel of record and self-represented parties.

RULE 9.5(e) CERTIFICATE

I certify that I have delivered this request for written reasons for judgment to the clerk of court for filing into the suit record, and I have contemporaneously provided a copy of this request to the ruling judge in chambers and to counsel for all parties and/or to self-represented parties by [insert method of delivery] on [insert date].

Ruling Judge: _______________________________

Chambers Address: _______________________________

Case Caption: _______________________________

Date(s) of trial or hearing: _______________________________

Certified this ___ day of _________, 20 ___.

____

[Insert typed or printed name]
Attorney for [insert name of party, if applicable]

Adopted April 1, 2002, effective April 1, 2002; amended June 2, 2003, effective July 1, 2003; amended October 29, 2003, effective January 4, 2004; amended November 3, 2004, effective January 1, 2005; amended November 3, 2008, effective January 1, 2009; amended November 20, 2009, effective January 1, 2010; amended November 21, 2011, effective January 1, 2012; amended May 15, 2013, effective June 1, 2013; amended December 11, 2018, effective January 1, 2019.

Rule 9.6

Rule 9.6. Form of the Pleadings; Civil Case Cover Sheet Form

All pleadings shall be typed or printed legibly, double-spaced, on legal-sized white paper, and written in the English language. Margins shall be 2″ at the top and 1″ on the sides and bottoms. Quotations and footnotes may be single-spaced. Once a matter is allotted, the docket number and the division or section assigned the matter shall be indicated in the caption.

At the commencement of any litigation involving an action for an offense or quasi-offense, counsel for the petitioner, counsel's representative, or the self-represented litigant, shall complete a Civil Case Cover Sheet Form authorized by the Supreme Court of Louisiana. The Civil Case Cover Sheet Form appears in Appendix 9.6.

Adopted April 1, 2002, effective April 1, 2002; amended November 20, 2009, effective January 1, 2010; November 27, 2012, effective January 1, 2013.

Rule 9.7

Rule 9.7. Signing of the Pleadings

Each pleading shall be signed by an attorney or by the self-represented party. The correct mailing address, street address, phone number, facsimile number, and e-mail address, if any, of the person signing the pleading, and in the case of an attorney, the Louisiana Bar Identification Number, shall appear below the signature.

Adopted April 1, 2002, effective April 1, 2002; amended November 20, 2009, effective January 1, 2010; amended November 21, 2011, effective January 1, 2012; amended April 29, 2014, effective June 1, 2014; amended May 18, 2016, effective July 1, 2016.

Rule 9.8

Rule 9.8. Exceptions and Motions

(a) Contradictory Exceptions and Motions. All exceptions and motions, including those incorporated into an answer, shall be accompanied by a proposed order requesting that the exception or motion be set for hearing. If the exceptor or mover fails to comply with this requirement, the court may strike the exception or motion, may set the matter for hearing on its own motion, or take other action as the court deems appropriate. To assist the court in scheduling the hearing, the exception or motion, and any opposition thereto, shall state: (1) whether or not the case is set for trial and, if so, the trial date; and (2) whether testimony will be offered at the hearing.

(b) Time between filing and hearing for motions for summary judgment is governed by La. Code Civ. Proc. art. 966.

(c) Time between filing and hearing. In cases other than juvenile and family law proceedings, no hearing on an exception or motion will be scheduled until at least fifteen calendar days after filing. A party seeking to have an exception or motion heard less than fifteen days after filing shall show good cause and shall state in the exception or motion the reasons why an expedited hearing is necessary.

(d) Ex parte motions. Paragraphs (a) and (b) do not apply to:

(1) unopposed motions;

(2) motions in which all affected parties have joined; or

(3) motions permitted by law or by these Rules to be decided ex parte.

Rule 9.8—Cont'd

Any motion that may be decided ex parte shall be accompanied by a proposed order, except a motion for the court to give in writing its findings of fact and reasons for judgment under La. Code Civ. Proc. art. 1917.

(e) Motions and Exceptions Referred to the Merits. If a party filing a motion or exception wishes to refer it to the merits, the party shall file an unopposed motion, accompanied by a proposed order, asking that it be referred to the merits. This Rule does not apply to motions for summary judgment (*see* Rule 9.10). If the court finds that the interests of justice would be served by referring the motion or exception to the merits, the court may do so.

(f) Unopposed motion. An "unopposed motion" is one to which all affected parties have consented. Before representing to the court that the motion is unopposed, the mover shall contact all parties affected by the motion and obtain their consent. The moving party shall certify in the motion that the consent requirement has been met.

Adopted April 1, 2002, effective April 1, 2002; amended June 2, 2003, effective July 1, 2003; amended October 29, 2003, effective January 4, 2004; amended November 3, 2008, effective January 1, 2009; amended November 20, 2009, effective January 1, 2010; amended April 20, 2010, effective June 1, 2010; amended April 29, 2014, effective June 1, 2014; amended October 7, 2015, effective January 1, 2016.

Rule 9.9

Rule 9.9. Memoranda Supporting or Opposing Exceptions and Motions

(a) This Rule does not apply to juvenile and family law proceedings. Due to the expedited nature of family law proceedings, time delays shall be at the discretion of the court.

(b) When a party files an exception or motion, that party shall concurrently furnish the trial judge and serve on all other parties a supporting memorandum that cites both the relevant facts and applicable law. The memorandum for motions and exceptions, other than motions for summary judgment, shall be served on all other parties so that it is received by the other parties at least fifteen calendar days before the hearing, unless the court sets a shorter time. The delays for motions for summary judgment filings are set forth in La. Code Civ. Proc. art. 966.

(c) A party who opposes an exception or motion shall concurrently furnish the trial judge and serve on all other parties an opposition memorandum so it is received at least eight calendar days before the scheduled hearing, except for motions for summary judgment, which delays are established by La. Code Civ. Proc. art. 966.

(d) The mover or exceptor may furnish the trial judge a reply memorandum, but only if the reply memorandum is furnished to the trial judge and served on all other parties so that it is received before 4:00 p.m. on a day that allows one full working day before the hearing, except for motions for summary judgment, which delays are established by La. Code Civ. Proc. art. 966. For example, if the hearing is set for Friday, the reply memorandum shall be received no later than 4:00 p.m. the preceding Wednesday. If the hearing is set for Monday, the reply memorandum shall be received no later than 4:00 p.m. the preceding Thursday.

(e) Parties who fail to comply with paragraphs (b) and (c) of this Rule may forfeit the privilege of oral argument. If a party fails to timely serve a memorandum, thus necessitating a continuance to give the opposing side a fair chance to respond, the court may order the late filing party to pay the opposing side's costs incurred on account of the untimeliness.

(f) Any party may, but need not, file a copy of the memorandum with the clerk of court. See Rule 9.4 and Appendix 9.4 to determine whether a particular judicial district requires that memoranda be filed with the clerk of court or sent directly to the presiding judge.

Rule 9.9—Cont'd

(g) Paragraphs (b)–(d) do not apply to the following motions:

(1) A motion for an extension of time to perform an act.

(2) A motion to continue a pre-trial conference, hearing, motion, or trial of an action.

(3) A motion to add or substitute parties.

(4) A motion to amend pleadings or to file supplemental pleadings.

(5) A motion to appoint a guardian, curator, or tutor.

(6) A motion to intervene.

(7) A motion to withdraw or substitute counsel of record (but any such motion shall comply with Rule 9.13).

(8) A motion to consolidate.

(9) Any unopposed motion or joint motion.

(10) A motion for the court to give in writing its findings of fact and reasons for judgment under La. Code Civ. Proc. art. 1917.

(11) A motion to compel a response to discovery when no response has been made.

(12) Any motions allowed to be granted ex parte under La. Code Civ. Proc. art. 963.

Any motion listed in (1) through (12) shall state the grounds in support, cite any applicable rule, statute, or other authority justifying the relief sought, and comply with Rule 9.8 to the extent applicable.

Adopted April 1, 2002, effective April 1, 2002; amended June 2, 2003, effective July 1, 2003; amended October 29, 2003, effective January 4, 2004; amended November 20, 2009, effective January 1, 2010; amended April 20, 2010, effective June 1, 2010; amended April 29, 2014, effective June 1, 2014; amended May 28, 2015, effective July 1, 2015; amended October 7, 2015, effective January 1, 2016.

Rule 9.10

Rule 9.10. Motions for Summary Judgment

(a) A memorandum in support of a motion for summary judgment shall contain:

(1) A list of the essential legal elements necessary for the mover to be entitled to judgment;

(2) A list of the material facts that the mover contends are not genuinely disputed; and

(3) A reference to the document proving each such fact, with the pertinent part containing proof of the fact designated.

(b) A memorandum in opposition to a motion for summary judgment shall contain:

(1) A list of the material facts that the opponent contends are genuinely disputed; and

(2) A reference to the document proving that each such fact is genuinely disputed, with the pertinent part designated.

Adopted April 1, 2002, effective April 1, 2002; amended June 2, 2003, effective July 1, 2003; amended October 29, 2003, effective January 4, 2004; amended November 20, 2009, effective January 1, 2010; amended May 28, 2015, effective July 1, 2015; amended October 7, 2015, effective January 1, 2016.

Rule 9.11

Rule 9.11. Executory Process

To assist the court, parties who file suit for executory process should clearly highlight or emphasize the language in the attached exhibits necessary for executory process, such as "confession of judgment" and "waiver of demand for payment."

Adopted April 1, 2002, effective April 1, 2002; amended June 2, 2003, effective July 1, 2003; amended November 20, 2009, effective January 1, 2010.

Comment

Failure to comply with Rule 9.11 may, at the discretion of the court, result in delay while pleadings are conformed to the requirements of this Rule.

Rule 9.12

Rule 9.12. Enrollment as Counsel of Record

All licensed Louisiana attorneys in good standing may enroll as counsel of record: (1) by oral notice made in open court when all parties or their counsel are present; or (2) by filing a written Notice of Enrollment or a written Notice of Limited Appearance in accordance with La. Code Civ. Proc. art. 853 with the clerk of court, with copies to all other enrolled counsel or self-represented parties and to the court.

A Notice of Limited Appearance shall specifically state the limitation of legal services by subject matter, proceeding, date, or time period in accordance with Rule 1.2(c) of the Rules of Professional Conduct. *See* forms in Appendix 9.12A (family law) and Appendix 9.12B (non-family law).

The applicable Appendix Form 9.12 shall be filed if an attorney is making a limited appearance, with or prior to the initial pleading or prior to the initial hearing. The Notice shall bear the signatures of both the appearing attorney and the client, unless the client is unavailable to sign at filing. If the Notice does not bear the client's signature, a certificate attesting to the scope of limited enrollment, signed by the client, shall be filed into the record within ten (10) days of the filing of the initial Notice of Limited Appearance.

Any pleading filed by an attorney making a limited appearance shall state in bold type on the signature page of that pleading: "Attorney for [client] for the limited purpose of [matter or proceeding]."

Adopted April 1, 2002, effective April 1, 2002; amended October 29, 2003, effective January 4, 2004; amended November 3, 2004, effective January 1, 2005; amended November 20, 2009, effective January 1, 2010; amended November 21, 2011, effective January 1, 2012; amended November 27, 2012, effective January 1, 2013; amended May 15, 2013, effective June 1, 2013.

Comments

Attorneys enrolling pro hac vice shall comply with Rule XVII, Section 13 of the Rules of the Louisiana Supreme Court.

Filing the initial petition or first responsive pleading constitutes enrollment, and no further notice of enrollment is needed, unless the attorney is making a limited appearance as authorized by Rule 1 2(c) of the Rules of Professional Conduct.

Rule 1.2(c) of the Rules of Professional Conduct allows an attorney to limit the scope of the representation if the limitation is reasonable and the client gives informed consent. *See also* Rule 1.0(c) of the Rules of Professional Conduct.

Rule 9.12—Cont'd

The use of standard forms for limited appearances makes the notices easily recognizable to judge, court staff, opposing parties, and the client. The form notices require the attorney to identify the scope of a limited representation with specificity.

Rule 9.13

Rule 9.13. Withdrawal as Counsel of Record

Enrolled attorneys have, apart from their own interests, continuing legal and ethical duties to their clients, all adverse parties, and the court. Accordingly, the following requirements govern any motion to withdraw as counsel of record:

(a) The withdrawing attorney who does not have written consent from the client shall make a good faith attempt to notify the client in writing of the withdrawal and of the status of the case on the court's docket. The attorney shall deliver or mail this notice to the client before filing any motion to withdraw.

(b) If the action or proceeding has been assigned to a particular section or division of the court, then the motion to withdraw shall be submitted to the judge presiding over that section or division.

(c) Any motion to withdraw shall include the following information:

(1) The motion shall state current or last-known street address and mailing address of the withdrawing attorney's client. The withdrawing attorney shall also furnish this information to the clerk of court.

(2) If a scheduling order is in effect, a copy of it shall be attached to the motion.

(3) The motion shall state whether any conference, hearing, or trial is scheduled and, if so, its date.

(4) The motion shall include a certificate that the withdrawing attorney has complied with paragraph (a) and with Rule 1.16 of the Rules of Professional Conduct, Louisiana State Bar Association, Articles of Incorporation, Art. 16. A copy of the written communication required by paragraph (a) shall be attached to the motion.

(5) If the motion is to withdraw upon completion of a limited appearance, the motion shall include a certification by the withdrawing attorney that the agreed upon limited services have been completed and that the withdrawing attorney has submitted all judgments or orders resulting from the limited appearance as ordered by the court. A copy of the relevant Notice of Limited Appearance shall be attached to the motion.

(d) The court may allow an attorney to withdraw by ex parte motion if:

(1) The attorney has been terminated by the client; or

(2) The attorney has secured the written consent of the client and of all parties or their respective counsel; or

(3) A limited appearance, as authorized by Rule 1.2(c) of the Rules of Professional Conduct and consented to by the client, has been completed, or

(4) The case has been concluded.

(e) The court may also allow an attorney to withdraw by ex parte motion if no hearing or trial is scheduled.

(f) If paragraph (d) does not apply, then an attorney may withdraw as counsel of record only after a contradictory hearing and for good cause. All parties and the withdrawing attorney's client shall be served with a copy of the motion and rule to show cause why it should not be granted.

Rule 9.13—Cont'd

(g) If counsel's withdrawal would delay a scheduled hearing or trial, the court will not allow the withdrawal unless exceptional circumstances exist or limited representation was undertaken pursuant to a Notice of Limited Appearance and completed.

(h) Paragraphs (a) through (f) do not apply to an ex parte motion to substitute counsel signed by both the withdrawing attorney and the enrolling attorney. The following rules govern such a motion:

(1) The court may grant the motion without a hearing. Movers shall furnish the court with a proposed order.

(2) Substitution of counsel will not, by itself, be good cause to alter or delay any scheduled matters or deadlines.

Adopted April 1, 2002, effective April 1, 2002; amended October 29, 2003, effective January 4, 2004; amended November 20, 2009, effective January 1, 2010; amended November 27, 2012, effective January 1, 2013.

Comments

Rule 9.13 is not intended to supersede the Rules of Professional Conduct regarding the presentation of false testimony to the court.

Rule 9.13(d)(3) provides for ex parte withdrawal by an attorney upon completion of a limited scope representation. It is intended to facilitate limited representation services as contemplated by Rule 1.2(c) of the Rules of Professional Conduct.

Rule 9.14

Rule 9.14. Fixing for Trial or Hearing; Scheduling Orders; Contact with Jurors

(a) The date on which a motion to fix for trial on the merits may be made, and the method of setting a date for trial or hearing of a matter, including deadlines for scheduling orders, pre-trial briefs, contact with jurors, or any other matter, shall be determined by each district court as set forth in Appendix 9.14.

(b) Any party may request in writing, or the court on its own motion may order, a La. Code Civ. Proc. art. 1551 scheduling conference between counsel and the court to which the case has been allotted. Within thirty days after receiving a request for a scheduling conference, the court shall schedule a conference for the purpose of addressing those matters set forth in La. Code Civ. Proc. art. 1551. The scheduling conference may be held by any appropriate means, including in person, by telephone, or teleconference.

Adopted April 1, 2002, effective April 1, 2002; amended November 20, 2009, effective January 1, 2010; amended April 20, 2010, effective June 1, 2010; amended November 18, 2010, effective January 1, 2011.

Comments

(a) La. R.S. 13:1303 requires that the Civil District Court of the Parish of Orleans prescribe the order of preference for the trial of cases. La. Code Civ. Proc. art. 1571(A)(1)(b) states that the district court should prescribe the order of preference "in accordance with the law."

(b) La. Code Civ. Proc. art. 1551 lists the matters that may be considered at scheduling conferences.

Rule 9.15

Rule 9.15. Subpoenas

(a) In cases other than juvenile and family law proceedings, a request for issuance of a subpoena shall be filed with the clerk of court at least ten days before the desired appearance date, unless a different deadline is set by the court in the pre-trial or other order.

Rule 9.15—Cont'd

(b) In the case of a settlement, counsel on whose client's behalf the witness has been asked to testify should make reasonable efforts to notify the witness.

Adopted April 1, 2002, effective April 1, 2002; amended November 20, 2009, effective January 1, 2010; amended November 21, 2011, effective January 1, 2012; amended November 27, 2012, effective January 1, 2013; amended April 29, 2014, effective June 1, 2014.

Comment

La. Code Civ. Proc. art. 1355.1 deals with the reissuance of subpoenas.

Rule 9.16

Rule 9.16. Agreements and Stipulations

The court may recognize agreements and stipulations between counsel concerning the conduct, trial, or continuance of a suit only if they are:

(1) written and filed in the record; or

(2) made in open court and entered on the minutes.

Adopted April 1, 2002, effective April 1, 2002; amended November 18, 2010, effective January 1, 2011.

Rule 9.17

Rule 9.17. Continuances

(a) The court may grant a continuance of a trial or hearing for good grounds. Among the factors the court will consider are the diligence and good faith of the moving party, the reasonableness of the grounds, the fairness to both parties and other litigants before the court, and the need for the orderly and prompt administration of justice.

(b) The court will grant a continuance in any case where the law so requires.

(c) If the court grants a continuance, each party is responsible for contacting its own witnesses.

Adopted April 1, 2002, effective April 1, 2002; amended November 20, 2009, effective January 1, 2010.

Comment

See La. Code Civ. Proc. arts. 1601–1605 regarding the grounds for a continuance.

Rule 9.18

Rule 9.18. Oral Arguments

Oral argument is a privilege, not a right, and is within the court's discretion.

Adopted April 1, 2002, effective April 1, 2002.

Rule 9.19

Rule 9.19. Preliminary Defaults

By moving for a preliminary default, the requesting attorney or party is certifying to the court that the defendant in the principal or incidental demand has been properly served and has failed to answer within the time prescribed by law.

Adopted April 1, 2002, effective April 1, 2002; amended June 2, 2003, effective July 1, 2003; amended November 20, 2009, effective January 1, 2010.

Rule 9.20

Rule 9.20. Appeals to the District Court

Appeals to the district court shall be randomly allotted.

Adopted April 1, 2002, effective April 1, 2002; amended November 20, 2009, effective January 1, 2010; amended April 20, 2010, effective June 1, 2010.

CHAPTER 10. DISCOVERY

Rule 10.0

Rule 10.0. Interrogatories

A party shall be allowed to serve upon any other party, without leave of court, thirty-five interrogatories, as allowed by La. Code Civ. Proc. art. 1457(B). A court may not restrict the parties to fewer than thirty-five interrogatories except by amendment to these Rules.

Adopted April 1, 2002, effective April 1, 2002; amended November 20, 2009, effective January 1, 2010.

Comment

See Nathaniel Gaines, et al. v. Avondale Industries, Inc., et al., Parish of Orleans, Civil District Court, Div. M, No. 95–1823, to the Court of Appeal, Fourth Circuit, No. 2001–C–0365, *writ denied* No. 2001–2348 (La. 11/16/01); 802 So.2d 616, holding that a local rule may not restrict the number of interrogatories to the defendants or plaintiffs in the aggregate.

Rule 10.1

Rule 10.1. Motions To Compel Discovery

(a) Before filing any motion to compel discovery, the moving party or attorney shall confer in person or by telephone with the opposing party or counsel for the purpose of amicably resolving the discovery dispute. The moving party or attorney shall attempt to arrange a suitable conference date with the opposing party or counsel and confirm the date by written notice sent at least five (5) days before the conference date, unless an earlier date is agreed upon or good cause exists for a shorter time period. If by telephone, the conference shall be initiated by the person seeking the discovery responses.

(b) No counsel for a party shall file, nor shall any clerk set for hearing, any motion to compel discovery unless accompanied by a "Rule 10.1 Certificate of Conference" as set forth below:

RULE 10.1. CERTIFICATE OF CONFERENCE

I, the undersigned party or attorney, certify to the court as follows:

If discovery conference is held:

The parties or counsel personally conducted a conference on [insert date]. At this conference, there was a substantive discussion of every item presented to the court in this motion and, despite their best efforts, the parties or counsel were unable to resolve the matters presented.

Certified this ___ day of _________, 20 ___.

____

Signature of Party or Attorney

If discovery conference is not held:

Rule 10.1—Cont'd

The moving party or counsel has personally attempted to contact the respondent or counsel to arrange a conference to resolve the matters presented in this motion as follows:

[Insert dates, times, methods of contact, and results here.]

Respondent or counsel has failed to respond or failed to confer in good faith in an attempt to resolve the matters presented.

Certified this ___ day of _____, 20 ___.

____

Signature of Party or Attorney

(c) If the court finds that the parties or counsel have failed to confer in good faith, or have willfully failed to confer, the court may impose, at its discretion, sanctions on the non-conferring party, including attorney fees and costs.

Adopted April 1, 2002, effective April 1, 2002; amended November 20, 2009, effective January 1, 2010; amended November 21, 2011, effective January 1, 2012.

CHAPTER 11. ALTERNATIVE DISPUTE RESOLUTION AND SPECIAL MASTERS

Rule 11.0

Rule 11.0. Louisiana Mediation Act

The district courts of Louisiana encourage and support the use of alternative dispute resolution to promote resolution of disputes and refer all counsel to the Louisiana Mediation Act La. R.S. 9:4101, et seq. Additionally, the district courts of Louisiana encourage and support the use of special masters in appropriate circumstances.

Adopted April 1, 2002, effective April 1, 2002.

Rule 11.1

Rule 11.1. Certification of No Opposition to Mediation

Before submitting a request for mediation under La. R.S. 9:4103(A), a party shall certify that opposing counsel has been contacted and does not object to mediation.

Adopted April 1, 2002, effective April 1, 2002; amended November 20, 2009, effective January 1, 2010.

Comments

(a) La. R.S. 13:4165 allows the court to appoint special masters in civil actions under the circumstances set forth therein.

(b) *See* La. R.S. 9:4103(A), which provides that, on motion of any party, a court may order the referral of a civil case for mediation. In the interest of judicial economy, these rules require a certificate of no opposition by opposing counsel before filing a request for court-ordered mediation under La. R.S. 9:4102(A).

CHAPTER 12. JURORS, COSTS, CHALLENGES, EXEMPTIONS

Rule 12.0

Rule 12.0. Deposit for Jury Costs

In a civil case, the court shall fix an amount to cover the costs related to the jury, clerk of court, and sheriff. The court may not require that the bond be filed or the costs paid more than 180 days before trial. The failure to pay these costs timely will constitute a waiver of trial by jury.

Adopted April 1, 2002, effective April 1, 2002; amended June 2, 2003, effective July 1, 2003; amended November 3, 2008, effective January 1, 2009; amended November 20, 2009, effective January 1, 2010; amended November 21, 2011, effective January 1, 2012.

Comments

(a) La. Code Civ. Proc. art. 1734 provides that the jury bond shall be filed no later than sixty days before trial. La. Code Civ. Proc. art. 1734.1 provides that the court may order, in lieu of the bond required in Article 1734, that a cash deposit for costs be made no later than thirty days prior to trial. Rule 12.0 provides further guidance by stating that the bond need not be filed or the costs need not be paid more than 180 days before trial. Of course, the jury bond may be filed at the time of filing, at the discretion of counsel.

(b) La. R.S. 13:3105 sets the compensation to jurors in civil cases in Orleans Parish at $25.00 per day. La. R.S. 13:3049 states that jurors shall be paid $25.00 per day and that they should be reimbursed at a mileage rate not less than $.16 a mile and not more than the rate in effect for state officials.

(c) *See* La. Code Civ. Proc. art. 1761, et seq., regarding the procedure for calling and examining jurors.

Rule 12.1

Rule 12.1. Central Jury Pool

There may be a central jury pool for civil cases. The central jury pool shall be administered by the Clerk of Court or the judicial administrator, if any has been appointed by the court, under the direct supervision of the court, in accordance with the following:

(a) Authorized personnel shall assemble the members of the general venire, present the orientation, call roll, and account for those members present and absent.

(b) The judges shall notify the clerk of court and the clerk of court shall notify the jury commission at least ninety days before the designated jury terms, which sections of the court will participate in each term. The jury commission shall select a general venire in a number directed by the judges. Authorized personnel shall randomly select from the general venire those persons who will comprise the central jury pool and shall determine the number of persons selected to compose the central jury pool based upon the number of civil jury trials remaining on the dockets.

(c) Authorized personnel shall select the required number of panels from the central jury pool. The panels shall be selected at random and indiscriminately from the central jury pool members then available. In civil cases, the number of jurors shall be determined by the judge presiding over the trial for which the panel is selected. If the need arises, the assigned judge may request additional persons from the central jury pool, who also shall be selected at random.

(d) Persons selected to serve on the central jury pool panel and not selected to serve on a jury shall be returned to the central jury pool.

Rule 12.1—Cont'd

(e) The chief judge, or his or her designee, shall qualify the members of the central jury pool.

(f) Any person requesting to be excused from jury service shall present the reasons in writing to the court, the clerk of court, or to the judicial administrator, when one has been appointed, who shall then communicate that request and the necessary information to the court, which shall determine whether to grant the request.

Adopted April 1, 2002, effective April 1, 2002; amended November 20, 2009, effective January 1, 2010.

Comment

See Supreme Court Rule XXV, Section 2, regarding Jury Service.

CHAPTER 13. CIVIL LITIGATION FILED BY INMATES [RENUMBERED]

Former Louisiana District Court Chapter 13, Civil Litigation Filed by Inmates, Rules 13.0 through 13.4, was redesignated as Title VI, Chapter 60, adopted April 20, 2010, effective June 1, 2010.

Rule 13.0. Petitions Filed by Offenders/Prisoners [Renumbered]

Rule 13.1. Declaration of Inmate Counsel [Renumbered]

Rule 13.2. In Forma Pauperis Offender/Prisoner Suits [Renumbered]

Rule 13.3. Offender/Prisoner In Forma Pauperis Applications [Renumbered]

Rule 13.4. Parole Revocation Appeals [Renumbered]

TITLE VI

RULES FOR LITIGATION FILED BY INMATES

CHAPTER 60. LITIGATION FILED BY INMATES

Rule 60.0

Rule 60.0. Compliance with Administrative Procedures in Actions Filed by Offenders/Prisoners

A. Any offender/prisoner, as defined in La. R.S. 15:1171–1179 (Corrections Administrative Remedy Procedure Act) (hereinafter "CARP") or La. R.S. 15:1181–1191 (Prison Litigation Reform Act) (hereinafter "PLRA"), shall initiate and exhaust the Administrative Remedy Procedure established by the Department of Corrections or the parish sheriff, if available, before filing an appeal or suit subject to the CARP or the PLRA, whichever is applicable.

B. To show compliance with the law and this Rule, any suit or appeal filed by an offender/prisoner subject to the CARP or the PLRA shall have attached to the appeal or suit a copy of the final agency decision.

C. Self-represented offenders/prisoners in the custody of the Department of Corrections appealing a decision of the Department or prison administration in accord with the CARP shall use the form IJR–1, "Petition for Judicial Review," available from the Department and the Clerk of Court for East Baton Rouge Parish, to apply for review of an administrative decision, excluding delictual actions for injury or damages. *See* Appendix 60.2.

D. The provisions of this section shall not apply to:

1. Appeals of judicial decisions;
2. Pending criminal matters;
3. Applications for post-conviction relief or habeas corpus applications attacking the petitioner's conviction.

Adopted April 20, 2010, effective June 1, 2010; amended November 18, 2010, effective January 1, 2011; amended November 21, 2011, effective January 1, 2012.

Rule 60.1

Rule 60.1. General Venue Statutes for Litigation by Inmates

A. Appeals of Administrative Decisions filed under the CARP shall be filed in the 19th Judicial District Court. Suits seeking monetary damages or based on delictual actions for injury caused by prison personnel are not subject to the CARP, but must be filed in accordance with La. La. Code Civ. Proc. arts. 851–893 in the exclusive venue set forth in La. R.S. 15:1184 (*see* Rule 60.3).

B. All Post-Conviction Relief actions shall be filed in the parish of conviction pursuant to La. Code Crim. Proc. art. 924.

C. Any ordinary civil actions, including torts or suits seeking monetary damages, shall be filed in accordance with the applicable venue statutes and the PLRA in the parish where prisoner was incarcerated at the time the action arose. Post-conviction relief applications and habeas petitions are excluded from the requirements of the PLRA and shall be filed in accord with the venue statutes applicable to such actions.

Rule 60.1—Cont'd

D. All Parole Revocation Complaints/Appeals are proper only in the 19th Judicial District Court, pursuant to La. R.S. 15:574.11.

Adopted April 20, 2010, effective June 1, 2010; amended November 18, 2010, effective January 1, 2011; amended November 21, 2011, effective January 1, 2012.

Rule 60.2

Rule 60.2. Proceedings in the 19th Judicial District Court

A. Proceedings that shall be filed in the 19th Judicial District Court include:

1. Appeals of administrative decisions pursuant to the CARP, venue for which is proper only in the 19th Judicial District Court for offenders/prisoners in the custody or under the supervision of the Department of Corrections. Administrative Appeals are defined in La. R.S. 15:1171, et seq., and La. R.S. 15:1181, et seq., and include actions against the Department of Corrections for judicial review (appeal) of an administrative decision, including but not limited to Prison Administrative Remedy Requests (that do not involve tortious conduct or request damages); Disciplinary Board Appeals; Lost Property Claims (that do not involve tortious conduct); Time Calculation or Good Time Complaints (even if urged as a Writ of Habeas Corpus); Duty Status Complaints (that do not involve medical care complaints or other tortious conduct); or any other complaints involving an internal prison grievance.

2. Parole Revocation Appeals pursuant to La. R.S. 15:574.11. *See also* Rule 60.8 for further procedures and forms required for Parole Revocations.

3. Ordinary civil actions or prisoner suits filed by prisoners, as defined in La. R.S. 15:1181 of the PLRA, filed against the Sheriff of East Baton Rouge or any employee thereof, when based on a cause of action that arose while the plaintiff was incarcerated in East Baton Rouge Parish or in the custody of the Sheriff of East Baton Rouge or any employee thereof. Such ordinary suits that involve a jury trial shall be heard and tried by the allotted judge.

B. Referral to Commissioners in the 19th Judicial District Court:

1. Proceedings set forth in A(1) and A(2), above, that are properly filed in the 19th Judicial District Court shall be randomly allotted to a section of court, and may then be referred to a commissioner for initial screening and further action in accordance with law.

2. Proceedings set forth in A(3), above, with consent of the parties and when the suit does not involve a jury trial.

Adopted April 20, 2010, effective June 1, 2010; amended November 18, 2010, effective January 1, 2011; amended November 21, 2011, effective January 1, 2012.

Rule 60.3

Rule 60.3. PLRA Civil Actions or Prisoner Suits Based on Delictual Actions of Government Officials or Employees

A. Suits against corrections officers or other governmental personnel that are based on personal injury or delictual actions of corrections officers or other government employees or officials filed by offenders/prisoners seeking monetary damages, injunction or related relief, whether in the custody of the Department of Corrections or the sheriff, shall be filed in the original jurisdiction of the district court of proper venue. Exclusive venue is addressed in La. R.S. 15:1184(F), of the PLRA.

Rule 60.3—Cont'd

B. Exhaustion of administrative remedies, when available, is required before filing suit in the parish of proper venue. *See* La. R.S. 15:1177(C) of the CARP and La. R.S. 15:1184(A)(2) of the PLRA.

Adopted April 20, 2010, effective June 1, 2010; amended November 18, 2010, effective January 1, 2011; amended November 21, 2011, effective January 1, 2012.

Rule 60.4

Rule 60.4. Additional Procedures in Actions by Prisoners Based on Delictual Actions of Governmental Officials or Employees

A. When a self-represented offender/prisoner files a complaint/petition that is not subject to judicial review under La. R.S. 15:1177, the inmate is required to follow the PLRA procedures and law in La. R.S. 15:1181, et seq. In addition, the offender/prisoner must follow the law and procedures for civil complaints set forth in the Louisiana Code of Civil Procedure, the Louisiana Civil Code, and any other applicable law, as well as the civil rules of the court of proper venue that are not in conflict with the PLRA or the Rules of this section.

B. Any ordinary petition filed pursuant to Chapter 9 of the Louisiana Rules for District Courts shall specifically comply with La. Code Civ. Proc. arts. 851–893, set forth specific facts to support the elements of each claim pursued, and designate a physical address not a post office box for each opposing party sufficient for service of pleadings.

C. Discovery Limitations

1. No discovery may be filed before service and until the court has had an opportunity to screen the petition to consider the petitioner's "strike" status, set the costs due, consider the mandatory venue, order service on the defendants, or dismiss the suit in accordance with the PLRA.

2. All discovery requests in prisoner suits shall be filed into the court record by sending the original to the clerk of court, in addition to sending a copy by mail to the opposing party or counsel therefor, and shall include a certificate of compliance with this Rule.

3. Once the defendant has made an appearance (filed an answer or motion), discovery in prisoner suits is governed by the Louisiana Code of Civil Procedure, the Louisiana Civil Code, the Louisiana Rules for District Courts, and other applicable Louisiana law, subject to the restrictions set forth in this section and pursuant to the PLRA.

D. Memoranda Required

Any pre-trial motion, rule, exception, etc., including those incorporated into an answer, shall have attached to it a supporting memorandum that cites both the relevant facts and the applicable law, and which includes a declaration that a copy of same has been provided to the opposing party or his or her counsel at a specific address. The memorandum shall be mailed to all other parties so that it is received by the other parties at least fifteen calendar days before the hearing, unless the court sets a shorter time. Any opposition briefs shall be filed with the clerk of court and delivered to the office of the assigned judge or commissioner presiding at least eight calendar days before the date of any hearing set. No motion, rule, exception, etc., shall be assigned for hearing until the above-required memorandum, as well as the name and address of opposing counsel, have been furnished to the judge or commissioner hearing the matter.

E. Pre-trial and Trial Matters

1. in accordance with statutory law, prisoners filing in forma pauperis may subpoena up to six witnesses for trial, but only after a proper pre-trial order has been completed by the plaintiff

Rule 60.4—Cont'd

and approved by the court as required hereinafter. For additional witnesses, *see* La. Code Civ Proc. art. 5185(A)(2)(a).

2. Pre-trial Conference

(a) Unless otherwise provided herein or by law, no suit requiring a trial on the merits may be assigned a trial date except at pre-trial conference. Any party desiring to assign a case for trial shall, after all issues have been joined and all contemplated motions, rules, exceptions, interrogatories, requests for admissions, or other discovery proceedings have been filed and answered, make a written request for pre-trial conference to the judge or commissioner to whom the case has been assigned.

(b) The party requesting the pre-trial conference shall certify in his or her request that all pre-trial matters have been completed and that the matter is ready for trial. If the party requesting the conference has any outstanding motions, exceptions, discovery, or other pre-trial matters, such pre-trial matters will be considered waived or withdrawn once a pre-trial conference is requested in writing.

(c) The self-represented prisoner requesting a pre-trial conference shall complete and attach his or her completed portion of the Self–Represented Prisoner–Plaintiff's Portion of the Pro–Trial Order, Appendix 60.4 hereto, to his or her request for a pre-trial conference, and certify that he or she has provided opposing counsel with a copy of the completed Pre–Trial Order and the specific address to which this copy was sent.

3. Jury Trial Requests

Any request for a jury trial and bond shall be made in accordance with the requirements of the Louisiana Code of Civil Procedure and Rule 12 of the Louisiana District Court Rules.

Adopted April 1, 2002, effective April 1, 2002. Amended November 3, 2004, effective January 1, 2005; amended November 3, 2008, effective January 1, 2009. Renumbered Rule 60.4 and amended April 20, 2010, effective June 1, 2010; amended November 18, 2010, effective January 1, 2011; amended November 21, 2011, effective January 1, 2012.

Rule 60.5

Rule 60.5. Declaration of Inmate Counsel Assistance

If the suit was prepared or filed by or with the help or advice of inmate counsel substitute, counsel substitute's name and D O C number shall be legibly printed on the appropriate line on the face of the petition. Failure to comply with this requirement may result in delay in the service and review of the petition. If no counsel substitute was involved in the preparation or filing of the petition, the plaintiff shall print "NONE" in the blank for the inmate counsel substitute's name.

Adopted April 1, 2002, effective April 1, 2002. Renumbered Rule 60.5 and amended April 20, 2010, effective June 1, 2010. Amended November 18, 2010, effective January 1, 2011; amended November 21, 2011, effective January 1, 2012.

Rule 60.6

Rule 60.6. In Forma Pauperis Offender/Prisoner Suits and PLRA Stays

A. La. R.S. 15:1186 governs in forma pauperis motions in actions filed pursuant to the CARP and the PLRA.

B. In ordinary civil suits governed by the PLRA, pursuant to La. R.S. 15:1186(B)(2), the order granting a prisoner's request to proceed in forma pauperis automatically stays all proceedings, including any service of process, until all court costs or fees due the clerk by the prisoner are paid. If

Rule 60.6—Cont'd

the prisoner does not pay the full court costs or fees within three years from when incurred, the suit shall be considered abandoned and dismissed without prejudice pursuant to subsection La. R.S. 15:1186(B)(2)(c).

C. A prisoner may not bring a civil action, or appeal a judgment in a civil action or proceeding, in forma pauperis if the prisoner has, on three or more prior occasions while incarcerated or detained in any facility, brought an action or appeal in a state court that was dismissed on the grounds it was frivolous, malicious, failed to state a cause of action, or failed to state a claim upon which relief may be granted pursuant to La. R.S. 15:1187. If a prisoner has at least three dismissals as described in La. R. S. 15:1187 that are not yet final, and further, if the prisoner is disqualified from proceeding as a pauper either in federal court by operation of 28 U.S.C. § 1915(g) or in the courts of another state by operation of a similar law of that state, then the court on its own motion may, or on motion of a party shall, stay all proceedings in any other prisoner suit or appeal in which the prisoner is proceeding as a pauper until such time as the dismissals become final, unless the court finds that the prisoner is in imminent danger of serious physical injury.

D. Actions filed in forma pauperis not governed by the CARP or the PLRA are governed by La. Code Civ. Proc. arts. 5181–5185. *See also* Louisiana Rules for District Courts, Rules 8.0–8.2.

E. Rules 8.1 and 8.2 of the Louisiana District Court Rules apply to suits brought by offenders/prisoners who proceed in forma pauperis.

Adopted November 3, 2008, effective January 1, 2009. Renumbered Rule 60.6 and amended April 20, 2010, effective June 1, 2010. Amended November 18, 2010, effective January 1, 2011; amended November 21, 2011, effective January 1, 2012.

Rule 60.7

Rule 60.7. Forms To Be Used for Offender/Prisoner In Forma Pauperis Applications

To proceed in forma pauperis, an offender/prisoner shall complete and file one of the following:

DISTRICT COURTS

For proceedings in district courts, including ordinary suits or other proceedings subject to the PLRA appeals, CARP appeals, and Parole Revocation appeals use the pauper form in Appendix 60.7A.

APPELLATE COURTS

For appeals to Louisiana Courts of Appeal, use the forms in Appendix 60.7 B.

Adopted April 1, 2002, effective April 1, 2002 as Rule 13.2. Amended November 3, 2008, effective January 1, 2009. Redesignated from Rule 13.2 to Rule 13.3, effective January 1, 2009. Renumbered Rule 60.7 and amended April 20, 2010, effective June 1, 2010. Amended November 18, 2010, effective January 1, 2011; amended November 21, 2011, effective January 1, 2012.

Rule 60.8

Rule 60.8. Parole Revocation Appeals

Parole is governed by La. R.S. 15:574.2, et seq. Venue for any action by an individual committed to the Department of Public Safety and Corrections contesting any action of the Board of Parole shall be in the Parish of East Baton Rouge pursuant to La. R.S. 15:574.11. Subject to the limitations set forth in La. R. S. 15:574.11, an offender/prisoner appealing the validity of his or her parole revocation

Rule 60.8—Cont'd

shall use the appellate form Appeal of Parole Revocation in Appendix 60.8 and attach to his or her petition a copy of the Order of Revocation provided to him or her by the Parole Board. Service, if ordered by the court, shall be requested on the Parole Board only. Within thirty days of service of the petition on the Parole Board, counsel for the Parole Board shall file a copy of the appellate record of the parole revocation maintained by the Department/Parole Board, and provide the petitioner with a copy of same. Any motions/exceptions requested to be heard before the merits of the appeal shall be filed within fifteen days of the filing of the appellate record. Thereafter, the matter will be reviewed and set for hearing on any motions/exceptions filed and/or alternatively for oral argument on the appeal, upon notice by the court to the parties, unless the court orders the appeal heard on the briefs.

Adopted November 3, 2008, effective January 2, 2009. Renumbered Rule 60.8 and amended April 20, 2010, effective June 1, 2010. Amended November 18, 2010, effective January 1, 2011.

Comments

This Chapter replaces former Chapter 13 of the Louisiana Rules for District Courts, which was entitled "Civil Litigation Filed by Inmates."

LOUISIANA CIVIL CODE

C.C. Art. 38

Art. 38. Domicile

The domicile of a natural person is the place of his habitual residence. The domicile of a juridical person may be either the state of its formation or the state of its principal place of business, whichever is most pertinent to the particular issue, unless otherwise specifically provided by law.

Acts 2008, No. 801, § 1, eff. Jan. 1, 2009. Amended by Acts 2012, No. 713, § 2.

Revision Comment—2008

This Article is new. It is based on Civil Code Article 38 (1870). The word "parish" is no longer used in the definition of "domicile." The suppression of "parish" will make the definition of domicile relevant for both in-state and out-of-state applications.

C.C. Art. 39

Art. 39. Domicile and residence

A natural person may reside in several places but may not have more than one domicile. In the absence of habitual residence, any place of residence may be considered one's domicile at the option of persons whose interests are affected.

Acts 2008, No. 801, § 1, eff. Jan. 1, 2009.

Revision Comments—2008

(a) This Article is new. It is based on Article 38, second paragraph, of the Louisiana Civil Code of 1870 and provisions of modern civil codes. *Cf.* Quebec Civil Code Art. 77 and 78; Greek Civil Code Art. 51; *cf.* Italian Civil Code Art. 44.

(b) For Louisiana jurisprudence illustrating the difference between domicile and residence, see *McClendon v. Bel*, 797 So.2d 700 (La. App. 1 Cir. 2000).

C.C. Art. 40

Art. 40. Domicile of spouses

Spouses may have either a common domicile or separate domiciles.

Acts 2008, No. 801, § 1, eff. Jan. 1, 2009.

Revision Comments—2008

(a) This Article is new; it is based on Article 82 of the Quebec Civil Code and Article 108.1 of the French Civil Code.

(b) Civil Code Article 98 declares: "Married persons owe each other fidelity, support, and assistance." Unlike the Quebec Civil Code, the Louisiana Civil Code does not impose on spouses the obligation to reside together.

C.C. Art. 40.1

Art. 40.1. [Blank]

C.C. Art. 41

Art. 41. Domicile of unemancipated minor

The domicile of an unemancipated minor is that of the parent or parents with whom the minor usually resides. If the minor has been placed by court order under the legal authority of a parent or other person, the domicile of that person is the domicile of the minor, unless the court directs otherwise.

The domicile of an unemancipated minor under tutorship is that of his tutor. In case of joint tutorship, the domicile of the minor is that of the tutor with whom the minor usually resides, unless the court directs otherwise.

Acts 2008, No. 801, § 1, eff. Jan. 1, 2009.

Revision Comment—2008

This Article is new. It is based on Civil Code Article 39 (1870), first clause, and Article 80 of the Quebec Civil Code. The first paragraph of this Article is applicable when the parents of the minor are married to each other and the minor is under parental authority. The second paragraph of this Article is applicable when the parents of the minor are divorced or widowed. That paragraph is also applicable when parents exercising parental authority have placed the minor under tutorship.

C.C. Art. 42

Art. 42. Domicile of interdict

The domicile of a full interdict is that of the curator. A limited interdict retains his domicile, unless otherwise provided in the judgment of interdiction.

Acts 2008, No. 801, § 1, eff. Jan. 1, 2009.

Revision Comment—2008

This Article is new. It is based on Civil Code Article 39 (1870), second clause and Article 81, second clause of the Quebec Civil Code.

C.C. Art. 43

Art. 43. Domicile of person under continued or permanent tutorship

The domicile of a person under continued or permanent tutorship is that of his tutor.

Acts 2008, No. 801, § 1, eff. Jan. 1, 2009.

Revision Comment—2008

This Article is new. It is intended to apply when a developmentally disabled person is under continued or permanent tutorship. See C.C. Arts. 354–362.

C.C. Art. 44

Art. 44. Change of domicile

Domicile is maintained until acquisition of a new domicile. A natural person changes domicile when he moves his residence to another location with the intent to make that location his habitual residence.

Acts 2008, No. 801, § 1, eff. Jan. 1, 2009.

Revision Comments—2008

(a) This Article is new. It is based on Civil Code Article 41 (1870).

(b) For the deletion of the word "parish," found in Civil Code Article 41 (1870), see comments under Article 38 (Rev. 2008). For the domicile of persons displaced from their place of residence by a gubernatorially declared state of emergency, see R.S. 18:101(F) and 451.3.

C.C. Art. 45

Art. 45. Proof of intent to change domicile

Proof of one's intent to establish or change domicile depends on the circumstances. A sworn declaration of intent recorded in the parishes from which and to which he intends to move may be considered as evidence of intent.

Acts 2008, No. 801, § 1, eff. Jan. 1, 2009.

Revision Comment—2008

This Article is new. It is based on Civil Code Articles 42 and 43 (1870).

C.C. Art. 46

Art. 46. Person holding temporary position

A person holding a temporary position away from his domicile retains his domicile unless he demonstrates a contrary intent.

Acts 2008, No. 801, § 1, eff. Jan. 1, 2009.

Revision Comment—2008

This Article is new. It is based on Civil Code Article 44 (1870) and broadens its principles to include positions other than public offices.

C.C. Art. 101

Art. 101. Termination of marriage

Marriage terminates upon:

The death of either spouse.

Divorce.

A judicial declaration of its nullity, when the marriage is relatively null.

C.C. Art. 101—Cont'd

The issuance of a court order authorizing the spouse of a person presumed dead to remarry, as provided by law.

Acts 1990, No. 1009, § 1, eff. Jan. 1, 1991.

Revision Comments—1990

(a) This Article reproduces the substance of the source provision, Article 136 of the Civil Code of 1870, omitting unnecessary material. It does not change the law, except as provided in comment (d), *infra.*

(b) The omission of the redundant phrase "legally obtained" that followed "divorce" in the source Article is not intended to change the law.

(c) The source Article's reference to the effect of separation from bed and board has been omitted because this revision does not provide for legal separation.

(d) This Article specifies a judicial declaration of nullity as a means of terminating only relatively null marriages because such a marriage is valid until its nullity is judicially declared. An absolutely null marriage, on the other hand, is null from its inception; so as a general rule no action, judicial or otherwise, is necessary to terminate it. See C.C. Art. 94 (1987).

(e) The last clause of this Article refers to R.S. 9:301 (1990).

C.C. Art. 102

Art. 102. Judgment of divorce; living separate and apart prior to rule

Except in the case of a covenant marriage, a divorce shall be granted upon motion of a spouse when either spouse has filed a petition for divorce and upon proof that the requisite period of time, in accordance with Article 103.1, has elapsed from the service of the petition, or from the execution of written waiver of the service, and that the spouses have lived separate and apart continuously for at least the requisite period of time, in accordance with Article 103.1, prior to the filing of the rule to show cause.

The motion shall be a rule to show cause filed after all such delays have elapsed.

Acts 1990, No. 1009, § 2, eff. Jan. 1, 1991. Amended by Acts 1991, No. 367, § 1; Acts 1993, No. 107, § 1; Acts 1995, No. 386, § 1; Acts 1997, No. 1380, § 1; Acts 2006, No. 743, § 1, eff. Jan. 1, 2007.

Revision Comments—1990

(a) This Article changes the law. A petition filed under this Article precedes the spouses' living separate and apart.

(b) A petition filed under this Article sufficiently states a cause of action for dissolution of marriage if it declares that the plaintiff desires to be divorced from the defendant, and alleges the jurisdictional facts called for by Article 10(A)(7) of the Code of Civil Procedure, and one or more of the bases for divorce venue specified in Article 3941 of the Code of Civil Procedure. See also C.C.P. Art. 3951 (added 1990). The petition need not allege marital breakdown, fault on the part of the other spouse, living separate and apart for a period of time, or any other basis for the plaintiff's demand.

(c) No answer need be made to a petition filed under this Article. The defense of reconciliation and the various procedural defenses implicit in this Article and Article 3952 et seq. of the Code of Civil Procedure (added 1990) should be raised at the hearing on the rule to show cause provided for in Code of Civil Procedure Article 3952 (added 1990).

(d) The one hundred eighty day waiting period required by this Article is not waivable.

C.C. Art. 102—Cont'd

(e) An action under this Article may be defeated by proof that the parties have reconciled during the one hundred eighty day period. See C.C. Art. 104, *infra* (rev.1990). What constitutes reconciliation under this Article and Article 103 is a question of fact to be decided in accordance with jurisprudential guidelines. See Millon v. Millon, 352 So.2d 325 (La.App. 4th Cir.1977); Jordan v. Jordan, 394 So.2d 1291 (La.App. 1st Cir.1981).

(f) Code of Civil Procedure Articles 3941 et seq. govern the procedures for obtaining a divorce under this Chapter.

(g) The rule to show cause required by this Article is the sole means whereby a final judgment of divorce may be obtained under this Article. In particular, a motion for summary judgment or judgment on the pleadings may not be employed for this purpose. C.C.P. Art. 969 (rev.1990).

(h) Under new Article 3954 of the Code of Civil Procedure (added 1990) an action under this Article is deemed abandoned if the motion for entry of judgment called for by this Article is not filed within one year of the service, or execution of a valid written waiver of service, of the original petition. [The time period was changed to two years in 1991.]

Revision Comment—1991

The reference to "execution of written waiver of the service" is added in order to coordinate this provision with new Article 3957 of the Code of Civil Procedure, added in 1991.

Editor's Notes

The second paragraph of Civil Code art. 102, providing that the motion for divorce shall be a "rule to show cause," apparently was inadvertently omitted from art. 102 when it was amended and reenacted by Acts 1991, No. 367, to add the provision for written waiver of service. The omission of that paragraph should not affect the action for divorce under C.C. art. 102, since the "rule to show cause" is still explicitly retained in C.C.P. arts. 3952, 3953, 3954, and 3956.

Rivette v. Rivette, 899 So.2d 873 (La. App. 3 Cir. 2005). A divorce action filed pursuant to C.C. art. 102 was dismissed upon the plaintiff's withdrawal of her action based upon "a period of reconciliation of the parties". The dismissal was granted, though opposed by the husband, because of the express requirement to live separate and apart for at least 180 days.

C.C. Art. 103

Art. 103. Judgment of divorce; other grounds

Except in the case of a covenant marriage, a divorce shall be granted on the petition of a spouse upon proof that:

(1) The spouses have been living separate and apart continuously for the requisite period of time, in accordance with Article 103.1, or more on the date the petition is filed.

(2) The other spouse has committed adultery.

(3) The other spouse has committed a felony and has been sentenced to death or imprisonment at hard labor.

(4) During the marriage, the other spouse physically or sexually abused the spouse seeking divorce or a child of one of the spouses, regardless of whether the other spouse was prosecuted for the act of abuse.

C.C. Art. 103—Cont'd

(5) After a contradictory hearing or consent decree, a protective order or an injunction was issued during the marriage against the other spouse to protect the spouse seeking the divorce or a child of one of the spouses from abuse.

Acts 1990, No. 1009, § 2, eff. Jan. 1, 1991. Amended by Acts 1991, No. 918, § 1; Acts 1997, No. 1380, § 1; Acts 2006, No. 743, § 1, eff. Jan. 1, 2007; Acts 2014, No. 316, § 1; Acts 2015, No. 221, § 1; Acts 2018, No. 265, § 1.

Revision Comments—1990

(a) Subparagraph (1) of this Article reproduces the substance of former R.S. 9:301 (1989) without change. It is intended to provide an alternative to an action under Article 102, *supra*, for spouses who have lived separate and apart for the requisite period of time and who do not wish to wait an additional six months to be divorced (as would be necessary if they instituted proceedings under Article 102 at the end of their period of living separate and apart).

(b) Subparagraphs (2) and (3) of this Article reproduce the first two grounds for immediate divorce contained in former Civil Code Article 139 (1870) without substantive change.

(c) Subparagraph (1) of this Article is not intended to change the prior jurisprudential rule that the one year living separate and apart required by former R.S. 9:301 (now this Article) must have been voluntary on the part of at least one of the parties. Adams v. Adams, 408 So.2d 1322 (La.1982).

C.C. Art. 103.1

Art. 103.1. Judgment of divorce; time periods

The requisite periods of time, in accordance with Articles 102 and 103 shall be as follows:

(1) One hundred eighty days where there are no minor children of the marriage.

(2) Three hundred sixty-five days when there are minor children of the marriage at the time the rule to show cause is filed in accordance with Article 102 or a petition is filed in accordance with Article 103.

Added by Acts 2006, No. 743, § 1, eff. Jan. 1, 2007. Amended by Acts 2010, No. 604, § 1, eff. June 25, 2010; Acts 2014, No. 316, § 1.

C.C. Art. 104

Art. 104. Reconciliation

The cause of action for divorce is extinguished by the reconciliation of the parties.

Acts 1990, No. 1009, § 2, eff. Jan. 1, 1991.

Revision Comment—1990

This Article codifies the prior jurisprudence holding that an action for divorce under former Civil Code Article 139 or R.S. 9:301 (now Article 103, *supra*) could be defeated by proof that the parties had reconciled. E.g., Whipple v. Smith, 428 So.2d 1114 (La.App. 1st Cir.1983), writ denied 433 So.2d 154 (La.1983); Humes v. McIntosh, 225 La. 390, 74 So.2d 167 (1954). What constitutes reconciliation is a question of fact to be decided in accordance with established jurisprudential guidelines. E.g., Millon v. Millon, 352 So.2d 325 (La.App. 4th Cir.1977). Under this revision reconciliation may also defeat a divorce action under new Civil Code Article 102, *supra*.

C.C. Art. 105

Art. 105. Determination of incidental matters

In a proceeding for divorce or thereafter, either spouse may request a determination of custody, visitation, or support of a minor child; support for a spouse; injunctive relief; use and occupancy of the family home or use of community movables or immovables; or use of personal property.

Acts 1990, No. 1009, § 2, eff. Jan. 1, 1991.

Revision Comments—1990

(a) This Article is new, but it does not change the law. It states in a single Article the general rule that either party to a divorce action may move the court to determine the incidental issues raised by the divorce.

(b) Under this Article a party may move the court to determine the relevant incidental issues either while the divorce action is pending, or for the post-divorce period, or both. This revision does not provide for an interlocutory judgment of separation (compare former C.C. Arts. 138, 139 (1870), R.S. 9:302 (repealed by this revision)); so it is not necessary to pretermit consideration of post-divorce dispositions until the final hearing on the divorce issue itself. The court may do so, however, in its discretion in order to afford the parties time to develop necessary evidence.

(c) In making a determination under this Article the court should consider the factors listed in the relevant provisions of Chapter 2 of this Title or of Title 9 of the Revised Statutes.

C.C. Art. 197

Art. 197. Child's action to establish paternity; proof; time period

A child may institute an action to prove paternity even though he is presumed to be the child of another man. If the action is instituted after the death of the alleged father, a child shall prove paternity by clear and convincing evidence.

For purposes of succession only, this action is subject to a peremptive period of one year. This peremptive period commences to run from the day of the death of the alleged father.

Acts 2005, No. 192, § 1, eff. June 29, 2005.

C.C. Art. 232

Art. 232. Parental authority

Either parent during the marriage has parental authority over his child unless otherwise provided by law.

Under extraordinary circumstances, such as if one parent is mentally incompetent, interdicted, or imprisoned, or is an absent person, the other parent has exclusive authority.

Acts 2015, No. 260, § 1, eff. Jan. 1, 2016.

C.C. Art. 233

Art. 233. Delegation of parental authority

Parents may delegate all or a part of their parental authority to others as provided by law.

C.C. Art. 233—Cont'd

Parents delegate a part of their parental authority to teachers and others to whom they entrust their child for his education, insofar as may be necessary.

Acts 2015, No. 260, § 1, eff. Jan. 1, 2016.

C.C. Art. 234

Art. 234. Parental authority; custody award

Parental authority continues during marriage, unless modified by a judgment awarding custody to one parent, by a joint custody implementation order, or by a judgment awarding custody to a third person.

An ascendant, other than a parent, who is awarded custody has parental authority. The authority of a third person who is awarded custody, other than an ascendant, is governed by the rules of tutorship, unless modified by court order.

Acts 2015, No. 260, § 1, eff. Jan. 1, 2016.

C.C. Art. 235

Art. 235. Termination of parental authority

Parental authority terminates upon the child's attaining the age of majority, upon the child's emancipation, or upon termination of the marriage of the parents of the child.

Acts 2015, No. 260, § 1, eff. Jan. 1, 2016.

C.C. Art. 246

Art. 246. Occasion for tutorship

The minor not emancipated is placed under the authority of a tutor after the dissolution of the marriage of his father and mother or the separation from bed and board of either one of them from the other.

Amended by Acts 1924, No. 72.

C.C. Art. 247

Art. 247. Kinds of tutorships

There are four sorts of tutorships:

Tutorship by nature;

Tutorship by will;

Tutorship by the effect of the law;

Tutorship by the appointment of the judge.

C.C. Art. 248

Art. 248. Modes of establishment of tutorships

Tutorship by nature takes place of right, but the natural tutor must qualify for the office as provided by law. In every other kind of tutorship the tutor must be confirmed or appointed by the court, and must qualify for the office as provided by law.

Amended by Acts 1960, No. 30, § 1, eff. Jan. 1, 1961.

C.C. Art. 249

Art. 249. Accountability of tutor

For every sort of tutorship, the tutor is accountable.

C.C. Art. 250

Art. 250. Persons entitled to tutorship

Upon the death of either parent, the tutorship of minor children belongs of right to the other. Upon divorce or judicial separation from bed and board of parents, the tutorship of each minor child belongs of right to the parent under whose care he or she has been placed or to whose care he or she has been entrusted; however, if the parents are awarded joint custody of a minor child, then the cotutorship of the minor child shall belong to both parents, with equal authority, privileges, and responsibilities, unless modified by order of the court or by an agreement of the parents, approved by the court awarding joint custody. In the event of the death of a parent to whom joint custody had been awarded, the tutorship of the minor children of the deceased belongs of right to the surviving parent.

All those cases are called tutorship by nature.

Amended by Acts 1924, No. 196; Acts 1981, No. 283, § 1; Acts 1982, No. 307, § 1, eff. Jan. 1, 1983; Acts 1983, No. 695, § 1.

C.C. Art. 252

Art. 252. Unborn and posthumous children

If a wife happens to be pregnant at the time of the death of her husband, no tutor shall be appointed to the child till after his birth; but, if it should be necessary, the judge may appoint a curator for the preservation of the rights of the unborn child, and for the administration of the estate which may belong to such child. At the birth of the posthumous child, such curator shall be of right the undertutor.

C.C. Art. 256

Art. 256. Children born outside of marriage

A. The mother is of right the tutrix of her child born outside of marriage not acknowledged by the father, or acknowledged by him without her concurrence.

B. After the death of the mother, if the father had not acknowledged the child prior to the mother's death, the court shall give first consideration to appointment as tutor either of her parents

C.C. Art. 256—Cont'd

or siblings who survive her and accept the appointment, and secondly, the father, always taking into consideration the best interests of the child.

C. If both parents have acknowledged their child born outside of marriage, the judge shall appoint as tutor the one by whose care the best interests of the child will be served. However, if the parents are awarded joint custody of such acknowledged child born outside of marriage, then the cotutorship of such child shall belong of right to both parents, with equal authority, privileges, and responsibilities, unless modified by order of the court or by an agreement of the parents, approved by the court awarding joint custody.

Amended by Acts 1974, No. 90, § 1; Acts 1979, No. 536, § 1; Acts 1983, No. 215, § 1, eff. Sept. 1, 1983; Acts 2016, No. 210, § 1.

C.C. Art. 257

Art. 257. Surviving parent's right of appointment

The right of appointing a tutor, whether a relation or a stranger, belongs exclusively to the father or mother dying last.

The right of appointing a tutor, whether a relation or a stranger, also belongs to a parent who has been named the curator for the other living spouse, when that other living spouse has been interdicted, subject only to the right of the interdicted parent to claim the tutorship should his incapacity be removed by a judgment of a court of competent jurisdiction.

This is called tutorship by will, because generally it is given by testament; but it may likewise be given by any declaration of the surviving father or mother, or the parent who is the curator of the other spouse, executed before a notary and two witnesses.

Amended by Acts 1974, No. 142, § 1.

C.C. Art. 258

Art. 258. Right of appointment where parents are divorced or separated

If the parents are divorced or judicially separated, only the one to whom the court has entrusted the care and custody of the children has a right to appoint a tutor for them as provided in Article 257. However, if the parents have been awarded joint custody of the children, then the right to appoint a tutor for them belongs to the parent dying last, but either parent may appoint a tutor of the property of the children as provided in Article 257. In the event that both parents appoint a tutor of the property of the children, the tutors shall separately administer that portion of the children's property which is attributable to the respective parent's estate. The court shall decide which tutor shall administer that portion of the children's property which is not attributable to either parent's estate.

Amended by Acts 1960, No. 30, § 1, eff. Jan. 1, 1961; Acts 1983, No. 695, § 1; Acts 1992, No. 680, § 1.

C.C. Art. 259

Art. 259. Option of acceptance of tutorship

The tutor by will is not compelled to accept the tutorship to which he is appointed by the father or mother.

C.C. Art. 259—Cont'd

But if he refuses the tutorship, he loses in that case all the legacies and other advantages, which the person who appointed him may have made in his favor under a persuasion that he would accept this trust.

C.C. Art. 261

Art. 261. Child born outside of marriage

The father or mother who is entitled to the tutorship of the child born outside of marriage, according to the provisions of Article 256, can choose a tutor for him, whose appointment, to be valid, must be approved by the judge.

Amended by Acts 1979, No. 607, § 1; Acts 2016, No. 210, § 1.

C.C. Art. 262

Art. 262. Appointment of several tutors; order of priority

If the parent who died last has appointed several tutors to the children, the person first mentioned shall be alone charged with the tutorship, and the second shall not be called to it, except in case of the death, absence, refusal, incapacity or displacing of the first, and in like manner as to the others in succession.

C.C. Art. 263

Art. 263. Qualified ascendants; collaterals by blood; surviving spouse

When a tutor has not been appointed to the minor by father or mother dying last, or if the tutor thus appointed has not been confirmed or has been excused, then the judge shall appoint to the tutorship, from among the qualified ascendants in the direct line, collaterals by blood within the third degree and the surviving spouse of the minor's mother or father dying last, the person whose appointment is in the best interests of the minor.

Amended by Acts 1976, No. 429, § 1.

C.C. Art. 270

Art. 270. Occasion for tutorship

When a minor is an orphan, and has no tutor appointed by his father or mother, nor any relations who may claim the tutorship by effect of law, or when the tutor appointed in some of the modes above expressed is liable to be excluded or disqualified, or is excused legally, the judge shall appoint a tutor to the minor.

Amended by Acts 1960, No. 30, § 1, eff. Jan. 1, 1961.

C.C. Art. 273

Art. 273. Necessity for appointment

In every tutorship there shall be an undertutor.

Amended by Acts 1960, No. 30, § 1, eff. Jan. 1, 1961.

C.C. Art. 278

Art. 278. Liability concerning minor's legal mortgage

The undertutor who fails or neglects to cause to be inscribed in the manner required by law, the evidence of the minor's legal mortgage against his tutor, shall be liable for all the damages which the minor may sustain in consequence of such failure or neglect; and this claim for damages shall not be prescribed so long as the minor's right of action exists against his tutor.

C.C. Art. 280

Art. 280. Termination of undertutorship

The duties of the undertutor are at an end at the same time with the tutorship.

C.C. Art. 292

Art. 292. Excuse by reason of office or function

The following persons are dispensed or excused from the tutorship by the privilege of their offices or functions:

1. The Governor and the Secretary of State;

2. The judges of the different courts of this State and the officers of the same;

3. The Mayor of the city of New Orleans;

4. The Collector of the Customs;

5. The officers and soldiers attached to the regular troops, whether on land or sea service, employed and in actual service in this State, and all the officers who are intrusted in this State with any mission from the Government, as long as they are employed;

6. Preceptors and other persons keeping public schools, as long as they remain in the useful and actual exercise of their profession;

7. Ministers of the gospel.

C.C. Art. 293

Art. 293. Waiver of excuse by subsequent acceptance of tutorship

The persons mentioned in the preceding article, who have accepted a tutorship posterior to their being invested with the offices, engaged in the service, or intrusted with the mission which dispenses from it, shall not be admitted to be excused on that account.

C.C. Art. 294

Art. 294. Subsequently acquired excuse

Those, on the contrary, who shall have been invested with offices, who shall have engaged in the service, or shall have been intrusted with commissions, posterior to their acceptation and administration of a tutorship, may, if they do not choose to continue to act as tutor, be excused from the tutorship, and apply for the appointment of another tutor to supply their place.

C.C. Art. 295

Art. 295. Excuse for remote relationship

No person, who is not a relation of the minor by consanguinity, or who is only related to him beyond the fourth degree, can be compelled to accept the tutorship.

C.C. Art. 296

Art. 296. Excuse for age

Every person who has attained the age of sixty-five years, may refuse to be a tutor.

The person who shall have been appointed prior to that age, may be excused from the tutorship at the age of seventy years.

C.C. Art. 297

Art. 297. Excuse for infirmity

Every person affected with a serious infirmity, may be excused from the tutorship, if this infirmity be of such nature as to render him incapable of transacting his own business.

He may even be discharged from the tutorship, if such infirmity has befallen him after his appointment.

C.C. Art. 298

Art. 298. Excuse for prior tutorships

The person who is appointed to two tutorships has a legal excuse for not accepting a third.

A parent who has been appointed to one tutorship shall not be compelled to accept a second tutorship, except it be that of his own children.

Amended by Acts 1974, No. 163, § 3.

C.C. Art. 299

Art. 299. Time to present excuse

The tutor, who has excuses to offer against his appointment, must propose them to the judge who has appointed him, within ten days after he has been acquainted with his appointment, or after the same shall have been notified to him, which period shall be increased one day for every ten miles distance from his residence to the place where his appointment was made, and after this delay he shall no longer be admitted to offer any excuse, unless he has sufficient reason to account for such delay.

C.C. Art. 300

Art. 300. Provisional administration pending consideration of excuse

During the time of the pendency of the litigation relative to the validity of his excuses, the tutor who is appointed shall be bound provisionally to administer as such, until he shall have been regularly discharged.

C.C. Art. 301

Art. 301. Parent's unconditional obligation of tutorship

The causes herein expressed, or any other, cannot excuse a parent from the obligation of accepting the tutorship of his children.

Amended by Acts 1974, No. 163, § 3.

C.C. Art. 308

Art. 308. Duty to apply for appointment

In every case where it is necessary to appoint a tutor to a minor, all those of his relations who reside within the parish of the judge, who is to appoint him, are bound to apply to such judge, in order that a tutor be appointed to the minor at farthest within ten days after the event which make [makes] such appointment necessary.

C.C. Art. 309

Art. 309. Minors exempt from taking application

Minor relations are not included in the provisions contained in the preceding article.

Amended by Acts 1974, No. 163, § 3.

C.C. Art. 310

Art. 310. Liability for failure to make application

Relations who have neglected to cause a tutor to be appointed, are responsible for the damages which the minor may have suffered.

This responsibility is enforced against relations in the order according to which they are called to the inheritance of the minor, so that they are responsible only in case of the insolvency of him or them who precede them in that order, and this responsibility is not *in solidum* between relations who have a right to the inheritance in the same degree.

C.C. Art. 311

Art. 311. Action for damages; prescription

The action which results from this responsibility can not be maintained by the tutor but within the year of his appointment.

If the tutor neglects to bring his action within that time, he is answerable for such neglect to the minor.

C.C. Art. 322

Art. 322. Minor's legal mortgage on tutor's property

The recording of the certificate of the clerk operates as a legal mortgage in favor of the minor for the amount therein stated, on all the immovable property of the natural tutor in the parish.

Amended by Acts 1960, No. 30, § 1, eff. Jan. 1, 1961.

C.C. Art. 333

Art. 333. Sale of mortgaged property by one claimant; inscription of legal mortgage of remaining minors

Whenever a special mortgage is given by a tutor to secure the rights of two or more minors, any of the minors, on attaining the age of majority or being emancipated, may cause the sale of the mortgaged property to satisfy the indebtedness of the tutor to him, after having discussed the other property of the debtor, in the following manner:

If the judge is of the opinion that the mortgaged property is sufficient to satisfy all of the demands of the major and minors, he shall order the sale of so much of the property as will satisfy the demand of the major, if susceptible of division, and the property so sold shall be free of the mortgage in favor of the remaining minors.

If the judge is of the opinion that the mortgaged property is not sufficient to meet the demands of the major and minors, or that it is not susceptible of division, he shall order the sale of the whole of the mortgaged property, and the release of the mortgage of the major and minors. The proceeds of the sale, after defraying the expenses thereof, shall be divided equally among the major and minors, giving each his virile share. The portion to be paid the minors shall be paid to their tutor.

When the judge orders the sale of the property, he shall order the inscription of the minor's legal mortgage in the manner heretofore provided. This inscription shall be made in the parish where the tutor resides within three days of the order, and in all other parishes where the tutor has immovable property within thirty days of the order.

Amended by Acts 1960, No. 30, § 1, eff. Jan. 1, 1961.

C.C. Art. 336

Art. 336. Alienation of minor's immovables

The prohibition of alienating the immovables of a minor, does not extend to the case in which a judgment is to be executed against him, or of a licitation made at the instance of the coheir, or other coproprietor.

Acts 1966, No. 496, § 1.

C.C. Art. 338

Art. 338. Interest

The sum which appears to be due by the tutor as the balance of his accounts, bears interest, without a judicial demand, from the day on which the accounts were closed.

The same rule applies to the balance due to the tutor.

Acts 1966, No. 496, § 1.

C.C. Art. 339

Art. 339. Agreements between tutor and minor

Every agreement which may take place between the tutor and the minor arrived at the age of majority, shall be null and void, unless the same was entered into after the rendering of a full account

C.C. Art. 339—Cont'd

and delivery of the vouchers, the whole being made to appear by the receipt of the person to whom the account was rendered, ten days previous to the agreement.

Acts 1966, No. 496, § 1.

C.C. Art. 340

Art. 340. Prescription of minor's action against tutor

The action of the minor against his tutor, respecting the acts of the tutorship, is prescribed by four years, to begin from the day of his majority.

Acts 1966, No. 496, § 1.

C.C. Art. 365

Art. 365. Emancipation

There are three kinds of emancipation: judicial emancipation, emancipation by marriage, and limited emancipation by authentic act.

Acts 2008, No. 786, § 1, eff. Jan. 1, 2009.

C.C. Art. 366

Art. 366. Judicial emancipation

A court may order for good cause the full or limited emancipation of a minor sixteen years of age or older. Full judicial emancipation confers all effects of majority on the person emancipated, unless otherwise provided by law. Limited judicial emancipation confers the effects of majority specified in the judgment of limited emancipation, unless otherwise provided by law.

Acts 2008, No. 786, § 1, eff. Jan. 1, 2009.

C.C. Art. 367

Art. 367. Emancipation by marriage

A minor sixteen or seventeen years of age is fully emancipated by marriage. Termination of the marriage does not affect emancipation by marriage. Emancipation by marriage may not be modified or terminated.

Acts 2008, No. 786, § 1, eff. Jan. 1, 2009. Amended by Acts 2019, No. 401, § 1.

C.C. Art. 368

Art. 368. Limited emancipation by authentic act

An authentic act of limited emancipation confers upon a minor age sixteen or older the capacity to make the kinds of juridical acts specified therein, unless otherwise provided by law. The act shall be executed by the minor, and by the parents of the minor, if parental authority exists, or by the tutor of the minor, if parental authority does not exist. All other effects of minority shall continue.

Acts 2008, No. 786, § 1, eff. Jan. 1, 2009.

C.C. Art. 369

Art. 369. Emancipation; when effective

Judicial emancipation is effective when the judgment is signed. Emancipation by marriage is effective upon marriage. Limited emancipation by authentic act is effective when the act is executed.
Acts 2008, No. 786, § 1, eff. Jan. 1, 2009.

C.C. Art. 370

Art. 370. Modification and termination of judicial emancipation

The court may modify or terminate its judgment of emancipation for good cause.

A judgment modifying or terminating a judgment of emancipation is effective toward third persons as to immovable property when the judgment is filed for registry in the conveyance records of the parish in which the property is situated, and as to movables when the judgment is filed for registry in the conveyance records of the parish or parishes in which the minor was domiciled at the time of the judgment.

A judgment modifying or terminating a judgment of emancipation does not affect the validity of an act made by the emancipated minor prior to the effective date of modification or termination.

The termination of judicial emancipation places the minor under the same authority to which he was subject prior to emancipation, unless otherwise ordered by the court for good cause shown.
Acts 2008, No. 786, § 1, eff. Jan. 1, 2009.

C.C. Art. 371

Art. 371. Modification or termination of limited emancipation by authentic act

The parties to an authentic act of limited emancipation may modify or terminate the limited emancipation by making a subsequent authentic act. In addition, a court, for good cause, may modify or terminate limited emancipation by authentic act.

An authentic act or judgment modifying or terminating limited emancipation by authentic act is effective toward third persons as to immovable property when the act or judgment is filed for registry in the conveyance records of the parish in which the property is situated and as to movables when the act or judgment is filed for registry in the conveyance records in the parish or parishes in which the minor was domiciled at the time of the act modifying or terminating limited emancipation by authentic act.

An authentic act or judgment modifying or terminating a prior act of limited emancipation does not affect the validity of a juridical act made by the minor prior to the effective date of modification or termination.

Acts 2008, No. 786, § 1, eff. Jan. 1, 2009.

C.C. Art. 389

Art. 389. Full interdiction

A court may order the full interdiction of a natural person of the age of majority, or an emancipated minor, who due to an infirmity, is unable consistently to make reasoned decisions

C.C. Art. 389—Cont'd

regarding the care of his person and property, or to communicate those decisions, and whose interests cannot be protected by less restrictive means.

Acts 2000, 1st Ex.Sess., No. 25, § 1, eff. July 1, 2001.

Revision Comments—2000

(a) This Article changes the law. Under prior law, full interdiction was appropriate when the defendant was "subject to an habitual state of imbecility, insanity or madness," or when the defendant "owing to any infirmity", was incapable of taking care of his person and administering his estate. See Civil Code Articles 389 and 422 (1870). This Article changes the law by making eligibility for interdiction dependent upon functional inability and is uncomplicated by considerations of "insanity", "madness", and the like.

(b) For a person to be interdicted under this Article, the inability to make reasoned decisions regarding the care of his person and his property must result from an infirmity, including among others, chronic substance abuse. Advanced age alone is not an infirmity. Consequently, a person who is merely caring for his person and property in an imprudent manner, but who does not suffer from an infirmity affecting his ability to make reasoned decisions, is not a candidate for full interdiction. However, categorizing the infirmity from which a person suffers is significantly less important than evaluating his functional ability to make reasoned decisions and to communicate those decisions. A decision is not unreasoned merely because it appears risky, unwise, or imprudent.

(c) A person lacks the ability to communicate reasoned decisions only when he cannot convey his thoughts in an understandable manner to other persons. Thus, a person who can consistently communicate his reasoned decisions through any form of verbal or nonverbal communication is not a candidate for full interdiction.

(d) A person is unable consistently to make reasoned decisions if, for example, he suffers from an infirmity which intermittently deprives him of reason. A person who experiences periodic deprivations of reason can inflict substantial harm to himself or his property during such bouts and is a candidate for full interdiction. In short, that a person suffering from an infirmity may experience lucid intervals does not render him ineligible for full interdiction.

(e) Full interdiction is a last resort and, as a result, is warranted only when a person's interests cannot be protected by less restrictive means. A person's interests can be protected by less restrictive means if, for example, his interests (1) are currently being protected by other legal arrangements, including a procuration, mandate, or trust, or (2) could be protected by other legal arrangements, including limited interdiction, see Civil Code Article 390 (Rev. 2000). If the court determines that less restrictive means can protect the defendant's interests, the court should deny full interdiction.

(f) Full interdiction is distinct from civil commitment. See Vance v. Ellerbe, 150 La. 388, 90 So. 735, 740 (1922). Civil commitment requires compliance with the standards and procedures set forth in the mental health law. See R.S. 28:1 through 28:173.

(g) The petitioner in a full interdiction proceeding shall prove by clear and convincing evidence all facts justifying interdiction. See Code of Civil Procedure Article 4548 (Rev. 2000).

C.C. Art. 390

Art. 390. Limited interdiction

A court may order the limited interdiction of a natural person of the age of majority, or an emancipated minor, who due to an infirmity is unable consistently to make reasoned decisions

C.C. Art. 390—Cont'd

regarding the care of his person or property, or any aspect of either, or to communicate those decisions, and whose interests cannot be protected by less restrictive means.

Acts 2000, 1st Ex.Sess., No. 25, § 1, eff. July 1, 2001.

Revision Comments—2000

(a) This Article reproduces the principle that a right not specifically restricted in the judgment of limited interdiction is retained by the limited interdict. See Civil Code Article 389.1 as enacted by Acts 1981, No. 167.

(b) A person is a candidate for limited interdiction if he is consistently unable to make reasoned decisions regarding the care of his person or property, or any aspect of either, or to communicate those decisions. If he is consistently unable to make reasoned decisions regarding the care of both his person and his property, or to communicate those decisions, he is a candidate for full interdiction.

(c) Various Louisiana laws, including Civil Code articles within this Title, refer to "interdicts" and "curators of interdicts." To the extent that doing so is consistent with the terms and purposes of the judgment of limited interdiction, such legislation should be applied to "limited interdicts" and to "curators of limited interdicts."

(d) A judgment of limited interdiction does not deprive a limited interdict of the capacity to make a disposition mortis causa. See Civil Code Articles 395 and 1482 (Rev. 2000).

C.C. Art. 391

Art. 391. Temporary and preliminary interdiction

When a petition for interdiction is pending, a court may order a temporary or preliminary interdiction when there is a substantial likelihood that grounds for interdiction exist and substantial harm to the health, safety, or property of the person sought to be interdicted is imminent.

Acts 2000, 1st Ex.Sess., No. 25, § 1, eff. July 1, 2001.

C.C. Art. 392

Art. 392. Curators

The court shall appoint a curator to represent the interdict in juridical acts and to care for the person or affairs of the interdict, or any aspect of either. The duties and powers of a curator commence upon his qualification. In discharging his duties, a curator shall exercise reasonable care, diligence, and prudence and shall act in the best interest of the interdict.

The court shall confer upon a curator of a limited interdict only those powers required to protect the interests of the interdict.

Acts 2000, 1st Ex.Sess., No. 25, § 1, eff. July 1, 2001.

C.C. Art. 393

Art. 393. Undercurators

The court shall appoint an undercurator to discharge the duties prescribed for him by law. The duties and powers of an undercurator shall commence upon qualification. In discharging his duties,

C.C. Art. 393—Cont'd

an undercurator shall exercise reasonable care, diligence, and prudence and shall act in the best interest of the interdict.

Acts 2000, 1st Ex.Sess., No. 25, § 1, eff. July 1, 2001.

C.C. Art. 394

Art. 394. Pre-interdiction juridical acts

Interdiction does not affect the validity of a juridical act made by the interdict prior to the effective date of interdiction.

Acts 2000, 1st Ex.Sess., No. 25, § 1, eff. July 1, 2001.

C.C. Art. 395

Art. 395. Capacity to make juridical acts

A full interdict lacks capacity to make a juridical act. A limited interdict lacks capacity to make a juridical act pertaining to the property or aspects of personal care that the judgment of limited interdiction places under the authority of his curator, except as provided in Article 1482 or in the judgment of limited interdiction.

Acts 2000, 1st Ex.Sess., No. 25, § 1, eff. July 1, 2001. Amended by Acts 2001, No. 509, § 1, eff. June 1, 2001; Acts 2003, No. 1008, § 1.

C.C. Art. 396

Art. 396. Effective date of judgment of interdiction

A judgment of interdiction has effect retroactive to the date of the filing of the petition for interdiction.

Acts 2000, 1st Ex.Sess., No. 25, § 1, eff. July 1, 2001.

C.C. Art. 397

Art. 397. Modification and termination of interdiction

The court may modify or terminate a judgment of interdiction for good cause. Interdiction terminates upon death of the interdict or by judgment of the court.

A judgment of preliminary interdiction granted after an adversarial hearing terminates thirty days after being signed, unless extended by the court for good cause for a period not exceeding thirty days. A judgment of temporary interdiction granted ex parte terminates ten days after being signed. On motion of the defendant or for extraordinary reasons shown at a contradictory hearing, the court may extend the judgment of temporary interdiction for one additional period not to exceed ten days.

Acts 2000, 1st Ex.Sess., No. 25, § 1, eff. July 1, 2001.

C.C. Art. 398

Art. 398. Effective date of modification or termination of a judgment of interdiction

An order modifying or terminating a judgment of interdiction is effective on the date signed by the court.

Acts 2000, 1st Ex.Sess., No. 25, § 1, eff. July 1, 2001.

C.C. Art. 399

Art. 399. Responsibility for wrongful filing of interdiction petition

A petitioner whose petition for interdiction is denied is liable for resulting damages caused to the defendant if the petitioner knew or should have known at the time of filing that any material factual allegation regarding the ability of the defendant consistently to make reasoned decisions or to communicate those decisions was false.

Acts 2000, 1st Ex.Sess., No. 25, § 1, eff. July 1, 2001.

C.C. Art. 2000

Art. 2000. Damages for delay measured by interest; no need of proof; attorney fees

When the object of the performance is a sum of money, damages for delay in performance are measured by the interest on that sum from the time it is due, at the rate agreed by the parties or, in the absence of agreement, at the rate of legal interest as fixed by R.S. 9:3500. The obligee may recover these damages without having to prove any loss, and whatever loss he may have suffered he can recover no more. If the parties, by written contract, have expressly agreed that the obligor shall also be liable for the obligee's attorney fees in a fixed or determinable amount, the obligee is entitled to that amount as well.

Acts 1984, No. 331, § 1, eff. Jan. 1, 1985. Amended by Acts 1985, No. 137, § 1, eff. July 3, 1985; Acts 1987, No. 883, § 1.

Editor's Notes

The Louisiana Supreme Court held that courts may inquire into the reasonableness of such attorney's fees, Central Progressive Bank v. Bradley, 502 So.2d 1017 (La.1987).

C.C. Art. 2315

Art. 2315. Liability for acts causing damages

A. Every act whatever of man that causes damage to another obliges him by whose fault it happened to repair it.

B. Damages may include loss of consortium, service, and society, and shall be recoverable by the same respective categories of persons who would have had a cause of action for wrongful death of an injured person. Damages do not include costs for future medical treatment, services, surveillance, or procedures of any kind unless such treatment, services, surveillance, or procedures are directly related to a manifest physical or mental injury or disease. Damages shall include any sales taxes paid by the owner on the repair or replacement of the property damaged.

Amended by Acts 1884, No. 71; Acts 1908, No. 120, § 1; Acts 1918, No. 159, § 1; Acts 1932, No. 159, § 1; Acts 1948, No. 333, § 1; Acts 1960, No. 30, § 1, eff. Jan. 1, 1961; Acts 1982, No. 202, § 1; Acts 1984, No. 397, § 1; Acts 1986, No. 211, § 1; Acts 1999, No. 989, § 1, eff. July 9, 1999; Acts 2001, No. 478, § 1.

Legislative intent and applicability—Acts 1999, No. 989

Sections 2 and 3 Acts 1999, No. 989 (§ 1 of which amended this article) provide:

"Section 2. The provisions of this Act are interpretative of Civil Code Article 2315 and are intended to explain its original intent, notwithstanding the contrary interpretation given in Bourgeois v. A.P. Green Indus., Inc., 97–3188 (La. 7/8/98); 716 So.2d 355, and all cases consistent therewith.

C.C. Art. 2315—Cont'd

"Section 3. The provisions of this Act shall be applicable to all claims existing or actions pending on its effective date and all claims arising or actions filed on and after its effective date."

Acts 1999, No. 989 became effective July 9, 1999.

C.C. Art. 2315.1

Art. 2315.1. Survival action

A. If a person who has been injured by an offense or quasi offense dies, the right to recover all damages for injury to that person, his property or otherwise, caused by the offense or quasi offense, shall survive for a period of one year from the death of the deceased in favor of:

(1) The surviving spouse and child or children of the deceased, or either the spouse or the child or children.

(2) The surviving father and mother of the deceased, or either of them if he left no spouse or child surviving.

(3) The surviving brothers and sisters of the deceased, or any of them, if he left no spouse, child, or parent surviving.

(4) The surviving grandfathers and grandmothers of the deceased, or any of them, if he left no spouse, child, parent, or sibling surviving.

B. In addition, the right to recover all damages for injury to the deceased, his property or otherwise, caused by the offense or quasi offense, may be urged by the deceased's succession representative in the absence of any class of beneficiary set out in Paragraph A.

C. The right of action granted under this Article is heritable, but the inheritance of it neither interrupts nor prolongs the prescriptive period defined in this Article.

D. As used in this Article, the words "child", "brother", "sister", "father", "mother", "grandfather", and "grandmother" include a child, brother, sister, father, mother, grandfather, and grandmother by adoption, respectively.

E. For purposes of this Article, a father or mother who has abandoned the deceased during his minority is deemed not to have survived him.

Added by Acts 1986, No. 211, § 2. Amended by Acts 1987, No. 675, § 1; Acts 1997, No. 1317, § 1, eff. July 15, 1997.

C.C. Art. 2315.2

Art. 2315.2. Wrongful death action

A. If a person dies due to the fault of another, suit may be brought by the following persons to recover damages which they sustained as a result of the death:

(1) The surviving spouse and child or children of the deceased, or either the spouse or the child or children.

(2) The surviving father and mother of the deceased, or either of them if he left no spouse or child surviving.

(3) The surviving brothers and sisters of the deceased, or any of them, if he left no spouse, child, or parent surviving.

C.C. Art. 2315.2—Cont'd

(4) The surviving grandfathers and grandmothers of the deceased, or any of them, if he left no spouse, child, parent, or sibling surviving.

B. The right of action granted by this Article prescribes one year from the death of the deceased.

C. The right of action granted under this Article is heritable, but the inheritance of it neither interrupts nor prolongs the prescriptive period defined in this Article.

D. As used in this Article, the words "child", "brother", "sister", "father", "mother", "grandfather", and "grandmother" include a child, brother, sister, father, mother, grandfather, and grandmother by adoption, respectively.

E. For purposes of this Article, a father or mother who has abandoned the deceased during his minority is deemed not to have survived him.

Added by Acts 1986, No. 211, § 2. Amended by Acts 1997, No. 1317, § 1, eff. July 15, 1997.

Editor's Notes

Landry v. Avondale Industries, Inc., 877 So.2d 970 (La. 2004). The wrongful death action was based upon mesothelioma allegedly contracted as a result of exposure to asbestos during the period 1959 to 1974, antedating our comparative fault law. The victim's death occurred in 2002 long after the effective date of comparative fault in August 1980. "We conclude the Louisiana's Comparative Fault Law applies to the plaintiff's wrongful death claim." "... the key relevant event giving rise to a claim for wrongful death for purposes of applying the comparative fault law is the victim's death."

Turner v. Thomas R. Busby and Zurich American Insurance Company, 883 So.2d 412 (La. 2004). Plaintiff had no wrongful death or survival action where decedent executed a formal acknowledgment of paternity of the plaintiff, but had no biological connection to him. Plaintiff was not a child of the decedent under C.C. arts. 2315.1 and 2315.2. Plaintiff relies on judgments fixing child's support in 1982, 1983, and 1984 that cannot now be challenged. C.C. art. 2004 is inapplicable because the judgments were the result of stipulations to pursuant to a criminal statute, R.S. 14:72.5.

C.C. Art. 2315.3

Art. 2315.3. Additional damages; child pornography

In addition to general and special damages, exemplary damages may be awarded upon proof that the injuries on which the action is based were caused by a wanton and reckless disregard for the rights and safety of the person through an act of pornography involving juveniles, as defined by R.S. 14:81.1, regardless of whether the defendant was prosecuted for his acts.

Added by Acts 2009, No. 382, § 1.

C.C. Art. 2315.4

Art. 2315.4. Additional damages; intoxicated defendant

In addition to general and special damages, exemplary damages may be awarded upon proof that the injuries on which the action is based were caused by a wanton or reckless disregard for the rights and safety of others by a defendant whose intoxication while operating a motor vehicle was a cause in fact of the resulting injuries.

Added by Acts 1984, No. 511, § 1.

C.C. Art. 2315.5

Art. 2315.5. Wrongful death and survival action; exception

Notwithstanding any other provision of law to the contrary, the surviving spouse, parent, or child of a deceased, who has been convicted of a crime involving the intentional killing or attempted killing of the deceased, or, if not convicted, who has been judicially determined to have participated in the intentional, unjustified killing or attempted killing of the deceased, shall not be entitled to any damages or proceeds in a survival action or an action for wrongful death of the deceased, or to any proceeds distributed in settlement of any such cause of action. In such case, the other child or children of the deceased, or if the deceased left no other child surviving, the other survivors enumerated in the applicable provisions of Articles 2315.1(A) and 2315.2(A), in order of preference stated, may bring a survival action against such surviving spouse, parent, or child, or an action against such surviving spouse, parent, or child for the wrongful death of the deceased.

An executive pardon shall not restore the surviving spouse's, parent's, or child's right to any damages or proceeds in a survival action or an action for wrongful death of the deceased.

Added by Acts 1987, No. 690, § 1. Amended by Acts 1991, No. 180, § 1.

C.C. Art. 2315.6

Art. 2315.6. Liability for damages caused by injury to another

A. The following persons who view an event causing injury to another person, or who come upon the scene of the event soon thereafter, may recover damages for mental anguish or emotional distress that they suffer as a result of the other person's injury:

(1) The spouse, child or children, and grandchild or grandchildren of the injured person, or either the spouse, the child or children, or the grandchild or grandchildren of the injured person.

(2) The father and mother of the injured person, or either of them.

(3) The brothers and sisters of the injured person or any of them.

(4) The grandfather and grandmother of the injured person, or either of them.

B. To recover for mental anguish or emotional distress under this Article, the injured person must suffer such harm that one can reasonably expect a person in the claimant's position to suffer serious mental anguish or emotional distress from the experience, and the claimant's mental anguish or emotional distress must be severe, debilitating, and foreseeable. Damages suffered as a result of mental anguish or emotional distress for injury to another shall be recovered only in accordance with this Article.

Added by Acts 1991, No. 782, § 1.

C.C. Art. 2315.7

Art. 2315.7. Liability for damages caused by criminal sexual activity occurring during childhood

In addition to general and special damages, exemplary damages may be awarded upon proof that the injuries on which the action is based were caused by a wanton and reckless disregard for the rights and safety of the person through criminal sexual activity which occurred when the victim was seventeen years old or younger, regardless of whether the defendant was prosecuted for his or her

C.C. Art. 2315.7—Cont'd

acts. The provisions of this Article shall be applicable only to the perpetrator of the criminal sexual activity.

Added by Acts 1993, No. 831, § 1, eff. June 22, 1993.

C.C. Art. 2315.8

Art. 2315.8. Liability for damages caused by domestic abuse

A. In addition to general and special damages, exemplary damages may be awarded upon proof that the injuries on which the action is based were caused by a wanton and reckless disregard for the rights and safety of a family or household member, as defined in R.S. 46:2132, through acts of domestic abuse resulting in serious bodily injury or severe emotional and mental distress, regardless of whether the defendant was prosecuted for his or her acts.

B. Upon motion of the defendant or upon its own motion, if the court determines that an action seeking damages under this Article is frivolous or fraudulent, the court shall award costs of court, reasonable attorney fees, and any other related costs to the defendant and any other sanctions and relief requested pursuant to Code of Civil Procedure Article 863.

Added by Acts 2014, No. 315, § 1. Amended by Acts 2018, No. 264, § 1.

C.C. Art. 2315.9

Art. 2315.9. Liability for damages caused by acts of terror

A. In addition to general and special damages, a prevailing plaintiff shall also be awarded court costs and reasonable attorney fees in the appropriate district or appellate court upon proof that the injuries on which the action is based were caused by an act of terror or terrorism resulting in injury to the person or damage to the person's property, regardless of whether the defendant was prosecuted for his acts.

B. The rights and remedies provided by this Article are in addition to any other rights and remedies provided by law.

C. As used in this Article, the terms shall be defined as follows:

(1) "Act of terror" or "terrorism" means the commission of any of the acts occurring primarily in this state and as enumerated in this Subparagraph, when the offender has the intent to intimidate or coerce the civilian population, influence the policy of a unit of government by intimidation or coercion, or affect the conduct of a unit of government by intimidation or coercion:

(a) Intentional killing of a human being.

(b) Intentional infliction of serious bodily injury upon a human being.

(c) Kidnapping of a human being.

(d) Aggravated arson upon any structure, watercraft, or movable.

(e) Aggravated criminal damage to property.

(2) "Terrorist" means a person who knowingly does any of the following:

(a) Commits an act of terror.

(b) Acts as an accessory before or after the fact, aids or abets, solicits, or conspires to commit an act of terror.

C.C. Art. 2315.9—Cont'd

(c) Lends material support to an act of terror.

D. Upon motion of the defendant or upon its own motion, if the court determines that any action alleging an act of terror is frivolous or fraudulent, the court shall award costs of court, reasonable attorney fees, and any other related costs to the defendant and any other sanctions and relief requested pursuant to Code of Civil Procedure Article 863.

E. An action under the provisions of this Article shall be subject to a liberative prescriptive period of two years.

Added by Acts 2015, No. 337, § 1.

C.C. Art. 2315.10

Art. 2315.10. Liability for death caused by hazing; additional damages

In addition to general and special damages, exemplary damages may be awarded upon proof that the death on which the action is based was caused by a wanton and reckless disregard for the rights and safety of the victim through an act of hazing, as defined by R.S. 17:1801, regardless of whether the defendant was prosecuted for his acts.

Added by Acts 2018, No. 481, § 1, eff. May 25, 2018.

C.C. Art. 2315.11

Art. 2315.11. Liability for damages caused by sexual assault

A. In addition to general and special damages, exemplary damages may be awarded upon proof that the injuries on which the action is based were caused by an act or acts of sexual assault in the workplace.

B. The provisions of this Article shall be applicable only to the perpetrator of the sexual assault.

C. Upon motion of the defendant or upon its own motion, if the court determines that an action seeking damages under this Article is frivolous or fraudulent, the court shall award costs of court, reasonable attorney fees, and any other related costs to the defendant and any other sanctions and relief requested pursuant to Code of Civil Procedure Article 863.

D. An action under the provisions of this Article shall be subject to a liberative prescriptive period provided for in Article 3496.2.

E. As used in this Article, sexual assault is as defined in R.S. 46:2184.

Added by Acts 2021, No. 411, § 1.

C.C. Art. 2316

Art. 2316. Negligence, imprudence or want of skill

Every person is responsible for the damage he occasions not merely by his act, but by his negligence, his imprudence, or his want of skill.

C.C. Art. 2317

Art. 2317. Acts of others and of things in custody

We are responsible, not only for the damage occasioned by our own act, but for that which is caused by the act of persons for whom we are answerable, or of the things which we have in our custody. This, however, is to be understood with the following modifications.

C.C. Art. 2317.1

Art. 2317.1. Damage caused by ruin, vice, or defect in things

The owner or custodian of a thing is answerable for damage occasioned by its ruin, vice, or defect, only upon a showing that he knew or, in the exercise of reasonable care, should have known of the ruin, vice, or defect which caused the damage, that the damage could have been prevented by the exercise of reasonable care, and that he failed to exercise such reasonable care. Nothing in this Article shall preclude the court from the application of the doctrine of res ipsa loquitur in an appropriate case.

Added by Acts 1996, 1st Ex.Sess., No. 1, § 1, eff. April 16, 1996.

Editor's Notes

Pepper v. Triplet, 864 So.2d 181 (La. 2004). Strict liability for a dog requires proof of unreasonable risk if injury, which satisfies the requirement "which the owner could have prevented ...". (Query: The quoted phrase might also serve to preclude liability for Acts of God.)

C.C. Art. 2318

Art. 2318. Acts of a minor

The father and the mother are responsible for the damage occasioned by their minor child, who resides with them or who has been placed by them under the care of other persons, reserving to them recourse against those persons. However, the father and mother are not responsible for the damage occasioned by their minor child who has been emancipated by marriage, by judgment of full emancipation, or by judgment of limited emancipation that expressly relieves the parents of liability for damages occasioned by their minor child.

The same responsibility attaches to the tutors of minors.

Amended by Acts 1984, No. 578, § 1; Acts 2008, No. 786, § 1, eff. Jan. 1, 2009.

C.C. Art. 2319

Art. 2319. Acts of interdicts

Neither a curator nor an undercurator is personally responsible to a third person for a delictual obligation of the interdict in his charge solely by reason of his office.

Acts 2000, 1st Ex.Sess., No. 25, § 2, eff. July 1, 2001.

Revision Comments—2000

(a) This Article is new and changes the law. This Article was revised by the legislature in 2000 as part of a comprehensive revision of Louisiana's interdiction laws. Under Article 2319 of the Civil Code of 1870, "(t)he curators of insane persons are answerable for the damage occasioned by those under their care". See Civil Code Article 2319 (1870). As revised, this Article shields curators and undercurators from vicarious liability for the torts of interdicts in their charge.

(b) Although a curator is not personally responsible for an interdict's torts solely by reason of the relationship, the curator may be liable for damages resulting from his own acts or omissions. For example, if a curator negligently supervises an interdict in his charge and, as a result, the interdict causes damages to himself or to a third party, the curator may be personally responsible for the resulting damages.

C.C. Art. 2320

Art. 2320. Acts of servants, students or apprentices

Masters and employers are answerable for the damage occasioned by their servants and overseers, in the exercise of the functions in which they are employed.

Teachers and artisans are answerable for the damage caused by their scholars or apprentices, while under their superintendence.

In the above cases, responsibility only attaches, when the masters or employers, teachers and artisans, might have prevented the act which caused the damage, and have not done it.

The master is answerable for the offenses and *quasi*-offenses committed by his servants, according to the rules which are explained under the title: *Of quasi-contracts, and of offenses and quasi-offenses.*

Last paragraph redesignated from C.C. art. 176 in 1990 by the Louisiana State Law Institute.

Editor's Notes

Cox v. Gaylord Container Corp., 897 So.2d 1 (La. App. 1 Cir. 2004). For an employer to be vicariously liable under C.C. art. 2320, it must be shown that the negligent act was one that the employer could have prevented. (This is contrary to a long standing jurisprudential interpretation of C.C. art. 2320 that did not recognize the "could have prevented" notion.)

C.C. Art. 2321

Art. 2321. Damage caused by animals

The owner of an animal is answerable for the damage caused by the animal. However, he is answerable for the damage only upon a showing that he knew or, in the exercise of reasonable care, should have known that his animal's behavior would cause damage, that the damage could have been prevented by the exercise of reasonable care, and that he failed to exercise such reasonable care. Nonetheless, the owner of a dog is strictly liable for damages for injuries to persons or property caused by the dog and which the owner could have prevented and which did not result from the injured person's provocation of the dog. Nothing in this Article shall preclude the court from the application of the doctrine of res ipsa loquitur in an appropriate case.

Amended by Acts 1996, 1st Ex.Sess., No. 1, § 1, eff. April 16, 1996.

Editor's Notes

See Note under C.C. art. 2317.1 as to Pepper v. Triplet.

Honeycutt v. State Farm Fire & Cas. Co., 890 So.2d 756 (La. App. 2 Cir. 2004). Res ipsa loquitur applied to action in negligence to recover damages caused by collision with cow. Strict liability applies only to dog owners.

C.C. Art. 2322

Art. 2322. Damage caused by ruin of building

The owner of a building is answerable for the damage occasioned by its ruin, when this is caused by neglect to repair it, or when it is the result of a vice or defect in its original construction. However, he is answerable for damages only upon a showing that he knew or, in the exercise of reasonable care, should have known of the vice or defect which caused the damage, that the damage could have been prevented by the exercise of reasonable care, and that he failed to exercise such

C.C. Art. 2322—Cont'd

reasonable care. Nothing in this Article shall preclude the court from the application of the doctrine of res ipsa loquitur in an appropriate case.

Amended by Acts 1996, 1st Ex.Sess., No. 1, § 1, eff. April 16, 1996.

C.C. Art. 2322.1

Art. 2322.1. Users of blood or tissue; a medical service

A. The screening, procurement, processing, distribution, transfusion, or medical use of human blood and blood components of any kind and the transplantation or medical use of any human organ, human tissue, or approved animal tissue by physicians, dentists, hospitals, hospital blood banks, and nonprofit community blood banks is declared to be, for all purposes whatsoever, the rendition of a medical service by each and every physician, dentist, hospital, hospital blood bank, and nonprofit community blood bank participating therein, and shall not be construed to be and is declared not to be a sale. Strict liability and warranties of any kind without negligence shall not be applicable to the aforementioned who provide these medical services.

B. In any action based in whole or in part on the use of blood or tissue by a healthcare provider, to which the provisions of Paragraph A do not apply, the plaintiff shall have the burden of proving all elements of his claim, including a defect in the thing sold and causation of his injuries by the defect, by a preponderance of the evidence, unaided by any presumption.

C. The provisions of Paragraphs A and B are procedural and shall apply to all alleged causes of action or other act, omission, or neglect without regard to the date when the alleged cause of action or other act, omission, or neglect occurred.

D. As used in this Article:

(1) "Healthcare provider" includes all individuals and entities listed in R.S. 9:2797, this Article, R.S. 40:1237.1 and R.S. 40:1231.1 whether or not enrolled with the Patient's Compensation Fund.

(2) "The use of blood or tissue" means the screening, procurement, processing, distribution, transfusion, or any medical use of human blood, blood products, and blood components of any kind, and the transplantation or medical use of any human organ, human or approved animal tissue, and tissue products or tissue components by any healthcare provider.

Added by Acts 1981, No. 611, § 1. Amended by Acts 1990, No. 1091, § 1; Acts 1999, No. 539, § 2, eff. June 30, 1999.

Application—Acts 1999, No. 539

Section 4 (as redesignated pursuant to the statutory revision authority of the Louisiana State Law Institute) of Acts 1999, No. 539 (§ 2 of which amended this article) provided:

"The provisions of this Act shall not affect any legal proceedings filed prior to the effective date of this Act."

C.C. Art. 2323

Art. 2323. Comparative fault

A. In any action for damages where a person suffers injury, death, or loss, the degree or percentage of fault of all persons causing or contributing to the injury, death, or loss shall be determined, regardless of whether the person is a party to the action or a nonparty, and regardless of the person's insolvency, ability to pay, immunity by statute, including but not limited to the provisions of R.S. 23:1032, or that the other person's identity is not known or reasonably ascertainable. If a

C.C. Art. 2323—Cont'd

person suffers injury, death, or loss as the result partly of his own negligence and partly as a result of the fault of another person or persons, the amount of damages recoverable shall be reduced in proportion to the degree or percentage of negligence attributable to the person suffering the injury, death, or loss.

B. The provisions of Paragraph A shall apply to any claim for recovery of damages for injury, death, or loss asserted under any law or legal doctrine or theory of liability, regardless of the basis of liability.

C. Notwithstanding the provisions of Paragraphs A and B, if a person suffers injury, death, or loss as a result partly of his own negligence and partly as a result of the fault of an intentional tortfeasor, his claim for recovery of damages shall not be reduced.

Amended by Acts 1979, No. 431, § 1, eff. Aug. 1, 1980; Acts 1996, 1st Ex.Sess., No. 3, § 1, eff. April 16, 1996.

C.C. Art. 2324

Art. 2324. Liability as solidary or joint and divisible obligation

A. He who conspires with another person to commit an intentional or willful act is answerable, in solido, with that person, for the damage caused by such act.

B. If liability is not solidary pursuant to Paragraph A, then liability for damages caused by two or more persons shall be a joint and divisible obligation. A joint tortfeasor shall not be liable for more than his degree of fault and shall not be solidarily liable with any other person for damages attributable to the fault of such other person, including the person suffering injury, death, or loss, regardless of such other person's insolvency, ability to pay, degree of fault, immunity by statute or otherwise, including but not limited to immunity as provided in R.S. 23:1032, or that the other person's identity is not known or reasonably ascertainable.

C. Interruption of prescription against one joint tortfeasor is effective against all joint tortfeasors.

Amended by Acts 1979, No. 431, § 1, eff. Aug. 1, 1980; Acts 1987, No. 373, § 1; Acts 1988, No. 430, § 1; Acts 1996, 1st Ex.Sess., No. 3, § 1, eff. April 16, 1996.

Editor's Notes

See Commentary, The Revision of Tort Law, in introductory pages of this volume.

C.C. Art. 2324.1

Art. 2324.1. Damages; discretion of judge or jury

In the assessment of damages in cases of offenses, quasi offenses, and quasi contracts, much discretion must be left to the judge or jury.

Added by Acts 1984, No. 331, § 3, eff. Jan. 1, 1985.

C.C. Art. 2324.2

Art. 2324.2. Reduction of recovery

A. When the recovery of damages by a person suffering injury, death, or loss is reduced in some proportion by application of Article 2323 or 2324 and there is a legal or conventional subrogation, then the subrogee's recovery shall be reduced in the same proportion as the subrogor's recovery.

B. Nothing herein precludes such persons and legal or conventional subrogees from agreeing to a settlement which would incorporate a different method or proportion of subrogee recovery for

C.C. Art. 2324.2—Cont'd

amounts paid by the legal or conventional subrogee under the Louisiana Worker's Compensation Act, R.S. 23:1021, et seq.

Added by Acts 1989, No. 771, § 1, eff. July 9, 1989.

C.C. Art. 2668

Art. 2668. Contract of lease defined

Lease is a synallagmatic contract by which one party, the lessor, binds himself to give to the other party, the lessee, the use and enjoyment of a thing for a term in exchange for a rent that the lessee binds himself to pay.

The consent of the parties as to the thing and the rent is essential but not necessarily sufficient for a contract of lease.

Acts 2004, No. 821, § 1, eff. Jan. 1, 2005.

C.C. Art. 2681

Art. 2681. Form

A lease may be made orally or in writing. A lease of an immovable is not effective against third persons until filed for recordation in the manner prescribed by legislation.

Acts 2004, No. 821, § 1, eff. Jan. 1, 2005.

C.C. Art. 2720

Art. 2720. Termination of lease with a fixed term

A lease with a fixed term terminates upon the expiration of that term, without need of notice, unless the lease is reconducted or extended as provided in the following Articles.

Acts 2004, No. 821, § 1, eff. Jan. 1, 2005.

C.C. Art. 2723

Art. 2723. Term of reconducted nonagricultural lease

The term of a reconducted nonagricultural lease is:

(1) From month to month in the case of a lease whose term is a month or longer;

(2) From day to day in the case of a lease whose term is at least a day but shorter than a month; and

(3) For periods equal to the expired term in the case of a lease whose term is less than a day.

Acts 2004, No. 821, § 1, eff. Jan. 1, 2005.

C.C. Art. 2727

Art. 2727. Termination of lease with an indeterminate term

A lease with an indeterminate term, including a reconducted lease or a lease whose term has been established through Article 2680, terminates by notice to that effect given to the other party by the party desiring to terminate the lease, as provided in the following Articles.

Acts 2004, No. 821, § 1, eff. Jan. 1, 2005.

C.C. Art. 2728

Art. 2728. Notice of termination; timing

The notice of termination required by the preceding Article shall be given at or before the time specified below:

(1) In a lease whose term is measured by a period longer than a month, thirty calendar days before the end of that period;

(2) In a month-to-month lease, ten calendar days before the end of that month;

(3) In a lease whose term is measured by a period equal to or longer than a week but shorter than a month, five calendar days before the end of that period; and

(4) In a lease whose term is measured by a period shorter than a week, at any time prior to the expiration of that period.

A notice given according to the preceding Paragraph terminates the lease at the end of the period specified in the notice, and, if none is specified, at the end of the first period for which the notice is timely.

Acts 2004, No. 821, § 1, eff. Jan. 1, 2005.

C.C. Art. 3299

Art. 3299. Judicial and legal mortgages

A judicial mortgage secures a judgment for the payment of money. A legal mortgage secures an obligation specified by the law that provides for the mortgage.

Acts 1992, No. 1132, § 2, eff. Jan. 1, 1993.

C.C. Art. 3300

Art. 3300. Creation of judicial mortgage

A judicial mortgage is created by filing a judgment with the recorder of mortgages.

Acts 1992, No. 1132, § 2, eff. Jan. 1, 1993.

C.C. Art. 3301

Art. 3301. Creation of legal mortgage

A legal mortgage is created by complying with the law providing for it.

Acts 1992, No. 1132, § 2, eff. Jan. 1, 1993.

C.C. Art. 3302

Art. 3302. Property burdened by judicial and legal mortgages

Judicial and legal mortgages burden all the property of the obligor that is made susceptible of mortgage by Paragraphs 1 through 4 of Article 3286 or that is expressly made subject to judicial or legal mortgage by other law.

Acts 1992, No. 1132, § 2, eff. Jan. 1, 1993.

C.C. Art. 3303

Art. 3303. Nature of judicial and legal mortgages

Judicial and legal mortgages are general mortgages. They are established over property that the obligor owns when the mortgage is created and over future property of the obligor when he acquires it.

Acts 1992, No. 1132, § 2, eff. Jan. 1, 1993.

C.C. Art. 3304

Art. 3304. Judgment; suspensive appeal

A judicial mortgage is not affected or suspended by a suspensive appeal or stay of execution of the judgment.

Acts 1992, No. 1132, § 2, eff. Jan. 1, 1993.

C.C. Art. 3359

Art. 3359. Duration of recordation of judicial mortgage

The effect of recordation of a judgment creating a judicial mortgage ceases ten years after the date of the judgment.

Acts 2005, No. 169, § 1, eff. July 1, 2006.

C.C. Art. 3362

Art. 3362. Method of reinscription

A person may reinscribe a recorded instrument creating a mortgage or pledge or evidencing a privilege by recording a signed written notice of reinscription. The notice shall state the name of the mortgagor or pledgor, or the name of the obligor of the debt secured by the privilege, as it appears in the recorded instrument, as well as the registry number or other appropriate recordation information of the instrument or of a prior notice of reinscription, and shall declare that the instrument is reinscribed.

Acts 2005, No. 169, § 1, eff. July 1, 2006. Amended by Acts 2014, No. 281, § 1, eff. Jan. 1, 2015.

C.C. Art. 3363

Art. 3363. Method of reinscription exclusive

The method of reinscription provided in this Chapter is exclusive. Neither an amendment of an instrument creating a mortgage or pledge, or evidencing a privilege, nor an acknowledgment of the existence of a mortgage, pledge, or privilege by the mortgagor, pledgor, or obligor, constitutes a reinscription of the instrument.

Acts 2005, No. 169, § 1, eff. July 1, 2006. Amended by Acts 2014, No. 281, § 1, eff. Jan. 1, 2015.

C.C. Art. 3364

Art. 3364. Effect of timely recordation of notice of reinscription

A notice of reinscription that is recorded before the effect of recordation ceases continues that effect for ten years from the date the notice is recorded.

Acts 2005, No. 169, § 1, eff. July 1, 2006.

C.C. Art. 3365

Art. 3365. Effect of notice recorded after cessation of effect of recordation

A notice of reinscription that is recorded after the effect of recordation of the instrument sought to be reinscribed has ceased, again produces the effects of recordation, but only from the time that the notice of reinscription is recorded. The effect of recordation pursuant to this Article shall continue for ten years from the date on which the notice of reinscription is recorded, and the instrument may be reinscribed thereafter from time to time as provided by Article 3362.

Reinscription pursuant to this Article does not require that the mortgage or pledge or evidence of privilege be again recorded, even if the original recordation has been cancelled.

Acts 2005, No. 169, § 1, eff. July 1, 2006. Amended by Acts 2014, No. 281, § 1, eff. Jan. 1, 2015.

C.C. Art. 3445

Art. 3445. Kinds of prescription

There are three kinds of prescription: acquisitive prescription, liberative prescription, and prescription of nonuse.

Acts 1982, No. 187, § 1, eff. Jan. 1, 1983.

C.C. Art. 3446

Art. 3446. Acquisitive prescription

Acquisitive prescription is a mode of acquiring ownership or other real rights by possession for a period of time.

Acts 1982, No. 187, § 1, eff. Jan. 1, 1983.

C.C. Art. 3447

Art. 3447. Liberative prescription

Liberative prescription is a mode of barring of actions as a result of inaction for a period of time.

Acts 1982, No. 187, § 1, eff. Jan. 1, 1983.

C.C. Art. 3448

Art. 3448. Prescription of nonuse

Prescription of nonuse is a mode of extinction of a real right other than ownership as a result of failure to exercise the right for a period of time.

Acts 1982, No. 187, § 1, eff. Jan. 1, 1983.

C.C. Art. 3449

Art. 3449. Renunciation of prescription

Prescription may be renounced only after it has accrued.

Acts 1982, No. 187, § 1, eff. Jan. 1, 1983.

C.C. Art. 3450

Art. 3450. Express or tacit renunciation

Renunciation may be express or tacit. Tacit renunciation results from circumstances that give rise to a presumption that the advantages of prescription have been abandoned.

Nevertheless, with respect to immovables, renunciation of acquisitive prescription must be express and in writing.

Acts 1982, No. 187, § 1, eff. Jan. 1, 1983.

C.C. Art. 3451

Art. 3451. Capacity to renounce

To renounce prescription, one must have capacity to alienate.

Acts 1982, No. 187, § 1, eff. Jan. 1, 1983.

C.C. Art. 3452

Art. 3452. Necessity for pleading prescription

Prescription must be pleaded. Except as otherwise provided by legislation, courts may not supply a plea of prescription.

Acts 1982, No. 187, § 1, eff. Jan. 1, 1983. Amended by Acts 2021, No. 259, § 1.

C.C. Art. 3453

Art. 3453. Rights of creditors and other interested parties

Creditors and other persons having an interest in the acquisition of a thing or in the extinction of a claim or of a real right by prescription may plead prescription, even if the person in whose favor prescription has accrued renounces or fails to plead prescription.

Acts 1982, No. 187, § 1, eff. Jan. 1, 1983.

C.C. Art. 3454

Art. 3454. Computation of time

In computing a prescriptive period, the day that marks the commencement of prescription is not counted. Prescription accrues upon the expiration of the last day of the prescriptive period, and if that day is a legal holiday, prescription accrues upon the expiration of the next day that is not a legal holiday.

Acts 1982, No. 187, § 1, eff. Jan. 1, 1983.

C.C. Art. 3455

Art. 3455. Computation of time by months

If the prescriptive period consists of one or more months, prescription accrues upon the expiration of the day of the last month of the period that corresponds with the date of the

C.C. Art. 3455—Cont'd

commencement of prescription, and if there is no corresponding day, prescription accrues upon the expiration of the last day of the period.

Acts 1982, No. 187, § 1, eff. Jan. 1, 1983.

C.C. Art. 3456

Art. 3456. Computation of time by years

If a prescriptive period consists of one or more years, prescription accrues upon the expiration of the day of the last year that corresponds with the date of the commencement of prescription.

Acts 1982, No. 187, § 1, eff. Jan. 1, 1983.

C.C. Art. 3457

Art. 3457. Prescription established by legislation only

There is no prescription other than that established by legislation.

Acts 1982, No. 187, § 1, eff. Jan. 1, 1983.

C.C. Art. 3458

Art. 3458. Peremption; effect

Peremption is a period of time fixed by law for the existence of a right. Unless timely exercised, the right is extinguished upon the expiration of the peremptive period.

Acts 1982, No. 187, § 1, eff. Jan. 1, 1983.

C.C. Art. 3459

Art. 3459. Application of rules of prescription

The provisions on prescription governing computation of time apply to peremption.

Acts 1982, No. 187, § 1, eff. Jan. 1, 1983.

C.C. Art. 3460

Art. 3460. Peremption need not be pleaded

Peremption may be pleaded or it may be supplied by a court on its own motion at any time prior to final judgment.

Acts 1982, No. 187, § 1, eff. Jan. 1, 1983.

C.C. Art. 3461

Art. 3461. Renunciation, interruption, or suspension ineffective

Peremption may not be renounced, interrupted, or suspended.

Acts 1982, No. 187, § 1, eff. Jan. 1, 1983.

C.C. Art. 3462

Art. 3462. Interruption by filing of suit or by service of process

Prescription is interrupted when the owner commences action against the possessor, or when the obligee commences action against the obligor, in a court of competent jurisdiction and venue. If action is commenced in an incompetent court, or in an improper venue, prescription is interrupted only as to a defendant served by process within the prescriptive period.

Acts 1982, No. 187, § 1, eff. Jan. 1, 1983.

Editor's Notes

See C.C. Art. 1799, interruption of prescription as to solidary obligors; and C.C. Art. 2324(C), as to joint tortfeasors. See also Brister v. Southern Baptist Hospitals, 555 So.2d 641 (La.App. 4th Cir.1989), noting that under C.C. Art. 1799 any interruption is effective as to all solidary obligors.

C.C. Art. 3463

Art. 3463. Duration of interruption; abandonment or discontinuance of suit

A. An interruption of prescription resulting from the filing of a suit in a competent court and in the proper venue or from service of process within the prescriptive period continues as long as the suit is pending.

B. Interruption is considered never to have occurred if the plaintiff abandons the suit, voluntarily dismisses the suit at any time either before the defendant has made any appearance of record or thereafter, or fails to prosecute the suit at the trial. The dismissal of a suit pursuant to a compromise does not constitute a voluntary dismissal.

Acts 1982, No. 187, § 1, eff. Jan. 1, 1983. Amended by Acts 1999, No. 1263, § 2, eff. Jan. 1, 2000; Acts 2018, No. 443, § 1; Acts 2021, No. 414, § 1.

Editor's Notes

Section 3 of Acts 1999, No. 1263 provides:

"The provisions of this Act shall become effective on January 1, 2000, and shall apply to all actions filed on or after January 1, 2000."

C.C. Art. 3464

Art. 3464. Interruption by acknowledgment

Prescription is interrupted when one acknowledges the right of the person against whom he had commenced to prescribe.

Acts 1982, No. 187, § 1, eff. Jan. 1, 1983.

C.C. Art. 3465

Art. 3465. Interruption of acquisitive prescription

Acquisitive prescription is interrupted when possession is lost.

The interruption is considered never to have occurred if the possessor recovers possession within one year or if he recovers possession later by virtue of an action brought within the year.

Acts 1982, No. 187, § 1, eff. Jan. 1, 1983.

C.C. Art. 3466

Art. 3466. Effect of interruption

If prescription is interrupted, the time that has run is not counted. Prescription commences to run anew from the last day of interruption.

Acts 1982, No. 187, § 1, eff. Jan. 1, 1983.

C.C. Art. 3467

Art. 3467. Persons against whom prescription runs

Prescription runs against all persons unless exception is established by legislation.

Acts 1982, No. 187, § 1, eff. Jan. 1, 1983.

C.C. Art. 3468

Art. 3468. Incompetents

Prescription runs against absent persons and incompetents, including minors and interdicts, unless exception is established by legislation.

Acts 1982, No. 187, § 1, eff. Jan. 1, 1983. Amended by Acts 1983, No. 173, § 3, eff. Jan. 1, 1984; Acts 1991, No. 107, § 1.

Comments—1983 Amendment

(a) This Article is new. It establishes the principle that prescription runs against absentees and incompetents, including minors and interdicts, unless exception is established by legislation.

(b) Article 3468 of the Louisiana Civil Code, as revised in 1982, followed prior law in declaring that prescription was suspended in favor of minors and interdicts, unless exception was established by legislation. In reality, exceptions had swallowed that rule. According to former Civil Code Article 3541 (1870), the liberative prescriptions of one, three, five, and thirty years ran against minors and interdicts. Aside from the liberative prescriptions of five years provided by C.C. Art. 3542 (1870) (Art. 3497 in this revision), which were specially suspended in favor of minors alone, only the liberative prescription of ten years was actually suspended in favor of minors and interdicts.

Similarly, special legislation provided that the prescription of nonuse of predial servitudes (C.C. Art. 763 (rev.1977)), and of mineral servitudes, (Mineral Code Article 58, R.S. 9:5805), ran against minors and interdicts, so that only the prescription of nonuse of personal servitudes was actually suspended in favor of minors and interdicts.

Likewise, the acquisitive prescriptions of immovables, ten and thirty years, ran against absentees, minors, and interdicts, (C.C. Arts. 3474 (rev. 1982) and 3541 (1870)) so that only the acquisitive prescription of movables, three and ten years, were actually suspended in favor of minors and interdicts.

(c) As a result of this revision, the following prescriptions which did not previously do so now run against minors and interdicts: (1) the ten year liberative prescription; (2) the prescription of nonuse of personal servitudes; and (3) the acquisitive prescriptions of movables, three and ten years. All other prescriptions, also run against minors, interdicts, and absentees unless an exception is established by legislation.

C.C. Art. 3469

Art. 3469. Suspension of prescription

Prescription is suspended as between: the spouses during marriage, parents and children during minority, tutors and minors during tutorship, and curators and interdicts during interdiction, and caretakers and minors during minority.

A "caretaker" means a person legally obligated to provide or secure adequate care for a child, including a tutor, guardian, or legal custodian.

Acts 1982, No. 187, § 1, eff. Jan. 1, 1983. Amended by Acts 1988, No. 676, § 1.

Editor's Notes

Section 2 of Acts 1988, No. 676 provides that: "This Act shall be applicable to all persons who attain majority on or after the effective date of this Act." Act 676 became effective September 9, 1988. See R.S. 40:1299.41(G), as to suspension of prescription by filing claim with Commissioner, and suspension of prescription as to solidary obligors; see also Brister v. Southern Baptist Hospitals, 555 So.2d 641 (La.App. 4th Cir.1989) holding that filing claim with Commissioner did not interrupt prescription as to late-added solidary obligor physician.

C.C. Art. 3470

Art. 3470. Prescription during delays for inventory; vacant succession

Prescription runs during the delay the law grants to a successor for making an inventory and for deliberating. Nevertheless, it does not run against a beneficiary successor with respect to his rights against the succession.

Prescription runs against a vacant succession even if an administrator has not been appointed.

Acts 1982, No. 187, § 1, eff. Jan. 1, 1983.

C.C. Art. 3471

Art. 3471. Limits of contractual freedom

A juridical act purporting to exclude prescription, to specify a longer period than that established by law, or to make the requirements of prescription more onerous, is null.

Acts 1982, No. 187, § 1, eff. Jan. 1, 1983.

C.C. Art. 3472

Art. 3472. Effect of suspension

The period of suspension is not counted toward accrual of prescription. Prescription commences to run again upon the termination of the period of suspension.

Acts 1982, No. 187, § 1, eff. Jan. 1, 1983.

C.C. Art. 3472.1

Art. 3472.1. Emergency suspension of prescription and peremption

A. Notwithstanding any other provisions of the law, in the event the governor declares a state of emergency or disaster pursuant to R.S. 29:721 through 772, the Supreme Court of Louisiana may

C.C. Art. 3472.1—Cont'd

enter an order or series of orders as deemed necessary and appropriate to suspend all prescriptive and peremptive periods for a period of time not to exceed ninety days. Thereafter, should the need for continuing suspension be necessary to preserve access to the courts, the governor may issue executive orders as deemed appropriate. The period of suspension authorized by the provisions of this Article shall terminate upon the earlier of an order of the Supreme Court of Louisiana or upon termination of the declared state of disaster or emergency. Nothing in this Article limits the authority of the governor or the legislature to act in accordance with its authority.

B. The right to file any pleading subject to the suspension as provided by Paragraph A of this Article shall terminate sixty days after the termination of the suspension as provided by Paragraph A of this Article.

Added by Acts 2020, 1st Ex.Sess., No. 3, § 1, eff. June 25, 2020.

C.C. Art. 3473

Art. 3473. Prescription of ten years

Ownership and other real rights in immovables may be acquired by the prescription of ten years.

Acts 1982, No. 187, § 1, eff. Jan. 1, 1983.

C.C. Art. 3474

Art. 3474. Incompetents

This prescription runs against absent persons and incompetents, including minors and interdicts.

Acts 1982, No. 187, § 1, eff. Jan. 1, 1983. Amended by Acts 1991, No. 107, § 1.

C.C. Art. 3475

Art. 3475. Requisites

The requisites for the acquisitive prescription of ten years are: possession of ten years, good faith, just title, and a thing susceptible of acquisition by prescription.

Acts 1982, No. 187, § 1, eff. Jan. 1, 1983.

C.C. Art. 3476

Art. 3476. Attributes of possession

The possessor must have corporeal possession, or civil possession preceded by corporeal possession, to acquire a thing by prescription.

The possession must be continuous, uninterrupted, peaceable, public, and unequivocal.

Acts 1982, No. 187, § 1, eff. Jan. 1, 1983.

C.C. Art. 3477

Art. 3477. Precarious possessor; inability to prescribe

Acquisitive prescription does not run in favor of a precarious possessor or his universal successor.

Acts 1982, No. 187, § 1, eff. Jan. 1, 1983.

C.C. Art. 3478

Art. 3478. Termination of precarious possession; commencement of prescription

A co-owner, or his universal successor, may commence to prescribe when he demonstrates by overt and unambiguous acts sufficient to give notice to his co-owner that he intends to possess the property for himself. The acquisition and recordation of a title from a person other than a co-owner thus may mark the commencement of prescription.

Any other precarious possessor, or his universal successor, may commence to prescribe when he gives actual notice to the person on whose behalf he is possessing that he intends to possess for himself.

Acts 1982, No. 187, § 1, eff. Jan. 1, 1983.

C.C. Art. 3479

Art. 3479. Particular successor of precarious possessor

A particular successor of a precarious possessor who takes possession under an act translative of ownership possesses for himself, and prescription runs in his favor from the commencement of his possession.

Acts 1982, No. 187, § 1, eff. Jan. 1, 1983.

C.C. Art. 3480

Art. 3480. Good faith

For purposes of acquisitive prescription, a possessor is in good faith when he reasonably believes, in light of objective considerations, that he is owner of the thing he possesses.

Acts 1982, No. 187, § 1, eff. Jan. 1, 1983.

C.C. Art. 3481

Art. 3481. Presumption of good faith

Good faith is presumed. Neither error of fact nor error of law defeats this presumption. This presumption is rebutted on proof that the possessor knows, or should know, that he is not owner of the thing he possesses.

Acts 1982, No. 187, § 1, eff. Jan. 1, 1983.

C.C. Art. 3482

Art. 3482. Good faith at commencement of prescription

It is sufficient that possession has commenced in good faith; subsequent bad faith does not prevent the accrual of prescription of ten years.

Acts 1982, No. 187, § 1, eff. Jan. 1, 1983.

C.C. Art. 3483

Art. 3483. Just title

A just title is a juridical act, such as a sale, exchange, or donation, sufficient to transfer ownership or another real right. The act must be written, valid in form, and filed for registry in the conveyance records of the parish in which the immovable is situated.

Acts 1982, No. 187, § 1, eff. Jan. 1, 1983.

C.C. Art. 3484

Art. 3484. Transfer of undivided part of an immovable

A just title to an undivided interest in an immovable is such only as to the interest transferred.

Acts 1982, No. 187, § 1, eff. Jan. 1, 1983.

C.C. Art. 3485

Art. 3485. Things susceptible of prescription

All private things are susceptible of prescription unless prescription is excluded by legislation.

Acts 1982, No. 187, § 1, eff. Jan. 1, 1983.

C.C. Art. 3486

Art. 3486. Immovables; prescription of thirty years

Ownership and other real rights in immovables may be acquired by the prescription of thirty years without the need of just title or possession in good faith.

Acts 1982, No. 187, § 1, eff. Jan. 1, 1983.

C.C. Art. 3487

Art. 3487. Restriction as to extent of possession

For purposes of acquisitive prescription without title, possession extends only to that which has been actually possessed.

Acts 1982, No. 187, § 1, eff. Jan. 1, 1983.

C.C. Art. 3488

Art. 3488. Applicability of rules governing prescription of ten years

The rules governing acquisitive prescription of ten years apply to the prescription of thirty years to the extent that their application is compatible with the prescription of thirty years.

Acts 1982, No. 187, § 1, eff. Jan. 1, 1983.

C.C. Art. 3489

Art. 3489. Movables; acquisitive prescription

Ownership and other real rights in movables may be acquired either by the prescription of three years or by the prescription of ten years.

Acts 1982, No. 187, § 1, eff. Jan. 1, 1983.

C.C. Art. 3490

Art. 3490. Prescription of three years

One who has possessed a movable as owner, in good faith, under an act sufficient to transfer ownership, and without interruption for three years, acquires ownership by prescription.

Acts 1982, No. 187, § 1, eff. Jan. 1, 1983.

C.C. Art. 3491

Art. 3491. Prescription of ten years

One who has possessed a movable as owner for ten years acquires ownership by prescription. Neither title nor good faith is required for this prescription.

Acts 1982, No. 187, § 1, eff. Jan. 1, 1983.

C.C. Art. 3492

Art. 3492. Delictual actions

Delictual actions are subject to a liberative prescription of one year. This prescription commences to run from the day injury or damage is sustained. It does not run against minors or interdicts in actions involving permanent disability and brought pursuant to the Louisiana Products Liability Act or state law governing product liability actions in effect at the time of the injury or damage.

Acts 1983, No. 173, § 1, eff. Jan. 1, 1984. Amended by Acts 1992, No. 621, § 1.

C.C. Art. 3493

Art. 3493. Damage to immovable property; commencement and accrual of prescription

When damage is caused to immovable property, the one year prescription commences to run from the day the owner of the immovable acquired, or should have acquired, knowledge of the damage.

Acts 1983, No. 173, § 1, eff. Jan. 1, 1984.

C.C. Art. 3493.10

Art. 3493.10. Delictual actions; two–year prescription; criminal act

Delictual actions which arise due to damages sustained as a result of an act defined as a crime of violence under Chapter 1 of Title 14 of the Louisiana Revised Statutes of 1950, except as provided in Article 3496.2, are subject to a liberative prescription of two years. This prescription commences to run from the day injury or damage is sustained.

Added by Acts 1999, No. 832, § 1. Amended by Acts 2016, No. 629, § 1.

C.C. Art. 3494

Art. 3494. Actions subject to a three-year prescription

The following actions are subject to a liberative prescription of three years:

C.C. Art. 3494—Cont'd

(1) An action for the recovery of compensation for services rendered, including payment of salaries, wages, commissions, professional fees, fees and emoluments of public officials, freight, passage, money, lodging, and board;

(2) An action for arrearages of rent and annuities;

(3) An action on money lent;

(4) An action on an open account; and

(5) An action to recover underpayments or overpayments of royalties from the production of minerals, provided that nothing herein applies to any payments, rent, or royalties derived from state-owned properties.

Acts 1983, No. 173, § 1, eff. Jan. 1, 1984. Amended by Acts 1984, No. 147, § 1, eff. June 25, 1984; Acts 1986, No. 1031, § 1; Acts 2018, No. 471, § 1.

C.C. Art. 3495

Art. 3495. Commencement and accrual of prescription

This prescription commences to run from the day payment is exigible. It accrues as to past due payments even if there is a continuation of labor, supplies, or other services.

Acts 1983, No. 173, § 1, eff. Jan. 1, 1984.

C.C. Art. 3496

Art. 3496. Action against attorney for return of papers

An action by a client against an attorney for the return of papers delivered to him for purposes of a law suit is subject to a liberative prescription of three years. This prescription commences to run from the rendition of a final judgment in the law suit or the termination of the attorney-client relationship.

Acts 1983, No. 173, § 1, eff. Jan. 1, 1984.

C.C. Art. 3496.1

Art. 3496.1. Action against a person for abuse of a minor

An action against a person for abuse of a minor is subject to a liberative prescriptive period of three years. This prescription commences to run from the day the minor attains majority, and this prescription, for all purposes, shall be suspended until the minor reaches the age of majority. This prescriptive period shall be subject to any exception of peremption provided by law.

Added by Acts 1988, No. 676, § 1. Amended by Acts 1992, No. 322, § 1.

C.C. Art. 3496.2

Art. 3496.2. Action against a person for sexual assault

A delictual action against a person for any act of sexual assault, as defined in R.S. 46:2184, is subject to a liberative prescription of three years. This prescription commences to run from the day the injury or damage is sustained or the day the victim is notified of the identity of the offender by

C.C. Art. 3496.2—Cont'd

law enforcement or a judicial agency, whichever is later. This prescriptive period shall be subject to any exception of peremption provided by law.

Added by Acts 2016, No. 629, § 1.

C.C. Art. 3497

Art. 3497. Actions subject to a five year prescription

The following actions are subject to a liberative prescription of five years:

An action for annulment of a testament;

An action for the reduction of an excessive donation;

An action for the rescission of a partition and warranty of portions; and

An action for damages for the harvesting of timber without the consent of the owner.

This prescription is suspended in favor of minors, during minority.

Acts 1983, No. 173, § 1, eff. Jan. 1, 1984. Amended by Acts 2009, No. 107, § 1.

C.C. Art. 3497.1

Art. 3497.1. Actions for arrearages of spousal support or of installment payments for contributions made to a spouse's education or training

An action to make executory arrearages of spousal support or installment payments awarded for contributions made by one spouse to the education or training of the other spouse is subject to a liberative prescription of five years.

Added by Acts 1984, No. 147, § 1, eff. June 25, 1984. Amended by Acts 1990, No. 1008, § 3, eff. Jan. 1, 1991; Acts 1997, No. 605, § 1, eff. July 3, 1997.

C.C. Art. 3498

Art. 3498. Actions on negotiable and nonnegotiable instruments

Actions on instruments, whether negotiable or not, and on promissory notes, whether negotiable or not, are subject to a liberative prescription of five years. This prescription commences to run from the day payment is exigible.

Acts 1983, No. 173, § 1, eff. Jan. 1, 1984. Amended by Acts 1992, No. 1133, § 1, eff. July 1, 1993; Acts 1993, No. 901, § 1, eff. July 1, 1993; Acts 1993, No. 948, § 6, eff. June 25, 1993.

Editor's Notes

Acts 1992, No. 1133, § 1, effective July 1, 1993, enacted Section 3–A, Six Year Prescription, of Chapter 4 of Title XXIV of Book III of the Louisiana Civil Code, effective July 1, 1993, consisting of C.C. art. 3498, as amended and reenacted by the same Act. Acts 1993, No. 901, § 2, effective July 1, 1993, and Acts 1993, No. 948, § 9, effective June 25, 1993, both repealed Section 3–A so that C.C. art. 3498, as amended by Acts 1992, No. 1133, never became effective.

C.C. Art. 3499

Art. 3499. Personal action

Unless otherwise provided by legislation, a personal action is subject to a liberative prescription of ten years.

Acts 1983, No. 173, § 1, eff. Jan. 1, 1984.

C.C. Art. 3500

Art. 3500. Action against contractors and architects

An action against a contractor or an architect on account of defects of construction, renovation, or repair of buildings and other works is subject to a liberative prescription of ten years.

Acts 1983, No. 173, § 1, eff. Jan. 1, 1984.

C.C. Art. 3501

Art. 3501. Prescription and revival of money judgments

A money judgment rendered by a trial court of this state is prescribed by the lapse of ten years from its signing if no appeal has been taken, or, if an appeal has been taken, it is prescribed by the lapse of ten years from the time the judgment becomes final.

An action to enforce a money judgment rendered by a court of another state or a possession of the United States, or of a foreign country, is barred by the lapse of ten years from its rendition; but such a judgment is not enforceable in this state if it is prescribed, barred by the statute of limitations, or is otherwise unenforceable under the laws of the jurisdiction in which it was rendered.

Any party having an interest in a money judgment may have it revived before it prescribes, as provided in Article 2031 of the Code of Civil Procedure. A judgment so revived is subject to the prescription provided by the first paragraph of this Article. An interested party may have a money judgment rendered by a court of this state revived as often as he may desire.

Acts 1983, No. 173, § 1, eff. Jan. 1, 1984.

C.C. Art. 3501.1

Art. 3501.1. Actions for arrearages of child support

An action to make executory arrearages of child support is subject to a liberative prescription of ten years.

Added by Acts 1997, No. 605, § 1, eff. July 3, 1997.

C.C. Art. 3502

Art. 3502. Action for the recognition of a right of inheritance

An action for the recognition of a right of inheritance and recovery of the whole or a part of a succession is subject to a liberative prescription of thirty years. This prescription commences to run from the day of the opening of the succession.

Acts 1983, No. 173, § 1, eff. Jan. 1, 1984.

C.C. Art. 3503

Art. 3503. Solidary obligors

When prescription is interrupted against a solidary obligor, the interruption is effective against all solidary obligors and their successors.

C.C. Art. 3503—Cont'd

When prescription is interrupted against a successor of a solidary obligor, the interruption is effective against other successors if the obligation is indivisible. If the obligation is divisible, the interruption is effective against other successors only for the portions for which they are bound.

Acts 1983, No. 173, § 1, eff. Jan. 1, 1984.

LOUISIANA REVISED STATUTES

§ 55. Days of public rest, legal holidays, and half-holidays

A. The following shall be days of public rest and legal holidays and half-holidays:

(1) The following shall be days of public rest and legal holidays: Sundays; January 1, New Year's Day; January 8, Battle of New Orleans; the third Monday in January, Dr. Martin Luther King, Jr.'s Birthday; January 19, Robert E. Lee Day; third Monday in February, Washington's Birthday; Good Friday; the last Monday in May, National Memorial Day; June 3, Confederate Memorial Day; July 4, Independence Day; August 30, Huey P. Long Day; the first Monday in September, Labor Day; the second Monday in October, Christopher Columbus Day; November 1, All Saints' Day; November 11, Veterans' Day; the fourth Thursday in November, Thanksgiving Day; December 25, Christmas Day; Inauguration Day in the city of Baton Rouge; provided, however, that in the parish of Orleans, the city of Baton Rouge, in each of the parishes comprising the second and sixth congressional districts, except the parish of Ascension, and in each of the parishes comprising the fourteenth and thirty-first judicial districts of the state, the whole of every Saturday shall be a legal holiday, and in the parishes of Catahoula, Caldwell, West Carroll, Concordia, East Carroll, Franklin, Madison, Morehouse, Ouachita, Richland, Tensas, Union, Jackson, Avoyelles, West Feliciana, Rapides, Natchitoches, Grant, LaSalle, Winn, Lincoln, and East Baton Rouge, the whole of every Saturday shall be a holiday for all banking institutions, and in the parishes of Sabine and Vernon each Wednesday and Saturday, from 12:00 o'clock noon until 12:00 o'clock midnight, shall be a half-holiday for all banking institutions. All banks and trust companies, however, may, each at its option, remain open and exercise all of its regular banking functions and duties upon January 8; Dr. Martin Luther King, Jr.'s Birthday; January 19; Washington's Birthday; Good Friday; National Memorial Day; June 3; August 30; Christopher Columbus Day; November 1; and Veterans' Day; and all banks and trust companies located in Ward 1 of the parish of Avoyelles may, each at its option, remain open and exercise all of its regular banking functions and duties until 12 o'clock noon on Saturdays; however, when on any of said last named days any bank or trust company does actually remain open it shall, as to transactions on such day, to exactly the same extent as if such day were not otherwise a legal holiday, be not subject to any of the provisions of R.S. 7:85 and 251 or any other laws of Louisiana covering the matters of maturity of negotiable instruments and demand, notice, presentment, acceptance, or protest thereof on legal holidays and half-holidays, and all instruments payable to or at such bank upon such day shall become due on such day; and provided, further, that the option of remaining open shall not, except as otherwise provided in this Paragraph, apply to Saturdays or Wednesdays which are holidays or half-holidays, or to Mardi Gras when the same has been declared a legal holiday; and provided still further that nothing in any law of this state shall in any manner whatsoever affect the validity of or render void or voidable the payment, certification, or acceptance of a check or other negotiable instrument or any other transaction by a bank in Louisiana because done on any holiday or half-holiday or because done on any day upon which such bank, if remaining open because of the option given it herein, if the payment, certification, acceptance, or other transaction could have been validly done on any other day.

(2) In all parishes of the state the governing authorities thereof shall have the option to declare the whole of every Saturday a holiday, and until the whole of Saturday is so declared a holiday in any parish, Saturday from 12 o'clock noon until 12 o'clock midnight shall be a half-holiday; provided that in the city of Baton Rouge and in the Parish of Orleans the whole of every Saturday is a holiday; provided further, that the governing authority of the Parish of Washington may declare the whole of Wednesday or the whole of Saturday a holiday, and if the Parish of Washington declares the whole of

R.S. 1:55—Cont'd

Wednesday a holiday, no part of Saturday shall be a holiday in that parish. In no parish shall the whole of Wednesday be a holiday when the immediately preceding day is a holiday.

(3) In the parishes of Orleans, St. Bernard, Jefferson, Plaquemines, St. Charles, St. James, St. John the Baptist, East Baton Rouge, Lafayette, St. Tammany, Iberia, St. Martin, Ascension, Washington, Calcasieu, Jefferson Davis, St. Landry, Evangeline, Cameron, Assumption, St. Mary, Acadia, Vermilion, Iberville, Pointe Coupee, West Baton Rouge, Lafourche, East Feliciana, and West Feliciana, and in all municipalities, Mardi Gras shall be a holiday when the governing authorities so declare by ordinance. The school boards of the parishes of Acadia and Lafayette may declare Mardi Gras and the International Rice Festival in Crowley a holiday for public school children of those parishes. In the parish of Washington, the Friday of the Washington Parish Free Fair shall be a legal holiday for the purpose of authorizing the clerk of court for the parish of Washington to close his office on that day.

(4) Whenever December 25, January 1, or July 4 falls on a Sunday, the next day is a holiday. When December 25, January 1, or July 4 falls on a Saturday, the preceding Friday is a holiday when the governing authorities so declare by ordinance, and if the local governing authorities declare the Friday preceding January 1st a legal holiday, such holiday shall be an optional holiday for banking institutions, and each bank may, each at its option remain open and exercise all of its regular banking functions under conditions set forth in Paragraph (1) of this Subsection.

(5) The governing authorities of all parishes in the state shall have the option to declare the second Friday of Holiday in Dixie a legal holiday. The school boards in all parishes shall have the option to declare such day a holiday for public school children.

(6) The third Monday in January, the birthday of Dr. Martin Luther King, Jr. for public schools; provided however, that a local school board shall decide to observe this holiday during a regularly scheduled school day with or without the necessity of adjourning school for all or any portion of the school day.

(7) The third Monday in February, the birthday of President George Washington for public schools; provided however, that a local school board shall decide to observe this holiday during a regularly scheduled school day with or without the necessity of adjourning school for all or any portion of the school day.

(8) The first Tuesday after the first Monday in November in even-numbered years for public schools in any parish where the parish governing authority has established a polling place at a public school.

B. Legal holidays shall be observed by the departments of the state as follows:

(1)(a) Insofar as may be practicable in the administration of the government, no employee shall work on New Year's Day, Dr. Martin Luther King, Jr.'s Birthday which shall be observed on the third Monday of January of each year or in conjunction with the day of the federal observance, Mardi Gras Day, Good Friday, Independence Day, Labor Day, Veterans' Day, Thanksgiving Day, Christmas Day, Inauguration Day once in every four years in the city of Baton Rouge, or the first Tuesday after the first Monday in November in even-numbered years.

(b) In addition, in the city court of Sulphur, the second Monday in October, Christopher Columbus Day shall be a legal holiday.

(2) Robert E. Lee Day, Washington's Birthday, National Memorial Day, Confederate Memorial Day, and Huey P. Long Day shall be observed only in such manner as the governor may proclaim,

R.S. 1:55—Cont'd

considering the pressure of the state's business; however, not more than two such legal holidays shall be proclaimed in any one year, one of which shall be National Memorial Day.

(3) The governor, by executive proclamation, may authorize the observance of such other holidays and half-holidays as he may deem in keeping with efficient administration. Whenever, in accordance with this Paragraph, the governor declares the Friday after Thanksgiving Day in November a holiday, such holiday shall be designated as Acadian Day and shall be observed in commemoration of the arrival in Louisiana of the Acadian people from the French colony Acadie following the ceding of that colony to England in 1713 and in recognition of the fact that much of the early economic and political development of Louisiana is directly attributable to the industry of the Acadian people, through cultivation of land, utilization of Louisiana's natural resources, and the interest of the Acadian people in political self-determination and American democracy.

(4) When one or more holidays or half-holidays fall on a full-time employee's regular day off, his holiday shall be the closest regularly scheduled workday preceding or following the legal holiday, as designated by the head of the agency. Employees whose regular work hours do not fall in the time period, or fall only partly within the time period, of the holiday shall receive a number of hours equivalent to the holiday through compensatory time or overtime. Part-time employees having a regular work schedule will receive benefits in a similar manner as full-time employees except that their benefits will be prorated to the number of hours normally worked.

(5) When time off is declared in case of natural emergencies, only those persons actually scheduled to work during the time period of the declaration shall receive the time off. Those persons who are scheduled to work during those hours and, because of the requirements of their job, do in fact work shall be entitled to compensatory time for those hours.

C. It shall be lawful to file and record suits, deeds, mortgages and liens, to issue and serve citations, to make sheriff's sales by virtue of any execution, and to take and to execute all other legal proceedings on Wednesday and Saturday holidays and half-holidays.

D. Notwithstanding the provisions of R.S. 6:65 or any other law to the contrary, all banking institutions and savings and loan associations located within the parishes of Terrebonne, Lafourche, Iberia, Pointe Coupee, West Baton Rouge, St. Mary, and Iberville, and all banking institutions located within the parishes of Lafayette and St. Landry, shall be closed during any year on Saturdays, Sundays, New Year's Day, Mardi Gras, Independence Day, Labor Day, Thanksgiving and Christmas; provided, however, that when New Year's Day, Independence Day or Christmas fall on a Sunday, said banking institutions and savings and loan associations shall be closed on the next day, and said financial institutions may, each at its option, remain open and exercise all of its regular functions and duties upon January eighth; January nineteenth; the third Monday in February, Washington's Birthday; Good Friday; the last Monday in May, National Memorial Day; June third; August thirtieth; the second Monday in October, Christopher Columbus Day; November first; and November eleventh, Veterans' Day; and further provided that when on any of said last named days any said financial institution does actually remain open it shall, as to transactions on such day, to exactly the same extent as if such day were not otherwise a legal holiday, be not subject to any of the provisions of R.S. 7:85 and 251, or any other laws of Louisiana, covering the matters of maturity of negotiable instruments and demands, notice, presentment, acceptance or protest thereof on legal holidays and half-holidays, and all instruments payable to or at such bank upon such day shall become due on such day; and provided further that the option of remaining open shall not apply to Saturdays or Wednesdays which are holidays or half-holidays, or to Mardi Gras when the same has been declared a legal holiday; and provided further that nothing in any law of this state shall in any manner

R.S. 1:55—Cont'd

whatsoever affect the validity of, or render void or voidable, the payment, certification of acceptance of a check or other negotiable instrument, or any other transaction by a bank in Louisiana because done on any holiday or half-holiday or because done on any day upon which such financial institution if remaining open because of the option given it herein, if the payment, certification, acceptance, or other transaction could have been validly done on any other day, provided, however, that in the parishes of Beauregard, Sabine, Vernon, Evangeline and DeSoto the banking institutions may elect to make the whole of Saturdays holidays and close, in lieu of half-holidays on Wednesdays and half-holidays on Saturdays.

E. (1)(a)(i) Each clerk of a district court, parish court, and city court shall close his office on the following days: New Year's Day, January first; Washington's Birthday, the third Monday in February; Good Friday; Memorial Day, the last Monday in May; the Fourth of July; Labor Day, the first Monday in September; All Saints' Day, November first; Veterans' Day, November eleventh; Thanksgiving Day, the fourth Thursday in November, and the next day, Friday; Christmas Eve Day; Christmas Day; and New Year's Eve Day, December thirty-first.

(ii) Whenever New Year's Day, the Fourth of July, or Christmas Day falls on a Saturday, the preceding Friday shall be a holiday. Whenever New Year's Day, the Fourth of July, or Christmas Day falls on a Sunday, the following Monday shall be a holiday.

(iii) In addition, in the city courts of Hammond and Sulphur, Ward Four, Mardi Gras and the day on which the national observance of Martin Luther King, Jr.'s birthday is celebrated shall be legal holidays and the clerk of court shall close his office on those days. In addition, in the city court of Sulphur, the second Monday in October, Christopher Columbus Day shall be a legal holiday and the clerk of city court shall close his office on that day. Notwithstanding any other law to the contrary, Mardi Gras shall be a legal holiday for the clerks of court for the parishes of East and West Feliciana, East Baton Rouge, Iberville, Pointe Coupee, West Baton Rouge, St. John the Baptist, St. Charles, Lafourche, St. Mary, Assumption, Terrebonne, St. Martin, Ascension, St. James, St. Tammany, St. Bernard, Jefferson Davis, Livingston, Acadia, Vermilion, Calcasieu, Orleans, Allen, and Tangipahoa.

(b) In addition, each clerk of a district court, parish court, and city court shall close his office on all of the legal holidays provided in Subparagraph (B)(1)(a) of this Section and on any day that the governor has proclaimed a legal holiday pursuant to Paragraph (B)(3) of this Section. Notwithstanding the provisions of Paragraph (2) of this Subsection, each clerk of a district court, parish court, and city court may close his office on any day an emergency situation has been declared by the governor or the local governing authority and governmental entities, including the courthouse, have been ordered to close.

(c) In addition, each clerk of a city court or parish court, with the approval of the chief judge of the court, may close his office on the day proclaimed by the governor or the local governing authority as a holiday in honor of Dr. Martin Luther King, Jr.'s birthday.

(d) In addition, each clerk of court in the parishes of St. James and St. John the Baptist shall close his office on any day upon which the governor has proclaimed a legal holiday. The provisions of this Section shall not apply to Inauguration Day once every four years or General Election Day every two years.

(e) In addition, in the parish of Vermilion, the Friday of the Cattle Festival in Abbeville shall be a legal holiday for the purpose of authorizing the clerk of court of the Fifteenth Judicial District Court and the clerk of court of the City Court of Abbeville to close their offices in observance of that day, unless there is an election that requires their office to remain open.

R.S. 1:55—Cont'd

(f) In addition, in the parish of Iberia, the Friday of the Sugar Cane Festival shall be a legal holiday for the purpose of authorizing the clerk of court of the Sixteenth Judicial District Court in the parish of Iberia to close offices in observance of that day, unless there is an election that requires the office to remain open.

(g) In addition, in the parish of St. Mary, the Friday of the Black Bear Festival shall be a legal holiday for the purpose of authorizing the clerk of court of the Sixteenth Judicial District Court in the parish of St. Mary to close offices in observance of that day, unless there is an election that requires the office to remain open.

(h) In addition, in the parish of Grant, the Friday of the Pecan Festival shall be a legal holiday for the purpose of authorizing the clerk of court of the Thirty–Fifth Judicial District Court in the parish of Grant to close offices in observance of that day, unless there is an election that requires the office to remain open.

(i) In addition, in the parish of Union, the Friday of the Watermelon Festival shall be a legal holiday for the purpose of authorizing the clerk of court of the Third Judicial District Court in the parish of Union to close offices in observance of that day, unless there are functions and duties related to an election that require the office to remain open.

(2) If an emergency situation develops which, in the judgment of the clerk of court, renders it hazardous or otherwise unsafe for employees of the office of the clerk to continue in the performance of their official duties or for the general public to conduct business with the clerk's office, the clerk, with prior approval from the clerk's chief judge or other person authorized to exercise his authority, may order the closing of his office for the duration of the hazardous or unsafe condition. No such closure shall be effective nor shall such period of closing be considered a legal holiday unless prior written approval or written confirmation from such chief judge or person acting on his behalf is received by the clerk of court. When the office is reopened, the clerk shall attach a statement setting forth the dates of closure, the hours of closure if applicable, the reasons for closure, and a statement that, pursuant to Paragraph (3) of this Subsection, these days or parts of days were legal holidays to every document, petition, or pleading filed in the office of the clerk on the first day or part of a day his office is open after being closed under the provisions of this Paragraph, whenever the petition or document relates to a cause of action, right of appeal, or other matter against which prescription could have run or time periods imposed by law could have expired.

(3) Only the enumerated holidays in Paragraph (1) of this Subsection, days of closure under Paragraph (2) of this Subsection, Mardi Gras only in those parishes in which the governing authority of the parish declares a holiday under authority of Paragraph (A)(3) of this Section, and all Saturdays and Sundays shall be considered as legal holidays for the purposes of Code of Civil Procedure Article 5059.

(4) The Municipal Court of New Orleans and the Traffic Court of New Orleans shall have the same legal holidays as the Civil District Court for the parish of Orleans and the Criminal District Court for the parish of Orleans.

(5) Notwithstanding any provision of this Section to the contrary, no court shall be required to be open if their respective clerk of court's office is closed pursuant to this Section.

F. Each institution of higher education in the state, through a representative appointed by it, shall designate a maximum of fourteen legal holidays per calendar year to be observed by all of its employees. If the institution does not elect to designate Veterans' Day as one of the fourteen legal holidays to be observed, an employee, who is a veteran as defined in R.S. 29:251.2, shall be allowed to

R.S. 1:55—Cont'd

attend activities or events related to Veterans' Day with compensation and for no more than four hours, when the designated day for observance by the state is on a regularly scheduled workday.

Amended by Acts 1950, No. 96, § 1; Acts 1950, No. 98, § 1; Acts 1952, No. 534, §§ 1, 2; Acts 1954, No. 593, § 1; Acts 1956, No. 463, § 1; Acts 1956, No. 549, § 1; Acts 1958, No. 210, § 1; Acts 1958, No. 270, § 1; Acts 1964, No. 158; Acts 1964, No. 250; Acts 1965, No. 159, § 1; Acts 1966, No. 45, § 1; Acts 1966, No. 137, § 1; Acts 1966, No. 152, § 1; Acts 1968, No. 48, §§ 1, 2; Acts 1968, No. 178, § 1; Acts 1968, No. 380, § 1; Acts 1968, No. 404, § 1; Acts 1968, No. 497, § 1; Acts 1970, No. 202, § 1; Acts 1970, No. 575, § 1; Acts 1972, No. 640, § 1; Acts 1973, No. 131, § 1; Acts 1975, No. 38, § 1; Acts 1976, No. 72, § 1; Acts 1976, No. 98, § 1, eff. July 9, 1976; Acts 1976, No. 111, § 1; Acts 1976, No. 493, § 1; Acts 1977, No. 505, § 1; Acts 1977, No. 668, § 1; Acts 1978, No. 69, § 1; Acts 1978, No. 163, § 1; Acts 1981, No. 171, § 1; Acts 1982, No. 148, § 1; Acts 1982, No. 255, § 1; Acts 1982, No. 627, § 1; Acts 1984, No. 79, § 1; Acts 1984, No. 464, § 1; Acts 1984, No. 643, § 1; Acts 1985, No. 838, § 1; Acts 1985, No. 1002, § 1; Acts 1986, No. 2, § 1; Acts 1986, No. 153, § 1; Acts 1986, No. 296, § 1; Acts 1986, No. 607, § 1; Acts 1988, No. 346, § 1; Acts 1989, No. 570, § 1; Acts 1991, No. 139, § 1; Acts 1991, No. 906, § 1; Acts 1992, No. 333, § 1; Acts 1992, No. 750, § 1; Acts 1992, No. 772, § 1; Acts 1993, No. 487, § 1; Acts 1993, No. 495, § 1; Acts 1993, No. 534, § 1; Acts 1993, No. 698, § 1; Acts 1995, No. 1021, § 1; Acts 1995, No. 1307, § 1; Acts 1996, 1st Ex.Sess., No. 22, § 1; Acts 1999, No. 257, § 1; Acts 1999, No. 279, § 1; Acts 1999, No. 733, § 1; Acts 2003, No. 354, § 1; Acts 2003, No. 409, § 1; Acts 2004, No. 474, § 1; Acts 2004, No. 740, § 1; Acts 2005, No. 45, § 1; Acts 2006, No. 734, § 1; Acts 2008, No. 788, § 1; Acts 2013, No. 220, § 1, eff. June 11, 2013; Acts 2014, No. 206, § 1; Acts 2014, No. 671, § 1; Acts 2015, No. 40, § 1; Acts 2016, No. 33, § 1; Acts 2016, No. 34, § 1, eff. May 10, 2016; Acts 2019, No. 316, § 1; Acts 2020, No. 264, § 1.

R.S. 9:196

§ 196. Limited tutorship by nature

A tutor who is entitled to tutorship by nature pursuant to the provisions of Section 2 of Chapter 1 of Title VIII of Book I of the Civil Code [1] and without qualification may perform or discharge any act affecting any right or interest of the minor which involves not more than ten thousand dollars actually received by the minor, notwithstanding court costs, attorney fees, and other expenses. For purposes of this Section, the natural tutor need not comply with the provisions of Code of Civil Procedure Articles 4061, 4265 through 4268, 4269.1, and 4270 through 4272.

Added by Acts 1997, No. 851, § 1; Acts 1997, No. 1243, § 1. Amended by Acts 2003, No. 600, § 1.

[1] C.C. art. 250 et seq.

R.S. 9:301

§ 301. Court may authorize spouse of military personnel presumed dead to remarry; judgment dissolves marriage

A. The spouse of a person presumed dead, as provided in R.S. 9:1441, may petition the district court of the parish in which the petitioner is domiciled for authority to contract another marriage. Upon the submission of proof that the petitioner is domiciled in the parish, and that the other spouse is presumed dead, the court may authorize petitioner to contract another marriage. The presumption of the death of petitioner's spouse may be proved as provided in R.S. 9:1443.

B. The judgment of court authorizing the petitioner to contract another marriage has the effect of terminating the marriage to the person presumed dead if he is alive at the time.

Added by Acts 1990, No. 1009, § 7, eff. Jan. 1, 1991.

R.S. 9:302

§ 302. Divorce proceedings; hearings in chambers; procedure

A. In addition to any hearing otherwise authorized by law to be held in chambers, the court by local rule, and only in those instances where good cause is shown, may provide that only with mutual

R.S. 9:302—Cont'd

consent, civil hearings before the trial court in divorce proceedings may be held in chambers. Such hearings shall include contested and uncontested proceedings and rules for spousal support, child support, visitation, injunctions, or other matters provisional and incidental to divorce proceedings.

B. A motion for hearing in chambers pursuant to this Section may be made by either party or upon the court's own motion.

C. Except for being closed to the public, the hearings held in chambers pursuant to this Section shall be conducted in the same manner as if taking place in open court. The minute clerk and court reporter shall be present if necessary to perform the duties provided by law.

D. The provisions of this Section shall not be construed to repeal or restrict the authority otherwise provided by law for any hearing to be held in chambers.

Added by Acts 1990, No. 1009, § 7, eff. Jan. 1, 1991.

PART III. CHILD CUSTODY

SUBPART A. EVALUATION AND MEDIATION

R.S. 9:331

§ 331. Custody or visitation proceeding; evaluation by mental health professional

A. The court may order an evaluation of a party or the child in a custody or visitation proceeding for good cause shown. The evaluation shall be made by a mental health professional selected by the parties or by the court. The court may render judgment for costs of the evaluation, or any part thereof, against any party or parties, as it may consider equitable.

B. The court may order a party or the child to submit to and cooperate in the evaluation, testing, or interview by the mental health professional. The mental health professional shall provide the court and the parties with a written report. The mental health professional shall serve as the witness of the court, subject to cross-examination by a party.

Acts 1993, No. 261, § 5, eff. Jan. 1, 1994.

R.S. 9:331.1

§ 331.1. Drug testing in custody or visitation proceeding

The court for good cause shown may, after a contradictory hearing, order a party in a custody or visitation proceeding to submit to specified drug tests and the collection of hair, urine, tissue, and blood samples as required by appropriate testing procedures within a time period set by the court. The refusal to submit to the tests may be taken into consideration by the court. The provisions of R.S. 9:397.2 and 397.3(A), (B), and (C) shall govern the admissibility of the test results. The fact that the court orders a drug test and the results of such test shall be confidential and shall not be admissible in any other proceedings. The court may render judgment for costs of the drug tests against any party or parties, as it may consider equitable.

Added by Acts 1999, No. 974, § 1.

R.S. 9:331.2

§ 331.2. Custody and visitation proceeding; parenting education programs

A. Upon the motion of any party, or on its own motion, the court may for good cause shown or upon agreement of the parties require the parties in a custody or visitation proceeding to attend and

R.S. 9:331.2—Cont'd

complete a court-approved program designed to educate and inform the parties of the needs of the children. The court may render judgment for the costs of the program, or any part thereof, against any party or parties as it may consider equitable. The instructor shall not be called as a witness in the custody or visitation proceeding without prior court approval.

B. If the court chooses to require participation in such a program, it shall adopt rules to accomplish the goals of Subsection A of this Section, which rules shall include but not be limited to the following:

(1) Criteria for evaluating a program provider and its instructors.

(2) Criteria to assure selected programs provide and incorporate into the provider's fee structure the cost of services to indigents.

(3) The amount of time a participant must take part in the program, which shall be a minimum of three hours.

(4) The time within which a party must complete the program.

C. For purposes of this Section, "instructor" means any psychiatrist, psychologist, professional counselor, social worker licensed under state law, or in any parish other than Orleans, means a person working with a court-approved, evidence-based nonprofit program, or a court-approved nonprofit program of an accredited university created for educating parents. All instructors must have received advanced training in instructing co-parenting or similar programs.

D. The program shall focus on the developmental needs of children, with emphasis on fostering the child's emotional health. The program shall be informative and supportive and shall direct people desiring additional information or help to appropriate resources. The course content shall contain but not be limited to the following subjects:

(1) The developmental stages of childhood, the needs of children at different ages, and age appropriate expectations of children.

(2) Stress indicators in children adjusting to divorce, the grief process, and avoiding delinquency.

(3) The possible enduring emotional effects of divorce on the child.

(4) Changing parental and marital roles.

(5) Recommendations with respect to visitation designed to enhance the child's relationship with both parents.

(6) Financial obligations of child rearing.

(7) Conflict management and dispute resolution.

E. Nonviolent acts or communications made during the program, which are otherwise relevant to the subject matter of a divorce, custody, or visitation proceeding, are confidential, not subject to disclosure, and may not be used as evidence in favor of or against a participant in the pending proceeding. This rule does not require the exclusion of any evidence otherwise discoverable merely because it is presented or otherwise made during the program.

R.S. 9:306. Added by Acts 1995, No. 766, § 1, eff. July 1, 1995. Amended by Acts 1999, No. 276, § 1; Acts 2019, No. 239, § 1. Redesignated as R.S. 9:331.2 by Acts 2019, No. 239, § 2.

§ 332. Custody or visitation proceeding; mediation

A. The court may order the parties to mediate their differences in a custody or visitation proceeding. The mediator may be agreed upon by the parties or, upon their failure to agree, selected

R.S. 9:331.2—Cont'd

by the court. The court may stay any further determination of custody or visitation for a period not to exceed thirty days from the date of issuance of such an order. The court may order the costs of mediation to be paid in advance by either party or both parties jointly. The court may apportion the costs of the mediation between the parties if agreement is reached on custody or visitation. If mediation concludes without agreement between the parties, the costs of mediation shall be taxed as costs of court. The costs of mediation shall be subject to approval by the court.

B. If an agreement is reached by the parties, the mediator shall prepare a written, signed, and dated agreement. A consent judgment incorporating the agreement shall be submitted to the court for its approval.

C. Evidence of conduct or statements made in mediation is not admissible in any proceeding. This rule does not require the exclusion of any evidence otherwise discoverable merely because it is presented in the course of mediation. Facts disclosed, other than conduct or statements made in mediation, are not inadmissible by virtue of first having been disclosed in mediation.

Acts 1993, No. 261, § 5, eff. Jan. 1, 1994.

SUBPART C. PROTECTIVE AND REMEDIAL PROVISIONS

R.S. 9:341

§ 341. Restriction on visitation

A. Whenever the court finds by a preponderance of the evidence that a parent has subjected any of his or her children or stepchildren to family violence, as defined in R.S. 9:362, or domestic abuse, as defined in R.S. 46:2132, has subjected any other household member, as defined in R.S. 46:2132, to a history of family violence as defined in R.S. 9:364(A), or has willingly permitted such abuse to any of his or her children or stepchildren despite having the ability to prevent it, the court shall allow only supervised visitation between the abusive parent and the abused child or children until such parent proves by a preponderance of the evidence at a contradictory hearing that the abusive parent has successfully completed a court-monitored domestic abuse intervention program, as defined in R.S. 9:362, since the last incident of domestic violence or family abuse. At the hearing, the court shall consider evidence of the abusive parent's current mental health condition and the possibility the abusive parent will again subject his children. stepchildren, or other household member to family violence or domestic abuse, or willingly permit such abuse to any of his or her children or stepchildren despite having the ability to prevent it. The court shall order visitation only if the abusive parent proves by a preponderance of the evidence that visitation would be in the best interest of the child, considering the factors in Civil Code Article 134, and would not cause physical, emotional, or psychological damage to the child. Should visitation be allowed, the court shall order such restrictions, conditions, and safeguards necessary to minimize any risk of harm to the child, including continued supervision. All costs incurred in compliance with the provisions of this Section shall be borne by the abusive parent.

B. Whenever the court finds by clear and convincing evidence that a parent has subjected any of his children, stepchildren, or any household member as defined in R.S. 46:2132, to sexual abuse, as defined in R.S. 14:403, or has willingly permitted such abuse to any of his or her children, stepchildren, or a household member, despite having the ability to prevent the abuse, the court shall prohibit all visitation and contact between the abusive parent and the children until such parent proves by a preponderance of the evidence at a contradictory hearing that he has successfully completed a treatment program designed for such sexual abusers. At the hearing, the court shall consider evidence of the abusive parent's current mental health condition and the possibility the

R.S. 9:341—Cont'd

abusive parent will repeat such conduct in the future. The court shall order visitation only if the abusive parent proves by a preponderance of the evidence that visitation would be in the best interest of the child, and that visitation would not cause physical, emotional, or psychological damage to the child. Should visitation be allowed, the court shall order such restrictions, conditions, and safeguards necessary to minimize any risk of harm to the child, including supervision of the visitation. All costs incurred in compliance with the provisions of this Section shall be the responsibility of the abusive parent.

C. When visitation has been restricted or prohibited by the court pursuant to Subsection A or B of this Section, and the court subsequently authorizes further restricted visitation, the parent whose visitation has been restricted shall not remove the child from the jurisdiction of the court except for good cause shown and with the prior approval of the court.

Acts 1993, No. 261, § 5, eff. Jan. 1, 1994. Amended by Acts 2018, No. 412, § 2, eff. May 23, 2018.

R.S. 9:342

§ 342. Bond to secure child custody or visitation order

For good cause shown, a court may, on its own motion or upon the motion of any party, require the posting of a bond or other security by a party to insure compliance with a child visitation order and to indemnify the other party for the payment of any costs incurred.

Acts 1993, No. 261, § 5, eff. Jan. 1, 1994.

R.S. 9:343

§ 343. Return of child kept in violation of custody and visitation order

A. Upon presentation of a certified copy of a custody and visitation rights order rendered by a court of this state, together with the sworn affidavit of the custodial parent, the judge, who shall have jurisdiction for the limited purpose of effectuating the remedy provided by this Section by virtue of either the presence of the child or litigation pending before the court, may issue a civil warrant directed to law enforcement authorities to return the child to the custodial parent pending further order of the court having jurisdiction over the matter.

B. The sworn affidavit of the custodial parent shall include all of the following:

(1) A statement that the custody and visitation rights order is true and correct.

(2) A summary of the status of any pending custody proceeding.

(3) The fact of the removal of or failure to return the child in violation of the custody and visitation rights order.

(4) A declaration that the custodial parent desires the child returned.

Acts 1993, No. 261, § 5, eff. Jan. 1, 1994.

R.S. 9:344

§ 344. Visitation rights of grandparents and siblings

A. If one of the parties to a marriage dies, is interdicted, or incarcerated, and there is a minor child or children of such marriage, the parents of the deceased, interdicted, or incarcerated party without custody of such minor child or children may have reasonable visitation rights to the child or

R.S. 9:344—Cont'd

children of the marriage during their minority, if the court in its discretion finds that such visitation rights would be in the best interest of the child or children.

B. When the parents of a minor child or children live in concubinage and one of the parents dies, or is incarcerated, the parents of the deceased or incarcerated party may have reasonable visitation rights to the child or children during their minority, if the court in its discretion finds that such visitation rights would be in the best interest of the child or children.

C. If one of the parties to a marriage dies or is incarcerated, the siblings of a minor child or children of the marriage may have reasonable visitation rights to such child or children during their minority if the court in its discretion finds that such visitation rights would be in the best interest of the child or children.

D. If the parents of a minor child of the marriage have lived apart for a period of six months, in extraordinary circumstances, the grandparents or siblings of the child may have reasonable visitation rights to the child during his minority, if the court in its discretion finds that such visitation rights would be in the best interest of the child. In determining the best interest of the child the court shall consider the same factors contained in Civil Code Article 136(D). Extraordinary circumstances shall include a determination by a court that a parent is abusing a controlled dangerous substance. Acts 1993, No. 261, § 5, eff. Jan. 1, 1994. Amended by Acts 1999, No. 1352, § 1; Acts 2012, No. 763, § 2, eff. June 12, 2012.

R.S. 9:345

§ 345. Appointment of attorney in child custody or visitation proceedings

A. In any child custody or visitation proceeding, the court, upon its own motion, upon motion of any parent or party, or upon motion of the child, may appoint an attorney to represent the child if, after a contradictory hearing, the court determines such appointment would be in the best interest of the child. In determining the best interest of the child, the court shall consider:

(1) Whether the child custody or visitation proceeding is exceptionally intense or protracted.

(2) Whether an attorney representing the child could provide the court with significant information not otherwise readily available or likely to be presented to the court.

(3) Whether there exists a possibility that neither parent is capable of providing an adequate and stable environment for the child.

(4) Whether the interests of the child and those of either parent, or of another party to the proceeding, conflict.

(5) Any other factor relevant in determining the best interest of the child.

B. The court shall appoint an attorney to represent the child if, in the contradictory hearing, any party presents a prima facie case that a parent or other person caring for the child has sexually, physically, or emotionally abused the child or knew or should have known that the child was being abused.

C. The order appointing an attorney to represent the child shall serve as his enrollment as counsel of record on behalf of the child.

D. Upon appointment as attorney for the child, the attorney shall interview the child, review all relevant records, and conduct discovery as deemed necessary to ascertain facts relevant to the child's custody or visitation.

R.S. 9:345—Cont'd

E. The appointed attorney shall have the right to make any motion and participate in the custody or visitation hearing to the same extent as authorized for either parent.

F. Any costs associated with the appointment of an attorney at law shall be apportioned among the parties as the court deems just, taking into consideration the parties' ability to pay. When the parties' ability to pay is limited, the court shall attempt to secure proper representation without compensation.

Acts 1993, No. 261, § 5, eff. Jan. 1, 1994.

R.S. 9:346

§ 346. Action for failure to exercise or to allow visitation, custody or time rights pursuant to court-ordered schedule; judgment and awards

A. An action for the failure to exercise or to allow child visitation, custody or time rights pursuant to the terms of a court-ordered schedule may be instituted against a parent. The action shall be in the form of a rule to show cause why such parent should not be held in contempt for the failure and why the court should not further render judgment as provided in this Section.

B. If the action is for the failure to exercise child visitation, custody or time rights pursuant to the terms of a court-ordered schedule, and the petitioner is the prevailing party, the defendant shall be held in contempt of court and the court shall award to the petitioner:

(1) All costs for counseling for the child which may be necessitated by the defendant's failure to exercise visitation, custody or time rights with the child.

(2) A reasonable sum for any actual expenses incurred by the petitioner by reason of the failure of the defendant to exercise rights pursuant to a court-ordered visitation, custody or time schedule.

(3) A reasonable sum for a caretaker of the child, based upon the hourly rate for caretakers in the community.

(4) All attorney fees and costs of the proceeding.

C. If the action is for the failure to allow child custody, visitation, or time rights pursuant to a court-ordered schedule, and the petitioner is the prevailing party, the defendant shall be held in contempt of court and the court shall award to the petitioner:

(1) A reasonable sum for any actual expenses incurred by the petitioner by the loss of his visitation, custody or time rights.

(2) Additional visitation, custody or time rights with the child equal to the time lost.

(3) All attorney fees and costs of the proceeding.

(4) All costs for counseling for the child which may be necessitated by the defendant's failure to allow visitation, custody, or time rights with the child.

D. The court may award a reasonable penalty to the petitioner against the defendant upon a finding that the failure to allow or exercise visitation, time or custody rights pursuant to the terms of a court-ordered visitation schedule was intended to harass the petitioner.

E. The court may award attorney fees and costs to the defendant if he is the prevailing party, based upon actual expenses incurred.

F. The court may require the prevailing party to submit proof showing the amounts to be awarded pursuant to this Section.

R.S. 9:346—Cont'd

G. It shall be a defense that the failure to allow or exercise child visitation rights pursuant to a court-ordered schedule was by mutual consent, beyond the control of the defendant, or for other good cause shown.

H. A pattern of willful and intentional violation of this Section, without good cause, may be grounds for a modification of a custody or visitation decree.

I. This Section applies to judicial orders involving sole or joint custody.

J. The action authorized by this Section shall be in addition to any other action authorized by law.

Added by Acts 2004, No. 519, § 1. Amended by Acts 2008, No. 671, § 2; Acts 2010, No. 277, § 1, eff. June 17, 2010.

R.S. 9:348

§ 348. Loss of visitation due to military service; compensatory visitation

A. As used in this Section, "active duty" shall mean a military service member under any of the following conditions:

(1) A service member on active duty pursuant to an executive order of the president of the United States, an act of the Congress of the United States, presidential recall, or the provisions of R.S. 29:7.

(2) A service member on orders including but not limited to annual training, active duty special work, or individual duty training.

(3) A service member on drill status.

(4) A service member subject to the Uniform Code of Military Justice or the Louisiana Code of Military Justice.

B. (1) When a service member on active duty is unable due to his military obligations to have visitation with a minor child as authorized by a court order, the service member may request a period of compensatory visitation with the child which shall be granted only if the court determines it is in the best interest of the child. Such compensatory visitation shall be negotiated, on a day-for-day basis for each day missed, for the number of compensatory days requested by the service member, not to exceed the total number of days missed. The custodial or domiciliary parent shall negotiate with the service member to develop an equitable schedule for the requested compensatory visitation.

(2)(a) If the parents cannot establish an equitable arrangement for compensatory visitation as required by this Section, the requesting parent may petition the court having jurisdiction to enforce the judicial order for visitation for a temporary alteration to the current visitation order by making an adjustment to require compensatory visitation for visitation days lost as a result of an obligation of active duty. The court may refer the parent to mediation under the provisions of R.S. 9:332.

(b) The court may render judgment for court costs against either party or may apportion such costs between the parties as it may consider equitable.

C. The provisions of this Section shall not apply if either party has a history of physically or sexually abusing a child.

Added by Acts 2006, No. 110, § 1.

SUBPART D. ACCESS TO RECORDS

R.S. 9:351

§ 351. Access to records of child

Notwithstanding any provision of law to the contrary, access to records and information pertaining to a minor child, including but not limited to medical, dental, and school records, shall not be denied to a parent solely because he is not the child's custodial or domiciliary parent.

Acts 1993, No. 261, § 5, eff. Jan. 1, 1994.

PART IV. POST–SEPARATION FAMILY VIOLENCE RELIEF ACT

R.S. 9:361

§ 361. Legislative findings

The legislature hereby reiterates its previous findings and statements of purpose set forth in R.S. 46:2121 and 2131 relative to family violence and domestic violence. The legislature further finds that the problems of family violence do not necessarily cease when the victimized family is legally separated or divorced. In fact, the violence often escalates, and child custody and visitation become the new forum for the continuation of the abuse. Because current laws relative to child custody and visitation are based on an assumption that even divorcing parents are in relatively equal positions of power, and that such parents act in the children's best interest, these laws often work against the protection of the children and the abused spouse in families with a history of family violence. Consequently, laws designed to act in the children's best interest may actually effect a contrary result due to the unique dynamics of family violence.

Added by Acts 1992, No. 1091, § 1.

R.S. 9:362

§ 362. Definitions

As used in this Part:

(1) "Abused parent" means the parent who has not committed family violence.

(2) "Court" means any district court, juvenile court, or family court having jurisdiction over the parents and/or child at issue.

(3) "Court-monitored domestic abuse intervention program" means a program, comprised of a minimum of twenty-six in-person sessions, that follows a model designed specifically for perpetrators of domestic abuse. The offender's progress in the program shall be monitored by the court. The provider of the program shall have all of the following:

(a) Experience in working directly with perpetrators and victims of domestic abuse.

(b) Experience in facilitating batterer intervention groups.

(c) Training in the causes and dynamics of domestic violence, characteristics of batterers, victim safety, and sensitivity to victims.

(4) "Family violence" includes but is not limited to physical or sexual abuse and any offense against the person as defined in the Criminal Code of Louisiana, except negligent injuring and defamation, committed by one parent against the other parent or against any of the children. Family

R.S. 9:362—Cont'd

violence does not include reasonable acts of self-defense utilized by one parent to protect himself or herself or a child in the family from the family violence of the other parent.

(5) "Injunction" means a temporary restraining order or a preliminary or a permanent court ordered injunction, as defined in the Code of Civil Procedure, which prohibits the violent parent from in any way contacting the abused parent or the children except for specific purposes set forth in the injunction, which shall be limited to communications expressly dealing with the education, health, and welfare of the children, or for any other purpose expressly agreed to by the abused parent. All such injunctions shall prohibit the violent parent, without the express consent of the abused parent, from intentionally going within fifty yards of the home, school, place of employment, or person of the abused parent and the children, or within fifty feet of any of their automobiles, except as may otherwise be necessary for court ordered visitation or except as otherwise necessitated by circumstances considering the proximity of the parties' residences or places of employment. Such injunctions shall be issued in the form of a Uniform Abuse Prevention Order and transmitted to the Louisiana Protective Order Registry, as required by this Part.

(6) "Sexual abuse" includes but is not limited to acts which are prohibited by R.S. 14:41, 42, 42.1, 43, 43.1, 43.2, 43.4, 78, 80, 81, 81.1, 81.2, 89 and 89.1.

(7) "Supervised visitation" means face-to-face contact between a parent and a child which occurs in the immediate presence of a supervising person approved by the court under conditions which prevent any physical abuse, threats, intimidation, abduction, or humiliation of either the abused parent or the child. The supervising person shall not be any relative, friend, therapist, or associate of the parent perpetrating family violence. With the consent of the abused parent, the supervising person may be a family member or friend of the abused parent. At the request of the abused parent, the court may order that the supervising person shall be a police officer or other competent professional. The parent who perpetrated family violence shall pay any and all costs incurred in the supervision of visitation. In no case shall supervised visitation be overnight or in the home of the violent parent.

Added by Acts 1992, No. 1091, § 1. Amended by Acts 1995, No. 888, § 1; Acts 1997, No. 1156, § 4; Acts 2014, No. 194, § 1; Acts 2014, No. 333, § 1.

R.S. 9:363

§ 363. Ordered mediation prohibited

Notwithstanding any other provision of law to the contrary, in any separation, divorce, child custody, visitation, child support, alimony, or community property proceeding, no spouse or parent who satisfies the court that he or she, or any of the children, has been the victim of family violence perpetrated by the other spouse or parent shall be court ordered to participate in mediation.

Added by Acts 1992, No. 1091, § 1.

R.S. 9:364

§ 364. Child custody; visitation

A. There is created a presumption that no parent who has a history of perpetrating family violence, as defined in R.S. 9:362, or domestic abuse, as defined in R.S. 46:2132, or has subjected any of his or her children, stepchildren, or any household member, as defined in R.S. 46:2132, to sexual abuse, as defined in R.S. 14:403, or has willingly permitted another to abuse any of his children or stepchildren, despite having the ability to prevent the abuse, shall be awarded sole or joint custody of

R.S. 9:364—Cont'd

children. The court may find a history of perpetrating family violence if the court finds that one incident of family violence has resulted in serious bodily injury or the court finds more than one incident of family violence.

B. The presumption shall be overcome only if the court finds all of the following by a preponderance of the evidence:

(1) The perpetrating parent has successfully completed a court-monitored domestic abuse intervention program as defined in R.S. 9:362, or a treatment program designed for sexual abusers, after the last instance of abuse.

(2) The perpetrating parent is not abusing alcohol or using illegal substances scheduled in R.S. 40:964.

(3) The best interest of the child or children, considering the factors listed in Civil Code Article 134, requires the perpetrating parent's participation as a custodial parent because of the other parent's absence, mental illness, substance abuse, or other circumstance negatively affecting the child or children.

C. The fact that the abused parent suffers from the effects of the abuse shall not be grounds for denying that parent custody.

D. If the court finds that both parents have a history of perpetrating family violence, custody shall be awarded solely to the parent who is less likely to continue to perpetrate family violence. In such a case, the court shall mandate completion of a court-monitored domestic abuse intervention program by the custodial parent. If necessary to protect the welfare of the child, custody may be awarded to a suitable third person pursuant to Civil Code Article 133, provided that the person would not allow access to a violent parent except as ordered by the court.

E. If the court finds that a parent has a history of perpetrating family violence, the court shall allow only supervised child visitation with that parent pursuant to R.S. 9:341.

F. If any court finds, by clear and convincing evidence, that a parent has sexually abused his or her child or children, the court shall prohibit all visitation and contact between the abusive parent and the children pursuant to R.S. 9:341.

Added by Acts 1992, No. 1091, § 1. Amended by Acts 1995, No. 888, § 1; Acts 2014, No. 194, § 1; Acts 2018, No. 412, § 2, eff. May 23, 2018.

R.S. 9:364.1

§ 364.1. Visitation with incarcerated parent

A. If the court authorizes visitation with an incarcerated parent, as part of such visitation order the court shall include restrictions, conditions, and safeguards as are necessary to protect the mental and physical health of the child and minimize the risk of harm to the child.

B. A court considering the supervised visitation of a minor child with an incarcerated parent shall consider the best interest of the child, including but not limited to:

(1) The length and quality of the prior relationship between the child and the parent.

(2) Whether the child is in need of guidance, enlightenment, or tutelage which can best be provided by the parent.

(3) The preference of the child if he is determined to be of sufficient maturity to express a preference.

R.S. 9:364.1—Cont'd

(4) The willingness of the relative to encourage a close relationship between the child and his parent or parents, including the willingness of the child's custodial parent, caretaker, or legal guardian to voluntarily take the child to the incarcerated parent's place of incarceration for supervised visitation.

(5) The mental and physical health of the child and the parent.

(6) The length of time that the child lived with the parent prior to the parent's incarceration.

(7) The desirability of maintaining the continuity of the relationship between the child and the incarcerated parent.

(8) The costs of travel and other expenses incurred by visitation at the place of incarceration, and who will bear responsibility for such costs.

(9) The effect upon the child of supervised visitation in the place of incarceration and the feasibility, if any, of alternative or additional use of technology for visitation pursuant to R.S. 9:357.

(10) Other testimony or evidence as the court may consider applicable.

Added by Acts 2014, No. 383, § 1.

R.S. 9:365

§ 365. Qualification of mental health professional

Any mental health professional appointed by the court to conduct a custody evaluation in a case where family violence is an issue shall have current and demonstrable training and experience working with perpetrators and victims of family violence.

Added by Acts 1992, No. 1091, § 1.

R.S. 9:366

§ 366. Injunctions

A. All separation, divorce, child custody, and child visitation orders and judgments in family violence cases shall contain an injunction as defined in R.S. 9:362. Upon issuance of such injunction, the judge shall cause to have prepared a Uniform Abuse Prevention Order as provided in R.S. 46:2136.2(C), shall sign such order, and shall immediately forward it to the clerk of court for filing on the day that the order is issued. The clerk of the issuing court shall transmit the Uniform Abuse Prevention Order to the Judicial Administrator's Office, Louisiana Supreme Court, for entry into the Louisiana Protective Order Registry, as provided in R.S. 46:2136.2(A), by facsimile transmission or direct electronic input as expeditiously as possible, but no later than the end of the next business day after the order is filed with the clerk of court. The clerk of the issuing court shall also send a copy of the Uniform Abuse Prevention Order, as provided in R.S. 46:2136.2(C), or any modification thereof, to the chief law enforcement officer of the parish where the person or persons protected by the order reside by facsimile transmission or direct electronic input as expeditiously as possible, but no later than the end of the next business day after the order is filed with the clerk of court. A copy of the Uniform Abuse Prevention Order shall be retained on file in the office of the chief law enforcement officer until otherwise directed by the court.

B. Any violation of the injunction, if proved by the appropriate standard, shall be punished as contempt of court, and shall result in a termination of all court–ordered child visitation.

Added by Acts 1992, No. 1091, § 1. Amended by Acts 1995, No. 888, § 1; Acts 2003, No. 750, § 3; Acts 2014, No. 317, § 1.

PART V. INJUNCTIONS AND INCIDENTAL ORDERS

R.S. 9:371

§ 371. Injunction against alienation or encumbrance; spouse's right to demand

A. In a proceeding for divorce, a spouse may obtain an injunction restraining or prohibiting the disposition or encumbrance of community property until further order of the court.

B. To be effective against a federally insured financial institution, an injunction granted under the provisions of this Section shall be served in accordance with the provisions of R.S. 6:285(C). An injunction granted pursuant to the provisions of this Section shall be effective only against accounts, safe deposit boxes, or other assets listed or held in the name of the following:

(1) One or both of the spouses named in the injunction.

(2) Another party or business entity specifically named in the injunction.

C. A federally insured financial institution shall not be liable for loss or damages resulting from its actions to comply with the injunction provided that the requirements of this Section have been met.

Added by Acts 1990, No. 1009, § 7, eff. Jan. 1, 1991. Amended by Acts 2012, No. 582, § 1.

R.S. 9:372

§ 372. Injunction against abuse; form; central registry

A. In a proceeding for divorce, a court may grant an injunction prohibiting a spouse from physically or sexually abusing the other spouse or a child of either of the parties.

B. Immediately upon rendering a decision granting relief provided in Subsection A of this Section, the judge shall cause to have prepared a Uniform Abuse Prevention Order, as provided in R.S. 46:2136.2(C), shall sign such order, and shall immediately forward it to the clerk of court for filing on the day that the order is issued.

C. The clerk of the issuing court shall transmit the Uniform Abuse Prevention Order to the Judicial Administrator's Office, Louisiana Supreme Court, for entry into the Louisiana Protective Order Registry, as provided in R.S. 46:2136.2(A), by facsimile transmission or direct electronic input as expeditiously as possible, but no later than the end of the next business day after the order is filed with the clerk of court. The clerk of the issuing court shall also send a copy of the Uniform Abuse Prevention Order, as provided in R.S. 46:2136.2(C), or any modification thereof, to the chief law enforcement officer of the parish where the person or persons protected by the order reside by facsimile transmission or direct electronic input as expeditiously as possible, but no later than the end of the next business day after the order is filed with the clerk of court. A copy of the Uniform Abuse Prevention Order shall be retained on file in the office of the chief law enforcement officer until otherwise directed by the court.

Added by Acts 1990, No. 1009, § 7, eff. Jan. 1, 1991. Amended by Acts 1997, No. 1156, § 4; Acts 2003, No. 750, § 3; Acts 2014, No. 317, § 1.

R.S. 9:372.1

§ 372.1. Injunction against harassment

In a proceeding for divorce, a court may grant an injunction prohibiting a spouse from harassing the other spouse.

Added by Acts 2003, No. 750, § 3.

R.S. 9:373

§ 373. Removal of personal property

A. In a proceeding for divorce, a court may grant an ex parte order requiring the sheriff or appropriate law enforcement officer to accompany a spouse to the family residence or another location designated by the court so that personal property specified in the order may be obtained by that spouse.

B. Personal property which may be obtained by a court order issued under this Section includes, but is not limited to, the following:

(1) Items of personal wearing apparel belonging to the petitioning spouse or belonging to any children in the custody of the spouse.

(2) Food and eating utensils necessary for the spouse or any children in the custody of the spouse.

(3) Any other item or items deemed necessary by the court for the safety or well-being of the spouse or any children in the custody of the spouse.

Added by Acts 1990, No. 1009, § 7, eff. Jan. 1, 1991.

R.S. 9:374

§ 374. Possession and use of family residence or community movables or immovables

A. When the family residence is the separate property of either spouse, after the filing of a petition for divorce or in conjunction therewith, the spouse who has physical custody or has been awarded temporary custody of the minor children of the marriage may petition for, and a court may award to that spouse, after a contradictory hearing, the use and occupancy of the family residence pending the partition of the community property or one hundred eighty days after termination of the marriage, whichever occurs first. In these cases, the court shall inquire into the relative economic status of the spouses, including both community and separate property, and the needs of the children, and shall award the use and occupancy of the family residence to the spouse in accordance with the best interest of the family. The court shall consider the granting of the occupancy of the family residence in awarding spousal support.

B. When the family residence is community property or is owned by the spouses in indivision, or the spouses own community movables or immovables, after or in conjunction with the filing of a petition for divorce or for separation of property in accordance with Civil Code Article 2374, either spouse may petition for, and a court may award to one of the spouses, after a contradictory hearing, the use and occupancy of the family residence and use of community movables or immovables pending partition of the property or further order of the court, whichever occurs first. In these cases, the court shall inquire into the relative economic status of the spouses, including both community and separate property, and the needs of the children, if any, and shall award the use and occupancy of the family residence and the use of any community movables or immovables to the spouse in accordance with the best interest of the family. If applicable, the court shall consider the granting of the occupancy of the family residence and the use of community movables or immovables in awarding spousal support.

C. A spouse who, in accordance with the provisions of Subsection A or B of this Section, uses and occupies or is awarded by the court the use and occupancy of the family residence, a community immovable occupied as a residence, or a community manufactured home as defined in R.S. 9:1149.2 and occupied as a residence, regardless of whether it has been immobilized, shall not be liable to the

R.S. 9:374—Cont'd

other spouse for rental for the use and occupancy, except as hereafter provided. If the court awards use and occupancy to a spouse, it shall at that time determine whether to award rental for the use and occupancy and, if so, the amount of the rent. The parties may agree to defer the rental issue for decision in the partition proceedings. If the parties agreed at the time of the award of use and occupancy to defer the rental issue, the court may make an award of rental retroactive to the date of the award of use and occupancy.

D. The court may determine whether a residence is separate or community property, or owned in indivision, in the contradictory hearing authorized under the provisions of this Section.

E. (1) In a proceeding for divorce or thereafter, a summary proceeding shall be undertaken by the court upon request of either party to allocate the use of community property, including monetary assets, bank accounts, savings plans, and other divisible movable property pending partition.

(2) The court shall determine allocation of community property after considering:

(a) The custody of the children and exclusive use and occupancy of the family residence.

(b) The total community property.

(c) The need of a spouse for funds to maintain a household prior to partition.

(d) The need of a spouse to receive legal representation during the course of the proceedings.

(3) Upon court order, each spouse shall provide the other a complete accounting of all allocated community property to demonstrate compliance with Civil Code Article 2369.3.

Added by Acts 1990, No. 1009, § 7, eff. Jan. 1, 1991. Amended by Acts 1995, No. 965, § 1; Acts 1997, No. 614, § 1; Acts 2001, No. 903, § 1; Acts 2001, No. 1082, § 1; Acts 2004, No. 668, § 1, eff. July 5, 2004; Acts 2008, No. 408, § 1; Acts 2009, No. 204, § 2.

R.S. 9:375

§ 375. Award of attorney fees

A. When the court renders judgment in an action to make executory past-due payments under a spousal or child support award, or to make executory past-due installments under an award for contributions made by a spouse to the other spouse's education or training, it shall, except for good cause shown, award attorney fees and costs to the prevailing party.

B. When the court renders judgment in an action to enforce child visitation rights it shall, except for good cause shown, award attorney fees and costs to the prevailing party.

Added by Acts 1990, No. 1009, § 7, eff. Jan. 1, 1991.

R.S. 9:572

§ 572. Person having parental authority; acts that may be performed without court approval

A person having parental authority may perform the following acts without court approval:

(1) Alienate any movable property of the minor if the sum to be received does not exceed fifteen thousand dollars.

(2) Encumber any property of the minor as security for his obligation if the secured obligation does not exceed fifteen thousand dollars.

R.S. 9:572—Cont'd

(3) Compromise a cause of action of the minor if the sum or value of the property to be paid or received does not exceed fifteen thousand dollars, excluding court costs, attorney fees, and other expenses.

(4) Make usual or customary donations of the corporeal, movable property of the minor, if the value of the minor's property transferred by the donation does not exceed one thousand dollars and the minor's property donated without court approval during parental authority does not exceed a total of fifteen thousand dollars.

(5) Obligate the minor if the obligation does not exceed fifteen thousand dollars.

Acts 2015, No. 260, § 3, eff. Jan. 1, 2016.

R.S. 9:2781

§ 2781. Open accounts; attorney fees; professional fees; open account owed to the state

A. When any person fails to pay an open account within thirty days after the claimant sends written demand therefor correctly setting forth the amount owed, that person shall be liable to the claimant for reasonable attorney fees for the prosecution and collection of such claim when judgment on the claim is rendered in favor of the claimant. Citation and service of a petition shall be deemed written demand for the purpose of this Section. If the claimant and his attorney have expressly agreed that the debtor shall be liable for the claimant's attorney fees in a fixed or determinable amount, the claimant is entitled to that amount when judgment on the claim is rendered in favor of the claimant. Receipt of written demand by the person is not required.

B. If the demand is forwarded to the person by first class mail to his last known address, a copy of the demand shall be introduced as evidence of written demand on the debtor.

C. If the demand is made by citation and service of a petition, the person shall be entitled to pay the account without attorney fees by delivering payment to the claimant or the claimant's attorney within ten days after service of the petition in city courts and fifteen days after service of the petition in all other courts.

D. For the purposes of this Section and Code of Civil Procedure Articles 1702 and 4916, "open account" includes any account for which a part or all of the balance is past due, whether or not the account reflects one or more transactions and whether or not at the time of contracting the parties expected future transactions. "Open account" shall include debts incurred for professional services, including but not limited to legal and medical services. For the purposes of this Section only, attorney fees shall be paid on open accounts owed to the state.

E. As used in this Section the following terms shall have the following meanings:

(1) "Person" means natural and juridical persons.

(2) "Reasonable attorney fees" means attorney fees incurred before judgment and after judgment if the judgment creditor is required to enforce the judgment through a writ of fieri facias, writ of seizure and sale, judgment debtor examination, garnishment, or other post-judgment judicial process.

F. If the judgment creditor incurs attorney fees after judgment on the principal demand associated with enforcement of the judgment, the judgment creditor may obtain judgment for those attorney fees and additional court costs by filing a rule to show cause along with an affidavit from counsel for the judgment creditor setting forth the attorney fees incurred. If the judgment debtor does not file with the court a memorandum in opposition at least eight days prior to the hearing on the rule, the court may award the attorney fees and court costs as prayed for without the necessity of

R.S. 9:2781—Cont'd

an appearance in court by counsel for the judgment creditor. The rule to show cause shall include notice to the judgment debtor of the consequences under this Subsection of not timely filing a memorandum in opposition. The amount of any post-judgment award of attorney fees and costs shall be added to the total to be recovered on the principal demand through any existing writ or garnishment proceedings.

Added by Acts 1976, No. 399, § 1. Amended by Acts 1977, No. 647, § 1; Acts 1981, No. 463, § 1; Acts 1983, No. 311, § 1; Acts 1985, No. 701, § 1; Acts 1986, No. 689, § 1; Acts 1987, No. 485, § 1; Acts 2001, No. 1075, § 1; Acts 2010, No. 695, § 1.

R.S. 9:2794

§ 2794. Physicians, dentists, optometrists, and chiropractic physicians; malpractice; burden of proof; jury charge; physician witness expert qualification

A. In a malpractice action based on the negligence of a physician licensed under R.S. 37:1261 et seq., a dentist licensed under R.S. 37:751 et seq., an optometrist licensed under R.S. 37:1041 et seq., or a chiropractic physician licensed under R.S. 37:2801 et seq., the plaintiff shall have the burden of proving:

(1) The degree of knowledge or skill possessed or the degree of care ordinarily exercised by physicians, dentists, optometrists, or chiropractic physicians licensed to practice in the state of Louisiana and actively practicing in a similar community or locale and under similar circumstances; and where the defendant practices in a particular specialty and where the alleged acts of medical negligence raise issues peculiar to the particular medical specialty involved, then the plaintiff has the burden of proving the degree of care ordinarily practiced by physicians, dentists, optometrists, or chiropractic physicians within the involved medical specialty.

(2) That the defendant either lacked this degree of knowledge or skill or failed to use reasonable care and diligence, along with his best judgment in the application of that skill.

(3) That as a proximate result of this lack of knowledge or skill or the failure to exercise this degree of care the plaintiff suffered injuries that would not otherwise have been incurred.

B. Any party to an action shall have the right to subpoena any physician, dentist, optometrist, or chiropractor for a deposition or testimony for trial, or both, to establish the degree of knowledge or skill possessed or degree of care ordinarily exercised as described in Subsection A of this Section without obtaining the consent of the physician, dentist, optometrist, or chiropractor who is going to be subpoenaed only if that physician, dentist, optometrist, or chiropractor has or possesses special knowledge or experience in the specific medical procedure or process that forms the basis of the action. The fee of the physician, dentist, optometrist, or chiropractor called for deposition or testimony, or both, under this Subsection shall be set by the court.

C. In medical malpractice actions the jury shall be instructed that the plaintiff has the burden of proving, by a preponderance of the evidence, the negligence of the physician, dentist, optometrist, or chiropractic physician. The jury shall be further instructed that injury alone does not raise a presumption of the physician's, dentist's, optometrist's, or chiropractic physician's negligence. The provisions of this Section shall not apply to situations where the doctrine of res ipsa loquitur is found by the court to be applicable.

D. (1) In a medical malpractice action against a physician, licensed to practice medicine by the Louisiana State Board of Medical Examiners under R.S. 37:1261 et seq., for injury to or death of a patient, a person may qualify as an expert witness on the issue of whether the physician departed

R.S. 9:2794—Cont'd

from accepted standards of medical care only if the person is a physician who meets all of the following criteria:

(a) He is practicing medicine at the time such testimony is given or was practicing medicine at the time the claim arose.

(b) He has knowledge of accepted standards of medical care for the diagnosis, care, or treatment of the illness, injury, or condition involved in the claim.

(c) He is qualified on the basis of training or experience to offer an expert opinion regarding those accepted standards of care.

(d) He is licensed to practice medicine by the Louisiana State Board of Medical Examiners under R.S. 37:1261 et seq., is licensed to practice medicine by any other jurisdiction in the United States, or is a graduate of a medical school accredited by the American Medical Association's Liaison Committee on Medical Education or the American Osteopathic Association.

(2) For the purposes of this Subsection, "practicing medicine" or "medical practice" includes but is not limited to training residents or students at an accredited school of medicine or osteopathy or serving as a consulting physician to other physicians who provide direct patient care, upon the request of such other physicians.

(3) In determining whether a witness is qualified on the basis of training or experience, the court shall consider whether, at the time the claim arose or at the time the testimony is given, the witness is board certified or has other substantial training or experience in an area of medical practice relevant to the claim and is actively practicing in that area.

(4) The court shall apply the criteria specified in Paragraphs (1), (2), and (3) of this Subsection in determining whether a person is qualified to offer expert testimony on the issue of whether the physician departed from accepted standards of medical care.

(5) Nothing in this Subsection shall be construed to prohibit a physician from qualifying as an expert solely because he is a defendant in a medical malpractice claim.

Added by Acts 1975, No. 807, § 1. Amended by Acts 1979, No. 545, § 1; Acts 1985, No. 709, § 1; Acts 1995, No. 821, § 1; Acts 1997, No. 623, § 1, eff. July 3, 1997; Acts 2003, No. 581, § 1, eff. June 27, 2003.

R.S. 9:2801

§ 2801. Partition of community property and settlement of claims arising from matrimonial regimes and co-ownership of former community property

A. When the spouses are unable to agree on a partition of community property or on the settlement of the claims between the spouses arising either from the matrimonial regime, or from the co-ownership of former community property following termination of the matrimonial regime, either spouse, as an incident of the action that would result in a termination of the matrimonial regime or upon termination of the matrimonial regime or thereafter, may institute a proceeding, which shall be conducted in accordance with the following rules:

(1)(a) Within forty-five days of service of a motion by either party, each party shall file a sworn detailed descriptive list of all community property, the fair market value and location of each asset, and all community liabilities. For good cause shown, the court may extend the time period for filing a detailed descriptive list. If a party fails to file a sworn detailed descriptive list timely, the other party may file a rule to show cause why its sworn detailed descriptive list should not be deemed to constitute a judicial determination of the community assets and liabilities. At the hearing of the rule to show cause, the court may either grant the request or, for good cause shown, extend the time

R.S. 9:2801—Cont'd

period for filing a sworn detailed descriptive list. If the court grants the request, no traversal shall be allowed.

(b) Each party shall affirm under oath that the detailed descriptive list filed by that party contains all of the community assets and liabilities then known to that party. Amendments to the descriptive lists shall be permitted. No inventory shall be required.

(2) Within sixty days of the date of service of the last filed detailed descriptive list, each party shall either traverse or concur in the inclusion or exclusion of each asset and liability and the valuations contained in the detailed descriptive list of the other party. For good cause shown, the court may extend the time period for a party to traverse or concur in the detailed descriptive list of the other party. The trial of the traverses may be by summary procedure. At the trial of the traverses, the court shall determine the community assets and liabilities; the valuation of assets shall be determined at the trial on the merits. The court, in its discretion, may by ordinary procedure try and determine at one hearing all issues, including those raised in the traverses.

(3) The court may appoint such experts pursuant to Articles 192 and 373 of the Louisiana Code of Civil Procedure as it deems proper to assist the court in the settlement of the community and partition of community property, including the classification of assets as community or separate, the appraisal of community assets, the settlement of the claims of the parties, and the allocation of assets and liabilities to the parties.

(4) The court shall then partition the community in accordance with the following rules:

(a) The court shall value the assets as of the time of trial on the merits, determine the liabilities, and adjudicate the claims of the parties.

(b) The court shall divide the community assets and liabilities so that each spouse receives property of an equal net value.

(c) The court shall allocate or assign to the respective spouses all of the community assets and liabilities. In allocating assets and liabilities, the court may divide a particular asset or liability equally or unequally or may allocate it in its entirety to one of the spouses. The court shall consider the nature and source of the asset or liability, the economic condition of each spouse, and any other circumstances that the court deems relevant. As between the spouses, the allocation of a liability to a spouse obligates that spouse to extinguish that liability. The allocation in no way affects the rights of creditors.

(d) In the event that the allocation of assets and liabilities results in an unequal net distribution, the court shall order the payment of an equalizing sum of money, either cash or deferred, secured or unsecured, upon such terms and conditions as the court shall direct. The court may order the execution of notes, mortgages, or other documents as it deems necessary, or may impose a mortgage or lien on either community or separate property, movable or immovable, as security.

(e) In the event that the allocation of an asset, in whole or in part, would be inequitable to a party, the court may order the parties to draw lots for the asset or may order the private sale of the asset on such terms and conditions as the court deems proper, including the minimum price, the terms of sale, the execution of realtor listing agreements, and the period of time during which the asset shall be offered for private sale.

(f) Only in the event that an asset cannot be allocated to a party, assigned by the drawing of lots, or sold at private sale, shall the court order a partition thereof by licitation. The court may fix the minimum bids and other terms and conditions upon which the property is offered at public sale. In the event of a partition by licitation, the court shall expressly state the reasons why the asset cannot be allocated, assigned by the drawing of lots, or sold at private sale.

R.S. 9:2801—Cont'd

B. Those provisions of a domestic relations order or other judgment which partitions retirement or other deferred work benefits between former spouses shall be considered interlocutory until the domestic relations order has been granted "qualified" status from the plan administrator and/or until the judgment has been approved by the appropriate federal or state authority as being in compliance with applicable laws. Amendments to this interlocutory judgment to conform to the provisions of the plan shall be made with the consent of the parties or following a contradictory hearing by the court which granted the interlocutory judgment. The court issuing the domestic relations order or judgment shall maintain continuing jurisdiction over the subject matter and the parties until final resolution.

C. In the absence of an agreement between the parties for an extension of time or the granting by the court of an extension for good cause, if a party fails to comply with any time limit provided in this Section, upon motion of the other party or upon its own motion, the court may award reasonable attorney fees and court costs to the other party for the filing of or the response to the motion. If the court rules, pursuant to Subparagraph (A)(1)(a) of this Section, that the other party's sworn detailed descriptive list be deemed to constitute the assets and liabilities of the community, then the court shall not award attorney fees and court costs to the other party.

Added by Acts 1982, No. 439, § 1. Amended by Acts 1986, No. 225, § 1; Acts 1992, No. 825, § 1; Acts 1993, No. 28, § 1; Acts 1995, No. 433, § 2; Acts 1995, No. 1008, § 1; Acts 1997, No. 35, § 2; Acts 2001, No. 493, § 1; Acts 2005, No. 415, § 1.

R.S. 9:2801.1

§ 2801.1. Community property; allocation and assignment of ownership

When federal law or the provisions of a statutory pension or retirement plan, state or federal, preempt or preclude community classification of property that would have been classified as community property under the principles of the Civil Code, the spouse of the person entitled to such property shall be allocated or assigned the ownership of community property equal in value to such property prior to the division of the rest of the community property. Nevertheless, if such property consists of a spouse's right to receive social security benefits or the benefits themselves, then the court in its discretion may allocate or assign other community property equal in value to the other spouse.

Added by Acts 2001, No. 642, § 1. Amended by Acts 2003, No. 1036, § 1.

R.S. 9:2801.2

§ 2801.2. Community property; valuation of goodwill

In a proceeding to partition the community, the court may include, in the valuation of any community-owned corporate, commercial, or professional business, the goodwill of the business. However, that portion of the goodwill attributable to any personal quality of the spouse awarded the business shall not be included in the valuation of a business.

Added by Acts 2003, No. 837, § 1. Amended by Acts 2004, No. 177, § 1.

R.S. 9:3150

§ 3150. Exclusiveness

This Chapter provides the exclusive remedies, warranties, and peremptive periods as between builder and owner relative to home construction and no other provisions of law relative to warranties

R.S. 9:3150—Cont'd

and redhibitory vices and defects shall apply. Nothing herein shall be construed as affecting or limiting any warranty of title to land or improvements.

Added by Acts 1986, No. 676, § 1. Amended by Acts 2003, No. 333, § 1.

Editor's Notes

Ciliberti v. Mistretta, 879 So.2d 789 (La. App. 1 Cir. 2004). Excellent and definitive discussion of the New Home Warranty Act (NHWA). Home buyer brought action against home seller for redhibition because the home purchased had a sewer blockage that made the house uninhabitable. Home seller filed third party demand against home builder for indemnity. The trial court dismissed the third party claim under the explicit terms of the NHWA indemnity and redhibition are not actions included in the Act. Both the home seller, who had purchased directly from the builder, and the home buyer were classified as "owners" under the Act so that the entire transaction was clearly subject to the provisions of the Act.

R.S. 9:3221

§ 3221. Assumption of responsibility by lessee; liability of owner

Notwithstanding the provisions of Louisiana Civil Code Article 2699, the owner of premises leased under a contract whereby the lessee assumes responsibility for their condition is not liable for injury caused by any defect therein to the lessee or anyone on the premises who derives his right to be thereon from the lessee, unless the owner knew or should have known of the defect or had received notice thereof and failed to remedy it within a reasonable time.

Amended by Acts 2004, No. 821, § 3, eff. Jan. 1, 2005.

R.S. 9:3500

§ 3500. Rates of legal and conventional interest; usury

A. Interest is either legal or conventional.

B. Legal interest is fixed at the following rates, to wit:

(1) At the rate fixed in R.S. 13:4202 on all sums which are the object of a judicial demand, whence this is called judicial interest; and

(2) On sums discounted at banks at the rate established by their charters.

C. (1) The amount of the conventional interest cannot exceed twelve percent per annum. The same must be fixed in writing; testimonial proof of it is not admitted in any case.

(2) Except in the cases herein provided, if any person shall pay on any contract a higher rate of interest than the above, as discount or otherwise, the same may be sued for and recovered within two years from the time of such payment.

(3)(a) The owner or discounter of any note or bond or other written evidence of debt for the payment of money, payable to order or bearer or by assignment, shall have the right to claim and recover the full amount of such note, bond, or other written evidence of debt and all interest not beyond twelve percent per annum interest that may accrue thereon, notwithstanding that the rate of interest or discount at which the same may be or may have been discounted has been beyond the rate of twelve percent per annum interest or discount.

(b) This provision shall not apply to the banking institutions of this state in operation under existing laws or to a consumer credit transaction as defined by the Louisiana Consumer Credit Law.

R.S. 9:3500—Cont'd

(4)(a) The owner of any promissory note, bond, or other written evidence of debt for the payment of money to order or bearer or transferable by assignment shall have the right to collect the whole amount of such promissory note, bond, or other written evidence of debt for the payment of money, notwithstanding such promissory note, bond, or other written evidence of debt for the payment of money may include a greater rate of interest or discount than twelve percent per annum; such obligation shall not bear more than twelve percent per annum after maturity until paid.

(b) This provision shall not apply to a consumer credit transaction as defined by the Louisiana Consumer Credit Law.

(c) Where usury is a defense to a suit on a promissory note or other contract of similar character, it is permissible for the defendant to show the usury whether same was given by way of discount or otherwise, by any competent evidence.

D. The provisions of this Article shall not apply to a loan made for commercial or business purposes or deferring payment of an obligation for commercial or business purposes.

C.C. art. 2924. Amended by Acts 1908, No. 68, § 1; Acts 1970, No. 315, § 1; Acts 1972, No. 454, § 9, eff. Jan. 1, 1973; Acts 1980, No. 402, § 2; Acts 1981, No. 574, § 1; Acts 1981, No. 639, § 1; Acts 1982, No. 142, § 1, eff. July 12, 1982; Acts 1984, No. 458, § 1; Acts 1987, No. 883, § 1; Acts 1989, No. 52, § 1; Acts 1989, No. 774, § 1, eff. July 9, 1989; Acts 1992, No. 1090, § 1, eff. Oct. 1, 1992; Acts 1997, No. 275, § 1, eff. June 17, 1997; Acts 1997, No. 1476, § 2, eff. Sept. 6, 1998. Redesignated from C.C. art. 2924 by Acts 2004, No. 743, § 2, eff. Jan. 1, 2005.

R.S. 9:5011

§ 5011. Privilege of succession creditor and particular legatee

A creditor of the succession of a deceased person has a privilege on all of the property left by the deceased, if the heirs or legatees have accepted the succession without an administration thereof. The creditor enjoys this privilege whether his claim is demandable or not, and whether it is liquidated or not.

A particular legatee who has not received the delivery of his legacy has a privilege on all of the property left by the deceased, if the residuary heirs or legatees have accepted the succession without an administration thereof.

The privileges provided by this section entitle the succession creditor to be paid out of the proceeds of the judicial sale of the property left by the deceased, and the particular legatee to compel the delivery of his legacy, with preference over the creditors of the heirs or legatees.

Added by Acts 1960, No. 31, § 5, eff. Jan. 1, 1961.

R.S. 9:5012

§ 5012. Privilege of creditor of heir or legatee

A creditor of an heir or residuary legatee who has accepted the succession of a deceased person without an administration thereof has a privilege on all of the property owned by the heir or legatee which was not acquired through the succession. The creditor enjoys this privilege whether his claim is demandable or not, and whether it is liquidated or not.

The privilege provided by this section entitles the creditor of the heir or residuary legatee to be paid out of the proceeds of the judicial sale of the property affected thereby, with preference over the succession creditors.

Added by Acts 1960, No. 31, § 5, eff. Jan. 1, 1961.

R.S. 9:5013

§ 5013. Effect of privileges

A. The privilege provided by R.S. 9:5011 or R.S. 9:5012, for a period of three months after the death of the deceased and whether recorded or not, shall affect the movables owned by the heirs or legatees at, but shall be subordinate to any mortgage granted or other privilege existing thereon prior to, the time the privilege to effect a separation of patrimony is sought to be enforced.

B. If the succession creditor, particular legatee, or creditor of the heir or legatee, as the case may be, files an affidavit of his claim for recordation in the mortgage office of the parish where the immovable property is situated within three months of the death of the deceased:

(1) The privileges provided by R.S. 9:5011 shall affect all immovables left by the deceased, including those alienated by the heirs or legatees, as provided by R.S. 9:5014; and

(2) The privilege provided by R.S. 9:5012 shall affect immovables not acquired through the succession and owned by the heir or legatee at, but shall be subordinate to any mortgage granted or other privilege existing thereon prior to, the time the privilege to effect a separation of patrimony is sought to be enforced.

Added by Acts 1960, No. 31, § 5, eff. Jan. 1, 1961.

R.S. 9:5014

§ 5014. Enforcement of privilege on immovables alienated by heirs or legatees

If an affidavit of his claim of privilege under R.S. 9:5011 has been filed for recordation as provided by R.S. 9:5013, a succession creditor or a particular legatee may enforce the privilege claimed against the immovable left by the deceased and alienated within three months of the death of the deceased, by a suit filed prior to the peremption of the inscription of his privilege against the then owner of the immovable and the heirs or legatees who have accepted the succession of the deceased.

Added by Acts 1960, No. 31, § 5, eff. Jan. 1, 1961.

R.S. 9:5015

§ 5015. Peremption of inscription of privilege of succession creditor or particular legatee

If no suit has been filed to enforce the privilege before, the inscription of either of the privileges provided by R.S. 9:5011 perempts three months from the date of any judgment of possession rendered without an administration of the succession of the deceased, or three months after the recordation of the privilege if the succession has not been opened judicially.

Added by Acts 1960, No. 31, § 5, eff. Jan. 1, 1961.

R.S. 9:5016

§ 5016. Peremption of inscription of privilege of creditor of heir or legatee

Unless the creditor institutes a suit to enforce his claim before, the inscription of the privilege provided by R.S. 9:5012 perempts three months after the date of any judgment of possession rendered without an administration of the succession of the deceased, or three months after the recordation of the privilege if the succession has not been opened judicially.

Added by Acts 1960, No. 31, § 5, eff. Jan. 1, 1961.

R.S. 9:5550

§ 5550. Definitions

The following words, phrases, and terms as used in this Part shall be defined and construed as follows:

(1) "Collateral mortgage" shall mean a mortgage that is given to secure a written obligation, such as a collateral mortgage note, negotiable or nonnegotiable instrument, or other written evidence of debt, that is issued, pledged, or otherwise used as security for another obligation. A collateral mortgage or collateral chattel mortgage may provide on its face that the mortgage is granted in favor of a designated mortgagee and any future holder or holders of the collateral mortgage note.

(2) "Vendor's privilege" shall mean a vendor's lien or vendor's privilege on immovable property that secures a written obligation, such as a collateral mortgage note, negotiable or nonnegotiable instrument, or other written evidence of debt.

Added by Acts 1989, No. 137, § 7, eff. Sept. 1, 1989. Amended by Acts 1991, No. 377, § 3, eff. Jan. 1, 1992.

R.S. 9:5551

§ 5551. Effective date of a collateral mortgage

A. A collateral mortgage becomes effective as to third parties, subject to the requirements of registry of the collateral mortgage, when a security interest is perfected in the obligation secured by the collateral mortgage in accordance with the provisions of Chapter 9 of the Louisiana Commercial Laws, R.S. 10:9–101 et seq.

B. A collateral mortgage takes its rank and priority from the time it becomes effective as to third parties. Once it becomes effective, as long as the effects of recordation continues in accordance with Articles 3328 through 3334 of the Civil Code, a collateral mortgage remains effective as to third parties (notwithstanding any intermediate period when the security interest in the secured obligation becomes unperfected) as long as the secured party or his agent or his successor retains possession of the collateral mortgage note or other written obligation, or the obligation secured by the mortgage otherwise remains enforceable according to its terms, by the secured party or his successor.

C. As long as the effects of registry of the collateral mortgage continue, in accordance with Articles 3328 through 3334 of the Civil Code, if there is a termination, remission, or release of possession of the written obligation, a collateral mortgage takes its rank and priority from the time a new security interest is perfected in the written obligation, regardless of whether the secured party is the original secured party, his successor, or a new or different secured party.

D. The provisions of this Section shall become effective on January 1, 1990.

Added by Acts 1989, No. 137, § 7, eff. Sept. 1, 1989; Acts 1989, No. 598, § 1, eff. Sept. 1, 1989. Amended by Acts 1990, No. 1079, § 3, eff. Sept. 1, 1990, at 12:01 A.M.; Acts 1991, No. 377, § 3, eff. Jan. 1, 1992; Acts 1995, No. 1087, § 3; Acts 2001, No. 128, § 4, eff. July 1, 2001 at 12:01 A.M.

R.S. 9:5552

§ 5552. Defenses to enforcement of a collateral mortgage

A. If the obligor of the written obligation that the collateral mortgage secures does not raise the following defenses or claim the extinction of the collateral mortgage, then the mortgagor may not raise as a defense to the enforcement or claim the extinction of the collateral mortgage for any cause,

R.S. 9:5552—Cont'd

other than forged signatures, based on the invalidity or unenforceability of the written obligation, or the extinction of the written obligation.

B. If neither the obligor of the written obligation that the collateral mortgage secures nor the mortgagor raises the following defenses or claims the extinction of the collateral mortgage, then, as long as the effects of registry continue in accordance with Article 3369 of the Civil Code, third persons may not raise as a defense to the enforcement or claim the extinction of the collateral mortgage for any cause, other than forged signatures, based on the invalidity or unenforceability of the written obligation, or the extinction of the written obligation.

Added by Acts 1989, No. 137, § 7, eff. Sept. 1, 1989.

R.S. 9:5553

§ 5553. Defenses to enforcement of a vendor's privilege

If the obligor of the written obligation that the vendor's privilege secures does not raise the following defenses or claim the extinction of the vendor's privilege, then, as long as the effects of recordation continue in accordance with Articles 3328 through 3334 of the Civil Code, third persons may not raise as a defense to the enforcement or claim the extinction of the vendor's privilege for any cause, other than forged signatures, based on: the invalidity of the written obligation; the extinction of the written obligation; or the lack of registry or any deficiency in registry of any transfer, assignment, or pledge of the written obligation from the original vendee.

Added by Acts 1989, No. 137, § 7, eff. Sept. 1, 1989; Acts 1989, No. 598, § 1, eff. Sept. 1, 1989. Amended by Acts 1995, No. 1087, § 3.

R.S. 9:5554

§ 5554. No requirement of registry of transfer, assignment, pledge, or security interest in or of the written obligation, collateral mortgage, or vendor's privilege

There is no requirement that there be registry of:

(1) Any evidence of pledge of the written obligation secured by a collateral mortgage or a vendor's privilege.

(2) Any transfer or assignment of the written obligation secured by a collateral mortgage or a vendor's privilege, or of the collateral mortgage or vendor's privilege.

(3) Any security interest in a collateral mortgage or vendor's privilege or written obligation secured by either.

Added by Acts 1989, No. 137, § 7, eff. Sept. 1, 1989. Amended by Acts 1990, No. 1079, § 3, eff. Sept. 1, 1990 at 12:01 A.M.

R.S. 9:5555

§ 5555. Executory process in the case of notes or other obligations not paraphed for identification with the mortgage

A. In accordance with Code of Civil Procedure Article 2636(8), there is no requirement that a note or other written obligation secured by a mortgage be paraphed for identification with the mortgage in order for the mortgagee to have the right to foreclose under the mortgage utilizing Louisiana executory process procedures. For purposes of executory process, the existence, amount,

R.S. 9:5555—Cont'd

terms, and maturity of the note or other written obligation not evidenced by an instrument paraphed for identification with the act of mortgage or privilege may be proved by affidavit or verified petition.

B. The affidavit or verified petition may be based upon personal knowledge or upon information and belief derived from the records kept in the ordinary course of business of the mortgagee, the creditor whose claim is secured by the privilege, or any other person. The affidavit or verified petition need not particularize or specifically identify the records or date upon which such knowledge, information or belief is based.

C. The affidavit shall be deemed to provide authentic evidence of the existence, amount, terms, and maturity of the obligation for executory process purposes.

Added by Acts 1991, No. 652, § 2, eff. Jan. 1, 1992. Amended by Acts 1993, No. 948, § 2, eff. Jan. 1, 1994; Acts 1995, No. 1087, § 3.

R.S. 9:5557

§ 5557. Obligation to grant release of mortgage

A. The provisions of this Section shall apply only to mortgages recorded prior to January 1, 2012.

B. Upon extinction of the mortgage, the mortgagor or his successor may request the mortgagee to provide a written act of release directing the recorder to erase the mortgage from his records. The mortgagee shall deliver the act of release to the mortgagor within sixty days of receiving the request. If the mortgagee fails to deliver the act timely and in a form susceptible of recordation, the mortgagor may, by summary proceedings instituted against the mortgagee in the parish where the mortgaged property is located, obtain a judgment ordering the mortgage to be erased from the records and for the costs, reasonable attorneys fees, and any damages he has suffered from the mortgagee's default.

C. This Section does not apply to a mortgage insofar as it secures payment of a note or other instrument paraphed for identification with the act of mortgage by the notary before whom it is executed.

Added by Acts 1991, No. 652, § 2, eff. Jan. 1, 1992. Amended by Acts 2011, No. 342, § 1, eff. Jan. 1, 2012.

R.S. 9:5604

§ 5604. Actions for professional accounting liability

A. No action for damages against any accountant duly licensed under the laws of this state, or any firm as defined in R.S. 37:71, whether based upon tort, or breach of contract, or otherwise, arising out of an engagement to provide professional accounting service shall be brought unless filed in a court of competent jurisdiction and proper venue within one year from the date of the alleged act, omission, or neglect, or within one year from the date that the alleged act, omission, or neglect is discovered or should have been discovered; however, even as to actions filed within one year from the date of such discovery, in all events such actions shall be filed at the latest within three years from the date of the alleged act, omission, or neglect.

B. The provisions of this Section are remedial and apply to all causes of action without regard to the date when the alleged act, omission, or neglect occurred. However, with respect to any alleged act, omission, or neglect occurring prior to September 7, 1990, actions must, in all events, be filed in a court of competent jurisdiction and proper venue on or before September 7, 1993, without regard to the date of discovery of the alleged act, omission, or neglect. The one-year and three-year periods of

R.S. 9:5604—Cont'd

limitation provided in Subsection A of this Section are peremptive periods within the meaning of Civil Code Article 3458 and, in accordance with Civil Code Article 3461, may not be renounced, interrupted, or suspended.

C. Notwithstanding any other law to the contrary, in all actions brought in this state against any accountant duly licensed under the laws of this state, or any firm as defined in R.S. 37:71, whether based on tort or breach of contract or otherwise arising out of an engagement to provide professional accounting service, the prescriptive and peremptive period shall be governed exclusively by this Section and the scope of the accountant's duty to clients and nonclients shall be determined exclusively by applicable Louisiana rules of law, regardless of the domicile of the parties involved.

D. The provisions of this Section shall apply to all persons whether or not infirm or under disability of any kind and including minors and interdicts.

E. The peremptive period provided in Subsection A of this Section shall not apply in cases of fraud, as defined in Civil Code Article 1953.

F. The peremptive periods provided in Subsections A and B of this Section shall not apply to any proceedings initiated by the State Board of Certified Public Accountants of Louisiana.

Added by Acts 1990, No. 683, § 1. Amended by Acts 1992, No. 611, § 1; Acts 1995, No. 190, § 1.

R.S. 9:5605

§ 5605. Actions for legal malpractice

A. No action for damages against any attorney at law duly admitted to practice in this state, any partnership of such attorneys at law, or any professional corporation, company, organization, association, enterprise, or other commercial business or professional combination authorized by the laws of this state to engage in the practice of law, whether based upon tort, or breach of contract, or otherwise, arising out of an engagement to provide legal services shall be brought unless filed in a court of competent jurisdiction and proper venue within one year from the date of the alleged act, omission, or neglect, or within one year from the date that the alleged act, omission, or neglect is discovered or should have been discovered; however, even as to actions filed within one year from the date of such discovery, in all events such actions shall be filed at the latest within three years from the date of the alleged act, omission, or neglect.

B. The provisions of this Section are remedial and apply to all causes of action without regard to the date when the alleged act, omission, or neglect occurred. However, with respect to any alleged act, omission, or neglect occurring prior to September 7, 1990, actions must, in all events, be filed in a court of competent jurisdiction and proper venue on or before September 7, 1993, without regard to the date of discovery of the alleged act, omission, or neglect. The one-year and three-year periods of limitation provided in Subsection A of this Section are peremptive periods within the meaning of Civil Code Article 3458 and, in accordance with Civil Code Article 3461, may not be renounced, interrupted, or suspended.

C. Notwithstanding any other law to the contrary, in all actions brought in this state against any attorney at law duly admitted to practice in this state, any partnership of such attorneys at law, or any professional law corporation, company, organization, association, enterprise, or other commercial business or professional combination authorized by the laws of this state to engage in the practice of law, the prescriptive and peremptive period shall be governed exclusively by this Section.

D. The provisions of this Section shall apply to all persons whether or not infirm or under disability of any kind and including minors and interdicts.

R.S. 9:5605—Cont'd

E. The peremptive period provided in Subsection A of this Section shall not apply in cases of fraud, as defined in Civil Code Article 1953.

Added by Acts 1990, No. 683, § 1. Amended by Acts 1992, No. 611, § 1.

Editor's Notes

Reeder v. North, 701 So.2d 1291 (La. 1997) holds that R.S. 9:5605 is absolutely peremptive and contra non valentem does not operate.

R.S. 9:5605.1

§ 5605.1. Theft of client funds; prescription

A. Notwithstanding the provisions of R.S. 9:5605, prescription of a claim of theft or misappropriation of funds of a client by the client's attorney shall be interrupted by the filing of a complaint with the Office of Disciplinary Counsel, Louisiana Attorney Disciplinary Board, by the client alleging the theft or misappropriation of the funds of the client.

B. The record of the hearing of the Office of Disciplinary Counsel, Louisiana Attorney Disciplinary Board, held to review the claim of theft or misappropriation of the funds of the client may be admissible as evidence in the civil action brought to recover the stolen or misappropriated funds, and in such action, the court may award reasonable attorney fees to the client.

Added by Acts 2003, No. 1154, § 1.

R.S. 9:5606

§ 5606. Actions for professional insurance agent liability

A. No action for damages against any insurance agent, broker, solicitor, or other similar licensee under this state, whether based upon tort, or breach of contract, or otherwise, arising out of an engagement to provide insurance services shall be brought unless filed in a court of competent jurisdiction and proper venue within one year from the date of the alleged act, omission, or neglect, or within one year from the date that the alleged act, omission, or neglect is discovered or should have been discovered. However, even as to actions filed within one year from the date of such discovery, in all events such actions shall be filed at the latest within three years from the date of the alleged act, omission, or neglect.

B. The provisions of this Section shall apply to all persons whether or not infirm or under disability of any kind and including minors and interdicts.

C. The peremptive period provided in Subsection A of this Section shall not apply in cases of fraud, as defined in Civil Code Article 1953.

D. The one-year and three-year periods of limitation provided in Subsection A of this Section are peremptive periods within the meaning of Civil Code Article 3458 and, in accordance with Civil Code Article 3461, may not be renounced, interrupted, or suspended.

Added by Acts 1991, No. 764, § 1. Amended by Acts 1999, No. 905, § 1.

R.S. 9:5607

§ 5607. Actions against a professional engineer, surveyor, professional interior designer, architect, real estate developer; peremptive periods

A. No action for damages against any professional engineer, surveyor, engineer intern, surveyor intern, or licensee as defined in R.S. 37:682, or any professional architect, landscape architect,

R.S. 9:5607—Cont'd

architect intern, or agent as defined in R.S. 37:141, or professional interior designer, or licensee as defined in R.S. 37:3171, or other similar licensee licensed under the laws of this state, or real estate developer relative to development plans which have been certified by a professional engineer or professional architect, whether based upon tort, or breach of contract, or otherwise arising out of an engagement to provide any manner of movable or immovable planning, construction, design, or building, which may include but is not limited to consultation, planning, designs, drawings, specifications, investigation, evaluation, measuring, or administration related to any building, construction, demolition, or work, shall be brought unless filed in a court of competent jurisdiction and proper venue at the latest within five years from:

(1) The date of registry in the mortgage office of acceptance of the work by owner; or

(2) The date the owner has occupied or taken possession of the improvement, in whole or in part, if no such acceptance is recorded; or

(3) The date the person furnishing such services has completed the services with regard to actions against that person, if the person performing or furnishing the services, as described herein, does not render the services preparatory to construction, or if the person furnishes such services preparatory to construction but the person furnishing such services does not perform any inspection of the work.

B. The provisions of this Section shall apply to all persons whether or not infirm or under disability of any kind and including minors and interdicts.

C. The five-year period of limitation provided for in Subsection A of this Section is a peremptive period within the meaning of Civil Code Article 3458 and in accordance with Civil Code Article 3461, may not be renounced, interrupted, or suspended.

D. The provisions of this Section shall take precedence over and supersede the provisions of R.S. 9:2772 and Civil Code Articles 2762 and 3545.

E. The peremptive period provided in Subsection A of this Section shall not apply in cases of fraud, as defined in Civil Code Article 1953.

F. The peremptive periods provided in Subsections A and B of this Section shall not apply to any proceedings initiated by the Louisiana Professional Engineering and Land Surveying Board or the State Board of Architectural Examiners.

Added by Acts 2003, No. 854, § 1. Amended by Acts 2006, No. 732, § 1.

R.S. 9:5608

§ 5608. Actions against home inspectors

A. No action for damages against any home inspector duly licensed under the laws of this state or against any home inspection company, whether based in tort, breach of contract, or otherwise, arising out of a home inspection or report performed or prepared by the home inspector shall be brought unless filed in a court of competent jurisdiction and proper venue within one year from the date the act, omission, or neglect is alleged to have occurred.

B. The prescriptive period provided in Subsection A of this Section shall not apply in cases of fraud, as defined in Civil Code Article 1953.

C. The prescriptive period provided in Subsection A of this Section shall not apply to any proceedings initiated by the Louisiana State Board of Home Inspectors.

R.S. 9:5608—Cont'd

D. The provisions of this Section shall not apply to the inspection of new homes which are subject to the provisions of R.S. 9:3141 et seq.

Added by Acts 2004, No. 437, § 1.

R.S. 9:5609

§ 5609. Contracts to buy or sell; peremption of the effect of recordation; prescription for actions

A. The effect of recording in the conveyance records of a contract to buy or sell an immovable shall cease one year from the date of its recordation, unless prior thereto one of the parties to the contract causes it to be reinscribed in the same manner as the reinscription of a mortgage as provided by Article 3362 of the Civil Code. Such a reinscription shall continue the effect of recordation for one year and its effect may be renewed from time to time thereafter in the same manner. Except as provided in Paragraph B, the effect of recordation shall thereafter cease upon the lapse of any continuous twelve-month period during which the contract is not reinscribed.

B. The filing of a notice of lis pendens of a suit to enforce a recorded contract to buy or sell the immovable that is then effective as provided in Paragraph A shall continue the effect of recordation in the manner and to the extent prescribed by Articles 3751 through 3753 of the Code of Civil Procedure, and reinscription of the contract shall thereafter not be required or have effect.

C. A contract recorded pursuant to Paragraph A shall be canceled from the records by the recorder upon the written request of any person after the effect of its inscription has ceased as herein provided or as provided by Article 3753 of the Code of Civil Procedure.

Added by Acts 2006, No. 701, § 1, eff. Aug. 15, 2007.

R.S. 9:5610

§ 5610. Actions against real estate appraisers, appraisal management companies, and real estate appraisal companies; prescriptive and peremptive periods

A. No action for damages against any real estate appraiser or appraisal management company duly licensed under the laws of this state, or against any real estate appraisal company, whether based in tort, breach of contract, or otherwise arising out of an agreement to perform real estate appraisal services or appraisal management company services, shall be brought unless filed in a court of competent jurisdiction and proper venue within one year from the date of the act, omission, or neglect, or within one year from the date that the alleged act, omission, or neglect is discovered or should have been discovered; however, even as to actions filed within one year from the date of such discovery, in all events such actions shall be filed at the latest within three years from the date of the act, omission, or neglect.

B. The provisions of this Section are remedial and apply to all causes of action without regard to the date when the alleged act, omission, or neglect occurred. However, with respect to any alleged act, omission, or neglect occurring prior to August 1, 2019, actions shall, in all events, be filed in a court of competent jurisdiction and proper venue on or before August 1, 2020, without regard to the date of discovery of the alleged act, omission, or neglect. The one-year period of limitation provided in Subsection A of this Section is prescriptive within the meaning of Civil Code Article 3447. The three-year period of limitation provided in Subsection A of this Section is a peremptive period within the meaning of Civil Code Article 3458 and, in accordance with Civil Code Article 3461, may not be renounced, interrupted, or suspended.

R.S. 9:5610—Cont'd

C. Notwithstanding any other law to the contrary, the prescriptive and peremptive period in all actions brought in this state against any real estate appraiser, appraisal management company, or real estate appraisal company shall be governed exclusively by the provisions of this Section.

D. The prescriptive period provided in Subsection A of this Section shall not apply in cases of fraud, as defined in Civil Code Article 1953.

E. The prescriptive period provided in Subsection A of this Section shall not apply to any proceedings initiated by the Louisiana Real Estate Appraisers Board.

Added by Acts 2019, No. 323, § 1, eff. Jan. 1, 2020.

Application; Actions Affected—Acts 2019, No. 323

Section 2 of Acts 2019, No. 323 provides:

"This Act shall not affect any action filed prior to the effective date of this Act."

Acts 2019, No. 323, is effective January 1, 2020.

R.S. 9:5622

§ 5622. Informalities in auction sales, two and five year prescription

All informalities of legal procedure connected with or growing out of any sale at public auction or at private sale of real or personal property made by any sheriff of the Parishes of this State, licensed auctioneer, or other persons authorized by an order of the courts of this State, to sell at public auction or at private sale, shall be prescribed against by those claiming under such sale after the lapse of two years from the time of making said sale, except where minors or interdicted persons were owners or part owners at the time of making it, and in the event of such ownership or part ownership by said minors or interdicted persons, the prescription thereon shall accrue after five years from the date of public adjudication or private sale thereof.

C.C. art. 3543. Amended by Acts 1932, No. 231; Acts 1960, No. 407, § 1. Redesignated as R.S. 9:5622 by Acts 1983, No. 173, § 2, eff. Jan. 1, 1984.

Editor's Notes

This section was redesignated as R.S. 9:5622 from C.C. art. 3543 by Acts 1983, No. 173, § 2, effective January 1, 1984.

R.S. 9:5628

§ 5628. Actions for medical malpractice

A. No action for damages for injury or death against any physician, chiropractor, nurse, licensed midwife practitioner, dentist, psychologist, optometrist, hospital or nursing home duly licensed under the laws of this state, or community blood center or tissue bank as defined in R.S. 40:1231.1(A), whether based upon tort, or breach of contract, or otherwise, arising out of patient care shall be brought unless filed within one year from the date of the alleged act, omission, or neglect, or within one year from the date of discovery of the alleged act, omission, or neglect; however, even as to claims filed within one year from the date of such discovery, in all events such claims shall be filed at the latest within a period of three years from the date of the alleged act, omission, or neglect.

B. The provisions of this Section shall apply to all persons whether or not infirm or under disability of any kind and including minors and interdicts.

R.S. 9:5628—Cont'd

C. The provisions of this Section shall apply to all healthcare providers listed herein or defined in R.S. 40:1231.1 regardless of whether the healthcare provider avails itself of the protections and provisions of R.S. 40:1231.1 et seq., by fulfilling the requirements necessary to qualify as listed in R.S. 40:1231.2 and 1231.4.

Added by Acts 1975, No. 808, § 1. Amended by Acts 1976, No. 214, § 1; Acts 1987, No. 915, § 1, eff. Sept. 1, 1987; Acts 1990, No. 501, § 1; Acts 1995, No. 818, § 1; Acts 1995, No. 983, § 1, eff. June 29, 1995; Acts 2001, No. 95, § 1.

Editor's Notes

See notes to C.C. art. 3462, supra. The one-year prescription of C.C. art. 3492 governs wrongful death actions for medical malpractice if victim dies after three-year period. Taylor v. Giddens, Sup.1993, 618 So.2d 834. The 3-year period is prescriptive, not peremptive, Hebert v. Drs. Memorial Hospital, 486 So.2d 717 (La. 1986).

Warren v. Louisiana Medical Mut. Ins. Co., 21 So.3d 186 (La. 2008). On rehearing the court implicitly overrules Giroir, 475 So.2d 1040 (La. 1985), and holds that the attempted late-adding of a survival claim and a wrongful death claim after prescriptive periods had run were prescribed and the relating-back effect of C.C.P. art. 1953 was inapplicable. It is emphasized that in Borel, 989 So.2d 42 (La. 2007), the court held that the provisions on suspension and prescription under the Medical Malpractice Act "apply to the exclusion of the general code articles on interruption of prescription against solidary obligors, just as the specific provisions of the Act regarding suspension of prescription applied to the exclusion of the general code article on interruption of prescription against joint tortfeasors under Borel." (This is long and complex litigation but the opinion gives a rather simple conclusion.)

Walker v. Bossier Medical Center, 873 So.2d 841 (La. App. 2 Cir. 2004). Writs granted, case remanded, per curiam, 894 So.2d 1095 (La. 2005). The three-year statutory prescription for medical malpractice claims was held to be an unconstitutional violation of due process for a patient who suffered from hepatitis C, a disease with a long latency period exceeding the prescriptive period. The court relied upon a footnote in Whitnell, 686 So.2d 23, in which the Supreme Court commented that it had not decided the constitutionality of R.S. 9:5628 as applied to long latency diseases.

Turner v. Willis Knighton Medical Center, 108 So.3d 60 (La. 2012). The Supreme Court found as a matter of law that prescription for the dismissal of a medical malpractice begins to run from the actual dismissal of the claim, rather than from the notice of dismissal. The ruling applies to the 90 day grace period continuing suspension of the prescriptive period on a medical malpractice action.

R.S. 9:5630

§ 5630. Actions by unrecognized successor against third persons

A. An action by a person who is a successor of a deceased person, and who has not been recognized as such in the judgment of possession rendered by a court of competent jurisdiction, to assert an interest in an immovable formerly owned by the deceased, against a third person, or his successors, who has acquired an interest in the immovable by onerous title from a person recognized as an heir or legatee of the deceased in the judgment of possession is prescribed in two years from the date of the rendering of the judgment of possession.

B. This Section establishes a liberative prescription, and shall be applied both retrospectively and prospectively; however, any person whose rights would be adversely affected by this Section, shall have one year from the effective date of this Section within which to assert the action described in Subsection A of this Section and if no such action is instituted within that time, such claim shall be forever barred.

C. "Third person" means a person other than one recognized as an heir or legatee of the deceased in the judgment of possession.

R.S. 9:5630—Cont'd

D. For the purposes of this Section, after thirty years from the date of recordation of a judgment of possession there shall be a conclusive presumption that the judgment was rendered by a court of competent jurisdiction.

Added by Acts 1981, No. 721, § 1. Amended by Acts 1982, No. 37, § 1; Acts 1984, No. 394, § 1, eff. July 6, 1984; Acts 1988, No. 312, § 1; Acts 2018, No. 122, § 1.

R.S. 9:5642

§ 5642. Sheriffs' deeds

Actions to set aside sheriffs' deeds are prescribed by five years, reckoning from their date. This prescription applies only where the owner knew that the sheriff was proceeding to sell his property and where the purchaser or those claiming under him went into possession under the deed and remained in actual, open, and peaceable possession as owner for five years, and where the purchaser paid consideration for the property which was then paid over by the sheriff to the creditors of the real owner of the property.

This prescription does not apply to any attempted sale of property, not belonging to the defendant in execution, nor does it apply to minors and interdicts.

R.S. 9:5801

§ 5801. Involuntary dismissal; failure to timely request service of citation

Notwithstanding the provisions of Civil Code Article 2324(C), interruption is considered never to have occurred as to a person named as a defendant who is dismissed from a suit because service of citation was not timely requested and the court finds that the failure to timely request service of citation was due to bad faith. Nonetheless, as to any other defendants or obligors, an interruption of prescription, as provided in Civil Code Article 3463, shall continue.

Added by Acts 1997, No. 518, § 3, eff. Jan. 1, 1998.

Editor's Notes

See Bordelon v. Medical Center of Baton Rouge, No. 03-C-0202, La. S.Ct. October 21, 2003, for a definitive analysis of the consequences of failure to request service of process within 90 days of filing suit.

R.S. 9:5828

§ 5828. Purpose; ratification

A. The legislature finds that the COVID–19 public health emergency created a statewide emergency disrupting and forcing the closure of certain courts and public offices and further resulting in the displacement of courts, offices, clients, and counsel. This Part is enacted for the benefit and protection of the state as a whole and its citizens, and to prevent injustice, inequity, and undue hardship to persons who were prevented by the COVID–19 public health emergency from timely access to courts and offices in the exercise of their legal rights, including the filing of documents and pleadings as authorized or required by law. Therefore, this Part shall be liberally construed to effect its purposes.

R.S. 9:5828—Cont'd

B. The action of the governor of this state in issuing Proclamation Number JBE 2020–30 and any extensions thereof are hereby approved, ratified, and confirmed subject to the provisions of this Part.

Added by Acts 2020, No. 162, § 1, eff. June 9, 2020.

R.S. 9:5829

§ 5829. Suspension and extension of prescription and peremption; exceptions

A. All prescriptions, including liberative, acquisitive, and the prescription of nonuse, abandonment periods, and all peremptive periods shall be subject to a limited suspension or extension during the time period of March 17, 2020, through July 5, 2020; however, the suspension or extension of these periods shall be limited and shall apply only if these periods would have otherwise expired during the time period of March 17, 2020, through July 5, 2020. The right to file a pleading or motion to enforce any right, claim, or action which would have expired during the time period of March 17, 2020, through July 5, 2020, shall expire on July 6, 2020.

B. The provisions of Subsection A of this Section shall not apply to any matter concerning the prescription of nonuse applicable to mineral servitudes, mineral royalty interests, and executive rights which shall be governed by the Louisiana Mineral Code and are not subject to the suspension provisions in this Section.

Added by Acts 2020, No. 162, § 1, eff. June 9, 2020.

R.S. 9:5830

§ 5830. Suspension of legal deadlines; extension of legal deadlines; contradictory hearing

A. All deadlines in legal proceedings that were suspended by Proclamation Number JBE 2020–30 and any extensions thereof shall be subject to a limited suspension or extension until July 6, 2020; however, the suspension or extension of these deadlines shall be limited and shall apply only if these deadlines would have otherwise expired during the time period of March 17, 2020, through July 5, 2020. The right to file a pleading or motion to enforce any deadline in legal proceedings which would have expired during the time period of March 17, 2020, through July 5, 2020, shall expire on July 6, 2020.

B. Notwithstanding the provisions of Subsection A of this Section and to the extent that deadlines in legal proceedings were not suspended by Proclamation Number JBE 2020–30 and any extensions thereof, if a deadline in a legal proceeding lapsed during the time period of March 17, 2020, through July 5, 2020, a party shall have the right to seek an extension or suspension of that deadline by contradictory motion or declaratory judgment. The party seeking the extension shall bear the burden of proving that either the party or his attorney was adversely affected by the COVID–19 public health emergency and, but for the adverse effects of the COVID–19 public health emergency, the legal deadline would have been timely met. For good cause shown, the court shall extend the deadline in the legal proceeding, but in no instance shall the extension be later than September 1, 2020.

C. Notwithstanding Subsections A and B of this Section, legal deadlines related to matters set forth in Louisiana Civil Code Book III, Title IX, Chapters 1 through 5 and Louisiana Code of Civil Procedure Book VII, Title XI, Chapters 1 and 2 shall not be suspended or extended beyond the time period provided for by Proclamation Number JBE 2020–30 and any extensions thereof.

Added by Acts 2020, No. 162, § 1, eff. June 9, 2020.

R.S. 12:308

§ 308. Registered agent; registered office; principal business establishment; keeping of records by foreign corporation

A. Each foreign corporation authorized to transact business in this state shall have and continuously maintain in this state:

(1) At least one registered agent, which agent may be any of the following:

(a) An individual resident in this state whose business office is identical with the corporation's registered office.

(b) An individual attorney or a partnership which is authorized to practice law in this state.

(c) A domestic corporation, domestic limited liability company, foreign corporation, or foreign limited liability company authorized to transact business in this state, which has a business office identical with such registered office, which is authorized by its articles or certificate of incorporation or organization to act as the agent of a corporation for service of process, and which has on file with the secretary of state both a certificate or amended certificate setting forth the names of at least two individuals in such office, each of whom is authorized to receive any process served on it as such agent and a notarized affidavit of acknowledgement and acceptance signed by each registered agent. The failure to attach a notarized affidavit of acknowledgement and acceptance as required by this Section shall not be a defense to proper service of process on the corporation.

(2) A registered office, which may, but need not, be the same as its business office in this state.

B. (1) A foreign corporation authorized to transact business in this state may change its registered office, its registered agent, or its principal business establishment in this state, upon filing in the office of the secretary of state a statement setting forth:

(a) The name of the corporation.

(b) If the address of its registered office is to be changed, the address to which the registered office is to be changed.

(c) If its registered agent is to be changed, the name of its successor registered agent. Attached thereto shall be a notarized affidavit of acknowledgement and acceptance signed by the successor registered agent.

(d) If its registered agent is an individual or a corporation, that the address of its registered office and the address of the business office of its registered agent, as changed, will be identical.

(e) If the address of the principal business establishment is to be changed, the address to which such principal business establishment is to be changed.

(2) The statement shall be executed by the corporation by its president or a vice president, and acknowledged by him and delivered to the secretary of state. If only the address of the registered office is changed, the statement need only be executed by the registered agent. If the secretary of state finds that the statement conforms to the provisions of this Chapter, he shall file the statement in his office, and upon such filing, the change of address of the registered office, or the appointment of a new registered agent, as the case may be, shall become effective.

C. A similar statement executed by the registered agent shall be filed in like manner within thirty days after any change in the name of a corporate or partnership registered agent.

D. Any registered agent of a foreign corporation may resign as such agent upon filing a written notice of his resignation, executed in duplicate, with the secretary of state, who shall forthwith mail a copy thereof to the corporation at its principal business office address. The appointment of such

R.S. 12:308—Cont'd

agent shall terminate upon the expiration of thirty days after receipt of such notice by the secretary of state. If the registered agent resigns, or if for any other reason the corporation ceases to maintain a registered agent, a successor agent shall be appointed, under the procedure set forth in Subsection B of this Section, within thirty days after termination of the tenure of the former agent.

E. If the corporation's registered office should be vacated, a new office shall be designated, under the procedure set forth in Subsection (B) of this Section, within thirty days. If such designation is not made, the office of the secretary of state may thereafter be treated as the registered office of the corporation by any person other than the corporation itself.

F. Every corporation shall keep at its principal place of business in or outside the state, records in written form or in any other form capable of being converted into written form within a reasonable time, showing correct accounts of its properties and business transactions in this state. These records shall include accounts of its assets and liabilities, receipts and disbursements, and gains and losses and, if the corporation is engaged in this state in a business which will subject it to liability for state severance taxes, a complete account of all severances produced from its operations in this state. Such records may be in written form or in any other form capable of being converted into written form within a reasonable time.

G. The secretary of state may prescribe and furnish forms for filing the statement of change and agent resignation.

Acts 1968, No. 105, § 1, eff. Jan. 1, 1969. Amended by Acts 1970, No. 50, §§ 24, 25, emerg. eff. June 18, 1970 at 5:05 P.M.; Acts 1974, No. 477, § 3; Acts 1976, No. 458, § 1; Acts 1982, No. 526, § 2, eff. Aug. 11, 1982; Acts 1987, No. 769, § 1; Acts 2003, No. 366, § 1; Acts 2017, No. 367, § 1; Acts 2019, No. 19, § 2, eff. May 28, 2019.

R.S. 13:850

§ 850. Facsimile transmission; filings in civil actions; fees; equipment and supplies

A. Any document in a civil action may be filed with the clerk of court by facsimile transmission. All clerks of court shall make available for their use equipment to accommodate facsimile filing in civil actions. Filing shall be deemed complete at the time the facsimile transmission is received by the clerk of court. No later than on the first business day after receiving a facsimile filing, the clerk of court shall transmit to the filing party via facsimile a confirmation of receipt and include a statement of the fees for the facsimile filing and filing of the original document. The facsimile filing fee and transmission fee are incurred upon receipt of the facsimile filing by the clerk of court and payable as provided in Subsection B of this Section. The facsimile filing shall have the same force and effect as filing the original document, if the filing party complies with Subsection B of this Section.

B. Within seven days, exclusive of legal holidays, after the clerk of court receives the facsimile filing, all of the following shall be delivered to the clerk of court:

(1) The original document identical to the facsimile filing in number of pages and in content of each page including any attachments, exhibits, and orders. A document not identical to the facsimile filing or which includes pages not included in the facsimile filing shall not be considered the original document.

(2) The fees for the facsimile filing and filing of the original document stated on the confirmation of receipt, if any.

(3) A transmission fee of five dollars.

R.S. 13:850—Cont'd

C. If the filing party fails to comply with any of the requirements of Subsection B of this Section, the facsimile filing shall have no force or effect. The various district courts may provide by court rule for other matters related to filings by facsimile transmission.

D. The clerk may purchase equipment and supplies necessary to accommodate facsimile filings out of the clerk's salary fund.

Added by Acts 1991, No. 463, § 1. Amended by Acts 1995, No. 1119, § 1; Acts 2012, No. 826, § 1; Acts 2016, No. 109, § 1.

Uniform Child Custody Jurisdiction and Enforcement Act

SUBPART A. GENERAL PROVISIONS

R.S. 13:1801

§ 1801. Short title

This Part may be cited as the Uniform Child Custody Jurisdiction and Enforcement Act.

Added by Acts 2006, No. 822, § 1, eff. Aug. 15, 2007.

R.S. 13:1802

§ 1802. Definitions

(1) "Abandoned" means left without provision for reasonable and necessary care or supervision.

(2) "Child" means an individual who has not attained eighteen years of age.

(3) "Child custody determination" means a judgment, decree, or other order of a court providing for the legal custody, physical custody, or visitation with respect to a child. The term includes a permanent, temporary, initial, and modification order. The term does not include an order relating to child support or other monetary obligation of an individual.

(4) "Child custody proceeding" means a proceeding in which legal custody, physical custody, or visitation with respect to a child is an issue. The term includes a proceeding for divorce, separation, neglect, abuse, dependency, guardianship, paternity, termination of parental rights, and protection from domestic violence, in which the issue may appear. The term does not include a proceeding involving juvenile delinquency, contractual emancipation, or enforcement under Subpart C of this Part.

(5) "Commencement" means the filing of the first pleading in a proceeding.

(6) "Court" means an entity authorized under the law of a state to establish, enforce, or modify a child custody determination.

(7)(a) "Home state" means the state in which a child lived with a parent or a person acting as a parent for at least six consecutive months immediately before the commencement of a child custody proceeding. In the case of a child less than six months of age, the term means the state in which the child lived from birth with any of the persons mentioned. A period of temporary absence of any of the mentioned persons is part of the period.

(b) When a parent or a person acting as a parent is required to evacuate this state with a minor child because of an emergency or disaster declared under the provisions of R.S. 29:721 et seq., or declared by federal authority, and for an unforeseen reason resulting from the effects of such

R.S. 13:1802—Cont'd

emergency or disaster is unable to return to this state for an extended period of time, this state shall be determined to be the home state if the child lived with his parents, a parent, or a person acting as his parent for a period of at least twelve consecutive months immediately preceding the time involved.

(8) "Initial determination" means the first child custody determination concerning a particular child.

(9) "Issuing court" means the court that makes a child custody determination for which enforcement is sought under this Act.

(10) "Issuing state" means the state in which a child custody determination is made.

(11) "Modification" means a child custody determination that changes, replaces, supersedes, or is otherwise made after a previous determination concerning the same child, whether or not it is made by the court that made the previous determination.

(12) "Person" means an individual, corporation, business trust, estate, trust, partnership, limited liability company, association, joint venture, government, governmental subdivision, agency, or instrumentality, public corporation, or any other legal or commercial entity.

(13) "Person acting as a parent" means a person, other than a parent, who:

(a) Has physical custody of the child or has had physical custody for a period of six consecutive months, including any temporary absence, within one year immediately before the commencement of a child custody proceeding; and

(b) Has been awarded legal custody by a court or claims a right to legal custody under the laws of this state.

(14) "Physical custody" means the physical care and supervision of a child.

(15) "State" means a state of the United States, the District of Columbia, Puerto Rico, the United States Virgin Islands, or any territory or insular possession subject to the jurisdiction of the United States.

(16) "Tribe" means an Indian tribe or band, or Alaskan Native village, which is recognized by federal law or formally acknowledged by a state.

(17) "Warrant" means an order issued by a court authorizing law enforcement officers to take physical custody of a child.

Added by Acts 2006, No. 822, § 1, eff. Aug. 15, 2007.

R.S. 13:1803

§ 1803. Proceedings governed by other law

This Part does not govern an adoption proceeding or a proceeding pertaining to the authorization of emergency medical care for a child.

Added by Acts 2006, No. 822, § 1, eff. Aug. 15, 2007.

R.S. 13:1804

§ 1804. Application to Indian tribes

A. A child custody proceeding that pertains to an Indian child as defined in the Indian Child Welfare Act, 25 USC § 1901 et seq. is not subject to this Act to the extent that it is governed by the Indian Child Welfare Act.

R.S. 13:1804—Cont'd

B. A court of this state shall treat a tribe as if it were a state of the United States for the purpose of applying Subparts A and B of this Part.

C. A child custody determination made by a tribe under factual circumstances in substantial conformity with the jurisdictional standards of this Act shall be recognized and enforced under Subpart C of this Part.

Added by Acts 2006, No. 822, § 1, eff. Aug. 15, 2007.

R.S. 13:1805

§ 1805. International application

A. A court of this state shall treat a foreign country as if it were a state of the United States for the purpose of applying Subparts A and B of this Part.

B. Except as otherwise provided in Subsection C of this Section, a child custody determination made in a foreign country under factual circumstances in substantial conformity with the jurisdictional standards of this Act shall be recognized and enforced under Subpart C of this Part.

C. A court of this state need not apply this Act if the child custody law of a foreign country violates fundamental principles of human rights.

Added by Acts 2006, No. 822, § 1, eff. Aug. 15, 2007.

R.S. 13:1806

§ 1806. Effect of child custody determination

A child custody determination made by a court of this state that had jurisdiction under this Act binds all persons who have been served in accordance with the laws of this state or notified in accordance with R.S. 13:1808 or who have submitted to the jurisdiction of the court, and who have been given an opportunity to be heard. As to those persons, the determination is conclusive as to all decided issues of law and fact except to the extent the determination is modified.

Added by Acts 2006, No. 822, § 1, eff. Aug. 15, 2007.

R.S. 13:1807

§ 1807. Priority

If a question of existence or exercise of jurisdiction under this Act is raised in a child custody proceeding, the question, upon request of a party, shall be given priority on the calendar and handled expeditiously.

Added by Acts 2006, No. 822, § 1, eff. Aug. 15, 2007.

R.S. 13:1808

§ 1808. Notice to persons outside state

A. Notice required for the exercise of jurisdiction when a person is outside this state may be given in a manner prescribed by the law of this state for service of process or by the law of the state in which the service is made. Notice shall be given in a manner reasonably calculated to give actual notice but may be by publication if other means are not effective.

R.S. 13:1808—Cont'd

B. Proof of service may be made in the manner prescribed by the law of this state or by the law of the state in which the service is made.

C. Notice is not required for the exercise of jurisdiction with respect to a person who submits to the jurisdiction of the court.

Added by Acts 2006, No. 822, § 1, eff. Aug. 15, 2007.

R.S. 13:1809

§ 1809. Appearance and limited immunity

A. A party to a child custody proceeding, including a modification proceeding, or a petitioner or respondent in a proceeding to enforce or register a child custody determination, is not subject to personal jurisdiction in this state for another proceeding or purpose solely by reason of having participated, or of having been physically present for the purpose of participating, in the proceeding.

B. A person who is subject to personal jurisdiction in this state on a basis other than physical presence is not immune from service of process in this state. A party present in this state who is subject to the jurisdiction of another state is not immune from service of process allowable under the laws of that state.

C. The immunity granted by Subsection A of this Section does not extend to civil litigation based on acts unrelated to the participation in a proceeding under this Act committed by an individual while present in this state.

Added by Acts 2006, No. 822, § 1, eff. Aug. 15, 2007.

R.S. 13:1810

§ 1810. Communication between courts

A. A court of this state may communicate with a court in another state concerning a proceeding arising under this Act.

B. The court may allow the parties to participate in the communication. If the parties are not able to participate in the communication, they shall be given the opportunity to present facts and legal arguments before a decision on jurisdiction is made.

C. Communication between courts on schedules, calendars, court records, and similar matters may occur without informing the parties. A record need not be made of the communication.

D. Except as otherwise provided in Subsection C of this Section, a record shall be made of a communication under this Section. The parties shall be informed promptly of the communication and granted access to the record.

E. For the purposes of this Section, "record" means information that is inscribed on a tangible medium or that is stored in an electronic or other medium and is retrievable in perceivable form.

Added by Acts 2006, No. 822, § 1, eff. Aug. 15, 2007.

R.S. 13:1811

§ 1811. Taking testimony in another state

A. In addition to other procedures available to a party, a party to a child custody proceeding may offer testimony of witnesses who are located in another state, including testimony of the parties

R.S. 13:1811—Cont'd

and the child, by deposition or other means allowable in this state for testimony taken in another state. The court on its own motion may order that the testimony of a person be taken in another state and may prescribe the manner in which and the terms upon which the testimony is taken.

B. A court of this state may permit an individual residing in another state to be deposed or to testify by telephone, audiovisual means, or other electronic means before a designated court or at another location in that state. A court of this state shall cooperate with courts of other states in designating an appropriate location for the deposition or testimony.

C. Documentary evidence transmitted from another state to a court of this state by technological means that do not produce an original writing may not be excluded from evidence on an objection based on the means of transmission.

Added by Acts 2006, No. 822, § 1, eff. Aug. 15, 2007.

R.S. 13:1812

§ 1812. Cooperation between courts; preservation of records

A. A court of this state may request the appropriate court of another state to:

(1) Hold an evidentiary hearing.

(2) Order a person to produce or give evidence pursuant to procedures of that state.

(3) Order that an evaluation be made with respect to the custody of a child involved in a pending proceeding.

(4) Forward to the court of this state a certified copy of the transcript of the record of the hearing, the evidence otherwise presented, and any evaluation prepared in compliance with the request.

(5) Order a party to a child custody proceeding or any person having physical custody of the child to appear in the proceeding with or without the child.

B. Upon request of a court of another state, a court of this state may hold a hearing or enter an order described in Subsection A of this Section.

C. Travel and other necessary and reasonable expenses incurred under Subsections A and B of this Section may be assessed against the parties according to the law of this state.

D. A court of this state shall preserve the pleadings, orders, decrees, records of hearings, evaluations, and other pertinent records with respect to a child custody proceeding until the child attains eighteen years of age. Upon appropriate request by a court or law enforcement official of another state, the court shall forward a certified copy of those records.

Added by Acts 2006, No. 822, § 1, eff. Aug. 15, 2007.

SUBPART B. JURISDICTION

R.S. 13:1813

§ 1813. Initial child custody jurisdiction

A. Except as otherwise provided in R.S. 13:1816, a court of this state has jurisdiction to make an initial child custody determination only if:

(1) This state is the home state of the child on the date of the commencement of the proceeding, or was the home state of the child within six months before the commencement of the proceeding and

R.S. 13:1813—Cont'd

the child is absent from this state but a parent or person acting as a parent continues to live in this state, or had been the child's home state within twelve months before commencement of the proceeding and the child is absent from the state because he was required to leave or was evacuated due to an emergency or disaster declared under the provisions of R.S. 29:721 et seq., or declared by federal authority, and for an unforeseen reason resulting from the effects of such emergency or disaster was unable to return to this state for an extended period of time.

(2) A court of another state does not have jurisdiction or a court of the home state of the child has declined to exercise jurisdiction on the ground that this state is the more appropriate forum under R.S. 13:1819 or 1820; and

(a) The child and the child's parents, or the child and at least one parent or a person acting as a parent, have a significant connection with this state other than mere physical presence.

(b) Substantial evidence is available in this state concerning the child's care, protection, training, and personal relationships.

(3) All courts having jurisdiction have declined to exercise jurisdiction on the ground that a court of this state is the more appropriate forum to determine the custody of the child under R.S. 13:1819 or 1820; or

(4) No court of any other state would have jurisdiction under the criteria specified in Paragraph (1), (2), or (3) of this Subsection.

B. Subsection A of this Section is the exclusive jurisdictional basis for making a child custody determination by a court of this state.

C. Physical presence of, or personal jurisdiction over, a party or a child is not necessary or sufficient to make a child custody determination.

Added by Acts 2006, No. 822, § 1, eff. Aug. 15, 2007.

R.S. 13:1814

§ 1814. Exclusive, continuing jurisdiction

A. Except as otherwise provided in R.S. 13:1816, a court of this state which has made a child custody determination consistent with R.S. 13:1813 or 1815 has exclusive, continuing jurisdiction over the determination until:

(1) A court of this state determines that neither the child, nor the child and one parent, nor the child and a person acting as a parent have a significant connection with this state and that substantial evidence is no longer available in this state concerning the child's care, protection, training, and personal relationships; or

(2) A court of this state or a court of another state determines that the child, the child's parents, and any person acting as a parent do not presently reside in this state.

B. A court of this state which has made a child custody determination and does not have exclusive, continuing jurisdiction under this Section may modify that determination only if it has jurisdiction to make an initial determination under R.S. 13:1813.

Added by Acts 2006, No. 822, § 1, eff. Aug. 15, 2007.

R.S. 13:1815

§ 1815. Jurisdiction to modify determination

Except as otherwise provided in R.S. 13:1816, a court of this state may not modify a child custody determination made by a court of another state unless a court of this state has jurisdiction to make an initial determination under R.S. 13:1813(A)(1) or (2) and:

(1) The court of the other state determines it no longer has exclusive, continuing jurisdiction under R.S. 13:1814 or that a court of this state would be a more convenient forum under R.S. 13:1819; or

(2) A court of this state or a court of the other state determines that the child, the child's parents, and any person acting as a parent do not presently reside in the other state.

Added by Acts 2006, No. 822, § 1, eff. Aug. 15, 2007.

R.S. 13:1816

§ 1816. Temporary emergency jurisdiction

A. A court of this state has temporary emergency jurisdiction if the child is present in this state and the child has been abandoned or it is necessary in an emergency to protect the child because the child, or a sibling or parent of the child, is subjected to or threatened with mistreatment or abuse.

B. If there is no previous child custody determination that is entitled to be enforced under this Act and a child custody proceeding has not been commenced in a court of a state having jurisdiction under R.S. 13:1813 through 1815, a child custody determination made under this Section remains in effect until an order is obtained from a court of a state having jurisdiction under R.S. 13:1813 through 1815. If a child custody proceeding has not been or is not commenced in a court of a state having jurisdiction under R.S. 13:1813 through 1815, a child custody determination made under this Section becomes a final determination, if it so provides and this state becomes the home state of the child.

C. If there is a previous child custody determination that is entitled to be enforced under this Act, or a child custody proceeding has been commenced in a court of a state having jurisdiction under R.S. 13:1813 through 1815, any order issued by a court of this state under this Section shall specify in the order a period that the court considers adequate to allow the person seeking an order to obtain an order from the state having jurisdiction under R.S. 13:1813 through 1815. The order issued in this state remains in effect until an order is obtained from the other state within the period specified or the period expires.

D. A court of this state which has been asked to make a child custody determination under this Section, upon being informed that a child custody proceeding has been commenced in, or a child custody determination has been made by a court of a state having jurisdiction under R.S. 13:1813 through 1815, shall immediately communicate with the other court. A court of this state which is exercising jurisdiction pursuant to R.S. 13:1813 through 1815, upon being informed that a child custody proceeding has been commenced in, or a child custody determination has been made by a court of another state under a statute similar to this Section shall immediately communicate with the court of that state to resolve the emergency, protect the safety of the parties and the child, and determine a period for the duration of the temporary order.

Added by Acts 2006, No. 822, § 1, eff. Aug. 15, 2007.

R.S. 13:1817

§ 1817. Notice; opportunity to be heard; joinder

A. Before a child custody determination is made under this Act, notice and an opportunity to be heard in accordance with the standards of R.S. 13:1808 shall be given to all persons entitled to notice under the laws of this state as in child custody proceedings between residents of this state, any parent whose parental rights have not been previously terminated, and any person having physical custody of the child.

B. This Act does not govern the enforceability of a child custody determination made without notice or an opportunity to be heard.

C. The obligation to join a party and the right to intervene as a party in a child custody proceeding under this Act are governed by the laws of this state as in child custody proceedings between residents of this state.

Added by Acts 2006, No. 822, § 1, eff. Aug. 15, 2007.

R.S. 13:1818

§ 1818. Simultaneous proceedings

A. Except as otherwise provided in R.S. 13:1816, a court of this state may not exercise its jurisdiction under this Subpart if, at the time of the commencement of the proceeding, a proceeding concerning the custody of the child has been commenced in a court of another state having jurisdiction substantially in conformity with this Act, unless the proceeding has been terminated or is stayed by the court of the other state because a court of this state is a more convenient forum under R.S. 13:1819.

B. Except as otherwise provided in R.S. 13:1816, a court of this state, before hearing a child custody proceeding, shall examine the court documents and other information supplied by the parties pursuant to R.S. 13:1821. If the court determines that a child custody proceeding has been commenced in a court in another state having jurisdiction substantially in accordance with this Act, the court of this state shall stay its proceeding and communicate with the court of the other state. If the court of the state having jurisdiction substantially in accordance with this Act does not determine that the court of this state is a more appropriate forum, the court of this state shall dismiss the proceeding.

C. In a proceeding to modify a child custody determination, a court of this state shall determine whether a proceeding to enforce the determination has been commenced in another state. If a proceeding to enforce a child custody determination has been commenced in another state, the court may:

(1) Stay the proceeding for modification pending the entry of an order of a court of the other state enforcing, staying, denying, or dismissing the proceeding for enforcement;

(2) Enjoin the parties from continuing with the proceeding for enforcement; or

(3) Proceed with the modification under conditions it considers appropriate.

Added by Acts 2006, No. 822, § 1, eff. Aug. 15, 2007.

R.S. 13:1819

§ 1819. Inconvenient forum

A. A court of this state which has jurisdiction under this Act to make a child custody determination may decline to exercise its jurisdiction at any time if it determines that it is an

R.S. 13:1819—Cont'd

inconvenient forum under the circumstances and that a court of another state is a more appropriate forum. The issue of inconvenient forum may be raised upon motion of a party, the court's own motion, or request of another court.

B. Before determining whether it is an inconvenient forum, a court of this state shall consider whether it is appropriate for a court of another state to exercise jurisdiction. For this purpose, the court shall allow the parties to submit information and shall consider all relevant factors, including:

(1) Whether domestic violence has occurred and is likely to continue in the future and which state could best protect the parties and the child.

(2) The length of time the child has resided outside this state.

(3) The distance between the court in this state and the court in the state that would assume jurisdiction.

(4) The relative financial circumstances of the parties.

(5) Any agreement of the parties as to which state should assume jurisdiction.

(6) The nature and location of the evidence required to resolve the pending litigation, including testimony of the child.

(7) The ability of the court of each state to decide the issue expeditiously and the procedures necessary to present the evidence.

(8) The familiarity of the court of each state with the facts and issues in the pending litigation.

C. If a court of this state determines that it is an inconvenient forum and that a court of another state is a more appropriate forum, it shall stay the proceedings upon condition that a child custody proceeding be promptly commenced in another designated state and may impose any other condition the court considers just and proper.

D. A court of this state may decline to exercise its jurisdiction under this Act if a child custody determination is incidental to an action for divorce or another proceeding while still retaining jurisdiction over the divorce or other proceeding.

Added by Acts 2006, No. 822, § 1, eff. Aug. 15, 2007.

R.S. 13:1820

§ 1820. Jurisdiction declined by reason of conduct

A. Except as otherwise provided in R.S. 13:1816, if a court of this state has jurisdiction under this Act because a person seeking to invoke its jurisdiction has engaged in unjustifiable conduct, the court shall decline to exercise its jurisdiction unless:

(1) The parents and all persons acting as parents have acquiesced in the exercise of jurisdiction;

(2) A court of the state otherwise having jurisdiction under R.S. 13:1813 through 1815 determines that this state is a more appropriate forum under R.S. 13:1819; or

(3) No court of any other state would have jurisdiction under the criteria specified in R.S. 13:1813 through 1815.

B. If a court of this state declines to exercise its jurisdiction pursuant to Subsection A of this Section, it may fashion an appropriate remedy to ensure the safety of the child and prevent a repetition of the unjustifiable conduct, including staying the proceeding until a child custody proceeding is commenced in a court having jurisdiction under R.S. 13:1813 through 1815.

R.S. 13:1820—Cont'd

C. If a court dismisses a petition or stays a proceeding because it declines to exercise its jurisdiction pursuant to Subsection A of this Section, it shall assess against the party seeking to invoke its jurisdiction necessary and reasonable expenses including costs, communication expenses, attorney fees, investigative fees, expenses for witnesses, travel expenses, and child care during the course of the proceedings, unless the party from whom fees are sought establishes that the assessment would be clearly inappropriate. The court may not assess fees, costs, or expenses against this state unless authorized by law other than this Act.

Added by Acts 2006, No. 822, § 1, eff. Aug. 15, 2007.

R.S. 13:1821

§ 1821. Information to be submitted to court

A. Subject to local law providing for the confidentiality of procedures, addresses, and other identifying information in a child custody proceeding, each party, in its first pleading or in an attached affidavit, shall give information, if reasonably ascertainable, under oath as to the child's present address or whereabouts, the places where the child has lived during the last five years, and the names and present addresses of the persons with whom the child has lived during that period. The pleading or affidavit shall state whether the party:

(1) Has participated, as a party or witness or in any other capacity, in any other proceeding concerning the custody of or visitation with the child and, if so, identify the court, the case number, and the date of the child custody determination, if any.

(2) Knows of any proceeding that could affect the current proceeding, including proceedings for enforcement and proceedings relating to domestic violence, protective orders, termination of parental rights, and adoptions and, if so, identify the court, the case number, and the nature of the proceeding.

(3) Knows the names and addresses of any person not a party to the proceeding who has physical custody of the child or claims rights of legal custody or physical custody of, or visitation with, the child and, if so, the names and addresses of those persons.

B. If the information required by Subsection A of this Section is not furnished, the court, upon motion of a party or its own motion, may stay the proceeding until the information is furnished.

C. If the declaration as to any of the items described in Paragraphs (1) through (3) of Subsection A is in the affirmative, the declarant shall give additional information under oath as required by the court. The court may examine the parties under oath as to details of the information furnished and other matters pertinent to the court's jurisdiction and the disposition of the case.

D. Each party has a continuing duty to inform the court of any proceeding in this or any other state that could affect the current proceeding.

E. If a party alleges in an affidavit or a pleading under oath that the health, safety, or liberty of a party or child would be jeopardized by disclosure of identifying information, the information shall be sealed and may not be disclosed to the other party or the public unless the court orders the disclosure to be made after a hearing in which the court takes into consideration the health, safety, or liberty of the party or child and determines that the disclosure is in the interest of justice.

Added by Acts 2006, No. 822, § 1, eff. Aug. 15, 2007.

R.S. 13:1822

§ 1822. Appearance of parties and child

A. In a child custody proceeding in this state, the court may order a party to the proceeding who is in this state to appear before the court in person with or without the child. The court may

R.S. 13:1822—Cont'd

order any person who is in this state and who has physical custody or control of the child to appear in person with the child.

B. If a party to a child custody proceeding whose presence is desired by the court is outside this state, the court may order that a notice given pursuant to R.S. 13:1808 include a statement directing the party to appear in person with or without the child and informing the party that failure to appear may result in a decision adverse to the party.

C. The court may enter any orders necessary to ensure the safety of the child and of any person ordered to appear under this Section.

D. If a party to a child custody proceeding who is outside this state is directed to appear under Subsection B of this Section or desires to appear personally before the court with or without the child, the court may require another party to pay reasonable and necessary travel and other expenses of the party so appearing and of the child.

Added by Acts 2006, No. 822, § 1, eff. Aug. 15, 2007.

SUBPART C. ENFORCEMENT

R.S. 13:1823

§ 1823. Definitions

A. "Petitioner" means a person who seeks enforcement of an order for return of a child under the Hague Convention on the Civil Aspects of International Child Abduction or enforcement of a child custody determination.

B. "Respondent" means a person against whom a proceeding has been commenced for enforcement of an order for return of a child under the Hague Convention on the Civil Aspects of International Child Abduction or enforcement of a child custody determination.

Added by Acts 2006, No. 822, § 1, eff. Aug. 15, 2007.

R.S. 13:1824

§ 1824. Enforcement under Hague Convention

Under this Subpart a court of this state may enforce an order for the return of the child made under the Hague Convention on the Civil Aspects of International Child Abduction as if it were a child custody determination.

Added by Acts 2006, No. 822, § 1, eff. Aug. 15, 2007.

R.S. 13:1825

§ 1825. Duty to enforce

A. A court of this state shall recognize and enforce a child custody determination of a court of another state if the latter court exercised jurisdiction in substantial conformity with this Act or the determination was made under factual circumstances meeting the jurisdictional standards of this Act and the determination has not been modified in accordance with this Act.

B. A court of this state may utilize any remedy available under other law of this state to enforce a child custody determination made by a court of another state. The remedies provided in this

R.S. 13:1825—Cont'd

Subpart are cumulative and do not affect the availability of other remedies to enforce a child custody determination.

Added by Acts 2006, No. 822, § 1, eff. Aug. 15, 2007.

R.S. 13:1826

§ 1826. Temporary visitation

A. A court of this state which does not have jurisdiction to modify a child custody determination may issue a temporary order enforcing:

(1) A visitation schedule made by a court of another state; or

(2) The visitation provisions of a child custody determination of another state that does not provide for a specific visitation schedule.

B. If a court of this state makes an order under Paragraph (2) of Subsection A of this Section, it shall specify in the order a period that it considers adequate to allow the petitioner to obtain an order from a court having jurisdiction under the criteria specified in Subpart B. The order remains in effect until an order is obtained from the other court or the period expires.

Added by Acts 2006, No. 822, § 1, eff. Aug. 15, 2007.

R.S. 13:1827

§ 1827. Registration of child custody determination

A. A child custody determination issued by a court of another state may be registered in this state, with or without a simultaneous request for enforcement, by sending to the appropriate court in this state:

(1) A letter or other document requesting registration.

(2) Two copies, including one certified copy, of the determination sought to be registered and a statement under penalty of perjury that to the best of the knowledge and belief of the person seeking registration, the order has not been modified.

(3) Except as otherwise provided in R.S. 13:1821, the name and address of the person seeking registration and any parent or person acting as a parent who has been awarded custody or visitation in the child custody determination sought to be registered.

B. On receipt of the documents required by Subsection A of this Section, the registering court shall:

(1) Cause the determination to be filed as a foreign judgment, together with one copy of any accompanying documents and information, regardless of their form.

(2) Serve notice upon the persons named pursuant to Paragraph (3) of Subsection A of this Section and provide them with an opportunity to contest the registration in accordance with this Section.

C. The notice required by Paragraph (2) of Subsection B of this Section shall state that:

(1) A registered determination is enforceable as of the date of the registration in the same manner as a determination issued by a court of this state.

(2) A hearing to contest the validity of the registered determination shall be requested within twenty days after service of notice.

R.S. 13:1827—Cont'd

(3) Failure to contest the registration will result in confirmation of the child custody determination and preclude further contest of that determination with respect to any matter that could have been asserted.

D. A person seeking to contest the validity of a registered order shall request a hearing within twenty days after service of the notice. At that hearing, the court shall confirm the registered order unless the person contesting registration establishes that:

(1) The issuing court did not have jurisdiction under Subpart B;

(2) The child custody determination sought to be registered has been vacated, stayed, or modified by a court having jurisdiction to do so under Subpart B; or

(3) The person contesting registration was entitled to notice, but notice was not given in accordance with the standards of R.S. 13:1808, in the proceedings before the court that issued the order for which registration is sought.

E. If a timely request for a hearing to contest the validity of the registration is not made, the registration is confirmed as a matter of law and the person requesting registration and all persons served shall be notified of the confirmation.

F. Confirmation of a registered order, whether by operation of law or after notice and hearing, precludes further contest of the order with respect to any matter that could have been asserted at the time of registration.

Added by Acts 2006, No. 822, § 1, eff. Aug. 15, 2007.

R.S. 13:1828

§ 1828. Enforcement of registered determination

A. A court of this state may grant any relief normally available under the law of this state to enforce a registered child custody determination made by a court of another state.

B. A court of this state shall recognize and enforce, but may not modify, except in accordance with Subpart B, a registered child custody determination of a court of another state.

Added by Acts 2006, No. 822, § 1, eff. Aug. 15, 2007.

R.S. 13:1829

§ 1829. Simultaneous proceedings

If a proceeding for enforcement under this Subpart is commenced in a court of this state and the court determines that a proceeding to modify the determination is pending in a court of another state having jurisdiction to modify the determination under Subpart B, the enforcing court shall immediately communicate with the modifying court. The proceeding for enforcement continues unless the enforcing court, after consultation with the modifying court, stays or dismisses the proceeding.

Added by Acts 2006, No. 822, § 1, eff. Aug. 15, 2007.

R.S. 13:1830

§ 1830. Expedited enforcement of child custody determination

A. A petition under this Subpart shall be verified. Certified copies of all orders sought to be enforced and of any order confirming registration shall be attached to the petition. A copy of a certified copy of an order may be attached instead of the original.

R.S. 13:1830—Cont'd

B. A petition for enforcement of a child custody determination shall state:

(1) Whether the court that issued the determination identified the jurisdictional basis it relied upon in exercising jurisdiction and, if so, what the basis was.

(2) Whether the determination for which enforcement is sought has been vacated, stayed, or modified by a court whose decision shall be enforced under this Act and, if so, identify the court, the case number, and the nature of the proceeding.

(3) Whether any proceeding has been commenced that could affect the current proceeding, including proceedings relating to domestic violence, protective orders, termination of parental rights, and adoptions and, if so, identify the court, the case number, and the nature of the proceeding.

(4) The present physical address of the child and the respondent if known.

(5) Whether relief in addition to the immediate physical custody of the child and attorney fees are sought, including a request for assistance from law enforcement officials and, if so, the relief sought.

(6) If the child custody determination has been registered and confirmed under R.S. 13:1827, the date and place of registration.

C. Upon the filing of a petition, the court shall issue an order directing the respondent to appear in person with or without the child at a hearing and may enter any order necessary to ensure the safety of the parties and the child. The hearing shall be held on the next judicial day after service of the order unless that date is impossible. In that event, the court shall hold the hearing on the first judicial day possible. The court may extend the date of hearing at the request of the petitioner.

D. An order issued under Subsection C of this Section shall state the time and place of the hearing and advise the respondent that at the hearing the court will order that the petitioner may take immediate physical custody of the child and the payment of fees, costs, and expenses under R.S. 13:1834, and may schedule a hearing to determine whether further relief is appropriate, unless the respondent appears and establishes that:

(1) The child custody determination has not been registered and confirmed under R.S. 13:1827 and that:

(a) The issuing court did not have jurisdiction under Subpart B;

(b) The child custody determination for which enforcement is sought has been vacated, stayed, or modified by a court having jurisdiction to do so under Subpart B; or

(c) The respondent was entitled to notice, but notice was not given in accordance with the standards of R.S. 13:1808, in the proceedings before the court that issued the order for which enforcement is sought; or

(2) The child custody determination for which enforcement is sought was registered and confirmed under R.S. 13:1827, but has been vacated, stayed, or modified by a court of a state having jurisdiction to do so under Subpart B.

Added by Acts 2006, No. 822, § 1, eff. Aug. 15, 2007.

R.S. 13:1831

§ 1831. Service of petition and order

Except as otherwise provided in R.S. 13:1833, the petition and order shall be served, by any method authorized by Louisiana law, upon respondent and any person who has physical custody of the child.

Added by Acts 2006, No. 822, § 1, eff. Aug. 15, 2007.

R.S. 13:1832

§ 1832. Hearing and order

A. Unless the court issues a temporary emergency order pursuant to R.S. 13:1816, upon a finding that a petitioner is entitled to immediate physical custody of the child, the court shall order that the petitioner may take immediate physical custody of the child unless the respondent establishes that:

(1) The child custody determination has not been registered and confirmed under R.S. 13:1827 and that:

(a) The issuing court did not have jurisdiction under Subpart B;

(b) The child custody determination for which enforcement is sought has been vacated, stayed, or modified by a court of a state having jurisdiction to do so under Subpart B; or

(c) The respondent was entitled to notice, but notice was not given in accordance with the standards of R.S. 13:1808, in the proceedings before the court that issued the order for which enforcement is sought; or

(2) The child custody determination for which enforcement is sought was registered and confirmed under R.S. 13:1827 but has been vacated, stayed, or modified by a court of a state having jurisdiction to do so under Subpart B.

B. The court shall award the fees, costs, and expenses authorized under R.S. 13:1834 and may grant additional relief, including a request for the assistance of law enforcement officials, and set a further hearing to determine whether additional relief is appropriate.

C. If a party called to testify refuses to answer on the ground that the testimony may be self-incriminating, the court may draw an adverse inference from the refusal.

D. A privilege against disclosure of communications between spouses and a defense of immunity based on the relationship of husband and wife or parent and child may not be invoked in a proceeding under this Subpart.

Added by Acts 2006, No. 822, § 1, eff. Aug. 15, 2007.

R.S. 13:1833

§ 1833. Warrant to take physical custody of child

A. Upon the filing of a petition seeking enforcement of a child custody determination, the petitioner may file a verified application for the issuance of a warrant to take physical custody of the child if the child is immediately likely to suffer serious physical harm or be removed from this state.

B. If the court, upon the testimony of the petitioner or other witness, finds that the child is imminently likely to suffer serious physical harm or be removed from this state, it may issue a warrant to take physical custody of the child. The petition shall be heard on the next judicial day after the warrant is executed unless that date is impossible. In that event, the court shall hold the hearing on the first judicial day possible. The application for the warrant shall include the statements required by R.S. 13:1830(B).

C. A warrant to take physical custody of a child shall:

(1) Recite the facts upon which a conclusion of imminent serious physical harm or removal from the jurisdiction is based.

(2) Direct law enforcement officers to take physical custody of the child immediately.

(3) Provide for the placement of the child pending final relief.

R.S. 13:1833—Cont'd

D. The respondent shall be served with the petition, warrant, and order immediately after the child is taken into physical custody.

E. A warrant to take physical custody of a child is enforceable throughout this state. If the court finds on the basis of the testimony of the petitioner or other witness that a less intrusive remedy is not effective, it may authorize law enforcement officers to enter private property to take physical custody of the child. If required by exigent circumstances of the case, the court may authorize law enforcement officers to make a forcible entry at any hour.

F. The court may impose conditions upon placement of a child to ensure the appearance of the child and the child's custodian.

Added by Acts 2006, No. 822, § 1, eff. Aug. 15, 2007.

R.S. 13:1834

§ 1834. Costs, fees, and expenses

A. The court shall award the prevailing party, including a state, necessary and reasonable expenses incurred by or on behalf of the party, including costs, communication expenses, attorney fees, investigative fees, expenses for witnesses, travel expenses, and child care during the course of the proceedings, unless the party from whom fees or expenses are sought establishes that the award would be clearly inappropriate.

B. The court may not assess fees, costs, or expenses against a state unless authorized by law other than this Act.

Added by Acts 2006, No. 822, § 1, eff. Aug. 15, 2007.

R.S. 13:1835

§ 1835. Recognition and enforcement

A court of this state shall accord full faith and credit to an order issued by another state and consistent with this Act which enforces a child custody determination by a court of another state unless the order has been vacated, stayed, or modified by a court having jurisdiction to do so under Subpart B.

Added by Acts 2006, No. 822, § 1, eff. Aug. 15, 2007.

R.S. 13:1836

§ 1836. Appeals

An appeal may be taken from a final order in a proceeding under this Subpart in accordance with expedited appellate procedures in other civil cases. Unless the court enters a temporary emergency order under R.S. 13:1816, the enforcing court may not stay an order enforcing a child custody determination pending appeal.

Added by Acts 2006, No. 822, § 1, eff. Aug. 15, 2007.

R.S. 13:1837

§ 1837. Role of prosecutor or public official

A. In a case arising under this Part or involving the Hague Convention on the Civil Aspects of International Child Abduction, the prosecutor or other appropriate public official may take any lawful

R.S. 13:1837—Cont'd

action, including resort to a proceeding under this Subpart or any other available civil proceeding to locate a child, obtain the return of a child, or enforce a child custody determination if there is:

(1) An existing child custody determination;

(2) A request to do so from a court in a pending child custody proceeding;

(3) A reasonable belief that a criminal statute has been violated; or

(4) A reasonable belief that the child has been wrongfully removed or retained in violation of the Hague Convention on the Civil Aspects of International Child Abduction.

B. A prosecutor or appropriate public official acting under this Section acts on behalf of the court and may not represent any party.

Added by Acts 2006, No. 822, § 1, eff. Aug. 15, 2007.

R.S. 13:1838

§ 1838. Role of law enforcement

At the request of a prosecutor or other appropriate public official acting under R.S. 13:1837, a law enforcement officer may take any lawful action reasonably necessary to locate a child or a party and assist a prosecutor or appropriate public official with responsibilities under R.S. 13:1837.

Added by Acts 2006, No. 822, § 1, eff. Aug. 15, 2007.

R.S. 13:1839

§ 1839. Costs and expenses

If the respondent is not the prevailing party, the court may assess against the respondent all direct expenses and costs incurred by the prosecutor or other appropriate public official and law enforcement officers under R.S. 13:1837 or 1838.

Added by Acts 2006, No. 822, § 1, eff. Aug. 15, 2007.

SUBPART D. MISCELLANEOUS PROVISIONS

R.S. 13:1840

§ 1840. Application and construction

In applying and construing this Part, consideration shall be given to the need to promote uniformity of the law with respect to its subject matter among states that enact it.

Added by Acts 2006, No. 822, § 1, eff. Aug. 15, 2007.

R.S. 13:1841

§ 1841. Severability clause

If any provision of this Act or its application to any person or circumstance is held invalid, the invalidity does not affect other provisions or applications of this Act which can be given effect without the invalid provision or application, and to this end the provisions of this Act are severable.

Added by Acts 2006, No. 822, § 1, eff. Aug. 15, 2007.

R.S. 13:1842

§ 1842. Transitional provision

A motion or other request for relief made in a child custody proceeding or to enforce a child custody determination which was commenced before August 15, 2007 is governed by the law in effect at the time the motion or other request was made.

Added by Acts 2006, No. 822, § 1, eff. Aug. 15, 2007.

R.S. 13:3041

§ 3041. Qualifications of juror in civil cases

A. It is the policy of this state that all qualified citizens have an obligation to serve on petit juries when summoned by the courts of this state, unless excused.

B. The qualifications of a juror in any civil case are as required by Article 401 of the Louisiana Code of Criminal Procedure.

C. The court may disqualify a prospective petit juror in accordance with Article 787 of the Louisiana Code of Criminal Procedure.

Amended by Acts 1966, No. 313, § 1, eff. Jan. 1, 1967; Acts 2003, No. 678, § 1, eff. Aug. 15, 2003.

Editor's Notes

See R.S. 13:3041, et seq., for full text.

R.S. 13:3201

§ 3201. Personal jurisdiction over nonresidents

A. A court may exercise personal jurisdiction over a nonresident, who acts directly or by an agent, as to a cause of action arising from any one of the following activities performed by the nonresident:

(1) Transacting any business in this state.

(2) Contracting to supply services or things in this state.

(3) Causing injury or damage by an offense or quasi offense committed through an act or omission in this state.

(4) Causing injury or damage in this state by an offense or quasi offense committed through an act or omission outside of this state if he regularly does or solicits business, or engages in any other persistent course of conduct, or derives revenue from goods used or consumed or services rendered in this state.

(5) Having an interest in, using or possessing a real right on immovable property in this state.

(6) Non-support of a child, parent, or spouse or a former spouse domiciled in this state to whom an obligation of support is owed and with whom the nonresident formerly resided in this state.

(7) Parentage and support of a child who was conceived by the nonresident while he resided in or was in this state.

(8) Manufacturing of a product or component thereof which caused damage or injury in this state, if at the time of placing the product into the stream of commerce, the manufacturer could have

R.S. 13:3201—Cont'd

foreseen, realized, expected, or anticipated that the product may eventually be found in this state by reason of its nature and the manufacturer's marketing practices.

B. In addition to the provisions of Subsection A, a court of this state may exercise personal jurisdiction over a nonresident on any basis consistent with the constitution of this state and of the Constitution of the United States.

Added by Acts 1964, No. 47, § 3. Amended by Acts 1977, No. 734, § 1, eff. July 21, 1977; Acts 1980, No. 764, § 2; Acts 1984, No. 398, § 1; Acts 1987, No. 418, § 1; Acts 1988, No. 273, § 1.

Comment—1987

The addition of Subsection (B) to this statute ensures that the long-arm process extends to the limits allowed by due process, while retaining a valuable list of specific examples of contacts sufficient to give rise to in personam jurisdiction.

Editor's Notes

Burnham v. Sup. Ct. of California, 110 S.Ct. 2105 (1990) holds that a state may exercise personal jurisdiction over a defendant personally served with process while temporarily in that state, in a suit unrelated to his activities in that state.

In Sunrise Shipping v. Universal Maritime, 700 So.2d 1135 (La. App. 4 Cir. 1997) the court said that personal jurisdiction is a question of law, to be reviewed de novo. The two-part test is to determine, first, whether there are minimum contacts, and second, if so, the fairness of trying the defendant in the forum state. General jurisdiction applies when the cause of action against the defendant does not arise out of the defendant's contacts with the state; specific jurisdiction applies when the cause of action arises out of contacts with the state.

In Young v. Bichan Partnership, 709 So.2d 794, (La. App. 5 Cir. 1997) a resident seller maintained an action against a nonresident buyer for breach of contract. Minimum contacts and fairness were satisfied. (All minimum contact and jurisdiction jurisprudence is reviewed.)

R.S. 13:3203

§ 3203. Venue

A suit on a cause of action described in R.S. 13:3201 may be instituted in the parish where the plaintiff is domiciled, or in any parish of proper venue.

Added by Acts 1964, No. 47, § 3. Amended by Acts 1997, No. 1056, § 2.

R.S. 13:3204

§ 3204. Service of process

A. In a suit under R.S. 13:3201, a certified copy of the citation or the notice in a divorce under Civil Code Article 102 and of the petition or a certified copy of a contradictory motion, rule to show cause, or other pleading filed by the plaintiff in a summary proceeding under Code of Civil Procedure Article 2592 shall be sent by counsel for the plaintiff, or by the plaintiff if not represented by counsel, to the defendant by registered or certified mail, or actually delivered to the defendant by commercial courier, when the person to be served is located outside of this state or by an individual designated by the court in which the suit is filed, or by one authorized by the law of the place where the service is made to serve the process of any of its courts of general, limited, or small claims jurisdiction.

B. If service of process cannot be made on the nonresident by registered or certified mail or by actual delivery, the court shall order that service of process be made on an attorney at law appointed to represent the defendant pursuant to Code of Civil Procedure Article 5091.

R.S. 13:3204—Cont'd

C. Service of process so made has the same legal force and validity as personal service on the defendant in this state.

D. For purposes of this Section, a "commercial courier" is any foreign or domestic business entity having as its primary purpose the delivery of letters and parcels of any type, and which:

(1) Acquires a signed receipt from the addressee, or the addressee's agent, of the letter or parcel upon completion of delivery.

(2) Has no direct or indirect interest in the outcome of the matter to which the letter or parcel concerns.

Added by Acts 1964, No. 47, § 3. Amended by Acts 1989, No. 120, § 1; Acts 1992, No. 787, § 1; Acts 1995, No. 205, § 1; Acts 1995, No. 331, § 1; Acts 1995, No. 943, § 1; Acts 1999, No. 395, § 2; Acts 2003, No. 619, § 1.

R.S. 13:3205

§ 3205. Default judgment; hearings; proof of service of process

No default judgment may be rendered against the defendant and no hearing may be held on a contradictory motion, rule to show cause, or other summary proceeding, except for actions pursuant to R.S. 46:2131 et seq., until thirty days after the filing in the record of the affidavit of the individual who has done any of the following:

(1) Mailed the process to the defendant, showing that it was enclosed in an envelope properly addressed to the defendant, with sufficient postage affixed, and the date it was deposited in the United States mail, to which shall be attached the return receipt of the defendant.

(2) Utilized the services of a commercial courier to make delivery of the process to the defendant, showing the name of the commercial courier, the date, and address at which the process was delivered to the defendant, to which shall be attached the commercial courier's confirmation of delivery.

(3) Actually delivered the process to the defendant, showing the date, place, and manner of delivery.

Added by Acts 1964, No. 47, § 3. Amended by Acts 2003, No. 619, § 1; Acts 2007, No. 140, § 2; Acts 2017, No. 419, § 2; Acts 2021, No. 174, § 2, eff. Jan. 1, 2022.

Comments—2017

This Section has been amended to substitute "preliminary default or final default judgment" for "default judgment" to make the provision more easily understood and to make the terminology consistent with related Articles in the Code of Civil Procedure. These amendments are intended to be stylistic only.

Editor's Notes

In Collier v. Fugler, 694 So.2d 553 (La. App. 2 Cir. 1997) default judgment against a nonresident was annulled because the affidavit of service required by R.S. 13:2305 was insufficient to show compliance with the service of process requirements, described in R.S. 13:3204, under the Louisiana long-arm statute, R.S. 13:4301.

R.S. 13:3206

§ 3206. "Nonresident" as used in R.S. 13:3201 through 3207

As used in R.S. 13:3201 through 3207, "nonresident" includes an individual, his executor, administrator, or other legal representative, who at the time of the filing of the suit is not domiciled in

R.S. 13:3206—Cont'd

this state, or a partnership, association, or any other legal or commercial entity, other than a corporation, not then domiciled in this state, or a corporation or limited liability company which is not organized under the laws of, and is not then licensed to do business in, this state.

Added by Acts 1964, No. 47, § 3. Amended by Acts 1997, No. 1056, § 2; Acts 1999, No. 145, § 3.

R.S. 13:3207

§ 3207. R.S. 13:3201–13:3206 provide additional remedies; no conflict with certain code and statutory provisions

R.S. 13:3201 through 13:3206 provide additional remedies, and do not in any way affect, conflict with, modify, or repeal any code article or statute providing any other remedy, including without being limited to any of the provisions of the Louisiana Code of Civil Procedure, R.S. 13:3471(1), R.S. 13:3472, R.S. 13:3474 and 13:3475, R.S. 13:3479 through 13:3482, R.S. 13:3914, or R.S. 22:1269.

Added by Acts 1964, No. 47, § 3.

R.S. 13:3471

§ 3471. Supplementary rules of service of process

The following rules supplement those governing the service of citation and other legal process in a civil action or proceeding contained in the Code of Civil Procedure:

(1)(a) If the foreign corporation or the foreign limited liability company is not one required by law to appoint an agent for the service of process, but has engaged in a business activity in this state, service of process in an action or proceeding on a cause of action resulting from such business activity in this state, or for any taxes due or other obligations arising therefrom, may be made on any employee or agent of the corporation or limited liability company of suitable age and discretion found in the state.

(b) If such employees or agents are no longer in the state, or cannot be found after diligent effort, the officer charged with the duty of making the service shall make his return to the court, stating the efforts made by him to secure service and the reason why he was unable to do so. Thereupon the court shall order that service shall be made on the secretary of state, or on some other individual in his office whom the secretary of state may designate to receive service of process.

(c) The secretary of state shall ascertain the domiciliary post office address of the corporation, or limited liability company and shall send the original papers served to the corporation or limited liability company by registered or certified mail, or by commercial courier as defined in R.S. 13:3204(D), when the corporation or person to be served is located outside of this state. The secretary of state shall retain in his office true copies of these papers, on which he shall note the date, the manner and other particulars of the service, and of the disposition made of the original papers.

(2) In an action or proceeding brought in a parish other than that of the domicile of a defendant, citation and all other legal process may be served on this defendant in the parish where the action or proceeding was brought, if the defendant can be served therein. Otherwise, the process may be sent by the clerk of the court from which it issued to any parish where the defendant may be found, and service may be made by the sheriff or a constable of the latter parish.

(3) When an action or proceeding is brought in the parish of the domicile of a defendant, and the latter is absent therefrom, service may be made on him in any parish of the state where he may be found.

R.S. 13:3471—Cont'd

(4) An acceptance of service shall be dated, and if no date is shown thereon, the acceptance takes effect from the date of its filing in court. No acceptance of service shall affect the delays allowed by law or by the local rules of court.

(5) The return of the serving officer on any citation or other legal process is conclusive, unless directly attacked. Such an attack may be made by rule in the action or proceeding, if made prior to judgment. If made after judgment, the return may be attacked only in a direct action to annul the judgment, which may be brought in the original action or proceeding.

If the defendant was actually served, the court may correct an error in the return by an amendment thereof, on a rule brought against and tried contradictorily with the defendant who was served, or any other party who may be affected by the amendment.

(6) Service of process on an inmate of a public institution may be made by the sheriff or any constable of the parish where the institution is situated.

(7) Service of process by a sheriff or constable shall be returned into the court which issued the process as soon as possible after the service is made. In addition thereto, the serving officer shall keep a complete record thereof in a book specially provided for that purpose. If the original return is lost or destroyed, the entries in this book shall be received and recognized in lieu thereof, subject to the provisions of R.S. 13:3471(5).

(8) Subsequent to service of the original petition in any civil action or proceeding, service of pleadings, documents, or notices that may be served by mail or delivery on an attorney of record may also be made by transmitting a copy to the attorney by electronic means at the number or addresses for receipt of electronic service expressly designated in a pleading or other writing for receipt of electronic service. Service by electronic means is complete upon transmission but is not effective and shall not be certified if the serving party learns the transmission did not reach the attorney to be served.

Amended by Acts 1950, No. 21, § 1; Acts 1954, No. 142, § 1; Acts 1960, No. 32, § 1, eff. Jan. 1, 1961; Acts 1983, No. 125, § 1; Acts 1989, No. 524, § 1; Acts 1999, No. 145, § 3; Acts 1999, No. 395, § 2; Acts 2010, No. 185, § 2; Acts 2012, No. 544, § 2.

R.S. 13:3472

§ 3472. Service on foreign corporation through secretary of state

In any case where service on a foreign corporation may be made through the secretary of state, under any law heretofore or hereafter enacted, such service may be made in person on the secretary of state anywhere in the state. Should the secretary of state be absent from his office, service may be made on the assistant secretary of state, or on some other individual in the office of the secretary of state designated by the latter to receive service of process in his absence, and such service has the same effect as if made upon the secretary of state personally.

Amended by Acts 1960, No. 32, § 1, eff. Jan. 1, 1961.

R.S. 13:3474

§ 3474. Operation of motor vehicle by non-resident as appointment of secretary of state as agent for service of process

The acceptance by non-residents of the rights and privileges conferred by existing laws to operate motor vehicles on the public highways of the state of Louisiana, or the operation by a non-resident or his authorized agent, employee or person for whom he is legally responsible of a motor

R.S. 13:3474—Cont'd

vehicle within the state of Louisiana, shall be deemed equivalent to an appointment by such non-resident of the secretary of state of Louisiana or his successor in office, to be his true and lawful attorney for service of process, as well as the attorney for service of process of the public liability and property damage insurer of the vehicle, if such insurer be a non-resident not authorized to do business in the state, upon whom or such insurer, may be served all lawful process in any action or proceeding against the non-resident, or such insurer, growing out of any accident or collision in which the non-resident may be involved while operating a motor vehicle in this state, or while same is operated by his authorized agent or employee. In the event of the death of such non-resident before service of process upon him, any action or proceeding growing out of such accident or collision may be instituted against the executors or administrators of such deceased non-resident, if there be such, and if not, then against his heirs or legatees, and service may be made upon them as provided in R.S. 13:3475. Process against the defendant or defendants, the non-resident, his executors or administrators, if there be such, and if not, then against his heirs or legatees, or the liability insurer of such vehicle, as the case may be, shall be of the same legal force and validity as if served upon such defendant personally.

Amended by Acts 1954, No. 136, § 1; Acts 1956, No. 138, § 1; Acts 1958, No. 345, § 1.

R.S. 13:3475

§ 3475. Service on secretary of state; sending or delivering notice and copies; filing receipt or affidavit; continuances

A. The service of the process authorized by R.S. 13:3474 shall be made by serving a copy of the petition and citation on the secretary of state, or his successor in office, and such service shall be sufficient service upon the defendant, the nonresident, the executors or administrators of the deceased nonresident, if there be such, and if not, then against his heirs or legatees, or the nonresident liability insurer of the vehicle, as the case may be; provided that notice of such service, together with a copy of the petition and citation, is forthwith sent by the plaintiff by registered mail or certified mail with receipt requested, or is actually delivered to the defendant and the defendant's returned receipt, in case notice is sent by registered or certified mail, or affidavit of the party delivering the petition and citation in case notice is made by actual delivery, is filed in the proceedings before judgment can be entered against the defendant. The court in which the action is pending may order such continuances as may be necessary to afford the defendant reasonable opportunity to defend the action.

B. For purposes of this Section, the return receipt indicating that the registered or certified mail was actually delivered, refused, or unclaimed, is satisfactory proof of service of process if mailed to the defendant's address as indicated on the defendant's safety responsibility personal accident report, SR10, or if such report was not timely filed with the Department of Public Safety and Corrections, if mailed to the defendant's address as indicated on the accident report filed with the department by the law enforcement officer who responded to the accident.

Amended by Acts 1956, No. 138, § 2; Acts 1977, No. 353, § 1; Acts 1990, No. 151, § 1.

R.S. 13:3479

§ 3479. Operation of water craft by non-resident as appointment of secretary of state as agent for service of process

The operation, navigation or maintenance by a non-resident or non-residents of a boat, ship, barge or other water craft in the state, either in person or through others, and the acceptance thereby by such non-resident or non-residents of the protection of the laws of the state for such water craft, or

R.S. 13:3479—Cont'd

the operation, navigation or maintenance by a non-resident or non-residents of a boat, ship, barge or other water craft in the state, either in person or through others, other than under the laws of the state, shall be deemed equivalent to an appointment by each such non-resident of the Secretary of State, or his successor in office or some other person in his office during his absence he may designate, to be the true and lawful attorney of each such non-resident for service of process, upon whom may be served all lawful process in any suit, action or proceeding against such non-resident or non-residents growing out of any accident or collision in which such non-resident or non-residents may be involved while, either in person or through others, operating, navigating or maintaining a boat, ship, barge or other water craft in the state; and such acceptance or such operating, navigating or maintaining in the state of such water craft shall be a signification of each such non-resident's agreement that any such process against him which is so served shall be of the same legal force and effect as if served on him personally.

Amended by Acts 1954, No. 137, § 1.

R.S. 13:3661

§ 3661. Attendance compulsory in civil cases; witnesses within state; deposit

A. Witnesses in civil cases who reside or who are employed in this state may be subpoenaed and compelled to attend trials or hearings wherever held in this state.

B. Witnesses who are subpoenaed to attend a trial or hearing shall be paid their travel expenses to and from the courthouse at a rate equal to the rate in effect for state officials and an attendance fee of fifty dollars for each day that the witness is required to appear in court.

C. No witness shall be subpoenaed to attend a trial or hearing unless the party who desires the testimony of the witness has deposited with the clerk of court the estimated attendance fee and travel expenses.

D. The witness shall be paid the attendance fee and travel expenses immediately by the clerk of court when the witness has answered the subpoena and has appeared for the purpose of testifying.

E. In cases of exceptional hardship, the court may increase the travel expenses paid to the witness.

Amended by Acts 1956, No. 300, § 1; Acts 1958, No. 303, § 1; Acts 1958, No. 527, § 1; Acts 1960, No. 32, § 1, eff. Jan. 1, 1961; Acts 1961, No. 25, § 1; Acts 1977, No. 606, § 1; Acts 1991, No. 145, § 1; Acts 2021, No. 259, § 3.

R.S. 13:3661.1

§ 3661.1. Departmental service of subpoenas on law enforcement officers and fire service personnel

A. Service of subpoenas on any law enforcement officer or fire service personnel, when not a party to the action, may be made through personal service on the law enforcement officer's or fire service personnel's ranking officers or their designated representative. This service shall be made at the district stations or departmental headquarters. The ranking officer, or his designated representative, shall sign for such subpoenas and shall be required to notify the law enforcement officer or fire service personnel named therein of receipt of said subpoenas.

B. This type of service shall be known as departmental subpoena service of law enforcement officers and fire service personnel, and shall not be construed to replace domiciliary or personal service for said officers or personnel, but shall be an additional method of service of subpoenas.

Added by Acts 1981, No. 255, § 1. Amended by Acts 1988, No. 969, § 1.

R.S. 13:3721

§ 3721. Parol evidence to prove debt or liability of deceased person; objections not waivable

Parol evidence shall not be received to prove any debt or liability of a deceased person against his succession representative, heirs, or legatees when no suit to enforce it has been brought against the deceased prior to his death, unless within one year of the death of the deceased:

(1) A suit to enforce the debt or liability is brought against the succession representative, heirs, or legatees of the deceased;

(2) The debt or liability is acknowledged by the succession representative as provided in Article 3242 of the Code of Civil Procedure, or by his placing it on a tableau of distribution, or petitioning for authority to pay it;

(3) The claimant has opposed a petition for authority to pay debts, or a tableau of distribution, filed by the succession representative, on the ground that it did not include the debt or liability in question; or

(4) The claimant has submitted to the succession representative a formal proof of his claim against the succession, as provided in Article 3245 of the Code of Civil Procedure.

The provisions of this section cannot be waived impliedly through the failure of a litigant to object to the admission of evidence which is inadmissible thereunder.

Amended by Acts 1960, No. 32, § 1, eff. Jan. 1, 1961.

R.S. 13:3722

§ 3722. Same; evidence required when parol evidence admissible

When parol evidence is admissible under the provisions of R.S. 13:3721 the debt or liability of the deceased must be proved by the testimony of at least one creditable witness other than the claimant, and other corroborating circumstances.

Amended by Acts 1960, No. 32, § 1, eff. Jan. 1, 1961.

FOREIGN DEPOSITIONS

LETTERS ROGATORY

R.S. 13:3821

§ 3821. Foreign depositions

Whenever any mandate, writ, or commission is issued out of any court of record in any other state or territory, district, or foreign jurisdiction, or whenever upon notice or agreement it is required to take the testimony of a witness or witnesses in this state, witnesses may be compelled to appear and testify in the same manner and by the same process and proceedings as may be employed for the purpose of taking testimony in proceedings pending in this state.

R.S. 13:3822

§ 3822. Same; interpretation and citation

R.S. 13:3821 and 3823 shall be so interpreted and construed as to effectuate its general purposes to make uniform the law of those states which enact it, and may be cited as the Uniform Foreign Depositions Law.

Amended by Acts 2014, No. 793, § 1.

R.S. 13:3823

§ 3823. Taking of depositions in another state, or in a territory, district, or foreign jurisdiction

A. (1) When an action is pending in this state, a deposition to obtain testimony or documents or other things may be taken in another state, or in a territory, district, or foreign jurisdiction on reasonable notice in writing to all parties, setting forth the time and place for taking the deposition, the name and address of each person to be examined, if known, and, if the name is not known, a general description sufficient to identify him or the particular class or group to which he belongs and the name or descriptive title of the person before whom the deposition will be taken.

(2) The deposition may be taken by any of the following:

(a) Before a person authorized to administer oaths in the place where the deposition is taken by the law thereof or by the law of this state or of the United States.

(b) Before a person commissioned by the court, and a person so commissioned shall have the power by virtue of his commission to administer any necessary oath.

(c) Pursuant to a letter rogatory issued by the court. A letter rogatory may be addressed "To the Appropriate Authority in", or "To the Appropriate Judicial Authority in" (here name the state or country).

(d) Pursuant to Article 1435 of the Code of Civil Procedure.

(e) In any manner stipulated by the parties before any person, at any time or place, upon any notice, and a person designated by the stipulation shall have the power by virtue of his designation to administer any necessary oath.

B. If a commission or a letter rogatory from a court in this state is required in another state, territory, district, or foreign jurisdiction, the party seeking the commission or letter rogatory shall apply for it by written motion. The commission or letter rogatory shall be issued ex parte if it is unopposed, or after notice and a contradictory hearing if it is opposed, and on terms that are just and appropriate. It is not requisite to the issuance of a commission or a letter rogatory that the taking of the deposition in any other manner is impracticable or inconvenient, and both a commission and a letter rogatory may be issued in proper cases. Evidence obtained in a foreign country in response to a letter rogatory need not be excluded merely for the reason that it is not a verbatim transcript or that the testimony was not taken under oath or for any similar departure from the requirements for depositions taken within this state.

C. When no action is pending, a court of this state may authorize a deposition to be taken in another state, or in a territory, district, or foreign jurisdiction, of any person regarding any matter that may be cognizable in any court of this state. The court may prescribe the manner in which and the terms upon which the deposition shall be taken.

Added by Acts 1966, No. 37, § 2. Amended by Acts 2014, No. 793, § 1.

R.S. 13:3824

§ 3824. Assistance to tribunals and litigants in another state, or in a territory, district, or foreign jurisdiction

A. A person who is domiciled or is found within this state may be compelled to give his testimony or statement or to produce documents or other things for use in a proceeding in a court in another state, territory, district, or foreign jurisdiction pursuant to:

(1) R.S. 13:3825.

R.S. 13:3824—Cont'd

(2) An order made upon the application of any interested person or in response to a letter rogatory. To the extent that the order does not prescribe otherwise, the practice and procedure shall be in accordance with that of the court of this state issuing the order. The order may direct that the testimony or statement be given, or document or other thing produced, before a person appointed by the court. The person appointed shall have power to administer any necessary oath.

B. A person within this state may voluntarily give his testimony or statement or produce documents or other things for use in a proceeding before a tribunal in another state, or in a territory, district, or foreign jurisdiction in any manner acceptable to him.

Added by Acts 1966, No. 37, § 2. Amended by Acts 2014, No. 793, § 1.

R.S. 13:3825

§ 3825. Louisiana Uniform Interstate Depositions and Discovery Act

A. Short Title. This Section may be cited as the "Louisiana Uniform Interstate Depositions and Discovery Act".

B. Definitions. In this Section:

(1) "Foreign jurisdiction" means a state other than this state.

(2) "Foreign subpoena" means a subpoena issued under authority of a court of record of a foreign jurisdiction.

(3) "Person" means an individual, corporation, business trust, estate, trust, partnership, limited liability company, association, joint venture, public corporation, government, or governmental subdivision, agency, or instrumentality, or other legal or commercial entity.

(4) "State" means a state of the United States, the District of Columbia, Puerto Rico, the United States Virgin Islands, or any territory or insular possession subject to the jurisdiction of the United States.

(5) "Subpoena" means a document, however denominated, issued under authority of a court of record requiring a person to do any of the following:

(a) Attend and give testimony at a deposition.

(b) Produce and permit inspection and copying of designated books, documents, records, electronically stored information, or tangible things in the possession, custody, or control of the person.

(c) Permit inspection of premises under the control of the person.

C. Issuance of Subpoena.

(1) To request issuance of a subpoena under this Section, a party must present the original or a certified copy of a foreign subpoena to the clerk of court of the parish in which discovery is sought to be conducted in this state. A request for the issuance of a subpoena under this Section does not constitute an appearance in the courts of this state.

(2) When a party presents a foreign subpoena to a clerk of court in this state, the clerk, in accordance with that court's procedure, shall promptly issue a subpoena for service upon the person to which the foreign subpoena is directed.

(3) A subpoena issued under Paragraph (2) of this Subsection must:

(a) Identify the caption and case number of the out-of-state case to which it relates and incorporate the terms used in the foreign subpoena.

R.S. 13:3825—Cont'd

(b) State the name of the court in this state which has issued it with an identifying number.

(c) Contain or be accompanied by the names, addresses, and telephone numbers of all counsel of record in the proceeding to which the subpoena relates and of any party not represented by counsel.

D. Service of Subpoena. A subpoena issued by a clerk of court under Subsection C of this Section must be served in compliance with the laws of this state, including Article 1355 of the Code of Civil Procedure.

E. Deposition, Production, and Inspection. The Code of Civil Procedure and any other laws or district court rules of this state governing a deposition, production of documents or other tangible items, or an inspection of premises apply to discovery under Subsection C of this Section.

F. Application to Court. An application to a court of this state for a protective order or for an order enforcing, quashing, or modifying a subpoena issued by a clerk of court under Subsection C of this Section must comply with the district court rules, the Code of Civil Procedure, and the Rules of Professional Conduct of this state and be submitted to the district court that issued the subpoena.

G. Uniformity of Application and Construction. In applying and construing this Section, consideration must be given to the need to promote uniformity of the law with respect to its subject matter among states that enact it.

Added by Acts 2014, No. 793, § 1.

R.S. 13:3881

§ 3881. General exemptions from seizure

A. The following income or property of a debtor is exempt from seizure under any writ, mandate, or process whatsoever, except as otherwise herein provided:

(1)(a) Seventy-five percent of his disposable earnings for any week, but in no case shall this exemption be less than an amount in disposable earnings which is equal to thirty times the federal minimum hourly wage in effect at the time the earnings are payable or a multiple or fraction thereof, according to whether the employee's pay period is greater or less than one week. However, the exemption from disposable earnings for the payment of a current or past due support obligation, or both, for a child or children is fifty percent of disposable earnings, and the exemption from seizure of the disposable earnings for the payment of a current or past due support obligation, or both, for a spouse or former spouse is sixty percent of the disposable earnings. For purposes of this Subsection, if the Department of Children and Family Services is providing support enforcement services to the spouse and a judgment or order for support includes an obligation for both a child or children and a spouse or former spouse, or in any case wherein the judgment or order does not clearly indicate which amount is attributable to support of the child or children and which amount is attributable to support of the spouse or former spouse, the support obligation shall be treated as if it is exclusively for the support of a child or children.

(b) The term "disposable earnings" means that part of the earnings of any individual remaining after the deduction from those earnings of any amounts required by law to be withheld and which amounts are reasonable and are being deducted in the usual course of business at the time the garnishment is served upon the employer for the purpose of providing benefits for retirement, medical insurance coverage, life insurance coverage and which amounts are legally due or owed to the employer in the usual course of business at the time the garnishment is served.

(2) That property necessary to the exercise of a trade, calling, or profession by which he earns his livelihood, which shall be limited to the following:

R.S. 13:3881—Cont'd

(a) Tools.

(b) Instruments.

(c) Books.

(d) One utility trailer.

(e) Repealed by Acts 2014, No. 322, § 2.

(3) The personal servitude of habitation and the usufruct under Article 223 of the Civil Code.

(4)(a) The clothing, bedding, linen, chinaware, nonsterling silverware, glassware, living room, bedroom, and dining room furniture, cooking stove, heating and cooling equipment, one noncommercial sewing machine, equipment for required therapy, kitchen utensils, pressing irons, washers, dryers, refrigerators, deep freezers, electric or otherwise, used by him or a member of his family.

(b) The family portraits.

(c) His military accoutrements.

(d) The musical instruments played or practiced on by him or a member of his family.

(e) The poultry, fowl, and one cow kept by him for the use of his family.

(f) All dogs, cats, and other household pets.

(g) All firearms, arms and ammunition, and accessories thereto, not exceeding a total maximum value of two thousand five hundred dollars, which may be used for any purpose.

(5) Any wedding or engagement rings worn by either spouse, provided the value of the ring does not exceed five thousand dollars.

(6) Federal earned income tax credit and the refundable portion of the child tax credit, except for seizure by the Department of Revenue or arrears in child support payments.

(7) Seven thousand five hundred dollars in equity value for one motor vehicle per household used by the debtor and his family household for any purpose. The equity value of the motor vehicle shall be based on the NADA retail value for the particular year, make, and model.

(8) Seven thousand five hundred dollars in equity value for one motor vehicle per household which vehicle is substantially modified, equipped, or fitted for the purposes of adapting its use to the physical disability of the debtor or his family and is used by the debtor or his family for the transporting of such person with a disability for any use.

(9) The proceeds from a property insurance policy received as a result of damage caused by a gubernatorially declared disaster to an asset considered exempt under this Section and that are held separately in an escrow account identified as insurance proceeds paid from the damage of an exempt asset shall be considered exempt to the same extent that the value of the underlying asset is considered exempt.

(10) Any consumer stimulus payments directly received by the debtor pursuant to federal law enacted to provide for COVID–19 relief, except for seizure of spousal or child support payments. This Paragraph shall not apply to payments received by the debtor as unemployment compensation.

B. (1) In cases instituted under the provisions of Title 11 of the United States Code, entitled "Bankruptcy", there shall be exempt from the property of the estate of an individual debtor only that property and income which is exempt under the laws of the state of Louisiana and under federal laws other than 11 U.S.C. 522(d).

R.S. 13:3881—Cont'd

(2) No property upon which a debtor has voluntarily granted a lien shall, to the extent of the balance due on the debt secured thereby, be subject to the provisions of this Chapter or be exempt from forced sale under process of law.

(3) Proceeds from the involuntary sale or distribution of personal property that is exempt from seizure under the laws of this state, made at or after the filing of a petition under any Chapter of Title 11 of the United States Code, shall remain exempt for purposes of state law exemptions, as applicable under 11 U.S.C. 522(b)(2)(A). For purposes of this Subsection, "involuntary sale" shall mean any non-consensual sale or disposition of property.

C. The state of Louisiana expressly waives any immunity from suit insofar as the garnishment of the nonexempt portion of the wages, salaries, commissions, or other compensation of public officials, whether elected or appointed, public employees, or contractors is concerned, of itself, its agencies, boards, commissions, political subdivisions, public corporations, and municipal corporations.

D. (1) Except as provided in Paragraph (2) of this Subsection and in R.S. 11:292, the following shall be exempt from all liability for any debt except alimony and child support: all pensions, all tax-deferred arrangements, annuity contracts, and all proceeds of and payments under all tax-deferred arrangements and annuity contracts, as defined in Paragraph (3) of this Subsection.

(2) No contribution to a tax-deferred arrangement or to an annuity contract, as defined in Paragraph (3) of this Subsection, shall be exempt if made less than one calendar year of the date of filing for bankruptcy, whether voluntary or involuntary, or the date writs of seizure are filed against the tax-deferred arrangement or annuity contract. A transfer from one tax-deferred arrangement to another or from one annuity contract to another shall not be considered a contribution for purposes of this Paragraph.

(3) The term "tax-deferred arrangement" includes all individual retirement accounts or individual retirement annuities of any variety or name, whether authorized now or in the future in the Internal Revenue Code of 1986, or the corresponding provisions of any future United States income tax law, including balances rolled over from any other tax- deferred arrangement as defined herein, money purchase pension plans, defined benefit plans, defined contribution plans, Keogh plans, simplified employee pension (SEP) plans, simple retirement account (SIMPLE) plans, Roth IRAs, or any other plan of any variety or name, whether authorized now or in the future in the Internal Revenue Code of 1986, or the corresponding provisions of any future United States income tax law, under which United States income tax on the tax-deferred arrangement is deferred. The term "annuity contract" shall have the same definition as defined in R.S. 22:912(B).

Added by Acts 1960, No. 32, § 6, eff. Jan. 1, 1961. Amended by Acts 1961, No. 25, § 1 eff. Jan. 1, 1961; Acts 1977, No. 360, § 1; Acts 1978, No. 563, § 1; Acts 1979, No. 596, § 1; Acts 1980, No. 764, § 9; Acts 1981, Ex.Sess., No. 36, § 8, eff. Nov. 19, 1981; Acts 1982, No. 670, § 1; Acts 1982, No. 704, § 1, eff. Aug. 2, 1982; Acts 1983, No. 108, § 1; Acts 1983, No. 178, § 1; Acts 1985, No. 532, § 1; Acts 1986, No. 303, § 2; Acts 1990, No. 495, § 1; Acts 1991, No. 155, § 1; Acts 1991, No. 796, § 1; Acts 1991, No. 856, § 1, eff. July 23, 1991; Acts 1992, No. 829, § 1; Acts 1999, No. 63, § 1; Acts 2003, No. 470, § 1; Acts 2004, No. 60, § 1; Acts 2004, No. 468, § 1, eff. June 24, 2004; Acts 2006, No. 601, § 1; Acts 2006, No. 753, § 1; Acts 2010, No. 634, § 2, eff. July 1, 2010; Acts 2014, No. 322, § 1; Acts 2014, No. 811, § 5, eff. June 23, 2014; Acts 2019, No. 197, § 1, eff. June 11, 2019; Acts 2020, No. 44, § 1, eff. June 4, 2020.

R.S. 13:3886

§ 3886. Request for notice of seizure on specific property; notification by sheriff; failure to notify

A. Any person desiring to be notified of the seizure of specific immovable property or of a fixture located upon specific immovable property shall file a request for notice of seizure in the

R.S. 13:3886—Cont'd

mortgage records of the parish where the immovable property is located. The request for notice of seizure shall state the legal description of the immovable property, the owner of the property, and the name and address of the person desiring notice of seizure. The person requesting notice of seizure shall pay the sum of ten dollars to the sheriff.

B. (1) Any interested person may request, by simple written application to the sheriff, that a written notice of seizure be given to any other person or persons. A fee of fifteen dollars for each person to be notified by mail, or twenty dollars for each person to be notified by service shall accompany the request for notice. After his receipt of the request and the appropriate fee, the sheriff shall, upon the seizure of the property, promptly give the requested notices.

(2) Additionally, in the event of seizure of immovable property or a fixture, the sheriff shall give written notice of the seizure and a list of the property seized to each person who, prior to the filing of the notice of seizure, has requested notice under the provisions of Subsection A and who has paid the fee required therein.

C. In the event of seizure of immovable property or a fixture, the sheriff shall request from the clerk of court, or the recorder of mortgages for the parish of Orleans, at least twenty-one days prior to the first scheduled sheriff's sale, a mortgage certificate effective as of the date and time of the filing of the notice of seizure. The mortgage certificate shall include any requests for notice of seizure. Upon receipt of the mortgage certificate the sheriff shall notify, at least ten days prior to the first scheduled sheriff's sale, those persons requesting notice of the seizure. The notice of seizure shall be by certified mail, return receipt requested, actual delivery, or any manner provided for service of citation, and shall include the name and address of the seizing creditor, the method of seizure and the sum owed, and the date of the first scheduled sheriff's sale.

D. Notices under this Section may be given by certified mail, return receipt requested, actual delivery, or by any manner provided by service of citation. Each notice shall be mailed or served at least ten days before the first scheduled date of the sheriff's sale, and shall include the time, date, and place of such sale.

E. Neither the clerk of court nor the sheriff, or any of their officers, agents, or employees, shall be held liable if a reasonable attempt has been made to mail or deliver the notice to the address provided in the request.

F. The failure of the sheriff to notify a person requesting notice of seizure shall not affect the rights of the seizing creditor nor invalidate the sheriff's sale.

Added by Acts 1982, No. 615, § 1. Amended by Acts 1989, No. 137, § 8, eff. Sept. 1, 1989; Acts 1991, No. 662, § 2, eff. Jan. 1, 1992; Acts 1992, No. 533, § 1; Acts 2005, No. 37, § 1.

R.S. 13:3886.1

§ 3886.1. Failure to notify

A. The failure to notify any lienholder or other interested person having an interest in the property shall not affect the rights of the seizing creditor nor invalidate the sheriff's sale; nor shall any lien, privilege, or other encumbrance that is inferior to the rank of the lien of the seizing creditor affect the property after the sheriff's adjudication. The exclusive remedy for any person affected by the provisions of this Subsection shall be to institute a claim by summary pleadings, within one year from the date of the sheriff's adjudication, proving that he has been damaged by the failure to notify him. In connection with any such claim, the court shall consider and the person claiming damages shall have the burden of proving all of the following:

R.S. 13:3886.1—Cont'd

(1) That his name and address were reasonably ascertainable through the exercise of reasonable diligence.

(2) That he lacked actual knowledge of the seizure.

(3) The respective ranking and amounts of all liens, privileges, and other encumbrances affecting the property as of the date of the sheriff's adjudication.

(4) The value of such respective rights.

(5) The value of the property as of the date of the sheriff's adjudication.

(6) The respective positions the parties would have occupied had the required notice been given.

(7) His ability and capacity to have obtained funds to purchase the property at the foreclosure sale had the required notice been given.

(8) That in such circumstances he would have bid on the property in such an amount as to have prevented him from suffering the alleged damages, either by such bid being successful or by such bid leading to a higher bid by another party.

B. In no event shall the claim of any such person exceed the value of the interest he possessed on the date of the sheriff's adjudication.

C. The provisions of this Section shall be applied both retrospectively and prospectively; however, any action for which the time period for bringing such action would otherwise be shortened by the provisions hereof shall be instituted within one year from July 17, 1991, and any suit not instituted within that time and any claims relating thereto shall be forever barred.

Added by Acts 1991, No. 662, § 3, eff. July 17, 1991.

Garnishment, Procedures

R.S. 13:3921

§ 3921. Judgment fixing portion subject to seizure, payment to creditor and processing fee

A. In every case in which the wage or salary of a laborer, wage earner, artisan, mechanic, engineer, fireman, carpenter, bricklayer, secretary, bookkeeper, clerk, employee on a commission basis, or employee of any nature and kind whatever, whether skilled or unskilled, shall be garnished either under attachment or fieri facias or as otherwise provided by law, a judgment shall be rendered by the court of competent jurisdiction in which the garnishment proceedings may be pending fixing the portion of such wage, salary, commission, or other compensation as may be exempt, as provided by law, and providing for the payment to the sheriff, marshal, or constable for processing prior to payment to the seizing creditor of whatever sum for which judgment may be obtained, out of the portion of such compensation which is not exempt. The sheriff, marshal, or constable shall apply and deduct their commission percentage as authorized by law from each garnishment payment upon receipt prior to remitting each payment to the seizing creditor.

B. Prior to releasing or terminating any garnishment under this Part because of amounts due under the garnishment have been paid or because the amount due as reflected in the statement furnished pursuant to R.S. 13:3923 has been reached, the garnishee or the sheriff, marshal, or constable shall make a reasonable effort to contact the seizing creditor, and obtain the current balance due.

C. The court shall also provide in the judgment for a processing fee of three dollars to be deducted by the employer from the nonexempt income of the employee for each pay period during

R.S. 13:3921—Cont'd

which the judgment of garnishment is in effect. The processing fee shall be for the costs of the employer in complying with the judgment of garnishment.

D. In garnishment proceedings in which the employee is a state officer or employee, the processing fee provided by Subsection C of this Section shall be paid into the state treasury and, in accordance with Article VII, Section 9 of the Constitution of Louisiana, shall be credited to the Bond Security and Redemption Fund.

Amended by Acts 1987, No. 777, § 1; Acts 1992, No. 984, § 4; Acts 2018, No. 261, § 1.

R.S. 13:3922

§ 3922. Hearing; evidence; prior acts

A judgment may be rendered by the court in which a garnishment proceeding is pending, with or without a hearing, if all competent evidence is presented to determine the amount of the person's earnings or the amount of any other assets, or both, and the court is satisfied of the existence of any judgment, writ of garnishment, or sale, transfer, or assignment of earnings, which remains unsatisfied. If any such act exists, it shall prime in enforcement any subsequent judgment, writ of garnishment, or sale, transfer, or assignment of earnings, and shall be satisfied out of the nonexempt portion of disposable earnings.

Amended by Acts 1980, No. 764, § 7; Acts 1988, No. 971, § 1.

R.S. 13:3923

§ 3923. One writ and one set of interrogatories sufficient, statement of sums due to be furnished to garnishee; installment payments; reopening case; retention of jurisdiction; cessation of seizure by garnishment upon termination of employment

It shall not be necessary that more than one writ of garnishment or one set of interrogatories be served in such cases, but the court shall render judgment for the monthly, semimonthly, weekly or daily payments to be made to the seizing creditor according to the manner best suited to the circumstances, until the indebtedness is paid. The garnisher shall serve upon the garnishee the citation, the petition, the garnishment interrogatories, the notice of seizure, and a statement of sums due under the garnishment, such statement to include, but not be limited to, the principal, interest, court costs incurred to date, and attorney's fee due under the judgment. The court, in its discretion, may reopen the case upon the motion of any party concerned for evidence affecting the proper continuance of such judgment, and the court shall retain jurisdiction to amend or set aside its judgment at any time in its discretion; however, all effects of the seizure by garnishment shall cease upon the termination of employment of the debtor with the garnishee, unless the debtor is reinstated or reemployed within one hundred eighty days after the termination. Should judgment by default be taken against any party garnishee, he may obtain a reopening of the case upon proper showing and within the discretion of the court.

Amended by Acts 1976, No. 359, § 1.

R.S. 13:3924

§ 3924. Interrogatories

The interrogatories to be served upon the garnishee shall include a question, or questions, the answer to which shall inform the court as to whether or not the defendant in the suit is employed by the garnishee, and, if not, where and by whom the defendant is presently employed and residing, if known to the garnishee, and, if employed by the garnishee, what his rate of compensation is, in what

R.S. 13:3924—Cont'd

manner it is paid, and whether or not there are other judgments or garnishments affecting such wage, salary or compensation, and, if so, the status thereof.

Amended by Acts 1982, No. 532, § 1, eff. July 22, 1982.

R.S. 13:3925

§ 3925. Indebtedness of employee to employer

A. If the employer answering such interrogatories should plead that the employee is indebted to the employer for other amounts due and owing, other than those specified in R.S. 13:3881, the employer shall make a full and complete disclosure of the status of such account to the creditor, in writing by certified mail, showing the time that the debt was incurred, the exact amount of the debt, the credits applied to the debt, the manner in which the debt is being liquidated as of the time of the service of the interrogatories, and all other pertinent facts. Thereafter, the seizing creditor shall have fifteen days to file an opposition to the court's consideration of the employee-employer debt as liquidated. Failure to file an opposition shall be considered a waiver of the seizing creditor's rights to oppose the court's consideration of the employee-employer debt as liquidated. If an opposition is filed with the court within the appropriate legal delays, the court may hear evidence affecting the issue of liquidation and shall render a judgment to determine whether the employee-employer debt should be considered liquidated, and thereby, allow payment to the employer of the non-exempt portion of the employee's salary, wage or commission at a specified rate in the same manner as if the employer were a judgment creditor having a prior garnishment.

B. It is the stated intention of this Section that the employer shall be presumed to be one holding a prior garnishment. It is the further intention of this Section, once an employee-employer debt is considered liquidated, either by waiver or judgment, that the retirement of such indebtedness be limited in the time within which such indebtedness should be considered paid and other equitable matters which the judge may consider so that the employee-employer debt be paid in full in order that other garnishments may attach.

C. The provisions of this Section shall not grant a preference over the enforcement of child support.

Amended by Acts 1991, No. 156, § 1.

R.S. 13:3926

§ 3926. Employee working on commission

If in response to such interrogatories the employer sets forth that the employee works on a commission basis, the employer shall make a full disclosure of the terms of employment, the amount of the commission and the method of payment of such commission and the dates on which settlements are made with the employee. The court thereupon shall render a judgment ordering a full accounting to be made at each date when such settlements are made and upon the filing of such accounting, the court shall fix the exempt portion and order the non-exempt portion paid in satisfaction of whatever judgment may be rendered.

R.S. 13:3927

§ 3927. Deposit to cover fee of employer's attorney; costs; return of deposit

Whenever a plaintiff suing out a writ of garnishment shall apply to the court for the issuance of such writ, the plaintiff shall deposit with the clerk of court the sum of fifteen dollars, as a fee for the attorney for the employer who answers such interrogatories. This sum may be charged and collected

R.S. 13:3927—Cont'd

as other costs. If no answer is filed by the garnishee, within the time provided by law, the attorney's fee so deposited shall be returned to the seizing creditor. If the court in its discretion should rule that no fee should be charged to the costs by such attorney for the employer, the fee shall likewise be returned to the seizing creditor. If the court should rule that a fee greater than fifteen dollars should be assessed, the court may fix the amount of such fee, which shall be charged to the costs of the suit.

Amended by Acts 1976, No. 359, § 1.

R.S. 13:3928

§ 3928. Priority of judgment, decree, or order of support

In any criminal or civil matter, a judgment, decree, order, or sentence of court, or a sale, transfer, or assignment of earnings by which a person is obligated to pay for the current or past due support, or both, of a child or children, or of a parent of a child or children if the Department of Children and Family Services is providing support enforcement services to the parent, shall prime in enforcement any prior or subsequent judgment, decree, order, or sentence of court, or sale, transfer, or assignment of earnings, and shall be satisfied out of the nonexempt portion of disposable earnings.

Added by Acts 1958, No. 479, § 1. Amended by Acts 1980, No. 764, § 8; Acts 1981, Ex.Sess., No. 36, § 7, eff. Nov. 19, 1981.

R.S. 13:4101

§ 4101. Mortgaged property in hands of receiver or liquidator

The appointment of a receiver or liquidator of a corporation shall not affect the right of a creditor to enforce by executory process a mortgage or security agreement importing a confession of judgment and affecting property owned by the corporation. If the receiver or liquidator is appointed prior to the institution of executory proceedings and the notice of appointment is recorded in the mortgage office in the parish in which the property is located and written notice of the appointment is received by the holder of the obligation that is sought to be enforced by executory process, then the receiver or liquidator shall be made defendant in the executory process proceedings. If the receiver or liquidator is not appointed prior to institution of executory proceedings or the notice of appointment is not recorded or if written notice of the appointment is not received by the creditor, then the receiver or liquidator need not be substituted as the defendant, and the seizure and sale of the encumbered property may be made in the same manner as if no receiver or liquidator had been appointed.

Amended by Acts 1960, No. 32, § 1, eff. Jan. 1, 1961; Acts 1982, No. 179, § 1; Acts 1989, No. 137, § 8, eff. Sept. 1, 1989.

Editor's Notes

Acts 1989, 1st Ex.Sess., No. 12, § 1, and Acts 1989, No. 135, § 12, provide for a Jan. 1, 1990 effective date for Chapter 9 of the Louisiana Commercial Laws (R.S. 10:9–101, et seq.). Acts 1989, No. 137, implementing Chapter 9, provides a Sept. 1, 1989 effective date for the affected Code of Civil Procedure articles and certain other amended statutes (see § 22 of Act 137). See Acts 1989, No. 135, §§ 10 and 11, and Acts 1989, No. 137, § 20 for provisions on application of security device laws prior to Jan. 1, 1990. See also Acts 1989, No. 598, § 9.

R.S. 13:4102

§ 4102. Executory process; bearer paper, movable or immovable property, authentic evidence; certification of documents

A. Whenever the holder of bearer paper, such as a note, bond, or other instrument evidencing an obligation secured by a mortgage or privilege on movable or immovable property, seeks to

R.S. 13:4102—Cont'd

foreclose by executory process, all requirements for authentic evidence regarding the transfer, assignment, pledge, or negotiation shall be inapplicable, provided that all other requirements for authentic evidence have been satisfied.

B. Whenever the holder of a note, bond, or other instrument evidencing an obligation secured by a mortgage or privilege on movable property seeks to foreclose by executory process, the transfer, assignment, pledge, or negotiation of such document by private act, duly acknowledged in any manner provided by law, shall be deemed to be authentic evidence and in compliance with Code of Civil Procedure Article 2636.

C. Whenever the holder of a note, bond, or other instrument evidencing an obligation secured by a mortgage or privilege on movable property approves the sale of the property from one person to another, such approval may be made by private act, duly acknowledged in any manner provided by law, and shall be deemed to be authentic evidence and in compliance with Code of Civil Procedure Article 2636.

D. (1) Whenever the law requires a certified copy of any document, including a photographic, photostatic, or miniature photographic copy or reproduction of such document, for purposes of executory process, a notary public who has the original or a copy of such document on file in his office, custodian of notarial records, or clerk of court shall note on the copy of the document that it is a correct copy and may include words such as "certified copy", "true copy", or any other words which reasonably indicate that the copy of the document is a certified copy, and the copy so certified shall be deemed authentic evidence.

(2) A document containing a certificate reading substantially as follows shall satisfy the requirements of (1) above and shall be deemed authentic:

"STATE OF LOUISIANA ________________, Louisiana

PARISH OF ________________ ________________, (Date)

I, ________________, (Custodian of Notarial Records, Clerk of Court, Notary Public) for the Parish of ________________, State of Louisiana, do hereby certify that the attached documents are true and correct copies of ________________, dated the ___ day of ________________, 19___, consisting of ___ pages (executed before, attached to ________________ executed before) ________________ ________________, a Notary Public of the Parish of ________________, State of Louisiana, the original or certified copy of which document(s) is on file in my office.

Name ________________________
Title
Address"

Added by Acts 1982, No. 178, § 1. Amended by Acts 1987, No. 855, § 1, eff. July 20, 1987.

R.S. 13:4103

§ 4103. Executory process against mortgaged corporation property; proof of authority to execute mortgage

A. The following shall be deemed to constitute authentic evidence for purposes of an executory proceeding to enforce a mortgage, chattel mortgage, or other security agreement against a corporate debtor:

(1) The consent of the shareholders evidenced as provided in R.S. 12:76 authorizing or ratifying the granting of such a mortgage, chattel mortgage, or other security agreement.

R.S. 13:4103—Cont'd

(2) An extract of the minutes of the meeting of the board of directors or other governing body of the corporation, or a written consent by the shareholders or directors of the corporation, signed and certified by the corporate secretary or any assistant secretary, setting forth the resolution or resolutions authorizing or ratifying the granting of such a mortgage or other security agreement or security interest, whether the specific transaction, mortgage, or security agreement or security interest is described with particularity, or more general authority is granted or ratified.

(3) A photocopy of the extract of minutes provided in Subsection (2) above, certified either by:

(a) A notary before whom the mortgage, chattel mortgage, or other security agreement was passed or acknowledged, or

(b) By the custodian of notarial archives for the parish of Orleans if the mortgage, chattel mortgage, or other security agreement, together with a certified copy of the extract of minutes, has been recorded in Orleans Parish, or by the clerk of the district court of any other parish in which the mortgage, chattel mortgage, or other security agreement, together with a certified copy of the extract of minutes, has been recorded.

B. The right of an interested party to question or attack the authority of the purported officer or agent to execute the mortgage is not affected in any manner by the provisions of this Section.

Amended by Acts 1960, No. 32, § 1, eff. Jan. 1, 1961; Acts 1974, No. 254, § 1; Acts 1982, No. 177, § 1; Acts 1986, No. 489, § 1; Acts 1991, No. 377, § 5, eff. Jan. 1, 1992; Acts 1993, No. 948, § 4, eff. June 25, 1993.

R.S. 13:4103.1

§ 4103.1. Executory process against mortgaged or secured limited liability company property; proof of authority to execute mortgage or security agreement

Any of the following shall be deemed to constitute authentic evidence for purposes of an executory proceeding to enforce a mortgage, collateral mortgage, or other security agreement against a limited liability company:

(1) A certified copy of the limited liability company's articles of organization filed with the secretary of state containing a grant of authority to one or more individuals to execute a mortgage or security agreement for and on behalf of the limited liability company, whether the specific transaction, mortgage, or security agreement is described with particularity or more general authority is granted.

(2) A written consent by all of the then members of the limited liability company, or such other persons as may have been delegated authority pursuant to R.S. 12:1318(B), signed and certified by any person named in the statement provided for in R.S. 12:1305(C)(5), or, if no such person or persons are so named, upon a certificate of a member, if management is reserved to the members, or a manager, if management is vested in one or more managers pursuant to R.S. 12:1312, of the limited liability company, authorizing or ratifying the grant of authority to one or more individuals to execute a mortgage or security agreement for and on behalf of the limited liability company, whether the specific transaction, mortgage, or security agreement is described with particularity or more general authority is granted or ratified.

(3) An extract of the minutes of the meeting of the then members of a limited liability company, or such other persons as may have been delegated authority pursuant to R.S. 12:1318(B), signed and certified by any person named in the statement provided for in R.S. 12:1305(C)(5), or, if no such person or persons are so named, signed and certified by a member, if management is reserved to the members, or manager, if management is vested in one or more managers pursuant to R.S. 12:1312, of the limited liability company, setting forth the resolution or resolutions authorizing or ratifying the

R.S. 13:4103.1—Cont'd

granting of a mortgage or security agreement, whether the specific transaction, mortgage, or security agreement is described with particularity or more general authority is granted or ratified.

Added by Acts 1993, No. 475, § 5, eff. June 9, 1993.

R.S. 13:4104

§ 4104. Variance between act of mortgage and note; correction

The right to an order for executory process shall exist when there is a variance between a notarial act of mortgage and the note or notes issued in connection therewith, when such variance is due to a clerical error and the fact that such variance is so due is certified on the note or notes or on the act of mortgage, or both, over the official signature of the notary before whom the mortgage was passed.

R.S. 13:4105

§ 4105. Notarial act acknowledging error, when sufficient

In any case where such variance exists and it is not possible to secure the certificate referred to in R.S. 13:4104, the right to an order for executory process will lie upon execution by the debtor or by his heirs, executors, administrators, or assigns, of a notarial act acknowledging the clerical error.

R.S. 13:4106

§ 4106. Deficiency judgment prohibited if sale made without appraisement

A. Unless otherwise provided by law, if a mortgagee or other creditor takes advantage of a waiver of appraisement of his property, movable, immovable, or both, by a debtor, and the proceeds of the judicial sale thereof are insufficient to satisfy the debt for which the property was sold, the debt nevertheless shall stand fully satisfied and discharged insofar as it constitutes a personal obligation of the debtor. The mortgagee or other creditor shall not have a right thereafter to proceed against the debtor or any of his other property for such deficiency, except as otherwise provided by law or as provided in the next subsection.

B. If a mortgage or pledge affects two or more properties, movable, immovable, or both, the judicial sale of any property so affected without appraisement shall not prevent the enforcement of the mortgage or pledge in rem against any other property affected thereby.

C. This Section is limited to judicial sales of mortgaged property and shall not apply to public or private sales of collateral subject to Chapter 9 of the Louisiana Commercial Laws or any similar statute.

Amended by Acts 1952, No. 20, § 1; Acts 1960, No. 32, § 1, eff. Jan. 1, 1961; Acts 1989, No. 137, § 8, eff. Sept. 1, 1989.

Editor's Notes

Acts 1989, 1st Ex.Sess., No. 12, § 1, and Acts 1989, No. 135, § 12, provide for a Jan. 1, 1990 effective date for Chapter 9 of the Louisiana Commercial Laws (R.S. 10:9–101, et seq.). Acts 1989, No. 137, implementing Chapter 9, provides a Sept. 1, 1989 effective date for the affected Code of Civil Procedure articles and certain other amended statutes (see § 22 of Act 137). See Acts 1989, No. 135, §§ 10 and 11, and Acts 1989, No. 137, § 20 for provisions on application of security device laws prior to Jan. 1, 1990. See also Acts 1989, No. 598, § 9.

R.S. 13:4107

§ 4107. R.S. 13:4106 cannot be waived; operation prospective

R.S. 13:4106 declares a public policy and the provisions thereof can not, and shall not be waived by a debtor, but it shall only apply to mortgages, contracts, debts or other obligations made, or arising on or after August 1, 1934.

R.S. 13:4108

§ 4108. Transactions which do not bar deficiency judgment

Notwithstanding any other law to the contrary, including but not limited to R.S. 13:4106 and 4107, none of the following actions by a mortgagee or other creditor shall prohibit the mortgagee or other creditor from obtaining a deficiency judgment against any debtor, guarantor, or surety, notwithstanding the fact that a sale of property or collateral may have occurred at a judicial sale without appraisal, at a public or private sale with or without appraisal, or at a judicial sale with a defective appraisal:

(1) A sale through the New York Stock Exchange, the American Stock Exchange, or the NASDAQ, of any pledged stock, bonds, or options registered or traded on such exchanges.

(2) A sale through the Chicago Commodity Exchange of any pledged options registered or traded on such exchange.

(3) A sale pursuant to an order of a United States Bankruptcy Court, or of a United States District Court sitting in bankruptcy.

(4) The mortgagee's or other creditor's exercise of its rights against property subject to a mortgage, pledge, privilege, security interest, or encumbrance in favor of such creditor, when the property or collateral is located outside the state of Louisiana, and the creditor has elected to proceed under the laws of the state, county, or territory where the property or collateral is then located to seize or sell such property or collateral.

(5) The collection or receipt of:

(a) Any proceeds of any pledged negotiable or nonnegotiable note;

(b) Any funds through the offset of any pledged deposit of cash, whether in the form of a demand deposit account with any institution insured by any agency of the federal government, certificate of deposit, or otherwise;

(c) Any proceeds of any pledge or assignment of accounts receivable; or

(d) Any proceeds of any pledge or assignment of the right to receive income under any lease or rent of movable property or immovable property.

(6) Collection or receipt of insurance proceeds under a simple or standard loss-payee clause.

(7) Collection or receipt of the return of any unearned premiums of any insurance policy.

Added by Acts 1986, No. 489, § 2. Amended by Acts 1989, No. 137, § 8, eff. Sept. 1, 1989.

Editor's Notes

Acts 1989, 1st Ex.Sess., No. 12, § 1, and Acts 1989, No. 135, § 12, provide for a Jan. 1, 1990 effective date for Chapter 9 of the Louisiana Commercial Laws (R.S. 10:9–101, et seq.). Acts 1989, No. 137, implementing Chapter 9, provides a Sept. 1, 1989 effective date for the affected Code of Civil Procedure articles and certain other amended statutes (see § 22 of Act 137). See Acts 1989, No. 135,

R.S. 13:4108—Cont'd

§§ 10 and 11, and Acts 1989, No. 137, § 20 for provisions on application of security device laws prior to Jan. 1, 1990. See also Acts 1989, No. 598, § 9.

R.S. 13:4108.1

§ 4108.1. Deficiency judgment when obligations based upon commercial transaction

A. As an exception to R.S. 13:4106 and 4107, if a mortgagee or other creditor holds a mortgage, pledge, security interest, or privilege which secures an obligation in a commercial transaction, the mortgagee or other creditor may collect from or pursue any debtor, guarantor, or surety for a deficiency judgment on the secured obligation whether or not the mortgagee or other creditor has foreclosed on all or any of the property and sold such property at a judicial, public, or private sale, with or without appraisal, regardless of the minimum bid, and whether or not the mortgagee or other creditor has acquired such property from any debtor, guarantor, or surety pursuant to a complete or partial giving in payment. However, other than with regard to a secured transaction subject to Chapter 9 of the Louisiana Commercial Laws, a mortgagee or other creditor may not pursue any debtor, guarantor, or surety for more than the secured obligation, minus the reasonably equivalent value of the property sold.

B. For the purpose of this Section, the terms "commercial transaction" and "reasonably equivalent value" shall have the following meanings:

(1) "Commercial transaction" means any transaction entered into primarily for business or commercial purposes.

(2) "Reasonably equivalent value" means the value that the owner and the mortgagee or other creditor of the property being sold or otherwise disposed of agree to attribute to the property for the purposes of reducing the secured debt.

Added by Acts 1986, No. 489, § 2. Amended by Acts 1989, No. 137, § 8, eff. Sept. 1, 1989.

Editor's Notes

Acts 1989, 1st Ex.Sess., No. 12, § 1, and Acts 1989, No. 135, § 12, provide for a Jan. 1, 1990 effective date for Chapter 9 of the Louisiana Commercial Laws (R.S. 10:9–101, et seq.). Acts 1989, No. 137, implementing Chapter 9, provides a Sept. 1, 1989 effective date for the affected Code of Civil Procedure articles and certain other amended statutes (see § 22 of Act 137). See Acts 1989, No. 135, §§ 10 and 11, and Acts 1989, No. 137, § 20 for provisions on application of security device laws prior to Jan. 1, 1990. See also Acts 1989, No. 598, § 9.

R.S. 13:4108.2

§ 4108.2. Deficiency judgment when obligations based on consumer transaction

A. Notwithstanding any other law to the contrary, including but not limited to R.S. 13:4106 and 4107, if a mortgagee or other creditor holds a mortgage, pledge, security interest, or privilege which secures an obligation in a consumer transaction, the mortgagee or other creditor may obtain a deficiency judgment on the secured obligation against the debtor for the amount of the secured obligation less the reasonably equivalent value of property acquired from the debtor without appraisal or any other legal proceeding concerning such property acquired, only if the mortgagee or other creditor has acquired such property from the debtor pursuant to a written agreement with the debtor to waive the debtor's rights to a judicial appraisal and sale and to voluntarily surrender title to the property to the creditor. The debtor must agree to the value to be attributed to the property transferred and must agree that a deficiency judgment for the amount of the secured obligations

R.S. 13:4108.2—Cont'd

minus such value may be obtained by the mortgagee or creditor without appraisal of or any other legal proceeding concerning the property transferred. The debtor may obtain an appraisal for the purpose of determining the value of the property and if he does so the value assigned to the property may not be less than three-fourths of the appraised value.

B. For the purposes of this Section, the following terms shall have the following meanings:

(1) "Consumer transaction" means any transaction entered into for personal, family, or household (noncommercial) purposes and particularly includes transactions that are secured by residential immovable property, but excluding secured transactions for consumer purposes that are subject to Chapter 9 of the Louisiana Commercial Laws.

(2) "Reasonably equivalent value" means the value which the owner and the mortgagee or other creditor expressly agree to attribute to the property transferred, as provided in Subsection A of this Section.

C. This Section shall not be construed as prohibiting a debtor from selling his property to a third party purchaser and signing a promissory note to a mortgagee or other creditor for all or part of the balance due on the secured debt.

D. Every agreement for a voluntary surrender of title to property in connection with a consumer transaction as defined above shall contain a statement which notifies the debtor in laymen's terms:

(1)(a) That he has a right to obtain an appraisal, and

(b) That the value of the property assigned has to be three-quarters of the appraised value, and

(2)(a) That by agreeing to the surrender of the property without judicial appraisal and sale, the debtor is waiving any rights he might have under the law to further judicial proceedings governing the judicial sale of his property,

(b) That he is waiving his right to a judicial appraisal and sale, and

(c) That the creditor may obtain a judgment to collect any remaining amount due under the obligation after subtracting the agreed upon value of the property.

Added by Acts 1988, No. 675, § 1, eff. July 15, 1988. Amended by Acts 1989, No. 137, § 8, eff. Sept. 1, 1989.

Editor's Notes

Acts 1989, 1st Ex.Sess., No. 12, § 1, and Acts 1989, No. 135, § 12, provide for a Jan. 1, 1990 effective date for Chapter 9 of the Louisiana Commercial Laws (R.S. 10:9–101, et seq.). Acts 1989, No. 137, implementing Chapter 9, provides a Sept. 1, 1989 effective date for the affected Code of Civil Procedure articles and certain other amended statutes (see § 22 of Act 137). See Acts 1989, No. 135, §§ 10 and 11, and Acts 1989, No. 137, § 20 for provisions on application of security device laws prior to Jan. 1, 1990. See also Acts 1989, No. 598, § 9.

R.S. 13:4108.3

§ 4108.3. Relation to Chapter 9 of the Louisiana Commercial Laws

The rights or absence thereof of a secured creditor to pursue and collect a deficiency from a debtor, guarantor, or surety in connection with a secured transaction subject to Chapter 9 of the Louisiana Commercial Laws (R.S. 10:9–101, et seq.) shall be exclusively subject to the provisions of Chapter 9.

Added by Acts 1989, No. 137, § 8, eff. Sept. 1, 1989.

R.S. 13:4108.3—Cont'd

Editor's Notes

Acts 1989, 1st Ex.Sess., No. 12, § 1, and Acts 1989, No. 135, § 12, provide for a Jan. 1, 1990 effective date for Chapter 9 of the Louisiana Commercial Laws (R.S. 10:9–101, et seq.). Acts 1989, No. 137, implementing Chapter 9, provides a Sept. 1, 1989 effective date for the affected Code of Civil Procedure articles and certain other amended statutes (see § 22 of Act 137). See Acts 1989, No. 135, §§ 10 and 11, and Acts 1989, No. 137, § 20 for provisions on application of security device laws prior to Jan. 1, 1990. See also Acts 1989, No. 598, § 9.

R.S. 13:4109

§ 4109. Executory process against property of insolvents; rights of persons holding special mortgages

Creditors holding special mortgages containing the pact de non alienando shall not lose their rights of executory process upon the property of their debtor, by reason of a cession of property, but in such cases the right shall continue and be exercised against the syndic, and when the cession takes place after the seizure under executory process it shall be continued against the provisional or definitive syndic.

R.S. 13:4110

§ 4110. Same; sale under first process where provisional or definitive syndic appointed

In all cases when executory process has issued and a surrender has been made and a provisional or definitive syndic has been appointed, the sale under the first process shall be effected the same as if no surrender has been made or syndic appointed.

R.S. 13:4111

§ 4111. Venue of executory proceeding against continuous tract of land in different parishes

An executory proceeding to enforce a mortgage or privilege affecting the whole of a continuous tract of land situated partly in different parishes, at the option of the plaintiff, may be brought at the domicile of the defendant, or in any parish where a portion of the tract is situated.

Added by Acts 1960, No. 32, § 6, eff. Jan. 1, 1961.

R.S. 13:4112

§ 4112. Actions to set aside or annul judicial sales in executory proceedings

No action may be instituted to set aside or annul the judicial sale of immovable property by executory process by reason of any objection to form or procedure in the executory proceedings, or by reason of the lack of authentic evidence to support the order and seizure, where the sheriff executing the foreclosure has either filed the proces verbal of the sale or filed the sale for recordation in the conveyance records of the parish. Any party seeking to annul or set aside a judicial sale of immovable property through executory proceedings filed for record before the adoption of this Section must do so within six months of September 12, 1975. Nothing herein shall be construed to affect legal defenses otherwise available to any person against whom a deficiency judgment is sought after the public sale of immovable property through executory proceedings.

Added by Acts 1975, No. 681, § 1.

R.S. 13:4163

§ 4163. Ex parte motion for legislative continuance or extension of time; legislators or employees engaged in legislative or constitutional convention activities

A. (1) A member of the legislature and a legislative employee shall have peremptory grounds for continuance or extension of a criminal case, civil case, or administrative proceeding as provided below. The continuance or extension shall be sought by written motion specifically alleging these grounds.

(2) For purposes of this Section, "legislative employee" means the clerk of the House of Representative, the secretary of the Senate, and an employee of the House of Representatives, the Senate, or the Legislative Bureau, when such person is employed full-time during the legislative session or during any other time in which the continuance or extension is being sought.

B. The peremptory grounds for continuance or extension is available to and for the benefit of a member or legislative employee and may only be asserted or waived by a member or employee.

C. (1) Such peremptory grounds are available for the continuance of any type of proceeding and the extension of any type of deadline pertaining to a criminal case, civil case, or administrative proceeding, if the presence, participation, or involvement of a member or employee is required in any capacity, including any pretrial or post-trial legal proceeding, during:

(a) Any time between thirty days prior to the original call to order and thirty days following the adjournment sine die of any session of the legislature.

(b) Any time between thirty days prior to convening and thirty days following adjournment sine die of any constitutional convention.

(c) Any time other than those provided in Subparagraph (a) or (b) of this Paragraph when such person is engaged in activities, including travel, in connection with or ordered by: (i) the legislature; (ii) any legislative committee or subcommittee appointed by the president of the Senate or the speaker of the House of Representatives; (iii) any committee or commission appointed by the governor or other person authorized to make such appointments; or (iv) any constitutional convention or commission.

(2) Such peremptory grounds are available to any member or employee enrolled as counsel of record when his participation is required. The availability of other counsel to assume the duties or responsibilities of counsel invoking the continuance or extension does not negate the peremptory nature of his motion.

D. (1) A motion for legislative continuance or extension filed by a legislative employee shall be accompanied by an affidavit, verifying such employment or service, executed by the presiding officer or the clerk or secretary of the respective house.

(2) A motion for legislative continuance or extension shall be filed at no cost to a member, employee, or a client of a member or employee.

E. (1)(a) If the grounds for a legislative continuance or extension are founded upon the convening of a regular legislative session or a constitutional convention, the motion for legislative continuance or extension shall be timely if filed no later than five calendar days prior to the hearing or proceeding to be continued.

(b) If the grounds for a legislative continuance or extension are founded upon any provision of Subparagraph (C)(1)(c) of this Section or upon the issuance of a call for an extraordinary session of the legislature, the motion for legislative continuance or extension shall be timely if filed no later than five calendar days prior to the hearing or proceeding to be continued or no later than two days

R.S. 13:4163—Cont'd

following the issuance of the notice of the meeting or of the call for the extraordinary legislative session, which ever occurs last.

(c) The provisions of this Paragraph shall not be applied so as to impede the peremptory nature of this Section.

(2) Within seventy-two hours of the filing of a motion for a legislative continuance or extension, the court or agency shall grant the continuance or extension ex parte as follows:

(a) If the grounds for the motion are pursuant to Subparagraph (C)(1)(a) or (b) of this Section, the continuance or extension shall be granted for a period of not less than sixty days from the date of adjournment sine die of the session of the legislature or of the constitutional convention.

(b) If the grounds for the motion are pursuant to Subparagraph (C)(1)(c) of this Section, the continuance or extension shall be granted for the day or days the member or employee is engaged in such activities.

F. (1) The provisions of this Section shall not apply to cases in the Supreme Court of Louisiana, criminal cases where the death penalty is sought, and administrative rulemaking authorized by R.S. 49:953.

(2) The provisions of this Section shall not apply to cases and proceedings wherein a member or employee is called as a witness, in which instances the provisions of R.S. 13:3667.1 and 3667.3 shall apply.

G. Any action taken against a person, including any sanction imposed on an attorney, who has filed a motion for legislative continuance or extension and which results from the failure of such person or attorney to appear or comply with an order of the court or agency or any deadline shall be considered an absolute nullity and shall be set aside by the court or agency upon the filing of a motion by the aggrieved person or attorney.

H. (1) Any person or attorney who has filed a motion for legislative continuance or extension which has been denied or which has not been granted within seventy-two hours of filing may apply directly to the Supreme Court of Louisiana for supervisory writs to review the action or inaction of the court or agency where the motion was filed.

(2) If a motion filed pursuant to Subsection G of this Section is denied, such denial shall be an appealable order.

I. (1) For sufficient cause shown, the court shall consider a motion for legislative continuance or extension at any time prior to the hearing or proceeding.

(2) The motion for a legislative continuance may be filed by electronic means such as facsimile transmission or electronic mail, or any other means authorized by law, provided that the mover shall provide all opposing counsel or parties with a copy of the motion, simultaneously with the transmission of the motion to the court.

Amended by Acts 1962, No. 78, § 1; Acts 1966, No. 186, § 2; Acts 1970, No. 681, § 1; Acts 1981, No. 332, § 1; Acts 1985, No. 276, § 1, eff. July 6, 1985; Acts 1990, No. 71, § 1, eff. June 27, 1990; Acts 1992, No. 408, § 1; Acts 2004, No. 873, § 1; Acts 2006, No. 690, § 2, eff. June 29, 2006; Acts 2008, No. 865, § 1; Acts 2016, No. 101, § 1; Acts 2017, No. 363, § 1, eff. June 23, 2017; Acts 2018, No. 180, § 1.

R.S. 13:4165

§ 4165. Special masters; appointment; duties and powers; compensation

A. Pursuant to the inherent judicial power of the court and upon its own motion and with the consent of all parties litigant, the court may enter an order appointing a special master in any civil

R.S. 13:4165—Cont'd

action wherein complicated legal or factual issues are presented or wherein exceptional circumstances of the case warrant such appointment. The consent of the parties litigant may be contingent upon any of the following:

(1) An estimate of the amount of the compensation of the special master.

(2) The identity of the special master.

(3) The court's anticipated specifications of the powers of the special master as defined by Subsection B of this Section.

B. The order appointing a special master may specify or limit the master's powers. Subject to such specifications or limitations, the master has and shall exercise the power to regulate all proceedings before him and to do all acts and take all measures necessary or proper for the efficient performance of his duties.

C. (1) The court may order the master to prepare a report upon the matters submitted to him and, if in the course of his duties he is required to make findings of facts or conclusions of law, the order may further require that the master include in his report information with respect to such findings or conclusions.

(2) The report shall be filed with the clerk of court and notice of such filing shall be served upon all parties.

(3) Within ten days after being served with notice of the filing of the report, any party may file a written objection thereto. After a contradictory hearing, the court may adopt the report, modify it, reject it in whole or in part, receive further evidence, or recommit it with instructions. If no timely objection is filed, the court shall adopt the report as submitted, unless clearly erroneous.

D. The master's compensation shall be reasonable, fixed by the court as limited by Subsection A of this Section, and taxed as costs of court.

E. Notwithstanding any other provision of law to the contrary, including Code of Evidence Article 706, the provisions of this Section shall provide the sole authority and procedure for the appointment, duties, powers, and compensation of a special master.

F. (1) For causes of action arising from a disaster within a parish declared by the president of the United States to be subject to a major disaster declaration under 42 U.S.C. 5121 through 5207 and certified for individual assistance in accordance with the provisions of 44 CFR 206.48(b), the judges with civil jurisdiction in any court of competent jurisdiction may en banc appoint one or more special masters for all causes of action related to first-party insurance property damage claims.

(2) Notwithstanding any other provision of law to the contrary, any order issued pursuant to this Subsection may provide for the appointment, duties, or compensation of the special master or masters in any manner directed by the court, and the court shall allow a party an opportunity to file a motion to opt out of the proceedings before the special master upon a showing of good cause.

(3) The appointment of a special master shall terminate upon determination by the appointing judges en banc.

(4) Each court in which a special master is appointed shall file an annual report of the preceding calendar year by February first of the following year, to the Louisiana Supreme Court, the House Committee on Civil Law and Procedure, and the Senate Committee on Judiciary A on the number, rate of compensation, duties, and assignments of each special master under its jurisdiction as well as the status of each cause of action assigned to each special master in the aggregate. The provisions of this Paragraph shall be applicable only to appointments made pursuant to this Subsection.

R.S. 13:4165—Cont'd

(5) An order pursuant to this Subsection shall comply with the requirements of Fed. Civ. R. 53 as to the appointment and disqualification of a master, except to the extent those requirements are specifically inconsistent with state law.

(6) Notwithstanding any other provision of law to the contrary, any order issued pursuant to this Subsection may provide for mandatory mediation with the goal of expedited dispute resolution using a qualified neutral mediator appointed and compensated in the manner directed by the court.

(7) Any special master appointed pursuant to this Subsection may waive the appointment. Orders initially issued pursuant to this Subsection after January 1, 2022, shall provide for an opt-out upon request of any party.

(8) Notwithstanding any provision of law to the contrary, no provision or policy form issued in this state may be construed to impair a court's authority under this Subsection, and no provision of this Subsection shall impair the jurisdiction or venue of any court of proper jurisdiction and venue in this state.

Added by Acts 1997, No. 580, § 1. Amended by Acts 2014, No. 521, § 1; Acts 2021, No. 318, § 1.

R.S. 13:4202

§ 4202. Rates of judicial interest

A. The rate of judicial interest resulting from a lawsuit pending or filed during the indicated periods shall be as follows:

(1) Prior to September 12, 1980, the rate shall be seven percent per annum.

(2) On and after September 12, 1980, until September 11, 1981, the rate shall be ten percent per annum.

(3) On and after September 11, 1981, until January 1, 1988, the rate shall be twelve percent per annum.

(4) On January 1, 1988, and for the entire year of 1988, the rate shall be nine and three-quarters percent per annum.

(5) On January 1, 1989, and for the entire year of both 1989 and 1990, the rate shall be eleven and one-half percent per annum.

(6) On January 1, 1991, and for the entire year of 1991, the rate shall be eleven percent per annum.

(7) On January 1, 1992, and for the entire year of 1992, the rate shall be nine percent per annum.

(8) On January 1, 1993, and for the entire year of both 1993 and 1994, the rate shall be seven percent per annum.

(9) On January 1, 1995, and for the entire year of 1995, the rate shall be eight and three-quarters percent per annum.

(10) On January 1, 1996, and for the entire year of 1996, the rate shall be nine and three-quarters percent per annum.

(11) On and after January 1, 1997, until August 1, 1997, the rate shall be nine and one-quarter percent per annum.

(12) On and after August 1, 1997, and for the remainder of 1997, the rate shall be seven and nine-tenths percent per annum.

R.S. 13:4202—Cont'd

(13) On January 1, 1998, and for the entire year of 1998, the rate shall be seven and six-tenths percent per annum.

(14) On January 1, 1999, and for the entire year of 1999, the rate shall be six and seventy-three-hundredths percent per annum.

(15) On January 1, 2000, and for the entire year of 2000, the rate shall be seven and two hundred eighty-five-thousandths percent per annum.

(16) On January 1, 2001, and for the entire year of 2001, the rate shall be eight and two hundred forty-one-thousandths percent per annum.

B. (1) On and after January 1, 2002, the rate shall be equal to the rate as published annually, as set forth below, by the commissioner of financial institutions. The commissioner of financial institutions shall ascertain, on the first business day of October of each year, the Federal Reserve Board of Governors approved "discount rate" published daily in the Wall Street Journal. The effective judicial interest rate for the calendar year following the calculation date shall be three and one-quarter percentage points above the discount rate as ascertained by the commissioner.

(2) The judicial interest rate for the calendar year following the calculation date shall be published in the December issue of the Louisiana Bar Journal, the December issue of the Louisiana Register, and in one newspaper of general circulation in each of the cities of Alexandria, Baton Rouge, Lake Charles, Lafayette, Monroe, New Orleans, and Shreveport. The notice in such newspapers shall be published on two separate occasions, with at least one week between publications, during the month of December. The publication in the Louisiana Register shall not be considered rulemaking, within the intendment of the Administrative Procedure Act, R.S. 49:950 et seq., and particularly R.S. 49:953.

C.C. art. 2924(B)(2) and (3) as amended by Acts 1997, No. 275, § 1, eff. June 17, 1997. Redesignated as R.S. 13:4202 pursuant to Acts 1997, No. 275, § 3, eff. June 17, 1997. Amended by Acts 2001, No. 841, § 1; Acts 2012, No. 825, § 1, eff. June 14, 2012.

R.S. 13:4231

§ 4231. Res judicata

Except as otherwise provided by law, a valid and final judgment is conclusive between the same parties, except on appeal or other direct review, to the following extent:

(1) If the judgment is in favor of the plaintiff, all causes of action existing at the time of final judgment arising out of the transaction or occurrence that is the subject matter of the litigation are extinguished and merged in the judgment.

(2) If the judgment is in favor of the defendant, all causes of action existing at the time of final judgment arising out of the transaction or occurrence that is the subject matter of the litigation are extinguished and the judgment bars a subsequent action on those causes of action.

(3) A judgment in favor of either the plaintiff or the defendant is conclusive, in any subsequent action between them, with respect to any issue actually litigated and determined if its determination was essential to that judgment.

C.C. art. 2286. Redesignated as R.S. 13:4231 by Acts 1984, No. 331, § 7, eff. Jan. 1, 1985. Amended by Acts 1990, No. 521, § 1, eff. Jan. 1, 1991.

Comments—1990

(a) R.S. 13:4231 makes a substantial change in the law. Under the present law a second action would be barred by the defense of res judicata only when the plaintiff seeks the same

R.S. 13:4231—Cont'd

relief based on the same cause or grounds. This interpretation of res judicata is too narrow to fully implement the purpose of res judicata which is to foster judicial efficiency and also to protect the defendant from multiple lawsuits. For example, in Mitchell v. Bertolla, 340 So. 2nd 287 (La.1976) the plaintiff sued unsuccessfully to rescind the lease for lesion beyond moiety and nonpayment of the rent, and then sued to rescind the same lease for fraud. The supreme court held that the second action was not barred by res judicata because it was based on a different cause (the legal principle upon which the demand is based).

Under new R.S. 13:4231 the second action would be barred because it arises out of the occurrence which was the subject matter of the prior litigation. The central inquiry is not whether the second action is based on the same cause or cause of action (a concept which is difficult to define) but whether the second action asserts a cause of action which arises out of the transaction or occurrence which was the subject matter of the first action. This serves the purpose of judicial economy and fairness by requiring the plaintiff to seek all relief and to assert all rights which arise out of the same transaction or occurrence. This prevents needless relitigation of the underlying facts and will free the defendant from vexatious litigation; and, by focusing on the transaction or occurrence which would be comparatively easy to determine, this proposal avoids the much more difficult problem of defining what constitutes "cause of action" is avoided. For purposes of res judicata it would not matter whether the cause of action asserted in the second action was the same as that asserted in the first or different as long as it arose out of the transaction or occurrence that was the subject matter of the first action.

(b) R.S. 13:4231 also changes the law by adopting the principle of issue preclusion. This principle serves the interests of judicial economy by preventing relitigation of the same issue between the same parties. For example, if a plaintiff brings an action against a defendant to recover for injuries sustained in an automobile accident, the judgment rendered in that action would preclude relitigation of any issue raised in a subsequent action brought by defendant against plaintiff to recover for his injuries sustained in the same accident provided that the issue had been actually litigated and essential to the judgment, e.g., fault of either party. This proviso insures that the issue would have been fully developed by the parties in the first action and makes it fair to hold the parties bound to that initial determination. Because a judgment rendered in the plaintiff's action can also have preclusive effect on an action by the defendant, Code of Civil Procedure Article 1061 has been amended to require the defendant to assert by reconventional demand all causes of action that he may have against the plaintiff that arise out of the transaction or occurrence that is the subject matter of the principal action.

(c) **Except as otherwise provided by law.** This makes it clear that the general principal of res judicata is subject to the exceptions set forth in R.S. 13:4232 and to any other exceptions that may be provided for in the substantive law as, for example, in cases of family matters.

(d) **Valid and final.** To have any preclusive effect a judgment must be valid, that is, it must have been rendered by a court with jurisdiction over subject matter and over parties, and proper notice must have been given. The judgment must also be a final judgment, that is, a judgment that disposes of the merits in whole or in part. The use of the phrase "final judgment" also means that the preclusive effect of a judgment attaches once a final judgment has been signed by the trial court and would bar any action filed thereafter unless the judgment is reversed on appeal. Having the res judicata effect of a judgment attach at the time of final judgment is rendered by the trial court is in accord with our present law on lis pendens, see Code of Civil Procedure Articles 531, 532.

R.S. 13:4231—Cont'd

(e) **Causes of action existing at the time of the final judgment.** This clause is important in determining the scope of res judicata and accords with the basic principle underlying the doctrine of res judicata that a plaintiff must assert all of his rights and claim all of his remedies arising out of the transaction or occurrence. Claims that arise or which he becomes aware of before trial, may be asserted through an amended or supplemental petition, and these claims will relate back to the time of the original filing if they arise out of the transaction or occurrence set forth in the original petition. Code of Civil Procedure Articles 1153, 1155. Alternatively, he may seek a reservation in the judgment of the right to bring another action. See R.S. 13:4232. A cause of action which arose after the rendition of the final judgment could not have been asserted earlier and would not be precluded by the judgment.

(f) **Extinguished and merged.** When the judgment is in favor of the plaintiff all causes of action that had been asserted are both extinguished and merged in the judgment. Any subsequent action by the plaintiff must be based on the judgment itself. Causes of action that had not been asserted by the plaintiff are extinguished and barred by the judgment.

R.S. 13:4232

§ 4232. Exceptions to the general rule of res judicata

A. A judgment does not bar another action by the plaintiff:

(1) When exceptional circumstances justify relief from the res judicata effect of the judgment;

(2) When the judgment dismissed the first action without prejudice; or,

(3) When the judgment reserved the right of the plaintiff to bring another action.

B. In an action for divorce under Civil Code Article 102 or 103, in an action for determination of incidental matters under Civil Code Article 105, in an action for contributions to a spouse's education or training under Civil Code Article 121, and in an action for partition of community property and settlement of claims between spouses under R.S. 9:2801, the judgment has the effect of res judicata only as to causes of action actually adjudicated.

Added by Acts 1990, No. 521, § 1, eff. Jan. 1, 1991. Amended by Acts 1991, No. 367, § 3.

Comment—1990

R.S. 13:4232 creates three exceptions to the general principle of res judicata set forth in R.S. 13:4231. First, it gives the court the discretion to grant relief from the judgment for exceptional circumstances. This discretion is necessary to allow the court to balance the principle of res judicata with the interests of justice. This discretion must be exercised on a case by case basis and such relief should be granted only in truly exceptional cases, otherwise the purpose of res judicata would be defeated. For the application of a similar principle see Federal Rule of Civil Procedure 60(b). Second, it gives the court the authority to reserve in the judgment the right of the plaintiff to bring a subsequent action. This would be particularly useful in custody, support and divorce actions and in cases involving injunctions and installment contracts. It could also be useful in cases where the plaintiff may be unsure whether he will suffer future injuries from the event which he is presently litigating, e.g., risk of contracting cancer from exposure to asbestos. See, Adams v. Johns–Manville Sales Corp., 783 F.2d 589 (5th Cir.1986); Jackson v. Johns–Manville Sales Corp., 781 F.2d 394 (5th Cir.1986). But it is not intended to apply in the case where the plaintiff has simply failed to assert a right or claim for damages through oversight or lack of proper preparation.

R.S. 13:4232—Cont'd

Comment—1991

Subsection B is added to this Section to make it clear that failure to raise related causes of action in any of the specified actions will not result in the actions that were not urged being barred by the subsequent judgment, if that judgment is silent as to the actions in question.

PART III. ENFORCEMENT OF FOREIGN JUDGMENTS ACT

R.S. 13:4241

§ 4241. Definition

In this Part "foreign judgment" means any judgment, decree, or order of a court of the United States or of any other court which is entitled to full faith and credit in this state.

Added by Acts 1985, No. 464, § 1.

R.S. 13:4242

§ 4242. Filing and status of foreign judgments

A copy of any foreign judgment authenticated in accordance with an act of congress or the statutes of this state may be annexed to and filed with an ex parte petition complying with Code of Civil Procedure Article 891 and praying that the judgment be made executory in a court of this state. The foreign judgment shall be treated in the same manner as a judgment of a court of this state. It shall have the same effect and be subject to the same procedures, and defenses, for reopening, vacating, or staying as a judgment of a court of this state and may be enforced in the same manner.

Added by Acts 1985, No. 464, § 1.

R.S. 13:4243

§ 4243. Notice of filing

A. At the time of the filing of the petition and foreign judgment, the judgment creditor shall file with the court an affidavit setting forth the name and last known address of the judgment debtor and the judgment creditor.

B. Promptly upon the filing of the petition, the foreign judgment, and the affidavit, the clerk shall send a notice by certified mail to the judgment debtor at the address given and shall make a note of the mailing in the record. The notice shall include the name and address of the judgment creditor and his attorney, if any. In addition, the judgment creditor may mail a notice of the filing to the judgment debtor and may file proof of mailing with the clerk. Failure to mail notice of filing by the clerk shall not affect the enforcement proceedings if proof of mailing by the judgment creditor has been filed.

C. No execution or other process for enforcement of a foreign judgment filed hereunder shall issue until thirty days after the mailing of the notice of the filing of the foreign judgment.

Added by Acts 1985, No. 464, § 1. Amended by Acts 1997, No. 1156, § 5; Acts 2003, No. 750, § 4.

R.S. 13:4244

§ 4244. Stay

A. If the judgment debtor proves on contradictory motion that an appeal from the foreign judgment is pending or will be taken, or that a stay of execution has been granted, the court shall stay

R.S. 13:4244—Cont'd

enforcement of the foreign judgment until the appeal is concluded, the time for appeal expires, or the stay of execution expires or is vacated, upon proof that the judgment debtor has furnished the security for the satisfaction of the judgment required by the state in which it was rendered.

B. If the judgment debtor proves on contradictory motion any ground upon which the execution of a judgment of a court of this state would be stayed, the court shall stay enforcement of the foreign judgment upon requiring security for satisfaction of the judgment as is required in this state.

Added by Acts 1985, No. 464, § 1.

R.S. 13:4245

§ 4245. Fees

Fees for filing and enforcing a foreign judgment shall be as provided by law.

Added by Acts 1985, No. 464, § 1.

R.S. 13:4246

§ 4246. Optional procedure

The right of a judgment creditor to bring an action to enforce the judgment under Article 2541 of the Code of Civil Procedure is preserved.

Added by Acts 1985, No. 464, § 1.

R.S. 13:4247

§ 4247. Short title

This Part may be cited as the "Enforcement of Foreign Judgments Act".

Added by Acts 1985, No. 464, § 1.

R.S. 13:4248

§ 4248. Foreign protective orders

A. A copy of any foreign protective order authenticated in accordance with an act of congress or the statutes of this state may be annexed to and filed with an ex parte petition praying that the protective order be made executory in this state. The address of the petitioner may remain confidential with the court.

B. At an ex parte hearing, the court shall make the protective order executory in this state, cause to have prepared a Uniform Abuse Prevention Order, as provided in R.S. 46:2136.2(C), shall sign such order, and shall forward it to the clerk of court for filing, all without delay.

C. The clerk of the issuing court shall transmit the order to the Louisiana Protective Order Registry, R.S. 46:2136.2(A), by facsimile transmission, mail, or direct electronic input, where available. The order shall be mailed and transmitted as expeditiously as possible, but no later than the end of the next business day after the order is filed with the clerk of court.

Added by Acts 1997, No. 1156, § 5. Amended by Acts 2003, No. 750, § 4.

R.S. 13:4359

§ 4359. Portion of price to be paid on adjudication

In all judicial sales when the terms of the sale are not fixed in the writ, judgment, or order of sale, before the advertisement the party provoking the sale may instruct the officer conducting the sale as to what portion of the purchase price is to be paid at the moment of adjudication. In default of such instruction, the officer may fix the amount, which in no case shall be less than ten per cent. The portion of the purchase price to be paid at the adjudication shall be stated in the advertisement.

Added by Acts 1960, No. 32, § 6, eff. Jan. 1, 1961.

R.S. 13:4363

§ 4363. Appointment of appraisers

A. Not less than seven days, exclusive of holidays, before the sale of seized property, the sheriff shall serve written notice on the debtor and on the seizing creditor, in the manner provided for the service of a citation, directing each to name an appraiser to value the property and to notify the sheriff of his appointment prior to the time stated in the notice, which shall be at least four days, exclusive of holidays, prior to the time of the sale. The appraisal of the debtor and seizing creditor shall be made and delivered to the sheriff at least two days, exclusive of holidays, prior to the time of the sale.

B. If there are two or more debtors or seizing creditors and these parties cannot agree as to which should act as or appoint an appraiser, and in any case where an appraisal is required prior to the judicial sale and which is not otherwise provided for in this Section, on the ex parte application of the sheriff or of any interested party, the court shall designate the party to act as or appoint the appraiser, and the notice required by Sub-section A of this Section shall be served on the party so designated.

Added by Acts 1960, No. 32, § 6, eff. Jan. 1, 1961. Amended by Acts 1978, No. 407, § 1; Acts 1981, No. 140, § 1; Acts 1982, No. 836, § 1.

R.S. 13:4441

§ 4441. Transfer of cases appealed to wrong court; retransfer

When an appeal is taken and perfected to an appellate court having no jurisdiction thereof, the court to which it is taken may transfer it to the court having jurisdiction thereof, instead of dismissing the appeal. The appellate court to which the appeal is transferred shall proceed as if the appeal had been taken to it originally.

If an appeal is transferred erroneously to the supreme court, the latter shall retransfer it to the court having appellate jurisdiction thereof. If an appeal is transferred by a district court erroneously to a court of appeal, the latter shall retransfer it to the district court to which it was taken originally, or to the supreme court if the latter has jurisdiction thereof.

This section applies to appeals in all cases, civil or criminal, to appeals over which a court of appeal has jurisdiction but which has been taken to the wrong court of appeal, and to all courts having appellate jurisdiction.

Amended by Acts 1960, No. 38, § 1, eff. June 20, 1960.

R.S. 13:4611

§ 4611. Punishment for contempt of court; defenses

Except as otherwise provided for by law:

(1) The supreme court, the courts of appeal, the district courts, family courts, juvenile courts and the city courts may punish a person adjudged guilty of a contempt of court therein, as follows:

(a) For a direct contempt of court committed by an attorney at law, by a fine of not more than one hundred dollars, or by imprisonment for not more than twenty-four hours, or both; and, for any subsequent contempt of the same court by the same offender, by a fine of not more than two hundred dollars, or by imprisonment for not more than ten days, or both;

(b) For disobeying or resisting a lawful restraining order, or preliminary or permanent injunction, by a fine of not more than one thousand dollars, or by imprisonment for not more than six months, or both.

(c) For a deliberate refusal to perform an act which is yet within the power of the offender to perform, by imprisonment until he performs the act; and

(d)(i) For any other contempt of court, including disobeying an order for the payment of child support or spousal support or an order for the right of custody or visitation, by a fine of not more than five hundred dollars, or imprisonment for not more than three months, or both.

(ii) In addition to or in lieu of the penalties provided by this Paragraph, the court may order that the person perform litter abatement work or community service in a court-approved program for each day he was to be imprisoned, provided that the total days of jail, litter abatement work, and community service do not exceed the maximum sentence provided by this Paragraph.

(iii) It is a defense as provided by R.S. 9:311.1 to a charge of contempt of court for failure to comply with a court order of child support if an obligor can prove that he was incarcerated during the period of noncompliance. This defense applies only to the time period of actual incarceration.

(e) In addition to or in lieu of the above penalties, when a parent has violated a visitation order, the court may order any or all of the following:

(i) Require one or both parents to allow additional visitation days to replace those denied the noncustodial parent.

(ii) Require one or both parents to attend a parent education course.

(iii) Require one or both parents to attend counseling or mediation.

(iv) Require the parent violating the order to pay all court costs and reasonable attorney fees of the other party.

(f) A pattern of willful and intentional violation of this Section, without good cause, may constitute a material change in circumstances warranting a modification of an existing custody or visitation order.

(g) The court may award attorney fees to the prevailing party in a contempt of court proceeding provided for in this Section.

(2) Justices of the peace may punish a person adjudged guilty of a direct contempt of court by a fine of not more than fifty dollars, or imprisonment in the parish jail for not more than twenty-four hours, or both.

(3) The court or justice of the peace, when applicable, may suspend the imposition or the execution of the whole or any part of the sentence imposed and place the defendant on unsupervised

R.S. 13:4611—Cont'd

probation or probation supervised by a probation office, agency, or officer designated by the court or justice of the peace, other than the division of probation and parole of the Department of Public Safety and Corrections. When the court or justice of the peace places a defendant on probation, the court or the justice of the peace may impose any specific conditions reasonably related to the defendant's rehabilitation, including but not limited to the conditions of probation as set forth in Code of Criminal Procedure Article 895. A term of probation shall not exceed the length of time a defendant may be imprisoned for the contempt, except in the case of contempt for disobeying an order for the payment of child support or spousal support or an order for the right of custody or visitation, when the term of probation may extend for a period of up to two years.

Added by Acts 1960, No. 32, § 6, eff. Jan. 1, 1961. Amended by Acts 1964, No. 241, § 1; Acts 1972, No. 664, § 1; Acts 1985, No. 43, § 1; Acts 1991, No. 508, § 2; Acts 1993, No. 429, § 1; Acts 1995, No. 517, § 1; Acts 1999, No. 57, § 1; Acts 2001, No. 425, § 2, eff. June 15, 2001; Acts 2004, No. 520, § 1; Acts 2006, No. 653, § 1; Acts 2014, No. 330, § 1; Acts 2016, No. 132, § 2; Acts 2017, No. 264, § 3, eff. Aug. 1, 2020.

R.S. 13:5101

§ 5101. Title and application

A. This Part shall be known and may be cited as the "Louisiana Governmental Claims Act".

B. This Part applies to any suit in contract or for injury to person or property against the state, a state agency, an officer or employee of the state or a state agency arising out of the discharge of his official duties or within the course and scope of his employment, or a political subdivision of the state, as defined herein, or against an officer or employee of a political subdivision arising out of the discharge of his official duties or within the course and scope of his employment. The provisions of this Part shall not supersede the provisions of R.S. 15:1171 et seq. or R.S. 15:1181 et seq.

Acts 1975, No. 434, § 1. Amended by Acts 1988, No. 781, § 1; Acts 1990, No. 284, § 1; Acts 1996, 1st Ex.Sess., No. 63, § 1, eff. May 9, 1996; Acts 2002, 1st Ex.Sess., No. 89, § 1, eff. April 18, 2002; Acts 2010, No. 301, § 1.

R.S. 13:5102

§ 5102. Definitions

A. As used in this Part, "state agency" means any board, commission, department, agency, special district, authority, or other entity of the state and, as used in R.S. 13:5106, any nonpublic, nonprofit agency, person, firm, or corporation which has qualified with the United States Internal Revenue Service for an exemption from federal income tax under Section 501(c)(3), (4), (7), (8), (10), or (19) of the Internal Revenue Code, and which, through contract with the state, provides services for the treatment, care, custody, control, or supervision of persons placed or referred to such agency, person, firm, or corporation by any agency or department of the state in connection with programs for treatment or services involving residential or day care for adults and children, foster care, rehabilitation, shelter, or counseling; however, the term "state agency" shall include such nonpublic, nonprofit agency, person, firm, or corporation only as it renders services to a person or persons on behalf of the state pursuant to a contract with the state. The term "state agency" shall not include a nonpublic, nonprofit agency, person, firm or corporation that commits a willful or wanton, or grossly negligent, act or omission. A nonpublic, nonprofit agency, person, firm or corporation otherwise included under the provisions of this Subsection shall not be deemed a "state agency" for the purpose of prohibiting trial by jury under R.S. 13:5105, and a suit against such agency, person, firm or corporation may be tried by jury as provided by law. "State agency" does not include any political subdivision or any agency of a political subdivision.

R.S. 13:5102—Cont'd

B. As the term is used in this Part, "political subdivision" means:

(1) Any parish, municipality, special district, school board, sheriff, public board, institution, department, commission, district, corporation, agency, authority, or an agency or subdivision of any of these, and other public or governmental body of any kind which is not a state agency.

(2) Any private entity, such as Transit Management of Southeast Louisiana, Inc. (TMSEL), including its employees, which on the behalf of a public transit authority was created as a result of Section 13(c) of the Urban Mass Transportation Act, requiring the terms of transit workers' collective bargaining agreements to be honored and provides management and administrative duties of such agency or authority and such entity is employed by no other agency or authority, whether public or private.

C. As the term is used in this Part, "suit" means civil actions as defined in Code of Civil Procedure Art. 421 whether instituted by principal or incidental demand.

Acts 1975, No. 434, § 1. Amended by Acts 1987, No. 329, § 1; Acts 1988, No. 781, § 1; Acts 1989, No. 706, § 1; Acts 2004, No. 704, § 1, eff. Sept. 1, 2004.

R.S. 13:5103

§ 5103. Determination of procedural questions

All procedural questions arising in suits on claims against the state, state agencies, or political subdivisions shall be determined, except as the contrary is specified in this Part, in accordance with the rules of law applicable to suits between private parties.

Acts 1975, No. 434, § 1.

R.S. 13:5104

§ 5104. Venue

A. All suits filed against the state of Louisiana or any state agency or against an officer or employee of the state or state agency for conduct arising out of the discharge of his official duties or within the course and scope of his employment shall be instituted before the district court of the judicial district in which the state capitol is located or in the district court having jurisdiction in the parish in which the cause of action arises.

B. All suits filed against a political subdivision of the state or against an officer or employee of a political subdivision for conduct arising out of the discharge of his official duties or within the course and scope of his employment shall be instituted before the district court of the judicial district in which the political subdivision is located or in the district court having jurisdiction in the parish in which the cause of action arises.

C. All suits filed against a coroner shall be instituted before the district court of the judicial district in which the coroner is elected.

D. All suits against the faculty or staff of the Louisiana State University Board of Supervisors, the Louisiana State Medical School, or the Louisiana State Health Sciences Center alleging administrative or supervisory negligence and arising out of the discharge of the duties of the faculty member or staff created pursuant to R.S. 17:1519 through 1519.8 shall be brought only in the parish where the medical care was actually provided to the patient.

Acts 1975, No. 434, § 1. Amended by Acts 1985, No. 306, § 1; Acts 1991, No. 622, § 1; Acts 1991, No. 660, § 1; Acts 1996, 1st Ex.Sess., No. 63, § 1, eff. May 9, 1996; Acts 1999, No. 640, § 1, eff. July 1, 1999; Acts 2000, 1st Ex.Sess., No. 127, § 1, eff. April 19, 2000; Acts 2009, No. 13, § 1.

R.S. 13:5105

§ 5105. Jury trial prohibited; demand for trial; costs

A. No suit against a political subdivision of the state shall be tried by jury. Except upon a demand for jury trial timely filed in accordance with law by the state or a state agency or the plaintiff in a lawsuit against the state or state agency, no suit against the state or a state agency shall be tried by jury.

B. Whenever a jury trial is demanded by the state, state agency, or the plaintiff in a lawsuit against the state or state agency, the party demanding the jury trial shall pay all costs of the jury trial including the posting of a bond or cash deposit for costs in accordance with Code of Civil Procedure Articles 1733 through 1734.1, inclusive.

C. Repealed by Acts 2016, No. 341, § 1, eff. June 2, 2016.

D. Notwithstanding the provisions of Subsection A, a political subdivision, by general ordinance or resolution, may waive the prohibition against a jury trial provided in Subsection A of this Section. Whenever the jury trial prohibition is waived by a political subdivision, and a jury trial is demanded by the political subdivision or the plaintiff in a suit against the political subdivision or against an officer or employee of the political subdivision, the demand for a jury trial shall be timely filed in accordance with law. The rights to and limitations upon a jury trial shall be as provided in Code of Civil Procedure Articles 1731 and 1732.

E. Notwithstanding the provisions of Subsection B of this Section, the state, a state agency, or state employee who is being indemnified and defended under R.S. 13:5108.1 or the Patients Compensation Fund shall not be required to post any bond, cash deposit, or other charge whatsoever to obtain a trial by jury. If the state, state agency, or state employee who is being indemnified and defended under R.S. 13:5108.1 or the Patients Compensation Fund is ordered to pay court costs, the state or the Patients Compensation Fund, as may be applicable, shall pay all jury costs directly associated with that trial within thirty days after mailing of the notice of judgment of the trial court.

Acts 1975, No. 434, § 1. Amended by Acts 1993, No. 993, § 1, eff. Jan. 1, 1994; Acts 1995, No. 598, § 1; Acts 1996, 1st Ex.Sess., No. 63, § 1, eff. May 9, 1996; Acts 2001, No. 249, § 1.

Editor's Notes

For a complex analysis of this prohibition of jury trials against the State, see Fontenot v. Patterson Ins., 997 So.2d 529 (La. 2008).

Arshad v. City of Kenner, 95 So.3d 477 (La. 2011). The Supreme Court held that a political subdivision may waive its statutory right for a nonjury trial only through an ordinance or a resolution waiving the right in all cases, not in a specific suit.

R.S. 13:5106

§ 5106. Limitations

A. No suit against the state or a state agency or political subdivision shall be instituted in any court other than a Louisiana state court.

B. (1) The total liability of the state and political subdivisions for all damages for personal injury to any one person, including all claims and derivative claims, exclusive of property damages, medical care and related benefits and loss of earnings, and loss of future earnings, as provided in this Section, shall not exceed five hundred thousand dollars, regardless of the number of suits filed or claims made for the personal injury to that person.

R.S. 13:5106—Cont'd

(2) The total liability of the state and political subdivisions for all damages for wrongful death of any one person, including all claims and derivative claims, exclusive of property damages, medical care and related benefits and loss of earnings or loss of support, and loss of future support, as provided in this Section, shall not exceed five hundred thousand dollars, regardless of the number of suits filed or claims made for the wrongful death of that person.

(3)(a) In any suit for personal injury against a political subdivision wherein the court, pursuant to judgment, determines that the claimant is entitled to medical care and related benefits that may be incurred subsequent to judgment, the court shall order that a reversionary trust be established for the benefit of the claimant and that all medical care and related benefits incurred subsequent to judgment be paid pursuant to the reversionary trust instrument. The reversionary trust instrument shall provide that such medical care and related benefits be paid directly to the provider as they are incurred. Nothing in this Paragraph shall be construed to prevent the parties from entering into a settlement or compromise at any time whereby medical care and related benefits shall be provided, but with the requirement of establishing a reversionary trust.

(b) Any funds remaining in a reversionary trust that is created pursuant to Subparagraph (3)(a) of this Subsection shall revert to the political subdivision that established the trust, upon the death of the claimant or upon the termination of the trust as provided in the trust instrument. The trustee may obtain the services of an administrator to assist in the administration of the trust. All costs, fees, taxes, or other charges imposed on the funds in the trust shall be paid by the trust. The trust agreement may impose such other reasonable duties, powers, provisions, and dispute resolution clauses as may be deemed necessary or appropriate. Disputes as to the administration of the trust can be appealed to the district court. Nothing in this Paragraph shall preclude the political subdivision from establishing other alternative funding mechanisms for the exclusive benefit of the claimant. The terms and conditions of the reversionary trust instrument or other alternative funding mechanism, prior to its implementation, must be approved by the court. The parties to the case may present recommendations to the court for the terms and conditions of the trust instrument or other funding mechanism to be included in the order. Upon request of either party, the court shall hold a contradictory hearing before granting a final order implementing the reversionary trust or the alternative funding mechanism.

(c) In any suit for personal injury against the state or a state agency wherein the court pursuant to judgment determines that the claimant is entitled to medical care and related benefits that may be incurred subsequent to judgment, all such medical care and related benefits incurred subsequent to judgment shall be paid from the Future Medical Care Fund as provided in R.S. 39:1533.2. Medical care and related benefits shall be paid directly to the provider as they are incurred. Nothing in this Subparagraph shall be construed to prevent the parties from entering into a settlement or compromise at any time whereby medical care and related benefits shall be provided but with the requirement that they shall be paid in accordance with this Subparagraph.

C. If the state or a state agency or political subdivision is held liable for damages for personal injury or wrongful death, the court shall determine:

(1) The amount of general damages exclusive of:

(a) Medical care.

(b) Related benefits.

(c) Loss of earnings and/or support.

(d) Loss of future earnings and/or support.

R.S. 13:5106—Cont'd

(2) The amount of medical care, related benefits and loss of earnings and/or support to date of judgment.

(3) Whether the claimant is in need of future medical care and related benefits and the amount thereof; and

(4) Whether there will be a loss of future earnings or support, and the amounts thereof.

D. (1) "Derivative claims" include but are not limited to claims for survival or loss of consortium.

(2) "Loss of earnings" and "loss of support" for the purpose of this Section means any form of economic loss already sustained by the claimant as a result of the injury or wrongful death which forms the basis of the claim. "Loss of future earnings" and "loss of future support" means any form of economic loss which the claimant will sustain after the trial as a result of the injury or death which forms the basis of the claim.

(3) "Medical care and related benefits" for the purpose of this Section means all reasonable medical, surgical, hospitalization, physical rehabilitation, and custodial services, and includes drugs, prosthetic devices, and other similar materials reasonably necessary in the provision of such services.

(4) "Reversionary trust" means a trust established by a political subdivision for the exclusive benefit of the claimant to pay the medical care and related benefits as they accrue, including without limitation reasonable and necessary amounts for all diagnosis, cure, mitigation, or treatment of any disease or condition from which the injured person suffers as a result of the injuries, and the *sequelae* thereof, sustained by the claimant on the date the injury was sustained. The trustee shall have the same fiduciary duties as imposed upon a trustee by the Louisiana Trust Code. Nothing herein shall limit the rights of claimants to contract with respect to attorney fees and costs.

E. The legislature finds and states:

(1) That judgments against public entities have exceeded ability to pay on current basis.

(2) That the public fisc is threatened by these judgments to the extent that the general health, safety, and welfare of the citizenry may be threatened.

(3) That the limitations set forth in this Section are needed to curb the trend of governmental liability abuses, to balance an individual's claim against the needs of the public interests and the common good of the whole society, and to avoid overburdening Louisiana's economy and its taxpaying citizens with even more new and/or increased taxes than are already needed for essential programs.

(4) That the purpose of this Section is not to reestablish any immunity based on the status of sovereignty but rather to clarify the substantive content and parameters of application of such legislatively created codal articles and laws and also to assist in the implementation of Article II of the Constitution of Louisiana.

F. The provisions of this Section shall not apply to claims arising under R.S. 40:1237.1 et seq.

Acts 1975, No. 434, § 1. Amended by Acts 1985, No. 452, § 1; Acts 1995, No. 828, § 2, eff. Nov. 23, 1995; Acts 1996, 1st Ex.Sess., No. 63, § 1, eff. May 9, 1996; Acts 2000, 1st Ex.Sess., No. 20, § 1, eff. July 1, 2000; Acts 2005, No. 1, § 1, eff. May 27, 2005; Acts 2010, No. 301, § 1; Acts 2018, No. 178, § 1.

Editor's Notes

Iles v. Ogden, 99 So.3d 1035 (La. App. 4 Cir. 2012). Special damages award for future medical and attendant care expenses was not payable in on lump sum but was payable only as the expenses were incurred, applying the applicable statute literally. R.S. 13:5106(B)(3)(c). (There is a concurring opinion detailing the applicable statutes with great specificity.)

R.S. 13:5107

§ 5107. Service of citation and process

A. (1) In all suits filed against the state of Louisiana or a state agency, citation and service may be obtained by citation and service on the attorney general of Louisiana, or on any employee in his office above the age of sixteen years, or any other proper officer or person, depending upon the identity of the named defendant and in accordance with the laws of this state, and on the department, board, commission, or agency head or person, depending upon the identity of the named defendant and in accordance with the laws of this state, and on the department, board, commission, or agency head or person, depending upon the identity of the named defendant and the identity of the named board, commission, department, agency, or officer through which or through whom suit is to be filed against.

(2) Service shall be requested upon the attorney general within ninety days of filing suit. This shall be sufficient to comply with the requirements of Subsection D of this Section and also Code of Civil Procedure Article 1201(C). However, the duty of the defendant served through the attorney general to answer the suit or file other responsive pleadings does not commence to run until the additional service required upon the department, board, commission, or agency head has been made.

B. In all suits filed against a political subdivision of the state, or any of its departments, offices, boards, commissions, agencies or instrumentalities, citation and service may be obtained on any proper agent or agents designated by the local governing authority and in accordance with the laws of the state provided that the authority has filed notice of the designation of agent for service of process with and paid a fee of ten dollars to the secretary of state, who shall maintain such information with the information on agents for service of process for corporations. If no agent or agents are designated for service of process, as shown by the lack of such designation in the records of the secretary of state, citation and service may be obtained on the district attorney, parish attorney, city attorney, or any other proper officer or person, depending upon the identity of the named defendant and in accordance with the laws of the state, and on the department, board, commission, or agency head or person, depending upon the identity of the named defendant and the identity of the named board, commission, department, agency, or officer through which or through whom suit is to be filed against.

C. In all suits in which title to lands or waterbottoms under the jurisdiction of the state land office is or may be at issue, and in all possessory actions, boundary disputes, trespass actions, actions involving alleged acquisitive prescription of immovable property, declaratory judgments, injunctions and concursus proceedings involving such lands or waterbottoms, citation and service of all pleadings also shall be made on the register of the state land office. In all suits in which property rights, mineral rights, or authorities under the jurisdiction of the State Mineral and Energy Board may also be at issue, citation and service of all pleadings shall also be made on the secretary of the Department of Natural Resources.

D. (1) In all suits in which the state, a state agency, or political subdivision, or any officer or employee thereof is named as a party, service of citation shall be requested within ninety days of the commencement of the action or the filing of a supplemental or amended petition which initially names the state, a state agency, or political subdivision or any officer or employee thereof as a party. This requirement may be expressly waived by the defendant in such action by any written waiver. If not waived, a request for service of citation upon the defendant shall be considered timely if requested on the defendant within the time period provided by this Section, notwithstanding insufficient or erroneous service.

(2) If service is not requested by the party filing the action within the period required in Paragraph (1) of this Subsection, the action shall be dismissed without prejudice, after contradictory

R.S. 13:5107—Cont'd

motion as provided in Code of Civil Procedure Article 1672(C), as to the state, state agency, or political subdivision, or any officer or employee thereof, upon whom service was not requested within the period required by Paragraph (1) of this Subsection.

(3) When the state, a state agency, or a political subdivision, or any officer or employee thereof, is dismissed as a party pursuant to this Section, the filing of the action, even as against other defendants, shall not interrupt or suspend the running of prescription as to the state, state agency, or political subdivision, or any officer or employee thereof; however, the effect of interruption of prescription as to other persons shall continue.

Acts 1975, No. 434, § 1. Amended by Acts 1983, No. 586, § 1; Acts 1985, No. 861, § 1, eff. July 23, 1985; Acts 1996, 1st Ex.Sess., No. 63, § 1, eff. May 9, 1996; Acts 1997, No. 518, § 1, eff. Jan. 1, 1998; Acts 2010, No. 55, § 1; Acts 2012, No. 770, § 1, eff. June 12, 2012; Acts 2014, No. 379, § 1, eff. May 30, 2014; Acts 2018, No. 242, § 1.

R.S. 13:5108

§ 5108. Prescription, immunity; pleas

The defendant in any suit filed against the state of Louisiana, a state agency or a political subdivision of the state shall not be entitled to file a plea of prescription or peremption barring such suit or the liability of the entity instituting the suit if the suit in contract or for injury to person or property is filed within the time fixed by law for such suits against private persons, or in other suits authorized by the legislature if the suit is filed within one year after the date on which the resolution authorizing it was adopted or within one year after the date on which the law authorizing it becomes effective.

Acts 1975, No. 434, § 1.

Editor's Notes

See also R.S. 13:5108.1 and 13:5108.2, indemnification of officers and employees of the state.

See Bordelon v. Medical Center of Baton Rouge, No. 03-C-0202, La. S.Ct. October 21, 2003, for a definitive analysis of the consequences of failure to request service of process within 90 days of filing suit.

R.S. 13:5109.1

§ 5109.1. Settlement of claims; prohibited terms

A. No settlement agreement of a claim against the state, a state agency, a political subdivision, or any employee or officer of the state, a state agency, or a political subdivision shall contain a provision prohibiting the disclosure by the claimant of the terms of or the facts associated with the underlying claim of the settlement agreement when the underlying claim is based on an allegation of sexual harassment or sexual assault of the claimant and public funds are paid, in whole or in part, as satisfaction of the terms of the settlement agreement.

B. (1) "Sexual assault" means any nonconsensual sexual contact including but not limited to any act provided in R.S. 15:541(24) or obscenity as provided by R.S. 14:106.

(2) "Sexual harassment" means unwelcome sexual advances, requests for sexual favors, and other verbal, physical, or inappropriate conduct of a sexual nature when the conduct explicitly or implicitly affects an individual's employment or the holding of office, unreasonably interferes with an individual's work performance, or creates an intimidating, hostile, or offensive work environment.

Added by Acts 2019, No. 35, § 1.

R.S. 13:5200

§ 5200. Declaration of purpose

A. The purpose of this Part is to improve the administration of justice in small noncriminal cases, and make the judicial system more available to and comprehensible by the public; to simplify practice and procedure in the commencement, handling, and trial of such cases in order that plaintiffs may bring actions in their own behalf, and defendants may participate actively in the proceedings rather than default; to provide an efficient and inexpensive forum with the objective of dispensing justice in a speedy manner; and generally to promote the confidence of the public in the overall judicial system by providing a forum for small claims.

B. In an effort to improve access to justice, the Louisiana Supreme Court has initiated an Online Dispute Resolution Pilot Project Program as provided in Part XVIII–A of this Chapter to include all small claims cases filed in the City Court of East St. Tammany beginning January 1, 2022, and continuing until the Louisiana Supreme Court or Louisiana Legislature terminates the program.

Added by Acts 1977, No. 710, § 1. Amended by Acts 2021, No. 281, § 1.

R.S. 13:5201

§ 5201. Small claims divisions

A. Each city court, now in existence or hereafter created, is authorized to establish by court rule one or more small claims divisions.

B. Such small claims divisions may be established in such areas of the territorial jurisdiction of the court as the judge or judges thereof deem appropriate to best serve the small claims litigants within the jurisdiction. Evening and Saturday hours of operations of a small claims division may also be established.

C. A small claims division so authorized is provided for the filing of matters within its subject matter jurisdiction as provided in R.S. 13:5202(A). A plaintiff filing suit on a claim within the jurisdiction of the division is authorized to file such suit in the division instead of on the regular civil docket of the court.

D. The clerk of court shall maintain a docket for the record of cases filed in the small claims division. At his option, small claims so identified may be entered in docket books maintained for the ordinary civil docket.

E. In the City Court of East St. Tammany, parties shall participate in the Online Dispute Resolution Pilot Project Program process pursuant to R.S. 13:5213 et seq.

Added by Acts 1977, No. 710, § 1. Amended by Acts 1979, No. 46, § 3, eff. Jan. 1, 1980; Acts 1987, No. 256, § 1; Acts 2021, No. 281, § 1.

R.S. 13:5202

§ 5202. Jurisdiction

A. A small claims division shall be a court not of record and shall have civil subject matter jurisdiction in cases where the amount in dispute does not exceed five thousand dollars, exclusive of interest, court costs, attorney fees, or penalties, whether provided by agreement or by law, provided that not more than ten parties plaintiff shall be joined in the same action pursuant to Article 463 of the Code of Civil Procedure and that there shall be no class certification pursuant to Articles 591 through 597 of the Code of Civil Procedure.

R.S. 13:5202—Cont'd

B. A small claims division shall have authority to grant any appropriate relief, including money damages and equitable relief. Injunctions and restraining orders shall not issue from a small claims division, except to arrest the execution of its own writ. Class actions, summary proceedings, and executory proceedings shall be prohibited.

C. The judges and clerks of the respective courts shall serve as the judges and clerks of the small claims divisions, except that an attorney appointed by the judges may serve as arbitrator as hereinafter provided.

D. Each court may by court rule establish mass filing limitations on all parties filing claims in the small claims divisions.

E. In the City Court of East St. Tammany, the small claims division shall have civil subject matter jurisdiction in cases where the amount in dispute is the same as the amount established for civil jurisdiction in a justice of the peace court, exclusive of interest, court costs, attorney fees, or penalties, whether provided by agreement or by law, provided that not more than ten parties plaintiff shall be joined in the same action pursuant to Code of Civil Procedure Article 463, and there shall be no class certification pursuant to Code of Civil Procedure Articles 591 through 597.

Added by Acts 1977, No. 710, § 1. Amended by Acts 1979, No. 46, § 3, eff. Jan. 1, 1980; Acts 1982, No. 286, § 1; Acts 1985, No. 298, § 1; Acts 1987, No. 256, § 1; Acts 1999, No. 312, § 1; Acts 2008, No. 195, § 1; Acts 2012, No. 209, § 1; Acts 2020, No. 205, § 1, eff. June 11, 2020.

R.S. 13:5203

§ 5203. Pleadings; citation; procedure; evidence; substantive law; depositions

A. The pleadings, citation, and procedure provided by Articles 4901 through 4904 of the Louisiana Code of Civil Procedure shall be applicable to a small claims division created under authority of this Part. The technical rules of evidence are relaxed, and all relevant evidence is admissible, including hearsay, provided the judge satisfies himself of its general reliability; and further provided that the judgment is founded upon competent evidence.

B. A small claims division shall conduct hearings upon small claims in such manner as to do substantial justice between the parties according to the rules of substantive law, and shall not be bound by the statutory provisions or rules governing practice, procedure, pleading, or evidence, except statutory provisions relating to privileged communications.

C. No depositions shall be taken and no interrogatories or other discovery proceedings shall be used under the small claims procedure.

Added by Acts 1977, No. 710, § 1. Amended by Acts 1979, No. 46, § 3, eff. Jan. 1, 1980; Acts 1987, No. 256, § 1.

R.S. 13:5204

§ 5204. Service of citation; extension of delay to answer

A. Service of citation or other process shall be by certified mail, with return receipt requested. However, should the receipt not be returned, or, if requested by a party filing the pleading who pays the service charge therefor, or if required by local court rule, service of pleadings may be made in accordance with the Louisiana Code of Civil Procedure.

B. Notwithstanding any other provision of law to the contrary, each citation or other process shall contain a notice which provides substantially as follows:

"ATTENTION!

R.S. 13:5204—Cont'd

THIS LAWSUIT IS FILED IN THE SMALL CLAIMS COURT.

THE ORDINARY RULES OF EVIDENCE DO NOT APPLY IN SMALL CLAIMS COURT.

IF YOU LOSE IN SMALL CLAIMS COURT, YOU HAVE NO RIGHT TO APPEAL THE COURT'S DECISION.

YOU MAY HAVE THIS CASE TRANSFERRED TO THE REGULAR CIVIL COURT IF YOU WISH. TO DO SO, YOU MUST FILE A WRITTEN NOTICE WITH THE CLERK OF THE SMALL CLAIMS COURT AND PAY THE APPROPRIATE TRANSFER FEE WITHIN TEN (10) DAYS OF RECEIVING THIS LETTER.

IF YOU ARE UNSURE OF WHAT TO DO, YOU SHOULD TALK WITH AN ATTORNEY ABOUT IT IMMEDIATELY."

C. (1) If the properly addressed certified mail return receipt reply form is signed by the addressee/defendant, then service shall be considered as personal service.

(2) If the properly addressed certified mail return receipt reply form is signed by a person other than the defendant then service shall be considered as domiciliary service.

(3) If the properly addressed certified mail return receipt reply form is returned and marked "refused" or "unclaimed" by the addressee then service is regarded as tendered and shall be considered as domiciliary service.

D. If service of the citation and original petition is made by domiciliary service as provided herein, service of the notice of judgment shall be made as provided by law, except if the certified mail is marked "unclaimed" or "refused", service of the notice of judgment shall be made by the sheriff, marshal, or constable having jurisdiction.

E. Repealed by Acts 1990, No. 76, § 2.

Added by Acts 1977, No. 710, § 1. Amended by Acts 1984, No. 216, § 1; Acts 1987, No. 256, § 1; Acts 1989, No. 86, § 1; Acts 1990, No. 76, § 1.

R.S. 13:5205

§ 5205. Fees

A. The plaintiff, upon filing a claim, shall pay as court costs a fee of thirty-five dollars for each party made defendant. No other prejudgment costs, except those required by R.S. 13:10.3, shall be required of the plaintiff so long as the action remains in a small claims division; provided that if the suit is amended or additional service of process is required, the court may require a fee of not more than twenty dollars for each additional service. Additionally, the court may require a fee of not more than twenty dollars for each subpoena issued. In accordance with the provisions of R.S. 49:225, no additional cost or fee shall be required when service of process is required to be made upon the secretary of state so long as the action remains in a small claims division.

B. Costs may be waived for an indigent party who complies with the provisions of Articles 5181 through 5188 of the Louisiana Code of Civil Procedure.

C. The filing fee of thirty-five dollars shall be paid to the judge of the court as a fee in lieu of all other fees in each such case; however, all costs and expenses incurred shall be paid from the filing fee, except as otherwise provided herein.

D. Repealed by Acts 1987, No. 256, § 2.

Added by Acts 1977, No. 710, § 1. Amended by Acts 1980, No. 118, § 1; Acts 1983, No. 211, § 1; Acts 1985, No. 312, § 1; Acts 1987, No. 256, § 1.

R.S. 13:5206

§ 5206. Reconventional demand beyond jurisdiction; filing in court of competent jurisdiction; transfer of proceedings from small claims division

A. If a defendant in a small claims action shall have a claim against the plaintiff in such action for an amount over the jurisdiction of the small claims division as set forth in R.S. 13:5202(A), but of a nature which may be asserted by a reconventional demand as authorized by Article 1061 of the Louisiana Code of Civil Procedure, the defendant may assert his claim in the manner provided by this Section, in order to secure consolidation for trial of the small claims action with his own claim.

B. At any time prior to trial in the small claims action, the defendant therein may commence an action against the plaintiff in a court of competent jurisdiction to assert a claim of the nature set forth by R.S. 13:5206(A), and file an affidavit that the reconventional demand is in excess of three thousand dollars with the judge of the small claims division in which the plaintiff has commenced the small claims action.

C. The defendant shall attach to the affidavit a true copy of his petition or reconventional demand so filed and shall pay the clerk of the small claims division a transmittal fee of ten dollars, in addition to the prescribed court costs for filing the reconventional demand, furnishing a copy of the affidavit and pleading to the plaintiff.

D. The judge of the small claims division shall order that the small claims division action be transferred to the ordinary docket of the court set forth in said affidavit, and he shall transmit to such court (if it is other than the court of the small claims division) copies of the citation and any pleadings in the small claims action, and the actions shall then be consolidated for trial in such other docket or court.

E. The plaintiff in the small claims action shall not be required to pay to the clerk of the court to which the action is so transferred any transmittal, appearance, or filing fee; although, upon adverse judgment, he may be taxed with costs as in the case of any other defendant.

Added by Acts 1977, No. 710, § 1. Amended by Acts 1987, No. 256, § 1; Acts 1999, No. 312, § 1.

R.S. 13:5207

§ 5207. Arbitration awards

A. The judge may refer small claims cases to an attorney at law who shall serve as arbitrator provided the parties agree to be bound by his arbitration. An attorney at law so appointed by the judge shall conduct the proceedings in the manner described in R.S. 13:5208(A), and, if authorized by rule of court, he may be entitled to reasonable compensation for his services to be paid from court funds if available.

B. The arbitrator's decision shall be reduced to writing and shall be final and binding upon all parties. Upon ex parte motion of any party, judgment may be granted in accordance with the arbitration award.

Added by Acts 1977, No. 710, § 1. Amended by Acts 1987, No. 256, § 1; Acts 1989, No. 301, § 1.

R.S. 13:5207.1

§ 5207.1. Request for arbitration

A. Upon filing an action in small claims court pursuant to R.S. 13:5203 et seq., a plaintiff may request in writing that the proceeding be referred for arbitration. Within ten days after service of a

R.S. 13:5207.1—Cont'd

small claims proceeding on any party, that party may request in writing that the proceeding be referred for arbitration.

B. Notice that a request for arbitration has been filed shall be served in accordance with R.S. 13:5204 and shall contain language in substantially the following form:

"ARBITRATION OF THIS MATTER HAS BEEN REQUESTED. YOU MAY PREVENT ARBITRATION AND HAVE THE MATTER TRIED IN SMALL CLAIMS COURT BY FILING A WRITTEN OBJECTION WITH THE CLERK OF THE SMALL CLAIMS COURT NO LATER THAN TEN DAYS FROM THE DATE ON WHICH YOU RECEIVE THIS NOTICE. COPIES OF THE WRITTEN OBJECTION SHOULD BE SENT TO ALL OTHER PARTIES IN THIS MATTER."

C. The party requesting arbitration shall cause notice of the request to be served on all other parties to the proceeding.

D. When a timely written request for arbitration has been filed, the clerk of court shall transfer the proceedings to arbitration unless a timely written objection to arbitration is filed by a party.

E. Any party may file with the clerk of court a written objection to arbitration within ten days after the date on which the party is served with notice of a request for arbitration. A copy of the written objection shall be served on all other parties to the proceeding. If any timely written objection is filed by any party, the proceeding shall be heard in small claims court.

F. Notwithstanding the provisions of this Section, a judge in a small claims proceeding retains the authority to refer the proceeding to an arbitrator as provided by R.S. 13:5207.

G. All costs of arbitration shall be borne by the litigants.

Added by Acts 1992, No. 489, § 1, eff. June 20, 1992.

R.S. 13:5208

§ 5208. Judge's role; judgment; new trial; stay; installment payments; enforcement

A. At trial, and after ascertaining that the case is properly lodged in the small claims division, it is the duty of the judge to conduct an informal hearing, and to develop all of the facts necessary and relevant to an impartial determination of the case. The judge may take testimony, raise defenses or claims of which the parties may be unaware, summon any party to appear as a witness in the suit upon his own motion, and do other acts which in his discretion appear necessary to effect a correct judgment and speedy disposition of the case. He may attempt to conciliate disputes and encourage fair settlements among the parties. The court may by local rule limit the role of attorneys in small claims division proceedings.

B. A judgment rendered in a small claims division becomes final and executory three days after it is signed, or notice of that judgment, if necessary, is mailed, unless within that period a motion for new trial is filed or the judge stays execution of that judgment in accordance with Subsection D of this Section.

C. Notice of judgment shall be mailed or served by the marshal, constable, or sheriff to a defendant against whom judgment is rendered if the citation was not served on or received by him personally and he failed to appear or answer. For purposes of this Part, the date of mailing such notice shall be considered the date the judgment is signed.

D. When judgment is to be rendered in an action pursuant to this Part, and the party against whom it is to be entered requests an inquiry, or on the judge's own motion, the judge may inquire

R.S. 13:5208—Cont'd

fully into the party's financial status and may stay execution and order partial payments in such amounts, over such periods, and upon such terms, which may include payment to the clerk of court, as deemed just under the circumstances. Upon a showing by a preponderance of the evidence that the party has failed to meet an installment payment without just excuse, the stay of execution shall be vacated. When a stay of execution has not been ordered or when a stay of execution has been vacated as provided in this Subsection, the party in whose favor the judgment has been entered may avail himself of all remedies available for the enforcement of the judgment provided by the Louisiana Code of Civil Procedure.

Added by Acts 1977, No. 710, § 1. Amended by Acts 1987, No. 256, § 1.

R.S. 13:5209

§ 5209. Waiver of right to appeal

A. A plaintiff who files a complaint in a small claims division shall be deemed to have waived his right to appeal unless the complaint is removed as provided in Subsection B below or is transferred as provided in R.S. 13:5206 above.

B. A defendant shall be deemed to have waived his right to appeal unless, within the time allowed for filing an answer to the complaint, he files a written motion seeking removal of the action to the ordinary civil docket of the court in which the complaint is filed, which motion shall be granted forthwith.

C. Upon removal as provided in Subsection B of this Section, a plaintiff shall not be required to pay for additional costs beyond those due under this Part; any such additional costs as may be lawfully assessed shall be paid by the defendant mover; the plaintiff, if judgment is rendered against him, shall not be cast in such additional costs.

Added by Acts 1977, No. 710, § 1. Amended by Acts 1987, No. 256, § 1.

R.S. 13:5210

§ 5210. State agencies

The provisions of this Part shall not apply to agencies of the state.

Added by Acts 1977, No. 710, § 1.

R.S. 13:5211

§ 5211. Clerk's role

If oral demand is made or written pleadings are filed, the clerk of the small claims division shall prepare the citation summoning the defendant to answer in accordance with the provisions of Article 4902 of the Louisiana Code of Civil Procedure. The clerk shall send notice to the defendant by certified mail, return receipt requested, or by service through the marshal, constable, or sheriff. In addition, the clerk is authorized to cooperate fully with the parties, which includes answering any questions that the parties may have concerning the small claims procedure, in identification of the proper parties to the suit, and in furnishing general information concerning appropriate evidence for trial. The clerk is neither authorized nor expected to provide legal advice.

Added by Acts 1977, No. 710, § 1. Amended by Acts 1979, No. 46, § 3, eff. Jan. 1, 1980; Acts 1987, No. 256, § 1.

R.S. 13:5212

§ 5212. Applicability of Part

The provisions of this Part, except as otherwise specifically provided by Book VIII of the Louisiana Code of Civil Procedure, shall govern and regulate the procedure in proceedings in small claims divisions of city courts.

Added by Acts 1987, No. 256, § 1.

R.S. 20:1

§ 1. Declaration of homestead; exemption from seizure and sale; debts excluded from exemption; waiver; certain proceeds from property insurance exempted

A. (1) The bona fide homestead consists of a residence occupied by the owner and the land on which the residence is located, including any building and appurtenances located thereon, and any contiguous tracts up to a total of five acres if the residence is within a municipality, or up to a total of two hundred acres of land if the residence is not located in a municipality.

(2) The homestead is exempt from seizure and sale under any writ, mandate, or process whatsoever, except as provided by Subsections C and D of this Section. This exemption extends to thirty-five thousand dollars in value of the homestead, except in the case of obligations arising directly as a result of a catastrophic or terminal illness or injury, in which case the exemption shall apply to the full value of the homestead based upon its value one year before such seizure. This homestead exemption from seizure and sale shall extend automatically to the proceeds from any property insurance policy received as a result of damage caused by a gubernatorially declared disaster to a homestead and that are held separately in an escrow account identified as insurance proceeds paid from the damage of a homestead for its repair or replacement.

(3) For the purposes of this Section, "catastrophic or terminal illness or injury" shall mean an illness or injury which creates uninsured obligations to health care providers of more than ten thousand dollars and which are greater than fifty percent of the annual adjusted gross income of the debtor, as established by an average of federal income tax returns for the three preceding years.

B. The exemption provided in Subsection A shall extend to the surviving spouse or minor children of a deceased owner and shall apply when the homestead is occupied as such and title to it is in either the husband or wife but not to more than one homestead owned by the husband or the wife. The exemption shall continue to apply to a homestead otherwise eligible while owned in indivision by the spouses, and occupied by either of them, when the community property regime of which the homestead is a part is dissolved by judgment which so provides, pursuant to R.S. 9:381 et seq., or Article 159 or 2375 of the Louisiana Civil Code. If either spouse becomes the sole owner and continues to occupy the homestead as such, the exemption as to that spouse shall be deemed to have continued uninterrupted.

C. This exemption shall not apply to any of the following debts:

(1) For the purchase price of property or any part of such purchase price.

(2) For labor, money, and material furnished for building, repairing, or improving the homestead.

(3) For liabilities incurred by any public officer, or fiduciary, or any attorney at law, for money collected or received on deposits.

(4) For taxes or assessments.

(5) For rent which bears a privilege upon said property.

(6) For the amount which may be due a homestead or building and loan association for a loan made by it on the security of the property; provided, that if at the time of making such loan the

R.S. 20:1—Cont'd

borrower be married, and not separated from bed and board from the other spouse, the latter shall have consented thereto.

(7) For the amount which may be due for money advanced on the security of a mortgage on said property; provided, that if at the time of granting such mortgage the mortgagor be married, and not separated from bed and board from the other spouse, the latter shall have consented thereto.

(8) For any obligation arising from the conviction of a felony or misdemeanor which has the possibility of imprisonment of at least six months.

D. The right to sell voluntarily any property that is exempt as a homestead shall be preserved, but no sale shall destroy or impair any rights of creditors thereon. Any person entitled to a homestead may waive same, in whole or in part, by signing a written waiver thereof; a copy of such waiver shall be provided to the homeowner; however, if the person is married, and not separated from bed and board from the other spouse, then the waiver shall not be effective unless signed by the latter, and all such waivers shall be recorded in the mortgage records of the parish where the homestead is situated. However, if the homestead is the separate property of one of the spouses, the homestead exemption may be waived by that spouse alone in any mortgage granted on the homestead, without the necessity of obtaining a waiver from the non-owning spouse. The waiver may be either general or special and shall have effect from the time of recording. The waiver shall not be required or permitted for the rendering of medical treatment, medical services, or hospitalization. Notwithstanding any other provision of law to the contrary, a waiver of exemption from seizure as to an exempted homestead shall automatically include insurance for that property to the extent subject to the creditor's mortgage or security interest.

Amended by Acts 1977, No. 446, § 1; Acts 1980, No. 249, § 1, eff. July 12, 1980; Acts 1999, No. 1365, § 1, eff. Jan. 1, 2000; Acts 2004, No. 481, § 1; Acts 2006, No. 601, § 2; Acts 2009, No. 201, § 2, eff. June 30, 2009.

R.S. 22:335

§ 335. Service of process; secretary of state as attorney

Every foreign or alien insurer shall appoint the secretary of state to be its true and lawful attorney in this state upon whom, or some other person in his office during his absence he may designate, all lawful process in any action or proceeding against such insurer may be served, which shall constitute service on such insurer. Such appointment shall continue in force so long as any contract or other liability of such insurer in this state shall remain outstanding. Whenever such process shall be served upon the secretary of state, he shall forthwith forward a copy of the process by registered or certified mail or by commercial courier as defined in R.S. 13:3204(D), when the person to be served is located outside of this state to the person designated for the purpose by the insurer.

Renumbered from R.S. 22:985 by Acts 2008, No. 415, § 1, eff. Jan. 1, 2009. Acts 1958, No. 125. Amended by Acts 1999, No. 395, § 4; Acts 2012, No. 544, § 3.

R.S. 22:1269

§ 1269. Liability policy; insolvency or bankruptcy of insured and inability to effect service of citation or other process; direct action against insurer

A. No policy or contract of liability insurance shall be issued or delivered in this state, unless it contains provisions to the effect that the insolvency or bankruptcy of the insured shall not release the insurer from the payment of damages for injuries sustained or loss occasioned during the existence of the policy, and any judgment which may be rendered against the insured for which the insurer is liable which shall have become executory, shall be deemed prima facie evidence of the insolvency of

R.S. 22:1269—Cont'd

the insured, and an action may thereafter be maintained within the terms and limits of the policy by the injured person, or his survivors, mentioned in Civil Code Art. 2315.1, or heirs against the insurer.

B. (1) The injured person or his survivors or heirs mentioned in Subsection A of this Section, at their option, shall have a right of direct action against the insurer within the terms and limits of the policy; and, such action may be brought against the insurer alone, or against both the insured and insurer jointly and in solido, in the parish in which the accident or injury occurred or in the parish in which an action could be brought against either the insured or the insurer under the general rules of venue prescribed by Code of Civil Procedure Art. 42 only; however, such action may be brought against the insurer alone only when at least one of the following applies:

(a) The insured has been adjudged bankrupt by a court of competent jurisdiction or when proceedings to adjudge an insured bankrupt have been commenced before a court of competent jurisdiction.

(b) The insured is insolvent.

(c) Service of citation or other process cannot be made on the insured.

(d) When the cause of action is for damages as a result of an offense or quasi-offense between children and their parents or between married persons.

(e) When the insurer is an uninsured motorist carrier.

(f) The insured is deceased.

(2) This right of direct action shall exist whether or not the policy of insurance sued upon was written or delivered in the state of Louisiana and whether or not such policy contains a provision forbidding such direct action, provided the accident or injury occurred within the state of Louisiana. Nothing contained in this Section shall be construed to affect the provisions of the policy or contract if such provisions are not in violation of the laws of this state.

C. It is the intent of this Section that any action brought under the provisions of this Section shall be subject to all of the lawful conditions of the policy or contract and the defenses which could be urged by the insurer to a direct action brought by the insured, provided the terms and conditions of such policy or contract are not in violation of the laws of this state.

D. It is also the intent of this Section that all liability policies within their terms and limits are executed for the benefit of all injured persons and their survivors or heirs to whom the insured is liable; and, that it is the purpose of all liability policies to give protection and coverage to all insureds, whether they are named insured or additional insureds under the omnibus clause, for any legal liability the insured may have as or for a tortfeasor within the terms and limits of the policy.

Renumbered from R.S. 22:655 by Acts 2008, No. 415, § 1, eff. Jan. 1, 2009. Acts 1958, No. 125. Amended by Acts 1962, No. 471, § 1; Acts 1988, No. 934, § 1, eff. Jan. 1, 1989; Acts 1989, No. 117, § 2; Acts 1992, No. 584, § 1; Acts 2010, No. 703, § 1, eff. Jan. 1, 2011.

Comment—1989

This Section has been amended to provide that the reference to C.C.P. Article 42 does not include the exceptions under C.C.P. Articles 71 through 85.

R.S. 22:1892

§ 1892. Payment and adjustment of claims, policies other than life and health and accident; vehicle damage claims; extension of time to respond to claims during emergency or disaster; penalties; arson-related claims suspension

A. (1) All insurers issuing any type of contract, other than those specified in R.S. 22:1811, 1821, and Chapter 10 of Title 23 of the Louisiana Revised Statutes of 1950, shall pay the amount of any

R.S. 22:1892—Cont'd

claim due any insured within thirty days after receipt of satisfactory proofs of loss from the insured or any party in interest. The insurer shall notify the insurance producer of record of all such payments for property damage claims made in accordance with this Paragraph.

(2) All insurers issuing any type of contract, other than those specified in R.S. 22:1811, R.S. 22:1821, and Chapter 10 of Title 23 of the Louisiana Revised Statutes of 1950, shall pay the amount of any third party property damage claim and of any reasonable medical expenses claim due any bona fide third party claimant within thirty days after written agreement of settlement of the claim from any third party claimant.

(3) Except in the case of catastrophic loss, the insurer shall initiate loss adjustment of a property damage claim and of a claim for reasonable medical expenses within fourteen days after notification of loss by the claimant. In the case of catastrophic loss, the insurer shall initiate loss adjustment of a property damage claim within thirty days after notification of loss by the claimant except that the commissioner may promulgate a rule for extending the time period for initiating a loss adjustment for damages arising from a presidentially declared emergency or disaster or a gubernatorially declared emergency or disaster up to an additional thirty days. Thereafter, only one additional extension of the period of time for initiating a loss adjustment may be allowed and must be approved by the Senate Committee on Insurance and the House Committee on Insurance, voting separately. Failure to comply with the provisions of this Paragraph shall subject the insurer to the penalties provided in R.S. 22:1973.

(4) All insurers shall make a written offer to settle any property damage claim, including a third-party claim, within thirty days after receipt of satisfactory proofs of loss of that claim.

(5) An insurer shall issue a copy of the insurer's field adjuster report, relative to the insured's property damage claim, to the insured within fifteen days of receiving a request for such from the insured.

B. (1)(a) Except as provided in Subparagraph (b) of this Paragraph, failure to make such payment within thirty days after receipt of such satisfactory written proofs and demand therefor or failure to make a written offer to settle any property damage claim, including a third-party claim, within thirty days after receipt of satisfactory proofs of loss of that claim, as provided in Paragraphs (A)(1) and (4) of this Section, respectively, or failure to make such payment within thirty days after written agreement or settlement as provided in Paragraph (A)(2) of this Section when such failure is found to be arbitrary, capricious, or without probable cause, shall subject the insurer to a penalty, in addition to the amount of the loss, of fifty percent damages on the amount found to be due from the insurer to the insured, or one thousand dollars, whichever is greater, payable to the insured, or in the event a partial payment or tender has been made, fifty percent of the difference between the amount paid or tendered and the amount found to be due as well as reasonable attorney fees and costs. Such penalties, if awarded, shall not be used by the insurer in computing either past or prospective loss experience for the purpose of setting rates or making rate filings.

(b) In the case of a presidentially or gubernatorially declared disaster, failure to make such payment within thirty days after receipt of such satisfactory written proofs and demand therefor or failure to make a written offer to settle any property damage claim, including a third-party claim, within thirty days after receipt of satisfactory proofs of loss of that claim, as provided in Paragraphs (A)(1) and (4) of this Section, respectively, or failure to make such payment within thirty days after written agreement or settlement as provided in Paragraph (A)(2) of this Section when such failure is found to be arbitrary, capricious, or without probable cause, shall subject the insurer to a penalty, in addition to the amount of the loss, of fifty percent damages on the amount found to be due from the insurer to the insured, or two thousand five hundred dollars, whichever is greater, payable to the insured, or in the event a partial payment or tender has been made, fifty percent of the difference

R.S. 22:1892—Cont'd

between the amount paid or tendered and the amount found to be due as well as reasonable attorney fees and costs or two thousand five hundred dollars, whichever is greater. The penalties, if awarded, shall not be used by the insurer in computing either past or prospective loss experience for the purpose of setting rates or making rate filings.

(2) The period set herein for payment of losses resulting from fire and the penalty provisions for nonpayment within the period shall not apply where the loss from fire was arson related and the state fire marshal or other state or local investigative bodies have the loss under active arson investigation. The provisions relative to time of payment and penalties shall commence to run upon certification of the investigating authority that there is no evidence of arson or that there is insufficient evidence to warrant further proceedings.

(3) The provisions relative to suspension of payment due to arson shall not apply to a bona fide lender which holds a valid recorded mortgage on the property in question.

(4) Whenever a property damage claim is on a personal vehicle owned by the third party claimant and as a direct consequence of the inactions of the insurer and the third party claimant's loss the third party claimant is deprived of use of the personal vehicle for more than five working days, excluding Saturdays, Sundays, and holidays, the insurer responsible for payment of the claim shall pay, to the extent legally responsible, for reasonable expenses incurred by the third party claimant in obtaining alternative transportation for the entire period of time during which the third party claimant is without the use of his personal vehicle. Failure to make such payment within thirty days after receipt of adequate written proof and demand therefor, when such failure is found to be arbitrary, capricious, or without probable cause shall subject the insurer to, in addition to the amount of such reasonable expenses incurred, a reasonable penalty not to exceed ten percent of such reasonable expenses or one thousand dollars whichever is greater together with reasonable attorneys fees for the collection of such expenses.

(5) When an insurance policy provides for the adjustment and settlement of first-party motor vehicle total losses on the basis of actual cash value or replacement with another of like kind and quality, and the insurer elects a cash settlement based on the actual cost to purchase a comparable motor vehicle, such costs shall be derived by using one of the following:

(a) A fair market value survey conducted using qualified retail automobile dealers in the local market area as resources. If there are no dealers in the local market area, the nearest reasonable market can be used.

(b) The retail cost as determined from a generally recognized used motor vehicle industry source; such as, an electronic database, if the valuation documents generated by the database are provided to the first-party claimant, or a guidebook that is available to the general public. If the insured demonstrates, by presenting two independent appraisals, based on measurable and discernable factors, including the vehicle's preloss condition, that the vehicle would have a higher cash value in the local market area than the value reflected in the source's database or the guidebook, the local market value shall be used in determining the actual cash value.

(c) A qualified expert appraiser selected and agreed upon by the insured and insurer. The appraiser shall produce a written nonbinding appraisal establishing the actual cash value of the vehicle's preloss condition.

(d) For the purposes of this Paragraph, local market area shall mean a reasonable distance surrounding the area where a motor vehicle is principally garaged, or the usual location of the vehicle covered by the policy.

(6)(a) For the purposes of this Paragraph the following terms have the meanings ascribed to them:

R.S. 22:1892—Cont'd

(i) "Damaged property" means a dwelling, structure, personal property, or any other property, except a vehicle, that requires repairs, replacement, restoration, or remediation to reestablish its former condition.

(ii) "Depreciation" means depreciation including but not limited to the cost of goods, materials, labor, and services necessary to replace, repair, or rebuild damaged property.

(b) An insurance policy covering damaged property may allow for depreciation.

(c) An insurance policy covering damaged property shall provide notice that depreciation may be deducted or withheld, in a form approved by the commissioner.

(d) If depreciation is applied to a loss for damaged property, the insurer shall provide a written explanation as to how the depreciation was calculated.

(e) Depreciation shall be reasonable and based on a combination of objective criteria and subjective assessment, including the actual condition of the property prior to loss.

C. (1) All claims brought by insureds, workers' compensation claimants, or third parties against an insurer shall be paid by check or draft of the insurer or, if offered by the insurer and the claimant requests, electronic transfer of funds to the order of the claimant to whom payment of the claim is due pursuant to the policy provisions, or his attorney, or upon direction of the claimant to one specified; however, the check or draft shall be made jointly to the claimant and the employer when the employer has advanced the claims payment to the claimant. The check or draft shall be paid jointly until the amount of the advanced claims payment has been recovered by the employer.

(2) No insurer shall intentionally or unreasonably delay, for more than three calendar days, exclusive of Saturdays, Sundays, and legal holidays, after presentation for collection, the processing of any properly executed and endorsed check or draft issued in settlement of an insurance claim.

(3) Any insurer violating this Subsection shall pay the insured or claimant a penalty of two hundred dollars or fifteen percent of the face amount of the check or draft, whichever is greater.

D. (1) When making a payment incident to a claim, no insurer shall require repairs be made to a motor vehicle, including window glass repairs or replacement, in a particular place or shop or by a particular entity.

(2) An insurer shall not recommend the use of a particular motor vehicle service or network of repair services without informing the insured or claimant that the insured or claimant is under no obligation to use the recommended repair service or network of repair services.

(3) An insurer shall not engage in any act or practice of intimidation, coercion, or threat to use a specified place of business for repair and replacement services.

(4) The commissioner may levy the following fines against any insurer that violates this Subsection:

(a) For a first offense, one thousand dollars.

(b) For a second offense within a twelve-month period, two thousand five hundred dollars.

(c) For a third or subsequent offense within a twelve-month period, five thousand dollars.

(5) A violation of this Subsection shall constitute an additional ground, under R.S. 22:1554, for the commissioner to refuse to issue a license or to suspend or revoke a license issued to any producer to sell insurance in this state.

E. (1) An insurer shall not require that repairs, replacement, restoration, or remediation be made to an insured's property by a particular preferred vendor or recommended contractor when making a payment on a residential or commercial property damage claim.

R.S. 22:1892—Cont'd

(2) An insurer shall not recommend the use of a particular preferred vendor or recommended contractor without informing the insured or claimant that the insured or claimant is under no obligation to use the preferred vendor or recommended contractor to complete repairs, replacement, restoration, or remediation of the insured's property.

F. (1) In the adjustment or settlement of first-party losses under fire and extended coverage policies, an insurer is required to include general contractor's overhead and profit in payments for losses when the services of a general contractor are reasonably foreseeable. This requirement applies to policies that provide for the adjustment and settlement of losses on a replacement cost basis and to policies that provide for the adjustment and settlement of losses on an actual cash value basis.

(2) The deduction of prospective contractor overhead, prospective contractor profit, and sales tax in determining the actual cash value of an adjustment or settlement is not allowed on replacement cost policies or on actual cash value policies.

G. On or after January 1, 2022, residential property insurance policies shall contain the following provision (with permission to substitute the word "company" with a more accurate descriptive term for the insurer):

"Appraisal. If you and this Company fail to agree as to the amount of loss, either party may demand that the amount of the loss be set by appraisal. If either party makes a written demand for appraisal, each party shall select a competent appraiser and notify the other party of their appraiser's identity within twenty days of receipt of the written demand for appraisal. The appraisers shall select a competent and impartial umpire; but, if after fifteen days the appraisers have not agreed upon who will serve as umpire, the umpire shall be appointed by a judge of the court of record in which the property is located. The appraisers shall then appraise the loss. If the appraisers submit written notice of an agreement as to the amount of the loss to this Company, the amount agreed upon shall set the amount of the loss. If the appraisers fail to agree within thirty days, the appraisers shall submit their differences along with any supporting documentation to the umpire, who shall appraise the loss. The appraisers may extend the time to sixty days for which they must agree upon the amount of loss or submit their differences and supporting documents to the umpire, if the extension is agreed to by the appraisers from both parties. A written agreement signed by the umpire and either party's appraiser shall set the amount of the loss, pursuant to the appraisal process, but shall not preclude either party from exercising its rights under the policy or the law. Each appraiser shall be paid by the party selecting that appraiser. Other expenses of the appraisal and the expenses of the umpire shall be divided and paid in equal shares by you and this Company. If there is an appraisal award, all applicable policy terms, limits, deductibles, and conditions will still apply. If you file a lawsuit relative to this policy against this Company prior to a demand for appraisal, the lawsuit will be held in abatement until the execution of an appraisal award."

Renumbered from R.S. 22:658 by Acts 2008, No. 415, § 1, eff. Jan. 1, 2009. Acts 1958, No. 125. Amended by Acts 1985, No. 778, § 1; Acts 1986, No. 132, § 1, eff. June 26, 1986; Acts 1988, No. 398, § 1; Acts 1989, No. 638, § 1; Acts 1990, No. 262, § 1, eff. July 4, 1990; Acts 1990, No. 955, § 1; Acts 1992, No. 879, § 1; Acts 1993, No. 163, § 1; Acts 1993, No. 585, § 1; Acts 2003, No. 790, § 1; Acts 2006, No. 404, § 1; Acts 2006, No. 813, § 1; Acts 2009, No. 488, § 1; Acts 2010, No. 1032, § 1; Acts 2012, No. 271, § 1; Acts 2018, No. 27, § 1; Acts 2019, No. 317, § 1; Acts 2021, No. 344, § 1; Acts 2021, No. 345, § 1.

R.S. 22:1907

§ 1907. Transacting business; constitutes appointment of agent for service of process; workers' compensation claims agent

A. The transacting of business in this state by a foreign or alien insurer without a certificate of authority is equivalent to an appointment by such insurer of the secretary of state and his successor

R.S. 22:1907—Cont'd

or successors in office to be its true and lawful attorney, upon whom may be served all lawful process in any action, suit, or proceeding maintained by the commissioner of insurance or arising out of such policy or contract of insurance, and the transacting of business by such insurer is a signification of its agreement that any such service of process is of the same legal force and validity as personal service of process in this state upon it.

B. Such service of process shall be made by delivering and leaving with the secretary of state or with some person in apparent charge of his office two copies thereof and the payment to him of such fees as may be prescribed by law. The secretary of state shall mail by registered mail or by commercial courier, as defined in R.S. 13:3204(D), when the person to be served is located outside of this state one of the copies of such process to the defendant at its last known principal place of business, and shall keep a record of all process so served upon him. Such service of process is sufficient if notice of such service and a copy of the process are sent within ten days thereafter by registered mail or by commercial courier, as defined in R.S. 13:3204(D), when the person to be served is located outside of this state by plaintiff's attorney to the defendant at its last known principal place of business, and the defendant's receipt, or receipt issued by the post office with which the letter is registered, showing the name of the sender of the letter and the name and address of the person to whom the letter is addressed, and the affidavit of the plaintiff's attorney showing compliance with this Section are filed with the clerk of the court in which such action is pending on or before the date the defendant is required to appear, or within such further time as the court may allow. However, no plaintiff or complainant shall be entitled to a judgment by default, or a judgment with leave to prove damages, or a judgment pro confesso under this Section until the expiration of thirty days from date of the filing of the affidavit of compliance.

C. (1) Service of process in any such action, suit, or proceeding shall, in addition to the manner provided in Subsection B of this Section, be valid if served as provided in Paragraph (2) of this Subsection upon any person within this state who, in this state on behalf of such insurer, is doing any of the following:

(a) Soliciting insurance.

(b) Making any contract of insurance or issuing or delivering any policies or written contracts of insurance.

(c) Collecting or receiving any premium for insurance.

(d) Acting as an agent for the sole purpose of operating a workers' compensation claims office established pursuant to R.S. 23:1161.1.

(2) A copy of such process shall be sent within ten days thereafter by registered mail by the plaintiff's attorney to the defendant at the last known principal place of business of the defendant, and the defendant's receipt, or the receipt issued by the post office with which the letter is registered, showing the name of the sender of the letter and the name and address of the person to whom the letter is addressed, and the affidavit of the plaintiff's attorney showing compliance with this Section shall be filed with the clerk of the court in which such action is pending on or before the date the defendant is required to appear, or within such further time as the court may allow.

D. Nothing in this Section shall limit or abridge the right to serve any process, notice, or demand upon any insurer in any other manner permitted by law.

Renumbered from R.S. 22:1253 by Acts 2008, No. 415, § 1, eff. Jan. 1, 2009. Acts 1958, No. 125. Amended by Acts 1968, No. 54, § 1; Acts 1990, No. 885, § 1; Acts 1999, No. 395, § 4; Acts 2012, No. 271, § 1.

R.S. 22:1973

§ 1973. Good faith duty; claims settlement practices; cause of action; penalties

A. An insurer, including but not limited to a foreign line and surplus line insurer, owes to his insured a duty of good faith and fair dealing. The insurer has an affirmative duty to adjust claims fairly and promptly and to make a reasonable effort to settle claims with the insured or the claimant, or both. Any insurer who breaches these duties shall be liable for any damages sustained as a result of the breach.

B. Any one of the following acts, if knowingly committed or performed by an insurer, constitutes a breach of the insurer's duties imposed in Subsection A of this Section:

(1) Misrepresenting pertinent facts or insurance policy provisions relating to any coverages at issue.

(2) Failing to pay a settlement within thirty days after an agreement is reduced to writing.

(3) Denying coverage or attempting to settle a claim on the basis of an application which the insurer knows was altered without notice to, or knowledge or consent of, the insured.

(4) Misleading a claimant as to the applicable prescriptive period.

(5) Failing to pay the amount of any claim due any person insured by the contract within sixty days after receipt of satisfactory proof of loss from the claimant when such failure is arbitrary, capricious, or without probable cause.

(6) Failing to pay claims pursuant to R.S. 22:1893 when such failure is arbitrary, capricious, or without probable cause.

C. In addition to any general or special damages to which a claimant is entitled for breach of the imposed duty, the claimant may be awarded penalties assessed against the insurer in an amount not to exceed two times the damages sustained or five thousand dollars, whichever is greater. Such penalties, if awarded, shall not be used by the insurer in computing either past or prospective loss experience for the purpose of setting rates or making rate filings.

D. The provisions of this Section shall not be applicable to claims made under health and accident insurance policies.

E. Repealed by Acts 1997, No. 949, § 2.

F. The Insurance Guaranty Association Fund, as provided in R.S. 22:2051 et seq., shall not be liable for any special damages awarded under the provisions of this Section.

Renumbered from R.S. 22:1220 by Acts 2008, No. 415, § 1, eff. Jan. 1, 2009. Added by Acts 1990, No. 308, § 1, eff. July 6, 1990. Amended by Acts 2006, 1st Ex.Sess., No. 12, § 1, eff. Feb. 23, 2006; Acts 2012, No. 271, § 1.

R.S. 23:921

§ 921. Restraint of business prohibited; restraint on forum prohibited; competing business; contracts against engaging in; provisions for

A. (1) Every contract or agreement, or provision thereof, by which anyone is restrained from exercising a lawful profession, trade, or business of any kind, except as provided in this Section, shall be null and void. However, every contract or agreement, or provision thereof, which meets the exceptions as provided in this Section, shall be enforceable.

(2) The provisions of every employment contract or agreement, or provisions thereof, by which any foreign or domestic employer or any other person or entity includes a choice of forum clause or

R.S. 23:921—Cont'd

choice of law clause in an employee's contract of employment or collective bargaining agreement, or attempts to enforce either a choice of forum clause or choice of law clause in any civil or administrative action involving an employee, shall be null and void except where the choice of forum clause or choice of law clause is expressly, knowingly, and voluntarily agreed to and ratified by the employee after the occurrence of the incident which is the subject of the civil or administrative action.

B. Any person, including a corporation and the individual shareholders of such corporation, who sells the goodwill of a business may agree with the buyer that the seller or other interested party in the transaction, will refrain from carrying on or engaging in a business similar to the business being sold or from soliciting customers of the business being sold within a specified parish or parishes, or municipality or municipalities, or parts thereof, so long as the buyer, or any person deriving title to the goodwill from him, carries on a like business therein, not to exceed a period of two years from the date of sale.

C. Any person, including a corporation and the individual shareholders of such corporation, who is employed as an agent, servant, or employee may agree with his employer to refrain from carrying on or engaging in a business similar to that of the employer and/or from soliciting customers of the employer within a specified parish or parishes, municipality or municipalities, or parts thereof, so long as the employer carries on a like business therein, not to exceed a period of two years from termination of employment. An independent contractor, whose work is performed pursuant to a written contract, may enter into an agreement to refrain from carrying on or engaging in a business similar to the business of the person with whom the independent contractor has contracted, on the same basis as if the independent contractor were an employee, for a period not to exceed two years from the date of the last work performed under the written contract.

D. For the purposes of Subsections B, C, E, F, J, K, and L of this Section, a person who becomes employed by a competing business, regardless of whether or not that person is an owner or equity interest holder of that competing business, may be deemed to be carrying on or engaging in a business similar to that of the party having a contractual right to prevent that person from competing.

E. Upon or in anticipation of a dissolution of the partnership, the partnership and the individual partners, including a corporation and the individual shareholders if the corporation is a partner, may agree that the partners shall refrain from carrying on or engaging in a similar business within the same parish or parishes, or municipality or municipalities, or within specified parts thereof, where the partnership business has been transacted, not to exceed a period of two years from the date of dissolution.

F. (1) Parties to a franchise may agree that:

(a) The franchisor shall refrain from selling, distributing, or granting additional franchises to sell or distribute, within defined geographic territory, those products or services which are the subject of the franchise.

(b) The franchisee shall:

(i) During the term of the franchise, refrain from competing with the franchisor or other franchisees of the franchisor or carrying on or engaging in any other business similar to that which is the subject of the franchise.

(ii) For a period not to exceed two years following severance of the franchise relationship, refrain from carrying on or engaging in any other business similar to that which is the subject of the franchise and from competing with or soliciting the customers of the franchisor or other franchisees of the franchisor.

(c) The employee if employed by a franchisor shall:

R.S. 23:921—Cont'd

(i) During the term of his employment by the franchisor, refrain from competing with his employer or any of the franchisees of his employer or carrying on or engaging in any other business similar to that which is the subject of the franchise.

(ii) For a period not to exceed two years following severance of the employment relationship between the franchisor and the employee, refrain from carrying on or engaging in any other business similar to that which is the subject of the franchise between the franchisor and its franchisees and from competing with or soliciting the customers of his employer or the franchisees of his employer.

(2) Except as provided in Paragraph (3) of this Subsection, neither a franchisee who is a party to a franchise agreement regulated under the Federal Trade Commission Franchise Disclosure Rule, 16 CFR 436, nor an employee of the franchisee shall be deemed to be an employee of the franchisor for any purpose. A voluntary agreement entered into between the United States Department of Labor and an employer shall not be used by a state department or agency as evidence or for any other purpose in an investigation or judicial or administrative determination, including whether an employee of a franchisee is also considered to be an employee of the franchisor.

(3) Pursuant to Chapter 10 and Chapter 11 of Title 23 of the Louisiana Revised Statutes of 1950, an employee of a franchisee may be deemed to be an employee of the franchisor only where the two entities share or co-determine those matters governing the essential terms and conditions of employment and directly and immediately control matters relating to the employment relationship such as hiring, firing, discipline, supervision, and direction.

(4) As used in this Subsection:

(a) "Franchise" means any continuing commercial relationship created by any arrangement or arrangements as defined in 16 CFR 436.1(h).

(b) "Franchisee" means any person who participates in a franchise relationship as a franchisee, partner, shareholder with at least a ten percent interest in the franchisee, executive officer of the franchisee, or a person to whom an interest in a franchise is sold, as defined in 16 CFR 436.1(h), provided that no person shall be included in this definition unless he has signed an agreement expressly binding him to the provisions thereof.

(c) "Franchisor" means any person who participates in a franchise relationship as a franchisor as defined in 16 CFR 436.1(k).

G. (1) An employee may at any time enter into an agreement with his employer that, for a period not to exceed two years from the date of the termination of employment, he will refrain from engaging in any work or activity to design, write, modify, or implement any computer program that directly competes with any confidential computer program owned, licensed, or marketed by the employer, and to which the employee had direct access during the term of his employment or services.

(2) As used in this Subsection, "confidential" means that which:

(a) Is not generally known to and not readily ascertainable by other persons.

(b) Is the subject of reasonable efforts under the circumstances to maintain its secrecy.

(3) As used in this Subsection, "computer program" means a plan, routine, or set of statements or instructions, including any subset, subroutine, or portion of instructions, regardless of format or medium, which are capable, when incorporated into a machine-readable medium, of causing a computer to perform a particular task or function or achieve a particular result.

(4) As used in this Subsection, "employee" shall mean any individual, corporation, partnership, or any other entity which contracts or agrees with an employer to perform, provide, or furnish any services to, for, or on behalf of such employer.

R.S. 23:921—Cont'd

H. Any agreement covered by Subsection B, C, E, F, G, J, K, or L of this Section shall be considered an obligation not to do, and failure to perform may entitle the obligee to recover damages for the loss sustained and the profit of which he has been deprived. In addition, upon proof of the obligor's failure to perform, and without the necessity of proving irreparable injury, a court of competent jurisdiction shall order injunctive relief enforcing the terms of the agreement. Any agreement covered by Subsection J, K, or L of this Section shall be null and void if it is determined that members of the agreement were engaged in ultra vires acts. Nothing in Subsection J, K, or L of this Section shall prohibit the transfer, sale, or purchase of stock or interest in publicly traded entities.

I. (1) There shall be no contract or agreement or provision entered into by an automobile salesman and his employer restraining him from selling automobiles.

(2)(a) For the purposes of this Subsection, "automobile" means any new or used motor-driven car, van, or truck required to be registered which is used, or is designed to be used, for the transporting of passengers or goods for public, private, commercial, or for-hire purposes.

(b) For the purposes of this Subsection, "salesman" means any person with a salesman's license issued by the Louisiana Motor Vehicle Commission or the Used Motor Vehicle and Parts Commission, other than a person who owns a proprietary or equity interest in a new or used car dealership in Louisiana.

J. A corporation and the individual shareholders of such corporation may agree that such shareholders will refrain from carrying on or engaging in a business similar to that of the corporation and from soliciting customers of the corporation within a specified parish or parishes, municipality or municipalities, or parts thereof, for as long as the corporation carries on a similar business therein, not to exceed a period of two years from the date such shareholder ceases to be a shareholder of the corporation. A violation of this Subsection shall be enforceable in accordance with Subsection H of this Section.

K. A partnership and the individual partners of such partnership may agree that such partners will refrain from carrying on or engaging in a business similar to that of the partnership and from soliciting customers of the partnership within a specified parish or parishes, municipality or municipalities, or parts thereof, for as long as the partnership carries on a similar business therein, not to exceed a period of two years from the date such partner ceases to be a partner. A violation of this Subsection shall be enforceable in accordance with Subsection H of this Section.

L. A limited liability company and the individual members of such limited liability company may agree that such members will refrain from carrying on or engaging in a business similar to that of the limited liability company and from soliciting customers of the limited liability company within a specified parish or parishes, municipality or municipalities, or parts thereof, for as long as the limited liability company carries on a similar business therein, not to exceed a period of two years from the date such member ceases to be a member. A violation of this Subsection shall be enforceable in accordance with Subsection H of this Section.

Amended by Acts 1962, No. 104, §§ 1, 2; Acts 1989, No. 639, § 1; Acts 1990, No. 137, § 1, eff. June 29, 1990; Acts 1990, No. 201, § 1; Acts 1991, No. 891, § 1; Acts 1995, No. 937, § 1, eff. June 28, 1995; Acts 1999, No. 58, § 1; Acts 2003, No. 428, § 1; Acts 2006, No. 436, § 1; Acts 2008, No. 399, § 1; Acts 2008, No. 711, § 1; Acts 2010, No. 164, § 1; Acts 2015, No. 404, § 1; Acts 2020, No. 121, § 1.

R.S. 35:200

§ 200. Limitation on actions

A. No action for damages against any notary public duly commissioned in any parish in this state, any partnership of such notaries public, or any professional corporation, company, organization,

R.S. 35:200—Cont'd

association, enterprise, or other commercial business or professional combination answerable for the damage occasioned by such notary public in the exercise of the functions of a notary public, whether based upon tort, or breach of contract, or otherwise, arising out of an engagement to provide notarial services shall be brought unless filed in a court of competent jurisdiction and proper venue within one year from the date of the alleged act, omission, or neglect, or within one year from the date that the alleged act, omission, or neglect is discovered or should have been discovered; however, even as to actions filed within one year from the date of such discovery, in all events such actions shall be filed at the latest within three years from the date of the alleged act, omission, or neglect.

B. The provisions of this Section are remedial and apply to all causes of action without regard to the date when the alleged act, omission, or neglect occurred. However, with respect to any alleged act, omission, or neglect occurring prior to July 1, 2004, actions shall, in all events, be filed in a court of competent jurisdiction and proper venue on or before July 1, 2007, without regard to the date of discovery of the alleged act, omission, or neglect. The one-year and three-year periods of limitation provided in Subsection A of this Section are peremptive periods within the meaning of Civil Code Article 3458 and, in accordance with Civil Code Article 3461, may not be renounced, interrupted, or suspended.

C. Notwithstanding any other law to the contrary, in all actions brought in this state against any notary public duly commissioned in this state, any partnership of such notaries public, or any professional corporation, company, organization, association, enterprise, or other commercial business or professional combination answerable for the damage occasioned by such notary public in the exercise of the functions of a notary public, the prescriptive and peremptive period shall be governed exclusively by this Section.

D. The provisions of this Section shall apply to all persons whether or not infirm or under disability of any kind and including minors and interdicts.

E. The peremptive period provided in Subsection A of this Section shall not apply in cases of fraud, as defined in Civil Code Article 1953.

F. The provisions of this Section shall not apply to notaries who are attorneys, who shall be subject to the provisions of R.S. 9:5605.

Added by Acts 1977, No. 451, § 2. Amended by Acts 2004, No. 77, § 1, eff. May 28, 2004.

R.S. 35:701

§ 701. Purpose; ratification

A. The legislature finds that the COVID–19 public health emergency created a statewide emergency disrupting the ability of notaries public to be in the physical presence of persons whose signatures the notary public was authenticating. This Chapter is enacted for the benefit and protection of the state as a whole and its citizens, to prevent injustice, inequity, undue hardship, and disruption of transactions to persons relying on the authentication of signatures of persons not in the physical presence of a notary public by a notary public who authenticated the signature through electronic means using audio-video communication. Therefore, this Chapter shall be liberally construed to effect its purposes.

B. The action of the governor of this state in issuing Section 6 of Proclamation Number 37 JBE 2020 and Part C of Section 5 of Proclamation Number 41 JBE 2020 is hereby approved, ratified, and confirmed subject to the provisions of this Chapter.

Added by Acts 2020, No. 131, § 1, eff. June 9, 2020.

R.S. 35:702

§ 702. Remote notarization authorized

A. Notwithstanding any law to the contrary, any act in which any person or witness appeared before a notary public using an electronic device or process which allowed all such persons and the notary public to communicate simultaneously by sight and sound and to which the electronic signatures of such persons, witnesses, and the notary public were affixed on or after March 11, 2020, and before May 1, 2020, shall have the same force and effect as if all persons, witnesses, and the notary public had been in the physical presence of each other.

B. The provisions of Subsection A of this Section shall not apply to any testament, trust instrument, donation inter vivos, matrimonial agreement, act modifying, waiving, or extinguishing an obligation of final spousal support, or any amendments to such acts, or authentic acts.

C. Any act which would constitute an authentic act but for the appearance of one or more necessary persons via electronic means, may still be valid as an act under private signature or an acknowledged act.

Added by Acts 2020, No. 131, § 1, eff. June 9, 2020.

R.S. 39:1538

§ 1538. Claims against the state

A. Claims against the state or any of its agencies to recover damages in tort for money damages against the state or its agencies for injury or loss of property, personal injury, or death caused by the negligent or wrongful act or omission of any employee of the agency while acting within the scope of his office or employment under circumstances in which the state or such agency, if a private person, would be liable to the claimant in accordance with the general laws of this state, may be prosecuted in accordance with the provisions specified in this Chapter. However, immunity for discretionary acts of executive, legislative, and judicial officers within the scope of their legally defined powers shall not be abridged.

B. The state and its agencies shall be liable for claims in the same manner and to the same extent as a private individual under like circumstances.

C. A judgment may be settled in accordance with R.S. 39:1535(B)(6).

D. In actions brought pursuant to this Section, process shall be served upon the head of the department concerned, the office of risk management, and the attorney general, as well as any others required by R.S. 13:5107. However, there shall be no direct action against the Self-Insurance Fund and claimants, with or without a final judgment recognizing their claims, shall have no enforceable right to have such claims satisfied or paid from the Self-Insurance Fund.

E. The division of administration, in cooperation with the attorney general as provided in R.S. 49:257(B), shall prepare a list of all final judgments against the state that are the result of a claim under Article XII, Section 10 of the Constitution of Louisiana and this Section and which remain unpaid. The list shall be updated quarterly, provided to the attorney general pursuant to R.S. 49:257(B), and information contained therein shall be included within the comprehensive annual financial report in a manner determined by the commissioner of administration.

Added by Acts 1980, No. 520, § 1, eff. July 1, 1980. Amended by Acts 2018, No. 627, § 1.

PART I. MEDICAL MALPRACTICE

R.S. 40:1231.1

§ 1231.1. Definitions and general applications

A. As used in this Part:

(1) "Ambulance service" means an entity under circumstances in which the provisions of R.S. 40:1237.1 are not applicable which operates either ground or air ambulances, using a minimum of two persons on each ground ambulance, at least one of whom is trained and registered at the level of certified emergency medical technician-basic, or at the intermediate or paramedic levels, or one who is a registered nurse, and using a minimum on any air ambulance of one person trained and registered at the paramedic level or a person who is a registered nurse, or any officer, employee, or agent thereof acting in the course and scope of his employment, including any student enrolled in a qualified emergency medical services educational program under the direct supervision of a licensed health care provider.

(2) "Authority" means the Residual Malpractice Insurance Authority established under Section 1231.7.

(3) "Board" means the Patient's Compensation Fund Oversight Board created in R.S. 40:1231.4(D).

(4) "Claimant" means a patient or representative or any person, including a decedent's estate, seeking or who has sought recovery of damages or future medical care and related benefits under this Part. All persons claiming to have sustained damages as a result of injuries to or death of any one patient are considered a single claimant.

(5) "Claims manager" means the claims manager appointed and employed by the board pursuant to R.S. 40:1231.4(D)(2)(g).

(6) "Community blood center" means any independent nonprofit nonhospital based facility which collects blood and blood products from donors primarily to supply blood and blood components to other health care facilities.

(7) "Court" means a court of competent jurisdiction and proper venue over the parties.

(8) "Executive director" means the executive director of the board, appointed and employed pursuant to R.S. 40:1231.4(D)(2)(f).

(9) "Health care" means any act or treatment performed or furnished, or which should have been performed or furnished, by any health care provider for, to, or on behalf of a patient during the patient's medical care, treatment, or confinement, or during or relating to or in connection with the procurement of human blood or blood components.

(10) "Health care provider" means a person, partnership, limited liability partnership, limited liability company, corporation, facility, or institution licensed or certified by this state to provide health care or professional services as a physician, hospital, nursing home, community blood center, tissue bank, dentist, a licensed dietician or licensed nutritionist employed by, referred by, or performing work under contract for, a health care provider or other person already covered by this Part, registered or licensed practical nurse or certified nurse assistant, offshore health service provider, ambulance service under circumstances in which the provisions of R.S. 40:1237.1 are not applicable, certified registered nurse anesthetist, nurse midwife, licensed midwife, nurse practitioner, clinical nurse specialist, pharmacist, optometrist, podiatrist, chiropractor, physical therapist, occupational therapist, psychologist, social worker, licensed professional counselor, licensed perfusionist, licensed respiratory therapist, licensed radiologic technologist, licensed clinical laboratory scientist, or

R.S. 40:1231.1—Cont'd

any nonprofit facility considered tax-exempt under Section 501(c)(3), Internal Revenue Code, pursuant to 26 U.S.C. 501(c)(3), for the diagnosis and treatment of cancer or cancer-related diseases, whether or not such a facility is required to be licensed by this state, or any professional corporation a health care provider is authorized to form under the provisions of Title 12 of the Louisiana Revised Statutes of 1950, or any partnership, limited liability partnership, limited liability company, management company, or corporation whose business is conducted principally by health care providers, or an officer, employee, partner, member, shareholder, or agent thereof acting in the course and scope of his employment.

(11) "Hospital" means any hospital as defined in R.S. 40:2102; any "nursing home" or "home" as defined in R.S. 40:2009.2; or any physician's or dentist's offices or clinics containing facilities for the examination, diagnosis, treatment or care of human illnesses.

(12) "Insurer" means the authority or the entity chosen to manage the authority or an insurer writing policies of malpractice insurance.

(13) "Malpractice" means any unintentional tort or any breach of contract based on health care or professional services rendered, or which should have been rendered, by a health care provider, to a patient, including failure to render services timely and the handling of a patient, including loading and unloading of a patient, and also includes all legal responsibility of a health care provider arising from acts or omissions during the procurement of blood or blood components, in the training or supervision of health care providers, or from defects in blood, tissue, transplants, drugs, and medicines, or from defects in or failures of prosthetic devices implanted in or used on or in the person of a patient.

(14) "Offshore health service provider" means any individual or entity which provides any health care service rendered by an emergency medical technician-basic, or at the intermediate or paramedic levels, or one who is a registered nurse, when such medical care is rendered on a fixed platform in Louisiana territorial waters or on the Outer Continental Shelf, adjacent to Louisiana territorial waters, or any instance on the Outer Continental Shelf where the applicable law, under the Outer Continental Shelf Lands Act, 43 U.S.C. 1331 et seq., would be the laws of the state of Louisiana.

(15) "Patient" means a natural person, including a donor of human blood, a donor or prospective donor of an organ or tissue, or blood components and a nursing home resident who receives or should have received health care from a licensed health care provider, under contract, expressed or implied.

(16) "Physician" means a person with an unlimited license to practice medicine in this state.

(17) "Proof of financial responsibility" as provided for in this Part shall be determined by the board in accordance with regulations promulgated under the Administrative Procedure Act.[1]

(18) "Representative" means the spouse, parent, guardian, trustee, attorney or other legal agent of the patient.

(19) "Risk" means any health care provider which shall apply for malpractice liability insurance coverage under the provisions of R.S. 40:1231.7.

(20) "Risk manager" means an insurance company with no less than an "A" rating according to the then current annual edition of Best's Insurance Reports or a domestic insurance company with assets in excess of ten million dollars chosen by the commissioner according to the public bid laws of the state, to manage the authority.

(21) "Tissue bank" means any independent nonprofit facility procuring and processing human organs or tissues for transplantation, medical education, research, or therapy.

(22) "Tort" means any breach of duty or any negligent act or omission proximately causing injury or damage to another. The standard of care required of every health care provider, except a hospital,

R.S. 40:1231.1—Cont'd

in rendering professional services or health care to a patient, shall be to exercise that degree of skill ordinarily employed, under similar circumstances, by the members of his profession in good standing in the same community or locality, and to use reasonable care and diligence, along with his best judgment, in the application of his skill.

B. Wherever necessary to the context of this Part the masculine shall mean and include the feminine and the singular shall mean and include the plural.

C. No liability shall be imposed upon any health care provider on the basis of an alleged breach of contract, whether by express or implied warranty, assuring results to be obtained from any procedure undertaken in the course of health care, unless such contract is expressly set forth in writing and signed by such health care provider or by an authorized agent of such health care provider.

D. A health care provider who fails to qualify under this Part is not covered by the provisions of this Part and is subject to liability under the law without regard to the provisions of this Part. If a health care provider does not so qualify, the patient's remedy will not be affected by the terms and provisions of this Part, except as hereinafter provided with respect to the suspension and the running of prescription of actions against a health care provider who has not qualified under this Part when a claim has been filed against the health care provider for review under this Part.

E. (1) Subject to R.S. 40:1231.8, a claimant having a claim under this Part for bodily injuries to or death of a patient on account of malpractice may file a complaint in any court of competent jurisdiction and proper venue. Upon filing the complaint in court for bodily injuries to or death of a patient on account of malpractice, said claimant shall send, by certified mail, return receipt requested, a copy of the complaint, and any amendments thereto, to the board. The claimant shall also promptly provide written notice to the board of the trial date upon receiving notice from the court scheduling a trial in such proceeding.

(2) No dollar amount or figure shall be included in the demand in any malpractice complaint, but the prayer shall be for such damages as are reasonable in the premises.

(3) This Section shall not prevent a person from alleging a requisite jurisdictional amount in a malpractice claim filed in a court requiring such an allegation.

(4) All claims and complaints submitted by a patient, claimant, or their representative, as a result of malpractice as defined in this Section, shall, once the parties have certified to the court that discovery is complete, be given priority on the court's docket, to the extent practicable, over any other civil action before the court, provided that the provisions of this Paragraph shall not supersede the provisions of Code of Civil Procedure Article 1573.

F. The provisions of this Part do not apply to any act of malpractice which occurred before September 1, 1975. The provisions of this Part that provide for the suspension and the running of prescription with respect to a health care provider who has not qualified under this Part, but against whom a claim has been filed under this Part, do not apply to any act of malpractice which occurred before September 1, 1981.

G. Notwithstanding the provisions of Subsection D of this Section, the running of prescription against a health care provider who is answerable in solido with a qualified health care provider against whom a claim has been filed for review under this Part shall be suspended in accordance with the provisions of R.S. 40:1231.8(A)(2)(a).

[Caveat: Acts 1991, No. 661, § 1, amended R.S. 40:1299.47(A)(2)(a) (redesignated as R.S. 40:1231.8 by H.C.R. No. 84 of the 2015 Regular Session) to provide that filing a request for review suspends prescription against all solidary obligors, whether health care providers or not.]

R.S. 40:1231.1—Cont'd

H. The provisions of this Part do not apply to any act of malpractice which occurred before September 1, 1975. The provisions of this Part that provide for the suspension of the running of prescription with respect to a health care provider who is answerable in solido with another health care provider apply to an act of malpractice which has been duly submitted for review prior to September 1, 1981 but in which the third health care provider panelist has not been selected. The provision for the suspension of the running of prescription does not apply to any act of malpractice which has not been duly submitted for review and which has prescribed on September 1, 1981.

I. Nothing in this Part shall be construed to make the patient's compensation fund liable for any sums except for those arising from medical malpractice. Notwithstanding any other law to the contrary, including but not limited to R.S. 13:5106, the provisions of this Part shall not apply to medical malpractice actions against the state or any political subdivision thereof with the exception of a hospital service district and a municipally owned hospital and any entities, organizations, or subsidiary owned, operated, or controlled by such a hospital service district or municipally owned hospital. However, this Part shall apply to any certified emergency medical technician—basic, or at the intermediate or paramedic level, employed by any political subdivision of the state, and to any medical advisor or registered nurse performing emergency medical services under contract with any political subdivision of the state.

J. The board shall appoint legal counsel for the Patient's Compensation Fund. It shall be the responsibility of the board to establish minimum qualifications and standards for lawyers who may be appointed to defend professional liability cases. The minimum qualifications and the appointments procedure shall be published at least annually in the Louisiana Bar Journal or such other publication as will reasonably assure dissemination to the membership of the Louisiana State Bar Association. The primary counsel may be permitted by the board to continue the professional liability litigation on behalf of the Patient's Compensation Fund where no conflict of interest exists or where there is no potential conflict of interest. The function of establishing reserves shall be carried out by the board.

K. The provisions of this Part shall not apply to any health care provider when performing the elective termination of an uncomplicated viable pregnancy.

L. Any cause of action for the unintentional acts or omissions arising from resuscitating a patient who has a declaration concerning life-sustaining procedures executed pursuant to R.S. 40:1151 et seq., a Louisiana Physician Order for Scope of Treatment executed pursuant to R.S. 40:1155.1 et seq., or a do not resuscitate order issued by a physician licensed in this state shall be governed by the provisions of this Part.

M. Any cause of action for an unintentional act or omission by an organ procurement organization to a donor or prospective donor of an anatomical gift, as defined in R.S. 17:2351, shall be governed by the provisions of this Section.

Redesignated from R.S. 40:1299.41 by H.C.R. No. 84 of the 2015 Regular Session. Added by Acts 1975, No. 817, § 1. Amended by Acts 1976, No. 183, §§ 1, 2; Acts 1976, No. 660, § 1, eff. Aug. 5, 1976; Acts 1977, No. 261, § 1; Acts 1981, No. 791, § 1, eff. Sept. 1, 1981; Acts 1981, No. 792, § 1, eff. Sept. 1, 1981; Acts 1984, No. 435, § 1, eff. July 6, 1984; Acts 1986, No. 141, § 1; Acts 1986, No. 208, § 1; Acts 1986, No. 498, § 1; Acts 1987, No. 187, § 1; Acts 1987, No. 567, § 2; Acts 1988, No. 735, § 1, eff. July 15, 1988; Acts 1990, No. 579, § 1; Acts 1990, No. 967, § 2, eff. Oct. 1, 1990; Acts 1991, No. 661, § 1; Acts 1991, No. 825, § 1; Acts 1992, No. 824, § 1; Acts 1992, No. 908, § 1; Acts 1997, No. 646, § 1; Acts 1999, No. 1309, § 8, eff. Jan. 1, 2000; Acts 2001, No. 108, § 1; Acts 2001, No. 486, § 4, eff. June 21, 2001; Acts 2001, No. 697, § 1; Acts 2002, 1st Ex.Sess., No. 86, § 1; Acts 2003, No. 431, § 1, eff. June 18, 2003; Acts 2003, No. 479, § 1; Acts 2003, No. 585, § 1; Acts 2003, No. 747, § 1; Acts 2004, No. 182, § 1; Acts 2006, No. 694, § 1; Acts 2008, No. 558, § 1; Acts 2009, No. 14, § 1; Acts 2010, No. 568, § 1; Acts 2010, No. 950, § 1; Acts 2012, No. 538, § 1, eff. June 5, 2012; Acts 2015, No. 323, § 1; Acts 2020, No. 201, § 1.

[1] R.S. 49:950 et seq.

R.S. 40:1231.8

§ 1231.8. Medical review panel

A. (1)(a) All malpractice claims against health care providers covered by this Part, other than claims validly agreed for submission to a lawfully binding arbitration procedure, shall be reviewed by a medical review panel established as hereinafter provided for in this Section. The filing of a request for review by a medical review panel as provided for in this Section shall not be reportable by any health care provider, the Louisiana Patient's Compensation Fund, or any other entity to the Louisiana State Board of Medical Examiners, to any licensing authority, committee, or board of any other state, or to any credentialing or similar agency, committee, or board of any clinic, hospital, health insurer, or managed care company.

(b) A request for review of a malpractice claim or a malpractice complaint shall contain, at a minimum, all of the following:

(i) A request for the formation of a medical review panel.

(ii) The name of only one patient for whom, or on whose behalf, the request for review is being filed; however, if the claim involves the care of a pregnant mother and her unborn child, then naming the mother as the patient shall be sufficient.

(iii) The names of the claimants.

(iv) The names of the defendant health care providers.

(v) The dates of the alleged malpractice.

(vi) A brief description of the alleged malpractice as to each named defendant health care provider.

(vii) A brief description of the alleged injuries.

(c) A claimant shall have forty-five days from the date of receipt by the claimant of the confirmation of receipt of the request for review in accordance with Subparagraph (3)(a) of this Subsection to pay to the board a filing fee in the amount of one hundred dollars per named defendant qualified under this Part.

(d) Such filing fee may be waived only upon receipt of one of the following:

(i) An affidavit of a physician holding a valid and unrestricted license to practice his specialty in the state of his residence certifying that adequate medical records have been obtained and reviewed and that the allegations of malpractice against each defendant health care provider named in the claim constitute a claim of a breach of the applicable standard of care as to each named defendant health care provider.

(ii) An in forma pauperis ruling issued in accordance with Code of Civil Procedure Article 5181 et seq. by a district court in a venue in which the malpractice claim could properly be brought upon the conclusion of the medical review panel process.

(e) Failure to comply with the provisions of Subparagraph (c) or (d) of this Paragraph within the specified forty-five day time frame in Subparagraph (c) of this Paragraph shall render the request for review of a malpractice claim invalid and without effect. Such an invalid request for review of a malpractice claim shall not suspend time within which suit must be instituted in Subparagraph (2)(a) of this Subsection.

(f) All funds generated by such filing fees shall be private monies and shall be applied to the costs of the Patient's Compensation Fund Oversight Board incurred in the administration of claims.

R.S. 40:1231.8—Cont'd

(g) The filing fee of one hundred dollars per named defendant qualified under this Part shall be applicable in the event that a claimant identifies additional qualified health care providers as defendants. The filing fee applicable to each identified qualified health care provider shall be due forty-five days from the mailing date of the confirmation of receipt of the request for review for the additional named defendants in accordance with Subparagraph (3)(a) of this Subsection.

(2)(a) The filing of the request for a review of a claim shall suspend the time within which suit must be instituted, in accordance with this Part, until ninety days following notification, by certified mail, as provided in Subsection J of this Section, to the claimant or his attorney of the issuance of the opinion by the medical review panel, in the case of those health care providers covered by this Part, or in the case of a health care provider against whom a claim has been filed under the provisions of this Part, but who has not qualified under this Part, until ninety days following notification by certified mail to the claimant or his attorney by the board that the health care provider is not covered by this Part. The filing of a request for review of a claim shall suspend the running of prescription against all joint and solidary obligors, and all joint tortfeasors, including but not limited to health care providers, both qualified and not qualified, to the same extent that prescription is suspended against the party or parties that are the subject of the request for review. Filing a request for review of a malpractice claim as required by this Section with any agency or entity other than the division of administration shall not suspend or interrupt the running of prescription. All requests for review of a malpractice claim identifying additional health care providers shall also be filed with the division of administration.

(b)(i) The request for review of a malpractice claim under this Section shall be deemed filed on the date the request is:

(aa) Sent, if the request is electronically sent by facsimile transmission or other authorized means, as provided by R.S. 9:2615(A), to the division of administration.

(bb) Mailed, if the request is delivered by certified or registered mail to the division of administration.

(cc) Received, if the request is delivered to the division of administration by any means other than as provided by Subitem (aa) or (bb) of this Item.

(ii) Upon receipt, the request shall be stamped with the filing date and certified by the division of administration. Filing of the request shall be complete only upon timely compliance with the provisions of Subparagraph (1)(c) or (d) of this Subsection. Upon receipt of any request, the division of administration shall forward a copy of the request to the board within five days of receipt.

(c) An attorney chairman for the medical review panel shall be appointed within one year from the date the request for review of the claim was filed. Upon appointment of the attorney chairman, the parties shall notify the board of the name and address of the attorney chairman. If the board has not received notice of the appointment of an attorney chairman within nine months from the date the request for review of the claim was filed, then the board shall send notice to the parties by certified or registered mail that the claim will be dismissed in ninety days unless an attorney chairman is appointed within one year from the date the request for review of the claim was filed. If the board has not received notice of the appointment of an attorney chairman within one year from the date the request for review of the claim was filed, then the board shall promptly send notice to the parties by certified or registered mail that the claim has been dismissed for failure to appoint an attorney chairman and the parties shall be deemed to have waived the use of the medical review panel. The filing of a request for a medical review panel shall suspend the time within which suit must be filed until ninety days after the claim has been dismissed in accordance with this Section.

R.S. 40:1231.8—Cont'd

(3) It shall be the duty of the board within fifteen days of the receipt of the claim by the board to:

(a) Confirm to the claimant by certified mail, return receipt requested, that the filing has been officially received and whether or not the named defendant or defendants have qualified under this Part.

(b) In the confirmation to the claimant pursuant to Subparagraph (a) of this Paragraph, notify the claimant of the amount of the filing fee due and the time frame within which such fee is due to the board, and that upon failure to comply with the provisions of Subparagraph (1)(c) or (d) of this Subsection, the request for review of a malpractice claim is invalid and without effect and that the request shall not suspend the time within which suit must be instituted in Subparagraph (2)(a) of this Subsection.

(c) Notify all named defendants by certified mail, return receipt requested, whether or not qualified under the provisions of this Part, that a filing has been made against them and request made for the formation of a medical review panel; and forward a copy of the proposed complaint to each named defendant at his last and usual place of residence or his office.

(4) The board shall notify the claimant and all named defendants by certified mail, return receipt requested, of any of the following information:

(a) The date of receipt of the filing fee.

(b) That no filing was due because the claimant timely provided the affidavit set forth in Item (1)(d)(i) of this Subsection.

(c) That the claimant has timely complied with the provisions of Item (1)(d)(ii) of this Subsection.

(d) That the required filing fee was not timely paid pursuant to Subparagraph (1)(c) of this Subsection.

(5) In the event that the board is unable to determine after forty-five days from the date of mailing of the notification, whether notification by certified mail, return receipt requested, provided for in Paragraphs (3) and (4) of this Subsection has been received by the claimant, or the notification is not claimed or is returned undeliverable, the board shall provide such notification by regular first class mail, which date of mailing shall have the effect of receipt of notice by certified mail for purposes of Subparagraphs (1)(c) and (d) of this Subsection.

(6) In the event the board receives a filing fee that was not timely paid pursuant to Subparagraph (1)(c) of this Subsection, then the board shall return, or refund the amount of, the filing fee to the claimant within thirty days of the date the board receives the untimely filing fee.

B. (1)(a)(i) No action against a health care provider covered by this Part, or his insurer, may be commenced in any court before the claimant's proposed complaint has been presented to a medical review panel established pursuant to this Section.

(ii) A certificate of enrollment issued by the board shall be admitted in evidence.

(b) However, with respect to an act of malpractice which occurs after September 1, 1983, if an opinion is not rendered by the panel within twelve months after the date of notification of the selection of the attorney chairman by the executive director to the selected attorney and all other parties pursuant to Paragraph (1) of Subsection C of this Section, suit may be instituted against a health care provider covered by this Part. However, either party may petition a court of competent jurisdiction for an order extending the twelve month period provided in this Subsection for good cause shown. After the twelve month period provided for in this Subsection or any court-ordered extension thereof,

R.S. 40:1231.8—Cont'd

the medical review panel established to review the claimant's complaint shall be dissolved without the necessity of obtaining a court order of dissolution.

(c) By agreement of all parties, the use of the medical review panel may be waived.

(d) By agreement of all parties and upon written request to the attorney chairman, an expedited medical review panel process may be selected. Unless otherwise specified in the provisions of Subsection N of this Section, the expedited process shall be governed by other provisions of this Section.

(2)(a) A health care provider, against whom a claim has been filed under the provisions of this Part, may raise peremptory exceptions of no right of action pursuant to Code of Civil Procedure Article 927(6) or any exception or defenses available pursuant to R.S. 9:5628 in a court of competent jurisdiction and proper venue at any time without need for completion of the review process by the medical review panel.

(b) If the court finds that the claim had prescribed or otherwise was perempted prior to being filed, the panel, if established, shall be dissolved upon the judgment becoming final. If the court grants the peremptory exception of no right of action as to all claimants, the panel, if established, shall be dissolved upon the judgment becoming final. If the court grants the peremptory exception of no right of action as to less than all claimants, the claimants as to whom the court granted the peremptory exception of no right of action shall be prohibited from participating in the panel process as a claimant.

(3) Ninety days after the notification to all parties by certified mail by the attorney chairman or the board of the dissolution of the medical review panel or ninety days after the expiration of any court-ordered extension as authorized by Paragraph (1) of this Subsection, the suspension of the running of prescription with respect to a qualified health care provider shall cease.

C. The medical review panel shall consist of three health care providers who hold unlimited licenses to practice their profession in Louisiana and one attorney. The parties may agree on the attorney member of the medical review panel. If no attorney for or representative of any health care provider named in the complaint has made an appearance in the proceedings or made written contact with the attorney for the plaintiff within forty-five days of the date of receipt of the notification to the health care provider and the insurer that the required filing fee has been received by the patient's compensation board as required by Subparagraph (A)(1)(c) of this Section, the attorney for the plaintiff may appoint the attorney member of the medical review panel for the purpose of convening the panel. Such notice to the health care provider and the insurer shall be sent by registered or certified mail, return receipt requested. If no agreement can be reached, then the attorney member of the medical review panel shall be selected in the following manner:

(1)(a) The office of the clerk of the Louisiana Supreme Court, upon receipt of notification from the board, shall draw five names at random from the list of attorneys who reside or maintain an office in the parish which would be proper venue for the action in a court of law. The names of judges, magistrates, district attorneys and assistant district attorneys shall be excluded if drawn and new names drawn in their place. After selection of the attorney names, the office of the clerk of the supreme court shall notify the board of the names so selected. It shall be the duty of the board to notify the parties of the attorney names from which the parties may choose the attorney member of the panel within five days. If no agreement can be reached within five days, the parties shall immediately initiate a procedure of selecting the attorney by each striking two names alternately, with the claimant striking first and so advising the health care provider of the name of the attorney so stricken; thereafter, the health care provider and the claimant shall alternately strike until both sides have stricken two names and the remaining name shall be the attorney member of the panel. If

R.S. 40:1231.8—Cont'd

either the plaintiff or defendant fails to strike, the clerk of the Louisiana Supreme Court shall strike for that party within five additional days.

(b) After the striking, the office of the board shall notify the attorney and all other parties of the name of the selected attorney.

(2) The attorney shall act as chairman of the panel and in an advisory capacity but shall have no vote. It is the duty of the chairman to expedite the selection of the other panel members, to convene the panel, and expedite the panel's review of the proposed complaint. The chairman shall establish a reasonable schedule for submission of evidence to the medical review panel but must allow sufficient time for the parties to make full and adequate presentation of related facts and authorities within ninety days following selection of the panel.

(3)(a) The plaintiff shall notify the attorney chairman and the named defendants of his choice of a health care provider member of the medical review panel within thirty days of the date of certification of his filing by the board.

(b) The named defendant shall then have fifteen days after notification by the plaintiff of the plaintiff's choice of his health care provider panelist to name the defendant's health care provider panelist.

(c) If either the plaintiff or defendant fails to make a selection of health care provider panelist within the time provided, the attorney chairman shall notify by certified mail the failing party to make such selection within five days of the receipt of the notice.

(d) If no selection is made within the five day period, then the chairman shall make the selection on behalf of the failing party. The two health care provider panel members selected by the parties or on their behalf shall be notified by the chairman to select the third health care provider panel member within fifteen days of their receipt of such notice.

(e) If the two health care provider panel members fail to make such selection within the fifteen day period allowed, the chairman shall then make the selection of the third panel member and thereby complete the panel.

(f) A physician who holds an unrestricted license to practice medicine by the Louisiana State Board of Medical Examiners and who is engaged in the active practice of medicine in this state, whether in the teaching profession or otherwise, shall be available for selection as a member of a medical review panel.

(g) Each party to the action shall have the right to select one health care provider and upon selection the health care provider shall be required to serve.

(h) When there are multiple plaintiffs or defendants, there shall be only one health care provider selected per side. The plaintiff, whether single or multiple, shall have the right to select one health care provider, and the defendant, whether single or multiple, shall have the right to select one health care provider.

(i) A panelist so selected and the attorney member selected in accordance with this Subsection shall serve unless for good cause shown may be excused. To show good cause for relief from serving, the panelist shall present an affidavit to a judge of a court of competent jurisdiction and proper venue which shall set out the facts showing that service would constitute an unreasonable burden or undue hardship. A health care provider panelist may also be excused from serving by the attorney chairman if during the previous twelve-month period he has been appointed to four other medical review panels. In either such event, a replacement panelist shall be selected within fifteen days in the same manner as the excused panelist.

R.S. 40:1231.8—Cont'd

(j) If there is only one party defendant which is not a hospital, community blood center, tissue bank, or ambulance service, all panelists except the attorney shall be from the same class and specialty of practice of health care provider as the defendant. If there is only one party defendant which is a hospital, community blood center, tissue bank, or ambulance service, all panelists except the attorney shall be physicians. If there are claims against multiple defendants, one or more of whom are health care providers other than a hospital, community blood center, tissue bank, or ambulance service, the panelists selected in accordance with this Subsection may also be selected from health care providers who are from the same class and specialty of practice of health care providers as are any of the defendants other than a hospital, community blood center, tissue bank, or ambulance service.

(4) When the medical review panel is formed, the chairman shall within five days notify the board and the parties by registered or certified mail of the names and addresses of the panel members and the date on which the last member was selected.

(5)(a) Before entering upon their duties, each voting panelist shall subscribe before a notary public the following oath:

"I, (name) do solemnly swear/affirm that I will faithfully perform the duties of medical review panel member to the best of my ability and without partiality or favoritism of any kind. I acknowledge that I represent neither side and that it is my lawful duty to serve with complete impartiality and to render a decision in accordance with law and the evidence."

(b) The attorney panel member shall subscribe to the same oath except that in lieu of the last sentence thereof the attorney's oath shall state:

"I acknowledge that I represent neither side and that it is my lawful duty to advise the panel members concerning matters of law and procedure and to serve as chairman."

(c) The original of each oath shall be attached to the opinion rendered by the panel.

(6) The party aggrieved by the alleged failure or refusal of another to perform according to the provisions of this Section may petition any district court of proper venue over the parties for an order directing that the parties comply with the medical review panel provisions of the medical malpractice act.

(7) A panelist or a representative or attorney for any interested party shall not discuss with other members of a medical review panel on which he serves a claim which is to be reviewed by the panel until all evidence to be considered by the panel has been submitted. A panelist or a representative or attorney for any interested party shall not discuss the pending claim with the claimant or his attorney asserting the claim or with a health care provider or his attorney against whom a claim has been asserted under this Section. A panelist or the attorney chairman shall disclose in writing to the parties prior to the hearing any employment relationship or financial relationship with the claimant, the health care provider against whom a claim is asserted, or the attorneys representing the claimant or health care provider, or any other relationship that might give rise to a conflict of interest for the panelists.

D. (1) The evidence to be considered by the medical review panel shall be promptly submitted by the respective parties in written form only.

(2) The evidence may consist of medical charts, x-rays, lab tests, excerpts of treatises, depositions of witnesses including parties, interrogatories, affidavits and reports of medical experts, and any other form of evidence allowable by the medical review panel.

(3) Depositions of the parties and witnesses may be taken prior to the convening of the panel.

R.S. 40:1231.8—Cont'd

(4) Upon request of any party, or upon request of any two panel members, the clerk of any district court shall issue subpoenas and subpoenas duces tecum in aid of the taking of depositions and the production of documentary evidence for inspection and/or copying.

(5) The chairman of the panel shall advise the panel relative to any legal question involved in the review proceeding and shall prepare the opinion of the panel as provided in Subsection G.

(6) A copy of the evidence shall be sent to each member of the panel.

E. Either party, after submission of all evidence and upon ten days notice to the other side, shall have the right to convene the panel at a time and place agreeable to the members of the panel. Either party may question the panel concerning any matters relevant to issues to be decided by the panel before the issuance of their report. The chairman of the panel shall preside at all meetings. Meetings shall be informal.

F. The panel shall have the right and duty to request and procure all necessary information. The panel may consult with medical authorities, provided the names of such authorities are submitted to the parties with a synopsis of their opinions and provided further that the parties may then obtain their testimony by deposition. The panel may examine reports of such other health care providers necessary to fully inform itself regarding the issue to be decided. Both parties shall have full access to any material submitted to the panel.

G. The panel shall have the sole duty to express its expert opinion as to whether or not the evidence supports the conclusion that the defendant or defendants acted or failed to act within the appropriate standards of care. After reviewing all evidence and after any examination of the panel by counsel representing either party, the panel shall, within thirty days, render one or more of the following expert opinions, which shall be in writing and signed by the panelists, together with written reasons for their conclusions:

(1) The evidence supports the conclusion that the defendant or defendants failed to comply with the appropriate standard of care as charged in the complaint.

(2) The evidence does not support the conclusion that the defendant or defendants failed to meet the applicable standard of care as charged in the complaint.

(3) That there is a material issue of fact, not requiring expert opinion, bearing on liability for consideration by the court.

(4) When Paragraph (1) of this Subsection is answered in the affirmative, that the conduct complained of was or was not a factor of the resultant damages. If such conduct was a factor, whether the plaintiff suffered: (a) any disability and the extent and duration of the disability, and (b) any permanent impairment and the percentage of the impairment.

H. Any report of the expert opinion reached by the medical review panel shall be admissible as evidence in any action subsequently brought by the claimant in a court of law, but such expert opinion shall not be conclusive and either party shall have the right to call, at his cost, any member of the medical review panel as a witness. If called, the witness shall be required to appear and testify. A panelist shall have absolute immunity from civil liability for all communications, findings, opinions and conclusions made in the course and scope of duties prescribed by this Part.

I. (1)(a) Each physician member of the medical review panel shall be paid at the rate of twenty-five dollars per diem, not to exceed a total of three hundred dollars for all work performed as a member of the panel exclusive of time involved if called as a witness to testify in a court of law regarding the communications, findings, and conclusions made in the course and scope of duties as a member of the medical review panel, and in addition thereto, reasonable travel expenses.

R.S. 40:1231.8—Cont'd

(b) The attorney chairman of the medical review panel shall be paid at the rate of one hundred dollars per diem, not to exceed a total of two thousand dollars for all work performed as a member of the panel exclusive of time involved if called as a witness to testify in a court of law regarding the communications, findings, and conclusions made in the course and scope of duties as a member of the medical review panel, and in addition thereto, reasonable travel expenses. Additionally, the attorney chairman shall be reimbursed for all reasonable out-of-pocket expenses incurred in performing his duties for each medical review panel. The attorney chairman shall submit the amount due him for all work performed as a member of the panel by affidavit, which shall attest that he has performed in the capacity of chairman of the medical review panel and that he was personally present at all the panel's meetings or deliberations.

(2)(a) The costs of the medical review panel shall be paid by the health care provider if the opinion of the medical review panel is in favor of said defendant health care provider.

(b) The claimant shall pay the costs of the medical review panel if the opinion of the medical review panel is in favor of the claimant. However, if the claimant is unable to pay, the claimant shall submit to the attorney chairman prior to the convening of the medical review panel an in forma pauperis ruling issued in accordance with Code of Civil Procedure Article 5181 et seq. by a district court in a venue in which the malpractice claim could properly be brought upon the conclusion of the medical review panel process. Upon timely receipt of the in forma pauperis ruling, the costs of the medical review panel shall be paid by the health care provider, with the proviso that if the claimant subsequently receives a settlement or receives a judgment, the advance payment of the medical review panel costs will be offset.

(c) In a medical malpractice suit filed by the claimant in which a unanimous opinion was rendered in favor of the defendant health care provider as provided in the expert opinion stated in Paragraph (G)(2) of this Section, the claimant who proceeds to file such a suit shall be required to post a cash or surety bond, approved by the court, in the amount of all costs of the medical review panel. Upon the conclusion of the medical malpractice suit, the court shall order that the cash or surety bond be forfeited to the defendant health care provider for reimbursement of the costs of the medical review panel, unless a final judgment is rendered finding the defendant liable to the claimant for any damages. If a final judgment is rendered finding the defendant liable to the claimant for any damages, the court shall order that the defendant health care provider reimburse the claimant an amount equal to the cost of obtaining the cash or surety bond posted by the claimant.

(d) In the event a medical review panel renders a unanimous opinion in favor of the claimant as provided in the expert opinions stated in Paragraphs (G)(1) and (4) of this Section, and the claimant has not timely submitted an in forma pauperis ruling to the panel's attorney chairman, and thereafter the defendant health care provider failed to settle the claim with the claimant resulting in the claimant filing a malpractice suit in a court of competent jurisdiction and proper venue against the defendant health care provider based on the same claim which was the subject of the unanimously adverse medical review panel opinion against the defendant health care provider, the defendant health care provider shall be required to post a cash or surety bond, approved by the court, in the amount of all costs of the medical review panel. Upon the conclusion of the medical malpractice suit, the court shall order that the cash or surety bond be forfeited to the claimant for reimbursement of the costs of the medical review panel, unless a final judgment is rendered finding that the defendant health care provider has no liability for damages to the claimant. If a final judgment is rendered finding that the defendant health care provider has no liability for damages to the claimant, the court shall order that the claimant reimburse the defendant health care provider an amount equal to the cost of obtaining the cash or surety bond posted by the defendant health care provider.

R.S. 40:1231.8—Cont'd

(3) If the medical review panel decides that there is a material issue of fact bearing on liability for consideration by the court, the claimant and the health care provider shall split the costs of the medical review panel. However, in those instances in which the claimant is unable to pay his share of the costs of the medical review panel, the claimant shall submit to the attorney chairman prior to the convening of the medical review panel an in forma pauperis ruling issued in accordance with Code of Civil Procedure Article 5181 et seq., by a district court in a venue in which the malpractice claim could properly be brought upon the conclusion of the medical review panel process. Upon timely receipt of the in forma pauperis ruling, the costs of the medical review panel shall be paid by the defendant health care provider with the proviso that if the claimant subsequently receives a settlement or receives a judgment, the advance payment of the claimant's share of the costs of the medical review panel will be offset.

(4) Upon the rendering of the written panel decision, if any one of the panelists finds that the evidence supports the conclusion that a defendant health care provider failed to comply with the appropriate standard of care as charged in the complaint, each defendant health care provider as to whom such a determination was made shall reimburse to the claimant that portion of the filing fee applicable to the claim against such defendant health care provider or if any one of the panelists finds that the evidence supports the conclusion that there is a material issue of fact, not requiring expert opinion, bearing on liability of such defendant health care provider for consideration by the court, each such defendant health care provider as to whom such a determination was made shall reimburse to the claimant fifty percent of that portion of the filing fee applicable to the claim against such defendant health care provider.

J. The chairman shall submit a copy of the panel's report to the board and all parties and attorneys by registered or certified mail within five days after the panel renders its opinion.

K. Repealed by Acts 2005, No. 127, § 2.

L. Where the medical review panel issues its opinion required by this Section, the suspension of the running of prescription shall not cease until ninety days following notification by certified mail to the claimant or his attorney of the issuance of the opinion as required by Subsection J of this Section.

M. Legal interest shall accrue from the date of filing of the complaint with the board on a judgment rendered by a court in a suit for medical malpractice brought after compliance with this Part.

N. (1)(a)(i) Parties seeking an expedited panel process pursuant to the provisions of Subparagraph (B)(1)(d) of this Section shall request such process in writing sixty days from the date of the letter of notification of the selection of the attorney chairman pursuant to Paragraph (C)(1) of of this Section. When a written request for an expedited medical review panel process has been made to the attorney chairman, the chairman shall establish a schedule for submission of evidence to the medical review panel within ninety days following selection of the third physician member of the panel so that a panel opinion is rendered within twelve months of the date of notification of the selection of the attorney chairman.

(ii) In accordance with Subsection J of this Section, the chairman shall submit a copy of the panel's report to the board and all parties and attorneys by registered or certified mail within five days after the panel renders its opinion. In accordance with Subsection L of this Section, where the medical review panel issues its opinion required by this Section, the suspension of the running of prescription shall not cease until ninety days following notification by certified mail to the claimant or his attorney of the issuance of the opinion as required by Subsection J of this Section.

R.S. 40:1231.8—Cont'd

(b)(i) No party may petition a court for an order extending the twelve month period provided in Subparagraph (B)(1)(b) of this Section. If an opinion is not rendered by the panel within the twelve month period established in this Subsection, suit may be instituted against the health care provider.

(ii) In accordance with Subparagraph (B)(1)(b) of this Section, after the twelve month period provided for in this Subsection, the medical review panel established to review the claimant's complaint shall be dissolved without the necessity of obtaining a court order of dissolution.

(iii) In accordance with Paragraph (B)(3) of this Section, ninety days after the notification to all parties by certified mail by the attorney chairman of the board of the dissolution of the medical review panel, the suspension of the running of prescription with respect to a qualified health care provider shall cease.

(2) During selection of the physician members of the medical review panel, the plaintiff shall notify the attorney chairman and the named defendants of his choice of a health care provider member of the medical review panel within ten days of the date of written request to the chairman for an expedited panel process. The named defendant shall then have five days after notification by the plaintiff of the plaintiff's choice of his health care provider panelist to name the defendant's health care provider panelist. If no selection is made within the five and ten day respective periods, then the chairman shall make the selection on behalf of the failing party. The two health care provider panel members selected by the parties or on their behalf shall be notified by the chairman to select the third health care provider panel member within fifteen days of their receipt of such notice from the chairman to make the selection. If no selection is made within the fifteen day period, then the chairman shall make the selection on behalf of the two health care provider panel members.

(3)(a) Within thirty days of the parties' written request for an expedited medical review panel process to the attorney chairman, the claimant shall provide all defendants with a list of the names and addresses of all known health care providers, including individuals and entities, who have treated the patient during the time period starting from three years prior to the date of the alleged malpractice up to and including the date that the list is provided. The claimant shall make a good faith effort to identify the treating health care providers.

(b) The claimant shall execute and provide all defendants with a HIPAA Compliant Authorization form to permit the defendants to obtain the medical records.

(c) An order to protect the medical records may be sought as provided in Code of Civil Procedure Article 1426 or the HIPAA regulations at 45 CFR 164.512(e) in a court of competent jurisdiction and proper venue.

(d) If an authorization is not provided or a protective order is not obtained within thirty days following the written request by the parties to the chairman for an expedited medical review panel process, the medical review panel shall lose its expedited status and no longer be governed by the provisions of this Subsection. The attorney chairman shall provide notice of this to the board and all parties by registered or certified mail.

(4)(a) The evidence to be considered by the medical review panel shall be promptly submitted by the respective parties in written form only, according to the schedule established by the chairman.

(b) The evidence may consist only of medical charts, x-rays or other film studies, lab tests, other diagnostic or medical tests, and a position paper submitted by or on behalf of each party.

(c) Neither interrogatories to nor depositions of the parties and witnesses may be taken prior to the convening of the panel.

(d) No party or panel member shall be permitted to request the clerk of any district court to issue subpoenas and subpoenas duces tecum in aid of the taking of depositions and the production of

R.S. 40:1231.8—Cont'd

documentary evidence. However, if a copy of the medical record is not produced by a health care provider within a reasonable period of time, not to exceed fifteen days, following a health care provider's receipt of a medical authorization executed by the claimant pursuant to Subparagraph (3)(b) of this Subsection then the party who forwarded the authorization to the health care provider may request the clerk of any district court to issue subpoenas and subpoenas duces tecum in aid of the production of the medical records.

(5) The attorney chairman, after submission of all evidence and upon ten days notice, shall convene the panel at a time and place agreeable to the members of the panel, but in no event shall the opinion be rendered later than twelve months from the date of notification of the selection of the attorney chairman by the executive director to the selected attorney and all other parties pursuant to Paragraph (C)(1) of this Section. Either party may informally question the panel concerning any matters relevant to issues to be decided by the panel before and after the issuance of their report. The panel deliberation and the questioning of the panel shall not be recorded. The chairman of the panel shall preside at all meetings.

(6) The panel shall have the sole duty to express its expert opinion as to whether or not the evidence supports the conclusion that the defendant or defendants acted or failed to act within the appropriate standards of care. After reviewing all evidence and after any examination of the panel by counsel representing either party, the panel shall, within thirty days, but in no event later than twelve months of the date of notification of the selection of the attorney chairman pursuant to Paragraph (C)(1) of this Section, render one or more of the following expert opinions, which shall be in writing and signed by the panelists, together with written reasons for their conclusions:

(a) The evidence supports the conclusion that the defendant or defendants failed to comply with the appropriate standard of care as charged in the complaint.

(b) The evidence does not support the conclusion that the defendant or defendants failed to meet the applicable standard of care as charged in the complaint.

(c) That there is a material issue of fact, not requiring expert opinion, bearing on liability for consideration by the court.

(7) The report of the expert opinion reached by the expedited medical review panel process pursuant to the provisions of this Subsection shall not be admissible as evidence in any action subsequently brought by the claimant in a court of law. Neither party shall have the right to call any member of the medical review panel as a witness. A panelist shall have absolute immunity from civil liability for all communications, findings, opinions and conclusions made in the course and scope of duties prescribed by this Part.

(8) The provisions of Subparagraphs (I)(2)(c) and (d) of this Section shall not apply to a medical review panel governed by the expedited medical review panel process.

Redesignated from R.S. 40:1299.47 by H.C.R. No. 84 of the 2015 Regular Session. Added by Acts 1975, No. 817, § 1. Amended by Acts 1976, No. 183, § 7; Acts 1977, No. 143, § 1; Acts 1979, No. 299, §§ 1, 2; Acts 1981, No. 791, § 1, eff. Sept. 1, 1981; Acts 1982, No. 235, § 1; Acts 1982, No. 236, § 1; Acts 1982, No. 674, § 1; Acts 1982, No. 768, § 1; Acts 1983, No. 402, § 1; Acts 1984, No. 435, § 5, eff. July 6, 1984; Acts 1986, No. 454, § 1, eff. July 2, 1986; Acts 1987, No. 567, § 2; Acts 1988, No. 755, § 1, eff. July 15, 1988; Acts 1990, No. 967, § 2, eff. Oct. 1, 1990; Acts 1991, No. 661, § 1; Acts 1991, No. 668, § 1; Acts 1992, No. 347, § 1, eff. June 17, 1992; Acts 1995, No. 1258, § 1; Acts 1997, No. 664, § 1; Acts 1997, No. 830, § 1; Acts 2002, 1st Ex.Sess., No. 86, § 1; Acts 2003, No. 484, § 1; Acts 2003, No. 644, § 1; Acts 2003, No. 961, § 1; Acts 2003, No. 1263, § 1, eff. July 7, 2003; Acts 2004, No. 306, § 1; Acts 2004, No. 309, § 1; Acts 2004, No. 311, § 1; Acts 2005, No. 127, § 1; Acts 2006, No. 323, § 1; Acts 2008, No. 558, § 1; Acts 2012, No. 802, § 1; Acts 2016, No. 275, § 1; Acts 2017, No. 294, § 1.

PART II. DOMESTIC ABUSE ASSISTANCE

R.S. 46:2131

§ 2131. Purposes

The purpose of this Part is to recognize and address the complex legal and social problems created by domestic violence. The legislature finds that existing laws which regulate the dissolution of marriage do not adequately address problems of protecting and assisting the victims of domestic abuse. The legislature further finds that previous societal attitudes have been reflected in the policies and practices of law enforcement agencies and prosecutors which have resulted in different treatment of crimes occurring between family members, household members, or dating partners and those occurring between strangers. It is the intent of the legislature to provide a civil remedy for domestic violence which will afford the victim immediate and easily accessible protection. Furthermore, it is the intent of the legislature that the official response of law enforcement agencies to cases of domestic violence shall stress the enforcement of laws to protect the victim and shall communicate the attitude that violent behavior is not excused or tolerated.

Added by Acts 1982, No. 782, § 2. Amended by Acts 2015, No. 85, § 1.

R.S. 46:2132

§ 2132. Definitions

As used in this Part:

(1) "Adult" means any person eighteen years of age or older, or any person under the age of eighteen who has been emancipated by marriage or otherwise.

(2) "Court" shall mean any court of competent jurisdiction in the state of Louisiana.

(3) "Domestic abuse" includes but is not limited to physical or sexual abuse and any offense against the person, physical or non-physical, as defined in the Criminal Code of Louisiana, except negligent injury and defamation, committed by one family member, household member, or dating partner against another. "Domestic abuse" also includes abuse of adults as defined in R.S. 15:1503 when committed by an adult child or adult grandchild.

(4) "Family members" means spouses, former spouses, parents and children, stepparents, stepchildren, foster parents, foster children, other ascendants, and other descendants. "Family member" also means the other parent or foster parent of any child or foster child of the offender. "Household members" means any person presently or formerly living in the same residence with the defendant and who is involved or has been involved in a sexual or intimate relationship with the defendant, or any child presently or formerly living in the same residence with the defendant, or any child of the defendant regardless of where the child resides. "Dating partner" means any person protected from violence under R.S. 46:2151. If a parent or grandparent is being abused by an adult child, adult foster child, or adult grandchild, the provisions of this Part shall apply to any proceeding brought in district court.

Added by Acts 1982, No. 782, § 2. Amended by Acts 1986, No. 154, § 1; Acts 1986, No. 459, § 1, eff. July 2, 1986; Acts 1993, No. 402, § 2; Acts 1997, No. 1156, § 7; Acts 1999, No. 1200, § 2; Acts 2001, No. 619, § 1; Acts 2010, No. 861, § 20; Acts 2015, No. 85, § 1; Acts 2017, No. 79, § 2; Acts 2020, No. 101, § 2; Acts 2020, No. 246, § 4.

R.S. 46:2133

§ 2133. Jurisdiction; venue; standing

A. Any court in the state of Louisiana which is empowered to hear family or juvenile matters shall have jurisdiction over proceedings appropriate to it under this Part.

B. Venue lies:

(1) In the parish where the marital domicile is located or where the household is located.

(2) In the parish where the defendant resides.

(3) In the parish where the abuse is alleged to have been committed.

(4) In the parish where the petitioner resides.

(5) In the parish where an action for annulment of marriage or for a divorce could be brought pursuant to Code of Civil Procedure Article 3941(A).

C. Notwithstanding the venue provisions of Subsection B of this Section, in a judicial district comprised of multiple parishes, if a court determines that it is in the interest of justice to afford the parties a more expeditious hearing than current docketing scheduling would permit, or to comply with the time provisions provided for by this Part, a judge or hearing officer may conduct a hearing in any parish within the judicial district.

D. An adult may seek relief under this Part by filing a petition with the court alleging abuse by the defendant. Any parent, adult household member, or district attorney may seek relief on behalf of any minor child or any person alleged to be incompetent by filing a petition with the court alleging abuse by the defendant. A petitioner's right to relief under this Part shall not be affected by leaving the residence or household to avoid further abuse.

Added by Acts 1982, No. 782, § 2. Amended by Acts 1984, No. 80, § 1; Acts 1986, No. 459, § 1, eff. July 2, 1986; Acts 1991, No. 361, § 1; Acts 1997, No. 1156, § 7; Acts 2016, No. 119, § 1.

R.S. 46:2134

§ 2134. Petition

A. A petition filed under the provisions of this Part shall contain the following:

(1) The name of each petitioner and each person on whose behalf the petition is filed, and the name, address, and parish of residence of each individual alleged to have committed abuse, if known; if the petition is being filed on behalf of a child or person alleged to be incompetent, the relationship between that person and the petitioner.

(2) The facts and circumstances concerning the alleged abuse.

(3) The relationship between each petitioner and each individual alleged to have committed abuse.

(4) A request for one or more protective orders.

(5) If desired, a request for a competent interpreter for a non-English-speaking principal party or witness to the proceeding.

B. The address and parish of each petitioner and each person on whose behalf the petition is filed may remain confidential with the court.

C. If the petition requests a protective order for a spouse and alleges that the other spouse has committed abuse, the petition shall state whether a suit for divorce is pending.

R.S. 46:2134—Cont'd

D. If the petition requests the issuance of an ex parte temporary restraining order, the petition shall contain a written affirmation signed and dated by each petitioner that the facts and circumstances contained in the petition are true and correct to the best knowledge, information, and belief of the petitioner, under penalty of perjury pursuant to R.S. 14:123. The affirmation shall be made before a witness who shall sign and print his name.

E. If a suit for divorce is pending, any application for a protective order shall be filed in that proceeding and shall be heard within the delays provided by this Part. Any decree issued in a divorce proceeding filed subsequent to a petition filed or an order issued pursuant to this Part may, in the discretion of the court hearing the divorce proceeding, supersede in whole or in part the orders issued pursuant to this Part. Such subsequent decree shall be forwarded by the rendering court to the court having jurisdiction of the petition for a protective order and shall be made a part of the record thereof. The findings and rulings made in connection with such protective orders shall not be res judicata in any subsequent proceeding.

F. A petitioner shall not be required to prepay or be cast with court costs or costs of service or subpoena for the filing of the petition or the issuance of a temporary restraining order or protective order pursuant to this Part, and the clerk of court shall immediately file and process the petition and temporary restraining order issued pursuant to this Part, regardless of the ability of the petitioner to pay court costs.

G. If the court orders the issuance of a temporary restraining order, the defendant may be cast for all costs.

Added by Acts 1982, No. 782, § 2. Amended by Acts 1990, No. 361, § 2, eff. Jan. 1, 1991; Acts 1997, No. 1156, § 7; Acts 2001, No. 430, § 2; Acts 2005, No. 191, § 1; Acts 2019, No. 406, § 2, eff. June 20, 2019; Acts 2021, No. 394, § 3.

R.S. 46:2135

§ 2135. Temporary restraining order

A. Upon good cause shown in an ex parte proceeding, the court may enter a temporary restraining order, without bond, as it deems necessary to protect from abuse the petitioner, any minor children, or any person alleged to be an incompetent. Any person who shows immediate and present danger of abuse shall constitute good cause for purposes of this Subsection. The court shall consider any and all past history of abuse, or threats thereof, in determining the existence of an immediate and present danger of abuse. There is no requirement that the abuse itself be recent, immediate, or present. The order may include but is not limited to the following:

(1) Directing the defendant to refrain from abusing, harassing, or interfering with the person or employment or going near the residence or place of employment of the petitioner, the minor children, or any person alleged to be incompetent, on whose behalf a petition was filed under this Part.

(2) Awarding to a party use and possession of specified jointly owned or leased property, such as an automobile.

(3) Granting possession to the petitioner of the residence or household to the exclusion of the defendant, by evicting the defendant or restoring possession to the petitioner where:

(a) The residence is jointly owned in equal proportion or leased by the defendant and the petitioner or the person on whose behalf the petition is brought;

(b) The residence is solely owned by the petitioner or the person on whose behalf the petition is brought; or

R.S. 46:2135—Cont'd

(c) The residence is solely leased by defendant and defendant has a duty to support the petitioner or the person on whose behalf the petition is brought.

(4) Prohibiting either party from the transferring, encumbering, or otherwise disposing of property mutually owned or leased by the parties, except when in the ordinary course of business, or for the necessary support of the party or the minor children.

(5) Awarding temporary custody of minor children or persons alleged to be incompetent.

(6) Awarding or restoring possession to the petitioner of all separate property and all personal property, including but not limited to telephones or other communication equipment, computers, medications, clothing, toiletries, social security cards, birth certificates or other forms of identification, tools of the trade, checkbooks, keys, automobiles, photographs, jewelry, or any other items or personal effects of the petitioner and restraining the defendant from transferring, encumbering, concealing, or disposing of the personal or separate property of the petitioner.

(7) Granting to the petitioner the exclusive care, possession, or control of any pets belonging to or under the care of the petitioner or minor children residing in the residence or household of either party, and directing the defendant to refrain from harassing, interfering with, abusing or injuring any pet, without legal justification, known to be owned, possessed, leased, kept, or held by either party or a minor child residing in the residence or household of either party.

B. If a temporary restraining order is granted without notice, the matter shall be set within twenty-one days for a rule to show cause why the protective order should not be issued, at which time the petitioner must prove the allegations of abuse by a preponderance of the evidence. The defendant shall be given notice of the temporary restraining order and the hearing on the rule to show cause by service of process as required by law within twenty-four hours of the issuance of the order.

C. During the existence of the temporary restraining order, a party shall have the right to return to the family residence once to recover his or her personal clothing and necessities, provided that the party is accompanied by a law enforcement officer to ensure the protection and safety of the parties.

D. If no temporary restraining order has been granted, the court shall issue a rule to show cause why the protective order should not be issued, and set the rule for hearing on the earliest day that the business of the court will permit, but in any case within ten days from the date of service of the petition, at which time the petitioner must prove the allegations of abuse by a preponderance of the evidence. The defendant shall be given notice by service of process as required by law.

E. If the hearing pursuant to Subsection B or D of this Section is continued, the court shall make or extend such temporary restraining orders as it deems necessary. Any continuance of a hearing ordered pursuant to Subsection B or D of this Section shall not exceed fifteen days, unless good cause is shown for further continuance.

F. The court may, in its discretion, grant an emergency temporary restraining order outside regular court hours.

G. Immediately upon entering a temporary restraining order, the judge shall cause to have prepared a Uniform Abuse Prevention Order, as provided in R.S. 46:2136.2(C), shall sign such order, and shall immediately forward it to the clerk of court for filing on the day that the order is issued.

H. The clerk of the issuing court shall transmit the Uniform Abuse Prevention Order to the judicial administrator's office, Louisiana Supreme Court, for entry into the Louisiana Protective Order Registry, as provided in R.S. 46:2136.2(A), by facsimile transmission or direct electronic input as expeditiously as possible, but no later than the end of the next business day after the order is filed with the clerk of court. The clerk of the issuing court shall also send a copy of the Uniform Abuse

R.S. 46:2135—Cont'd

Prevention Order, as provided in R.S. 46:2136.2(C), or any modification thereof, to the chief law enforcement officer of the parish where the person or persons protected by the order reside by facsimile transmission or direct electronic input as expeditiously as possible, but no later than the end of the next business day after the order is filed with the clerk of court. A copy of the Uniform Abuse Prevention Order shall be reviewed by the law enforcement agency and shall be retained on file in the office of the chief law enforcement officer until otherwise directed by the court.

I. The initial rule to show cause hearing required pursuant to Subsection B or D may be conducted by a hearing officer who is qualified and selected in the same manner provided in R.S. 46:236.5(C). The hearing officer shall be subject to the applicable limitations and shall follow the applicable procedures provided in R.S. 46:236.5(C). The hearing officer shall make recommendations to the court as to the action that should be taken in the matter.

J. Upon filing a petition for a temporary restraining order, regardless of whether the court grants the temporary restraining order, the clerk of court shall notify the petitioner of his right to initiate criminal proceedings and shall inform the petitioner that the granting of a temporary restraining order pursuant to the provisions of this Section does not automatically file criminal charges against the defendant.

Added by Acts 1982, No. 782, § 2. Amended by Acts 1983, No. 406, § 1; Acts 1983, No. 407, § 1; Acts 1984, No. 77, § 1; Acts 1997, No. 1156, § 7; Acts 1999, No. 1200, § 2; Acts 1999, No. 1336, § 1; Acts 2003, No. 750, § 6; Acts 2006, No. 777, § 2; Acts 2008, No. 411, § 1, eff. June 21, 2008; Acts 2009, No. 427, § 1; Acts 2014, No. 317, § 3; Acts 2015, No. 85, § 1; Acts 2018, No. 206, § 5; Acts 2019, No. 417, § 1.

R.S. 46:2136

§ 2136. Protective orders; content; modification; service

A. The court may grant any protective order or approve any consent agreement to bring about a cessation of domestic abuse as defined in R.S. 46:2132, or the threat or danger thereof, to a party, any minor children, or any person alleged to be incompetent, which relief may include but is not limited to:

(1) Granting the relief enumerated in R.S. 46:2135.

(2) Where there is a duty to support a party, any minor children, or any person alleged to be incompetent living in the residence or household, ordering payment of temporary support or provision of suitable housing for them, or granting possession to the petitioner of the residence or household to the exclusion of the defendant, by evicting the defendant or restoring possession to the petitioner where the residence is solely owned by the defendant and the petitioner has been awarded the temporary custody of the minor children born of the parties.

(3) Awarding temporary custody of or establishing temporary visitation rights and conditions with regard to any minor children or person alleged to be incompetent.

(4)(a) Ordering either a medical or mental health evaluation or both of the perpetrator to be conducted by an independent court-appointed evaluator who qualifies as an expert in the field of domestic abuse. The evaluation shall be conducted by a person who has no family, financial, or prior medical or mental health relationship with the perpetrator or his attorney of record.

(b) After a medical or mental health evaluation has been completed and a report issued, the court may order counseling or other medical or mental health treatment as deemed appropriate.

B. A protective order may be rendered pursuant to this Part if the court has jurisdiction over the parties and subject matter and either of the following occurs:

R.S. 46:2136—Cont'd

(1) The parties enter into a consent agreement.

(2) Reasonable notice and opportunity to be heard is given to the person against whom the order is sought sufficient to protect that person's right to due process.

C. Any protective order issued within this state or outside this state that is consistent with Subsection B of this Section shall be accorded full faith and credit by the courts of this state and enforced as if it were the order of the enforcing court.

D. (1) On the motion of any party, the court, after notice to the other parties and a hearing, may modify a prior order to exclude any item included in the prior order, or to include any item that could have been included in the prior order.

(2) On the motion of any party, after a hearing, the court may modify the effective period of a protective order pursuant to Paragraph (F)(2) of this Section.

E. A protective order made under this Part shall be served on the person to whom the order applies in open court at the close of the hearing, or in the same manner as a writ of injunction.

F. (1) Except as provided in Paragraph (2) of this Subsection, any final protective order or approved consent agreement shall be for a fixed period of time, not to exceed eighteen months, and may be extended by the court, after a contradictory hearing, in its discretion. Such protective order or extension thereof shall be subject to a devolutive appeal only.

(2)(a) For any protective order granted by the court which directs the defendant to refrain from abusing, harassing, or interfering with the person as provided in R.S. 46:2135(A)(1), the court may grant the order to be effective for an indefinite period of time as provided by the provisions of this Paragraph on its own motion or by motion of the petitioner. The indefinite period shall be limited to the portion of the protective order which directs the defendant to refrain from abusing, harassing, or interfering with the person as provided in R.S. 46:2135(A)(1).

(b) The hearing for this motion shall be conducted concurrently with the hearing for the rule to show cause why the protective order should not be issued.

(c) Any motion to modify the indefinite effective period of the protective order as provided in Subparagraph (a) of this Paragraph may be granted only after a good faith effort has been made to provide reasonable notice of the hearing to the victim, the victim's designated agent, or the victim's counsel, and either of the following occur:

(i) The victim, the victim's designated agent, or the victim's counsel is present at the hearing or provides written waiver of such appearance.

(ii) After a good faith effort has been made to provide reasonable notice of the hearing, the victim could not be located.

G. Immediately upon granting a protective order or approving any consent agreement, the judge shall cause to have prepared a Uniform Abuse Prevention Order, as provided in R.S. 46:2136.2(C), shall sign such order, and shall immediately forward it to the clerk of court for filing on the day that the order is issued.

H. The clerk of the issuing court shall transmit the Uniform Abuse Prevention Order to the judicial administrator's office, Louisiana Supreme Court, for entry into the Louisiana Protective Order Registry, as provided in R.S. 46:2136.2(A), by facsimile transmission or direct electronic input as expeditiously as possible, but no later than the end of the next business day after the order is filed with the clerk of court. The clerk of the issuing court shall also send a copy of the Uniform Abuse Prevention Order, as provided in R.S. 46:2136.2(C), or any modification thereof, to the chief law enforcement officer of the parish where the person or persons protected by the order reside by

R.S. 46:2136—Cont'd

facsimile transmission or direct electronic input as expeditiously as possible, but no later than the end of the next business day after the order is filed with the clerk of court. A copy of the Uniform Abuse Prevention Order shall be reviewed by the law enforcement agency and shall be retained on file in the office of the chief law enforcement officer until otherwise directed by the court.

I. At the proceeding, regardless of whether the court grants the protective order, the court shall notify the petitioner of his right to initiate criminal proceedings and shall inform the petitioner that the granting of a protective order pursuant to the provisions of this Section does not automatically file criminal charges against the defendant.

Added by Acts 1982, No. 782, § 2. Amended by Acts 1994, 3rd Ex.Sess., No. 22, § 2; Acts 1997, No. 1156, § 7; Acts 1999, No. 1200, § 2; Acts 2003, No. 750, § 6; Acts 2008, No. 411, § 1, eff. June 21, 2008; Acts 2012, No. 197, § 2; Acts 2014, No. 317, § 3; Acts 2015, No. 85, § 1; Acts 2017, No. 381, § 4, eff. June 23, 2017; Acts 2018, No. 206, § 5; Acts 2018, No. 697, § 1; Acts 2019, No. 417, § 1.

R.S. 46:2136.1

§ 2136.1. Costs paid by abuser

A. All court costs, attorney fees, costs of enforcement and modification proceedings, costs of appeal, evaluation fees, and expert witness fees incurred in maintaining or defending any proceeding concerning domestic abuse assistance in accordance with the provisions of this Part shall be paid by the perpetrator of the domestic violence, including all costs of medical and psychological care for the abused adult, or for any of the children, necessitated by the domestic violence.

B. However, if the court determines the petition was frivolous, the court may order the nonprevailing party to pay all court costs and reasonable attorney fees of the other party.

Added by Acts 1997, No. 1156, § 7. Amended by Acts 2006, No. 777, § 2; Acts 2008, No. 411, § 1, eff. June 21, 2008; Acts 2018, No. 264, § 4.

R.S. 46:2136.2

§ 2136.2. Louisiana Protective Order Registry

A. In order to provide a statewide registry for abuse prevention orders to prevent domestic abuse, dating violence, stalking, and sexual assault and to aid law enforcement, prosecutors, and the courts in handling such matters, there shall be created a Louisiana Protective Order Registry administered by the judicial administrator's office, Louisiana Supreme Court. The judicial administrator's office shall collect the data transmitted to it from the courts, law enforcement, and private process servers of the state and enter it into the Louisiana Protective Order Registry as expeditiously as possible.

B. The Louisiana Protective Order Registry encompasses temporary restraining orders, protective orders, preliminary injunctions, permanent injunctions, and court-approved consent agreements resulting from actions brought pursuant to R.S. 46:2131 et seq., R.S. 46:2151, R.S. 46:2171 et seq., R.S. 46:2181 et seq., R.S. 9:361 et seq., R.S. 9:372, Children's Code Article 1564 et seq., Code of Civil Procedure Article 3607.1, or peace bonds pursuant to Code of Criminal Procedure Article 30(B), or as part of the disposition, sentence, or bail condition of a criminal matter pursuant to Code of Criminal Procedure Articles 327.1, 335.1, 335.2, or 871.1 as long as such order is issued for the purpose of preventing violent or threatening acts or harassment against, contact or communication with, or physical proximity to, another person to prevent domestic abuse, stalking, dating violence, or sexual assault.

R.S. 46:2136.2—Cont'd

C. The courts of this state shall use a uniform form for the issuance of any protective or restraining order, which form shall be developed, approved, and distributed by the judicial administrator's office, shall be titled the "Uniform Abuse Prevention Order".

D. The clerk of the issuing court shall immediately send a copy of the order or any modification thereof to the Louisiana Protective Order Registry and to the chief law enforcement officer of the parish in which the person or persons protected by the order reside as expeditiously as possible but no later than by the end of the next business day after the order is filed with the clerk of court. Transmittal of the Uniform Abuse Prevention Order shall be made by facsimile transmission or direct electronic input as expeditiously as possible, but no later than the end of the next business day after the order is filed with the clerk of court.

E. Upon formation, the registry shall immediately implement a daily process of expungement of records and names of the parties in all cases where either a temporary restraining order expires without conversion to an injunction or, after an evidentiary hearing, it is determined that a protective order is not warranted.

F. The judicial administrator's office shall make the Louisiana Protective Order Registry available to state and local law enforcement agencies, district attorney offices, the Department of Children and Family Services, office of children and family services, child support enforcement section, the Louisiana Department of Health, bureau of protective services, the office of elderly affairs, elderly protective services, the office of the attorney general, and the courts.

Added by Acts 1997, No. 1156, § 7. Amended by Acts 1999, No. 213, § 1; Acts 2003, No. 750, § 6; Acts 2004, No. 674, § 1; Acts 2012, No. 255, § 7; Acts 2014, No. 317, § 3; Acts 2014, No. 318, § 3; Acts 2014, No. 355, § 2; Acts 2015, No. 242, § 3; Acts 2018, No. 679, § 3.

R.S. 46:2136.3

§ 2136.3. Prohibition on the possession of firearms by a person against whom a protective order is issued

A. Any person against whom the court has issued a permanent injunction or a protective order pursuant to a court-approved consent agreement or pursuant to the provisions of R.S. 9:361 et seq., R.S. 9:372, R.S. 46:2136, 2151, or 2173, Children's Code Article 1570, Code of Civil Procedure Article 3607.1, or Code of Criminal Procedure Articles 30, 320, or 871.1 shall be prohibited from possessing a firearm or carrying a concealed weapon for the duration of the injunction or protective order if both of the following occur:

(1) The permanent injunction or protective order includes a finding that the person subject to the permanent injunction or protective order represents a credible threat to the physical safety of a family member, household member, or dating partner.

(2) The permanent injunction or protective order informs the person subject to the permanent injunction or protective order that the person is prohibited from possessing a firearm pursuant to the provisions of 18 U.S.C. 922(g)(8) and this Section.

B. For the provisions of this Section, "firearm" means any pistol, revolver, rifle, shotgun, machine gun, submachine gun, black powder weapon, or assault rifle which is designed to fire or is capable of firing fixed cartridge ammunition or from which a shot or projectile is discharged by an explosive.

C. Whoever violates the provisions of this Section shall be in violation of and subject to the penalties set forth in R.S. 14:79.

Added by Acts 2014, No. 195, § 2. Amended by Acts 2015, No. 440, § 3; Acts 2017, No. 84, § 3; Acts 2018, No. 367, § 2, eff. Oct. 1, 2018.

R.S. 46:2138

§ 2138. Assistance; clerk of court; domestic abuse advocate

A. The clerk of court shall make forms available for making application for protective orders under this Part, provide clerical assistance to the petitioner when necessary, advise indigent applicants of the availability of filing in forma pauperis, provide the necessary forms, as supplied by the judicial administrator's office, Louisiana Supreme Court, and provide the services of a notary, where available, for completion of the affidavit required in R.S. 46:2134(D).

B. Domestic abuse advocates may provide clerical assistance to petitioners in making an application for a protective order in accordance with this Part.

C. For purposes of this Section, "domestic abuse advocate" means an employee or representative of a community based shelter providing services to victims of family violence or domestic abuse.

Added by Acts 1982, No. 782, § 2. Amended by Acts 1983, No. 195, § 1; Acts 1997, No. 1156, § 7; Acts 2011, No. 234, § 1.

R.S. 46:2139

§ 2139. Other relief not affected

The granting of any relief authorized under this Part shall not preclude any other relief authorized by law.

Added by Acts 1982, No. 782, § 2.

R.S. 46:2140

§ 2140. Law enforcement officers; duties

A. If a law enforcement officer has reason to believe that a family or household member or dating partner has been abused and the abusing party is in violation of a temporary restraining order, a preliminary or permanent injunction, or a protective order issued pursuant to R.S. 9:361 et seq., R.S. 9:372, R.S. 46:2131 et seq., R.S. 46:2151, R.S. 46:2171 et seq., Children's Code Article 1564 et seq., Code of Civil Procedure Articles 3604 and 3607.1, or Code of Criminal Procedure Articles 30, 327.1, 335.1, 335.2, and 871.1, the officer shall immediately arrest the abusing party.

B. If a law enforcement officer has reason to believe that a family or household member or dating partner has been abused, and the abusing party is not in violation of a restraining order, a preliminary or permanent injunction, or a protective order, the officer shall immediately use all reasonable means to prevent further abuse, including:

(1) Arresting the abusive party with a warrant or without a warrant pursuant to Code of Criminal Procedure Article 213, if probable cause exists to believe that a felony has been committed by that person, whether or not the offense occurred in the officer's presence.

(2) Arresting the abusive party in case of any misdemeanor crime which endangers the physical safety of the abused person whether or not the offense occurred in the presence of the officer. If there is no cause to believe there is impending danger, arresting the abusive party is at the officer's discretion.

(3) Assisting the abused person in obtaining medical treatment necessitated by the battery; arranging for, or providing, or assisting in the procurement of transportation for the abused person to a place of shelter or safety.

R.S. 46:2140—Cont'd

(4) Notifying the abused person of his right to initiate criminal or civil proceedings; the availability of the protective order, R.S. 46:2136; and the availability of community assistance for domestic violence victims.

C. (1) When a law enforcement officer receives conflicting accounts of domestic abuse or dating violence, the officer shall evaluate each account separately to determine if one party was the predominant aggressor.

(2) In determining if one party is the predominant aggressor, the law enforcement officer may consider any other relevant factors, but shall consider the following factors based upon his or her observation:

(a) Evidence from complainants and other witnesses.

(b) The extent of personal injuries received by each person.

(c) Whether a person acted in self-defense.

(d) An imminent threat of future injury to any of the parties.

(e) Prior complaints of domestic abuse or dating violence, if that history can be reasonably ascertained by the officer.

(f) The future welfare of any minors who are present at the scene.

(g) The existence of a temporary restraining order, a preliminary or permanent injunction, or a protective order issued pursuant to R.S. 9:361 et seq., R.S. 9:372, R.S. 46:2131 et seq., R.S. 46:2151, R.S. 46:2171 et seq., Children's Code Article 1564 et seq., Code of Civil Procedure Articles 3604 and 3607.1, or Code of Criminal Procedure Articles 30, 327.1, 335.1, 335.2, and 871.1. The officer shall presume that the predominant aggressor is the person against whom the order was issued.

(3)(a) If the officer determines that one person was the predominant aggressor in a felony offense, the officer shall arrest that person. The arrest shall be subject to the laws governing arrest, including the need for probable cause as otherwise provided by law.

(b) If the officer determines that one person was the predominant aggressor in a misdemeanor offense, the officer shall arrest the predominant aggressor if there is reason to believe that there is impending danger or if the predominant aggressor is in violation of a temporary restraining order, a preliminary or permanent injunction, or a protective order issued pursuant to R.S. 9:361 et seq., R.S. 9:372, R.S. 46:2131 et seq., R.S. 46:2151, R.S. 46:2171 et seq., Children's Code Article 1564 et seq., Code of Civil Procedure Articles 3604 and 3607.1, or Code of Criminal Procedure Articles 30, 327.1, 335.1, 335.2, and 871.1. If there is no threat of impending danger or no violation of a temporary restraining order, a preliminary or permanent injunction, or a protective order, the officer may arrest the predominant aggressor at the officer's discretion, whether or not the offense occurred in the presence of the officer. An arrest pursuant to the provisions of this Subparagraph shall be subject to the laws governing arrest, including the need for probable cause as otherwise provided by law. The exceptions provided for in this Section shall apply.

(4) As used in this Subsection:

(a) "Dating violence" has the meaning as defined in R.S. 46:2151(C).

(b) "Domestic abuse" has the meaning as defined in R.S. 46:2132(3).

Added by Acts 1985, No. 442, § 1, eff. July 12, 1985. Amended by Acts 2003, No. 750, § 6; Acts 2004, No. 882, § 1; Acts 2014, No. 317, § 3; Acts 2015, No. 85, § 1.

R.S. 46:2141

§ 2141. Reporting

Whenever a law enforcement officer investigates an allegation of domestic abuse, whether or not an arrest is made, the officer shall make a written report of the alleged incident, including a statement of the complainant, and the disposition of the case.

Added by Acts 1985, No. 442, § 1, eff. July 12, 1985.

R.S. 46:2142

§ 2142. Immunity

Any law enforcement officer reporting in good faith, exercising due care in the making of an arrest or providing assistance pursuant to the provisions of R.S. 46:2140 and 2141 shall have immunity from any civil liability that otherwise might be incurred or imposed because of the report, arrest, or assistance provided.

Added by Acts 1985, No. 442, § 1, eff. July 12, 1985.

CHAPTER 28–A. PROTECTION FROM DATING VIOLENCE ACT

R.S. 46:2151

§ 2151. Dating violence

A. A victim of a dating partner, as defined in Subsection B of this Section, shall be eligible to receive all services, benefits, and other forms of assistance provided by Chapter 28 of this Title.[1]

B. For purposes of this Section, "dating partner" means any person who is involved or has been involved in a sexual or intimate relationship with the offender characterized by the expectation of affectionate involvement independent of financial considerations, regardless of whether the person presently lives or formerly lived in the same residence with the offender. "Dating partner" shall not include a casual relationship or ordinary association between persons in a business or social context.

C. For purposes of this Section, "dating violence" includes but is not limited to physical or sexual abuse and any offense against the person as defined in the Criminal Code of Louisiana, except negligent injury and defamation, committed by one dating partner against the other.

Added by Acts 2001, No. 1180, § 1. Amended by Acts 2003, No. 750, § 6; Acts 2017, No. 84, § 3.

[1] R.S. 46:2121 et seq.

LOUISIANA CODE OF EVIDENCE

CHAPTER 1. GENERAL PROVISIONS

C.E. Art. 101

Art. 101. Scope

This Code governs proceedings in the courts of Louisiana to the extent and with the exceptions stated in Article 1101.

Added by Acts 1988, No. 515, § 1, eff. Jan. 1, 1989.

C.E. Art. 102

Art. 102. Purpose and construction

These articles shall be construed to secure fairness and efficiency in administration of the law of evidence to the end that the truth may be ascertained and proceedings justly determined.

Added by Acts 1988, No. 515, § 1, eff. Jan. 1, 1989.

C.E. Art. 103

Art. 103. Rulings on evidence

A. Effect of erroneous ruling. Error may not be predicated upon a ruling which admits or excludes evidence unless a substantial right of the party is affected, and

(1) Ruling admitting evidence. When the ruling is one admitting evidence, a timely objection or motion to admonish the jury to limit or disregard appears of record, stating the specific ground of objection; or

(2) Ruling excluding evidence. When the ruling is one excluding evidence, the substance of the evidence was made known to the court by counsel.

B. Record of ruling. The court may add any other or further statement which shows the character of the evidence, the form in which it was offered, the objection made, and the ruling thereon.

C. Hearing of jury. In jury cases, proceedings shall be conducted, to the extent practicable, so as to prevent inadmissible evidence from being suggested to the jury by any means, such as making statements or asking questions in the hearing of the jury.

Added by Acts 1988, No. 515, § 1, eff. Jan. 1, 1989.

C.E. Art. 104

Art. 104. Preliminary questions

A. Questions of admissibility generally. Preliminary questions concerning the competency or qualification of a person to be a witness, the existence of a privilege, or the admissibility of evidence shall be determined by the court, subject to the provisions of Paragraph B. In making its determination it is not bound by the rules of evidence except those with respect to privileges.

C.E. Art. 104—Cont'd

B. Relevancy conditioned on fact. Subject to other provisions of this Code, when the relevancy of evidence depends upon the fulfillment of a condition of fact, the court shall admit it upon, or subject to, the introduction of evidence sufficient to support a finding of the fulfillment of the condition.

C. Hearing of jury. Hearings on matters to be decided by the judge alone shall be conducted out of the hearing of the jury when the interests of justice require. Hearings on the admissibility of confessions or admissions by the accused or evidence allegedly unlawfully obtained shall in all cases be conducted out of the hearing of the jury, but when there has been a ruling prior to trial, it shall not be necessary to conduct another hearing as to admissibility before presentation of the evidence to a jury.

D. Weight and credibility. The preliminary determination by the court that evidence is admissible does not limit the right of a party to introduce evidence relevant to weight or credibility at the trial.

Added by Acts 1988, No. 515, § 1, eff. Jan. 1, 1989.

C.E. Art. 105

Art. 105. Limited admissibility

When evidence which is admissible as to one party or for one purpose but not admissible as to another party or for another purpose is admitted, the court, upon request, shall restrict the evidence to its proper scope and instruct the jury accordingly. Failure to restrict the evidence and instruct the jury shall not constitute error absent a request to do so.

Added by Acts 1988, No. 515, § 1, eff. Jan. 1, 1989.

CHAPTER 2. JUDICIAL NOTICE

C.E. Art. 201

Art. 201. Judicial notice of adjudicative facts generally

A. Scope of Article. This Article governs only judicial notice of adjudicative facts. An "adjudicative fact" is a fact normally determined by the trier of fact.

B. Kinds of facts. A judicially noticed fact must be one not subject to reasonable dispute in that it is either:

(1) Generally known within the territorial jurisdiction of the trial court; or

(2) Capable of accurate and ready determination by resort to sources whose accuracy cannot reasonably be questioned.

C. When discretionary. A court may take judicial notice, whether requested or not.

D. When mandatory. A court shall take judicial notice upon request if supplied with the information necessary for the court to determine that there is no reasonable dispute as to the fact.

E. Opportunity to be heard. A party is entitled upon timely request to an opportunity to be heard as to the propriety of taking judicial notice and the tenor of the matter noticed. In the absence of prior opportunity to be heard, the request may be made after judicial notice has been taken.

F. Time of taking notice. A party may request judicial notice at any stage of the proceeding but shall not do so in the hearing of a jury. Before taking judicial notice of a matter in its instructions to the jury, the court shall inform the parties before closing arguments begin.

C.E. Art. 201—Cont'd

G. Instructing jury. In a civil case, the court shall instruct the jury to accept as conclusive any fact judicially noticed. In a criminal case, the court shall instruct the jury that it may, but is not required to, accept as conclusive any fact judicially noticed.

Added by Acts 1988, No. 515, § 1, eff. Jan. 1, 1989.

C.E. Art. 202

Art. 202. Judicial notice of legal matters

A. Mandatory. A court, whether requested to do so or not, shall take judicial notice of the laws of the United States, of every state, territory, and other jurisdiction of the United States, and of the ordinances enacted by any political subdivision within the court's territorial jurisdiction whenever certified copies of the ordinances have been filed with the clerk of that court.

B. Other legal matters. (1) A court shall take judicial notice of the following if a party requests it and provides the court with the information needed by it to comply with the request, and may take judicial notice without request of a party of:

(a) Proclamations of the President of the United States and the governor of this state.

(b) Rules of boards, commissions, and agencies of this state that have been duly published and promulgated in the Louisiana Register.

(c) Ordinances enacted by any political subdivision of the State of Louisiana.

(d) Rules which govern the practice and procedure in a court of the United States or of any state, territory, or other jurisdiction of the United States, and which have been published in a form which makes them readily accessible.

(e) Rules and decisions of boards, commissions, and agencies of the United States or of any state, territory, or other jurisdiction of the United States which have been duly published and promulgated and which have the effect of law within their respective jurisdictions.

(f) Law of foreign countries, international law, and maritime law.

(2) A party who requests that judicial notice be taken and the court, if notice is taken without request shall give reasonable notice during trial to all other parties.

C. Information by court. The court may inform itself of any of the foregoing legal matters in such manner as it may deem proper, and the court may call upon counsel to aid it in obtaining such information.

D. Time of taking notice. Judicial notice of the foregoing legal matters may be taken at any stage of the proceeding, provided that before taking judicial notice of a matter in its instructions to the jury, the court shall inform the parties before closing arguments begin.

E. Question for court. The determination of the foregoing legal matters shall be made by the court.

Added by Acts 1988, No. 515, § 1, eff. Jan. 1, 1989.

CHAPTER 3. EFFECT IN CIVIL CASES OF PRESUMPTIONS AND PRIMA FACIE EVIDENCE

C.E. Art. 301

Art. 301. Scope of Chapter

This Chapter applies only to civil cases. It defines and clarifies the foundation, weight, and other effects of presumptions and prima facie evidence or proof as used in legislation but does not apply where more specific legislation provides otherwise. It does not create new presumptions, nor does it apply to or directly affect mixed questions of law and fact, such as the inference of negligence arising from the doctrine of res ipsa loquitur.

Added by Acts 1997, No. 577, § 1.

C.E. Art. 302

Art. 302. Definitions

The following definitions apply under this Chapter:

(1) The "burden of persuasion" is the burden of a party to establish a requisite degree of belief in the mind of the trier of fact as to the existence or nonexistence of a fact. Depending on the circumstances, the degree of belief may be by a preponderance of the evidence, by clear and convincing evidence, or as otherwise required by law.

(2) A "predicate fact" is a fact or group of facts which must be established for a party to be entitled to the benefits of a presumption.

(3) A "presumption" is an inference created by legislation that the trier of fact must draw if it finds the existence of the predicate fact unless the trier of fact is persuaded by evidence of the nonexistence of the fact to be inferred. As used herein, it does not include a particular usage of the term "presumption" where the content, context, or history of the statute indicates an intention merely to authorize but not to require the trier of fact to draw an inference.

(4) An "inference" is a conclusion that an evidentiary fact exists based on the establishment of a predicate fact.

Added by Acts 1997, No. 577, § 1.

C.E. Art. 303

Art. 303. Conclusive presumptions

A "conclusive presumption" is a rule of substantive law and is not regulated by this Chapter.

Added by Acts 1997, No. 577, § 1.

C.E. Art. 304

Art. 304. Rebuttable presumptions

Presumptions regulated by this Chapter are rebuttable presumptions and therefore may be controverted or overcome by appropriate evidence.

Added by Acts 1997, No. 577, § 1.

C.E. Art. 305

Art. 305. Effect of presumptions if there is no controverting evidence

If the trier of fact finds the existence of the predicate fact, and there is no evidence controverting the fact to be inferred, the trier of fact is required to find the existence of the fact to be inferred.

Added by Acts 1997, No. 577, § 1.

C.E. Art. 306

Art. 306. Effect of presumptions if there is controverting evidence

If the trier of fact finds the existence of the predicate fact, and if there is evidence controverting the fact to be inferred, it shall find the existence of the inferred fact unless it is persuaded by the controverting evidence of the nonexistence of the inferred fact.

Added by Acts 1997, No. 577, § 1.

C.E. Art. 307

Art. 307. Jury instructions

In jury cases, upon request, the jury shall be instructed of the existence of a presumption and instructed as to its effect in accordance with Articles 305 and 306.

Added by Acts 1997, No. 577, § 1.

C.E. Art. 308

Art. 308. Effect of the term "prima facie" in legislation

A. Legislation providing that a document or other evidence is prima facie evidence or proof of all or part of its contents or of another fact establishes a presumption under this Chapter. When, however, the content, context, or history of the legislation indicates an intention not to shift the burden of persuasion, such legislation establishes only an inference and in a jury case, the court on request shall instruct the jury that if it finds the existence of the predicate fact it may but need not find the inferred fact.

B. Other uses of the term "prima facie", such as those that merely provide for the admissibility of specified evidence, do not create presumptions or inferences and are not regulated by this Chapter.

Added by Acts 1997, No. 577, § 1.

CHAPTER 4. RELEVANCY AND ITS LIMITS

C.E. Art. 401

Art. 401. Definition of "relevant evidence"

"Relevant evidence" means evidence having any tendency to make the existence of any fact that is of consequence to the determination of the action more probable or less probable than it would be without the evidence.

Added by Acts 1988, No. 515, § 1, eff. Jan. 1, 1989.

C.E. Art. 402

Art. 402. Relevant evidence generally admissible; irrelevant evidence inadmissible

All relevant evidence is admissible, except as otherwise provided by the Constitution of the United States, the Constitution of Louisiana, this Code of Evidence, or other legislation. Evidence which is not relevant is not admissible.

Added by Acts 1988, No. 515, § 1, eff. Jan. 1, 1989.

C.E. Art. 403

Art. 403. Exclusion of relevant evidence on grounds of prejudice, confusion, or waste of time

Although relevant, evidence may be excluded if its probative value is substantially outweighed by the danger of unfair prejudice, confusion of the issues, or misleading the jury, or by considerations of undue delay, or waste of time.

Added by Acts 1988, No. 515, § 1, eff. Jan. 1, 1989.

C.E. Art. 404

Art. 404. Character evidence generally not admissible in civil or criminal trial to prove conduct; exceptions; other criminal acts

A. **Character evidence generally.** Evidence of a person's character or a trait of his character, such as a moral quality, is not admissible in a civil or criminal proceeding for the purpose of proving that he acted in conformity therewith on a particular occasion, except:

(1) Character of accused. Evidence of a pertinent trait of his character, such as a moral quality, offered by an accused, or by the prosecution to rebut the character evidence; provided that such evidence shall be restricted to showing those moral qualities pertinent to the crime with which he is charged, and that character evidence cannot destroy conclusive evidence of guilt.

(2) Character of victim. (a) Except as provided in Article 412, evidence of a pertinent trait of character, such as a moral quality, of the victim of the crime offered by an accused, or by the prosecution to rebut the character evidence; provided that in the absence of evidence of a hostile demonstration or an overt act on the part of the victim at the time of the offense charged, evidence of his dangerous character is not admissible; provided further that when the accused pleads self-defense and there is a history of assaultive behavior between the victim and the accused and the accused lived in a familial or intimate relationship such as, but not limited to, the husband-wife, parent-child, or concubinage relationship, it shall not be necessary to first show a hostile demonstration or overt act on the part of the victim in order to introduce evidence of the dangerous character of the victim, including specific instances of conduct and domestic violence; and further provided that an expert's opinion as to the effects of the prior assaultive acts on the accused's state of mind is admissible; or

(b) Evidence of a character trait of peacefulness of the victim offered by the prosecution in a homicide case to rebut evidence that the victim was the first aggressor;

(3) Character of witness. Evidence of the character of a witness, as provided in Articles 607, 608, and 609.

B. **Other crimes, wrongs, or acts.** (1) Except as provided in Article 412, evidence of other crimes, wrongs, or acts is not admissible to prove the character of a person in order to show that he acted in conformity therewith. It may, however, be admissible for other purposes, such as proof of motive, opportunity, intent, preparation, plan, knowledge, identity, absence of mistake or accident,

C.E. Art. 404—Cont'd

provided that upon request by the accused, the prosecution in a criminal case shall provide reasonable notice in advance of trial, of the nature of any such evidence it intends to introduce at trial for such purposes, or when it relates to conduct that constitutes an integral part of the act or transaction that is the subject of the present proceeding.

(2) In the absence of evidence of a hostile demonstration or an overt act on the part of the victim at the time of the offense charged, evidence of the victim's prior threats against the accused or the accused's state of mind as to the victim's dangerous character is not admissible; provided that when the accused pleads self-defense and there is a history of assaultive behavior between the victim and the accused and the accused lived in a familial or intimate relationship such as, but not limited to, the husband-wife, parent-child, or concubinage relationship, it shall not be necessary to first show a hostile demonstration or overt act on the part of the victim in order to introduce evidence of the dangerous character of the victim, including specific instances of conduct and domestic violence; and further provided that an expert's opinion as to the effects of the prior assaultive acts on the accused's state of mind is admissible.

Added by Acts 1988, No. 515, § 1, eff. Jan. 1, 1989. Amended by Acts 1994, 3rd Ex.Sess., No. 51, § 1; Acts 2016, No. 357, § 1.

C.E. Art. 405

Art. 405. Methods of proving character

A. Reputation. Except as provided in Article 412, in all cases in which evidence of character or a trait of character of a person is admissible, proof may be made by testimony as to general reputation only. On cross-examination of the character witness, inquiry is allowable into relevant specific instances of conduct.

B. Specific instances of conduct. In cases in which character or a trait of character of a person is an essential element of a charge, claim, or defense, such as in a prosecution for defamation or when there is a defense of entrapment, proof may also be made of specific instances of his conduct.

C. Foundation. Before a person may be permitted to testify to the reputation of another person, a foundation must be established that the witness is familiar with that reputation.

Added by Acts 1988, No. 515, § 1, eff. Jan. 1, 1989.

C.E. Art. 406

Art. 406. Habit; routine practice; methods of proof

Evidence of the habit of a person or of the routine practice of an organization, whether corroborated or not and regardless of the presence of eyewitnesses, is relevant to prove that the conduct of the person or organization on a particular occasion was in conformity with the habit or routine practice. The evidence may consist of testimony in the form of an opinion or evidence of specific instances of conduct sufficient in number to warrant a finding that the habit existed or that the practice was routine.

Added by Acts 1988, No. 515, § 1, eff. Jan. 1, 1989.

C.E. Art. 407

Art. 407. Subsequent remedial measures

In a civil case, when, after an event, measures are taken which, if taken previously, would have made the event less likely to occur, evidence of the subsequent measures is not admissible to prove

C.E. Art. 407—Cont'd

negligence or culpable conduct in connection with the event. This Article does not require the exclusion of evidence of subsequent measures when offered for another purpose, such as proving ownership, authority, knowledge, control, or feasibility of precautionary measures, or for attacking credibility.

Added by Acts 1988, No. 515, § 1, eff. Jan. 1, 1989.

C.E. Art. 408

Art. 408. Compromise and offers to compromise

A. Civil cases. In a civil case, evidence of (1) furnishing or offering or promising to furnish, or (2) accepting or offering or promising to accept, anything of value in compromising or attempting to compromise a claim which was disputed as to either validity or amount, is not admissible to prove liability for or invalidity of the claim or its amount. Evidence of conduct or statements made in compromise negotiations is likewise not admissible. This Article does not require the exclusion of any evidence otherwise admissible merely because it is presented in the course of compromise negotiations. This Article also does not require exclusion when the evidence is offered for another purpose, such as proving bias or prejudice of a witness, negativing a contention of undue delay, or proving an effort to obstruct a criminal investigation or prosecution.

B. Criminal cases. This Article does not require the exclusion in a criminal case of evidence of the actions or statements described in Paragraph A, above, or of a giving or offer to give anything of value by the accused in direct or indirect restitution to a victim.

Added by Acts 1988, No. 515, § 1, eff. Jan. 1, 1989.

C.E. Art. 409

Art. 409. Payment of medical and similar expenses

In a civil case, evidence of furnishing or offering or promising to pay expenses or losses occasioned by an injury to person or damage to property is not admissible to prove liability for the injury or damage nor is it admissible to mitigate, reduce, or avoid liability therefor. This Article does not require the exclusion of such evidence when it is offered solely for another purpose, such as to enforce a contract for payment.

Added by Acts 1988, No. 515, § 1, eff. Jan. 1, 1989.

C.E. Art. 410

Art. 410. Inadmissibility of pleas, plea discussions, and related statements

A. General rule. Except as otherwise provided in this Article, evidence of the following is not, in any civil or criminal proceeding, admissible against the party who made the plea or was a participant in the plea discussions:

(1) A plea of guilty or of nolo contendere which was later withdrawn or set aside;

(2) In a civil case, a plea of nolo contendere;

(3) Any statement made in the course of any court proceeding concerning either of the foregoing pleas, or any plea discussions with an attorney for or other representative of the prosecuting authority regarding either of the foregoing pleas; or

C.E. Art. 410—Cont'd

(4) Any statement made in the course of plea discussions with an attorney for or other representative of the prosecuting authority which do not result in a plea of guilty or which result in a plea of guilty later withdrawn or set aside.

B. Exceptions. However, such a statement is admissible:

(1) In any proceeding wherein another statement made in the course of the same plea or plea discussions has been introduced and the statement ought in fairness be considered contemporaneously with it; or

(2) In a criminal proceeding for perjury or false statement if the statement was made by the defendant under oath, on the record and in the presence of counsel.

Added by Acts 1988, No. 515, § 1, eff. Jan. 1, 1989.

C.E. Art. 411

Art. 411. Liability insurance

A. Although a policy of insurance may be admissible, the amount of coverage under the policy shall not be communicated to the jury unless the amount of coverage is a disputed issue which the jury will decide.

B. The existence of insurance coverage shall not be communicated to the jury unless any of the following apply:

(1) A factual dispute related to an issue of coverage is an issue which the jury will decide.

(2) The existence of insurance coverage would be admissible to attack the credibility of a witness pursuant to Article 607.

(3) The cause of action is brought against the insurer pursuant to R.S. 22:1973 or against the insurer alone pursuant to R.S. 22:1269(B)(1)(a) through (f).

C. The identity of the insurer shall not be communicated to the jury unless the identity of the insurer would be admissible to attack the credibility of a witness pursuant to Article 607.

D. In all cases brought against an insurer pursuant to R.S. 22:1269 or 1973, at the opening and closing of the trial, the court shall read instructions to the jury that there is insurance coverage for the damages claimed by the plaintiff.

Added by Acts 1988, No. 515, § 1, eff. Jan. 1, 1989. Amended by Acts 2020, 1st Ex.Sess., No. 37, § 3, eff. Jan. 1, 2021.

C.E. Art. 412

Art. 412. Victim's past sexual behavior in sexual assault cases; trafficking offenses

A. (1) Opinion and reputation evidence; sexual assault cases. When an accused is charged with a crime involving sexually assaultive behavior, reputation or opinion evidence of the past sexual behavior of the victim is not admissible.

(2) Other evidence; exceptions. When an accused is charged with a crime involving sexually assaultive behavior, evidence of specific instances of the victim's past sexual behavior is also not admissible except for:

(a) Evidence of past sexual behavior with persons other than the accused, upon the issue of whether or not the accused was the source of semen or injury; provided that such evidence is limited

C.E. Art. 412—Cont'd

to a period not to exceed seventy-two hours prior to the time of the offense, and further provided that the jury be instructed at the time and in its final charge regarding the limited purpose for which the evidence is admitted; or

(b) Evidence of past sexual behavior with the accused offered by the accused upon the issue of whether or not the victim consented to the sexually assaultive behavior.

B. **(1) Opinion and reputation evidence; trafficking.** When an accused is charged with a crime involving human trafficking or trafficking of children for sexual purposes, reputation or opinion evidence of the past sexual behavior of the victim is not admissible.

(2) Evidence of specific instances of the victim's past sexual behavior is not admissible unless the evidence is offered by the prosecution in a criminal case to prove a pattern of trafficking activity by the defendant.

C. **Motion.** (1) Before the person, accused of committing a crime that involves sexually assaultive behavior, human trafficking, or trafficking of children for sexual purposes, may offer under Subparagraph (A)(2) or (B)(2) of this Article evidence of specific instances of the victim's past sexual behavior, the accused shall make a written motion in camera to offer such evidence. The motion shall be accompanied by a written statement of evidence setting forth the names and addresses of persons to be called as witnesses.

(2) The motion and statement of evidence shall be served on the state which shall make a reasonable effort to notify the victim prior to the hearing.

D. **Time for a motion.** The motion shall be made within the time for filing pre-trial motions specified in Code of Criminal Procedure Article 521, except that the court shall allow the motion to be made at a later date, if the court determines that:

(1) The evidence is of past sexual behavior with the accused, and the accused establishes that the motion was not timely made because of an impossibility arising through no fault of his own; or

(2) The evidence is of past sexual behavior with someone other than the accused, and the accused establishes that the evidence or the issue to which it relates is newly discovered and could not have been obtained earlier through the exercise of due diligence.

E. **Hearing.** (1) If the court determines that the statement of evidence contains evidence described in Subparagraph (A)(2) or (B)(2), the court shall order a hearing which shall be closed to determine if such evidence is admissible. At such hearing the parties may call witnesses.

(2) The victim, if present, has the right to attend the hearing and may be accompanied by counsel.

(3) If the court determines on the basis of the hearing described in Subparagraph (E)(1) that the evidence which the accused seeks to offer is relevant and that the probative value of such evidence outweighs the danger of unfair prejudice, such evidence may be admissible in the trial to the extent an order made by the court specifies evidence which may be offered and areas with respect to which the victim may be examined or cross-examined. Introduction of such evidence shall be limited to that specified in the order.

(4) Any motion made under Subparagraph C and any statement of evidence, brief, record of a hearing, or like material made or used in connection with the motion shall be kept in a separate, sealed package as part of the record in the case. Nothing in this Article shall preclude the use of the testimony at such hearing in a subsequent prosecution for perjury or false swearing.

C.E. Art. 412—Cont'd

F. **Past sexual behavior defined.** For purposes of this Article, the term "past sexual behavior" means sexual behavior other than the sexual behavior with respect to which the offense of sexually assaultive behavior is alleged.

G. The rules of admissibility of evidence provided by this Article shall also apply to civil actions brought by the victim which are alleged to arise from sexually assaultive behavior, human trafficking, or trafficking of children for sexual purposes by the defendant, whether or not convicted of such crimes.

Added by Acts 1988, No. 515, § 1, eff. Jan. 1, 1989. Amended by Acts 2014, No. 564, § 5; Acts 2016, No. 357, § 1.

C.E. Art. 412.1

Art. 412.1. Victim's attire in sexual assault cases

A. When an accused is charged with the crime of aggravated or first degree rape, forcible or second degree rape, simple or third degree rape, sexual battery, or second degree sexual battery, the manner and style of the victim's attire shall not be admissible as evidence that the victim encouraged or consented to the offense; however, items of clothing or parts thereof may be introduced in order to establish the presence or absence of the elements of the offense and the proof of its occurrence.

B. The rules of admissibility of evidence provided by this Article shall also apply to civil actions brought by the victim which are alleged to arise from the crimes of aggravated or first degree rape, forcible or second degree rape, simple or third degree rape, sexual battery, or second degree sexual battery committed by the defendant, whether or not convicted of such crimes.

Added by Acts 1992, No. 725, § 1. Amended by Acts 2004, No. 676, § 4; Acts 2015, No. 184, § 7; Acts 2016, No. 357, § 1.

C.E. Art. 412.2

Art. 412.2. Evidence of similar crimes, wrongs, or acts in sex offense cases

A. When an accused is charged with a crime involving sexually assaultive behavior, or with acts that constitute a sex offense involving a victim who was under the age of seventeen at the time of the offense, evidence of the accused's commission of another crime, wrong, or act involving sexually assaultive behavior or acts which indicate a lustful disposition toward children may be admissible and may be considered for its bearing on any matter to which it is relevant subject to the balancing test provided in Article 403.

B. In a case in which the state intends to offer evidence under the provisions of this Article, the prosecution shall, upon request of the accused, provide reasonable notice in advance of trial of the nature of any such evidence it intends to introduce at trial for such purposes.

C. This Article shall not be construed to limit the admission or consideration of evidence under any other rule.

Added by Acts 2001, No. 1130, § 1. Amended by Acts 2004, No. 465, § 1.

C.E. Art. 412.3

Art. 412.3. Statements made by victims of trafficking during investigations

If a victim of human trafficking or trafficking of children for sexual purposes is also a defendant in any case arising from unlawful acts committed as part of the same trafficking activity, any

C.E. Art. 412.3—Cont'd

inculpatory statement made by the victim as a result of questioning by any person then known by the victim to be a law enforcement officer is inadmissible against the victim, except pursuant to Article 801 of this Code or in any prosecution of the victim for perjury, at a trial of the victim for the unlawful acts committed by the victim as part of the same trafficking activity if all of the following conditions exist:

(1) The victim cooperates with the investigation and prosecution, including the giving of a use-immunity statement as directed by the prosecuting attorney.

(2) The victim testifies truthfully at any hearing or trial related to the trafficking activity, or agrees, either in writing or on the record, to testify truthfully at any hearing or trial related to the trafficking activity in any prosecution of any other person charged with an offense arising from the same trafficking activity, regardless of whether the testimony is unnecessary due to entry of a plea by the other person.

(3) The victim has agreed in writing to receive services or participate in a program that provides services to victims of human trafficking or trafficking of children for sexual purposes, if such services are available.

Added by Acts 2014, No. 564, § 5.

C.E. Art. 412.4

Art. 412.4. Evidence of similar crimes, wrongs, or acts in domestic abuse cases and cruelty against juveniles cases

A. When an accused is charged with a crime involving abusive behavior against a family member, household member, or dating partner or with acts which constitute cruelty involving a victim who was under the age of seventeen at the time of the offense, evidence of the accused's commission of another crime, wrong, or act involving assaultive behavior against a family member, household member, or dating partner or acts which constitute cruelty involving a victim who was under the age of seventeen at the time of the offense, may be admissible and may be considered for its bearing on any matter to which it is relevant, subject to the balancing test provided in Article 403.

B. In a case in which the state intends to offer evidence under the provisions of this Article, the prosecution shall, upon request of the accused, provide reasonable notice in advance of trial of the nature of any such evidence it intends to introduce at trial for such purposes.

C. This Article shall not be construed to limit the admissibility or consideration of evidence under any other rule.

D. For purposes of this Article:

(1) "Abusive behavior" means any behavior of the offender involving the use or threatened use of force against the person or property of a family member, household member, or dating partner of the alleged offender.

(2) "Dating partner" means any person who is involved or has been involved in a sexual or intimate relationship with the offender characterized by the expectation of affectionate involvement independent of financial considerations, regardless of whether the person presently lives or formerly lived in the same residence with the offender. "Dating partner" shall not include a casual relationship or ordinary association between persons in a business or social context.

(3) "Family member" means spouses, former spouses, parents and children, stepparents, stepchildren, foster parents, foster children, other ascendants, and other descendants. "Family member" also means the other parent or foster parent of any child or foster child of the offender.

C.E. Art. 412.4—Cont'd

(4) "Household member" means any person presently or formerly living in the same residence with the offender and who is involved or has been involved in a sexual or intimate relationship with the offender, or any child presently or formerly living in the same residence with the offender, or any child of the offender regardless of where the child resides.

Added by Acts 2016, No. 399, § 1. Amended by Acts 2017, No. 84, § 4; Acts 2020, No. 101, § 3.

C.E. Art. 412.5

Art. 412.5. Evidence of similar crimes, wrongs, or acts in certain civil cases

A. In any civil action alleging acts of domestic abuse as defined in R.S. 46:2132, family violence as defined in R.S. 9:362, or sexual abuse as defined in R.S. 9:362, evidence of the defendant's commission of a crime, wrong, or act involving acts of domestic abuse, family violence, or sexual abuse may be admissible and may be considered for its bearing on any matter to which it is relevant subject to the balancing test provided in Article 403.

B. A plaintiff in a tort action intending to offer evidence under the provisions of this Article shall provide reasonable notice in advance of trial of the nature of such evidence.

C. The provisions of this Article shall not be construed to preclude or limit the introduction or consideration of any evidence otherwise authorized under law.

Added by Acts 2018, No. 228, § 1, eff. May 15, 2018.

C.E. Art. 413

Art. 413. Settlement or tender

Any amount paid in settlement or by tender shall not be admitted into evidence unless the failure to make a settlement or tender is an issue in the case.

Added by Acts 1988, No. 515, § 1, eff. Jan. 1, 1989.

C.E. Art. 414

Art. 414. Workers' compensation payments

Evidence of the nature and extent of a workers' compensation claim or of payment of past or future workers' compensation benefits shall not be admissible to a jury, directly or indirectly, in any civil proceeding with respect to a claim for damages relative to the same injury for which the workers' compensation benefits are claimed or paid. Such evidence shall be admissible and presented to the judge only.

Added by Acts 1990, No. 973, § 2.

C.E. Art. 415

Art. 415. Act of contacting or retaining an attorney

In any criminal proceeding, the act of contacting or retaining an attorney shall not be admissible against any individual or entity, unless such act falls within an established exception for crime or fraud.

Added by Acts 1993, No. 626, § 1.

CHAPTER 5. TESTIMONIAL PRIVILEGES

C.E. Art. 501

Art. 501. Scope of privileges

Privileges as recognized in this Chapter are evidentiary in nature, do not of themselves create causes of action or other substantive rights, and are applicable to proceedings enumerated in Article 1101. Nothing in this Chapter is intended to regulate the content or waiver of constitutional rights, nor inferences to be drawn from their invocation.

Added by Acts 1992, No. 376, § 1, eff. Jan. 1, 1993.

C.E. Art. 502

Art. 502. Waiver of privilege

A. Waiver. A person upon whom the law confers a privilege against disclosure waives the privilege if he or his predecessor while holder of the privilege voluntarily discloses or consents to disclosure of any significant part of the privileged matter. This rule does not apply if the disclosure itself is privileged.

B. Disclosure under compulsion or without opportunity to claim. A claim of privilege is not defeated by a disclosure which was compelled or made without opportunity to claim the privilege.

C. Joint holders. Where two or more persons are joint holders of a privilege, a waiver of the right of one joint holder to claim the privilege does not affect the right of another joint holder to claim the privilege.

Added by Acts 1992, No. 376, § 1, eff. Jan. 1, 1993.

C.E. Art. 503

Art. 503. Comment on or inference from claim of privilege; instructions; exception

A. Comment, inference, and instructions.

(1) The claim of privilege, whether in the present proceeding or upon a prior occasion, is not a proper subject of comment by judge or counsel. No inferences may be drawn therefrom.

(2) In jury cases, proceedings shall be conducted, to the extent practicable, so as to facilitate the making of claims of privilege without the knowledge of the jury.

(3) Upon request, any party against whom the jury might draw an adverse inference from a claim of privilege is entitled to an instruction that no inference may be drawn therefrom.

B. Exception in non-criminal proceedings. In non-criminal proceedings, under exceptional circumstances in the interest of justice, if a claim of privilege is sustained counsel may comment thereon, and, upon request, the court shall instruct the trier of fact that it may draw all reasonable inferences therefrom.

Added by Acts 1992, No. 376, § 1, eff. Jan. 1, 1993.

C.E. Art. 504

Art. 504. Spousal confidential communications privilege

A. Definition. A communication is "confidential" if it is made privately and is not intended for further disclosure unless such disclosure is itself privileged.

C.E. Art. 504—Cont'd

B. Confidential communications privilege. Each spouse has a privilege during and after the marriage to refuse to disclose, and to prevent the other spouse from disclosing, confidential communications with the other spouse while they were husband and wife.

C. Confidential communications; exceptions. This privilege does not apply:

(1) In a criminal case in which one spouse is charged with a crime against the person or property of the other spouse or of a child of either.

(2) In a civil case brought by or on behalf of one spouse against the other spouse.

(3) In commitment or interdiction proceedings as to either spouse.

(4) When the communication is offered to protect or vindicate the rights of a minor child of either spouse.

(5) In cases otherwise provided by legislation.

Added by Acts 1992, No. 376, § 1, eff. Jan. 1, 1993.

C.E. Art. 505

Art. 505. Spousal witness privilege

In a criminal case or in commitment or interdiction proceedings, a witness spouse has a privilege not to testify against the other spouse. This privilege terminates upon the annulment of the marriage, legal separation, or divorce of the spouses. This privilege does not apply in a criminal case in which one spouse is charged with a crime against the person of the other spouse or a crime against the person of a child including but not limited to the violation of a preliminary or permanent injunction or protective order and violations of R.S. 14:79.

Added by Acts 1992, No. 376, § 1, eff. Jan. 1, 1993. Amended by Acts 2006, No. 191, § 1.

C.E. Art. 506

Art. 506. Lawyer-client privilege

A. Definitions. As used in this Article:

(1) "Client" is a person, including a public officer, corporation, partnership, unincorporated association, or other organization or entity, public or private, to whom professional legal services are rendered by a lawyer, or who consults a lawyer with a view to obtaining professional legal services from the lawyer.

(2) "Representative of the client" is:

(a) A person having authority to obtain professional legal services, or to act on advice so obtained, on behalf of the client.

(b) Any other person who makes or receives a confidential communication for the purpose of effectuating legal representation for the client, while acting in the scope of employment for the client.

(3) "Lawyer" is a person authorized, or reasonably believed by the client to be authorized, to practice law in any state or nation.

(4) "Representative of the lawyer" is a person engaged by the lawyer to assist the lawyer in the lawyer's rendition of professional legal services.

(5) A communication is "confidential" if it is not intended to be disclosed to persons other than:

C.E. Art. 506—Cont'd

(a) Those to whom disclosure is made in furtherance of obtaining or rendering professional legal services for the client.

(b) Those reasonably necessary for the transmission of the communication.

(c) When special circumstances warrant, those who are present at the behest of the client and are reasonably necessary to facilitate the communication.

B. General rule of privilege. A client has a privilege to refuse to disclose, and to prevent another person from disclosing, a confidential communication, whether oral, written, or otherwise, made for the purpose of facilitating the rendition of professional legal services to the client, as well as the perceptions, observations, and the like, of the mental, emotional, or physical condition of the client in connection with such a communication, when the communication is:

(1) Between the client or a representative of the client and the client's lawyer or a representative of the lawyer.

(2) Between the lawyer and a representative of the lawyer.

(3) By the client or his lawyer, or a representative of either, to a lawyer, or representative of a lawyer, who represents another party concerning a matter of common interest.

(4) Between representatives of the client or between the client and a representative of the client.

(5) Among lawyers and their representatives representing the same client.

(6) Between representatives of the client's lawyer.

C. Exceptions. There is no privilege under this Article as to a communication:

(1)(a) If the services of the lawyer were sought or obtained to enable or aid anyone to commit or plan to commit what the client or his representative knew or reasonably should have known to be a crime or fraud.

(b) Made in furtherance of a crime or fraud.

(2) Which was with a client now deceased relevant to an issue between parties who claim through that client, regardless of whether the claims are by testate or intestate succession or by transaction inter vivos.

(3) Which is relevant to an issue of breach of duty by a lawyer to the client or by a client to the client's lawyer.

(4)(a) Which is relevant to an issue of authenticity or capacity concerning a document which the lawyer signed as a witness or notary.

(b) Concerning the testimony of a representative of a lawyer regarding a communication relevant to an issue of authenticity or capacity concerning a document to which the representative is a witness or notary.

(5) Which is relevant to a matter of common interest between or among two or more clients if the communication was made by any of them or their representative to a lawyer or his representative retained or consulted in common, when subsequently offered by one client against the other in a civil action.

(6) Concerning the identity of the lawyer's client or his representative, unless disclosure of the identity by the lawyer or his representative would reveal either the reason for which legal services were sought or a communication which is otherwise privileged under this Article.

C.E. Art. 506—Cont'd

D. Who may claim privilege. The privilege may be claimed by the client, the client's agent or legal representative, or the successor, trustee, or similar representative of a client that is a corporation, partnership, unincorporated association, or other organization, whether or not in existence. The person who was the lawyer or the lawyer's representative at the time of the communication is presumed to have authority to claim the privilege on behalf of the client, former client, or deceased client.

Added by Acts 1992, No. 376, § 1, eff. Jan. 1, 1993.

C.E. Art. 507

Art. 507. Subpoena of lawyer or his representative in criminal cases

A. General rule. Neither a subpoena nor a court order shall be issued to a lawyer or his representative to appear or testify in any criminal investigation or proceeding where the purpose of the subpoena or order is to ask the lawyer or his representative to reveal information about a client or former client obtained in the course of representing the client unless the court after a contradictory hearing has determined that the information sought is not protected from disclosure by any applicable privilege or work product rule; and all of the following:

(1) The information sought is essential to the successful completion of an ongoing investigation, prosecution, or defense.

(2) The purpose of seeking the information is not to harass the attorney or his client.

(3) With respect to a subpoena, the subpoena lists the information sought with particularity, is reasonably limited as to subject matter and period of time, and gives timely notice.

(4) There is no practicable alternative means of obtaining the information.

B. Waiver. Failure to object timely to non-compliance with the terms of this Article constitutes a waiver of the procedural protections of this Article, but does not constitute a waiver of any privilege.

C. Binding effect of determination; notice to client. The determination that a lawyer-client privilege is not applicable to the testimony shall not bind the client or former client unless the client or former client was given notice of the time, place, and substance of the hearing and had an opportunity fully to participate in that hearing.

D. Exceptions. This Article shall not apply in habitual offender proceedings when a lawyer is called as a witness for purposes of identification of his client or former client, or in post-conviction proceedings when a lawyer is called as a witness on the issue of ineffective assistance of the lawyer.

E. The procedural provisions and protections afforded by Paragraph A of this Article shall extend to lawyers serving as prosecutors in state, parish, or municipal courts, whether those functions are exercised in the name of the state of Louisiana or any parish or municipality, and whether the lawyer is the attorney general or assistant attorney general, a district attorney or assistant district attorney, or a parish or municipal prosecutor, and shall extend to lawyers employed by either house of the Louisiana Legislature.

Added by Acts 1992, No. 376, § 1, eff. Jan. 1, 1993. Amended by Acts 2007, No. 23, § 1.

C.E. Art. 508

Art. 508. Subpoena of lawyer or his representative in civil cases

A. General rule. Neither a subpoena nor a court order shall be issued to a lawyer or his representative to appear or testify in any civil or juvenile proceeding, including pretrial discovery, or

C.E. Art. 508—Cont'd

in an administrative investigation or hearing, where the purpose of the subpoena or order is to ask the lawyer or his representative to reveal information about a client or former client obtained in the course of representing the client unless, after a contradictory hearing, it has been determined that the information sought is not protected from disclosure by any applicable privilege or work product rule; and all of the following:

(1) The information sought is essential to the successful completion of an ongoing investigation, is essential to the case of the party seeking the information, and is not merely peripheral, cumulative, or speculative.

(2) The purpose of seeking the information is not to harass the attorney or his client.

(3) With respect to a subpoena, the subpoena lists the information sought with particularity, is reasonably limited as to subject matter and period of time, and gives timely notice.

(4) There is no practicable alternative means of obtaining the information.

B. Waiver. Failure to object timely to non-compliance with the terms of this Article constitutes a waiver of the procedural protections of this Article, but does not constitute a waiver of any privilege.

C. Binding effect of determination; notice to client. The determination that a lawyer-client privilege is not applicable to the testimony shall not bind the client or former client unless the client or former client was given notice of the time, place, and substance of the hearing and had an opportunity fully to participate in that hearing.

D. Scope. Nothing in this Article is intended to affect the provisions of Code of Civil Procedure Articles 863 and 1452(B).

E. The procedural provisions and protections afforded by Paragraph A of this Article shall extend to lawyers representing the state or any political subdivision, whether the lawyer is the attorney general or assistant attorney general, a district attorney or assistant district attorney, a parish attorney or assistant parish attorney; or a municipal or city attorney or assistant municipal or assistant city attorney; and shall extend to lawyers employed by either house of the Louisiana Legislature.

Added by Acts 1992, No. 376, § 1, eff. Jan. 1, 1993. Amended by Acts 2007, No. 23, § 1.

C.E. Art. 509

Art. 509. Work product rule not affected

Nothing in this Chapter shall be construed as derogating from the protection afforded by the rules relating to work product.

Added by Acts 1992, No. 376, § 1, eff. Jan. 1, 1993.

C.E. Art. 510

Art. 510. Health care provider-patient privilege

A. Definitions. The definitions of health care provider, physician, psychotherapist, and their representatives as provided in this Article include persons reasonably believed to be such by the patient or his representative. As used in this Article:

(1)(a) "Confidential communication" is the transmittal or acquisition of information not intended to be disclosed to persons other than:

C.E. Art. 510—Cont'd

(i) A health care provider and a representative of a health care provider.

(ii) Those reasonably necessary for the transmission of the communication.

(iii) Persons who are participating in the diagnosis and treatment under the direction of the physician or psychotherapist.

(iv) A patient's health care insurer, including any entity that provides indemnification to a patient.

(v) When special circumstances warrant, those who are present at the behest of the patient, physician, or psychotherapist and are reasonably necessary to facilitate the communication.

(b) "Confidential communication" includes any information, substance, or tangible object, obtained incidental to the communication process and any opinion formed as a result of the consultation, examination, or interview and also includes medical and hospital records made by health care providers and their representatives.

(2) "Health care provider" is a person or entity defined as such in R.S. 13:3734(A), and includes a physician and psychotherapist as defined below, and also includes a person who is engaged in any office, center, or institution referred to as a rape crisis center, who has undergone at least forty hours of sexual assault training and who is engaged in rendering advice, counseling, or assistance to victims of sexual assault.

(3) "Health condition" is a physical, mental, or emotional condition, including a condition induced by alcohol, drugs, or other substance.

(4) "Patient" is a person who consults or is examined or interviewed by another for the purpose of receiving advice, diagnosis, or treatment in regard to that person's health.

(5) "Physician" is a person licensed to practice medicine in any state or nation.

(6) "Psychotherapist" is:

(a) A physician engaged in the diagnosis or treatment of a mental or emotional condition, including a condition induced by alcohol, drugs, or other substance.

(b) A person licensed or certified as a psychologist under the laws of any state or nation.

(c) A person licensed as a licensed professional counselor or social worker under the laws of any state or nation.

(7) "Representative" of a physician, psychotherapist, or other health care provider is:

(a) A person acting under the supervision, direction, control, or request of a physician, psychotherapist, or health care provider engaged in the diagnosis or treatment of the patient.

(b) Personnel of a "hospital", as defined in R.S. 13:3734(A)(3), whose duties relate to the health care of patients or to maintenance of patient records.

(8) "Representative of a patient" is any person who makes or receives a confidential communication for the purpose of effectuating diagnosis or treatment of a patient.

B. (1) General rule of privilege in civil proceedings. In a non-criminal proceeding, a patient has a privilege to refuse to disclose and to prevent another person from disclosing a confidential communication made for the purpose of advice, diagnosis or treatment of his health condition between or among himself or his representative, his health care provider, or their representatives.

(2) Exceptions. There is no privilege under this Article in a noncriminal proceeding as to a communication:

C.E. Art. 510—Cont'd

(a) When the communication relates to the health condition of a patient who brings or asserts a personal injury claim in a judicial or worker's compensation proceeding.

(b) When the communication relates to the health condition of a deceased patient in a wrongful death, survivorship, or worker's compensation proceeding brought or asserted as a consequence of the death or injury of the deceased patient.

(c) When the communication is relevant to an issue of the health condition of the patient in any proceeding in which the patient is a party and relies upon the condition as an element of his claim or defense or, after the patient's death, in any proceeding in which a party deriving his right from the patient relies on the patient's health condition as an element of his claim or defense.

(d) When the communication relates to the health condition of a patient when the patient is a party to a proceeding for custody or visitation of a child and the condition has a substantial bearing on the fitness of the person claiming custody or visitation, or when the patient is a child who is the subject of a custody or visitation proceeding.

(e) When the communication made to the health care provider was intended to assist the patient or another person to commit or plan to commit what the patient knew or reasonably should have known to be a crime or fraud.

(f) When the communication is made in the course of an examination ordered by the court with respect to the health condition of a patient, the fact that the examination was so ordered was made known to the patient prior to the communication, and the communication concerns the particular purpose for which the examination was made, unless the court in its order directing the examination has stated otherwise.

(g)(i) When the communication is made by a patient who is the subject of an interdiction or commitment proceeding to his current health care provider when such patient has failed or refused to submit to an examination by a health care provider appointed by the court regarding issues relating to the interdiction or commitment proceeding, provided that the patient has been advised of such appointment and the consequences of not submitting to the examination.

(ii) Notwithstanding the provisions of Subitem (i) of this Item, in any commitment proceeding, the court-appointed physician may review the medical records of the patient or respondent and testify as to communications therein, but only those which are essential to determine whether the patient is dangerous to himself, dangerous to others, or unable to survive safely in freedom or protect himself from serious harm. However, such communications shall not be disclosed unless the patient was informed prior to the communication that such communications are not privileged in any subsequent commitment proceedings. The court-appointed examination shall be governed by Item B(2)(f).

(h) When the communication is relevant in proceedings held by peer review committees and other disciplinary bodies to determine whether a particular health care provider has deviated from applicable professional standards.

(i) When the communication is one regarding the blood alcohol level or other test for the presence of drugs of a patient and an action for damages for injury, death, or loss has been brought against the patient.

(j) When disclosure of the communication is necessary for the defense of the health care provider in a malpractice action brought by the patient.

(k) When the communication is relevant to proceedings concerning issues of child abuse, elder abuse, or the abuse of persons with disabilities or persons who are incompetent.

C.E. Art. 510—Cont'd

(*l*) When the communication is relevant after the death of a patient, concerning the capacity of the patient to enter into the contract which is the subject matter of the litigation.

(m) When the communication is relevant in an action contesting any testament executed or claimed to have been executed by the patient now deceased.

C. (1) **General rule of privilege in criminal proceedings.** In a criminal proceeding, a patient has a privilege to refuse to disclose and to prevent another person from disclosing a confidential communication made for the purpose of advice, diagnosis or treatment of his health condition between or among himself, his representative, and his physician or psychotherapist, and their representatives.

(2) **Exceptions.** There is no privilege under this Article in a criminal case as to a communication:

(a) When the communication is relevant to an issue of the health condition of the accused in any proceeding in which the accused relies upon the condition as an element of his defense.

(b) When the communication was intended to assist the patient or another person to commit or plan to commit what the patient knew or reasonably should have known to be a crime or fraud.

(c) When the communication was made in the course of an examination ordered by the court in a criminal case to determine the health condition of a patient, provided that a copy of the order was served on the patient prior to the communication.

(d) When the communication is a record of the results of a test for blood alcohol level or drugs taken from a patient who is under arrest, or who was subsequently arrested for an offense related to the test.

(e) When the communication is in the form of a tangible object, including a bullet, that is removed from the body of a patient and which was in the body as a result of the crime charged.

(f) When the communication is relevant to an investigation of or prosecution for child abuse, elder abuse, or the abuse of persons with disabilities or persons who are incompetent.

D. **Who may claim the privilege.** In both civil and criminal proceedings, the privilege may be claimed by the patient or by his legal representative. The person who was the physician, psychotherapist, or health care provider or their representatives, at the time of the communication is presumed to have authority to claim the privilege on behalf of the patient or deceased patient.

E. **Waiver.** The exceptions to the privilege set forth in Paragraph B(2) shall constitute a waiver of the privilege only as to testimony at trial or to discovery of the privileged communication by one of the discovery methods authorized by Code of Civil Procedure Article 1421 et seq., or pursuant to R.S. 40:1165.1 or R.S. 13:3715.1.

F. **Medical malpractice.** (1) There shall be no health care provider-patient privilege in medical malpractice claims as defined in R.S. 40:1231.1 et seq. as to information directly and specifically related to the factual issues pertaining to the liability of a health care provider who is a named party in a pending lawsuit or medical review panel proceeding.

(2) In medical malpractice claims information about a patient's current treatment or physical condition may only be disclosed pursuant to testimony at trial, pursuant to one of the discovery methods authorized by Code of Civil Procedure Article 1421 et seq., pursuant to R.S. 40:1165.1 or R.S. 13:3715.1.

G. **Sanctions.** Any attorney who violates a provision of this Article shall be subject to sanctions by the court.

Added by Acts 1992, No. 376, § 1, eff. Jan. 1, 1993. Amended by Acts 1993, No. 988, § 2; Acts 1995, No. 1250, § 3; Acts 1997, No. 643, § 1; Acts 1999, No. 747, § 1; Acts 1999, No. 1309, § 11, eff. Jan. 1, 2000; Acts 2001, No. 486, § 6, eff. June 21, 2001; Acts 2014, No. 811, § 32, eff. June 23, 2014.

C.E. Art. 511

Art. 511. Communications to clergymen

A. Definitions. As used in this Article:

(1) A "clergyman" is a minister, priest, rabbi, Christian Science practitioner, or other similar functionary of a religious organization, or an individual reasonably believed so to be by the person consulting him.

(2) A communication is "confidential" if it is made privately and not intended for further disclosure except to other persons present in furtherance of the purpose of the communication.

B. General rule of privilege. A person has a privilege to refuse to disclose and to prevent another person from disclosing a confidential communication by the person to a clergyman in his professional character as spiritual adviser.

C. Who may claim the privilege. The privilege may be claimed by the person or by his legal representative. The clergyman is presumed to have authority to claim the privilege on behalf of the person or deceased person.

Added by Acts 1992, No. 376, § 1, eff. Jan. 1, 1993. Amended by Acts 2003, No. 1187, § 2.

C.E. Art. 512

Art. 512. Political vote

Every person has a privilege to refuse to disclose the tenor of his vote at a political election conducted by secret ballot unless the vote was cast illegally.

Added by Acts 1992, No. 376, § 1, eff. Jan. 1, 1993.

C.E. Art. 513

Art. 513. Trade secrets

A person has a privilege, which may be claimed by him or his agent or employee, to refuse to disclose, and to prevent another person from disclosing, a trade secret owned by him, if the allowance of the privilege will not tend to conceal fraud or otherwise work injustice. When disclosure is directed, the judge shall take such protective measure as the interests of the holder of the privilege and of the parties and the furtherance of justice may require.

Added by Acts 1992, No. 376, § 1, eff. Jan. 1, 1993.

C.E. Art. 514

Art. 514. Identity of informer

A. General rule of privilege. The United States, a state, or subdivision thereof has a privilege to refuse to disclose, and to protect another from required disclosure of, the identity of a person who has furnished information in order to assist in an investigation of a possible violation of a criminal law.

B. Who may claim the privilege. The privilege may be claimed by the prosecuting authority or an appropriate representative of the public entity to which the information was furnished.

C. Inapplicability of privilege. No privilege shall be recognized if:

C.E. Art. 514—Cont'd

(1) The informer appears as a witness for the government and testifies with respect to matters previously disclosed in confidence.

(2) The identity of the informer has been disclosed to those who have cause to resent the communication by either the informer or the prosecution, or in a civil case, a person with authority to claim the privilege.

(3) The party seeking to overcome the privilege clearly demonstrates that the interest of the government in preventing disclosure is substantially outweighed by exceptional circumstances such that the informer's testimony is essential to the preparation of the defense or to a fair determination on the issue of guilt or innocence.

(4) In a criminal case, the prosecution objects.

D. Order to disclose identity. If the court orders disclosure of the identity of an informer and the prosecution opposes the disclosure, the court:

(1) In a criminal case, shall enter one of the following orders exclusively:

(a) An order suppressing the evidence concerning which the identity of the informer has been ordered.

(b) An order declaring a mistrial.

(2) In a civil case, may make any order justice requires.

Added by Acts 1995, No. 1040, § 1.

C.E. Art. 515

Art. 515. Accountant–client privilege

A. Definitions. As used in this Article:

(1) "Client" is a person, including a public officer, corporation, partnership, unincorporated association, or other organization or entity, public or private, to whom professional services are rendered by an accountant, or who consults an accountant with a view to obtaining professional services from the accountant.

(2) "Representative of the client" is either of the following:

(a) A person having authority to obtain professional services from an accountant, or to act on advice so obtained, on behalf of the client.

(b) Any other person who makes or receives a confidential communication for the purpose of effectuating representation by an accountant for the client, while acting in the scope of employment for the client.

(3) "Accountant" is the holder of a license issued pursuant to the Louisiana Accountancy Act and shall include all persons and entities within the definition of licensee in R.S. 37:73(8).

(4) "Representative of the accountant" means a person engaged by the accountant to assist the accountant in the accountant's rendition of professional services.

(5) "Confidential communication" is any communication not intended to be disclosed to persons other than:

(a) Those to whom disclosure is made in furtherance of obtaining or rendering professional accounting services for the client.

C.E. Art. 515—Cont'd

(b) Those reasonably necessary for the transmission of the communication.

(c) When special circumstances warrant, those who are present at the behest of the client and are reasonably necessary to facilitate the communication.

B. General rule of privilege. A client has a privilege to refuse to disclose, and to prevent another person from disclosing, a confidential communication, whether oral, written, or otherwise, made for the purpose of facilitating the rendition of professional accounting services to the client, as well as the perceptions, observations, and the like, of the mental, emotional, or physical condition of the client in connection with such a communication. This privilege includes the protection of other confidential information or material obtained by the accountant from the client for the purpose of rendering professional services. This privilege exists when the communication is:

(1) Between the client or a representative of the client and the client's accountant or a representative of the accountant.

(2) Between the accountant and a representative of the accountant.

(3) By the client or his accountant or a representative of either, to an accountant or lawyer, or representative of an accountant or lawyer, who represents another party concerning a matter of common interest.

(4) Between representatives of the client or between the client and a representative of the client.

(5) Among accountants and their representatives representing the same client.

(6) Between representatives of the client's accountant.

C. Exceptions. There is no privilege under this Article as to a communication:

(1)(a) If the services of the accountant were sought or obtained to enable or aid anyone to commit or plan to commit what the client or his representative knew or reasonably should have known to be a crime or fraud.

(b) Made in furtherance of a crime or fraud.

(2) Which was with a client now deceased relevant to an issue between parties who claim through that decedent, regardless of whether the claims are by testate or intestate succession or by transaction inter vivos.

(3) Which is relevant to an issue of breach of duty by an accountant to the client or by a client to the client's accountant.

(4)(a) Which is relevant to an issue of authenticity or capacity concerning a document which the accountant signed as a witness or notary.

(b) Concerning the testimony of a representative of an accountant regarding a communication relevant to an issue of authenticity or capacity concerning a document to which the representative is a witness or notary.

(5) Which is relevant to a matter of common interest between or among two or more clients if the communication was made by any of them or their representative to an accountant or his representative retained or consulted in common, when subsequently offered by one client against the other in a civil action.

(6) Concerning the identity of the accountant's client or his representative, unless disclosure of the identity by the accountant or his representative would reveal either the reason for which accounting services were sought or a communication which is otherwise privileged under this Article.

C.E. Art. 515—Cont'd

(7) Concerning information required to be disclosed by the standards of the public accounting profession in reporting on the examination of financial statements whose proceedings are protected from discovery pursuant to R.S. 37:86.

(8) Concerning disclosures in investigations or proceedings of the State Board of Certified Public Accountants of Louisiana pursuant to the provisions of Part I of the Louisiana Accountancy Act whose proceedings are protected from discovery pursuant to R.S. 37:86.

(9) Concerning disclosures in ethical investigations of an accountant conducted by private professional organizations whose proceedings are protected from discovery pursuant to R.S. 37:86 or in the course of quality or peer reviews.

(10) In any domestic proceeding including the partition of community property and the settlement of claims arising from matrimonial regimes, spousal support, and child support.

D. Who may claim privilege. The privilege may be claimed by the client, the client's agent or accountant, or the successor, trustee, or similar representative of a client that is a corporation, partnership, unincorporated association, or other organization, whether or not in existence. The person who was the accountant or the accountant's representative at the time of the communication is presumed to have authority to claim the privilege on behalf of the client, former client, or deceased client.

E. Scope. Nothing in this Article is intended to affect the absolute privileges against disclosure contained in R.S. 37:86(B) through (E).

Added by Acts 2001, No. 954, § 1. Amended by Acts 2003, No. 152, § 1.

C.E. Art. 516

Art. 516. Subpoena of accountant or his representative in criminal cases

A. General rule. Neither a subpoena nor a court order shall be issued to an accountant or his representative to appear or testify in any criminal investigation or proceeding when the purpose of the subpoena or order is to ask the accountant or his representative to reveal information about a client or former client obtained in the course of representing the client unless the party issuing the subpoena executes and attaches to the subpoena an affidavit that:

(1) The information sought is essential to the successful completion of an ongoing investigation, prosecution, or defense.

(2) The purpose of seeking the information is not to harass the accountant or the client.

(3) With respect to a subpoena, the subpoena lists the information sought with particularity, is reasonably limited as to subject matter and period of time, and gives timely notice.

(4) There is no practicable alternative means of obtaining the information.

B. Waiver. Failure to object timely to noncompliance with the terms of this Article constitutes a waiver of the procedural protections of this Article, but does not constitute a waiver of any privilege.

C. Binding effect of determination; notice to client. The determination that an accountant-client privilege is not applicable to the testimony shall not bind the client or former client unless the client or former client was given notice of the subpoena.

D. Exceptions. This Article shall not apply in habitual offender proceedings when an accountant is called as a witness for purposes of identification of his client or former client.

C.E. Art. 516—Cont'd

E. Scope. Nothing in this Article is intended to affect the absolute privileges against disclosure contained in R.S. 37:86(B) through (E).

Added by Acts 2001, No. 954, § 1.

C.E. Art. 517

Art. 517. Subpoena of accountant; civil, juvenile, administrative proceedings

A. General rule. Neither a subpoena nor a court order shall be issued to an accountant or his representative to appear or testify in any civil or juvenile proceeding, including pretrial discovery, or in an administrative investigation or hearing, except proceedings by the State Board of Accountancy as provided in the Louisiana Accountancy Act, where the purpose of the subpoena or order is to ask the accountant or his representative to reveal information about a client or former client obtained in the course of representing the client unless the court determines, after a contradictory hearing held after service of actual notice to the accountant and the client at least ten days prior to the contradictory hearing, that the information sought is not protected from disclosure by any applicable privilege or work product rule and all of the following apply:

(1) The information sought is essential to the successful completion of an ongoing investigation, is essential to the case of the party seeking the information, and is not merely peripheral, cumulative, or speculative.

(2) The purpose of seeking the information is not to harass the accountant or his client.

(3) With respect to a subpoena, the subpoena lists the information sought with particularity, is reasonably limited as to subject matter and period of time, and gives timely notice.

(4) There is no practicable alternative means of obtaining the information.

B. Waiver. Failure to object timely to noncompliance with the terms of this Article constitutes a waiver of the procedural protections of this Article, but does not constitute a waiver of any privilege.

C. Binding effect of determination; notice to client. The determination that an accountant-client privilege is not applicable to the testimony shall not bind the client or former client unless the client or former client was given notice within the time period set forth in Subsection A of this Section, of the time, place, and substance of the hearing and had an opportunity fully to participate in that hearing.

D. Scope. Nothing in this Article is intended to affect the absolute privileges against disclosure in R.S. 37:86(B) through (E).

Added by Acts 2001, No. 954, § 1.

C.E. Art. 518

Art. 518. Trained peer support member privilege

A. (1) A trained peer support member shall not, without consent of the emergency responder making the communication, be compelled to testify about any communication made to the trained peer support member by the emergency responder while receiving peer support services. The trained peer support member shall be designated as such by the emergency service agency or entity, prior to the incident that results in receiving peer support services. The privilege only applies when the communication was made to the trained peer support member.

(2) The privilege does not apply to any of the following if:

C.E. Art. 518—Cont'd

(a) The trained peer support member was an initial responding emergency responder, a witness, or a party to the incident which prompted the delivery of peer support services to the emergency responder.

(b) A communication reveals the intended commission of a crime or harmful act and such disclosure is determined to be necessary by the trained peer support member to protect any person from a clear, imminent risk of serious mental or physical harm or injury, or to forestall a serious threat to the public safety.

B. For purposes of this Section, a "trained peer support member" is an emergency responder or civilian volunteer of an emergency service agency or entity, who has received training in Critical Incident Stress Management to provide emotional and moral support to an emergency responder who needs those services as a result of an incident in which the emergency responder was involved while acting in his official capacity. A "trained peer support member" also includes a volunteer counselor or other mental health services provider who has been designated by the emergency service agency or entity to provide emotional and moral support and counseling to an emergency responder who needs those services as a result of an incident in which the emergency responder was involved while acting in his official capacity.

Added by Acts 2003, No. 1137, § 1.

C.E. Art. 519

Art. 519. Subpoena of judge or his representative in civil and criminal cases

A. General rule. Neither a subpoena nor a court order shall be issued to a judge or his representative to appear or testify in any civil, criminal, or juvenile proceeding, including pretrial discovery or an administrative hearing, unless, after a contradictory hearing, it has been determined that the information sought is not protected from disclosure by the judicial deliberative process privilege, and all of the following:

(1) The information sought is essential to the case of the party seeking the information and is not merely peripheral, cumulative, or speculative.

(2) The purpose of seeking the information is not to harass the judge, nor for the mere purpose of seeking recusal of the judge.

(3) With respect to a subpoena, the subpoena lists the information sought with particularity, is reasonably limited as to subject matter and period of time, and gives timely notice.

(4) There is no practical alternative means of obtaining the information.

B. Waiver. Failure to object timely to a party's non-compliance with the provisions of this Article constitutes a waiver of the procedural protections of this Article, but does not constitute a waiver of any privilege.

C. The procedural provisions of and the protections afforded by Paragraph A of this Article shall extend to any judge of any court provided for by Article V of the Constitution of Louisiana and to any commissioner or special master of such court.

Added by Acts 2012, No. 563, § 1, eff. June 5, 2012.

CHAPTER 6. WITNESSES

C.E. Art. 601

Art. 601. General rule of competency

Every person of proper understanding is competent to be a witness except as otherwise provided by legislation.

Added by Acts 1988, No. 515, § 1, eff. Jan. 1, 1989.

C.E. Art. 602

Art. 602. Lack of personal knowledge

A witness may not testify to a matter unless evidence is introduced sufficient to support a finding that he has personal knowledge of the matter. Evidence to prove personal knowledge may, but need not, consist of the testimony of the witness himself. This Article is subject to the provisions of Article 703, relating to opinion testimony by expert witnesses.

Added by Acts 1988, No. 515, § 1, eff. Jan. 1, 1989.

C.E. Art. 603

Art. 603. Oath or affirmation

Before testifying, every witness shall be required to declare that he will testify truthfully, by oath or affirmation administered in a form calculated to awaken his conscience and impress his mind with his duty to do so.

Added by Acts 1988, No. 515, § 1, eff. Jan. 1, 1989.

C.E. Art. 604

Art. 604. Interpreters

An interpreter is subject to the provisions of this Code relating to qualification as an expert and the administration of an oath or affirmation that he will make a true translation.

Added by Acts 1988, No. 515, § 1, eff. Jan. 1, 1989.

C.E. Art. 605

Art. 605. Disqualification of judge as witness

The judge presiding at the trial may not testify in that trial as a witness. No objection need be made in order to preserve the point.

Added by Acts 1988, No. 515, § 1, eff. Jan. 1, 1989.

C.E. Art. 606

Art. 606. Disqualification of juror as witness

A. At the trial. A member of the jury may not testify as a witness before that jury in the trial of the case in which he is sitting as a juror. If he is called so to testify, the opposing party shall be afforded an opportunity to object out of the presence of the jury.

C.E. Art. 606—Cont'd

B. Inquiry into validity of verdict or indictment. Upon an inquiry into the validity of a verdict or indictment, a juror may not testify as to any matter or statement occurring during the course of the jury's deliberations or to the effect of anything upon his or any other juror's mind or emotions as influencing him to assent to or dissent from the verdict or indictment or concerning his mental processes in connection therewith, except that a juror may testify on the question whether any outside influence was improperly brought to bear upon any juror, and, in criminal cases only, whether extraneous prejudicial information was improperly brought to the jury's attention. Nor may his affidavit or evidence of any statement by him concerning a matter about which he would be precluded from testifying be received for these purposes.

Added by Acts 1988, No. 515, § 1, eff. Jan. 1, 1989.

C.E. Art. 607

Art. 607. Attacking and supporting credibility generally

A. Who may attack credibility. The credibility of a witness may be attacked by any party, including the party calling him.

B. Time for attacking and supporting credibility. The credibility of a witness may not be attacked until the witness has been sworn, and the credibility of a witness may not be supported unless it has been attacked. However, a party may question any witness as to his relationship to the parties, interest in the lawsuit, or capacity to perceive or to recollect.

C. Attacking credibility intrinsically. Except as otherwise provided by legislation, a party, to attack the credibility of a witness, may examine him concerning any matter having a reasonable tendency to disprove the truthfulness or accuracy of his testimony.

D. Attacking credibility extrinsically. Except as otherwise provided by legislation:

(1) Extrinsic evidence to show a witness' bias, interest, corruption, or defect of capacity is admissible to attack the credibility of the witness.

(2) Other extrinsic evidence, including prior inconsistent statements and evidence contradicting the witness' testimony, is admissible when offered solely to attack the credibility of a witness unless the court determines that the probative value of the evidence on the issue of credibility is substantially outweighed by the risks of undue consumption of time, confusion of the issues, or unfair prejudice.

Added by Acts 1988, No. 515, § 1, eff. Jan. 1, 1989.

C.E. Art. 608

Art. 608. Attacking or supporting credibility by character evidence

A. Reputation evidence of character. The credibility of a witness may be attacked or supported by evidence in the form of general reputation only, but subject to these limitations:

(1) The evidence may refer only to character for truthfulness or untruthfulness.

(2) A foundation must first be established that the character witness is familiar with the reputation of the witness whose credibility is in issue. The character witness shall not express his personal opinion as to the character of the witness whose credibility is in issue.

(3) Inquiry into specific acts on direct examination while qualifying the character witness or otherwise is prohibited.

C.E. Art. 608—Cont'd

B. Particular acts, vices, or courses of conduct. Particular acts, vices, or courses of conduct of a witness may not be inquired into or proved by extrinsic evidence for the purpose of attacking his character for truthfulness, other than conviction of crime as provided in Articles 609 and 609.1 or as constitutionally required.

C. Cross-examination of character witnesses. A witness who has testified to the character for truthfulness or untruthfulness of another witness may be cross-examined as to whether he has heard about particular acts of that witness bearing upon his credibility.

Added by Acts 1988, No. 515, § 1, eff. Jan. 1, 1989.

C.E. Art. 609

Art. 609. Attacking credibility by evidence of conviction of crime in civil cases

A. General civil rule. For the purpose of attacking the credibility of a witness in civil cases, no evidence of the details of the crime of which he was convicted is admissible. However, evidence of the name of the crime of which he was convicted and the date of conviction is admissible if the crime:

(1) Was punishable by death or imprisonment in excess of six months under the law under which he was convicted, and the court determines that the probative value of admitting this evidence outweighs its prejudicial effect to a party; or

(2) Involved dishonesty or false statement, regardless of the punishment.

B. Time limit. Evidence of a conviction under this Article is not admissible if a period of more than ten years has elapsed since the date of the conviction.

C. Effect of pardon or annulment. Evidence of a conviction is not admissible under this Article if the conviction has been the subject of a pardon, annulment, or other equivalent procedure explicitly based on a finding of innocence.

D. Juvenile adjudications. Evidence of juvenile adjudications of delinquency is generally not admissible under this Article.

E. Pendency of appeal. The pendency of an appeal therefrom does not render evidence of a conviction inadmissible. When evidence of a conviction is admissible, evidence of the pendency of an appeal is also admissible.

F. Arrest, indictment, or prosecution. Evidence of the arrest, indictment, or prosecution of a witness is not admissible for the purpose of attacking his credibility.

Added by Acts 1988, No. 515, § 1, eff. Jan. 1, 1989.

C.E. Art. 609.1

Art. 609.1. Attacking credibility by evidence of conviction of crime in criminal cases

A. General criminal rule. In a criminal case, every witness by testifying subjects himself to examination relative to his criminal convictions, subject to limitations set forth below.

B. Convictions. Generally, only offenses for which the witness has been convicted are admissible upon the issue of his credibility, and no inquiry is permitted into matters for which there has only been an arrest, the issuance of an arrest warrant, an indictment, a prosecution, or an acquittal.

C.E. Art. 609.1—Cont'd

C. Details of convictions. Ordinarily, only the fact of a conviction, the name of the offense, the date thereof, and the sentence imposed is admissible. However, details of the offense may become admissible to show the true nature of the offense:

(1) When the witness has denied the conviction or denied recollection thereof;

(2) When the witness has testified to exculpatory facts or circumstances surrounding the conviction; or

(3) When the probative value thereof outweighs the danger of unfair prejudice, confusion of the issues, or misleading the jury.

D. Effect of pending post-conviction relief procedures. The pendency of an appeal or other post-conviction relief procedures does not render the conviction inadmissible, but may be introduced as bearing upon the weight to be given the evidence of the conviction.

E. Effect of pardon or annulment. When a pardon or annulment, based upon a finding of innocence, has been granted, evidence of that conviction is not admissible to attack the credibility of the witness.

F. Juvenile adjudications. Evidence of juvenile adjudications of delinquency is generally not admissible under this Article, except for use in proceedings brought pursuant to the habitual offender law, R.S. 15:529.1.

Added by Acts 1988, No. 515, § 1, eff. Jan. 1, 1989. Amended by Acts 1994, 3rd Ex.Sess., No. 23, § 3.

C.E. Art. 610

Art. 610. Religious beliefs or opinions

Except as provided in Article 613, evidence of the beliefs or opinions of a witness on matters of religion is not admissible for the sole purpose of showing that by reason of their nature his credibility is impaired or enhanced.

Added by Acts 1988, No. 515, § 1, eff. Jan. 1, 1989.

C.E. Art. 611

Art. 611. Mode and order of interrogation and presentation

A. Control by court. Except as provided by this Article and Code of Criminal Procedure Article 773, the parties to a proceeding have the primary responsibility of presenting the evidence and examining the witnesses. The court, however, shall exercise reasonable control over the mode and order of interrogating witnesses and presenting evidence so as to:

(1) Make the interrogation and presentation effective for the ascertainment of the truth;

(2) Avoid needless consumption of time; and

(3) Protect witnesses from harassment or undue embarrassment.

B. Scope of cross-examination. A witness may be cross-examined on any matter relevant to any issue in the case, including credibility. However, in a civil case, when a party or person identified with a party has been called as a witness by an adverse party to testify only as to particular aspects of the case, the court shall limit the scope of cross-examination to matters testified to on direct examination, unless the interests of justice otherwise require.

C.E. Art. 611—Cont'd

C. Leading questions. Generally, leading questions should not be used on the direct examination of a witness except as may be necessary to develop his testimony and in examining an expert witness on his opinions and inferences. However, when a party calls a hostile witness, a witness who is unable or unwilling to respond to proper questioning, an adverse party, or a witness identified with an adverse party, interrogation may be by leading questions. Generally, leading questions should be permitted on cross-examination. However, the court ordinarily shall prohibit counsel for a party from using leading questions when that party or a person identified with him is examined by his counsel, even when the party or a person identified with him has been called as a witness by another party and tendered for cross-examination.

D. Scope of redirect examination; recross examination. A witness who has been cross-examined is subject to redirect examination as to matters covered on cross-examination and, in the discretion of the court, as to other matters in the case. When the court has allowed a party to bring out new matter on redirect, the other parties shall be provided an opportunity to recross on such matters.

E. Rebuttal evidence. The plaintiff in a civil case and the state in a criminal prosecution shall have the right to rebut evidence adduced by their opponents.

Added by Acts 1988, No. 515, § 1, eff. Jan. 1, 1989.

C.E. Art. 612

Art. 612. Writing used to refresh memory

A. Civil cases. In a civil case, any writing, recording, or object may be used by a witness to refresh his memory while testifying. If a witness asserts that his memory is refreshed he must then testify from memory independent of the writing, recording, or object. If, before or during testimony, a witness has used or uses a writing, recording, or object to refresh his memory for the purpose of testifying in court, an adverse party is entitled, subject to Paragraph C, to have the writing, recording, or object produced, if practicable, at the hearing, to inspect it, to examine the witness thereon, and to introduce in evidence those portions which relate to the testimony of the witness. If production of the writing, recording, or object at the hearing is impracticable, the court may make any appropriate order, including one for inspection.

B. Criminal cases. In a criminal case, any writing, recording, or object may be used by a witness to refresh his memory while testifying. If a witness asserts that his memory is refreshed he must then testify from memory independent of the writing, recording, or object. If while testifying a witness uses a writing, recording, or object to refresh his memory an adverse party is entitled, subject to Paragraph C, to inspect it, to examine the witness thereon, and to introduce in evidence those portions which relate to the testimony of the witness.

C. Claim of irrelevance. If it is claimed that a writing or recording contains matters not related to the subject matter of the testimony the court shall examine it in camera, excise any portions not so related, and order delivery of the remainder to the party entitled thereto. Any portion withheld over objections shall be preserved and made available to the appellate court in the event of an appeal.

D. Failure to produce. If a writing, recording, or object is not produced or delivered pursuant to an order under this Article, the court shall make any order justice requires, except that in criminal cases when the prosecution elects not to comply, the order shall only be one excluding the testimony or, if the court in its discretion determines that the interests of justice so require, declaring a mistrial.

Added by Acts 1988, No. 515, § 1, eff. Jan. 1, 1989.

C.E. Art. 613

Art. 613. Foundation for extrinsic attack on credibility

Except as the interests of justice otherwise require, extrinsic evidence of bias, interest, or corruption, prior inconsistent statements, conviction of crime, or defects of capacity is admissible after the proponent has first fairly directed the witness' attention to the statement, act, or matter alleged, and the witness has been given the opportunity to admit the fact and has failed distinctly to do so.

Added by Acts 1988, No. 515, § 1, eff. Jan. 1, 1989.

C.E. Art. 614

Art. 614. Calling and questioning of witnesses by court

A. Calling by court. The court, at the request of a party or if otherwise authorized by legislation, may call witnesses, and all parties are entitled to examine witnesses thus called.

B. Questioning by court. The court may question witnesses, whether called by itself or by a party.

C. Objections. Objections to the calling of witnesses by the court or to questioning of witnesses by it may be made at the time or at the next available opportunity when the jury is not present.

D. Exception. In a jury trial, the court may not call or examine a witness, except upon the express consent of all parties, which consent shall not be requested within the hearing of the jury.

Added by Acts 1988, No. 515, § 1, eff. Jan. 1, 1989.

C.E. Art. 615

Art. 615. Exclusion of witnesses

A. As a matter of right. On its own motion the court may, and on request of a party the court shall, order that the witnesses be excluded from the courtroom or from a place where they can see or hear the proceedings, and refrain from discussing the facts of the case with anyone other than counsel in the case. In the interests of justice, the court may exempt any witness from its order of exclusion.

B. Exceptions. This Article does not authorize exclusion of any of the following:

(1) A party who is a natural person.

(2) A single officer or single employee of a party which is not a natural person designated as its representative or case agent by its attorney.

(3) A person whose presence is shown by a party to be essential to the presentation of his cause such as an expert.

(4) The victim of the offense or the family of the victim.

C. Violation of exclusion order. A court may impose appropriate sanctions for violations of its exclusion order including contempt, appropriate instructions to the jury, or when such sanctions are insufficient, disqualification of the witness.

Added by Acts 1988, No. 515, § 1, eff. Jan. 1, 1989. Amended by Acts 1999, No. 783, § 2, eff. Jan. 1, 2000.

CHAPTER 7. OPINIONS AND EXPERT TESTIMONY

C.E. Art. 701

Art. 701. Opinion testimony by lay witnesses

If the witness is not testifying as an expert, his testimony in the form of opinions or inferences is limited to those opinions or inferences which are:

(1) Rationally based on the perception of the witness; and

(2) Helpful to a clear understanding of his testimony or the determination of a fact in issue.

Added by Acts 1988, No. 515, § 1, eff. Jan. 1, 1989.

C.E. Art. 702

Art. 702. Testimony by experts

A. A witness who is qualified as an expert by knowledge, skill, experience, training, or education may testify in the form of an opinion or otherwise if:

(1) The expert's scientific, technical, or other specialized knowledge will help the trier of fact to understand the evidence or to determine a fact in issue;

(2) The testimony is based on sufficient facts or data;

(3) The testimony is the product of reliable principles and methods; and

(4) The expert has reliably applied the principles and methods to the facts of the case.

B. This Article shall also govern expert witnesses on the issue of memory and eyewitness identification. In a criminal case, if a party seeks to offer the testimony of a memory and eyewitness identification expert under this Article, such expert testimony may be considered for admission only if all provisions of Paragraph A of this Article are satisfied. A memory and eyewitness identification expert's testimony may not be admitted under this Article if there is physical or scientific evidence that corroborates the eyewitness identification of the defendant. An expert's testimony admitted under this Paragraph shall not offer an opinion as to whether a witness's memory or eyewitness identification is accurate.

Added by Acts 1988, No. 515, § 1, eff. Jan. 1, 1989. Amended by Acts 2014, No. 630, § 1; Acts 2019, No. 115, § 1, eff. June 5, 2019.

C.E. Art. 703

Art. 703. Bases of opinion testimony by experts

The facts or data in the particular case upon which an expert bases an opinion or inference may be those perceived by or made known to him at or before the hearing. If of a type reasonably relied upon by experts in the particular field in forming opinions or inferences upon the subject, the facts or data need not be admissible in evidence.

Added by Acts 1988, No. 515, § 1, eff. Jan. 1, 1989.

C.E. Art. 704

Art. 704. Opinion on ultimate issue

Testimony in the form of an opinion or inference otherwise admissible is not to be excluded solely because it embraces an ultimate issue to be decided by the trier of fact. However, in a criminal case, an expert witness shall not express an opinion as to the guilt or innocence of the accused.

Added by Acts 1988, No. 515, § 1, eff. Jan. 1, 1989.

C.E. Art. 705

Art. 705. Disclosure of facts or data underlying expert opinion; foundation

A. Civil cases. In a civil case, the expert may testify in terms of opinion or inference and give his reasons therefor without prior disclosure of the underlying facts or data, unless the court requires otherwise. The expert may in any event be required to disclose the underlying facts or data on cross-examination.

B. Criminal cases. In a criminal case, every expert witness must state the facts upon which his opinion is based, provided, however, that with respect to evidence which would otherwise be inadmissible such basis shall only be elicited on cross-examination.

Added by Acts 1988, No. 515, § 1, eff. Jan. 1, 1989.

C.E. Art. 706

Art. 706. Court appointed experts

A. Civil cases. In a civil case, the court may on its own motion or on the motion of any party enter an order to show cause why expert witnesses should not be appointed, and may request the parties to submit nominations. The court may appoint any expert witnesses agreed upon by the parties, and may appoint expert witnesses of its own selection. An expert witness shall not be appointed by the court unless he consents to act. A witness so appointed shall be informed of his duties by the court in writing, a copy of which shall be filed with the clerk, or at a conference in which the parties shall have opportunity to participate. A witness so appointed shall advise the parties of his findings, if any; his deposition may be taken by any party; and he may be called to testify by the court or any party.

B. Disclosure of appointment. In a civil case, in the exercise of its discretion, the court may authorize disclosure to the jury of the fact that the court appointed the expert witness.

C. Parties' experts of own selection. Nothing in this Article limits the parties in calling expert witnesses of their own selection.

D. Criminal cases. In a criminal case, the court may appoint an expert witness only when specifically authorized by statute, or as constitutionally required.

Added by Acts 1988, No. 515, § 1, eff. Jan. 1, 1989.

CHAPTER 8. HEARSAY

C.E. Art. 801

Art. 801. Definitions

The following definitions apply under this Chapter:

C.E. Art. 801—Cont'd

A. **Statement.** A "statement" is:

(1) An oral or written assertion; or

(2) Nonverbal conduct of a person, if it is intended by him as an assertion.

B. **Declarant.** A "declarant" is a person who makes a statement.

C. **Hearsay.** "Hearsay" is a statement, other than one made by the declarant while testifying at the present trial or hearing, offered in evidence to prove the truth of the matter asserted.

D. **Statements which are not hearsay.** A statement is not hearsay if:

(1) Prior statement by witness. The declarant testifies at the trial or hearing and is subject to cross-examination concerning the statement, and the statement is:

(a) In a criminal case, inconsistent with his testimony, provided that the proponent has first fairly directed the witness' attention to the statement and the witness has been given the opportunity to admit the fact and where there exists any additional evidence to corroborate the matter asserted by the prior inconsistent statement;

(b) Consistent with his testimony and is offered to rebut an express or implied charge against him of recent fabrication or improper influence or motive;

(c) One of identification of a person made after perceiving the person; or

(d) Consistent with the declarant's testimony and is one of initial complaint of sexually assaultive behavior.

(e) A statement made by the victim of a sexually-oriented criminal offense to a healthcare provider during the course of a forensic medical examination as defined in R.S. 15:622 and the healthcare provider has documented that statement in writing during the course of the forensic medical examination.

(2) Personal, adoptive, and authorized admissions. The statement is offered against a party and is:

(a) His own statement, in either his individual or a representative capacity;

(b) A statement of which he has manifested his adoption or belief in its truth; or

(c) A statement by a person authorized by him to make a statement concerning the subject.

(3) Relational and privity admissions. The statement is offered against a party, and the statement is:

(a) A statement by an agent or employee of the party against whom it is offered, concerning a matter within the scope of his agency or employment, made during the existence of the relationship;

(b) A statement by a declarant while participating in a conspiracy to commit a crime or civil wrong and in furtherance of the objective of the conspiracy, provided that a prima facie case of conspiracy is established;

(c) In a civil case, a statement by a declarant when the liability, obligation, or duty of the party against whom it is offered is derivatively based in whole or in part upon a liability, obligation, or duty of the declarant, or when the claim or right asserted by that party is barred or diminished by a breach of duty by the declarant, and when the statement would be admissible if offered against the declarant as a party in an action involving that liability, obligation, or breach of duty;

(d) In a civil case, a statement by a declarant when a right, title, or interest in any property or claim asserted by the party against whom it is offered requires a determination that a right, title, or

C.E. Art. 801—Cont'd

interest exists or existed in the declarant during the time that that party now claims the declarant was the holder of the right, title, or interest, and when the statement would be admissible if offered against the declarant as a party in an action involving that right, title, or interest;

(e) A statement by a declarant offered against the party in an action for damages arising from the death of that declarant; or

(f) A statement by a minor child offered against a party in an action to recover for injury to that child, or against the person responsible for the child in an action to recover damages for losses caused by the child.

(4) Things said or done. The statements are events speaking for themselves under the immediate pressure of the occurrence, through the instructive, impulsive and spontaneous words and acts of the participants, and not the words of the participants when narrating the events, and which are necessary incidents of the criminal act, or immediate concomitants of it, or form in conjunction with it one continuous transaction.

E. Optical disk imaging system. "Optical disk imaging system" means a storage system that utilizes non-erasable Write Once Read Many (WORM) optical storage technology to record information on an optical disk with the use of laser technology, and that utilizes laser technology to retrieve and read previously stored information.

Added by Acts 1988, No. 515, § 1, eff. Jan. 1, 1989. Amended by Acts 1995, No. 346, § 1; Acts 1995, No. 1300, § 1; Acts 2004, No. 694, § 1; Acts 2019, No. 237, § 1.

C.E. Art. 802

Art. 802. Hearsay rule

Hearsay is not admissible except as otherwise provided by this Code or other legislation.

Added by Acts 1988, No. 515, § 1, eff. Jan. 1, 1989.

C.E. Art. 803

Art. 803. Hearsay exceptions; availability of declarant immaterial

The following are not excluded by the hearsay rule, even though the declarant is available as a witness:

(1) Present sense impression. A statement describing or explaining an event or condition made while the declarant was perceiving the event or condition, or immediately thereafter.

(2) Excited utterance. A statement relating to a startling event or condition made while the declarant was under the stress of excitement caused by the event or condition.

(3) Then existing mental, emotional, or physical condition. A statement of the declarant's then existing state of mind, emotion, sensation, or physical condition (such as intent, plan, motive, design, mental feeling, pain, and bodily health), offered to prove the declarant's then existing condition or his future action. A statement of memory or belief, however, is not admissible to prove the fact remembered or believed unless it relates to the execution, revocation, identification, or terms of declarant's testament.

(4) Statements for purposes of medical treatment and medical diagnosis in connection with treatment. Statements made for purposes of medical treatment and medical diagnosis in connection with treatment and describing medical history, or past or present symptoms, pain, or sensations, or

C.E. Art. 803—Cont'd

the inception or general character of the cause or external source thereof insofar as reasonably pertinent to treatment or diagnosis in connection with treatment.

(5) **Recorded recollection.** A memorandum or record concerning a matter about which a witness once had knowledge but now has insufficient recollection to enable him to testify fully and accurately, shown to have been made or adopted by the witness when the matter was fresh in his memory and to reflect that knowledge correctly. If admitted, the memorandum or record may be read into evidence and received as an exhibit but may not itself be taken into the jury room. This exception is subject to the provisions of Article 612.

(6) **Records of regularly conducted business activity.** A memorandum, report, record, or data compilation, in any form, including but not limited to that which is stored by the use of an optical disk imaging system, of acts, events, conditions, opinions, or diagnoses, made at or near the time by, or from information transmitted by, a person with knowledge, if made and kept in the course of a regularly conducted business activity, and if it was the regular practice of that business activity to make and to keep the memorandum, report, record, or data compilation, all as shown by the testimony of the custodian or other qualified witness, unless the source of information or the method or circumstances of preparation indicate lack of trustworthiness. This exception is inapplicable unless the recorded information was furnished to the business either by a person who was routinely acting for the business in reporting the information or in circumstances under which the statement would not be excluded by the hearsay rule. The term "business" as used in this Paragraph includes business, institution, association, profession, occupation, and calling of every kind, whether or not conducted for profit. Public records and reports which are specifically excluded from the public records exception by Article 803(8)(b) shall not qualify as an exception to the hearsay rule under this Paragraph.

(7) **Absence of entry in records of regularly conducted business activity.** Evidence that a matter is not included in the memoranda, reports, records, or data compilations, in any form, kept in accordance with the provisions of Paragraph (6), to prove the nonoccurrence or nonexistence of the matter, if the matter was of a kind of which a memorandum, report, record, or data compilation was regularly made and preserved unless the sources of information or other circumstances indicate lack of trustworthiness.

(8) **Public records and reports.** (a) Records, reports, statements, or data compilations, in any form, of a public office or agency setting forth:

(i) Its regularly conducted and regularly recorded activities;

(ii) Matters observed pursuant to duty imposed by law and as to which there was a duty to report; or

(iii) Factual findings resulting from an investigation made pursuant to authority granted by law. Factual findings are conclusions of fact reached by a governmental agency and may be based upon information furnished to it by persons other than agents and employees of that agency.

(b) Except as specifically provided otherwise by legislation, the following are excluded from this exception to the hearsay rule:

(i) Investigative reports by police and other law enforcement personnel or the notification of administrative sanctions form which records the administrative sanctions proceedings conducted pursuant to Code of Criminal Procedure Article 899.1 or R.S. 15:574.7.

(ii) Investigative reports prepared by or for any government, public office, or public agency when offered by that or any other government, public office, or public agency in a case in which it is a party.

(iii) Factual findings offered by the prosecution in a criminal case.

C.E. Art. 803—Cont'd

(iv) Factual findings resulting from investigation of a particular complaint, case, or incident, including an investigation into the facts and circumstances on which the present proceeding is based or an investigation into a similar occurrence or occurrences.

(9) Records of vital statistics. Records or data compilations, in any form, of birth, filiation, adoption, or death, including fetal death, still birth, and abortion, or of marital status, including divorce and annulment, if the report thereof was made to a public office pursuant to requirements of law, and any record included within the Louisiana Vital Statistics Laws.

(10) Absence of public record or entry. To prove the absence of a record, report, statement, or data compilation, in any form, or the nonoccurrence or nonexistence of a matter of which a record, report, statement, or data compilation, in any form, was regularly made and preserved by a public office or agency, evidence in the form of a certification in accordance with Article 902, or testimony, that diligent search failed to disclose the record, report, statement, or data compilation, or entry.

(11) Records of religious organizations. Statements of births, marriages, divorces, deaths, filiation, ancestry, relationship by blood or marriage, or other similar facts of personal or family history, contained in a regularly kept record of a religious organization.

(12) Marriage, baptismal, and similar certificates. Statements of fact contained in a certificate that the maker performed a marriage or other ceremony or administered a sacrament, made by a clergyman, public official, or other person authorized by the rules or practices of a religious organization or by law to perform the act certified, and purporting to have been issued at the time of the act or within a reasonable time thereafter.

(13) Family records. Statements of fact concerning personal or family history contained in family Bibles, genealogies, charts, engravings on rings, inscriptions on family portraits, engravings on urns, crypts, or tombstones, or the like.

(14) Records of documents affecting an interest in property. Records of documents purporting to establish or affect an interest in property to the extent that their admission is authorized by other legislation.

(15) Statements in documents affecting an interest in property. A statement contained in a document purporting to establish or affect an interest in property if the matter stated was relevant to the purpose of the document, unless dealings with the property since the document was made have been inconsistent with the truth of the statement or the purport of the document.

(16) Statements in ancient documents. Statements in a document in existence thirty years or more the authenticity of which is established, or statements in a recorded document as provided by other legislation.

(17) Market reports, commercial publications. Market quotations, tabulations, lists, directories, or other published compilations, generally used and relied upon by the public or by persons in particular occupations.

(18) Learned treatises. To the extent called to the attention of an expert witness upon cross-examination or, in a civil case, relied upon by him in direct examination, statements contained in published treatises, periodicals, or pamphlets on a subject of history, medicine, or other science or art, established as a reliable authority by the testimony or admission of the witness or by other expert testimony or by judicial notice. If admitted, such a statement may be read into evidence and received as an exhibit but may not be taken into the jury room.

(19) Reputation concerning personal or family history. Reputation, arising before the controversy, among members of his family by blood, adoption, or marriage, or among his associates, or in the community, concerning a person's birth, adoption, marriage, divorce, death, filiation,

C.E. Art. 803—Cont'd

relationship by blood, adoption, or marriage, ancestry, or other similar fact of his personal or family history.

(20) Reputation concerning boundaries or general history. Reputation in a community, arising before the controversy, as to boundaries of or customs affecting lands in the community, and reputation as to events of general history important to the community or state or nation in which located.

(21) Reputation as to character. Reputation of a person's character among his associates or in the community.

(22) Judgment of previous conviction. Evidence of a final judgment, entered after a trial or upon a plea of guilty (but not upon a plea of nolo contendere), adjudging a person guilty of a crime punishable by death or imprisonment in excess of six months, to prove any fact essential to sustain the judgment. This exception does not permit the prosecutor in a criminal prosecution to offer as evidence the judgment of conviction of a person other than the accused, except for the purpose of attacking the credibility of a witness. The pendency of an appeal may be shown but does not affect admissibility.

(23) Judgment as to personal, family, or general history, or boundaries. Judgments as proof of matters of personal, family, or general history, or boundaries, essential to the judgment, if the same would be provable by evidence of reputation.

(24) Testimony as to age. A witness' testimony as to his own age.

Added by Acts 1988, No. 515, § 1, eff. Jan. 1, 1989. Amended by Acts 1995, No. 346, § 1; Acts 1995, No. 1300, § 1; Acts 2004, No. 26, § 4; Acts 2012, No. 158, § 1.

C.E. Art. 803.1

Art. 803.1. Hearsay exceptions; foreign records of regularly conducted activity

A. (1) Except as otherwise provided by this Code, in a criminal proceeding, a foreign record of regularly conducted activity, or a copy of such record, shall not be excluded as evidence by the hearsay rule if a foreign certification attests to the following:

(a) Such record was made, at or near the time of the occurrence of the matters set forth, by or from information transmitted by, a person with knowledge of those matters; and

(b) Such record was kept in the course of a regularly conducted business activity; and

(c) The business activity made such a record as a regular practice; and

(d) If such record is not the original, such record is a duplicate of the original, unless the source of information or the method or circumstances of preparation indicate lack of trustworthiness.

(2) A party intending to offer in evidence pursuant to this Article a foreign record of regularly conducted activity shall provide written notice of that intention to each other party not less than ten days prior to trial. A motion opposing admission in evidence of such record shall be made by the opposing party and determined by the court before trial. Failure by a party to file such motion before trial shall constitute a waiver of objection to such record or duplicate, but the court for cause shown may grant relief from the waiver.

B. As used in this Article:

C.E. Art. 803.1—Cont'd

(1) "Foreign record of regularly conducted activity" means a memorandum, report, record, or data compilation, in any form, of acts, events, conditions, opinions, or diagnoses, maintained by a business domiciled in a jurisdiction outside the territorial limits of the state of Louisiana.

(2) "Foreign certification" means a written declaration made and signed in a jurisdiction outside the territorial limits of the state of Louisiana by the custodian of a business record of regularly conducted activity or another qualified person that, if falsely made, would subject the maker to criminal penalty under the laws of the state of Louisiana.

(3) "Business" includes a business, institution, association, profession, occupation, and calling of every kind, whether or not conducted for profit.

Added by Acts 2008, No. 178, § 1.

C.E. Art. 804

Art. 804. Hearsay exceptions; declarant unavailable

A. Definition of unavailability. Except as otherwise provided by this Code, a declarant is "unavailable as a witness" when the declarant cannot or will not appear in court and testify to the substance of his statement made outside of court. This includes situations in which the declarant:

(1) Is exempted by ruling of the court on the ground of privilege from testifying concerning the subject matter of his statement;

(2) Persists in refusing to testify concerning the subject matter of his statement despite an order of the court to do so;

(3) Testifies to a lack of memory of the subject matter of his statement;

(4) Is unable to be present or to testify at the hearing because of death or then existing physical or mental illness, infirmity, or other sufficient cause; or

(5) Is absent from the hearing and the proponent of his statement has been unable to procure his attendance by process or other reasonable means. A declarant is not unavailable as a witness if his exemption, refusal, claim of lack of memory, inability, or absence is due to the procurement or wrongdoing of the proponent of his statement for the purpose of preventing the witness from attending or testifying.

B. Hearsay exceptions. The following are not excluded by the hearsay rule if the declarant is unavailable as a witness:

(1) Former testimony. Testimony given as a witness at another hearing of the same or a different proceeding, if the party against whom the testimony is now offered, or, in a civil action or proceeding, a party with a similar interest, had an opportunity and similar motive to develop the testimony by direct, cross, or redirect examination. Testimony given in another proceeding by an expert witness in the form of opinions or inferences, however, is not admissible under this exception.

(2) Statement under belief of impending death. A statement made by a declarant while believing that his death was imminent, concerning the cause or circumstances of what he believed to be his impending death.

(3) Statement against interest. A statement which was at the time of its making so far contrary to the declarant's pecuniary or proprietary interest, or so far tended to subject him to civil or criminal liability, or to render invalid a claim by him against another, that a reasonable man in his position would not have made the statement unless he believed it to be true. A statement tending to

C.E. Art. 804—Cont'd

expose the declarant to criminal liability and offered to exculpate the accused is not admissible unless corroborating circumstances clearly indicate the trustworthiness of the statement.

(4) Statement of personal or family history. (a) A statement, made before the controversy, concerning the declarant's own birth, adoption, marriage, divorce, filiation, relationship by blood, adoption, or marriage, ancestry, or other similar fact of personal or family history, even though declarant had no means of acquiring personal knowledge of the matter stated; or

(b) A statement, made before the controversy, concerning the foregoing matters, and death also, of another person, if the declarant was related to the other by blood, adoption, or marriage or was so intimately associated with the other's family as to be likely to have accurate information concerning the matter declared.

(5) Complaint of sexually assaultive behavior. A statement made by a person under the age of twelve years and the statement is one of initial or otherwise trustworthy complaint of sexually assaultive behavior.

(6) Other exceptions. In a civil case, a statement not specifically covered by any of the foregoing exceptions if the court determines that considering all pertinent circumstances in the particular case the statement is trustworthy, and the proponent of the evidence has adduced or made a reasonable effort to adduce all other admissible evidence to establish the fact to which the proffered statement relates and the proponent of the statement makes known in writing to the adverse party and to the court his intention to offer the statement and the particulars of it, including the name and address of the declarant, sufficiently in advance of the trial or hearing to provide the adverse party with a fair opportunity to prepare to meet it. If, under the circumstances of a particular case, giving of this notice was not practicable or failure to give notice is found by the court to have been excusable, the court may authorize a delayed notice to be given, and in that event the opposing party is entitled to a recess, continuance, or other appropriate relief sufficient to enable him to prepare to meet the evidence.

(7)(a) Forfeiture by wrongdoing. A statement offered against a party that has engaged or acquiesced in wrongdoing that was intended to, and did, procure the unavailability of the declarant as a witness.

(b) A party seeking to introduce statements under the forfeiture by wrongdoing hearsay exception shall establish, by a preponderance of the evidence, that the party against whom the statement is offered, engaged or acquiesced in the wrongdoing.

Added by Acts 1988, No. 515, § 1, eff. Jan. 1, 1989. Amended by Acts 1995, No. 346, § 1; Acts 1995, No. 1300, § 1; Acts 1997, No. 577, § 2; Acts 2004, No. 26, § 4; Acts 2009, No. 7, § 1; Acts 2010, No. 543, § 1.

C.E. Art. 805

Art. 805. Hearsay within hearsay

Hearsay included within hearsay is not excluded under the hearsay rule if each part of the combined statements conforms with an exception to the hearsay rule provided by legislation. Added by Acts 1988, No. 515, § 1, eff. Jan. 1, 1989.

C.E. Art. 806

Art. 806. Attacking and supporting credibility of declarant

When a hearsay statement, or a statement defined in Article 801(D)(2)(c) or (D)(3), has been admitted in evidence, the credibility of the declarant may be attacked, and if attacked may be

C.E. Art. 806—Cont'd

supported, by any evidence which would be admissible for those purposes if declarant had testified as a witness. Evidence of a statement or conduct by the declarant at any time, offered to attack the declarant's credibility, is not subject to any requirement that he may have been afforded an opportunity to deny or explain. If the party against whom a hearsay statement has been admitted calls the declarant as a witness, the party is entitled to examine him on the statement as a witness identified with an adverse party.

Added by Acts 1988, No. 515, § 1, eff. Jan. 1, 1989.

CHAPTER 9. AUTHENTICATION AND IDENTIFICATION

C.E. Art. 901

Art. 901. Requirement of authentication or identification

A. General provision. The requirement of authentication or identification as a condition precedent to admissibility is satisfied by evidence sufficient to support a finding that the matter in question is what its proponent claims.

B. Illustrations. By way of illustration only, and not by way of limitation, the following are examples of authentication or identification conforming with the requirements of this Article:

(1) Testimony of witness with knowledge. Testimony that a matter is what it is claimed to be.

(2) Nonexpert opinion on handwriting. Nonexpert opinion as to the genuineness of handwriting, based upon familiarity not acquired for purposes of the litigation.

(3) Comparison by trier or expert witness. Comparison by the trier of fact or by expert witnesses with specimens which have been authenticated.

(4) Distinctive characteristics and the like. Appearance, contents, substance, internal patterns, or other distinctive characteristics, taken in conjunction with circumstances.

(5) Voice identification. Identification of a voice, whether heard firsthand or through mechanical or electronic transmission or recording, by opinion based upon hearing the voice at any time under circumstances connecting it with the alleged speaker.

(6) Telephone conversations. Telephone conversations, by evidence that a call was made to the number assigned at the time by the telephone company to a particular person or business, if:

(a) In the case of a person, circumstances, including self-identification, show the person answering to be the one called; or

(b) In the case of a business, the call was made to a place of business and the conversation related to business reasonably transacted over the telephone.

(7) Public records or reports. Evidence that a writing authorized by law to be recorded or filed and in fact recorded or filed in a public office, or a purported public record, report, statement, or data compilation, in any form, is from the public office where items of this nature are kept.

(8) Ancient documents or data compilation. Evidence that a document or data compilation, in any form:

(a) Is in such condition as to create no suspicion concerning its authenticity;

(b) Was in a place where it, if authentic, would likely be; and

(c) Has been in existence thirty years or more at the time it is offered.

C.E. Art. 901—Cont'd

(9) Process or system. Evidence describing a process or system used to produce a result and showing that the process or system produces an accurate result.

(10) Methods provided by legislation. Any method of authentication or identification provided by Act of Congress or by Act of the Louisiana Legislature.

Added by Acts 1988, No. 515, § 1, eff. Jan. 1, 1989.

C.E. Art. 902

Art. 902. Self-authentication

Extrinsic evidence of authenticity as a condition precedent to admissibility is not required with respect to the following:

(1) Domestic public documents under seal. A document bearing a seal, including electronically generated documents logically associated with electronically generated seals, purporting to be that of the United States, or of any state, district, commonwealth, territory, or insular possession thereof, or the Panama Canal Zone, or the Trust Territory of the Pacific Islands, or of a political subdivision, department, officer, or agency thereof, and a signature purporting to be an attestation or execution.

(2) Domestic public documents not under seal. (a) Domestic public documents generally. A document purporting to bear the signature in his official capacity of an officer or employee of any entity included in Paragraph (1) of this Article, having no seal, if a public officer having a seal and having official duties in the district or political subdivision of the officer or employee certifies under seal that the signer has the official capacity and that the signature is genuine.

(b) Certified Louisiana public documents. A purported record, book, paper, or other document of the State of Louisiana, or of a department, board, or agency thereof or of a political subdivision of the state or a department, board, or agency of such a subdivision when certified as being the original by an officer or employee who identifies his official position and who either has custody of the document or who is otherwise authorized to make such a certification.

(3) Foreign public documents. A document purporting to be executed or attested in his official capacity by a person authorized by the laws of a foreign country to make the execution or attestation, and accompanied by a final certification as to the genuineness of the signature and official position (a) of the executing or attesting person, or (b) of any foreign official whose certificate of genuineness of signature and official position relates to the execution or attestation or is in a chain of certificates of genuineness of signature and official position relating to the execution or attestation. A final certification may be made by a secretary of embassy or legation, consul general, consul, vice consul, or consular agent of the United States, or a diplomatic or consular official of the foreign country assigned or accredited to the United States. If reasonable opportunity has been given to all parties to investigate the authenticity and accuracy of official documents, the court may, for good cause shown, order that they be treated as presumptively authentic without final certification or permit them to be evidenced by an attested summary with or without final certification.

(4) Presumptions under Acts of Congress and the Louisiana Legislature. Any signature, document, or other matter declared by Act of Congress or by Act of the Louisiana Legislature to b presumptively or prima facie genuine or authentic.

(5) Official publications. Books, pamphlets, or other publications purporting to be issued by public authority.

(6) Newspapers and periodicals. Printed materials purporting to be newspapers or periodicals.

C.E. Art. 902—Cont'd

(7) Trade inscriptions and the like. Inscriptions, signs, tags, or labels purporting to have been affixed in the course of business and indicating ownership, control, or origin.

(8) Authentic acts, acknowledged acts, and other instruments attested by witnesses. (a) Authentic acts, acts under private signature duly acknowledged, and instruments attested by witnesses and accompanied by affidavits, as provided by Louisiana law, whether executed in Louisiana or elsewhere. (b) Documents executed in a jurisdiction other than Louisiana accompanied by a certificate of acknowledgment executed in the manner provided by the laws of that jurisdiction by a notary public or other officer authorized by law to take acknowledgments.

(9) Commercial paper and related documents. Commercial paper, signatures thereon, and documents relating thereto to the extent provided by general commercial law.

(10) Labor reports. A copy of a report from the Louisiana Workforce Commission, or from any state or federal reporting agency, which is in the possession of a field officer of the support enforcement services program, office of children and family services, Department of Children and Family Services, introduced as evidence in any child or spousal support proceeding. "Field officer" means any person designated or authorized as a field officer pursuant to the provisions of R.S. 46:236.1.8.

(11) Certified records of a regularly conducted business activity in criminal cases. In criminal cases, the original or a copy of a record of a regularly conducted business activity that meets the requirements of Article 803(6), as shown by a certification of the custodian or another qualified person, and that complies with Louisiana law, including R.S. 13:3733 through 3733.2, or a rule prescribed by the Louisiana Supreme Court. Before the trial or hearing, the proponent shall give an adverse party reasonable written notice of the intent to offer the record and shall make the record and certification available for inspection so that the party has a fair opportunity to challenge it.

Added by Acts 1988, No. 515, § 1, eff. Jan. 1, 1989. Amended by Acts 1997, No. 604, § 1; Acts 2010, No. 238, § 5; Acts 2010, No. 541, § 1; Acts 2017, No. 409, § 1.

C.E. Art. 903

Art. 903. Subscribing witness' testimony unnecessary

The testimony of a subscribing witness is not necessary to authenticate a writing unless required by the laws of the jurisdiction whose laws govern the validity of the writing.

Added by Acts 1988, No. 515, § 1, eff. Jan. 1, 1989.

C.E. Art. 904

Art. 904. Self-authentication of copies of public documents

When an original public document is deemed authentic without proof by extrinsic evidence as provided in Article 902(1), (2), or (3), a purported copy of the document also shall be deemed authentic when certified as true or correct by the custodian or other person authorized to make that certification, by certificate complying with Article 902(1), (2), or (3).

Added by Acts 1988, No. 515, § 1, eff. Jan. 1, 1989.

C.E. Art. 905

Art. 905. Self-authentication of other public records

A. Self-authentication. Extrinsic evidence of authenticity as a condition precedent to admissibility is not required with respect to a document purporting to be a document authorized by law to be

C.E. Art. 905—Cont'd

recorded or filed and actually recorded or filed in a public office, including data compilations in any form, when it is certified as being true or correct by the custodian or other person authorized to make the certification, by certificate complying with Article 902(1), (2), or (3) and when, by statute, it is made to be presumptively or prima facie genuine or authentic.

B. Copy of original document described in Paragraph A. A document which purports to be a copy of an original document described in Paragraph A shall be deemed as authentic as the original when certified as true or correct by the custodian or other person authorized to make the certification, by certificate complying with Article 902(1), (2), or (3).

C. Copy of other public records. A document which purports to be a copy of an original document, other than a document described in Paragraph A, which is recorded or filed in a public office, including a data compilation in any form, shall be prima facie evidence that the copy accurately reflects the contents of the document which is filed or recorded when the copy is certified as true or correct by the custodian or other person authorized to make the certification, by certificate complying with Article 902(1), (2), or (3).

Added by Acts 1988, No. 515, § 1, eff. Jan. 1, 1989.

CHAPTER 10. CONTENTS OF WRITINGS, RECORDINGS, AND PHOTOGRAPHS

C.E. Art. 1001

Art. 1001. Definitions

For purposes of this Chapter the following definitions are applicable:

(1) Writings and recordings. "Writings" and "recordings" consist of letters, words, numbers, sounds, or their equivalent, set down by handwriting, typewriting, printing, photostating, photographing, magnetic impulse, mechanical or electronic recording, or other form of data compilation.

(2) Photographs. "Photographs" include still photographs, X-ray films, video tapes, motion pictures, and their equivalents.

(3) Original. An "original" of a writing or recording is the writing or recording itself or any counterpart intended to have the same effect by a person executing or issuing it. An "original" of a photograph includes the negative or any print therefrom. If data are stored in or copied onto a computer or similar device, including any portable or hand-held computer or electronic storage device, any printout or other output readable by sight, shown to reflect the data accurately, is an "original".

(4) Optical disk imaging system. An "optical disk imaging system" is a storage system that utilizes non-erasable Write Once Read Many (WORM) optical storage technology to record information on an optical disk with the use of laser technology, and that utilizes laser technology to retrieve and read previously stored information.

(5) Duplicate. A "duplicate" is a counterpart produced by the same impression as the original, or from the same matrix, or by means of photography, including enlargements and miniatures, or by mechanical or electronic re-recording, or electronic imaging, or by chemical reproduction, or by an optical disk imaging system, or by other equivalent techniques, which accurately reproduces the original.

(6) Electronic imaging. "Electronic imaging" is the process of storing and retrieving any record, document, data, or other information through the use of electronic data processing, or computerized, digital, or optical scanning, or other electronic imaging system.

Added by Acts 1988, No. 515, § 1, eff. Jan. 1, 1989. Amended by Acts 1995, No. 346, § 1; Acts 2001, No. 941, § 1; Acts 2003, No. 1135, § 1, eff. July 2, 2003.

C.E. Art. 1002

Art. 1002. Requirement of original

To prove the content of a writing, recording, or photograph, the original writing, recording, or photograph is required, except as otherwise provided by this Code or other legislation.

Added by Acts 1988, No. 515, § 1, eff. Jan. 1, 1989.

C.E. Art. 1003

Art. 1003. Admissibility of duplicates

A duplicate is admissible to the same extent as an original unless:

(1) A genuine question is raised as to the authenticity of the original;

(2) In the circumstances it would be unfair to admit the duplicate in lieu of the original; or

(3) The original is a testament offered for probate, a contract on which the claim or defense is based, or is otherwise closely related to a controlling issue.

Added by Acts 1988, No. 515, § 1, eff. Jan. 1, 1989. Amended by Acts 2001, No. 941, § 1.

C.E. Art. 1003.1

Art. 1003.1. Electronic duplicates

A duplicate may not be deemed inadmissible or excluded from evidence solely because it is in electronic form or is a reproduction of electronically imaged or stored records, documents, data, or other information.

Added by Acts 2001, No. 941, § 1.

C.E. Art. 1004

Art. 1004. Admissibility of other evidence of contents

The original is not required, and other evidence of the contents of a writing, recording, or photograph is admissible if:

(1) Originals lost or destroyed. All originals are lost or have been destroyed, unless the proponent lost or destroyed them in bad faith;

(2) Original not obtainable. No original can be obtained by any available judicial process or procedure;

(3) Original in possession of opponent. At a time when an original was under the control of the party against whom offered, he was put on notice, by the pleadings or otherwise, that the contents would be a subject of proof at the hearing, and he does not produce the original at the hearing;

(4) Collateral matters. The writing, recording, or photograph is not closely related to a controlling issue; or

(5) Impracticality of producing original. The original, because of its location, permanent fixture, or otherwise, cannot as a practical matter be produced in court; or the cost or other consideration to be incurred in securing the original is prohibitive and it appears that a copy will serve the evidentiary purpose.

Added by Acts 1988, No. 515, § 1, eff. Jan. 1, 1989.

C.E. Art. 1005

Art. 1005. Public records

The contents of an official record, or of a document authorized to be recorded or filed and actually recorded or filed, including data compilations in any form, if otherwise admissible, may be proved by copy, certified as correct in accordance with Article 902 or testified to be correct by a witness who has compared it with the original. If a copy which complies with the foregoing cannot be obtained by the exercise of reasonable diligence, then other evidence of the contents may be given.

Added by Acts 1988, No. 515, § 1, eff. Jan. 1, 1989.

C.E. Art. 1006

Art. 1006. Summaries

The contents of otherwise admissible voluminous writings, recordings, or photographs which cannot conveniently be examined in court may be presented in the form of a chart, summary, or calculation. The originals, or duplicates, shall be made available for examination or copying, or both, by other parties at a reasonable time and place. The court may order that they be produced in court.

Added by Acts 1988, No. 515, § 1, eff. Jan. 1, 1989.

C.E. Art. 1007

Art. 1007. Testimony or written admission of party

Contents of writings, recordings, or photographs may be proved by the testimony or, in a civil case, deposition of the party against whom offered or by his written admission, without accounting for the nonproduction of the original.

Added by Acts 1988, No. 515, § 1, eff. Jan. 1, 1989.

C.E. Art. 1008

Art. 1008. Functions of court and jury

When the admissibility of other evidence of contents of writings, recordings, or photographs under these articles depends upon the fulfillment of a condition of fact, the question whether the condition has been fulfilled is ordinarily for the court to determine in accordance with the provisions of Article 104. However, when an issue is raised (1) whether the asserted writing ever existed, or (2) whether another writing, recording, or photograph produced at the trial is the original, or (3) whether other evidence of contents correctly reflects the contents, the issue is for the trier of fact to determine as in the case of other issues of fact.

Added by Acts 1988, No. 515, § 1, eff. Jan. 1, 1989.

CHAPTER 11. MISCELLANEOUS RULES

C.E. Art. 1101

Art. 1101. Applicability

A. Proceedings generally; rule of privilege.

(1) Except as otherwise provided by legislation, the provisions of this Code shall be applicable to the determination of questions of fact in all contradictory judicial proceedings and in proceedings to

C.E. Art. 1101—Cont'd

confirm a default judgment. Juvenile adjudication hearings in non-delinquency proceedings shall be governed by the provisions of this Code applicable to civil cases. Juvenile adjudication hearings in delinquency proceedings shall be governed by the provisions of this Code applicable to criminal cases.

(2) Furthermore, except as otherwise provided by legislation, Chapter 5 of this Code with respect to testimonial privileges applies to all stages of all actions, cases, and proceedings where there is power to subpoena witnesses, including administrative, juvenile, legislative, military courts-martial, grand jury, arbitration, medical review panel, and judicial proceedings, and the proceedings enumerated in Paragraphs B and C of this Article.

B. Limited applicability. Except as otherwise provided by Article 1101(A)(2) and other legislation, in the following proceedings, the principles underlying this Code shall serve as guides to the admissibility of evidence. The specific exclusionary rules and other provisions, however, shall be applied only to the extent that they tend to promote the purposes of the proceeding.

(1) Worker's compensation cases.

(2) Child custody cases.

(3) Revocation of probation hearings.

(4) Preliminary examinations in criminal cases, and the court may consider evidence that would otherwise be barred by the hearsay rule.

(5) All proceedings before mayors' courts and justice of the peace courts.

(6) Peace bond hearings.

(7) Extradition hearings.

(8) Hearings on motions and other summary proceedings involving questions of fact not dispositive of or central to the disposition of the case on the merits, or to the dismissal of the case, excluding in criminal cases hearings on motions to suppress evidence and hearings to determine mental capacity to proceed.

C. Rules inapplicable. Except as otherwise provided by Article 1101(A)(2) and other legislation, the provisions of this Code shall not apply to the following:

(1) The determination of questions of fact preliminary to admissibility of evidence when the issue is to be determined by the court under Article 104.

(2) Proceedings with respect to release on bail.

(3) Disposition hearings in juvenile cases.

(4) Sentencing hearings except as provided in Code of Criminal Procedure Article 905.2 in capital cases.

(5) Small claims court proceedings except as provided in R.S. 13:5203 and 13:5207.

(6) Proceedings before grand juries except as provided by Code of Criminal Procedure Article 442.

D. Discretionary applicability. Notwithstanding the limitations on the applicability of this Code stated in Paragraphs A, B, and C of this Article, in all judicial proceedings a court may rely upon the provisions of this Code with respect to judicial notice, authentication and identification, and proof of contents of writings, recordings, and photographs as a basis for admitting evidence or making a finding of fact.

Added by Acts 1988, No. 515, § 1, eff. Jan. 1, 1989. Amended by Acts 1988, 2nd Ex.Sess., No. 7, § 1, eff. Jan. 1, 1989; Acts 1992, No. 376, § 3, eff. Jan. 1, 1993.

C.E. Art. 1102

Art. 1102. Title

This Code may be known and cited as the "Louisiana Code of Evidence."

Added by Acts 1988, No. 515, § 1, eff. Jan. 1, 1989.

C.E. Art. 1103

Art. 1103. Repealed by Acts 1995, No. 1300, § 2

C.E. Art. 1104

Art. 1104. State v. Prieur; pretrial; burden of proof

The burden of proof in a pretrial hearing held in accordance with State v. Prieur, 277 So.2d 126 (La. 1973), shall be identical to the burden of proof required by Federal Rules of Evidence Article IV, Rule 404.

Added by Acts 1994, 3rd Ex.Sess., No. 51, § 2.

LOUISIANA CHILDREN'S CODE

Ch.C. Art. 1301.1

Art. 1301.1. Short title

This Chapter may be cited as the "Uniform Interstate Family Support Act".

Acts 2015, No. 80, § 1, eff. July 1, 2015.

Ch.C. Art. 1302.1

Art. 1302.1. Basis for jurisdiction over nonresident

A. In a proceeding to establish or enforce a support order or to determine parentage of a child, a tribunal of this state may exercise personal jurisdiction over a nonresident individual or the individual's guardian, curator, or tutor, if:

(1) The individual is personally served with citation, summons, or notice within this state;

(2) The individual submits to the jurisdiction of this state by consent in a record, by entering a general appearance, or by filing a responsive document having the effect of waiving any contest to personal jurisdiction;

(3) The individual resided with the child in this state;

(4) The individual resided in this state and provided prenatal expenses or support for the child;

(5) The child resides in this state as a result of the acts or directives of the individual;

(6) The individual engaged in sexual intercourse in this state and the child may have been conceived by that act of intercourse;

(7) The individual asserted parentage of a child in the putative father registry maintained in this state by the Louisiana Department of Health, office of public health; or

(8) There is any other basis consistent with the constitutions of this state and the United States for the exercise of personal jurisdiction.

B. The basis for personal jurisdiction set forth in Paragraph A or in any other law of this state may not be used to acquire personal jurisdiction for a tribunal of this state to modify a child support order of another state unless the requirements of Article 1306.11 are met, or, in the case of a foreign support order, unless the requirements of Article 1306.15 are met.

Acts 2015, No. 80, § 1, eff. July 1, 2015.

RULES OF SUPREME COURT OF LOUISIANA

For complete text of Supreme Court Rules, see Volume 8 of West's Louisiana Statutes Annotated—Revised Statutes, West's Louisiana Rules of Court Pamphlet, or Louisiana Statutes & Court Rules on Westlaw.

Sup.Ct.Rule VII

RULE VII. BRIEFS

Section 1. Not less than one original and fifteen legible copies of each brief must be filed. Briefs may be printed or produced by any duplicating or copying process which produces a clear black image on white paper, or they may be typewritten. Carbon copies and photocopies produced on wet copiers are not acceptable.

Section 2. Briefs may be printed or lithographed in pamphlet or book form 6 × 9 inches in size, or they may be typewritten or otherwise produced on either letter or legal size white. Except for matters customarily single-spaced and indented, all typewritten briefs must be double-spaced. With the exception of matters which are customarily indented, margins of at least ¾ inch, but no more than 1¼ inches, shall be maintained on the left, right and bottom of all pages. Margins of no less than 1½ inches, but no more than 2 inches, shall be maintained at the top of each page. Briefs shall be bound in at least two places along the top margin (metal fasteners or staples are preferred). No part of the text of the brief shall be obscured by the binding. No less than 11 point typeface, but no more than 12 point typeface, shall be used.

Briefs in civil cases shall not exceed 25 legal size pages or 35 letter size pages, exclusive of the cover page and the index of authorities. Briefs in criminal cases shall not exceed 35 legal size pages or 50 letter size pages, exclusive of the cover page and the index of authorities. Briefs in criminal capital cases shall not exceed 85 legal size pages or 115 letter size pages, exclusive of the cover page and the index of authorities.

Section 3. Briefs shall state on the front cover or the first page the following: (1) the words, SUPREME COURT OF LOUISIANA; (2) the docket number of the case in this court; (3) the title of the case as it appears on the docket of this court; (4) the name or title of the court and the name of the parish from which the case came, a statement whether it came on appeal or in response to a writ, and the name of the judge who rendered the decision or ruling complained of (for example: "Appeal from the Thirty-Fifth Judicial District Court, Parish of Napoleon, John Smith, District Judge", or "Writ of Review to the Court of Appeal, Blank Circuit, Parish of Napoleon"); (5) a statement showing on whose behalf the brief is filed, and whether as plaintiff, defendant, intervenor, amicus curiae, or otherwise, and whether as appellant, appellee, applicant, petitioner, relator or respondent, and whether the brief is original or supplemental, and whether in support of or opposition to a motion, writ, rehearing, or otherwise, or on the merits; and (6) the name of the attorney or attorneys, with address and telephone number, by whom the brief is filed, and a designation of the party or parties represented.

Section 4. The brief for the appellant, applicant or relator, as the case may be, shall set forth (1) an index of the authorities cited; (2) a concise statement of the case; (3) a specification of the alleged errors complained of; and (4) an argument free from unnecessary repetition and confined strictly to the issue or issues of the case.

Sup.Ct.Rule VII—Cont'd

Section 5. The brief for the appellee, or respondent, as the case may be, shall contain an index of the authorities cited and such statement of the case and such argument as may be deemed necessary.

Section 6. When a brief is filed for a criminal review, the argument on the assignment of error must include a suitable reference by page number, or by any more precise method of location, to the place(s) in the transcript which contains the basis for the alleged error. If the party fails to do so, the court may disregard that argument. The court may consider as abandoned any assignment of error which has not been briefed.

Section 7. The language used in any brief or document filed in this court must be courteous, and free from insulting criticism of any person, individually or officially, or of any class or association of persons, or of any court of justice, or other institution. Any violation of this rule shall subject the author or authors of the brief or document to the humiliation of having the brief or document returned, and to punishment for contempt of the authority of the court.

Section 8.

(a) In all cases in which a writ application has been granted, except those specially assigned for argument under (c) below, the brief of the applicant or relator shall be filed not later than twenty-five days after the date that the writ is granted, and the brief of the respondent shall be filed not later than forty-five days after the date that the writ is granted. In all appeals, the brief of the appellant shall be filed not later than thirty days after the lodging of the record in this court and the brief of the appellee shall be filed not later than sixty days after the lodging of the record in this court. The briefing schedule for disciplinary proceedings will be governed by Supreme Court Rule 19, Section 11(G). In all instances, the briefs shall be accompanied by a certificate showing that a copy was delivered or mailed to the opposing counsel, or to the opposing litigant or litigants, if not represented by counsel.

(b) Failure to file briefs timely in accordance with the above provision shall forfeit the right of the party, so failing, to orally argue the case before the Court. In its discretion, the Court may nonetheless allow oral argument by a party who has failed to file briefs timely. The other party or parties, if they have complied, shall be entitled to oral argument. However, all parties must file briefs in every criminal case.

(c) In cases specially assigned for argument, this rule shall be complied with, if possible. But if the time between the date of fixing and argument be insufficient to render a strict compliance feasible, it shall nevertheless be the duty of counsel to deliver briefs to their opponents at the earliest time practicable.

Revision Note—1979

The practice of this court is to require that briefs be filed in all criminal cases, since constitutional issues may arise if counsel for a criminal defendant fails to perform this duty of representation. The rule change is in accordance with this practice.

Section 9. Briefs sent through the mail shall be deemed timely filed if mailed on or before the due date. If the brief is received by mail on the first legal day following the expiration of the delay, there shall be a rebuttable presumption that it was timely filed. In all cases where the presumption does not apply, the timeliness of the mailing shall be shown only by an official United States postmark or by official receipt or certificate from the United States Postal Service, or bonafide commercial mail services such as Federal Express or United Parcel Service, made at the time of mailing which indicates the date thereof. Any other date stamp, such as a private commercial mail meter stamp, or label from an Automated Postal Center, shall not be used to establish timeliness.

Sup.Ct.Rule VII—Cont'd

Applications forwarded by private delivery or courier service shall be deemed timely filed only if received by the clerk on or before the last day of the delay for filing.

Revision Note—1978

In addition to an official postmark, permissible proof of date of mailing includes:

(1) A certificate of mailing, which may be obtained for a small additional charge per letter by depositing ordinary mail with the postal clerk and requesting said certificate;

(2) A receipt for certified mail secured from the postal clerk at time of mailing; and

(3) A receipt for registered mail secured from the postal clerk at time of mailing.

Section 10. An extension of time within which to file a brief will be granted at the discretion of the court and only in cases in which good cause is shown through written motion filed with the clerk of court on or before the date the brief would ordinarily be due under the appropriate rule. If an extension is granted on behalf of appellant, an extension of time is automatically accorded for the filing of the brief on behalf of appellee, and no action to obtain such an extension shall be necessary on the part of the appellee or his counsel. An extension will not be granted if the hearing and determination of the case will be retarded.

Section 11. [Redesignated as Section 11.1, effective March 29, 2006.]

Section 11.1. Supplemental briefs on the merits, or briefs in support of or in opposition to motions, may be filed at any time. However, a brief filed without leave after the matter is argued or submitted may not be considered.

Section 11.2. Citation of Supplemental Authorities.

If pertinent and significant authorities come to a party's attention after all original and reply briefs have been filed – or after oral argument but before decision – a party may promptly advise the clerk by letter, with a copy to all other parties, setting forth the citations. The letter shall be limited to: (a) the name and citation of the opinion or authority; (b) the issue raised by the case which is pertinent to the issues raised in the case pending before this Court; and (c) a citation to the page number of where this point has been raised in briefs before this Court or, if not raised in briefs and dealt with in oral argument only, where and how this issue arose during oral argument. The body of the letter shall not exceed 350 words. Any response must be made promptly and must be similarly limited. No response to the response shall be allowed. This Section 11.2 letter shall not contain argument; if a party desires to make an argument or to exceed 350 words, the party shall file a motion for permission to file a supplemental brief pursuant to Section 11.1 of this Rule.

Section 12. Brief of an amicus curiae.

A brief of an amicus curiae may be filed only by leave of court granted upon motion and notice to the parties. The amicus curiae brief shall be conditionally filed with the motion for leave. A motion for leave to file an amicus curiae brief must include consideration of and satisfaction of at least one of the following criteria:

(1) Amicus has an interest in some other case involving a similar question;

(2) There are matters of fact or law that might otherwise escape the court's attention; or

(3) The amicus has substantial, legitimate interests that will likely be affected by the outcome of the case and which interests will not be adequately protected by those already party to the case.

An amicus curiae brief which does not meet these criteria, or which merely repeats the position(s) taken by a party, burdens the staff and facilities of the court and its filing is not favored.

Sup.Ct.Rule VII—Cont'd

A motion for leave to file an amicus curiae brief, and the conditionally filed amicus curiae brief, shall be filed within the time allowed for the filing of a brief by the party whose position as to affirmance or reversal the amicus brief will support. The motion for leave to file an amicus brief shall not exceed 5 pages in length; an amicus curiae brief shall not exceed 15 legal size pages or 20 letter size pages in length.

No reply brief of an amicus curiae and no brief of an amicus curiae in support of a petition for rehearing will be accepted.

Amended and effective April 10, 1974; Sept. 18, 1975; Oct. 31, 1975; Jan. 1, 1978; Oct. 4, 1979; March 13, 1989; amended Nov. 19, 1991, effective Dec. 1, 1991; April 27, 1992, effective Sept. 1, 1992; amended and effective June 29, 1995; amended Nov. 9, 1995, effective Jan. 1, 1996; amended and effective Nov. 30, 1995; Jan. 29, 1996; March 21, 2002; March 29, 2006; Nov. 16, 2015.

Advisory Committee Notes

Source: Rule IX, Supreme Court; Rule IX, Uniform Rules of the Courts of Appeal, 1963 Revision.

Explanatory Comment: The chief changes are: (1) all briefs may be typewritten; (2) all briefs become due within 30 days and 60 days of docketing.

The other main changes are the elimination of detailed requirements for standard format in briefs. A general conformity by way of legible and convenient briefs is the emphasis.

Sup.Ct.Rule VII Appendix

RULE VII APPENDIX

The Clerk of the Supreme Court shall be entitled to receive the filing fee set forth in Rule IV for the filing of any motion for leave to file an amicus curiae brief in this Court. This fee shall not be assessed by the Clerk when the motion for leave is presented by the State of Louisiana.

Added and effective June 29, 1995; amended June 28, 2013, effective July 1, 2013.

Sup.Ct.Rule VIII

RULE VIII. ORAL ARGUMENT

Section 1. The appellant or appellants, applicant or applicants, relator or relators, as the case may be, shall have the right to open and close the argument. When there are two or more appellants, applicants, or relators in the same case, the court shall decide, when the case is called for argument, who shall open and who shall close the argument, unless the parties agree upon the one who shall open and upon the one who shall close the argument.

Section 2. (A) Forty minutes, divided equally between the opposing parties, will be allowed for oral argument in lawyer discipline cases and all criminal cases except capital cases, unless additional time is requested, for good cause, and allowed in advance of argument.

(B) Sixty minutes, divided equally between the opposing parties, will be allowed for oral argument in civil cases, unless additional time is requested, for good cause, and allowed in advance of argument.

(C) Sixty minutes, divided equally between the opposing parties, will be allowed for oral argument in cases in which the Judiciary Commission recommends the discipline of a judge, unless additional time is requested, for good cause, and allowed in advance of argument.

Sup.Ct.Rule VIII—Cont'd

(D) Eighty minutes, divided equally between the opposing parties, will be allowed for oral argument in capital cases, unless additional time is requested, for good cause, and allowed in advance of argument.

The court in its discretion may prescribe a shorter period of oral argument for a case or a class of case. Furthermore, the court in its discretion may limit oral argument in any case in which the argument becomes repetitive or irrelevant to the issue or issues before the court.

Section 3. When, in the citation of authorities, a law book is referred to which is not in the consultation room or in the state library, the attorney citing the book must produce it and leave it with the clerk of court until the case is decided.

Section 4. Oral argument will not be allowed in support of or in opposition to:

a. An application for a rehearing.

b. An application for a writ of review to the court of appeal.

c. An application for a supervisory or remedial writ.

Section 5. Repealed effective Nov. 12, 1997.

Amended and effective Nov. 12, 1997.

Sup.Ct.Rule IX

RULE IX. REHEARINGS

Section 1. An application for rehearing must be filed with the Clerk, along with the filing fee set forth in Rule IV, on or before the fourteenth calendar day after the mailing of the notice of judgment, and no extension of time therefor will be granted. Nine copies of the application shall be filed with the original. A copy of the application shall be mailed or delivered to opposing counsel.

Section 2. An application for rehearing properly mailed on or before the last day of the delay shall be deemed timely filed. If the application is received by mail on the first legal day following the expiration of the delay, there shall be a rebuttable presumption that it was timely filed. In all cases where the presumption does not apply, the timeliness of the mailing shall be shown only by an official United States postmark or by official receipt or certificate from the United States Postal Service, or bonafide commercial mail services such as Federal Express or United Parcel Service, made at the time of mailing which indicates the date thereof. Any other date stamp, such as a private commercial mail meter stamp, or label from an Automated Postal Center, shall not be used to establish timeliness.

Applications forwarded by private delivery or courier service shall be deemed timely filed only if received by the clerk on or before the last day of the delay for filing.

Revision Note—1978

In addition to an official postmark, permissible proof of date of mailing includes:

(1) A certificate of mailing, which may be obtained for a small additional charge per letter by depositing ordinary mail with the postal clerk and requesting said certificate;

(2) A receipt for certified mail secured from the postal clerk at time of mailing; and

(3) A receipt for registered mail secured from the postal clerk at time of mailing.

Section 3. If the applicant for rehearing desires further time for filing of brief in support of his application, he shall request additional time in his application and the court may grant or refuse such delay in its discretion.

Sup.Ct.Rule IX—Cont'd

Section 4. When a rehearing is granted, the case may be specially fixed for argument. When called, the case may be argued orally, on the briefs already filed, with such additional or supplemental briefs as the parties may see fit to file before the argument and resubmission of the case on rehearing. When a rehearing is granted, the court may order it submitted on the briefs previously filed and such supplemental briefs as the parties may wish to file.

Section 5. When a case has been decided on rehearing, another application for rehearing will not be considered unless the applicant has not theretofore applied for and been granted a rehearing or unless the court, in deciding the case on rehearing, has expressly reserved to the unsuccessful party or parties the right to apply for another rehearing.

Section 6. An application for rehearing will not be considered when the court has merely granted or denied an application for a writ of certiorari or a remedial or other supervisory writ, or when the judgment of this court is merely overruling a motion to dismiss an appeal or a motion to recall or rescind a rule nisi, or when, for any reason, the judgment has not finally disposed of the case in this court, or when an election case has been decided as provided by Rule X, Section 5(c).

Amended and effective April 10, 1974; May 27, 1976; Jan. 1, 1978; amended March 13, 1989; amended April 27, 1992, effective Sept. 1, 1992; amended and effective Nov. 11, 1993; amended Nov. 9, 1995, effective Jan. 1, 1996; June 28, 2013, effective July 1, 2013; amended and effective Nov. 16, 2015.

Advisory Committee Notes

Source: Rule XI, Supreme Court. See also Rule XI, Uniform Rules of the Courts of Appeal, 1963 Revision.

Sup.Ct.Rule X

RULE X. WRIT APPLICATIONS

Section 1. Writ Grant Considerations.

(a) The grant or denial of an application for writs rests within the sound judicial discretion of this court. The following, while neither controlling nor fully measuring the court's discretion, indicate the character of the reasons that will be considered, one or more of which must ordinarily be present in order for an application to be granted:

1. **Conflicting Decisions.** The decision of a court of appeal conflicts with a decision of another court of appeal, this court, or the Supreme Court of the United States, on the same legal issue.

2. **Significant Unresolved Issues of Law.** A court of appeal has decided, or sanctioned a lower court's decision of, a significant issue of law which has not been, but should be, resolved by this court.

3. **Overruling or Modification of Controlling Precedents.** Although the decision of the court of appeal is in accord with the controlling precedents of this court, the controlling precedents should be overruled or substantially modified.

4. **Erroneous Interpretation or Application of Constitution or Laws.** A court of appeal has erroneously interpreted or applied the constitution or a law of this state or the United States and the decision will cause material injustice or significantly affect the public interest.

5. **Gross Departure From Proper Judicial Proceedings.** The court of appeal has so far departed from proper judicial proceedings or so abused its powers, or sanctioned such a departure or abuse by a lower court, as to call for an exercise of this court's supervisory authority.

Sup.Ct.Rule X—Cont'd

(b) The application for writs shall address, in concise fashion, why the case is appropriate for review under the considerations stated in subsection (a) above, in accordance with Section 3 or 4 of this rule.

Section 2. Writ Applications; General Filing Requirements.

(a) An application for any writ, and all documents and exhibits in connection therewith, shall be filed in duplicate with the clerk of this court, and will not be considered by the court or by any member of the court unless it is so filed with and regularly allotted by the clerk. Seven additional copies of the application shall be filed, except that additional copies are not required for pro se writs in criminal matters. The additional copies shall include the trial court's judgment and reasons for judgment, if the reasons were written or transcribed, and the court of appeal opinion, if any, and may also include any other pleadings or exhibits attached to the original and duplicate.

(b) To the extent practicable, the original and duplicate applications and copies, either or all of which may be produced through a permanent duplicating process, shall be prepared on white, legal size paper and shall be double-spaced. With the exception of matters which are customarily indented, margins of at least ¾ inch, but no more than 1¼ inches, shall be maintained on the left, right and bottom of all pages. Margins of no less than 1½ inches, but no more than 2 inches, shall be maintained at the top of each page. Applications shall be bound in at least two places along the top margin (metal fasteners or staples are preferred). No part of the text of the application shall be obscured by the binding. No less than 11 point typeface, but no more than 12 point typeface, shall be used. The pages in the application shall be consecutively numbered, except that exhibits and attachments may be indexed and tabbed on the right side of the page.

(c) A copy of the application shall be mailed or delivered to all counsel and unrepresented parties. In cases where a remedial writ is sought, a copy of the application shall also be mailed or delivered to the respondent judge. Where a court of appeal has taken any action in a case, either by judgment on appeal or by granting or denying writs, a copy of the application to this court shall be simultaneously filed with the clerk of that court of appeal, which copy need include only the memorandum directed to this court.

(d) The application shall be signed by the applicant or applicant's attorney of record. The applicant or the applicant's attorney of record shall verify the allegations of the application and certify that a copy of the application has been mailed or delivered to the appropriate court of appeal (if required by Section 2(c) of this rule), to the respondent judge in the case of a remedial writ, and to all other counsel and unrepresented parties. The names, addresses and telephone numbers of all counsel and unrepresented parties involved in the case, together with the name of the party or parties each counsel represents, shall be listed in the verification or an attachment thereto.

All duplicate originals and copies of writ applications filed in this court shall include a completed writ application filing sheet. Satisfactory completion of the writ application filing sheet shall satisfy the verification requirements of this subsection. The completed writ application filing sheet should follow the cover sheet in writ applications. The writ application filing sheet is published in the Appendices to the Rules of the Supreme Court of Louisiana.

(e) In all applications requesting a stay order or other priority consideration, the applicant must certify that all counsel and unrepresented parties have been notified by telephone or other equally prompt means of communication that said writ application has been or is about to be filed in this Court and said application must be served forthwith on all parties at interest or their counsel, by a means equal to the means used to effect filing in this Court. (That is, if filing in this Court is by overnight mail, the same means shall be sufficient for service on all parties at interest. If filing is by hand to this Court, service must be made on all parties at interest by an equally prompt method.)

Sup.Ct.Rule X—Cont'd

All duplicate originals and copies of priority writ applications shall include, in addition to a completed writ application filing sheet, a completed civil or criminal priority filing sheet. The civil or criminal priority filing sheet shall precede the writ application filing sheet in the writ application. The civil and criminal priority filing sheets are published in the Appendices to the Rules of the Supreme Court of Louisiana.

The applicant shall immediately notify the Court if the need for expedited consideration changes due to settlement, continuance or any other circumstance. Failure to notify the Court shall subject the applicant to punishment for contempt of the authority of the Court.

Section 3. Writ Applications; Civil; Contents.

In civil cases, a writ application shall be accompanied by the filing fee set forth in R.S. 13:126 and shall contain:

1. An index of all items contained therein;
2. A statement of which of the considerations set forth in Section 1(a) of this rule is present in the case;
3. A memorandum, not exceeding 25 pages in length, containing:

   (a) A concise statement of the case summarizing the nature of the case and prior proceedings;

   (b) An assignment of errors in the opinion, judgment, ruling or order complained of;

   (c) A summary of the argument which should be a succinct but accurate and clear condensation of the argument actually made within the body of the memorandum; it should not be a mere repetition of the headings under which the argument is arranged.

   (d) An argument of each assignment of error on the facts and law, addressing particularly why the case is appropriate for review under the considerations stated in Section 1(a) of this rule.
4. A verification, as required by Section 2(d) of this rule;
5. An appendix containing a copy of the trial court's judgment, order or ruling and reasons for judgment, if reasons were written or transcribed, and the court of appeal's order and opinion, if any, including rulings and opinions on rehearing or applications therefor.
6. Other pleadings or documents shall not be filed, unless their inclusion is essential to demonstrate why the application should be granted. Other pleadings or documents shall be bound separately from the writ application and shall not exceed twenty-five pages.
7. The Clerk will not accept for filing any other pleadings or documents if the twenty-five page limit is exceeded. The applicant shall have seven days from the date the filing is rejected to file other pleadings or documents that conform to this rule, along with the filing fee set forth in Rule IV.
8. Briefs filed in the court of appeal shall not be attached. The court may require the submission of any additional documents or information that it deems useful to its consideration of the application.
9. Applications in cases where an application has been previously filed and is pending may refer to the documents or exhibits attached to the previous application without the necessity of filing additional copies.

Official Comments (2007)

Excessive and irrelevant pleadings and documents included with writ applications are burdensome to the court and are strongly discouraged. In cases where the applicant believes the inclusion of exhibits are absolutely necessary to his or her argument, the

Sup.Ct.Rule X—Cont'd

applicant should limit the scope of those materials to ensure they relate to the subject matter of the application. For example, if an applicant attaches a deposition, it should be limited to those pages which clearly relate to the subject matter of the application. Ordinarily, there is no need to attach pleadings filed in the lower courts, such as petitions, answers, exceptions, appellate briefs, etc. In no event shall the applicant file more than twenty-five pages of other pleadings or documents. The filing of condensed deposition or trial transcripts, reducing multi-page exhibits to one page, and other artifices designed to circumvent the twenty-five page limit are prohibited and will be grounds for rejecting the other pleadings and documents. If the court determines additional materials are necessary for its review, the court may request supplementation.

* * *

Section 5. Writ Applications; Time for Filing.

(a) An application seeking to review a judgment of the court of appeal either after an appeal to that court, or after that court has granted relief on an application for supervisory writs (but not when the court has merely granted an application for purposes of further consideration), or after a denial of an application, shall be made within thirty days of the mailing of the notice of the original judgment of the court of appeal; however, if a timely application for rehearing has been filed in the court of appeal in those instances where a rehearing is allowed, the application shall be made within thirty days of the mailing of the notice of denial of rehearing or the judgment on rehearing. No extension of time therefor will be granted.

(b) When an application is sought to review the action or inaction of a trial court in (a) a case in which the court of appeal does not have supervisory jurisdiction, i.e., a criminal case in which a death sentence has been imposed or in which a conviction and sentence were imposed before July 1, 1982, or (b) a case in which the court of appeal has supervisory jurisdiction but the applicant seeks to file an application directly or simultaneously in this court (which application will not ordinarily be considered by this court absent extraordinary circumstances), the trial court shall fix a reasonable time within which the application shall be filed in this court, and the trial court may in the court's discretion stay further proceedings. Upon proper showing, the trial court or this court may by order extend the time for such filing. Any application not filed in this court within the time so fixed or extended may not be considered, in the absence of showing that the delay in filing was not due to the applicant's fault.

(c) An application for a writ to review a decision of the court of appeal on an objection to a candidacy or on an election contest, shall be made, as provided by R.S. 18:1409 and 1413, within forty-eight hours, including Sundays and other legal holidays, after judgment is rendered by the court of appeal; however, if the forty-eighth hour falls on a Sunday or other legal holiday, then noon of the next legal day shall be deemed to be the expiration of the time interval.

If the application is granted, the case shall be promptly heard and decided. No application for a rehearing of the case shall be entertained.

(d) An application properly mailed shall be deemed timely filed if mailed on or before the last day of the delay for filing. If the application is received by mail on the first legal day following the expiration of the delay, there shall be a rebuttable presumption that it was timely filed. In all cases where the presumption does not apply, the timeliness of the mailing shall be shown only by an official United States postmark or cancellation stamp or by official receipt or certificate from the United States Postal Service, or bonafide commercial mail services such as Federal Express or United Parcel Service, made at the time of mailing which indicates the date thereof. Any other date stamp, such as a private commercial mail meter stamp, or label from an Automated Postal Center, shall not be used to establish timeliness.

Sup.Ct.Rule X—Cont'd

Applications forwarded by private delivery or courier service shall be deemed timely filed only if received by the clerk on or before the last day of the delay for filing.

Revision Note—1978

In addition to an official postmark, permissible proof of date of mailing includes:

(1) A certificate of mailing, which may be obtained for a small additional charge per letter by depositing ordinary mail with the postal clerk and requesting said certificate;

(2) A receipt for certified mail secured from the postal clerk at time of mailing; and

(3) A receipt for registered mail secured from the postal clerk at time of mailing.

Section 6. Writ Applications; Oppositions.

Any party may file and serve an opposition memorandum, setting forth reasons why the application should not be granted. The opposition must be filed within fifteen days of the filing of the application unless the time for filing is extended by order of the court. The opposition memorandum should be as brief as possible, and must not exceed twenty-five pages in length.

Other pleadings or documents shall not be filed with the opposition memorandum, unless their inclusion is essential to demonstrate why the application should not be granted. In the event any other pleadings or documents are filed, they shall be bound separately from the opposition memorandum and shall not exceed twenty-five pages.

The Clerk will not accept for filing any other pleadings or documents if the twenty-five page limit is exceeded. The applicant shall have seven days from the date the filing is rejected to file other pleadings or documents that conform to this rule.

When the application requests emergency action or a stay order, any party desiring to oppose such action should file the opposition to such action immediately upon receipt of a copy of the application.

Oppositions serve an important purpose in assisting the court in the exercise of its discretionary jurisdiction. As such, the court encourages the filing of oppositions.

Section 7. Reply to Opposition.

The court does not encourage the filing of reply memoranda. Nonetheless, any party who feels the filing of a reply is essential to the court's consideration of the writ application may file and serve a reply memorandum in response to an opposition. The reply memorandum must be filed within ten days of the filing of the opposition and shall be accompanied by the filing fee set forth in Rule IV. The reply memorandum shall not exceed seven pages in length, inclusive of exhibits and other documents. No response to a reply memorandum shall be allowed.

Section 8. Oral Argument; Briefs; Record; Peremptory Relief

(a) When a writ has been granted, the record shall be lodged with the clerk of court forthwith. The case shall be placed on the calendar for oral argument and briefs shall be required in accordance with Rule VII, Section 8(a), unless at or after the time the writ is granted the court provides otherwise. In lieu of filing a brief, the applicant may, within the time prescribed by Rule VII, Section 8(a), file fifteen additional copies of the application (with or without the supporting exhibits) and any memorandum or brief filed in support of the application.

(b) At the time the writ is granted, the court may order peremptory relief. A party affected may apply for rehearing within the delay provided by Rule IX and the court may, with or without application, stay the relief granted to permit consideration of any such application.

Reenacted June 17, 1991, effective July 1, 1991; amended April 27, 1992, effective Sept. 1, 1992; amended and effective Oct. 2, 1992; Oct. 20, 1992; amended Nov. 9, 1995, eff. Jan. 1, 1996; amended Dec. 18, 1997, effective March 1, 1998; Sept. 9, 1999, effective Oct. 15, 1999; March 28, 2007, effective June 1, 2007; April 26, 2007, effective June 1, 2007; amended effective Jan. 21, 2011; amended June 28, 2013, effective July 1, 2013; amended effective Oct. 12, 2015; Nov. 16, 2015.

Sup.Ct.Rule XXXVI

RULE XXXVI. [UNTITLED]

If a justice of the Supreme Court of Louisiana or a judge of a court of appeal, district, family, juvenile, parish, city, traffic or municipal court of the State of Louisiana recuses himself/herself in a proceeding before that justice's or judge's court, that justice or judge shall, unless otherwise prohibited by law or applicable Supreme Court Rule, provide in writing the factual basis for recusal within fifteen days of the rendering of the order of recusal.

Adopted June 4, 2002, effective Sept. 1, 2002.

UNIFORM RULES
COURTS OF APPEAL

For complete text of Uniform Rules of Courts of Appeal, see Volume 8 of West's Louisiana Statutes Annotated—Revised Statutes, West's Louisiana Rules of Court Pamphlet, or Louisiana Statutes & Court Rules on Westlaw.

Adopted March 19, 1982

Effective July 1, 1982

As amended

Courts of Appeal Rule 1–1

Rule 1–1. Promulgation and Effective Date of Rules; Amendments

1–1.1. Promulgation and Effective Date

The Rules of Court shall be promulgated by posting a copy to the Louisiana Courts of Appeal websites and published in the manner which the court deems most effective and practicable. They shall become effective on July 1, 1982.

Amended effective April 15, 2010.

1–1.2. Amendments

Amendments of these Rules shall be promulgated and published in the same manner, and shall become effective as of the date fixed therein.

Courts of Appeal Rule 1–2

Rule 1–2. Title and Scope of Rules

These Rules shall govern practice and procedure in all appeals and in all writ applications to the Louisiana Courts of Appeal, and shall be known as the "Uniform Rules of Louisiana Courts of Appeal."

Courts of Appeal Rule 1–3

Rule 1–3. Scope of Review

The scope of review in all cases within the appellate and supervisory jurisdiction of the Courts of Appeal shall be as provided by LSA–Const. Art. 5, § 10(B), and as otherwise provided by law. The Courts of Appeal will review only issues which were submitted to the trial court and which are contained in specifications or assignments of error, unless the interest of justice clearly requires otherwise.

Courts of Appeal Rule 1–4

Rule 1–4. Sessions of Court

Unless the court orders otherwise, each Court of Appeal will hold sessions at its legal domicile.

Courts of Appeal Rule 1–5

Rule 1–5. Panels

The court ordinarily will sit in rotating panels, each composed of 3 Judges, as may be directed by the Chief Judge. In civil cases, when a judgment or ruling of a trial court is to be modified or reversed and one judge dissents, the case shall be reargued or resubmitted before a panel of at least 5 Judges if required by the constitution or by the local rules of the particular appellate circuit. When an appeal is taken from an election case objecting to candidacy or contesting an election, the case shall be heard by the court as directed by law. When authorized by law, or when the court deems it necessary to promote justice or expedite the business of court, the court may sit in panels of more than 3 judges or en banc.

Amended effective Oct. 7, 1991; amended Oct. 6, 2003.

Courts of Appeal Rule 2–12

Rule 2–12. Briefs

2–12.1. Filing

Each party shall file an original and 7 copies of the brief in every case. All parties must file briefs in every criminal appeal.

Amended Oct. 3, 1994, effective Jan. 1, 1995.

2–12.2. Preparation of Briefs

A. The provisions of this Section shall apply to briefs submitted in appeals and to briefs or supporting memoranda submitted in connection with motions, applications for supervisory writs and applications for rehearing.

B. Briefs may be printed, typewritten, or produced by any copying or duplicating process which produces a clear black image on white paper. Illegible copies and photocopies produced on wet copiers are not acceptable. Briefs may be typewritten or otherwise acceptably produced on either letter or legal-size, white, unglazed, opaque paper, with a margin of 1" on each side, using only one side of each page. The text of briefs shall be double-spaced except for matters which are customarily single-spaced. The pages in the briefs shall be numbered consecutively.

C. The language used in the brief shall be courteous, free from vile, obscene, obnoxious, or offensive expressions, and free from insulting, abusive, discourteous, or irrelevant matter or criticism of any person, class of persons or association of persons, or any court, or judge or other officer thereof, or of any institution. Any violation of this Subsection shall subject the author, or authors, of the brief to punishment for contempt of court, and to having such brief returned.

D. The preparation of briefs shall be subject to the following requirements and limitations:

(1) Original briefs on 8 1/2″ × 14″ paper shall not exceed thirty-one pages; reply briefs on such paper shall not exceed thirteen pages. Original briefs on 8 1/2″ × 11″ paper shall not exceed forty-one pages; reply briefs on such paper shall not exceed eighteen pages. These limitations do not include pages containing the table of contents required by Rule 2–12.4, Subsection A(1) and the table of authorities required by Rule 2–12.4, Subsection A(2).

(2) The size type in all briefs will be: (a) Roman or Times New Roman 14 point or larger computer font, normal spacing; or (b) no more than 10 characters per inch typewriter print. A

Courts of Appeal Rule 2–12—Cont'd

margin of at least one inch at the top and bottom of each page shall be maintained. Footnotes may be single-spaced but shall not be used to circumvent the spirit of this rule.

(3) A motion for leave to file a brief in excess of the page limitation of this rule must be filed at least ten days in advance of the due date of the brief. Such a motion will be granted only for extraordinary and compelling reasons.

Amended April 3, 1986, effective July 1, 1986; amended Oct. 5, 1992; amended Oct. 3, 1994, effective Jan. 1, 1995; amended March 22, 2001, effective Jan. 1, 2002; amended Oct. 7, 2013, effective Jan. 1, 2014.

2–12.3. Cover Inscription

Briefs shall state on the cover or on the title page the following:

(a) the title of the court to which it is directed;

(b) the docket number of the case in the court;

(c) the title of the case as it appears on the docket of the court;

(d) the name or title of the court and the parish from which the case came;

(e) the name of the judge who rendered the judgment or ruling complained of;

(f) a statement as to whether the case comes before the court on appeal or in response to a writ.

(g) a statement identifying the party on whose behalf the brief is filed and the party's status before the court;

(h) the nature of the brief, whether original, in reply, or supplemental;

(i) the name of counsel, with address and telephone number, by whom the brief is filed, and a designation of the parties represented, and a designation of "appeal counsel";

(j) the designation of whether the case is a civil, criminal, juvenile, or special proceeding (state particular type of proceeding).

2–12.4. Appellant's Brief

A. The brief of the appellant shall contain, under appropriate headings and in the order indicated:

(1) a table of contents with page references;

(2) a table of authorities, including cases alphabetically arranged, statutes and other authorities, with references to the pages of the brief where the authorities are cited;

(3) a jurisdictional statement setting forth the constitutional and statutory basis for the court to exercise appellate jurisdiction, with citations to applicable provisions. The jurisdictional statement shall also include the dates of the judgment appealed and of the motion and order for appeal to establish the timeliness of the appeal and the following, as applicable:

(a) an assertion that the appeal is from a final appealable judgment and, if the appealability is dependent upon a designation by the trial court, a reference to the specific page numbers of the record where the designation and reasons for the designation are to be found, or

(b) an assertion that the appeal is from an interlocutory judgment or order which is appealable as expressly provided by law, or

(c) an assertion of information establishing the court of appeal's jurisdiction on some other basis;

Courts of Appeal Rule 2–12—Cont'd

(4) a concise statement of the case indicating the nature of the case, the action of the trial court and the disposition;

(5) assignments of alleged errors;

(6) a listing of issues presented for review;

(7) a statement of facts relevant to the assignments of error and issues for review, with references to the specific page numbers of the record;

(8) a short summary of the argument, *i.e.*, a succinct, clear and accurate statement of the arguments made in the body of the brief;

(9) the argument, which shall contain:

(a) appellant's contentions, with reference to the specific page numbers of the record and citations to the authorities on which the appellant relies,

(b) for each assignment of error and issue for review, a concise statement of the applicable standard of review, which may appear in the discussion or under a separate heading placed before the discussion, and

(c) for each assignment of error and issue for review which required an objection or proffer to preserve, a statement that the objection or proffer was made, with reference to the specific page numbers of the record; and

(10) a short conclusion stating the precise relief sought.

B. (1) A copy of the judgment, order, or ruling complained of, and a copy of either the trial court's written reasons for judgment, transcribed oral reasons for judgment, or minute entry of the reasons, if given, shall be appended to the brief of the appellant. If reasons for judgment were not given, the brief shall so declare.

(2) Citation of Louisiana cases shall be in conformity with Section VIII of the Louisiana Supreme Court General Administrative Rules. Citations of other cases shall be to volume and page of the official reports (and when possible to the unofficial reports). It is recommended that where United States Supreme Court cases are cited, all three reports be cited, e.g., *Miranda v. Arizona*, 384 U.S. 436, 86 S.Ct. 1602, 16 L.Ed.2d 694 (1966).

(3) The court may disregard the argument on an assignment of error or issue for review if suitable reference to the specific page numbers of the record is not made.

(4) All assignments of error and issues for review must be briefed. The court may consider as abandoned any assignment of error or issue for review which has not been briefed.

Amended April 3, 1986, effective July 1, 1986; amended Oct. 3, 1994, effective Jan. 1, 1995; amended Oct. 2, 2006, effective Nov. 1, 2006; amended Oct. 7, 2013, effective Jan. 1, 2014; amended April 10, 2014, effective May 1, 2014.

2–12.5. Appellee's Brief

The brief of the appellee shall contain appropriate and concise responses and arguments to the contentions and arguments of the appellant and shall conform to the requirements for the appellant's brief set forth in Rule 2–12. 4, except that the following need not be included unless the appellee is dissatisfied with the appellant's statements:

(1) the jurisdictional statement, Rule 2–12–4, Subsection A(3);

(2) the statement of the case, Rule 2–12–4, Subsection A(4);

(3) assignments of alleged errors, Rule 2–12–4, Subsection A(5);

(4) the listing of issues, Rule 2–12.4, Subsection A(6);

(5) the statement of facts, Rule 2–12.4, Subsection A(7);

Courts of Appeal Rule 2–12—Cont'd

(6) the statement of the standard of review, Rule 2–12.4, Subsection A(9)(b);

(7) the statement of the objection or proffer, Rule 2–12.4, Subsection A(9)(c); and

(8) a copy of the judgment or order and a copy of the trial court's written or transcribed oral reasons, Rule 2–12.4, Subsection B(1).

Amended Oct. 2, 2006, effective Nov. 1, 2006; amended Oct. 7, 2013, effective Jan. 1, 2014; amended April 10, 2014, effective May 1, 2014.

2–12.6. Reply Brief

The appellant may file a reply brief, if he has timely filed an original brief, but it shall be strictly confined to rebuttal of points urged in the appellee's brief. No further briefs may be filed except by leave of court.

2–12.6.1. Citation of Supplemental Authorities

A. If pertinent and significant authorities come to a party's attention after all original and reply briefs have been filed—or after oral argument but before decision—a party may promptly advise the clerk by letter, with a copy to all other parties, setting forth the citations.

B. The letter shall be limited to: (1) the name and citation of the opinion or authority; (2) the issue raised by the case which is pertinent to the issues raised in the case pending before this Court; and (3) a citation to the page number of where this point has been raised in briefs before this Court or, if not raised in briefs and dealt with in oral argument only, where and how this issue arose during oral argument. The letter shall not include attachments, including but not limited to the documents cited within the letter.

C. The body of the letter shall not exceed two pages (letter size). Any response must be made promptly and must be similarly limited. This section 2–12.6.1 letter shall not contain argument; if a party desires to make an argument or to exceed two pages (letter size), the party shall file a motion for permission to file a supplemental brief.

Adopted April 6, 2006. Amended April 10, 2014, effective May 1, 2014.

2–12.7. Time to File

The brief of the appellant shall be filed not later than 25 calendar days after the filing of the record in the court, and the brief of the appellee shall be filed not later than 45 calendar days after the filing of the record in the court. The reply brief, if any, of the appellant shall be filed not later than 10 calendar days after the appellee's brief is filed.

Unless otherwise directed by the court in the notice of lodging, in the case of a timely order of appeal being obtained by a litigant subsequent to an earlier order of appeal obtained by a different litigant, the brief on behalf of the litigant whose order of appeal bears the earlier date shall be due in point of time under the provisions of the appropriate rule regarding the appellant. The brief on behalf of the litigant whose order of appeal bears the later date shall be due in point of time under the provisions of the appropriate rule regarding the appellee.

Amended Oct. 7, 2002.

2–12.8. Extensions of Time

An extension of time within which to file the brief may be granted by the court for good cause shown on written motion filed with the clerk of the court on or before the date the brief was due. If an extension of time is granted to an appellant to file the original brief, time for filing the appellee's brief is extended for a period of twenty days from the date of the extended time granted the appellant, without the necessity of a motion or request by the appellee. To preserve the right to oral

Courts of Appeal Rule 2–12—Cont'd

argument, an appellee must file the brief within the extended twenty-day period, whether or not the appellant's brief is timely filed. An extension of time may not be granted if such extension will retard the hearing or determination of the case.

Amended Oct. 5, 1987, effective Dec. 1, 1987.

2–12.9. Specially-assigned Cases

In cases specially assigned for argument, the briefs shall be filed as ordered by the court.

2–12.10. Briefs on Motions or Writ Applications

Briefs in support of motions or applications for writs shall be filed with the motion or writ application. Briefs in opposition thereto shall be filed prior to decision by the court, or as may be ordered by the court.

2–12.11. Amicus Curiae Briefs

Amicus curiae briefs may be filed only upon motion by the applicant and order of the court. The motion shall identify the interest of the applicant, state that the applicant has read the briefs of the parties, and state specific reasons why applicant's brief would be helpful to the court in deciding the cases. An amicus curiae may not request oral argument.

2–12.12. Untimely Briefs; Sanctions

If the brief on behalf of any party is not filed by the date that the brief is due, the party's right to oral argument shall be forfeited. The court may also impose other sanctions including, but not limited to, dismissal of the appeal when the appellant does not file a brief as provided for in Rule 2–8.6.

2–12.13. Non-conforming Briefs; Sanctions

Briefs not in compliance with these Rules may be stricken in whole or in part by the court, and the delinquent party or counsel of record may be ordered to file a new or amended brief.

Courts of Appeal Rule 2–13

Rule 2–13. Filing of Papers; Timeliness

All papers and required copies to be filed in a Court of Appeal shall be legible and shall be filed with the clerk. Filing may be accomplished by delivery or by mail addressed to the clerk. The filing of such papers shall be deemed timely when the papers are mailed on or before the due date. If the papers are received by mail on the first legal day following the expiration of the delay, there shall be a rebuttable presumption that they were timely filed. In all cases where the presumption does not apply, the timeliness of the mailing shall be shown only by an official United States postmark or cancellation stamp or by official receipt or certificate from the United States Postal Service or bonafide commercial mail services such as Federal Express or United Parcel Service, made at the time of mailing which indicates the date thereof. Any other dated stamp, such as a private commercial mail meter stamp, shall not be used to establish timeliness.

Amended Oct. 7, 2002; amended Oct. 2, 2006, effective Nov. 1, 2006; amended April 10, 2014, effective May 1, 2014.

Courts of Appeal Rule 2–15

Rule 2–15. Oral Argument

2–15.1. Order of Argument

The appellant shall have the right to open and close the argument. Where there are 2 or more appellants in the same case, the court will decide when the case is called for argument who shall open and who shall close the argument, unless the parties agree upon the order of presentation.

2–15.2. Length of Time

The parties shall be allowed a period of time not to exceed 40 minutes, divided equally between opposing parties, unless additional time is allowed by the court for sound reason, or the court deems additional time is needed for proper presentation of the case. Counsel is not required to use all of the allotted time. The time for argument may be shortened in the discretion of the court. When there is a conflict of interests between appellants or between appellees, the court will decide upon the apportionment of the time allowed them for argument, unless they agree upon the apportionment.

2–15.3. Reading From Briefs

Argument should not be read from a prepared text. Counsel shall not be permitted to read from briefs, except matters, such as quotations, which are customarily read.

2–15.4. Textual Materials and Exhibits

(a) Textual Materials. A book, treatise, or other textual material not conveniently available to the court, used as authority during argument by counsel, shall, on request of court, be deposited with the court until the case is decided. By leave of court, a photocopy of the pertinent material may be substituted in lieu of the book, the treatise, or other textual material.

(b) Exhibits for Demonstration. All models, maps, charts, diagrams, or other exhibits used for purposes of illustration, demonstration, or explanation during oral argument before the court (but not made a part of the record) and deposited thereafter with the court shall be removed by the party or counsel responsible for such use and deposit within 30 days after written notice given by the clerk. Failure to remove timely shall authorize the clerk to destroy the exhibit or make other disposition thereof as the court may deem proper.

Courts of Appeal Rule 2–18

Rule 2–18. Rehearing

2–18.1. Application for Rehearing

An application for rehearing shall state with particularity contentions of the applicant and shall contain a concise argument in support of the application. Except by permission of court, an application for rehearing shall not exceed 10 pages. An original and 4 copies of the application for rehearing shall be filed. Oral argument in support of the application will not be permitted.

2–18.2. Time to File

(A) In cases governed by the Code of Criminal Procedure, an application for rehearing must be filed with the clerk on or before fourteen days after the rendition of the judgment.

(B) In cases governed by the Code of Civil Procedure, an application for rehearing must be filed with the clerk on or before fourteen days after transmission of the notice of the judgment.

Courts of Appeal Rule 2–18—Cont'd

(C) No extension of time for filing an application for rehearing shall be granted.

Amended effective August 30, 1983; amended effective October 6, 2014.

2–18.3. Support Brief

The applicant shall file an original and 4 copies of a brief in support of the application for rehearing at the time the application for rehearing is filed.

Amended Oct. 3, 1994, effective Jan. 1, 1995.

2–18.4. Additional Time for Brief

If the applicant for rehearing needs additional time for filing a brief in support of the application, an extension of time within which to file the brief may be granted by the court for good cause shown on written motion filed with the clerk of the court at the time the application for rehearing is filed. The act of filing the motion to extend the time within which to file the brief does not extend the time; an extension is effective only as ordered by the Court.

Amended April 10, 2014, effective May 1, 2014.

2–18.5. Granting of Rehearing

When a rehearing is granted, the case shall be submitted, with or without oral argument, as ordered by the court.

2–18.6. Repetitive Applications

When a case has been decided on rehearing, another application for a rehearing will not be considered unless the applicant has not theretofore been granted a rehearing, or unless the court has expressly granted the right to apply for another rehearing.

2–18.7. When Rehearing Will Be Considered

An application for rehearing will be considered in cases where the court has:

(A) Granted a writ application on the merits;

(B) Dismissed an appeal; or

(C) Ruled on the merits of an appeal.

Amended Oct. 2, 1989, effective Jan. 1, 1990; amended Oct. 3, 1994, effective Jan. 1, 1995.

Courts of Appeal Rule 4–1

Rule 4–1. Application for Writs

An application for writs of any kind, and all documents and exhibits in connection therewith, shall be filed in an original and 3 duplicate copies with the clerk of the Court of Appeal, and shall not be considered by the court or any judge of the court unless it is properly filed with the clerk.

Application for Post-conviction Relief. The applicant shall use the uniform application for post-conviction relief (see Appendix A). Inexcusable failure of the applicant to comply with this Rule may subject the applicant to dismissal of the application, or to other sanctions of the court.

Amended March 29, 1983, effective May 1, 1983; amended Oct. 3, 1994, effective Jan. 1, 1995.

Courts of Appeal Rule 4–2

Rule 4–2. Notice of Intention

The party, or counsel of record, intending to apply to the Court of Appeal for a writ shall give to opposing parties or opposing counsel of record, notice of such intention; notice simultaneously shall be

Courts of Appeal Rule 4–2—Cont'd

given to the judge whose ruling is at issue, by requesting a return date to be set by the judge within the time period provided for in Rule 4–3.

Amended Oct. 2, 2000; amended effective April 15, 2010.

Courts of Appeal Rule 4–3

Rule 4–3. Time to File; Extension of Time

The judge who has been given notice of intention as provided by Rule 4–2 shall immediately set a reasonable return date within which the application shall be filed in the appellate court. The return date in civil cases shall not exceed 30 days from the date of notice, as provided in La. C.C.P. art. 1914. In criminal cases, unless the judge orders the ruling to be reduced to writing, the return date shall not exceed 30 days from the date of the ruling at issue. When the judge orders the ruling to be reduced to writing in criminal cases, the return date shall not exceed 30 days from the date the ruling is signed. In all cases, the judge shall set an explicit return date; an appellate court will not infer a return date from the record.

Upon proper showing, the trial court or the appellate court may extend the time for filing the application upon the filing of a motion for extension of return date by the applicant, filed within the original or an extended return date period. An application not filed in the appellate court within the time so fixed or extended shall not be considered, in the absence of a showing that the delay in filing was not due to the applicant's fault. The application for writs shall contain documentation of the return date and any extensions thereof; any application that does not contain this documentation may not be considered by the appellate court.

Amended Oct. 3, 1994, effective Jan. 1, 1995; amended Oct. 2, 2000; amended Oct. 6, 2003; amended Nov. 7, 2003, effective Nov. 10, 2003.

Courts of Appeal Rule 4–4

Rule 4–4. Stay of Proceedings

(A) When an application for writs is sought, further proceedings may be stayed at the trial court's discretion. Any request for a stay of proceedings should be presented first to the trial court. The filing of, or the granting of, a writ application does not stay further proceedings unless the trial court or appellate court expressly orders otherwise.

(B) When expedited consideration by an appellate court is requested, including, but not limited to, a request for a stay order, the application shall include on the cover a statement in bold print that such consideration is sought and a statement within the application itself, entitled "REQUEST FOR EXPEDITED CONSIDERATION", setting forth justification for the request and a specific time within which action by the appellate court is sought by the applicant. The "REQUEST FOR EXPEDITED CONSIDERATION" shall be included as a separate page and properly noted in the index. The applicant shall notify the appellate court immediately of any change in the status of the case.

(C) In all applications requesting a stay order or other priority consideration, the applicant must certify in affidavit form that the trial court and all counsel and unrepresented parties have been notified by telephonic or other equally prompt means of communication that said writ application has been or is about to be filed and that said application has been served forthwith on the trial court and all parties at interest or their counsel, by means equal to the means used to effect filing with the appellate court. (That is, if filing with the appellate court is by overnight mail, the same means shall

Courts of Appeal Rule 4–4—Cont'd

be employed for service on the trial court and all parties at interest or their counsel. If filing is by hand to the appellate court, service must be made on the trial court and all parties at interest or their counsel by an equally prompt means.)

Amended Oct. 3, 1994, effective Jan. 1, 1995; amended Oct. 2, 1995, effective Jan. 1, 1996.

Courts of Appeal Rule 4–5

Rule 4–5. Contents of Application

A. The original application for writs shall be signed by the applicant or counsel of record, and shall contain an affidavit verifying the allegations of the application and certifying that a copy has been delivered or mailed to the respondent judge and to opposing counsel, and to any opposing party not represented by counsel. The affidavit shall list all parties and all counsel, indicating the parties each represents. The affidavit also shall list the addresses and telephone numbers (if available) of the respondent judge, opposing counsel and any opposing party not represented by counsel.

B. The original and duplicates shall be legible and shall have the pages of the application and attached documents and exhibits consecutively numbered. The entire submission shall be hole punched and bound in two places along the top margin, preferably with 4 ¼ inch metal file fasteners such that no part of the text on any page is obscured, and in sections consisting of no more than 250 pages. No tabs shall be used in lieu of consecutive page numbering and no tabs or extensions shall be placed outside the paper dimensions. Documents within the bound submission shall not contain any staples, clips or other fasteners.

C. The submission shall contain these items:

(1) an index of all items contained therein;

(2) a concise statement of the grounds on which the jurisdiction of the court is invoked;

(3) a concise statement of the case, including the status of the case at the time the writ application is filed, in order to reflect any trial dates or hearing dates that are pending;

(4) the issues and questions of law presented for determination by the court;

(5) the assignments or specifications of errors and a memorandum in support of the application, in accordance with Rules 2–12.2 and 2–12.10, and a prayer for relief;

(6) a copy of the judgment, order, or ruling complained of (if by written judgment, order, or ruling);

(7) a copy of the judge's reasons for judgment, order, or ruling (if written);

(8) a copy of each pleading on which the judgment, order, or ruling was founded, including the petition(s) in civil cases and the indictment or the bill of information in criminal cases;

(9) a copy of any opposition and any attachments thereto filed by a party in the trial court or a statement by the relator that no opposing written document was filed;

(10) a copy of pertinent court minutes;

(11) the notice of intent and return date order required by Rules 4–2 and 4–3; and

(12) a separate page entitled "REQUEST FOR EXPEDITED CONSIDERATION" and indexed as such shall be included if the applicant seeks expedited relief or a stay order as required by Rule 4–4(B) and a corresponding affidavit as required by Rule 4–4(C).

D. If any trial or hearing date is set after a writ application is filed or if any trial or hearing date included in a filed writ application is changed or continued, the applicant shall notify the court by facsimile or by e-mail, if directed by the Court of Appeal, of the setting, change, or continuance of the hearing date no later than three business days after the setting, change or continuance. The filed

Courts of Appeal Rule 4–5—Cont'd

writ application shall be supplemented with this information not later than one week after the setting, change or continuance.

Amended March 26, 1992, effective April 1, 1992; amended Oct. 3, 1994, effective Jan. 1, 1995; amended Oct. 2, 1995, effective Jan. 1, 1996; amended Oct. 2, 2000; amended March 14, 2002, effective Jan. 1, 2003; amended Oct. 2, 2006, effective Nov. 1, 2006; amended effective April 15, 2010; amended April 10, 2014, effective May 1, 2014.

Courts of Appeal Rule 4–6

Rule 4–6. Notices of Disposition of an Application for Writs

(A) The clerk shall transmit a copy of the court of appeal's disposition of an application for writs in each particular case to

(1) The applicant;

(2) The opposing party or parties respondent;

(3) The trial judge whose ruling has been complained of;

(4) The trial court clerk; and.

(5) Any party who has requested, before disposition, a copy of such disposition.

If a party is not represented by a counsel of record, the clerk shall transmit a copy of the disposition to the litigant at the United States mailing address shown in the application or in care of the trial court clerk where no such address of the litigant is shown.

(B) Where circumstances require prompt notice of the court's disposition of an application for writs, the clerk shall transmit the disposition in accordance with Rule 2–20, but may also give prompt notice of the disposition by telephone and/or by email or facsimile transmission to those who are to receive the notice via United States mail.

Amended Oct. 2, 1989, effective Jan. 1, 1990; Sept. 30, 2012, eff. Jan. 1, 2013.

Courts of Appeal Rule 4–7

Rule 4–7. Action on Writ Application

In exercise of its supervisory jurisdiction, the court may act peremptorily on the application, if circumstances warrant such action, with or without a response by the opposing party. The court alternatively may order a response by the opposing party and/or a per curiam by the trial court or may assign the case for argument and/or submission on any day that the court shall select.

Amended Oct. 2, 1989, effective Jan. 1, 1990; amended Oct. 3, 1994, effective Jan. 1, 1995.

Courts of Appeal Rule 4–8

Rule 4–8. Applicability of Rules

The Rules of the court pertaining to appeals and not conflicting with Rules specifically pertaining to applications for writs, when applicable and insofar as practicable, shall govern writ applications and the disposition thereof.

Courts of Appeal Rule 4–9

Rule 4–9. Rehearing

Rules 2–18.1 through 2–18.7 apply to requests for rehearings related to writ applications.

Adopted Oct. 3, 1994, effective Jan. 1, 1995.

Courts of Appeal Rule 5–1

Rule 5–1. Cases Designated for Expedited Handling

In recognition of the need for confidentiality and expeditious consideration of writs and appeals in certain types of cases involving minors, the following cases shall be afforded preferential treatment and consideration:

(a) Cases set forth in LSA–Ch.C. art. 337, including:

(1) Title VI. Child in Need of Care

(2) Title VII. Families in Need of Services

(3) Title VIII. Delinquency

(4) Title X. Involuntary Termination of Parental Rights

(5) Title XI. Surrender of Parental Rights

(6) Title XII. Adoption of Children

(7) Title XV, Chapter 7. Protection of Terminally Ill Children

(b) Cases in which there is a modification of an existing custody decree or custody arrangement, including but not limited to:

(1) change of domiciliary parent

(2) change of custodial time

(3) change in or to sole custody

(4) rendition of an initial custody decree changing custody in fact

(c) Cases involving intercountry adoption of children, as set forth in Title XII–A of the Children's Code.

Adopted April 13, 2000.

Courts of Appeal Rule 5–2

Rule 5–2. Confidentiality

To ensure the confidentiality of a minor who is a party to or whose interests are the subject matter in the proceedings listed in Rule 5–1(a) or (c) above, initials shall be used in all filings and in opinions rendered by the court of appeal to protect the minor's identity.

Adopted April 13, 2000.

Courts of Appeal Rule 5–3

Rule 5–3. Procedures in Cases Designated for Expedited Handling

The following procedures shall apply in cases designated for expedited treatment, unless a case is given special assignment by the court pursuant to Rule 2–11.2:

(a) Once a return date is set by the trial court, no extension shall be granted by the trial court or the court of appeal except upon a showing of extraordinary circumstances.

(b) Appeals and writ applications in such cases shall be assigned by preference to the next docket or cycle following any required briefing schedule.

(c)(1) In appeals taken in such cases, the brief of the appellant shall be filed not later than 15 calendar days after the filing of the record, and the brief of the appellee shall be filed not later than

Courts of Appeal Rule 5–3—Cont'd

30 calendar days after the filing of the record. The reply brief, if any, of the appellant shall be filed not later than 5 calendar days after the appellee's brief is filed.

(2) In such civil cases, if an appellant does not file a brief within the time prescribed by this rule or any extension thereof granted by the court as provided by this rule or Rule 2–12.8, a notice shall be mailed by the clerk to counsel for the appellant, or to the appellant if not represented, that the appeal shall be dismissed 10 days thereafter unless a brief is filed in the meantime. If an appellant does not file a brief within 10 days after such notice is mailed, the appeal shall be dismissed as abandoned. Provided, however, that irrespective of the time limit provided in this rule for the appellee to file a brief, the appellee's brief shall be filed within 15 days from the due date shown on the notice of abandonment.

(d) When an application for writs is sought in such cases to review the actions of a trial court, the trial court shall fix a reasonable time within which the application shall be filed in the appellate court, not to exceed 15 days from the date of the ruling at issue. Only upon a showing of extraordinary hardship shall the trial court or an appellate court extend the time for filing the application; and such an extension, if any, must be sought by the applicant, in writing, within the original or an extended return date period.

(e) Appeals and writs in these cases shall be considered by priority and the court shall render such opinions expeditiously to allow release on or before the next regularly scheduled opinion release date following the cycle or docket in which the case was submitted.

(f) Rehearing applications in compliance with URCA 2–18 shall be decided by preference by the court.

Adopted April 13, 2000; amended Oct. 1, 2001.

Courts of Appeal Rule 5–4

Rule 5–4. Applicability of Rules

All other Rules or laws regulating writs or appeals, not inconsistent with the foregoing, shall apply.

Adopted April 13, 2000.

INDEX TO
CODE OF CIVIL PROCEDURE

References are to Articles

SUCCESSIONS